E-Business and E-Commerce Management

Visit the *E-Business and E-Commerce Management, third edition* Companion Website with Grade Tracker at www.pearsoned.co.uk/chaffey to find valuable **student** learning material including:

- Multiple choice questions with Grade Tracker function to test your learning and monitor your progress
- Study Guide to reinforce key ideas and topics
- Smarter Online Searching Guide
- Links to relevant sites on the web
- An online glossary to explain key terms
- A blog with a collection of articles and links

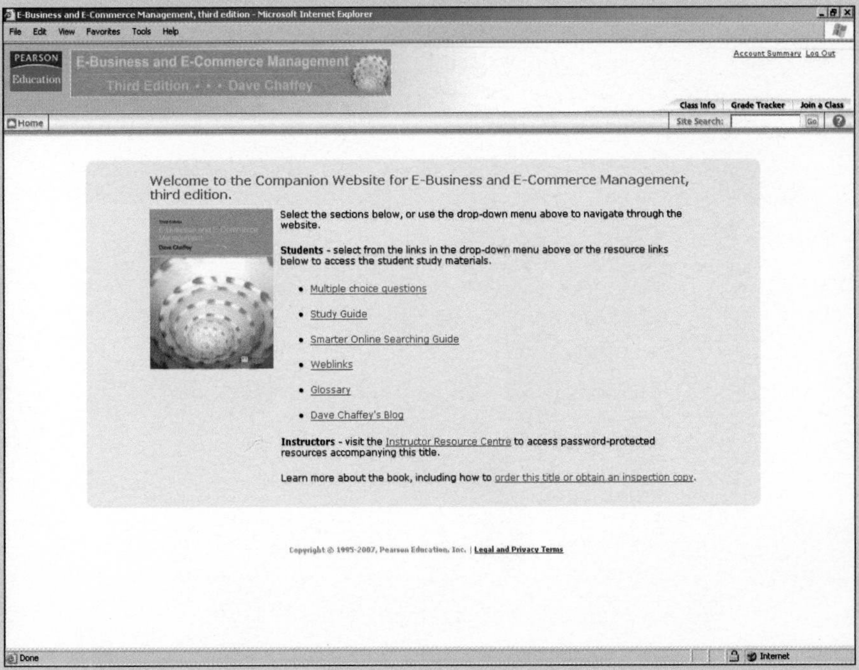

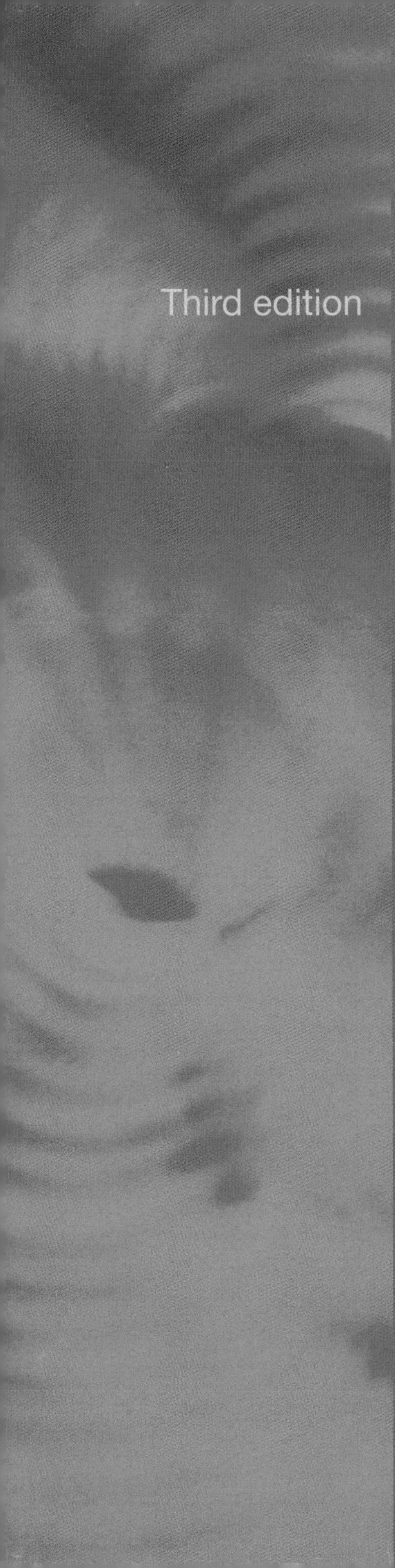

Third edition

E-Busin
and E-Co
Manageme

Strategy, Implementation an

Pearson Education Limited
Edinburgh Gate
Harlow
Essex CM20 2JE
England

and Associated C

Visit us on the
www.pears

First
Sec
T

Dave Chaffey

FT Prentice Hall
FINANCIAL TIMES

An imprint of Pearson Education
Harlow, England • London • New York • Boston • San Francisco • Toronto
Sydney • Tokyo • Singapore • Hong Kong • Seoul • Taipei • New Delhi
Cape Town • Madrid • Mexico City • Amsterdam • Munich • Paris • Milan

ompanies throughout the world

World Wide Web at:
oned.co.uk

ublished 2002
ond edition published 2004
hird edition published 2007

ISBN-13: 978-0-273-70752-3
ISBN-10: 0-273-70752-3

British Library Cataloguing-in-Publication Data
A catalogue record for this book is available from the British Library.

Library of Congress Cataloging-in-Publication Data
A catalog record for this book is available from the Library of Congress.

10 9 8 7 6 5 4 3 2 1
10 09 08 07 06

Typeset in 9/12 pt Stone Serif by 30
Printed and bound by Graficas Estella, Bilbao, Spain

The publisher's policy is to use paper manufactured from sustainable forests.

Brief contents

Contents

Supporting resources

Visit www.pearsoned.co.uk/chaffey to find valuable online resources

Companion Website with Grade Tracker for students

- Multiple choice questions with Grade Tracker function to test your learning and monitor your progress
- Study Guide to reinforce key ideas and topics
- Smarter Online Searching Guide
- Links to relevant sites on the web
- An online glossary to explain key terms
- A blog with a collection of articles and links

For instructors

- A module guide to help plan lectures
- Complete, downloadable Instructor's Manual including additional FT case studies
- PowerPoint slides that can be downloaded and used for presentations

Also: The Companion Website provides the following features:

- Search tool to help locate specific items of content
- Online help and support to assist with website usage and troubleshooting

For more information please contact your local Pearson Education sales representative or visit www.pearsoned.co.uk/chaffey

Preface

In 1849 a group of settlers travelling west towards the promised land, California, entered a then unnamed valley. The valley presented a harsh environment with a barrier of mountains to the west making the way forward unclear. Some of the settlers lost their lives as they sought to find a route west before eventually reaching California and what was to become one of the most prosperous places on Earth. As the group left the valley, one of the women in the group turned and said 'Goodbye, Death Valley' and hence the valley got its name.

The route to e-business success is also not straightforward and similarly fraught with difficulties of selecting the correct strategic direction and surviving in an increasingly harsh competitive environment. Not all who follow the route survive. However, the competitive drivers to follow this route, such as demand from customers and adoption by competitors make this journey essential. The rewards are evident from those adopters who identified the opportunity early and steered their companies in the right direction.

Flagship e-businesses with headquarters in California such as eBay and Google.com are now leading global brands with turnovers of billions of dollars, yet this has happened less than 300 years since the first modern settlers arrived.

This book is intended to equip current and future managers with some of the knowledge and practical skills to help them navigate their organization towards e-business. It is your guide to how all types of companies can prosper through e-business.

A primary aim of this book is to identify and review the key management decisions required by organizations moving to e-business and consider the process by which these decisions can be taken. Key questions are the following: What approach to e-business strategy do we follow? How much do we need to invest in e-business? Which processes should be our e-business priorities? Should we adopt new business and revenue models? What are the main changes that need to be made to the organization to facilitate e-business?

Given the broad scope of e-business, this book takes an integrative approach drawing on new and existing approaches and models from many disciplines including information systems, strategy, marketing, supply and value chain management, operations and human resources management.

What is e-business management?

Electronic business (e-business)
All electronically mediated information exchanges, both within an organization and with external stakeholders supporting the range of business processes.

As we will see in *Chapter 1*, electronic business (e-business) is aimed at enhancing the competitiveness of an organization by deploying innovative information and communications technology throughout an organization and beyond, through links to partners and customers. It does not simply involve using technology to automate existing processes, but should also involve using technology to help change these processes. To be successful in managing e-business, a breadth of knowledge is needed of different business processes and activities from across the value chain such as marketing and sales, through new product development, manufacturing and inbound and outbound logistics. Organizations also need to manage the change required by new processes and technology through what have traditionally been support activities such as human resources management.

From this definition, it is apparent that e-business involves looking at how electronic communications can be used to enhance all aspects of an organization's supply chain management. It also involves optimizing an organization's value chain, a related concept that describes the different value-adding activities that connect a company's supply side with its demand side. The e-business era also involves management of a network of interrelated value chains or value networks.

Supply chain management (SCM)
The coordination of all supply activities of an organization from its suppliers and partners to its customers.

Value chain
A model for analysis of how supply chain activities can add value to products and services delivered to the customer.

Value networks
The links between an organization and its strategic and non-strategic partners that form its external value chain.

What is e-commerce management?

To this point we have exclusively used the term 'e-business', but what of 'e-commerce'? Both these terms are applied in a variety of ways; to some they mean the same, to others they are quite different. As explained in *Chapter 1*, what is most important is that they are applied consistently within organizations so that employees and external stakeholders are clear about how the organization can exploit electronic communications. The distinction made in this book is to use 'electronic commerce' (e-commerce) to refer to all types of electronic transactions between organizations and stakeholders whether they are financial transactions or exchanges of information or other services. These e-commerce transactions are either buy-side e-commerce or sell-side e-commerce and the management issues involved with each aspect are considered separately in *Part 2* of the book. 'E-business' is applied as a broader term encompassing e-commerce but also including all electronic transactions within an organization.

Management of e-commerce involves prioritizing buy-side and sell-side activities and putting in place the plans and resources to deliver the identified benefits. These plans need to focus on management of the many risks to success, some of which you may have experienced when using e-commerce sites, from technical problems such as transactions that fail, sites that are difficult to use or are too slow, through to problems with customer service or fulfilment, which also indicate failure of management.

Electronic commerce (e-commerce)
All electronically mediated information exchanges between an organization and its external stakeholders.

Buy-side e-commerce
E-commerce transactions between an organization and its suppliers and other partners.

Sell-side e-commerce
E-commerce transactions between an organization and its customers.

How is this book structured?

The overall structure of the book shown in *Figure P.1* follows a logical sequence: introducing e-business terms, concepts and history of development in *Part 1*; reviewing alternative strategic approaches and applications of e-business in *Part 2*; and how strategy can be implemented in *Part 3*. Within this overall structure, differences in how electronic communications are used to support different business processes are considered separately. This is achieved by distinguishing between how electronic communications are used, from buy-side e-commerce aspects of supply chain management in *Chapters 6* and *7*, to the marketing perspective of sell-side e-commerce in *Chapters 8* and *9*. *Figure P.1* shows the emphasis of perspective for the particular chapters.

Part 1: Introduction (Chapters 1–4)

Part 1 introduces e-business and e-commerce. It seeks to clarify basic terms and concepts by looking at different interpretations of terms and applications through case studies.

- *Chapter 1: Introduction to e-business and e-commerce*. Definition of the meaning and scope of e-business and e-commerce. Introduction to business use of the Internet – what are the benefits and barriers to adoption and how widely used is it?
- *Chapter 2: E-commerce fundamentals*. Introduction to new business models and marketplace structures enabled by electronic communications.
- *Chapter 3: E-business infrastructure*. Background on the hardware, software and telecommunications that need to be managed to achieve e-business.
- *Chapter 4: E-environment*. Describes the macro-environment of an organization that presents opportunities and constraints on strategy and implementation.

Part 2: Strategy and applications (Chapters 5–9)

In *Part 2* of the book approaches to developing e-business strategy and applications are reviewed for the organization as a whole (*Chapter 5*) and with an emphasis on buy-side e-commerce (*Chapters 6* and *7*) and sell-side e-commerce (*Chapters 7* and *8*).

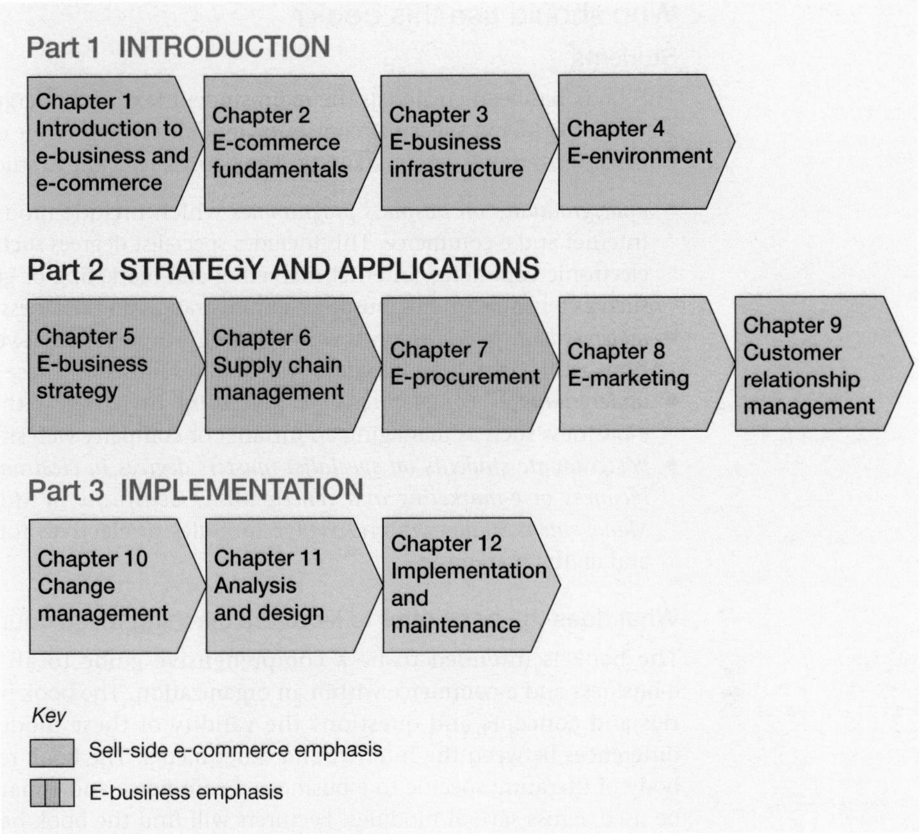

Figure P.1 Structure of the book

- *Chapter 5: E-business strategy.* Approaches to developing e-business strategy. Differences from traditional strategic approaches. Relation to IS strategy.
- *Chapter 6: Supply chain management.* A supply chain perspective on strategy with examples of how technology can be applied to increase supply chain and value chain efficiency.
- *Chapter 7: E-procurement.* Evaluation of the benefits and practical issues of adopting e-procurement.
- *Chapter 8: E-marketing.* A sell-side e-commerce perspective to e-business, reviewing differences in marketing required through digital media. Structured around developing an e-marketing plan.
- *Chapter 9: Customer relationship management.* Reviews marketing techniques that apply e-commerce for acquiring and retaining customers.

Part 3: Implementation (Chapters 10–12)

Management of e-business implementation is described in *Part 3* of the book in which we examine practical management issues involved with creating and maintaining e-business solutions.

- *Chapter 10: Change management.* How to manage the organizational, human and technology changes required in the move to e-business.
- *Chapter 11: Analysis and design.* We discuss the main issues of analysis and design raised by e-commerce systems that need to be discussed by managers and solutions providers.
- *Chapter 12: Implementation and maintenance.* How should e-commerce systems be managed and monitored once they are live?

Who should use this book?

Students

This book has been created as the main student text for undergraduate and postgraduate students taking specialist courses or modules which cover e-business, e-commerce information systems or e-marketing. The book is relevant to students who are:

- *undergraduates on business programmes* which include modules on the use of the Internet and e-commerce. This includes specialist degrees such as electronic business, electronic commerce, Internet marketing and marketing or general business degrees such as business studies, business administration and business management;
- *undergraduate project students* who select this topic for final-year projects or dissertations – this book is an excellent source of resources for these students;
- *undergraduates completing work placement* involved with different aspects of e-business such as managing an intranet or company web site;
- *postgraduate students on specialist masters degrees in electronic commerce, electronic business or e-marketing and generic MBA, Certificate in Management, Diploma in Management Studies* which involve modules or electives for electronic commerce and digital marketing.

What does the book offer to lecturers teaching these courses?

The book is intended to be a comprehensive guide to all aspects of deploying e-business and e-commerce within an organization. The book builds on existing theories and concepts and questions the validity of these models in the light of the differences between the Internet and other media. The book references the emerging body of literature specific to e-business, e-commerce and e-marketing. As such, it can be used across several modules. Lecturers will find the book has a good range of case studies, activities and exercises to support their teaching. These activities assist in using the book for student-centred learning as part of directed study. Web links given in the text and at the end of each chapter highlight key information sources for particular topics.

Practitioners

There is also much of relevance in this book for the industry professional, including:

- *Senior managers and directors* seeking to apply the right e-business and e-commerce approaches to benefit their organization.
- *Information systems managers* who are developing and implementing e-business and e-commerce strategies.
- *Marketing managers* responsible for defining an e-marketing strategy and implementing and maintaining the company web site.
- *Supply chain, logistics and procurement managers* wanting to see examples of best practice in using e-commerce for supply chain management.
- *Technical project managers or webmasters* who may understand the technical details of building a site, but have a limited knowledge of business or marketing fundamentals.

Student learning features

A range of features have been incorporated into this book to help the reader get the most out of it. They have been designed to assist understanding, reinforce learning and help readers find information easily. The features are described in the order you will encounter them.

At the start of each chapter

- *Chapter at a glance*: a list of main topics, 'focus on' topics and case studies.
- *Learning outcomes*: a list describing what readers can learn through reading the chapter and completing the activities.
- *Management issues*: a summary of main issues or decisions faced by managers related to the chapter topic area.
- *Web support*: additional material on the Companion Web Site.
- *Links to other chapters*: a summary of related topics in other chapters.
- *Introductions*: succinct summaries of the relevance of the topic to marketing students and practitioners together with content and structure.

In each chapter

- *Activities*: Short activities in the main text that develop concepts and understanding, often by relating to student experience or through reference to web sites. Model answers are provided to activities at the end of the chapter where applicable.
- *Case studies*: Real-world examples of issues facing companies that implement e-business. Questions at the end of the case study highlight the main learning points from that case study (*see p. xix*).
- *Running case studies*: The B2B Company and The B2C Company. These two cases are used throughout the book in activities to encourage students to think about solutions to commonly faced management decisions relating to a particular topic. Managers can substitute their own organization to reflect on how they are approaching an issue. The two companies are introduced in Chapter 1 (pp. 25–29).
- *'Focus on' sections*: More detailed coverage of specific topics of interest.
- *Questions for debate*: Suggestions for discussion of significant issues for managers involved with the transformation required for e-business.
- *Definitions*: When significant terms are first introduced the main text contains succinct definitions in the margin for easy reference.
- *Web links*: Where appropriate, web addresses are given for further information, particularly those to update information.
- *Chapter summaries*: Intended as revision aids and to summarize the main learning points from the chapter.

At the end of each chapter

- *Self-assessment exercises*: short questions which will test understanding of terms and concepts described in the chapter.
- *Discussion questions*: require longer essay-style answers discussing themes from the chapter, and can be used for essays or as debate questions in seminars.
- *Essay questions*: conventional essay questions.
- *Examination questions*: typical short-answer questions found in exams and can also be used for revision.
- *References*: these are references to books, articles or papers referred to within the chapter.
- *Further reading*: supplementary texts or papers on the main themes of the chapter. Where appropriate a brief commentary is provided on recommended supplementary reading on the main themes of the chapters.
- *Web links*: these are significant sites that provide further information on the concepts and topics of the chapter. All web site references within the chapter, for example company sites, are not repeated here. The web site address prefix 'http://' is omitted from www links for clarity.

At the end of the book

- *Glossary*: a list of all definitions of key terms and phrases used within the main text.
- *Index*: all key words and abbreviations referred to in the main text.

Learning techniques

The book is intended to support a range of learning styles. It can be used for an active or student-centred learning approach whereby students attempt the activities through reflecting on questions posed, answering questions and then comparing to a suggested answer at the end of the chapter. Alternatively, students can proceed straight to suggested answers in a more traditional learning approach, which still encourages reflection about the topic.

Module guide

The table below presents one mapping of how the book could be used in different weekly lectures and seminars through the core eleven weeks of a module where the focus is on management issues of e-business and e-commerce.

A fullset of PowerPoint slides and accompanying notes to assist lecturers in preparing lectures is available on the lecturer's side of the Companion Web Site.

Enhancements for the third edition

The effective chapter structure of the second edition has been retained, but many other changes have been incorporated based on lecturer and student feedback. The main changes are:

- In-depth cases written specifically for this book illustrating best practices and the challenges of e-business from well-known global e-businesses such as Amazon, the BBC and eBay to European and Asian e-retailers such as Tesco.com, dabs.com and start-ups such as North West Supplies and Zopa.com. A full listing of cases is given in *Table A*. Mini case studies and examples within each chapter have also been updated;
- References to new e-business technology web service delivery (including service oriented architecture) and 'Web 2.0' applications including blogging, Really Simple Syndication (RSS), instant messaging, podcasting, digital TV and mobile marketing (*Chapter 3*);
- Updates on the legal constraints from data protection and privacy laws and accessibility legislation (*Chapter 4*);
- Content on e-business strategy updated to reflect latest thinking on customer-centric online marketing using customer personas and journeys as part of multi-channel marketing (*Chapters 5, 8* and *9*);
- Supply chain management and e-procurement (*Chapters 6* and *7*) updated to reference current approaches to online B2B marketplaces and new techniques such as RFID;
- *Chapter 9* on relationship marketing now has an electronic customer relationship management (e-CRM) oriented approach and includes more detail on techniques used by e-retailers and e-mail marketers such as lifetime value and Recency–Frequency–Monetary (RFM) value analysis;
- Greater depth on online marketing communications techniques including affiliate marketing, search engine marketing, online PR and viral marketing (*Chapter 9*);
- The challenges of managing e-business security has more coverage in the areas of hacking, viruses, spam, identity theft and managing employee Internet access;
- Coverage on the latest approaches to using web analytics to measure and improve e-commerce (*Chapter 12*).

Table A In-depth case studies in *E-Business and E-Commerce Management*, 3rd edition

Chapter	*Case Study*
1 Introduction to e-business and e-commerce	1.1 North West Supplies extends its reach online 1.2 eBay – the world's largest e-business
2 E-commerce fundamentals	2.1 The impact of B2B reverse auctions 2.2 Lastminute.com – an international dot-com survivor 2.3 Zopa launches a new lending model
3 E-business infrastructure	3.1 New architecture or just new hype?
4 E-environment	4.1 Next-generation broadband 4.2 The implications of globalization for consumer attitudes 4.3 How do industry analysts affect technology adoption
5 E-business strategy	5.1 Capital One creates value through e-business 5.2 Setting the Internet revenue contribution at Sandvik Steel 5.3 Boo hoo – learning from the largest European dot-com failure
6 Supply chain management	6.1 Shell Chemicals redefines its customers' supply chains 6.2 Tesco develops buy-side e-commerce system for supply chain management 6.3 RFID: keeping track starts its move to a faster track
7 E-procurement	7.1 Cambridge Consultants reduce costs through e-procurement 7.2 Covisint – a typical history of a B2B marketplace?
8 E-marketing	8.1 The e-volution of easyJet's online revenue contribution 8.2 The new Napster changes the music marketing mix
9 Customer relationship management	9.1 Tesco.com increases product range and uses triggered communications to support CRM
10 Change management	10.1 Smoothing the workflow through business process management 10.2 Sharing knowledge at the BBC using Internet technologies
11 Analysis and design	11.1 Dabs.com refines its web store 11.2 Building an e-business fortress
12 Implementation and maintenance	12.1 Learning from Amazon's culture of metrics

Table B Module guide

Week	*Lecture topic*	*Seminar or tutorial topics*		*Notes*
1.	LI. Introduction to e-business and e-commerce	Activity 1.1 Case Study 1.1 Case Study 1.2 Debate 1.1	Introduction NW Supplies eBay E-business *vs* IS	Chapter 1 Chapter 3 (technical introduction)
2.	L2. E-commerce microenvironment	Activity 2.1 Case Study 2.2 Case Study 2.3 Debate 2.1	Introduction Lastminute.com Zopa.com Online intermediaries	Chapter 2
3.	L3. E-commerce macroenvironment	Activity 4.1 Case Study 4.2 Debate 4.2	Introduction Globalization E-government	Chapters 3 and 4
4.	L4. E-business strategy: (a) Situation analysis and objective setting	Activity 5.2 Case Study 5.1 Debate 5.1	B2C/B2B analysis Capital One E-business responsibility	Chapter 5
5.	L5. E-business strategy: (b) Strategy and tactics	Activity 5.4 Case Study 5.2 Debate 5.2	B2C/B2B Strategies Boo.com Board-level representation	Chapter 5
6.	L6. E-business applications: (a) Supply chain management	Activity 6.1 Case Study 6.1 Case Study 6.2 Debate 6.1	Introduction Shell Chemical Tesco Value chain	Chapter 6
7.	L7. E-business applications: (b) E-procurement	Activity 7.1 Case Study 7.1 Case Study 7.2 Debate 7.2	Introduction Cambridge Consultants Covisint B2B exchanges	Chapter 7
8.	L8. E-business applications: (c) E-marketing	Activity 8.2 Case Study 8.1 Case Study 8.2 Debate 8.1	Competitor benchmarking easyJet The new Napster E-marketing planning	Chapter 8
9.	L9. E-business applications: (d) e-CRM	Activity 9.1 Case Study 9.1 Debate 9.1	Introduction Tesco.com Permission marketing	Chapter 9
10.	L10. Change management	Activity 10.1 Case Study 10.1 Case Study 10.2 Debate 10.1	Introduction Smoothing the workflow through BPM Sharing knowledge at the BBC E-business function	Chapter 10
11.	L11. Evaluation and maintenance	Activity 12.1 Case Study 11.1 Case Study 12.1 Debate 12.2	Introduction Dabs.com Amazon Standards control	Chapter 12

The author's timeline

	1960	
1963	Born	Black and white television
	1970	
1976		Colour television
	1980	
1982 1985	BSc, Imperial College, London	First used computer-programmed mainframe using punched cards
1988	PhD, University of Leeds	Wrote PhD on mainframe
1989	Project Manager in software house developing GIS for marketing planning	First used PC
	1990	
1991	Software Engineering Manager for company producing packaged and bespoke engineering software	Sent first e-mail
1994	Project Manager for customer-facing financial services systems	Started using World Wide Web
1995	Senior Lecturer, Business Information Systems, Derbyshire Business School, University of Derby	First ordered book online
1997	Delivering CIM Internet Marketing seminars	Built first web site
1998	*Groupware, Workflow and Intranets* published	Mobile phone
1999	*Business Information Systems* published	
	2000	
2000	*Internet Marketing* published	Interactive digital TV
2000	MSc E-commerce course launched at Derby	WAP phone
2003	Nominated by CIM as one of 50 'gurus' to have 'shaped the future of marketing' along with Philip Kotler and Michael Porter!	
2004	Recognized by the Department of Trade and Industry, NOP World and E-consultancy as one of the 'Top 100 hundred people commended by the industry as key influencers and drivers, who have driven the development and growth of e-commerce in the UK over the last ten years'.	
2005	Second edition of *E-marketing Excellence* published	Blogging and RSS on www.davechaffey.com

This timeline supports *Activity 3.2*. This considers the diffusion of technological innovation at home and in the workplace. The author first started using a computer regularly when he was 18, yet his 4-year-old daughter is already an Internet user. Readers can compare their own adoption of computer technology at home and at work. How do you think the use of the Internet and its successors for e-commerce and e-entertainment will change as successive generations become increasingly computer-literate?

Guided tour

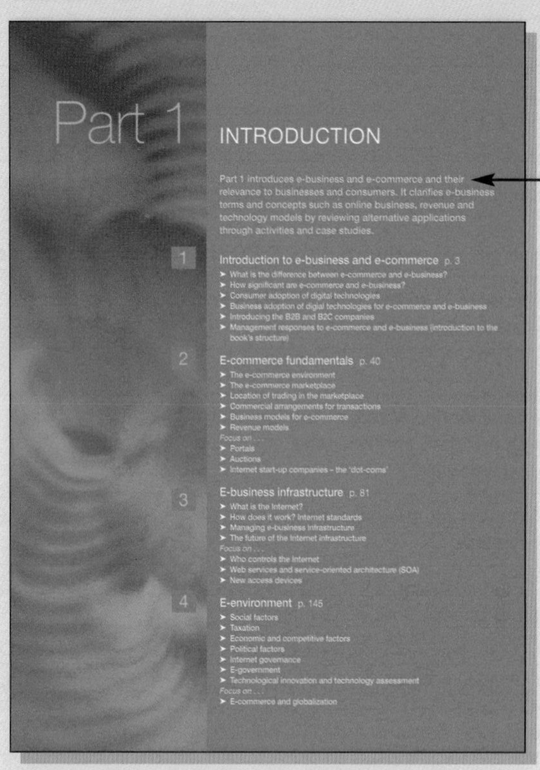

Part 1

INTRODUCTION

Part 1 introduces e-business and e-commerce and their relevance to businesses and consumers. It clarifies e-business terms and concepts such as online business, revenue and technology models by reviewing alternative applications through activities and case studies.

1 Introduction to e-business and e-commerce p. 3
- What is the difference between e-commerce and e-business?
- How significant are e-commerce and e-business?
- Consumer adoption of digital technologies
- Business adoption of digial technologies for e-commerce and e-business
- Introducing the B2B and B2C companies
- Management responses to e-commerce and e-business (introduction to the book's structure)

2 E-commerce fundamentals p. 40
- The e-commerce environment
- The e-commerce marketplace
- Location of trading in the marketplace
- Commercial arrangements for transactions
- Business models for e-commerce
- Revenue models

Focus on . . .
- Portals
- Auctions
- Internet start-up companies – the 'dot-coms'

3 E-business infrastructure p. 81
- What is the Internet?
- How does it work? Internet standards
- Managing e-business infrastructure
- The future of the Internet infrastructure

Focus on . . .
- Who controls the Internet
- Web services and service-oriented architecture (SOA)
- New access devices

4 E-environment p. 145
- Social factors
- Taxation
- Economic and competitive factors
- Political factors
- Internet governance
- E-government
- Technological innovation and technology assessment

Focus on . . .
- E-commerce and globalization

Part introduction
Each part of the book is summarised with a brief list of chapter contents and 'focus on' issues.

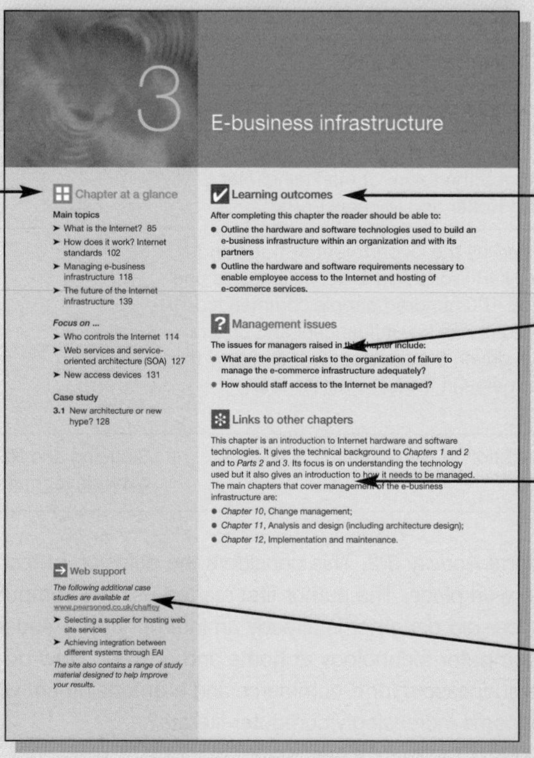

3

E-business infrastructure

Chapter at a glance

Main topics
- What is the Internet? 85
- How does it work? Internet standards 102
- Managing e-business infrastructure 118
- The future of the Internet infrastructure 139

Focus on ...
- Who controls the Internet 114
- Web services and service-oriented architecture (SOA) 127
- New access devices 131

Case study
3.1 New architecture or new hype? 128

Web support

The following additional case studies are available at www.pearsoned.co.uk/chaffey
- Selecting a supplier for hosting web site services
- Achieving integration between different systems through EAI

The site also contains a range of study material designed to help improve your results.

Learning outcomes

After completing this chapter the reader should be able to:
- Outline the hardware and software technologies used to build an e-business infrastructure within an organization and with its partners
- Outline the hardware and software requirements necessary to enable employee access to the Internet and hosting of e-commerce services.

Management issues

The issues for managers raised in this chapter include:
- What are the practical risks to the organization of failure to manage the e-commerce infrastructure adequately?
- How should staff access to the Internet be managed?

Links to other chapters

This chapter is an introduction to Internet hardware and software technologies. It gives the technical background to *Chapters 1* and *2* and to *Parts 2* and *3*. Its focus is on understanding the technology used but it also gives an introduction to how it needs to be managed. The main chapters that cover management of the e-business infrastructure are:
- *Chapter 10*, Change management;
- *Chapter 11*, Analysis and design (including architecture design);
- *Chapter 12*, Implementation and maintenance.

Chapter at a glance
This feature summarises the main topics of the chapter and the case studies.

Learning outcomes
These are set out clearly at the start of each chapter.

Management issues
These list the strategic and practical implications of each topic and case study.

Links to other chapters
To highlight the connections between chapters.

Web support
To highlight additional support material available on the Companion Website.

Focus on
'Focus on' sections contain more detailed coverage of key areas.

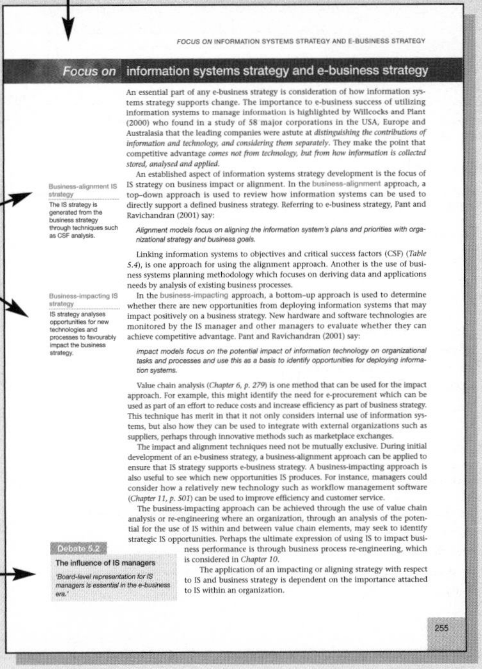

Key terms
These are explained through the text in a margin glossary.

Debate
Topical issues or statements to stimulate class-room discussion.

Mini Case Study
Extra smaller case studies have been added in this edition to give students more examples of e-commerce within business.

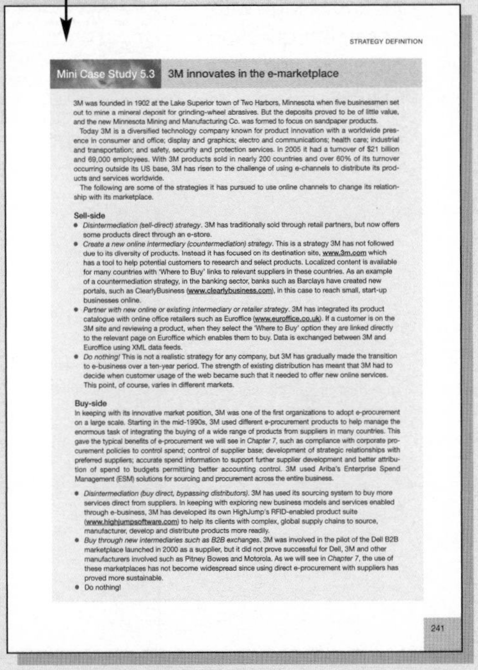

Activity
To test students' understanding of key topics.

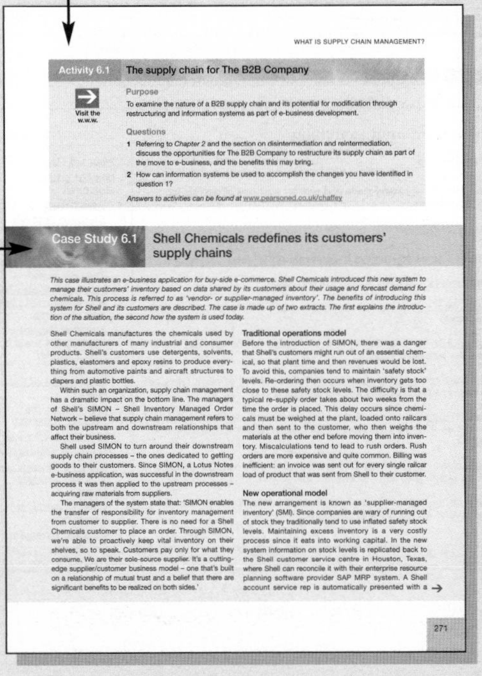

Case study
Integrated throughout the text, with many taken from the *Financial Times*, illustrating current examples of e-commerce and its application.

Essay, Discussion and Examination questions
These provide engaging activities for students and lecturers in and out of the classroom.

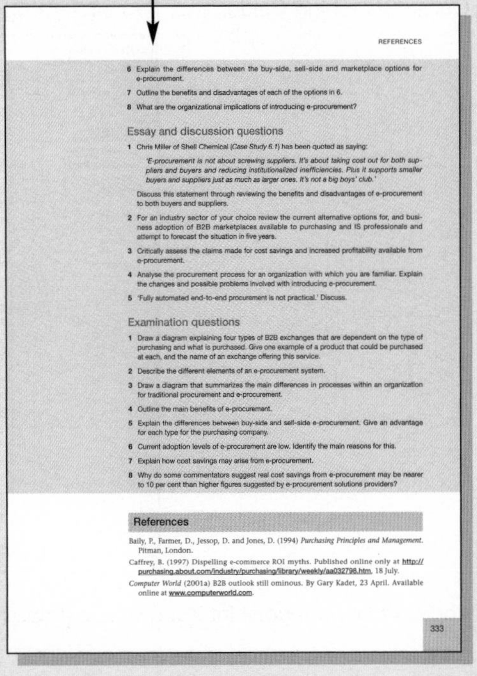

Guided tour continued

The Access Code included in this book unlocks a range of valuable online learning resources to help you pass your course. Go to www.pearsoned.co.uk/chaffey to get started!

Test your knowledge with self-assessment questions, save your score and track your progress.

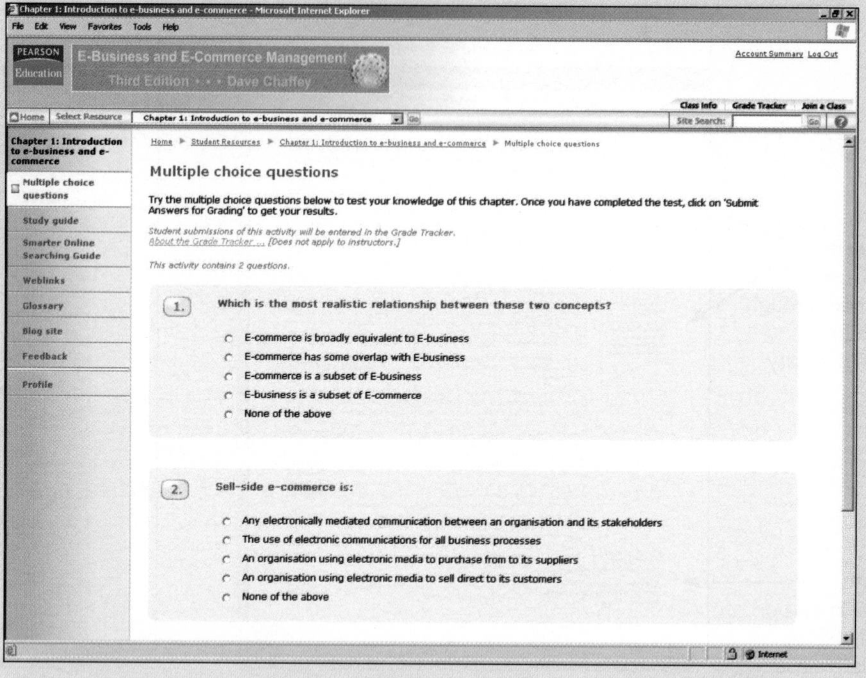

Save time in researching what you need from the web with the Smarter Online Searching Guide.

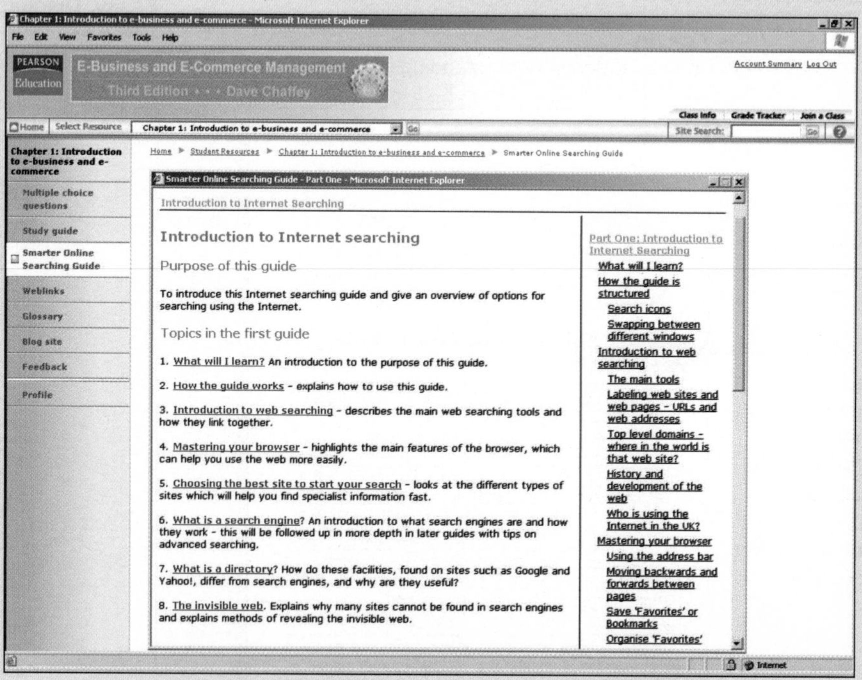

And take advantage of interactive study materials, glossary and flashcards to improve your grade.

Author's acknowledgements

The author would like to thank the team at Pearson Education in Harlow for their help in the creation of this book. I would particularly like to thank the reviewers who undertook detailed reviews for the second and third editions – these reviews have been important in shaping the book: Magdy Abdel-Kader, University of Essex; Poul Andersen, Aarhus Business School, Denmark; Michelle Bergadaa, University of Geneva, Switzerland; Bruce Bowhill, University of Portsmouth; Yaw Busia, University of Middlesex; Janet French, Barking College; Ulf Hoglind, Orebro University, Sweden; Britt-Marie Johansson, University of Jonkoping, Sweden; Tuula Mittila, University of Tampere, Finland; Barry Quinn, University of Ulster; Gerry Rogers, EdExcel Qualifications Leader; Chandres Tejura, University of North London; Ian Watson, University of Northumbria; Steve Wood, Liverpool John Moores University.

Thanks also to these reviewers who were involved at earlier stages with this book: Fintan Clear, Brunel University; Neil Doherty, Loughborough University; Jean-Noel Ezingeard, Henley Management College; Dr Felicia Fai, University of Bath; Lisa Harris, Brunel University; Sue Hartland, Gloucestershire Business School at Cheltenham and Gloucester College of Higher Education; Mike Healy, University of Westminster; Eric van Heck, Rotterdam School of Management, The Netherlands; Dipak Khakhar, Lund University, Sweden; Robert Proops, University of Westminster; Professor Michael Quayle, University of Glamorgan; Richard Riley, University of Central England; Gurmak Singh, University of Wolverhampton; John Twomey, Brunel University; Gerry Urwin, Coventry University.

Publisher's acknowledgements

We are grateful to the following for permission to reproduce copyright material:

Figures 1.1, 1.4, 2.1, 2.3, 3.5, 3.7, 3.9, 3.13, 3.14, 4.10, 4.12, 5.5, 5.17, 6.4a, 7.6, 8.5, 8.9, 8.13, 9.2 and Tables 12.7 and 12.8 from *Internet Marketing: Strategy, Implementation and Practice, 2nd Edition*, Financial Times Prentice Hall, Copyright © 2003 Pearson Education Ltd. (Chaffey, D. *et al.* 2003); Tables 1.2 and 4.2 from *Omnibus Survey*, Office for National Statistics, reproduced under the terms of the Click-Use Licence (ONS 2005); Figures 1.3, 1.7, 2.5, 2.6, 2.9, 2.11, 2.12, 2.13, 3.9, 5.3, 5.13, 5.18, 5.20, 5.21, 6.6, 7.2, 7.4, 7.5, 7.8, 7.9, 7.10, 8.7, 8.18, 9.9, 11.11, 11.16, 12.2, 12.4, Fig. p. 589 and 12.13 screenshot frames reprinted with permission from Microsoft Corporation; Figure 1.3 screenshot from www.dubit.co.uk reprinted by permission of Dubit Limited; Figure 1.5 from MORI Technology Tracker, January 2006, reprinted by permission of Ipsos MORI; Figures 1.6 and 1.9 from *Business in the Information Age – International Benchmarking Study 2002*, reproduced under the terms of the Click-Use Licence (DTI 2002); Figure 1.7 screenshot from www.northwestsupplies.co.uk reprinted by permission of North West Supplies Ltd.; Figures 1.8 and 6.8 from *Information Society Benchmarking Report*, © European Communities 2005, http://europa.eu.int/information_society, reprinted by permission of the European Communities (eEurope 2005); Figure 1.10 adapted from Structure is not organization in *McKinsey Quarterly*, 1980, McKinsey & Co., Inc. (Waterman, R. H., Peters, T. J. and Phillips, J. R. 1980); Table 2.2 from Nielsen//NetRatings NetView data, UK, home data, including Internet Applications, December 2005, reprinted by permission of Nielsen//NetRatings; Table 2.4 reprinted from *New Marketing: Transforming the Corporate Future*, M. McDonald and H. Wilson, Copyright 2002, with permission from Elsevier (McDonald, M. and Wilson, H. 2002); Table 2.5 adapted from The all-in-one market in *Harvard Business Review*, May-June, reprinted by permission of Harvard Business School Publishing Corporation (Nunes, P. *et al.* 2000); Figure 2.12 screenshot from www.e-consultancy.com reprinted by permission of E-consultancy.com Ltd.; Figure 2.13 screenshot from www.firebox.com with thanks to www.firebox.com; Table 3.2 republished with permission of CRC Press LLC – Journals, from Road map to the e-revolution by P. Kampas in *Information Systems Management*, Spring, 2000; permission conveyed through Copyright Clearance Center, Inc. (Kampas, P. 2000); Table 3.6 adapted from *Keynote KUK 40 Index October 2005*, reprinted by permission of Keynote Systems, Inc.; Figures 3.10a and 3.10b adapted from Information system integration in *Communications of the ACM*, Vol. 43, No. 6, 2000, pp.33-38, ACM Press Books and Journals, Copyright © 2000 ACM, Inc., reprinted by permission, and reproduced by kind permission of the author (Hasselbring, W. 2000); Figure 4.2 data from www.itu.int/ITU-D/ict/statistics reproduced with the kind permission of ITU; Figure 4.3 from eMORI Technology Tracker, www.mori.com/technology/trackerdata.shtml, reprinted by permission of Ipsos MORI; Table 4.3 from UK leads the way in online shopping, European Interactive Advertising Association press release published 12 January, reprinted by permission of EIAA (EIAA 2006); Table 4.4 from 2005 - The Year of the Identity Fraud!, CIFAS press release published 30 January, reproduced with the permission of CIFAS, the UK's fraud prevention service (CIFAS 2006); Figures 4.6, 6.9 and 6.10 from *Business in the Information Age – International Benchmarking Study 2004*, reproduced under the terms of the Click-Use Licence (DTI 2004); Figure 4.8 from *International E-Economy Benchmarking the World's Most Effective*

Policies for the E-Economy, report published 19 November, reproduced under the terms of the Click-Use Licence (Booz Allen Hamilton 2002); Figure 4.9 adapted from Economist Intelligence Unit data, © 2005, Economist Intelligence Unit, reprinted by permission of The Economist; Figure 5.3 screenshot from www.britishairways.com reprinted by permission of British Airways plc; Figure 5.12 from *Mastering Information Management*, Financial Times Prentice Hall, reprinted by permission of Pearson Education Ltd. (Marchand, D. *et al.* eds 2000); Figure 5.13 screenshot from www.capitalone.co.uk reprinted by permission of Capital One Bank (Europe) plc; Figure 5.14 from PricewaterhouseCoopers *Trendsetter Barometer Report, Quarter 2*, 2000, www.barometersurveys.com, Copyright © 2000 PricewaterhouseCoopers; Figure 5.20 screenshot from www.smile.co.uk reprinted by permission of The Co-operative Bank; Figure 5.21 screenshot from www.dabs.com reprinted by permission of dabs.com; Figures 7.2, 7.4, 7.5, 7.8 screenshots from Tranmit plc website, www.tranmit.co.uk, reproduced by kind permission of Tranmit plc; Table 7.3 adapted from Reducing the costs of goods sold: role of complexity, design relationships in *McKinsey Quarterly*, Vol. 2, 1997, pp. 212-215, www.mckinsey-quarterly.com, McKinsey & Co., Inc. (Kluge, J. 1997); Table 7.7 adapted from E-hubs: the new B2B marketplaces in *Harvard Business Review*, May-June, reprinted by permission of Harvard Business School Publishing Corporation (Kaplan, S. and Sawhney, M. 2000); Figure 7.10 screenshot from www.supply2.gov.uk reprinted by permission of supply2gov.uk, supplier route to government; Figure 8.2 adapted from *Marketing Communications: an integrated approach, 2nd Edition*, Kogan Page (Smith, P.R. 1999); Figures 8.3, 8.15, 10.2, 10.3, 10.6 and 10.8 from Managing an E-commerce team. Integrating digital marketing into your organization, author: Dave Chaffey, reprinted by permission of E-consultancy.com Ltd. (E-consultancy 2005); Table 8.4 adapted from M. de Kare-Silver, *EShock 2000. The Electronic Shopping Revolution: Strategies for Retailers and Manufacturers*, pub 2000, Macmillan Business, reproduced with permission of Palgrave Macmillan and the author (de Kare-Silver, M. 2000); Table 8.6 from *Annual Report*, reprinted by permission of Napster, LLC (Napster 2005); Figure 8.18 screenshot from www.napster.co.uk reprinted by permission of Napster, LLC; Table 9.3 data from www.iab.net/xmos, reprinted by permission of Interactive Advertising Bureau; Table 9.4 from information in E-loyalty: Your secret weapon on the web in *Harvard Business Review*, July-August, reprinted by permission of Harvard Business School Publishing Corporation (Reicheld, F. and Schefter, P. 2000); Figure 9.9 Google screenshot – search for email security, reprinted by permission of Google, Inc., Google™ is a trademark of Google, Inc.; Figure 9.11 reprinted by permission of Epsilon Interactive, http://www.epsiloninteractive.com; Figure 9.12 adapted from Putting the service-profit chain to work in *Harvard Business Review*, March-April, reprinted by permission of Harvard Business School Publishing Corporation (Heskett, J. *et al.* 1994); Table 10.6 adapted from How risky is your company? in *Harvard Business Review*, May-June, reprinted by permission of Harvard Business School Publishing Corporation (Simons, R. 1999); Figure 10.7 adapted from Organizing for digital marketing in *The McKinsey Quarterly*, No. 4, 1996, pp. 183-192, www.mckinsey-quarterly.com, McKinsey & Co., Inc. (Parsons, A., Zeisser, M. and Waitman, R. 1996); Figure 11.1 adapted from *Groupware, Workflow and Intranets – Re-engineering the Enterprise with Collaborative Software, 1st Edition*, Digital Press, Woburn, MA, reprinted by permission of Elsevier Science (Chaffey, D. J. 1998); Figure 11.11 screenshot of RS Components homepage supplied courtesy of RS Components, http://rswww.com; Figure 11.17 from *Department of Trade and Industry Information Security Breaches Survey. Executive Summary 2006*, reproduced under the terms of the Click-Use Licence (DTI 2006); Figure 11.18 Code Red (CRv2) Spread Animation, CAIDA/UC San Diego, Copyright © 2001 The Regents of the University of California, reprinted by permission of The Regents of the University of California; Figures 11.19 and 11.21 from *Department of Trade and*

Industry Information Security Breaches Survey, reproduced under the terms of the Click-Use Licence (DTI 2006); Figure 11.20 reprinted by permission of Marshal Ltd.; Figure 11.22 from Threat Statistics reprinted by permission of MessageLabs (MessageLabs 2006); Table 12.3 adapted from *Business Information Systems: Technology, Development and Management, 2nd Edition*, Financial Times Prentice Hall, reprinted by permission of Pearson Education Ltd. (Bocij, P. *et al.* 2002); Table 12.4 adapted from *Software Testing: A Craftsman's Approach*, reproduced by permission of Routledge/Taylor & Francis Group, LLC and the author (Jorgensen, P. C. 1995); Table 12.6 reprinted by permission of ABC ELECTRONIC, www.abce.org.uk.

Mini Case Study 2.1 with thanks to www.firebox.com; Case Study 5.1 reprinted by permission of Capital One Bank (Europe) plc; Mini Case Study 5.4 reprinted by permission of The Co-operative Bank; Case Study 8.2 reprinted by permission of Napster, LLC.

Waterfront for the use of 'Betfair profits with C2C online gambling service' by Dave Chaffey from www.betfair.com; Peter Davies of Menter Môn (www.mentormon.com) for the use of 'North-West Supplies extends its reach online' by Peter Davies for the Opportunity Wales project; Zopa Ltd. for the use of 'Zopa launches a new lending model'; The Henley Centre for extracts from www.TheHenleyCentre.com; British Airways for the use of 'BA asks "Have you clicked yet?"' from the 'Have you clicked yet?' print ad campaign; 3M for the use of '3M innovates in the e-marketplace' by Dave Chaffey; RS Components Ltd. for the use of 'Cambridge Consultants reduce costs through e-procurement' taken from RS Components White Paper, www.rswww.com; George Karibian, CEO/Founder of Euroffice Ltd. for the use of 'Euroffice segment office supplies purchasers using "touch marketing funnel" approach' by Dave Chaffey; Tesco Stores Limited for the use of 'Tesco.com increases product range and use triggered communications to support CRM' by Dave Chaffey; and Amazon.co.uk for the use of 'Learning from Amazon's culture of metrics' by Dave Chaffey.

Case Study 2.1 A bid to save money for the government, © *Financial Times*, 29 January 2003; Case Study 3.1 New Architecture or just new hype?, © *Financial Times*, 8 March 2006; Case study 4.1 Where high-speed access is going mainstream, © *Financial Times*, 6 June 2004; Case Study 4.2 Extract from An optimist's vision of tomorrow's technology, © *Financial Times*, 6 June 2006; Case Study 5.2 Boo.com collapses as investors refuse funds, © *Financial Times*, 19 May 2000; Chapter 5 p.341 and 342 Buried treasure © *FT-IT*, 10 December 2003; Case Study 6.2 Retailers website allows suppliers to closely monitor product demand, © *FT-IT*, 3 May 2000; Case Study 6.3 RFID: Keeping track starts its move to a faster track, © *FT.com*, 20 April 2005; Case Study 10.1 Smoothing the workflow, © *FT.com*, 15 May 2003; Case Study 10.2 Encouraging information sharing, © *FT.com*, 24 January 2006; Case Study 11.2 A different approach to protection, © *FT.com*, 8 November 2005.

In some instances we have been unable to trace the owners of copyright material, and we would appreciate any information that would enable us to do so.

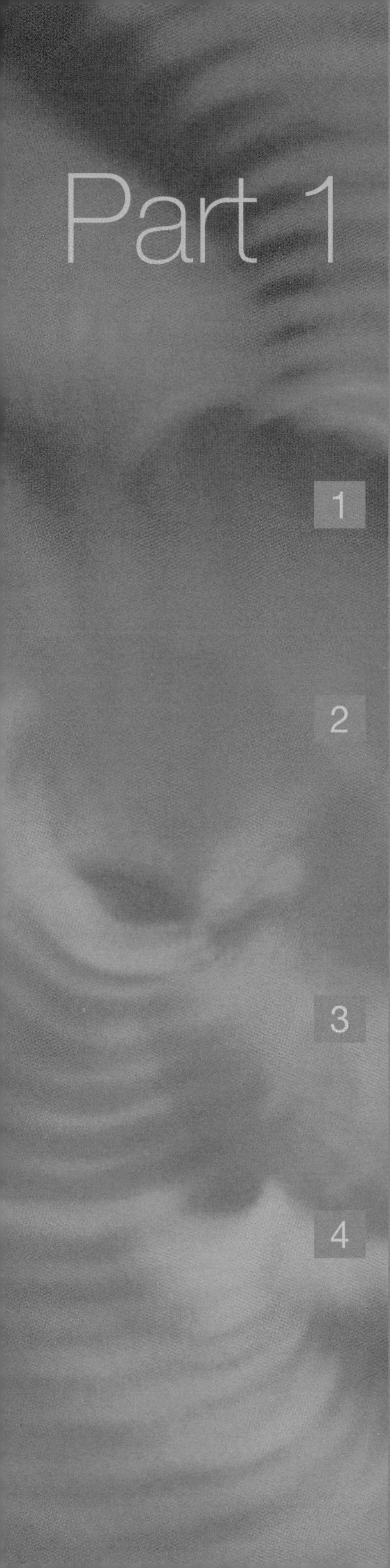

Part 1

INTRODUCTION

Part 1 introduces e-business and e-commerce and their relevance to businesses and consumers. It clarifies e-business terms and concepts such as online business, revenue and technology models by reviewing alternative applications through activities and case studies.

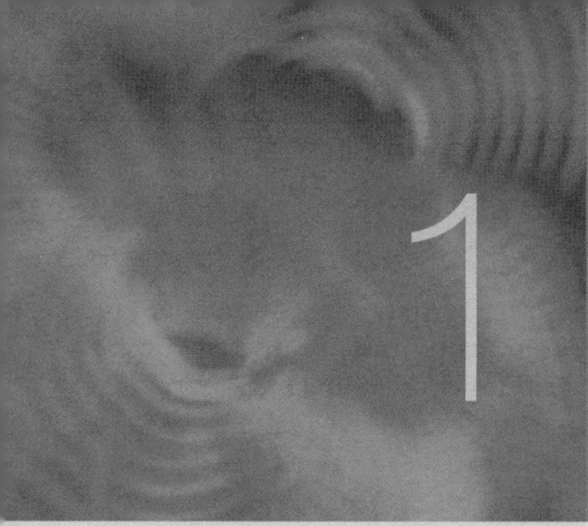

1 Introduction to e-business and e-commerce

Chapter at a glance

Main topics

Case studies

Web support

The following additional case studies are available at www.pearsoned.co.uk/chaffey

- SME adoption of sell-side e-commerce
- Death of the dot-com dream
- Encouraging SME adoption of sell-side e-commerce

The site also contains a range of study material designed to help improve your results.

Learning outcomes

After completing this chapter the reader should be able to:

- Define the meaning and scope of e-business and e-commerce and their different elements
- Summarize the main reasons for adoption of e-commerce and e-business and barriers that may restrict adoption
- Use resources to define the extent of adoption of the Internet as a communications medium for consumers and businesses
- Outline the business challenges of introducing e-business and e-commerce to an organization.

Management issues

The issues for managers raised in this chapter include:

- How do we explain the scope and implications of e-business and e-commerce to staff?
- What is the full range of benefits of introducing e-business and what are the risks?
- How great will the impact of the Internet be on our business? What are the current and predicted adoption levels?

Links to other chapters

The main related chapters are:

- *Chapter 2* examines the principal e-commerce business and marketplace models in more detail;
- *Chapter 3* introduces the technical infrastructure of software and hardware that companies must incorporate to achieve e-commerce;
- *Chapter 5* describes approaches to e-business strategy introduced in *Chapter 1*.

Introduction

The 'dot-com era' is now fast receding into the past. In 2006, the global number of Internet users passed 1 billion for the first time and in many countries over half the adult population is online. You can see how many Internet users there are as a proportion of the population in your country by completing *Activity 1.1*. But despite the commercial Internet and web having existed for well over 15 years, throughout the world, managers are still grappling with turning the e-business concept into a business reality. The essence of successfully managing e-business, which we will review in *E-Business and E-Commerce Management*, is to take full advantage of the business opportunities while managing the risks. In this book we will explore the techniques managers can use to assess the relevance of different e-business opportunities arising from increased use of electronic communications such as the Internet, World Wide Web and wireless communications and then devise and implement strategies to exploit these opportunities. We will also study how to manage more practical risks such as delivering a satisfactory service quality, maintaining customer privacy and managing security.

In this chapter we start by considering some of the main opportunities and risks of e-business. We then introduce the scope of e-business and e-commerce. We will also look at some of the drivers and barriers to adoption of e-business services which need to be understood by all managers to help encourage adoption of these services. Finally, we will introduce the two case study organizations which we use to illustrate e-business concepts and challenges in every chapter and look at some of the organizational challenges of managing e-business using the classic McKinsey 7S strategy framework.

The Internet
'The Internet' refers to the physical network that links computers across the globe. It consists of the infrastructure of network servers and communication links between them that are used to hold and transport information between the client PCs and web servers.

World Wide Web (WWW)
The most common technique for publishing information on the Internet. It is accessed through web browsers which display web pages of embedded graphics and HTML/XML-encoded text.

Wireless communications
Electronic transactions and communications conducted using mobile devices such as laptops, personal digital assistants (PDAs) and mobile phones (and fixed access platforms) with different forms of wireless connection.

Disruptive Internet technologies
New Internet-based communications approaches which change the way in which information about products is exchanged, which impact the basis for competition in a marketplace.

E-business opportunities

E-business has introduced new opportunities for small and large organizations to compete in the global marketplace. Many commentators have noted that one of the biggest changes introduced by electronic communications is how approaches to transmitting and transforming information can be used for competitive advantage. For example, Evans and Wurster of Harvard argue in their classic 1997 paper 'Strategies and the new economics of information' that there are three characteristics of information which, when combined with disruptive Internet technologies, can have a major impact on a marketplace. These characteristics of information are:

1 *Reach.* Conventionally, 'reach' refers to the potential number of customers a business can interact with. The Internet enables reach to be increased nationally and internationally at low cost through making content available via search engines. 'Reach' also refers to the number of different categories and products a consumer interface (e.g. store, catalogue or web site) can cover: witness the large range of products available through e-businesses such as Amazon, eBay and Kelkoo.com and existing companies such as easyJet.com and Tesco.com which have used the web to extend their product range.

2 ***Richness***. This is a characteristic of the information itself. The Internet enables more detailed information about products, prices and availability to be made available. It also enables more interactivity and customization to engage customers and to provide more up-to-date information. But, Evans and Wurster also note that richness is limited by bandwidth (the volume of information that can be transmitted using a communications link in a given time), the accuracy or reliability of information and its security.

3 *Affiliation*. This refers to the effectiveness of links with partners. In an online context, an organization which has the most and richest links with other compatible organizations will be able to gain a larger reach and influence. Consider how e-businesses such as eBay, Google and Yahoo! have successfully formed partnerships or acquired other companies to provide new diverse information services such as social networking, mapping, voice communications and online photography, to name just a few.

In markets such as car sales which have been transformed by the Internet, understanding how to improve reach, richness and affiliation is crucial. This is not because a large proportion of people buy cars online, but rather they research which make, model and supplier online. In many developed economies over half of purchasers of executive cars now research their purchase online.

With the increase in availability of information about products, services and providers for potential customers, there are now great opportunities to acquire new customers online, particularly since many consumers and business people now naturally turn to the web when researching products and services. Look at the examples in *Table 1.1* of the volume of searches for these generic, broad keywords. The numbers in the table are huge in any country, but most users also narrow their searches using phrases like 'free online banking', 'cuba holidays' and 'ski jackets'. This enables online suppliers to target their messages to consumers looking for these products in the search engines through advertising services such as Google and Overture (Yahoo! Search Marketing).

Table 1.1 Volume of searches for single keywords in a single month

Keyword	*Estimated Google Adwords clicks (Position 1.0)*	*Total estimated UK searches on Google*	*Overture UK searches*
Online banking	120	72,000	142,324
HSBC	730	438,000	197,577
Holidays	12,000	720,000	1,041,441
Thomas Cook	230	138,000	67,228
Clothing	6,600	3,960,000	327,988
Debenhams	100	60,000	292,839
CRM	79	47,400	17,562
Oracle	270	162,000	6,476

Notes:
1. Google estimates from Google Traffic Estimator for UK January 2006, available through Google Adwords. Total Google searches based on assuming that on average Position 1 ad slot receives 5% clickthrough rate, so total searches 20 times this (actual clickthrough will vary by key phrase, e.g. highest for brands).
2. Yahoo! Search UK (formerly Overture) advertising network main search sources included Yahoo!, MSN and Wanadoo. Includes both singular and plural.
3. Both include automated software-generated searches and repeated searches by the same user.

There are also significant opportunities for many businesses to build closer relationships with their existing customers (and suppliers) online to help achieve customer retention. Encouraging use of online, e-business services by customers and suppliers can significantly reduce costs while providing a new, convenient channel for purchase and customer service. Through providing high-quality online services, organizations can build lasting relationships with their stakeholders. While it is sometimes said that '*online, your customers are only a mouse click away from your competitors*', this is a simplification, and encouraging use of online services can help achieve 'soft lock-in'. This means that a customer or supplier continues to use a service since they find the service valuable and they have also invested a lot of time in learning the service or integrating it with their systems and there are some costs in switching. Think of different online services you use for different purposes. How often do you switch between them? Of course, the ideal is that the service meets the needs of its users so well and delivers value such that they are satisfied and do not consider switching.

Soft lock-in
Customers or suppliers continue to use online services because of the switching costs.

Some companies in every sector have demonstrated success. In Europe, the low-cost airlines such as easyJet and Ryanair have succeeded in migrating the majority of their customers to online booking in the space of a few years, while acquiring many new customers. Other companies have also used the Internet to gain competitive advantage. For example, the supermarket Tesco has launched a market-leading e-commerce service for customers and also uses the Internet extensively for purchasing.

E-business risks

But we also have to remember the risks of introducing e-business services which vary from strategic risks to practical risks. One of the main strategic risks is making the wrong decision about e-business investments. In every business sector, some companies have taken advantage of e-business and gained a competitive advantage. But others have invested in e-business without achieving the hoped-for returns, either because the execution of the plan was flawed, or simply because the planned approaches used for their market were inappropriate. The impact of the Internet and technology varies by industry. As Andy Grove, Chairman of Intel, one of the early adopters of e-business has noted, every organization needs to ask whether, for them:

> *The Internet is a typhoon force, a ten times force, or is it a bit of wind? Or is it a force that fundamentally alters our business?* (Grove, 1996)

This statement still seems to encapsulate how managers must respond to digital technologies; the impact will vary through time from minor for some companies to significant for others, and an appropriate response is required.

As well as the strategic risks, there are also many practical risks to manage which, if ignored, can lead to bad customer experiences and bad news stories which lead to damage to the reputation of the company. In the section on e-business opportunities, we reviewed the concept of soft lock-in; however, if the customer experience of a service is very bad, they will stop using it, and switch to other online options. Examples of poor online customer experience which you may be familiar with include:

- Web sites that fail because of a spike in visitor traffic after a peak-hour TV advertising campaign.
- Hackers penetrating the security of the system and stealing credit card details.
- A company e-mails customers without receiving their permission, so annoying customers and potentially breaking privacy and data protection laws.
- Problems with fulfilment of goods ordered online, meaning customer orders go missing or are delayed and the customer never returns.
- E-mail customer-service enquiries from the web site don't reach the right person and are ignored.

Activity 1.1 Consumer Internet adoption

Visit the w.w.w.

Purpose

To examine the growth of Internet use by consumers and to review the variation in different countries.

Activity

Visit ClickZ Stats (www.clickz.com/stats/) which includes aggregates of estimates from different sources of Internet adoption in different sectors and in countries. The 'Web Worldwide section' (www.clickz.com/stats/web_worldwide/) has a compilation of usage for different countries. Another source of information about variation in use of communications technologies in different countries is the statistics from the International Telecommunications Union (www.itu.int/ITU-D/ict/statistics/) .

Questions

1 What is the proportion of Internet access in your country and neighbouring countries?

2 Which factors explain the variation in Internet adoption.

3 To what extent do you think this level of access will change in the future?

We will return to this theme later in the chapter in the section on the drivers and barriers to e-commerce adoption by consumers and businesses.

Answers to activities can be found at www.pearsoned.co.uk/chaffey.

What is the difference between e-commerce and e-business?

The rapid advancement of technology and its application to business has been accompanied by a range of new terminology and jargon. The use of the term 'electronic commerce' has been supplemented by additional terms such as e-business, e-marketing, and more specialist terms such as e-CRM, e-tail and e-procurement. Do we need to be concerned about the terminology? The short answer is no; Mougayer (1998) noted that it is understanding the services that can be offered to customers and the business benefits that are obtainable through e-business that are important. However, labels are convenient in defining the *scope* of the changes we are looking to make within an organization through using electronic communications. Managers need to communicate the extent of changes they are proposing through introducing digital technologies to employees, customers and partners. Complete *Activity 1.2* to start unravelling the different terms through looking at how General Electric, one of the world's largest companies has embraced e-business.

Activity 1.2 Understanding e-commerce and e-business

Purpose

To encourage discussion of what is understood by 'e-commerce' and 'e-business' and their significance to managers.

Activity

Read the extract below and then answer the questions which follow. Although this is now a dated example, it is still useful as a historic document showing the different aspects of e-business that a business must address. In one of his last AGM speeches for General Electric (Welch, 2001), Jack Welch made these comments about GE's adoption of e-business.

> *Like the Amazons of the world, we started out with what we call 'e-Sell', primarily distributing our products on the Internet. Moving our traditional customers to the Web for much more efficient transactions has been very successful. And in 2000 we sold $8 billion in goods and services online, a number that'll grow to $20 billion this year, making this 123-year-old institution one of the biggest, if not the biggest, e-Business company in the world.*
>
> *On what we call the 'e-Buy' side, we followed the same path, adopting many of the dot.com ideas on auctions, having a global network of Six Sigma suppliers. The concept of reverse auctions was right in the GE sweet spot and we wasted no time in spreading the new technology across our businesses. We now run global auctions daily – $6 billion worth last year, $12 billion this year, generating over $600 million in savings for the company in 2001.*
>
> *But the biggest breakthrough of all was what we call 'e-Make' and that didn't come from the dot.coms. They had little infrastructure and few processes. e-Make came from learning what the Internet could do for internal processes and seeing the enormous advantage Digitization can give a big old company that actually makes things, particularly one with Six Sigma methodology already deeply entrenched in its veins. By digitizing our processes from customer service to travel and living, we'll take over a billion dollars of cost out of our operations this year alone.*
>
> *Last year I told you I believed e-Business was neither 'old economy' nor 'new economy', but simply new technology. I'm more sure of that today. If we needed confirmation that this technology was made for us, we got it. GE was named last year 'e-Business of the Year' by InternetWeek magazine and awarded the same title last week by WORTH magazine.*
>
> *Digitization is, in fact, a game changer for GE. And, with competition cutting back because of the economy, this is the time for GE to widen the digital gap, to further improve our competitive position. We will do that by increasing our spending on information technology by 10% to 15% this year despite the weak economy.*

Note: the Six Sigma concept of process quality improvement is described in more detail at www.isixsigma.com, and reverse auctions are explored in *Chapters 2* and *7*.

Questions

1 Identify the different components of e-business described in this speech and assess their relative impact on the organization.

2 Where do other 'e' terms such as e-CRM, e-marketing, e-logistics, e-procurement, e-tail and e-government fit within this description?

Answers to activities can be found at www.pearsoned.co.uk/chaffey

E-commerce defined

Electronic commerce (e-commerce)
All electronically mediated information exchanges between an organization and its external stakeholders.

Electronic commerce (e-commerce) is often thought simply to refer to buying and selling using the Internet; people immediately think of consumer retail purchases from companies such as Amazon. But e-commerce involves much more than electronically mediated *financial* transactions between organizations and customers. Many commentators refer to e-commerce as *all* electronically mediated transactions between an organization and any third party it deals with. By this definition, non-financial transactions such as customer requests for further information would also be considered to be part of e-commerce. Kalakota and Whinston (1997) refer to a range of different perspectives for e-commerce:

1 *A communications perspective* – the delivery of information, products/services or payment by electronic means.
2 *A business process perspective* – the application of technology towards the automation of business transactions and workflows.

3 *A service perspective* – enabling cost cutting at the same time as increasing the speed and quality of service delivery.
4 *An online perspective* – the buying and selling of products and information online.

The UK government used a broad definition when explaining the scope of e-commerce to industry:

> *E-commerce is the exchange of information across electronic networks, at any stage in the supply chain, whether within an organization, between businesses, between businesses and consumers, or between the public and private sector, whether paid or unpaid.* (Cabinet Office, 1999)

These definitions show that electronic commerce is not solely restricted to the actual buying and selling of products, but also includes pre-sale and post-sale activities across the supply chain.

E-commerce is facilitated by a range of digital technologies that enable electronic communications. These technologies include Internet communications through web sites and e-mail as well as other digital media such as wireless or mobile and media for delivering digital television such as cable and satellite. We will explain the characteristics of these technologies and some of the challenges in managing them in *Chapter 3*.

When evaluating the strategic impact of e-commerce on an organization, it is useful to identify opportunities for buy-side and sell-side e-commerce transactions as depicted in *Figure 1.1*, since systems with different functionalities will need to be created in an organization to accommodate transactions with buyers and with suppliers.

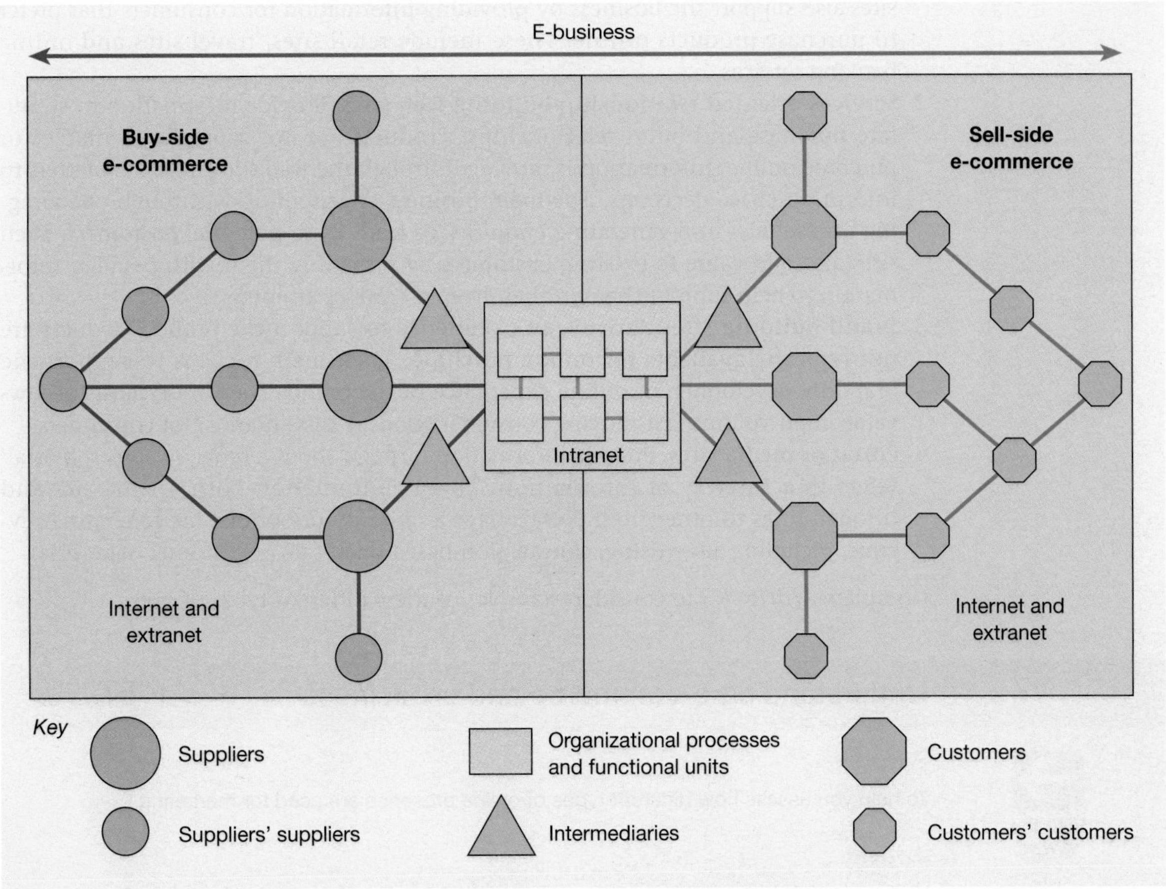

Figure 1.1 **The distinction between buy-side and sell-side e-commerce**

Buy-side e-commerce
E-commerce transactions between a purchasing organization and its suppliers.

Sell-side e-commerce
E-commerce transactions between a supplier organization and its customers.

Buy-side e-commerce refers to transactions to procure resources needed by an organization from its suppliers. In *Chapter 6, Case Study 6.1* reviews how Shell has developed an e-business capability that enables buy-side e-commerce for its customers. Sell-side e-commerce refers to transactions involved with selling products to an organization's customers. So e-commerce transactions between organizations can be considered from two perspectives: sell-side from the perspective of the selling organization and buy-side from the perspective of the buying organization.

Different types of sell-side e-commerce

Sell-side e-commerce doesn't only involve selling products such as books and CDs online, but also involves using Internet technologies to market services using a range of techniques we will explore in *Chapters 8* and *9*. Not every product is suitable for sale online, so the way in which a web site is used to market products will vary. It is useful to consider the four main types of online presence for sell-side e-commerce, which each have different objectives and are appropriate for different markets. Note that these are not clear-cut categories of web sites since any company may combine these types, but with a change in emphasis according to the market they serve. As you review web sites, note how organizations have different parts of the site focusing on these functions of sales transactions, services, relationship-building, brand-building and providing news and entertainment. The four main types of site are:

1. **Transactional e-commerce sites**. These enable purchase of products online. The main business contribution of the site is through sale of these products. The sites also support the business by providing information for consumers that prefer to purchase products offline. These include retail sites, travel sites and online banking services.
2. **Services-oriented relationship-building web sites**. Provide information to stimulate purchase and build relationships. Products are not typically available for purchase online. Information is provided through the web site and e-newsletters to inform purchase decisions. The main business contribution is through encouraging offline sales and generating enquiries or leads from potential customers. Such sites also add value to existing customers by providing them with detailed information to help support them in their lives at work or at home.
3. **Brand-building sites**. Provide an experience to support the brand. Products are not typically available for online purchase. Their main focus is to support the brand by developing an online experience of the brand. They are typical for low-value, high-volume fast-moving consumer goods (FMCG brands) for consumers.
4. **Portal or media sites**. Provide information or news about a range of topics. 'Portal' refers to a gateway of information. This is information both on the site and through links to other sites. Portals have a diversity of options for generating revenue, including advertising, commission-based sales, sale of customer data (lists).

Complete *Activity 1.3* to consider examples of these different types of sites.

Activity 1.3 Understanding e-commerce and e-business

Visit the w.w.w.

Purpose

To help you assess how different types of online presence are used for marketing.

Activity

Visit each of the sites below and then place them into one of the four categories of online presence according to their primary focus:

1 Transactional e-commerce site.
2 Services-oriented relationship-building web site.
3 Brand-building site.
4 Portal or media site.

You should also indicate their secondary focus in terms of these four site types.

Example sites

- Business site: Silicon (www.silicon.com)
- Bank, e.g. HSBC (www.hsbc.com)
- Lingerie manufacturer, e.g. Gossard (www.gossard.com)
- Management consultants such as PricewaterhouseCooper (www.pwcglobal.com) and Accenture (www.accenture.com)
- Beverage manufacturers, e.g. Tango (www.tango.com), Guinness (www.guinness.com).
- Travel company, Thomas Cook (www.thomascook.com)
- An end-product manufacturer such as Vauxhall (www.vauxhall.co.uk)
- Consumer site, Yahoo! (www.yahoo.com)
- Online retailer such as Amazon (www.amazon.com).

Answers to activities can be found at www.pearsoned.co.uk/chaffey

Supply chain management

When distinguishing between buy-side and sell-side e-commerce we are looking at different aspects of managing an organization's supply chain. Supply chain management (SCM) is the coordination of all supply activities of an organization from its suppliers and delivery of products to its customers. The opportunities for using e-commerce to streamline and restructure the supply chain are described in more detail in *Chapter 6*. The value chain is a related concept that describes the different value-adding activities that connect a company's supply side with its demand side. We can identify an *internal* value chain within the boundaries of an organization and an *external* value chain where these activities are performed by partners. Note that in the era of e-business a company will manage many interrelated value chains, so in *Chapter 6* we also consider the concept of a value network.

Supply chain management (SCM)
The coordination of all supply activities of an organization from its suppliers and partners to its customers.

Value chain
A model for analysis of how supply chain activities can add value to products and services delivered to the customer.

Value network
The links between an organization and its strategic and non-strategic partners that form its external value chain.

Business or consumer models of e-commerce transactions

It is now commonplace to describe e-commerce transactions between an organization and its stakeholders according to whether they are with consumers (business-to-consumer – B2C) or other businesses (business-to-business – B2B).

Figure 1.2 gives examples of different companies operating in the business-to-consumer (B2C) and business-to-business (B2B) spheres.

Often companies such as BP or Dell Computer will have products that appeal to both consumers and businesses, so will have different parts of their site to appeal to these audiences. *Figure 1.2* also presents two additional types of transaction, those where consumers transact directly with other consumers (C2C) and where they initiate trading with companies (C2B). Note that the C2C and C2B monikers are less widely used (e.g. *Economist*, 2000), but they do highlight significant differences between Internet-based commerce and earlier forms of commerce. Consumer-to-consumer interactions (also known as peer-to-peer or person-to-person (P2P) were relatively rare, but are now very common in the form of the community components such as discussion groups or forums on B2C or B2B sites. Indeed, P2P transactions are

Business-to-consumer (B2C)
Commercial transactions between an organization and consumers.

Business-to-business (B2B)
Commercial transactions between an organization and other organizations (interorganizational marketing).

To: Consumer of content/service ↓ / From: Supplier of content/service →	*Consumer or citizen*	*Business (organization)*	*Government*
Consumer or citizen	**Consumer-to-Consumer (C2C)** • eBay • Peer-to-Peer (Skype) • Blogs and communities • Product recommendations • Social networks: MySpace, Bebo	**Business-to-Consumer (B2C)** • Transactional: Amazon • Relationship-building: BP • Brand-building: Unilever • Media owner – News Corp • Comparison intermediary: Kelkoo, Pricerunner	**Government-to-Consumer (G2C)** • National government transactional: Tax – inland revenue • National government information • Local government services
Business (organization)	**Consumer-to-Business (C2B)** • Priceline • Consumer-feedback, communities or campaigns	**Business-to-Business (B2B)** • Transactional: Euroffice • Relationship-building: BP • Media Owned: Emap business publications • B2B marketplaces: EC21	**Government-to-Business (G2B)** • Government services and transactions: tax • Legal regulations
Government	**Consumer-to-Government (C2G)** • Feedback to government through pressure group or individual sites	**Business-to-Government (B2G)** • Feedback to government businesses and non-governmental organizations	**Government-to-Government (G2G)** • Inter-government services • Exchange of information

Figure 1.2 Summary and examples of transaction alternatives between businesses, consumers and governmental organizations

Consumer-to-consumer (C2C)
Informational or financial transactions between consumers, but usually mediated through a business site.

Consumer-to-business (C2B)
Consumers approach the business with an offer.

Figure 1.3 Dubit C2C site for a youth audience (www.dubit.co.uk)

the main basis for some online business models for e-businesses such as Betfair (see *Mini Case Study 1.1*) and eBay (www.ebay.com, see Case Study 1.2) which are still run on a business basis, and some blogs which are not run by companies, but by individuals. Another example of a C2C site, shown in *Figure 1.3*, is the youth social network Dubit (www.dubit.co.uk) which is also used by FMCG brands to research youth market trends and engage opinion-formers. Hoffman and Novak (1996) suggest that C2C interactions are a key characteristic of the Internet that is important for companies to take into account. Finally, the diagram also includes government and public services organizations which deliver online or e-government services. As well as the models shown in *Figure 1.3*, it has also been suggested that employees should be considered as a separate type of consumer through the use of intranets, which are referred to as employee-to-employee or E2E.

Social network
A site-facilitating exchange of text, audio or visual content.

Mini Case Study 1.1 Betfair profits with C2C online gambling service

Online gaming has become incredibly popular with eSuperbrands (2005) reporting that there are over 2,400 online gaming and gambling sites worldwide, generating over £12 billion in profit.

Betfair has introduced a novel form of betting which replaces the typical role of the bookmaker such as Ladbrokes or William Hill who provide fixed odds and take their own risk on the outcome. With Betfair, all bets placed are with other Betfair customers rather than with Betfair which has no risks on the outcome. As with all forms of gambling, there is a risk of corruption 'throwing the bet'; to reduce this risk Betfair has a transparent approach where evidence of corruption may be shared with the governing body of a sport.

Through providing an online service, there are additional aspects of its proposition:

- You can either place bets conventionally or request your own odds.
- You can choose the odds you want to play at.
- You can bet whilst the game is in play.

Betfair's revenue model

Betfair charges a commission (typically 5%) on each player's net winnings on a market. If a player loses, there is no commission. There is a discount on commission, the more bets you place, to encourage and reward regular punters.

Betfair's growth

This outline history of Betfair shows how it has extended its product range and partnerships to support its growth:

2000 – The Sporting Exchange Ltd launches Betfair.com from Russell Square, London.
2001 – Betfair matches £1 million in seven days for the first time.
2002 – Betfair announces a merger with competitor Flutter and sponsorship of Fulham Football Club.
2003 – Betfair launches sites in German, Danish, Greek, Italian, Swedish, Norwegian, Finnish and Chinese.
2004 – Betfair launches Betfair poker, which today has 60,000 registered players. Betfair signs joint venture with Australia's Publishing and Broadcasting Limited.
2005 – Betfair sponsors the Channel 4 Ashes Cricket coverage and records the highest-ever single market turnover, matching £36 million on the Fifth Ashes Test Match alone! Betfair signs exclusive deal with Yahoo! UK and Ireland to launch a simplified betting exchange as well as a co-branded betting exchange.
2006 – Tens of millions of pounds were matched between punters during the 2006 World Cup. Betfair reported that for the year ending 30 April 2005, it had 650 employees and an annual turnover in excess of £100 million with operating profit of £22 million. International revenues are growing most rapidly and contributed 23 per cent of exchange revenues compared with 18 per cent last year. Principal regions include Australia, south-east Asia, continental Europe and the Nordic countries.

Source: eSuperbrands (2005) and corporate site (www.betfaircorporate.com)

E-government defined

E-government
The application of e-commerce technologies to government and public services for citizens and businesses.

E-government refers to the application of e-commerce technologies to government and public services. In the same way that e-business can be understood as transactions with customers (citizens), suppliers and internal communications, e-government covers a similar range of applications:

- *Citizens* – facilities for dissemination of information and use of online services at local and national levels. For example, at a local level you can find out when refuse is collected and at national level it is possible to fill in tax returns.
- *Suppliers* – government departments have a vast network of suppliers. The potential benefits (and pitfalls) of electronic supply chain management and e-procurement described in *Chapters 6* and *7* apply are equally valid for government.
- *Internal communications* – this includes information collection and dissemination and e-mail and workflow systems for improving efficiency within government departments.

E-government is now viewed as important within government in many countries. The European Union has set up 'i2010' (*European Information society in 2010*) whose aims include

> *providing an integrated approach to information society and audio-visual policies in the EU, covering regulation, research, and deployment and promoting cultural diversity.* (eEurope, 2005)

E-business defined

Electronic business (e-business)
All electronically mediated information exchanges, both within an organization and with external stakeholders supporting the range of business processes.

Given that *Figure 1.1* depicts different types of e-commerce, what then is e-business? Let's start from the definition by IBM (www.ibm.com/e-business), which was one of the first suppliers to use the term in 1997 to promote its services:

> *e-business (e'biz'nis) – the transformation of key business processes through the use of Internet technologies.*

Today, IBM calls the e-business services it provides for its clients 'on-demand' web services, as explained in *Chapter 3*.

You will find that the term 'e-business' is used in two main ways within organizations. The first is as a concept which can be applied to strategy and operations. For example, *'our organization needs an improved e-business strategy (or e-business technology)'*. Secondly, 'e-business' is used as an adjective to describe businesses that mainly operate online, i.e. they have no physical presence on the high streets and seek to minimize customer service and support through enabling 'web self-service', i.e. customers serve themselves before, during and after sales. In the dot-com era e-businesses used to be known as 'pure-plays'. Amazon (www.amazon.com) and eBay (www.ebay.com, *Case Study 1.3*) are the world's two biggest e-businesses.

Information and communication technology (ICT or IT)
The software applications, computer hardware and networks used to create e-business systems.

In an international benchmarking study analysing the adoption of e-business in SMEs the Department of Trade and Industry emphasizes the application of technology (information and communications technologies (ICTs)) in the full range of business processes, but also emphasizes how it involves innovation. DTI (2000) describes e-business as follows:

> *when a business has fully integrated information and communications technologies (ICTs) into its operations, potentially redesigning its business processes around ICT or completely reinventing its business model . . . e-business, is understood to be the integration of all these activities with the internal processes of a business through ICT.* (DTI, 2000)

Referring back to *Figure 1.1*, the key business processes referred to in the IBM and DTI definitions are the organizational processes or units in the centre of the figure. They include research and development, marketing, manufacturing and inbound and outbound logistics. The buy-side e-commerce transactions with suppliers and the sell-side e-commerce transactions with customers can also be considered to be key business processes.

Debate 1.1

How new is the e-business concept?

'E-business is just a new label – there is no distinction between the role of e-business and traditional information systems management.'

Figure 1.4 presents some alternative viewpoints of the relationship between e-business and e-commerce. In *Figure 1.4(a)* there is a relatively small overlap between e-commerce and e-business. From *Figure 1.1* we can reject *Figure 1.4(a)* since the overlap between buy-side and sell-side e-commerce is significant. *Figure 1.4(b)* seems to be more realistic, and indeed many commentators seem to consider e-business and e-commerce to be synonymous. It can be argued, however, that *Figure 1.4(c)* is most realistic since e-commerce does not refer to many of the transactions *within* a business, such as processing a purchasing order, that are part of e-business.

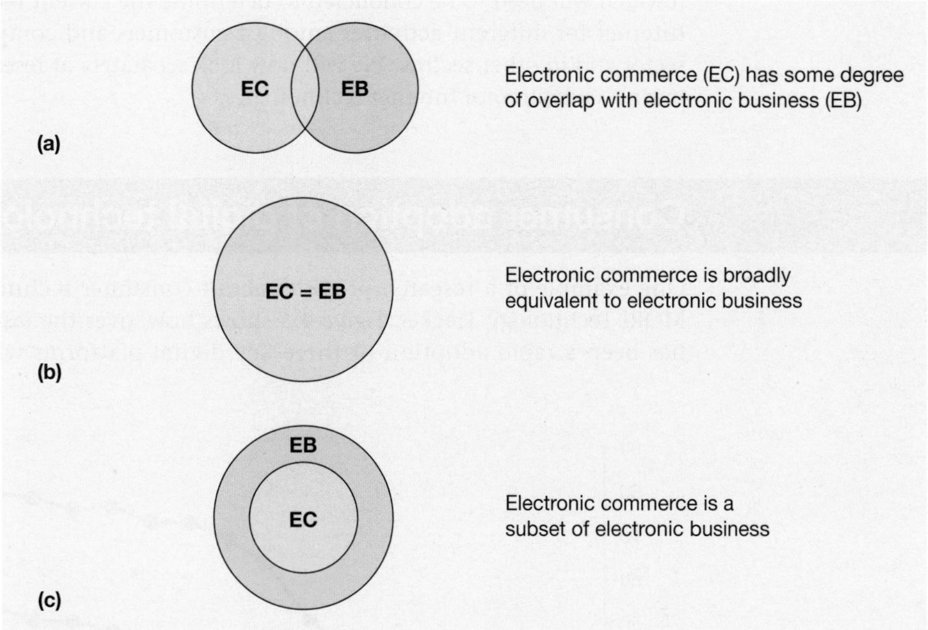

Figure 1.4 **Three definitions of the relationship between e-commerce and e-business**

So e-commerce can best be conceived of as a subset of e-business and this is the perspective we will use in this book. Since the interpretation in *Figure 1.4(b)* is equally valid, what is important within any given company is that managers involved with the implementation of e-commerce/e-business are agreed on the scope of what they are trying to achieve!

In *Chapter 8* we go on to consider how e-marketing, a concept now used by many marketing professionals, relates to the concepts of e-business and e-commerce.

Intranet
A private network within a single company using Internet standards to enable employees to share information using e-mail and web publishing.

Intranets and extranets

The majority of Internet services are available to any business or consumer that has access to the Internet. However, many e-business applications that access sensitive company information require access to be limited to qualified individuals or partners. If information is restricted to employees inside an organization, this is an intranet. If

Extranet
Formed by extending an intranet beyond a company to customers, suppliers and collaborators.

access is extended to some others, but not everyone beyond the organization, this is an **extranet**. Whenever you log on to an Internet service such as that for an e-retailer or online news site, this is effectively an extranet arrangement, although the term is most often used to mean a business-to-business application such as the Shell SIMON capability described in *Case Study 6.1* where certain customers or suppliers are given shared access. We will look at examples of intranets and extranets in *Chapter 3*.

How significant are e-commerce and e-business?

As managers, we need to assess the impact of e-commerce and e-business on our marketplace and organizations. How should we respond? How much do we need to invest? What are our priorities and how quickly do we need to act? Answering these questions is an essential part of formulating an e-business and e-marketing strategy and is considered in more detail in *Part 2*. To answer these questions marketing research will need to be conducted to determine the current levels of adoption of the Internet for different activities amongst customers and competitors in our market sector and in other sectors. We will now look separately at research on consumer and business adoption of Internet technologies.

Consumer adoption of digital technologies

One example of a research provider about consumer technology adoption is the MORI Technology Tracker. *Figure 1.5* shows how, over the last 10 years or so, there has been a rapid adoption of three key digital platforms which enable access to

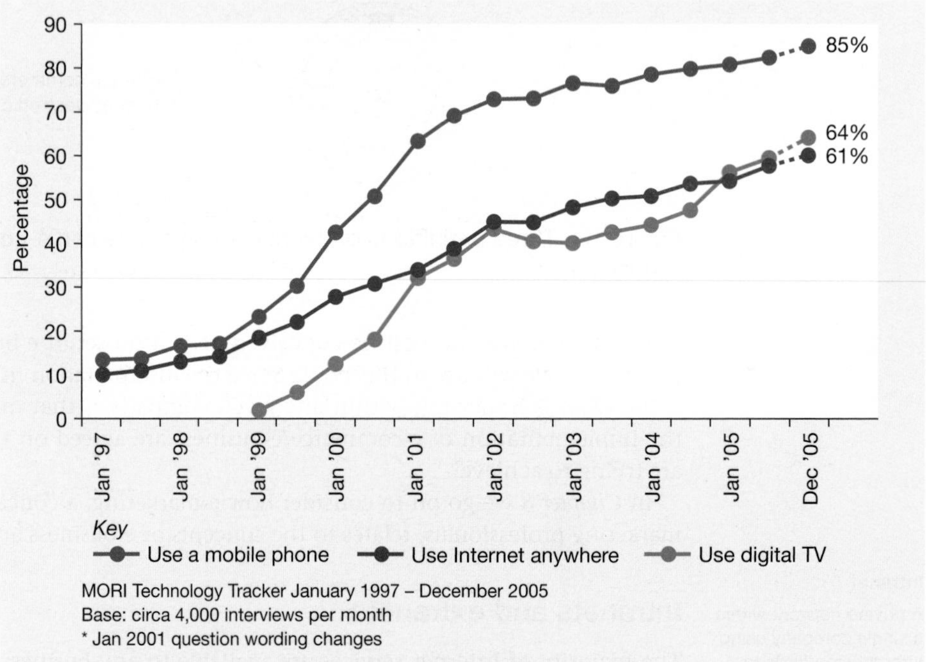

Figure 1.5 UK rate of adoption of different digital media
Source: MORI Technology Tracker, January 2006. See www.mori.com/technology/techtracker.shtml for latest details

e-commerce services. We will explain the different access technologies in more depth in *Chapter 3*.

Since figures published in books date, I encourage you to complete *Activity 1.4* which illustrates some other sources of information for consumer adoption in different countries.

Activity 1.4 E-commerce adoption by consumers and businesses

Visit the w.w.w.

Purpose

To examine estimates of the current and future size of e-commerce trade and critically review the validity of these estimates.

Activity

Using a search engine, or the recommended resources below, research consumer and business demand for online services.

(a) ClickZ Stats (www.clickz.com/stats/) is an aggregator site that compiles estimates from different industry analysts of e-commerce activity in different sectors and countries.

(b) Europa Eurostat (http://europa.eu.int/comm/eurostat) aggregates research about e-commerce adoption completed by the European Union. Data are in the 'Industry, trade and services', 'Information Society Initiative' category.

1 Consumer demand

(a) Summarize the demand for access to the Internet in your country in millions of users and use historical data to show how this has varied through time. How does access vary between home and work?

(b) What are the current levels and future projections for consumer demand for online retail and e-government services?

2 Business demand

(a) Summarize the business demand for access to the Internet in your country as a proportion of all business and calculate the annual percentage growth and show how this has varied between years.

(b) What are the future projections for total B2B demand?

Answers to activities can be found at www.pearsoned.co.uk/chaffey

Drivers of consumer Internet adoption

Table 1.2 gives an indication of the main types of activities the Internet is used for, which suggests what drives consumer Internet adoption. The popularity of e-mail use and general browsing show that socializing and entertainment are common online activities. From a commercial perspective, you can see from the table that using the Internet to inform buying decisions is a common activity – almost twice as common as actually purchasing online. This again shows the importance to consumers and the businesses they interact with of non-commercial transactions. Online purchase transactions are more common amongst the younger age groups, suggesting a barrier to online purchase in the older age groups.

Online value proposition (OVP)
A statement of the benefits of online services reinforces the core proposition and differentiates from an organization's offline offering and those of competitors.

We will see in *Chapter 4* on strategy development for e-business how it is important that companies offering e-commerce services create a clear online value proposition (OVP) to encourage customers to use online services. Typical benefits of online services are summarized by the 'Six Cs', a simple mnemonic to show different types of customer value:

1 *Content* – In the mid-1990s it was often said that 'content is king'. Well, relevant rich content is still king. This means more detailed, in-depth information to

Table 1.2 Internet usage activities in the UK, 2003/04 (percentages) – adults who have used the Internet in the last three months

	16–34	*35–54*	*55 and over*	*All adults*
Using e-mail	83	84	85	84
Searching for information about goods or services	80	84	74	80
Searching for information about travel and accommodation	63	74	70	69
General browsing or surfing	76	66	49	67
Buying goods, tickets or services	51	52	42	50
Internet banking	34	39	33	36
Activities related specifically to employment	39	37	17	35
Reading or downloading online news	37	34	25	34
Activities related to an education course	38	23	11	28
Playing or downloading music	37	18	12	25
Other educational activities	26	26	18	25
Downloading other software	27	22	18	23
Listening to web radios	20	13	9	15
Other financial services	7	9	9	8

Source: *Omnibus Survey*, Office for National Statistics, in ONS (2005), Table 13.12, p. 179 www.statistics.gov.uk/downloads/theme_social/Social_Trends35/Social_Trends_ 35_Ch13.pdf

support the buying process for transactional or relationship-building sites or branded experiences to encourage product usage for FMCG brands.

2 *Customization* – In this case mass customization of content, whether received as web site pages such as '*Amazon recommends*' or e-mail alerts, and commonly known as 'personalization'.

3 *Community* – The Internet liberates consumers to discuss anything they wish through forums, chat-rooms and blog comments. We will explore these techniques more in *Chapters 2* and *3*.

4 *Convenience* – This is the ability to select, purchase and in some cases use products from your desktop at any time: the classic 24 × 7 × 365 availability of a service. Online usage of products is, of course, restricted to digital products such as music or other data services. Amazon has advertised offline using creative showing a Christmas shopper battling against a gale-swept street clutching several bags to reinforce the convenience message.

5 *Choice* – The web gives a wider choice of products and suppliers than via conventional distribution channels. The success of online intermediaries such as Kelkoo (www.kelkoo.com) and Screentrade (www.screentrade.com) is evidence of this. Similarly, Tesco.com provides Tesco with a platform to give consumers a wider choice of products (financial, travel, white goods) with more detailed information than are physically available in-store.

6 *Cost reduction* – The Internet is widely perceived as a relatively low-cost place of purchase. Often customers expect to get a good deal online as they realize that online traders have a lower cost-base as they have lower staff and distribution costs than a retailer that runs a network of high-street stores. A simple price differential is a key approach to encouraging usage of online services. In the late 1990s, low-cost airline easyJet encouraged the limited change behaviour required from phone booking to online booking by offering a £2.50 discount on online flight bookings.

Note that the 7 Cs of Rayport and Jaworski (2003) provide a similar framework of Context, Content, Community, Customization, Communication, Connection and Commerce.

Barriers to consumer Internet adoption

An indication of some of the barriers to using the Internet, in particular for consumer purchases, is clear from a survey (Booz Allen Hamilton, 2002) of perceptions in different countries. It noted that consumer barriers to adoption of the Internet included:

- No perceived benefit
- Lack of trust
- Security problems
- Lack of skills
- Cost.

These factors combine to mean that there is a significant group in each national population of around a third of the adult population that does not envisage ever using the Internet. Clearly, the lack of demand for Internet services from this group needs to be taken into account when forecasting future demand. It is not sufficient to simply extrapolate past rates of Internet adoption growth, since in many developed countries it appears that penetration within households is reaching a plateau as saturation of services amongst those who require them is reached. Taking the UK as an example of possible saturation of fixed PC-based Internet access, National Statistics (2005) reports that in the UK just under one third (32 per cent) of adults had never used the Internet as of May 2005. Of those who had not used the Internet, 43 per cent stated that they did not want to use, or had no need for, or no interest, in the Internet; 38 per cent had no Internet connection; and 33 per cent felt they lacked knowledge or the confidence to use it. These adults were also asked which of four statements best described what they thought about using the Internet. Over half (55 per cent) of non-users chose the statement '*I have not really considered using the Internet before and I am not likely to in the future.*' This core group of Internet non-users represented 17 per cent of all adults in the UK.

More detail on the levels of adoption by consumers for different types of activities using these technologies are presented at the start of *Chapter 4*.

Business adoption of digital technologies for e-commerce and e-business

In this section we look at the drivers encouraging and barriers restricting e-commerce adoption from the organization's perspective. You will see that the levels of adoption vary markedly according to business size.

Drivers of business Internet adoption

Business adoption of e-commerce and e-business is driven by benefits to different parts of their organization. First and foremost, they are concerned how the benefits of e-business will impact on profitability. The two main ways in which this can be achieved are:

1. Potential for increased revenue arising from increased reach to a larger customer base and encouraging loyalty and repeat purchases among existing customers.
2. Cost reduction achieved through delivering services electronically. Reductions include staff costs, transport costs and costs of materials such as paper.

An international study of companies in the UK, the Republic of Ireland, France, Germany, Italy, Sweden, Australia, the USA, Canada and Japan sought to evaluate some of the reasons why companies adopt e-commerce (DTI, 2002). Although the DTI surveys are now dated, the responses still provide a useful insight to the issues that many small and medium businesses discuss today. The different drivers were rated as shown in *Figure 1.6*.

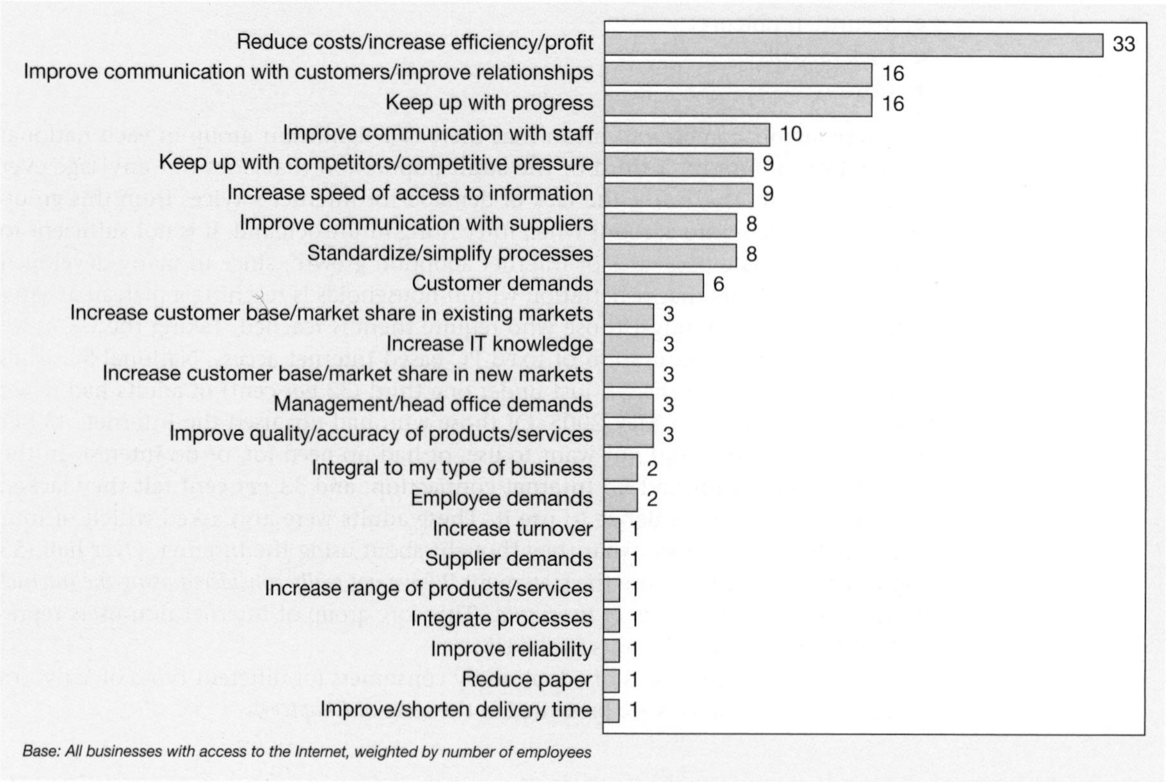

Figure 1.6 Attitudes to business benefits of online technologies
Source: DTI (2002)

The 2000 survey (DTI, 2000) identified two different types of drivers as follows:

Cost/efficiency drivers

1 Increasing speed with which supplies can be obtained
2 Increasing speed with which goods can be dispatched
3 Reduced sales and purchasing costs
4 Reduced operating costs.

Competitiveness drivers

5 Customer demand
6 Improving the range and quality of services offered
7 Avoid losing market share to businesses already using e-commerce.

This survey suggested that the cost/efficiency drivers and competitiveness drivers are of similar importance. The survey also reports on scores for non-adopters, and unsurprisingly all these benefits are rated significantly lower. In the 2001 survey (DTI, 2001), the main difference between adopters and non-adopters was in their perception of using the Internet as a communications tool. Adopters rated the Internet significantly better for communication both with the workforce and with customers.

Table 1.3 Summary of factors most important in encouraging Internet adoption amongst e-retailers

Factor influencing adoption	*A*	*B*	*C*
1 Internet target segment	3	2	1
2 Internet strategy	1	1	6
3 Internet marketplace	4	5	2
4 Infrastructure and development capability	2	3	5
5 Internet communications	5	6	4
6 Cost of Internet trading	8	9	10
7 Internet cost opportunity	6	8	7
8 Market development opportunity	7	4	3
9 Concerns	9	10	9
10 Consumer preferences	10	7	8

A = Internet adoption (static web site), B = active web site, C = online sales (transactional site)

Based on a compilation from separate tables in Doherty *et al.* (2003)

Brochureware

Brochureware describes a web site in which a company has migrated its existing paper-based promotional literature on to the Internet without recognizing the differences required by this medium.

An example of an analysis performed to identify the barriers and drivers for adoption of Internet technologies for one market is that from Doherty *et al.* (2003). These authors researched the drivers and barriers to retailers' adoption to determine the most important factors. *Table 1.3* summarizes the ranking in importance for different degrees of Internet adoption from static **brochureware**, through an active web site containing product information (B) to a transactional site where items can be purchased (C). You can see that the two most important factors which correlate with adoption are 'Internet target segment', i.e. customers in their market are typically adopters of the Internet, and 'Internet strategy', i.e. a defined Internet strategy is in place. This suggests, as would be expected, that companies that do not have a coherent Internet or e-business strategy are less likely to use higher levels of Internet

Table 1.4 Tangible and intangible benefits from e-commerce and e-business

Tangible benefits	*Intangible benefits*
• Increased sales from new sales leads giving rise to increased revenue from: – new customers, new markets – existing customers (repeat-selling) – existing customers (cross-selling). • Marketing cost reductions from: – reduced time in customer service – online sales – reduced printing and distribution costs of marketing communications. • Supply-chain cost reductions from: – reduced levels of inventory – increased competition from suppliers – shorter cycle time in ordering. • Administrative cost reductions from more efficient routine business processes such as recruitment, invoice payment and holiday authorization.	• Corporate image communication • Enhancement of brand • More rapid, more responsive marketing communications including PR • Faster product development lifecycle enabling faster response to market needs • Improved customer service • Learning for the future • Meeting customer expectations to have a web site • Identifying new partners, supporting existing partners better • Better management of marketing information and customer information • Feedback from customers on products

services. Many larger organizations that have responded to the challenge of e-business have created a separate e-commerce plan and separate resources to implement it. This book covers what needs to go into such a plan and the issues to consider when implementing it.

When reviewing potential benefits, it is useful to identify both tangible benefits (for which monetary savings or revenues can be identified) and intangible benefits (for which it is more difficult to calculate cost savings). The types of potential benefits are summarized in *Table 1.4* (page 21).

Now read *Case Study 1.1* which illustrates the benefits of setting up an online operation for a small or medium enterprise (SME). It also highlights some of the challenges of managing an online business and highlights the need for continued investment to refine online services and the marketing needed to attract visitors to the web site.

Case Study 1.1 North West Supplies extends its reach online

North West Supplies (*Figure 1.7*) was launched as a business in March 1999 when Andrew Camwell, a member of the RAF Volunteer Reserve at the time, spotted a gap in the UK market for mail-order supplies of military garments to people active in the Volunteer Reserve and the Air Cadet Force. Andrew, his wife Carys, and her sister Elaine Hughes, started running a mail order business out of shop premises in the village of Cemaes Bay.

The Web store at www.northwestsupplies.co.uk has been on-line since November 2002. As it can take several months for a Web site to be indexed by search engines, NWS used pay per click advertising (PPC – see *Chapter 9*) as a method of very quickly increasing the Web site's presence in the major search engines. This marketing method proved successful. The directors were pleasantly surprised as they had previously been somewhat dubious about the prospect of the Internet generating sales in their sector. Within six months of running the Web site, the company had increased turnover by £20,000, but further advances would incur a high advertising cost. Following an eCommerce Review by Opportunity Wales, the company decided to tackle the issues by implementing search engine optimization (SEO – see *Chapter 9*) and a site re-design which included:

Figure 1.7 **North West Supplies Ltd site (www.northwestsupplies.co.uk)**

Source: Opportunity Wales

- *Improved graphic design* – this was to be changed to a more professional and up-to-date look.
- *Best, featured and latest products* – the introduction of a dynamic front page to entice customers to re-visit the site on a regular basis. The contents of this page would feature the best sellers, and latest or featured products.
- *Reviews and ratings* – to provide confidence to consumers and allow some kind of interaction with them, this would allow users to review products they have purchased and give them a star rating.
- *Cross-selling* – when customers view a product there may be other products or categories that may be of interest or complementary, hence there was a proposal to allow staff to link products and categories so that these would be displayed.
- *Segmentation* – the site would be split into two sections emphasizing the segmentation of product lines into military wear and outdoor wear sectors, thus being less confusing, and easier to use for the respective users (see front page screenshot under 'Best, featured and latest products').
- *Navigation by sub-categories* – as the product range had expanded, the additional pages created in each category made it harder for customers to find specific items or made them have to browse many pages before finding a suitable product. The introduction of sub-categories would provide a clear link to the areas of interest and contain fewer pages to browse, thus helping the customer to make a choice more easily and more quickly. A new search tool and order tracking were also seen as important parts of the online customer experience (*Chapter 8*).

Benefits

The owners describe the benefits of the improvements to the site as follows:

- *Increased Direct Sales – 'The new launch increased sales and appealed to a broader audience – young and old'*. The annual turnover of the business has increased from £250,000 to £350,000 and this is mainly attributable to the new Web site. The high-profile launch aimed at existing customers, the greater visibility in search engines, and the greater usability of the site have all contributed to this.
- *Improved Promotion of the Whole Range of Stock – 'We started selling stuff that we hadn't sold before'* – The changes in navigation, particularly division into two market segments (military and outdoors) and greater use of sub-categories, meant that products were easier to find and hence easier to buy, leading to increased sales of products that had previously been slow sellers.
- *New Customers – 'We now send more items abroad'* – The better performance of the site in search engines has led to an increase in orders from new customers and from abroad. The company now has regular sales to Canada, Australia, New Zealand and various European states. 60% of orders are from new customers – not bad for a business that initially set up on the premise of a niche market for UK based cadet forces.
- *Adding Value to the Brand – 'New corporate clients could look at our Web site and see we weren't fly-by-night and that we meant business'*. Improvements to the design have raised confidence levels in visitors and this has led to increased sales. But perhaps more significantly, the professional image of the site was a good boost to confidence for potential business partners in the emerging business-to-business division that started to trade as North Star Contracts.

Question

Discuss the new opportunities and risks that need to be managed by North West Supplies with the increased importance of its online channel to market.

Barriers to e-business and e-commerce adoption

While it can be seen that there are many tangible and intangible benefits from developing e-commerce and e-business services, there have been variable levels of uptake in different countries and within different types of business. Look at *Figure 1.8*. This shows that across Europe, although the vast majority of businesses have access to the Internet they are not using it for particular e-business applications. Around 40% of small and medium enterprises (SMEs) do not have a web site and the majority do not use intranets, extranets, online purchasing or e-government services. This shows that over 15 years after the first adoption of the World Wide Web, there are still great opportunities for further use of e-business services. By the same token, it suggests there are considerable barriers to using some e-business services and it is important to understand the reasons behind this.

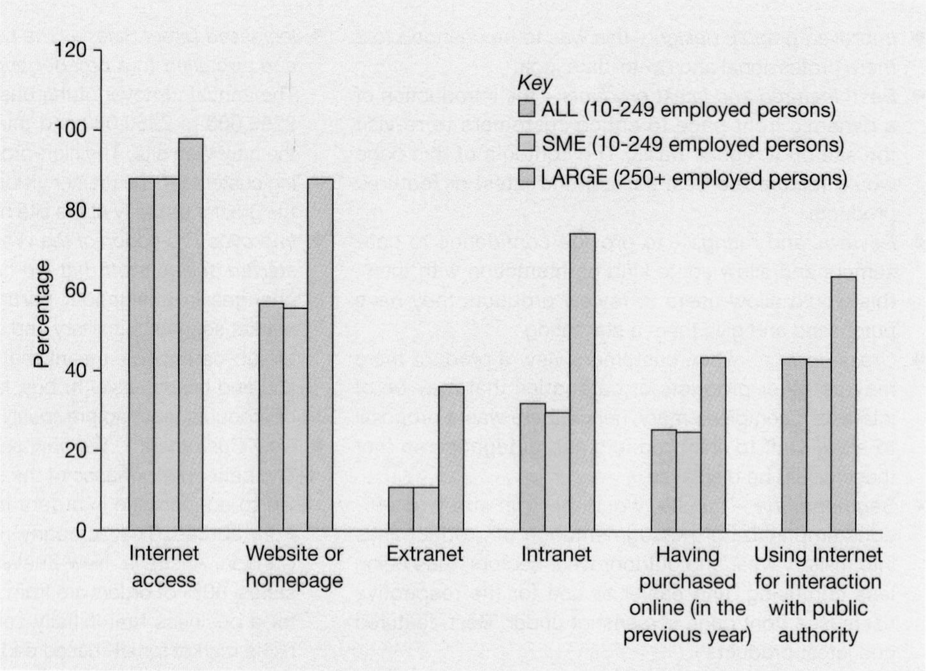

Figure 1.8 Adoption of Internet and e-business services across Europe

Source: Eurostat, Community Survey on ICT usage in enterprises, eEurope (2005) Information Society Benchmarking Report, © European Communities 2005, http://europa.eu.int/information_society

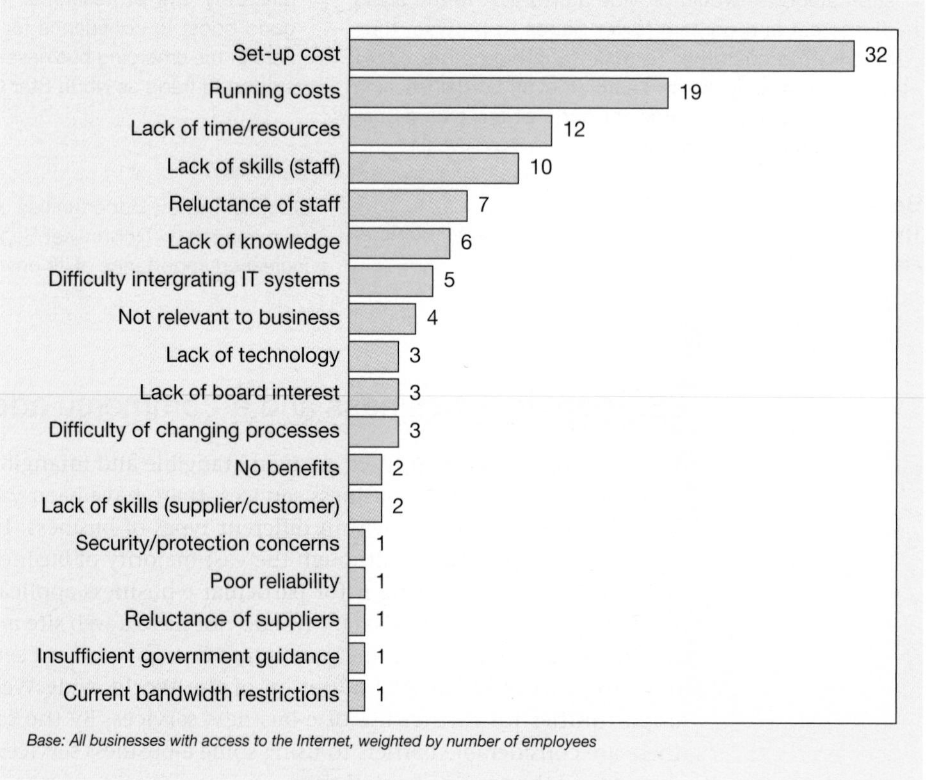

Figure 1.9 Barriers to development of online technologies

Source: DTI (2002)

Total cost of ownership (TCO)
TCO refers to the total cost for a company operating a computer system or other investment. This includes not only the purchase or leasing cost, but also the cost of all the services needed to maintain the system and support the end-user.

The DTI (2002) study also evaluated some of the barriers to B2B e-commerce (*Figure 1.9*). You can see that reasons of cost are the most important factors considered to be barriers to online adoption. This suggests the importance of managers assessing e-business to develop a cost–benefit analysis that considers both the initial investment costs and the ongoing costs that form the total cost of ownership (TCO) against the value created from the tangible and intangible benefits. The difficulties in implementation which we will review later in this book such as the lack of the right resources or difficulty in integrating systems are also indicated by the figure.

Debate 1.2

Limited SME adoption of e-business

'Adoption of e-business by established SMEs is generally less than that in larger businesses. This is principally a consequence of the negative attitude of managing directors and CEOs to the business benefits of information and communication technology.'

Introducing the B2B and B2C companies

The significance of e-commerce and e-business will vary between all businesses and organizations in terms of adoption by customers in their marketplace and the timing and amount of investment needed. In particular, as we have seen, adoption is likely to vary between businesses and consumers. For this reason it has become conventional to consider business-to-business (B2B) e-commerce and business-to-consumer (B2C) e-commerce separately.

Due to their differences, throughout this book we shall distinguish between B2B and B2C e-commerce. To prompt readers to think about the differences between e-commerce management decisions required for B2B and B2C e-commerce and to give a common theme through the book we shall also consider two typical companies. These generic companies will be referred to as 'The B2B Company', a medium-to-large company selling paints and chemicals used for coating products manufactured by other companies, and 'The B2C Company', a smaller company selling kitchenware to consumers. *Activity 1.5* introduces these companies as the basis for activities later in the book.

Activity 1.5 Introducing The B2B Company and The B2C Company

Purpose

To introduce the running case companies used for activities throughout the book. Key e-business issues faced by these companies are highlighted and related to the relevant section later in the book.

The B2B Company

The B2B Company is an international company employing 600 people worldwide, including 300 at its head office. Its annual turnover is approximately £100 million and it was established in 1955.

Products

There are two different types of products:

1 *Composites* – sold to other businesses to be incorporated in their products. For example, products are used in the mouldings and coatings for boats, trains, planes and cars. There are about 200 top customers who are responsible for the majority of revenue in this area.

→

These orders are usually delivered by tanker load, with some customers receiving several loads each week. There are about 800 smaller customers who purchase in quantities measured in drums. There are over 100 product variants of composites for different applications (see www.globalcomposites.com for market information).

2 *Speciality polymers* – the polymer technology is incorporated into graphic arts for use in paper and board applications (such as overprint varnishes on cereal packets and glossy magazines). There are about 10 key speciality polymer customers. These polymers are also ordered in bulk.

Table 1.5 Key e-business issues for The B2B Company

Key issue	*Description*	*Activities and details*
Reverse auctions	Should the company participate in B2B reverse auctions?	See *Case Study 2.1*
Using intermediary sites to promote products	Every country has a range of sites that can be used to connect a company to its market	*Activity 2.6*
Adoption of intranets and extranets	Techniques to use to overcome limited use of intranets and extranets by employees and third parties respectively	*Activity 3.3*
Assessing ISP performance	Ensuring a reliable quality of service for online customers in terms of site availability and download speed	*Activity 3.5*
Opportunities for using ASPs	Using application service providers to provide its e-business services	*Activity 3.7*
Global variation in Internet provision	International companies such as The B2B Company will need to assess demand for their online services in different countries	*Activity 4.3*
Internal analysis of e-business capabilities	Techniques such as SWOT and applications portfolio analysis	*Activity 5.2*
Assessing the significance of digital channels	As part of strategy, the potential for different types of online services must be carefully analysed	*Activity 5.3*
Supply chain management	What are the options for The B2B Company to restructure its links to its suppliers?	*Activity 6.1*
E-procurement	What are the arguments for using e-procurement? What are the typical problems? How can integration occur?	*Activities 7.1, 7.6*
Customer acquisition	What techniques can be used to gain new customers using new media?	*Activity 9.1*
Customer retention	Which techniques can be used to encourage repeat business using new media?	*Activity 9.4*
Process redesign	Techniques for redesigning processes and corresponding user interfaces are described in these activities	*Activities 11.2, 11.6*
Intranet content creation	Implementation and changeover issues for an intranet	*Activities 12.4, 12.5*

Distribution

Products are sold through independent distributors in over 90 countries worldwide. For example, in Europe, agents exist in Albania, Austria, Belarus, Belgium, Bulgaria, Croatia, the Czech Republic, Estonia, France, Germany, Greece, Hungary, Iceland, Italy, Latvia, Lithuania, Moldova, the Netherlands, Poland, Portugal, Romania, Russia, Scandinavia, Slovakia, Spain, Switzerland, Turkey, the UK and Ireland, and Ukraine. The company grew during the 1990s through joint ventures or acquisitions of manufacturing facilities in France, the Middle East, South Africa, the USA, Scandinavia and the Czech Republic.

Competitors

There are two major European competitors which have not adopted e-commerce and a single US competitor which recently introduced an e-commerce system.

Current web site

The current web site is informational, not transactional – orders cannot be placed online. However, questions about the company or its products can be entered into an online form that is sent to the company by e-mail. The web site content contains details of the company history and an overview of its products. More detailed technical data sheets are available for visitors who register their contact details such as name, role and company. These details can be used to contact potential customers by sales staff. Contact points in the different countries are available, but no localized content is available for the different regions.

Current information systems

The company currently use an ERP system specifically developed for their market to manage information on customers, orders, inventory and logistics. It is not currently used for procurement. The ERP system is managed from a central-server database with a separate software application used to access it by users. This requires a software application to be installed on each desktop. It also has EDI links to suppliers rather than Internet-based EDI links. This will need to be integrated with the e-commerce solution. Lotus Notes (Domino) is used to provide web access to the technical data sheets and other documents – it is used as a content management system for some web content. It is also used for competitive intelligence – sales reps file reports on customer visits and other marketplace changes.

Table 1.5 lists the main issues faced by The B2B Company and similar companies, together with activities that explore these issues further.

Enterprise resource planning (ERP) systems
Enterprise applications used to manage information about organizational resources such as raw materials, products, staff and customers as part of delivery of a product or service.

Electronic data interchange (EDI)
The exchange, using digital media, of structured business information, particularly for sales transactions such as purchase orders and invoices between buyers and sellers.

Example companies

The B2B Company is a fictitious company used for activities throughout this book. Similar companies that can be referred to to gain an idea of the company and its markets are: Dow Derakane (www.dow.com/derakane), Scott Bader (www.scottbader.com) and Owens Corning (www.owenscorning.com).

The B2C Company

The B2C Company is a small company that was established in 1984 and has 80 staff. Approximately half the staff are in production and the other half are divided between management, administration and retail. It manufactures kitchenware and sells these products and similar items from other manufacturers through its network of shops.

Products

The B2C Company manufactures and sells plastic kitchenware such as storage containers, plates, bags and kitchen implements.

Distribution

It opened its first shop on the trading estate where it manufactures its products and has since opened thirty other shops in towns within the country. It also sells its products through traditional outlets such as department stores, supermarkets and small specialist retailers. Finally, it has sold its products by mail order for about ten years. No products are currently sold abroad.

Competitors

The B2C Company has three major national competitors, two of which have adopted e-commerce, and a major European competitor which also has an e-commerce system.

Current web site

The web site is a transactional web site enabling online purchase of hundreds of items in categories such as Kitchenware, Kitchen Electrical and Food Storage. It is possible to browse for products, search by keyword and search by product code. Products are added to a shopping basket and then taken to an online checkout, using the metaphor of traditional shopping which has been widely adopted online. A map of stores around the country is available. Customer service is provided through a page detailing contact points and a customer support form.

Current information systems

Intershop (www.intershop.com) is used as the commerce management system for the company – it is used to modify the online product catalogue. Details for web-site customers

Table 1.6 Key e-business issues for The B2C Company

Key issue	*Description*	*Activities and details*
Representation on intermediary sites	B2C manufacturers and retailers must decide how to best use third-party sites to promote their products online	*Activity 2.3*
Infrastructure risk assessment	An introduction to the type of problem that may be encountered if the e-business systems are not adequately managed	*Activity 3.1*
Understanding enablers and barriers to consumer adoption	Through understanding these factors which affect usage of the Internet, the company can encourage usage	*Activity 4.2*
E-business strategies	What are the different strategies and how should they be selected?	*Activity 5.4*
Customer acquisition	What techniques can be used to gain new customers using new media?	*Activity 9.1*
Customer retention	Which techniques can be used to encourage repeat business using new media?	*Activity 9.4*
Delivering customer service	How can customer service be delivered online?	*Activity 9.5*
Managing change	Which changes to the organization's structure, processes and personnel may be required	*Activities 10.1, 10.2, 10.3, 10.4*
Risk management	Assessing the possible problems of e-business implementations, and devising solutions	*Activity 10.8*
Data structures	A simple example of the data structures used for an e-commerce site is provided	*Activity 11.3*
Content creation and review	The HTML coding used for creating a simple page is reviewed. The stages involved in content review are also covered	*Activities 12.2, 12.5*
Measuring e-business effectiveness	Which measures should be used to assess the effectiveness of e-business strategy and implementation?	*Activity 12.7*

are stored in a separate database from those for mail-order customers. Analysis of the customers for marketing purposes is difficult since it requires export of data to Excel for analysis and staff do not have the right level of skill for analysis. The site does not currently use a content management system, so changes made by the marketing department need to be sent to an external agency before being added to the site and this can be costly and time-consuming. The company uses Sage for its accounts together with specialist manufacturing software. No e-procurement system is used.

Table 1.6 lists the main issues faced by The B2C Company and similar companies, together with activities that explore these issues further.

Example companies

The B2C Company is a fictitious company used for activities throughout this book. Similar companies that can be referred to to gain an idea of the company and its markets are: Cooking.com (www.cooking.com), Lakeland Limited (www.lakelandlimited.com) and Tupperware (www.tupperware.com).

Questions

1 For each of the two companies, summarize the business benefits of e-commerce and e-business using the simple mnemonic of the 6 Cs (Bocij *et al.*, 2005), that is, cost reduction, new capability, communication, control, customer service and competitive advantage. You should mark each benefit as to whether it is an advantage arising from buy- or sell-side e-commerce or enhancement of e-business processes. Alternatively, you may wish to consider a not-for-profit organization such as a charity, local government or the health service which can be considered to be B2C.

2 Discuss the differences in benefits between the B2B and B2C organizations.

Answers to activities can be found at www.pearsoned.co.uk/chaffey

Management responses to e-commerce and e-business

A primary aim of this book is to consider the management issues when businesses look to take advantage of the opportunities afforded by e-commerce and e-business. How should an e-business strategy be developed? To what extent can we use existing business and IS strategy models? What are the main changes that need to be made to the organization as part of implementing the strategy? These issues are explored in more detail in *Part 2*. Before we can develop e-business strategy a foundation is needed. This is provided in *Part 1* of the book.

Part 1: Introduction

Part 1 describes the background to e-business as follows:

- *Chapter 1: Introduction to e-business and e-commerce*. Definition of the meaning and scope of e-business and e-commerce. Introduction to business use of the Internet – what are the benefits and barriers to adoption and how widely used is it?
- *Chapter 2: E-commerce fundamentals*. Introduction to new business models and marketplace structures enabled by electronic communications.
- *Chapter 3: E-business infrastructure*. Background on the hardware, software and telecommunications that need to be managed to achieve e-business.

- *Chapter 4: E-environment.* Describes the macro-environment of an organization that presents opportunities for and constraints on strategy and implementation.

Part 2: Strategy and applications

In *Part 2* of the book approaches to developing e-business strategy are covered by reviewing how e-business strategy and applications should be developed for the organization as a whole (*Chapter 5*) and with an emphasis on the buy-side (*Chapters 6* and *7*) and the sell-side (*Chapters 7* and *8*).

- *Chapter 5: E-business strategy.* Approaches to developing e-business strategy. Differences from traditional strategic approaches. Relation to IS strategy.
- *Chapter 6: Supply chain management.* A supply chain perspective on strategy with examples of how technology can be applied to increase supply chain and value chain efficiency.
- *Chapter 7: E-procurement.* Evaluation of the benefits of adopting e-procurement.
- *Chapter 8: E-marketing.* A sell-side e-commerce perspective to e-business reviewing differences in marketing required through digital media.
- *Chapter 9: Customer relationship management.* Using e-commerce as part of acquiring, retaining and extending the range of products sold to customers.

Here we introduce some of the strategy issues involved with e-business using the classic McKinsey 7S strategy instrument (Waterman *et al.*, 1980). This is summarized in diagrammatic form in *Figure 1.10* and in table form in *Table 1.7* to highlight some aspects that need to be managed when developing an e-business strategy and that are covered in this text (*Activity 1.6*).

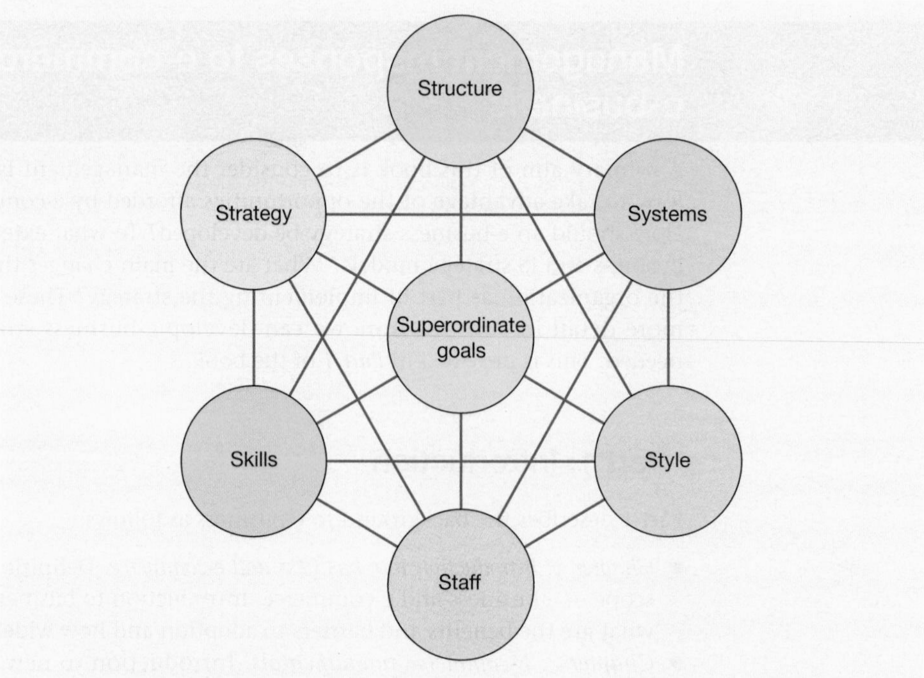

Figure 1.10 **The McKinsey 7S framework**

Source: Adapted from Waterman *et al.* (1980)

Table 1.7 The application to 7S strategic framework to e-business and e-commerce management

Element of 7S model	*Relevance to Internet marketing capability*	*Key issues*
Strategy	The contribution of e-business and e-commerce in influencing and supporting organizations' strategy	• Gaining appropriate budgets and demonstrating/delivering value and ROI (return on investment) from budgets. Annual planning approach • Techniques for using e-commerce to impact organization strategy • Techniques for aligning e-commerce strategy with organizational and marketing strategy
Structure	The modification of organizational structure to support e-business	• Integration of e-commerce/IT team with other management, marketing (corporate communications, brandmarketing, direct marketing) and operations staff • Use of cross-functional teams and steering groups • Insourcing vs outsourcing
Systems	The development of specific processes, procedures or information systems to support e-business	• Managing/sharing customer and supply chain information • Integration of the web into marketing campaign planning • Managing content quality for different audiences • Unified reporting of e-commerce effectiveness • In-house vs external best-of-breed vs external integrated technology solutions
Staff	The breakdown of staff in terms of their background, age and sex and characteristics such as IT vs marketing, use of contractors/ consultants	• Insourcing vs outsourcing • Achieving senior management buy-in/involvement with digital marketing • Staff recruitment and retention • Virtual working • Staff development and training
Style	Includes both the way in which key managers behave in achieving the organization's goals and the cultural style of the organization as a whole	• Relates to role of the e-business team in influencing strategy – is it dynamic and influential or conservative and looking for a voice?
Skills	Distinctive capabilities of key staff, but can be interpreted as specific skill-sets of team members	• Staff skills in specific areas: supplier selection, project management, content management, specific e-marketing approaches (search engine marketing, affiliate marketing, e-mail marketing, online advertising) and supply chain management
Superordinate goals	The guiding concepts of the organization which are also part of shared values and culture. The internal and external perception of these goals may vary	• Improving the perception of the importance and effectiveness of the digital marketing team amongst senior managers and staff it works with (marketing generalists and IT)

Activity 1.6 Applying the 7S framework to e-business initiatives

Visit the w.w.w.

Purpose

To illustrate some of the key strategy issues of implementing e-business.

Question

Take either the B2B or the B2C Company or an organization you are familiar with and consider organizational changes that may be required for each of the 7 Ss. Which factors do you feel are ignored by the 7 Ss?

Answers to activities can be found at www.pearsoned.co.uk/chaffey

Part 3: Implementation

E-business management is described in *Part 3* of the book where we examine practical management issues involved with creating and implementing e-business solutions.

- *Chapter 10*: *Change management*. How to manage the organizational, human and technology change required in the move to e-business.
- *Chapter 11*: *Analysis and design*. We discuss the main issues of analysis and design raised by e-commerce systems that need to be discussed by managers and solutions providers.
- *Chapter 12*: *Implementation and maintenance*. How should e-commerce systems be managed and monitored once they are live?

To complete this chapter, read *Case Study 1.2* for the background on the success factors which have helped build one of the world's biggest e-businesses.

Case Study 1.2 eBay – the world's largest e-business

This case summarizes the strategic approach used by eBay to take advantage of increased consumer adoption of the Internet. It summarizes their objectives, strategy and proposition and some of the risks that need management.

Context

It's hard to believe that one of the most celebrated dot-coms has now celebrated its tenth birthday. Pierre Omidyar, a 28-year-old French-born software engineer living in California coded the site while working for another company, eventually launching the site for business on Monday, 4 September 1995 with the more direct name 'Auction Web'. Legend reports that the site attracted no visitors in its first 24 hours. The site became eBay in 1997 and site activity is rather different today; peak traffic in 2004 was 890 million page views per day and 7.7 gigabits of outbound data traffic per second. At the end of 2005, if eBay was a country, it would have the 9th largest population with its 157 million eBayers.

Mission

eBay describes its purpose as to 'pioneer new communities around the world built on commerce, sustained by trust, and inspired by opportunity'.

At the time of writing eBay comprises three major businesses:

1. *The eBay Marketplace*. The mission for the core eBay business is to 'create the world's online marketplace'. eBay's SEC filing notes some of the success factors for this business for which eBay seeks to manage the functionality, safety, ease-of-use and reliability of the trading platform.
2. *PayPal*. The mission is to 'create the new global standard for online payments'. This online payments company was acquired in 2003.
3. *Skype Internet telephony*. This company was acquired in 2005.

This case focuses on the best-known of the three, the eBay Marketplace.

Revenue model

The vast majority of eBay's revenue is for the listing and commission on completed sales. For PayPal purchases an additional commission fee is charged. Margin on each transaction is phenomenal since once the infrastructure is built, incremental costs on each transaction are tiny – all eBay is doing is transmitting bits and bytes between buyers and sellers.

Advertising and other non-transaction net revenues represent a relatively small proportion of total net revenues and the strategy is that this should remain the case. Advertising and other net revenues totalled $94.3 million in 2004 (just 3% of net revenue).

Proposition

The eBay Marketplace is well known for its core service which enables sellers to list items for sale on an auction or fixed-price basis, giving buyers the opportunity to bid for and purchase items of interest.

Software tools are provided, particularly for frequent traders including Turbo Lister, Seller's Assistant, Selling Manager and Selling Manager Pro, which help automate the selling process, the Shipping Calculator, Reporting tools, etc. Today over sixty per cent of listings are facilitated by software, showing the value of automating posting for frequent trading.

Fraud is a significant risk factor for eBay. BBC (2005) reported that around 1 in 10,000 transactions within the

UK were fraudulent. 0.0001% is a small percentage, but scaling this up across the number of transactions, it is a significant volume.

eBay has developed 'Trust and Safety Programs' which are particularly important to reassure customers since online services are prone to fraud. For example, the eBay feedback forum can help establish credentials of sellers and buyers. There is also a Safe Harbor data protection method and a standard purchase protection system.

According to the SEC filing, eBay summarizes the core messages to define its proposition as follows:

For buyers:

- Selection
- Value
- Convenience
- Entertainment.

For sellers:

- Access to broad markets
- Efficient marketing and distribution costs
- Ability to maximize prices
- Opportunity to increase sales.

Competition

Although there are now few direct competitors of online auction services in many countries, there are many indirect competitors. SEC (2005) describes competing channels as including online and offline retailers, distributors, liquidators, import and export companies, auctioneers, catalogue and mail-order companies, classifieds, directories, search engines, products of search engines, virtually all online and offline commerce participants (consumer-to-consumer, business-to-consumer and business-to-business) and online and offline shopping channels and networks.

BBC (2005) reports that eBay is not complacent about competition. It has already pulled out of Japan due to competition from Yahoo! and within Asia and China is also facing tough competition from Yahoo! which has a portal with a broader range of services and is more likely to attract subscribers.

Before the advent of online auctions, competitors in the collectables space included antique shops, car boot sales and charity shops. Anecdotal evidence suggests that all of these are now suffering at the hands of eBay. Some have taken the attitude of 'if you can't beat 'em, join 'em'. Many smaller traders that previously ran antique or car boot sales are now eBayers. Even charities such as Oxfam now have an eBay service where they sell high-value items contributed by donors online. Other retailers such as Vodafone have used eBay as a means to distribute certain products within their range.

Objectives and strategy

The overall eBay aims are to increase the gross merchandise volume and net revenues from the eBay Marketplace. More detailed objectives are defined to achieve these aims, with strategies focusing on:

1. *Acquisition* – increasing the number of newly registered users on the eBay Marketplace.
2. *Activation* – increasing the number of registered users that become active bidders, buyers or sellers on the eBay Marketplace.
3. *Activity* – increasing the volume and value of transactions that are conducted by each active user on the eBay Marketplace.

The focus on each of these three areas will vary according to strategic priorities in particular local markets.

eBay marketplace growth is also driven by defining approaches to improving performance in these areas. First, category growth is achieved by increasing the number and size of categories within the marketplace, for example: Antiques, Art, Books and Business & Industrial. Second, formats for interaction. The traditional format is auction listings, but it has been refined now to include the 'Buy-It-Now' fixed-price format. Another format is the 'Dutch auction' format, where a seller can sell multiple identical items to the highest bidders. eBay Stores was developed to enable sellers with a wider range of products to showcase their products in a more traditional retail format. eBay say they are constantly exploring new formats, for example through the acquisition in 2004 of mobile.de in Germany and Marktplaats.nl in the Netherlands, as well as the investment in craigslist, the US-based classified ad format. Another acquisition is Rent.com, which enables expansion into the online housing and apartment rental category. Finally, marketplace growth is achieved through delivering specific sites localized for different geographies as follows. You can see there is still potential for greater localization, for example in parts of Scandinavia, Eastern Europe and Asia.

Localized eBay marketplaces:

Australia	India	South Korea
Austria	Ireland	Spain
Belgium	Italy	Sweden
Canada	Malaysia	Switzerland
China	The Netherlands	Taiwan
France	New Zealand	The United Kingdom
Germany	The Philippines	The United States
Hong Kong	Singapore	

In its SEC filing, success factors eBay believes are important to enable it to compete in its market include:

- ability to attract buyers and sellers;
- volume of transactions and price and selection of goods;
- customer service; and
- brand recognition.

It also notes that for its competitors, other factors it believes are important are:

- community cohesion, interaction and size;
- system reliability;

→

- reliability of delivery and payment;
- web site convenience and accessibility;
- level of service fees; and
- quality of search tools.

This implies that eBay believes it has optimized these factors, but its competitors still have opportunities for improving performance in these areas which will make the market more competitive.

Risk management

The SEC filing lists the risks and challenges of conducting business internationally as follows:

- regulatory requirements, including regulation of auctioneering, professional selling, distance selling, banking and money transmitting;
- legal uncertainty regarding liability for the listings and other content provided by users, including uncertainty as a result of less Internet-friendly legal systems, unique local laws, and lack of clear precedent or applicable law;
- difficulties in integrating with local payment providers, including banks, credit and debit card associations, and electronic fund transfer systems;

	Year ended 31 December (in thousands, except per share amounts)				
	2000	*2001*	*2002*	*2003*	*2004*
Consolidated statement of income data:					
Net revenues	$ 431,424	$ 748,821	$ 1,214,100	$ 2,165,096	$ 3,271,309
Cost of net revenues	95,453	134,816	213,876	416,058	614,415
Gross profit	335,971	614,005	1,000,224	1,749,038	2,656,894
Operating expenses:					
Sales and marketing	166,767	253,474	349,650	567,565	857,874
Product development	55,863	75,288	104,636	159,315	240,647
General and administrative	73,027	105,784	171,785	302,703	415,725
Patent litigation expense	—	—	—	29,965	—
Payroll tax on employee stock options	2,337	2,442	4,015	9,590	17,479
Amortization of acquired intangible assets	1,433	36,591	15,941	50,659	65,927
Merger-related costs	1,550	—	—	—	—
Total operating expenses	300,977	473,579	646,027	1,119,797	1,597,652
Income from operations	34,994	140,426	354,197	629,241	1,059,242
Interest and other income, net	46,337	41,613	49,209	37,803	77,867
Interest expenses	(3,374)	(2,851)	(1,492)	(4,314)	(8,879)
Impairment of certain equity investments	—	(16,245)	(3,781)	(1,230)	—
Income before cumulative effect of accounting change, income taxes and minority interests	77,957	162,943	398,133	661,500	1,128,230
Provision for income taxes	(32,725)	(80,009)	(145,946)	(206,738)	(343,885)
Minority interests	3,062	7,514	(2,296)	(7,578)	(6,122)
Income before cumulative effect of accounting change	48,294	90,448	249,891	447,184	778,223
Cumulative effect of accounting change, net of tax	—	—	—	(5,413)	—
Net income	$ 48,294	$ 90,448	$ 249,891	$ 441,771	$ 778,223

	Year ended 31 December (in millions)				
	2000	*2001*	*2002*	*2003*	*2004*
Supplemental operating data:					
US and international marketplace segments:					
Confirmed registered users	22.5	42.4	61.7	94.9	135.5
Active users	—	17.8	27.7	41.2	56.1
Number of non-stores listings	264.7	419.1	629.7	955.0	1,339.9
Number of stores listings	—	4.0	8.6	16.0	72.7
Gross merchandise volume	$ 5,422	$ 9,319	$ 14,868	$ 23,779	$ 34,168

- differing levels of retail distribution, shipping and communications infrastructures;
- different employee/employer relationships and the existence of workers' councils and labour unions;
- difficulties in staffing and managing foreign operations;
- longer payment cycles, different accounting practices, and greater problems in collecting accounts receivable;
- potentially adverse tax consequences, including local taxation of fees or of transactions on web sites;
- higher telecommunications and Internet service provider costs;
- strong local competitors;
- different and more stringent consumer protection, data protection and other laws;
- cultural ambivalence towards, or non-acceptance of, online trading;
- seasonal reductions in business activity;
- expenses associated with localizing products, including offering customers the ability to transact business in the local currency;
- laws and business practices that favour local competitors or prohibit foreign ownership of certain businesses;
- profit repatriation restrictions, foreign currency exchange restrictions, and exchange rate fluctuations;
- volatility in a specific country's or region's political or economic conditions; and
- differing intellectual property laws and taxation laws.

Results

eBay's community of confirmed registered users has grown from around 2 million at the end of 1998 to more than 94 million at the end of 2003 and to more than 135 million at 31 December 2004. It is also useful to identify active users who contribute revenue to the business as a buyer or seller. eBay had 56 million active users at the end of 2004, defined as any users who have bid, bought or listed an item during a prior 12-month period.

Financial results are presented in the table opposite.

Sources: BBC (2005), SEC (2005)

Question

Assess how the characteristics of the digital media and the Internet together with strategic decisions taken by its management team have supported eBay's continued growth.

Summary

1 Electronic commerce traditionally refers to electronically mediated buying and selling.

2 Sell-side e-commerce involves all electronic business transactions between an organization and its customers, while buy-side e-commerce involves transactions between an organization and its suppliers.

3 'Electronic business' is a broader term, referring to how technology can benefit all internal business processes and interactions with third parties. This includes buy-side and sell-side e-commerce and the internal value chain.

4 The monetary value of e-commerce for business-to-business (B2B) transactions greatly exceeds that for business-to-consumer transactions (B2C).

5 The main business drivers for introducing e-commerce and e-business are opportunities for increased revenues and reducing costs, but many other benefits can be identified that improve customer service and corporate image.

6 Consumer adoption of the Internet is limited by lack of imperative, cost of access and security fears. Business adoption tends to be restricted by perceptions of cost, making return on investment difficult to quantify.

7 Introducing new technology is not all that is required for success in introducing e-commerce and business. Clearly defined objectives, creating the right culture for change, mix of skills, partnerships and organizational structure are arguably more important.

Exercises

Answers to these exercises are available online at www.pearsoned.co.uk/chaffey

Self-assessment questions

1 Distinguish between e-commerce and e-business.

2 Explain what is meant by buy-side and sell-side e-commerce.

3 Describe the different services that can be offered to customers via a web presence.

4 Summarize the consumer and business adoption levels in your country. What seem to be the main barriers to adoption?

5 Outline the reasons why a business may wish to adopt e-commerce.

6 What are the main differences between business-to-business and business-to-consumer e-commerce?

7 Summarize the impact of the introduction of e-business on different aspects of an organization.

8 What is the relevance of intermediary sites such as Kelkoo (www.kelkoo.com) to the B2C company?

Essay and discussion questions

1 Discuss the following question with reference to how an organization should react to the Internet. *'Is the Internet a typhoon force, a ten times force, or is it a bit of wind? Or is it a force that fundamentally alters our business?'*. (Andy Grove, Chairman of Intel)

2 Suggest how a organization can evaluate the impact of the Internet on its business. Is it a passing fad or does it have a significant impact?

3 'Similar benefits and barriers exist for the adoption of sell-side e-commerce for both B2B and B2C organizations.' Discuss.

4 'In most countries the Internet will never be used by more than 50 per cent of the population, so its impact on businesses will be limited.' Discuss.

5 'Confusion over the meaning of the terms e-commerce and e-business will limit the adoption of e-business in many businesses.' Discuss.

6 Analyse *Figure 1.4* commenting on:
- the overall percentage of sales for e-commerce predicted for 2004 across all markets;
- the variation in percentage of sales for e-commerce predicted for 2004 in different markets;
- the growth rates indicated over the four years of predictions;
- the implications for the developing world.

Examination questions

1 Explain the relationship between the concepts of e-commerce and e-business.

2 Distinguish between buy-side and sell-side e-commerce and give an example of the application of each.

3 Summarize three reasons why a company may wish to introduce e-commerce.

4 Describe three of the main barriers to adoption of e-commerce by consumers and suggest how a company could counter these.

5 Outline the internal changes a company may need to make when introducing e-business.

6 Summarize the differences between adoption of Internet access for consumers and businesses and give reasons for these differences.

7 Name three risks to a company that introduces buy-side e-commerce.

8 Name three risks to a company that introduces sell-side e-commerce.

References

BBC (2005) eBay's 10-year rise to world fame. By Robert Plummer. Story from BBC News, 2 September http://news.bbc.co.uk/go/pr/fr/-/l/hi/business/42075/10.stm.

Bocij, P., Chaffey, D., Greasley, A. and Hickie, S. (2005) *Business Information Systems. Technology, Development and Management*, 3rd edn. Financial Times Prentice Hall, Harlow.

Booz Allen Hamilton (2002) *International E-Economy Benchmarking the World's Most Effective Policies for the E-Economy*. Report published 19 November 2002, London.

Cabinet Office (1999) E-commerce@its.best.uk. A Performance and Innovation Unit report – September. UK Cabinet Office. Available online at: www.cabinet-office.gov.uk/innovation/1999/ecommerce/ec.body.pdf.

Doherty, N., Ellis-Chadwick, F and Hart, C. (2003) An analysis of the factors affecting the adoption of the Internet in the UK retail sectors. *Journal of Business Research*, 56, 887–97.

DTI (2000) *Business in the Information Age – International Benchmarking Study 2000*. UK Department of Trade and Industry.

DTI (2001) *Business in the Information Age – International Benchmarking Study 2001*. UK Department of Trade and Industry.

DTI (2002) *Business in the Information Age – International Benchmarking Study 2002*. UK Department of Trade and Industry.

Economist (2000) E-commerce survey. Define and sell. *Supplement*, 26 February, pp. 6–12.

eEurope (2005) Information Society Benchmarking Report. From eEurope (2005) initiative. Published at: http://europa.eu.int/information society/eeurope/i2010/docs/ benchmarking/051222%20Final%20Benchmarking%20Report.pdf.

eSuperbrands (2005) *eSuperbrands 2006.Your Guide to Some of the Best Brands on the Web*. Superbrands Ltd, London.

Evans, P. and Wurster, T.S. (1997) Strategy and the new economics of information. *Harvard Business Review*, September–October, 70–82.

Grove, A. (1996) *Only the Paranoid Survive*. Doubleday, New York.

Hoffman, D.L. and Novak, T.P. (1996) Marketing in hypermedia computer-mediated environments: conceptual foundations, *Journal of Marketing*, 60 (July), 50–68.

Kalakota, R. and Whinston, A. (1997) *Electronic Commerce. A Manager's Guide*. Addison-Wesley, Reading, MA.

Mougayer, M. (1998) E-commerce? E-business? Who e-cares? *Computer World* web site (www.computerworld.com), 2 November.

ONS (2005) *Social Trends* 35, 2005 edition.

Rayport, J. and Jaworski, B. (2003) *Introduction to E-Commerce*, 2nd edn. McGraw-Hill, NY.

SEC (2005) United States Securities and Exchange Commission submission form 10-n e-Bay submission for the fiscal year ended 31 December 2004.

Waterman, R.H., Peters, T.J. and Phillips, J.R. (1980) Structure is not organization. *McKinsey Quarterly* in-house journal. McKinsey & Co., New York.

Welch, J. (2001) CEO of GE speech to Annual Shareowners Meeting, Atlanta, GA, 25 April.

Further reading

Chaffey, D., Ellis-Chadwick, F., Mayer, R. and Johnston, K. (2006) *Internet Marketing: Strategy, Implementation and Practice*, 2nd edn. Financial Times Prentice Hall, Harlow. Chapters 10 and 11 highlight the differences between B2C and B2B e-commerce.

Web links

Sites giving general information on market characteristics of the Internet

ClickZ Experts (www.clickz.com/experts/) An excellent collection of articles on online marketing communications. US-focused.

ClickZ Stats (www.clickz.com/stats/) The definitive source of news on Internet developments, and reports on company and consumer adoption of the Internet and characteristics in Europe and worldwide. A searchable digest of most analyst reports.

DaveChaffey.com (www.davechaffey.com) A blog containing updates and articles on all aspects of e-business and e-commerce structured according to the chapters in Dave Chaffey's books.

Europa European Commission Statistics (http://europa.eu.int/comm/enterprise/ict/index_en.htm) Technology For Innovation / ICT Industries and E-Business. Reports evaluating e-business activity across the European Union.

E-consultancy.com (www.e-consultancy.com) UK-focused portal with extensive supplier directory, best-practice white papers and forum.

Guide to Smarter Internet Searching (www.pearsoned.co.uk/chaffey) is a detailed explanation from the author of this book on how to use the Internet more effectively to search for business and academic sources. Includes a description of an advanced searching approach using Google.

Ofcom (www.ofcom.org.uk/research/) The Office of Communication has reports on adoption of digital media including telecommunications and the Internet (including broadband adoption), digital television and wireless services.

University-sponsored research projects on e-business and e-commerce

Centre for E-business @ MIT (http://ebusiness.mit.edu) Created by MIT Sloan School of Management, contains summaries of over 50 research projects.

eCommerce Innovation Centre (www.ecommerce.ac.uk) News, case studies and research coordinated from the University of Cardiff.

NetAcademy on Electronic Markets (www.electronicmarkets.org) Research compiled in *Electronic Markets – The International Journal of Electronic Commerce and Business Media.*

Sloan Center for Internet Retailing (http://ecommerce.vanderbilt.edu) Originally founded in 1994 as Project 2000 by Tom Novak and Donna Hoffman at School of Management, Vanderbilt University, to study marketing implications of the Internet. Useful links/papers.

Trade magazines

E-commerce Times (www.ecommercetimes.com) has 'daily news e-business news and analysis'.

E-commerce news for IT managers (www.internetnews.com/ec-news) Content structured in different business and technical categories.

New Media Age (www.newmediazero.com/nma) is a weekly new media magazine, with partial content online.

Revolution magazine (www.revolutionmagazine.com) is also a weekly UK magazine on new media – mainly sell-side e-commerce. Fully archived on site.

Portals for encouraging e-business adoption and start-ups

Note that these now refer to information management and commerce strategy rather than e-business/e-commerce/online as they did five years ago.

Australian Government Information Management Office (www.agimo.gov.au) Formerly, the Australian National Office for the Information Economy.

Business.gov.sg (www.business.gov.sg) Singapore government portal for encouragement of e-business.

Clearly Business (www.clearlybusiness.com) Independent UK site funded by Barclays Bank.

New Zealand Government E-Commerce (www.ecommerce.govt.nz) Information on e-commerce policy and initiatives.

UK CIO Council (www.cio.gov.uk) The UK government now has a Chief Information Office tasked with managing e-government for 'ensuring that IT supports the business transformation of Government itself so that we can provide better, more efficient, public services'.

US Office of Electronic Government and Technology (www.estrategy.gov) US agency facilitating e-government in the USA.

UK Office of Government Commerce (www.ogc.gov.uk) Information on e-government and e-procurement.

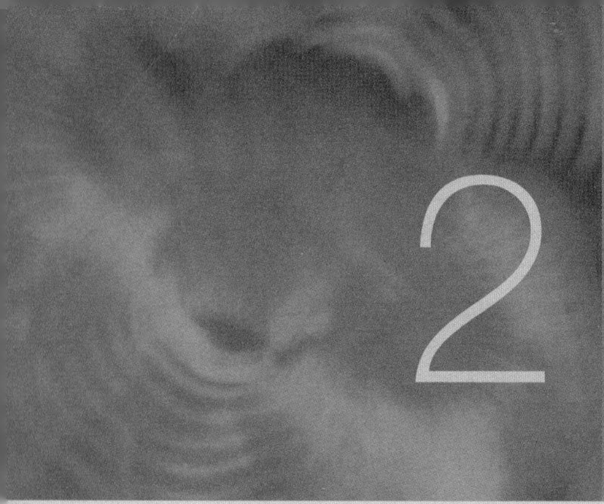

2 E-commerce fundamentals

Chapter at a glance

Main topics

Web support

The following additional case studies are available at www.pearsoned.co.uk/chaffey

- ➤ Dynamic pricing at GlaxoSmithKline
- ➤ Ahold explores new ways to reach customers
- ➤ The implications of broadband access
- ➤ Learning from the dot-coms

The site also contains a range of study material designed to help improve your results.

Learning outcomes

After completing this chapter the reader should be able to:

- **Evaluate changes in business relationships between organizations and their customers enabled by e-commerce**
- **Identify the main business and marketplace models for electronic communications and trading**
- **Describe different revenue models and transaction mechanisms available through online services.**

Management issues

The fundamentals of e-commerce imply these questions for managers:

- **What are the implications of changes in marketplace structures for how we trade with customers and other partners?**
- **Which business models and revenue models should we consider in order to exploit the Internet?**
- **What will be the importance of online intermediaries and marketplace hubs to our business and what actions should we take to partner these intermediaries?**

Links to other chapters

The main related chapters are:

- *Chapter 3* explains the hardware and software infrastructure enabling these new business models;
- *Chapters 4* and *5* consider appropriate strategic responses to these new models and paradigms;
- *Chapter 6* explores new models of the value chain in more detail;
- *Chapter 7* explores the effect of new intermediaries and marketplaces on procurement.

Introduction

Disruptive technologies
New technologies that prompt businesses to reappraise their strategic approaches.

Destination site
Typically a retailer or manufacturer site with sales and service information. Intermediaries such as media sites may be destination sites for some.

Online intermediaries
Web sites which help connect web users with content they are seeking on destination sites. Include new online intermediaries such as search engines and shopping comparison sites and traditional brokers, directories and newspaper and magazine publishers that now have an online presence.

Portal
An intermediary site focused on providing a gateway to other information on other sites, but often also providing its own content and services. Examples includes search engines, ISPs, and online newspapers and magazines.

Electronic communications are **disruptive technologies** that have already caused major changes in industry structure, marketplace structure and business models. Consider a B2B organization such as 'The B2B Company'. Traditionally it has sold its products through a network of distributors. With the advent of e-commerce it now has the opportunity to bypass distributors and trade directly with customers via a destination web site, and it also has the opportunity to reach customers through new B2B marketplaces. Similarly, for The B2C Company, an e-retail **destination site** has the opportunity to market its products through **online intermediaries** such as search engines, price comparison sites and media-owned sites or **portals**. Knowledge of the opportunities and threats presented by these changes is essential to those involved in defining business, marketing and information systems strategy. In this chapter we introduce a number of frameworks that will be applied throughout the remainder of the book when considering the e-commerce and e-business strategies that companies should adopt in response to the Internet. To conclude the chapter, we evaluate the Internet start-ups – the dot-coms launched in response to the opportunities provided by new business models, and see what lessons can be learnt from the dot-com failures.

The chapter starts by considering the different participants and constraints in the e-commerce environment. We then look at how electronic communications have facilitated restructuring of the relationships between members of the electronic marketplace – a key feature of e-commerce. Electronic communications have also given rise to many exciting new business models and we investigate the potential of these also.

Throughout this chapter we mainly consider the sell-side elements of e-commerce rather than the e-business as a whole. This approach has been chosen since the focus is mainly on how an organization can restructure relationships on the downstream side of its supply chain. A review of the entire supply chain is completed in *Chapter 6*.

The e-commerce environment

All organizations operate within an environment that influences the way in which they conduct business. Strategy development is strongly influenced by considering the environment the business operates in. *Figure 2.1* illustrates some of the elements that may influence the way in which an organization operates. For e-commerce strategy, the most significant influences are those of the immediate marketplace that is shaped by the needs of customers and how services are provided to them through competitors and intermediaries and via upstream suppliers. Wider influences are provided by local and international economic conditions and legislation together with whatever business practices are acceptable to society. Finally, technological innovations are vital in providing opportunities to provide superior services to competitors or through changing the shape of the marketplace. For example, a web site with *personalization facilities* (*Chapter 9, p. 426*) can provide information tailored for a customer that offers advantages beyond a competitor's offerings. What are the implications of these environmental influences for a company? If you look at the top 100

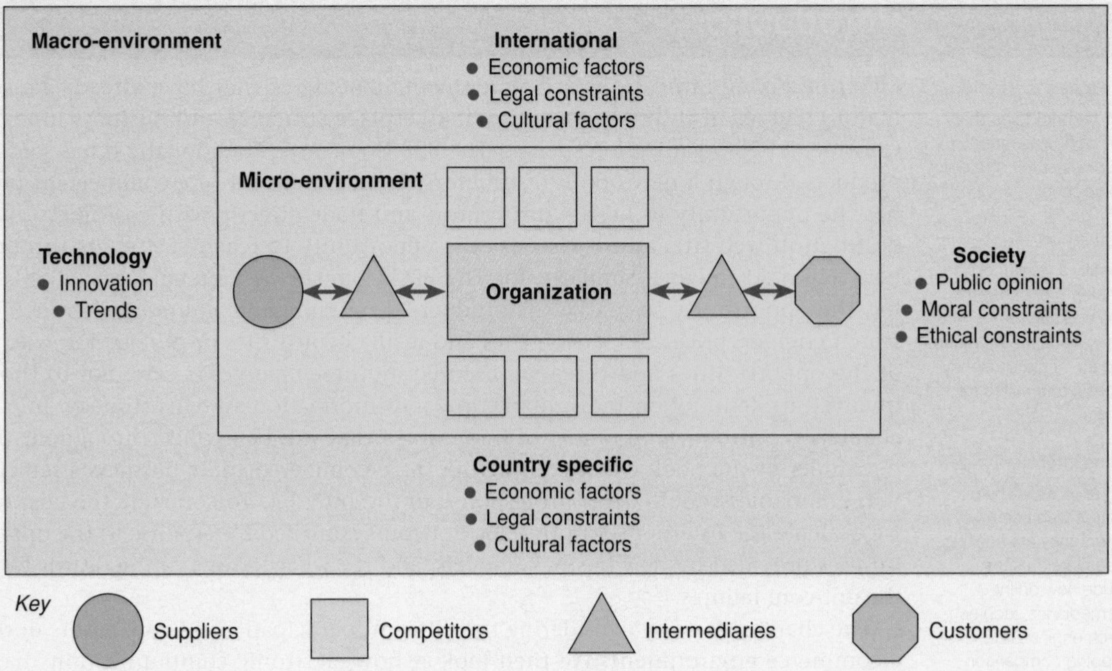

Figure 2.1 **The environment in which e-business services are provided**

companies from 50 years ago in your country you will probably find that less than a quarter of them remain in the top 100; many may even have ceased to exist. There are many reasons why this may be the case, but a key issue will be failure to monitor and respond to environmental influences. Given that these influences vary rapidly and will have a major impact on the success of a company, it is important that the current environment be monitored and future environmental trends be anticipated. This is an important role of *knowledge management* (*Chapter 10, p. 486*). Not only must employees be charged with monitoring these environmental factors, but it must be possible to disseminate this information so that decision makers can take appropriate action. In a later chapter we examine some of the issues of the *e-commerce environment* (*Chapter 4, p. 146*) in more detail using the SLEPT framework to examine Social, Legal, Economic, Political and Technological issues. Now complete *Activity 2.1* to review the importance of these environmental influences.

Activity 2.1 Why are environmental influences important?

Purpose

To emphasize the importance of monitoring and acting on a range of environmental influences.

Activity

For each of the environmental influences shown in *Figure 2.1*, give examples of why it is important to monitor and respond in an e-business context. For example, the personalization mentioned in the text is part of why it is important to respond to technological innovation.

Answers to activities can be found at www.pearsoned.co.uk/chaffey

The e-commerce marketplace

In this section we look at how electronic communications have changed relationships between the different participants of commercial transactions. Since the nature of these changes according to whether the transaction is between business and consumer or between businesses (inter-organizational), we start by reviewing differences between these types of transactions. We then look at how the channel structures of organizations have been changed through the process of disintermediation and reintermediation. Locations for trading and mechanisms of commercial exchange in the electronic marketplace are then reviewed. Management teams have difficult decisions to take about which of these new models of trading is relevant to them, so we take a questioning approach, looking at some examples that have worked and some that haven't.

Restructuring of the supply chain and value chain is not discussed in this chapter since it is covered later (*Chapter 6, p. 277*).

Business or consumer model?

Business-to-consumer – (B2C)
These transactions are between an organization and consumers.

Business-to-business – (B2B)
These transactions are between an organization and other organizations.

As introduced in *Chapter 1*, it is commonplace to identify e-business opportunities in terms of whether an organization is transacting with consumers (**business-to-consumer – B2C**) or other businesses (**business-to-business – B2B**). *Activity 2.2* shows why studies of e-commerce often distinguish between B2B and B2C – the characteristics of trading in each environment are quite different in terms of devising strategy and marketing techniques.

Business-to-business transactions predominate over the Internet, in terms of value, if not frequency. *Figure 2.2* helps explain why this is the case. It shows that there are many more opportunities for B2B transactions than for B2C, both between an organi-

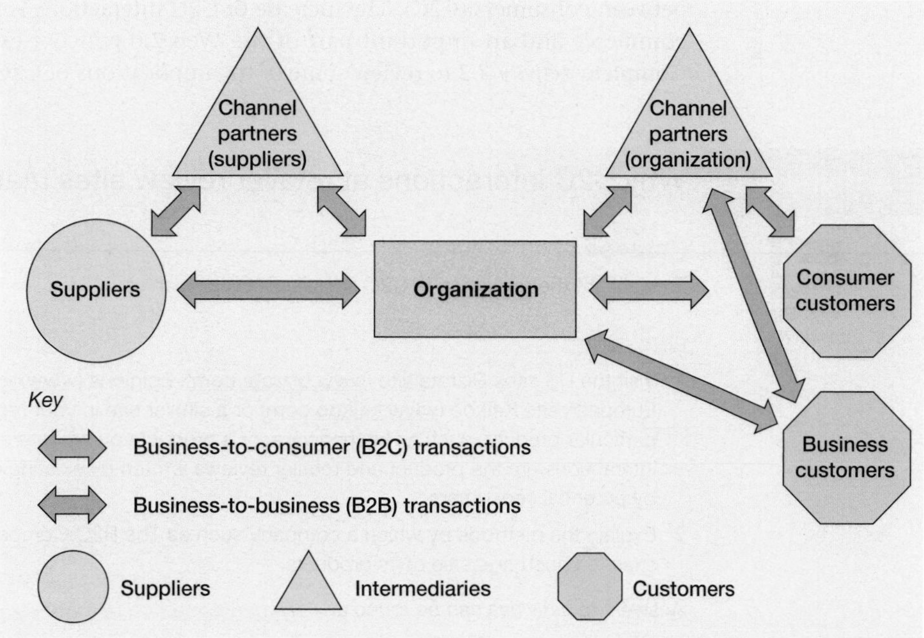

Figure 2.2 **B2B and B2C interactions between an organization, its suppliers and its customers**

zation and its suppliers, together with intermediaries, and through distributors such as agents and wholesalers with customers.

Activity 2.2 Why distinguish between B2B and B2C?

Purpose

To introduce the differences between B2B and B2C e-commerce that must be taken into consideration when devising strategy and tactics

Activity

Consider how you think the characteristics summarized in the first column of *Table 2.1* differ for B2C and B2B. Refer to *Figure 2.2* when completing your answer.

Table 2.1 **Differences in characteristics between B2B and B2C e-commerce**

Characteristic	*B2C*	*B2B*
Proportion of adopters with access		
Complexity of buying decisions		
Channel		
Purchasing characteristics		
Product characteristic		

Answers to activities can be found at www.pearsoned.co.uk/chaffey

Figure 1.2 gives examples of different companies operating in the business-to-consumer (B2C) and business-to-business (B2B) spheres and also direct interactions between consumers (C2C). The increase of C2C interactions is a key feature of online commerce and an important part of the Web 2.0 concept explained in *Chapter 3*. Complete *Activity 2.3* to review some of the implications of C2C interactions.

Activity 2.3 Why C2C interactions at retailer review sites matter for retailers

Visit the w.w.w.

Purpose

To highlight the relevance of C2C sites to B2C companies.

Questions

1 Visit the US sites Bizrate site (www.bizrate.com), Epinions (www.epinions.com) the European site Kelkoo (www.kelkoo.com) or a similar site in your region. Choose a particular product, such as kitchenware, or a product you are interested in. The C2C interactions are the product and retailer reviews written by existing customers and read by potential consumers.

2 Explain the methods by which a company such as The B2C Company should use such sites to encourage sale of its products.

Answers to activities can be found at www.pearsoned.co.uk/chaffey

Marketplace channel structures

Channel structures describe the way a manufacturer or selling organization delivers products and services to its customers. The distribution channel will consist of one or more intermediaries such as wholesalers and retailers. For example, a music company is unlikely to distribute its CDs directly to retailers, but will use wholesalers who have a large warehouse of titles which are then distributed to individual branches according to demand. Of course today, they can distribute digital tracks straight to online retailers such as iTunes and Napster, a major change to their channel strategy. Companies selling business products often have a longer distribution channel involving more intermediaries.

The relationship between a company and its channel partners shown in *Figure 2.2* can be dramatically altered by the opportunities afforded by the Internet. This occurs because the Internet offers a means of bypassing some of the channel partners. This process is known as **disintermediation** or 'cutting out the middleman'.

Disintermediation
The removal of intermediaries such as distributors or brokers that formerly linked a company to its customers.

Figure 2.3 illustrates disintermediation in a graphical form for a simplified retail channel. Further intermediaries such as additional distributors may occur in a business-to-business market. *Figure 2.3(a)* shows the former position where a company marketed and sold its products by 'pushing' them through a sales channel. *Figures 2.3(b)* and *(c)* show two different types of disintermediation in which the wholesaler *(b)* or the wholesaler and retailer *(c)* are bypassed, allowing the producer to sell and promote direct to the consumer. The benefits of disintermediation to the producer are clear – it is able to remove the sales and infrastructure cost of selling through the channel. Benjamin and Weigand (1995) calculate that, using the sale of quality shirts as an example, it is possible to make cost savings of 28 per cent in the case of *(b)* and 62 per cent for case *(c)*. Some of these cost savings can be passed on to the customer in the form of cost reductions.

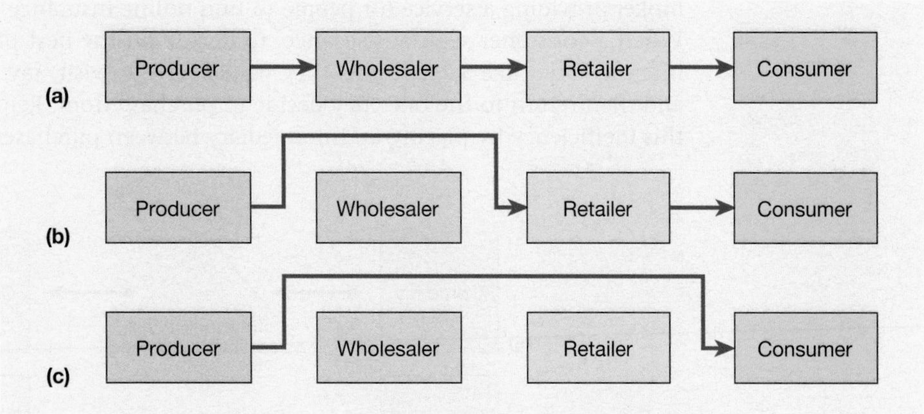

Figure 2.3 Disintermediation of a consumer distribution channel showing (a) the original situation, (b) disintermediation omitting the wholesaler, and (c) disintermediation omitting both wholesaler and retailer

Vauxhall (www.vauxhall.co.uk), the UK part of General Motors, provides a good example of the response to the opportunities provided by new electronic channels. The initial aims for this web site were not limited to online sales generation. Indeed, a wholesale replacement of dealerships was not envisaged. Additional aims included raising the profile and branding awareness of Vauxhall and lead generation for dealerships (such as brochure and test drive requests). To achieve these aims online approaches used include differential pricing ('Vauxhall Internet Price'), an online sales support tool ('Vauxhall Advisor') and an e-mail newsletter. *CIO* (*Chief Information Officer*) (2002) reported that in November 2001, eGM – a group created in 1999 to manage e-business projects and processes throughout General Motors – was dismantled and rolled back into GM's traditional business units. While sceptics may point to this as evidence of disappointing results from e-business, the article reports that GM executives, including CEO Rick Wagoner and *CIO*'s Ralph Szygenda, say the changes at eGM are not indicative of a wholesale retreat from e-business:

> *The intent from the beginning was to create a separate function for two to three years to drive [e-business capabilities] across GM. The dismantling of the eGM group is seen as a sign of success, with e-business now an integral part of the company's fabric.*

GM managers also point to the role of the Internet in generating leads for dealer sales. Since September 2001, the GM BuyPower US web site has delivered an average of more than 2,000 leads to dealers per day with 20 per cent of dealer leads generated through BuyPower converting into sales. This pattern of the incorporation of e-business back into traditional structures is commonplace amongst the advanced adopters of e-business who have successfully integrated e-business into their organizations.

Reintermediation
The creation of new intermediaries between customers and suppliers providing services such as supplier search and product evaluation.

Although disintermediation has occurred, **reintermediation** is perhaps a more significant phenomenon resulting from Internet-based communications. *Figure 2.4* illustrates this concept. Let us take the example of car insurance in the UK market. In *Figure 2.4(a)* we commence with the traditional situation in which many sales were through brokers such as the Automobile Association (www.theaa.co.uk). With disintermediation (*Figure 2.4(b)*) there was the opportunity to sell direct, initially via call centres as with Direct Line (www.directline.co.uk) and then more recently by their transactional web site. Purchasers of products still needed assistance in the selection of products and this led to the creation of new intermediaries, the process referred to as reintermediation (*Figure 2.4(c)*).

In the UK Screentrade (www.screentrade.co.uk) is an example of a new entrant broker providing a service for people to find online insurance at a competitive price. When a consumer selects insurance, to decide on the best price and offer without intermediaries like Screentrade, they would have to visit, say, five different insurers and then return to the one they decide to purchase from. Reintermediation removes this inefficiency by placing an intermediary between purchaser and seller. This inter-

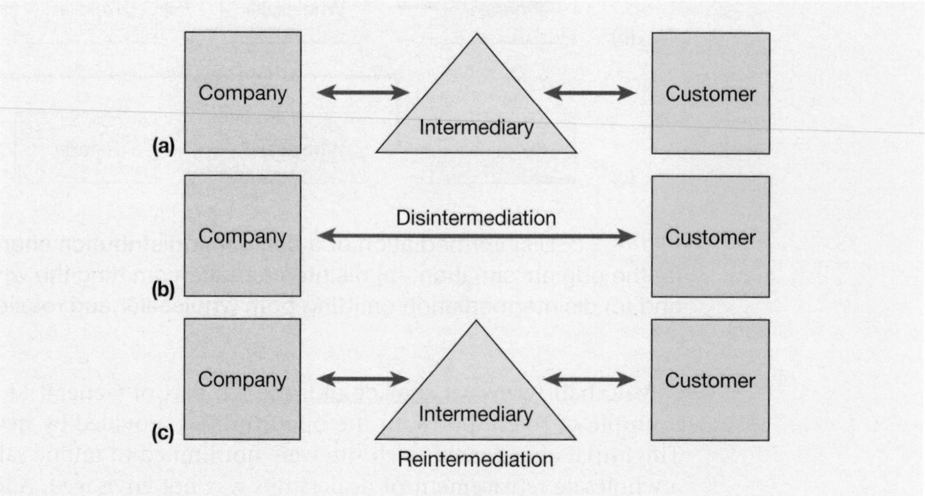

Figure 2.4 **From original situation (a) to disintermediation (b) and reintermediation (c)**

mediary performs the price evaluation stage of fulfilment since its database has links updated from prices contained within the databases of different suppliers. Screentrade was purchased by Lloyds TSB, a traditional financial services provider, but is still positioned as independent from its parent.

What are the implications of reintermediation for the e-commerce manager? First, it is necessary to make sure that your company, as a supplier, is represented with the new intermediaries operating within your chosen market sector. This implies the need to integrate, using the Internet, databases containing price information with those of different intermediaries. Forming partnerships or setting up sponsorship with some intermediaries can give better online visibility compared to competitors. Second, it is important to monitor the prices of other suppliers within this sector (possibly by using the intermediary web site for this purpose). Third, it may be appropriate to create your own intermediary, for example DIY chain B&Q has set up its own intermediary to help budding DIYers, but is positioned separately from its owners. Such tactics to counter or take advantage of reintermediation are sometimes known as countermediation. Screentrade is another example of countermediation, except that here the strategy of Lloyds TSB was to use the lower-risk approach of purchasing an existing online intermediary rather than creating its own intermediary. A further example is Opodo (www.opodo.com) which has been set up by nine European airlines including Air France, BA, KLM and Lufthansa. Such collaboration would have been inconceivable just a short time ago.

Debate 2.1

Countermediation

'The advent of e-commerce means that marketers cannot rely on the online presence of existing intermediaries – instead they must create their own online intermediaries.'

Countermediation
Creation of a new intermediary by an established company.

Different types of online intermediary

There are many different types of intermediary in addition to the broker intermediaries such as Screentrade that simplify the purchase and sale of goods. Bizrate (*see Figure 2.3*) is a further type of intermediary, in this case bringing consumers together.

Sarkar *et al.* (1996) identify many different types of new intermediaries (mainly from a B2C perspective) which they refer to as 'cybermediaries'. Hagel and Rayport (1997) use 'infomediary' specifically to refer to sale of customer information.

Infomediary
A business whose main source of revenue derives from capturing consumer information and developing detailed profiles of individual customers for use by third parties.

Some of the main new intermediaries identified by Sarkar *et al.* (1996) were:

- Directories (such as Yahoo!, Excite).
- Search engines (AltaVista, Infoseek).
- Malls (BarclaySquare, Buckingham Gate).
- Virtual resellers (own-inventory and sell-direct, e.g. Amazon, CDNow).
- Financial intermediaries (offering digital cash and cheque payment services, such as Digicash).
- Forums, fan clubs and user groups (referred to collectively as 'virtual communities').
- Evaluators (sites which perform review or comparison of services)

It is interesting to review how the role of online intermediaries has changed since this time. Directories are now less important and have mainly merged with search engines since search is now the preferred form of access through the search engines that have risen to the top of the pile, namely Google, Yahoo! and MSN. Online shopping malls, which were online equivalents of the offline phenomenon, did not prove effective since there was no consumer benefit in visit a shopping mall retailer when you could go direct to the retailer's web site. Instead, sites in the evaluator category such as the price comparison search engines we mentioned earlier in this chapter such as Kelkoo and Pricerunner have become important destinations since they enable a choice of many suppliers across many categories based on price. Price comparison sites are also known as *aggregators* (particularly for financial services comparison sites such as www.moneysupermarket.com) since they aggregate product information from different sources. E-retailers such as Amazon have remained important, but many such as CDNow have failed, to be replaced by new e-business such as CDWow (www.cdwow.com) and Play.com (www.play.com). Many of the forms of digital currency such as Digicash and E-cash did not prove popular. Instead, PayPal (www.paypal.com) became popular and was purchased by eBay (www.ebay.com, see *Case Study 1.2*). The C2C category described by Sarkar *et al.* has proved important with forums and chatrooms developing to support different audiences. For the younger age group, HabboHotel (www.habbohotel.com) has proved popular in many countries. Another major new C2C category that has exploded in popularity since the previous edition of this book is the blog.

Blogs

Blog
An online diary or news source prepared by an individual or a group of people.

Weblogs or '**blogs**' give an easy method of regularly publishing web pages which are best described as online journals, diaries or news or events listings. They may include feedback (traceback) comments from other sites or contributors to the site. Frequency can be hourly, daily, weekly or less frequently, but daily updates are typical.

An example of a useful blog which can keep marketing professionals up-to-date about Internet marketing developments is www.marketingvox.com which is coupled with daily e-mail digests of stories posted. Another example, with news items and articles structured according to the chapters of a book is Davechaffey.com (www.davechaffey.com, *Figure 2.5*). Business blogs are created by people within an organization. They can be useful in showing the expertise of those within the organization, but need to be carefully controlled to avoid releasing damaging information. An example of a business blog used to showcase the expertise of its analysts is the Jupiter Research Analyst Weblogs (http://weblogs.jupiterresearch.com). Technology companies like Sun Microsystems and Microsoft have several hundreds of bloggers and have a policy to control them to make positive comments. There are many free services which enable anyone to blog (for example www.blogger.com which was purchased by Google

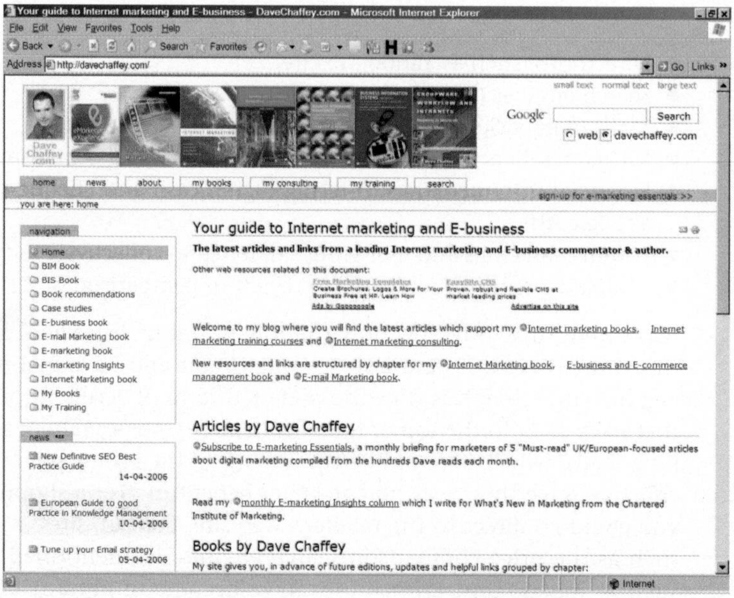

Figure 2.5 **Dave Chaffey's blog site (www.davechaffey.com)**

in 2003). Blogs were traditionally accessed through online tools (e.g. www.bloglines.com, www.blogpulse.com) or software readers (www.rssreader.com) but were incorporated into mainstream software in 2006. We will review the importance of the related technology Really Simple Syndication (RSS) in *Chapter 3*.

Activity 2.4 highlights the alternative revenue models available to these new intermediaries, in this case an evaluator, and speculates on their future.

Activity 2.4 Kelkoo.com, an example of revenue models for new intermediaries

Visit the w.w.w.

Purpose

To provide an example of the services provided by cybermediaries and explore their viability as businesses.

Background

Kelkoo, which describes itself as 'the leading shopping search engine', is also known as a price comparison site. It receives a commission on each sale made by a visitor to its site from the retailer or merchant selling the product. Kelkoo (www.kelkoo.com) has been profitable since 2002. According to the Kelkoo Investor Relations site, it now operates in 10 European countries and in 2004 received over 8.5 million unique users monthly (over 3 million in the UK) from users across Europe. In April 2004 Kelkoo was acquired by Yahoo! Inc. and is now a wholly owned subsidiary. In Europe it retains the Kelkoo brand, but elsewhere the shopping comparison technology acquired by Yahoo! has been used to 'power' its own shopping service as shown in *Figure 2.6*.

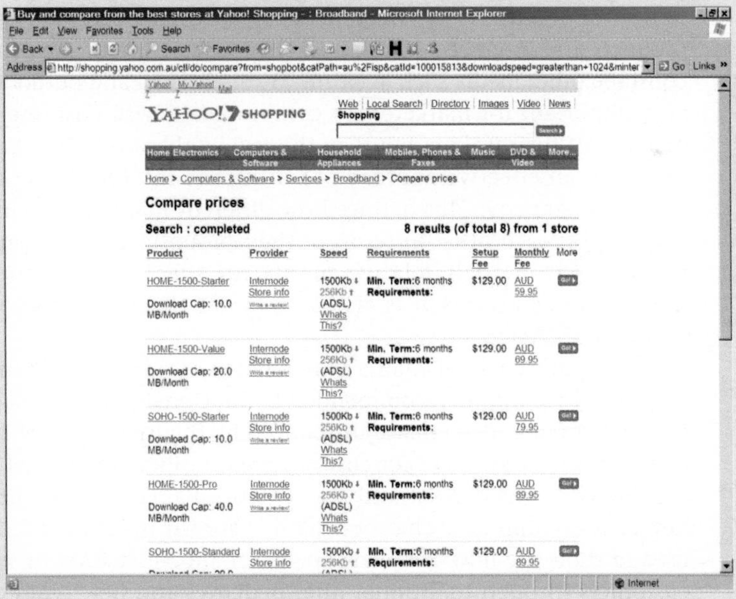

Figure 2.6 Yahoo! Shopping Australia, a price comparison site based on the Kelkoo.com shopping comparison technology (http://shopping.yahoo.com.au)

Questions

1 Visit the Kelkoo web site (www.kelkoo.com; see *Figure 2.6*) and search for this book, a CD or anything else you fancy. Explain the service that is being offered to customers.

→

2 Write down the different revenue opportunities for this site (some may be evident from the site, but others may not; write down your own ideas also).

3 Given that there are other competing sites in this intermediary category such as PriceRunner (www.pricerunner.com), assess the future of this online business using press releases and comments from other sites such as Moreover (www.moreover.com).

Answers to activities can be found at www.pearsoned.co.uk/chaffey

A further type of intermediary is the *virtual marketplace* or virtual trading community. These are of vital importance in the B2B marketplace. From the supplier's or manufacturer's perspective they provide a new channel for selling their products. If the marketplace is set up by major players in an industry such as the Covisint marketplace originally created by Ford, GM and DaimlerChrysler (www.covisint.com) it will probably be essential to trade with key customers via this method, since this will be a prerequisite for trading with the customer. From the viewpoint of the B2B customer procuring supplies, the virtual marketplace offers the opportunity for lower prices as pricing becomes more transparent, giving rise to greater price competition. The form of these marketplaces is considered in more detail in *Focus on electronic B2B marketplaces* (*Chapter 7, p. 325*).

The importance of multi-channel marketplace models

Customer journey
A description of modern multi-channel buyer behaviour as consumers use different media to select suppliers, make purchases and gain customer support.

Multi-channel marketing strategy
Defines how different marketing channels should integrate and support each other in terms of their proposition development and communications based on their relative merits for the customer and the company.

In the previous section we discussed new types of online channels and intermediaries, but it needs to be stressed that in many categories, purchasers use a combination of channels. As consumers follow their customer journeys as they select products and interact with brands, they do not use the Internet in isolation – they consume other media such as print, TV, direct mail and outdoor. These media are still very important for marketers to communicate with customers who still spend the majority of their waking hours in the real world rather than the virtual world. It follows that an effective approach to using the Internet is as part of a multi-channel marketing strategy. This defines how different marketing channels should integrate and support each other in terms of their proposition development and communications based on their relative merits for the customer and the company. The multi-channel approach is also a common theme throughout this book and we return to in *Chapter 4*.

Developing 'channel chains' which help us understand multi-channel behaviour is a powerful technique recommended by McDonald and Wilson (2002) for analysing the changes in a marketplace introduced by the Internet. A channel chain shows different customer journeys for customers with different channel preferences. It can be used to assess the current and future performance of these different customer journeys. An example of a channel chain is shown in *Figure 2.7*. A market map can be used to show the flow of revenue between a manufacturer or service provider and its customers through traditional intermediaries and new types of intermediaries. For example, Thomas and Sullivan (2005) give the example of a US multi-channel retailer that used cross-channel tracking of purchases through assigning each customer a unique identifier to calculate channel preferences as follow: 63% bricks-and-mortar store only, 12.4% Internet-only customers, 11.9% catalogue-only customers, 11.9% dual-channel customers and 1% three-channel customers. This shows the future potential for further growth and suggests that different strategies need to be developed to appeal to each group.

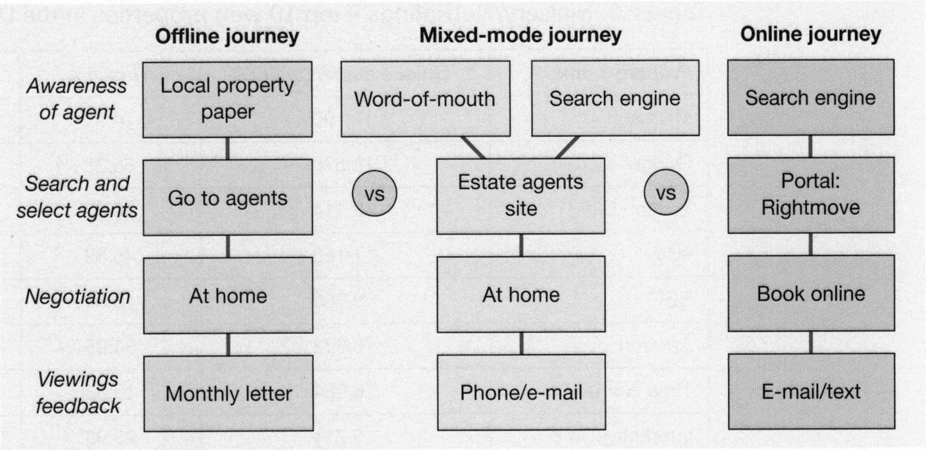

Figure 2.7 **Example channel chain map for consumers selecting an estate agent to sell their property**

Focus on portals

At the time that Sarkar *et al.* (1996) described the different types of 'cybermediaries' listed above, there were many separate web sites offering these types of services. But over the past 10 years or more, there has been a consolidation into three major portals which are popular in most countries. These are Google (www.google.com), Yahoo! (www.yahoo.com) and MSN (www.msn.com). In this section, we review the role of these portals and also look at other types of more specialized portals which are also important in understanding how to reach customers online.

Portal
A web site that acts as a gateway to information and services available on the Internet by providing search engines, directories and other services such as personalized news or free e-mail.

The concept of the portal has evolved to reflect the range of services offered by some cybermediaries. The term 'portal' originated with reference to sites that were the default home pages of users. In other words, when users started their web browser, the first page they saw was their personal home page. When users use a newly installed browser it will be set up so that the home page is that of the company that produces it. In the case of Microsoft this is usually www.msn.com (the Microsoft Network) and for AOL it is www.aol.com.

Portals are significant since they are the prime real estate of the Internet. Inspection of the most visited sites in Europe (*Table 2.2*) shows that the top ten in the UK are all portals.

The large reach of the sites in *Table 2.2* shows why portals are important to companies looking to use keyword advertising, banner advertising or sponsorship to promote their products. This topic is discussed further in *Chapter 9*. *Activity 2.5* illustrates different ways portals look to gain revenue through the example of Yahoo!

Types of portals

Portals vary in scope and the services they offer, so naturally terms have evolved to describe the different types of portals. It is useful, in particular for marketers, to understand these terms since they act as a checklist that companies are represented on the different types of portals. *Table 2.3* shows different types of portals. It is apparent that there is overlap between the different types of portal. Yahoo!, for instance, is a horizontal portal since it offers a range of services, but it has also been developed as a geographical portal for different countries and, in the USA, even for different cities.

Table 2.2 **Nielsen//NetRatings – top 10 web properties in the UK, December 2005**

Property name	*Unique audience (000)*	*Reach%*	*Time per person*
Microsoft	17,790	74.71	02:30:05
Google	15,570	65.38	00:28:37
Yahoo!	12,114	50.87	00:53:25
eBay	11,150	46.82	01:56:08
BBC	9,653	40.54	00:37:21
Amazon	8,322	34.95	00:21:02
Time Warner	6,984	29.33	02:53:37
InterActiveCorp	5,711	23.98	00:10:13
Apple Computer	5,342	22.43	00:55:02
RealNetworks	4,984	20.93	00:27:14

Source: Nielsen//NetRatings Netview data, UK, home data, including Internet Applications, December 2005

Activity 2.5 Portal services and revenue models – the Yahoo! example

Visit the w.w.w.

Purpose

To illustrate the range and depth of services available at leading portals and how this contributes to revenue models.

Background

Yahoo! has arguably the widest range of services of any portal and it has been successful in growing revenue and achieving profitability despite tough competition from Google and MSN. You can see the success of the Yahoo! revenue models from its financial results. At the time of writing the third edition, revenues for the year ended 31 December, 2005 had just been $5,258 million, a 47 per cent increase compared to $3,575 million for 2004. The majority of this revenue comes from advertising ('Marketing services revenue' was $4,594 million for 2005, a 47 per cent increase compared to $3,127 million for 2004). Fees revenue was $664 million for 2005, a 48 per cent increase compared to $447 million for 2004. Gross profit for 2005 was $3,225 million, a 42 per cent increase compared to $2,276 million for 2004.

Question

Visit the Yahoo! site relevant to your country (from www.yahoo.com) and identify the range of services offered. Which are pure services, and which are basically providing information from other sources? You can update on the level of revenue from these services at the Yahoo! Investor Relations portal (http://yahoo.client.shareholder.com/).

Tip

To answer this question you may find it useful to refer to *Figure 2.10* where different business and revenue models are summarized.

Answers to activities can be found at www.pearsoned.co.uk/chaffey

Table 2.3 **Different types of portal**

Type of portal	*Characteristics*	*Example*
Access portal	Associated with ISP	• Wanadoo (www.wanadoo.com) and now (www.orange.co.uk) • AOL (www.aol.com)
Horizontal or functional portal	Range of services: search engines, directories, news recruitment, personal information management, shopping, etc.	• Yahoo! (www.yahoo.com) • MSN (www.msn.com) • Google (www.google.com) which for a long period just focused on search
Vertical	A vertical portal covers a particular market such as construction with news and other services	• Construction Plus (www.constructionplus.co.uk) • Chem Industry (www.chemindustry.com) • Barbour Index for B2B resources (www.barbour-index.com) • E-consultancy (www.e-consultancy.com) • Focuses on e-business resources
Media portal	Main focus is on consumer or business news or entertainment	• BBC (www.bbc.co.uk) • Guardian (www.guardian.co.uk) • ITWeek (www.itweek.co.uk)
Geographical (region, country, local)	May be: • horizontal • vertical	• Google country versions • Yahoo! country and city versions • Craigslist (www.craigslist.com) • Countyweb (www.countyweb.com)
Marketplace	May be: • horizontal • vertical • geographical	• EC21(www.ec21.com) • eBay (www.eBay.com)
Search portal	Main focus is on search	• Google (www.google.com) • Ask Jeeves (www.ask.com)
Media type	May be: • voice • video Delivered by streaming media or downloads of files	• BBC (www.bbc.co.uk) • Silicon (www.silicon.com)

The importance of search engines

Search engines are a key type or element of portals for organizations marketing their services online, since today they are the primary method of finding information about a company and its products. Research compiled by Searchenginewatch (www.searchenginewatch.com) shows that over 90 per cent of web users state that they use search engines to find information online. Their importance can also be seen from the volumes of searches in *Table 1.1* and volume of users from *Table 2.2*. Search engines also offer a **directory** of different web sites. We explain how search engines work in *Chapter 3* and in *Chapter 9* explain how companies can market themselves on the search engines through search engine optimization and paid search marketing.

Search engines, spiders and robots
Automatic tools known as 'spiders' or 'robots' index registered sites. Users search this by typing keywords and are presented with a list of pages.

Directories or catalogues
Structured listings of registered sites in different categories.

Location of trading in the marketplace

Electronic marketplace
A virtual marketplace such as the Internet in which no direct contact occurs between buyers and sellers.

While traditional marketplaces have a physical location, an Internet-based market has no physical presence – it is a virtual marketplace. Rayport and Sviokla (1996) used this distinction to coin a new term: electronic marketplace. This has implications for the way in which the relationships between the different actors in the marketplace occur.

The new electronic marketspace has many alternative virtual locations where an organization needs to position itself to communicate and sell to its customers. Thus one tactical marketing question is: 'What representation do we have on the Internet?' One aspect of representation that needs to be considered is the different types of marketplace location. Berryman *et al.* (1998) identified a useful framework for this, identifying three different types of location. Seller-controlled sites are the main home page of the company and are e-commerce-enabled. Buyer-controlled sites are intermediaries which have been set up so that it is the buyer who initiates the market making. This can occur through procurement posting where a purchaser specifies what they wish to purchase, it is sent by e-mail to suppliers registered on the system and then offers are awaited. Aggregators involve a group of purchasers combining to purchase a multiple order, thus reducing the purchase cost. Neutral sites are independent evaluator intermediaries that enable price and product comparison.

The framework of Berryman *et al.* (1998) has been updated by McDonald and Wilson (2002) who introduce two additional locations for purchase which are useful (*Table 2.4*):

Table 2.4 **Different places for online representation**

Place of purchase	*Examples of sites*
A. Seller-controlled	• Vendor sites, i.e. home site of organization selling products, e.g. www.dell.com
B. Seller-oriented	• Intermediaries controlled by third parties to the seller such as distributors and agents, e.g. Opodo (www.opodo.com) represents the main air carriers
C. Neutral	• Intermediaries not controlled by buyer's industry, e.g. EC21 (www.ec21.com) • Product-specific search engines, e.g. CNET (www.computer.com) • Comparison sites, e.g. MoneySupermarket (www.moneysupermarket.com) • Auction space, e.g. eBay (www.ebay.com)
D. Buyer-oriented	• Intermediaries controlled by buyers, e.g. Covisint used to represent the major motor manufacturers (www.covisint.com) although they now don't use a single marketplace, but each manufacturer uses the technology to access its suppliers direct • Purchasing agents and aggregators
E. Buyer-controlled	• Web-site procurement posting on company's own site, e.g. GE • Trading Process Network (www.gxs.com)

Source: Adapted from McDonald and Wilson (2002)

A *Seller-controlled sites* are those that are the main site of the supplier company and are e-commerce-enabled.

B *Seller-oriented sites* are controlled by third parties, but represent the seller rather than providing a full range of options.

C *Neutral sites* are independent evaluator intermediaries that enable price and product comparison and will result in the purchase being fulfilled on the target site.
D *Buyer-oriented sites* are controlled by third parties on behalf of the buyer.
E *Buyer-controlled sites* usually involve either procurement posting on buyer-company sites or those of intermediaries that have been set up in such a way that it is the buyer who initiates the market making.

We will see in *Chapter 7* that the most successful intermediaries such as Covisint are those which are not independent, but are seller-oriented or seller-controlled. *Activity 2.6* gives examples of intermediaries which could be used to promote a company operating in a specialist market such as The B2B Company.

Activity 2.6 Intermediary selection for The B2B Company

Visit the w.w.w.

Purpose

To assess the potential benefit of using different forms of intermediary for a B2B company.

Question

Using a search engine such as Google (www.google.com), identify different types of intermediary which could be involved in selling plastic composites or coatings – one of the main products of The B2B Company. Key phrases to use are: 'composites suppliers', 'composites manufacturers'.

Answers to activities can be found at www.pearsoned.co.uk/chaffey

Evans and Wurster (1999) have argued that there are three aspects of navigation that are key to achieving competitive advantage online. These should be considered when selecting intermediaries. The three aspects are:

- *Reach*. Evans and Wurster say: *'It [reach] means, simply, how many customers a business can connect with and how many products it can offer to those customers.'* Reach can be increased by moving from a single site to representation with a large number of different intermediaries. Allen and Fjermestad (2001) suggest that niche suppliers can readily reach a much wider market due to search-engine marketing (*Chapter 8*). Evans and Wurster also suggest reach refers to the range of products and services that can be offered since this will increase the number of people the company can appeal to.
- *Richness*. This is the depth or detail of information which is both collected about the customer and provided to the customer. The latter is related to the richness of product information and how well it can be personalized to be relevant to the individual needs.
- *Affiliation*. This refers to whose interest the selling organization represents – consumers or suppliers – and stresses the importance of forming the right partnerships. This particularly applies to retailers. The authors suggest that successful online retailers will provide customers who provide them with the richest information on comparing competitive products. They suggests this tilts the balance in favour of the customer.

It is also useful to consider the scale of e-commerce when evaluating the long-term potential of an e-commerce site and in particular *business-to-business marketplaces or exchanges* (*Chapter 7, p. 325*). Has the facility been set up by a single supplier or by multiple suppliers? Can it support many customers or is it available to a limited number of customers? Such questions need to be asked by companies developing an e-business strategy since it will govern who it is best to partner, both for procurement and for sales. Such questions are answered from a strategic perspective in later chapters. *Figure 2.8* shows three alternatives across the continuum of trading for trading within the electronic marketspace.

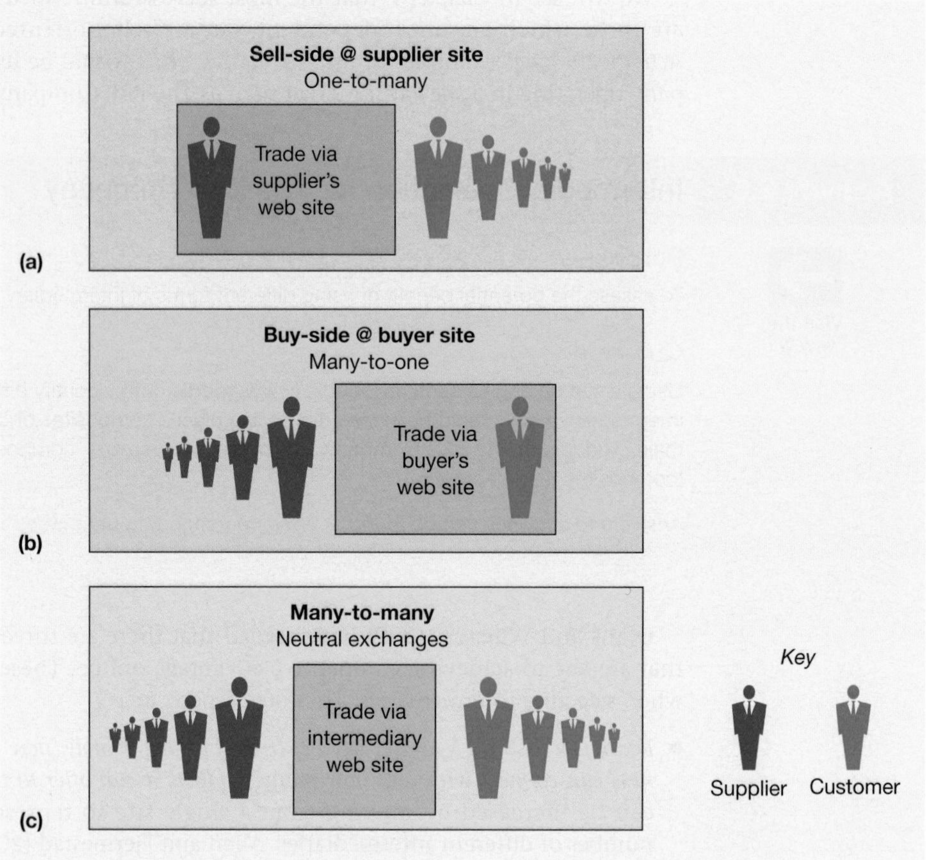

Figure 2.8 Variations in the location and scale of trading on e-commerce sites

The options can be summarized as follows:

- Sell-side at supplier's site (typically one supplier to many customers). *Examples*: most e-tailers such as Amazon (www.amazon.com) or Dell (www.dell.com).
- Sell-side at distribution portal (some suppliers to many customers).
- Buy-side at buyer's site (many (or some) suppliers to a single customer). *Examples*: first to set this up was General Electric Trading Post Network, now the GE subsidiary Global eXchange Services (www.gxs.com).
- Buy-side at procurement portal (many suppliers to selected customers).
- Neutral exchanges, marketplaces or hubs (many suppliers to many customers). *Examples*: VertMarkets (www.vertmarkets.com) and Global Composite (www.globalcomposites.com).

Commercial arrangements for transactions

Markets can also be considered from another perspective – that of the type of commercial arrangement that is used to agree a sale and price between the buyer and supplier. The main types of commercial arrangements are shown in *Table 2.5*.

Table 2.5 Commercial mechanisms and online transactions

Commercial (trading) mechanism	*Online transaction mechanism of Nunes et al. (2000)*
1 **Negotiated deal** *Example*: can use similar mechanism to auction as on Commerce One (www.commerceone.net)	Negotiation – bargaining between single seller and buyer. Continuous replenishment – ongoing fulfilment of orders under pre-set terms
2 **Brokered deal** *Example*: intermediaries such as screentrade (www.screentrade.co.uk)	Achieved through online intermediaries offering auction and pure markets online
3 **Auction** *Example*: C2C: eBay (www.ebay.com) B2B: Industry to Industry (http://business.ebay.co.uk/)	Seller auction – buyers' bids determine final price of sellers' offerings. Buyer auction – buyers request prices from multiple sellers. Reverse – buyers post desired price for seller acceptance
4 **Fixed-price sale** *Example*: all e-tailers	Static call – online catalogue with fixed prices. Dynamic call – online catalogue with continuously updated prices and features
5 **Pure markets** *Example*: electronic share dealing	Spot – buyers' and sellers' bids clear instantly
6 **Barter** *Example*: www.intagio.com and www.bartercard.co.uk	Barter – buyers and sellers exchange goods. According to the International Reciprocal Trade Association (www.irta.com) barter trade was over $9 billion in 2002

Source: Adapted and reprinted by permission of *Harvard Business Review* from table on pp. 2–3 from 'The all-in-one-market', by Nunes, P., Kambil, A. and Wilson, D., in *Harvard Business Review*, May–June, 2000. Copyright © 2000 by the Harvard Business School Publishing Corporation, all rights reserved

It can be seen from *Table 2.5* that each of these commercial arrangements is similar to traditional arrangements. Although the mechanism cannot be considered to have changed, the relative importance of these different options has changed with the Internet. Owing to the ability to rapidly publish new offers and prices, auction has become an important means of selling on the Internet. A turnover of several billion dollars has been achieved by eBay from consumers offering items such as cars and antiques. Many airlines have successfully trialled auctions to sell seats remaining on an aircraft just before a flight, and this has led to the site **www.lastminute.com** which can broker or link to such offers.

An example of a completely new commercial mechanism that has been made possible through the web is provided by priceline.com (**www.priceline.com**). This travel site is characterized by its unique and proprietary 'Name Your Own Price™' buying service. Here, users enter the price they wish to pay for airline tickets, hotel rooms or car hire together with their credit card details. If priceline.com can match the user's price and other terms with inven-

Debate 2.2

Innovative business models

'The new business models associated with the dot-com era were, in fact, existing models in an online context. Business models and revenue models have not changed.'

tory available from its participating suppliers, the deal will go ahead. This business model has been successful in the USA where priceline.com Incorporated, a NASDAQ-listed company (PCLN), had a user base of more than 16 million at the end of 2002 and a turnover of $1 billion. The brand has also been licensed overseas. In the UK, priceline.com has three core services: airline tickets, hotels and car hire, and a similar service has been launched in Asia (*Figure 2.9*).

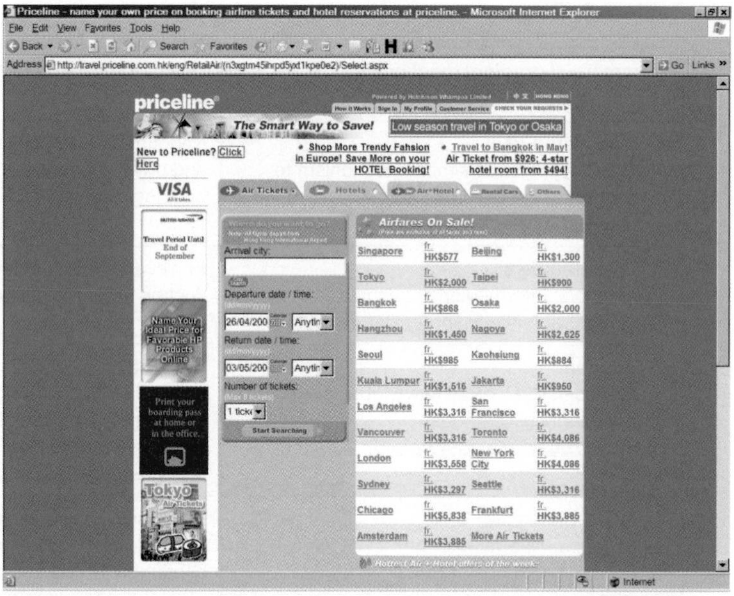

Figure 2.9 **Priceline Hong Kong service (www.priceline.com.hk)**

Focus on auctions

With the success of eBay (**www.ebay.com**), auctions have been highlighted as one of the new business models for the Internet. But how do auctions work, what infrastructure is required and what is the potential for B2B auctions? In this section we will address some of these issues.

Auctions involve determination of the basis for product or service exchange between a buyer and seller according to particular trading rules that help select the best match between the buyer and seller from a number of participants.

Klein (1997) identifies different roles for auction:

1 *Price discovery* – an example of price discovery is in the traditional consumer auction involving bidding for antiques. Antiques do not have standardized prices, but the auction can help establish a realistic market price through a gathering of buyers.
2 *Efficient allocation mechanism* – the sale of items that are difficult to distribute through traditional channels falls into this category. Examples include 'damaged inventory' that has a limited shelf life or is only available at a particular time such as aircraft flight or theatre tickets. Lastminute.com (**www.lastminute.com**) has specialized in disposal of this type of inventory in Europe, not always by means of auctions.
3 *Distribution mechanism* – as a means of attracting particular audiences.

4 *Coordination mechanism* – here the auction is used to coordinate the sale of a product to a number of interested parties; an example is the broadband spectrum licences for 3G telecoms in the UK (www.spectrumauctions.gov.uk).

Offer

A commitment by a trader to *sell* under certain conditions.

Bid

A commitment by a trader to *purchase* under certain conditions.

To understand auctions it is important to distinguish between offers and bids. An **offer** is a commitment for a trader to sell under certain conditions such as a minimum price. A **bid** is made by a trader to buy under certain conditions such as a commitment to purchase at a particular price.

There are many potential combinations of the sequence of bids and offers and these have been described by Reck (1997). Despite the combinations two main types of auction can be identified:

1 *Forward, upward or English auction (initiated by seller)*. These are the types of auctions available on consumer sites such as eBay. For these auctions, the seller sets the rules and the timing, and then invites potential bidders. Increasing bids are placed within a certain time limit and the highest bid will succeed provided the reserve (minimum) price is exceeded. The forward auction can also potentially be used to perform price discovery in a market.
2 *Reverse, downward or Dutch auction (initiated by buyer)*. These are more common on business-to-business marketplaces. For these auctions, the buyer sets the rules and the timing. Here, the buyer places a request for tender or quotation (RFQ) and many suppliers compete, decreasing the price, with the supplier whom the buyer selects getting the contract. This will not necessarily be the lowest price since other factors such as quality and capability to deliver will be taken into account. Companies may use reverse auctions to:
   - rationalize suppliers in a particular spending category;
   - source new components in an area they are unfamiliar with.

Some marketplaces also offer a basic exchange where buyers and sellers can offer and bid, but without the constraints of an auction. The scale of some auctions is shown by the auction activity of large manufacturers such as DaimlerChrysler. Through 2001 there were over 512 online auction bidding events processed for DaimlerChrysler on vendor-supported portal Covisint (www.covisint.com) amounting to approximately €10 billion, that is, a third of their total procurement volume. In May 2001, DaimlerChrysler staged the largest online bidding event ever, with an order volume of €3.5 billion in just four days. As well as savings in material purchasing prices, DaimlerChrysler also reduced throughput times in purchasing by 80 per cent (Covisint, 2002).

Note that Covisint (www.covisint.com) is no longer a marketplace, rather it is a neutral supplier of technology owned by Compuware. The original vision of a neutral B2B marketplace has not transpired. Instead, each manufacturer or company requiring B2B services uses e-business technology to source materials. So the e-business messaging technology has proved successful, but the B2B auction marketplace model has not. In 2006, Covisint technogies had 266,000 users in more than 30,000 companies in 96 countries. Although it doesn't now exist as a single marketplace, many manufacturers still use this technology for procurement. For example, in January 2006, GM announced that it was going to continue using Covisint for links with its 18,000 worldwide suppliers.

Emiliani (2001) reviews the implications of B2B reverse auctions in detail and *Case Study 2.1* shows how auctions can be used in a B2B context.

Case Study 2.1 The impact of B2B reverse auctions

FT

This case explains the process of a reverse auction and the types of products suitable for purchase by this method. The benefits of reverse auctions are explored through many examples from different sectors including purchases by government departments.

A dozen people sit in a room staring at the projection of a computer screen on the wall.

For 20 minutes or so nothing much happens. 'It's a little like watching paint dry', says Steve Dempsey, government partner with the consulting firm Accenture.

But suddenly someone miles away, linked via the internet, makes a bid. A pale blue dot registers at the top of the screen. Soon others follow, different colours representing different companies. An e-auction, aimed at cutting the price the public sector pays for anything from paper to computer equipment to air freight, is under way.

Reverse auctions – where companies bid their way down to the lowest price at which they are prepared to supply – are a commonplace tool in parts of the private sector. Operating a little like eBay in reverse, they are a way for buyers to negotiate, online, with suppliers to source a range of goods – those whose quality and nature can be defined with absolute clarity.

Accenture has run more than 1,500 such auctions in the private sector in businesses as diverse as the oil and chemical industries, industrial equipment, marketing and foodstuffs. More than 125 different commodities have been bought and sold this way, including fork lift trucks, coffee, foil, fuel, filters, pallets, pipes and structural steel. Auctions have also included services, such as temporary staff and contracts for earth removal.

The approach has now come to the public sector and has been greeted with enthusiasm by the Office for Government Commerce, which is charged with lopping £1bn off the government's £13bn civil procurement bill over three years.

'E-auctions are not suitable for everything', Mr Dempsey says. The product has to be a commodity – one where the purchaser can specify precisely what standards the desired good or service has to meet. It could not, for example, be used to buy in the services of lawyers or consultants, or something where the purchaser has to design the service or innovate. But about a third of all commodities are suitable for auction, Mr Dempsey says. For the government, that may mean hundreds of millions of pounds' worth of goods a year.

The auctions it has conducted in the private sector have produced average savings of 17 per cent on the historic price of previous contracts, Accenture claims.

In the public sector, only the Driver and Vehicle Licensing Agency, Royal Mail and the Police Information Technology Organization have used the reverse auction approach – buying computer supplies and security watermarked paper, for example. The four auctions, however, have each produced savings of between 22 per cent and 25 per cent on the previous contract.

The reason, Mr Dempsey argues, is twofold: the field of suppliers can be widened from those who traditionally do business with government; and the auction takes place in real time, increasing the competition on suppliers to find their lowest price.

The process works by the purchaser spelling out precisely what is needed, advertising the requirement and then drawing up an approved list of those who can meet it. Potentially, Mr Dempsey says, that opens up the market to small and medium-sized companies that might not normally see the government as a customer. The parameters of the auction are then set, the suppliers trained – and battle commences. Usually auctions are set to last 30 minutes but are extended for 10 minutes each time a bid comes in during the last five minutes. An average auction runs for about 90 minutes, although some have lasted for several hours.

'You can really feel the tension and excitement', Mr Dempsey says. A company may, for example, have excess stocks of what the government needs. Or it may have a hole in its production run, or a sales target that the contract fills. 'It creates real time, dynamic competition between suppliers', he says. 'It's a real marketplace.' The DVLA, for example, saved more than £200,000 buying several tons of watermarked paper. It is now working on a similar e-auction for millions of the envelopes it uses every year. The Royal Mail, having saved £550,000 on its first two e-auctions, is in the process of buying more than £20m of air freight space to shift air mails.

Paul Cattroll of the DVLA says the reaction of suppliers is mixed. Some feel that it has forced them to reduce their profit margins. 'But it is an opportunity for the government to get better value for money for the taxpayer', he says.

Despite the need to prepare the auction carefully, Accenture argues that the process can prove quicker than traditional procurement, while cutting the administrative cost for both purchaser and provider.

E-auctions have been slow to take off in the public sector because there was a question mark over whether they breached European Union procurement rules. Another barrier is that government contracts tend to run for many years.

But over time e-auctions could become commonplace. The DVLA and Royal Mail, having tried them on a pilot basis, both plan to use them again. And the Office of

Government Commerce, happy they now fit within EU procurement rules, is encouraging other government departments to use them.

Source: A bid to save money for the government. By Nicholas Timmins. *Financial Times*, 29 January 2003.

Questions

1 Summarize the operation of a B2B reverse auction from both the buyer's and seller's perspective.

2 Which types of products are suitable for purchase by reverse auction?

3 Explain the benefits of reverse auction to purchasers.

4 What are the implications to selling companies of the reverse auction?

Business models for e-commerce

Business models
A summary of how a company will generate revenue, identifying its product offering, value-added services, revenue sources and target customers.

A review of the different **business models** made available through e-commerce is of relevance to existing companies, but in particular, start-up companies. Venkatram (2000) points out that existing businesses need to use the Internet to build on current business models, while at the same time experimenting with new business models. New business models may be important to gain a competitive advantage over existing competitors, while at the same time heading off similar business models created by new entrants. More commonly, they may simply offer a different revenue stream through advertising or charging for services in a new way. For start-ups or dot-coms the viability of a business model will be crucial to funding from venture capitalists. But what is a business model? Timmers (1999) defines a 'business model' as:

> *An architecture for product, service and information flows, including a description of the various business actors and their roles; and a description of the potential benefits for the various business actors; and a description of the sources of revenue.*

It can be suggested that a business model for e-commerce requires consideration of the marketplace from several different perspectives:

- Does the company operate in the B2B or B2C arena, or a combination?
- How is the company positioned in the value chain between customers and suppliers?
- What is its value proposition and for which target customers?
- What are the specific revenue models that will generate different income streams?
- What is its representation in the physical and virtual world, e.g. high-street presence, online only, intermediary, mixture?

Timmers (1999) identifies no less than 11 different types of business model that can be facilitated by the web. You will notice that many of these are in common with the intermediary types identified by Sarkar which we reviewed earlier in the chapter:

1 *E-shop* – marketing of a company or shop via the web;
2 *E-procurement* – electronic tendering and procurement of goods and services;
3 *E-malls* – a collection of e-shops such as Indigo Square (www.indigosquare.com);
4 *E-auctions* – these can be B2C, e.g. eBay (www.ebay.com), or predominantly B2B, e.g. QXL (www.qxl.com);
5 *Virtual communities* – these can be B2C communities such as iVillage (www.ivillage.co.uk) or B2B communities such as Vertical Net (www.vertical.net); these are important for their potential in e-marketing and are described in the section on virtual communities in *Chapter 9*;

6 *Collaboration platforms* – these enable collaboration between businesses or individuals, e.g. E-groups, now part of Yahoo! (www.yahoo.com) services;
7 *Third-party marketplaces* – marketplaces are described in *Focus on electronic B2B marketplaces* in *Chapter 7*;
8 *Value-chain integrators* – offer a range of services across the value chain;
9 *Value-chain service providers* – specialize in providing functions for a specific part of the value chain, such as the logistics company UPS (www.ups.com);
10 *Information brokerage* – provide information for consumers and businesses, often to assist in making the buying decision or for business operations or leisure;
11 *Trust and other services* – examples of trust services include include Internet Shopping is Safe (ISIS) (http://www.imrg.org/isis) or TRUSTe (www.truste.org) which authenticate the quality of service provided by companies trading on the web.

Pant and Ravichandran (2001) have also produced a similar list of business models.

Now complete *Activity 2.7* to assess whether it is possible to simplify these business models and read *Case Study 2.1* to see examples of new revenue models that can be used by a forward-looking retailer.

Activity 2.7 Exploring business models

Purpose

To explore the different types of business model available on the web and suggest a structure for evaluating business models.

Question

Identify overlap between the different business models identified by Timmers (1999). Can you group the different business models into different types of services? Do you think these business models operate in isolation?

Answers to activities can be found at www.pearsoned.co.uk/chaffey

Figure 2.10 suggests a different perspective for reviewing alternative business models. There are three different perspectives from which a business model can be viewed. Any individual organization can operate in different categories, as the examples below show, but most will focus on a single category for each perspective. Such a categorization of business models can be used as a tool for *formulating e-business strategy* (*Chapter 5, p. 233*). The three perspectives, with examples, are:

1 *Marketplace position perspective*. The book publisher here is the manufacturer, Amazon is a retailer and Yahoo! is both a retailer and a marketplace intermediary.
2 *Revenue model perspective* (*p. 63*). The book publisher can use the web to sell direct and Yahoo! and Amazon can take commission-based sales. Yahoo! also has advertising as a revenue model.
3 *Commercial arrangement perspective* (*p. 57*). All three companies offer fixed-price sales, but, in its place as a marketplace intermediary, Yahoo! also offers alternatives.

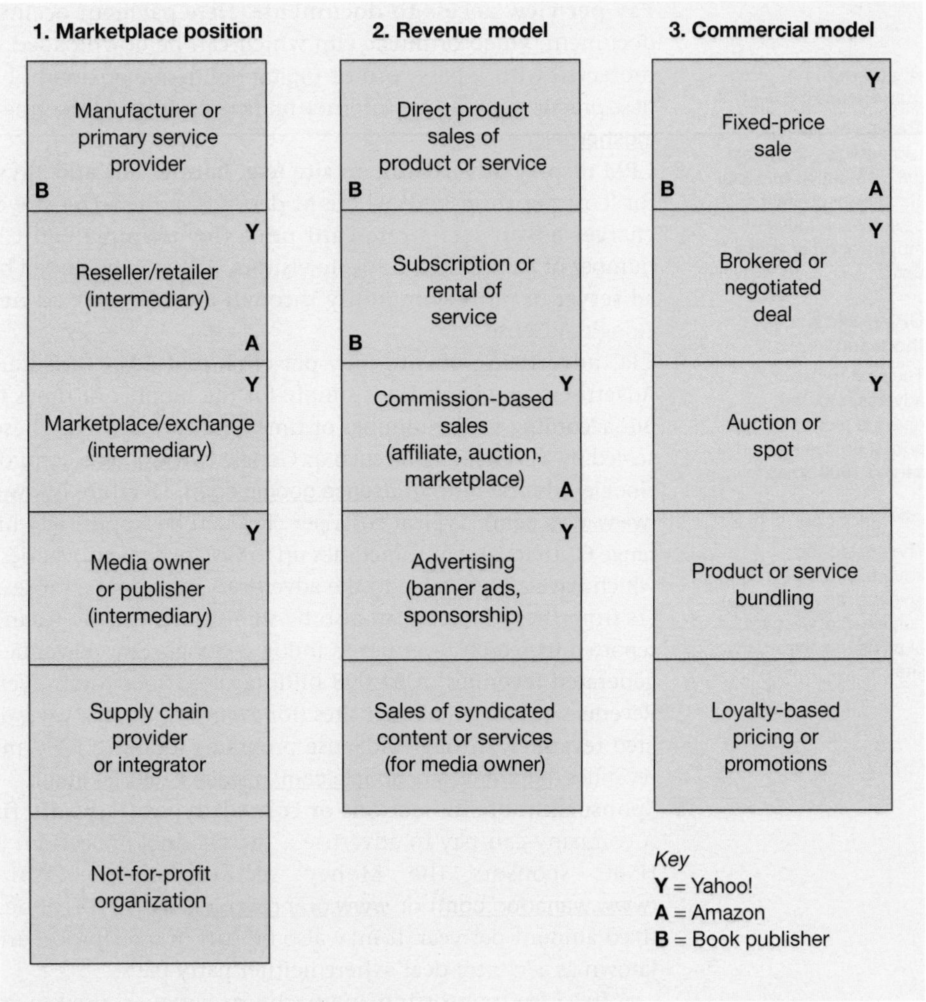

Figure 2.10 **Alternative perspectives on business models**

Revenue models

Revenue models
Describe methods of generating income for an organization.

Revenue models specifically describe different techniques for generation of income. For existing companies, revenue models have revolved largely around the income from sales of products or services. This may be either for selling direct from the manufacturer or supplier of the service or through an intermediary who will take a cut of the selling price. Both of these revenue models are, of course, still crucial in online trading. There may, however, be options for other methods of generating revenue; perhaps a manufacturer may be able to sell advertising space or sell digital services that were not previously possible.

Publisher revenue models

For a publisher, the main types of revenue model which are possible include:

1 **Subscription access to content.** A range of documents can be accessed for a period of a month or typically a year. For example, I subscribe to the *FT* (www.ft.com) for access to the digital technology section for around €80 per year.

2 **Pay-per-view access to documents.** Here payment occurs for single access to a document, video or music clip which can be downloaded. It may or may not be protected with a password or digital rights management. I pay to access detailed best-practice guides on Internet marketing from Marketing Sherpa (www.marketingsherpa.com).

Digital rights management (DRM)
The use of different technologies to protect the distribution of digital services or content such as software, music, movies or other digital data.

3 **CPM display advertising on site (e.g. banner ads and skyscrapers).** CPM stands for 'cost per thousand' where M denotes 'mille'. The site owner such as FT.com charges advertisers a rate card price (for example €50 CPM) according to the number of its ads shown to site visitors. Ads may be served by the site owner's own ad server or more commonly through a third-party ad network service such as Google AdSense.

CPM (cost per thousand)
The cost to the advertiser (or the revenue received by the publisher) when an ad is served 1000 times.

4 **CPC advertising on site (pay-per-click text ads).** CPC stands for 'cost per click'. Advertisers are charged not simply for the number of times their ads are displayed, but according to the number of times they are viewed. These are typically text ads served by a search engine such as Google (www.google.com) or on a network such as Google Adsense (http://adsense.google.com), Overture (www.overture.com) or MIVA (www.miva.com). Typical costs per click can be surprisingly high, i.e. they are in the range €0.10 to €4, but sometimes up to €20 for some categories such as 'life insurance' which have a high value to the advertiser. The revenue for search engines or publishers from these sources can also be significant. For the financial year 2005, Google reported its search revenues as follows: Google Sites Revenues – Google-owned sites generated revenues of $1.098 billion, or 57% of total revenues; Google Network Revenues – Google's partner sites (for example, my site: www.davechaffey.com) generated revenues, through AdSense programs totalling $799 million, or 42% of total revenues (http://investor.google.com/ releases/2005Q4.html).

CPC (cost per click)
The cost to the advertiser (or the revenue received by the publisher) of each click of a link to a third-party site.

5 **Sponsorship of site sections or content types (typically fixed fee for a period).** A company can pay to advertise a site channel or section. For example, the bank HSBC sponsors the Money section on the Wanadoo/Orange portal (www.wanadoo.com) or www.orange.co.uk. This type of deal is often struck for a fixed amount per year. It may also be part of a reciprocal arrangement, sometimes known as a 'contra-deal' where neither party pays.

A fixed-fee sponsorship approach was famously used in 2005 by Alex Tew, a 21-year-old considering going to university in the UK who was concerned about paying off his university debts. This is no longer a concern since he earned $1,000,000 in 4 months when he set up his Million Dollar Homepage (www.milliondollarhomepage.com). In fact, he may no longer need to go to university... His page (*Figure 2.11*) is divided into 100-pixel blocks (each measuring 10 × 10 pixels) of which there are 10,000 giving 1,000,000 pixels in total. Alex spent £50 on buying the domain name (www.milliondollarhomepage.com) and a basic web-hosting package. He designed the site himself but it began as a blank page. Jealous? I am, but it's a great concept and a good PR approach was used. His friends and family paid the first $1,000 dollars, which he spent on a press release. The BBC reported him as saying: 'It snowballed. As I made money, more people talked about it and the more people talked about it, the more money I made.' He also had the idea of auctioning the last pixels. US$38,100 was reportedly bid and received for a 100-pixel ad from Million Dollar Weightloss!

6 **Affiliate revenue (CPA, but could be CPC).** Affiliate revenue is commission-based, for example I display Amazon books on my site DaveChaffey.com (www.davechaffey.com) and receive around 5% of the cover price as a fee from Amazon. Such an arrangement is sometimes known as cost per acquisition (CPA). Increasingly this approach is replacing CPM or CPC approaches where the advertiser has more negotiating power. For example, in 2005 the manufacturing company Unilever negotiated CPA deals with online publishers where it paid for

CPA (cost per acquisition)
The cost to the advertiser (or the revenue received by the publisher) for each outcome such as a lead or sale generated after a click to a third-party site.

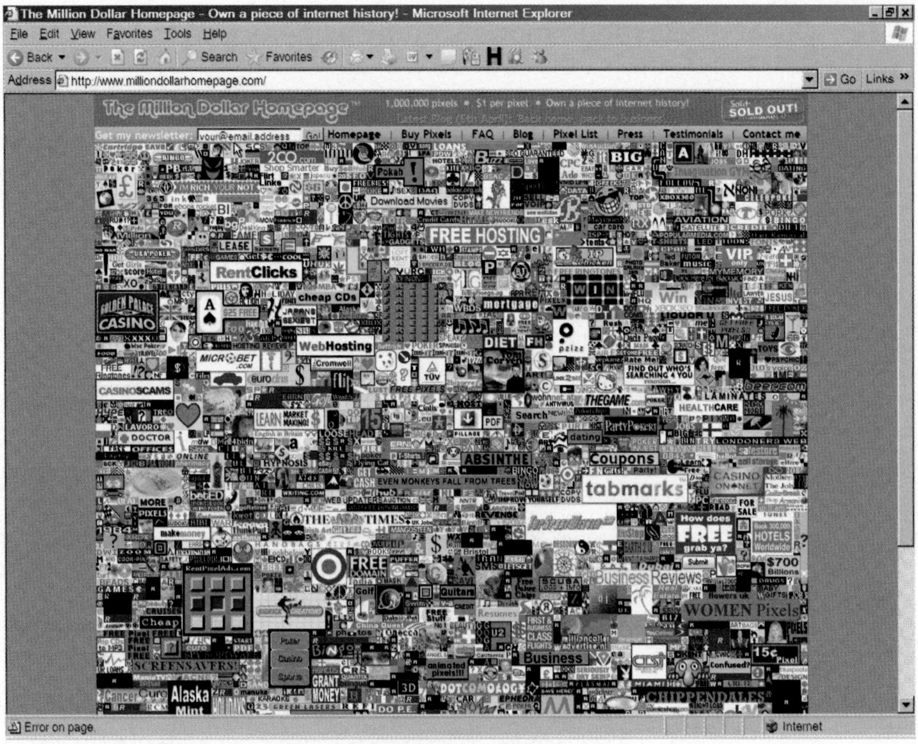

Figure 2.11 Alex Tew's Million Dollar Home Page (www.milliondollarhomepage.com)

every e-mail address captured by a campaign rather than a traditional CPM deal. However, it depends on the power of the publisher, who will often receive more revenue overall for CPM deals. After all, the publisher cannot influence the quality of the ad creative or the incentivization to click which will affect the clickthrough rate on the ad and so the CPM.

7 **Subscriber data access for e-mail marketing.** The data a site owner has about its customers are also potentially valuable since it can send different forms of e-mail to its customers if they have given their permission that they are happy to receive e-mail from either the publisher or third parties. The site owner can charge for adverts placed in its newletter or can deliver a separate message on behalf of the advertiser (sometimes known as list rental). A related approach is to conduct market research with the site customers.

Considering all of these approaches to revenue generation together, the site owner will seek to use the best combination of these techniques to maximize the revenue. To assess how effective different pages or sites in their portfolio are at generating revenue, they will use two approaches. The first is eCPM, or effective cost per thousand. This looks at the total they can charge (or cost to advertisers) for each page or site. Through increasing the number of ad units on each page this value will increase. This is why you will see some sites which are cluttered with ads. The other alternative to assess page or site revenue-generating effectiveness is revenue per click (RPC), which is also known as 'earnings per click' (EPC). This is particularly important for affiliate marketers who make money through commission when their visitors click through to third-party retail sites such as Amazon, and then purchase there.

Activity 2.8 explores some of the revenue models that are possible.

Activity 2.8 Revenue models at e-business portals

Visit the w.w.w.

Purpose

To illustrate the range of revenue-generating opportunities for an online publisher. This site looks at three alternative approaches for publishing, referencing three different types of portal.

Question

Visit each of the sites in this category. You should:

1 Summarize the revenue models which are used for each site by looking at the information for advertisers and affiliates.

2 What are the advantages and disadvantages of the different revenue models for the site audience and the site owner?

3 Given an equivalent audience, which of these sites do you think would generate the most revenue? You could develop a simple spreadsheet model based on the following figures:

- *Monthly site visitors*: 100,000, 0.5% of these visitors clickthrough to affiliate sites where 2% go on to buy business reports or services at an average order value of €100;
- *Monthly page views*: 1,000,000, average of three ads displayed for different advertisers at €20 CPM (we are assuming all ad inventory is sold, which is rarely true in reality);
- *Subscribers to weekly newsletter*: 50,000. Each newsletter broadcast four times per month has four advertisers each paying at a rate of €10 CPM.

Note: These are not actual figures for any of these sites.

The sites are:

- E-consultancy (www.e-consultancy.com), *Figure 2.12*.
- Net Imperative (www.netimperative.com)
- Marketing Sherpa (www.marketingsherpa.com).

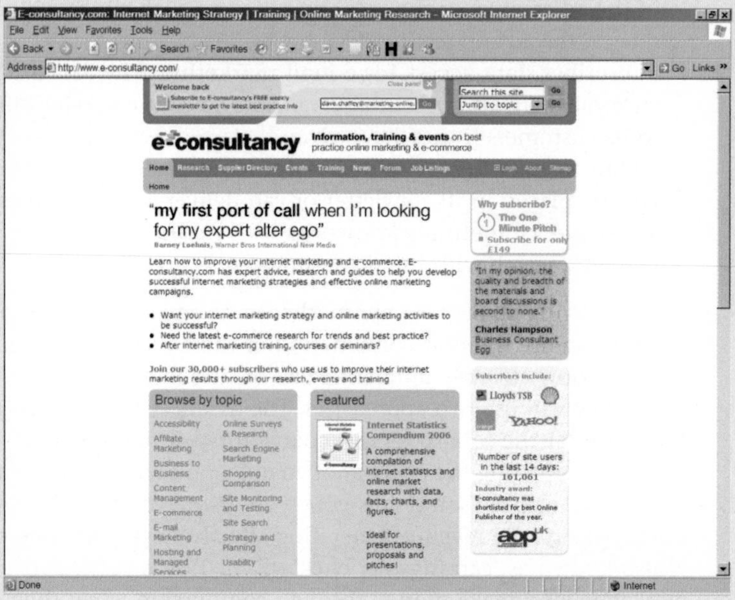

Figure 2.12 E-consultancy (www.e-consultancy.com)

Answers to activities can be found at www.pearsoned.co.uk/chaffey

Focus on Internet start-up companies – the 'dot-coms'

To conclude the chapter, we evaluate the new Internet start-ups – the 'dot-coms' launched in response to the opportunities of new business and revenue models opened up by the Internet in the mid-to-late 1990s. We also consider what lessons can be learnt from the dot-com failures. The emphasis of e-business and e-commerce management is deliberately placed on how electronic communications will impact on existing organizations. But, much of the media coverage of e-commerce in this new medium is on how start-ups are faring. In this section, we consider some of the core attributes of start-up companies. We also reflect on the impact of the 'dot-com' phenomenon on existing organizations.

Dot-coms
Businesses whose main trading presence is on the Internet.

Internet start-ups were first referred to as **'dot-coms'** in the late 1990s since their business model is firmly based on the Internet medium and their web address typically ends in 'dot-com'. The best-known example is probably Amazon.com (www.amazon.com); others include Yahoo! (www.yahoo.com) and CDNow (www.cdnow.com). Note that the extent to which their business presence and operations are on the Internet is dependent on the type of services offered. For Yahoo!, the majority of its services are offered online, although promotion of the services is necessary in the 'real world', since most of its audience spend more time in the real world than in the virtual world – this is the most effective medium for communicating its services. For dot-com e-tailers such as Amazon that sell physical products that have to be distributed to customers, their offline operations are very important to delivering customer satisfaction. As will be seen in the section on *logistics* (*Chapter 6, p. 274*) a major factor affecting Amazon's profitability is how its products are distributed from different warehouses. Furthermore, Amazon has also opened some physical retail units to compete with existing book retailers.

From 'bricks and mortar' to 'clicks and mortar'

Bricks and mortar
A traditional organization with limited online presence.

'Clicks and mortar'
A business combining an online and offline presence.

Clicks only or Internet pureplay
An organization with principally an online presence.

These expressions were introduced in 1999/2000 to refer to traditional **'bricks and mortar'** enterprises with a physical presence, but limited Internet presence. In the UK, an example of a 'bricks and mortar' store would be the bookseller Waterstones (www.waterstones.co.uk), which when it ventured online would become **'clicks and mortar'**. Significantly, in 2001 Waterstones decided it was most cost-effective to manage the Internet channel through a partnership with Amazon (www.amazon.co.uk). In 2006 it reversed this decision and set up its own independent site once more. As mentioned above, some virtual merchants such as Amazon that need to operate warehouses and shops to sustain growth have also become 'clicks and mortar' companies. An Internet 'pureplay' which only has an online representation is referred to as **'clicks only'**. A pureplay typically has no retail distribution network. They may have phone-based customer service, as is the case with office supplier Euroffice (www.euroffice.co.uk), or not, as is the case with financial services provider Zopa (www.zopa.com), or may offer phone service for more valuable customers, as is the case with hardware provider dabs.com (www.dabs.com).

Assessing dot-com businesses

Dot-com companies were often perceived as dynamic and successful owing to the rapid increase in visitors to sites, or sales, or due to initial valuations on stock markets. In reality, it was difficult to assess the success of these companies since despite positive indications in terms of sales or audience, the companies were often not profitable.

Boo.com is an interesting case of the potential and pitfalls of an e-commerce start-up and criteria for success, or one could say of 'how not to do it'. The boo.com site was launched in November 1999 following two significant delays in launching and in January 2000 it was reported that 100 of its 400 employees had been made redundant due to disappointing initial revenues of about £60,000 in the Christmas period. Boo faced a high 'burn rate' because of the imbalance between promotion and site development costs and revenues. As a consequence, it appeared to change its strategy by offering discounts of up to 40 per cent on fashions from the previous season. Closure followed in mid-2000 and the boo.com brand was purchased by an American entrepreneur who still continues to use the brand, as you can see on www.boo.com. Boo.com features as a case study in *Chapter 5*.

Burn rate

The speed at which dot-coms spend investors' money.

Boo.com sold upmarket clothing brands such as North Face, Paul Smith and Helly Hansen. Its founders were all under 30 and included Kajsa Leander, an ex-model. Investors provided a reported £74 million in capital. This enthusiasm is partly based on the experience of two of the founders in creating bokus.com, a relatively successful online bookseller.

As with all new companies, it is difficult for investors to assess the long-term sustainability of start-ups. There are a number of approaches that can be used to assess the success and sustainability of these companies. There have been many examples where it has been suggested that dot-com companies have been overvalued by investors who are keen to make a fast return from their investments. There were some clear anomalies if traditional companies are compared to dot-coms. *Table 2.6* gives an example from the travel industry where in 2000 the market capitalization of Lastminute was approaching that of travel company Thomson which had a much higher turnover and profitability. You can read more about the fate of lastminute.com in *Case Study 2.2*.

Table 2.6 **Comparison between a traditional company and a dot-com, June 2000**

	Thomson Travel	*lastminute.com*		
Formed	1965	1998		
Turnover	FY 2000	FY 2000	FY 2002	6 months to 31 March 2005 (sold after this)
	£3 billion	£2.6 million	£18.4m gross profit (on total transaction value of £124.2m)	£83m gross profit (on total transaction value of £512m)
Profit/loss	£77 million	–£6 million	–£53 million	–£43 million
Market capitalization	£980 million	£700 million	£200 million	c£580 million

Valuing Internet start-ups

Desmet *et al.* (2000) apply traditional discounted cash flow techniques to assess the potential value of Internet start-ups or dot-coms. They point out that traditional techniques do not work well when profitability is negative, but revenues are growing rapidly. They suggest that for new companies the critical factors to model when considering the future success of a company are:

1 The cost of acquiring a customer through marketing.
2 The contribution margin per customer (before acquisition cost).

3 The average annual revenues per year from customers and other revenues such as banner advertising and affiliate revenues.
4 The total number of customers.
5 The customer churn rate.

Churn rate
The proportion of customers (typically subscribers) that no longer purchase a company's products in a time period.

As would be expected intuitively, modelling using these variables indicates that for companies with a similar revenue per customer, contribution margin and advertising costs, it is the churn rate that will govern their long-term success. To look at this another way, given the high costs of customer acquisition for a new company, it is the ability to retain customers for repeat purchases which governs the long-term success of companies. This then forces dot-com retailers to compete on low prices with low margins to retain customers.

A structured evaluation of the success and sustainability of UK Internet start-ups has been undertaken by management consultancy Bain and Company in conjunction with *Management Today* magazine and was described in Gwyther (1999). Six criteria were used to assess the companies as follows.

1 Concept

This describes the strength of the business model. It includes:

- potential to generate revenue including the size of the market targeted;
- 'superior customer value', in other words how well is the proposition of the service differentiated from that of competitors;
- first-mover advantage.

2 Innovation

This criterion looks at another aspect of the business concept, which is the extent to which the business model merely imitates existing real-world or online models. Note that imitation is not necessarily a problem if it is applied to a different market or audience. For example, UK auction company QXL.com (www.qxl.com) has applied the existing model of US companies such as eBay (www.ebay.com) and Ubid (www.ubid.com) to the UK and European market with a focus on so-called white goods. QXL was started by Tim Jackson, a former journalist, who is a multi-millionaire on paper following the valuation of QXL.com at £280 million on its first day of trading. The company whose products are evaluated on the intermediary should review the criteria for assessing quality and be sure it will be compared favourably to competitors on the site.

3 Execution

A good business model does not, of course, guarantee success. If there are problems with aspects of the implementation of the idea, then the start-up will fail. Aspects of execution that can be seen to have failed for some companies are:

- promotion – online or offline techniques are insufficient to attract sufficient visitors to the site;
- performance, availability and security – some sites have been victims of their own success and have not been able to deliver fast access to the sites or technical problems have meant that the service is unavailable or insecure. Some sites have been unavailable despite large-scale advertising campaigns due to delays in creating the web site and its supporting infrastructure;
- fulfilment – the site itself may be effective, but customer service and consequently brand image will be adversely affected if products are not dispatched correctly or promptly.

4 Traffic

This criterion is measured in terms of page impressions and online revenues. Page impressions or visits are not necessarily an indication of success but are dependent on the business model. After the viability of the business model, how it will be promoted is arguably the most important aspect for a start-up. A critical volume of revenue-generating users of a service is required to repay the investment in these companies. Promotion from zero base is difficult and costly if there is a need to reach a wide audience. An important decision is the investment in promotion and how it is split between online and offline techniques. Perhaps surprisingly, to reach the mass market, traditional advertising seems to be required to get the message about the service across clearly to the numbers required. Boo has had major TV and newspaper campaigns. Online promotion through banner ads may also be included in the campaign. Some of the other companies such as lastminute.com and QXL.com have been able to grow without the initial investment in advertising. These have grown more organically, helped by favourable word of mouth and mentions in newspaper features supported by some traditional advertising. Promotion for all these companies seems to indicate that the Internet medium is simply adding an additional dimension to the communications mix and that traditional advertising is still required.

5 Financing

This describes the ability of the company to attract venture capital or other funding to help execute the idea. It is particularly important given the cost of promoting these new concepts.

6 Profile

This is the ability of the company to generate favourable publicity and to create awareness within its target market.

Case Study 2.2 lastminute.com – an international dot-com survivor

This case illustrates the fortunes of lastminute.com, a start-up which used the Internet to introduce an innovative service. The case describes the service and its growth. Success factors in achieving growth and threats to growth throughout the history of the company are described.

lastminute.com was a European innovation, since at launch, no equivalent site existed in the USA. Its business model is based on commission from selling 'distressed inventories' which will have no value if they are not sold immediately. This includes hotel rooms, airline and theatre tickets. In the first half of 2005, the breakdown of product sales (total transaction value on which lastminute gain commission) was as follows:

- Hotels £96 million
- Holidays £163 million
- Flights £158 million
- Car hire £71 million
- Non-travel, e.g. theatre tickets £24 million
- Total £512 million

lastminute explain TTV as follows: Total transaction value ('TTV') does not represent statutory turnover. Where lastminute.com acts as agent or cash collector, TTV represents the price at which products or services have been sold across the Group's various platforms. In other cases, for example the reservation of restaurant tables, a flat fee is earned, irrespective of the value of products or services provided. In such cases TTV represents the flat fee commission earned. Where lastminute.com acts as principal, TTV represents the price at which goods or services are sold across the Group's various platforms.

Turnover for H1 2005 was £222 million with gross profit of £83 million. For the Group as a whole, the number of active customers increased in the half year to 1.69 million compared with 0.99 million in the first half of 2004 (71 per cent growth). There were over 10 million e-mail subscribers and 7 million cumulative customers, although not all were active customers. Active customers purchased 3.6 million items in the half-year, an increase of 49 per cent over the previous year. This gives an average order value of £142 (512 divided by 3.6).

As Table 2.6 shows, although the turnover and gross profit of lastminute.com did improve until the point of takeover, it did not achieve profitability in all markets (it did in the UK for its travel business). It did make great steps in reducing is customer acquisition costs which were £7.30 prior to takeover (£5.69 in the UK) in its final financial report as an independent company. Note 'customer acquisition costs' are calculated in the financial report as all external media spend divided by the number of unique customers. This is effectively media spend per customer, not customer acquisition costs. Since this figure includes repeat customers it would be expected that this number would fall naturally in more mature markets.

In 2005, lastminute had relationships with 13,600 supliers including Lufthansa, Air France, Alitalia, bmi british midland, United Airlines, Virgin Atlantic Airways, Starwood Hotels and Resorts Worldwide, The Savoy Group, Sol Melia, Six Continents, JMC, Disneyland Paris, Kempinski Hotels, English National Ballet, The Royal Albert Hall, The Way Ahead Box Office and Conran Restaurants.

In terms of its brand, lastminute says:

lastminute.com seeks to differentiate itself by generating some of the lowest prices for many travel and entertainment deals, and by packaging and delivering products and services, such as restaurant reservations, entertainment tickets and gifts, in convenient, novel and distinctive ways. It also aims to inspire its customers to try something different. Since 1998 the company believes that it has developed a distinctive brand, which communicates spontaneity and a sense of adventure, attracting a loyal community of registered subscribers.

At 30 September 2001, there were over 4 million registered subscribers, with a total transaction value on the site of £124 million. Of these subscribers, there have only been 536,000 customers since inception. However, lastminute.com is working hard at increasing the conversion rate of new subscribers to customers. This increased from 5.5% to 13.9% between 2000 and 2001. The preferences of users for the type of service required are held on a database and then matched against the offers of suppliers to the site. The choice of suppliers is one of the key differences between an intermediary site such as this and one hosted by a single supplier or travel agency. Enhancements in 2001, to help increase conversion rate included:

- 9 times faster image download time;
- completely redesigned home page and navigation;
- smarter search capability including a mapping search tool to find restaurants, hotels and entertainment options in your local area;
- 200% product supply increase with over 100,000 offers available at any given time;
- new 'MySpace' category with personalized offers and e-mail alerts;
- new 'Staying In' category with food and in-home entertainment delivery options.

The company was founded by Brent Hoberman, 31, and Martha Lane-Fox, 27, both Oxford graduates. Hoberman suggested the idea in 1996 while working at Spectrum, a company specializing in new media strategies. At the time, Lane-Fox said that the idea was too complex and would need thousands of suppliers to be effective. Hoberman and Lane-Fox raised £600,000 to get the company going and achieved many high-profile backers such as France Telecom, Deutsche Telecom, Sony Music Entertainment, the British Airports Authority and Intel and venture capital company Arts Alliance Advisers. One problem was the domain name which had been registered by a Sardinian businessman. Both founders were adamant that their site had to be called this and the Sardinian was happy to sell it for several hundred thousand pounds. This can be compared to the owner of Jungle.com, a Californian who sold it for £235,000 to the site's founder.

The company hoped to use the money from flotation to increase access to the service by offering access to its service by WAP mobile and has signed deals with BT Cellnet and Orange to help achieve this. Other site improvements will also be made – Lane-Fox has been quoted as saying 'We've spent a lot of money improving the back-end, but we want to do more with the front-end.' The improvements to the 'back-end' have been necessary to avoid problems with customer service. Writing in *Computer Weekly*, 2 March 2000, Anne Hyland reported that several customers had money deducted from their account without purchasing any products from the site. For example, Charlotte Brett, a London customer has had £50 deducted from her account on three occasions in January and February 2000. The money was recredited to her account, but Ms Brett was quoted as saying 'I am a very angry customer; in my experience they have failed on the three key areas of technology, customer service and Internet capability'. Brent Hoberman said the problems were caused by its third-party credit-authority firm.

What of the future threats and opportunities for the company? In a *Guardian* interview with Jamie Doward on 27 February 2000 Lane-Fox was asked about the threat of a major ticket site setting up its own site. Lane-Fox dismissed this possibility: 'Companies can't do it on their own web site because they fear cannibalization', and she says of first-mover advantage: 'you still have to set the company up and we're starting to get critical mass in Europe'. lastminute.com have opened offices in London, Paris, Munich and Stockholm to help achieve this. Towards the end of 2001, nine European airlines including Air France, BA, KLM and Lufthansa responded to lastminute.com with the launch of Opodo (which stands for →

OPportunities tO DO (www.opodo.com) which has been set up by nine European airlines. By April 2002, Opodo had become the third most important travel site in the UK, but it appears that the lastminute.com brand is now well established and it is unlikely to be displaced.

To help counter this competition, lastminute.com completed 14 acquisitions between 2003 and 2005, lastminute.com now owns and operates online brands including holidayautos.com, travelprice.com, degriftour.com, travelselect.com, travel4less.co.uk, eXhilaration.co.uk, medhotels.com, first-option.co.uk, gemstonetravel.com, onlinetravel.com and lastminute.de.

2005: The end of lastminute.com as an independent organization

In July 2005, lastminute.com was purchased by Sabre Holdings Corporation (www.sabre-holdings.com/investor), best known as the world's largest electronic global distribution system (GDS), connecting travel agents and travel suppliers with travellers and also the owner of online travel service Travelocity (www.travelocity.com). It was acquired for £577 million, including gross debt of approximately £79 million and estimated cash at bank of £72 million.

Lastminute is now an international e-business with separate web sites for the UK, Ireland, France, Belgium, the Netherlands, Germany, Italy, Spain, Sweden, Australia, New Zealand, Japan, USA, Norway and Denmark.

Source: lastminute.com Investors Relations web site (http://cws.huginonline.com/L/131840/last_index.html)

Questions

1 Explain the business and revenue model for lastminute.com and assess the potential for profitability.

2 Summarize the measures which are used to assess the effectiveness of an e-business such as lastminute.com (such as subscribers, conversion rate and total transaction value). How do they relate to each other?

3 Explain the relative success of lastminute.com and Thomson Travel using the six criteria listed above.

4 What action do you consider the founders of the company should take to ensure the future success of lastminute.com?

The dot-com bubble bursts

The media played a key role in the dot-com story. Initially the media helped produce stratospheric prices for dot-coms by tempting investors with instant gains when companies went through IPOs (Independendent Public Offerings). The media could then also report on the newsworthy spectacle of the failure of many of these businesses. As failure of more and more dot-coms was reported this also impacted on the share prices of the more successful dot-coms such as Yahoo! and even other technology stocks. Popular analogies for the dot-com collapse are the bursting of the South Sea Company's bubble in 1720 and the wilting of the fortunes invested in tulips in the 17th century.

Why dot-coms failed

At the end of *Chapter 5* we review the reasons for failed e-business strategies and in *Case Study 5.2,* examine the reasons for one of the most spectacular dot-com failures – Boo.com. We will see that in many cases it was a case of an unsound business strategy, or ideas before their time. Many of the dot-coms were founded on innovative ideas which required a large shift in consumer behaviour. A rigorous demand analysis would have shown that, at the time, there were relatively few Internet users, with the majority on dial-up connections, so there wasn't the demand for these services. We see in the Boo.com example that there were also failings in implementation, with technology infrastructure resulting in services that were simply too slow.

Remember, though, that many companies that identified a niche and carefully controlled their growth did survive, of which 'boys' toys site' Firebox is a great example.

Mini Case Study 2.1 Firebox.com survives the dot-com boom and bust

Firebox.com *Figure 2.13* opened its virtual doors in 1998 as hotbox.co.uk, an internet retailer which was founded by university flatmates Michael Smith and Tom Boardman. Initially operating out of Cardiff, the company saw rapid initial growth due to the success of the founders' invention, the Shot Glass Chess Set. In the summer of 1999 the company moved to London and relaunched as Firebox.com.

Figure 2.13 **www.firebox.com**

eSuperbrands (2005) describes Firebox products as 'unique, unusual and quirky products from around the world'. Examples include glowing alarm clocks, light sabres, duct tape wallets and, of course, lava lamps. With many traditional retailers and other niche players operating in this sector now, Firebox positions itself as being one of the first outlets for innovative products. Firebox makes use of the collaborative nature of the web with C2C interactions where Firebox.com customers describe their experiences with products and even send in photos and videos of them in action!

Initially a 'pureplay' Internet-only business, Firebox is now a multi-channel retailer, providing a mail order service via its catalogue, corporate products (sales promotion and staff incentives for Yahoo, Oracle, Five, Siemens and Abbey and wholesale and trade suppliers) who distribute niche products to other online and offline e-retailers.

Firebox received £500,000 of investment from New Media Spark, with further funding from private investors. Sales have grown 156% a year from £262,000 in 2000 to £4.4m in 2003 and £8 million in 2004 from 175,000 orders. In the same year, it received 4.5 million page impressions and 680,000 monthly

→

unique visitors, according to the Nielsen//Netratings panel (eSuperbrands, 2005). Firebox.com became profitable in 2001.

One of the reasons for the success of Firebox is the way it has embraced traditional channels to market. Silicon.com (2004) reports that Head of PR Charlie Morgan explained:

> *In a market place that was fast becoming cluttered there was a strong need to both expand the customer base and ensure that Firebox itself grew as a brand. By building in a programme of catalogue drops, Firebox aimed to recruit many new customers who had not thought of the internet as a purchasing medium, increase turnover and of course grow the brand.*

At Christmas 2003, Firebox.com sent out more than 1 million catalogues, resulting in 10,000 new customers which the company regards as an impressive return, since several hundred thousand of these catalogues were sent to already-existing customers. During a three-month promotion the catalogues drove more than £600,000-worth of sales.

Source: Company web site, About Us, eSuperbrands (2005) and Silicon.com (2004). With thanks to www.firebox.com

The impact of the dot-com phenomenon on traditional organizations

The failure of so many dot-coms has accounted for much adverse publicity in the media and e-commerce and e-business were perhaps perceived by some as a fad. However, for every story about dot-com failure there is perhaps an untold story of e-business success. In the background, traditional companies have continued to adopt new technologies. The changes made by existing business are aptly summed up by David Weymouth, Barclays Bank chief information officer, who says (Simons, 2000):

> *There is no merit in becoming a dot-com business. Within five years successful businesses will have embraced and deployed at real-scale across the whole enterprise the processes and technologies that we now know as dot-com.*

What then is the legacy of the dot-com phenomenon? What can we learn from the dot-com successes and failures? We look at the strategic reasons for many dot-com failures in Chapter 4 and *Case Study 5.2* on Boo.com highlights many of the classic problems of dot-com businesses.

The following guidelines can be suggested for managers developing e-commerce strategy for their own companies:

1 Explore new business and revenue models.
2 Perform continuous scanning of the marketplace and respond rapidly.
3 Set up partner networks to use the expertise and reputation of specialists.
4 Remember that the real world is still important for product promotion and fulfilment.
5 Carefully examine the payback and return on investment of new approaches.

As a conclusion to this chapter, consider *Case Study 2.3* which highlights the issues faced by a relatively new e-business launched in 2005.

Case Study 2.3 Zopa launches a new lending model

This case shows how it is still possible to develop radical new online business models. It shows how an online business can be launched without large-scale expenditure on advertising and how it needs to be well targeted at its intended audience.

Context

It might be thought that innovation in business models was left behind in the dot-com era, but still fledgling businesses are launching new online services. Zopa is an interesting example launched in March 2005.

Zopa is an online service which enables borrowers and lenders to bypass the big high-street banks. It is an example of a consumer-to-consumer exchange intermediary. It illustrates the challenges and opportunities of launching a new business online, especially a business with a new business model.

Zopa stands for 'zone of possible agreement' which is a term from business theory. It refers to the overlap between one person's bottom line (the lowest they're prepared to receive for something they are offering) and another person's top line (the most they're prepared to pay for something). In practice, this approach underpins negotiations about the majority of types of products and services.

The business model

The exchange provides a matching facility between people who want to borrow with people who want to lend. Significantly, each lender's money is parcelled out between at least 50 borrowers. Zopa revenue is based on charging borrowers 1 per cent of their loan as a fee, and from commission on any repayment protection insurance that the borrower selects. At the time of writing, Zopa estimated it needs to gain just a 0.2 per cent share of the UK loan market to break even, which it could achieve within 18 months of launch.

The main benefit for borrowers is that they can borrow relatively cheaply over shorter periods for small amounts. This is the reverse of banks, where if you borrow more and for longer it gets cheaper. The service will also appeal to borrowers who have difficulty gaining credit ratings from traditional financial services providers.

For lenders, higher returns are possible than through traditional savings accounts if there are no bad debts. These are in the range of 20 to 30% higher than putting money in a deposit account, but of course, there is the risk of bad debt. Lenders choose the minimum interest rate that they are prepared to accept after bad debt has been taken into account for different markets within Zopa. Borrowers are placed in different risk categories with different interest rates according to their credit histories (using the same Equifax-based credit ratings as used by the banks) and lenders can decide which balance of risk against return they require.

Borrowers who fail to pay are pursued through the same mechanism as banks use and also get a black mark against their credit histories. But, for the lender, their investment is not protected by any compensation scheme, unless they have been defrauded.

The *Financial Times* reported that banks don't currently see Zopa as a threat to their high-street business. One financial analyst said Zopa was 'one of these things that could catch on but probably won't'.

Zopa does not have a contact centre. According to its web site, enquiries to Zopa are restricted to e-mail in order to keep its costs down. However, there is a service promise of answering e-mails within 3 hours during working hours.

Although the service was launched initially in the UK in 2005, *Financial Times* (2005) reported that Zopa has 20 countries where people want to set up franchises. These include the US, where Zopa has a team trying to develop the business through the regulatory hurdles. Other countries include China, New Zealand, India and some South American countries.

About the founders

The three founders of Zopa are chief executive Richard Duvall, chief financial officer James Alexander and David Nicholson, inventor of the concept and business architect. All were involved with Egg, with Richard Duvall creating the online bank for Prudential in 1998. Mr Alexander had been strategy director at Egg after joining in 2000, and previously had written the business plan for Smile, another online bank owned by the Co-operative Bank. The founders were also joined by Sarah Matthews from Egg who was Egg's brand development director.

Target market

The idea for the business was developed from market research that showed there was a potential market of 'freeformers' to be tapped.

Freeformers are typically not in standard employment, rather they are self-employed or complete work that is project-based or freelance. Examples include consultants and entrepreneurs. Consequently, their incomes and lifestyles may be irregular, although they may still be assessed as creditworthy. According to James Alexander, 'they're people who are not understood by banks, which value stability in people's lives and income over everything else'. Institute of Directors (IOD) (2005) reported that the research showed that freeformers had 'much less of a spending model of money and much more of an asset model'.

→

Surprisingly, the research indicated a large number of freeformers. *New Media Age* reported Duvall as estimating that in the UK there may be around 6 million freeformers (of a population of around 60 million). Duvall is quoted as saying: 'it's a group that's growing really quickly. I think in 10 or 15 years time most people will work this way. It's happening right across the developed world. We've been doing some research in the US and we think there are some 30 or 40 million people there with these attitudes and behaviours.'

Some of the directors see themselves as freeformers: they have multiple interests and do not only work for Zopa; James Alexander works for one day a week in a charity and Sarah Matthews works just 3 days a week for Zopa. You can see example personas of typical borrowers and lenders on the web site: www.zopa.com/Zopa Web/public/ how/zopamembers.shtml.

From reviewing the customer base, lenders and borrowers are often united by a desire to distance themselves from conventional institutions. James Alexander says: 'I spend a lot of time talking to members and have found enormous goodwill towards the idea, which is really like lending to family members or within a community.' But he also says that some of the lenders are simply entrepreneurs who have the funds, understand portfolio diversification and risk and are lending on Zopa alongside other investments.

Business status

The *Financial Times* (2005) reported that Zopa had just 300 members at launch, but within 4 months it had 26,000 members. According to James Alexander, around 35 per cent are lenders, who between them have £3m of capital waiting to be distributed. The company has not, to date, revealed how much has been lent, but average loans have been between £2,000 and £5,000. Moneyfacts.co.uk isn't showing any current accounts with more than 5 per cent interest, but Zopa is a riskier product, so you'd expect better rates. Unlike a deposit account, it's not covered by any compensation schemes.

Marketing communications

The launch of Zopa has been quite different from Egg and other dot-coms at the turn of the millennium. Many companies at that time invested large amounts in offline media such as TV and print to rapidly grow awareness and to explain their proposition to customers.

Instead, Zopa has followed a different communications strategy, which has relied on word of mouth and PR with some online marketing activities where the cost of customer acquisition can be controlled. The launch of such a model and the history of its founders makes it relatively easy to have major pieces about the item in relevant newspapers and magazines such as *The Guardian*, *The Financial Times*, *The Economist* and the Institute of Directors house magazine, which its target audience may read. Around launch, IOD (2005) reports that Duvall's PR agency, Sputnik, achieved 200 million opportunities for the new company to be read about. Of course, not all coverage is favourable: many of the articles explored the risk of lending and the viability of the start-up. However, others have pointed out that the rates for the best-rated 'A category' borrowers are better than any commercial loan offered by a bank and for lenders, rates are better than any savings account. The main online marketing activities that Zopa uses are search engine marketing and affiliate marketing.

Funding

Zopa initially received funding from two private equity groups, Munich-based Wellington Partners and Benchmark Capital of the US. Although the model was unique within financial services, its appeal was increased by the well-publicized success of other peer-to-peer Internet services such as Betfair, the gambling web site, and eBay, the auction site.

Sources: *Financial Times* (2005), *New Media Age* (2005), Institute of Directors (2005), Zopa web site (www.zopa.com) and blog http://blog.zopa.com.

Question

Imagine you are a member of the team at the investors reviewing the viability of the Zopa business. On which criteria would you assess the future potential of the business and the returns in your investment based on Zopa's position in the marketplace and its internal capabilities?

Summary

1 The constantly changing e-business environment should be monitored by all organizations in order to be able to respond to changes in social, legal, economic, political and technological factors together with changes in the immediate marketplace that occur through changes in customer requirements and competitors' and intermediaries' offerings.

2 The e-business marketplace involves transactions between organizations and consumers (B2C) and other businesses (B2B). Consumer-to-consumer (C2C) and consumer-to-business categories (C2B) can also be identified.

3 The Internet can cause *disintermediation* within the marketplace as an organization's channel partners such as wholesalers or retailers are bypassed. Alternatively, the Internet can cause *reintermediation* as new intermediaries with a different purpose are formed to help bring buyers and sellers together in a *virtual marketplace* or marketspace. Evaluation of the implications of these changes and implementation of alternative *countermediation* strategies is important to strategy.

4 Trading in the marketplace can be sell-side (seller-controlled), buy-side (buyer-controlled) or at a neutral marketplace.

5 A business model is a summary of how a company will generate revenue identifying its product offering, value-added services, revenue sources and target customers. Exploiting the range of business models made available through the Internet is important to both existing companies and start-ups.

6 The Internet may also offer opportunities for new revenue models such as commission on affiliate referrals to other sites or banner advertising.

7 The opportunities for new commercial arrangements for transactions include negotiated deals, brokered deals, auctions, fixed-price sales and pure spot markets, and barters should also be considered.

8 The success of dot-com or Internet start-up companies is critically dependent on their business and revenue models and traditional management practice.

Exercises

Answers to these exercises are available online at www.pearsoned.co.uk/chaffey

Self-assessment questions

1 Outline the main options for trading between businesses and consumers.

2 Explain the concepts of disintermediation and reintermediation with reference to a particular industry; what are the implications for a company operating in this industry?

3 Describe the three main alternative locations for trading within the electronic marketplace.

4 What are the main types of commercial transactions that can occur through the Internet or in traditional commerce?

5 E-business involves re-evaluating value chain activities. What types of changes can be introduced to the value chain through e-business?

6 List the different business models identified by Timmers (1999).

7 Describe some alternative revenue models for a web site from a magazine publisher.

8 Draw a diagram summarizing the different types of online marketplace.

Essay and discussion questions

1 'Disintermediation and reintermediation occur simultaneously within any given market.' Discuss.

2 For an organization you are familiar with, examine the alternative business and revenue models afforded by the Internet and assess the options for the type and location of e-commerce transitions.

3 For a manufacturer or retailer of your choice, analyse the balance between partnering with portals and providing equivalent services from your web site.

4 Contrast the market potential for B2B and B2C auctions.

5 Select an intermediary site and assess how well it makes use of the range of business models and revenue models available to it through the Internet.

Examination questions

1 Explain disintermediation and reintermediation using examples.

2 Describe three different revenue models for a portal such as Yahoo!.

3 What is meant by buy-side, sell-side and marketplace-based e-commerce?

4 What are the different mechanisms for online auctions?

5 Describe two alternative approaches for using e-business to change a company's value chain.

6 Explain what a business model is and relate it to an Internet pureplay of your choice.

7 Outline the elements of the e-business environment for an organization and explain its relevance to the organization.

8 Give three different transaction types that an industry marketplace could offer to facilitate trade between buyers and suppliers.

References

Allen, E. and Fjermestad, J. (2001) E-commerce marketing strategies: a framework and case analysis. *Logistics Information Management*, 14(1/2), 14–23.

Benjamin, R. and Weigand, R. (1995) Electronic markets and virtual value-chains on the information superhighway. *Sloan Management Review*, Winter, 62–72.

Berryman, K., Harrington, L., Layton-Rodin, D. and Rerolle, V. (1998) Electronic commerce: three emerging strategies. *The McKinsey Quarterly*, no. 1, 152–9.

CIO (2002) GM Shifts Gears. Article by Derek Slater, 1 April. Available online at: www.cio.com/archive/040102/matters_content.html.

Covisint (2002) E-business at DaimlerChrysler is paying off: savings exceed present investment. Press release on www.covisint.com, 4 February 2002.

Desmet, D., Francis, T., Hu, A., Koller, M. and Riedel, G. (2000) Valuing dot coms. *The McKinsey Quarterly*, no. 1. Available online at www.mckinseyquarterly.com.

Emiliani, V. (2001) Business-to-business online auctions: key issues for purchasing process improvement. *Supply Chain Management: An International Journal*, 5(4) 176–86

eSuperbrands (2005) eSuperbrands 2006. *Your Guide to Some of the Best Brands on the Web.* Superbrands Ltd, London.

Evans, P. and Wurster, T.S. (1999) Getting real about virtual commerce. *Harvard Business Review*, November, 84–94.

Financial Times (2005) Lending exchange bypasses high street banks. Paul J. Davies, 22 August. *Financial Times*.

Gwyther, M. (1999) Jewels in the web. *Management Today*, November, 63–9.

Hagel, J. and Rayport, J. (1997) The new infomediaries. *McKinsey Quarterly*, no. 4, 54–70.

Institute of Directors (2005) Profile – Richard Duvall. IOD House magazine, *Director*, pp. 51–5.

Klein, S. (1997) Introduction to electronic auctions. *International Journal of Electronic Markets*, 4(7), 3–6.

McDonald, M. and Wilson, H. (2002) *New Marketing: Transforming the Corporate Future*. Butterworth-Heinemann, Oxford.

New Media Age (2005) Personal lender, Dominic Dudley, *New Media Age*, 18 August.

Nunes, P., Kambil, A. and Wilson, D. (2000). The all-in-one market. *Harvard Business Review*, May–June, 2–3.

Pant, S. and Ravichandran, T. (2001) A framework for information systems planning for e-business. *Logistics Information Management*, 14(1), 85–98.

Rayport, J. and Sviokla, J. (1996) Exploiting the virtual value-chain. *McKinsey Quarterly*, no. 1, 20–37.

Reck, M. (1997) Trading characteristics of electronic auctions. *International Journal of Electronic Markets*, 4(7), 17–23.

Sarkar, M., Butler, B. and Steinfield, C. (1996) Intermediaries and cybermediaries. A continuing role for mediating players in the electronic marketplace. *Journal of Computer Mediated Communication*, 1(3). Online-only journal, no page numbers.

Silicon.com (2004) Ecommerce sites: 'Long live ... the catalogue'? 23 November. Author, Will Sturgeon (www.silicon.com)

Simons, M. (2000) Setting the banks alight. *Computer Weekly*, 20 July, 6.

Thomas, J. and Sullivan, U. (2005) Managing marketing communications with multichannel customers, *Journal of Marketing*, 69 (October), 239–51.

Timmers, P. (1999) *Electronic Commerce Strategies and Models for Business-to-Business Trading*. Series on Information Systems, Wiley, Chichester.

Venkatram, N. (2000) Five steps to a dot-com strategy: how to find your footing on the web. *Sloan Management Review*, Spring, 15–28.

Further reading

Deise, M., Nowikow, C., King, P. and Wright, A. (2000) *Executive's Guide to E-Business. From Tactics to Strategy*. Wiley, New York. Introductory chapters consider buy- and sell-side options and later chapters look at value-chain transformation.

Fingar, P., Kumar, H. and Sharma, T. (2000) *Enterprise E-Commerce*. Meghan-Kiffler Press, Tampa, FL. These authors present a model of the different actors in the e-marketplace that is the theme throughout this book.

Novak, T.P. and Hoffman, D.L. (2002) Profitabilty on the web: business models and revenue streams. Vanderbilt position paper. Available online at http://elab.vanderbilt.edu/research/manuscripts/index.htm.

Timmers, P. (1999) *Electronic Commerce Strategies and Models for Business-to-Business Trading*. Series on Information Systems, Wiley, Chichester. Provides coverage of value-chain analysis and business model architectures in Chapter 3.

Turban, E., Lee, J., King, D. and Chung, H. (2000) *Electronic Commerce: A Managerial Perspective*. Prentice-Hall, Upper Saddle River, NJ. Chapter 1 introduces industry structures and models for e-commerce.

Varianini, V. and Vaturi, D. (2000) Marketing lessons from e-failures. *The McKinsey Quarterly*, no. 4, 86–97. Available online at www.mckinseyquarterly.com.

Web links

Computer Weekly (www.computerweekly.com) Has case studies and features of new business models.

Business 2.0 (www.business2.com) Has regular features on the business model of the new economy.

E-business Forum (www.ebusinessforum.com) Provides business intelligence information on e-business adoption from the Economic Intelligence Forum.

International Journal of Electronic Markets (www.electronicmarkets.org) Is published by the Institute for Media and Communications Management, University of St Gallen, Switzerland.

Journal of Computer Mediated Communication (http://jcmc.indiana.edu/) On the web quarterly since June 1995.

Mohansawhney.com (www.mohansawhney.com) Papers from e-business specialist, Mohanbir Sawhney of Kellogg School of Management, Northwestern University, Evanston IL, USA.

Silicon.com (www.silicon.com) Has commentary on new business models and interviews with companies involved with change.

3 E-business infrastructure

Chapter at a glance

Main topics

Focus on ...

Case study

Web support

The following additional case studies are available at www.pearsoned.co.uk/chaffey

- Selecting a supplier for hosting web site services
- Achieving integration between different systems through EAI

The site also contains a range of study material designed to help improve your results.

Learning outcomes

After completing this chapter the reader should be able to:

- **Outline the hardware and software technologies used to build an e-business infrastructure within an organization and with its partners**
- **Outline the hardware and software requirements necessary to enable employee access to the Internet and hosting of e-commerce services.**

Management issues

The issues for managers raised in this chapter include:

- **What are the practical risks to the organization of failure to manage the e-commerce infrastructure adequately?**
- **How should staff access to the Internet be managed?**

Links to other chapters

This chapter is an introduction to Internet hardware and software technologies. It gives the technical background to *Chapters 1* and *2* and to *Parts 2* and *3*. Its focus is on understanding the technology used but it also gives an introduction to how it needs to be managed. The main chapters that cover management of the e-business infrastructure are:

- *Chapter 10*, Change management;
- *Chapter 11*, Analysis and design (including architecture design);
- *Chapter 12*, Implementation and maintenance.

Introduction

E-business infrastructure
The architecture of hardware, software, content and data used to deliver e-business services to employees, customers and partners.

Defining an adequate e-business infrastructure is vital to all companies adopting e-business. The infrastructure directly affects the quality of service experienced by users of the systems in terms of speed and responsiveness. E-business infrastructure refers to the combination of hardware such as servers and client PCs in an organization, the network used to link this hardware and the software applications used to deliver services to workers within the e-business and also to its partners and customers. Infrastructure also includes the architecture of the networks, hardware and software and where it is located. Finally, infrastructure can also be considered to include the data and documents accessed through e-business applications. A key decision with managing this infrastructure is which elements are located within the company and which are managed externally as third-party managed applications, data servers and networks.

It is also important that the e-business infrastructure and the process of reviewing new technology investments be flexible enough to support changes required by the business to compete effectively. For example, for the media there are many new technologies being developed which were described from 2005 onwards as Web 2.0 and IPTV (television delivered over the broadband Internet). We will look at these approaches later in this chapter, but for now let's look at an example of where the implications of new technologies are not heeded. In a speech to the American Society of Newspaper editors in April 2005, Rupert Murdoch of News Corporation said:

> *Scarcely a day goes by without some claim that new technologies are fast writing newsprint's obituary. Yet, as an industry, many of us have been remarkably, unaccountably complacent. Certainly, I didn't do as much as I should have after all the excitement of the late 1990s. I suspect many of you in this room did the same, quietly hoping that this thing called the digital revolution would just limp along.*
>
> *Well it hasn't ... it won't .... And it's a fast developing reality we should grasp as a huge opportunity to improve our journalism and expand our reach.* (News Corporation, 2005)

We refer above to an *adequate* e-business infrastructure, but what does this mean? For the manager in the e-business, this is a key question. While it is important to be able to understand some of the technical jargon and concepts when talking to third-party suppliers of hardware, software and services, what is of crucial importance is to be aware of some of the limitations (and also the business potential) of the infrastructure. Through being aware of these problems, managers of an organization can work with their partners to ensure a good level of service is delivered to everyone, internal and external, who is using the e-business infrastructure. To highlight some of the problems that may occur if the infrastructure is not managed correctly, complete *Activity 3.1*. It illustrates how companies should think about risks and solutions to these risks.

Activity 3.1 Infrastructure risk assessment for The B2C Company

Purpose

To indicate potential problems to customers, partners and staff of the e-business if technical infrastructure is not managed adequately.

Activity

Make a list of the potential problems for users of e-business services developed by The B2C Company. You should consider problems faced by users of e-business applications who are either internal or external to the organization. Base your answer on problems you have experienced on a web site that can be related to network, hardware and software failures or problems with data quality.

Answers to activities can be found at www.pearsoned.co.uk/chaffey

Figure 3.1 summarizes how the different components of e-business architecture referred to in this chapter relate to each other. They can be conceived of as different layers with defined interfaces between each layer. The different layers can best be understood in relation to a typical task performed by a user of an e-business system. For example, an employee who needs to book a holiday will access a specific human resources application or program that has been created to enable the holiday to be booked (Level I in *Figure 3.1*). This application will enable a holiday request to be entered and will forward the application to their manager and human resources department for approval. To access the application, the employee will use a web browser such as Microsoft Internet Explorer using an operating system such as Microsoft Windows XP or Apple OS X (Level II in *Figure 3.1*). This systems software will then request transfer of the information about the holiday request across a network or transport layer (Level III in *Figure 3.1*). The information will then be stored in computer memory (RAM) or in long-term magnetic storage on a web server (Level IV in *Figure 3.1*). The information itself which makes up the web pages or content viewed by the employee and the data about their holiday request are shown as a separate layer (Level V in *Figure 3.1*), although it could be argued that this is the first or second level in an e-business architecture.

Figure 3.1 is similar to other models of e-business or information systems infrastructure from other authors which describe the different elements, but with arguably less logical relationships between layers. Zwass (1998) describes a framework for the Internet consisting of three main elements:

1 *Infrastructure*. The hardware, software, databases and telecommunications.
2 *Services*. Software-based services such as search engines, digital money and security systems.
3 *Products and services*. The web sites of individual companies and marketplaces.

Kampas (2000) describes a five-level model of what he refers to as 'the information system function chain':

1 *Storage/physical*. Memory and disk hardware components (equivalent to Level IV in *Figure 3.1*).
2 *Processing*. Computation and logic provided by the processor (processing occurs at Levels I and II in *Figure 3.1*).
3 *Infrastructure*. This refers to the human and external interfaces and also the network, referred to as 'extrastructure'. (This is Level III in *Figure 3.1*, although the human or external interfaces are not shown there.)
4 *Application/content*. This is the data processed by the application into information. (This is Level V in *Figure 3.1*.)
5 *Intelligence*. Additional computer-based logic that transforms information to knowledge. (This is also part of the application layer I in *Figure 3.1*.)

Each of these elements of infrastructure presents separate management issues which we will consider separately. In this chapter, infrastructure management issues are introduced, while more detailed discussion of management solutions is presented in *Chapters 10, 11* and *12*.

We start our coverage of e-business infrastructure by considering the technical infrastructure for the Internet, extranets, intranets and the World Wide Web which are Levels II and III in *Figure 3.1*. As you will know, The World Wide Web is an interlinked publishing medium for displaying graphic and text information. This information is stored on web server computers and then accessed by users who run web browser programs such as Microsoft Internet Explorer, Apple Safari or Mozilla Firefox which display the information and allow users to select links to access other web sites.

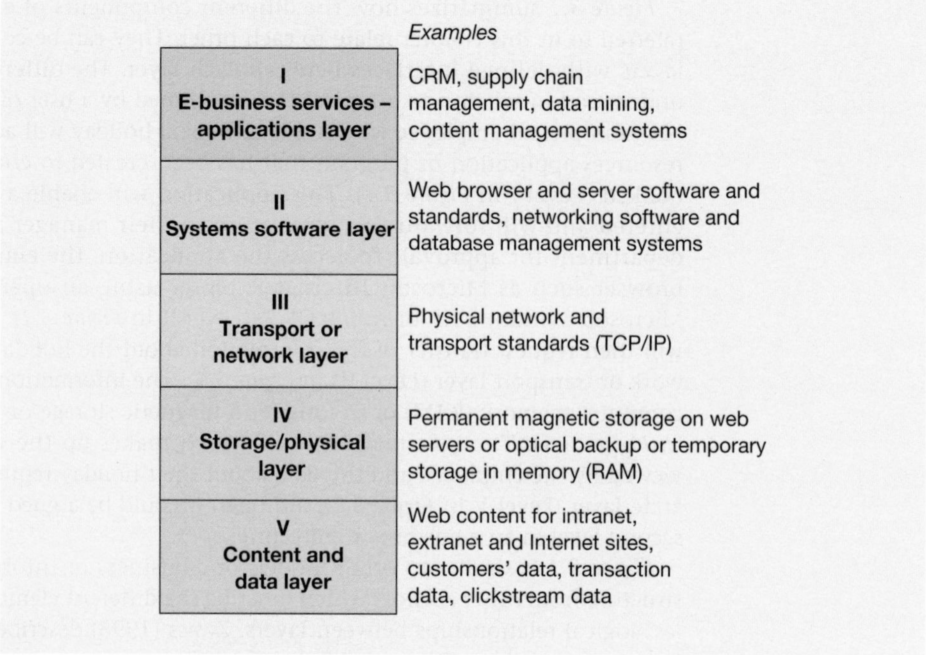

Figure 3.1 A five-layer model of e-business infrastructure

We then look at how these facilities work by reviewing the standards that are used to enable electronic communications, including communications standards such as TCP/IP and EDI and publishing standards such as HTML and XML.

In the second part of the chapter, some management issues of hosting e-business services are then reviewed, specifically management of Level I applications and services by external parties and how to manage staff access to the Internet. Finally, we focus on how new access platforms such as mobile phones and interactive digital TV will change the way the Internet is used in the future (Level II in *Figure 3.1*).

We return to some issues of e-business infrastructure management later in this book. *Table 3.1* provides a summary of the main issues facing businesses and where they are covered in this chapter and later in the book.

Table 3.1 Key management issues of e-business infrastructure

Main issue	*Detail*	*Where covered?*
Which type of e-business applications do we develop?	For example, supply chain management, e-procurement, secure online ordering, customer relationship management	*Chapter 5* sections on e-business services and stage models *Chapters 7,8 and 9* on specific e-business applications
Which technologies do we use?	For example, e-mail, web-based ordering *vs* EDI	This chapter introduces different technologies at different levels of *Figure 3.1* *Chapter 4* discusses adoption of new technologies

Main issue	*Detail*	*Where covered?*
How do we achieve quality of service in applications?	Requirements are: business fit, security, speed, availability and errors	Section on ISPs in this chapter. *Chapter 11* on design *Chapter 12* on implementation
Where do we host applications?	Internal or external sourcing and hosting?	Focus on ASPs section in this chapter Managing partnerships section in *Chapter 9* on SCM
Application integration	Integration of e-business solutions with: – legacy systems – partner systems – B2B exchanges and intermediaries	Section on integrating information systems into supply chain management in *Chapter 6*
Which access platforms do we support? Which development technologies and standards do we use?	Mobile access, interactive digital TV, e.g. CGI, Perl, Cold Fusion, ActiveX	Focus on access devices in this section in *Chapter 12*
How do we manage content and data quality?	How are content and data updated so that they are up-to-date, accurate, easy to find and easy to interpret?	Web content management is introduced in this chapter and in more detail in *Chapters 11* and *12*
How do we manage employee access to the Internet?	Staff can potentially waste time using the Internet or can act illegally	Covered in *Chapter 11* in Focus on e-business security
How do we secure data?	Content and data can be deleted in error or maliciously	Safeguards are described in *Chapter 11*

What is the Internet?

Client/server
The client/server architecture consists of *client* computers, such as PCs, sharing resources such as a database stored on a more powerful *server* computer.

Internet service provider (ISP)
A provider providing home or business users with a connection to access the Internet. They can also host web-based applications.

Backbones
High-speed communications links used to enable Internet communications across a country and internationally.

The **Internet** enables communication between millions of connected computers worldwide. Information is transmitted from client PCs whose users request services to server computers that hold information and host business applications that deliver the services in response to requests. Thus, the Internet is a large-scale **client/server** system.

Figure 3.2 shows how the client PCs within homes and businesses are connected to the Internet via local **Internet service providers (ISPs)** which, in turn, are linked to larger ISPs with connection to the major national and international infrastructure or **backbones**. In the UK, at the London Internet Exchange in the Docklands area of east London, a facility exists to connect multiple backbones of the major ISPs within the UK onto a single high-speed link out of the UK into Europe and to the world. These high-speed links can be thought of as the motorways on the 'information superhighway', while the links provided from ISPs to consumers are equivalent to slow country roads.

The Internet timeline

The Internet is only the latest of a series of developments in the way that the human race has used technology to disseminate information. Kampas (2000) identifies ten stages that are part of five 'megawaves' of change. The first six stages are summarized in *Table 3.2*. It is evident that many of the major advances in the use of information

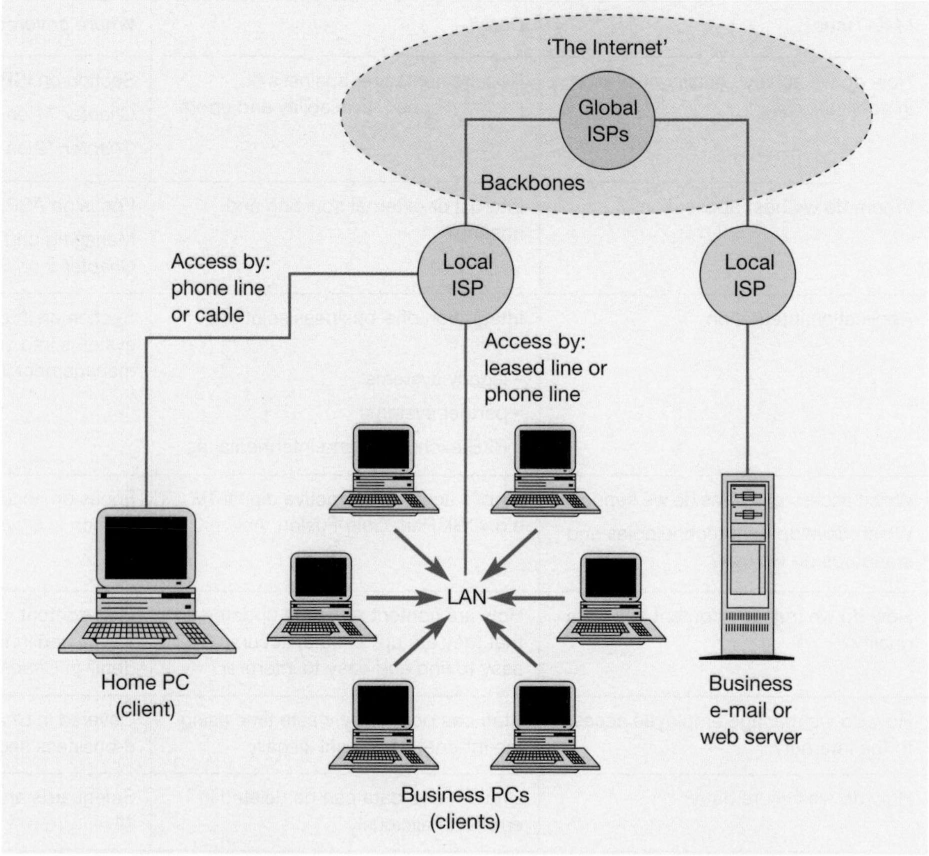

Figure 3.2 **Physical and network infrastructure components of the Internet (Levels IV and III in *Figure 3.1*)**

Table 3.2 **Six stages of advances in the dissemination of information**

Stage	*Enabling technology*	*Killer applications* and impact*
1 Documentation: 3500 BC to AD 1452	Written language and the development of clay tablets in Mesopotamia	Taxes, laws and accounting giving rise to the development of civilization and commerce
2 Mass publication: 1452 to 1946	The Gutenburg press of movable metal type	Demand for religious and scientific texts resulting in scientific advances and ideological conflicts
3 Automation: 1946 to 1978	Electric power and switching technologies (vacuum tubes and transistors)	Code breaking and scientific calculations. Start of information age
4 Mass interaction: 1978 to 1985	Microprocessor and personal computer	Spreadsheets and word processing
5 Infrastructuralization: 1985 to 1993	Local- and wide-area networks, graphical user interfaces	E-mail and enterprise resource planning
6 Mass communication: 1993 to *c*.2005	Internet, World Wide Web, Java	Mass information access for communications and purchasing

**Very* useful applications which will encourage adoption of a technology.

Source: Adapted and republished with permission of CRC Press LLC from table on pp. 8–22 from '*Road map to the e-revolution*', by Kampas, P., in *Information Systems Management Journal*, Spring 2000, Auerbach Publications, Copyright © 2000 by CRC Press LLC; permission conveyed through Copyright Clearance Center, Inc.

Activity 3.2 The development of the Internet

Purpose

To highlight reasons for the development of the Internet as a vital enabler for business.

Questions

Referring to *Figure 3.3*:

1. Give reasons why the Internet took a long time to develop into today's essential business tool.
2. Develop your own timeline of significant events on the Internet. A key source is the Hobbes Internet timeline (www.isoc.org/guest/zakon/Internet/History/HIT.html) or that of Gillies and Cailliau (2000). See the author's timeline (*p. xxi*). See also the Focus on new access devices section (*p. 131*). You may want to speculate on how timelines will differ for future generations.

Answers to activities can be found at www.pearsoned.co.uk/chaffey

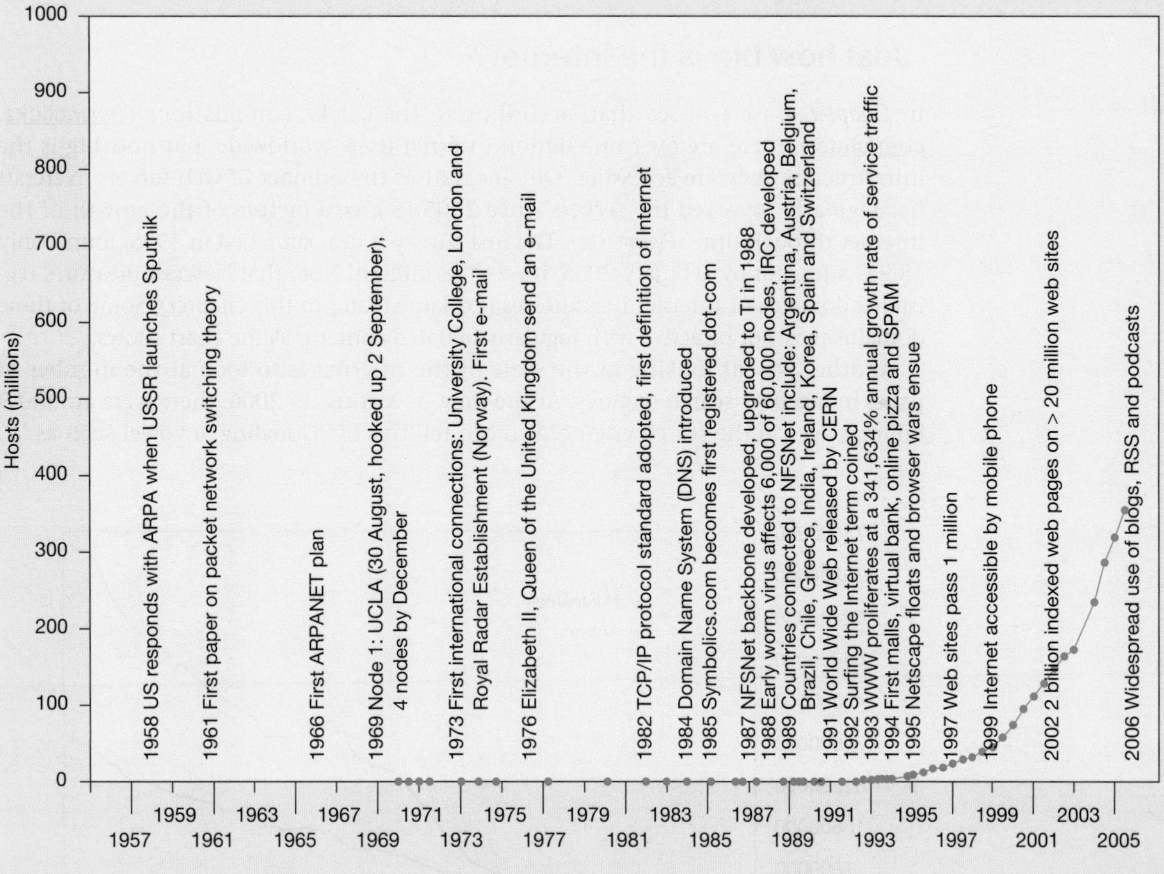

Figure 3.3 **A five-layer model of e-business infrastructure**

have happened within the last hundred years. This indicates that the difficulty of managing technological change is likely to continue. Kampas goes on to speculate on the impact of access to lower-cost, higher-bandwidth technologies.

The history and origin of the Internet as a business tool is surprising since it has taken a relatively long time to become an essential part of business. It started life at the end of the 1960s as the ARPAnet research and defence network in the USA that linked servers used by key military and academic collaborators. It was established as a network that would be reliable even if some of the links were broken. This was achieved since data and messages sent between users were broken up into smaller packets and could follow different routes. Read Gillies and Cailliau (2000) for a detailed description of the history of the Internet.

Although the Internet was subsequently extended worldwide and was used extensively by academic and defence communities, it has only recently been catapulted into mainstream business and consumer use. *Activity 3.2* examines this relatively slow development.

It is the advent of the World Wide Web, which was invented by Tim Berners-Lee of CERN to help share research easily, that is responsible for the massive growth in business use of the Internet. (See Berners-Lee (1999) for a description of the invention of the web.) The World Wide Web provides a publishing medium which makes it easy to publish and read information using a web browser and also to link to related information. (See section *What is the World Wide Web? p. 95.*)

Just how big is the Internet?

In *Chapter 4*, we will see that, according to the ClickZ compilations (**www.clickz.com/stats/**), there are over one billion Internet users worldwide, but how big is the infrastructure they are accessing. One measure is the number of web servers. Netcraft has regularly surveyed the servers since 2005 to give a picture of the growth of the Internet through time (*Figure 3.4*). The first survey it ran, launched in 1995, found only 18,957 sites, but by February 2006, it was 178 million! Note that Netcraft measures registered domains or Internet IP addresses (explained later in this chapter). Some of these domains may not be active with regularly updated content, as the chart shows.

Another way at looking at the scale of the Internet is to look at the number of pages indexed by search engines. At the time of writing, in 2006, there were around 9 billion pages in the search engine. You can tell this by 'Googling' a vowel such as 'a'.

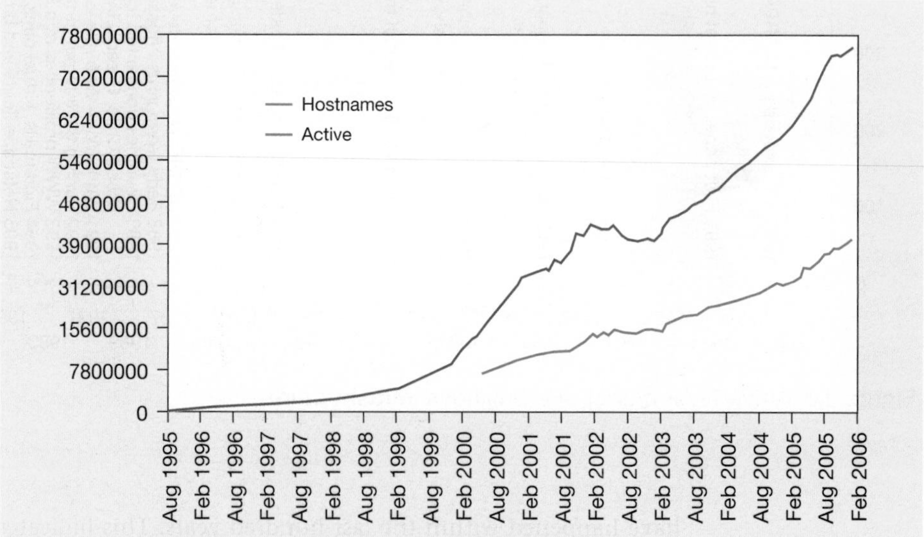

Figure 3.4 **The Netcraft index of number of servers**

Source: Netcraft Web Server Survey. http://news.netcraft.com/archives/web_server_survey.html. Netcraft, http://netcraft.com

At the time, however, Google was readying an enhanced technology known as 'Big Daddy' which was reputed to index 24 billion pages. The next time you Google, Google 'a' and see the latest figure for the number of pages indicated on the top right of the search engine results page.

Intranets and extranets

Intranet
A private network within a single company using Internet standards to enable employees to share information using e-mail and web publishing.

Extranet
Formed by extending an intranet beyond a company to customers, suppliers and collaborators.

The majority of Internet services are available to any business or consumer that has access to the Internet. However, many e-business applications that access sensitive company information require access to be limited to favoured individuals or third parties. If information is limited to those inside an organization, this is an **intranet**. If access is extended to some others, but not everyone beyond the organization, this is an **extranet**. The relationship between these terms is illustrated in *Figure 3.5*. Extranets can be accessed by authorized people outside the company such as collaborators, suppliers or major customers, but information is not available to everyone with an Internet connection – only those with password access. Note that 'intranet' is sometimes loosely used to refer to extranets.

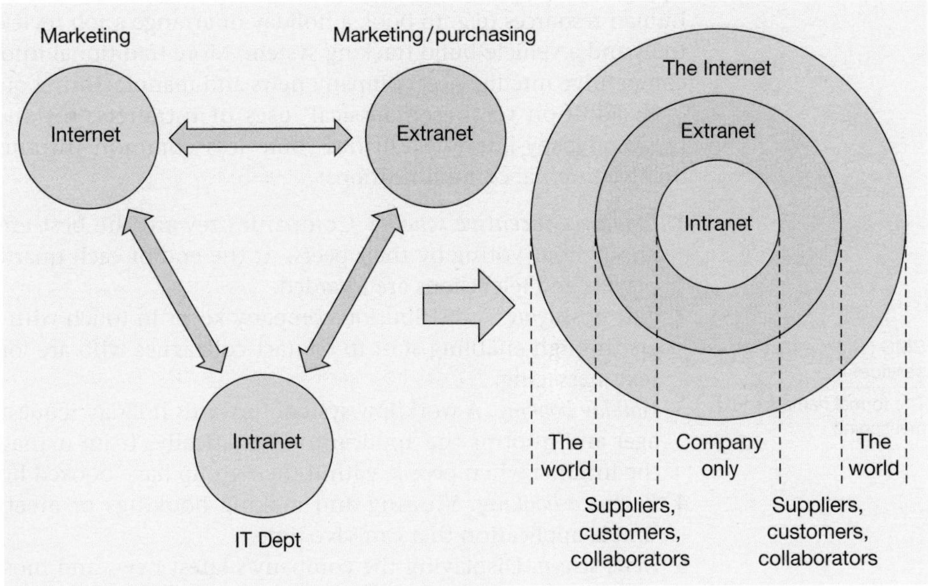

Figure 3.5 **The relationship between intranets, extranets and the Internet**

Intranet applications

Intranets are used extensively for supporting sell-side e-commerce from within the marketing function. They are also used to support core supply-chain management activities as described in the next section on extranets. A marketing intranet has the following advantages:

- Reduced product lifecycles – as information on product development and marketing campaigns is rationalized we can get products to market faster.
- Reduced costs through higher productivity, and savings on hard copy.
- Better customer service – responsive and personalized support with staff accessing customers over the web.
- Distribution of information through remote offices nationally or globally.

Intranets are also used for internal marketing communications since they can include the following types of information:

- Staff phone directories
- Staff procedures or quality manuals
- Information for agents such as product specifications, current list and discounted prices, competitor information, factory schedules, and stocking levels, all of which normally have to be updated frequently and can be costly
- Staff bulletin or newsletter
- Training courses.

Intranets can be used for much more than publishing information. Web browsers also provide an access platform for business applications which were traditionally accessed using separate software programs. This can help reduce the **total cost of ownership (TCO)** of delivering and managing information systems. Applications delivered through a web-based intranet or extranet can be cheaper to maintain since no installation is required on the end-user's PC, upgrades are easier and there are fewer problems with users reconfiguring software on their PC. For example, at Chrysler Corporation the Dashboard intranet aims to increase the productivity of 40,000 employees by simplifying information access while reducing TCO. Applications include tools for workgroups to collaborate on projects, self-service human resources (e.g. to book a holiday or arrange a job review), financial modelling tools and a vehicle-build tracking system. More traditional information is available to competitive intelligence, company news and manufacturing quality statistics.

Total cost of ownership (TCO)
The sum of all cost elements of managing information systems for end-users, including purchase, support *and* maintenance.

In addition to these 'classical' uses of intranets, intranet developer Odyssey (www.odyssey-i.com) identifies some less common intranet applications which involve internal communications:

1 *Employee incentive scheme*. Companies reward the best employees according to anonymous voting by their peers. At the end of each quarter, prizes such as DVD players and televisions are awarded.
2 *Text messaging*. A distribution company keeps in touch with its sales staff and drivers through enabling staff to contact colleagues who are 'on the road' using **SMS** text messaging.
3 *Holiday booking*. A workflow system forwards holiday requests to the relevant manager and informs the applicant automatically. Team managers can also check on the intranet when people within their group have booked holidays.
4 *Resource booking*. Viewing and making bookings of meeting rooms is another simple application that can save time.
5 *News screen*. Displaying the company's latest news and most recent achievements on a dedicated screen can give a focal point to a waiting room or foyer area.
6 *Integrated external resources*. Route planning, mapping or traffic news sites can be integrated into the intranet to save time for staff. One example of this is a housing authority that stores its list of properties on the intranet. Each house has a link to a mapping site (e.g. Multimap, www.multimap.com) which will display the location of the property based on its postcode).

SMS (short message services)
The formal name for text messaging.

In a survey of 275 managers responsible for an intranet featured in CIO (2002), the main benefits mentioned by managers were:

1 Improved information sharing (customer service), 97%
2 Enhanced communications and information sharing (communications), 95%
3 Increased consistency of information (customer service), 94%
4 Increased accuracy of information (customer service), 93%
5 Reduced or eliminated processing, 93%
6 Easier organizational publishing, 92%.

It is apparent that benefits focus on information delivery, suggesting that management of information quality is a key to successful use of intranets. Notice that cost saving is not referred to directly in the list of benefits. Direct cost reduction can be achieved through reduced cost of printing and indirectly though reduced staff time needed to access information. However, intranets represent a substantial investment, so careful consideration of the return on investment is required. David Viney, who has managed implementation of intranets at PricewaterhouseCoopers, British Airways and Centrica PLC estimates that for a large implementation of more than 10,000 staff, the cost could average £250 per user or seat (Viney, 2003). He suggests this cost breaks down into four categories: software (content management systems), hardware (servers to store content and applications), integration of information sources and applications and process change (staff costs and opportunity costs associated within implementation). He also suggests that if the portal project involves integration with ERP systems, this could add £150 per seat.

The management challenges of implementing and maintaining an intranet are similar to those of an extranet. In the next section, we examine five key management issues of extranets. Each of these issues also applies to intranets.

A suitable technology is also required to enable staff to manage their own content. For large sites, it is not practical for all changes to web content to be sent through to a webmaster to update the pages. Think about a large site such as the BBC site (www.bbc.co.uk) which has around 400,000 pages indexed in Google (the search '+a site:www.bbc.co.uk' finds all pages containing the letter 'a' on this site). Many of these pages are news stories which must be updated in real time. The only practical method is to provide journalists and other content providers with access to a system which allows them to add and edit web pages. Such a system is known as a **content management system (CMS)**. As explained in more detail in *Chapter 12*, a CMS is a means of managing the updating and publication of information on any web site, whether intranet, extranet or Internet.

Content management system (CMS)
Software used to manage creation, editing and review of web-based content.

Extranet applications

Although an extranet may sound complex, from a user point of view, it is straightforward. If you have bought a book or CD online and have been issued with a username and password to access your account, then you have used an extranet. This is a consumer extranet. Extranets are also used to provide online services which are restricted to business customers. If you visit the Ifazone (www.ifazone.com) extranet of financial services company Standard Life, which is designed for the independent financial advisers who sell its products, you will see that the web site only has three initial options – log-in, register and demonstrations. The Ifazone extranet is vital to Standard Life since ninety per cent of business is now introduced through this source. This usage of the term 'extranet', referring to electronic business-to-business communications is most typical (see for example, Vlosky *et al.*, 2000). Hannon (1998) concurs, and also notes the relationship of extranets with intranets, he describes an extranet as

> *any network connected to another network for the purpose of sharing information and data. An extranet is created when two businesses connect their respective intranets for business communication and transactions.*

For example, Dell provides Premier Dell.com (formerly Premier Pages) for its business customers. This is how Dell describes the service to customers:

> *Premier Dell.com is your customized procurement portal. A powerful tool created for you to more efficiently manage all phases of computer ownership: purchasing, asset management and product support.*
>
> *Beyond mere customer service or e-commerce, Premier Dell.com empowers organizations to take control. Your organization's Premier Dell.com procurement portal may include a customized online computer store, purchasing and asset management reports and tools,*

system specific technical information, links to useful information throughout Dell's extensive website and more. All the information you need to do business with Dell, in one place, available to you 24 hours a day, 7 days a week. 'Easy as Dell'.

Source: http://premier.dell.com/premier/demo

Vlosky *et al.* (2000) refer to these business benefits of an extranet:

1 *Information sharing in secure environment.* Information needed to support business through a range of business partners can be shared using an extranet. Vlosky *et al.* (2000) give the example of advertising agency Saatchi using an extranet to allow their advertisers to access draft advertising material during a project. Information for suppliers is often shared by providing a log-in to a database which shows demand for products.
2 *Cost reduction.* Operating processes can be made more efficient through an extranet. The example given by these authors is Merisel, a $3.5 billion computer hardware reseller reducing its order processing costs by 70%. Such cost reductions are achieved by reducing the number of people involved in placing orders and the need to rekey information from paper documents.
3 *Order processing and distribution.* The authors refer to an 'electronic integration effect'. For example, an extranet can connect a retailer's point of sales terminals to a supplier's delivery system, ensuring prompt replenishment of goods sold. This potentially means less lost sales because of out-of-stock items and a lower inventory holding is needed.
4 *Customer service.* Improving levels of service is one of the main benefits of the Premier Dell.com extranet described above although it also has the other benefits listed above. Distributors or agents of companies can also find information such as customized pricing or advertising materials. For example, 3M provides open web access to individual customers to find information about its office products such as Post-it notes and transparent films (www.3m.com/uk/office), but it also offers an extranet for distributors such as Spicers (www.spicers.net) and Euroffice (www.euroffice.co.uk).

Many of the management issues involved with managing extranets are similar to those for intranets. These are five key questions that need to be asked when reviewing an existing extranet or when creating a new extranet:

1 *Are the levels of usage sufficient?* Extranets require a substantial investment, but as with a public-facing web site, efforts need to be made to encourage usage since we are asking the users of the service to change their behaviour. It is in the organization's interest to encourage usage, to achieve a return on their investment and achieve the cost savings and efficiencies intended. Take the example of the Standard Life Ifazone referred to above. Many financial advisers may be comfortable with their existing way of selling products using the phone and post. Education will be needed to explain the benefits of the extranet and incentives such as increased commission may also be used.
2 *Is it effective and efficient?* Controls must be put in place to assess how well it is working and improve its performance. Return on investment should be assessed. For example, visitors levels can be measured for different types of audiences and the level of usage for accessing different types of information can be assessed. The direct and indirect cost savings achieved through each extranet transaction can be calculated to help assess effectiveness. For example, 3M, manufacturer of many products including office products such as Post-it notes, has an extranet to connect to the office supply retailers (see www.3m.com/uk/easy). Retailers download the latest price lists and promotional information such as product pictures. Each digital download represents a significant saving in comparison to shipping physical items to the retailer.

3 *Who has ownership of the extranet?* Functions with an interest in an extranet include IT (technical infrastructure), Finance (setting payments and exchanging purchase orders and invoices), Marketing (providing marketing materials and sales data to distributors or providing services to customers) and Operations Management (exchanging information about inventory). Clearly the needs of these different parties must be resolved and management controls established.
4 *What are the levels of service quality?* Since an extranet will become a vital part of an organization's operating process, a problem with the speed or availability of the extranet could cause loss of a lot of money; it is arguably more important than the public-facing Internet site.
5 *Is the quality of the information adequate?* The most important attributes of information quality is that it is up-to-date and accurate. Vlosky *et al.* (2000) point out the importance of liability if information is inaccurate or the extranet crashes.

It will be seen in *Chapter 6* that extranets are used extensively to support supply chain management as resources are ordered from suppliers and transformed into products and services delivered to customers. At Marshall Industries, for example, when a new customer order is received across the extranet it automatically triggers a scheduling order for the warehouse (transferred by intranet), an order acknowledgement for the customer and a shipping status when the order is shipped (Mougayer, 1998). To enable different applications within a company such as a sales ordering system and an inventory control system to interoperate with each other and databases in other companies, requires an internal company intranet to be created that can then communicate across an extranet with applications on another company intranet. To enable different applications on the intranet to communicate, middleware is used by systems integrators.

Middleware
Software used to facilitate communications between business applications including data transfer and control.

This middleware technology that is used to connect together different business applications and their underlying databases across extranets is now also referred to as enterprise application integration (EAI) (*Internet World*, 1999). Such applications include a sales-order processing system and a warehousing system. It now also includes software programs from different organizations.

Enterprise application integration (EAI)
Software used to facilitate communications between business applications including data transfer and control.

A final example of the use of an extranet on a global basis is that of Mecalux (www.mecalux.com). Mecalux, based in Barcelona, is involved in the design, manufacture and assembly of storage systems, from the simple slotted angle rack to sophisticated self-supporting warehouses. Since it was formed in 1996, the company has expanded and has offices in Argentina, Germany, the UK, France, Portugal, Singapore and Mexico. One of the challenges of this expansion was to improve communications between its representatives around the world and to supply them with the information needed to improve customer service. The management team decided they wanted to create a paperless company where information flows freely in all locations around the world. This makes it easier for the engineers to have the information necessary to respond to any customer's requirements. The extranet created to solve this problem has, for example, enabled representatives in Singapore to tap into data held on the server in Spain to check the availability of the product and get the specifications (such as measurements and price) to a local customer in the shortest possible timeframe. The solution also permits technicians and engineers to collaborate on ideas and work together on future designs from anywhere in the world.

Firewalls

Firewall
A specialized software application mounted on a server at the point where the company is connected to the Internet. Its purpose is to prevent unauthorized access into the company from outsiders.

Firewalls are necessary when creating an intranet or extranet to ensure that outside access to confidential information does not occur. Firewalls are usually created as software mounted on a separate server at the point where the company is connected to the Internet. Firewall software can then be configured to only accept links from trusted domains representing other offices in the company. A firewall has implications for e-marketing since staff accessing a web site from work may not be able to access some content such as graphics plug-ins.

The use of firewalls within the infrastructure of a company is illustrated in *Figure 3.6*. It is evident that multiple firewalls are used to protect information on the company. The information made available to third parties over the Internet and extranet is partitioned by another firewall using what is referred to as the 'demilitarized zone' (DMZ). Corporate data on the intranet are then mounted on other servers inside the company.

The design of security measures for e-business is reviewed in the *Focus on security design* (*Chapter 11, p. 540*).

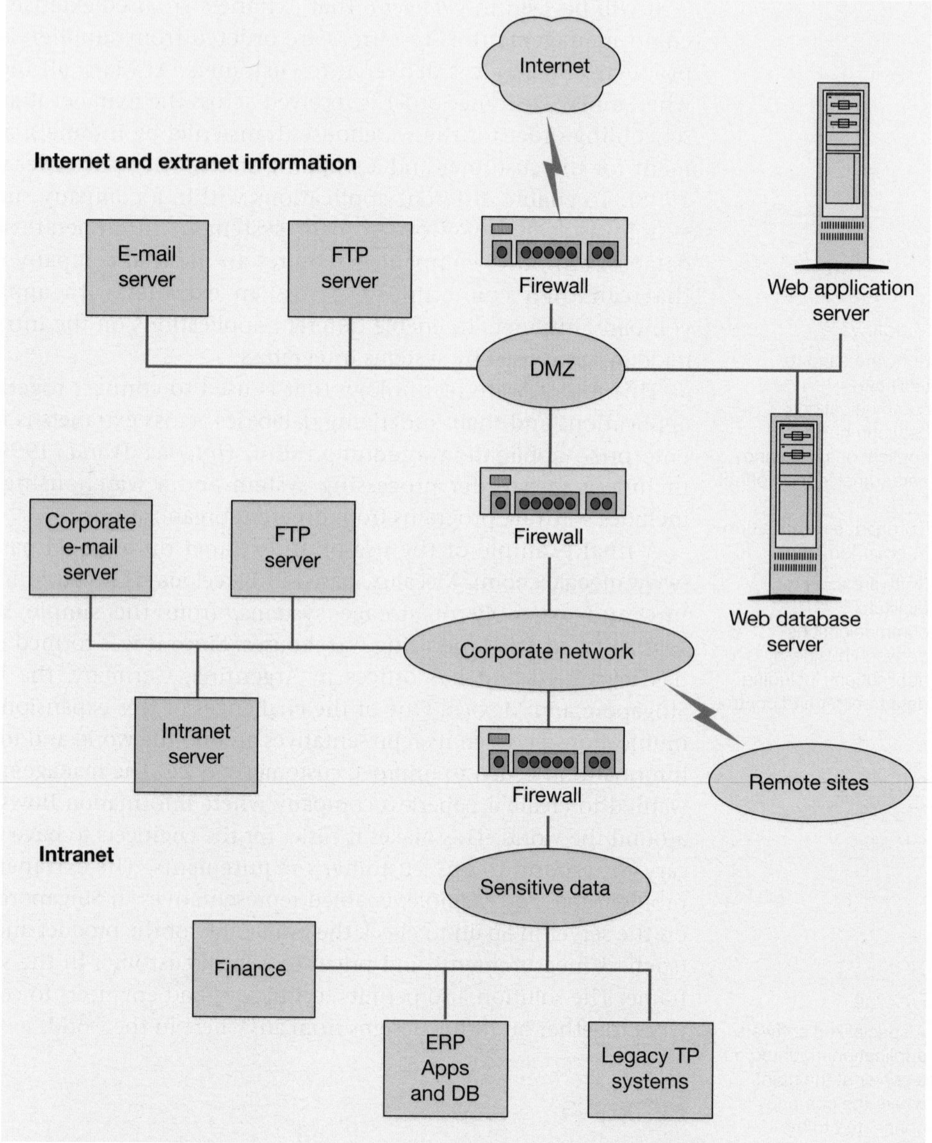

Figure 3.6 Firewall positions within the e-business infrastructure of the B2B company

Encouraging use of intranets and extranets

Although intranets and extranets have many benefits for the business, they often represent a change to existing methods of working for business people. As such, encouraging their usage is often a challenge. In many ways, this challenge is similar to encouraging customers to use open-access web sites. A common issue with intranets is that they may be launched to a great fanfare, but, if their content is neglected, their usage will dwindle. Common warning signs identified in the KM Column (2002) are:

- Staff usage of the intranet is low, and not growing.
- The majority of content is out-of-date, incomplete or inaccurate.
- The intranet is very inconsistent in appearance, particularly across sections managed by different groups.
- Almost all information on the intranet is reference material, not news or recent updates.
- Most sections of the intranet are used solely to publicize the existence of the business groups within the organization.

To explore solutions to limited usage of intranets and extranets, complete *Activity 3.3.*

Activity 3.3

Overcoming limited use of intranets and extranets in The B2B Company

Purpose

To illustrate solutions to limited usage of intranets and extranets.

Activity

The B2B Company has found that after an initial surge of interest in its intranet and extranet, usage has declined dramatically. Many of the warning signs mentioned in the KM (2002) article listed above are evident. The e-business manager wants to achieve these aims:

1. Increase usage.
2. Produce more dynamic content.
3. Encourage more clients to order (extranet).

Answers to activities can be found at www.pearsoned.co.uk/chaffey

World Wide Web (WWW)
The most common technique for publishing information on the Internet. It is accessed through web browsers which display web pages of embedded graphics and HTML/XML-encoded text.

Hyperlink
A method of moving between one web site page and another, indicated to the user by an image or text highlighted by underlining and/or a different colour.

What is the World Wide Web?

The World Wide Web, or 'web' for short, provides a standard method for exchanging and publishing information on the Internet. If we take the analogy of television, then the Internet would be equivalent to the broadcasting equipment such as masts and transmitters, and the World Wide Web is equivalent to the content of different TV programmes. The medium is based on standard document formats such as HTML (Hypertext Markup Language, *p. 106* and *Chapter 12, pp. 574–8*), which can be thought of as similar to a word-processing format such as that used for Microsoft Word documents. This standard has been widely adopted since:

- it offers hyperlinks which allow users to move readily from one document or web site to another – the process known as 'surfing';
- HTML supports a wide range of formatting, making documents easy to read on different access devices;

- graphics and animations can be integrated into web pages;
- interaction is possible through HTML-based forms that enable customers to supply their personal details for more information on a product, perform searches, ask questions or make comments.

It is the combination of web browsers and HTML that has proved so successful in establishing widespread business use of the Internet. The use of these tools provides a range of benefits including:

- it is easy to use since navigation between documents is enabled by clicking on hyperlinks or images. This soon becomes a very intuitive way of navigation which is similar across all web sites and applications;
- it can provide a graphical environment supporting multimedia which is popular with users and gives a visual medium for advertising;
- the standardization of tools and growth in demand means information can be exchanged with many businesses and consumers.

Web browsers and servers

Web browsers
Browsers such as Mozilla Firefox or Microsoft Internet Explorer provide an easy method of accessing and viewing information stored as web documents on different servers.

Web servers
Store and present the web pages accessed by web browsers.

Static web page
A page on the web server that is invariant.

Web browsers are software such as Microsoft Internet Explorer and Mozilla Firefox which we use to access the information on the WWW that is stored on web servers.

Web servers are used to store, manage and supply the information on the WWW. The main web browsers are Microsoft Internet Explorer and Mozilla Firefox. Browsers display the text and graphics accessed from web sites and provide tools for managing information from web sites.

Figure 3.7 indicates the process by which web browsers communicate with web servers. A request from the client PC is executed when the user types in a web address, clicks on a hyperlink or fills in an online form such as a search. This request is then sent to the ISP and routed across the Internet to the destination server using the mechanism described in the section on *protocols* in networking standards, below. The server then returns the requested web page if it is a static (fixed) web page, or, if it requires reference to a database, such as a request for product information, it will

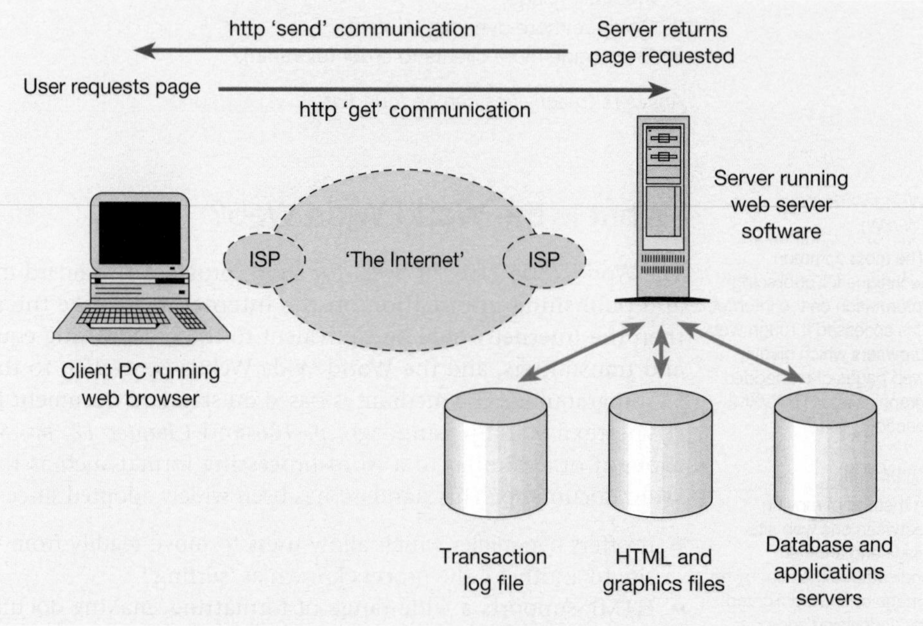

Figure 3.7 Information exchange between a web browser and web server

pass the query on to a database server and will then return this to the customer as a dynamically created web page. Information on all page requests is stored in a transaction log file which records the page requested, the time it was made and the source of the enquiry. This information can be analysed to assess the success of the web site, as explained in *Chapter 12* (*p. 612*).

Dynamic web page
A page that is created in real time, often with reference to a database query, in response to a user request.

Transaction log files
A web-server file that records all page requests.

Web 2.0 concept
Web 2.0 refers to a collection of web services which facilitate certain behaviours online such as community participation and user-generated content, rating and tagging.

Web 2.0

Since 2004, the Web 2.0 concept has increased in prominence amongst web-site owners and developers. The main technologies and principles of Web 2.0 have been explained in an influential article by Tim O'Reilly (O'Reilly, 2005). It is important to realize that Web 2.0 isn't a new web standard or a 'paradigm shift' as the name implies, rather it's an evolution of technologies and communications approaches which have grown in importance since 2004–5. The main characteristics of Web 2.0 are that it typically involves:

- Web services or interactive applications hosted on the web such as Flickr (www.flickr.com), Google maps (http://maps.google.com) or blogging services such as Blogger.com or Typepad (www.typepad.com);
- Supporting participation – many of the applications are based on altruistic principles of community participation;
- Encouraging creation of user-generated content – blogs are the best example of this. Another example is the collaborative encyclopedia Wikipedia (www.wikipedia.com);
- Enabling rating of content and online services – services such as delicious (http://del.icio.us) and traceback comments on blogs support this. These services are useful given the millions of blogs that are available – rating and tagging (categorizing) content help indicate the relevance and quality of the content;
- Ad funding of neutral sites – web services such as Google Mail/GMail and many blogs are based on contextual advertising such as Google Adsense or Overture/Yahoo! Content Match;
- Data exchange between sites through XML-based data standards. RSS is based on XML, but has relatively little semantic markup to describe the content. An attempt by Google to facilitate this which illustrates the principle of structured information exchange and searching is Google Base (http://base.google.com). This allows users to upload data about particular services such as training courses in a standardized format based on XML. New classes of content can also be defined;
- Rapid application development using interactive technology approaches known as AJAX (Asynchronous JavaScript and XML). The best-known Ajax implementation is Google Maps which is responsive since it does not require refreshes to display maps.

Debate 3.1

Web 2.0

'Web 2.0 is simply a new label for a range of web technologies and consumer behaviours that have existed since the 1990s. They don't represent a "paradigm shift".'

Internet-access software applications

Over its lifetime, many tools have been developed to help find, send and receive information across the Internet. Web browsers used to access the World Wide Web are the latest of these applications. These tools are summarized in *Table 3.3*. In this section we will briefly discuss the relevance of some of the more commonly used tools to the modern organization. The other tools have either been superseded by the use of the World Wide Web or are of less relevance from a business perspective.

The application of the Internet for marketing in this book concentrates on the use of e-mail and the World Wide Web since these tools are now most commonly used by businesses for digital marketing. Many of the other tools such as IRC and newsgroups, which formerly needed special software to access them, are now available from the WWW.

Table 3.3 **Applications of different Internet tools**

Internet tool	*Summary*
Electronic mail or e-mail	Sending messages or documents, such as news about a new product or sales promotion between individuals.
Instant Messaging (IM) and Internet Relay Chat (IRC)	These are synchronous communications tools for text-based 'chat' between different users who are logged on at the same time. IM from providers such as AOL, Yahoo and MSN has largely replaced IRC and provides opportunities for advertising to users.
Usenet newsgroups	Forums to discuss a particular topic such as a sport, hobby or business area. Traditionally accessed by special newsreader software, but can now be accessed via a web browser from www.deja.com (now part of Google – www.google.com).
FTP file transfer	The File Transfer Protocol is used as a standard for moving files across the Internet. FTP is still used for marketing applications such as downloading files such as product price lists or specifications. Also used to upload HTML files to web servers.
Gophers, Archie and WAIS	These tools were important before the advent of the web for storing and searching documents on the Internet. They have largely been superseded by the web which provides better searching and more sophisticated document publishing.
Telnet	This allows remote access to computer systems. For example a retailer could check to see whether an item was in stock in a warehouse using a telnet application.
Blogs	Web-based publishing of regularly updated information in an online diary type format using tools such as Blogger.com or Typepad.
Really Simple Syndication (RSS)	An XML-based content distribution format commonly used for accessing blog information.
Podcasting	A method of downloading and playing audio or visual clips for portable devices such as the iPod or MP3 players or fixed devices.
Voice over Internet Protocol (VOIP)	Technology for digitally transmitting voice over a LAN or Internet.
World Wide Web	Widely used for publishing information and running business applications over the Internet accessed through browsers such as Internet Explorer, Firefox, Safari and Opera.
IPTV	Digital TV channels are made available via broadband Internet either as streamed live broadcasts or as archived broadcasts of TV programmes.
BitTorrent	A peer-to-peer file-sharing technology used to enable sharing of large audio and video files.

Electronic mail or e-mail

E-mail is well known as a method of sending and receiving electronic messages. It has been available across the Internet for over 20 years. E-mails are typically written and read in a special mail reader program that in a large company is often part of a groupware package such as Lotus Notes, Microsoft Exchange or Novell Groupwise. Smaller companies or individuals may use lower-cost or free mail programs such as Microsoft Outlook Express, Eudora or Pegasus mail. A relatively recent innovation is the use of web sites which provide free e-mail facilities and do not require any special software other than a web browser. Hotmail (**www.hotmail.com**) and Yahoo! mail (**www.yahoo.com**) are the best known of these. Kennedy (2001) gives a practical description of Internet-based e-mail.

E-mail is now vital as a method of communicating internally and externally with customers, suppliers and partners. Since many e-mails are received and sent by companies, management of e-mail is a major management issue for the e-business. For example, ZDNet (2000) reported that Dell receives 50,000 e-mail messages a month and 100,000 order status requests a month from customers. It is thought that globally 4 billion e-mail messages are sent daily as well as 300 million SMS messages. For Dutch electronics company Philips International, 110,000 users within the firm create 7 million e-mails and 700 Gb of data a week. A large company with an average of 8,000 corporate e-mail users spends more than £1 million a year as users try to find and retrieve old e-mail messages, often from archives.

Inbound e-mail
E-mail received from outside the organization such as customer and supplier enquiries.

Outbound e-mail
E-mail sent from the company to other organizations.

E-mail management involves developing procedures and using systems to ensure that inbound and outbound e-mail is processed efficiently. Inbound e-mail should be routed to the correct person. E-mails may be sent from a customer to a company requesting information such as product specifications or quotations. Autoresponders or mail-bots are used to notify customers that their response is being dealt with. For example, an e-mail sent to products@company_name.com could automatically dispatch a summary of a company's products.

Outbound e-mail may be used on an *ad hoc* basis or as part of a standardized method of keeping customers informed, such as through a regular e-mail newsletter. Managing inbound and outbound e-mail is an important issue for customer service delivery (*Chapter 9, p. 421*).

Issues with managing e-mail security and employee usage are covered in Chapter 11 in the Focus on e-business security section.

Blogs

'Blogs' (short for web logs) give an easy method of publishing web pages, particularly those with news or events listings. Blogs give an easy method of publishing web pages which can be best described as online journals, diaries or news or events listings. An example of a business blog used to showcase the expertise of its analysts is the Jupiter Research Analyst Weblogs (http://weblogs.jupiterresearch.com). The use of blogs for business is showcased at Rick Bruner's http://www.businessblogconsulting. com. Many technology businesses such as Google, Microsoft and Sun now have employee bloggers who discuss new technologies online and this needs to be carefully controlled in case they pre-announce a new technology or highlight a problem with their technology. However, these blogs are now valuable in informing the journalists who indirectly promote their companies. A Euro RSCG Magnet study showed that over half of journalists used blogs to inform their stories, with around 25% using them for their day-to-day work. Of course, the figure is higher in technology publications sectors.Charles Arthur (www.charlesarthur.com), contributor to the Guardian Online in a posting 'Why I'm not reading PR emails to get news stories any more' says:

> *I'm not going to read things that are obviously press releases because the possibility of it just being annoying or irrelevant is too great; I'm going to go to my aggregator instead, because I've chosen every feed there for its potential interest. I pay more attention to my RSS feeds because they're sources I've chosen, rather than the e-mails I get from PR companies.*

As well as professional bloggers, there are many free services which enable anyone to keep their diary online (for example www.blogger.com which was purchased by Google in 2003, Movable Type (www.movabletype.com) and WordPress (www.wordpress.com).

Really Simple Syndication (RSS)

The last technology we will review in this section is arguably the most exciting. I'm excited by the potential of this technology and believe that in the long term it will both complement and rival e-mail as a communications medium.

From a technology viewpoint, Really Simple Syndication (RSS), also sometimes known as 'Rich Site Summary', is an Internet standard for publishing and exchanging content using XML. From a practical viewpoint it enables two things. First, content can be syndicated or published on one site that originates on another site. Second, and of much greater interest to the e-mail marketer, it is a relatively new method of distributing messages to subscribers.

At the time of writing, most consumers and few business people have heard of RSS – it is mainly used by journalists and analysts as a convenient way to keep up-to-date with press releases. Initially, the RSS messages were received by specialist software which could be downloaded for free such as RSS Reader (**www.rssreader.com**) or sites which receive feeds such as Bloglines (**www.bloglines.com**). These RSS readers, or aggegators, poll for RSS at a defined interval, often once an hour.

RSS will not become widespread until it is incorporated into standard software, but this will happen. In 2006 you could receive RSS feeds within your web browser and once they are included as a different type of inbox within e-mail packages, I believe they will be much more widely used. Currently, though, the proposition of RSS against e-mail isn't strong enough for most audiences, although it is superior for some such as journalists and technology followers. I also think improvements to the RSS readers to incorporate features similar to e-mail packages, such as rules and keyword-based filters will help manage the volume of RSS,

RSS has been embraced by major publishers such as the BBC and if you visit the BBC web site, you can see its potential. It enables you to subscribe to very specific content that interests you and then provides you with an alert when a new story is published. For example, I subscribe to the e-commerce news channel and that for Arsenal, my football team. In this arrangement subscription does not require opt-in, it just requires a request of the feed. So RSS is potentially a threat to the permission marketing model since there is no data exchange and it is easy for subscribers to switch them on and off.

More technical information on RSS is available at: **www.rss-specifications.com/rss-submission.htm.**

RSS will become much more widely adopted when it extends beyond specialist readers to the still ubiquitous Internet Explorer and Outlook products. Going forward, e-mail marketers need to manage the risk of reduced use of permission-based e-mail as customers realize the benefits of RSS, i.e.

1 More granular control of communications (e.g. choose content updates from any channel on the BBC site such as the e-commerce section (see BBC site for explanation of RSS consumer proposition).
2 Can switch on and off without registration (reduces control of marketers). Someone could subscribe to holiday offers within a 2-week period from a travel web site for instance.
3 Little or no spam since messages are pulled to the reader from the server (currently – although ads may be placed within a feed).

There are certainly disadvantages to RSS from the consumer viewpoint. That it requires a separate inbox or reader to set up and monitor has deterred many. It also only suits certain types of information – published as single alerts – it is mainly used for short stories and press releases. It has not traditionally been used in a newsletter type format with an edited collection of stories, but this is possible within the specification.

RSS is a threat to e-mail marketers since typically users profile and qualify themselves before opt-in to e-mail. With RSS this permission marketing isn't necessary since it is a pull service where the user retrieves information from the web site hosting the RSS feed. They just subscribe to the feed without the need to share any information with the organization. This has been the typical model to date, but Silverpop has recently launched RSS Direct which uses a more familiar e-mail permission marketing model where the user provides information before signing up to feeds. I'm sure many e-mail marketing service providers will move to offer this service and indeed the data capture technology looks straightforward – simply placing a data capture form with which to configure the feeds – so could also be implemented in-house.

It will be interesting to see how this plays out over the next couple of years. Will marketers provide free access to RSS to maximize volume of subscribers, but be limited by their capability to profile and target customers? Alternatively, they could use the permission-based opt-in RSS model which will have lower volume, but improved profiling and targeting.

RSS certainly presents opportunities for new types of communications. As the BBC site shows, subscribers can access much more specific, more timely information and from the content provider's point of view, all they have to do is to publish it on the site and subscribers will be notified. Marketers will have to think how the page layout of the template can be used to achieve wider objectives, such as generating awareness, interaction and response such as sign-up to e-mail subscription. In some sectors RSS has potential – updating about new holiday offers (perhaps you will just switch it on for a 2-week period, for example to just show holiday deals in Cuba), books from a favourite author or new gadgets from a favourite supplier.

In reality, I think more complex e-mail/RSS communications preferences will be offered to consumers. Perhaps, certain types of high-value information will only be offered through e-mail.

Voice over IP (VoIP)

Voice over IP (VOIP)
Voice data is transferred across the Internet – it enables phone calls to be made over the Internet.

Voice over IP (VoIP) is a relatively new approach which can be used for transmitting voice over a LAN or on a wider scale. You will remember that IP stands for Internet Protocol and so VoIP enables phone calls to be made over the Internet. IP enables a single network to handle all types of communications needs of an organization, i.e. data, voice and multimedia. VoIP (pronounced 'voyp') is proving increasingly popular for reducing the cost of making phone calls both within an office and for calls between offices, particularly internationally. IOD (2005) estimates that after initial investment, the cost of managing a converged VoIP communications system could be 50 per cent lower than managing separate voice and data systems. In the longer term it will also be used by major telecommunications companies such as AT&T and BT to replace their existing voice networks with IP networks.

In addition to the cost-reduction benefits, other benefits include:

- Click-to-call – users click the number they want from an on-screen directory to call.
- Call forwarding and conferencing to people at other locations
- Unified messaging. E-mails, voicemails and faxes all integrated into a single inbox
- Hot-desking – calls are routed to staff wherever they log-in – on-site or off-site
- Cost control – review and allocation of costs between different businesses is more transparent.

To implement VoIP several options are available to managers:

1 **Peer-to-peer.** The best-known peer-to-peer solution is Skype (purchased by eBay in 2005) which offers free calls or video-conferencing between Internet-connected PCs that are enabled with a headset (sometimes called 'softphones'). A service called SkypeOut enables calls to landlines or mobile phones at a reduced cost compared to traditional billing. This service is only really suited to smaller businesses, but could be used in larger businesses for some staff who call abroad frequently to bypass the central system.
2 **Hosted service.** This principle is similar to hosted software from application service providers (ASPs). Here, a company makes use of a large centralized IP-based

system shared between many companies. This potentially reduces costs, but some companies might be concerned about outsourcing their entire phone directory.

3 **Complete replacement of all telephone systems.** This is potentially costly and disruptive in the short term, but new companies or relocating companies may find this the most cost-effective solution.

4 **Upgrading existing telephone systems to use VoIP**. Typically, the best compromise for existing companies.

How does it work? Internet standards

We have introduced the general terms and concepts that describe the operation of the Internet and the World Wide Web. In this section we look in more detail at the standards that have been adopted to enable information transfer. Knowledge of these terms is useful for anyone involved in the management of e-commerce since discussion with suppliers may involve them. The technical infrastructure of the Internet is controlled by several bodies which are reviewed at the end of this chapter.

Networking standards

Internet standards are important in that they are at the heart of definitions of the Internet. According to Leiner *et al.* (2000), on 24 October 1995 the Federal Networking Council unanimously passed a resolution defining the term 'Internet'.

> *Internet' refers to the global information system that – (i) is logically linked together by a globally unique address space based on the Internet Protocol (IP) or its subsequent extensions/follow-ons; (ii) is able to support communications using the Transmission Control Protocol/Internet Protocol (TCP/IP) suite or its subsequent extensions/follow-ons, and/or other IP-compatible protocols; and (iii) provides, uses or makes accessible, either publicly or privately, high level services layered on the communications and related infrastructure described herein.*

TCP/IP

TCP/IP
The Transmission Control Protocol is a transport layer protocol that moves data between applications. The Internet Protocol is a network layer protocol that moves data between host computers.

TCP/IP development was led by Robert Kahn and Vince Cerf in the late 1960s and early 1970s and, according to Leiner *et al.* (2000), four ground rules controlled Kahn's early work on this protocol. These four ground rules highlight the operation of the TCP/IP protocol:

1 Distinct networks would be able to communicate seamlessly with other networks.

2 Communications would be on a best-effort basis, that is, if a data packet did not reach the final destination, it would be retransmitted from the source until successful receipt.

3 Black boxes would be used to connect the networks; these are now known as 'gateways' and 'routers' and are produced by companies such as Cisco and 3Com. In order to keep them simple there would be no information retained by the 'gateways'.

4 There would be no global control of transmissions – these would be governed by the requester and sender of information.

It can be seen that simplicity, speed and independence from control were at the heart of the development of the TCP/IP standards.

The data transmissions standards of the Internet such as TCP/IP are part of a larger set of standards known as the Open Systems Interconnection (OSI) model. This defines a layered model that enables servers to communicate with other servers and clients. When implemented in software, the combined layers are referred to as a 'protocol stack'. The seven layers of the OSI model are:

- *Application.* The program such as a web browser that creates and receives messages.
- *Presentation.* These protocols are usually part of the operating system.
- *Session.* This includes data-transfer protocols such as SMTP, HTTP and FTP.
- *Transport.* This layer ensures the integrity of data transmitted. Examples include the Internet TCP and Novell SPX.
- *Network.* Defines protocols for opening and maintaining links between servers. The best known are the Internet IP protocol and Novell IPX.
- *Data link.* Defines the rules for sending and receiving information.
- *Physical.* Low-level description of physical transmission methods.

The postal service is a good analogy for the transmission of data around the Internet using the TCP/IP protocol. Before we send mail, we always need to add a destination address. Likewise, the IP acts as an addressed envelope that is used to address a message to the appropriate IP address of the receiver (*Figure 3.8*).

The Internet is a packet-switched network that uses TCP/IP as its protocol. This means that, as messages or packets of data are sent, there is no part of the network that is dedicated to them. This is like the fact that when your letters and parcels are sent by post they are mixed with letters and parcels from other people. The alternative type of network is the circuit-switched network such as phone systems where the line is dedicated to the user for the duration of the call. Taking the analogy further, the transmission media of the Internet such as telephone lines, satellite links and optical cables are the equivalent of the vans, trains and planes that are used to carry post. Transmission media for the Internet include analogue media such as phone lines and faster, digital media such as Integrated Service Digital Network technology (ISDN) and more recently Asynchronous Digital Subscriber Line (ADSL).

In addition to the transmission media, components of the network are also required to direct or route the packets or messages via the most efficient route. On the Internet these are referred to as 'routers' or 'hubs', and are manufactured by companies such as Cisco and 3Com. The routers are the equivalent of postal sorting offices which decide the best route for mail to take. They do not plan the entire route of the message, but rather they direct it to the next router that seems most appropriate given the destination and current network traffic.

Some addressing information goes at the beginning of your message; this information gives the network enough information to deliver the packet of data. The IP address of a receiving server is usually in the form 207.68.156.58 which is a numerical representation of a better-known form such as www.microsoft.com. Each IP address is unique to a given organization, server or client, in a similar way to postal codes referring to a small number of houses. The first number refers to the top-level domain in the network, in this case .com. The remaining numbers are used to refer to a particular organization.

IP address
The unique numerical address of a computer.

Once the Internet message is addressed, the postal analogy is not so apt since related information is not sent across the Internet in one large message. For reasons of efficiency, information sent across IP networks is broken up into separate parts called packets. The information within a packet is usually between 1 and 1,500 characters long. This helps to route information most efficiently and fairly with different packets sent by different people gaining equal priority. The transmission control protocol TCP performs the task of splitting up the original message into packets on dispatch and reassembling it on receipt. Combining TCP and IP, you can think of an addressed IP envelope containing a TCP envelope which in turn contains part of the original message that has been split into a packet (*Figure 3.8*).

Packet
Each Internet message such as an e-mail or http request is broken down into smaller parts for ease of transmission.

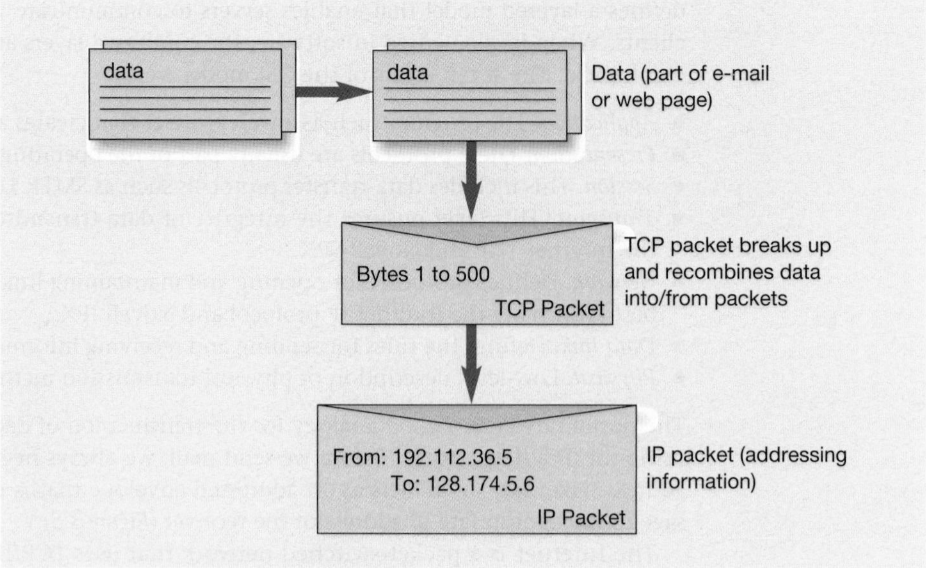

Figure 3.8 **The TCP/IP protocol**

The HTTP protocol

HTTP (Hypertext Transfer Protocol)
HTTP is a standard which defines the way information is transmitted across the Internet between web browsers and web servers.

HTTP, the Hypertext Transfer Protocol is the standard used to allow web browsers and servers to transfer requests for delivery of web pages and their embedded graphics. When you click on a link while viewing a web site, your web browser will request information from the server computer hosting the web site using HTTP. Since this protocol is important for delivering the web pages, the letters http:// are used to prefix all web addresses. HTTP messages are divided into HTTP 'get' messages for requesting and web page and HTTP 'send' message as shown in *Figure 3.8*. The web pages and graphics transferred in this way are transferred as packets, which is why web pages do not usually download gradually but come in jumps as different groups of packets arrive.

The inventor of http, Tim Berners-Lee, describes its purpose as follows (Berners-Lee, 1999):

> *HTTP rules define things like which computer speaks first, and how they speak in turn. When two computers agree they can talk, they have to find a common way to represent their data so they can share it.*

Uniform resource locators (URLs)

Uniform (universal) resource locator (URL)
A web address used to locate a web page on a web server.

Web addresses refer to particular pages on a web server which is hosted by a company or organization. The technical name for web addresses is **uniform (or universal) resource locators (URLs)**. URLs can be thought of as a standard method of addressing, similar to postcodes or ZIP codes, that make it straightforward to find the name of a site.

Web addresses always start with 'http://', so references to web sites in this book and in most promotional material from companies omit this part of the URL. Indeed, when using modern versions of web browsers, it is not necessary to type this in as part of the web page location since it is added automatically by the web browser. Although the vast majority of sites start with 'www', this is not universal, so it is necessary to specify this.

Web addresses are structured in a standard way as follows:

http://www.domain-name.extension/filename.html

In this book we conventionally omit the 'http://' for URLs that start with 'www', but include it for all others.

Domain names

Domain name

The domain name refers to the name of the web server and it is usually selected to be the same as the name of the company, e.g. www.<company-name>.com, and the extension will indicate its type.

The domain name refers to the name of the web server and is usually selected to be the same as the name of the company, and the extension will indicate its type. The extension is known as the global top-level domain (gTLD). There are also some 250 country-code top-level domains (ccTLD).

Common gTLDs are:

- **.com** represents an international or American company such as www.travelagency.com
- **.co.uk** represents a company based in the UK such as www.thomascook.co.uk
- **.ac.uk** is a UK university (e.g. www.leeds.ac.uk), while **.edu** is a US university such as www.mit.edu
- **.org.uk** and **.org** are for not-for-profit organizations (e.g. www.greenpeace.org)
- **.net** is a network provider such as www.virgin.net

The 'filename.html' part of the web address refers to an individual web page, for example 'products.html' for a web page summarizing a company's products. When a web address is typed in without a filename, for example www.bt.com, the browser automatically assumes the user is looking for the home page, which by convention is referred to as index.html. When creating sites, it is therefore vital to name the home page index.html. The file index.html can also be placed in sub-directories to ease access to information. For example, to access a support page a customer would type www.bt.com/support.

Note that gTLDs are continuously under review and in 2000 ICANN, the Internet Corporation for Assigned Names and Numbers (www.icann.org), granted seven new gTLDs. These became available from June 2001 and included .biz for business, .name to be used by individuals, .museum, .pro for professionals, .aero for aviation, .coop for cooperatives and .info. The new names have not been widely used by existing businesses with existing domain names, but do offer alternatives for new businesses. According to another view, existing companies such as Amazon will attempt to register with the new domain such as '.biz' which will not help to increase the availability of gTLD names.

ICANN is also involved in domain name arbitration. Its first case involved an individual who offered the name WorldWrestlingFederation.com to the World Wrestling Federation. The WWF won since it was considered the individual was 'cybersquatting'. In another case, Penguin Books stated that it had a claim to www.penguin.org which had been registered by an individual. But in this case Penguin lost since the respondent argued convincingly that he was known as Penguin and his wife as Mrs Penguin!

Domain name registration

If a company wants to establish a web presence it needs to register a domain name that is unique to it. Domain names can be registered via an ISP or at more favourable rates direct from the domain name services:

1 InterNIC – www.internic.net: registration and information about sites in the .com, .org and .net domains.

2 Nomination – www.nomination.uk.com: is an alternative registration service for the UK, allowing you to register in the (uk.com) pseudo-domain.
3 Nominet – www.nominet.org.uk: main co.uk site

The registration process is straightforward. It is usually performed by agencies that will register through their Internet service provider, which in turn will use one of the ICANN-accredited domain name registrars. (See www.internic.net/alpha.html for a list for all countries.)

Web presentation and data exchange standards

Content
The design, text and graphical information that forms a web page. Good content is the key to attracting customers to a web site and retaining their interest or achieving repeat visits.

The information, graphics and interactive elements that make up the web pages of a site are collectively referred to as content. Different standards exist for text, graphics and multimedia. The saying 'content is king' is often applied to the World Wide Web, since the content will determine the experience of the customer and whether he or she will return to a web site in future.

HTML (Hypertext Markup Language) – display of unstructured text content

HTML (Hypertext Markup Language)
A standard web-page presentation format used to define the text and layout of web pages. HTML files usually have the extension .HTML or .HTM.

Web-page text has many of the formatting options available in a word processor. These include applying fonts, emphasis (bold, italic, underline) and placing information in tables. Formatting is possible since the web browser applies these formats according to instructions that are contained in the file that makes up the web page. This is usually written in HTML or Hypertext Markup Language. HTML is an international standard established by the World Wide Web Consortium (and published at www.w3.org) intended to ensure that any web page authored according to the definitions in the standard will appear the same in any web browser. HTML files can be authored in an ordinary text editor such as the Notepad program available with Microsoft Windows. Modern word processors also have an option to save formatted information in the HTML format. Alternatively, many software utilities are available to simplify writing HTML.

A brief example of HTML is given for a simplified home page for The B2B Company in *Figure 3.9*. The HTML code used to construct pages has codes or instruction tags such as <TITLE>. to indicate to the browser what is displayed. The <TITLE>. tag indicates what appears at the top of the web browser window. Each starting tag has a corresponding end tag usually marked by a '/', for example, <B>plastics</B> to embolden 'plastics'.

The simplicity of HTML compared to traditional programming languages makes it possible for simple web pages to be developed by non-specialists such as marketing assistants, particularly if templates for more complex parts of the page are provided. Interactive forms and brochures and online sales are more complex and usually require some programming expertise, although tools are available to simplify these. See detailed information on creating HTML pages (*Chapter 12*).

XML (eXtensible Markup Language) – display and exchange of structured text and data

Meta-data
A definition of the structure and content of a collection of data or documents. 'Data about data'.

While HTML has proved powerful in providing a standard method of displaying information that was easy to learn, it is largely presentational. HTML only had a limited capability for describing the data on web pages. A capability for summarizing the content of pages is an example of meta-data. 'Meta' is part of the ancient Greek lan-

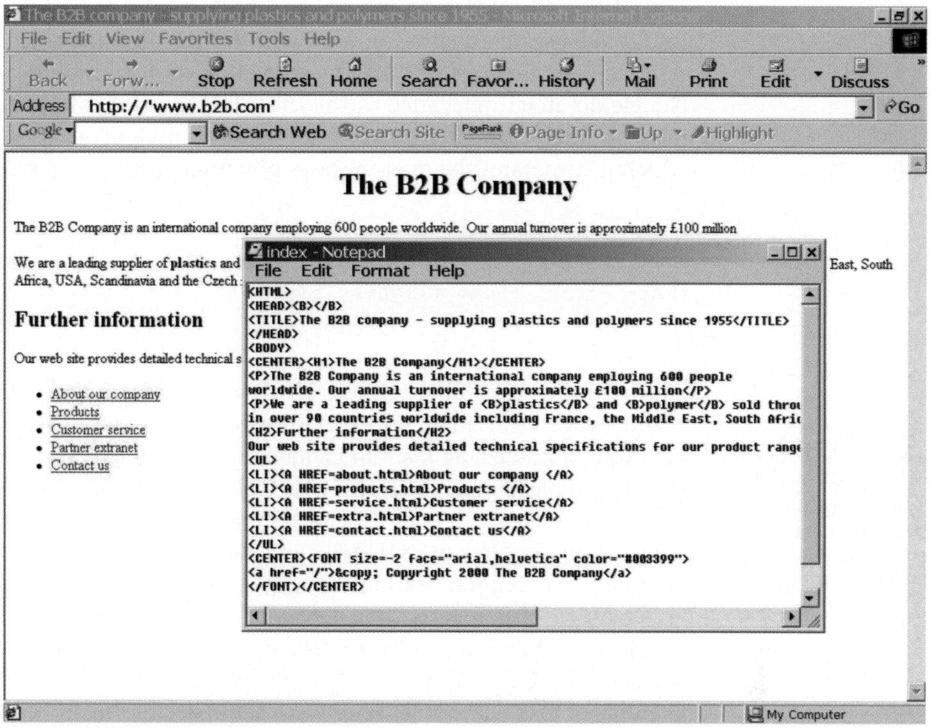

Figure 3.9 Home page index.html for The B2B Company in a web browser showing HTML source in text editor

guage, and in an information management context can be summarized as providing a description or definition about a topic or item.

HTML meta-tags
Standard HTML codes used to specify the content and characteristics of the document.

HTML also has a limited capability for describing documents through **HTML meta-tags**. These are presented at the start of the document in the header area. As the example below shows they can be used to specify a document's author, last update and type of content. This uses only some examples of meta-tags; the full definition and an introduction to HTML are available from the World Wide Web consortium at www.w3.org/MarkUp.

```
<HEAD>
 <TITLE>An intranet document example</TITLE>
 <META name="author" content="Dave Chaffey">
 <META name="keywords" content="phone directory, address
 book">
 <META name="description" content="An online phone book">
 <META name="date" content="2005-11-06T08:49:37+00:00">
</HEAD>
```

One application of meta-tags and an illustration of meta-data is that they are used by search engines to identify the content of documents. Early search engines such as AltaVista ranked documents higher in their listings which had meta-keywords that corresponded to the words typed into the search engine by its user. This led to abuse by companies that might include the name of their competitor or repeat keywords several times in the meta-tags, a process known as 'search engine spamming'. As a result, most search engines now attach limited importance to the keyword meta-tags – in fact Google does not use them at all. However, most search engines including Google do attach relevance to the <TITLE> tag, so it is important that this does not just contain a company name. For example, easyJet.com uses the following title tag which incorporates the main phrases potential visitors may type into a search engine.

```
<title>easyJet.com - easyjet low cost airline, easy jet, flight,
air fares, cheap flights</title>
```

XML or eXtensible Markup Language
Standard for transferring structured data, unlike HTML which is purely presentational.

The limited capability within HTML for meta-data and data exchange have been acknowledged and, in an effort coordinated by the World Wide Web Consortium, the first **XML** or **eXtensible Markup Language** was produced in February 1998. This is not strictly a replacement for HTML since HTML and XML can coexist – they are both markup languages. To help developers use HTML and XML together a new standard, confusingly known as XHTML, was adopted. XHTML and XML are based on Standardized General Markup Language (SGML). The key word describing XML is 'extensible'. This means that new markup tags can be created that facilitate the searching and exchange of information. For example, product information on a web page could use the XML tags <NAME>, <DESCRIPTION>, <COLOUR> and <PRICE>. Example of tags relevant to a product catalogue are shown below.

Example XML for online marketplace catalogue

This example is a standard for publishing catalogue data. It can be seen that specific tags are used to identify:

- Product ID
- Manufacturer
- Long and short description
- Attributes of product and associated picture.

There is no pricing information in this example.

```
<CatalogData>
<Product>
<Action Value5"Delete"/>
<ProductID>118003-008</ProductID>
</Product>
<Product Type5"Good" SchemaCategoryRef5"C43171801">
<ProductID>140141-002</ProductID>
<UOM><UOMCoded>EA</UOMCoded></UOM>
<Manufacturer>Compaq</Manufacturer>
<LeadTime>2</LeadTime>
<CountryOfOrigin>
<Country><CountryCoded>US</CountryCoded></Country>
</CountryOfOrigin>
<ShortDescription xml:lang5"en">Armada M700 PIII 500
12GB</ShortDescription>
<LongDescription xml:lang5"en">
```

```
This light, thin powerhouse delivers no-compromise
performance in a sub-five pound form factor. Size and
Weight(HxWxD): 12.4 X 9.8 X 1.1 in 4.3 – 4.9 lbs
(depending on configuration) Processor: 500-MHZ Intel
Pentium III Processor with 256K integrated cache Memory:
128MB of RAM, expandable to 576MB Hard Drive: 12.0GB
Removable SMART Hard Drive Display Graphics: 14.1-inch
color TFT with 1024 x 768 resolution (up to 16M colors
internal) Communication: Mini-PCI V.90 Modem/Nic Combo
Operating System: Dual Installation of Microsoft Windows
95 &amp; Microsoft Windows 98
</LongDescription>
<ProductAttachment>
<AttachmentURL>file:\5931.jpg</AttachmentURL>
<AttachmentPurpose>PicName</AttachmentPurpose>
<AttachmentMIMEType>jpg</AttachmentMIMEType>
</ProductAttachment>
<ObjectAttribute>
<AttributeID> Processor Speed</AttributeID>
<AttributeValue>500MHZ</AttributeValue>
</ObjectAttribute>
<ObjectAttribute>
<AttributeID>Battery Life</AttributeID>
<AttributeValue>6 hours</AttributeValue>
</ObjectAttribute>
</Product>
```

An XML implementation typically consists of three parts: the XML document, a document type definition (DTD) and a stylesheet (XSL), which are usually stored as separate files. We need a simple example to understand how these relate. Let's take the example of a bookstore cataloguing different books. You will see from this example that it is equivalent to using a database such as Microsoft Access to define database fields about the books and then store and display their details.

The XML document contains the data items, in this case the books, and it references the DTD and XSL files:

Data items: The XML document <books.xml>

```
<?xml version="1.0"?>
<!DOCTYPE Bookstore SYSTEM "books.dtd">
<?xml-stylesheet type="text/html" href="books.xsl"?>

<Bookstore>
<Book ID="101">
  <Author>Dave Chaffey</Author>
  <Title>E-business and E-commerce Management</Title>
  <Date>30 November 2003</Date>
```

→

```
  <ISBN>0273683780</ISBN>
  <Publisher>Pearson Education</Publisher>
</Book>
<Book ID="102">
  <Author>Dave Chaffey</Author>
  <Title>Total E-mail Marketing</Title>
  <Date>20 February 2003</Date>
  <ISBN>0750657545</ISBN>
  <Publisher>Butterworth Heinemann</Publisher>
</Book>
</Bookstore>
```

Note: The tags such as Bookstore, Book and author are defined for this particular application. They are defined in a separate Data Type Definition document which is shown below.

The DTD referenced at the start of the XML document defines the data items associated with the root element, which in this case is the Bookstore:

Data definition: Document Type Definition <books.dtd>

```
<!ELEMENT BookStore (Book)*>
<!ELEMENT Book (Title, Author+, Date, ISBN, Publisher)>

<!ATTLIST Book ID #REQUIRED>
<!ELEMENT Title (#PCDATA)>
<!ELEMENT Author (#PCDATA)>
<!ELEMENT Date (#PCDATA)>
<!ELEMENT ISBN (#PCDATA)>
<!ELEMENT Publisher (#PCDATA)>
```

Notes:
The Bookstore can contain many books *
Bookstore is known as the 'Root element'.
+ Allows for one or more author.
PCDATA stands for Parsed character data, i.e. A text string, further validation of fields could be used REQUIRED shows that this field is essential.

The XSL document uses HTML tags to instruct the browser how the data within XML file should be displayed. Separation of data from their presentation method makes this a more powerful approach than combining the two since different presentation schemes such as with and without graphics can readily be switched between according to user preference.

Presentation: Document Style Sheet File <books.xsl>

```
<?xml version='1.0'?>
<xsl:stylesheet xmlns:xsl="http://www.w3.org/TR/WD-xsl">
<xsl:template match="/">
  <html> <body>
    <table cellpadding="2" cellspacing="0" border="1"
    bgcolor="#FFFFD5">  <tr>
       <th>Title</th>
       <th>Author</th>
       <th>Publisher</th>
       <th>Date</th>
       <th>ISBN</th>
    </tr> <xsl:for-each select="Bookstore/Book">
    <tr><td><xsl:value-of select="Title"/></td>
       <td><xsl:value-of select="Author"/></td>
       <td><xsl:value-of select="Publisher"/></td>
       <td><xsl:value-of select="Date"/></td>
       <td><xsl:value-of select="ISBN"/></td>
       </tr> </xsl:for-each>
    </table>
  </body> </html>
</xsl:template>
</xsl:stylesheet>
```

Note: The style sheet uses standard HTML tags to display the data

This stylesheet would display the data as follows:

Display of data through browser

Title	Author	Publisher	Date	ISBN
E-business and E-commerce Management	Dave Chaffey	Pearson Education	30 November 2003	0273683780
Total E-mail Marketing	Dave Chaffey	Butterworth Heinemann	20 February 2003	0750657545

Examples of XML applications

One widely adopted XML application is the Dublin Core meta-data initiative (DCMI) (www.dublincore.org), so called since the steering group first met in Dublin, Ohio in 1995, has been active in defining different forms of meta-data to support information access across the Internet. An important part of this initiative is in defining a standard method of referencing web documents and other media resources. If widely adopted this would make it much more efficient to search for a document produced by a particular author in a particular language in a particular date range. Up to now, it has mainly been applied within content management systems to assist in knowledge management for data on intranets and extranets rather than on the public Internet.

The significance of XML is indicated by its use for facilitating supply chain management. For example, Microsoft's BizTalk server (www.microsoft.com/biztalk) for B2B application integration is based on XML. Since this is a proprietary standard, an open standard 'RosettaNet' (www.rosettanet.org) has been created by a consortium of many of the world's leading information technology, electronic components and semiconductor manufacturing companies such as Intel, Sony and Nokia.

BizTalk server enables different enterprise applications such as SAP and JDEdwards to exchange information as part of improved supply chain management. Microsoft summarize the benefits of Biztalk as:

1. Reduced 'time to value', i.e. development time and cost of application integration
2. Easy integration with virtually any application or technology
3. Scalability to any size of application
4. Support for industry standards such as EDI, XML and Simple Object Access Protocol (SOAP)
5. Reliable document delivery including 'once only' delivery of documents, comprehensive document tracking, and logging and support for failover (automatic recovery of documents from a backup system)
6. Secure document exchange – this is not an integral feature of XML but has been built into this application
7. Automation for complex business processes
8. Management and monitoring of business processes
9. Automated trading partner management
10. Reduced complexity in development.

Another widely adopted application of XML is ebXML (www.ebxml.org). This standard has been coordinated by Oasis (www.oasis-open.org) which is an international not-for-profit consortium for promoting Internet standards. The original project was intended to define business exchange using five standards:

- business processes (support for different activities and transactions involved in buying and selling online)
- core data components
- collaboration protocol agreements
- messaging
- registries and repositories.

Oasis defines three types of transactions that form business processes:

1. *Business Transaction.* A single business transaction between two partners, such as placing an order or shipping an order.
2. *Binary Collaboration.* A sequence of these business transactions, performed between two partners, each performing one role.
3. *MultiParty Collaboration.* A series of binary collaborations composed of a collection of business partners.

One application developed using ebXML is to enable different accounting packages to communicate with online order processing systems. This new standard has been recognised by 85% of the accounting industry, the World Wide Web Consortium and the United Nations. In addition, over 120 national and international accounting software vendors have confirmed that they are developing interfaces. Exchequer Software Ltd (www.exchequer.com) is the first company to embed this new technology in its products, which means it receives orders via e-mail directly into its own accounting system. This has resulted in a reduction of 30% in processing costs and a sales increase of 40%. The e-business module of the accounting software can be used to provide a remotely hosted e-commerce shopping cart system with regular updates of stock details, pricing matrices, account information and transactional data, such as outstanding orders and invoices.

Governments are also using XML to standardize data transfer between departments. Examples of the UK government's draft schema, for example for transfer of patient records, are at www.govtalk.gov.uk.

Semantic web standards

Semantic web
Interrelated content including data with defined meaning, enabling better exchange of information between computers and between people and computers.

Agents
Software programs that can assist humans by automatically gathering information from the Internet or exchanging data with other agents based on parameters supplied by the user.

The semantic web is a concept promoted by the World Wide Web Consortium (www.w3.org) to improve on the current World Wide Web. One of the greatest strengths of the web, the ability to easily create web pages and link them together, is also one of its greatest weaknesses. Finding information on a particular topic through searching is inexact since there is no standard way of describing the content of web pages. Furthermore, data cannot readily be exchanged between software agents running on different computers. The semantic web is a new form of web content which is intended to overcome these problems.

The applications of the semantic web are best illustrated through examples. Berners-Lee *et al.* (2001) give the example of a patient seeking medical treatment for a particular condition. They envisage a patient having a personal software agent (effectively a search engine) which is used to find the best source of treatment. The patient's agent will interact with the doctor's agent which will describe the symptoms and search pages from different health-care providers which detail their services. The patient's agent will then give them the different treatment options in terms of cost, effectiveness, waiting time and location. Similarly, a personal agent could be used to find the best flight or a business agent could be used to participate in a reverse auction.

Graphical images (GIF and JPEG files)

GIF (Graphics Interchange Format)
A graphics format and compression algorithm best used for simple graphics.

JPEG (Joint Photographics Experts Group)
A graphics format and compression algorithm best used for photographs.

Plug-in
An add-on program to a web browser, providing extra functionality such as animation.

Graphics produced by graphic designers or captured using digital cameras can be readily incorporated into web pages as images. GIF (Graphics Interchange Format) and JPEG (Joint Photographics Experts Group) refer to the two standard file formats most commonly used to present images on web pages. GIF files are limited to 256 colours and are best used for small simple graphics such as banner adverts, while JPEG is best used for larger images where image quality is important, such as photographs. Both formats use image compression technology to minimize the size of downloaded files.

Animated graphical information (GIFs and plug-ins)

GIF files can also be used for interactive banner adverts. Plug-ins are additional programs, sometimes referred to as 'helper applications', that work in association with the web browser to provide features not present in the basic web browser. The best known plug-ins are probably the one for Adobe Acrobat that is used to display documents in .pdf format (www.adobe.com) and the Macromedia Flash and Shockwave products for producing interactive graphics (www.macromedia.com).

Audio and video standards

Traditionally sound and video, or 'rich media', have been stored as the Microsoft standards .wav and .avi. A newer sound format for music is mp3. These formats are used on some web sites, but they are not appropriate for sites such as the BBC

Streaming media
Sound and video that can be experienced within a web browser before the whole clip is downloaded.

(www.bbc.co.uk), since the user would have to wait until the whole clip downloads before hearing or viewing it. Streaming media are now used for many multimedia sites since they enable video or audio to start playing within a few seconds – it is not necessary for the whole file to be downloaded before it can be played. Formats for streaming media have been established by Real Networks (www.realnetworks.com).

Focus on who controls the Internet

In Chapter 4 we will look briefly at how governments promote and control, through laws, the use of the Internet in their jurisdiction. In this section, we look at the growth of the Internet as a global phenomenon and how the standards described in the previous section were devised. The Internet is quite different from all previous communication media since it is much less easy for governments to control and shape its development. Think of print, TV, phone and radio and you can see that governments can exercise a fair degree of control on what they find acceptable. With the Internet, governments can have a say, but their control is diminished.

Internet governance
Control of the operation and use of the Internet.

Esther Dyson (1998) has been influential in advising on the impact of Internet on society, she describes Internet governance as the control put in place to manage the growth of the Internet and its usage. Governance is traditionally undertaken by government, but the global nature of the Internet makes it less practical for a government to control cyberspace. Dyson says:

> *Now, with the advent of the Net, we are privatizing government in a new way – not only in the traditional sense of selling things off to the private sector, but by allowing organizations independent of traditional governments to take on certain 'government' regulatory roles. These new international regulatory agencies will perform former government functions in counterpoint to increasingly global large companies and also to individuals and smaller private organizations who can operate globally over the Net.*

Dyson (1998) describes different layers of jurisdiction. These are:

1 Physical space comprising individual countries in which their own laws such as those governing taxation, privacy and trading and advertising standards hold.
2 ISPs – the connection between the physical and virtual worlds.

There are a number of established non-profit-making organizations that control different aspects of the Internet. These are sometimes called 'supra-governmental' organizations since their control is above government level. We will explore each of these in turn.

The Internet Corporation for Assigned Names and Numbers (ICANN, www.icann.org)

The Internet Corporation for Assigned Names and Numbers (ICANN) is the non-profit body formed for domain name and IP address allocation and management. It is perhaps the most public of the Internet control organizations since domain names or web addresses are one of the most tangible aspects of the Internet for users. These were previously controlled through US government contract by IANA (Internet Assigned Numbers Authority) and other entities. According to the ICANN Fact Sheet (www.icann.org/general/fact-sheet.htm):

> *In the past, many of the essential technical coordination functions of the Internet were handled on an ad hoc basis by US government contractors and grantees, and a wide network of volunteers. This informal structure represented the spirit and culture of the research community in*

which the Internet was developed. However, the growing international and commercial importance of the Internet has necessitated the creation of a technical management and policy development body that is more formalized in structure, more transparent, more accountable, and more fully reflective of the diversity of the world's Internet communities.

The independence of such bodies raises several questions, such as who funds them and who they answer to – are they regulated? Incredibly, in 2002 ICANN had just 14 staff and a 19-member volunteer board of directors with Dr Vinton Cerf, who many consider as 'father of the Internet' as its chairman. Funding is through the fees charged for domain registration by commercial companies that register these domains. The policy statements on the sites suggest that ICANN policy is influenced by various stakeholders, but the main control is an independent review body of ten academics, lawyers from countries as diverse as New Zealand, Argentina, Peru, Denmark, Japan and, of course, the USA.

The Internet Society (www.isoc.org)

The Internet Society (ISOC) is a professional membership society formed in 1992. In 2002 it had more than 150 organization and 11,000 individual members in over 182 countries. It summarizes its aims as

To provide leadership in addressing issues that confront the future of the Internet, and is the organization home for the groups responsible for Internet infrastructure standards, including the Internet Engineering Task Force (IETF) and the Internet Architecture Board (IAB).

A key aspect of the society's mission statement (www.isoc.org/isoc/mission) is:

To assure the open development, evolution and use of the Internet for the benefit of people throughout the world.

Detailed points of the aims of its mission are that it:

1. *Facilitates open development of standards, protocols, administration and the technical infrastructure of the Internet*
2. *Supports education in developing countries specifically, and wherever the need exists*
3. *Promotes professional development and opportunities for association to Internet leadership*
4. *Provides reliable information about the Internet*
5. *Provides forums for discussion of issues that affect Internet evolution, development and use – technical, commercial, societal, etc.*
6. *Fosters an environment for international cooperation, community, and a culture that enables self-governance to work*
7. *Serves as a focal point for cooperative efforts to promote the Internet as a positive tool to benefit all people throughout the world*
8. *Provides management and coordination for on-strategy initiatives and outreach efforts – humanitarian, educational, societal, etc.*

It can be seen that although it focuses on technical issues of standards and protocols, it is also conscious of how these will affect global society.

The Internet Engineering Task Force (IETF www.ietf.org)

This is one of the main technical bodies. It is an international community of network designers, operators, vendors and researchers concerned with the development of the Internet's architecture and its transport protocols such as IP. Significant subgroups are the Internet Architecture Board, a technical advisory group of ISOC with a wide range of responsibilities and the Internet Engineering Steering Group, which is responsible for overseeing the activities of the IETF and the Internet standards process.

An interesting feature of the IETF, in common with the other organizations, is that it operates using electronic communications as much possible, without recourse to meetings. The IETF has just three main meetings per year. New technical specifications are largely agreed through e-mail and discussion forums.

The World Wide Web Consortium (www.w3.org)

This organization is responsible for web standards. Its director is Tim Berners-Lee who effectively invented the World Wide Web in the late 1990s while working at CERN, the European Particle Physics Laboratory in Geneva. He wrote the first WWW client (browser) and the first WWW server along with most of the communications software, defining URLs, HTTP and HTML. Today, it focuses on improving publishing standards such as HTML and XML. XML is an important development in forming what the WWW organization refers to as the 'semantic web' – see **www.w3.org/Consortium/Points** for details. The consortium also aims to promote accessibility to the web for those with disabilities – for instance, it is working on a voice-based browser. It is another relatively small organization, with fewer than 100 full-time staff in different countries.

Telecommunications Information Networking Architecture Consortium TINA-C (www.tina.com)

This consortium is somewhat different from the others in that it takes a higher-level view of how applications communicate over communications networks. It does not define detailed standards. Its principles are based on an object-oriented approach to enable easier integration of systems. In its terms:

> *The purpose of these principles is to insure interoperability, portability and reusability of software components and independence from specific technologies, and to share the burden of creating and managing a complex system among different business stakeholders, such as consumers, service providers, and connectivity providers.*

Although it has been established since the 1990s, it has had limited success in establishing solutions which are branded as 'TINA-compliant'.

How can companies influence or take control of Internet standards?

As well as the supra-governmental organizations which we have reviewed above, it can be argued that companies seek control of the Internet to gain competitive advantage. For example, Microsoft used what have been judged as anti-competitive tactics to gain a large market share for its browser, Internet Explorer. In a five-year period, it achieved over 75% market share, which has given it advantages in other areas of e-commerce such as advertising revenue through its portal MSN (**www.msn.com**) and retail, through its sites such as travel site Expedia (**www.expedia.com**). Microsoft has also sought to control standards such as HTML and has introduced rival standards or variants of other standards (for example, VBScript rather than JavaScript and C# rather than Java). The control exerted by Microsoft is criticized by many and has been found to be anti-competitive in law (see **http://news.bbc.co.uk/1/hi/business/700084.stm** for a summary of the judgment).

The existence of global Internet standards bodies such as those described above arguably means that it is less likely that one company can develop proprietary standards, although Microsoft has been successfully using this approach for many years. Today, companies such as Microsoft have to lobby independent organizations such as the World Wide Web Consortium to have their input into standards such as XML. Businesses can protect their interests in the Internet by lobbying these organizations or governments, or subscribing as members and having employees involved with development of standards. Even SMEs can be involved. Exchequer software, referred to in the XML section above, which has 75 employees, has been able to obtain competitive advantage through being closely involved with the development of XML standards for accounting software.

Many remain worried about the future control of the Internet by companies; the 'World of Ends' campaign (www.worldofends.com) illustrates some of the problems where control can limit consumer choice and stifle innovation.

Open-source software

Open-source software
Is developed collaboratively, independent of a vendor, by a community of software developers and users.

It could be argued that commercial pressure enabled rapid development of practical solutions, examples including Javascript and Cookies (Netscape), .Net (Microsoft) and Java (Sun Microsystems). The use of **open-source software** such as the Linux operating system, Apache web servers or the Plone content management system (www.plone.org) has partly developed as a response to one organization gaining too much control. Proponents of open source also proclaim that it can also result in better-quality software as many users and developers are involved in quality control. The Open Source organization (www.opensource.org) explains the benefits as follows:

> *The basic idea behind open source is very simple: When programmers can read, redistribute, and modify the source code for a piece of software, the software evolves. People improve it, people adapt it, people fix bugs. And this can happen at a speed that, if one is used to the slow pace of conventional software development, seems astonishing.*
>
> *We in the open source community have learned that this rapid evolutionary process produces better software than the traditional closed model, in which only a very few programmers can see the source and everybody else must blindly use an opaque block of bits.*

Table 3.4 summarizes some of the main advantages and disadvantages of open-source software. To gain an appreciation of the issues faced by a technical manager pondering the open-source dilemma, complete Activity 3.4.

Table 3.4 Three advantages and three disadvantages of open-source software

Advantages of open-source software	*Counter-argument*
1 Effectively free to purchase	Cost of migration from existing systems may be high and will include costs of disruption and staff training
2 Lower cost of maintenance since upgrades are free	There is not a specific counter-argument for this, but see the disadvantages below
3 Increased flexibility	Organizations with the resources can tailor the code. Frequent patches occur through collaborative development.
Disadvantages of open-source software	*Counter-argument*
1 Has less functionality than commercial software	Simplicity leads to ease of use and fewer errors. Many functions not used by the majority of users
2 More likely to contain bugs compared to commercial software since not tested commercially	Evidence does not seem to suggest this is the case. The modular design needed by collaborative development enables problems to be isolated and resolved
3 Poor quality of support	Organizations with the resource can fix problems themselves since they have access to the code. Companies such as IBM, SuSe and RedHat do offer support for Linux for a fee.

Activity 3.4 Selecting open-source software

Visit the w.w.w.

Purpose

The final activity for this chapter looks at a common issue facing technical managers: should they adopt standard software promoted by the largest companies or open-source software or cheaper software from other vendors?

Questions

1 For the different alternatives facing a technical manager below, assess:

(a) Which is most popular (research figures).

(b) The benefits and disadvantages of the Microsoft solution against the alternatives.

2 Make recommendations, with justifications, of which you would choose for a small–medium or large organization.

A. Operating system: Microsoft Windows 2000/Windows XP or Linux (open source) for server and desktop clients.

B. Browser: Internet Explorer browser or rivals such as Netscape and Opera (www.opera.com).

C. Programming language for dynamic e-commerce applications: Microsoft ASP.Net *or* independent languages/solutions such as PHP/MySQL and Perl.

Answers to activities can be found at www.pearsoned.co.uk/chaffey

Managing e-business infrastructure

As explained at the start of the chapter, e-business infrastructure comprises the hardware, software, content and data used to deliver e-business services to employees, customers and partners.

In this part of the chapter we look at the management of e-business infrastructure by reviewing different perspectives on the infrastructure. These are:

1 *Hardware and systems software infrastructure*. This refers mainly to the hardware and network infrastructure discussed in the previous sections. It includes the provision of clients, servers, network services and also systems software such as operating systems and browsers (Layers II, III and IV in *Figure 3.1*).
2 *Applications infrastructure*. This refers to the applications software used to deliver services to employees, customers and other partners (Layer I in *Figure 3.1*).

A further perspective is the management of data and content (Layer V in *Figure 3.1*) which is reviewed in more detail in the third part of this book.

Managing hardware and systems software infrastructure

Management of the technology infrastructure requires decisions on Layers II, III and IV in *Figure 3.1*.

Layer II – Systems software

The key management decision is standardization throughout the organization. Standardization leads to reduced numbers of contacts for support and maintenance and can reduce purchase prices through multi-user licences. Systems software choices occur for the client, server and network. On the client computers, the decision will be which browser software to standardize on, for example Microsoft Explorer, Netscape Communicator or more specialized software such as the Lotus Notes client or the Opera browser (www.opera.com). Standardized plug-ins such as Adobe Acrobat to access .pdf files should also be installed across the organization. The systems software for the client will also be decided on; this will probably be a variant of Microsoft Windows, but alternatives such as Sun Microsystems' Solaris or Linux may also be considered. When considering systems software for the server, it should be remembered that there may be many servers in the global organization, both for the Internet and intranets. Using standardized web-server software such as Apache will help maintenance. Networking software will also be decided on; this could be Microsoft-sourced or from other suppliers such as Sun Microsystems or Novell.

Layer III – Transport or network

Decisions on the network will be based on the internal company network, which for the e-business will be an intranet, and for the external network either an extranet or VPN (*p. 131*) or links to the public Internet. The main management decision is whether internal or external network management will be performed by the company or outsourced to a third party. Outsourcing of network management is common. Standardized hardware is also needed to connect clients to the Internet, for example, a modem card or external modem in home PCs or a network interface card (NIC) to connect to the company (local-area) network for business computers.

Layer IV – Storage

The decision on storage is similar to that for the transport layer. Storage can be managed internally or externally. This is not an either/or choice. For example, intranet and extranet are commonly managed internally while Internet storage such as the corporate web site is commonly managed externally or at an application service provider (*p. 127*). However, intranets and extranets can also be managed externally.

We will now consider decisions involving third-party service providers of the hardware and systems software infrastructure.

Internet service providers

Service providers are usually referred to as 'ISPs' or 'Internet service providers'. Providers who also provide some specialized web content to users such as America Online (AOL) or Compuserve are sometimes distinguished as OSPs or online service providers. ISPs are telecommunications companies which provide access to the Internet for home and business users. ISPs have two main functions. First, they provide a link to a company or individual which enables them to access the World Wide Web and send Internet e-mail. Second, they host web sites or publish a company's web site content to enable other companies or consumers access to it. Note that as well as these basic services many ISPs have extended their services to become applications service providers (ASPs, *p. 127*).

ISP connection methods

Figure 3.2 shows the way in which companies or home users connect to the Internet. The diagram is greatly simplified in that there are several tiers of ISPs. A user may connect to one ISP which will then transfer the request to another ISP which is connected to the main Internet backbone.

Dial-up connection
Access to the Internet via phone lines using analogue modems.

Broadband connection
Access to the Internet via phone lines using a digital data transfer mechanisim.

Home access to the Internet is still predominantly based on a dial-up connection using a modem with a maximum access speed of 56 kbps. Most ISPs now charge fees for unlimited access via dial-up connections or broadband and this has enabled many to become profitable. For example, Wanadoo, in the 6 months to 30 June 2002 recorded access revenues across Europe of €460 million. This compared to advertising revenues €40 million and merchant affiliate revenue of €17 million.

Increasingly, consumers are purchasing broadband connections using digital modems with an access speed of up to 10 times faster than dial-up (512 kbps). These use a technology known as ADSL or asymmetric digital subscriber line, which means that the traditional phone line can be used for digital data transfer. It is asymmetric since download speeds are typically higher than upload speeds. Small and medium businesses can also benefit from faster continuous access than was previously possible.

The higher speeds available through broadband together with a continuous 'always on' connection seem likely to transform the use of the Internet. Information access is more rapid and it becomes more practical to access richer content such as digital video. The increased speed increases usage of the Internet. *The Financial Times* (2002) reported that South Korea is the world's most highly penetrated broadband market with nearly 14 connections per 100 inhabitants, more than double the penetration of the second country in world rankings, Canada, which has a penetration of 6.2 inhabitants out of every 100. The UK has over a million broadband connections, equating to a household penetration of close to 4 per cent. Average usage of the Internet in Korea is 1,340 minutes per month compared to 382 minutes in the UK. The high usage stems partly from Korean broadband being fast enough for video on demand and playing online games.

Issues in management of ISP relationships

The primary issue in managing ISPs is to ensure a satisfactory service quality at a reasonable price. Organizations hosting events have to have web sites with the capacity to deal with large increases in traffic volume. The official site of the Wimbledon tennis tournament (www.wimbledon.org) in 2000 received 2.3 billion hits in a fortnight compared to 942 million hits the previous year, with the site busiest during the fifth set of the semi-final between André Agassi and Pat Rafter, registering 963,948 hits a minute. The official Euro 2000 web site (www.euro2000.org), recorded around a billion hits during the tournament. For these large sites, a single server is not used – the Euro 2000 site was hosted in 10 locations with traffic balanced so that each user went to the closest and fastest location. We will now examine the elements of service quality – speed, availability and security.

Speed of access

Speed of access of a customer, employee or partner to services on an e-business server is determined by both the speed of server and the speed of the network connection to the server. The speed of the site governs how quick the response is to a request for information from the end-user. This will be dependent on the speed of the server machine on which the web site is hosted and how quickly the server processes the information. If there are only a small number of users accessing information on the server, then there will not be a noticeable delay on requests for pages. If, however, there are thousands of users requesting information at the same time then there may be a delay and it is important that the combination of web server software and hardware can cope. Web server software will not greatly affect the speed at which requests are answered. The speed of the server is mainly controlled by the amount of primary storage (for example, 1024 Mb RAM memory is faster than 512 Mb RAM) and the speed of the magnetic storage (hard disk). Many of the search-engine web sites now store all their index data in RAM since this is faster than reading data from the hard disk. Companies will pay ISPs according to the capabilities of the server. An important point is whether the server is dedicated or shared. Clearly, if content on a server is shared with other sites hosted on the same server then performance will be affected by demand loads on these other sites. For high-traffic sites servers may be located across several computers with many processors to spread the demand load. Such arrangements are sometimes referred to as 'web farms'. New methods of hosting content, summarized by Spinrad (1999), have been introduced to improve the speed of serving web pages. These methods involve distributing content on servers around the globe. Two rival schemes emerging are Akamai Freeflow (www.akamaitech.net) and Sandpiper Networks Footprint (www.sandpiper.com). These are used by companies such as Yahoo!, Apple and other 'hot-spot' sites likely to receive many hits.

Dedicated server
Server only contains content and applications for a single company.

The speed is also governed by the speed of the network connection, commonly referred to as the network 'bandwidth'. The bandwidth of a web site's connection to the Internet and the bandwidth of the customer's connection to the Internet will affect the speed with which web pages and associated graphics load onto the customer's PC. The term is so called because of the width of range of electromagnetic frequencies an analogue or digital signal occupies for a given transmission medium.

Bandwidth
Indicates the speed at which data are transferred using a particular network medium. It is measured in bits per second (bps).

Bandwidth gives an indication of the speed at which data can be transferred from a web server along a particular medium such as a network cable or phone line. In simple terms bandwidth can be thought of as the size of a pipe along which information flows. The higher the bandwidth, the greater the diameter of the pipe, and the faster information is delivered to the user.

The bandwidth required for acceptable quality of service is proportional to the complexity of the data. For example, more bandwidth is required to download a graphical image in one second compared to downloading a page of text in one second.

Bandwidth measures (see box) are in bits per second where one character or digit, such as the number '1', would be equivalent to 8 bits. So a modem operating at 57,600 bits per second (57.6 kbps) will transfer information at 7,200 characters per second (57,600/8). When selecting an ISP it is important to consider the bandwidth of the connection between the ISP and the Internet. Choices may be:

- ISDN – 56 kbps up to 128 kbps
- Frame relay – 56 kbps up to a T1 communications channel (1.55 Mbps)
- Dedicated point-to-point – 56 kbps up to T3 (45 Mbps): connected to the Internet backbone.

Bandwidth measures

Kbps one kilobit per second or 1,000 bps (a modem operates at up to 56.6 kbps)

Mbps one megabit per second or 1,000,000 bps (company networks operate at 10 or more Mbps)

Gbps one gigabit per second or 1,000,000,000 bps (fibre-optic or satellite links operate at Gbps)

A medium-to-large business connects to an ISP using a high-speed phone line such as a T1 line. A T1 line can handle approximately 1.5 million bits per second, while a smaller business will use a normal phone line using a modem that can usually handle a maximum of 56,600 bits per second, or ISDN, which is up to twice as fast.

Some ISPs are not connected directly to the Internet backbone but are linked to it via other providers. Their service will be slower than those directly connected to the main Internet backbone since information has to 'jump' several different network links.

Table 3.5 shows that the top five sites with the lowest download speeds tend to have a much lower page size or 'weight' compared with the slower sites from 95 to 100. This shows that the performance of a site is not simply dependent on the hosting with the ISP, but depends on how the site is designed. Such a system is known as a content management system (CMS). As explained in more detail in *Chapter 12*, a CMS is a means of managing the updating and publication of information on any web site, whether intranet, extranet or Internet. The CMS used can also make a big difference. However, viewing these slower sites over a broadband connection shows that this is perhaps less of an issue than in the days when the majority, rather than the minority, were dial-up Internet users.

Table 3.5 **Variation in download speed (for a 56.6 kbps modem) and page size for the top five and bottom five UK sites week starting 6 October 2005**

	Web site	*Avg. download speed*	*Page size*
1	Thomas Cook	4.65 s	18.46 kb
2	British Airways	5.15 s	23.46 kb
3	Next On-Line Shopping	5.64 s	26.90 kb
4	easyJet	6.09 s	27.88 kb
5	NTL	6.66 s	29.77 kb
95	Nokia UK	37.60 s	180.98 kb
96	The Salvation Army	37.68 s	171.07 kb
97	Rail Track	38.14 s	111.00 kb
98	workthing.com	38.77 s	187.35 kb
99	Orange	40.01 s	194.16 kb
100	FT.com	44.39 s	211.55 kb

Source: Site Confidence (www.siteconfidence.co.uk)

A major factor for a company to consider when choosing an ISP is whether the server is *dedicated* to one company or whether content from several companies is located on the same server. A dedicated server is best, but it will attract a premium price.

Availability

Availability refers to the amount of time that a web site is available to customers. For a company offering 24-hour, 7-day services, it should be 100 per cent. However, inspection of *Table 3.6* shows that this is often not the case. For an e-commerce site, such as travel site E-bookers, a large amount of revenue could be lost if availability drops below 100 per cent. Of course, this will not only be revenue lost from customers unable to complete their transactions, but also revenue lost from potential or current customers who are unlikely to use the site in the future because of the disruption they have faced.

Table 3.6 Variation in download and availability of top UK sites, October 2005

	Download (secs)	*Availability (%)*
Google.co.uk	0.28	99.91
Yahoo.co.uk	0.45	99.91
BBC.co.uk	0.59	99.82
Barclays	2.80	99.24
MSN.co.uk	0.65	99.78
Worst	10.00	99.51

Source: Adapted from *Keynote KUK 40 Index October 2005*. Copyright © 2005 Keynote Systems Inc., The Internet Performance Authority, San Mateo, CA

Service-level agreements

Service-level agreement
A contractual specification of service standards a contractor must meet.

To ensure the best speed and availability a company should check the service-level agreements (SLAs) carefully when outsourcing web site hosting services. The SLA will define confirmed standards of availability and performance measured in terms of the *latency* or network delay when information is passed from one point to the next (such as London to New York). The SLA also includes notification to the customer detailing when the web service becomes unavailable with reasons why and estimates of when the service will be restored. Further information on SLAs is available at www.uk.uu.net/support/sla/. *Activity 3.5* gives sources where individuals or companies can monitor the performance of their ISP.

Security

Security is another important issue in service quality. How to control security was referred to in the earlier section on firewalls and is considered in detail in the *Focus on security design* (*Chapter 11, p. 540*).

Activity 3.5 Assessing ISP performance

Visit the w.w.w.

Purpose

To highlight management issues in monitoring and controlling ISP performance.

Activity

1 Several UK Internet magazines such as *Internet Works* (www.iwks.com) or *Internet Magazine* (www.internet-magazine.com) provide monthly performance assessments of different ISPs. Services for companies to assess their performance are also provided by Keynote (www.keynote.com), Zeus (www.zeus.co.uk and http://webperf.net) and Mercury Interactive (www.mercuryinteractive.com).

Visit the sites of these suppliers and review the variation of the ISPs in terms of different factors. Which is the fastest, which is the slowest? How does your ISP fare?

- Long-term availability trend for web server.
- Variation of download rate from web server.
- E-mail server availability and response.
- FTP server availability and response.

→

2 Imagine you are in charge of e-commerce at The B2B Company. You have an existing web site hosted by a small ISP, but customers are complaining about the speed of the web site and you are concerned about the ISP going out of business. You also want to move to a transactional web site. You have decided to select a new ISP which you hope will provide a better quality of service for customers and will provide a better long-term solution. You require a single supplier for ease of management, although the supplier may subcontract some services.

Questions

1 List the services you would require.
2 What are the key factors on which you will judge the ISP?

Answers to activities can be found at www.pearsoned.co.uk/chaffey

Managing employee access to the Internet and e-mail

This is covered in *Chapter 11* in the *Focus on e-business security* section.

Managing e-business applications infrastructure

E-business applications infrastructure
Applications that provide access to services and information inside and beyond an organization.

Management of the e-business applications infrastructure concerns delivering the right applications to all users of e-business services. The issue involved is one that has long been a concern of IS managers, namely to deliver access to integrated applications and data that are available across the whole company. Traditionally businesses have developed applications silos or islands of information, as depicted in *Figure 3.10(a)*. This shows that these silos may develop at three different levels: (1) there may be different technology architectures used in different functional areas, giving rise to the problems discussed in the previous section, (2) there will also be different applications and separate databases in different areas and (3) processes or activities followed in the different functional areas may also be different.

These applications silos are often a result of decentralization or poorly controlled investment in information systems, with different departmental managers selecting different systems from different vendors. This is inefficient in that it will often cost more to purchase applications from separate vendors, and also it will be more costly to support and upgrade. Even worse is that such a fragmented approach stifles decision making and leads to isolation between functional units. An operational example of the problems this may cause is if a customer phones a B2B company for the status of a bespoke item they have ordered, where the person in customer support may have access to their personal details but not the status of their job, which is stored on a separate information system in the manufacturing unit. Problems can also occur at tactical and strategic levels. For example, if a company is trying to analyse the financial contribution of customers, perhaps to calculate lifetime values, some information about customers' purchases may be stored in a marketing information system, while the payments data will be stored in a separate system within the finance department. It may prove difficult or impossible to reconcile these different data sets.

Enterprise resource planning (ERP) applications
Software providing integrated functions for major business functions such as production, distribution, sales, finance and human resources management.

To avoid the problems of a fragmented applications infrastructure, companies attempted throughout the 1990s to achieve the more integrated position shown in *Figure 3.10(b)*. Here the technology architecture, applications, data architecture and process architecture are uniform and integrated across the organization. To achieve this many companies turned to enterprise resource planning (ERP) vendors such as SAP, Baan, PeopleSoft and Oracle.

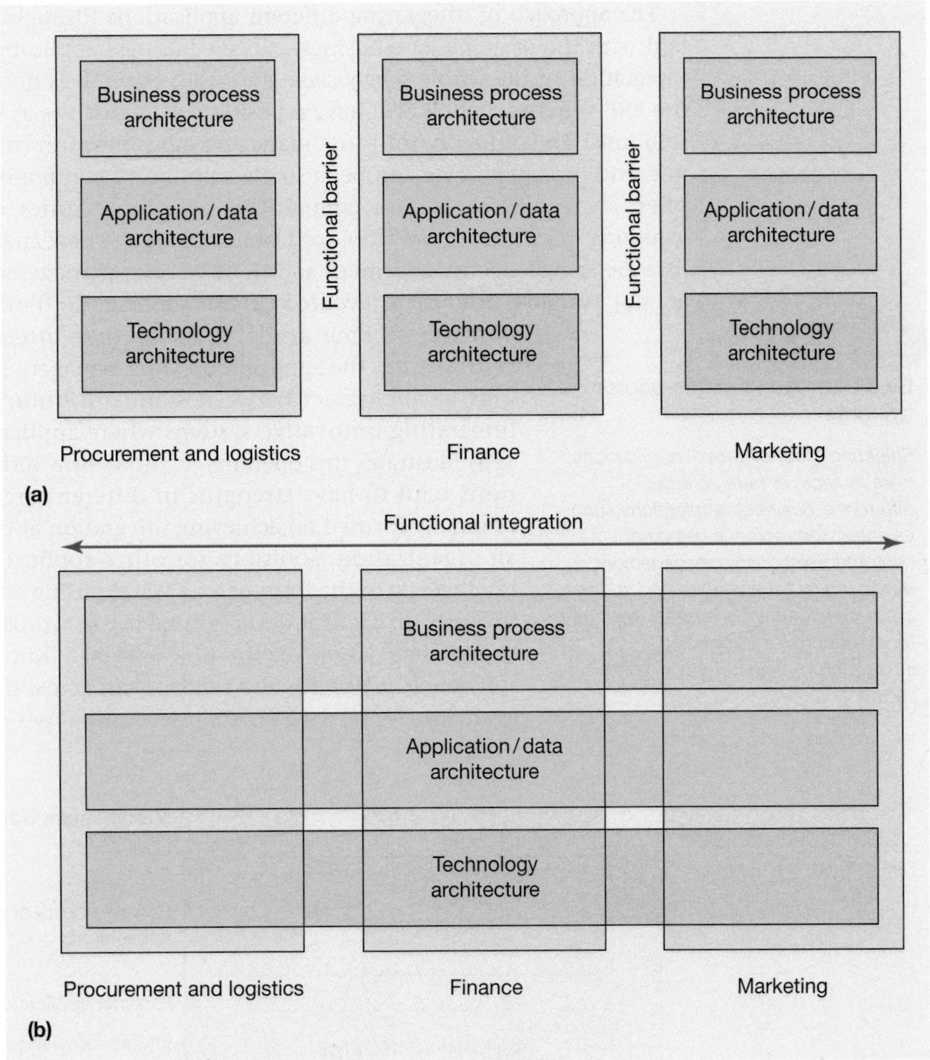

Figure 3.10 (a) Fragmented applications infrastructure, (b) integrated applications infrastructure

Source: Adapted from Hasselbring (2000)

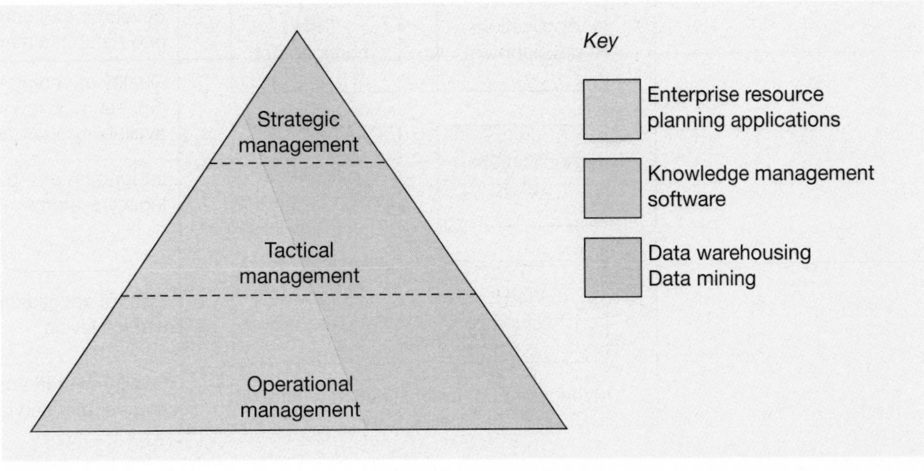

Figure 3.11 Differing use of applications at levels of management within companies

The approach of integrating different applications through ERP is entirely consistent with the principle of e-business, since e-business applications must facilitate the integration of the whole *supply chain* and *value chain*. It is noteworthy that many of the ERP vendors such as SAP have repositioned themselves as suppliers of e-business solutions! The difficulty for those managing e-business infrastructure is that there is not, and probably never can be, a single solution of components from a single supplier. For example, to gain competitive edge, companies may need to turn to solutions from innovators who, for example, support new channels such as WAP, or provide knowledge management solutions or sales management solutions. If these are not available from their favoured current supplier, do they wait until these components become available or do they attempt to integrate new software into the application? Thus managers are faced with a precarious balancing act between standardization or core product and integrating innovative systems where applicable. *Figure 3.11* (*page 125*) illustrates this dilemma. It shows how different types of applications tend to have strengths in different areas. ERP systems were originally focused on achieving integration at the operational level of an organization. Solutions for other applications such as business intelligence in the form of data warehousing and data mining tended to focus on tactical decision making based on accessing the operational data from within ERP systems. Knowledge management software (*Chapter 10*) also tends to cut across different levels of management. *Figure 3.11* only shows some types of applications, but it

Debate 3.2

Best of breed *vs* single-source systems

Selecting 'best-of-breed' applications from multiple system vendors for different e-business applications such as enterprise resource planning, customer relationship management, transactional e-commerce and supply chain management is a better approach for an effective e-business infrastructure than using a single-vendor solution.

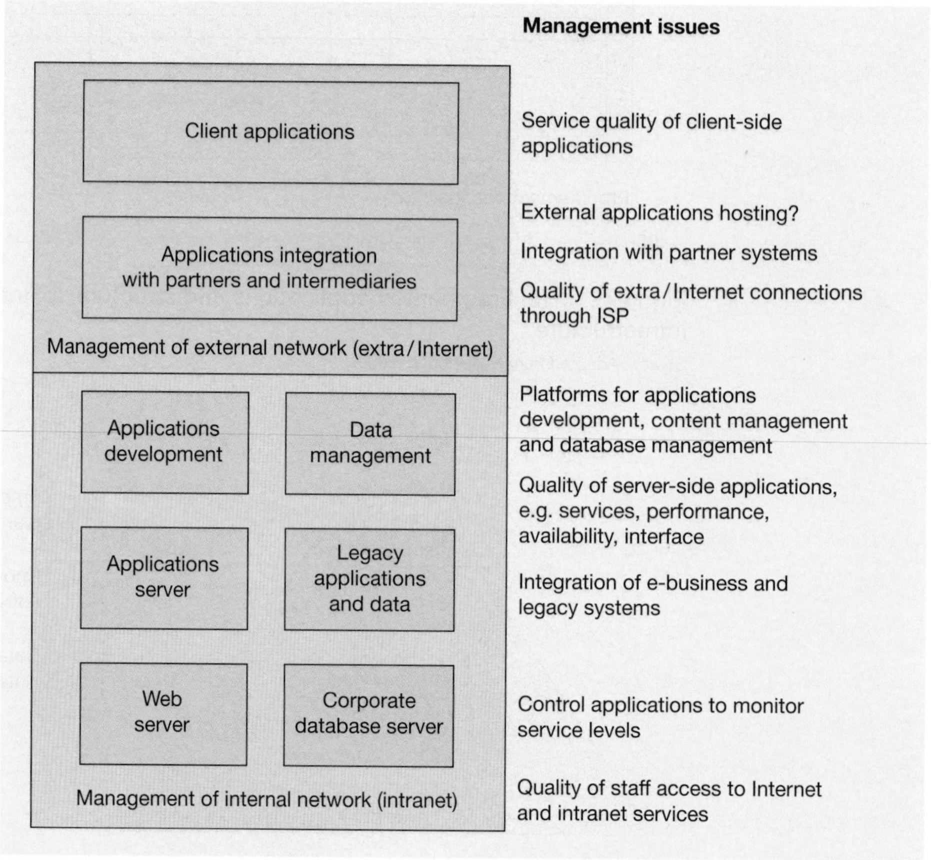

Figure 3.12 **Elements of e-business infrastructure that require management**

shows the trial of strength between the monolithic ERP applications and more specialist applications looking to provide the same functionality.

In this section we have introduced some of the issues of managing e-business infrastructure. These are examined in more detail later in the book. *Figure 3.12* summarizes some of these management issues and is based on the layered architecture introduced at the start of this section with applications infrastructure at the top and technology infrastructure towards the bottom.

Focus on web services and service-oriented architecture (SOA)

Web services
Business applications and software services are provided through Internet and web protocols with the application managed on a separate server to where it is accessed through a web browser on an end users's computer.

'Web services' refers to a highly significant model for managing software and data within the e-business age. The web services model involves managing and performing all types of business processes and activities through accessing web-based services rather than running a traditional executable application on the processor of your local computer. For example, rather than running a word processor such as Microsoft Word on your local computer through starting 'Word.exe', a web-service model would involve visiting a web site which hosts the application and completing your word processing there. At the time of writing, Google had just purchased Writely (www.writely.com), so by the time you read this, it is likely that Google will be offering full word processing and probably later spreadsheet and presentation web services. 'Office Live' is an initiative from Microsoft that will deliver this capability in future – today the best example is 'Outlook Live' which is an online version of the Outlook e-mail software. Indeed if you use Hotmail, Yahoo! Mail or Google GMail you are using a web service.

Utility computing
IT resources and in particular software and hardware are utilized on a pay-per-use basis and are managed externally as 'managed services'.

Application server provider
An application server provides a business application on a server remote from the user.

On-demand computing
This term was coined by IBM to describe managed services.

A related concept to web services is utility computing. Utility computing involves treating all aspects of IT as a commodity service such as water, gas or electricity where payment is according to usage. This includes not only software which may be used on a pay-per-use basis, but also using hardware. An earlier term is 'applications service providers' (ASP) which is less widely used now. Yet another term used to describe this concept is 'on-demand computing'. This term, which was coined by IBM, has a broader meaning since IBM refers to it as an extension of the e-business concept.

Think of examples of web services that you or businesses use, and you will soon see how important they are for both personal and business applications. Examples include:

- Web mail readers
- E-commerce account and purchasing management facilities such as Amazon.com
- Many services from Google such as Google Maps, GMail, Picasa and Google Analytics
- Customer relationship management applications from Salesforce.com and Siebel/Oracle
- Supply chain management solutions from SAP, Oracle and Covisint
- E-mail and web security management from companies like MessageLabs.

From the point of view of managing IT infrastructure these changes are dramatic since traditionally companies have employed their own information systems support staff to manage different types of business applications such as e-mail. A web service provider offers an alternative where the application is hosted remotely or off-site on a server operated by an ASP. Costs associated with upgrading and configuring new software on users' client computers and servers are dramatically decreased.

Activity 3.6 illustrates the decision-making process involved with using the web services approach and highlights the advantages and disadvantages of this approach.

Activity 3.6 Opportunities for using web services by The B2B Company

Purpose

To highlight the advantages and disadvantages of the web services approach.

Question

Develop a balanced case for the managing director explaining the web services approach and summarizing its advantages and disadvantages.

Answers to activities can be found at www.pearsoned.co.uk/chaffey

Service-oriented architecture (SOA)

Service-oriented architecture
A service-oriented architecture is a collection of services that communicate with each other as part of a distributed systems architecture comprising different services.

The technical architecture used to build web services is formerly known as a 'service-oriented architecture'. This is an arrangement of software processes or agents which communicate with each other to deliver the business requirements.

The main role of a service within SOA is to provide functionality. This is provided by three characteristics:

1 An interface with the service which is platform-independent (not dependent on a particular type of software or hardware). The interface is accessible through applications development approaches such as Microsoft .Net or Java and accessed through protocols such as SOAP (Simple Object Access Protocol) which is used for messages, i.e. instructions and returned results to be exchanged between services.
2 The service can be dynamically located and invoked. One service can query for the existence of another service through a service directory – for example an e-commerce service could query for the existence of a credit card authorization service.
3 The service is self-contained. That is, the service cannot be influenced by other services, rather it will return a required result to a request from another service, but will not change state. Within web services, messages and data are typically exchanged between services using XML.

The examples of web services we mentioned above have given above all imply a user interacting with the web service. But with the correct business rules and models to follow, there is no need for human intervention and different applications and databases can communicate with each other in real time. A web service such as Kelkoo.com which was discussed in *Chapter 2* exchanges information with all participating merchants through XML using an SOA. The concept of the semantic web mentioned above and business applications of web services such as CRM, SCM and ebXML are also based on an SOA approach.

Read *Case Study 3.1* to explore the significance and challenges of SOA further.

Case Study 3.1 New architecture or just new hype?

Depending on whom you listen to, it could be the most important shift in corporate computing since the advent of the internet – or it could be just the latest excuse for technology companies to hype their products in a dismal market.

'We believe it's the Next Big Thing', says Henning Kagermann, chairman of SAP, Europe's biggest software company.

'It's the new fashion statement', counters Mark Barrenechea, chief technology officer of Computer Associates. 'I'm sceptical.'

The 'it' in question goes by the ungainly name of 'service-oriented architecture', or SOA for short. According to the big software companies, its impact on computing will be as big as the client–server revolution of the early

1990s, or the arrival of web-based applications with the internet.

'Every five or 10 years, we see this in the industry', says John Wookey, the executive in charge of Oracle's Project Fusion, the giant effort to re-engineer all of the software applications inherited as a result of that company's various acquisitions.

For those with ambitions to dominate the next phase of corporate software – SAP, Oracle, IBM and Microsoft – it represents an important turning-point. 'When these transitions occur you have your best opportunity to change the competitive landscape', adds Mr Wookey.

Yet for customers, the benefits and costs of this next transformation in the underlying computing architecture are still hard to ascertain.

Bruce Richardson, chief research officer at AMR Research, draws attention to the unexpected costs that came with the rise of client–server computing: the soaring hardware and software expenses, the difficulty of supporting such a wide array of machines, and the cost of dealing with security flaws.

'That ended up being a huge bill', he notes.

It is hardly surprising that enterprise software companies – those that create the heavy-duty software that big corporations and governments use to run their operations – are so eager to latch on to the next big thing.

An industry still in its infancy is facing potential disruptive upheaval. New licensing models and ways of delivering software, along with open-source approaches to development and distribution, are turning the young software industry on its head.

At the same time, the maturity of existing applications and the technology platform on which they run has left the best-established enterprise software companies stuck in a period of slow growth.

That is fertile soil for extravagant marketing claims to take root in.

Even if SOA risks being over-hyped, however, it still seems likely to represent an important step forward for today's often monolithic corporate IT systems.

By harnessing industry-wide technology standards that have been in development since the late 1990s, it promises at least a partial answer to one of the biggest drawbacks of the current computing base: a lack of flexibility that has driven up the cost of software development and forced companies to design their business processes around the needs of their IT systems, rather than the other way around.

Software executives say that the inability to redesign IT systems rapidly to support new business processes, and to link those systems to customers and suppliers, was one of the main reasons for the failure of one of the great early promises of the internet – seamless 'B2B', or business-to-business, commerce.

'It's what killed the original [B2B] marketplaces', says Shai Agassi, who heads SAP's product and technology development.

SAP is certainly further ahead than others in the race to build a more flexible computing platform. While Oracle and Microsoft are busy trying to create coherent packages of software applications from the corporate acquisitions they have made, SAP is halfway through a revamp of its technology that could give it a lead of two years or more.

'If they're right, it will be a huge thing for them', says Charles Di Bona, software analyst at Sanford C. Bernstein.

Underlying the arrival of SOA has been the spread of so-called web services standards – such as the mark-up language XML and communications protocol SOAP – that make it easier for machines to exchange data automatically.

This holds the promise of automating business processes that run across different IT systems, whether inside a single company or spanning several business partners: a customer placing an order in one system could automatically trigger production requests in another and an invoice in a third.

Breaking down the different steps in a business process in this way, and making them available to be recombined quickly to suit particular business needs, is the ultimate goal of SOA. Each step in the process becomes a service, a single reusable component that is 'exposed' through a standard interface.

The smaller each of these software components, the more flexibility users will have to build IT systems that fit their particular needs.

SAP has created 300 services so far; that number will rise to 3,000 by the end of this year, says Mr Agassi. Through NetWeaver, the set of 'middleware' tools that provide the glue, it has also finalised much of the platform to deliver this new set of services. The full 'business process platform' will be complete by the end of next year, SAP says.

'The factory is running – we have all the tools ready now', says Peter Graf, head of solution marketing at SAP. To get customers to start experimenting with the new technology, he adds, 'we need to come up with killer apps'.

The first full-scale demonstration will come from a project known as Mendecino, under which SAP and Microsoft have been working to integrate their 'back-end' and 'front-end' systems and which is due to be released in the middle of this year.

By linking them to the widely used components of Microsoft's Office desktop software, SAP's corporate applications will become easier to use, says Mr Graf: for instance, when a worker enters a holiday in his or her Outlook calendar, it could automatically trigger an approval request to a manager and cross-check with a system that records holiday entitlements.

While such demonstrations may start to show the potential of SOA, however, the real power of this architectural shift is likely to depend on a much broader ecosystem of software developers and corporate users.

'People want to extend their business processes to get closer to customers', says Mr Richardson at AMR. To do that through the 'loosely coupled' IT systems promised by SOA will require wider adoption of the new technology architecture.

A number of potential drawbacks stand in the way.

Along with uncertainty about the ultimate cost, points out Mr Richardson, is concern about security: what safeguards will companies need before they are willing to let valuable corporate data travel outside their own IT systems, or before they open up their own networks to code developed elsewhere?

A further question is whether SOA can fulfil one of its most important promises: that the technology platforms being created by SAP and others will stimulate a wave of innovation in the software industry, as developers rush to create new and better applications, many of them suited to the specific needs of particular industries or small groups of companies.

That depends partly on whether companies such as SAP can create true technology 'ecosystems' around their platforms, much as Microsoft's success in desktop software depended on its ability to draw developers to its desktop software platform.

'We were told three years ago that we didn't know how to partner', says Mr Agassi at SAP, before dismissing such criticism as 'quite funny', given what he says was the success of its earlier software applications in attracting developers. 'We are more open than we have ever been, we are more standards-based than we have ever been', he adds – a claim that is contested by Oracle, which has tried to make capital from the fact that its German rival's underlying technology still depends on a proprietary computing language, ABAP.

However, even if the future SOA-enabled platforms succeed in stimulating a new generation of more flexible corporate software, one other overriding issue remains: rivals such as SAP and Oracle will see little to gain from linking their rival platforms to each other. Full inter-operability will remain just a dream.

'To make SOA real, you have to have a process start in one system and end in another, with no testing or certification needed', says Mr Barrenechea at Computer Associates – even if those systems are rivals ones from SAP and Oracle.

The software giants, he says, 'have to be motivated to make it work'.

According to Mr Agassi, companies will eventually 'have to choose' which of the platforms they want to use as the backbone for their businesses.

The web services standards may create a level of inter-operability between these different backbones, but each will still use its own 'semantics', or way of defining business information, to make it comprehensible to other, connected systems.

Like a common telephone network, the standards should make it easier to create connections, but they can do nothing if the people on either end of the line are talking a different language.

If different companies in the same industry, or different business partners, adopt different software platforms, there will still be a need for the expensive manual work to link the systems together.

'You will have to spend the same amount of money on systems integrators that you spend today', says Mr Graf.

Despite that, the new service-oriented technology should still represent a leap forward from today's monolithic IT systems. Even the sceptics concede that the gains could be substantial. It should lead to 'better [software] components and better interfaces – which equals better inter-operability', says Mr Barrenechea.

As with any sales pitch from the technology industry, however, it is as well to be wary of the hype.

Source: Richard Waters in San Francisco FT.com. Published: 7 March 2006

Question

Discuss the extent to which SOA will reduce reliance on a single provider of enterprise software and increase flexibility in deploying new applications and functionality.

Electronic data interchange (EDI)
The exchange, using digital media, of structured business information, particularly for sales transactions such as purchase orders and invoices between buyers and sellers.

Financial EDI
Aspect of electronic payment mechanism involving transfer of funds from the bank of a buyer to the bank of a seller.

EDI

Transactional e-commerce predates the World Wide Web and service-oriented architecture by some margin. In the 1960s, **electronic data interchange (EDI)**, **financial EDI** and **electronic funds transfer (EFT)** over secure private networks became established modes of intra- and inter-company transaction. In this section, we briefly cover EDI to give a historical context. The idea of standardized document exchange can be traced back to the 1948 Berlin Airlift, where a standard form was required for efficient management of items flown to Berlin from many locations. This was followed by electronic transmission in the 1960s in the US transport industries. The EDIFACT (Electronic Data Interchange for Administration, Commerce and Transport) standard was later produced by a joint United Nations/European committee to enable international trading. There is also a similar X12 EDI standard developed by the ANSI Accredited Standards Committee.

Electronic funds transfer (EFT)
Automated digital transmission of money between organizations and banks.

Clarke (1998) considers that EDI is best understood as the replacement of paper-based purchase orders with electronic equivalents, but its applications are wider than this. The types of documents exchanged by EDI include business transactions such as orders, invoices, delivery advice and payment instructions as part of EFT. There may also be pure information transactions such as a product specification, for example engineering drawings or price lists. Clarke (1998) defines EDI as:

> *the exchange of documents in standardised electronic form, between organisations, in an automated manner, directly from a computer application in one organisation to an application in another.*

DTI (2000) describes EDI as follows:

> *Electronic data interchange (EDI) is the computer-to-computer exchange of structured data, sent in a form that allows for automatic processing with no manual intervention. This is usually carried out over specialist EDI networks.*

It is apparent from these definitions that EDI is one form, or a subset of, electronic commerce. A key point is that direct communication occurs between applications (rather than between computers). This requires information systems to achieve the data processing and data management associated with EDI and integration with associated information systems such as sales order processing and inventory control systems.

According to IDC (1999), revenues for EDI network services were already at $1.1 billion in 1999 and forecast to reach over $2 billion by 2003. EDI is developing through new standards and integration with Internet technologies to achieve **Internet EDI**. IDC (1999) predicts that Internet EDI's share of EDI revenues will climb from 12 per cent to 41 per cent over the same period.

Internet EDI
Use of EDI data standards delivered across non-proprietary IP networks.

Value-added network (VAN)
A secure wide-area network that uses proprietary rather than Internet technology.

Virtual private networks (VPN)
A secure, encrypted (tunnelled) connection between two points using the Internet, typically created by ISPs for organizations wanting to conduct secure Internet trading.

Internet EDI enables EDI to be implemented at lower costs since, rather than using proprietary, so-called **value-added networks (VANs)**, it uses the same EDI standard documents, but using lower-cost transmission techniques through **virtual private networks (VPNs)** or the public Internet. Reported cost savings are up to 90 per cent (*EDI Insider*, 1996). *EDI Insider* estimated that this cost differential would cause an increase from the 80,000 companies in the United States using EDI in 1996 to hundreds of thousands. Internet EDI also includes EDI-structured documents being exchanged by e-mail or in a more automated form using FTP.

It is apparent that there is now a wide choice of technologies for managing electronic transactions between businesses. The Yankee Group (2002) refers to these as 'transaction management (TXM)' technologies which are used to automate machine-to-machine information exchange between organizations. These include:

> *document and data translation, transformation, routing, process management, Electronic data interchange (EDI), eXtensible Mark-up Language (XML), Web services ... Value-added networks, electronic trading networks, and other hosted solutions are also tracked in the TXM market segment.*

Focus on new access devices

In this section we introduce two alternative access platforms to PC-based Internet access, which provide many similar advantages. These two other access devices or platforms are interactive digital TV and mobile or wireless access to the Internet. The advent of such new technologies for customers to access content poses a difficult dilemma for organizations that have adopted e-commerce since, to be competitive, the decision to adopt must be made before the extent of its impact is apparent. These issues apply, in particular, to business-to-consumer companies since the content made available for new access devices has mainly been targeted at consumers. Imagine you are the e-commerce manager or brand manager at The B2C Company: what would be the benefits and drawbacks of updating your e-commerce systems to support these new platforms? The benefits of deciding to invest could include:

- Early-mover advantage
- Learning about the technology
- Customer acquisition
- Customer retention
- Improving corporate or brand image.

However, it will be difficult to estimate the number of new customers who may be acquired and the profitability of the project may be sacrificed to achieve the other benefits above. As new technologies become available, companies need to assess the technology, understand the services that may be relevant to their customers and work out a strategy and implementation plan. It also becomes necessary to support development across multiple platforms, for example retailers such as WH Smith Online use a database to generate book catalogue content for display on web, mobile or interactive digital TV platforms.

Although it may appear there is a divergence in access devices from PC to phone to TV, in the long term most commentators expect technology convergence to occur. Mougayer (1998) identifies different types of convergence:

Technology convergence
A trend in which different hardware devices such as TVs, computers and phones merge and have similar functions.

- *Infrastructure convergence* – this is the increase in the number of delivery media channels for the Internet such as phone lines, microwave (mobile phones), cable and satellite. These are now often being used in combination.
- *Information appliance (technology) convergence* – the use of different hardware devices to access and deliver the content of the Internet.
- *Supplier convergence* – the overlap between suppliers such as Internet service providers, online access providers and more traditional media suppliers such as the telecommunications and cable companies.

Mobile access devices

Mobile technologies are not new; it has been possible for many years to access the Internet for e-mail using a laptop connected via a modem. The need for a large device to access the Internet was overcome with the development of personal digital assistants (PDAs) such as the Palm Computing Palm VII or Psion and mobile phones that accessed the Internet via a wireless connection. When wireless devices are used for e-commerce applications, this is referred to as mobile commerce or m-commerce.

Mobile commerce or m-commerce
Electronic transactions and communications conducted using mobile devices such as laptops, PDAs and mobile phones, and typically with a wireless connection.

The characteristics that mobile or wireless connections offer to their users can be summarized by the supposedly idyllic image used in many adverts of a user accessing the Internet via a laptop or phone from a field, riverbank or mountain-top. They provide ubiquity (can be accessed from anywhere), reachability (their users can be reached when not in their normal location) and convenience (it is not necessary to have access to a power supply or a fixed-line connection). In addition to these obvious benefits, there are additional benefits that are less obvious: they provide security – each user can be authenticated since each wireless device has a unique identification code, their location can be used to tailor content, and they provide a degree of privacy compared with a desktop PC – looking for a new job on a wireless device might be better than under the gaze of a boss. An additional advantage that will shortly be available is that of instant access or being 'always-on'; here there is no need to dial up a wireless connection. The proposition or consumer benefits for mobile commerce are summarized in *Table 3.7*.

Table 3.7 **Summary of mobile or wireless Internet access consumer proposition**

Element of proposition	*Evaluation*
No fixed location	The user is freed from the need to access via the desktop, making access possible when commuting, for example
Location-based services	Mobiles can be used to give geographically based services, e.g. an offer in a particular shopping centre. Future mobiles will have global positioning services integrated
Instant access/convenience	The latest General Packet Radio Service (GPRS) and 3G services are always on, avoiding the need for lengthy connection
Privacy	Mobiles are more private than desktop access, making them more suitable for social use or for certain activities such as an alert service for looking for a new job
Personalization	As with PC access, personal information and services can be requested by the user, although these often need to be set up via PC access
Security	In the future mobiles may become a form of wallet, but thefts of mobiles make this a source of concern

In addition to offering voice calls, mobile phones have increasingly been used for e-mail and Short Message Service (SMS), commonly known as 'texting'. SMS is effectively a simple form of e-mail that enables messages to be transferred between mobile phones. According to MobileCommerceWorld (2002) 1.3 billion text messages were sent in December 2001, bringing the total number of messages sent in 2001 in the UK to 12.2 billion. This suggests an average of nearly 300 messages per person annually and a much higher figure for some users! In 2002, telecoms providers launched picture messaging or multimedia messaging services, which it was hoped would capitalize on the interest in texting.

In 1999 the first of a new generation of mobile phones such as the Nokia 7110 were introduced – these offered the opportunity to access the Internet. They are known as 'Wireless Application Protocol' or WAP phones, or in more common parlance web-enabled or Internet phones. What these phones offer is the facility to access information on web sites that has been specially tailored for display on the small screens of mobile phones. There was a tremendous amount of hype about these phones since they seemed to provide all the benefits that have been provided by the World Wide Web, but in a mobile form. Levels of product purchase by mobile phone and content access have proved very low in comparison with the Internet, even for standardized products such as books and CDs. Many m-commerce providers such as Sweden's M-box went into receivership. However, analysts expect that with new access platforms, such as 3G, this will change. Taking the example of travel, which is the leading e-commerce category in Europe by revenue for the fixed Internet, analysts IDC (2002) estimated that by 2005, 23 million Europeans would buy travel products and services using their mobile phones.

Wireless Application Protocol (WAP)
WAP is a technical standard for transferring information to wireless devices, such as mobile phones.

The Japanese experience with i-Mode suggests that with a suitable access device which supports colour images, the impact of 3G could be significant. MobileCommerceWorld (2001) reports that Japanese i-Mode users spend an average of ¥2,614 (US$21.60) each month on wireless content and m-commerce. Mobile-phone ringtones and other music downloads are the most popular i-Mode purchases, followed by other paid-for information services such as dating. The strength of the proposition is indicated since over 30 million Japanese were using this service less than two years after its launch.

i-Mode
A mobile access platform that enables display of colour graphics and content subscription services.

In the longer term 4G broadband mobile communications are under development and are expected to be introduced first in Japan, as early as 2006. As would be

4G
Fourth-generation wireless, expected to deliver wireless broadband at 20–40 Mbps (about 10–20 times the current rates of ADSL broadband service).

expected, the main distinction over 3G is transmission rates. 4G is currently estimated to yield increases reaching 20–40 Mbps (about 10–20 times the current rates of ADSL broadband service).

Wi-Fi ('wireless-fidelity') mobile access

Wi-Fi ('wireless fidelity')
A high-speed wireless local-area network enabling wireless access to the Internet for mobile, office and home users.

'Wi-Fi' is the shorthand often used to describe a high-speed wireless local-area network. Most Wi-Fi networks use a standard protocol known as *802.11 a,b or g*, which offers speeds of up to 11 Mbps, which is relatively fast compared to ADSL, although this depends on signal strength. Wi-Fi can be deployed in an office or home environment where it removes the need for cabling and adds flexibility. However, it has attracted most attention for its potential for offering wireless access in cities and towns without the need for a fixed connection. The Intel Centrino mobile chip launched in 2003 offers facilities to make Wi-Fi access easier for laptop users.

In 2002 some airports, cafés and hotels started offering Wi-Fi 'hotspots' which allowed customers access to the Internet from their laptops or other mobile devices without the need to connect using a wire. This helped differentiate themselves from other services without this facility.

There was extensive media coverage of Wi-Fi when it was launched and, as is often the case with new technologies, the technology does not appear to satisfy a well-established demand. *The Guardian* (2003) quotes Lars Godell, a telecoms analyst at Forrester Research. In a recent research note, he said

> *It's as if the dotcom boom and bust never happened – this bubble seems ready to burst. I agree there is some need, but think there has been very pointed exaggeration of the need for internet access around the clock, and on top of that the willingness to pay for it. And that is the critical issue when you create a business plan.*

He also noted that 'The usage rates of wireless Lan have been appallingly low'. He cites the case of Amsterdam's Schiphol airport, through which 41 million passengers pass every year, but where there are only a dozen Wi-Fi hotspot users a day. Other hotspot operators confirm, in private, that they see similarly low usage numbers.

Despite the media hype about public wireless networks it appears as if the main applications for wireless networks are at home and at work. According to IDC, people are connecting wirelessly at home rather than taking to Wi-Fi via a hotspot. In a survey of 2,500 users of mobile devices, IDC found that 34 per cent of those who use Wi-Fi connect to a wireless network at home, compared with 27 per cent at work. The use of wireless LANs (WLANs) is also increasing at work. Note that this increased usage has security limitations since with Wi-Fi encryption is limited and communications can potentially be intercepted or 'sniffed' by anyone in the vicinity with appropriate scanning software. For WLANs additional hardware is needed. For example, home users need to buy a wireless router (sometimes with firewall included) which connects to the Internet and shares the Internet and local network access with all PCs in the house which contain wireless cards to receive the signal. Other devices can also be used: for example music or video streamed from the Internet can be played on appropriate devices. Transmission is limited in home applications to around 100m line-of-sight.

Bluetooth

Bluetooth
A wireless standard for transmission of data between devices over short ranges (less than 100 m).

Bluetooth is another wireless technology, this time used for short-range data transmission between devices. Applications of Bluetooth include wireless keyboards and beaming data between a PDA and a desktop or a laptop and a printer. Transmission distances between Bluetooth-enabled devices were initially limited to 10 m, but can now be up to 100 m, so there is now the option for using the technology for networking like

Wi-Fi. However, Bluetooth is significantly slower than the main Wi-Fi standard at 723 kbps, so usage for WLANs will be less common.

From a marketing application viewpoint we are only just starting to see this technique used (many phones don't have Bluetooth). While individuals can exchange a business card or use their phone as a modem which links by Bluetooth to their mobile, a much more exciting application is BlueCasting. This technique was used with the launch of the latest Coldplay album where a London-based campaign involved 13,000 fans downloading free pre-release video clips, never-seen-before interviews, audio samples and exclusive images onto their mobile, via Bluetooth from Transvision screens at mainline train stations. In this campaign, 87,000 unique handsets were 'discovered' and 13,000 people opted in to receive the material, a response rate of 15%. The busiest day was Saturday 4 June – two days before the official album launch date – when over 8,000 handsets were discovered and over 1,100 users opted in to receive a video file. The Bluecast systems can deliver time-sensitive content, so, for example, in the morning the user would get an audio clip of the tracks 'Fix You' and be prompted to tune in to Radio One, but in the afternoon the clip would be the same but the user would be prompted to watch Jonathan Ross on BBC1.

And yes, in case you're wondering, the first cases of Bluejacking other phones, Bluetooth viruses and Bluespamming have already been reported. It has been suggested that use of Bluetooth for business purposes represents a security risk through a process known as 'Bluesnarfing'. An example of this often referred to is that, if you so wished, you could go to an airport passenger lounge and scan the diaries or contacts on passengers' different laptop, phone or PDA contacts.

Next-generation mobile services

UMTS (Universal Mobile Telecommunications System)
The standard for 3G mobile access.

GSM (Global System for Mobile communications)
The most widely used digital mobile phone systems in Europe before the emergence of 3G.

Figure 3.13 summarizes these new standards for accessing the mobile Internet. For each new technology there is an envelope between the lowest and highest possible transmission speeds. Very often the hype is based on the upper limit, but when implemented only the lower limit is achieved. Note that the UMTS standard for 3G is now often referred to as 'Wideband CDMA' or W-CDMA.

In 2001 new services became available on GPRS (General Packet Radio Service). This is approximately five times faster than GSM and is an 'always-on' service which is charged according to usage. Display is still largely text-based and based on the WAP protocol. Uptake of these services was limited due to the need for new handsets and

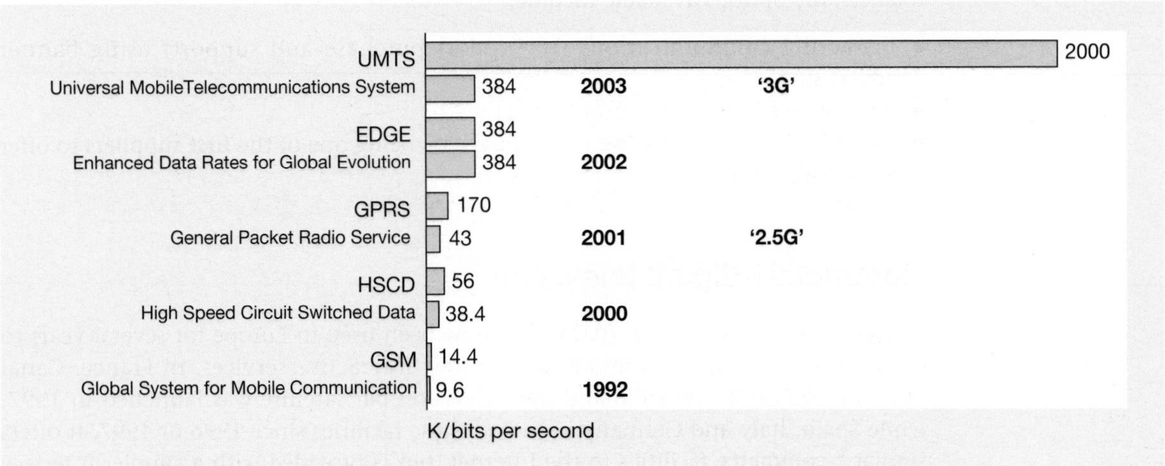

Figure 3.13 Mobile access technologies

3G

Third generation of mobile phone technology based on UMTS standard with high-speed data transfer enabling video calling and download.

EDGE (Evolved Data for GSM Evolution)

Intermediate mobile standard between GSM and UMTs.

the cost of data services. In March 2003 a completely new generation of services known as '3G' became available based on UMTS (*Figure 3.14*). With this, delivery of video downloads and chat becomes possible, enabling instant access or 'always-on'.

In the UK auctions for the licence to operate on these frequencies have exceeded £20 billion – such is the perceived importance of these services to the telecommunications companies. Many commentators now believe it will be difficult for the companies to recoup this money and this has resulted in large falls in their share prices. Charges for new 3G services and handsets will initially be several times those for GSM services and this is bound to limit the initial uptake. A new realism seems to be afoot in the telecoms industry, partly as a result of limited uptake of services such as WAP and picture messaging.

BBC (2003) reported that John Erskine, the head of network operator O_2, said:

> *3G is no longer a field of dreams adhering to the philosophy that if you built it, users will come. Now the attitudes are more pragmatic and led by market demand.*

Jean-François Pontal of Orange concurred (BBC, 2003), saying:

> *We might suggest ways customers might like to use services but at the end of the day they will be defined and deployed by the street. The next big thing is here already, in clubs, warehouses and bedroom.*

Debate 3.3

Predicting the future of the mobile Internet

'Future-generation mobile access devices using such technologies as 3G will supersede PCs as the main consumer access device for the Internet within 5 years.'

Pre-orders for 65,000 phones at the 'soft launch' of 3G in March 2003 show that there are many early adopters of the technology; it remains to be seen whether the remainder of the population will be convinced.

Strategies for mobile commerce

Repurposing

Developing content for a new access platform which was previously used for a different platform such as the web.

Different types of strategy can be identified for two main different types of players. For portal and media owners the options are to migrate their own portal to WAP/SMS (the option followed by Excite and The *Guardian*) or to partner with other WAP portals and provide content for these. Alternatively, they may decide the cost of repurposing is too high and they may wait for users to access the web with 3G devices which will require less repurposing since the screen resolution is higher. Revenue models may include sponsorship or subscription for individual content items or be on a subscription basis. Options for advertising are also being explored – www.247europe.com is one of the first companies to offer WAP-based advertisements. For destination sites such as banks and retailers, the options available include:

- marketing communications (to support purchase and support) using banner advertising
- e-commerce (sale of products on-site)
- brand building – improving brand image by being one of the first suppliers to offer an innovative service.

Interactive digital television

Interactive digital television (iDTV) has now been used in Europe for several years to deliver broadcasting to homes and offer new interactive services. In France, Canal Plus launched iDTV in 1996 and the Télévision par satellite was launched in 1997, while Spain, Italy and Germany have had these facilities since 1996 or 1997. It offers similar e-commerce facilities to the Internet, but is provided with a simpler interface that can be operated from a remote control. The system has attracted a limited number of advertisers and retailers compared to the Internet since start-up costs are higher. The amount of information available from providers is lower because of limited bandwidth on-site and because costs are higher.

In the UK, there are several providers and levels of access to interactive digital TV rival those of the Internet. All three main new media are tracked by IpsosMORI Technology Tracker (www.mori.com/technology). In January 2003, in the UK, the level of access in new media was reported as:

- Own mobile phone (77%)
- Use Internet anywhere (48%)
- Have digital TV (40%).

The importance of digital TV is indicated by these data. This medium rivals the Internet in its reach and tends to be used by different demographic groupings. Research by Jupiter MMXI (2002) suggests a similar picture in the rest of Europe to that in the UK, although access levels are currently lower. Total digital TV penetration is set to increase from 20 per cent in 2002 up to 52 per cent in 2006. The research indicates that by the end of 2006 more European households will be watching digital television than using the Internet.

Table 3.8 summarizes the proposition for interactive digital TV. It is evident that it is more similar to PC-based Internet access than to mobile access. A key difference is that TV viewing is more likely to involve several members of a family while PC usage is more individual. This may cause conflict in use of some individualized iDTV services.

Table 3.8 **Summary of interactive digital TV consumer proposition**

Element of proposition	*Evaluation*
Instant access/convenience	Interactive services are available quite rapidly, but return-path connections using phone lines for purchase are slower
Personalization	This is less practical for PC and mobile since there are usually several viewers
Security	Credit card details can be held by the iDTV provider, making it theoretically unnecessary to repeatedly enter personal details

Curry (2001) has proposed three alternative types of interactivity that online marketers can exploit:

1 *Distribution interactivity*. Here the user controls when the content is delivered. Video-on-demand is an example of this. Using personal video recorders such as TiVO is a further example, since users can choose to watch content at a later time and possibly omit adverts.
2 *Information interactivity*. Here the user can select different information. Curry gives the example of teletext and games which are together the most popular interactive TV activity. A further example is where a viewer of an advert can access a micro-site with further information on the advert. Information can be exchanged via a return path such as completing a competition. This provides an improved option for direct response advertising in comparison to traditional TV.
3 *Participation activity*. This is where the user can select different options during a programme such as choosing a different camera angle in a football match or different news stories. There is no return path in this case.

Return path
An interaction where the customer sends information to the provider using a phone line or cable.

Taking the UK as an example, there are several providers. For example, Sky Digital is viewed by over 6 million subscribers and has content from banks such as HSBC and

Woolwich and retailers such as Woolworths, Dixons and Carphone Warehouse. This is known as a 'walled garden service' since it is not open-access like the Internet. The online shopping service was formerly branded as 'Open', but has been rebranded as Sky Active since 2001. Although there are few reported figures of the overall use of these services, individual examples indicate some early success: HSBC registered 80,000 customers within 3 weeks, of whom 20,000 were new. Domino Pizza had 10,000 requests in the first 10 days. Curry (2001) reviews the success of online shopping on the Open platform; he reports that while 80% have heard of the Open platform, only 50% have used it and just 10% have bought through it. In contrast, he reports that 50% of Internet users have bought online and have spent more, more often.

The other main UK iDTV providers are cable providers ntl and Telewest and the digital terrestrial or FreeView service provided through a conventional aerial connected to a satellite box (formerly ITV Digital).

How does interactive digital TV work?

Figure 3.14 shows that a set-top box is an important component of the interactive digital TV system. This is used to receive and decode the message from a satellite dish or cable that is then displayed on a conventional TV. The set-top box also includes a modem that is used to pass back selections made on the interactive shopping channel to the company across the Internet.

Services include:

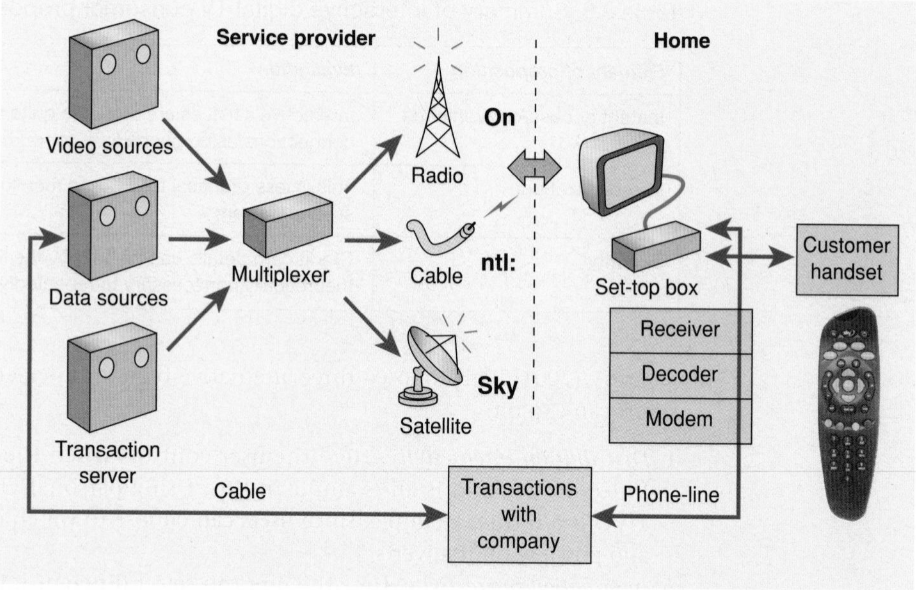

Figure 3.14 **Components of an interactive digital TV system**

- Interactive advertising where users can request more information or sign up for a promotion giving direct feedback on the success of an advert. One of the first, in Spring 2000, was for 'Chicken Tonite'. Direct sales are not permitted. There is a problem with viewers losing attention in subsequent ads, so interactive adverts are always last.
- Enhanced TV: this includes home shopping, banking, travel bookings and e-mail with video on demand.

When a company decides how to respond to iDTV several levels of commitment can be identified:

- *Promotion* – using interactive ads
- *Content* – repurpose web site
- *Content* – new interactive services
- *E-commerce* – perhaps for a limited range of products.

There is also the issue of which platform(s) to support in different countries.

IPTV

Digital TV channels are made available via broadband Internet either as streamed live broadcasts or as archived broadcasts of TV programs.

From 2005 onwards, the market share of proivders of digital TV delivered via satellite or cable is likely to decline with the adoption of **IPTV**. IPTV enables digital TV channels to be made available via broadband Internet either as streamed live broadcasts or as archived broadcasts of TV programmes. This will be particularly popular with households that use a computer known as a 'home media centre' to replace their television.

An example of the application of IPTV is the BBC imp (**www.bbc.co.uk/imp/**) 2005–6 trial which was due to be made more widely available in 2006. Viewers were given the opportunity to access TV and radio programmes from the last seven days, using a peer-to-peer (P2P) distribution technology to legally distribute programmes. In the UK, SKY launched a similar system for movie subscribers in 2006.

BitTorrent

A peer-to-peer file-sharing technology used to enable sharing of large audio and video files.

These facilities use a similar technological approach to **BitTorrent** which was developed in 2002 to enable sharing of large audio and video files. The BitTorrent protocol breaks a large file into smaller segments and these are then downloaded by different client computers. Once downloaded, a fragment can then be uploaded by other computers to form a 'P2P swarm'. Fragments are then reassembled by BitTorrent software on a user's computer. BitTorrent has become very popular with home users (and unpopular with copyright holders such as movie studios) and it is thought it may account for a sizeable proportion of Internet traffic and will be a major strain on Internet performance in the future.

The future of the Internet infrastructure

For many first-time and regular users, the Internet is seen as frustrating because of its speed. Of course, the poor performance is, to an extent, a consequence of the success of the Internet in attracting over half a billion users. The advent of widespread broadband access is also likely to dispel the reputation for poor performance. The performance delivered through the infrastructure has also improved, with response times such as those monitored by Keynote (*Table 3.6*) significantly faster than 2 or 3 years ago. Action to further improve this situation takes the form of projects by government departments such as Education and Defence, together with business initiatives. The Internet 2 project is coordinated by the University Corporation for Advanced Internet Development (UCAID), an association formed by 34 international universities in 1996. UCAID's Internet 2 project (**www.internet2.edu**) is mainly directed at software aspects of the infrastructure. These include the concept of 'teleimmersion' where different people can occupy virtual space from different locations. The development of broadband access will also enable improved use of multimedia. On a more fundamental level, UCAID is reviewing how improvements in the standards of the Internet such as IPv6 can be used in Internet 2. IPv6 is a revision of the IP protocol and is intended to give better performance and increase the number of addresses available. This could enable, for example, walking through a prototype building to discuss its merits. Other initiatives from the United States include new high-speed network backbones such as Abilene, the National Science

Foundation's Very High Speed Backbone Network Service (VBNS) and new defence networks to link military organizations. To promote the work of Abilene an Internet 2 Land Speed Record has been devised (http://lsr.internet2.edu). In November 2002, the record was increased when 6.7 gigabytes of data (approximately two DVD movies) were transferred across 10,978 kilometres of network in less than one minute. The transfer was accomplished at an average speed of more than 923 megabits per second. By 2005, using IPv6, a team consisting of members from the University of Tokyo, the WIDE Project, Microsoft Corporation, and others accomplished a transfer of 585 gigabytes of data across 30,000 kilometres of network in about 30 minutes at an average rate of 6.96 gigabits per second.

Summary

1 The Internet is a global communications network that is used to transmit the information published on the World Wide Web (WWW) in a standard format based on Hypertext Markup Language (HTML) using different standard protocols such as HTTP and TCP/IP.

2 Companies deliver e-business services to employees and partners through web servers which are often hosted at third-party companies known as 'Internet service providers' (ISPs). Web servers will be linked to applications servers, database servers and legacy applications to deliver these services.

3 Consumers and business users access these e-business services using web browser software, with connections to the Internet also managed by an ISP through which they can access web servers.

4 Intranets are private networks used inside companies to share information. Internet-based tools such as e-mail, FTP and the World Wide Web are all used as methods of sharing this information. Not all Internet users can access intranets since access is restricted by firewalls and password controls. Extranets are similar to intranets, but they are extended beyond the company to third parties such as suppliers, distributors or selected customers.

5 Standards to enable delivery of information include:
- Communications standards such as TCP/IP and HTTP.
- Text information standards such as HTML, XML and WML.
- Graphical information standards such as GIF and JPEG.
- Multimedia standards such as Shockwave, Flash and streaming audio and video.

6 Managing staff access to the Internet involves taking decisions about the number of staff with access and how much time can be permitted and the nature of monitoring used for e-mails and web pages.

7 Managers need to decide on internal or external management of the technology and applications infrastructure of an organization.

8 Electronic data interchange (EDI) involves the structured transfer of information, particularly for online B2B purchasing transactions. It can now occur over the Internet as Internet EDI.

9 Applications service providers are increasingly important as businesses look to reduce infrastructure costs and improve e-business service delivery through external hosting of applications and data outside an organization.

10 Managers of e-commerce services need to monitor the adoption of new access devices for the Internet including mobile phones and interactive digital TV. An e-commerce infrastructure should be designed to readily enable new access media to be supported as they develop.

Exercises

Self-assessment questions

1 What is the difference between the Internet and the World Wide Web?

2 Describe the two main functions of an Internet service provider (ISP). How do they differ from applications service providers?

3 Distinguish between intranets, extranets and the Internet.

4 Describe the standards involved when a web page is served from a web server to a user's web browser.

5 What are the management issues involved with enabling staff access to a web site?

6 Explain the following terms:
HTML HTTP XML FTP

7 What is the difference between static web content written in HTML and dynamic content developed using a scripting language such as JavaScript?

8 What software and hardware are required to access the Internet from home?

Essay and discussion questions

1 'Without the development of the World Wide Web by Tim Berners-Lee, the Internet is unlikely to have become a commercial medium.' Discuss.

2 'In the future the distinction between intranets, extranets and the Internet for marketing purposes is likely to disappear.' Discuss.

3 Discuss the merits and disadvantages of locating company e-business services inside a company, in comparison with outsourcing to an ISP or ASP.

4 You are consultant to a small retailer interested in setting up a transactional e-commerce site. Create a summary guide for the company about the stages that are necessary in the creation of a web site and the management issues involved.

Examination questions

1 You have been tasked with arranging Internet access for other employees in your company. Summarize the hardware and software needed.

2 How would you explain to a friend what they need to purchase to access the World Wide Web using the Internet? Explain the hardware and software needed.

3 Explain the term 'electronic data interchange'. Is it still relevant to companies?

4 Describe how the following tools would be used by a company hosting a web site:
HTML FTP RSS

5 The existence of standards such as HTML and HTTP has been vital to the success and increased use of the World Wide Web. Explain why.

6 What benefits to a business-to-business company does the XML standard offer beyond those of HTML?

7 Explain why the e-business coordinator of a company might investigate the use of applications service providers.

8 Explain the differences between intranet, extranet and the Internet from an e-business perspective.

References

BBC (2003) Mobile bosses cautious over 3G, By Jane Wakefield. *BBC News*. London. Monday 24 February. Available online at: http://news.bbc.co.uk/1/hi/technology/2787787.stm.

Berners-Lee, T. (1999) *Weaving the Web. The Past, Present and Future of the World Wide Web by its Inventor*. Orion Publishing, London.

Berners-Lee, T., Hendler, J. and Lassila, O. (2001) The Semantic Web. *Scientific American*, May. Published online at: www.sciam.com.

CIO (2002) Measuring the ROIs of Intranets – Mission Possible? By Toby Ward. *CIO Magazine*, October. Available online at: www.cio.com/research/intranet/study 2002.html.

Clarke, R. (1998) *Electronic Data Interchange* (EDI): An Introduction. www.anu.edu.au/people/Roger.Clarke/EC/EDIIntro.html.

Curry, A. (2001) What's next for interactive television. *Interactive marketing*, 3(2), October/December, 128–40.

DTI (2000) *Business in the Information Age – International Benchmarking Study 2000*. UK Department of Trade and Industry.

DTI (2003) *Business in the Information Age – International Benchmarking Study 2002*. UK Department of Trade and Industry. Available online at: www.ukonlineforbusiness.gov.uk/benchmaking 2002.

Dyson, E. (1998) *Release 2.1 A Design for Living in the Digital Age*. Penguin, London.

EDI Insider (1996) Internet EDI: separating hope from hype. EDI Insider, 1(1), Washington Publishing Company, Washington DC, www.wpc-edi.com/Insider/Articles/V1/I-1B.html.

Financial Times (2002) UK broadband report looks to Korean lead, by Robert Budden. *Financial Times*, 9 October.

Gillies, J. and Cailliau, R. (2000) *How the Web Was Born*. Oxford University Press, New York.

Guardian (2003) Mail out of order, The Guardian Online, 27 February. Available online at: www.guardian.co.uk/online/story/0,3605,903312,00.html.

Hannon, N. (1998) *The Business of the Internet*. Course Technology, New York.

Hasselbring, W. (2000) Information system integration. *Communications of the ACM*, 43(6), 33–8.

IDC (1999) *Reinventing EDI: Electronic Data Interchange Services Market Review and Forecast*, 1998–2003. International Data Corporation, Framingham, MA.

IDC (2002) Online travel services set to boost mobile commerce. IDC Research press release, 23 January, www.idc.com.

Internet World (1999) Enterprise application integration – middleware apps scale firewalls. *Internet World*, 17 May.

IOD (2005) Voice Over IP. Institute of Directors (www.iod.com), February, London.

Jupiter MMXI (2002) Low cost set top boxes kick start Digital TV market in Europe. Press release, 7 March, (http://uk.jupitermmxi.com/xp/uk/press/releases/pr 030702.xml).

Kampas, P. (2000) Road map to the e-revolution. *Information Systems Management Journal*, Spring, 8–22.

Kennedy, A. (2001) *The Internet. The Rough Guide*. Rough Guides, London.

KM Column (2002) September 2002 issue: Sixteen steps to a renewed corporate intranet. Published by Step Two Designs at www.steptwo.com.au/papers/kmc renewintranet/index.html.

Leiner, B., Cerf, V., Clark, D., Kahn, R., Kleinrock, L., Lynch, D., Postel, J., Roberts, J. and Wolff, S. (2000) *A Brief History of the Internet*. The Internet Society, www.isoc.org/internet-history/brief.html, continuously updated document.

MobileCommerceWorld (2001) i-Mode users spending more on content. 26 November, press release based on data from Infocom, www.mobilecommerceworld.com.

MobileCommerceWorld (2002) British SMS records smashed in December. 24 January, press release based on data from the mobile data association, www.mobilecommerce-world.com.

Mougayer, W. (1998) *Opening Digital Markets – Battle Plans and Strategies for Internet Commerce*, 2nd edn. CommerceNet Press, McGraw-Hill, New York.

News Corporation (2005). Press release. Speech by Rupert Murdoch to the American Society of Newspaper Editors, 13 April. www.newscorp.com/news/ news 247.html.

O'Reilly, T. (2005) What is Web 2? Design patterns and business models for the next generation of software. Web article, 30 September. O'Reilly Publishing, Sabagtopol, CA.

Spinrad, P. (1999). The new cool. Akamai overcomes the Internet's hotspot problem. *Wired*, 7 August, 152–4.

Viney, D. (2003) Intranet portal guide (Online article: www.viney.com/DFV).

Vlosky, R., Fontenot, R., and Blalock, L. (2000) Extranets: impacts on business practices and relationships. *Journal of Business and Industrial Marketing*, 15(6), 438–57.

Yankee Group (2002). E-business evolution: transaction management costs, benefits, and market development. *Yankee Group Research Report 2002*. Available online at: www.sterlingcommerce.com/go/yankeegroup/yankeeWP 07-02.pdf.

ZDNet (2000) www.zdnet.co.uk/itweek/specials/2000/ ecommerce2.

Zwass, V. (1998) Structure and macro-level impacts of electronic commerce: from technological infrastructure to electronic marketplaces. In *Emerging Information Technologies*, ed. K. Kendall, Sage, Thousand Oaks, CA.

Further reading

Berners-Lee, T. (1999) *Weaving the Web. The Past, Present and Future of the World Wide Web by its Inventor*. Orion Publishing, London. A fascinating, readable description of how the concept of the web was developed by the author with his thoughts on its future development.

Gillies, J. and Cailliau, R. (2000) *How the Web Was Born*. Oxford University Press, New York. Another readable book, this time, despite the title, on the whole history of the Internet.

Web links

A brief history of the Internet (www.isoc.org/internet-history/brief.html) Updated history by key players in its design – Barry M. Leiner, Vinton G. Cerf, David D. Clark.

CIO Magazine (www.cio.com/research/intranet) Intranet and extranet research centre.

Clearly Business (www.clearlybusiness.com/e-business) Business portal channel intended to support SMEs in moving online. Explains stages and tools involved in plain language.

Digital Future Reports (www.digitalcenter.org) USC Annenberg School Center for the Digital Future.

Free Online Dictionary of Computing (www.foldoc.org) Comprehensive non-commercial site with succinct definitions supported by Imperial College London. Particularly good for Internet standards.

Google (www7.scu.edu.au/programme/fullpapers/1921/com1921.htm) Interesting, but technical article on Google, 'The anatomy of a large-scale hypertextual web search engine'.

Howstuffworks (www.howstuffworks.com) Good explanations with diagrams of many Internet technologies.

Intranet Focus (www.intranetfocus.com) Best-practice guidelines and links on intranets, portals and content management systems.

Intranet Journal (www.intranetjournal.com) Articles on intranet management.

IT Toolbox (www.ittoolbox.com) Guidelines, articles on e-business, ERP, CRM and data warehousing.

Mobile Commerce World (www.mobilecommerceworld.com) Industry news.

RosettaNet (www.rosettanet.org) Organization promoting exchange of B2B data.

UK Online For Business (www.ukonlineforbusiness.gov.uk) Government portal.

WapInsight (www.wapinsight.com) News and definitions of all mobile commerce developments.

Whatis.com (www.whatis.com) Succinct explanations of technical terms.

XMLEDI (www.xmledi.com/.net) Organization promoting use of XML to support EDI.

XML.com (www.xml.com) XML resources.

4 E-environment

Chapter at a glance

Web support

The following additional case studies are available at www.pearsoned.co.uk/chaffey

- ➤ Singapore government creates 'intelligent island'
- ➤ Variations in take-up of online services for Orient Overseas Container Line (OOCL)
- ➤ Is there a future for print?
- ➤ The wired GP

The site also contains a range of study material designed to help improve your results.

Learning outcomes

After completing this chapter the reader should be able to:

- Identify the different elements of an organization macro-environment that impact on an organization's e-business and e-marketing strategy
- Assess the impact of legal, privacy and ethical constraints or opportunities on a company
- Assess the role of macro-economic factors such as economics, governmental e-business policies, taxation and legal constraints.

Management issues

The issues for managers raised in this chapter include:

- What are the constraints such as legal issues placed on developing and implementing an e-business strategy by the e-environment?
- What factors influence the adoption of digital media and how can we estimate future demand for online services?
- How can trust and privacy be assured for the customer while seeking to achieve marketing objectives of customer acquisition and retention?

Links to other chapters

The main related chapters are:

- *Chapter 2* E-commerce fundamentals – introduces the different elements of the e-environment;
- The strategic approaches outlined in *Part 2 (Chapters 5, 6* and *8)* require consideration of the constraints placed on strategy by the e-environment.

Introduction

In *Chapter 2* we introduced the importance of monitoring changes in the environment and how they impact on an organization. *Table 4.1* presents the main marketplace or macro-environmental factors and the micro-environmental factors that directly affect an organization.

Table 4.1 Factors in the macro- and micro-environment of an organization

Macro-environment	*Micro-environment (e-marketplace)*
Social	The organization
Legal, ethical and taxation	Its customers
Economic	Its suppliers
Political	Its competitors
Technological	Intermediaries
Competitive	The public at large

In this chapter we concentrate on the role of the macro-environmental forces. Aspects of the micro-environment or e-marketplace such as competitors, suppliers and intermediaries are the focus of *Chapters 2* and *4* and *Part 2* of this book. We will review the macro-environmental factor using the widely used SLEPT framework. SLEPT stands for Social, Legal, Economic, Political and Technological factors. Often, these factors are known as the PEST factors, but we use SLEPT since it is useful to stress the importance of the law in influencing Internet marketing practices. The SLEPT factors are:

- *Social factors* – these include the influence of consumer perceptions in determining usage of the Internet for different activities.
- *Legal and ethical factors* – determine the method by which products can be promoted and sold online. Governments, on behalf of society, seek to safeguard individuals' rights to privacy.
- *Economic factors* – variations in the economic performance in different countries and regions affect spending patterns and international trade.
- *Political* – national governments and transnational organizations have an important role in determining the future adoption and control of the Internet and the rules by which it is governed.
- *Technological factors* – changes in technology offer new opportunities to the way products can be marketed.

For each factor we look at new issues raised for managers responsible for e-commerce trading. For those actively involved in the implementation of e-business, and in particular sell-side e-commerce, factors associated with buyer behaviour are also important when implementing e-commerce. These are covered separately in the section *The online buying process* (*Chapter 9, p. 400*).

Now complete *Activity 4.1* to reflect on some of the macro-environmental factors that have to be considered by the e-business manager.

Activity 4.1 Introduction to social, legal and ethical issues

List all the social, legal and ethical issues that the manager of a sell-side e-commerce web site needs to consider to avoid damaging relationships with users of his or her site or which may leave the company facing prosecution. You can base your answer on issues which may concern you, your friends or your family when accessing a web site.

Answers to activities can be found at www.pearsoned.co.uk/chaffey.

The issues identified in *Activity 4.1* and others such as economic and competitive pressures tend to change rapidly, particularly dynamic factors associated with advances in technology.

An indication of the challenge of assessing the macro-environment factors is presented in *Figure 4.1*. This figure of the 'waves of change' shows how fluctuations in the characteristics of different aspects of the environment vary at different rates through time. The manager has to constantly scan the environment and assess which changes are relevant to their sphere of influence. Changes in social culture and particularly pop culture (what's hot and what's not) tend to be very rapid. Introduction of new technologies and changes in their popularity tend to be frequent too and need to be assessed. Governmental and legal changes tend to happen over longer timescales although, since this is only a generalization, new laws can be introduced relatively fast. The trick for Internet marketers is to identify those factors which are important in the context of Internet marketing which are critical to competitiveness and service delivery and monitor these. We believe it is the technological and legal factors which are most important to the Internet marketer, so we focus on these.

Organizations that either do not monitor these environmental factors, or those that do not respond to them adequately will not remain competitive and may fail.

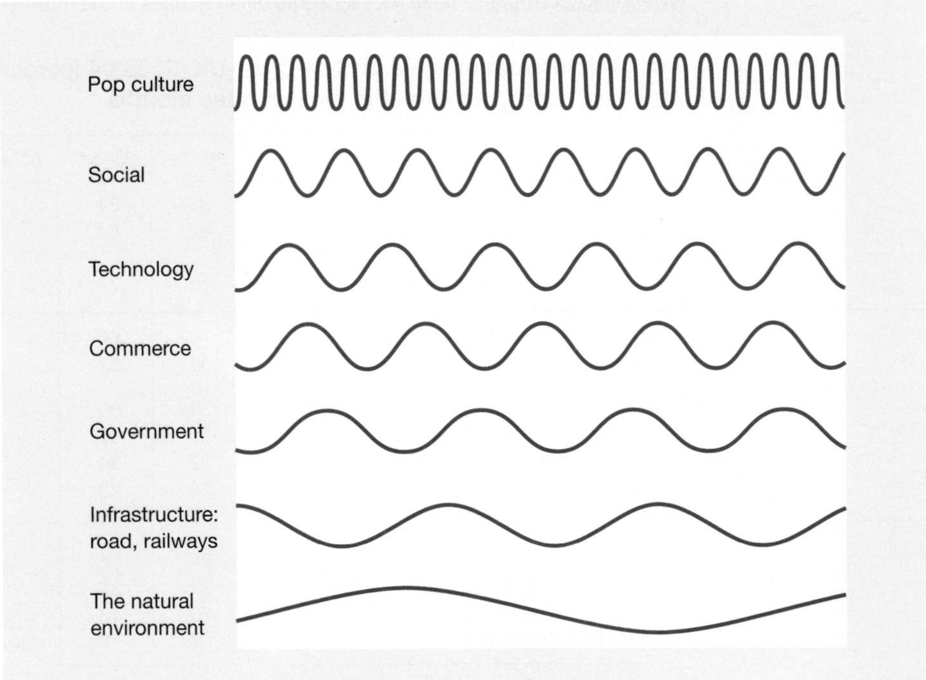

Figure 4.1 'Waves of change' – different timescales for change in the environment

Environmental scanning
The process of continuously monitoring the environment and events and responding accordingly.

The process of monitoring the environment is usually referred to as environmental scanning. This often occurs as an *ad hoc* process in which many employees and managers will monitor the environment and will, perhaps, respond appropriately. The problem with the *ad hoc* approach is that if there is not a reporting mechanism then some major changes may not be apparent to managers. Environmental analysis is required to evaluate different information and respond accordingly.

Social and legal factors

In this section we look at the social and cultural impacts of the Internet. These are important from a marketing perspective since they govern demand for Internet services and propensity to purchase online. Further aspects of the social influence of the Internet are described in the references to the Information Society Initiative in this chapter and in the *Focus on online buyer behaviour and the virtual communities* section (*Chapter 9, p. 000 and p. 000*). Complete *Activity 4.2* to start to review some of the social issues associated with the Internet.

Activity 4.2 Understanding enablers and barriers to consumer adoption

Visit the w.w.w.

Purpose

To identify reasons why consumers may be encouraged online or may resist.

Activity

Access a recent survey in your country of attitudes to the Internet. In particular, you should concentrate on reasons why customers have used the Internet or have not used the Internet at all. A compilation of research about the Internet and technology adoption is available at www.clickz.com/stats. *Table 4.2* highlights different uses of the Internet in the UK.

Table 4.2 Internet usage activities in the UK, 2003/04 (percentages) – adults who have used the Internet in the last three months

	16–34	*35–54*	*55 and over*	*All adults*
Using email	83	84	85	84
Searching for information about goods or services	80	84	74	80
Searching for information about travel and accommodation	63	74	70	69
General browsing or surfing	76	66	49	67
Buying goods, tickets or services	51	52	42	50
Internet banking	34	39	33	36
Activities related specifically to employment	39	37	17	35
Reading or downloading online news	37	34	25	34
Activities related to an education course	38	23	11	28
Playing or downloading music	37	18	12	25
Other educational activities	26	26	18	25
Downloading other software	27	22	18	23
Listening to web radios	20	13	9	15
Other financial services	7	9	9	8

Source: Omnibus Survey, Office for National Statistics, in ONS (2005), Table 13.12, p. 179. www.statistics.gov.uk/downloads/theme_social/Social_Trends35/Social_ Trends_35_Ch13.pdf

1 Summarize and explain the reasons for the levels of usage of the medium for different activities.
2 What are the main enablers and barriers to higher levels of adoption of these different activities and which actions should organizations take to increase adoption?

Alternatively, devise an *ad hoc* survey to investigate attitudes to and use of the Internet using friends, family or classmates as respondents. Example questions might include the following. What have you bought online? If not, why not? How many hours do you spend online each month? How many e-mails do you receive or send? What stops you using the Internet more? What aspects of the Internet are you concerned about?

Answers to activities can be found at www.pearsoned.co.uk/chaffey

Factors governing Internet adoption

It is useful for e-business managers to understand the different factors that affect how many people actively use the Internet. If these are understood for customers in a target market, action can be taken to overcome some of these barriers. For example, marketing communications can be used to reduce fears about the value proposition, ease of use and security. Chaffey *et al.* (2006) suggest that the following factors are important in governing adoption:

1 *Cost of access.* This is certainly a barrier for those who do not already own a home computer: a major expenditure for many households. The other main costs are the cost of using an ISP to connect to the Internet and the cost of using the media to connect (telephone or cable charges). Free access would certainly increase adoption and usage.
2 *Value proposition.* Customers need to perceive a need to be online – what can the Internet offer that other media cannot? Examples of value propositions include access to more supplier information and possibly lower prices. In 2000, company advertisements started to refer to 'Internet prices'.
3 *Ease of use.* This includes the ease of first connecting to the Internet using the ISP and the ease of using the web once connected.
4 *Security.* While this is only, in reality, a problem for those who shop online, the perception generated by news stories may be that if you are connected to the Internet then your personal details and credit card details may not be secure. It will probably take many years for this fear to diminish as using the Internet slowly becomes established as a standard way of purchasing goods.
5 *Fear of the unknown.* Many will simply have a general fear of the technology and the new media, which is not surprising since much of the news about the Internet non-adopters will have heard will concern pornography, fraud and privacy infringements.

An attempt has been made to quantify the magnitude of barriers to access in a UK government-sponsored survey (Booz Allen Hamilton, 2002) of different countries. Barriers for individuals noted by the survey included:

- No perceived benefit
- Lack of trust
- Security problems
- Lack of skills
- Cost.

The authors of the report note that:

significant (national) variation exists in what citizens perceive to be the most important barriers to further use, and in governments' chosen role in tackling those barriers. Using the internet and ICTs in education seems to be a significant driver of citizens' confidence in their own skills. Several governments, notably Italy and France, have attempted to tackle the skill issue later in life through a range of courses in computer skills.

As expected, there is a strong correlation between Internet use and PC penetration. Countries such as Sweden have encouraged home use most actively through government initiatives, in this case the 'PC REFORM' programme. This appears to exert more influence than cost, since in leading countries such as Sweden and Australia, cost is relatively high.

Assessing demand for e-commerce services

To set realistic strategic objectives such as online revenue contributions for digital channels, as described in *Chapter 5*, e-commerce managers need to understand the level of customer access and activity in each marketplace. What is the key customer profile information that managers must collect using market research? For each customer segment and for each digital channel such as Internet, interactive digital TV or mobile we need to know the proportion of customers who:

1 have access to the channel
2 are influenced by using the channel
3 purchase using the channel.

This information can be gathered as secondary research by the researcher by accessing many online data sources. Primary research can be used to better understand these characteristics in the target market. We will now review each of these three factors which affect demand for e-commerce services, and start by reviewing these factors for consumers in the B2C marketplace.

Internet access

E-commerce provides a global marketplace, and this means we must review access and usage of the Internet channel at many different geographic levels: from worldwide to within a single country.

On a worldwide basis, a relatively small proportion of the population has access to the Internet. The compilation of statistics prepared by ClickZ (**www.clickz.com/stats/web_worldwide/**) suggests that despite rapid growth from the mid-1990s to about one billion users by 2005/06 this only represents less than 20% of the global population although there are initiatives such as the $100 PC that are intended to redress this.

If we look at individual countries, the proportion of consumers and businesses accessing the Internet is startling. If we take the United Kingdom, National Statistics (2005) showed that by 2005 over 55% of households had access to the Internet. To look at the scale of variation between different countries and continents complete *Activity 4.3*.

Demographic characteristics
Variations in attributes of the populations such as age, sex and social class.

Of course, within each country, adoption of the Internet will also vary significantly according to individual **demographic characteristics** such as sex, age and social class or income. This analysis is important as part of the *segmentation* of different groups within a target market. Since these factors will vary throughout each

Activity 4.3 Global variation in Internet provision

Visit the w.w.w.

Visit the web site of the International Telecommunications Union (ITU) (**www.itu.int/ITU-D/ict/statistics**). Choose Internet indicators. This presents data on Internet and PC penetration in over 200 countries. A summary of the indicators for different continents is presented in *Figure 4.2*.

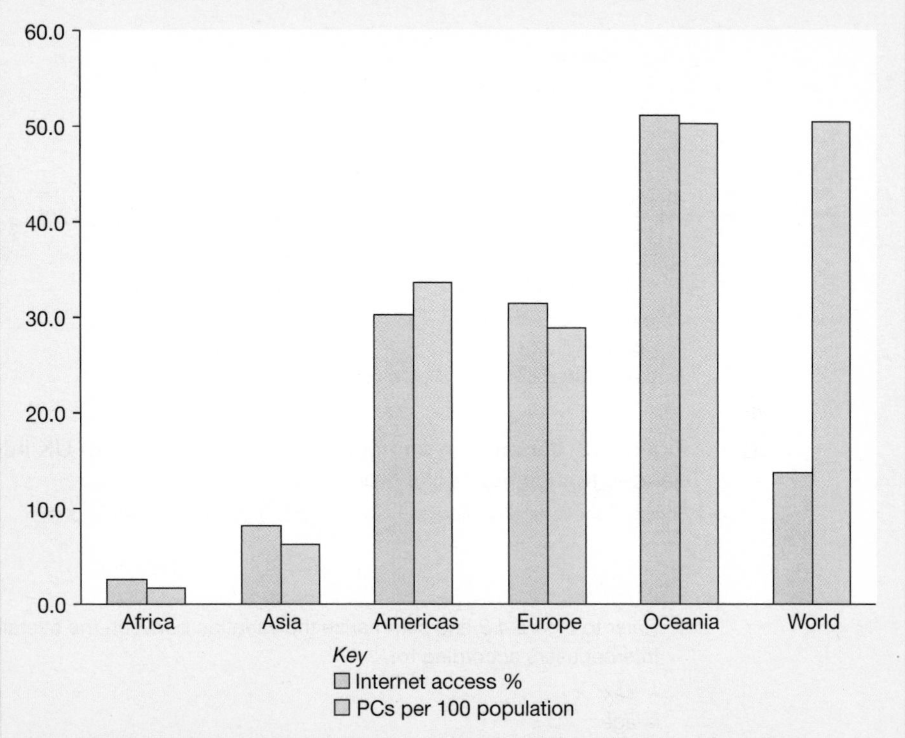

Figure 4.2 **Global variation in number of PCs per hundred population and percentage Internet access in 2004**
Source: ITU (www.itu.int/ITU-D/ict/statistics/)

Questions

1. Find your country and compare the number of PCs per hundred population and percentage Internet access compared with other countries in your region and on a global basis.
2. Now attempt to explain reasons for the disparity between your country and other countries.
3. Can you see your country equalling or exceeding the USA in terms of these indicators?

Note that PCs are recorded as PCs per hundred population. This figure may be skewed in developed countries by people with more than one PC (e.g. at home and at work).

No suggested answer supplied.

country there will also be regional differences. Access is usually much higher in capital cities. Now complete *Activity 4.4* to gain an appreciation of reasons for variation in adoption.

Activity 4.4 Adoption of the Internet according to demographic characteristics

Visit the w.w.w.

Purpose

To highlight variation in Internet access according to individual consumer characteristics. Web update: see www.mori.com/technology/trackerdata.shtml for up-to-date data on demographics in the UK.

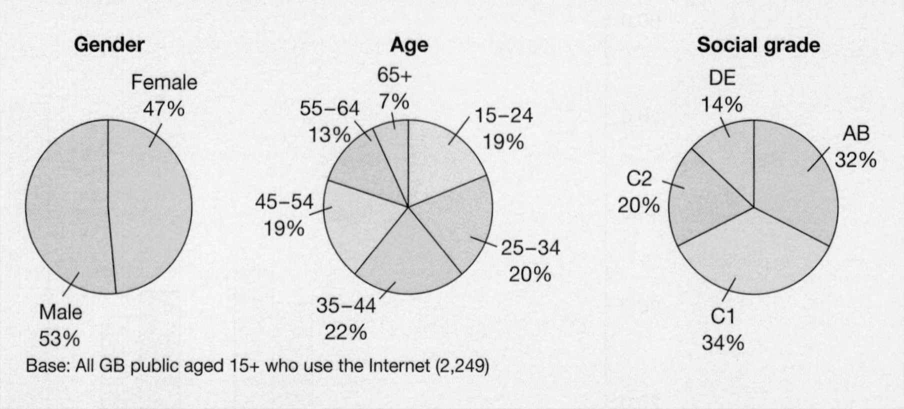

Figure 4.3 **Variation in demographic characteristics of UK Internet users: (a) gender, (b) age, (c) social grade.**

Source: eMori Technology Tracker – www.mori.com/technology/trackerdata.shtml

Questions

1. Refer to *Figure 4.3* and summarize the variation between the overall UK population and Internet users according to:
   - sex
   - age
   - social group.
2. Attempt to explain this variation and suggest how it may change in the future.

Answers to activities can be found at www.pearsoned.co.uk/chaffey

From *Activity 4.4* it can be seen that the stereotype of the typical Internet user as male, around 30 years of age and with high disposable income no longer holds true. Many females and more senior 'silver surfers' are also active.

To fully understand online customer access we also need to consider the users' access location, access device and 'webographics', which can help target certain types of customers and are an important constraint on *site design*. 'Webographics' is a term coined by Grossnickle and Raskin (2001). According to these authors webographics includes:

- Usage location (in most countries, many users access either from home or from work, with home being the more popular choice)
- Access device (browser and computer platform; remember that interactive TV and mobile access are becoming more important)
- Connection speed
- ISP
- Experience level
- Usage type
- Usage level.

Broadband adoption

Competition in the marketplace amongst broadband providers has caused a great increase in the Internet access options available for consumers and small businesses.

A September 2004 report from National Statistics Online showed increases in broadband subscriptions from 17 per cent of all connections in July 2003 to 31 per cent after 12 months. A milestone was reached in July 2004, as high-speed connections surpassed unmetered dial-up access in the UK. Just 29 per cent of UK users connected via unlimited dial-up in July 2004 compared to 35 per cent a year prior. Some UK users are also using limited dial-up with a fixed number of hours per month. Similarly, Ofcom (2004) produced a media consumption report showing the importance of broadband and wireless technologies. Ofcom found that in the UK, there are around 50,000 new broadband subscribers every week (ADSL and cable) with the 5 million broadband subscriber milestone passed in mid-September 2004 (that's one-third of Internet households).

The increased speed and the 'always-on' broadband connection have helped increase Internet usage. Note though, that while broadband was originally introduced as an 'always-on', high-speed connection, some Internet service providers (both ADSL and cable companies) have offered lower-speed options while others have capped usage at a fixed number of hours per month or limits on amount of data transferred.

For example, in 2005, one ISP offered three levels of speed which are compared to download speeds relative to an analogue modem as follows:

- Silver £17.99 per month. 256 kbps – up to 5 times faster
- Gold £24.99 per month. 512 kbps – up to 10 times faster
- Platinum £29.99 per month. 1 Mbps – up to 20 times faster.

Another provider offered a fixed 512 kbps download speed, but at different prices for different amounts of data downloaded:

- £17.99 per month for 512k (10× speed) connection – 1 GB monthly usage allowance (light user)
- £24.99 per month for 512k (10× speed) connection – 15 GB monthly usage allowance (heavy user)
- £29.99 per month for 512k (10× speed) connection – unlimited monthly usage allowance (very heavy user).

But what are these broadband services used for? An interesting look at the future for Europe is provided by *Case Study 4.1* which shows how the broadband Internet is used in South Korea, which has the highest broadband penetration in the world.

Case Study 4.1 Next-generation broadband

At lunchtime on South Korea's presidential election day 18 months ago, internal party exit polls showed that Lee Hoi-chang, the conservative candidate, was on course for victory. Yet history shows that, by the end of December 19 2002, Roh Moo-hyun, the liberal outsider, was elected president.

What happened in those few hours to propel Mr Roh to power? Many people believe the answer lies partly in cyberspace. Microsoft Korea noticed a surge of traffic on its instant messaging service during the afternoon of polling day. 'People were messaging each other, urging friends to vote', says K.R. Choi, marketing manager of Microsoft Korea.

Mr Roh had done much of his campaigning over the internet, calculating it was the best way to communicate with the young and liberal people whose backing he needed. The tactic paid off in spectacular fashion as his online community of supporters roamed chatrooms and message boards, urging young websurfers to vote for him.

The role of the internet in Mr Roh's victory demonstrated the power of South Korea's world-leading →

broadband network, with more than 10 million subscribers, or 70 per cent of homes, enjoying high-speed access to the web. This compares with about 50 per cent of households in Canada, the second most advanced market and 23 per cent in the US.

Not only does South Korea have the highest broadband penetration, it also has the highest-speed service. Whereas most copper wire ADSL (asymmetric digital subscriber line) connections in Europe operate at speeds of less than 1 megabit (million bits) per second, in South Korea both KT and Hanaro, the two biggest service providers, offer standard ADSL at up to 8 Mbps. Both companies also offer very high speed, or VDSL, services that can already reach 20 Mbps and will eventually hit 50 Mbps. Already, 5.8m KT customers, or 27 per cent of its subscribers, have upgraded to VDSL. The service costs Won50,000 ($43) a month, compared to Won30,000–Won40,000 for ordinary ADSL.

Politics is just one of many parts of South Korean society transformed by broadband. Whereas in most countries, online services remain the preserve of a relatively small, tech-savvy elite, in South Korea they are fast becoming mainstream.

E-commerce is growing sharply, despite a slump in the country's domestic economy: everyday activities such as banking, bill payments and tax affairs are routinely conducted over the internet, and increasing numbers watch television and films over the web, taking advantage of the higher-speed connections.

Stephen Ward, consultant manager of the telecommunications group at Deloitte, the consultancy, says there are six main reasons for South Korea's successful uptake of broadband.

Government policy. At least $14bn of public funds were invested in the broadband network. 'Korea was a late starter to industrialisation, so we were determined to be a leader in the age of knowledge-based economies', says Paek Ki-hun, director of the country's ministry of communication.

Competition. Several rival internet service providers were set up to challenge the dominance of Korea Telecom, the incumbent fixed-line operator. This drove down prices and widened availability, both through ADSL connections and cable. A wave of consolidation has since reduced competition but prices remain the lowest among the advanced countries of the Organisation for Economic Co-operation and Development.

Culture. 'Koreans tend to be early adopters of technology and more significantly are fast followers', says Mr Ward. 'They are always conscious of the need not to get left behind by the Japanese and the young have a great desire to conform with the gadget-carrying norm of their peers.'

Population density. South Korea is one of the world's most urbanised and densely-populated countries, with many people living in high-rise apartment blocks. This creates the economies of scale required to provide broadband cheaply. In new apartment blocks, high-speed internet connections are fitted automatically during construction, as if it were as indispensable a utility as water and electricity.

PC rooms. Before broadband became widespread in homes, many people relied on the country's 30,000 high-street internet cafes for access to the web. This got people hooked on high-speed connections, driving demand for household subscriptions. Even today, the so-called PC 'Bangs' – Korean for 'room' – are packed with teens playing online games or exploring chat rooms.

Online games. Just as e-mail first awoke the world to the possibilities of the internet, it was online games that demonstrated the benefits of broadband to millions of young Koreans. The country's online games market grew by 67 per cent last year to $646m, more than double the size of the music industry.

Mr Ward says the same combination of factors have not been present in any other market, which is why South Korea's broadband penetration is much higher than any other country.

Asked to describe the benefits of broadband to South Korea, Han Jun-ho, a 25-year-old computer science student, gives an example of how it has changed the way he studies. 'When my professor is absent, he delivers his class online. We can download it from his homepage whenever we want. Last week, I filmed a presentation in a studio and sent it to my classmates over the web.'

Kim Min-sun, a 25-year-old statistics student, says her favourite use of broadband is watching television. 'I have classes in the evening, so I often miss my favourite TV programme. But I can watch it on the internet when I get home because most programmes are available on broadcasters' websites. My mother also uses the internet a lot. There is an online community in her apartment block. Residents discuss problems over the internet, share information and get to know each other better.'

Source: Where high-speed access is going mainstream. By Andrew Ward. Published: 6 June 2004 http://news.ft.com/cms/s/2086ed22-b4a6-11d8-81c6-000e2511c801,dwp_uuid=cd03ba9c-f814-11d8-8b09-00000e2511c8.html

Question

Based on the article, assess how widespread high-speed broadband access will affect society and business-to-consumer commerce in your country.

According to *The Register* (2004), the main reason for consumer broadband adoption is accessing pornography. Asked the main reason for getting broadband by ISP Homecall in a survey of 5,000 adults, 23 per cent of Britons admitted that pornography was the main reason, while other factors were significantly lower (12 per cent cited access to music videos, 8 per cent access to movie trailers, 9 per cent for radio and 5 per cent social factors, such as the ability to share photos and information with friends and family).

However, the National Statistics (2005) paints a slightly different picture due to the nature of the questions asked! The most common use of the Internet amongst adults was e-mail (85 per cent) and finding information about goods or services (82 per cent). The most frequent place of access was the person's own home (82 per cent), followed by their workplace (42 per cent).

Despite the growth in Internet usage, it is surprising that in many countries there are a significant proportion of people who do not have Internet access. The same survey showed that in July 2004, 37 per cent of adults had never used the Internet while 21 per cent of adults said they would never use it. This will limit the adoption of e-commerce until such users are replaced by younger users brought up as dependent on the Internet!

Consumers influenced by using the online channel

Online buyer behaviour
An assessment of how consumers and business people use the Internet in combination with other communications channels when selecting and buying products and services.

To help develop effective online services, we need to understand customers' **online buyer behaviour** (this topic is considered in more depth in *Chapter 9, p. 400*). As we saw in *Figure 4.1*, finding information about goods and services is a popular online activity, but each organization needs to capture data about online influence in the buying process for their own market. We can understand significant features of online buyer behaviour from research summarized in the AOL-sponsored BrandNewWorld (2004) which study showed that:

1. The Internet is a vital part of the research process with 73% of Internet users agreeing that they now spend longer researching products. The purchase process is generally now more considered and is more convoluted.
2. The Internet is used at every stage of the research process from the initial scan to the more detailed comparison and final check before purchase.
3. Consumers are more informed from a multiplicity of sources; price is not exclusively the primary driver.
4. Online information and experience (and modified opinions about a brand or product) also translates into offline purchase. This is an important but sometimes underestimated role of e-commerce (*Figure 4.4*).

There is also a wide variation in influence according to type of product, so it is important to assess the role of the web in supporting buying decisions for a particular market. Understanding the potential reach of a web site and its role in influencing purchase is clearly important in setting e-marketing budgets. A different perspective on this is indicated by *Figure 4.4* which shows the proportion of people who purchase offline after online research.

Psychographic segmentation
A breakdown of customers according to different characteristics.

Another way for organizations to help them better understand their online customers is for marketers to develop **psychographic segmentations**. Specialized psychodemographic profiles have been developed for web users, for example see the box 'Psychographic segmentation for transactional e-commerce' for an example of this type of segmentation applied to online purchase behaviour. Which profile do you fit?

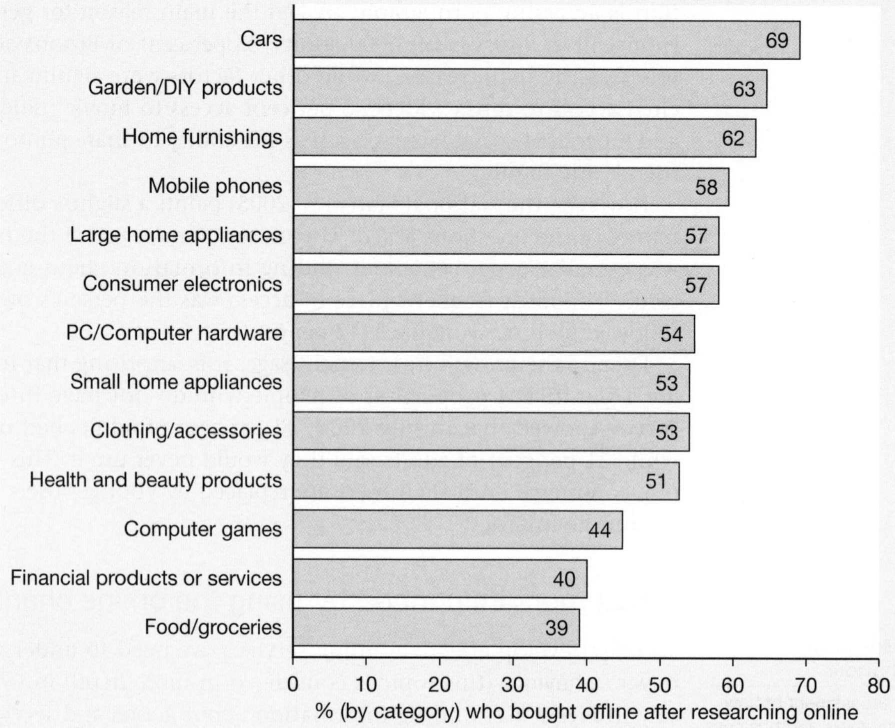

Figure 4.4 Percentage by category who bought offline after researching online
Source: BrandNewWorld: AOL UK / Anne Molen (Cranfield School of Management) / Henley Centre, 2004

Psychographic segmentation for transactional e-commerce

Market research firm BMRB (2004) has developed this segmentation which is used to represent different attitudes to purchasing online.

1 **Realistic enthusiasts (14% 2004, 15% 1999)** – characterized by an enthusiastic approach toward e-commerce but they typically like to see the product in real life before making a purchase and they often consider that finding the product to purchase is a difficult process. Examples of this include a willingness to use the Internet for purchases in excess of £500, they are prepared to purchase products from an unknown company and consider the convenience of Internet shopping to be more important than price.
2 **Confident brand shoppers (18% 2004, 16% 1999)** – members of this group are happy to use the Internet for the next time they want to make a purchase in excess of £500 with this confidence stemming from the importance they lay on purchasing well known brands and the necessity to shop around.
3 **Carefree spenders (19% 2004, 15% 1999)** – These consumers are prepared to purchase from unknown companies and do not consider that purchases should be restricted to well known brands. Furthermore, they are willing to make the purchase without seeing the product first.
4 **Cautious shoppers (14% 2004, 20% 1999)** – these shoppers are not likely to purchase goods through an online auction, have concerns over the quality of products they purchase and would like to see the product prior to making a purchase.
5 **Bargain hunters (21% 2004, 16% 1999)** – this group would buy from an unknown company or any web site as long as it was the cheapest and is driven not by the convenience of the medium but by price.

6 Unfulfilled (14% 2004, 17% 1999) – this group finds it too difficult to find the products they wish to purchase on the Internet, they would not buy from any web site or through an auction and they think it takes too long for products purchased online to be delivered.

Purchased online

Increasing numbers of consumers are now purchasing online, but research on behaviour suggests it takes time for individuals to build up confidence to purchase. Frequency of purchase is also increased through adoption of the broadband Internet. *Figure 4.5* shows that initially Internet users may restrict themselves to searching for information or using e-mail. As their confidence grows their use of the Internet for purchase is likely to increase with a move to higher value items and more frequent purchases. This is often coupled with the use of broadband. For this reason, there is still good potential for e-retail sales, even if the percentage of the population with access to the Internet plateaus.

You can see from *Figure 4.5* that Internet users take longer to become confident to purchase more expensive and more complex products. Many of us will initially have purchased a book or DVD online, but today we buy more expensive electronic products or financial services. *Figure 4.4* shows that the result is a dramatic difference in online consumer behaviour for different products according to their price and complexity. For some products such as travel and cinema and theatre tickets, the majority buy online, while for many others such as clothes and insurance fewer people purchase online. However, consistent with the trend in *Figure 4.5*, there is now less difference between the products than there was two or three years ago. The figure suggests that the way companies should use digital technologies for marketing their products will vary markedly according to product type. In some, such as cars and complex financial products such as mortgages, the main role of online marketing will be to support research, while for other standardized products like

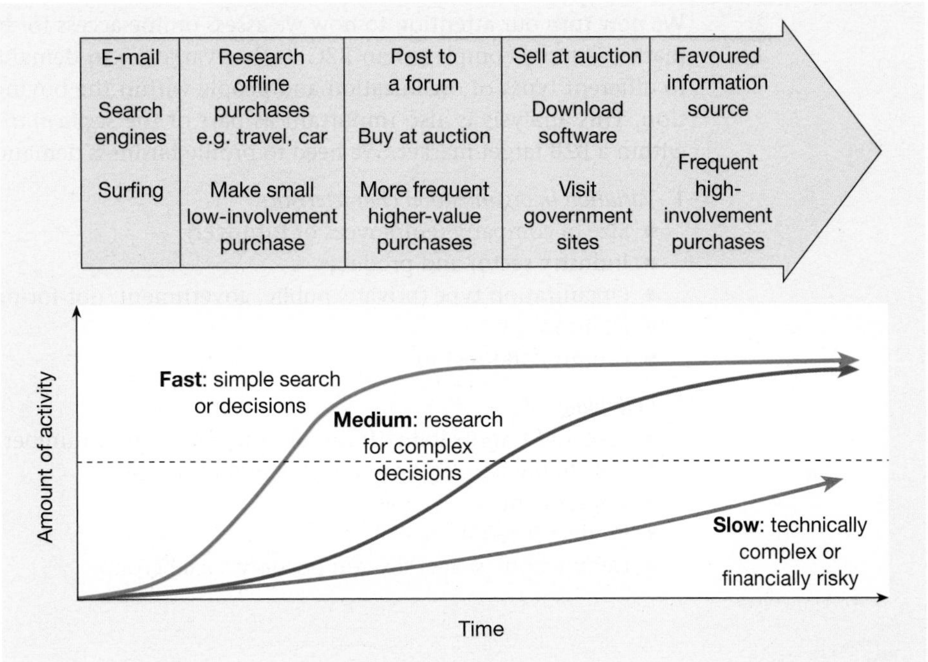

Figure 4.5 **Development of experience in Internet usage**

books and CDs there will be a dual role for the web in supporting research and enabling purchase.

The extent of adoption also varies significantly by country according to other political, economic and cultural factors. *Table 4.3* shows that there is a marked difference between the amount spent online in different countries. It also shows the potential for further growth in e-commerce in countries where e-commerce adoption has been lower.

Table 4.3 **Variation in amount spent and number of purchases in Europe**

Country	*Amount spent online per Internet shopper*	*Average number of items bought online per Internet shopper*
UK	£875 (€1285)	12
Denmark	£734 (€1078)	9
Norway	£731 (€1074)	7
Belgium	£477 (€701)	4
Netherlands	£417 (€612)	3
Germany	£405 (€594)	10
Sweden	£393 (€577)	5
Spain	£355 (€521)	2
Italy	£306 (€449)	3
France	£254 (€373)	6

Source: EIAA (2006)

Online demand for business services

We now turn our attention to how we assess online access for business users. The B2B market is more complex than B2C in that variation in demand will occur according to different types of organization and people within the buying unit in the organization. This analysis is also important as part of the *segmentation* of different groups within a B2B target market. We need to profile business demand according to:

1 *Variation in organization characteristics*
- Size of company (employees or turnover)
- Industry sector and products
- Organization type (private, public, government, not-for-profit)
- Division
- Country and region.

2 *Individual role*
- Role and responsibility from job title, function or number of staff managed
- Role in buying decision (purchasing influence)
- Department
- Product interest
- Demographics: age, sex and possibly social group.

B2B profiles

We can profile business users of the Internet in a similar way to consumers by assessing:

1 *The percentage of companies with access.* In the business-to-business market, Internet access levels are higher than for business-to-consumer. The DTI International Benchmarking Study for 2004 (DTI, 2004) shows that around 95% of businesses in the majority of countries surveyed have Internet access although this figure masks lower levels of access for SMEs (small and medium enterprises) and particularly micro-businesses. Understanding access for different members of the organizational buying unit amongst their customers is also important for marketers. Although the Internet seems to be used by many companies we also need to ask whether it reaches the right people in the buying unit. The answer is 'not necessarily' – access is not available to all employees. This can be an issue if marketing to particular types of staff who have shared PC access, such as healthcare professionals for example.

2 *Influenced online.* In B2B marketing, the high level of access is consistent with a high level of using the Internet to identify suppliers. As for consumer e-commerce, the Internet is important in identifying online suppliers rather than completing the transaction online. This is particularly the case in the larger companies.

3 *Purchase online.* The DTI (2004) survey reveals that there is a large variation the proportion of businesses in different countries who order online (*Figure 4.6*) with the figure substantially higher in countries such as Sweden and Germany in comparison to Italy and France for example. This shows the importance of understanding differences in the environment for e-commerce in different countries since this will dramatically affect the volume of leads and orders generated through e-channels. It also suggests the importance of education and persuasion in encouraging partners to migrate to these new electronic channels.

In summary, to estimate online revenue contribution to determine the amount of investment in e-business we need to research the number of connected customers, the percentage whose offline purchase is influenced online and the number who buy online.

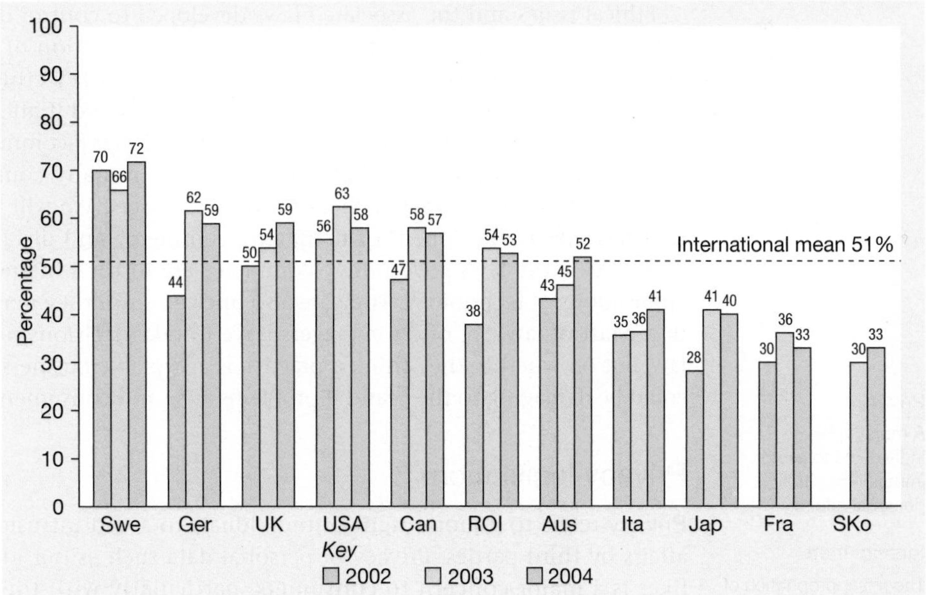

Figure 4.6 Percentage of businesses that order online

Source: DTI (2004), Fig 7.3a

Adoption of e-business by small and medium enterprises

Daniel *et al.* (2002) researched e-business adoption in UK SMEs and found a similar staged progression to those reviewed in *Chapter 5*. They noted four clusters – firms in the first cluster (developers) were actively developing services, but were limited at the time of research. The other clusters are (2) communicators, those where e-mail is being used to communicate internally and within customers and suppliers; (3) web presence and (4) transactors.

The luxury of sufficient resources to focus on the planning and implementing an Internet strategy isn't open to many small businesses and is likely to explain why they have not been such enthusiastic adopters of e-business.

A useful guide to risks and rewards of e-business for SMEs has been produced by *Computer Weekly* (2004). The author suggests that the level of risk and reward can be assessed through a combination of four factors.

1 *Revenue*. This suggests comparison of the importance of online channels for direct or indirect revenue. If revenue becomes significant, then steps must be put in place to avoid outages leading to loss.
2 *Reputation*. Again, if a significant proportion of trade is online, there is a reputational damage if the web site becomes defaced or unavailable.
3 *Strategic importance*. How important is the web site (and electronic transactions) to you? Would there be a significant impact if it were to become unavailable?
4 *Regulatory compliance*. If a company is processing or storing data which are subject to legislative control (e.g. customer or employee data) then the penalties or reputational damage from not providing adequate safeguards may be high if the data are compromised.

Ethical issues of sell-side e-commerce

Ethical standards
Practice or behaviour which is morally acceptable to society.

Ethical standards are personal or business practices or behaviour which are generally considered acceptable by society. A simple test is that acceptable ethics can be described as moral or just and unethical practices as immoral or unjust.

Ethical issues and the associated laws developed to control the ethical approach to Internet marketing constitute an important consideration of the Internet business environment for marketers. Privacy of consumers is a key ethical issue on which we will concentrate since many laws have been enacted and it affects all types of organization regardless of whether they have a transactional e-commerce service. A further ethical issue for which laws have been enacted in many countries is providing an accessible level of Internet services for disabled users. We will also review other laws that have been developed for managing commerce and distance-selling online. In many cases, the laws governing e-commerce are in their infancy and lag behind the applications of technology. They are also unclear, since they may not have been tested in a court of law. So, often managers have to take decisions not based solely on the law, but on whether they think a practice is acceptable business practice or whether it could be damaging to the brand if problems arise and consumers complain.

Privacy
A moral right of individuals to avoid intrusion into their personal affairs.

Identity theft
The misappropriation of the identity of another person without their knowledge or consent.

Privacy legislation

Privacy refers to a moral right of individuals to avoid intrusion into their personal affairs by third parties. Privacy of personal data such as our identities, likes and dislikes is a major concern to consumers, particularly with the dramatic increase in identity theft. This is clearly a concern for many consumers when using e-commerce services since they believe their privacy and identity may be compromised. This is not unfounded. According to *The Guardian* (2003), quoting the Credit Industry Fraud Avoidance System (CIFAS), the UK's fraud prevention service, it is the fastest-growing white-collar crime, generating a criminal cashflow of £10m a day. In 1999, there were 20,264 reported cases of identity theft in the UK; by 2003, the figure was 101,000 and by 2005, there were 355,000 identity-related frauds in total, although 'only' 81,000 involved a false identity. *Table 4.4* shows the breakdown.

Table 4.4 **Identity fraud categories in the UK**

CIFAS category	*Jan to Dec 2004*	*Jan to Dec 2005*	*% change*
Category 1 – False identity	69,512	80,894	16.37
Category 2 – Victim of impersonation	50,455	56,200	11.39
Category 3 – Application fraud facility granted	19,865	22,466	13.09
Category 4 – Application fraud facility refused	162,911	153,290	–5.91
Category 5 – Conversion*	875	1,140	30.29
Category 6 – First-party fraud	41,588	41,313	–0.66
Category 7 – Aiding and abetting	27	47	74.07
Category 8 – Insurance claims fraud	802	488	–39.15

*Sale of assets subject to a credit agreement where the lender retained title to the asset.

Source: CIFAS (2006)

While identity theft is traumatic for the person who has their identity stolen, in the majority of cases, they will *eventually* be able to regain any lost funds through their financial services providers. This is not necessarily the case for the e-retailer. In the second part of 2005, CIFAS members reported 178,800 cases of identify theft, of which 22% resulted in a loss to their members.

Why personal data are valuable for e-businesses

While there is much natural concern amongst consumers about their online privacy, information about these consumers is very useful to marketers. Through understanding their customers' needs, characteristics and behaviours it is possible to create more personalized, targeted communications such as e-mails and web-based personalization about related products and offers which help increase sales. How should marketers respond to this dilemma? An obvious step is to ensure that marketing activities are consistent with the latest data protection and privacy laws. Although compliance with the laws may sound straightforward, in practice different interpretations of the law are possible and since these are new laws they have not been tested in court. As a result, companies have to take their own business decision based on the business benefits of applying particular marketing practices, against the financial and reputational risks of less strict compliance.

Effective e-commerce requires a delicate balance to be struck between the benefits the individual customer will gain to their online experience through providing personal information and the amount and type of information that they are prepared for companies to hold about them.

What are the main information types used by the Internet marketer which are governed by ethics and legislation? The information needs are:

1 *Contact information.* This is the name, postal address, e-mail address and, for B2B companies, web site address.
2 *Profile information.* This is information about a customer's characteristics that can be used for segmentation. They include age, gender and social group for consumers, and company characteristics and individual role for business customers. The specific types of information and how they are used is referenced in *Chapters 2* and *6*. The willingness of consumers to give this information and the effectiveness of incentives have been researched in Australian consumers by Ward *et al.* (2005). They found that consumers are willing to give non-financial data if there is an appropriate incentive.
3 *Behavioural information (on a single site).* This is purchase history, but also includes the whole buying process. Web analytics (*Chapter 12*) can be used to assess the web and e-mail content accessed by individuals.
4 *Behavioural information (across multiple sites).* This can potentially show how a user accesses multiple sites and responds to ads across sites.

Table 4.5 summarizes how these different types of customer information are collected and used through technology.

Table 4.5 **Types of information collected online and related technologies**

Type of information	*Approach and technology used to capture and use information*
Contact information	Collected through online forms in response to an incentive for the customer. Stored in databases linking to web site. Cookies are used to remember a specific person on subsequent visits
Profile information	Also collected through online forms. Cookies can be used to assign a person to a particular segment by linking the cookie to a customer database record and then offering content consistent with their segment
Behavioural information on a single site	Purchase histories are stored in the sales order database. Web analytics software analyses clickstreams of the sequence of web pages visited stored in a web log file. A single pixel GIF is used to assess whether a reader had opened an e-mail. Cookies are also used for monitoring visitor behaviour during a site visit and on subsequent visits
Behavioural information across multiple sites	Web analytics can also indicate the previous site visited by a customer. Banner advertising networks and ISPs can potentially assess all sites visited

Ethical issues concerned with personal information ownership have been usefully summarised by Mason (1986) into four areas:

- *Privacy* – what information is held about the individual?
- *Accuracy* – is it correct?
- *Property* – who owns it and how can ownership be transferred?
- *Accessibility* – who is allowed to access this information, and under which conditions?

Fletcher (2001) provides an alternative perspective, raising these issues of concern for both the individual and the marketer:

- *Transparency* – who is collecting what information?
- *Security* – how is information protected once it has been collected by a company?
- *Liability* – who is responsible if data are abused?

All of these issues arise in the next section which reviews actions marketers should take to achieve privacy and trust.

Data protection legislation is enacted to protect the individual, to protect their privacy and to prevent misuse of their personal data. Indeed, the first article of the European Union directive 95/46/EC on which legislation in individual European countries is based, specifically refers to personal data. It says:

> *Member states shall protect the fundamental rights and freedoms of natural persons [i.e. a named individual at home or at work], and in particular their right to privacy with respect to the processing of personal data.*

Personal data
Any information about an individual stored by companies concerning their customers or employees.

In the UK, the enactment of the European legislation is the Data Protection Act 1984, 1998 (DPA). It is managed by the 'Information Commissioner' and summarized at www.informationcommissioner.gov.uk. This law is typical of what has evolved in many countries to help protect personal information. Any company that holds personal data on computers or on file about customers or employees must be registered with the data protection registrar (although there are some exceptions which may exclude small businesses). This process is known as notification.

Notification
The process whereby companies register with the data protection registrar to inform about their data holdings.

The guidelines on the eight data protection principles are produced by legal requirements of the 1998 UK Data Protection Act, on which this overview is based. These principles state that personal data should be:

1 Fairly and lawfully processed.

In full: *'Personal data shall be processed fairly and lawfully and, in particular, shall not be processed unless – at least one of the conditions in Schedule 2 is met; and in the case of sensitive personal data, at least one of the conditions in Schedule 3 is also met.'*

The Information Commissioner has produced a 'fair processing code' which suggests how an organization needs to achieve 'fair and lawful processing' under the details of schedules 2 and 3 of the Act. This requires:

Data controller
Each company must have a defined person responsible for data protection.

Data subject
The legal term to refer to the individual whose data are held.

- Appointment of a data controller who is a person with defined responsibility for data protection within a company.
- Clear details in communications such as on a web site or direct mail of how a 'data subject' can contact the data controller or a representative.
- Before data processing 'the data subject has given his consent' or the processing must be necessary either for a 'contract to which the data subject is a party' (for example as part of a sale of a product) or because it is required by other laws. Consent is defined in the published guidelines as *'any freely given specific and informed indication of his wishes by which the data subject signifies his agreement to personal data relating to him being processed'*.
- Sensitive personal data require particular care, these include
  - the racial or ethnic origin of the data subject;
  - political opinions;
  - religious beliefs or other beliefs of a similar nature;
  - membership of a trade union;
  - physical or mental health or condition;
  - sexual life;
  - the commission or alleged commission or proceedings of any offence.
- No other laws must be broken in processing the data.

2 Processed for limited purposes.

In full: *'Personal data shall be obtained only for one or more specified and lawful purposes, and shall not be further processed in any manner incompatible with that purpose or those purposes.'*

This implies that the organization must make it clear why and how the data will be processed at the point of collection. For example, an organization has to explain how your data will be used if you provide your details on a web site when entering a prize draw. You would also have to agree (give *consent*) for further communications from the company.

Figure 4.7 suggests some of the issues that should be considered when a data subject is informed of how the data will be used. Important issues are:

- Whether future communications will be sent to the individual (explicit consent is required for this in online channels, which is clarified by the related Privacy and Electronic Communications Regulation Act which is referred to below);
- Whether the data will be passed on to third parties (again explicit consent is required);
- How long the data will be kept for.

3 Adequate, relevant and not excessive.

In full: *'Personal data shall be adequate, relevant and not excessive in relation to the purpose or purposes for which they are processed.'*

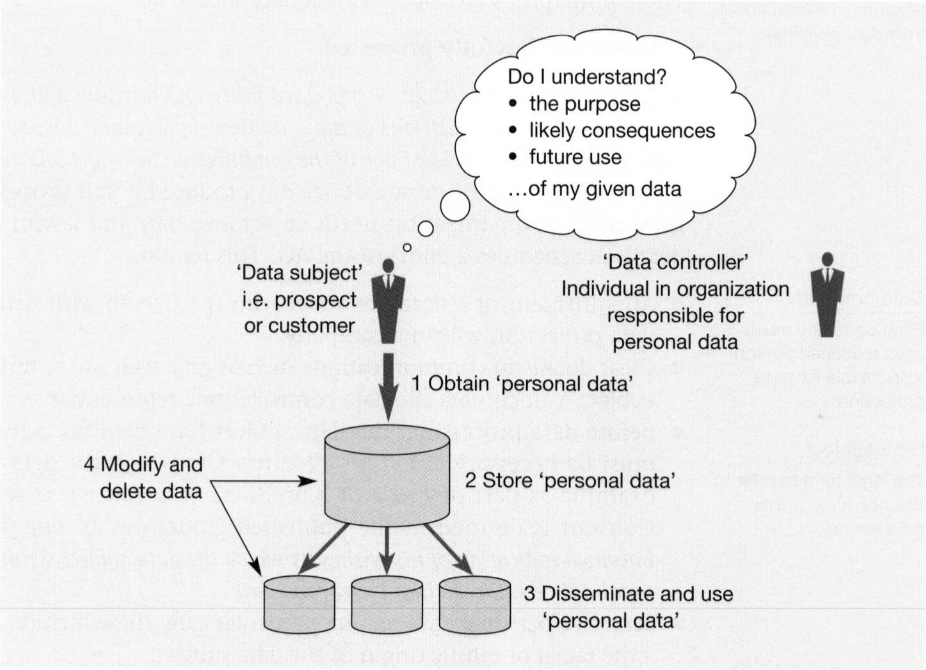

Figure 4.7 **Information flows that need to be understood for compliance with data protection legislation**

This specifies that the minimum necessary amount of data is requested for processing. There is difficulty in reconciling this provision between the needs of the individual and the needs of the company. The more details that an organization has about a customer, the better they can understand that customer and so develop products and marketing communications specific to that customer which they are more likely to respond to.

4 Accurate.

In full: *'Personal data shall be accurate and, where necessary, kept up to date.'*

It is clearly also in the interest of an organization in an ongoing relationship with a partner that the data is kept accurate and up-to-date. The guidelines on the Act suggests that additional steps should be taken to check data are accurate, in case they are in error, for example due to mis-keying by the data subject, or the organization or for some other reason. Inaccurate data is defined in the guidelines as: 'incorrect or misleading as to any matter of fact'.

The guidelines go on to discuss the importance of keeping information up-to-date. This is only necessary where there is an ongoing relationship and the rights of the individual may be affected if they are not up-to-date. This implies, for example that a credit-checking agency should keep credit scores up-to-date.

5 Not kept longer than necessary.

In full: *'Personal data processed for any purpose or purposes shall not be kept for longer than is necessary for that purpose or those purposes.'*

The guidelines state: *'To comply with this Principle, data controllers will need to review their personal data regularly and to delete the information which is no longer required for their purposes.'*

It might be in a company's interests to 'clean data' so that records that are not relevant are archived or deleted, for example if a customer has not purchased for ten years. However, there is the possibility that the customer may still buy again, in which case the information would be useful.

If a relationship between the organization and the data subject ends, then data should be deleted. This will be clear in some instances, for example when an employee leaves a company their personal data should be deleted. With a consumer who has purchased products from a company this is less clear since frequency of purchase will vary, for example, a car manufacturer could justifiably hold data for several years.

6 Processed in accordance with the data subject's rights.

In full: *'Personal data shall be processed in accordance with the rights of data subjects under this Act.'*

Subject access request
A request by a data subject to view personal data from an organization.

One aspect of the data subject's rights is the option to request a copy of their personal data from an organization; this is known as a 'subject access request'. For payment of a small fee such as £10 or £30, an individual can request information which must be supplied by the organization within 40 days. This includes all information on paper files and on computer. If you requested this information from your bank there might be several boxes of transactions!

Other aspects of a data subject's rights which the law upholds are designed to prevent or control processing which:

- causes damage or distress (for example repeatedly sending mailshots to someone who has died);
- is used for direct marketing (for example, in the UK consumers can subscribe to the mail, e-mail or telephone preference service to avoid unsolicited mailings, e-mails or phone calls). This invaluable service is provided by the Direct Marketing Association (www.dmaconsumers.org). If you subscribe to these services organizations must check against these 'exclusion lists' before contacting you. If they don't, and some don't, they are breaking the law.
- is used for automatic decision taking – automated credit checks, for example, may result in unjust decisions on taking a loan – these can be investigated if you feel the decision is unfair.

7 Secure.

In full: *'Appropriate technical and organisational measures shall be taken against unauthorised or unlawful processing of personal data and against accidental loss or destruction of, or damage to, personal data.'*

This guideline places a legal imperative on organizations to prevent unauthorized internal or external access to information and also its modification or destruction. Of course, most organizations would want to do this anyway since the information has value to their organization. Techniques for managing data security are discussed in *Chapter 11*.

Of course, the cost of security measures will vary according to the level of security required. The Act allows for this through this provision:

(i) Taking into account the state of technological development at any time and the cost of implementing any measures, the measures must ensure a level of security appropriate to: (a) the harm that might result from a breach of security; and (b) the nature of the data to be protected. (ii) The data controller must take reasonable steps to ensure the reliability of staff having access to the personal data.

8 Not transferred to countries without adequate protection.

In full: *'Personal data shall not be transferred to a country or territory outside the European Economic Area, unless that country or territory ensures an adequate level of protection of the rights and freedoms of data subjects in relation to the processing of personal data.'*

Transfer of data beyond Europe is likely for multinational companies. This principle prevents export of data to countries that do not have sound data processing laws. If the transfer is required in concluding a sale or contract or if the data subject agrees to it, then transfer is legal.

Anti-spam legislation

Spam
Unsolicited e-mail (usually bulk-mailed and untargeted).

Laws have been enacted in different countries to protect individual privacy and with the intention of reducing spam or unsolicited commercial e-mail (UCE). Originally, the best-known 'spam' was tinned meat (a contraction of 'spiced ham'), but a modern version of this acronym is *'Sending Persistent Annoying e-Mail'*. Spammers rely on sending out millions of e-mails in the hope that even if there is only a 0.01% response they may make some money, if not get rich.

Anti-spam laws do not mean that e-mail cannot be used as a marketing tool. As explained below, opt-in is the key to successful e-mail marketing. Before starting an e-mail dialogue with customers, according to law in Europe, America and many countries in the Asia–Pacific region, companies must ask customers to provide their e-mail address and then give them the option of 'opting into' further communications. Ideally, they should proactively opt in by checking a box. E-mail lists can also be purchased where customers have opted in to receive e-mail. Data held about individuals are commonly used for marketing products to potential or existing customers through e-mail.

Cold list
Data about individuals that are rented or sold by a third party.

House list
Data about existing customers used to market products to encourage future purchase.

Legal opt-in e-mail addresses and customer profile information are available for purchase or rental from a database traditionally known by marketers as a 'cold list', so-called because the company that purchases the data from a third party does not know you. Your name will also potentially be stored on an opt-in house list within companies you have purchased from where you have given your consent to be contacted by the company or given additional consent to be contacted by its partners.

Regulations on privacy and electronic communications

While the Data Protection Directive 95/46 and Data Protection Act afford a reasonable level of protection for consumers, they were quickly superseded by advances in technology and the rapid growth in SPAM. As a result, in 2002 the European Union passed the Act '2002/58/EC Directive on Privacy and Electronic Communications' to complement previous data protection law. This act is significant from an information technology perspective since it applies specifically to electronic communications such as e-mail and the monitoring of web sites.

As with other European laws, this law was implemented differently in different countries. Some countries considered infringements more seriously. A company which is in breach of the Directive in Italy is threatened by fines of up to €66,000 while in the UK the maximum fine is £5,000. It is clearly important for managers to have access to legal advice which applies not only to their country, but also to other European countries.

In the US in January 2004, a new federal law known as the CAN-SPAM Act was introduced to assist in the control of unsolicited e-mail. CAN-SPAM stands for 'Controlling the Assault of Non-Solicited Pornography and Marketing Act' (an ironic juxtaposition between pornography and marketing). This harmonized separate laws in different US states, but was less strict than laws in some states such as California. The Act requires unsolicited commercial e-mail messages to be labelled (though not by a standard method) and to include opt-out instructions and the sender's physical address. It prohibits the use of deceptive subject lines and false headers in such messages. Anti-spam legislation in other countries can be accessed at **www.spamlaws.com**.

While such laws are clearly in consumers' interests, some companies see the practice as restrictive. In 2002, ten companies including IBM, Oracle and VeriSign, who refer to themselves as the 'Global Privacy Alliance (GPA)', lobbied the EU saying that it put too much emphasis on the protection of individuals' privacy, and not enough on ensuring the free flow of information between companies! In the USA, there is a privacy initiative aimed at education of consumers and business (**www.ftc.gov/privacy**), but legislation is limited.

In Australia the law is known as privacy law (**www.privacy.gov.au**).

As an example of European privacy law enacted specifically to control electronic communications related to e-commerce, we will now review the implications for managers of the UK enactment of 2002/58/EC Directive on Privacy and Electronic Communications. This came into force in the UK on 11 December 2003 as the Privacy and Electronic Communications Regulations (PECR) Act. The law is published at: **www.hmso.gov.uk/si/si2003/20032426.htm**. Consumer marketers in the UK also need to heed the Code of Advertising Practice from the Advertising Standards Agency (ASA CAP code, **www.asa.org.uk/the codes**). This has a broadly similar aims and places similar restrictions on marketers to the PECR law.

Privacy and Electronic Communications Regulations Act

A law intended to control the distribution of e-mail and other online communications including cookies.

It is a surprisingly accessible and commonsense document – many marketers will be practising similar principles already. Clauses 22 to 24 are the main clauses relevant to e-mail communications. We will summarize the main implications of the law by picking out key phrases. The new PECR law:

1 **Applies to consumer marketing using e-mail or SMS text messages.** 22(1) applies to *'individual subscribers'*. 'Individual subscribers' means consumers, although the Information Commissioner has stated that this may be reviewed in future to include business subscribers as is the case in some other countries such as Italy and Germany.

   Although this sounds like great news for business-to-business (B2B) marketers and some take the view *'great, the new law doesn't apply to us'*, it could be dangerous. There has been adjudication by the Advertising Standards Agency which found against a B2B organization which had unwittingly e-mailed consumers from what they believed was an in-house list of B2B customers.

2 **Is an 'opt-in' regime.** The new law applies to *'unsolicited communications'* (22(1)). It was introduced with a view to reducing spam, although we all know its impact

Opt-in

A customer proactively agrees or consents to receive further communications.

will be limited on spammers beyond Europe. The relevant phrase is part of 22(2) where the recipient must have *'previously notified the sender that he consents'* or has proactively agreed to receiving commercial e-mail. This is opt-in. Opt-in can be achieved online or offline through asking people whether they want to receive e-mail. Online this is often done through a tick box. In fact, the PECR law does not mandate a tick box option (except for receiving communications from third parties) provided consent is clearly indicated, such as by pressing a button.

The approach required by the law has, in common with many aspects of data protection and privacy law, been used by many organizations for some time. In other words, sending unsolicited e-mails was thought to be unethical and also not in the best interests of the company because of the risk of annoying customers. In fact, the law conforms to an established approach known as 'permission marketing', a term coined by US commentator Seth Godin (1999) (see *Chapter 9, p. 395*).

Debate 4.1

How far should opt-in go?

'Companies should always use an "opt-in" privacy policy for
(a) e-mailing prospects and customers
(b) monitoring web site visitors using site analysis software
(c) identifying repeat visitors using cookie.'

Permission marketing

Customers agree (opt in) to be involved in an organization's marketing activities, usually as a result of an incentive.

Opt-out

A customer declines the offer to receive further information.

3 **Requires an opt-out option in all communications.** An opt-out or method of 'unsubscribing' is required so that the recipient does not receive future communications. In a database this means that a 'do not e-mail' field must be created to avoid e-mailing these customers. The law states that a 'simple means of refusing' future communications is required both when the details were first collected and in each subsequent communication.

4 **Does not apply to existing customers when marketing similar products.** This commonsense clause (22(3)(a)) states that previous opt-in is not required if the contact details were obtained during the course of the sale or negotiations for the sale of a product or service. This is sometimes known as 'soft opt-in'. While this is great news for retailers, it is less clear where this leaves not-for-profit organizations such as charities or public sector organizations where the concept of a sale does not apply.

   Clause 22(3)(b) adds that when marketing to existing customers the marketer may market 'similar products and services only'. Case law will help in clarifying this. For example, for a bank, it is not clear whether a customer with an insurance policy could be targeted for a loan.

5 **Contact details must be provided.** It is not sufficient to send an e-mail with a simple signoff from 'The Marketing team' or 'Web team' with no further contact details. The law requires a name, address or phone number to whom a recipient can complain.

6 **The 'From' identification of the sender must be clear.** Spammers aim to disguise the e-mail originator. The law says that the identity of the person who sends the communication must not be 'disguised or concealed' and that a valid address to 'send a request that such communications cease' should be provided.

7 **Applies to direct marketing communications.** The communications that the legislation refers to are for 'direct marketing'. This suggests that other communications involved with customer service such as an e-mail about a monthly phone statement are not covered, so the opt-out choice may not be required here.

8 **Restricts the use of cookies.** Some privacy campaigners consider that the user's privacy is invaded by planting cookies or electronic tags on the end-user's computer. The concept of the cookie and its associated law is not straightforward, so it warrants separate discussion.

Cookies

Cookies are small text files stored on an end-user's computer to enable web sites to identify them.

Understanding cookies

A 'cookie' is a data file placed on your computer that identifies an individual computer. Cookie derives from the Unix operating system term 'magic cookie' which meant something passed between routines or programs that enables the receiver to perform some operation.

Types of cookies

The main cookie types are:

- Persistent cookies – these stay on a user's computer between multiple sessions and are most valuable for marketers to identify repeat visits to sites.
- Temporary or session cookies – single session – useful for tracking within pages of a session such as on an e-commerce site.
- First-party cookies – served by the site you are currently using – typical for e-commerce sites. These can be persistent or session cookies.
- Third-party cookies – served by another site to the one you are viewing – typical for portals where an ad network will track remotely or where the web analytics software places a cookie. These are typically persistent cookies.

Persistent cookies
Cookies that remain on the computer after a visitor session has ended. Used to recognize returning visitors.

Session cookies
Cookies used to manage a single visitor session.

First-party cookies
Served by the site you are currently using – typical for e-commerce sites.

Third-party cookies
Served by another site to the one you are viewing – typical for portals where an ad network will track remotely or where the web analytics software places a cookie.

Cookies are stored as individual text files in a directory on a personal computer. There is usually one file per web site. For example: dave_chaffey@british-airways.txt. This file contains encoded information as follows:

*FLT_VIS |K:bapzRnGdxBYUU|D:Jul-25-1999| british-airways.com/ 0 425259904 293574 26 1170747936 29284034 **

The information in the cookie file is essentially just an identification number and a date of the last visit although other information can be stored.

Cookies are specific to a particular browser and computer, so if a user connects from a different computer such as at work or starts using a different browser, the web site will not identify him or her as a similar user.

What are cookies used for?

Common marketing applications of cookies include:

A *Personalizing a site for an individual*. Cookies are used to identify individual users and retrieve their preferences from a database according to an identifier stored in the cookie.
For example, I subscribe to the E-consultancy service (www.e-consultancy.com) for the latest information about e-business; each time I return I do not have the annoyance of having to log in because it remembers my previous visit. Many sites feature a 'Remember Me' option which implies using a cookie to remember a returning visitor. Retailers such as Amazon can use cookies to recognize returning visitors and can recommend related books purchased by other readers. This approach generally has benefits for both the individual (it is a hassle to sign in again and relevant content can be delivered) and the company (tailored marketing messages can be delivered).

B *Online ordering systems*. This enables a site such as Tesco.com to track what is in your basket as you order different products.

C *Tracking within a site*. Web analytics software such as Webtrends (www.webtrends.com) which analyses statistics on visitors to web sites relies on persistent cookies to find the proportion of repeat visitors to a web site. Webtrends and other tools increasingly use first-party cookies since they are more accurate and less likely to be blocked. Marketers should check whether use of first-party cookies is possible on their site.

→

D *Tracking across sites.* Advertising networks use cookies to track the number of times a particular computer user has been shown a particular banner advertisement; they can also track adverts served on sites across an ad network. There was an individual rights outcry in the late 1990s when Doubleclick was using this to profile customers. Doubleclick no longer operates an ad network, partly because of this.

Affiliate networks and pay-per-click ad networks such as Google Adwords and Yahoo! Search services (Overture) may also use cookies to track through from a click on a third-party site to a sale or lead being generated on a destination or merchant site. These approaches tend to use third-party cookies. For example, if conversion tracking is enabled in Google Adwords, Google sets a cookie when a user clicks through on an ad. If this user buys the product, then the purchase confirmation page will include script code supplied by Google to make a check for a cookie placed by Google. If there is a match, the sale is attributed to Adwords. An alternative approach using third-party tracking is that different online campaigns have different tracking parameters or codes within the links through to the destination site and when the user arrives on a site from a particular source (such as Google Adwords) this is identified and a cookie is set. When purchase confirmation occurs, this can then be attributed back to the original source, e.g. Google Adwords and the particular referrer.

Owing to the large investments now made in pay-per-click marketing and affiliate marketing by many companies, this is the area of most concern for marketers since the tracking can become inaccurate. However, sale should still occur even if the cookies are blocked or deleted, so the main consequence is that the ROI of online advertising or pay-per-click marketing may look lower than expected. In affiliate marketing, this phenomemon may benefit the marketer in that payment may not need to be made to the third party if a cookie has been subsequently deleted (or blocked) between the time of original clickthrough and sale.

Privacy issues with cookie use

The problem for Internet marketers is that, despite these important applications, blocking by browsers, such as Internet Explorer, or security software and deletion by users has increased dramatically. In 2005 Jupiter Research claimed that 39% of online users may be deleting cookies from their primary computer monthly, although this is debated.

Many distrust cookies since they indicate a 'big brother' is monitoring your actions. Others fear that their personal details or credit card details may be accessed by other web sites. This is very unlikely since all that cookies contain is a short identifier or number that is used to link you to your record in a database. Anyone who found the cookie wouldn't be able to log on to the database without your password. Cookies do not contain passwords, credit card information or any personal details as many people seem to think. These are held on the site servers protected by firewalls and usernames and passwords. In most cases, the worst that someone can do who gets access to your cookies is to find out which sites you have been visiting.

It is possible to block cookies if the user finds out how to block them, but this is not straightforward and many customers either do not know or do not mind that their privacy may be infringed. In 2003 an interesting survey on the perception and behaviour with regards to cookies was conducted on cookie use in the UK (RedEye, 2003). Of the 1,000 respondents:

- 50% had used more than one computer in the last three months;
- 70% said that their computer was used by more than one person;
- 94% said they either accepted cookies or did not know what they were, although 20% said they only accepted session cookies;
- 71% were aware of cookies and accepted them. Of these, only 18% did not know how to delete cookies, and 55% of them were deleting them on a monthly basis;
- 89% knew what cookies were and how to delete them and said that they had deleted them once in the last three months.

Legal constraints on cookies

The new PECR law limits the use of cookie. It states:

> *a person shall not use an electronic communications network to store information, or to gain access to information stored, in the terminal equipment of a subscriber or user unless the following requirements are met.*

The requirements are:

> *(a) the user is provided with clear and comprehensive information about the purposes of the storage of, or access to, that information; and*
> *(b) is given the opportunity to refuse the storage of or access to that information.*

Privacy statement
Information on a web site explaining how and why an individual's data are collected, processed and stored.

(a) suggests that it is important that there is a clear **privacy statement** and (b) suggests that opt-in to cookies is required. In other words, on the first visit to the site, a box would have to be ticked to agree to the use of cookies. This was thought by many commentators to be a curious provision since this facility is already available in the web browser. A further provision clarifies this. The law states: *'where such storage or access is strictly necessary for the provision of an information society service requested by the subscriber or user'*. This indicates that for an e-commerce service session cookies are legitimate without the need for opt-in. It is arguable whether the identification of return visitors is 'strictly necessary' and this is why some sites have a 'remember me' tick box next to the log-in. Through doing this they are compliant with the law. Using cookies for tracking return visits alone would seem to be outlawed, but we will have to see how case law develops over the coming years before this is resolved.

Viral e-mail marketing

Viral marketing
In an online context, 'Forward to a friend' e-mail used to transmit a promotional message from one person to another. 'Online word of mouth.'

One widespread business practice that is not covered explicitly in the PECR law is '**viral marketing**'. The network of people referred to in the definition is more powerful in an online context where e-mail is used to transmit the virus – rather like a cold or flu virus. The combination of the viral offer and the transmission medium is sometimes referred to as the 'viral agent'. Different types of viral marketing are reviewed in *Chapter 9, p. 423*.

There are several initiatives that are being taken by industry groups to reassure web users about threats to their personal information. The first of these is TRUSTe (**www.truste.org**), sponsored by IBM and with sites validated by PricewaterhouseCoopers and KPMG. The validators will audit the site to check each site's privacy statement to see whether it is valid. For example, a privacy statement will describe:

- how a site collects information;
- how the information is used;
- who the information is shared with;
- how users can access and correct information;
- how users can decide to deactivate themselves from the site or withhold information from third parties.

A UK accreditation initiative aimed at *reassurance* coordinated by the Internet Media in Retail Group is ISIS, a trade group for e-retailers (Internet Shopping is Safe) (**www.imrg.org/ISIS**). Another initiative, aimed at *education* is GetSafeOnline (**www.getsafeonline.org**) which is a site created by government and business to educate consumers to help them understand and manage their online privacy and security.

Government initiatives will also define best practice in this area and may introduce laws to ensure guidelines are followed. In the UK, the Data Protection Act covers some of these issues and the 1999 European Data Protection Act also has draft laws to help maintain personal privacy on the Internet.

We conclude this section on privacy legislation with a checklist summary of the practical steps that are required to audit a company's compliance with data protection and privacy legislation. Companies should:

1 Follow privacy and consumer protection guidelines and laws in all local markets. Use local privacy and security certification where available.
2 Inform the user, before asking for information:
   - who the company is;
   - what personal data are collected, processed and stored;
   - what is the purpose of collection.
3 Ask for consent for collecting sensitive personal data, and it is good practice to ask before collecting any type of data.
4 Reassure customers by providing clear and effective privacy statements and explaining the purpose of data collection.
5 Let individuals know when 'cookies' or other covert software are used to collect information about them.
6 Never collect or retain personal data unless it is strictly necessary for the organization's purposes. For example, a person's name and full address should not be required to provide an online quotation. If extra information is required for marketing purposes this should be made clear and the provision of such information should be optional.
7 Amend incorrect data when informed and tell others. Enable correction on-site.
8 Only use data for marketing (by the company, or third parties) when a user has been informed this is the case and has agreed to this. (This is opt-in.)
9 Provide the option for customers to stop receiving information. (This is opt-out.)
10 Use appropriate security technology to protect the customer information on your site.

Other e-commerce legislation

Sparrow (2000) identified eight areas of law which need to concern online marketers. Although laws have been refined since this point, this is still a useful framework for considering the laws to which digital marketers are subject.

1 Marketing your e-commerce business

Domain name
The domain name refers to the name of the web server and it is usually selected to be the same as the name of the company, e.g. www.<company-name>.com, and the extension will indicate its type.

At the time of writing, Sparrow used this category to refer to purchasing a domain name for its website. There are now other legal constraints that also fall under this category.

A Domain name registration

Most companies are likely to own several domains, perhaps for different product lines, countries or specific marketing campaigns. Domain name disputes can arise when an individual or company has registered a domain name which another company claims they have the right to. This is sometimes referred to as 'cybersquatting'.

One of the best known cases was brought in 1998 by Marks & Spencer and other high street retailers, since another company, 'One In a Million Limited', had registered names such as marks&spencer.com, britishtelecom.net and sainsbury.com. It then tried to sell these names for a profit. The companies already had sites with more familiar addresses such as marksandspencers.co.uk, but had not taken the precaution of registering all related domains with different forms of spelling and different top-level domains such as .net. Unsurprisingly, an injunction was issued against One in a Million which was no longer able to use these names.

The problem of companies' names being misappropriated was common during the 1990s, but companies still need to be sure to register all related domain names for each brand since new top-level domain names are created through time such as .biz and .eu.

If you are responsible for web sites, you need to check that domain names are automatically renewed by your hosting company (as most are today). For example, the .co.uk domain must be renewed every two years. Companies that don't manage this process potentially risk losing their domain name since another company could potentially register it if the domain name lapsed.

B Using competitor names and trademarks in meta-tags (for search engine optimisation)

Meta-tags, which are part of the HTML code of a site, are used to market web sites by enabling them to appear more prominently in search engines as part of search engine optimization (SEO) (see *Chapter 9*). Some companies have tried putting the name of a competitor company name within the meta-tags. This is not legal since case law has found against companies that have used this approach. A further issue of marketing-related law is privacy law for e-mail marketing which was considered in the previous section.

C Using competitor names and trademarks in pay-per-click advertising

A similar approach can potentially be used in pay-per-click marketing (see *Chapter 9*) to advertise on competitors' names and trademarks. For example, if a search user types 'Dell laptop' can an advertiser bid to place an ad offering an 'HP laptop'? There is less case law in this area and different findings have occurred in the US and France (such advertising is not permitted in France).

Pay-per-click (PPC) search marketing
A company pays for text adverts to be displayed on the search engine results pages when a specific key phrase is entered by the search users. It is so called because the marketer pays for each time the hypertext link in the ad is clicked on.

D Accessibility law

Web accessibility refers to enabling all users of a web site to interact with it regardless of disabilities they may have or the web browser or platform they are using to access the site. The visually impaired or blind is the main audience that designing an accessible web site can help.

Many countries now have specific accessibility legislation. This is often contained within disability and discrimination acts. In the UK, the relevant act is the Disability and Discrimination Act 1995.

Accessibility legislation
Legislation intended to protect users of web sites with disabilities including visual disability.

Internet standards organizations such as the World Wide Web Consortium have been active in promoting guidelines for web accessibility (www.w3.org/WAI). This site describes such common accessibility problems as:

> *images without alternative text; lack of alternative text for imagemap hot-spots; misleading use of structural elements on pages; uncaptioned audio or undescribed video; lack of alternative information for users who cannot access frames or scripts; tables that are difficult to decipher when linearized; or sites with poor color contrast.*

A tool provided to assess the WWW standards is BOBBY (http://bobby.cast.org).

A case that highlights the need for web site accessibility is that brought by Bruce Maguire, a blind Internet user who uses a refreshable Braille display, against the Sydney Organizing Committee for the Olympic Games in 2000. Maguire successfully demonstrated deficiencies in the site which prevented him using it adequately, which were not successfully remedied. He was protected under the 1992 Australian Disability Discrimination Act and the defendant was ordered to pay AU$20,000. This was the first case brought in the world, and it showed organizations in all companies that they could be guilty of discrimination if they did not audit their sites against accessibility guidelines since many countries such as the USA and UK have similar discrimination acts. Such acts are now being amended in many countries to specifically refer to online discrimination.

2 Forming an electronic contract (contract law and distance-selling law)

We will look at two aspects of forming an electronic contract.

Country of origin principle

The contract formed between a buyer and a seller on a web site will be subject to the laws of a particular country. In Europe, many such laws are specified at the regional (European Union) level, but are interpreted differently in different countries. This raises the issue of which law applies – is it that for the buyer, for example located in Germany or the seller (merchant), whose site is based in France? Although this has been unclear, in 2002, attempts were made by the EU to adopt the *'country of origin principle'*. This means that the law for the contract will be that where the merchant is located.

Distance-selling law

Sparrow (2000) advises different forms of disclaimers to protect the retailer. For example, if a retailer made an error with the price or product details in error, then the retailer is not bound to honour a contract, since it was only displaying the products as 'an invitation to treat', not a fixed offer.

A well known case was when an e-retailer offered televisions for £2.99 due to an error in pricing a £299 product. Numerous purchases were made, but the e-retailer claimed that a contract had not been established simply by accepting the online order, although the customers did not see it that way! Unfortunately no legal precedent was established in this case since the case did not come to trial.

Disclaimers can also be used to limit liability if the web-site service causes a problem for the user, such as a financial loss resulting from an action based on erroneous content. Furthermore, Sparrow suggests that terms and conditions should be developed to refer to issues such as timing of delivery and damage or loss of goods.

The distance-selling directive also has a bearing on e-commerce contracts in the European Union. It was originally developed to protect people using mail-order (by post or phone). The main requirements, which are consistent with what most reputable e-retailers would do anyway, are that e-commerce sites must contain easily accessible content which clearly states:

- The company's identity including address
- The main features of the goods or services
- Prices information, including tax and, if appropriate, delivery costs
- The period for which the offer or price remains valid
- Payment, delivery and fulfilment performance arrangements
- Right of the consumer to withdraw, i.e. cancellation terms
- The minimum duration of the contract and whether the contract for the supply of products or services is to be permanent or recurrent, if appropriate
- Whether an equivalent product or service might be substituted and confirmation as to whether the seller pays the return costs in this event.

After the contract has been entered into, the supplier is required to provide written confirmation of the information provided. An e-mail confirmation is now legally binding provided both parties have agreed that e-mail is an acceptable form for the contract. It is always advisable to obtain an electronic signature to confirm that both parties have agreed the contract, and this is especially valuable in the event of a dispute. The default position for services is that there is no cancellation right once services begin.

3 Making and accepting payment

For transactional e-commerce sites, the relevant laws are those referring to liability between a credit card issuer, the merchant and the buyer. Merchants need to be aware of their liability for different situations such as the customer making a fraudulent transaction.

4 Authenticating contracts concluded over the Internet

'Authentication' refers to establishing the identity of the purchaser. For example, to help prove a credit card owner is the valid owner, many sites now ask for a 3-digit authentication code which is separate from the credit card number. This helps reduce the risk of someone buying fraudulently who has, for instance, found a credit card number from a traditional shopping purchase. Using digital signatures is another method of helping to prove the identity of purchasers (and merchants).

5 E-mail risks

One of the main risks with e-mail is infringing an individual's privacy. Specific laws have been developed in many countries to reduce the volume of unsolicited commercial e-mail or spam, as explained in the previous section on privacy.

A further issue with e-mail is defamation. This is where someone makes a statement that is potentially damaging to an individual or a company. A well known example from 2000 involved a statement made on the Norwich Union Healthcare internal e-mail system in England which was defamatory towards a rival company, WPA. The statement falsely alleged that WPA was under investigation and that regulators had forced them to stop accepting new business. The posting was published on the internal e-mail system to various members of Norwich Union Healthcare staff. Although this was only on an internal system, it was not contained and became more widespread. WPA sued for libel and the case was settled in an out-of-court settlement when Norwich Union paid £415,000 to WPA. Despite this, such cases are relatively rare.

6 Protecting intellectual property (IP)

Intellectual property rights (IPR)
Protect the intangible property created by corporations or individuals that is protected under copyright, trade secret and patent laws.

Intellectual property rights (IPR) protect designs, ideas and inventions and includes content and services developed for e-commerce sites. Closely related is copyright law which is designed to protect authors, producers, broadcasters and performers through ensuring they see some returns from their works every time they are experienced. The European Directive of Copyright (2001/29/EC) came into force in many countries in 2003. This is a significant update to the law which covers new technologies and approaches such as streaming a broadcast via the Internet.

IP can be misappropriated in two senses online.

First, an organization's IP may be misappropriated and you need to protect against this. For example, it is relatively easy to copy web content and republish on another site, and this practice is not unknown amongst smaller businesses. Reputation management services can be used to assess how an organization's content, logos and trademarks are being used on other web sites.

Trademark
A trademark is a unique word or phrase that distinguishes your company. The mark can be registered as plain or designed text, artwork or a combination. In theory, colours, smells and sounds can also be trademarks.

Secondly, an organization may misappropriate content inadvertently. Some employees may infringe copyright if they are not aware of the law. Additionally, some methods of designing transactional web sites have been patented. For example, Amazon has patented its 'One-click' purchasing option, which is why you do not see this labelling and process on other sites.

7 Advertising on the Internet

Advertising standards that are enforced by independent agencies such as the UK's Advertising Standards Authority also apply in the Internet environment (although they are traditionally less strongly policed, leading to more 'edgy' creative executions online).

8 Data protection

Data protection has been referred to in depth in the previous section.

Activity 4.6 Achieving legal compliance

Purpose

To examine approaches by which organizations can monitor changes to the law.

Question

Identify different options for companies to monitor and comply with emerging e-commerce law. You should consider options for different sizes of company.

Answers to activities can be found at www.pearsoned.co.uk/chaffey

Taxation

How to change tax laws to reflect globalization through the Internet is a problem that many governments have grappled with. The fear is that the Internet may cause significant reductions in tax revenues to national or local governments if existing laws do not cover changes in purchasing patterns. In Europe, the use of online betting in lower-tax areas such as Gibraltar has resulted in lower revenues to governments in the countries where consumers would have formerly paid gaming tax to the government via a betting shop. Large UK bookmakers such as William Hill and Victor Chandler are offering Internet-based betting from 'offshore' locations such as Gibraltar. The lower duties in these countries offer the companies the opportunity to make betting significantly cheaper than if they were operating under a higher-tax regime. This trend has been dubbed LOCI or 'location-optimized commerce on the Internet' by Mougayer (1998). Meanwhile, the government of the country from which a person places the bet will face a drop in its tax revenues. In the UK the government has sought to reduce the revenue shortfall by reducing the differential between UK and overseas costs.

The extent of the taxation problem for governments is illustrated by the US ABC News (2000), which reported that between $300 million and $3.8 billion of potential tax revenue was lost by authorities in 2000 in the USA as more consumers purchased online. The revenue shortfall occurs because online retailers need to impose sales or use tax only when goods are being sent to a consumer who lives in a state (or country) where the retailer has a bricks-and-mortar store. Buyers are supposed to pay voluntarily the appropriate sales taxes when buying online, but this rarely happens in practice. This makes the Internet a largely tax-free area in the USA.

Since the Internet supports the global marketplace it could be argued that it makes little sense to introduce tariffs on goods and services delivered over the Internet. Such instruments would, in any case, be impossible to apply over products delivered electronically. This position is currently that of the USA. In the document 'A Framework for Global Electronic Commerce', President Clinton stated that:

> *The United States will advocate in the World Trade Organization (WTO) and other appropriate international fora that the Internet be declared a tariff-free zone.*

Tax jurisdiction

Tax jurisdiction determines which country gets tax income from a transaction. Under the pre-electronic commerce system of international tax treaties, the right to tax was divided between the country where the enterprise that receives the income is resident ('residence country') and that from which the enterprise derives that income ('source country'). In 2002, the EU enacted two laws (Council Directive 2002/38/EC and

Council Regulation (EC) 792/2002) on how Value Added Tax (VAT) was to be charged and collected for electronic services. These were in accordance with the principles agreed within the framework of the Organisation for Economic Co-operation and Development (OECD) at a 1998 conference in Ottawa. These principles establish that the rules for consumption taxes (such as VAT) should result in taxation in the jurisdiction where consumption takes place. These laws helped to make European countries more competitive in e-commerce. An announcement from the EU explained:

> *Under the new rules, EU suppliers will no longer be obliged to levy VAT when selling products on markets outside the EU, thereby removing a significant competitive handicap. Previous EU rules, drawn up before e-commerce existed, oblige EU suppliers to levy VAT when supplying digital products even in countries outside the EU.*
>
> *The proposals are designed to eliminate an existing competitive distortion by subjecting non-EU suppliers to the same VAT rules as EU suppliers when they are providing electronic services to EU customers, something which EU businesses have been actively seeking.*
>
> *The VAT rules for non-EU suppliers selling to business customers in the Union (at least 90% of the market), will remain unchanged, with the VAT paid by the importing company under self-assessment arrangements.*

The OECD also agreed that a simplified online registration scheme, as now adopted by the European Council, is the only viable option today for applying taxes to e-commerce sales by non-resident traders. The tax principles are as follows in the UK interpretation of this law implemented in 2003 for these electronic services:

- supply of web sites or web-hosting services
- downloaded software (including updates of software)
- downloaded images, text or information, including making databases available
- digitized books or other electronic publications
- downloaded music, films or games
- electronic auctions or
- Internet service packages.

The UK VAT rules are as follows:

- if the supplier (residence) and the customer (source) are both in the UK, VAT will be chargeable;
- exports to private customers in the EU will attract either UK VAT or local VAT;
- exports outside the EU will be zero-rated (but tax may be levied on imports);
- imports into the UK from the EU or beyond will attract local VAT, or UK import tax when received through customs (for which overseas suppliers need to register);
- services attract VAT according to where the supplier is located. This is different from products and causes anomalies if online services are created. For example, a betting service located in Gibraltar enabled UK customers to gamble at a lower tax rate than with the same company in the UK. This law has since been reviewed.

The situation is more complex where a company has transnational offices, these examples from HMRC (2003) also illustrate the logic behind the new legislation:

> ***Example 1**: A UK business purchases digitised software from an Irish supplier for use only in its branch in the Channel Islands. Although the supply is received in the UK where the business belongs, it is used outside the EU and is outside the scope of UK (and EU) VAT.*
>
> ***Example 2**: A USA business purchases web-hosting services for its international business, including its UK branch. Although the supply is received in the USA, to the extent that it is used in the UK, it is subject to UK VAT.*
>
> ***Example 3**: A UK business purchases downloaded information from another UK business for use both in its UK headquarters and its Canadian branch. Although the supply is received in the UK, to the extent it is used in Canada, it is outside the scope of UK VAT. UK VAT is due only to the extent of use by the UK headquarters.*

Freedom-restrictive legislation

Although governments enact legislation in order to protect consumer privacy on the Internet, as described in the previous section, it is also worth noting that some individuals and organizations believe that legislation may also be too restrictive. In the UK, a new Telecommunications Act and Regulation of Investigatory Powers Act (RIP) took several years to enact since companies were concerned to ensure security and to give security forces the ability to monitor all communications passing through ISPs. This was fiercely contested due to cost burdens placed on infrastructure providers and in particular the Internet service providers (ISPs), and of course many citizens and employees may not be happy about being monitored either!

The Freedom House (www.freedomhouse.org) is a human rights organization created to reduce censorship since it believes government censorship laws may be too restrictive. It notes in a report (Freedom House, 2000) that governments in many countries, both developed and developing, are increasingly censoring online content. Only 69 of the countries studied have completely free media, while 51 have partly free media and 66 countries suffer heavy government censorship. Censorship methods include implementing licensing and regulation laws, applying existing print and broadcast restrictions to the Internet, filtering content and direct censoring after dissemination. In Asia and the Middle East, governments frequently cite protection of morality and local values as reasons for censorship. Countries where Internet access is mostly or totally controlled by the authorities include Azerbaijan, Belarus, Burma, China, Cuba, Iran, Iraq, Kazakhstan, Kyrgyzstan, Libya, North Korea, Saudi Arabia, Sierra Leone, Sudan, Syria, Tajikistan, Tunisia, Turkmenistan, Uzbekistan and Vietnam. Even the US government tried to control access to certain Internet sites with the Communications Decency Act in 1996, but this was unsuccessful. Refer to *Activity 4.7* to discuss these issues.

Activity 4.7 Government and company monitoring of electronic communications

Purpose

To examine the degree to which governments and organizations should monitor electronic communications.

Activity

Write down the arguments for and against each of these statements, debate individually or as a group to come to a consensus:

1. '*This house believes that organizations have no right to monitor employees' use of e-mail or the web*.' Use Moreover (www.moreover.com) to research recent cases where employees have been dismissed for accessing or sending e-mails or web content that is deemed unsuitable. Is this just used as an excuse for dismissing staff?
2. '*This house believes that governments have no right to monitor all Internet-based communications passing through ISPs*.' Use Moreover (www.moreover.com) to research action taken by the government of your country to monitor and control Internet communications.

What action do you think managers in a company should take with regard to monitoring employee access? Should laws be set at a national level or should action be taken by individual companies?

Answers to activities can be found at www.pearsoned.co.uk/chaffey

Economic and competitive factors

The economic health and competitive environment in different countries will determine the e-commerce potential of each. Managers developing e-commerce strategies in multinational companies will initially target the countries that are most developed in the use of the technology. A comprehensive framework for assessing an 'e-economy' has been developed by Booz Allen Hamilton (2002). The report authors define the e-economy as

E-economy
The dynamic system of interactions between a nation's citizens, the businesses and government that capitalize upon online technology to achieve a social or economic good.

the dynamic system of interactions between a nation's citizens, the businesses and government that capitalize upon online technology to achieve a social or economic good.

The framework is based upon four layers of environment, readiness, uptake and use, and impact, and three major stakeholder groups: citizens, businesses and government, as shown in *Figure 4.8*.

A review of how different governments have tried to improve the health of their e-economies is presented in the sections later in this chapter on political factors and e-government.

Knowledge of different economic conditions is also part of budgeting for revenue from different countries. For example, Fisher (2000) notes that the Asian market for e-commerce is predicted to triple within three years. However, within this marketplace there are large variations. Relative to income, the cost of a PC is still high in

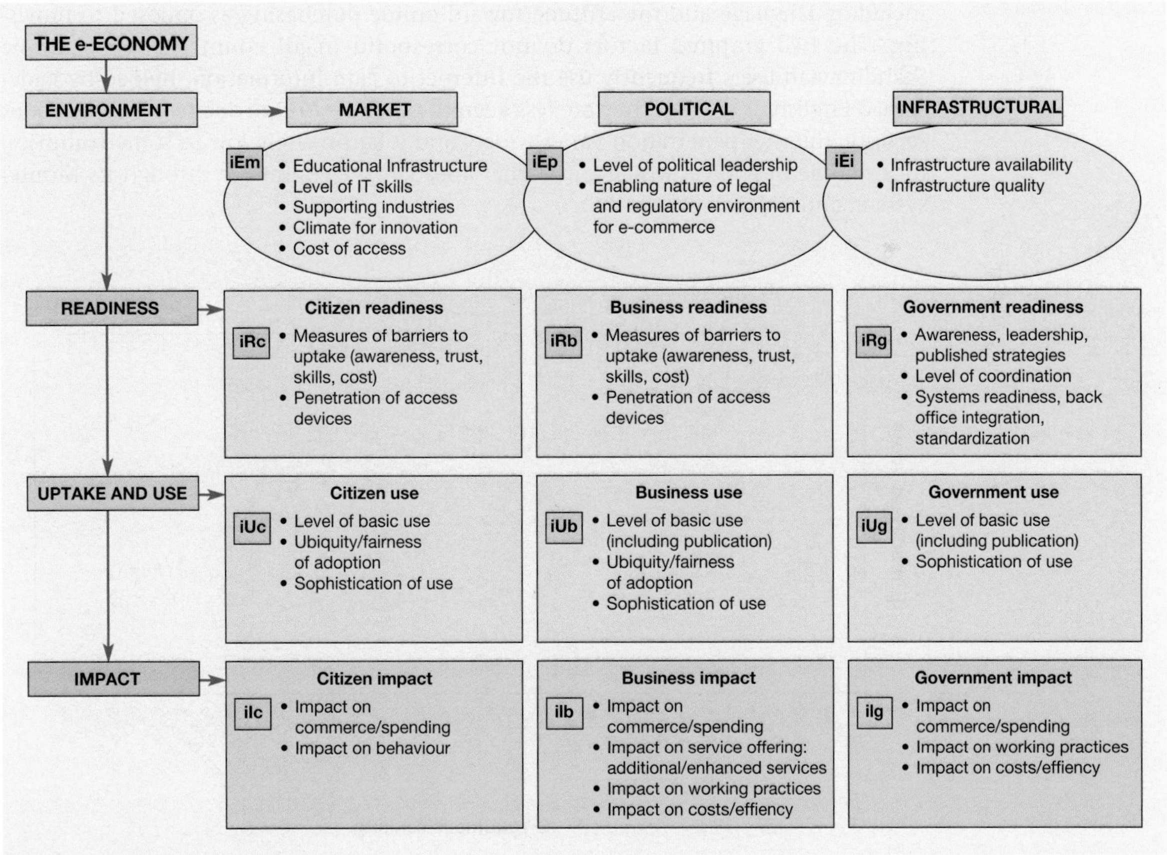

Figure 4.8 A framework describing the e-economy

Source: Booz Allen Hamilton (2002). *International E-Economy: Benchmarking The World's Most Effective Policy for the E-Economy*. Report published 19 November, London. www.e-envoy.gov.uk/oee/oee/nsf/sections/summit_benchmarking/$file/indexpage.htm © Crown copyright 2002.

many parts of Asia for people on low incomes. Fisher (2000) suggests that there will be a division between information 'haves' and 'have-nots' and, as we will see in the section on *Political factors*, this is dependent on government factors. In China there is regulation of foreign ownership of Internet portals and ISPs which could hamper development. User access to certain content is also restricted. Despite this, access in China is doubling every 6 months and at this rate China could have the largest user base within 10 years!

The trend towards globalization can arguably insulate a company to some extent from fluctuations in regional markets, but is, of course, no protection from a global recession. Managers can also study e-commerce in these leading countries to help predict future e-commerce trends in their own country.

We saw earlier in this chapter that there are wide variations in the level of use of the Internet in different continents and countries, particularly for consumer use. According to Roussel (2000), economic, regulatory and cultural issues are among the factors affecting use of the Internet for commercial transactions. The relative importance of these means e-commerce will develop differently in every country. Roussel (2000) rated different countries according to their readiness to use the Internet for business. This was based on two factors – propensity for e-commerce and Internet penetration. To calculate the propensity of a country for e-commerce transactions, the business environment was evaluated using the Economic Intelligence Unit (www.eiu.com) rating of countries according to 70 different indicators, such as the strength of the economy, political stability, the regulatory climate, taxation policies and openness toward trade and investment. Cultural factors were also considered, including language and the attitude toward online purchasing as opposed to browsing. The two graphed factors do not correspond in all countries, for example Scandinavian users frequently use the Internet to gain information, helped by widespread English usage, but they are less keen to purchase online due to concerns about security. Internet penetration varies widely and is surprisingly low in some countries, for example in France, which was earlier a leader in e-commerce through its Minitel system, and in Japan (*Figure 4.9*).

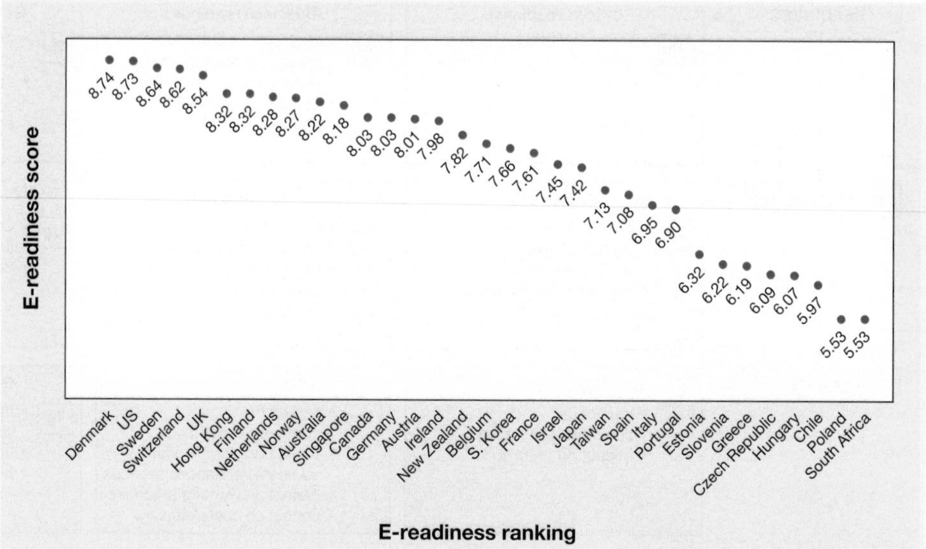

Figure 4.9 Leaders and laggards in e-commerce

Source: © 2005 Adapted from Economist Intelligence Unit data © 2005, Economist Intelligence Unit

Focus on e-commerce and globalization

Globalization
The increase of international trading and shared social and cultural values.

Globalization refers to the move towards international trading in a single global market place and also to blurring of social and cultural differences between countries. Some perceive it as 'Westernization' or even 'Americanization'. We saw in *Chapter 1* that for both SMEs such as North West Supplies and larger organizations such as easyJet and Cisco, electronic communications gives the opportunity for increasing the reach of the company to achieve sales around the world.

Quelch and Klein (1996) point out some of the obvious consequences for organizations that wish to compete in the global marketplace; they say a company must have:

- *a 24-hour order taking and customer service response capability;*
- *regulatory and customs-handling experience to ship internationally;*
- *in-depth understanding of foreign marketing environments to assess the advantages of its own products and services.*

Localization
Tailoring of web site information for individual countries or regions.

Language and cultural understanding may also present a problem and a smaller or medium-sized company is unlikely to possess the resources to develop a multi-language version of its site or employ staff with sufficient language skills. On the other hand, Quelch and Klein (1996) note that the growth of the use of the Internet for business will accelerate the trend of English becoming the lingua franca of commerce. Tailoring e-commerce services for individual countries or regions is referred to as localization. A web site may need to support customers from a range of countries with:

- different product needs;
- language differences;
- cultural differences.

The importance of localization is highlighted by a report by Common Sense Advisory (2002). According to them, for many US Fortune 500 firms, non-US revenue – or what they refer to as 'xenorevenue' – accounts for 20 to more than 50 per cent of their global income. A similar situation is likely to exist for non-US multinational organizations.

Don Da Palma, the author of the report, adds:

> *This fact alone makes it easy to see the value in catering to buyers in global markets with localized products and services in their language. Still, localization expenditures are minuscule – 2.5% and lower of non-US revenue – compared to the benefits of gaining market share and customer loyalty.*

It may be necessary to vary:

- The language that content is provided in.
- Tone and style of copy.
- Site design – certain colours or images may be unsuitable or less effective in some countries.
- Range of product offerings.
- Product pricing.
- Promotional offers used to encourage acquisition of customer e-mail address (see *Chapter 9*). This may be affected by local data protection, taxation and trading laws.
- Local contact points.

Localization will address all these issues. It may be that products will be similar in different countries and localization will simply involve providing a local-language version of a web site. However, in order to be effective, this often needs more than translation, since different promotion concepts may be needed for different countries. An example of a business-to-consumer site with extensive localization is Durex (www.durex.com) and a business-to-business site is 3M (www.3m.com). Durex localizes content for many countries since language and the way in which sexual issues can be discussed will vary greatly between different countries. 3M, however, only localizes content in local language for some countries such as France, Germany and Spain. Consider large multinational companies such as 3M, Ford and GlaxoSmithKline for which localization is a significant strategic issue for e-commerce. The decision on the level of localization will need to be taken on a regional or country basis to prioritize different countries according to the size of the market and the importance of having localization. Since the cost of localization is high it may only generate a return on investment for the largest markets. To explore the implications of globalization for consumer-oriented companies, refer to *Case Study 4.2*.

Case Study 4.2 The implications of globalization for consumer attitudes

The article starts by discussing anti-globalization. It then explores the implications of variations in the characteristics of different cultures on businesses providing services to them. At the end of the article, research about attitudes to globalization is summarized, along with its implications for businesses trading internationally.

Globalisation, or maybe more specifically, anti-globalisation issues, are never far from the headlines, whether it's coverage of the latest anti-WTO demonstration or news that McDonalds has replaced Ronald McDonald in France with Asterix – in a move to 'appease anti-globalisation protesters' (BBC News, 22 January 2002).

But what does globalisation actually mean? Stemming from the application of free market principles it has manifested the belief that the world is small and that consumers are becoming more and more alike, thus allowing companies to use the same advertising and marketing across regions and countries. Such a doctrine has enabled companies to act global and think global, much to the distaste of the anti-globalisation lobbies. Indeed, in 1985 it was Friends of the Earth that coined the slogan 'think global, act local' in its desire to counter such global forces – particularly with regards to environmental issues.

However, such 'glocalisation' [global localisation] makes a lot of sense for multinational companies operating today and planning new market entry, for a number of reasons. Firstly, the term globalisation for many Europeans is virtually synonymous with that of 'Americanisation'. For some this has negative connotations of materialism, loss of native culture and the encroachment of the English language. At its extreme, it drives many of the anti-globalisation activists. Thus there is real risk that companies will damage their brand and reputation if they don't recognise the importance of localization when considering market entry.

Secondly, consumers are as different as they are similar – local and regional cultures have a profound effect in shaping consumer demand. These differences are potentially more interesting than the similarities, in that they can allow product and service differentiation as well as new approaches to segmentation and marketing communications. To take advantage of such opportunities, businesses have to have a clear insight into how and why consumers in one market may differ from ones in another.

Feelings of anti-Americanisation are a strong undercurrent in Europe. Businesses have to plan how to counter such a groundswell of feeling if planning on entering new markets – given that some 50% of Europeans believe that 'our society is too Americanised' and such an attitude has increased over the past 10 years. While the degree of agreement varies within Europe (e.g. 67% of Spaniards agreeing with the statement, as compared with 44% of Brits) it is a significant influence of customer behaviour. To compound matters, multinational companies are the least trusted of 27 entities when European consumers have been asked to state which they trust to be honest and fair.

As a result, not only have we seen an increase in consumer activism (such as anti-WTO protests, growth of the slow food movement in Europe etc.), but also we have seen global brands coming under threat from emergent local brands which are gaining in currency. We would expect this to continue. This is not to say that there is no room for global brands! Many global brands have successfully tapped into local culture and tastes and recognised the need to either modify the product/service completely or change different elements of the offer and how it is ultimately marketed. Thus companies expanding into new geographic markets have to ensure that their strategies are based on a real understanding of regional and local markets.

Globalisation is not making the world a smaller, homogeneous place. While this presents many opportunities for businesses, it also implies a need for a clear understanding of what shapes consumer needs and desires in the different nations. Not surprising perhaps that many businesses found the notion of a 'globalised' world compelling given the significant implications for researching a multitude of different markets in terms of time and money budgets. Similarly, it is easy to understand the temptation of taking well-established national stereotypes and assuming that they are representative of the truth.

Recent attitudinal studies in Europe and the US undertaken by The Henley Centre show the complexity of attempting to categorise consumers on a broad scale. Let's take an example. At one level, results show that all consumers take pride in their family, so a global advertising campaign using the 'family' as a theme may feel like safe territory. To some extent it is. Dig down a bit deeper, however, and you find that different people define 'family' in very different ways, so what people take pride in will be subtly different. At a country level, many more differences expose themselves.

Businesses wanting to broaden their geographic reach have to consider at a strategic level what level of understanding of consumer needs they require. Generalisations are important and are a good place to start, but it is critical to then delve further – national stereotypes are too simplistic. Differences, rather than similarities, have to be considered, and interrogated in terms of how these will impact customer needs.

Source: The Henley Centre (www.henleycentre.com)

Question

Based on this article and your experiences, debate the question: 'Site localization is essential for each country for an e-commerce offering to be successful in that country.'

The implications of e-commerce for international B2B trading

Hamill and Gregory (1997) highlight the strategic implications of e-commerce for international business-to-business trading. They note that there will be increasing standardization of prices across borders as businesses become more aware of price differentials. Secondly, they predict that the importance of traditional intermediaries such as agents and distributors will be reduced by Internet-enabled direct marketing and sales.

Larger organizations typically already compete in the global marketplace, or have the financial resources to achieve this. But what about the smaller organization? Most governments are looking to encourage SMEs to use electronic commerce to tap into the international market. Advice from governments must reassure SMEs wishing to export. Hamill and Gregory (1997) identify the barriers to SME internationalization shown in *Table 4.6*. Complete *Activity 4.8* to look at the actions that can be taken to overcome these barriers.

More recent research suggests SMEs have been relatively slow to adopt the Internet. Research by Arnott and Bridgewater (2002) also suggests limited usage of the Internet. The authors test the level of sophistication by which SMEs are using the Internet (see stage models in *Chapter 5*). They find that the majority of firms are using the Internet for information provision rather than interactive, relationship-building or transactional facilities. They find that smaller firms are using significantly fewer Internet tools than their larger counterparts. Quayle (2002) has assessed issues considered by SMEs to be strategically important. In the UK 298 SMEs were surveyed. Issues of marketing, leadership and waste reduction were given highest priority and supplier development, financial management, time to market and supply chain management were medium priority. Perhaps unsurprisingly, the lowest priority was given to technology, research and development, e-commerce, customer management and purchasing – all closely related to e-business.

Activity 4.8 Overcoming SME resistance to international e-commerce

Purpose

To highlight barriers to exporting amongst SMEs and suggest measures by which they may be overcome by governments.

Activity

For each of the four barriers to internationalization given in *Table 4.6* suggest the management reasons why the barriers may exist and actions that governments can take to overcome these barriers. Evaluate how well the government in your country communicates the benefits of e-commerce through education and training.

Table 4.6 **Issues in SME resistance to exporting**

Barrier	*Management issues*	*How can barrier be overcome?*
1 Psychological		
2 Operational		
3 Organizational		
4 Product/market		

Source: Barriers from Hamill and Gregory (1997) and Poon and Jevons (1997)

Answers to activities can be found at www.pearsoned.co.uk/chaffey

Political factors

The political environment is shaped by the interplay of government agencies, public opinion, consumer pressure groups such as CAUCE (the Coalition against Unsolicited E-mail), www.cauce.org, and industry-backed organizations such as TRUSTe (www.truste.org) that promote best practice amongst companies. The political environment is one of the drivers for establishing the laws to ensure privacy and to achieve taxation, as described in previous sections.

Political action enacted through government agencies to control the adoption of the Internet can include:

- promoting the benefits of adopting the Internet for consumers and business to improve a country's economic prosperity;
- enacting legislation to protect privacy or control taxation, as described in previous sections;
- providing organizations with guidelines and assistance for compliance with legislation (in the UK, this is coordinated by the Communications and Information Industries Directorate (www.dti.gov.uk/cii/cii));
- setting up international bodies to coordinate the Internet such as ICANN (the Internet Corporation for Assigned Names and Numbers, www.icann.com) and other independent organizations controlling Internet technology described in *Chapter 3*.

Political involvement in many of these activities is intended to improve the economic competitiveness of countries or groups of countries. Quayle (2002) summarizes six strands of the UK government strategy for e-commerce which are intended to increase industry competitiveness:

1 Establish a brand in e-commerce both domestically and internationally.
2 Transform existing businesses.
3 Foster e-commerce creation and growth.
4 Expand the e-commerce talent pool (skills).
5 Provide leadership in international e-commerce policy development.
6 Government online should be a priority.

These goals are typical for many countries and specific targets are set for the proportion of people and businesses that have access, including public access points for those who cannot currently afford the technology. Managers who are aware of these initiatives can tap into sources of funding for development or free training to support their online initiatives. Alternatively, there may be incentives such as tax breaks for business or consumer adoption of the Internet and technology companies can also take advantage of these.

One interesting example of political intervention from 2005 is the backing of a new European Internet search engine to rival Google and Yahoo by French president Jacques Chirac. In a speech in Reims, Mr Chirac said: 'We're engaged in a global competition for technological supremacy. In France, in Europe, it's our power that's at stake.' The 'multimedia search engine for the Internet' was initially developed by French group Thomson and Deutsche Telekom. The plans are a reflection of the often-expressed concern over US 'cultural imperialism' and its impact on French culture. The French government also funded an initiative to create an online digital library to rival one planned by Google.

Some other examples of the role of government organizations in promoting and regulating e-commerce are given by these examples from the European Commission (EC):

Information society
A society with widespread access and transfer of digital information within business and the community.

- The EC Information Society initiative (http://europa.eu.int/information_society/index_en.htm) was launched in 1998 with the aims of increasing public awareness of the impact of the information society and stimulating people's motivation and ability to participate (reducing social exclusion); increasing socio-economic benefits and enhancing the role of Europe in influencing the global Information Society. Information Society was defined by the UK INSINC working party on social inclusion in the information society in 1997 as:

  > *A society characterised by a high level of information intensity in the everyday life of most citizens, in most organizations and workplaces; by the use of common or compatible technology for a wide range of personal, social, educational and business activities; and by the ability to transmit and receive digital data rapidly between places irrespective of distance.*

  UNESCO (the United Nations Educational, Scientific and Cultural Organization) has also been active in advancing the Information Society in less developed countries (http://portal.unesco.org/ci).
- The European Community has set up 'i2010' (*European Information Society in 2010*) whose aims include

  > *providing an integrated approach to information society and audio-visual policies in the EU, covering regulation, research, and deployment and promoting cultural diversity.* (eEurope, 2005)

- In 1998 new data protection guidelines were enacted to help protect consumers and increase the adoption of e-commerce by reducing security fears. In the new millennium cross-Europe laws have been enacted to control online consumer privacy, electronic selling and taxation.

Booz Allen Hamilton (2002) reviews approaches used by governments to encourage use of the Internet. They identify five broad themes in policy:

1 *Increasing the penetration of 'access devices'.* Approaches include either home access through Sweden's PC Tax Reform, or in public places, as in France's programme to

develop 7,000 access points by 2003. France also offer a tax incentive scheme, where firms can make tax-free gifts of PCs to staff for personal use.

2 *Increasing skills and confidence of target groups*. These may target potentially excluded groups, as with France's significant €150 million campaign to train the unemployed. Japan's IT training programmes use existing mentors.
3 *Establishing 'driving licences' or 'passport' qualifications*. France, Italy and the UK have schemes which grant simple IT qualifications, particularly at low-skilled groups such as the long-term unemployed.
4 *Building trust, or allaying fears*. An example of this in the US is the 1998 Child Online Protection Act which used schemes to provide 'kitemark'-type verification, or certification of safe services.

Internet governance

5 *Direct marketing campaigns*. According to the report, only the UK, with its UK Online campaign, is marketing directly to citizens on a large scale.

Internet governance
Control of the operation and use of the Internet.

Internet governance describes the control put in place to manage the growth of the Internet and its usage. Governance is traditionally undertaken by government, but the global nature of the Internet makes it less practical for a government to control cyberspace. Dyson (1998) says:

> *Now, with the advent of the Net, we are privatizing government in a new way – not only in the traditional sense of selling things off to the private sector, but by allowing organizations independent of traditional governments to take on certain 'government' regulatory roles. These new international regulatory agencies will perform former government functions in counterpoint to increasingly global large companies and also to individuals and smaller private organizations who can operate globally over the Net.*

The US approach to governance, formalized in the Framework for Global Electronic Commerce in 1997, is to avoid any single country taking control.

Dyson (1998) describes different layers of jurisdiction. These are:

1 Physical space comprising each individual country where its own laws such as those governing taxation, privacy and trading and advertising standards hold.
2 ISPs – the connection between the physical and virtual worlds.
3 Domain name control (**www.icann.net**) and communities.
4 Agencies such as TRUSTe (**www.truste.org**).

The organizations that manage the infrastructure, which were described in *Chapter 3*, also have a significant role in governance.

E-government

E-government
The application of e-commerce technologies to government and public services.

E-government is distinct from Internet governance. We introduced e-government in *Chapter 1*, where we noted that it is a major strategic priority for many countries in Europe and the remainder of the world. To achieve the potential cost savings, some governments have set targets for both buy- and sell-side e-government. In the UK, the government's main target was:

> *That by 2005, 100% of dealings with Government should be capable of being delivered electronically, where there is a demand.*

Although this target is to be applauded, one can view this as the UK government's dot-com investment. Although many services have been created, adoption rates tend to be low (see, for example, *Figure 1.8*) and the government is having to invest in marketing usage of these services.

In Australia, the National Office for the Information Economy, NOIE (www.noie.gov.au), has created a strategic framework which has the following themes. This summarizes the types of actions that many governments are taking to encourage e-business within their countries.

1 *Access, participation and skills* – Encouraging all sectors of the community to actively participate in the information economy
2 *Adoption of e-business* – The government is working to provide more efficient communication between businesses to help improve the productivity of the Australian economy. A priority focus for 2002/03 is to promote the uptake of electronic procurement and broader electronic business processes, especially by small and medium enterprises.
3 *Confidence, trust and security* – The government is working to build public trust and confidence in going online, and addressing barriers to consumer confidence in e-commerce and other areas of online content and activity.
4 *e-Government strategies and implementation* – The use of new technologies for government information provision, service delivery and administration has the potential to transform government. This transformation will improve the lives of Australians. NOIE provides a framework and coordinates all government approaches to support Commonwealth agency efforts in this area.
5 *Environment for information economy firms* – Provide research on the environmental variables that drive innovation and growth in the information economy and underpin its future development.
6 *International dimensions* – NOIE, in cooperation with other government bodies, represents Australia in world forums where decisions are made that may affect national interests in the information economy.

Booz Allen Hamilton (2002) report that the leading countries in e-government are Sweden, Australia and Germany. In Sweden, for example, local authorities allow public participation via the Internet in council meetings. However, the report notes that:

> *Generally, delivery of services on the internet has been approached as an opportunity to automate services over an additional channel rather than opportunity for service innovation, and so comprehensive process redesign is only just beginning to emerge.*
>
> *Many innovative schemes (such as e-voting) remain at the pilot stage and as a result, evidence for real impact is scarce. Furthermore, with currently low levels of uptake of e-government services compared to offline channels, even in the leading countries, tangible impact on costs and efficiency is yet to be felt.*
>
> *A rare example of both process redesign and tangible efficiency gains is Italy's e-procurement platform, Consip. Another example is the German student loan authority, which has moved to paperless administration with savings of 4.5mn Euro annually.*

Debate 4.2

Getting value from e-government

'Efforts by national governments to deliver e-government services for citizens represent a massive waste of public money, given the limited demand for these services.'

Technological innovation and technology assessment

One of the great challenges of managing e-commerce is the need to be able to assess which new technological innovations can be applied to give competitive advantage. For example, personalization technology is intended to enhance customers' online experience and increase their loyalty. However, a technique such as personalization requires a large investment in software and hardware technology such as Broadvision or Engage to be able to implement it effectively. How does the manager decide whether to proceed and which solution to adopt? The manager may have read several articles in the trade and general press which have highlighted the issue and then faces a difficult decision as to whether to:

- ignore the use of the technique, perhaps because it is felt to be too expensive, untried, or the manager simply doesn't believe the benefits will outweigh the costs;
- enthusiastically adopt the technique without a detailed evaluation since the hype alone convinces the manager that the technique should be adopted;
- evaluate the technique and then take a decision whether to adopt it according to the evaluation.

Depending on the attitude of the manager, this behaviour can be summarized as:

1 Cautious, 'wait-and-see' approach.
2 Risk-taking, early-adopter approach.
3 Intermediate approach.

This diffusion–adoption process (represented by the bell curve in *Figure 4.10*) was identified by Rogers (1983) who classified those trialling new products as innovators, early adopters, early majority, late majority, or laggards.

Early adopters
Companies or departments that invest in new technologies and techniques.

Figure 4.10 can be used in two main ways as an analytical tool to help managers. First, it can be used to understand the stage customers have reached in adoption of a technology, or any product. For example, the Internet is now a well established tool and in many developed countries we are into the late majority phase of adoption with larger numbers of users of services. This suggests it is essential to use this medium for marketing purposes. But if we look at WAP technology it can be seen that we are in the innovator phase, so investment now may be wasted since it is not clear how many will adopt the product. Second, managers can look at adoption of a new technique by other businesses – from an organizational perspective. For example, an online supermarket could look at how many other e-tailers have adopted personalization to evaluate whether it is worthwhile adopting the technique.

An alternative graphic representation of diffusion of innovation has been specifically developed by technology analyst Gartner for assessing the maturity, adoption and business application of specific technologies (*Figure 4.11*). Gartner (2005) recog-

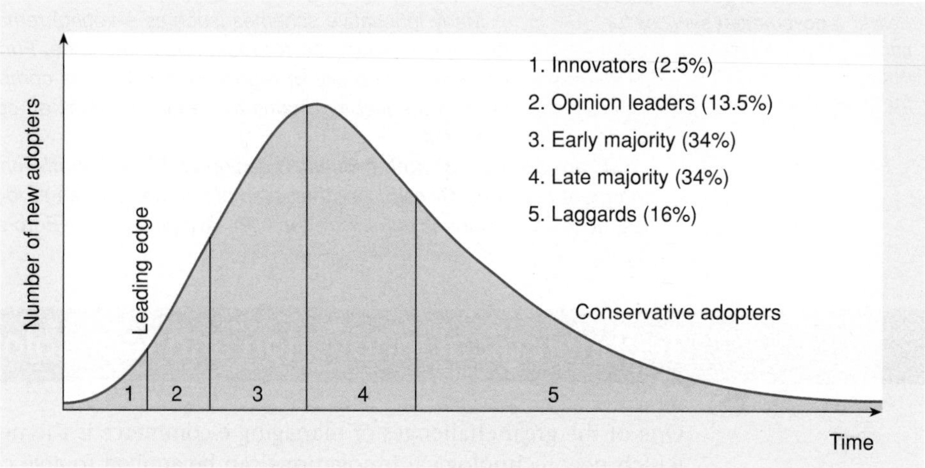

Figure 4.10 **Diffusion–adoption curve**

Hype cycle
A graphic representation of the maturity, adoption and business application of specific technologies.

nizes the following stages within a **hype cycle**, an example of which is given in *Figure 4.11* for trends current in 2005:

1. ***Technology Trigger*** *– The first phase of a hype cycle is the 'technology trigger' or breakthrough, product launch or other event that generates significant press and interest.*
2. ***Peak of Inflated Expectations*** *– In the next phase, a frenzy of publicity typically generates over-enthusiasm and unrealistic expectations. There may be some successful applications of a technology, but there are typically more failures.*
3. ***Trough of Disillusionment*** *– Technologies enter the 'trough of disillusionment' because they fail to meet expectations and quickly become unfashionable. Consequently, the press usually abandons the topic and the technology.*
4. ***Slope of Enlightenment*** *– Although the press may have stopped covering the technology, some businesses continue through the 'slope of enlightenment' and experiment to understand the benefits and practical application of the technology.*
5. ***Plateau of Productivity*** *– A technology reaches the 'plateau of productivity' as the benefits of it become widely demonstrated and accepted. The technology becomes increasingly stable and evolves in second and third generations. The final height of the plateau varies according to whether the technology is broadly applicable or benefits only a niche market.*

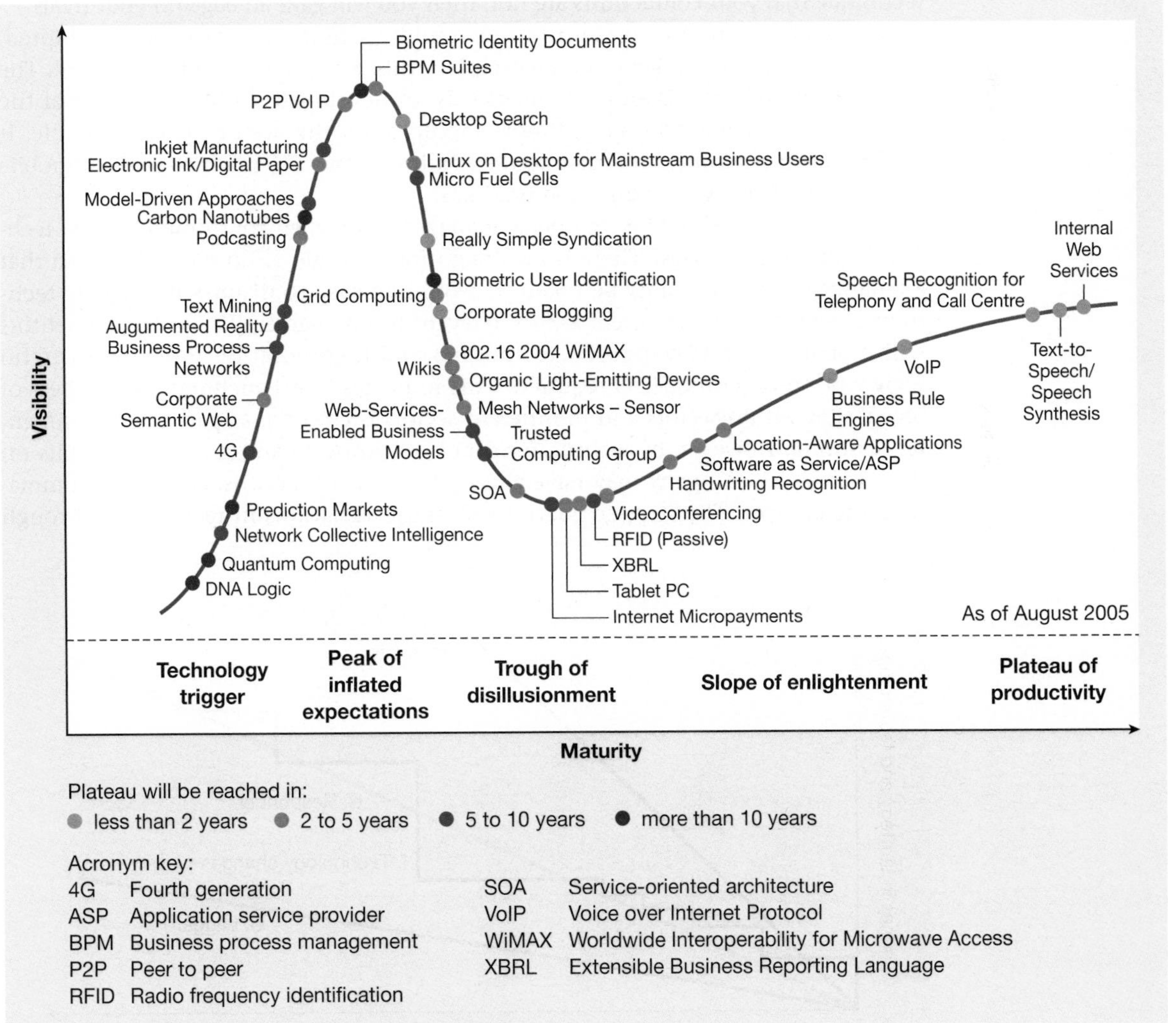

Figure 4.11 Example of a Gartner hype cycle
Source: Gartner (2005) Gartner's Hype Cycle Special Report for 2005

Trott (1998) looks at this organizational perspective to technology adoption. He identifies different requirements that are necessary within an organization to be able to respond effectively to technological change or innovation. These are:

- *Growth orientation* – a long-term rather than short-term vision
- *Vigilance* – the capability of environment scanning
- *Commitment to technology* – willingness to invest in technology
- *Acceptance of risk* – willingness to take managed risks
- *Cross-functional cooperation* – capability for collaboration across functional areas
- *Receptivity* – the ability to respond to externally developed technology
- *Slack* – allowing time to investigate new technological opportunities
- *Adaptability* – a readiness to accept change
- *Diverse range of skills* – technical and business skills and experience.

The problem with being an early adopter (as an organization) is that the leading edge of using new technologies is often also referred to as the 'bleeding edge' due to the risk of failure. New technologies will have bugs, may integrate poorly with the existing systems, or the marketing benefits may simply not live up to their promise. Of course, the reason for risk taking is that the rewards are high – if you are using a technique that your competitors are not, then you will gain an edge on your rivals.

It may also be useful to identify how rapidly a new concept is being adopted. When a product or service is adopted rapidly this is known as 'rapid diffusion'. The access to the Internet is an example of this. In developed countries the use of the Internet has become widespread more rapidly than the use of TV, for example. It seems that in relation to Internet access and interactive TV, Internet-enabled mobile phones are relatively slow-diffusion products!

So, what action should e-commerce managers take when confronted by new techniques and technologies? There is no straightforward rule of thumb, other than that a balanced approach must be taken. It would be easy to dismiss many new techniques as fads, or classify them as 'not relevant to my market'. However, competitors will probably be reviewing new techniques and incorporating some, so a careful review of new techniques is required. This indicates that benchmarking of 'best of breed' sites within sectors and in different sectors is essential as part of environmental scanning. However, by waiting for others to innovate and review the results on their web site, a company may have already lost 6 to 12 months. *Figure 4.12* summarizes the choices. The stepped curve I shows the variations in technology through

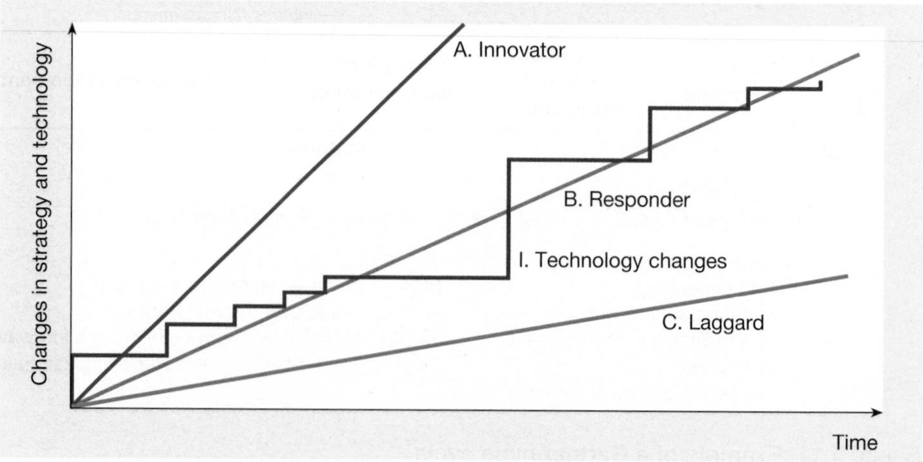

Figure 4.12 Alternative responses to changes in technology

time. Some may be small incremental changes such as a new operating system, others such as the introduction of personalization technology are more significant in delivering value to customers and so improving business performance. Line A is a company that is using innovative business techniques, that adopts technology early, or is even in advance of what the technology can currently deliver. Line C shows the conservative adopter whose use of technology lags behind the available potential. Line B, the middle ground, is probably the ideal situation where a company monitors new ideas as early adopters trial them and then adopts those that will have a positive impact on the business.

As a conclusion to this chapter we look in *Case Study 4.3* at the use of portable books as a new technology. How does a manager in the media industry respond to this?

Case Study 4.3 How do industry analysts affect technology adoption?

FT

This case study focuses on the views of George Colony, chairman and chief executive of analysts Forrester Research. It looks at different future innovations and illustrates the way analysts have trenchant viewpoints. The questions are to prompt discussion of the value of such research to a business and how it can best be applied.

By 2007, 70 per cent of the world's computer programming activity will be in developing countries. Companies such as Accenture, EDS and International Business Machines will go out of business unless they adapt, by farming out their programming to countries such as India and China and concentrating on high-value project management work.

George Colony, chairman and chief executive of Forrester Research, delights in such challenging predictions. He founded Forrester in 1983, with a brief to examine new aspects of computer technology and how they would affect business. 'Our main quality is courage, not being afraid of making decisive statements, as long as we can back them up', he says.

So, in typically trenchant style, he dismisses Microsoft's latest operating system, Windows XP, as unfit for corporate use. 'It is not ready for prime time. Too many bugs. It would be a big mistake for any large corporations to adopt it', he says.

It is no wonder that, according to Mr Colony, Bill Gates hates him, though Microsoft continues to be a client. He shrugs: 'People can keep old versions of Windows. One of my main pieces of advice to companies is that if a technology works, keep it. Doesn't matter if it is rats on wheels that makes it work.'

Rats on wheels would have to run very fast to keep up with the rate of technical innovation Forrester demands from business. Before and throughout the late 1990s technology boom, Forrester was among leading consultancies advocating the immediate adoption of new technologies, from the internet to customer relationship management systems. 'Technology changes everything', Mr Colony is fond of saying, with the corollary that organisations failing to heed technological change will fall behind.

Despite technology companies' recent setbacks, innovation in the sector has not slowed, he contends. 'The next battle ground for technology will be my watch.' Over the next few years, he says, the internet will extend beyond the 500m personal computers connected to it now to encompass billions of wireless devices.

'Soon, the average person will have between one and four devices on their body connected to the internet. A watch. A pacemaker. A drug delivery system. A pulse monitor', he predicts. Mr Colony's sweeping visions of the technological future have not been dimmed, either, by the damage done to analysts' reputations by the internet boom. Forrester was certainly buoyed by the dotcom bubble but has not emerged well from its wreckage, having lost three-quarters of its market capitalisation.

As dotcoms sought to persuade investors of the value of their big new idea, they needed some intellectual validation. That is where the analysts came in. The business community was bombarded with predictions of astronomical growth in online markets and seeming endorsements of the business plans of scores of online hopefuls.

When the bubble burst, many of the predictions that had been used to shore up the likes of eToys and Boo.com were shown to be unrealistic.

Analysts at investment banks came in for the worst criticism – but Mr Colony accepts that independent analysis companies also suffered a serious blow to their reputations. 'I was struck by the lack of depth in what was going on at the time. Too many companies became cheerleaders', he says.

Forrester's research was quoted widely by keen dotcoms. Webvan, the internet grocer that burned through $1bn (£700m) in its brief existence, noted in its 1999 initial public offering filing: 'Forrester Research estimates that online grocery spending in the US will grow from $235m in 1998 to $10.8bn by 2003.' Forrester, however, later revised these estimates, nearly halving its 2003 forecast to $5.8bn.

The now-defunct Pets.com also cited Forrester in its 1999 listing document, saying: 'Forrester Research estimates that online purchases made by consumers in the US will grow from $20bn in 1999 to $184bn by 2004, representing a compound annual growth rate of 56 per cent.' Forrester's forecast was that in 2000, online retail sales would be worth $32bn in the US; the real figure, according to the US Census Bureau, turned out to be 25 per cent less.

Though his company's research was cited by failures such as Webvan and Pets.com, Mr Colony accepts no responsibility for their demise, saying that their business plans were flawed. He also seeks to distance his company from 'other internet (analyst) companies', claiming that these had a greater proportion of dotcoms among their clients, therefore an interest in talking up the boom and so consistently overestimated the prospects of many dotcom sectors. These participants in the 'irrational exuberance' of the turn of the century ended, he says, by sullying their reputations. Forrester, he argues, did not fall into that camp. 'We were not cheerleaders. There were no pompoms out among our analysts. We are analysts: very large corporations make very big decisions based on our guidance. We have to be objective', he says.

These standards, he contends, were maintained throughout the period. For evidence, he points to a report published by Forrester in January 2000 predicting that spiralling costs would cause most dotcoms to fail and that consolidation would begin at the end of that year's first quarter. The dotcom crash started in March 2000.

An internal audit of Forrester's research carried out after the market peaked showed its figures were often conservative, according to Mr Colony. For instance, Forrester forecast in 1998 that $251bn of business in the US would be carried out online in 2000; in 1999, it revised this figure upwards to $406bn; according to the US Census Bureau, the real figure was much higher, at $620bn.

Forrester gets its estimates right about 65 to 80 per cent of the time, the audit concluded. 'That is a pretty good average', Mr Colony says.

Others cast doubt on his assurance. Noah Yasskin, European director of research at rival technology researcher Jupiter Media Metrix, questions the validity of internal audits: 'It all depends on what you measure. It is rather controversial, how you measure your own numbers.' Whatever their lapses, analyst companies still find technology research lucrative ground. It is not difficult to see why: technology plays a bigger part than ever in business and yet most senior executives in large companies have little idea about new technical developments.

The sigh of relief from traditional company executives when the dotcom bubble burst was almost audible. Many thought their scepticism about the role of new technology had been vindicated and no longer felt any pressure to think about technology investment. Mr Colony shakes his head, warning that companies that switch their attention from new technology will be lost. 'Technology is hard – and few people understand it. It is like a different language. But companies have no choice but to learn it.'

Mr Colony divides executives into ties, turtlenecks and T-shirts: directors, marketing departments and technology workers. As the bubble burst, the first two categories retreated from technology. They need to come back, he argues, to marry business acumen with the possibilities technology opens up. The T-shirts will also have to change, he says.

'I am astounded by the lack of vision of the technologists. The PC arrived and the IT department fought it. The internet arrived and the IT department fought it. Companies need the whole view, both the business strategy vision and the technical savvy.'

Of course, he would say that. Though he denies cheerleading for the technology sector, Mr Colony's success is wholly bound up with information technology. As the dotcoms and technology start-ups went to the wall, and established technology companies were forced into profit warnings, technology analysis companies also suffered.

Forrester cut 220 jobs in the last year, leaving 455 staff worldwide. 'Whatever else we do, we are a business and we have to make a profit', says Mr Colony. Forrester recorded net income of $18.1m for 2001, down from $21.6m in 2000, on revenues of $159m, roughly flat with the previous year.

Forrester's fortunes clearly depend on more than just the reputations of its analysts. Only when IT budgets stop shrinking will the prospects perk up for companies such as Forrester, which rely on large companies' need for advice on IT spending.

Though he estimates that companies overspent on technology by more than $65bn during the boom, Mr Colony remains bullish even on the near-term prospects for the sector. This year, he thinks, will see technology companies grow at 3.9 per cent; next, growth will return to double digits, at 10.4 per cent, and the following year hit 12.5 per cent. By his own estimation, he has about a 70 per cent chance of being right.

Source: Fiona Harvey, *An optimist's vision of tomorrow's technology*. Interview with George Colony, Forrester Research, *Financial Times*, 2 April 2002

Questions

1 Referring to the article, evaluate whether reports from independent industry analysts such as Forrester represent a useful tool for managers to assess whether their company should adopt new technologies or business practices.

2 What steps could be taken by managers to make best use of these reports?

Summary

1 Environmental scanning and analysis are necessary in order that a company can respond to environmental changes and act on legal and ethical constraints on its activities.

2 Environmental constraints are related to the micro-environment variables reviewed in *Chapter 5* and the macro-environment variables in this chapter using the SLEPT mnemonic.

3 Social factors that must be understood as part of the move to the Information Society include buyer behaviour characteristics such as access to the Internet and perceptions about it as a communications tool.

4 Ethical issues include the need to safeguard consumer privacy and security of personal information. Privacy issues include collection and dissemination of customer information, cookies and the use of direct e-mail.

5 Legal factors to be considered by e-commerce managers include: accessibility, domain name registration, copyright and data protection legislation.

6 Economic factors considered in the chapter are the regional differences in the use of the Internet for trade. Different economic conditions in different markets are considered in developing e-commerce budgets.

7 Political factors involve the role of governments in promoting e-commerce, but also trying to control it.

8 Rapid variation in technology requires constant monitoring of adoption of the technology by customers and competitors and appropriate responses.

Exercises

Self-assessment questions

1 Why is environmental scanning necessary?

2 Give an example how each of the macro-environment factors may directly drive the content and services provided by a web site.

3 Summarize the social factors that govern consumer access to the Internet. How can companies overcome these influences once people venture online?

4 What actions can e-commerce managers take to safeguard consumer privacy and security?

5 What are the general legal constraints that a company acts under in any country?

6 How do governments attempt to control the use of the Internet?

7 Summarize adoption patterns across the continents.

8 How should innovation be managed?

→

Essay and discussion questions

1 You recently started a job as e-commerce manager for a bank. Produce a checklist of all the different legal and ethical issues that you need to check for compliance on the existing web site of the bank.

2 How should the e-commerce manager monitor and respond to technological innovation?

3 Benchmark different approaches to achieving and reassuring customers about their privacy and security using three or four examples for a retail sector such as travel, books, toys or clothing.

4 'Internet access levels will never exceed 50% in most countries.' Discuss.

5 Select a new Internet access technology (such as phone, kiosks or TV) that has been introduced in the last two years and assess whether it will become a significant method of access.

6 Assess how the eight principles of the UK Data Protection Act (www.dataprotection.gov.uk) relate to actions an e-commerce manager needs to take to ensure legal compliance of their site.

Examination questions

1 Explain the concept of a 'virtual community'. What are the benefits to the organization that hosts it?

2 Explain the different layers of governance of the Internet.

3 Summarize the macro-environment variables a company needs to monitor.

4 Explain the purpose of environmental scanning.

5 Give three examples of how web sites can use techniques to protect the user's privacy.

6 What are the three key factors which affect consumer adoption of the Internet?

7 Explain the significance of the diffusion–adoption concept to the adoption of new technologies to:
   (a) Consumers purchasing technological innovations.
   (b) Businesses deploying technological innovations.

8 What action should an e-commerce manager take to ensure compliance with ethical and legal standards of their site?

References

ABC News (2000) *Ecommerce Causes Tax Shortfall in US*. News story on ABC.com, 27 July. http://abcnews.go.com/sections/business/DailyNews/internettaxes000725.html.

Arnott, D. and Bridgewater, S. (2002) Internet, interaction and implications for marketing. *Marketing Intelligence and Planning*, 20(2), 86–95.

BMRB (2004) *Internet Monitor*, November. BMRB International, Manchester. Available online at www.bmrb.co.uk.

Booz Allen Hamilton (2002) *International E-Economy Benchmarking the World's Most Effective Policies for the E-Economy*. Report published 19 November, London. www.e-envoy.gov.uk/oee/oee.nsf/sections/esummit-benchmarking/$file/indexpage.htm.

BrandNewWorld (2004) AOL Research published at www.brandnewworld.co.uk.

Chaffey, D., Mayer, R., Johnston, K. and Ellis-Chadwick, F. (2006) *Internet Marketing: Strategy, Implementation and Practice*, 3rd edn. Financial Times Prentice Hall, Harlow.

CIFAS (2006) Press release, 30 January 2006. 2005 – The Year of the Identity Fraud! www.cifas.org.uk/press_20060130.asp.

Common Sense Advisory (2002) 'Beggars at the globalization banquet'. White Paper available at: www.commonsenseadvisory.com. Editor: Don Da Palma. No locale given.

Computer Weekly (2004) Assessing the real risk of being online. *Computer Weekly*. Article by Stewart King. Thursday 9 December. www.computerweekly.com.

Daniel, L., Wilson, H. and Myers, A. (2002) Adoption of e-commerce by SMEs in the UK. Towards a stage model. *International Small Business Journal*, 20(3), 253–70.

DTI (2004) Business in the Information Age – International Benchmarking Study 2004. UK Department of Trade and Industry. www.ukonlineforbusiness.gov.uk.

Dyson, E. (1998) *Release 2.1. A Design for Living in the Digital Age*. Penguin, London.

eEurope (2005) Information Society Benchmarking Report. From eEurope (2005) initiative. Published at: http://europa.eu.int/information_society/eeurope/i2010/docs/benchmarking/051222%20Final%20Benchmarking%20Report.pdf.

EIAA (2006) UK leads the way in online shopping, European Interactive Advertising Association Press release published 12 January. www.eiaa.net/news/eiaa-articles-details.asp?lang=1&id=85.

Fisher, A. (2000) Gap widens between the 'haves' and 'have-nots'. *Financial Times, 5* December.

Fletcher, K. (2001) Privacy: the Achilles heel of the new marketing. *Interactive Marketing*, 3(2), 128–40.

Freedom House (2000) *Censoring dot-gov report*. 17 April. www.freedomhouse.org/news/pr041700.html, New York.

Gartner (2005) Gartner's Hype Cycle Special Report for 2005. Report summary available at www.gartner.com: ID Number: G00130115.

Godin, S. (1999) *Permission Marketing*. Simon and Schuster, New York.

Grossnickle, J. and Raskin, O. (2001) *The Handbook of Online Marketing Research, Knowing Your Customer Using the Net*. McGraw-Hill, New York.

Guardian (2003) Hijacked your bank balance, your identity, your life. *The Guardian*, 25 October, www.guardian.co.uk/weekend/story/0,3605,1069646,00.html.

Hamill, J. and Gregory, K. (1997) Internet marketing in the internationalisation of UK SMEs. *Journal of Marketing Management*, 13, 9–28.

HMRC (2003) Electronically supplied services and broadcasting services: New EU rules

HMRC Reference: VAT Info Sheet 01/03. HM Revenue and Customs.

Mason, R. (1986) Four ethical issues of the information age. *MIS Quarterly*, March.

Mougayer, W. (1998) *Opening Digital Markets – Battle Plans and Strategies for Internet Commerce*, 2nd edn. CommerceNet Press, McGraw-Hill, New York.

National Statistics (2005) UK National Statistics Omnibus Survey – Internet access section, May, www.statistics.gov.uk.

Ofcom (2004) *UK Communications Market Report 2004*. UK Office of Communications. www.ofcom.org.uk/research/industry market research/m i index/cm/cmpdf/?a=87101.

Poon, S. and Jevons, C. (1997) Internet-enabled international marketing: a small business network perspective. *Journal of Marketing Management*, 13, 29–41.

Quayle, M. (2002) E-commerce: the challenge for UK SMEs in the twenty-first century. *International Journal of Operation and Production Management*, 22(10), 1148–61.

Quelch, J. and Klein, L. (1996) The Internet and international marketing. *Sloan Management Review*, Spring, 61–75.

RedEye (2003) A study into the accuracy of IP and cookie-based online management information. The RedEye Report. Available at www.redeye.com.

The Register (2004) One in four Brits on net for porn. Andrew Orlowski, December. *The Register*. www.theregister.co.uk/2004/12/08/brit net filth/.

Rogers, E. (1983) *Diffusion of Innovations*, 3rd edn. Free Press, New York.

Roussel, A. (2000) Leaders and laggards in B2C commerce. Gartner Group report, 4 August. SPA-11-5334 www.gartner.com.

Sparrow, A. (2000) *E-Commerce and the Law. The Legal Implications of Doing Business Online.* Financial Times Executive Briefings, London.

Trott, P. (1998) *Innovation Management and New Product Development.* Financial Times Prentice Hall, Harlow.

Ward, S., Bridges, K. and Chitty, B. (2005) Do incentives matter? An examination of on-line privacy concerns and willingness to provide personal and financial information. *Journal of Marketing Communications*, 11(1), 21–40.

Further reading

Booz Allen Hamilton (2002) *International E-Economy Benchmarking. The World's Most Effective Policies for the E-Economy.* Report published 19 November, London. A detailed study (177-page report) reviewing government attempts to influence use of the Internet by citizens and businesses.

Dibb, S., Simkin, L., Pride, W. and Ferrell, O. (2000) *Marketing. Concepts and Strategies*, 4th edn. Houghton Mifflin, Boston. In Chapter 2, the authors introduce the different elements of the marketplace from a marketing perspective.

Dyson, E. (1998) *Release 2.1. A Design for Living in the Digital Age.* Penguin, London. Chapters 5 (Governance), 8 (Privacy), 9 (Anonymity) and 10 (Security) are of particular relevance.

Garfinkel, S. (2000) *Database Nation.* O'Reilly, San Francisco. This book is subtitled 'The death of privacy in the 21st century' and this is the issue on which it focuses (includes Internet- and non-Internet-related privacy).

Slevin, J. (2000) *The Internet and Society.* Polity Press, Oxford. A book about the Internet that combines social theory, communications analysis and case studies from both academic and applied perspectives.

Web links

Dave Chaffey's link directory (www.davechaffey.com) A directory of e-business-related audience Internet adoption and usage links is maintained by Dave Chaffey to support this book.

Guide to Smarter Internet Searching (www.pearsoned.co.uk/chaffey) A detailed explanation from the author of this book on how to use the Internet more effectively to search for business and accademic sources. Includes a description of an advanced searching approach using Google.

The Oxford Internet Institute (OII) (www.oii.ox.ac.uk) Research institute focused on the study of the impact of the Internet on society.

OECD (www.oecd.org/eco/wp/onlinewp.htm#2000) OECD global development of e-commerce working papers. No. 252 is e-commerce paper.

Online audience usage data

- **ClickZ Internet research** (www.clickz.com/stats/) An aggregator of worldwide research about Internet adoption.
- **Comscore** (www.comscore.com) A similar audience panel to Nielsen//Netratings, but mainly US.
- **Hitwise** (www.hitwise.com) Formerly an Australian service, now operating in many countries. Press releases provide popularity of portals and destination sites in different categories.

- **Ipsos MORI** (www.mori.com) Ipsos MORI Technology Tracker. (www.mori.com/technology/trackerdata.shtml) provides a free summary of UK digital media adoption.
- **Nielsen Media Netratings** (www.netratings.com) In 'Top Rankings' section publishes user universe and top properties in different countries.

Privacy

- **Australian Privacy Commissioner** (www.privacy.gov.au) Information on privacy laws in Australia such as the Privacy Act and the Telecommunications Act.
- **European Data Protection resources** (http://europa.eu.int/comm/justice_home/fsj/privacy/index_en.htm) These laws are coordinated centrally, but interpreted differently in different countries.
- **Federal Trade commission** (www.ftc.gov/privacy) US privacy initiatives.
- **GetSafeOnline** (www.getsafeonline.org) Site created by government and business to educate consumers to help them understand and manage their online privacy and security.
- **Home Office Identify theft web site** (www.identitytheft.org) An awareness site created by the government.
- **iCompli** (www.icompli.co.uk) Portal and e-newsletter about privacy and data protection compliance.
- **Information Commissioner** (www.informationcommisioner.gov.uk) Site explaining law for UK consumers and businesses.
- **Marketing Law** (www.marketinglaw.co.uk) Useful e-mail update on latest privacy law developments.
- **Outlaw** (www.out-law.com) Compilation of latest technology-related law.
- **Office of Electronic Government and Technology** (www.estrategy.gov) US agency facilitating e-government in the USA.
- **Privacy International** (www.privacyinternational.org) A human rights group formed in 1990 as a watchdog on surveillance and privacy invasions by governments and corporations.

Part 2 STRATEGY AND APPLICATIONS

In *Part 2* of the book approaches to developing e-business strategy and applications are reviewed for the organization as a whole (*Chapter 5*), with an emphasis on buy-side e-commerce (*Chapters 6* and *7*) and sell-side e-commerce (*Chapters 8* and *9*).

5 E-business strategy

Chapter at a glance

Main topics

Focus on ...

Case studies

Web support

The following additional case study is available at www.pearsoned.co.uk/chaffey

- Evolving business models in the Internet car sales market

The site also contains a range of study material designed to help improve your results.

Learning outcomes

After completing this chapter the reader should be able to:

- Follow an appropriate strategy process model for e-business
- Apply tools to generate and select e-business strategies
- Outline alternative strategic approaches to achieve e-business.

Management issues

Consideration of e-business strategy raises these issues for management:

- How does e-business strategy differ from traditional business strategy?
- How should we integrate e-business strategy with existing business and information systems strategy?
- How should we evaluate our investment priorities and returns from e-business?

Links to other chapters

The main related chapters to this chapter are summarized in *Figure 5.1*. They are as follows:

- *Chapters 6* and *7* review the specific enactment of e-business strategy to supply chain and procurement management processes;
- *Chapters 8* and *9* explain how e-marketing and customer relationship management relate to the concept of e-business, and e-commerce and e-marketing planning are approached;
- *Chapters 10, 11* and *12* look at practical aspects of the implementation of e-business strategy.

Introduction

Developing an e-business strategy requires a fusion of existing approaches to business, marketing, supply chain management and information systems strategy development. In addition to traditional strategy approaches, commentators have exhorted companies to apply innovative techniques to achieve competitive advantage. Around the start of the new millennium, many articles, fuelled by the dot-com hype of the time, urged CEOs to 'innovate or die'. For many existing companies this has not been necessary or desirable. Those companies that have successfully managed the transformation to e-business such as Cisco, Dell, General Motors, HSBC and IBM, and, in Europe, easyJet and British Telecom, have done so by applying traditional strategy approaches. At the same time there have been many start-ups featured as cases in previous chapters such as eBay, Lastminute.com and Zopa.com that have succeeded through innovative business models. But these companies also have succeeded through applying established principles of business strategy, planning and risk management.

In this chapter we seek to show how an e-business strategy can be created through following these established principles, but also through careful consideration of how to best identify and exploit the differences introduced by new electronic channels. In a nutshell, e-business isn't just about defining *'how to do business online'*, it defines *'how to do business differently online'*. The e-business strategy defines how.

We start the chapter by considering an appropriate strategy process model to follow as a framework for developing e-business strategy. The chapter is structured around this four-stage strategy process model:

1 Strategic evaluation.
2 Strategic objectives.
3 Strategy definition.
4 Strategy implementation.

For each of these components of strategy, management actions are reviewed with the emphasis on development of e-business strategy.

E-business strategy

Strategy
Definition of the future direction and actions of a company defined as approaches to achieve specific objectives.

Strategy defines the future direction and actions of an organization or part of an organization. Johnson and Scholes (1999) define corporate strategy as:

> *the direction and scope of an organization over the long-term: which achieves advantage for the organization through its configuration of resources within a changing environment to meet the needs of markets and to fulfil stakeholder expectations.*

Lynch (2000) describes strategy as an organization's sense of purpose. However, he notes that purpose alone is not strategy; plans or actions are also needed.

E-business strategies share much in common with corporate, business and marketing strategies. These quotes summarizing the essence of strategy could equally apply to each strategy:

- 'Is based on current performance in marketplace.'
- 'Defines how we will meet our objectives.'
- 'Sets allocation of resources to meet goals.'
- 'Selects preferred strategic options to compete within a market.'
- 'Provides a long-term plan for the development of the organization.'

Johnson and Scholes (1999) note that organizations have different levels of strategy, particularly for larger or global organizations. These are summarized within *Figure 5.1*. They identify *corporate strategy* which is concerned with the overall purpose and scope of the organization, *business unit strategy* which defines how to compete successfully in a particular market and *operational strategies* which are concerned with achieving corporate and business unit strategies. Additionally, there are what can be described as *functional strategies* that describe how the corporate and business unit strategies will be operationalized in different functional areas or business processes. Functional or process strategies refer to marketing, supply chain management, human resources, finance and information systems strategies. Where does **e-business strategy** fit? *Figure 5.1* does not show at which level e-business strategy should be defined, since for different organizations this must be discussed and agreed. We can observe that there is a tendency for e-business strategy to be incorporated within the functional strategies, for example within a marketing plan or logistics plan, or as part of information systems (IS) strategy. A danger with this approach is that e-business strategy may not be recognized at a higher level within organizational planning. A distinguishing feature of organizations that are leaders in e-business, such as Cisco, Dell, HSBC, easyJet and General Electric, is that e-business is an element of corporate strategy development.

E-business strategy
Definition of the approach by which applications of internal and external electronic communications can support and influence corporate strategy.

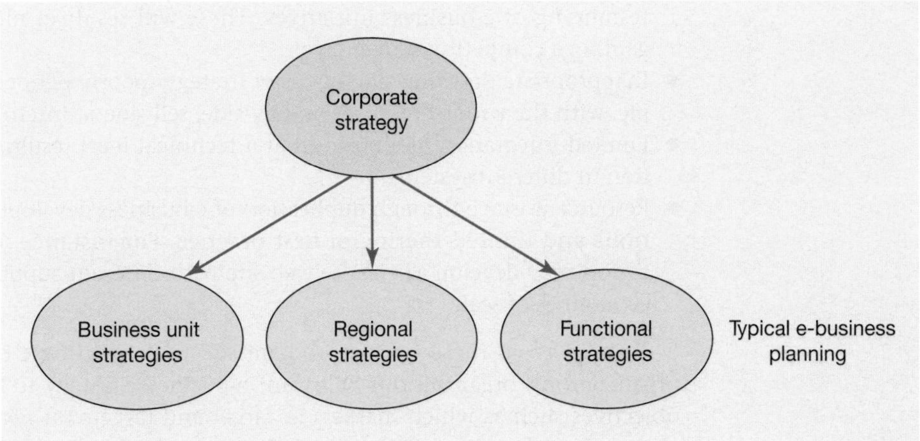

Figure 5.1 Different forms of organizational strategy

There is limited research on how businesses have integrated e-business strategy into existing strategy, although authors such as Doherty and McAulay (2002) have suggested it is important that e-commerce investments be driven by corporate strategies.

Research of retail banks by Hughes (2001) suggests that, in the early phases of e-business development, there is no clarity in e-commerce strategy at a senior level.

In one of the responding companies interviewees comment that:

> *My perception would be that they are not leading e-commerce as actively as they are other parts of change within the organisation.*
>
> (Organisation development manager, case 1)

Another comments:

> *There is a lack of understanding of the new technology and its implications by the executive team: Whereas if it's a life and pensions decision they can take that because it's in their blood. If it's a technology decision, it's much more difficult.*
>
> (Marketing manager, case 1)

However, problems in defining strategy can occur, even though clear control is evident. In company 3 the importance of senior involvement is stressed:

> *The ability to drive forward a project without a very high level sponsor is doomed to failure really.* [In our organization] *The allocation of budgets is decided at the highest level.*

In organization 3, three senior managers are responsible for driving e-commerce: the chief executive, the head of the electronic channel and the technology director. However, the marketing manager feels that the marketing function has not been sufficiently central in e-commerce development:

> *What marketing is trying to do is say there should be a strong consumer voice within there who can think about it purely from the marketing side. We're trying to make sure that we've got strong representation.*

The imperative for e-business strategy

Think about the implications if e-business strategy is not clearly defined. The following may result:

- Missed opportunities from lack of evaluation of opportunities or insufficient resourcing of e-business initiatives. These will result in more savvy competitors gaining a competitive advantage;
- Inappropriate direction of e-business strategy (poorly defined objectives, for example, with the wrong emphasis on buy-side, sell-side or internal process support);
- Limited integration of e-business at a technical level resulting in silos of information in different systems;
- Resource wastage through duplication of e-business development in different functions and limited sharing of best practice. For instance, each business unit or region may develop a separate web site with different suppliers without achieving economies of scale.

To help avoid these typical problems of implementing e-business in traditional organizations, organizations will want e-business strategy to be based on corporate objectives such as which markets to target and targets for revenue generation from electronic channels. As Rowley (2002) has pointed out, it is logical that e-business strategy should support corporate strategy objectives and it should also support functional marketing and supply chain management strategies.

However, these corporate objectives should be based on new opportunities and threats related to electronic network adoption, which are identified from environment analysis and objectives defined in an e-business strategy. So it can be said that e-business strategy should not only support corporate strategy, but should also influence it. *Figure 5.2* explains how e-business strategy should relate to corporate and functional strategies. It also shows where these topics are covered in this book.

E-channel strategies
Define how a company should set specific objectives and develop specific differential strategies for communicating with its customers and partners through electronic media such as the Internet, e-mail and wireless media.

E-channel strategies

An important aspect of e-business strategies is that they create new **'e-channel strategies'** for organizations.

E-channel strategies define specific goals and approaches for using electronic channels. This is to prevent simply replicating existing processes through e-channels, which will create efficiencies but will not exploit the full potential for making an organization more effective through e-business. Without specific goals and strategies to communicate the benefit of e-channels for customers and partners, adoption of

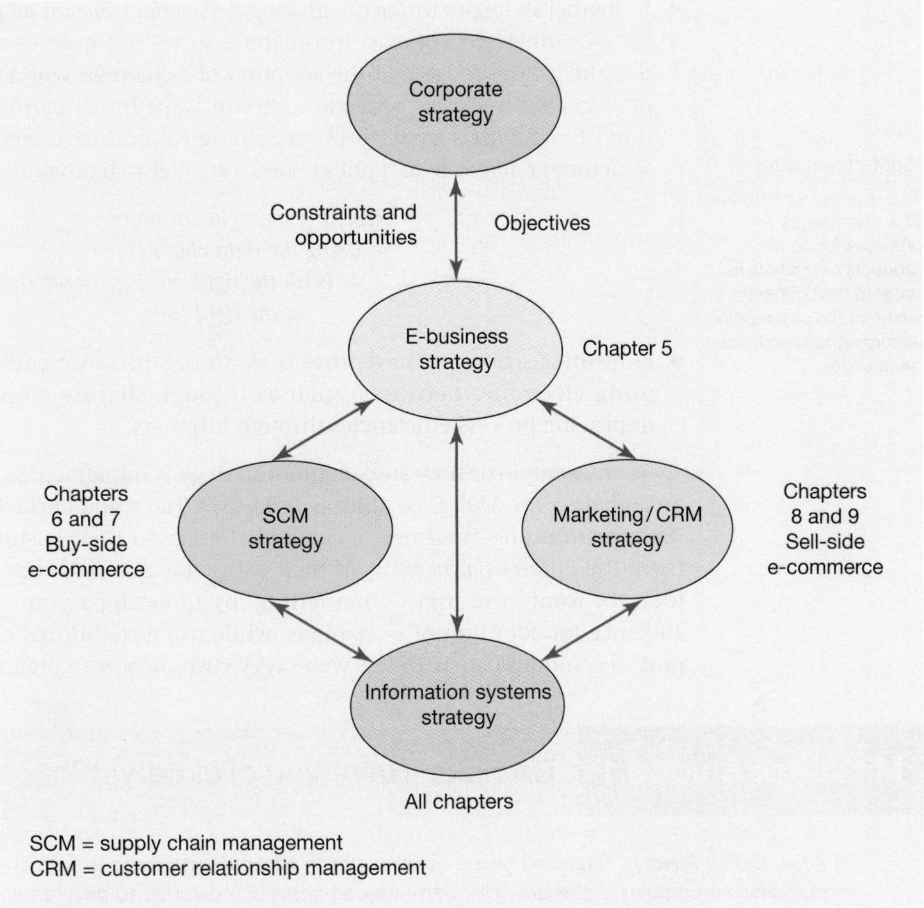

Figure 5.2 **Relationship between e-business strategy and other strategies**

the new channels will be slow relative to a structured approach. We will see in the section on objective setting that key metrics about online contribution can be set which suggest the percentage and value of leads, sales, services and purchases that are facilitated through e-commerce transactions. E-channel strategies also need to define how electronic channels are used in conjunction with other channels as part of a **multi-channel e-business strategy**. This multi-channel e-business strategy defines how different marketing and supply chain channels should integrate and support each other in terms of their proposition development and communications based on their relative merits for the customer and the company. Finally, we also need to remember that e-business strategy also defines how an organization gains value internally from using electronic networks, such as sharing employee knowledge and improving process efficiencies through intranets. Myers *et al.* (2004) provide a useful summary of the decisions required about multi-channel marketing.

Multi-channel e-business strategy
Defines how different marketing and supply chain channels should integrate and support each to drive business efficiency and effectiveness.

The characteristics of a multi-channel e-business strategy are:

- E-business strategy is a *channel strategy*;
- *Specific e-business objectives* need to be set to benchmark adoption of e-channels;
- E-business strategy defines how we should:
  1 *Communicate the benefits* of using e-channels
  2 *Prioritize audiences or partners targeted* for e-channel adoption
  3 *Prioritize products sold or purchased* through e-channel
  4 *Achieve our e-channel targets;*

- E-channel strategies thrive on creating *differential value* for all parties to a transaction;
- *But* e-channels do not exist in isolation, so we still need to manage *channel integration* and acknowledge that the adoption of e-channels will not be appropriate for all products or services or generate sufficient value for all partners. This selective adoption of e-channels by business according to product or stakeholder preference is sometimes referred to as 'right-channelling'. Right-channelling can be summarized as:

  - *Reaching the right customer*
  - *Using the right channel*
  - *With the right message or offering*
  - *At the right time;*

- E-business strategy also defines how an organization *gains value internally* from using electronic networks, such as through sharing employee knowledge and improving process efficiencies through intranets.

Right-channelling

This is selective adoption of e-channels by business for some products or markets in order to best generate value for the organization according to stakeholder preferences.

As an example of how an e-channel strategy is implemented and communicated to an audience, see *Mini Case Study 5.1*: BA asks 'Have you clicked yet?' This shows how BA communicates their new e-channel strategy to their customers in order to show them the differential benefits of their using the channel, and so change their behaviour. BA would use 'right-channelling' by targeting a younger, more professional audience for adoption of e-channels, while using traditional channels of phone and post to communicate with less web-savvy customers who prefer to use these media.

Mini Case Study 5.1 BA asks 'Have you clicked yet?'

In 2004, British Airways, launched online services which allowed customers to take control of the booking process so combining new services with reduced costs. BA decided to develop a specific online ad campaign to create awareness and encourage usage of its Online Value Proposition (OUP). BA's UK marketing manager said about the objective:

> *British Airways is leading the way in innovating technology to simplify our customers' journey through the airport. The role of this campaign was to give a strong message about what is now available online, over and above booking tickets.*

The aim of the campaign was to develop a campaign that educated and changed the way in which BA's customers behave before, during and after they travel. The campaign focused on the key benefits of the new online services – speed, ease and convenience – and promoted the ability to check in online and print out a boarding pass. The two main target audiences were quite different, early adopters and those who use the web occasionally, but don't rely on it. Early adopters were targeted on sites such as T3.co.uk, Newscientist.com and DigitalHomeMag.com. Occasional users were reached through ads on sites such as JazzFM.com, Vogue.com and Menshealth.com.

Traditional media used to deliver the 'Have you clicked yet?' message included print, TV and outdoor media. The print ad copy, which details the OVP was:

> *Your computer is now the airport. Check in online, Print your own boarding pass, choose your seat, change your booking card and even find hire cars and hotels. Simple.*

A range of digital media were used, including ATMs, outdoor LCD transvision screens such as those in London rail stations which included BlueCasting where commuters could receive a video on their Bluetooth-enabled mobile phone, and digital escalator panels. More than 650,000 consumers interacted with the ATM screen creative. Online ads included overlays and skyscrapers which showed a consumer at this computer, printing out a ticket and walking across the screen to the airport. Such rich-media campaigns generated 17 per cent clickthrough and 15% interaction. The web site used in the campaign is shown in *Figure 5.3*.

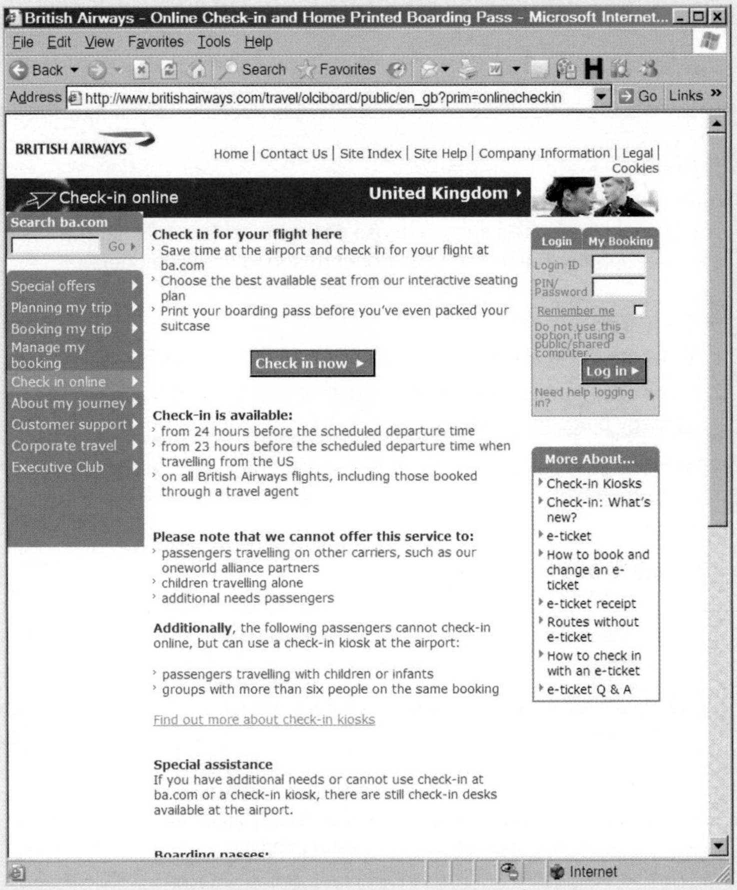

Figure 5.3 BA communicates their online value proposition (www.britishairways.com)

Source: Based on *Revolution* (2005)

Strategy process models for e-business

Strategy process model
A framework for approaching strategy development.

Before developing any type of strategy, a management team needs to agree the process they will follow for generating and then implementing the strategy. A **strategy process model** provides a framework that gives a logical sequence to follow to ensure inclusion of all key activities of e-business strategy development. It also ensures that e-business strategy can be evolved as part of a process of continuous improvement.

Before the advent of e-business, many strategy process models had been developed for each of the strategies described above. To what extent can management teams apply these models to e-business strategy development? Although strategy process models differ in emphasis and terminology, they all have common elements. Complete *Activity 5.1* to discuss what these common elements are.

Debate 5.1

E-business responsibility

'A single person with specific e-business responsibility is required for every medium-to-large business. It is not sufficient for this to be the responsibility of a non-specialist manager.'

Activity 5.1 Selecting an e-business strategy process model

Purpose

To identify the applicability of existing strategy process models to e-business.

Activity

Review three or four strategy process models that you have encountered in other modules. These could be models such as those shown in *Table 5.1*. Note that columns in this table are independent – each row does not correspond across models.

Questions

1 What are the strengths and weaknesses of each model?

2 What common features do the models share? List the key elements of an appropriate strategy process model.

Answers to activities can be found at www.pearsoned.co.uk/chaffey

Table 5.1 **Alternative strategy process models**

Lynch (2000) *Sequential corporate strategy model*	Johnson and Scholes (1999) *Parallel corporate strategy model*	McDonald (1999) *Sequential marketing strategy model*	Smith (1999) *SOSTAC™ Sequential marketing strategy model* (see Chapter 8)
Environment analysis (e.g. marketplace, customers, competitors). Resource analysis (e.g. human, financial and operational)	Strategic analysis (environment, resources, expectations, objectives and culture)	Situation review (marketing audit, SWOT analysis, assumptions)	Situation analysis
Vision, mission and objectives	Strategic choice (generation of options, evaluation of options, selection of strategy)	Goal setting (mission, corporate objectives)	Objective setting
Strategy development	Strategic implementation (resource planning, people and systems, organization structure)	Strategy formulation (marketing objectives and strategy, estimate expected results, identify alternative plans and mixes)	Strategy
Strategy implementation		Resource allocation and monitoring (budget, first-year implementation plan)	Tactics Actions Control

Through considering alternative strategy process models such as those of *Table 5.1*, common elements are apparent:

1 Internal and external environment scanning or analysis is needed. Scanning occurs both during strategy development and as a continuous process in order to respond to competitors.

2 A clear statement of vision and objectives is required. Clarity is required to communicate the strategic intention both to employees and the marketplace. Objectives are also vital to act as a check as to whether the strategy is successful!

3 Strategy development can be broken down into strategy option generation, evaluation and selection. An effective strategy will usually be based on reviewing a range of alternatives and selecting the best on its merits.
4 After strategy development, enactment of the strategy occurs as strategy implementation.
5 Control is required to monitor operational and strategy effectiveness problems and adjust the operations or strategy accordingly.

Additionally, the models suggest that these elements, although generally sequential, are also iterative and require reference back to previous stages. In reality there is overlap between these stages.

To what extent, then, can this traditional strategy approach be applied to e-business? We will now review some suggestions for how e-business strategy should be approached.

Hackbarth and Kettinger (2000) suggest a four-stage 'strategic e-breakout' model with stages of:

1 Initiation
2 Diagnosis of the industry environment
3 Breakout to establish a strategic target
4 Transition or plotting a migration path.

This model emphasizes the need to innovate away from traditional strategic approaches by using the term 'breakout' to show the need for new *marketplace structures* and *business/revenue models* (*Chapter 2*). A weakness of this approach is that it does not emphasize objective setting and control. However, Hackbarth and Kettinger's paper is valuable in detailing specific e-business strategy development activities. For example, the authors suggest that company analysis and diagnosis should review the firm's capabilities with respect to the customers, suppliers, business partnerships and technologies.

Deise *et al.* (2000) present a novel approach to developing e-business strategy. Their approach is based on work conducted for clients of management consultants PricewaterhouseCoopers. They suggest that the focus of e-business strategy will vary according to the evolutionary stage of e-business. Initially the focus will involve the enhancement of the selling channels (sell-side e-commerce), this then tends to be followed by value-chain integration (buy-side e-commerce), and creation of a value network. We will return to this issue of emphasis in the section on strategy definition (*p. 233*).

Rowley (2002) suggests that strategy formulation for e-business has much in common with strategy development for other business contexts. The stages she suggests, which are adapted from Lord (2000), are as follows. (1) Acquire e-business competence by making key appointments or establishing outsourcing arrangements with partners. (2) Establish channel and 'acclimatize start-up community' or develop prototype projects. (3) Extend applications and increase community dependence by implementing larger-scale supply chain management and CRM systems. (4) Optimize Internet contribution to core business – a maturity stage where e-business is continuously improved.

Venkatram (2000) suggests a five-stage strategy process for what he describes as a 'dot-com strategy', for existing businesses looking to make use of new digital media. The five stages are presented as five questions for a management team:

1 *What is your strategic vision?* This includes consideration of business models and how to achieve differentiation.
2 *How do you govern dot-com operations?* Governance is divided into operational decisions (production, sourcing, logistics, marketing and human resources) and the trade-off with financial decisions (investment logic, funding sources and performance criteria, i.e. objectives).

3 *How do you allocate key resources for the dot-com operations?* To operationalize the e-business, which of these techniques are used for resourcing: commit internal resources, form strategic alliances or outsource?
4 *What is your operating infrastructure for the dot-com operations?* Venkatram emphasizes the importance of the infrastructure in adding value to the customer through functionality, personalization and ensuring privacy.
5 *Is your management team aligned for the dot-com agenda?* This considers the responsibilities and structures used for executing the other aspects of the strategy such as vision, resourcing and infrastructure.

It could be argued that questions 2 to 5 are more about strategy implementation, but they are key questions of e-business change management that need to be

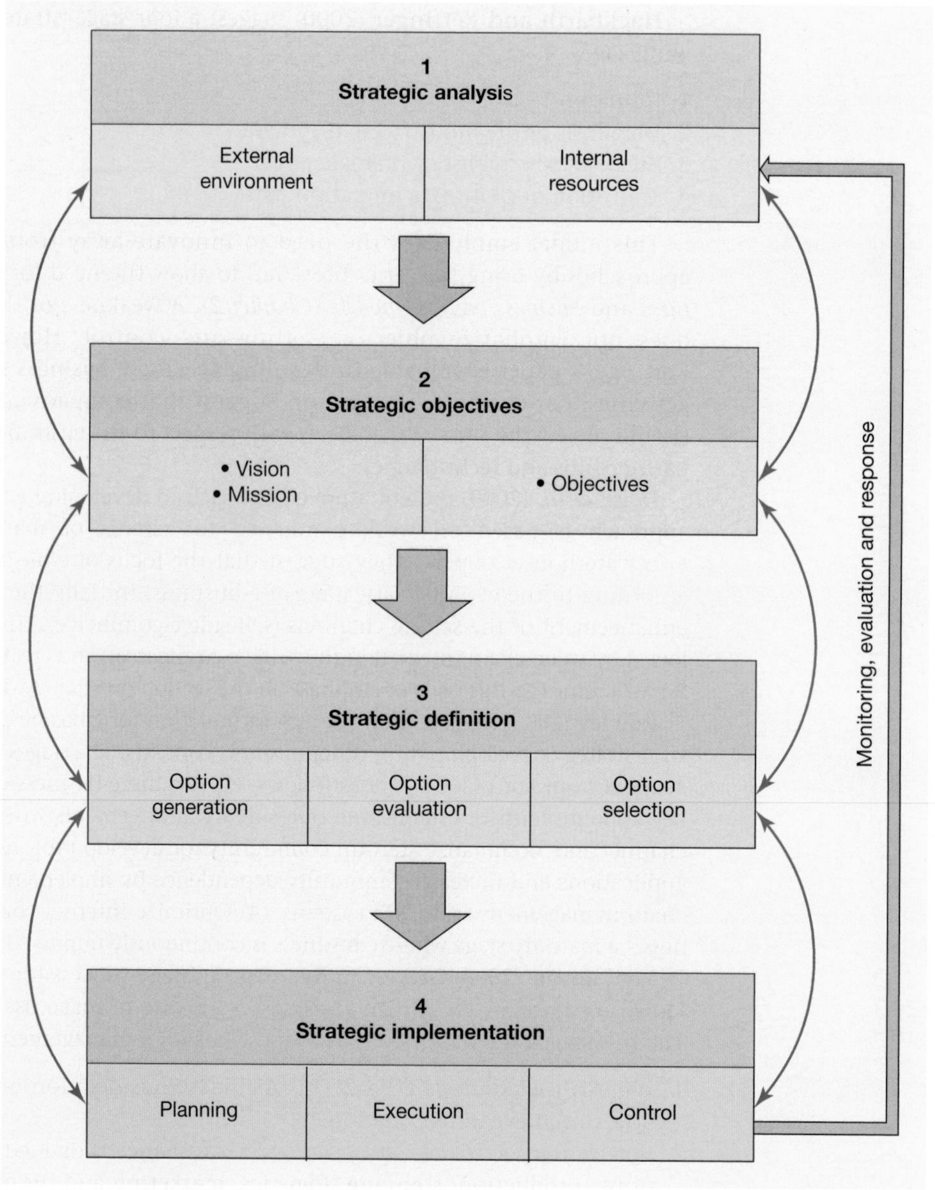

Figure 5.4 **A generic strategy process model**

answered. Venkatram (2000) also highlights the need to continuously scan the environment and so revise the strategy; he says:

> *We need to abandon calendar-driven models of strategy perfected under the predictable conditions of the Industrial Age. We should embrace the philosophy of experimentation since the shape of future business models is not obvious.*

Plant (2000), following examination of 40 US and European organizations, suggests that the e-commerce strategy (buy-side and sell-side) should devise approaches for seven dimensions made up of four positional factors (technology, service, market, brand) and three bonding (internal) factors (leadership, infrastructure, organizational learning).

Bringing together the ideas of these pioneering authors on e-business we can note that it does appear that existing strategy elements such as environment analysis, objective setting and strategy definition are naturally still required. However, there is greater emphasis on restructuring and resourcing through using new technology to build an infrastructure and supporting knowledge management (*Chapter 10, p. 485*) to achieve quality customer service. Based on existing models and a review of newer models, this chapter is structured according to a generic four-stage strategy process model depicted in *Figure 5.4* opposite.

Note the use of two-way arrows in *Figure 5.4* to indicate that each stage is not discrete, but rather it involves referring backwards or forwards to other strategy elements. Each strategy element will have several iterations. The arrows in *Figure 5.4* highlight an important distinction in the way in which strategy process models are applied. Referring to the work of Mintzberg and Quinn (1991), Lynch (2000) distinguishes between prescriptive and emergent strategy approaches. In the **prescriptive strategy** approach he identifies three elements of strategy – strategic analysis, strategic development and strategy implementation, and these are linked together sequentially. Strategic analysis is used to develop a strategy, and it is then implemented. In other words, the strategy is prescribed in advance. Alternatively, the distinction between the three ele-

Prescriptive strategy
The three core areas of strategic analysis, strategic development and strategy implementation are linked together sequentially.

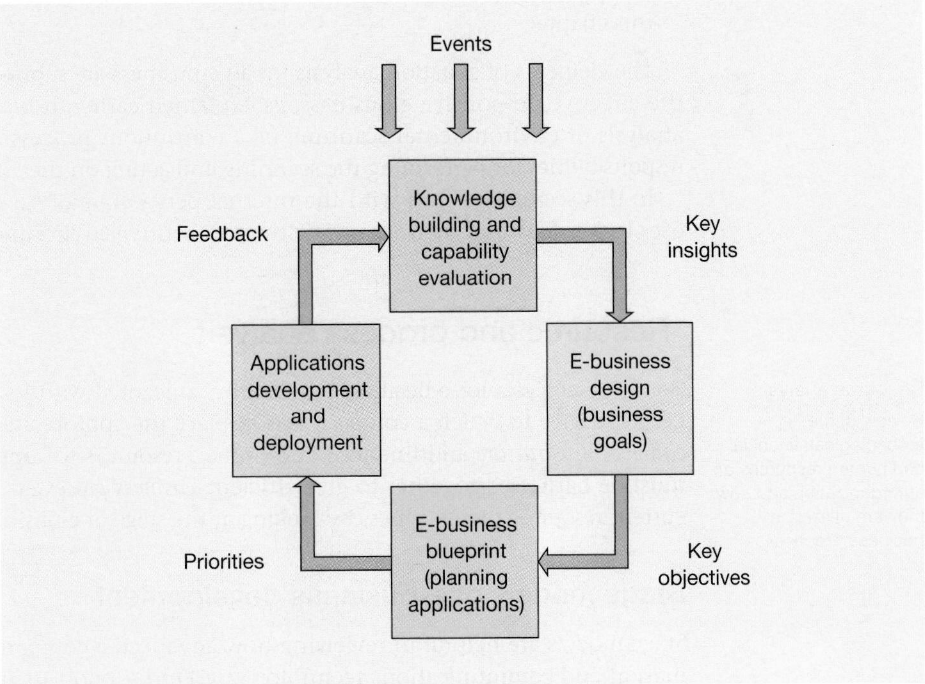

Figure 5.5 Dynamic e-business strategy model
Source: Adapted from description in Kalakota and Robinson (2000)

Emergent strategy
Strategic analysis, strategic development and strategy implementation are interrelated and are developed together.

ments of strategy may be less clear. This is the **emergent strategy** approach where strategic analysis, strategic development and strategy implementation are interrelated. Lynch (2000) does point out, however, that strategic analysis can be regarded as distinctive and usually occurs before strategy development and implementation. Johnson and Scholes (1999) seek to highlight the emergent strategy approach. It can be suggested that the emergent strategy approach is an essential part of any e-business strategy to enable response in a highly dynamic environment.

Kalakota and Robinson (2000) recommend a dynamic emergent strategy process specific to e-business. The elements of this approach are shown in *Figure 5.5* (*page 211*). It essentially shares similar features to *Figure 5.4*, but with an emphasis on responsiveness with continuous review and prioritization of investment in new applications.

We will now examine each of the main strategy elements of *Figure 5.4* in more detail.

Strategic analysis

Strategic analysis
Collection and review of information about an organization's internal processes and resources and external marketplace factors in order to inform strategy definition.

Strategic analysis or situation analysis involves review of:

- the internal resources and processes of the company to assess its e-business capabilities and results to date in the context of a review of its activity in the marketplace;
- the immediate competitive environment (micro-environment), including customer demand and behaviour, competitor activity, marketplace structure and relationships with suppliers and partners;
- the wider environment (macro-environment) in which a company operates; this includes economic development and regulation by governments in the forms of law and taxes together with social and ethical constraints such as the demand for privacy. These macro-environment factors, including the social, legal, economic and political factors, were reviewed in *Chapter 4* and are not considered further in this chapter.

The elements of situation analysis for an e-business are summarized in *Figure 5.6*. For the effective, responsive e-business, as explained earlier, it is essential that situation analysis or environmental scanning be a continuous process with clearly identified responsibilities for performing the scanning and acting on the knowledge acquired.

In this section we start with the internal perspective of how a company currently uses technology and then we review the competitive environment.

Resource and process analysis

Resource analysis
Review of the technological, financial and human resources of an organization and how they are utilized in business processes.

Resource analysis for e-business is primarily concerned with its e-business capabilities, i.e. the degree to which a company has in place the appropriate *technological and applications infrastructure* and financial and human resources to support it. These resources must be harnessed together to give efficient *business processes*. We start by looking at current resources for e-business by looking at the stage of e-business development.

Stage models of e-business development

Stage models are helpful in reviewing how advanced a company is in its use of information and communications technology (ICT) to support its processes. Stage models have traditionally been popular in the analysis of the current application of business information systems (BIS) within an organization. For example, the six-stage model

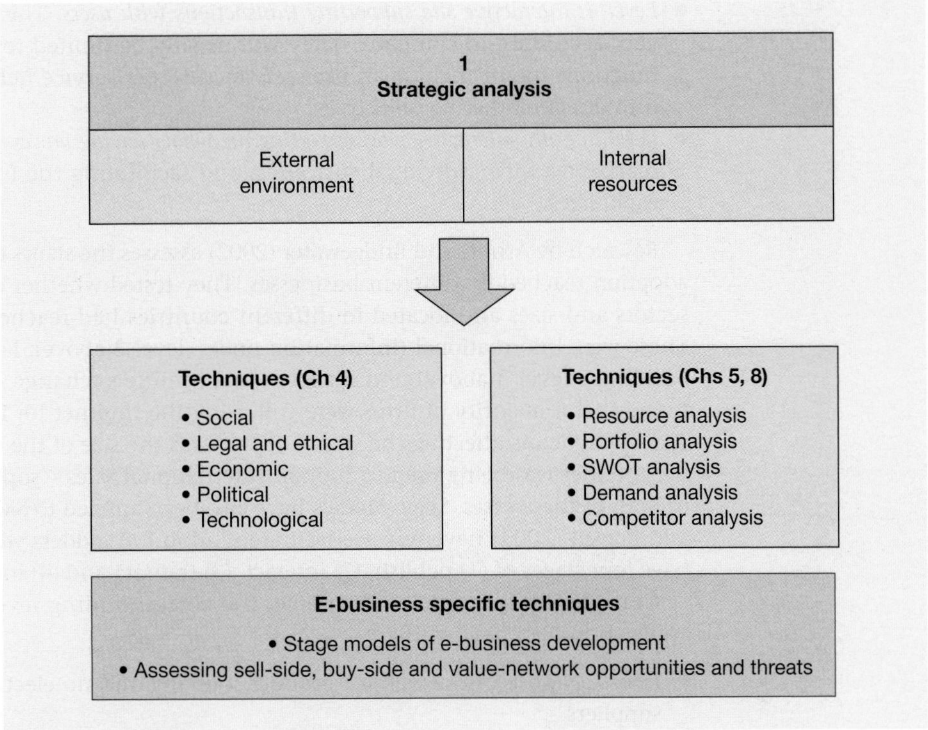

Figure 5.6 Elements of strategic situation analysis for the e-business

of Nolan (1979) refers to the development of use of information systems within an organization from initiation with simple data processing through to a mature adoption of BIS with controlled, integrated systems.

When assessing the current use of ICT within a company it is instructive to analyse the extent to which an organization has implemented the technological infrastructure and support structure to achieve e-business. In an early model focusing on sell-side web site development, Quelch and Klein (1996) developed a five-stage model referring to the development of sell-side e-commerce. For existing companies the stages are:

1 Image and product information
2 Information collection
3 Customer support and service
4 Internal support and service
5 Transactions.

Considering sell-side e-commerce, Chaffey *et al.* (2006) suggest there are six choices for a company deciding on which *marketing services* to offer via an online presence:

- *Level 0: No web site or presence on web.*
- *Level 1: Basic web presence.* Company places an entry in a web site, listing company names such as www.yell.co.uk to make people searching the web aware of the existence of the company or its products. There is no web site at this stage.
- *Level 2: Simple static informational web site.* Contains basic company and product information, sometimes referred to as 'brochureware'.
- *Level 3: Simple interactive site.* Users are able to search the site and make queries to retrieve information such as product availability and pricing. Queries by e-mail may also be supported.

- *Level 4: Interactive site supporting transactions with users.* The functions offered will vary according to company. They will usually be limited to online buying. Other functions might include an interactive customer service helpdesk which is linked into direct marketing objectives.
- *Level 5. Fully interactive site supporting the whole buying process.* Provides relationship marketing with individual customers and facilitating the full range of marketing exchanges.

Research by Arnott and Bridgewater (2002) assesses the stages of sell-side e-commerce adoption reached by different businesses. They tested whether companies of different sectors and sizes and located in different countries had reached one of three stages. These were informational (information only – level 2 above), facilitating (relationship building – level 3 above) and transactional (online exchange – level 4 above). They found that a majority of firms were still using the Internet for information provision. The main factors affecting the stage adopted was the size of the company and whether the Internet was being used to support international sales – sophistication was greater in both of these cases. Stage models have also been applied to SME businesses and Levy and Powell (2003) have reviewed different adoption ladders which broadly speaking have four stages of (1) publish, (2) interact, (3) transact and (4) integrate.

Considering buy-side e-commerce, the corresponding levels of *product sourcing* applications can be identified:

- *Level I.* No use of the web for product sourcing and no electronic integration with suppliers.
- *Level II.* Review and selection from competing suppliers using intermediary web sites, B2B exchanges and supplier web sites. Orders placed by conventional means.
- *Level III.* Orders placed electronically through EDI, via intermediary sites, exchanges or supplier sites. No integration between organization's systems and supplier's systems. Rekeying of orders necessary into procurement or accounting systems.
- *Level IV.* Orders placed electronically with integration of company's procurement systems.
- *Level V.* Orders placed electronically with full integration of company's procurement, manufacturing requirements planning and stock control systems.

In *Chapter 6, (p. 269)*, the case of BHP Steel is an illustration of such a stage model.

A staged model which focuses on these buy-side applications of e-commerce is shown in *Table 5.2*. The DTI likens the process of adoption to moving up the steps of a ladder. Companies start off using e-mail to communicate internally and with suppliers (step 1), before moving to offering product information and availability checking (step 2), online ordering (step 3), online payment (step 4), online progress tracking (step 5) and, finally, when the e-business is achieved, all stages are integrated (step 6).

We should remember that typical stage models of web-site development such as those described above are most appropriate to companies whose products can be sold online through transactional e-commerce. In fact, stage models could be developed for a range of different types of online presence and business models each with different objectives. In *Chapter 1*, in the section *'What is the difference between e-commerce and e-business?'*, we identified the four major different types of online presence for marketing: 1. transactional e-commerce site, 2. services-oriented relationship-building web site, 3. brand-building site and 4. portal or media site. A stage model for increasing sophistication in each of these areas can be defined. As a summary to this section *Table 5.2* presents a synthesis of stage models for e-business development. Organizations can assess their position on the continuum between stages 1 and 4 for the different aspects of e-business development shown in the column on the left.

Table 5.2 **A stage model for e-business development**

	1 Web presence	*2 E-commerce*	*3 Integrated e-commerce*	*4 E-business*
Services available	Brochureware or interaction with product catalogues and customer service	Transactional e-commerce on buy-side or sell-side	Buy- and sell-side integrated with enterprise resource planning (ERP) or legacy systems. Personalization of services	Full integration between all internal organizational processes and elements of the value network
Organizational scope	Isolated departments, e.g. marketing department	Cross-organizational	Cross-organizational	Across the enterprise and beyond ('extraprise')
Transformation	Technological infrastructure	Technology and new responsibilities identified for e-commerce	Internal business processes and company structure	Change to e-business culture, linking of business processes with partners
Strategy	Limited	Sell-side e-commerce strategy, not well integrated with business strategy	E-commerce strategy integrated with business strategy using a value-chain approach	E-business strategy incorporated as part of business strategy

When companies devise the strategies and tactics to achieve their objectives they may return to the stage models to specify which level of innovation they are looking to achieve in the future.

Applications portfolio analysis

Analysis of the current portfolio of business applications within a business is used to assess current information systems capability and also to inform future strategies. A widely applied framework is that of McFarlan and McKenney (1993) with the modifications of Ward and Griffiths (1996). *Figure 5.7* illustrates the results of a portfolio analysis for The B2B Company applied within an e-business context. It can be seen that current applications such as human resources, financial management and production-line management systems will continue to support the operations of the business and will not be a priority for future investment. In contrast, to achieve competitive advantage, applications for maintaining a dynamic customer catalogue online, online sales and collecting marketing intelligence about customer buying behaviour will become more important. Applications such as procurement and logistics will continue to be of importance in an e-business context. Of course, the analysis will differ greatly according to the type of company; for a professional services company or a software company, its staff will be an important resource, hence systems that facilitate the acquisition and retention of quality staff will be strategic applications.

Portfolio analysis is also often used to select the most appropriate future Internet projects. It is applied in this way in the *strategy definition* section: *Decision 1: E-business priorities*.

A weakness of the portfolio analysis approach is that today applications are delivered by a single e-business software or *enterprise resource planning* application. Given this, it is perhaps more appropriate to define the services that will be delivered to external and internal customers through deploying information systems.

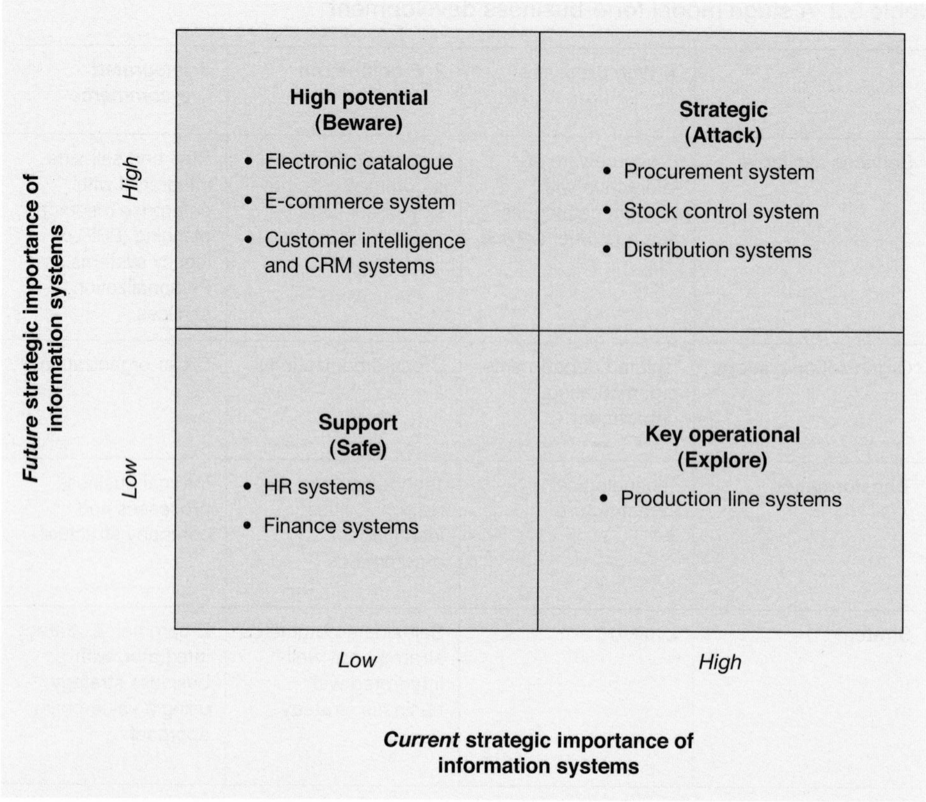

Figure 5.7 **Summary applications of a portfolio analysis for The B2B Company**

In addition to portfolio analysis, organizations should also review the capability of their *technology infrastructure* such as hardware and networking facilities to deliver these applications.

Organizational and IS SWOT analysis

SWOT analysis
Strengths, weaknesses, opportunities and threats.

SWOT analysis is a relatively simple yet powerful tool that can help organizations analyse their internal resources in terms of strengths and weaknesses and match them against the external environment in terms of opportunities and threats. In an e-business context, a SWOT analysis of e-business-specific issues can combine SWOT related to corporate, marketing, supply chain and information systems, or a separate SWOT can be performed for each. SWOT analysis is of greatest value when it is used not only to analyse the current situation, but also as a tool to formulate strategies. To achieve this it is useful once the strengths, weaknesses, opportunities and threats have been listed to combine them as shown in *Figure 5.8*, which shows an example SWOT analysis for The B2B Company. The approaches such as mini–maxi are read in order of approach to external factors and then approach to internal factors. So 'mini–maxi' means minimize external factors, maximize internal factors. It can be suggested that the mini–mini and mini–maxi sectors should be paid greatest attention since these are the key deficiencies of the company. *Activity 5.2* examines how the analyses summarized in *Figures 5.7* and *5.8* could inform strategy for The B2B Company.

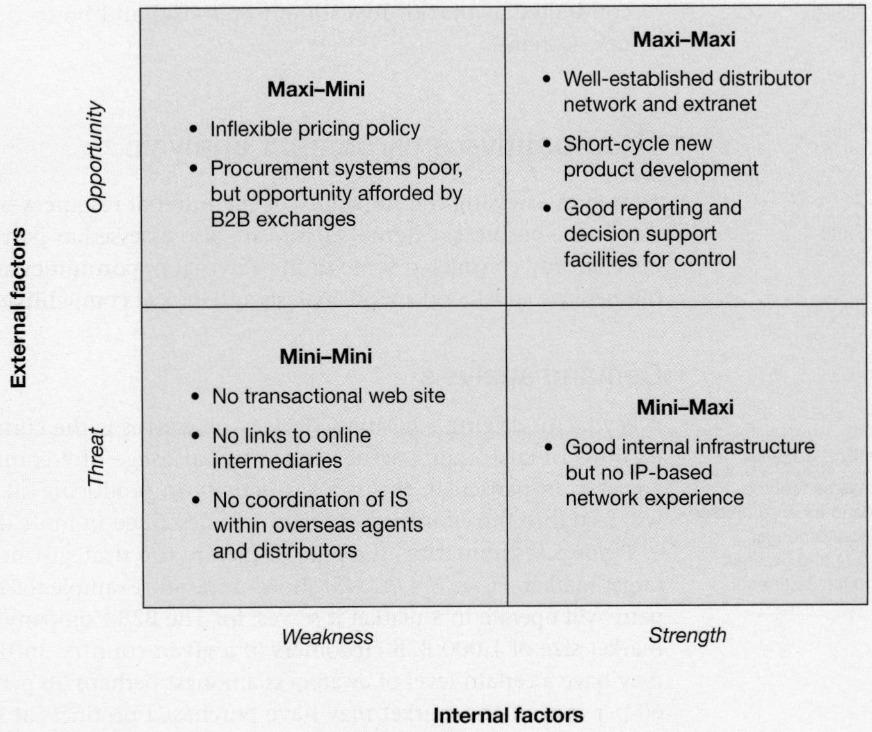

Figure 5.8 **SWOT analysis for The B2B Company**

Activity 5.2 Using portfolio and SWOT analysis to inform e-business strategy at The B2B Company

Purpose

Figure 5.7 and *Figure 5.8* can be used to identify priorities for deploying resources from a limited budget for e-business and to avoid errors resulting from a 'big-bang approach' where different applications are implemented simultaneously.

Activity

Review the two figures and suggest which e-business applications in *Figure 5.7* and *Figure 5.8* are most appropriate on a scale from P1 (high priority for immediate implementation) to P3 (of strategic significance, but not requiring immediate implementation).

Answers to activities can be found at www.pearsoned.co.uk/chaffey

Human and financial resources

Resource analysis will also consider these two factors:

1 *Human resources*. To take advantage of the opportunities identified in strategic analysis the right resources must be available to deliver e-business solutions. The importance of having a human resources approach that enables the recruitment and retention of staff is examined in *Chapter 10, 'Change management'*. The need for new structures and cultures to achieve e-business is also covered.

2 *Financial resources.* Assessing financial resources for information systems is usually conducted as part of investment appraisal and budgeting for enhancements to new systems.

Competitive environment analysis

As well as assessing the suitability of the internal resources of an organization for the move to e-business, external factors are also assessed as part of strategic analysis. We have already considered some of the external opportunities and threats for a business, but here we consider demand analysis and look at competitive threats in more detail.

Demand analysis

Demand analysis
Assessment of the demand for e-commerce services amongst existing and potential customer segments.

A key factor driving e-business strategy objectives is the current level and future projections of customer, partner and internal usage of e-commerce services, **demand analysis**. In particular, this is a key activity in producing an e-marketing plan which will feed into the e-business strategy. It is described in more detail in *Chapter 8*.

Figure 5.9 summarizes the type of picture the strategist needs to build up for each target market. *Figure 8.4 (p. 345)* shows a specific example for the car market. Any company will operate in a market it serves: for The B2B Company there may be a potential market size of 1,000 B2B customers in a given country. In this market the company may have a certain level of awareness amongst perhaps 80 per cent of the marketplace, 60 per cent of the market may have purchased products at some point, and current market share (by customers) may be 30 per cent. This demand for products then needs to be considered relative to the number of companies that have Internet access and particular employees who are actively using the web for e-commerce.

For buy-side e-commerce a company also needs to consider the e-commerce services its suppliers offer: how many offer services for e-commerce and where they are located (e.g. direct with suppliers, in customer solutions or marketplaces – *Chapter 7, p. 325*).

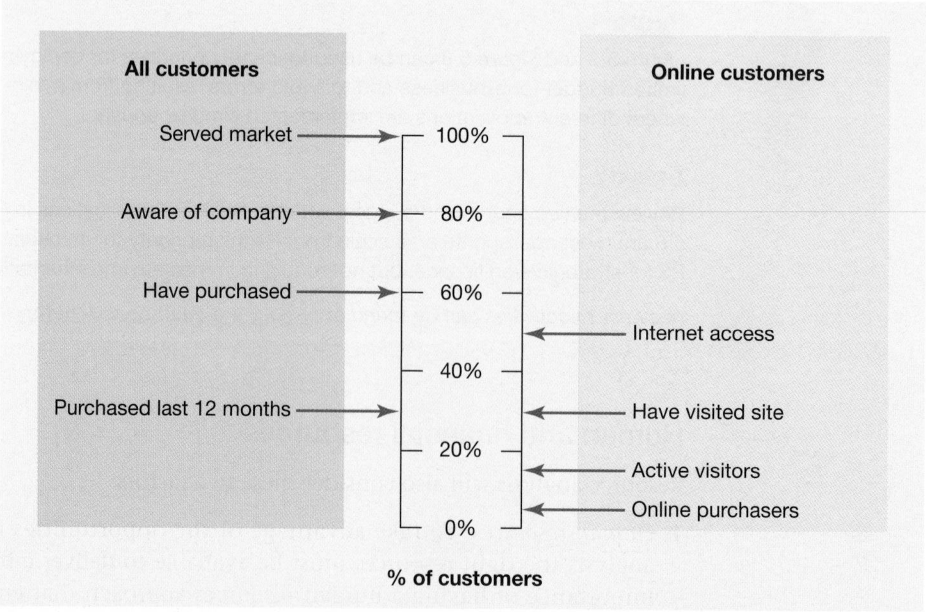

Figure 5.9 Customer demand for e-marketing services for The B2B Company

Assessing competitive threats

Michael Porter's classic 1980 model of the five main competitive forces that affect a company still provides a valid framework for reviewing threats arising in the e-business era. It is instructive to assess how the Internet may change the competitive environment. *Table 5.3* summarizes the impact of the Internet on the five competitive forces. This table is a summary of the analysis by Michael Porter of the impact of the Internet on business using the five forces framework (Porter, 2001).

Table 5.3 **Impact of the Internet on the five competititive forces**

Bargaining power of buyers	*Bargaining power of suppliers*	*Threat of substitute products and services*	*Barriers to entry*	*Rivalry amongst existing competitors*
• The power of online buyers is increased since they have a wider choice and prices are likely to be forced down through increased customer knowledge and price transparency, i.e. switching behaviour is encouraged. • For a B2B organization, forming electronic links with customers may deepen a relationship and it may increase switching costs, leading to 'soft lock-in'.	• When an organization purchases, the bargaining power of its suppliers is reduced since there is wider choice and increased commoditization due to e-procurement and e-marketplaces. • The reverse arguments also apply as for bargaining power of buyers.	• Substitution is a significant threat since new digital products or extended products can be more readily introduced. • The introduction of new substitute products and services should be carefully monitored to avoid erosion of market share. • Internet technology enables faster introduction of products and services. • This threat is related to new business models which are covered in a later section in this chapter.	• Barriers to entry are reduced, enabling new competitors, particularly for retailers or service organizations that have traditionally required a high-street presence or a mobile sales force. • New entrants must be carefully monitored to avoid erosion of market share. • Internet services are easier to imitate than traditional services, making it easy for 'fast followers'.	• The Internet encourages commoditization which makes it less easy to differentiate products. • Rivalry becomes more intense as product lifecycles shorten and lead times for new product development decrease. • The Internet facilitates the move to the global market, increasing the number of competitors.

Placed in an e-business context, *Figure 5.10* shows the main threats updated to place emphasis on the competitive threats to the e-business. Threats have been grouped into buy-side (upstream supply chain), sell-side (downstream supply chain) and competitive threats. The main difference from the five forces model of Porter (1980) is the distinction between competitive threats from intermediaries (or partners) on the buy-side and sell-side. We will now review these e-business threats in more detail.

Competitive threats

1 Threat of new e-commerce entrants

For traditional 'bricks and mortar' companies (*Chapter 2, p. 67*) this has been a common threat for retailers selling products such as books and financial services. For example, in Europe, traditional banks have been threatened by the entry of completely new start-up competitors such as First-e (www.first-e.com, which did not prove to be a viable business) or traditional companies from a different geographic market that use the Internet to facilitate their entry into an overseas market. Citibank (www.citibank.com, which successfully operates in the UK, has used this approach. ING, another existing financial services group, formed in 1991 and based in the Netherlands, has also used the Internet to facilitate market development. In May 2003, ING (www.ing.com) launched the online bank ING Direct in the UK (www.ingdirect.co.uk). Since its launch in 1997 ING Direct has gained over 10 million customers worldwide through its online banking operations in the USA, France, Italy, Germany, Spain, Australia and Canada. These new entrants have been able to succeed in a short time since they do not have the cost of developing and maintaining a distribution network to sell their products and these products do not require a manufacturing base. In other words, the *barriers to entry* are low. However, to succeed, new entrants need to be market leaders in executing marketing and customer service. The costs of achieving these will be high. These could perhaps be described as *barriers to success* rather than barriers to entry. This competitive threat is less common in vertical business-to-business markets involving manufacture and process industries such as the chemical or oil industry since the investment barriers to entry are much higher.

2 Threat of new digital products

This threat can occur from established or new companies. The Internet is particularly good as a means of providing information-based services at a lower cost. The greatest threats are likely to occur where digital product fulfilment can occur over the Internet, as is the case with delivering share prices, digital media content or software. This may not affect many business sectors, but is vital in some such as newspaper, magazine and book publishing, and music and software distribution. In photography, Kodak has responded to a major threat of reduced demand for traditional film by increasing its range of digital cameras to enhance this revenue stream and by providing online services for customers to print and share digital photographs. The extent of this threat can be gauged by a review of product in the context of *Figure 5.10*.

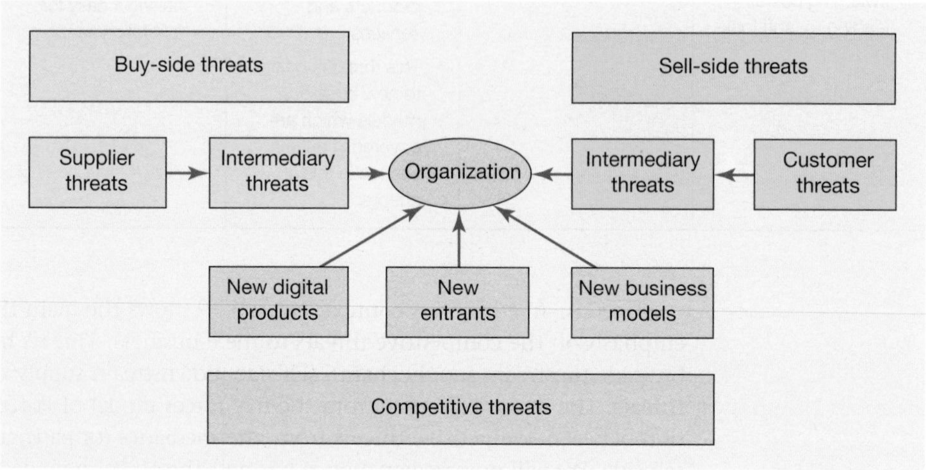

Figure 5.10 **Competitive threats acting on the e-business**

3 Threat of new business models

This threat can also occur from established or new companies. It is related to the competitive threat in that it concerns new methods of service delivery. The threats from existing competitors will continue, with the Internet perhaps increasing rivalry since price comparison is more readily possible and the rival e-businesses can innovate and undertake new product development and introduce alternative business and revenue models with shorter cycle times than previously. This again emphasizes the need for continual environment scanning. See the section on business and revenue models in *Chapter 2* for examples of strategies that can be adopted in response to this threat.

Sell-side threats

1 Customer power and knowledge

This is perhaps the single biggest threat posed by electronic trading. The bargaining power of customers is greatly increased when they are using the Internet to evaluate products and compare prices. This is particularly true for standardized products for which offers can be compared for different suppliers through price comparison engines provided by intermediaries such as Kelkoo (www.kelkoo.com) or PriceRunner (www.pricerunner.com). For commodities, auctions on business-to-business exchanges can also have a similar effect of driving down price. Purchase of some products that have not traditionally been thought of as commodities may become more price-sensitive. This process is known as 'commoditization'. Examples of goods that are becoming commoditized are electrical goods and cars. The issue of online pricing is discussed in *Chapter 8*.

Commoditization
The process whereby product selection becomes more dependent on price than differentiating features, benefits and value-added services.

Soft lock-in
Electronic linkages between supplier and customer increase switching costs.

In the business-to-business arena, a further issue is that the ease of use of the Internet channel makes it potentially easier for customers to swap between suppliers – switching costs are lower. With the Internet, which offers a more standard method for purchase through web browsers, the barriers to swapping to another supplier will be lower. With a specific EDI (electronic data interchange) link that has to be set up between one company and another, there may be reluctance to change this arrangement (soft lock-in due to switching costs). Commentators often glibly say 'online, your competitor is only a mouse click away', but it should be remembered that soft lock-in still exists on the web – there are still barriers and costs to switching between suppliers since once a customer has invested time in understanding how to use a web site to select and purchase a particular type of products, they may not want to learn another service.

2 Power of intermediaries

A significant downstream channel threat is the potential loss of partners or distributors if there is a channel conflict resulting from *disintermediation* (*Chapter 2, p. 45*). For example, a car distributor could switch to an alternative manufacturer if its profitability were threatened by direct sales from the manufacturer. *The Economist* (2000) reported that to avoid this type of conflict, Ford US is now using dealerships as part of the e-commerce solution and is still paying commission when sales are achieved online. This also helps protect their revenue from the lucrative parts and services market.

An additional downstream threat is the growth in number of intermediaries (another form of partners) to link buyers and sellers. These include consumer portals such as Bizrate (www.bizrate.com) and business-to-business exchanges such as EC21 (www.ec21.com). This threat links to the rivalry between competitors. If a company's competitors are represented on a portal while the company is absent or, worse still, they are in an exclusive arrangement with a competitor, then this can potentially exclude a substantial proportion of the market. For example, in the billion-dollar market involved in the verification of consumer products and business shipments such as oil, chemicals and grain, Integrated Testing Services (www.itsgroup.com) found that its main rival, the Swiss SGS Group (Société Générale de Surveillance, www.sgsgroup.com) had signed an exclusive arrangement for verification of cars on the Carbuster site. Despite its vintage, SGS has proved adaptable to the new trading environment and has set up its own verification portal (SGS Online certification, www.sgsonline.com) which offers a Gold Seal 'kitemark' that is indicative of 'an extremely good likelihood that sellers so rated would satisfy their buyers' requirements on pre-defined aspects of quality, quantity or delivery'. This is an example of countering new intermediaries, sometimes referred to as a 'countermediation strategy'. Through seizing opportunities SGS has pre-empted threats from existing competitors such as ITS and start-ups such as UK-based Clicksure.

Buy-side threats

1. Power of suppliers

This can be considered as an opportunity rather than a threat. Companies can insist, for reasons of reducing cost and increasing supply chain efficiency, that their suppliers use electronic links such as EDI or Internet EDI to process orders. Additionally, the Internet tends to reduce the power of suppliers since barriers to migrating to a different supplier are reduced, particularly with the advent of *business-to-business exchanges*. However, if suppliers insist on proprietary technology to link companies, then this creates 'soft lock-in' due to the cost or complexity of changing suppppliers.

2. Power of intermediaries

Threats from buy-side intermediaries such as business-to-business exchanges are arguably less than those from sell-side intermediaries, but risks arising from using these services should be considered. These include the cost of integration with such intermediaries, particularly if different standards of integration are required for each. They may pose a threat from increasing commission once they are established.

From the review above, it should be apparent that the extent of the threats will be dependent on the particular market a company operates in. Generally the threats seem to be greatest for companies that currently sell through retail distributors and have products that can be readily delivered to customers across the Internet or by parcel. *Case Study 5.1* highlights how one company has analysed its competitive threats and developed an appropriate strategy.

Competitor analysis

Competitor analysis for e-business
Review of e-business services offered by existing and new competitors and adoption by their customers.

Competitor analysis is also a key aspect of e-business situation analysis, but since it is also a key activity in producing an e-marketing plan which will feed into the e-business strategy this is also described in more detail in *Chapter 8*.

Resource-advantage mapping

Core competencies
Resources, including skills or technologies, that provide a particular benefit to customers.

Customer value
Value dependent on product quality, service quality, price and fulfilment time.

Once the external opportunities and internal resources have been reviewed, it is useful to map the internal resource strengths against external opportunities, to identify, for example, where competitors are weak and can be attacked. To identify internal strengths, definition of core competencies is one approach. Lynch (2000) explains that core competencies are the resources, including knowledge, skills or technologies that provide a particular benefit to customers, or increase customer value relative to competitors. Customer value is defined by Deise *et al.* (2000) as dependent on product quality, service quality, price and fulfilment time. So, to understand core competencies we need to understand how the organization is differentiated from competitors in these areas. Benchmarking e-commerce services of competitors, as described in *Chapter 8*, is important here. The cost-base of a company relative to its competitors' is also important since lower production costs will lead to lower prices. Lynch (2000) argues that core competencies should be emphasized in objective setting and strategy definition.

Strategic objectives

Strategic objectives
Statement and communication of an organization's mission, vision and objectives.

Defining and communicating an organization's **strategic objectives** is a key element of any strategy process model since (1) the strategy definition and implementation elements of strategy must be directed at how best to achieve the objectives and (2) the overall success of e-business strategy will be assessed by comparing actual results against objectives and taking action to improve strategy. (3) Clear, realistic objectives help communicate the goals and significance of an e-business initiative to employees and partners. Note that objective setting typically takes place in parallel with strategic analysis, defining a vision and strategy for e-business as part of an iterative process.

Figure 5.11 highlights some of the key aspects of strategic objective setting that will be covered in this section.

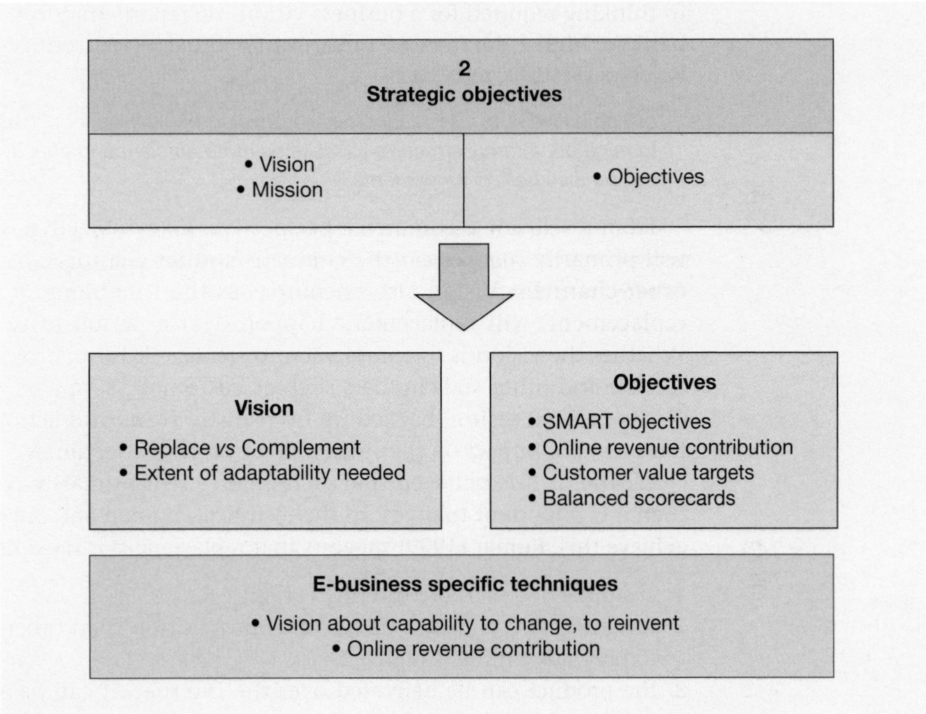

Figure 5.11 **Elements of strategic objective setting for the e-business**

Defining vision and mission

Corporate vision is defined in Lynch (2000) as 'a mental image of the possible and desirable future state of the organization'. It provides a backdrop for the development of purpose and strategy of the organization. Defining company vision in the context of e-business will be based on managers' view of the future relevance of the Internet to their industry. **Scenario-based analysis** is a useful approach to discussing alternative visions of the future prior to objective setting. Lynch (2000) explains that scenario-based analysis is concerned with possible models of the future of an organization's environment. He says:

Scenario-based analysis
Models of the future environment are developed from different starting points.

> *The aim is not to predict, but to explore a set of possibilities; scenarios take different situations with different starting points.*

He distinguishes qualitative scenario-based planning from quantitative prediction based on demand analysis, for example. In an e-business perspective, scenarios that could be explored include:

1 One player in our industry becomes dominant through use of the Internet ('Amazoning' the sector).
2 Major customers do not adopt e-commerce due to organizational barriers.
3 Major disintermediation (*Chapter 2*) occurs in our industry.
4 B2B marketplaces do or do not become dominant in our industry.
5 New entrants or substitute products change our industry.

Through performing this type of analysis, better understanding of the drivers for different views of the future will result, new strategies can be generated and strategic risks can be assessed. It is clear that the scenarios above will differ between worst-case and best-case scenarios.

Simons (2000a), in referring to the vision of Barclays Bank, illustrates the change in thinking required for e-business vision. He reports that to execute the vision of the bank 'a high tolerance of uncertainty' must be introduced. The group CEO of Barclays (Matt Barrett) said:

> *our objective is to use technology to develop entirely new business models ... while transforming our internal structure to make us more efficient and effective. Any strategy that does not achieve both is fundamentally flawed.*

From a sell-side e-commerce perspective, a key objective is whether the Internet will primarily *complement* the company's other channels or whether it will *replace* other channels. Vision also encompasses the timeframe or the rate of change of replacement: will replacement happen over a period of two years or ten years? Whether the vision is to complement or replace it is important to communicate this to staff and other stakeholders such as customers, suppliers and shareholders. The clarity of such vision, backed up by realistic plans and actions has been shown to have a major impact on the stock market value of companies.

Clearly, if it is believed that e-commerce will primarily replace other channels, then it is important to invest in the technical, human and organizational resources to achieve this. Kumar (1999) suggests that replacement is most likely to happen when:

1 customer access to the Internet is high;
2 the Internet can offer a better value proposition than other media (i.e. propensity to purchase online is high);
3 the product can be delivered over the Internet (it can be argued that this is not essential for replacement);
4 the product can be standardized (user does not usually need to view to purchase).

If at least two of Kumar's conditions are met there may be a replacement effect. For example, purchase of travel services or insurance online fulfils criteria 1, 2 and 4. As a consequence, physical outlets for these products may no longer be viable since the service can be provided in a cheaper, more convenient form online. The closure of British Airways travel retail units and AA shops is indicative of this change, with the business being delivered completely by phone or online sales channel. The extent to which these conditions are met will vary through time, for example as access to the Internet and propensity to purchase online increase. A similar test is de Kare-Silver's (2000) *Electronic Shopping Test* (*Chapter 8, p. 354*).

A similar vision of the future can be developed for buy-side activities such as procurement. A company can have a vision for how e-procurement and e-enabled supply chain management (SCM) will complement or replace paper-based procurement and SCM over a future time period.

How can e-business create business value?

As Chaffey and Wood (2004) have emphasized, much of the organizational value created by e-business is due to more effective use of information. The strategic importance of business information management in an organization can be reviewed and communicated as part of vision using *Figure 5.12*. This analytic tool, devised by Professor Don Marchand, shows different ways in which information can create value for organizations.

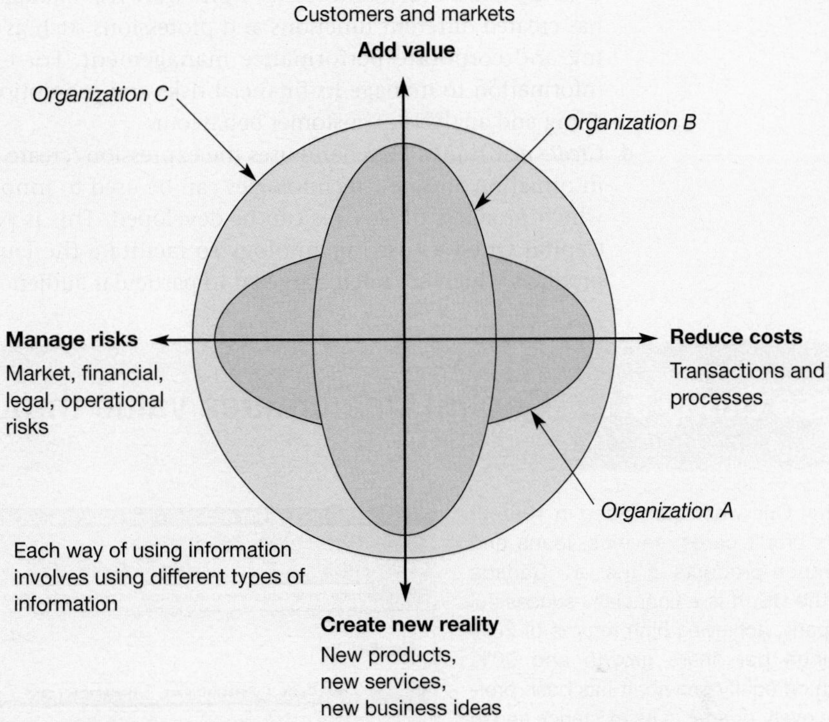

Figure 5.12 **An evaluation tool relating information to business value. An organization's use of information on each axis can be assessed from 1 (low use of information) to 10 (high use of information)**

Source: Marchand *et al*. eds (1999)

The main methods are:

1 *Adding value*. Value is added through providing better-quality products and services to an organization's customers. Information can be used to better understand customer characteristics, needs and their level of satisfaction with services. Information is also used to sense and respond to markets. Information about trends in demands, competitor products and activities must be monitored so organizations can develop strategies to compete in the marketplace. For example, all organizations will use databases to store personal characteristics of customers and details of their transaction history which shows when they have purchased different products, responded to marketing campaigns or used different online services. Analysis of these databases using data mining can then be used to understand customer preferences and market products that better meet their needs. Companies can use sense and respond communications. The classic example of this is the personalization facilities provided by Amazon where personal recommendations are provided.

Sense and respond communications
Organizations use technology to monitor consumers' preferences indicated by their responses to web sites or e-mail communications in order to target them with relevant, peronalized and targeted communications.

2 *Reduce costs*. Cost reduction through information is achieved through making the business processes shown in *Figure 5.10* more efficient. Efficiency is achieved through using information to source, create, market and deliver services using fewer resources than previously. Technology is applied to reduce paperwork, reduce the human resources needed to operate the processes through automation and improve internal and external communications. Capital One (*Case Study 5.1*) has used Internet technology so that customers can apply for and service their credit cards online – the concept of 'web self-service'.

3 *Manage risks*. Risk management is a well-established use of information within organizations. Marchand (1999) notes how risk management within organizations has created different functions and professions such as finance, accounting, auditing and corporate performance management. For example, Capital One uses information to manage its financial risks and promotions through extensive modelling and analysis of customer behaviour.

4 *Create new reality*. Marchand uses the expression 'create new reality' to refer to how information and new technologies can be used to innovate, to create new ways in which products or services can be developed. This is particular apt for e-business. Capital One has used technology to facilitate the launch of flexible new credit products which are micro-targeted to particular audiences.

Case Study 5.1 Capital One creates value through e-business

Capital One was established in 1995. It offers credit cards, savings, loans and insurance products in the UK, Canada and the US. It is a financially successful company, achieving high returns of 20% earnings per share growth and 20% return on equity growth. It has been profitable every quarter in its existence and in less than ten years it achieved net income of over $1 billion.

Capital One uses what it calls an Information-Based Strategy (IBS), which brings marketing, credit, risk, operations, and IT together to enable flexible decision making. It describes IBS as 'a rigorously scientific test-and-learn methodology that has enabled us to excel at product innovation, marketing and risk management – the essentials of success in consumer financial services'. For customers it aims to offer financial solutions tailored to individual customers' needs. It does this through mass-customization: offering different rates and fees structures to different customers depending on their risk status. Its mission can be summarized as to deliver the right product, at the right price, to the right customer, at the right time through continual testing, learning and innovation.

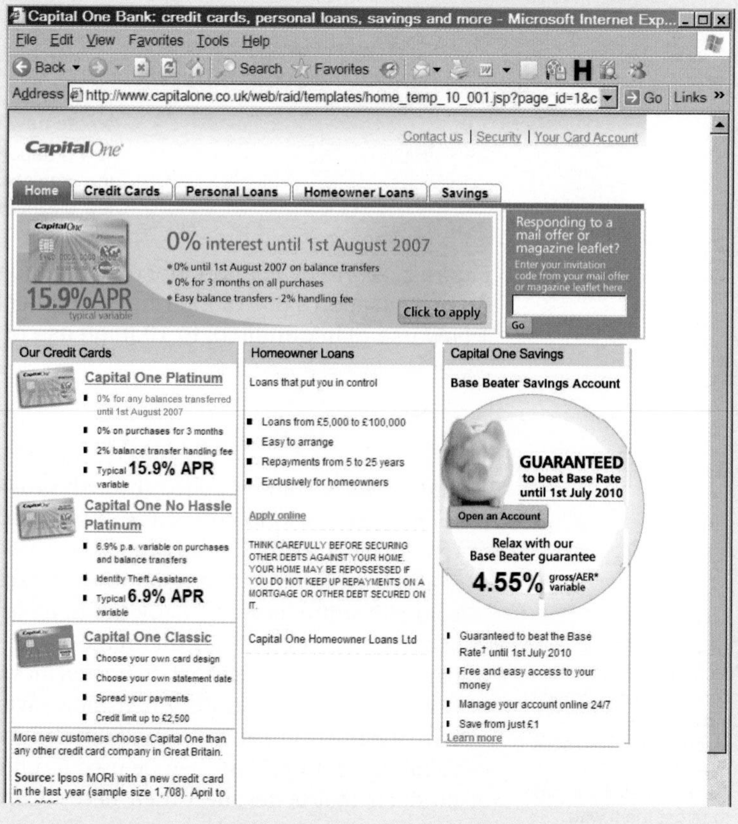

Figure 5.13 **Capital One web site (www.capitalone.co.uk)**

The scale of use of information is indicated by different operations in the business. In corresponding with customers, *The Banker* reported that Capital One sends out one billion items of mail per year and handles 90 million inbound calls, 300 million outbound calls, 230 million Internet impressions and 40 million transactions per day. Together with its subsidiaries, the company had 45.8 million managed accounts and $60.7bn in managed loans outstanding as of June 2003.

The information-based strategy is managed by the Chief Information Officer, Gregor Bailar. He is in charge of operations related to computer systems, analysis of customer data, data protection, setting data standards, business continuity and information security.

According to *The Banker*, Gregor says:

CIOs today need to be technology alchemists. They need to be strong in professional technical methodologies so that their conversation is a disciplined one but, at the same time, they need to understand the business, be it banking, credit cards or loans.

Their job is not to know the future of technology, nor the latest and greatest of delivery networks, but to be focused on balancing the set of business needs, and choosing or creating the best possible solutions that can be provided from a technical perspective.

On the one hand, the CIO has to be an advocate for the business into the technology world, and on the other hand, the voice of technology in the best respect of how it can respond to the business. This is a relatively new role and the challenge is to interpret and prioritise correctly the business needs and make the technology systems really responsive.

The CIO is expected to be involved not only in strategy development, but also in business and product innovation. Now, more than ever, CIOs are being held accountable for driving the business value, not just for keeping the lights blinking on the computers.

Capital One uses their web site (*Figure 5.13*) both as a tool to acquire new customers and to service existing customers

Source: Based on company annual reports and an article in *The Banker* (2003). Reproduced by permission of Captial One Bank (Europe) plc.

Question

Explain with reference to *Figure 5.13* how Capital One has achieved competitive advantage through creating value through e-business.

Objective setting

The relationship between objectives, strategies and performance measures is illustrated by the e-business strategic plan for The B2B Company in *Table 5.4*. Each of the performance indicators should also have a timeframe in which to achieve these objectives. Despite the

Table 5.4 **Objectives, strategies and performance indicators for The B2B Company (in order of priority)**

Objectives	*Strategies to achieve goals*	*Key performance indicators (critical success factors)*
1 Develop revenue from new geographical markets	1 Create e-commerce facility for standard products and assign agents to these markets	1 Achieve combined revenue of £1m by year-end online revenue contribution of 70%
2 Increase revenue from smaller-scale purchases from retailers	2 Create e-commerce facility for standard products	2 Increase sales through retailers from 15% to 25% of total by year 2 Online revenue contribution of 30%
3 Ensure retention of key account customers	3 Attain soft lock-in by developing extranet facilities and continued support from sales reps	3 Retain five key account customers. Online revenue contribution of 100% from these five
4 Improve efficiency of sourcing raw materials	4 Develop e-procurement system	4 Reduce cost of procurement by 5% by year-end, 10% by year 2 Achieve 80% of puchasing online
5 Reduce time to market and costs for new product development	5 Use collaboration and project management tools	5 Reduce cost and time to market by average of 10% by year 3
6 Protect and increase efficiency of distributor and partner network	6 Create partner extranet and aim for paperless support	6 Reduce cost of sales in each of five main geographical markets by 30%

dynamism of e-business, some of the goals that require processes to be re-engineered cannot be achieved immediately. Prioritization of objectives, in this case from 1 to 6, can help in communicating the e-business vision to staff and also when allocating resources to achieve the strategy. Objectives should be *SMART* and should include both efficiency and effectiveness measures. Put simply, efficiency is 'doing the thing right' – it defines whether processes are completed using the least resources and in the shortest time possible. Effectiveness is 'doing the right thing'. 'Doing the right thing' means conducting the right activities and applying the best strategies for competitive advantage. From a process viewpoint it is producing the required outputs and outcomes, in other words meeting objectives. When organizations set goals for e-business and e-commerce, there is a tendency to focus on the efficiency metrics such as time to complete a process and reducing costs. Such measures often do not capture the overall value that can be derived from e-business. Effectiveness measures will assess how many customers or partners are using the e-business services and the incremental benefits that contribute to profitability. For example, an airline such as BA.com could use its e-channel services to reduce costs (increased efficiency), but could be facing a declining share of online bookers (decreased effectiveness). Effectiveness may also refer to the relative importance of objectives for revenue generation through online sales and improving internal process or supply chain efficiency. It may be more effective to focus on the latter.

Efficiency
Minimizing resources or time needed to complete a process: 'Doing the thing right'.

Effectiveness
Meeting process objectives, delivering the required outputs and outcomes: 'doing the right thing'.

Performance management system
A process used to evaluate and improve the efficiency and effectiveness of an organization and its processes.

As for improving any aspect of business performance, performance management systems are needed to monitor, analyse and refine the performance of an organization. The use of systems such as web analytics in achieving this is covered in *Chapter 12*.

The online revenue contribution

Online or Internet revenue contribution (ORC)
An assessment of the direct or indirect contribution of the Internet to sales, usually expressed as a percentage of overall sales revenue.

By considering the demand analysis, competitor analysis and factors such as those defined by Kumar (1999) an Internet or online revenue contribution (ORC) objective can be set. This key e-business objective states the percentage of company revenue *directly* generated through online transactions. However, for some companies such as B2B service companies, it is unrealistic to expect a high direct online contribution. In this case, an *indirect* online contribution can be stated; this is where the sale is influenced by the online presence but purchase occurs using conventional channels, for example a customer selecting a product on a web site and then phoning to place the order. Online revenue contribution objectives can be specified for different types of products, customer segments and geographic markets. They can also be set for different digital channels such as web, mobile or interactive digital TV.

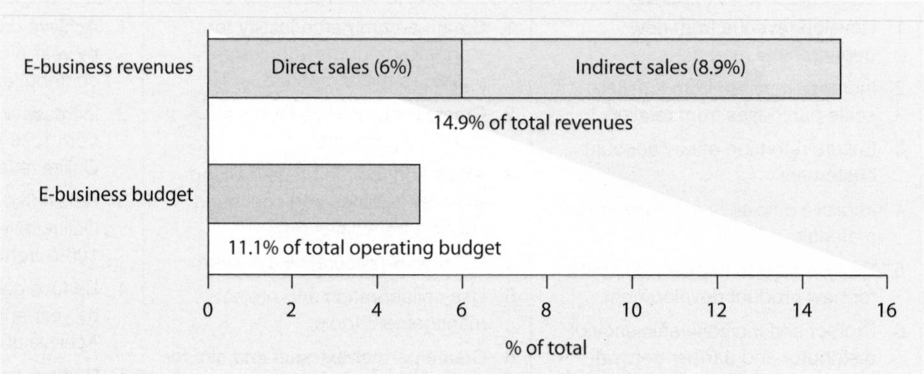

Figure 5.14 Direct and indirect Internet contributions for fast-growth companies in the USA

Source: PricewaterhouseCoopers (2000)

Figure 5.14 shows a historical example of how these objectives can be presented and measured for a company. Here the data were an average across 441 fast-growth US companies with revenues from $1 million to $50 million surveyed by PricewaterhouseCoopers (2000). Owing to the importance of online revenue contributions, this topic is also covered in *Chapter 8, p. 350,* and Figure 8.5 shows how online revenue contributions have to be estimated for the future in order to resource e-business appropriately.

Another important type of high-level contribution objective is the e-channel service contribution. This gives an indication of the proportion of service-type processes that are completed using electronic channels. Examples include e-service (proportion of customers who use web self-service), e-procurement (proportion of different types of purchases bought online) and administrative process facilities used via an intranet or extranet.

E-channel service contribution

The proportion of service-type processes that are completed using electronic channels.

An example of objective setting within a particular company, then at a relatively early stage of adoption, is provided by *Case Study 5.2* and for different industries in *Activity 5.3*.

Case Study 5.2 Setting the Internet revenue contribution at Sandvik Steel

Sandvik Steel, a company selling into many international markets provides a good illustration of how Internet revenue contribution can be used to set objectives for different geographical markets.

When dotcom mania was at its height, so-called old economy companies, such as Sweden's Sandvik, tended to be overshadowed as the brash new online stars took the limelight.

But now that the collapse of internet and other technology stocks has injected a harsh dose of reality into the stock market and business scene, many established names are back in favour again.

As the experience of Sandvik, founded in 1862, shows, skilful use of the internet can lead to huge improvements in links with customers and suppliers, bringing considerable cost savings.

Based north of Stockholm in Sandviken, the company's activities seem remote from the virtual world of the internet. It makes cutting tools, specialty steels and mining and construction equipment.

However, the group is a long-time advocate of IT. Its annual IT budget is some SKr1bn.

'We first formulated our IT strategy in 1969', says Clas Ake Hedstrom, the chief executive. 'We didn't foresee the internet.' Only recently, he adds, has IT moved from serving the company to benefiting customers.

Transferring its 30-year-old IT experience to the age of the web requires more than a deep understanding of technology, says Arnfinn Fredriksson, director of internet business development at the group's Coromant tooling business.

'The major challenges are not IT and systems, but 'soft' things such as attitudes, insights and getting people to understand and accept that this is part of their daily work.' This means focusing hard on business needs and cutting through the internet hype.

Sandvik Steel, the specialty steel operation, also goes beyond transactions to find solutions for its customers. Its extranet enables users to obtain worldwide stock information, catalogues and training aids, as well as take part in online discussions.

At both Coromant and Sandvik Steel, e-business activities are mainly directed towards enhancing links with customers. 'Customer value comes when our product is used, not when it is purchased', Mr Fredriksson says.

Thus, Coromant allows customers not only to buy tools over the web but also to design their own products – within parameters set by Coromant – and receive advice on how best to use them.

Choosing the right cutting tools and using them effectively can save around 10 per cent of the total cost of manufactured components. The e-business strategy had to take account of this.

It also had to avoid channel conflict, the bypassing of its traditional sales outlets. Most Coromant tools are sold directly to customers, but 40 per cent goes through resellers. Moreover, there are big regional variations; more than 80 per cent of sales in the Nordic region are direct, while most North American sales are indirect.

The company's approach was to work with the traditional sales channels. 'So many companies try to bypass traditional channels and lose sales and relationships', Mr Fredriksson says.

It is the relationship with the customer – including greater personalisation and an extended reach into global markets – which will be the most important pillar of its e-business strategy in the long term, he says.

This is what provides real competitive advantage. Shifting existing customers to the internet, winning new ones and saving costs are also important. But other companies will be doing the same.

At present, only a small part of Coromant's orders are transacted over the web. Nordic countries are leading the way. Around 20 per cent of all orders from Denmark are online and 31 per cent of those from Sweden.

The proportion in the US, however, is only 3 per cent, since most business goes through distributors and is conducted by EDI (electronic data interchange), the pre-internet means of e-commerce.

Over the next six months, the company hopes to raise the US figure to 40 per cent. Mr Fredriksson hopes that in two years, between 40 and 50 per cent of total orders will come via the web.

To enhance its online service to customers, Coromant plans to offer each one a personalised web page. This will enable the company to offer new products, materials and advice on productivity improvements. Training will also be part of this expanded web offering, which Coromant aims to have in place later this year.

For both Coromant and Sandvik Steel, the value of the web lies in strengthening and expanding relationships with customers. In the case of Coromant, with some 25,000 standard products, there are numerous customers buying low volumes. With Sandvik Steel, however, a small number of customers buys a high volume of products.

'Our aim is to have 200 key customers using the extranet at the end of June', says Annika Roos, marketing manager at Sandvik Steel. 'By the end of December, we want a confirmation from at least 80 per cent of key customers that they consider the extranet to be a major reason to deal with Sandvik.'

By putting the internet at the heart of its business, the Sandvik group intends to penetrate deeply into the minds and ambitions of its customers. 'The challenge is not just doing e-business, it is becoming an e-business', she adds.

Source: Andrew Fisher, Sandvik Steel, 4 June 2001

Questions

1 Summarize Sandvik Steel's e-business strategy as described in the article.

2 Suggest why the proportion of online purchases varies in the different countries in which Sandvik trades.

Activity 5.3 Assessing the significance of digital channels

Purpose

To illustrate the issues involved with assessing the suitability of the Internet for e-commerce.

Activity

For each of the following products and services assess the suitability of the Internet for delivery of the product or service and position it on the grid in *Figure 5.15* with justification and make estimates in *Table 5.5* for the direct and indirect online revenue contribution in five and ten years' time for different products in your country. Choose specific products within each category.

No suggested answer supplied.

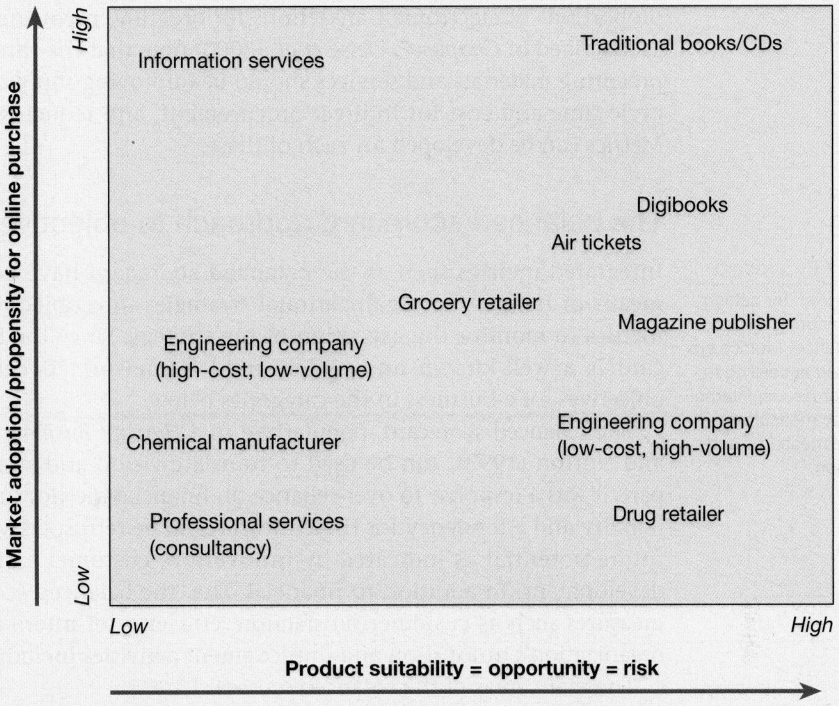

Figure 5.15 Grid of product suitability against market adoption for transactional e-commerce (online purchases)

Table 5.5 Vision of online revenue contribution for The B2B Company

Products/services	*Now*	*2 years*	*5 years*	*10 years*
Example: Cars, US Direct online sales Indirect online sales	 5% 50%	 10% 70%	 25% 90%	 50% 95%
Financial services Direct online sales Indirect online sales				
Clothing Direct online sales Indirect online sales				
Business office supplies Direct online sales Indirect online sales				

An equivalent buy-side measure to the online revenue contribution is the proportion of procurement that is achieved online. This can be broken down into the proportions of electronic transactions for ordering, invoicing, delivery and payment, as described in *Chapter 7*. Deise *et al.* (2000) note that the three business objectives for procuring materials and services should be improving supplier performance, reducing cycle time and cost for indirect procurement, and reducing total acquisition costs. Metrics can be developed for each of these.

The balanced scorecard approach to objective setting

Balanced scorecard
A framework for setting and monitoring business performance. Metrics are structured according to customer issues, internal efficiency measures, financial measures and innovation.

Integrated metrics such as the **balanced scorecard** have become widely used as a means of translating organizational strategies into objectives and then providing metrics to monitor the execution of the strategy. Since the balanced business scorecard is a well-known and widely used framework, it can be helpful to define objectives for e-business in the categories below.

The balanced scorecard, popularized in a *Harvard Business Review* article by Kaplan and Norton (1993), can be used to translate vision and strategy into objectives. In part, it was a response to over-reliance on financial metrics such as turnover and profitability and a tendency for these measures to be retrospective rather than looking at future potential as indicated by innovation, customer satisfaction and employee development. In addition to financial data, the balanced scorecard uses operational measures such as customer satisfaction, efficiency of internal processes and also the organization's innovation and improvement activities including staff development.

The main areas of the balanced scorecard are:

1 *Customer concerns*. These include time (lead time, time to quote, etc.), quality, performance, service and cost. Example measures from Halifax Bank from Olve *et al.* (1999): satisfaction of mystery shoppers visiting branches and from branch customer surveys.
2 *Internal measures*. Internal measures should be based on the business processes that have the greatest impact on customer satisfaction: cycle time, quality, employee skills, productivity. Companies should also identify critical core competencies and try to guarantee market leadership. Example measures from Halifax Bank: ATM availability (%), conversion rates on mortgage applications (%), arrears on mortgage (%).
3 *Financial measures*. Traditional measures such as turnover, costs, profitability and return on capital employed. For publicly quoted companies this measure is key to shareholder value. Example measures from Halifax Bank: gross receipts (£), mortgage offers (£), loans (£).
4 *Learning and growth: innovation and staff development*. Innovation can be measured by change in value through time (employee value, shareholder value, percentage and value of sales from new products). Examples: management performance, training performance, new product development.

For each of these four areas management teams will define objectives, specific measures, targets and initiatives to achieve these targets. For some companies, such as Skandia Life, the balanced scorecard becomes much more than a performance measurement system and provides a framework for the entire business strategy process. Olve *et al.* (1999) make the point that a further benefit of the scorecard is that it does not solely focus on outcomes, but also considers measures that are performance drivers that should positively affect the outcomes. For example, investment in technology and in employee training are performance drivers.

More recently, as the scorecard has been widely used, it has been suggested that it provides a useful tool for aligning business and IS strategy, see for example der Zee and de Jong (1999).

Table 5.6 outlines how the balanced scorecard could be deployed in The B2B Company to support its e-business strategy. A more detailed example how the balanced scorecard can be used for specific e-business processes such as Internet marketing is given in *Chapter 8*.

Table 5.6 An example of an e-business balanced scorecard for The B2B Company

Scorecard component	*Objective metric*
Customer perspective	Customer acquisition rate (leads generated online) Customer retention rate (% using online services) Customer satisfaction index
Process	Average time for new product development (months) Procurement lead times Sales cycle lead time
Financial	Revenue contribution from online channel Margin from online channel Cost savings from partners using different e-services
Innovation and employee development	Number of new product releases per year Training hours attended per employee: target 30 hours/year

Strategy definition

Strategy definition
Formulation, review and selection of strategies to achieve strategic objectives.

The definition of strategy is driven by the objectives and vision referred to in the previous sections. As strategy is formulated based on vision and objectives, so it is necessary to frequently revisit and revise them.

In this section the key strategic decisions faced by a management team developing e-business strategy are reviewed. For each of the areas of strategy definition that we cover, managers will generate different options, review them and select them as shown in *Figure 5.16*. As you read through the six key decisions think about how these decisions are going to vary according to the many different organizational characteristics: B2C, B2B, physical products or intangible services or mixed, size of organization, stage in product lifecycle, market penetration, not-for-profit. What strategy decisions would be taken for organizations you are familiar with?

Decision 1: E-business channel priorities

The e-business strategy must be directed according to the priority of different strategic objectives such as those in *Table 5.4*. If the priorities are for the *sell-side downstream channel*, as are objectives 1 to 3 in *Table 5.4*, then the strategy must be to direct resources at these objectives. For a B2B company that is well known in its marketplace worldwide and cannot offer products to new markets, an initial investment on *buy-side channel upstream channel* e-commerce and value chain management may be more appropriate.

E-business channel strategy priorities can be summarized in the words of Gulati and Garino (2000) *'Getting the right mix of bricks and clicks'*. This expression usually refers to sell-side e-commerce. The general options for the mix of 'bricks and clicks' are shown in *Figure 5.17*. A similar figure was produced by de Kare-Silver (2000) who suggests that strategic e-commerce alternatives for companies should be selected according to the percentage of the target market who can be persuaded to migrate to

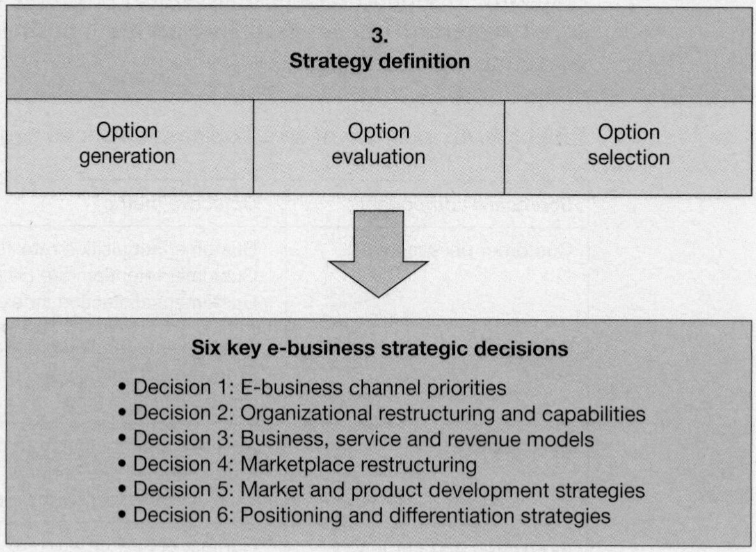

Figure 5.16 Elements of strategy definition for the e-business

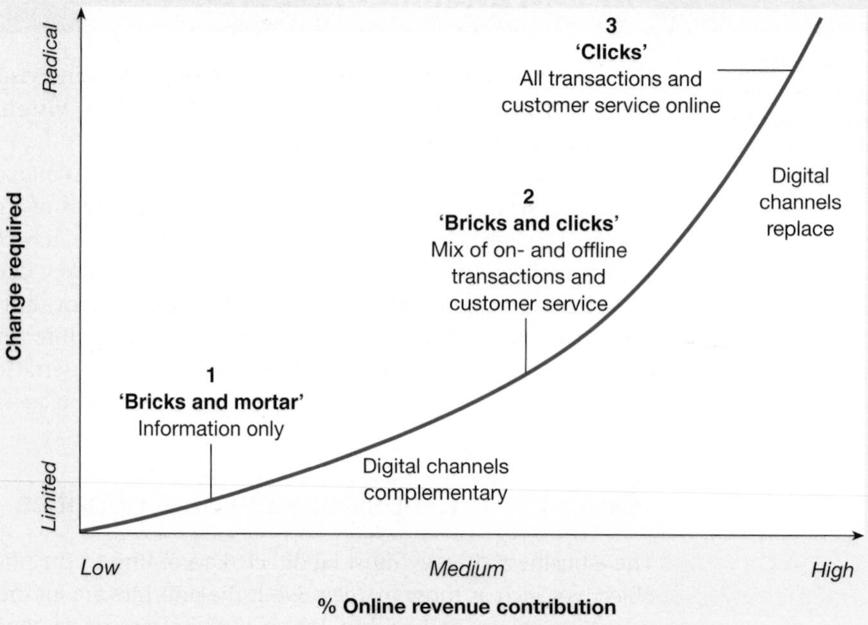

Figure 5.17 Strategic options for a company in relation to the importance of the Internet as a channel

use the e-channel and the benefits to the company of encouraging migration in terms of anticipated sales volume and costs for initial customer acquisition and retention.

In the terminology of de Kare-Silver (2000) the strategic alternatives given in *Figure 5.15* range from those where there is a limited response to the medium such as 'information only' or 'subsume' in business through to spinning off the electronic

Internet pureplay
A company trading online that has limited or no physical presence such as retail units.

commerce part of the company into a 'separate business' or even 'switching fully' to an Internet-based business. Internet-only businesses, particularly start-ups, are sometimes referred to as **'Internet pureplays'**. Although the 'switch-fully' alternative may seem unlikely for many businesses, companies are moving along the curve in this direction. In the UK, the Automobile Association and British Airways have closed the majority of their retail outlets since orders are predominately placed via the Internet or by phone. This makes sense for both of these companies, since no physical products are supplied at point of sale. But both of these companies still make extensive use of the phone channel since its interactivity is needed for many situations. Essentially they have followed a 'bricks and clicks' approach, indeed most businesses require some human element of service.

The transition to a service that is clicks-only is unlikely for the majority of companies. Where a retailer is selling a product such as a mobile phone or electronic equipment many consumers naturally want to compare the physical attributes of products or gain advice from the sales person. Companies selling mobile phones and related tariffs such as the Carphone Warehouse, Phones4U and the network providers such as O_2, Orange, T-Mobile and Vodafone still have a strong high-street presence and the majority of their sales are in-store.

Even dot-coms such as lastminute.com have set up a call centre and experimented with a physical presence in airports or train stations since this helps it to reach a key audience and has benefits in promoting the brand.

Right-channelling

Prioritization of different communications channels to achieve different e-business objectives is an important aspect of e-business strategy. It is necessary to identify which strategies will be pursued, set objectives for them and then define approaches to encourage customers to adopt the appropriate channel. This approach is commonplace and is often referred to as **'right-channelling'**. Right-channelling involves devising a contact strategy and tactics, support by technology to reach:

- *The Right Person*
- *At the Right Time*
- *Using the Right Communications Channel*
- *With a Relevant Offer, Product or Message*

Some examples of right-channelling are given in *Table 5.7*.

Assessing different e-business projects

Typically, there will be a range of different e-business service alternatives to be evaluated. Limited resources will dictate that only some applications are practical. Portfolio analysis can be used to select the most suitable projects – it was introduced in the section on resource and process analysis. For example, Daniel *et al.* (2001) suggest that potential e-commerce opportunities should be assessed for the value of the opportunity to the company against its ability to deliver. Typical opportunities for Internet marketing strategy for an organization which has a brochureware site might be:

- online catalogue facility;
- e-CRM system – lead generation system;
- e-CRM system – customer service management;
- e-CRM system – personalization of content for users;
- partner relationship management extranet for distributors/agents;
- transactional e-commerce facility.

Table 5.7 Examples of 'right-channelling' applications

Right-channelling example	*Application and tactics to achieve channel adoption*	*Typical sector and company examples*
1 Sell to and serve SMEs through online channels.	Using the Internet for sales and service through an extranet to lower-sales-volume SME customers who cannot be serviced direct through account managers. Customer channel adoption encouraged by convenience and lack of other options.	B2B. Hardware: Dell, software services such as MessageLabs Antivirus; anti-spam and e-mail management services. Commercial banks such as HSBC.
2 Account-managed relationships with larger companies offline, either direct or through partner companies.	The converse of strategy 1. Using face-to-face and phone meetings with large, high-sales-volume clients through account managers. Customer channel adoption encouraged by personal service and capability to negotiate service levels and buying options.	B2B. Account managers at Dell for larger clients. Bank 'relationship managers' who discuss financial management with 'higher-wealth' individuals.
3 Encourage consumers to buy through online channels.	Customers buying online have lower cost of sale. However, there is a risk of customers' evaluating competitor offerings and lower conversion rates during the sales process. Customer channel adoption encouraged by reduced 'Internet prices' compared to offline channels and explaining proposition of more choice, more convenience.	Insurance companies such as DirectLine.com and morethan.com. Retailers such as Tesco and Comet.
4 Provide offline conversion to sale options during sales process.	Offer a phone call-back or live chat facility (*Figure 5.18*) from within web sales process since strategy 3 may involve lower conversion rates than an in-store or call-centre customer interaction. Customer channel adoption encouraged by providing clear contact numbers on site (but not on home page, when part-way through customer journey).	Insurance companies such as DirectLine.com and morethan.com.
5 Migrate customers to web self-service.	Customers are encouraged to use the web to manage their accounts which results in a lower cost-to-serve for the company. E-mail notification and e-billing. Customer channel adoption encouraged by marketing campaigns which encourage e-channel adoption, possibly including savings on service.	B2C. Service providers such as mobile phone companies, utility companies, banks and government (tax returns).
6 Selective service levels for different customer types.	With integrated CRM systems (*Chapter 9*), companies can determine, in real time, the value of customers and then assess where they are placed in queue or which call-centre they are directed to.	Most companies would not publicly admit to this, but the practice is common amongst financial services companies, mobile phone network providers and some pureplays.

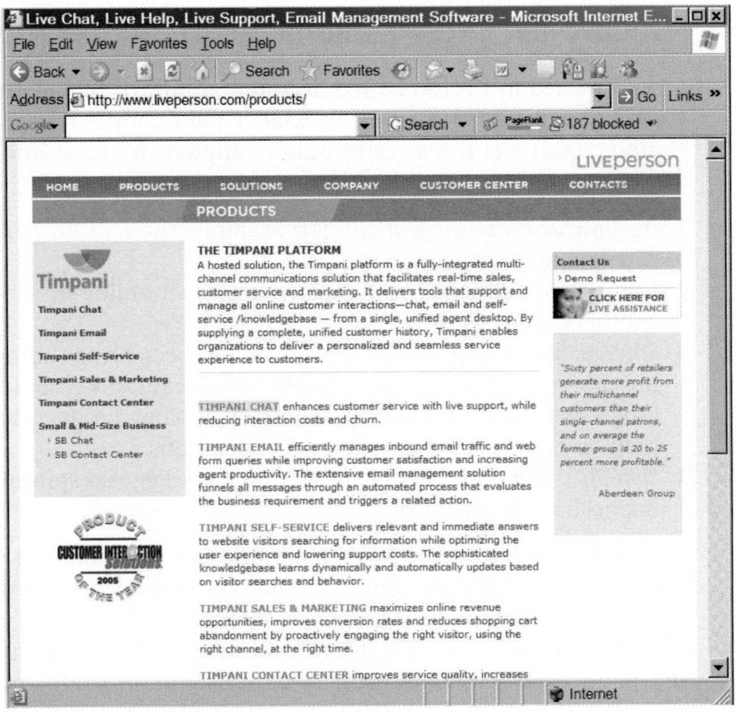

Figure 5.18 Liveperson – an example of a service to assist with 'right-channelling'
Source: www.liveperson.com

Such alternatives can then be evaluated in terms of their risk against reward. *Figure 5.7* shows a possible evaluation of strategic options. It is apparent that with limited resources, the e-CRM lead generation, partner extranet and customer services options offer the best mix of risk and reward.

For information systems investments, the model of McFarlan and McKenney (1993) has been used extensively to assess the future strategic importance applications in a portfolio. This model has been applied to e-commerce applications by Daniel *et al.* (2001) and earlier in this chapter.

A further portfolio analysis suggested by McDonald and Wilson (2002) is a matrix of attractiveness to customer against attractiveness to company, which will give a similar result to the risk–reward matrix. Finally, Tjan (2001) has suggested a matrix approach of viability (return on investment) against fit (with the organization's capabilities) for Internet applications. He presents the following metrics for assessing viability of each application. For 'fit' these are:

- Alignment with core capabilities
- Alignment with other company initiatives
- Fit with organizational structure
- Fit with company's culture and value
- Ease of technical implementation.

For 'viability' the metrics are:

- Market value potential (return on investment)
- Time to positive cash flow
- Personnel requirement
- Funding requirement.

Decision 2: Organizational restructuring and capabilities

Closely related to Decision 1 is a decision on how the company should restructure or change its capabilities in order to achieve the priorities set for e-business. Gulati and Garino (2000) identify a continuum of approaches from integration to separation. The choices are:

1 *In-house division* (*integration*). For example, the RS Components Internet Trading Channel (www.rswww.com).
2 *Joint venture* (*mixed*). The company creates an online presence in association with another player.
3 *Strategic partnership* (*mixed*). This may also be achieved through purchase of existing dot-coms, for example, in the UK Great Universal Stores acquired e-tailer Jungle.com for its strength in selling technology products and strong brand while John Lewis purchased Buy.com's UK operations.
4 *Spin-off* (*separation*). For example, the bank Egg is a spin-off from the Prudential financial services company.

Referring back to *Figure 5.17*, the in-house division or joint venture will be typical for the clicks-and-mortar approach while the strategic partnership or spin-off is more likely to be used to create a clicks-only operation.

Gulati and Garino (2000) give the advantages of the integration approach as being able to use existing brands, being able to share information and achieving economies of scale (e.g. purchasing and distribution efficiencies). They say the spin-off approach gives better focus, more flexibility for innovation and the possibility of funding through flotation. For example, Egg has been able to create a brand distinct from Prudential and has developed new revenue models such as retail sales commission. Gulati and Garino say that separation is preferable in situations where:

- a different customer segment or product mix will be offered online
- differential pricing is required between online and offline
- there is a major channel conflict
- the Internet threatens the current business model
- additional funding or specialist staff need to be attracted.

Additionally, from a technology viewpoint it may be quicker to develop a new infrastructure rather than integrating with an existing one, but again economies of scale are lost.

An example of the integration approach is provided by Barclays Bank. Simons (2000b) reported that Barclays wanted to double its profits in three years through a radical transformation of its business processes. It created an 'e-enablement task force' and the plan involved revising IS strategy, significant outsourcing and investments in customer relationship management systems. The impetus for this strategy is the threat of new rivals such as Egg, Cahoot, Smile and Intelligent Finance. The group CIO of Barclays (David Weymouth) said:

> *the transformation requires a fundamental shift in operating model internally ...* [Benchmarking had shown] *a dramatic gap between our potential opportunities in this area and our actions thus far.*

It is seen that changes in organization structure range from setting up a new department, through setting up a new strategic business unit to creating autonomous companies.

Within a business there are many issues for changing internal capabilities; these options are considered in more depth in *Chapter 10, 'Change management'*.

Decision 3: Business, service and revenue models

Business model
A summary of how a company will generate revenue, identifying its product offering, value-added services, revenue sources and target customers.

Revenue models
Describe methods of generating income for an organisation.

A further aspect of Internet strategy formulation closely related to product development options is the review of opportunities from new business and revenue models, (first introduced in *Chapter 2*). As well as new business and revenue models, constantly reviewing innovation in services to improve the quality of experience offered is important for e-businesses. We also discuss this later in the context of positioning and differentiation. For example, holiday company Thomson (www.thomson.co.uk), innovates to improve the quality of the purchase experience. Innovations have included: travel guides to destinations, video tours of destinations and hotels, 'build your own' holidays and the use of e-mail alerts and RSS (Really Simple Syndication, *Chapter 3*) feeds with holiday offers. Such innovations can help differentiate from competitors and increase loyalty to a brand online.

Evaluating new models and approaches is important since if companies do not review opportunities to innovate then competitors and new entrants certainly will. Andy Grove of Intel famously said: *'Only the paranoid will survive'*, alluding to the need to review new revenue opportunities and competitor innovations. A willingness to test and experiment with new business models is also required. Dell is another example of a tech company that regularly reviews and modifies its business model, as shown in Mini Case Study 5.2. Companies at the bleeding edge of technology such as Google and Yahoo! constantly innovate through acquiring other companies. For example, Google purchased linguistic analysis company Applied Semantics in 2003 to improve its search results algorithm; it developed social networking site Orkut (www.orkut.com) in 2004 (based on a concept developed during the staff's research time) and Google Earth (via Keyhole Inc). Yahoo! has purchased eGroups, later to become Yahoo! Groups and more recently photo sharing and tagging service Flickr (www.flickr.com) and shared bookmark tagging service (www.del.cio.us). Microsoft will also acquire companies where appropriate, but in the areas mentioned above has tended to pursue a 'fast-follower' strategy based on internally developed technology. For example, many of these services are available through MSN Spaces (http://spaces.msn.com), a rival service to social network site MySpace (www.myspace.com) which was purchased by News Corporation in 2005.

These companies also invest in internal research and development (witness Google Labs (http://labs.google.com), Microsoft Research (http://research.microsoft.com) and Yahoo! Research (http://research.yahoo.com)) and continuously develop and trial new services.

Early (first) mover
An early entrant into the marketplace.

The case study on Tesco.com in *Chapter 6* also highlights how innovation in the Tesco business model has been facilitated through online channels.

Mini Case Study 5.2 Innovation in the Dell business model

One example of how companies can review and revise their business model is provided by Dell Computer. Dell gained early-mover advantage in the mid-1990s when it became one of the first companies to offer PCs for sale online. Its sales of PCs and peripherals grew from the mid-1990s with online sales of $1 million per day to 2000 sales of $50 million per day. Based on this success it has looked at new business models it can use in combination with its powerful brand to provide new services to its existing customer base and also to generate revenue through new customers. In September 2000, Dell announced plans to become a supplier of IT consulting services through linking with enterprise resource planning specialists such as software suppliers, systems integrators and business consulting firms. This venture enabled Dell's Premier B2B customer extranet to be integrated into the procurement component

→

of ERP systems such as SAP and Baan, thus avoiding the need for rekeying and reducing costs. Dell Business Solutions is now an important contributor to its business.

In a separate initiative, Dell launched a B2B marketplace (formerly www.dellmarketplace.com) in mid-2000 aimed at discounted office goods and services procurements including PCs, peripherals, software, stationery and travel. This strategic option did not prove sustainable, but it was able to test a model and then move on – it closed the marketplace after just 4 months! This was Dell's dot.com disaster. However, it does offer Dell Outlet, a relatively low-cost purchase method for returned, refurbished PCs.

To sound a note of caution, flexibility in the business model should not be to the company's detriment through losing focus on the core business. A 2000 survey of CEOs of leading UK Internet companies such as Autonomy, Freeserve, NetBenefit and QXL (Durlacher, 2000) indicates that although flexibility is useful this may not apply to business models. The report states:

> *A widely held belief in the new economy in the past, has been that change and flexibility is good, but these interviews suggest that it is actually those companies who have stuck to a single business model that have been to date more successful. CEOs were not moving far from their starting vision, but that it was in the marketing, scope and partnerships where new economy companies had to be flexible.*

So with all strategy options, managers should also consider the 'do-nothing option'. Here a company will not risk a new business model, but will adopt a 'wait-and-see' or 'fast-follower' approach to see how competitors perform and respond rapidly if the new business model proves sustainable.

Finally, we can note that companies can make less radical changes to their revenue models through the Internet which are less far-reaching, but may nevertheless be worthwhile. For example:

- Transactional e-commerce sites (for example Tesco.com and lastminute.com) can sell advertising space or run co-branded promotions on site or through their e-mail newsletters or lists to sell access to their audience to third parties.
- Retailers or media owners can sell-on white-labelled services through their online presence such as ISP, e-mail services or photo-sharing services.
- Companies can gain commission through selling products which are complementary (but not competitive to their own). For example, a publisher can sell its books through an affiliate arrangement through an e-retailer.

Decision 4: Marketplace restructuring

A related issue to reviewing new business and revenue models is to consider the options created through *disintermediation* and *reintermediation* (*Chapter 2, pp. 45–6*) within a marketplace. For all options tactics will be needed to manage the channel conflicts that may occur as a result of restructuring.

We will take the example of 3M (www.3m.com), manufacturer of tens of thousands of products such as Post-it notes and reflective Scotchlite film. These options can be reviewed from both a buy-side and a sell-side perspective.

Mini Case Study 5.3 3M innovates in the e-marketplace

3M was founded in 1902 at the Lake Superior town of Two Harbors, Minnesota when five businessmen set out to mine a mineral deposit for grinding-wheel abrasives. But the deposits proved to be of little value, and the new Minnesota Mining and Manufacturing Co. was formed to focus on sandpaper products.

Today 3M is a diversified technology company known for product innovation with a worldwide presence in consumer and office; display and graphics; electro and communications; health care; industrial and transportation; and safety, security and protection services. In 2005 it had a turnover of $21 billion and 69,000 employees. With 3M products sold in nearly 200 countries and over 60% of its turnover occurring outside its US base, 3M has risen to the challenge of using e-channels to distribute its products and services worldwide.

The following are some of the strategies it has pursued to use online channels to change its relationship with its marketplace.

Sell-side

- *Disintermediation (sell-direct) strategy*. 3M has traditionally sold through retail partners, but now offers some products direct through an e-store.
- *Create a new online intermediary (countermediation) strategy*. This is a strategy 3M has not followed due to its diversity of products. Instead it has focused on its destination site, www.3m.com which has a tool to help potential customers to research and select products. Localized content is available for many countries with 'Where to Buy' links to relevant suppliers in these countries. As an example of a countermediation strategy, in the banking sector, banks such as Barclays have created new portals, such as ClearlyBusiness (www.clearlybusiness.com), in this case to reach small, start-up businesses online.
- *Partner with new online or existing intermediary or retailer strategy*. 3M has integrated its product catalogue with online office retailers such as Euroffice (www.euroffice.co.uk). If a customer is on the 3M site and reviewing a product, when they select the 'Where to Buy' option they are linked directly to the relevant page on Euroffice which enables them to buy. Data is exchanged between 3M and Euroffice using XML data feeds.
- *Do nothing!* This is not a realistic strategy for any company, but 3M has gradually made the transition to e-business over a ten-year period. The strength of existing distribution has meant that 3M had to decide when customer usage of the web became such that it needed to offer new online services. This point, of course, varies in different markets.

Buy-side

In keeping with its innovative market position, 3M was one of the first organizations to adopt e-procurement on a large scale. Starting in the mid-1990s, 3M used different e-procurement products to help manage the enormous task of integrating the buying of a wide range of products from suppliers in many countries. This gave the typical benefits of e-procurement we will see in *Chapter 7*, such as compliance with corporate procurement policies to control spend; control of supplier base; development of strategic relationships with preferred suppliers; accurate spend information to support further supplier development and better attribution of spend to budgets permitting better accounting control. 3M used Ariba's Enterprise Spend Management (ESM) solutions for sourcing and procurement across the entire business.

- *Disintermediation (buy direct, bypassing distributors)*. 3M has used its sourcing system to buy more services direct from suppliers. In keeping with exploring new business models and services enabled through e-business, 3M has developed its own HighJump's RFID-enabled product suite (www.highjumpsoftware.com) to help its clients with complex, global supply chains to source, manufacturer, develop and distribute products more readily.
- *Buy through new intermediaries such as B2B exchanges*. 3M was involved in the pilot of the Dell B2B marketplace launched in 2000 as a supplier, but it did not prove successful for Dell, 3M and other manufacturers involved such as Pitney Bowes and Motorola. As we will see in *Chapter 7*, the use of these marketplaces has not become widespread since using direct e-procurement with suppliers has proved more sustainable.
- Do nothing!

Decision 5: Market and product development strategies

Deciding on which markets to target is a key strategic consideration for Internet marketing strategy in the same way as it is key to marketing strategy. Managers of e-business strategy have to decide whether to use new technologies to change the scope of their business to address new markets and new products. As for Decision 1, the decision is a balance between fear of the do-nothing option and fear of poor return on investment for strategies that fail. The model of Ansoff (1957) is still useful as a means for marketing managers to discuss market and product development using electronic technologies. This decision is considered from an e-marketing perspective in *Chapter 8*. The market and product development matrix (*Figure 5.19*) can help identify strategies to grow sales volume through varying what is sold (the product dimension on the horizontal axis of *Figure 5.19*) and who it is sold to (the market dimension on the *y*-axis). Specific objectives need to be set for sales generated via these strategies, so this decision relates closely to that of objective setting. Let's now review these strategies in more detail.

1 *Market penetration*. This strategy involves using digital channels to sell more existing products into existing markets. The Internet has great potential for achieving sales growth or maintaining sales by the market penetration strategy. As a starting point, many companies will use the Internet to help sell existing products into existing markets, although they may miss opportunities indicated by the strategies in other parts of the matrix. *Figure 5.19* indicates some of the main ways in which the Internet can be used for market penetration:

- *Market share growth* – companies can compete more effectively online if they have web sites that are efficient at converting visitors to sale and mastery of the online

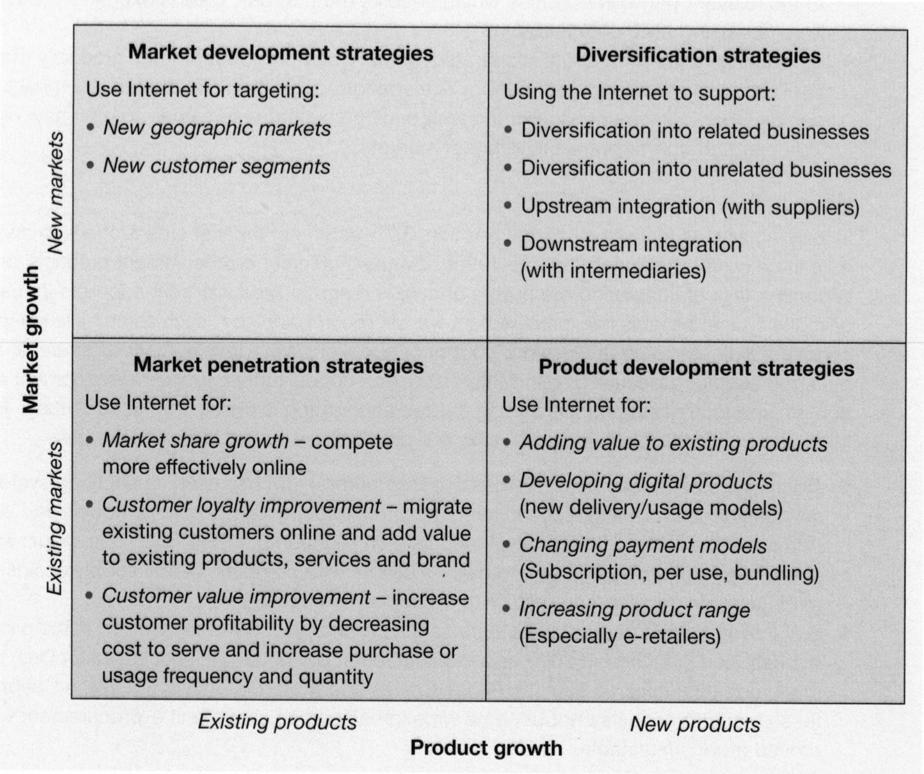

Figure 5.19 Using the Internet to support different growth strategies

marketing communications techniques reviewed in *Chapter 9* such as search engine marketing, affiliate marketing and online advertising.

- *Customer loyalty improvement* – companies can increase their value to customers and so increase loyalty by migrating existing customers online (see Mini Case Study 5.1 on BA earlier in the chapter) by add value to existing products, services and brand by developing their online value proposition (see Decision 6).
- *Customer value improvement* – the value delivered by customers to the company can be increased by increasing customer profitability by decreasing cost to serve (and so price to customers) and at the same time increasing purchase or usage frequency and quantity. These combined effects should drive up sales.

2 *Market development.* Here online channels are used to sell into new markets, taking advantage of the low cost of advertising internationally without the necessity for a supporting sales infrastructure in the customer's country. The Internet has helped low-cost airlines such as easyJet and Ryanair to enter new markets served by their routes cost-effectively. This is a relatively conservative use of the Internet, but is a great opportunity for SMEs to increase exports at a low cost, but it does require overcoming the barriers to exporting.

Existing products can also be sold to new market segments or different types of customers. This may happen simply as a by-product of having a web site. For example, RS components (www.rswww.com), a supplier of a range of MRO (maintenance, repair and operations) items, found that 10% of the web-based sales were to individual consumers rather than traditional business customers. The UK retailer Argos found the opposite was true with 10% of web-site sales from businesses, when their traditional market was consumer-based. EasyJet also has a section of its web site to serve business customers. The Internet may offer further opportunities for selling to market sub-segments that have not be previously targeted. For example, a product sold to large businesses may also appeal to SMEs they have previously been unable to reach because of the cost of sales via a specialist sales force. Alternatively, a product targeted at young people could also appeal to some members of an older audience and vice versa. Many companies have found that the audience and customers of their web site are quite different from their traditional audience.

3 *Product development.* The web can be used to add value to or extend existing products for many companies. For example, a car manufacture can potentially provide car performance and service information via a web site. But truly new products or services that can be delivered by the Internet only apply for some types of products. These are typically digital media or information products, for example online trade magazine *Construction Weekly* has diversified to a B2B portal CN Plus (www.cnplus.co.uk) which has new revenue streams. Similarly, music and book publishing companies have found new ways to deliver products through the new development and usage model such as subscription and pay per use as explained in *Chapter 8* in the section on the Product element of the marketing mix. Retailers can extend their product range and provide new bundling options online also.

4 *Diversification.* In this sector, new products are developed which are sold into new markets. The Internet alone cannot facilitate these high-risk business strategies, but it can facilitate them at lower costs than have previously been possible. The options include:

- *Diversification into related businesses* (for example, a low-cost airline can use the web site and customer e-mails to promote travel-related services such as hotel booking, car rental or travel insurance at relatively low costs).
- *Diversification into unrelated businesses* – again the web site can be used to promote less-related products to customers – this is the approach used by the Virgin brand, although it is relatively rare.

- *Upstream integration* – with suppliers – achieved through data exchange between a manufacturer or retailer with its suppliers to enable a company to take more control of the supply chain.
- *Downstream integration* – with intermediaries – again achieved through data exchange with distributors such as online intermediaries.

The danger of diversification into new product areas is illustrated by the fortunes of Amazon, which was infamous for limited profitability despite multi-billion-dollar sales. Phillips (2000) reported that for books and records, Amazon sustained profitability through 2000, but it is following a strategy of product diversification into toys, tools, electronics and kitchenware. This strategy gives a problem through the cost of promotion and logistics to deliver the new product offerings. Amazon is balancing this against its vision of becoming a 'one-stop shop' for online shoppers.

Target marketing strategy
Evaluation and selection of appropriate segments and the development of appropriate offers.

A closely related issue is the review of how a company should change its **target marketing strategy**. This starts with segmentation, or identification of groups of customers sharing similar characteristics. Targeting then involves selectively communicating with different segments. This topic is explored further in *Chapter 8*. Some examples of customer segments that are commonly targeted online include:

- *the most profitable customers* – using the Internet to provide tailored offers to the top 20 per cent of customers by profit may result in more repeat business and cross-sales;
- *larger companies (B2B)* – an extranet could be produced to service these customers, and increase their loyalty;
- *smaller companies (B2B)* – large companies are traditionally serviced through sales representatives and account managers, but smaller companies may not warrant the expense of account managers. However, the Internet can be used to reach smaller companies more cost-effectively. The number of smaller companies that can be reached in this way may be significant, so although individual revenue of each one is relatively small, the collective revenue achieved through Internet servicing can be large;
- *particular members of the buying unit (B2B)* – the site should provide detailed information for different interests which supports the buying decision, for example technical documentation for users of products, information on savings from e-procurement for IS or purchasing managers and information to establish the credibility of the company for decision makers;
- *customers who are difficult to reach using other media* – an insurance company looking to target younger drivers could use the web as a vehicle for this;
- *customers who are brand-loyal* – services to appeal to brand loyalists can be provided to support them in their role as advocates of a brand as suggested by Aaker and Joachimstiler (2000);
- *customers who are not brand-loyal* – conversely, incentives, promotion and a good level of service quality could be provided by the web site to try and retain such customers.

Mini Case Study 5.4 smile taps a new market for the Co-op

The benefits and risks of market and product development are highlighted by the creation of **smile** (www.smile.co.uk), an Internet-specific bank (*Figure 5.20*) set up by the Co-operative Bank in the UK. **smile** opened for business in October 1999 and in its first year added 200,000 customers at a rate of 20,000 per month. Significantly, 80% of these customers were market development in the context of the parent, since they were not existing Co-op Bank customers and typically belonged to a higher income segment. The risks of the new approach to banking were highlighted by the cost of innovation; with it being estimated that in its first year, costs of creation and promotion of **smile** increased overall costs of the Co-op Bank by 5%. However, within five years **smile** was on target, profitable and growing strongly, and continues to do so today.

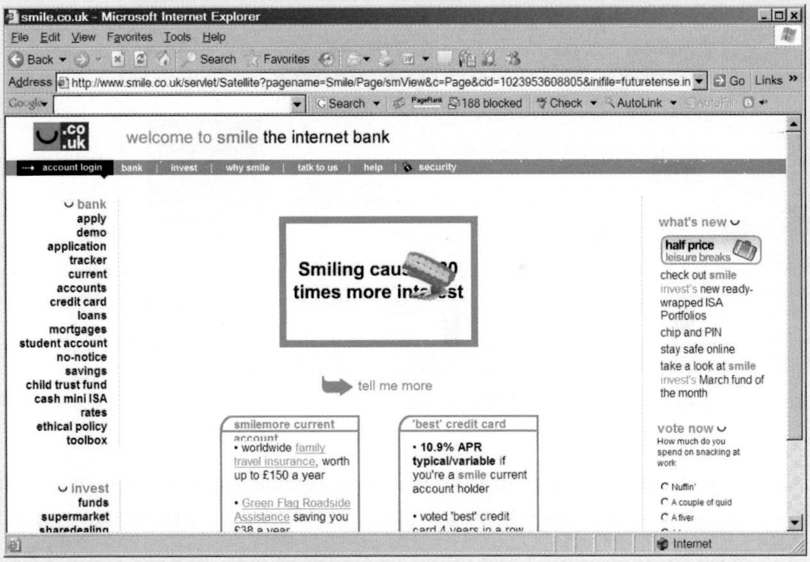

Figure 5.20 **smile (www.smile.co.uk)**

Source: Reprinted by permission of The Co-operative Bank

Decision 6: Positioning and differentiation strategies

Companies can position their products relative to competitors according to four main variables: product quality, service quality, price and fulfilment time. As mentioned earlier, Deise *et al.* (2000) suggest it is useful to review these through an equation of how they combine to influence customer perceptions of value or brand:

$$\text{Customer value (brand perception)} = \frac{\text{Product quality} \times \text{Service quality}}{\text{Price} \times \text{Fulfilment time}}$$

Strategies should review the extent to which increases in product and service quality can be matched by decreases in price and time. We will now look at some other opinions of positioning strategies for e-businesses. As you read through, refer back to the customer value equation to note similarities and differences.

Chaston (2000) argues that there are four options for strategic focus to position a company in the online marketplace. He says that these should build on existing strengths, but can use the online facilities to enhance the positioning as follows:

- *Product performance excellence*. Enhance by providing online product customization.
- *Price performance excellence*. Use the facilities of the Internet to offer favourable pricing to loyal customers or to reduce prices where demand is low (for example, British Midland Airlines uses auctions to sell underused capacity on flights).
- *Transactional excellence*. A site such as software and hardware e-tailer Dabs.com (*Figure 5.21*) (www.dabs.com) offers transactional excellence through combining pricing information with dynamic availability information on products listing number in stock, number on order and when expected.

Figure 5.21 **Dabs.com (www.dabs.com)**

- *Relationship excellence.* Personalization features to enable customers to review sales order history and place repeat orders; for example RS Components (www.rswww.com).

These positioning options have much in common with Porter's competitive strategies of cost leadership, product differentiation and innovation (Porter, 1980). Porter has been criticized since many commentators believe that to remain competitive it is necessary to combine excellence in all of these areas. It can be suggested that the same is true for sell-side e-commerce. These are not mutually exclusive strategic options, rather they are prerequisites for success. Customers will probably not judge on a single criterion, but on multiple criteria. This is the view of Kim *et al.* (2004) who concluded that for online businesses, *'integrated strategies that combine elements of cost leadership and differentiation will outperform cost leadership or differentiation strategies'*.

The type of criteria on which customers judge performance can be used to benchmark the proposition. *Table 5.8* summarizes criteria typically used for benchmarking. It can be seen that the criteria are consistent with the strategic postioning options of Chaston (2000). Significantly, the retailers with the best overall score at the time of writing, such as Tesco (grocery retail), smile (online banking) and Amazon (books), are also perceived as the market leaders and are strong in each of the scorecard categories. These ratings have resulted from strategies that enable the investment and restructuring to deliver customer performance.

Plant (2000) also identifies four different positional e-strategic directions which he refers to as technology leadership, service leadership, market leadership and brand leadership. The author acknowledges that these are not exclusive. It is interesting that this author does not see price differentiation as important, rather he sees brand and service as important to success online.

Online value proposition (OVP)
A statement of the benefits of online services reinforces the core proposition and differentiates from an organization's offline offering and those of competitors.

In *Chapter 8* we look further at how segmentation, positioning and creating differential advantage through. We also see how the differential advantage and positioning of an e-commerce service can be clarified and communicated by developing an **online value proposition (OVP)**.

To conclude this section on e-business strategies, complete *Activity 5.4* for a different perspective on e-business strategies.

Table 5.8 Example scorecard criteria for rating e-tailers

Scorecard category	*Scorecard criteria*
1 Ease of use	• Demonstrations of functionality. • Simplicity of account opening and transaction process. • Consistency of design and navigation. • Adherence to proper user interaction principles. • Integration of data providing efficient access to information commonly accessed by consumers.
2 Customer confidence	• Availability, depth and breadth of customer service options, including phone, e-mail and branch locations. • Ability to resolve accurately and readily a battery of telephone calls and e-mails sent to customer service, covering simple technical and industry-specific questions. • Privacy policies, service guarantees, fees and explanations of fees. • Each ranked web site is monitored every 5 minutes, 7 days a week, 24 hours a day for speed and reliability of both public and secure (if available) areas. • Financial strength, technological capabilities and independence, years in business, years online and membership organizations.
3 On-site resources	• Availability of specific products. • Ability to transact in each product online. • Ability to seek service requests online.
4 Relationship services	• Online help, tutorials, glossary and frequently asked questions. • Advice. • Personalization of data. • Ability to customize a site. • Re-use of customer data to facilitate future transactions. • Support of business and personal needs such as tax reporting or repeated buying. • Frequent-buyer incentives.
5 Overall cost	• A basket of typical services and purchases. • Added fees due to shipping and handling. • Minimum balances. • Interest rates.

Activity 5.4 E-business strategies for The B2C Company

Purpose

To evaluate the suitability of different e-business strategies.

Introduction

Many industry analysts such as the Gartner Group, Forrester, IDC Research and the 'big five' consulting firms are suggesting e-business strategies. Many of these will not have been trialled extensively, so a key management skill becomes evaluating suggested approaches from reports and then selecting appropriate measures.

Questions

1. Review the summaries of the approaches recommended by IDC Research below (Picardi, 2000). Which elements of these strategies would you suggest are most relevant to The B2C Company?
2. Alternatively, for a company with which you are familiar review the six strategy definition choices presented in the previous section.

Summary of IDC approach to e-business strategies

Picardi (2000) identifies six strategies for sell-side e-commerce. The approaches are interesting since they also describe the timeframe in which response is required in order to remain competitive.
The six strategies are:

1 **Attack e-tailing**. As suggested by the name, this is an aggressive competitive approach that involves frequent comparison with competitors' prices and then matching or bettering them. This approach is important on the Internet because of the transparency of pricing and availability of information made possible through shopping comparison sites such as ShopSmart (www.shopsmart.com) and Kelkoo (www.kelkoo.com). As customers increasingly use these facilities then it is important that companies ensure their price positioning is favourable. High-street white-goods retailers have long used the approach of matching competitors' prices, but the Internet enables this to be achieved dynamically. Shopping sites such as Buy.com (www.buy.com) and Evenbetter.com (www.evenbetter.com) can now find the prices of all comparable items in a category but also guarantee that they will beat the lowest price of any competing product. These sites have implemented real-time adjustments in prices with small increments based on price policy algorithms that are simply not possible in traditional retailing.

2 **Defend e-tailing**. This is a strategic approach that traditional companies can use in response to 'attack e-tailing'. It involves differentiation based on other aspects of brand beyond price. The IDC research quoted by Picardi (2000) shows that while average prices for commodity goods on the Internet are generally lower, less than half of all consumers purchase the lowest-priced item when offered more information from trusted sources, i.e. price dispersion may actually increase online. Reasons why the lowest price may not always result in the sale are:

- Ease of use of site and placing orders (e.g. Amazon One-Click makes placing an order with Amazon much easier than using a new supplier).
- Ancillary information (e.g. book reviews contributed by other customers enhances Amazon service).
- After-sales service (prompt, consistent fulfilment and notification of dispatch from Amazon increases trust in the site).
- Trust with regard to security and customer privacy.

These factors enable Amazon to charge more than competitors and still achieve the greatest sales volume of online booksellers. In summary, trust becomes the means of differentiation and loyalty. As a result, price comparison sites are being superseded by sites that independently rate the overall service such as Gomez (www.gomez.com) or use customers' opinions to rate the service such as Bizrate (www.bizrate.com) and Epinions (www.epinions.com).

3 **E2E (end-to-end) integration**. This is an efficiency strategy that uses the Internet to decrease costs and increase product quality and shorten delivery times. This strategy is achieved by moving towards an automated supply chain (*Chapter 8*) and internal value chain. A key issue in moving towards the automated supply chain is determining which process should be owned internally, which should be achieved via partnerships, and which should be outsourced.

4 **Market creation**. Picardi (2000) defines market creation as *'the business of supplying market clearing and ancillary services in cyberspace, resulting in the creation of an integrated ecosystem of suppliers'*. The term 'ecosystem' was coined in the new millennium to emphasize the move from relatively static supply chains with defined suppliers, partners and customers for an organization to a more dynamic environment in which such links are formed more readily. In tangible terms, this strategy involves integrating and continuously revising supply chains with market-maker sites such as business-to-business exchanges (*Chapter 8*).

5 **Customer as designer**. This strategy uses the technology to enable customers to personalize products, again as a means of differentiation. This approach is particularly suited to information products, but manufactured products such as cars can now be specified to a fine degree of detail by the customer.

6 **Open-source value creation**. The best-known example of this is the creation and commercial success of the operating system Linux by over 300,000 collaborators worldwide. Picardi (2000) suggests that organizations will make more use of external resources to solve their problems.

Answers to activities can be found at www.pearsoned.co.uk/chaffey

Strategy implementation

Strategy implementation
Planning, actions and controls needed to achieve strategic goals.

Strategy implementation includes all tactics used to achieve strategic objectives. The main tactics and actions required are summarized in *Figure 5.22*. These actions are described in more detail in the remainder of *Part 2* and in *Part 3* as indicated in the figure and also *Table 5.7*.

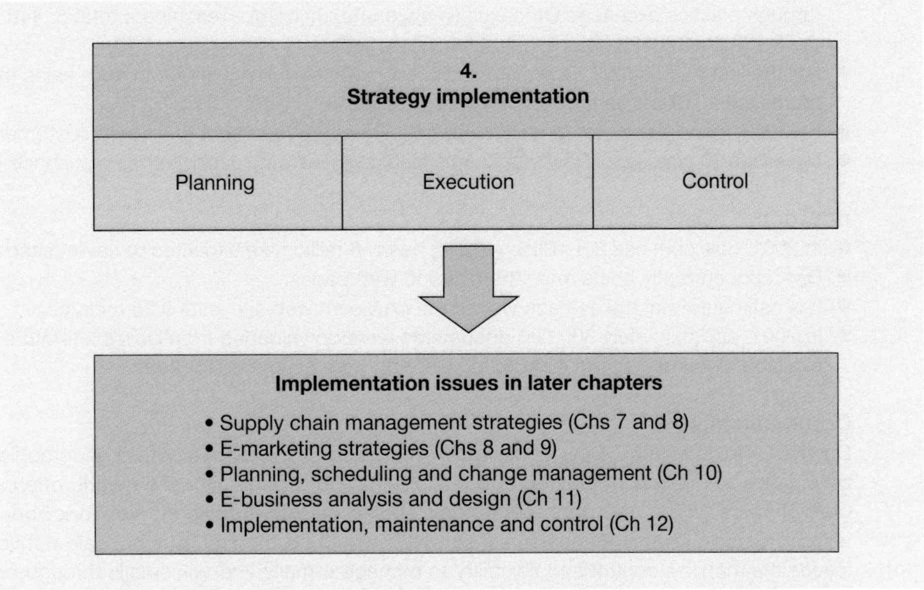

Figure 5.22 **Elements of strategy implementation for the e-business**

Chapter 10 focuses on approaches to managing the change associated with change management. *Figure 10.1* summarizes different implementation marketing activities that need to be completed by an online retailer structured according to customer acquisition, conversion and retention activities.

Mini Case Study 5.5 E-business implementation at Dow Chemical

Damanpour (2001) suggests that the main factors needed for success in e-business implementation are: flexibility and speed, collaboration and execution, and demand fulfilment (integration of supply chain). Dow Chemical provides a good example of a successful implementation based on this approach and resulting from an e-business strategy of combining use of their own site with independent e-marketplaces to communicate with existing and potential customers. Their e-business strategy documented at www.dow.com/ebusiness has been recognized by many industry awards. The results in 2001 which demonstrates Dow's success in managing e-business partnerships include the following.

→

Creation of industry exchanges

- Approximately 200 customer ERP connections exist, covering North America, Europe, Latin America and some Pacific countries.
- Dow has conducted more than 1,400 transactions through chemical exchange, Elemica (www.elemica.com), transacting with BASF, Bayer, Ciba, HB Fuller and Procter & Gamble on the sell-side; and with BASF, Bayer, Celanese, CHEMCENTRAL, Ciba, Degussa, Shell and Solvay on the buy-side.
- Elemica has linked with several e-marketplaces in a 'hub-to-hub strategy' that extends the online reach of Elemica's members. New alliances include Transwide, Omnexus, Quadrem and Rubber Network.
- Compared to 2001, Dow Plastics has more than doubled the number of customer transactions made through plastics exchange Omnexus (www.omnexus.com) – reaching a total of 448 transactions for the first half of 2002.
- For the first half of 2002, Dow has facilitated more than $10.5 million in resin sales through Omnexus, representing 19 per cent of Omnexus total sales.
- By 2003, Dow intends to connect electronically with 80 per cent of its core customer base.
- More than 30 per cent of Dow's Latin American revenues were generated via e-channels by year-end 2001.

dow.com

- In 2001, dow.com had 3.8 million visitors; nearly 5 million are expected to have visited the site in 2002.
- Dow.com currently hosts more than 17,000 web pages.
- It is estimated that the average visit to the dow.com web site lasts 9.26 minutes.
- In 2001, approximately 300,000 documents were downloaded from Dow's Literature Library of 40,000 available documents, and 400,000 downloads were estimated for 2002.

Communicating

DowNET – in June 2001, Dow unveiled DowNET, a solution that overcomes geographic and connectivity boundaries to provide employees and customers with a single global network, offering the best attributes of voice, video and data technology. Based on EDS Intelligent Network Foundation (INF) and utilizing Cisco Systems technologies, DowNET would be the first, global-scale network to allow employees the mobility, control and flexibility to manage e-mails and voicemails through both the telephone and computer, send fax documents, as well as access files and LAN services on a 24/7 basis via voice-over Internet protocol (VoIP) technology.

Source: www.dow.com/ebusiness/e_lead/results.htm

Failed e-business strategies

There are many case studies of successes with e-business strategy, but unsurprisingly there are few companies that want to have their mistakes detailed in public. However, the names of failures are well known: Boo (clothing retail – see *Case Study 5.3*), eToys (retail), CDNow (retail), Peapod (online grocer), VerticalNet (online B2B marketplaces) and Mondus (B2B marketplaces). Behind these well-known names, there are many other Internet companies that have failed or that have merged and many existing companies that invested in e-commerce without achieving a satisfactory return on investment. For example, bookseller Waterstones, which has 200 bookstores in the UK, spent several million euro on developing its Waterstones Online service, but then changed its strategy to partnership with Amazon (www.amazon.co.uk) because it failed to stop Amazon becoming dominant in the online book retail market. By 2002, Amazon UK had achieved book sales of around £150m compared to Waterstones' total turnover of around £400 million.

What then can be learned from these failures which can also be applied to all companies looking to implement e-business? The story of the failure of Boo has become a best-seller since it was one of the first dot-coms to fail in May 2000. You can read the exciting, but ultimately sad story in *Case Study 5.3.*

There are usually more fundamental problems resulting in failure of Internet companies. Miller (2003) has reviewed these misjudgements from an analysis of many Internet failures. He believes that the biggest mistake companies made was to *'massively overestimate the speed at which the marketplace would adopt dot com innovations'*. Furthermore, it was assumed that new innovations would rapidly displace existing product offerings, for example online grocery shopping would rapidly replace conventional grocery shopping. Even Tesco.com, one of the most successful online retailers achieves a single-digit percentage of its retail sales from the Internet – and this has taken several years to achieve. Other reasons mentioned by Miller include:

- *Timing errors:* for example, services for download of digital entertainment that were offered before high-speed broadband Internet access was widely available. The learning is that insufficient research had been conducted about demand for online products in terms of the Access:Use:Buy framework introduced in *Chapter 4.*
- *Lack of creativity*: many services copied existing business models, or other online retail services. The learning is that insufficient research had been conducted about competitor differentiators and capabilities and whether these would be sufficient to encourage consumers to switch providers.
- *Offering free services*: many services were offered free to gain site visitors and registration. If a good free facility was provided it then became difficult to encourage payment for marginally better services. This is a difficult balance to get right. A straightforward example is provided by Webshots.com which provides a comprehensive image library and screensaver for free, but hopes to gain revenue from those who wish to download many images.
- *Over-ambition.* To achieve investor funding amongst many competing companies, some entrepreneurs exaggerated the demand for their products and the growth.

Beyond these reasons, we can also point to classic mistakes that start-up and existing businesses have always made and will continue to make from all stages of the strategy process described in this chapter. These include:

- *Situation analysis* – insufficient rigour in researching demand for new products and competitive forces.
- *Objective setting* – setting unrealistic objectives or, worse still, not setting clear objectives.
- *Strategy definition* – poor decisions about business and revenue models, target markets, product differentiation, pricing, distribution, etc.
- *Implementation* – problems with customer service quality, infrastructure and change management, as described in *Chapter 10.*

E-business strategy implementation success factors for SMEs

Of course, government statistics show that a high proportion of new businesses fail within 2 to 3 years of start-up regardless of whether they are online or offline and good planning practice and financial risk management are important in both.

An assessment of success factors for e-business strategy implementation in SMEs has been produced by Jeffcoate *et al.* (2002). They suggest these 11 critical success factors, which can also be usefully applied to larger organizations:

1. *Content.* The effective presentation of a products or services.
2. *Convenience.* The usability of the web site.
3. *Control.* The extent to which organizations have defined processes that they can manage.

4 *Interaction*. The means of relationship building with individual customers.
5 *Community*. The means of relationship building with groups of like-minded individuals or organizations.
6 *Price sensitivity*. The sensitivity of a product or service to price competition on the Internet.
7 *Brand image*. The ability to build up a credible brand name for e-commerce.
8 *Commitment*. A strong motivation for using the Internet and the will to innovate.
9 *Partnership*. The extent to which an e-commerce venture uses partnerships (value chain relationships) to leverage Internet presence and expand its business.
10 *Process improvement*. The extent to which companies can change and automate business processes.
11 *Integration*. The provision of links between underlying IT systems in support of partnership and process improvement.

As a counterpoint to *Case Study 5.3*, consider *Mini Case Study 2.1* which shows how SME Firebox.com has survived and prospered.

Case Study 5.3 Boo hoo – learning from the largest European dot-com failure

Context

'*Unless we raise $20 million by midnight, boo.com is dead*'. So said boo.com CEO Ernst Malmsten, on 18 May 2000. Half the investment was raised, but this was too little, too late, and at midnight, less than a year after its launch, Boo.com closed. The headlines in the *Financial Times*, the next day read: '*Boo.com collapses as investors refuse funds. Online sports retailer becomes Europe's first big Internet casualty.*'

The Boo.com case remains a valuable case study for all types of businesses, since it doesn't only illustrate the challenges of managing e-commerce for a clothes retailer, but rather highlights failings in e-commerce strategy and management that can be made in any type of organization.

Company background

Boo.com was a European company founded in 1998 and operating out of a London head office, which was founded by three Swedish entrepreneurs, Ernst Malmsten, Kajsa Leander and Patrik Hedelin. Malmsten and Leander had previous business experience in publishing where they created a specialist publisher and had also created an online bookstore, bokus.com, which in 1997 became the world's third largest book e-retailer behind Amazon and Barnes & Noble. They became millionaires when they sold the company in 1998. At Boo.com, they were joined by Patrik Hedelin who was also the financial director at bokus, and at the time they were perceived as experienced European Internet entrepreneurs by the investors who backed them in their new venture.

Company vision

The vision for Boo.com was for it to become the world's first online global sports retail site. It would be a European brand, but with a global appeal. Think of it as a sports and fashion retail version of Amazon. At launch it would open its virtual doors in both Europe and America with a view to 'amazoning the sector'. Note though that in contrast, Amazon did not launch simultaneously in all markets. Rather it became established in the US before providing local European distribution through acquisition and re-branding of other e-retailers in the United Kingdom for example.

The boo.com brand name

According to Malmsten *et al*. (2001), the boo brand name originated from filmstar 'Bo Derek', best known for her role in the movie *10*. The domain name 'bo.com' was unavailable, but adding an 'o', they managed to procure the domain 'boo.com' for $2,500 from a domain name dealer. According to Rob Talbot, director of marketing for Boo.com, Boo were '*looking for a name that was easy to spell across all the different countries and easy to remember ... something that didn't have a particular meaning*'.

Target market

The audience targeted by Boo.com can be characterized as 'young, well-off and fashion-conscious' 18-to-24-year-olds. The concept was that globally the target market would be interested in sports and fashion brands stocked by Boo.com.

The market for clothing in this area was viewed as very large, so the thought was that capture of only a small part of this market was required for Boo.com to be successful. The view at this time on the scale of this market and the basis for success is indicated by *New Media Age* (1999) where it was described as

The $60b USD industry is dominated by Gen X'ers who are online and according to market research in need of knowing what is in, what is not and a way to receive such goods quickly. If boo.com becomes known as the place to keep up with fashion and can supply the latest trends then there is no doubt that there is a market, a highly profitable one at that, for profits to grow from.

The growth in market was also supported by retail analysts, with Verdict predicting online shopping in the United Kingdom to grow from £600 million in 1999 to £12.5 billion in 2005.

However, *New Media Age* (2005) does note some reservations about this market, saying

Clothes and trainers have a high rate of return in the mail order/home shopping world. Twenty year olds may be online and may have disposable income but they are not the main market associated with mail order. To date there is no one else doing anything similar to boo.com.

The Boo.com proposition

In their proposal to investors, the company stated that 'their business idea is to become the world-leading Internet-based retailer of prestigious brand leisure and sportswear names'. They listed brands such as Polo, Ralph Lauren, Tommy Hilfiger, Nike, Fila, Lacoste and Adidas. The proposition involved sports and fashion goods alongside each other. The thinking was that sports clothing has more standardized sizes with less need for a precise fit than designer clothing.

The owners of Boo.com wanted to develop an easy-to-use experience which re-created the offline shopping experience as far as possible. As part of the branding strategy, an idea was developed of a virtual salesperson, initially named Jenny and later Miss Boo. She would guide users through the site and give helpful tips. When selecting products, users could drag them on to models, zoom in and rotate them in 3D to visualize them from different angles. The technology to achieve this was built from scratch along with the stock control and distribution software. A large investment was required in technology with several suppliers being replaced before launch which was 6 months later than promised to investors, largely due to problems with implementing the technology.

Clothing the mannequin and populating the catalogue was also an expensive challenge. For 2000, about $6 million was spent on content about spring/summer fashion wear. It cost $200 to photograph each product, representing a monthly cost of more than $500,000.

Although the user experience of Boo.com is often criticized for its speed, it does seem to have had that wow factor that influenced investors. Analyst Nik Margolis, writing in *New Media Age* (1999), illustrates this by saying:

What I saw at boo.com is simply the most clever web experience I have seen in quite a while. The presentation of products and content are both imaginative and offer an experience. Sure everything loads up fast in an office but I was assured by those at boo.com that they will keep to a limit of 8 seconds for a page to download. Eight seconds is not great but the question is will it be worth waiting for?

Of course, today, the majority of European users have broadband, but in the late 1990s the majority were on dial-up and had to download the software to view products.

Communicating the Boo.com proposition

Early plans referred to extensive 'high-impact' marketing campaigns on TV and newspapers. Public relations were important in leveraging the novelty of the concept and human side of the business – Leander was previously a professional model and had formerly been Malmsten's partner. This PR was initially focused within the fashion and sportswear trade and then rolled out to publications likely to be read by the target audience. The success of this PR initiative can be judged by the 350,000 e-mail pre-registrations who wanted to be notified of launch. For the launch Malmsten *et al*. (2001) explains that '*with a marketing and PR spend of only $22.4 million we had managed to create a worldwide brand*'.

To help create the values of the Boo.com brand, *Boom*, a lavish online fashion magazine, was created, which required substantial staff for different language versions. The magazine wasn't a catalogue which directly supported sales, rather it was a publishing venture competing with established fashion titles. For existing customers the Look Book, a 44-page print catalogue was produced which showcased different products each month.

The challenges of building a global brand in months

The challenges of creating a global brand in months are illustrated well by Malmsten *et al*. (2001). After an initial round of funding, including investment from JP Morgan, LMVH Investment and the Benetton family, which generated around $9 million, the founders planned towards launch by identifying thousands of individual tasks, many of which needed to be completed by staff yet to be recruited. These tasks were divided into twenty-seven areas of responsibility familiar to many organizations including office infrastructure, logistics, product information, pricing, front-end applications, call centres, packaging, suppliers, designing logos, advertising//PR, legal issues, and recruitment. At its zenith, Boo.com had 350 staff, with over one hundred in London and new offices in, Munich, New York, Paris and Stockholm. Initially boo.com was available in UK English, US English, German, Swedish, Danish and Finnish with localized versions for France, Spain and Italy added after launch. The →

web site was tailored for individual countries using the local language and currency and also local prices. Orders were fulfilled and shipped out of one of two warehouses: one in Louisville, Kentucky and the other in Cologne, Germany. This side of the business was relatively successful with on-time delivery rates approaching 100% achieved.

Boo possessed classic channel conflicts. Initially, it was difficult getting fashion and sports brands to offer their products through Boo.com. Manufacturers already had a well-established distribution network through large high-street sports and fashion retailers and many smaller retailers. If clothing brands permitted Boo.com to sell their clothes online at discounted prices, then this would conflict with retailers' interests and would also portray the brands in a negative light if their goods were in an online 'bargain bucket'. A further pricing issue is where local or *zone pricing* in different markets exists, for example lower prices often exist in the US than Europe and there are variations in different European countries.

Making the business case to investors

Today it seems incredible that investors were confident enough to invest $130 million in the company and, at the high point, the company was valued at $390 million. Yet much of this investment was based on the vision of the founders to be a global brand and achieve 'first-mover advantage'. Although there were naturally revenue projections, these were not always based on an accurate detailed analysis of market potential. Immediately before launch, Malmsten *et al.* (2001) explains a meeting with would-be investor Pequot Capital, represented by Larry Lenihan who had made successful investments in AOL and Yahoo! The Boo.com management team were able to provide revenue forecasts, but unable to answer fundamental questions for modelling the potential of the business, such as '*How many visitors are you aiming for? What kind of conversion rate are you aiming for? How much does each customer have to spend? What's your customer acquisition cost. And what's your payback time on customer acquisition cost?*' When these figures were obtained, the analyst found them to be 'far-fetched' and reputedly ended the meeting with the words. '*I'm not interested. Sorry for my bluntness, but I think you're going to be out of business by Christmas.*'

When the site launched on 3 November 1999, around 50,000 unique visitors were achieved on the first day, but there were only 4 in 1,000 placed orders (a 0.25% conversion rate). Showing the importance of modelling conversion rate accurately in modelling business potential. This low conversion rate was also symptomatic of problems with technology. It also gave rise to negative PR. One reviewer explained how he waited: '*Eighty-one minutes to pay too much money for a pair of shoes that I still have to wait a week to get?*' These rates did improve as problems were ironed out – by the end of the week 228,848 visits had resulted in 609 orders with a value of $64,000. In the 6 weeks from launch, sales of $353,000 were made and conversion rates had more than doubled to 0.98% before Christmas. However, a relaunch was required within 6 months to cut download times and to introduce a 'low-bandwidth version' for users using dial-up connections. This led to conversion rates of nearly 3% on sales promotion. Sales results were disappointing in some regions with US sales accounting for 20% compared to the planned 40%.

The management team felt that further substantial investment was required to grow the business from a presence in 18 countries and 22 brands in November to 31 countries and 40 brands the following spring. Turnover was forecast to rise from $100 million in 2000/01 to $1350 million by 2003/04 which would be driven by $102.3 million in marketing in 2003/04. Profit was forecast to be $51.9 million by 2003/4.

The end of Boo.com

The end of Boo.com came on 18 May 2000, when investor funds could not be raised to meet the spiralling marketing, technology and wage bills.

Source: Prepared by Dave Chaffey from original sources including Malmsten *et al.* (2001) and *New Media Age* (1999).

Questions

1. Which strategic marketing assumptions and decisions arguably made Boo.com's failure inevitable? Contrast these with other dot-com era survivors that are still in business, for example lastminute.com, Egg.com and Firebox.com
2. Using the framework of the marketing mix, appraise the marketing tactics of Boo.com in the areas of Product, Pricing, Place, Promotion, Process, People and Physical Evidence.
3. In many ways, the vision of Boo's founders were 'ideas before their time'. Give examples of e-retail techniques used to create an engaging online customer experience which Boo adopted that are now becoming commonplace.

Focus on information systems strategy and e-business strategy

An essential part of any e-business strategy is consideration of how information systems strategy supports change. The importance to e-business success of utilizing information systems to manage information is highlighted by Willcocks and Plant (2000) who found in a study of 58 major corporations in the USA, Europe and Australasia that the leading companies were astute at *distinguishing the contributions of information and technology, and considering them separately*. They make the point that competitive advantage *comes not from technology, but from how information is collected stored, analysed and applied.*

Business-alignment IS strategy
The IS strategy is generated from the business strategy through techniques such as CSF analysis.

An established aspect of information systems strategy development is the focus of IS strategy on business impact or alignment. In the **business-alignment** approach, a top–down approach is used to review how information systems can be used to directly support a defined business strategy. Referring to e-business strategy, Pant and Ravichandran (2001) say:

> *Alignment models focus on aligning the information system's plans and priorities with organizational strategy and business goals.*

Linking information systems to objectives and critical success factors (CSF) (*Table 5.4*), is one approach for using the alignment approach. Another is the use of business systems planning methodology which focuses on deriving data and applications needs by analysis of existing business processes.

Business-impacting IS strategy
IS strategy analyses opportunities for new technologies and processes to favourably impact the business strategy.

In the **business-impacting** approach, a bottom–up approach is used to determine whether there are new opportunities from deploying information systems that may impact positively on a business strategy. New hardware and software technologies are monitored by the IS manager and other managers to evaluate whether they can achieve competitive advantage. Pant and Ravichandran (2001) say:

> *impact models focus on the potential impact of information technology on organizational tasks and processes and use this as a basis to identify opportunities for deploying information systems.*

Value chain analysis (*Chapter 6, p. 279*) is one method that can be used for the impact approach. For example, this might identify the need for e-procurement which can be used as part of an effort to reduce costs and increase efficiency as part of business strategy. This technique has merit in that it not only considers internal use of information systems, but also how they can be used to integrate with external organizations such as suppliers, perhaps through innovative methods such as marketplace exchanges.

The impact and alignment techniques need not be mutually exclusive. During initial development of an e-business strategy, a business-alignment approach can be applied to ensure that IS strategy supports e-business strategy. A business-impacting approach is also useful to see which new opportunities IS produces. For instance, managers could consider how a relatively new technology such as workflow management software (*Chapter 11, p. 501*) can be used to improve efficiency and customer service.

The business-impacting approach can be achieved through the use of value chain analysis or re-engineering where an organization, through an analysis of the potential for the use of IS within and between value chain elements, may seek to identify strategic IS opportunities. Perhaps the ultimate expression of using IS to impact business performance is through business process re-engineering, which is considered in *Chapter 10*.

The application of an impacting or aligning strategy with respect to IS and business strategy is dependent on the importance attached to IS within an organization.

Debate 5.2

The influence of IS managers

'Board-level representation for IS managers is essential in the e-business era.'

Elements of IS strategy

Developing an IS strategy for e-business involves many different perspectives, rather than a single perspective such as hardware technologies or applications to deploy. Ward and Griffiths (1996) suggest an IS strategy plan contains three elements:

1 *Business information strategy*. How information will support the business. This will include applications to manage particular types of business.
2 *IS functionality strategy*. Which services are provided?
3 *IS/IT strategy*. Earlier in this book we have referred to providing a suitable *technological, applications and process infrastructure* (*Chapter 3, p. 118*).

The advent of e-business clearly increases the strategic importance of information systems resources of an organization. However, developing an IS strategy to achieve e-business goals is complex because it can be viewed from many different perspectives (*Table 5.9*). This table is essentially a checklist of different aspects of IS strategy that have to be implemented by an IS manager in the e-business. Many of these aspects are solutions to business and technical problems that are described in *Parts 2* and *3* of this book as summarized in the table.

Table 5.9 **Different elements of IS strategy**

IS strategy element	*What needs to be specified*	*Approaches to aid selected tactics (applications)*	*Specification*
1 Business contribution perspective (*Chapter 5*)	How applications achieve e-business objectives	Impact and alignment Portfolio analysis Investment types	Implementation of key systems
2 Information management strategy (*Chapter 10*)	Strategy for integrated information and knowledge management	Audit information management and knowledge management requirements by internal and external resources Security audit	Committee to standardize company information Enterprise resource planning, knowledge management, data ware housing, intranet and extranet projects
3 Applications perspective (*Chapters 3* and *11*)	Priorities for applications acquisition	Portfolio analysis Investment appraisal	As above
4 Process perspective (supply chain perspective to e-business) (*Chapters 6* and *11*)	How do applications and infrastructure support processes and value chain activities? Are new processes required?	Process mapping and analysis Value chain analysis	Enterprise resource planning integrated with transactional e-commerce
5 Departmental (functional) perspective (*Chapters 3* and *10*)	Which applications support different departments?	Portfolio analysis	Standardization of applications
6 Infrastructure perspective (*Chapters 3* and *11*)	Network capacity and service levels	Cost/benefit feasibility study of applications	Managing total cost of ownership Outsourcing
7 Communications perspective (*Chapter 9*)	Using technology to improve process efficiency and customer service quality	Audit communications volume and complexity Prioritize	E-mail, groupware and workflow systems Knowledge management

8 User services perspective (*Chapter 9*)	Helpdesk services for internal and external system users	Audit service levels, impact on business and then prioritize	Outsourcing Enquiry management systems
9 Customer and partner relationship management perspective (*Chapters 6* and *9*)	Investment in systems for managing customer and partner relationships	Customer relationship management and partner relationship management systems Use of standards for integration: EDI and XML	CRM facilities on web site Integration
10 Resourcing perspective (*Chapter 10*)	How are relevant IS skills acquired and developed?	Skills audit and industry comparison End-user computing	Technology partners Outsourcing Recruitment tactics E-learning and skills transfer
11 Change management perspective (*Chapter 10*)	How organizational culture and structure change to achieve e-business are managed	Apply existing change management approaches	Risk management Project management
12 Internal integration perspective (*Chapters 3* and *11*)	Overall applications architecture across the value chain	Analyse information access constraints, rekeying	Enterprise resource planning
13 External integration perspective (*Chapters 3* and *11*)	How are links between internal applications and partners managed?	Analyse ease of setting up links, prioritize	Outsourcing to systems integrator Standardization through ERP Integration of IS systems with buy- and sell side intermediaries
14 Legal constraints approach (*Chapter 4*)	How do we ensure company stays within international legal and ethical constraints?	Seek specialist advice, e.g. www.itcompliance.com	Specialist lawyers and privacy statements

We will now consider one of the most important issues facing IS managers in more detail.

Investment appraisal

In the e-business context, investment appraisal can refer to:

1 Overall levels of spending on information systems to support e-business.
2 Decisions about which business applications to invest in (portfolio analysis).
3 Assessment of the cost/benefit for individual applications.

Overall levels of spending on information systems to support e-business

Figure 5.14 suggests that companies should aim to invest in e-business in line with the objectives set. Since e-business investment is only 11.1 per cent compared to revenues of 14.9 per cent, this suggests that companies are underinvesting in e-commerce. The PricewaterhouseCoopers (2000) analysis also breaks down revenue and spending for product and service companies. Service companies achieve 20.6 per cent of total revenues online while product companies achieve 9 per cent of their revenues online. In terms of spending, service companies spend 10 per cent of operating budget on IT, split 57 per cent for IT personnel and 43 per cent for hardware and software. Product companies spend just 3.1 per cent of operating budget, split 44 per cent for IT personnel and 56 per cent for hardware and software. Lower revenues in these companies seems consistent with lower investment. Hackbarth and Kettinger (2000) suggest that one element of e-business strategy development is whether to focus on the sell-side or the buy-side for applications development.

Decisions about which business applications to invest in

A portfolio analysis such as that illustrated for The B2C Company in *Figure 5.7* can also be used to decide priorities for application by selecting those that fall within the strategic and turnaround categories for further investment. Relative priorities and the amount of investment in different applications can also be assisted if priorities for e-business objectives have been assigned, as is the case with *Table 5.4*.

Traditionally investments in information systems have been categorized according to their importance and contribution to the organization. For example, Robson (1997) describes four types of BIS investment:

1 *Operational value investment.* These investments are in systems that are key to the day-to-day running of the organization, such as transaction processing systems for processing orders received by phone or a workflow system for managing booking staff training and leave. Such systems are often valuable in increasing efficiency or reducing costs, but they do not contribute directly to the performance of the business.
2 *Strategic value investment.* Strategic investments will enhance the performance of a business and should help in developing revenue. A customer relationship management system would be a strategic investment. This will be intended to increase customer loyalty, resulting in additional sales from existing customers.
3 *Threshold investment.* These are investments in BIS that a company must make to operate within a business. Investments may have a negative return on investment but are needed for competitive survival.
4 *Infrastructure investment.* These can be substantial investments which result in gain in the medium-to-long term. Typically this includes investment in internal networks, electronic links with suppliers, customers and partners and investment in new hardware such as client PCs and servers.

As part of developing e-business strategies, companies can prioritize potential information systems investments in the above categories according to their impact on the business. A similar approach is to specify the applications portfolio described in the section on situation analysis. It is evident that priority should be given to applications that fall into the strategic and high-potential categories in *Figure 5.7*. Now complete *Activity 5.5*.

Activity 5.5 E-business investment types

Purpose

To gain an appreciation of how to prioritize IS investments.

Questions

1 Referring to the four investment categories of Robson (1997), discuss in groups which category the following investments would fit into:

(a) E-procurement system
(b) Transactional e-commerce web site
(c) Contract with ISP to host web server and provide Internet connectivity for staff
(d) Workflow system to manage complex customer orders (e.g. processing orders)
(e) Upgrading a company network.

2 Assume you only had sufficient funds to invest in two of these options. Which two would you choose?

Answers to activities can be found at www.pearsoned.co.uk/chaffey

The productivity paradox

Productivity paradox
Research results indicating a poor correlation between organizational investment in information systems and organizational performance measured by return on equity.

All discussion of investment appraisals in information systems should acknowledge the existence of the productivity paradox. Studies in the late 1980s and 1990s summarized by Brynjolfsson (1993) and Strassman (1997) suggest that there is little or no correlation between a company's investment in information systems and its business performance measured in terms of profitability or stock returns. Strassman's work, based on a study of 468 major North American and European firms, showed a random relationship between IT spending per employee and return on equity.

To the present day, there has been much dispute about the reality of the productivity paradox. Carr (2003) suggests that information technology has become commoditized to such an extent that it no longer delivers a competitive advantage. Carr says:

> *What makes a resource truly strategic – what gives it the capacity to be the basis for a sustained competitive advantage is not ubiquity, but scarcity. You only gain an edge over rivals by having something that they can't have or can't do. By now the core functions of IT – data storage, data processing and data transport have become available and affordable to all ... They are becoming costs of doing business that must be paid by all but provide distinction to none.*

While many would agree that the technology such as PCs, servers and communications technologies have become commoditized, it is arguable whether technology cannot provide distinction. Carr's argument is consistent with the productivity paradox concept, since although IT investments may help in increasing productivity, this does not necessarily yield a competitive advantage if all competitors are active in making similar IT investments. As the *Financial Times* (2003) puts it:

> *Productivity gains that are easily replicated across an industry usually end up in the hands of customers. Only when gains remain unique to a company do managers get a say in how to distribute the spoils – between customers (in the form of lower prices or higher quality), shareholders (higher profits) and workers (increased pay).*

Today, most authors such as Brynjolfsson and Hitt (1998) refute the productivity paradox and conclude that it results from mismeasurement, the lag occurring between initial investment and payback and the mismanagement of information systems projects. More recent detailed studies such as that by Sircar *et al.* (2000) confirm the findings of Brynjolfsson and Hitt (1998). They state that:

> *Both IT and corporate investments have a strong positive relationship with sales, assets, and equity, but not with net income. Spending on IS staff and staff training is positively correlated with firm performance, even more so than computer capital.*

In conclusion they state:

> *The value of IS staff and staff training was also quite apparent and exceeded that of computer capital. This confirms the positions of several authors, that the effective use of IT is far more important than merely spending on IT.*

The disproportionate allocation of spend to implementation was highlighted by the *Financial Times* (2003) which said:

> *Prof Brynjolfsson and colleagues found that of the $20m total cost of an enterprise resource planning (ERP) system, only about $3m goes to the software supplier and perhaps $1m towards the acquisition of new computers. The $16m balance is spent on business process redesign, external consultants, training and managerial time. The ratio between IT investment and this 'supporting' expenditure varies across projects and companies. But, over a range of IT projects, Prof Brynjolfsson believes that a 10:1 ratio is about right. Returns on these investments commonly take 5 years to materialise.*

The 10:1 ratio between total investment in new information management practices and IT, mentioned in the extract, also shows that applying technology is only a relatively small part in achieving returns – developing the right approaches to process innovation, business models and change management are more important, and arguably more difficult and less easy to replicate. Some leading companies have managed to align investment in e-business with their business strategies to achieve these unique gains. For example, Wal-Mart Stores, Dell, Intel and easyJet have combined extensive use of technology with strategic innovation. For example, Dell has used a range of IT-enabled techniques mentioned earlier in the chapter such as online ordering, the Dell Premier extranet for large purchasers, vendor-managed inventory, adaptive supply chains, build-to-order to gain competitive advantage.

So, in summary research into the productivity paradox highlights the importance of considering the information, people and technology resources together when planning for e-business strategy and implementation. It also suggests that e-business contributes to productivity gains only when combined with investments in process redesign, organizational change management and innovation.

Summary

1 E-business strategy process models tend to share the following characteristics:
   - Continuous internal and external environment scanning or analysis are required.
   - Clear statement of vision and objectives is required.
   - Strategy development can be broken down into formulation and selection, a key emphasis being assessing the differential benefits provided by e-channels for company and stakeholders and then selecting the most appropriate channels for different business activities and partners ('right-channelling').
   - After strategy development, enactment of the strategy occurs as strategy implementation.
   - Control is required to detect problems and adjust the strategy accordingly.
   - They must be responsive to changes in the marketplace.

2 In this chapter a four-stage model is used as a framework for e-business strategy development. Key e-business issues within this framework are outlined below.

3 *Strategic analysis*. Continuous scanning of the micro- and macro-environment of an organization are required, with particular emphasis on the changing needs of customers, actions and business models of competitors, and opportunities afforded by new technologies. Techniques include resource analysis, demand analysis and competitor analysis, applications portfolio analysis, SWOT analysis and competitive environment analysis.

4 *Strategic objectives.* Organizations must have a clear vision on wh media will complement or replace other media, and their capacit Clear objectives must be defined and in particular goals for the on contribution should be set.

5 *Strategy definition.* Six key elements of e-business strategy that were reviewed are:

- E-business priorities – significance to organization (replace or complement) and emphasis on buy-side or sell-side.
- Form of restructuring required.
- Business and revenue models.
- Marketplace restructuring.
- Market and product development strategies.
- Positioning and differentiation strategies.

6 Strategy implementation. Detailed in the remainder of *Part 2* and in *Part 3*.

7 Information systems strategy should use a combination of impact and alignment techniques to govern e-business strategy. IS strategy can take a number of perspectives, of which those that focus on information or knowledge management and technological and applications infrastructure are most important.

Exercises

Self-assessment questions

1 What are the key characteristics of an e-business strategy model?

2 Select a retailer or manufacturer of your choice and describe what the main elements of its situation analysis should comprise.

3 For the same retailer or manufacturer suggest different methods and metrics for defining e-business objectives.

4 For the same retailer or manufacturer assess different strategic options to adopt for e-business.

Essay and discussion questions

1 Evaluate the range of restructuring options for an existing 'bricks-and-mortar' organization to move to 'bricks-and-clicks' or 'clicks-only' contributing a higher online revenue.

2 Explain the main strategy definition options or decisions available to an organization intending to become an e-business.

3 Between 1994 and 1999 Amazon lost more than $500m, but at the end of this period its valuation was still more than $20bn. At the start of 2000 Amazon.com underwent its first round of job cuts, sacking 150 staff or 2 per cent of its worldwide workforce. Later in 2000 its valuation dropped to less than half.

Write an essay on the strategy of Amazon.com exploring its history, different criteria for success and its future. See the *Wired Magazine* archive for profiles of Amazon (www.wired.com).

4 Analyse the reasons for the failure of the original boo.com. Research and assess the sustainability of the new boo.com business model.

5 What can existing businesses learn from the business approaches of the dot-com organizations? →

6 What are the similarities and differences between the concepts of business process re-engineering (BPR) and e-business? Will the e-business concept face the same fate as BPR?

7 Discuss this statement by David Weymouth, Barclays Bank chief information officer (Simons, 2000b):

> *There is no merit in becoming a dot-com business. Within five years successful businesses will have embraced and deployed at real-scale across the whole enterprise, the processes and technologies that we now know as dot-com.*

8 Compare and contrast different approaches to developing e-business strategy.

Examination questions

1 Define the main elements of an e-business strategy.

2 You are the incumbent e-business manager for a domestic airline. What process would you use to create objectives for the organization? Suggest three typical objectives and how you would measure them.

3 Explain the productivity paradox and its implications for managers.

4 What choices do executives have for the scope and timeframe of implementing e-business?

References

Aaker, D. and Joachimsthaler, E. (2000) *Brand Leadership*. Free Press, New York.

Ansoff, H. (1957) Strategies for diversification. *Harvard Business Review*, September–October, 113–24.

Arnott, D. and Bridgewater, S. (2002) Internet, interaction and implications for marketing. *Marketing Intelligence and Planning*, 20(2), 86–95.

Banker (2003) Why does the CIO have so many hats? *The Banker*, 2 December, 2003. http://www.thebanker.com/news/fullstory.php/aid/921/Why does the CIO have so many hats .html?PHPSESSID=6127f5720bc3f4cb3bd386bf1f31087a.

Brynjolfsson, E. (1993) The productivity paradox of information technology. *Communications of the ACM*, 36(12), 67–77.

Brynjolfsson, E. and Hitt, L. (1998) Beyond the productivity paradox. *Communications of the ACM*, 41(8), 49–55.

Carr, N. (2003) IT doesn't matter. *Harvard Business Review*, May, 5–12.

Chaffey, D. and Wood, S. (2004) *Business Information Management, Improving Performance Using Information Systems*. Financial Times Prentice Hall, Harlow.

Chaffey, D., Mayer, R., Johnston, K. and Ellis-Chadwick, F. (2006) *Internet Marketing: Strategy, Implementation and Practice*, 3rd edn. Financial Times Prentice Hall, Harlow.

Chaston, I. (2000) *E-Marketing Strategy*. McGraw-Hill, Maidenhead.

Damanpour, F. (2001) E-business, e-commerce, evolution: perspective and strategy. *Managerial Finance*, 27(7), 16–33.

Daniel, E., Wilson, H., McDonald, M. and Ward, J. (2001) *Marketing Strategy in the Digital Age*. Financial Times Prentice Hall, Harlow.

Deise, M., Nowikow, C., King, P. and Wright, A. (2000) *Executive's Guide to E-Business. From Tactics to Strategy*. Wiley, New York.

de Kare-Silver, M. (2000) *EShock 2000. The Electronic Shopping Revolution: Strategies for Retailers and Manufacturers*. Macmillan, London.

der Zee, J. and de Jong, B. (1999) Alignment is not enough: integrating business and information technology management with the balanced business scorecard. *Journal of Management Information Systems*, 16(2), 137–57.

Doherty, N. and McAulay, L. (2002) Towards the formulation of a comprehensive framework for the evaluation of investments in sell-side e-commerce. *Evaluation and Program Planning*, 25, 159–65.

Durlacher (2000) Trends in the UK new economy. *Durlacher Quarterly Internet Report*, November, pp. 1–12.

Economist (2000) Enter the ecosystem. 11 November.

Financial Times (2003) Buried treasure. *Financial Times*. Article by Simon London, 10 December.

Gulati, R. and Garino, J. (2000) Getting the right mix of bricks and clicks for your company. *Harvard Business Review*, May–June, 107–14.

Hackbarth, G. and Kettinger, W. (2000) Building an e-business strategy. *Information Systems Management*, Summer, 78–93.

Hughes, S. (2001) Market orientation and the response of UK financial services companies to changes in market conditions as a result of e-commerce. *International Journal of Bank Marketing*, 19(6), 222–31.

Jeffcoate, J., Chappell, C. and Feindt, S. (2002) Best practice in SME adoption of e-commerce. *Benchmarking: An International Journal*, 9, 122–32.

Johnson, G. and Scholes, K. (1999) *Exploring Corporate Strategy*. Prentice Hall Europe, Hemel Hempstead.

Kalakota, R. and Robinson, M. (2000) *E-Business. Roadmap for Success*. Addison-Wesley, Reading, MA.

Kaplan, R.S. and Norton, D.P. (1993) Putting the balanced scorecard to work. *Harvard Business Review*, September–October, 134–42.

Kim, E., Nam, D. and Stimpert, D. (2004) The applicability of Porter's generic strategies in the digital age: assumptions, conjectures and suggestions. *Journal of Management*, 30, 569–89.

Kumar, N. (1999) Internet distribution strategies: dilemmas for the incumbent. *Financial Times*, Special Issue on Mastering Information Management, no. 7, Electronic Commerce.

Levy, M. and Powell, P. (2003) Exploring SME Internet adoption: towards a contingent model. *Electronic Markets*, 13(2): 173–81. www.electronicmarkets.org.

Lord, C. (2000) The practicalities of developing a successful e-business strategy. *Journal of Business Strategy*, 21(2), 40–7.

Lynch, R. (2000) *Corporate Strategy*. Financial Times Prentice Hall, Harlow.

Malmsten, E., Portanger, E. and Drazin, C. (2001) *Boo Hoo. A Dot.com Story from Concept to Catastrophe*. Random House, London.

Marchand, D. (1999) Hard In choices for senior managers. In *Mastering Information Management*, D. Marchand, T. Davenport and T. Dickson (eds). Financial Time Prentice Hall, Harlow, 187–92.

McDonald, M. (1999) Strategic marketing planning: theory and practice. In *The CIM Marketing Book*, 4th edn, (ed.) M. Baker Butterworth-Heinemann, Oxford, 50–77.

McDonald, M. and Wilson, H. (2002) *New Marketing: Transforming the Corporate Future*. Butterworth-Heinemann, Oxford.

McFarlan, F. and McKenney, J. (1993) *Corporate Information Systems Management*. Prentice Hall, London.

Miller, T. (2003) Top ten lessons from the Internet shakeout. Article on Webmergers.com. Available online at: www.webmergers.com/data/article.php?id=48.

Mintzberg, H. and Quinn, J. (1991) *The Strategy Process*, 2nd edn. Prentice-Hall, Upper Saddle River, NJ.

Myers, J., Pickersgill, A, and Van Metre, E. (2004) Steering Customers to the Right Channels. *McKinsey Quarterly*, no. 4.

New Media Age (1999) Will boo.com scare off the competition? By Budd Margolis. *New Media Age*. 22 July. Online only. www.nma.co.uk.

New Media Age (2005) Delivering the goods. By Nic Howell. *New Media Age*, 5 May.

Nolan, R. (1979) Managing the crisis in data processing. *Harvard Business Review*, March–April, 115–26.

Olve, N., Roy, J. and Wetter, M. (1999) *Performance Drivers. A Practical Guide to Using the Balanced Scorecard*. Wiley, Chichester.

Pant, S. and Ravichandran, T. (2001) A framework for information systems planning for e-business. *Logistics Information Management*, 14(1), 85–98.

Phillips, S. (2000) Retailer's crown jewel is a unique customer database. *Financial Times*, 4 December.

Picardi, R. (2000) *EBusiness Speed: Six Strategies for eCommerce Intelligence*. IDC Research Report. IDC, Framingham, MA.

Plant, R. (2000) *ECommerce: Formulation of Strategy*. Prentice-Hall, Upper Saddle River, NJ.

Porter, M. (1980) *Competitive Strategy*. Free Press, New York.

Porter, M. (2001) Strategy and the Internet. *Harvard Business Review*, March, 62–78.

PricewaterhouseCoopers (2000) Trendsetter Barometer Report, Q2, 2000. Available online only at www.barometersurveys.com.

Quelch, J. and Klein, L. (1996) The Internet and international marketing. *Sloan Management Review*, Spring, 60–75.

Revolution (2005) Campaign of the Month, by Emma Rigby, *Revolution*. October, 69.

Robson, W. (1997) *Strategic Management and Information Systems: An Integrated Approach*. Pitman, London.

Rowley, J. (2002) Synergy and strategy in e-commerce. *Marketing Intelligence and Planning*, 20(4), 215–20.

Simons, M. (2000a) Barclays gambles on web big bang. *Computer Weekly*, 13 July, 1.

Simons, M. (2000b) Setting the banks alight. *Computer Weekly*, 20 July, 6.

Sircar, S., Turnbow, J. and Bordoloi, B. (2000) A framework for assessing the relationship between information technology investments and firm performance. *Journal of Management Information Systems*, Spring, 16(4), 69–98.

Smith, P. (1999) *Marketing Communications: An Integrated Approach*, 2nd edn. Kogan Page, London.

Strassman, P. (1997) *The Squandered Computer*. Information Economics Press, New Canaan, CT.

Tjan, A. (2001) Finally, a way to put your Internet portfolio in order. *Harvard Business Review*, February, 78–85.

Venkatraman, N. (2000) Five steps to a dot-com strategy: how to find your footing on the web. *Sloan Management Review*, Spring, 15–28.

Ward, J. and Griffiths, P. (1996) *Strategic Planning for Information Systems*. Wiley, Chichester.

Willcocks, L. and Plant, R. (2000) Business Internet strategy – moving to the net. In L. Willcocks and C. Sauer (eds), *Moving to E-Business*. Random House, London, 19–46.

Further reading

Deise, M., Nowikow, C., King, P. and Wright, A. (2000) *Executive's Guide to E-Business. From Tactics to Strategy*. Wiley, New York. An excellent practitioner's guide.

Gulati, R. and Garino, J. (2000) Getting the right mix of bricks and clicks for your company. *Harvard Business Review*, May–June, 107–14. A different perspective on the six strategy decisions given in the strategic definition section, with a road map through the decision process.

Hackbarth, G. and Kettinger, W. (2000) Building an e-business strategy. *Information Systems Management*, Summer, 78–93. An information systems perspective to e-business strategy.

Porter, M. (2001) Strategy and the Internet. *Harvard Business Review*, March, 63–78. Michael Porter defends his existing models in the new economy context.

Willcocks, L. and Sauer, C. (2000) *Introduction to Moving to e-business*. Random House, London, 1–18. Combines traditional IS strategy-based approaches with up-to-date case studies.

Web links

BRINT.com (www.brint.com): a business researcher's interests. Extensive portal with articles on e-business, e-commerce, knowledge management, change management and IS strategy.

CIO Magazine e-commerce resource centre (www.cio.com/forums/ec) One of the best online magazines from a business/technical perspective – see other research centres also, e.g. intranets, knowledge management.

DaveChaffey.com (www.davechaffey.com/E-business) Updates by the author about all aspects of e-business, including strategy.

E-commerce innovation centre (www.ecommerce.ac.uk) at Cardiff University. Interesting case studies for SMEs and basic explanations of concepts and terms.

E-commerce Times (www.ecommercetimes.com) An online newspaper specific to e-commerce developments.

Financial Times Digital Business (http://news.ft.com/reports/digitalbusiness) Excellent monthly articles based on case studies.

E-commerce About.com (www.ecommerce.about.com) Portal about all aspects of e-commerce.

E-consultancy (www.e-consultancy.com) E-business portal with links to news and white papers on other sites.

IT Toolbox (www.ittoolbox.com) Guidelines and articles on e-business including ERP, CRM and data warehousing.

Mohansawney.com (www.mohansawney.com). Case studies and white papers from one of the leading US authorities on e-commerce.

US Center for e-business (www.ebusiness.mit.edu) Useful collection of articles.

6 Supply chain management

Chapter at a glance

Web support

The following additional case studies are available at www.pearsoned.co.uk/chaffey

- A short history of the Sainsburys approach to e-fulfilment models
- The Telecoms supply chain

The site also contains a range of study material designed to help improve your results.

Learning outcomes

After completing this chapter the reader should be able to:

- Identify the main elements of supply chain management and their relationship to the value chain and value networks
- Assess the potential of information systems to support supply chain management and the value chain.

Management issues

The issues for the manager:

- Which technologies should we deploy for supply chain management and how should they be prioritized?
- Which elements of the supply chain should be managed within and beyond the organization and how can technology be used to facilitate this?

Links to other chapters

The main related chapters are:

- *Chapter 1* introduces the supply chain as a key element of e-business;
- *Chapter 7* considers the e-procurement part of the supply chain in more detail.

Introduction

In the end business all comes down to supply chain vs supply chain.

(Robert Rodin, then CEO of Marshall Industries, one of the largest global distributors of electronic components, 1999)

Supply chain management is essentially the optimization of material flows and associated information flows involved with an organization's operations. To manage these material and information flows e-business applications are today essential to synchronize demand and supply and manage procurement, warehouse inventory and product distribution.

Supply chain management is presented as the premier application of e-business in *Part 2* of this book since it is a unifying concept that incorporates both e-procurement (*Chapter 7*) and sell-side e-commerce (*Chapters 8* and *9*). By applying information systems, companies can enhance or radically improve many aspects of the supply chain. In the context of *Figure 1.1*, which was used to introduce the concept of e-business, supply chain management can be enhanced through buy-side e-commerce, internal communications, relationships with partners and sell-side e-commerce. E-business technologies enable information flows to be redefined to facilitate the sharing of information between partners, often at lower costs than were previously possible. For example in *Case Study 6.1*, we see how Shell Chemicals has developed a vendor-managed inventory (VMI) system to enable delivery of supplies to be more responsive to customers' demands.

Much of the excitement generated by the e-business concept concerns the benefits that companies can achieve through increasing the efficiency of the whole supply chain. Companies such as Tesco (*Case Study 6.2*), that have enthusiastically embraced technology to manage the supply chain, have been reaping the benefits for many years.

What is supply chain management?

Supply chain management (SCM)
The coordination of all supply activities of an organization from its suppliers and partners to its customers.

Upstream supply chain
Transactions between an organization and its suppliers and intermediaries, equivalent to buy-side e-commerce.

Downstream supply chain
Transactions between an organization and its customers and intermediaries, equivalent to sell-side e-commerce.

Supply chain network
The links between an organization and all partners involved in multiple supply chains.

Supply chain management (SCM) involves the coordination of all supply activities of an organization from its suppliers and delivery of products to its customers (*Figure 6.1*). *Figure 6.1* introduces the main players in the supply chain. In *Figure 6.1(a)* the main members of the supply chain are the organizations that manufacture a product and/or deliver a service.

For most commercial and not-for-profit organizations we can distinguish between **upstream supply chain** activities which are equivalent to buy-side e-commerce and **downstream supply chain** activities which correspond to sell-side e-commerce. In this chapter and the next we focus mainly on improving the efficiency of upstream supply chain activities, while in *Chapters 8* and *9* the emphasis is on the marketing aspects of improving downstream supply chain activities.

Remember also from *Figure 1.1* that supply chain management includes not only supplier and buyer, but also the intermediaries such as the supplier's suppliers and the customer's customers (*Figure 6.1(b)*). Indeed, *Figure 6.1(b)* is a simplification of some companies which may have first-tier suppliers, second-tier and even third-tier suppliers or first-, second- and higher-tier customers. Because each company effectively has many individual supply chains for different products, the use of the term 'chain' is limiting and **supply chain network** is a more accurate reflection of the links between an organization and its partners. The existence of this network increases the need for electronic communications technology to manage and optimize this network.

Technology is vital to supply chain management since managing relationships with customers, suppliers and intermediaries is based on the flow of information and

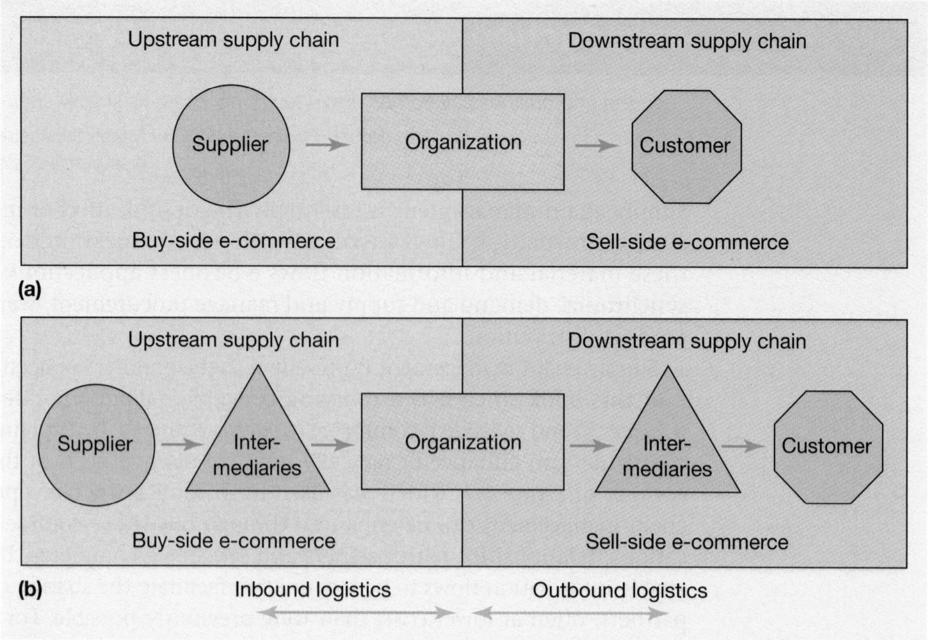

Figure 6.1 **Members of the supply chain: (a) simplified view, (b) including intermediaries**

the transactions between these parties. The main strategic thrust of enhancing the supply chain is to provide a superior value proposition to the customer, of which efficient consumer response is one method; see the box *Efficient consumer response*. As explained in *Chapter 5* improving customer value involves improving product

Efficient consumer response (ECR)

The ECR concept was developed for the food retailing business in the USA but since then it has been applied to other products and in other countries. It was originally developed by David Jenkins, then chairman of Shaw's supermarkets, to compete with other players such as Wal-Mart. *Table 6.1* shows that some of the aims and strategic approaches generated by ECR can also apply to business customers.

Table 6.1 **Objectives and strategies for effective consumer response (ECR)**

Objective	*Strategy*
Timely, accurate, paperless information flow	Revision of organization processes supported by information systems
Smooth, continual product flow matched to variations in consumption levels	See strategies below
Optimize productivity of retail space and inventory	Efficient store assortments
Optimize for time and cost in the ordering process	Efficient replacement
Maximize efficiency of promotions	Promotions are integrated into entire supply chain planning
Maximize effectiveness of new product development (NPD)	NPD process improved and better forward planning with other partners

quality, customer service quality and/or reducing price and fulfilment times. An alternative emphasis is on increasing efficiency in obtaining resources from a supplier organization or distributing products to customers. This emphasis is about reducing operational costs and so increasing profitability.

Using technology to support supply chain management – an example

A good example of how the introduction of information systems can be used to improve supply chain management is provided by BHP Steel, an Australian firm. Its use of PC-based technology for supply chain management dates back to the 1980s and e-business represents a change of emphasis rather than a radically new approach. Chan and Swatman (2000) assess the stages in implementation of e-commerce for this company. It highlights that electronic supply chain management and indeed 'e-business' are well established in large companies. The authors identify three phases:

1 *Early implementation*: *1989–1993*. This was a PC-based EDI purchasing system. At this stage, objectives were to (1) reduce data errors to 0, (2) reduce administration costs, (3) improve management control, (4) reduce order lead time. Benefits of this phase included rationalization of suppliers to 12 major partnerships (accounting for 60% of invoices); 80% of invoices placed electronically by 1990; 7,000 items were eliminated from the warehouse, to be sourced directly from suppliers, on demand. Shorter lead times in the day-to-day process – from 10 days to 26 hours for items supplied through a standard contract and from 42 days to 10 days for direct-purchase items. At this stage the main barriers to the implementation were technological.
2 *Electronic trading gateway: 1990–1994*. This was again EDI-based, but involved a wider range of parties both externally (from suppliers through to customers) and internally (from marketing, sales, finance, purchasing and legal). The aim was to provide a combined upstream and downstream supply chain solution to bring benefits to all parties. The main learning from this process was the difficulty of getting customers involved – only four were involved after 4 years, although an industry-standard method for data exchange was used. This was surprising since suppliers had been enthusiastic adopters. From 1994, there was no further uptake of this system.
3 *The move towards Internet commerce: 1996 onwards*. The Internet was thought to provide a lower-cost alternative to traditional EDI for smaller suppliers and customers, through using a lower-cost value-added network. So, one objective of the project was to extend the reach of electronic communications with supply chain partners. The second was to broaden the type of communications to include catalogue ordering, freight forwarding and customer ordering. The strategy divided transactions into three types: (1) strategic (high volume, high value, high risk) – a dedicated EDI line was considered most appropriate; (2) tactical (medium volume, value and risk) EDI or Internet EDI was used; (3) consumer transactions (low volume, value and risk) – a range of lower-cost Internet-based technologies could be used. One example of the benefits has been reducing test certificates for products from AU$3 to 30 cents. The main barriers to implementation at this stage have been business issues, i.e. convincing third parties of the benefits of integration and managing the integration process.

A simple model of a supply chain

An organization's supply chain can be viewed from a systems perspective as the acquisition of resources (inputs) and their transformation (process) into products and services (outputs) which are then delivered to customers. Such a perspective indicates that as part of moving to e-business, organizations can review the transformation process and optimize it in order to deliver products to customers with greater efficiency and lower cost. Note that the position of the systems boundary for SCM extends beyond the organization – it involves improving not only internal processes, but also processes performed in conjunction with suppliers, distributors and customers. However, this process perspective misses the strategic importance of supply chain management – it also provides great opportunities to improve product performance and deliver superior value to the customer. As a result, supply chain management can dramatically have an impact on the profitability of a company through reducing operating costs and increasing customer satisfaction and so loyalty and revenue.

Since *Figure 6.1* is a grossly simplified version of most supply chains, a more representative supply chain is illustrated in *Figure 6.2* which shows the supply chain for The B2B Company. Complete the introductory activity (*Activity 6.1*) to consider the issues involved in modifying the supply chain in response to e-business. Note that although this example is based on a business-to-business scenario, supply chain management is also vital to the management of business-to-consumer and service companies. With service companies such as financial services, the resources managed tend not to be physical but human, financial and information resources. However, the same principles of using e-commerce technology to enhance supply chain activities can be applied.

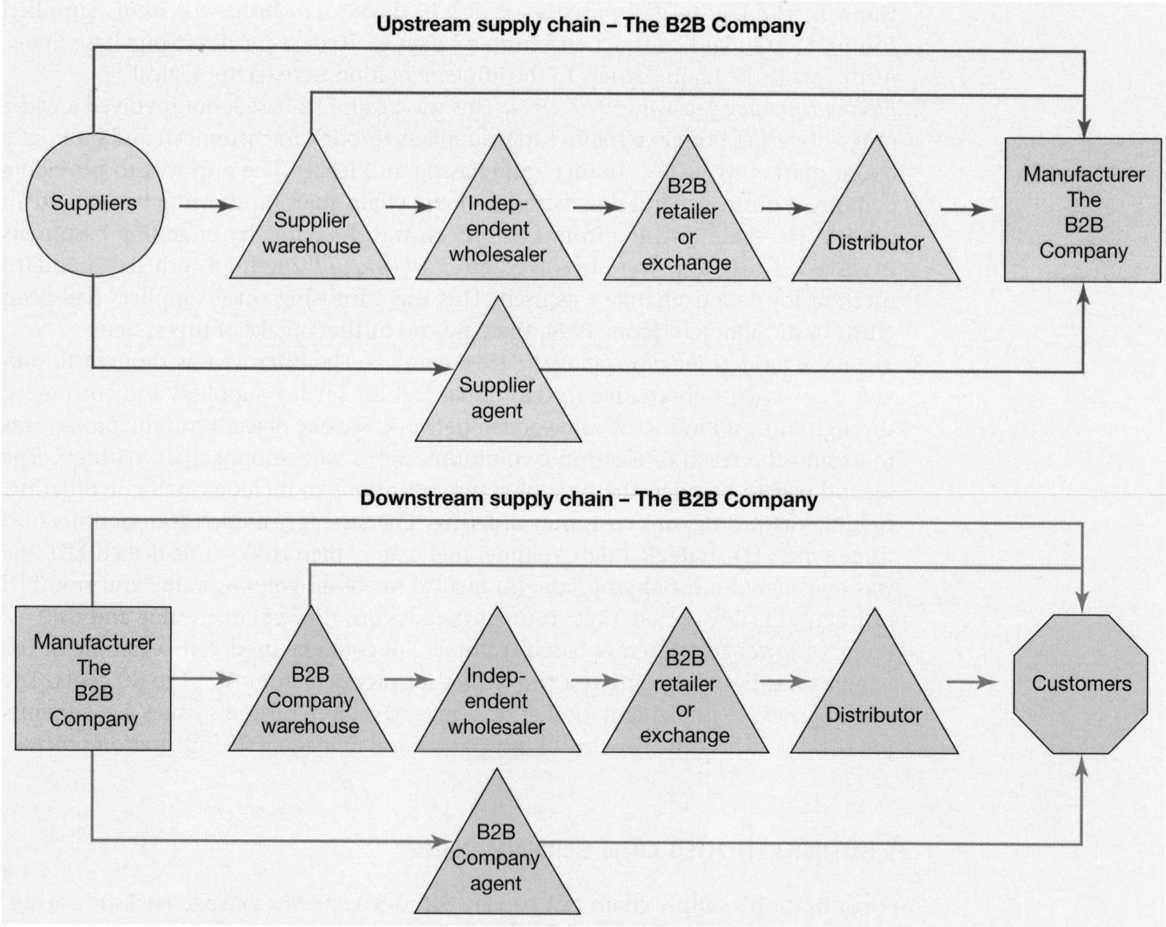

Figure 6.2 **A typical supply chain (an example from The B2B Company)**

Activity 6.1 The supply chain for The B2B Company

Visit the w.w.w.

Purpose

To examine the nature of a B2B supply chain and its potential for modification through restructuring and information systems as part of e-business development.

Questions

1 Referring to *Chapter 2* and the section on disintermediation and reintermediation, discuss the opportunities for The B2B Company to restructure its supply chain as part of the move to e-business, and the benefits this may bring.

2 How can information systems be used to accomplish the changes you have identified in question 1?

Answers to activities can be found at www.pearsoned.co.uk/chaffey

Case Study 6.1 Shell Chemicals redefines its customers' supply chains

This case illustrates an e-business application for buy-side e-commerce. Shell Chemicals introduced this new system to manage their customers' inventory based on data shared by its customers about their usage and forecast demand for chemicals. This process is referred to as 'vendor- or supplier-managed inventory'. The benefits of introducing this system for Shell and its customers are described. The case is made up of two extracts. The first explains the introduction of the situation, the second how the system is used today.

Shell Chemicals manufactures the chemicals used by other manufacturers of many industrial and consumer products. Shell's customers use detergents, solvents, plastics, elastomers and epoxy resins to produce everything from automotive paints and aircraft structures to diapers and plastic bottles.

Within such an organization, supply chain management has a dramatic impact on the bottom line. The managers of Shell's SIMON – Shell Inventory Managed Order Network – believe that supply chain management refers to both the upstream and downstream relationships that affect their business.

Shell used SIMON to turn around their downstream supply chain processes – the ones dedicated to getting goods to their customers. Since SIMON, a Lotus Notes e-business application, was successful in the downstream process it was then applied to the upstream processes – acquiring raw materials from suppliers.

The managers of the system state that: 'SIMON enables the transfer of responsibility for inventory management from customer to supplier. There is no need for a Shell Chemicals customer to place an order. Through SIMON, we're able to proactively keep vital inventory on their shelves, so to speak. Customers pay only for what they consume. We are their sole-source supplier. It's a cutting-edge supplier/customer business model – one that's built on a relationship of mutual trust and a belief that there are significant benefits to be realized on both sides.'

Traditional operations model

Before the introduction of SIMON, there was a danger that Shell's customers might run out of an essential chemical, so that plant time and then revenues would be lost. To avoid this, companies tend to maintain 'safety stock' levels. Re-ordering then occurs when inventory gets too close to these safety stock levels. The difficulty is that a typical re-supply order takes about two weeks from the time the order is placed. This delay occurs since chemicals must be weighed at the plant, loaded onto railcars and then sent to the customer, who then weighs the materials at the other end before moving them into inventory. Miscalculations tend to lead to rush orders. Rush orders are more expensive and quite common. Billing was inefficient: an invoice was sent out for every single railcar load of product that was sent from Shell to their customer.

New operational model

The new arrangement is known as 'supplier-managed inventory' (SMI). Since companies are wary of running out of stock they traditionally tend to use inflated safety stock levels. Maintaining excess inventory is a very costly process since it eats into working capital. In the new system information on stock levels is replicated back to the Shell customer service centre in Houston, Texas, where Shell can reconcile it with their enterprise resource planning software provider SAP MRP system. A Shell account service rep is automatically presented with a →

re-supply plan. If the plan indicates that stocking levels at the customer site are low, the rep fills out an electronic purchase order and initiates a new shipment to the customer. Previously, the customer would have had to explicitly initiate each new order. Now, once a month (not once per railcar load!), an invoice is generated. The invoice is based on consumption figures, not shipments.

Using the new SIMON application that the customer accesses from a Notes client, the customer can find out:

- the amount of product consumed in the past 24 hours
- the amount of new product that arrived and was unloaded in the same period
- current and anticipated production schedules, and known changes to those schedules
- status of these orders and shipments
- estimated dates of arrival and shipment weights
- receipt and unloading dates
- current stock and consumption levels
- a comparison of metered and calculated consumption from a 'Reconciliation' tab,
- the mutually-agreed-upon plan for management of inventory from a 'Site level agreements' tab.

Through access to this information Shell customers receive the following benefits. The use of SIMON:

- eliminates expensive excess inventory, which means an increase in working capital
- facilitates timely, low-cost 're-synching' of the supply chain
- ensures product is on site whenever needed
- ensures quicker response times to changing conditions
- reduces transaction costs (e.g. invoices and data entry)
- eliminates erratic order patterns
- reduces order processing overhead
- streamlines financial statements and reconciliation processes.

SIMON was first introduced to 23 of Shell's largest, most strategic customer accounts during summer 1996 and now supports over 50 accounts. Within 12 months, Shell experienced a $20 million increase in additional product sales, and Shell stated that its customers were reporting increased flexibility in its acquisition and delivery processes. Shell also stated that there were more sole supplier accounts as a result of this system, suggesting it is giving rise to some lock-in. In the second phase, Shell extended SIMON to its suppliers, enabling suppliers to manage the inventories of items they provided to Shell so that Shell could achieve similar benefits to its customers.

Implementation

SIMON is described by Shell as a Notes-based corporate extranet acting as a customer inventory management system. This represents a change from the industry standard practice of using electronic data interchange (EDI) forms, telephone orders and paper invoices to communicate with customers. However, EDI didn't give Shell the flexibility it needed to accommodate data on exceptions and processes. The company invested roughly $200,000 and two months to set up the Shell Inventory Management Order Network at the first site. A server in the customer's purchasing department replicates changes to Shell's internal SIMON server. Those changes are available to Shell account representatives via a token ring network.

Source: Adapted from the IBM e-business web site case study (www.ibm.com/ebusiness)

SIMON 10 years on

In 2004, the Shell house magazine showed how the SIMON system is still in use nearly 10 years later and how it is used for supply chain management.

The Shell Chemicals Channel Captain programme provides customers with integrated inventory management. For Bayer in the US, the coordination and management of all phenol and acetone deliveries by one supplier offers both supply chain efficiencies and potential for competitive advantage.

As a supplier-managed inventory analyst for Shell Chemical LP, Denise Covin begins each day checking SIMON (Supplier Inventory Management Order Network). A Shell-developed software programme, SIMON allows Covin to see the status of product shipments and reconcile product supply and demand so that her customer, Bayer Corporation, has a continuous supply of phenol and acetone for its BPA plant in Baytown, Texas.

What's unique about Covin's role is that she coordinates the entire supply chain inventory management process, working closely with the customer and even coordinating product delivery requests with another supplier, to manage Bayer's inventory.

While the Channel Captain service has been offered to numerous bulk supply customers around the world for several years, the relationship with Bayer is unique because it is the first to involve product deliveries by barge to the company's Business Process Automation (BPA) manufacturing facility.

In an industry often driven by spot market price advantage and future delivery schedules, the Channel Captain service is more than an inventory management system. It's a working relationship between Shell Chemical LP and the customer to cut costs from within the total supply chain.

'It is costly to have extra inventory in your supply process', says Phenol/Acetone sales manager Chuck Walker. 'The Channel Captain programme enables us to better understand inventory requirements and have only the product needed by the customer in the supply chain, thus helping us to better manage inventory and reduce carrying costs. The objective of the service is to realise increased value and savings to both parties in the supply management process.'

The key to the success of the Channel Captain service is close cooperation between the Shell Chemical people and their supply chain counterparts at the customer. In the case of Bayer, Shell Chemicals LP people worked closely with the customer to define the working relationship process and to identify key people involved and their responsibilities within the overall supply chain process.

'It's important to have people at all levels, within both companies, involved so everyone is aligned with the same vision', says Matt Vandergrifft, Phenol/Acetone supply chain manager. 'This is not simply a process that takes a job from the customer's purchasing group and transfers it to Shell. Instead, we as supplier literally manage the inventory and billing process, so people on both sides get involved at different levels of the supply chain.'

Shell customer relationship coordinators, like Covin, use SIMON to get daily inventory readings, consumption forecasts, product receipts and current customer consumption in order to supply inventory on an as-needed basis. She also places product orders and coordinates delivery with another phenol and acetone supplier.

Barge delivery is a complicated process that can be impacted by weather, dock issues and ship channel traffic conditions.

'This is a customer who needs product on a just-in-time basis. Product flows very rapidly and there is not a lot of slack in the system', she says.

It means, among other things, watching the weather. 'If there is a potential problem with fog, we may opt to load the barge ahead of time and reposition closer to the delivery location to get it to the customer on time. We must be able to keep the process moving regardless of any contingency.'

Covin works closely with production and shipping colleagues at the Deer Park phenol/acetone plant near Houston to make sure product is in the correct tanks for loading onto barges, and to coordinate movement of product at the docks.

If a barge is delayed due to weather conditions, dock congestion or any other reason, she's in contact with the barge company, logistics and supply people, as well as Bayer's purchasing and logistics people, to keep everyone informed.

Product transfers occur several times per week, so timing and close coordination for both loading and deliveries is critical. Deer Park production specialist Carl Pittman, who coordinates movement of product, says: 'We've developed a good team that works together to make sure both Bayer and Shell needs are met.'

The Shell Chemical LP customer service and production teams meet their customer counterparts on a quarterly basis for a general round table discussion, to foster good communications and to continually streamline the process.

'SIMON may appear on paper to be a computerised system that provides information, but the expertise really lies with the people who understand the value and know how to use the system effectively', Walker adds.

Shell began the Channel Captain arrangements with Bayer in 2002. That same year, it was one of only twelve of Bayer's 4,000-plus suppliers to receive a Superior Supplier award for service quality and value provided. Only one other raw material supplier received the honour.

Duke Stiddard, procurement manager of raw materials for Bayer in Pittsburgh, Pennsylvania, says the Channel Captain service is more than just saving money. 'It's a concept that says Shell will share in your business and help you better manage your inventory processes. We don't view our relationship as ending at the point of barge delivery.

'The service separates Shell from other suppliers', Stiddard continues. 'A lot of people talk about doing this, but very few implement it. For Bayer, our low inventory is the biggest benefit. We don't have inventory in our system until we consume it.

'Obviously, as a result, we save time and energy around scheduling and logistics. Plus, our people are free to work on other things', he adds.

The relationship is a win–win for both supplier and customer. 'If we can streamline the supply management process and save the customer money at the same time, it goes a long way to help them have a competitive advantage in the marketplace', says Walker.

Source: *Shell Chemicals Magazine*, Spring 2004: www.shellchemicals.com/magazine/1,1098,957-article_id=159,00.html

Questions

1. The SIMON system supports both 'upstream and downstream' business relationships. Explain how this relates to *Figure 1.1* and whether you would consider it an e-commerce system or an e-business system.
2. Draw a table summarizing the before and after implementation roles for Shell and their customers (downstream side).
3. This description of SIMON is explained from the Shell perspective. Using your answer to question 2, state whether you think the customer truly benefits, or is Shell transferring some of its workload to the customer?
4. Visit the Shell Chemicals web site (www.shellchemicals.com). How are the benefits of these facilities explained?

What is logistics?

Logistics is a concept closely related to supply chain management. According to the Institute of Logistics and Transportation (www.iolt.org):

> *Logistics is the time-related positioning of resource, or the strategic management of the total supply chain. The supply chain is a sequence of events intended to satisfy a customer. It can include procurement, manufacture, distribution, and waste disposal, together with associated transport, storage and information technology.*

This definition of logistics is broad, reflecting its provenance. More typically, logistics is used to refer not to all supply chain activities, but specifically to the management of logistics or inbound and outbound logistics, (*Figure 6.1*). Logistics is essential to the efficient management of the supply chain, for example resource management and transport are integral parts of the supply chain, not only between supply chain processes, but within these processes.

Inbound logistics
The management of material resources entering an organization from its suppliers and other partners.

Outbound logistics
The management of resources supplied from an organization to its customers and intermediaries such as retailers and distributors.

To understand why supply chain management plays an important role in modern management thinking, read the box *Developments in supply chain management*.

Developments in supply chain management

In order to understand how e-commerce can be used to enhance supply chain and logistics management it is useful to consider the historical context of management approaches to supply chain management and how information systems have been used to support them. The following stages can be identified:

1960s/70s: Physical distribution management (PDM)

Physical distribution management (PDM) focused upon the physical movement of goods by treating stock management, warehousing, order processing and delivery as related rather than separate activities. Although information systems were developed to manage these processes they were often paper-based and not integrated across different functions. However, some leading companies started using EDI at this time. PDM was essentially about the management of finished goods but not about the management of materials and processes that impacted upon the distribution process. PDM was superseded by logistics management which viewed manufacturing storage and transport from raw material to final consumer as integral parts of a total distribution process.

1970s/80s: Logistics management (materials requirement planning (MRP) and just-in-time – JIT)

The just-in-time philosophy (JIT) is still a relatively recent development of logistics management, its aim being to make the process of raw materials acquisition, production and distribution as efficient and flexible as possible in terms of material supply and customer service. Minimum order quantities and stock levels were sought by the customer and therefore manufacturers had to introduce flexible manufacturing processes and systems that interfaced directly with the customer who could call an order directly against a prearranged schedule with a guarantee that it would be delivered on time. Materials Requirement Planning systems were important in maintaining resources at an optimal level. The Design for Manufacture technique was used to simplify the number of components required for manufacture. However, none of the above methods looked at the management of the total supply chain. An associated phenomenon is lean production and lean supply where supply chain efficiency is aimed at eliminating waste and minimizing inventory and work in progress.

1980s/90s: Supply chain management and efficient consumer response (ECR)

Effective management of the supply chain involved much closer integration between the supplier, customer and intermediaries and in some instances involved one organization in the channel taking over functions that were traditionally the domain of the intermediary. Bottlenecks or undersupply/oversupply can have a significant impact on an organization's profitability. The two primary goals of supply chain management are to maximize the efficiency and effectiveness of the total supply chain for the benefit of all the players, not just one section of the channel, and to maximize the opportunity for customer purchase by ensuring adequate stock levels at all stages of the process. These two goals impact upon the sourcing of raw materials and stockholding. A recent phenomenon has been the rapid growth in global sourcing of supplies from preferred suppliers, particularly amongst multinational or global organizations. The Internet will provide increased capability for smaller players to globally source raw materials and therefore improve their competitivness. Quelch and Klein (1996) argue that the Internet will revolutionize the dynamics of international commerce and in particular lead to the more rapid internationalization of small and medium-sized enterprises. The web will reduce the competitive advantage of economies of scale in many industries, making it easier for smaller companies to compete on a worldwide basis. New integrated information systems such as the SAP enterprise resource planning (ERP) system have helped manage the entire supply chain. ERP systems include modules which are deployed throughout the business and interface with suppliers. Technology has enabled the introduction of faster, more responsive and flexible ordering, manufacturing and distribution systems, which has diminished even further the need for warehouses to be located near to markets that they serve.

1990s/2000s: Technological interface management (TIM)

According to Hamill and Gregory (1997) the challenge facing suppliers, intermediaries and customers in the supply chain will shift from a focus on physically distributing goods to a process of collection, collation, interpretation and dissemination of vast amounts of information. Enterprise resource planning systems are continuously being updated to support direct data interfaces with suppliers and customers, for example to support EDI. A more recent development is interfacing of ERP systems with B2B intermediary sites or exchanges such as Commerce One (www.commerceone.com). See the Focus on B2B exchanges in *Chapter 7* for further discussion of these. SAP has also created the mySAP facility to help customers manage and personalize their interactions with these exchanges. XML (*Chapter 3*) is increasingly used as the technical means by which technological interface management is achieved. (The critical resource possessed by these new intermediaries will be information rather than inventory. Hagel and Rayport (1997) take this a stage further by suggesting that customer information capture will serve customers rather than vendors in future. Currently customers leave a trail of information behind them as they visit sites and make transactions. This data can be captured and then used by suppliers and agents to improve targeting of offers. However, as customers become more aware of the value of information and as technology on the Internet enables them to protect private information relating to site visits and transactions, then the opportunity grows for intermediaries to act as customer agents and not supplier agents.)

Push and pull supply chain models

Push supply chain
A supply chain that emphasizes distribution of a product to passive customers.

A change in supply chain thinking, and also in marketing communications thinking, is the move from push models of selling to pull models or to combined push–pull approaches. The push model is illustrated by a manufacturer who perhaps develops an innovative product and then identifies a suitable target market. A distribution channel is then created to push the product to the market. This situation is shown in *Figure 6.3(a)* where it can be characterized by the statement 'This is a great product, now who shall we sell it to?' or the quip about the original Model T Ford – 'You can have any colour, so long as it is black.' The typical motivation for a push approach is to optimize the production process for cost and efficiency.

Pull supply chain
An emphasis on using the supply chain to deliver value to customers who are actively involved in product and service specification.

The alternative approach consistent with ECR is the **pull model**, which is focused on the customer's needs and starts with analysis of their requirements through market research and close cooperation with customers and suppliers in new product development *(Figure 6.3(b))*. Here the supply chain is constructed to deliver value to the customer by reducing costs and increasing service quality. *Figure 6.3(b)* shows how there are much closer links between the elements of the supply chain through use of technology such as EDI to minimize document transfer and rekeying. This approach can be characterized by the question 'What do our customers demand in the ideal product and service?'. Modern car manufacturers now not only provide a choice of colour, but thousands of permutations of trim and accessories backed up by service promises such as three-year warranties. The typical motivation for a pull approach is to optimize the production process for customer response, cost and efficiency. It will be apparent that such an approach is also consistent with management thinking about the similar concept of the value chain as illustrated in the *Focus on the value chain* section.

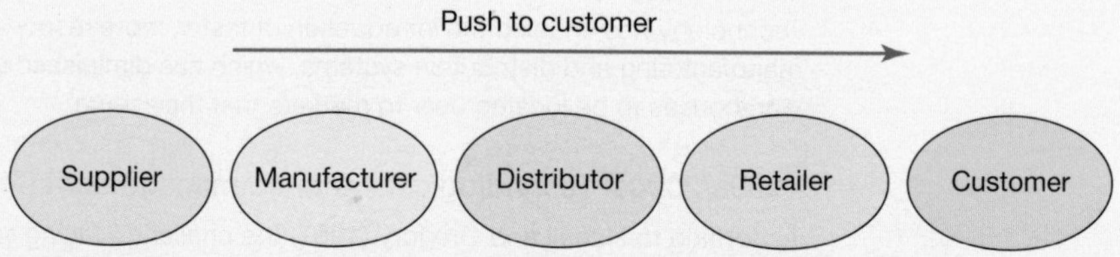

Typical aim:	Optimize the production process for cost and efficiency.
Typical characteristics:	Manufacturer-led new product development, poor data integration through limited use of technology, long cycle and response times, and high inventory levels.
Use of IS:	Independent data management by supply chain members. Limited use of EDI.

(a)

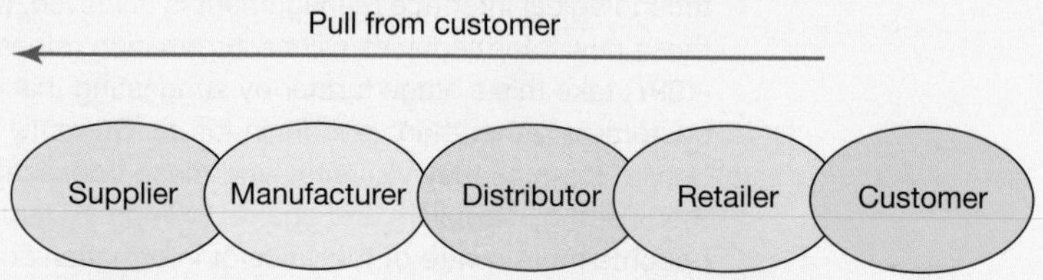

Typical aim:	Enhance product and service quality.
Typical characteristics:	Market research driven, technology used to achieve research and data integration, short cycle and response times, low inventory levels.
Use of IS:	Integrated internal systems, information sharing between supply chain members. Extensive use of EDI and e-commerce, often through B2B exchanges and intermediaries.

(b)

Figure 6.3 **Push and pull approaches to supply chain management**

Focus on the value chain

Value chain
A model that considers how supply chain activities can add value to products and services delivered to the customer.

Michael Porter's **value chain (VC)** is a well-established concept for considering key activities that an organization can perform or manage with the intention of adding value for the customer as products and services move from conception to delivery to the customer (Porter, 1980). The value chain is a model that describes different value-adding activities that connect a company's supply side with its demand side. We can identify an *internal* value chain within the boundaries of an organization and an *external* value chain where activities are performed by partners. By analysing the different parts of the value chain managers can redesign internal and external processes to improve their efficiency and effectiveness. Benefits for the customer are created by reducing cost *and* adding value to customers:

- *within each* element of the value chain such as procurement, manufacture, sales and distribution;
- *at the interface between* elements of the value chain such as between sales and distribution.

In equation form this is:

Value = (Benefit of each VC activity – Its cost) +
(Benefit of each interface between VC activities – Its cost)

Electronic communications can be used to enhance the value chain by making value chain activities such as procurement more efficient (see *Chapter 7*) and also enabling data integration between activities. For example, if a retailer shares information electronically with a supplier about demand for its products, this can enhance the value chain of both parties since the cycle time for ordering can be reduced, resulting in lower inventory holding and hence lower costs for both. *Case Study 6.1* illustrates this point.

Traditional value chain analysis (*Figure 6.4(a)*) distinguishes between *primary activities* that contribute directly to getting goods and services to the customer (such as inbound logistics, including procurement, manufacturing, marketing and delivery to

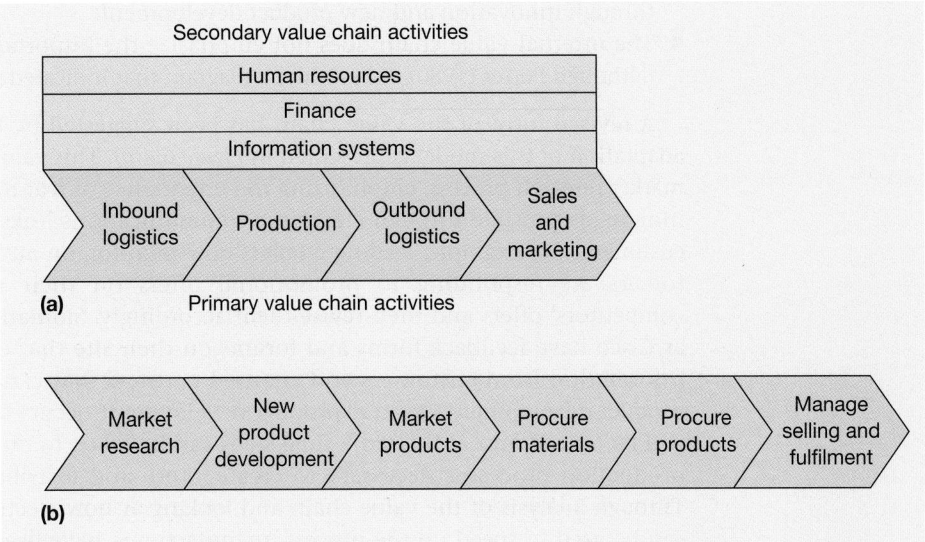

Figure 6.4 Two alternative models of the value chain: (a) traditional value chain model, (b) revised value chain model
Source: Figure 6.4(b) adapted from Deise *et al*. (2000)

> **Debate 6.2**
>
> **New value chain models**
>
> *'The traditional value chain model of Michael Porter (Figure. 6.4 (a)) is no longer useful, as a framework for value chain management. Instead, Figure. 6.4 (b) is more appropriate.'*

buyers, and support and servicing after sale) and *support activities* which provide the inputs and infrastructure that allow the primary activities to take place. Support activities include finance, human resources and information systems. It can be argued that, with the advent of e-business, the support activities offer much more than support; indeed, having effective information systems and management of human resources contributes critically to the primary activities. Michael Porter now acknowledges that this is the case.

Internet technologies can reduce production times and costs by increasing the flow of information as a way to *integrate* different value chain activities. Through doing this the value chain can be made more efficient and services delivered to customers more readily. Rayport and Sviokla (1996) contend that the Internet enables value to be created by gathering, organizing, selecting, synthesizing and distributing information. They refer to a separate parallel virtual value chain mirroring the physical value chain. The *virtual value chain* involves electronic commerce used to mediate traditional value chain activities such as market research, procurement, logistics, manufacture, marketing and distributing. The processing is machine-based or 'virtual' rather than paper-based. The situation is not truly virtual in that human intervention is still required in many value chain activities such as procurement. The 'virtuality' of the virtual value chain will increase as software agents increasingly perform these activities.

Restructuring the internal value chain

Traditional models of the value chain (such as *Figure 2.11* and *Figure 6.4(a)*) have been re-evaluated with the advent of global electronic communications. It can be suggested that there are some key weaknesses in the traditional value chain model:

- It is most applicable to manufacturing of physical products as opposed to providing services.
- It is a one-way chain involved with pushing products to the customer (see section on *Push and pull supply chain models*); it does not highlight the importance of understanding customer needs through market research and responsiveness through innovation and new product development.
- The internal value chain does not emphasize the importance of value networks (although Porter (1980) did produce a diagram that indicated network relationships).

A revised form of the value chain has been suggested by Deise *et al.* (2000); an adaptation of this model is presented in *Figure 6.4(b)*. This value chain starts with the market research process, emphasizing the importance of real-time environment scanning made possible through electronic communications links with distributors and customers. For example, leading e-tailers now monitor, on an hourly basis, how customers are responding to promotional offers on their web site and review competitors' offers and then revise them accordingly. Similarly, manufacturers such as Cisco have feedback forms and forums on their site that enable them to collect information from customers and channel partners that can feed through to new product development. As new product development occurs the marketing strategy will be refined and at the same time steps can be taken to obtain the resources and production processes necessary to create, store and distribute the new product. Through analysis of the value chain and looking at how electronic communications can be used to speed up the process, manufacturers have been able to significantly reduce time to market from conception of a new product idea through to launch on the market. For example, car manufacturers have reduced time to market from over 5 years to 18 months. At the same time the use of technology increases value chain efficiency, for example it enables customers to specify their needs through a web site or a kiosk in a car dealership and then the car will be manufactured to order.

In addition to changes in the efficiency of value chain activities, electronic commerce also has implications for whether these activities are achieved internally or externally. These changes have been referred to as value chain *disaggregation* (Kalakota and Robinson, 2000) or *deconstruction* (Timmers, 1999) and value chain *reaggregation* (Kalakota and Robinson, 2000) or *reconstruction* (Timmers, 1999). Value chain disaggregation can occur through deconstructing the primary activities of the value chain. Each of the elements can be approached in a new way, for instance by working differently with suppliers. In value chain reaggregation the value chain is streamlined to increase efficiency between each of the value chain stages. Indeed, Timmers (1999) notes that the conventional wisdom of the value chain as a separate series of discrete steps may no longer be tenable as steps such as inbound logistics and operations become more tightly integrated through technology. We have only touched upon changes to the structure of the value chain here, since there is great similarity with the changes possible in the structure of the supply chain. This is evaluated in more depth in the sections on vertical integration and models for redefining the value chain.

The value stream

Value stream
The combination of actions required to deliver value to the customer as products and services.

The **value stream** is a concept closely related to the value chain. The difference is that it considers different types of tasks that are involved with adding value and looks at how the efficiency of these tasks can be improved. Womack and Jones (1998) define the value stream as:

> *the set of all the specific actions required to bring a specific product through the three critical management tasks of any business:*
>
> 1 *the problem-solving task* [the processes of new product development and production launch]
> 2 *the information management task* [the processes of order taking, scheduling to delivery]
> 3 *the physical transformation task* [the processes of transforming raw materials to finished product delivered to customers].

Tasks 2 and 3 are traditional value chain activities (*Figure 6.4(a)*), but task 1 is not.

Returning to the definition of customer value from Deise *et al.* (2000) shown in the equation below, we can see that the lean thinking approach proposed by Womack and Jones is aimed at adding value by cutting out waste in each of these three management tasks. By reducing new product development and production times and costs, organizations can then either increase customer value by decreasing fulfilment time or, if they wish do it, by decreasing price, and/or increasing product and service quality. Clearly e-commerce plays a key role in decreasing time to market and production times and costs.

$$\text{Customer value (brand perception)} = \frac{\text{Product quality} \times \text{Service quality}}{\text{Price} \times \text{Fulfilment time}}$$

Value chain analysis

This is an analytical framework for decomposing an organization into its individual activities and determining value added at each stage. In this way the organization can then assess how effectively resources are being used at the various points within the value chain. The relevance for information systems is that for each element in the value chain it may be possible to use IS to increase the efficiency of resource usage in that area. In addition, IS may be used *between* value chain activities to increase organizational efficiency.

How can an organization positively impact on its value chain by investing in new or upgraded information systems? Porter and Millar (1985) propose the following five-step process.

- *Step 1.* Assess the information intensity of the value chain (i.e. the level and usage of information *within* each value chain activity and *between* each level of activity). The higher the level of intensity and/or the higher the degree of reliance on good-quality information, the greater the potential impact of new information systems.
- *Step 2.* Determine the role of IS in the industry structure (for example, banking will be very different from mining). It is also important here to understand the information linkages between buyers and suppliers within the industry and how they and competitors might be affected by and react to new information technology.
- *Step 3.* Identify and rank the ways in which IS might create competitive advantage (by impacting on one of the value chain activities or improving linkages between them). High-cost or critical activity areas present good targets for cost reduction and performance improvement.
- *Step 4.* Investigate how IS might spawn new businesses (for example, the Sabre computerized reservation system spawned a multi-billion-dollar software company which now has higher earnings than the original core airline business).
- *Step 5.* Develop a plan for taking advantage of IS. A plan must be developed which is business-driven rather than technology-driven. The plan should assign priorities to the IS investments (which of course should be subjected to an appropriate cost–benefit analysis).

In the five-step analysis above we have mainly been looking at how value chain analysis can be applied to the internal value chain. Such a process can also be applied to an organization's external value chain. Womack and Jones (1998) refer to the related concept of *value stream analysis*. This considers how the whole production and delivery process can be made more efficient. To conduct this analysis, they suggest that companies should map every activity that occurs in creating new products and delivering products or services to customers and then categorize them as:

1. Those that create value as perceived by the customer.
2. Those which create no value, but are required by product development or production systems and so cannot immediately be eliminated.
3. Those that don't add value, so can be immediately eliminated.

Having performed this analysis, plans for removing the category 3 activities can be made and managers can then concentrate on eliminating category 2 activities and enhancing category 1 activities. Womack and Jones give the example of the value stream for a cola can. Even a superficially simple product such as canned cola can have many activities involved in its production. Indeed there are several value streams: that in producing the can itself, those to produce the contents from beet field to sugar and corn field to caramel and those to produce the packaging. Taking the example of the can itself, value stream analysis can be performed to identify the stages in production as follows:

1. Mine bauxite.
2. Reduction mill.
3. Smelter.
4. Hot rolling mill.

5 Cold rolling mill.
6 Can maker.
7 Bottler.
8 Regional distribution centre (RDC).
9 Retail unit storage.
10 Home storage.

In value stream analysis, efficiency for each of the stages above will be calculated. For example, at stage 7, the bottler (adding the drink to the can), Womack and Jones (1998) give times of incoming storage four days, processing time one minute, finished storage five weeks. The need for such analysis is shown by the delays in the whole process which give incoming storage of five months, finished storage of six months, but processing time of only three hours. This gives a total cycle time of nearly a year from mine to home. Clearly, if information management can be used to reduce these storage times, it can create large savings in terms of reduced storage capacities. The benefits are evident for a retailer such as Tesco (*Case Study 6.2*) that has already undertaken value stream analysis and deployed e-commerce in the Tesco Information Exchange to reduce its storage in the RDC and in-store to only two and three days respectively. It has also been able to move to a system of continuous replenishment in 24 hours. Orders made by a Tesco store on a Monday night are delivered from suppliers via the RDCs to arrive before the store opens Wednesday morning!

Value networks

Reduced time to market and increased customer responsiveness are not simply the result of reviewing the efficiency of internal processes and how information systems are deployed, but also result through consideration of how partners can be involved to outsource some processes that have traditionally been considered to be part of the internal value chain of a company. Porter's original work considered not only the internal value chain, but also the **external value chain** or **network**. Since the 1980s there has been a tremendous increase in outsourcing of both core value chain activities and support activities. As companies outsource more and more activities, management of the links between the company and its partners becomes more important. Deise *et al.* (2000) describe value network management as:

Value network
The links between an organization and its strategic and non-strategic partners that form its external value chain.

> *the process of effectively deciding what to outsource in a constraint-based, real-time environment based on fluctuation.*

Electronic communications have enabled this shift to outsourcing, enabling the transfer of information necessary to create, manage and monitor partnerships. These links are mediated not only directly through the company, but also through intermediaries known as 'value chain integrators' or directly between partners. As a result the concept of managing a value network of partners has become commonplace.

Figure 6.5, which is adapted from the model of Deise *et al.* (2000), shows some of the partners of a value network that characterizes partners as:

1 Supply-side partners (upstream supply chain) such as suppliers, business-to-business exchanges, wholesalers and distributors.
2 Partners that fulfil primary or core value chain activities. The number of core value chain activities that will have been outsourced to third parties will vary with different companies and the degree of virtualization of the organization. In some companies the management of inbound logistics may be outsourced, in others different aspects of the manufacturing process. In the virtual organization all core activities may be outsourced.

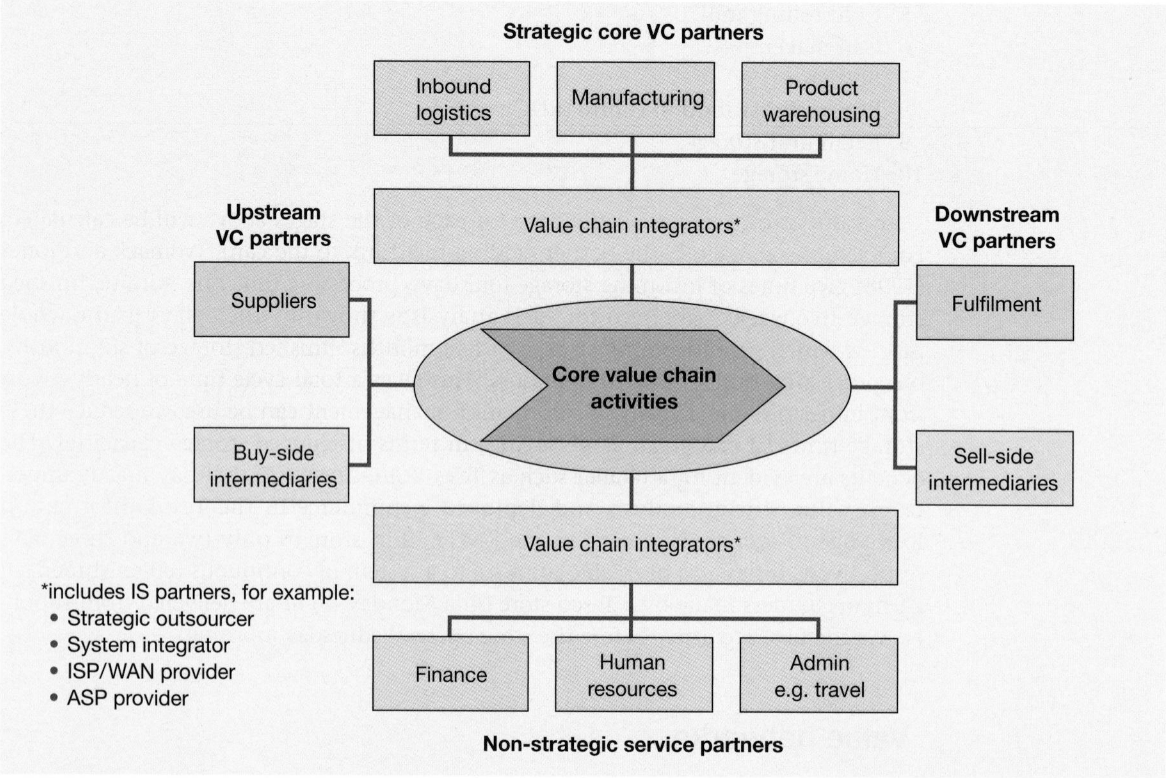

Figure 6.5 Members of the value network of an organization (adapted from Deise *et al.* 2000)

3 Sell-side partners (downstream supply chain) such as business-to-business exchanges, wholesalers, distributors and customers (not shown, since conceived as distinct from other partners).
4 Value chain integrators or partners who supply services that mediate the internal and external value chain. These companies typically provide the electronic infrastructure for a company and include strategic outsourcing partners, system integrators, ISP/WAN providers and ASP providers.

The similarity between elements of the value network of *Figure 6.5* and the supply chain of The B2B Company of *Figure 6.2* will be apparent. But the value network offers a different perspective that is intended to emphasize:

- The electronic interconnections between partners and the organization and directly between partners that potentially enables real-time information exchange between partners.
- The dynamic nature of the network. The network can be readily modified according to market conditions or in response to customer demands. New partners can readily be introduced into the network and others removed if they are not performing well.
- Different types of links can be formed between different types of partners. For example, EDI links may be established with key suppliers, while e-mail links may suffice for less-significant suppliers.

The Waterstones' book chain (**www.waterstones.co.uk**) provides an example of the importance of developing a value network of infrastucture partners. Field (2000) describes how initially the web site was designed and hosted a single company, Hyperlink, and offered book searching among 1.2 million books, secure ordering, diary, Waterstones' Club and online chat. But Field states that, according to Andrew

Hatton, project manager, the technology was holding the company back, particularly as Amazon continued to use its huge market capitalization to invest in web interface and back-end fulfilment systems. Using an in-house-developed application and web server, the site was unable to deliver new functionality quickly or cost-effectively since the supplier had to perform a time-consuming software upgrade to meet Halton's request for the site's pages to change more rapidly. Waterstones decided to expand the network of suppliers to get best-of-breed suppliers. Partners included numerous hardware and software vendors, as well as integration and design consultants; these included Siemens, web site designers Brainstormers and e-commerce integrator Nvision. Nvision achieved the key back-end integration to link the new solution to Waterstones' existing business systems in 12 weeks. The integrator performed a 'SWOT' (strength, weakness, opportunities, threats) analysis to identify the market opportunities for an online bookstore, and these were then matched against Waterstones' existing capabilities, both on the web site and in the supply chain.

In this section, we refer to wholesale outsourcing of the elements of a value network to third parties. In fact, the options are more complex than this. The different types of partnership that can be formed are described in more detail in the later section on *Managing partnerships*. Remember also that outsourcing does imply cost reduction. Michael Dell relates that Dell do not see outsourcing as getting rid of a process that does not add value, rather they see it as a way of *'coordinating their activity to create the most value for customers'* (Magretta, 1998). Dell has improved customer service by changing the way it works with both its suppliers and distributors to build a computer to the customer's specific order within just six days.

Towards the virtual organization

Davidow and Malone (1992) describe a virtual corporation as follows:

> *To the outside observer, it will appear almost edgeless, with permeable and continuously changing interfaces between company, supplier and customer. From inside the firm, the view will be no less amorphous, with traditional offices, departments, and operating divisions constantly reforming according to need. Job responsibilities will regularly shift.*

Virtual organization
An organization which uses information and communications technology to allow it to operate without clearly defined physical boundaries between different functions. It provides customized services by outsourcing production and other functions to third parties.

An implication of increasing outsourcing of core activities is that companies will move towards the **virtual organization**. Benjamin and Wigand (1995) state that *'it is becoming increasingly difficult to delineate accurately the borders of today's organizations'*. A further implication of the introduction of electronic networks such as the Internet is that it becomes easier to outsource aspects of the production and distribution of goods to third parties (Kraut *et al.*, 1998). This can lead to the boundaries between supplier and organization becoming blurred. Employees may work in any time zone and customers are able to purchase tailored products from any location. The absence of any rigid boundary or hierarchy within the organization should lead to a more responsive and flexible company with greater market orientation.

Virtual organizations can also be viewed as a way of transforming existing organizations. Malcolm Warner is a professor of organization behaviour at the Judge Institute of Management Studies, University of Cambridge, who has defined a virtual organization, in this context, as follows:

> *Put simply, it is an organisational form that enables companies to reduce their physical assets (large headquarters, centralised plants and so on), relying instead on small decentralised units linked by a strong communications network. In other words, the old physical constraints of the plant and office building are broken down, and activities of co-ordination and control, which used to take place face-to-face, are now handled remotely 'over the wire'.* (Warner, 2001)

He suggests that companies such as Accenture, British Airways, Lotus and Dell are all experimenting with different characteristics of virtual organizations. These characteristics include:

- *Lack of physical structure*: virtual organizations have little or no physical existence.
- *Reliance on knowledge*: the lack of physical facilities and contacts mean that knowledge is the key driving force of the virtual organization.
- *Use of communications technologies*: it follows that virtual organizations tend to rely on information technology.
- *Mobile work*: the reliance on communications technologies means that the traditional office or plant is no longer the only site where work is carried out. Increasingly, the office is wherever the worker is.
- *Boundaryless and inclusive*: virtual companies tend to have fuzzy boundaries.
- *Flexible and responsive*: virtual organizations can be pulled together quickly from disparate elements, used to achieve a certain business goal and then dismantled again.

An alternative viewpoint on features of a virtual organization (Kraut *et al.*, 1998) is:

1. Processes transcend the boundaries of a single firm and are not controlled by a single organizational hierarchy.
2. Production processes are flexible with different parties involved at different times.
3. Parties involved in the production of a single product are often geographically dispersed.
4. Given this dispersion, coordination is heavily dependent on telecommunications and data networks.

Virtualization
The process of a company developing more of the characteristics of the virtual organization.

Here, all companies tend to have some elements of the virtual organization. As these characteristics increase this is known as **virtualization**. Malone *et al.* (1987) argued that the presence of electronic networks tends to lead to virtualization since the governance and coordination of business transactions can be conducted effectively at lower costs.

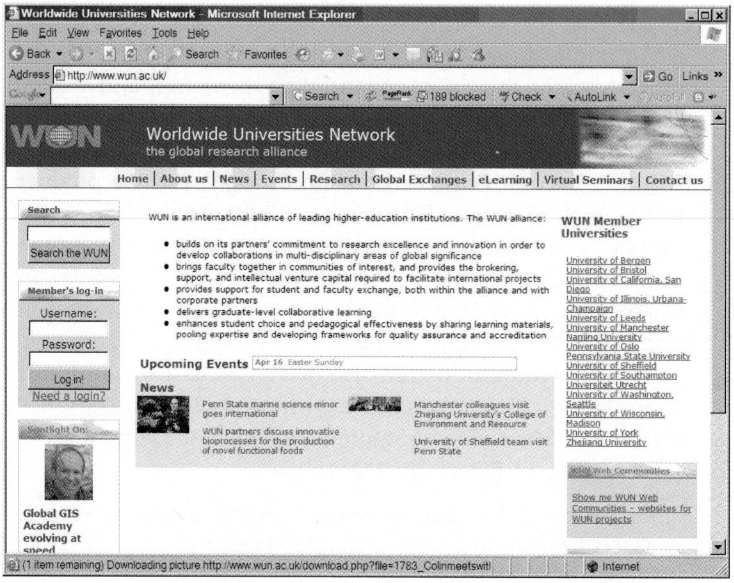

Figure 6.6 **The Worldwide Universities Network showing member institutions (www.wun.ac.uk)**

A final example of a virtual organization is the Worldwide Universities Network, which provides collaboration for research and e-learning facilities (*Figure 6.6*). Although this initiative appears successful, note that the Global University Alliance (www.gua.com), an e-learning initiative featured in the previous edition of this book has not proved tenable. This service, launched in 2000, provided distance learning education to a worldwide market including centres in China and Korea. The suppliers include around ten educational institutions in the United States, the United Kingdom, Australia and New Zealand. Through collaborating in this way, the institutions hoped to be able to pool funds for marketing the service and reach a wider audience than they could individually. Learners would benefit from a wider choice of specialized courses and lower costs than from travelling for education or going to a single provider. While the concept appeared logical, practical implementation of marketing and delivering such a service which is entirely virtual proved untenable. This was a dot-com disaster for the universities involved, but perhaps it was just an idea before its time.

Options for restructuring the supply chain

As part of strategy definition for e-business, managers will consider how the structure of the supply chain can be modified. These choices are not primarily based on Internet technology choices, rather they are mainly choices that have existed for many years. What Internet technology provides is a more efficient enabler and lower-cost communications within the new structures.

Supply chain management options can be viewed as a continuum between internal control of the supply chain elements and external control of supply chain elements through outsourcing. The two end elements of the continuum are usually referred to as 'vertical integration' and 'virtual integration'. The intermediate situation is sometimes referred to as 'vertical disintegration' or 'supply chain disaggregation'. This continuum is illustrated in *Figure 6.7*.

Vertical integration
The extent to which supply chain activities are undertaken and controlled within the organization.

Virtual integration
The majority of supply chain activities are undertaken and controlled outside the organization by third parties.

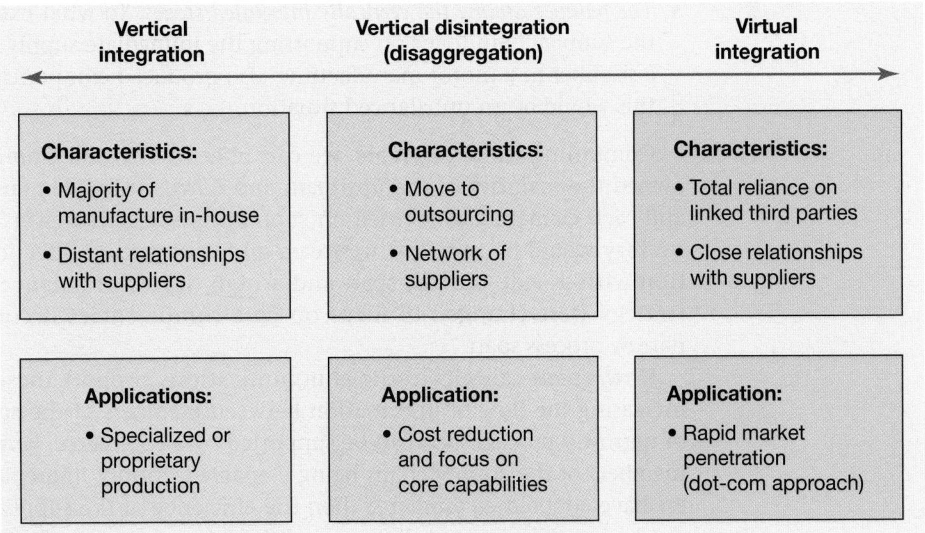

Figure 6.7 The characteristics of vertical integration, vertical disintegration and virtual integration

Debate 6.2

Virtual integration and outsourcing of core processes

'The success of companies such as Dell in outsourcing core business processes and in virtual integration suggests that all companies need to adopt this model in order to be competitive.'

There was a general trend during the second half of the twentieth century from vertical integration through vertical disintegration to virtual integration. A good example is provided by the car manufacturing industry where traditionally car plants would be located near to a steelworks so that the input to the car plant would be raw materials, with finished cars produced as the output. Other components of the car such as the engine and passenger equipment would also be manufactured by the company. In addition, other value chain activities such as marketing would also largely be performed in-house. There has been a gradual move to sourcing more and more components such as lights, upholstery and trim and even engines to third parties. Marketing activities such as web site development, brochure fulfilment and advertising campaigns are now largely outsourced to marketing agencies. Another example is the purchase by pharmaceutical companies of pharmacy benefit managers (companies that manage drug distribution with private and company health schemes). By acquiring these companies which are part of a pharmaceutical company's downstream supply chain the aim is to 'get closer to the customer' while at the same time favourably controlling the distribution of the company's own drugs.

Hayes and Wheelwright (1994) provide a useful framework that summarizes choices for an organization's vertical integration strategy. The three main decisions are:

1 *The direction of any expansion.* Should the company aim to direct ownership at the upstream or downstream supply chain? The pharmaceuticals companies referred to above have decided to buy into the downstream part of the supply network (downstream vertical integration). This is sometimes referred to as an *offensive* strategic move since it enables the company to increase its power with respect to customers. Alternatively, if the pharmaceuticals company purchased other research labs this would be upstream-directed vertical integration which is strategically *defensive*.
2 *The extent of vertical integration.* How far should the company take downstream or upstream vertical integration? Originally car manufacturers had a high degree of vertical integration, but more recently they have moved from a *wide process span* to a *narrow process span*. This change is the main way in which e-business can impact upon vertical integration by assisting the change from wide to narrow process span.
3 *The balance among the vertically integrated stages.* To what extent does each stage of the supply chain focus on supporting the immediate supply chain? For example, if a supplier to a motor manufacturer also produced components for other industries this would be an unbalanced situation.

Combining these concepts, we can refer to The B2B Company (*Figure 6.2*). If it owned the majority of the upstream and downstream elements of the supply chain and each element was focused on supporting the activities of The B2B Company, its strategy would be to follow upstream and downstream directions of vertical integration with a wide process span and a high degree of balance. Alternatively, if the strategy were changed to focus on core competencies it could be said to have a narrow process span.

How, then, can electronic communications support these strategies? Through increasing the flow of information between members of the supply chain, a strategy of narrower process span can be supported by e-commerce. However, this relies on all members of the supply chain being e-enabled. If only immediately upstream suppliers have adopted e-commerce then the efficiency of the supply chain as a whole will not be greatly increased. It may be difficult for a manufacturer to encourage companies further up the supply chain to adopt e-commerce. So companies undertaking offensive or defensive strategies will be in a better position to stipulate adoption of e-commerce, and so increase the overall efficiency of the supply chain. As we saw in

Case Study 1.1, a company such as Shell helps e-enable the supply chain by sharing information in its own databases with customers to increase the efficiency of the supply chain.

Our next example in the manufacture of personal computers also illustrates the concept of the two different supply chain products well. Complete *Activity 6.2* to review the benefits of each approach.

Activity 6.2 Supply chain models in personal computer manufacture

Activity

1. Review the approaches of the two companies illustrated below. Which tends to vertical integration and which tends to virtual integration?
2. Produce a table summarizing the benefits and disadvantages of each approach. Which do you think is the better approach?
3. How can information systems facilitate each approach?

Approach 1 IBM during the 1980s and early 1990s

Manufacture of many components by IBM plants in different locations including IBM processors, IBM hard disks, IBM cases and IBM monitors and even IBM mice. Distribution to companies by IBM logistics.

Approach 2 Dell during the 1990s and 2000s

Manufacture of all components by third parties in different locations including Intel processors, Seagate hard disks, Sony monitors and Microsoft mice. Assembly of some components in final product by third parties, e.g. adding appropriate monitor to system unit for each order. For more information on Dell see Magretta (1998).

Answers to activities can be found at www.pearsoned.co.uk/chaffey

Using e-business to restructure the supply chain

In this section we start by reviewing the extent of adoption of different types of information systems to support supply chain management as part of e-business strategy. The benefits of implementing these technologies are also described. We then consider, through referring to case studies, how companies can use technologies to support the management of the upstream and downstream supply chain.

Adoption rates of e-business applications

How popular are the e-business technologies we have been describing in this chapter? The final DTI International Benchmarking Study (DTI, 2004) showed that around 95% of businesses in the majority of countries surveyed have Internet access, although this figure masks lower levels of access for SMEs (small and medium-sized enterprises) and particularly micro-businesses. However, within this, there is a large variation between countries in the proportion that order online (*Figure 4.6*) with the figure substantially higher in countries such as Sweden and Germany in comparison to Italy and France for example.

In 2006, the UK launched the Supplier Route to Government Portal (www.supply2.gov.uk) as part of its e-government initiative, this is an online marketplace for public-sector procurement valued at less than £100,000. Registered users can receive daily e-mail alerts about contracts appropriate to them, search for contracts online and post details of their offerings.

A European Union report (eEurope, 2005) also shows surprisingly low rates of adoption of different types of e-business applications. *Figure 6.8* shows the popularity of different e-business applications. Despite the benefits of these applications discussed in this and other chapters, adoption is surprisingly low, particularly amongst smaller companies that use manual systems or systems based on desktop spreadsheet, database or accounting systems.

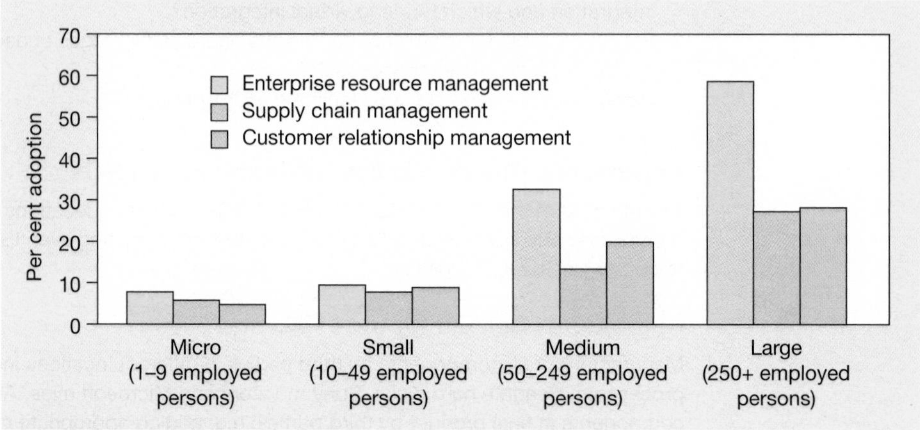

Figure 6.8 Popularity of different e-business applications in Europe according to company size *Source*: eEurope (2005)

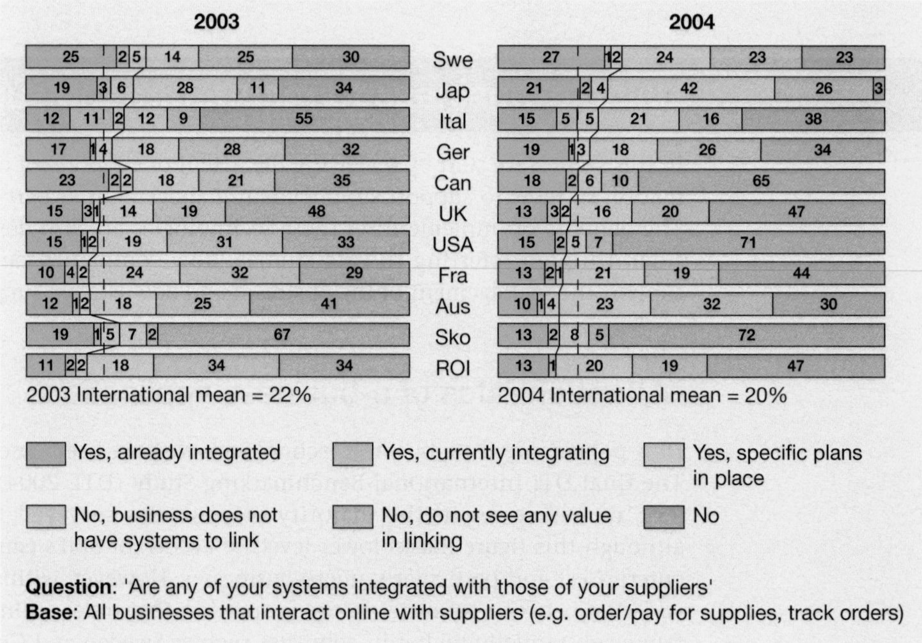

Figure 6.9 Proportion of businesses that integrate with their suppliers, or plan to
Source: DTI (2004), Fig. 7.5b

The DTI International Benchmarking Study (DTI, 2004) also assessed the extent of adoption of integration of systems with suppliers. *Figure 6.9* shows that again there is a large proportion of companies without fully integrated SCM systems. A similar situation is evident for downstream integration with customers.

The study also enquired as to the barriers to adoption, unsurprisingly across countries the costs (both fixed implementation costs and variable running costs) were cited as a major factor (*Figure 6.10*). Concerns about the change management and disruption in implementing the new e-business system were also voiced. People factors tended to be more important in some countries (e.g. France, Sweden, South Korea, Japan and Australia than cost which was considered more important in other countries (the USA, Canada, the UK and the Republic of Ireland). However, due to increased outsourcing as a practice, in the latest study skills were less of a barrier than in previous studies.

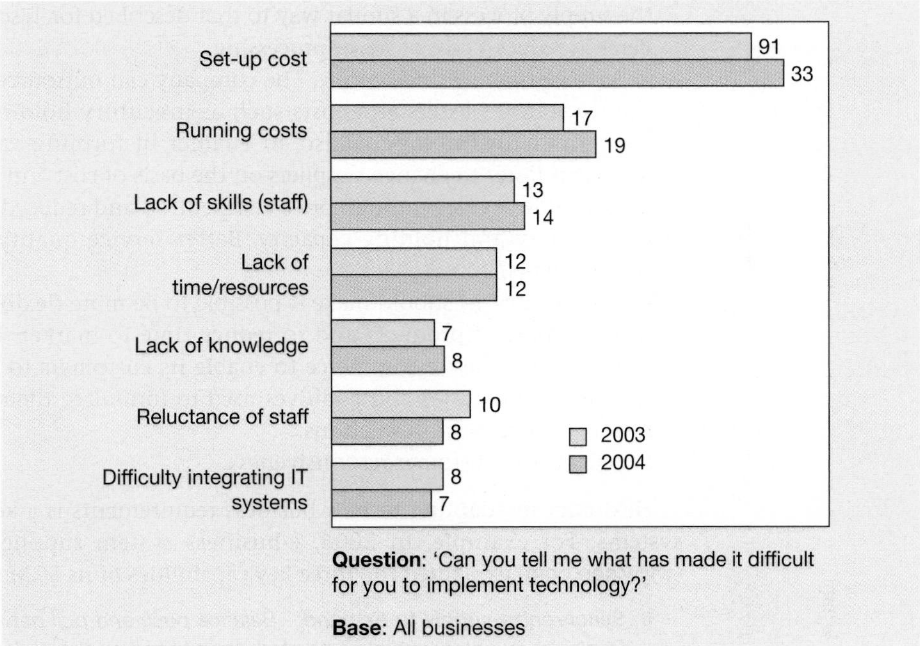

Figure 6.10 **Barriers to implementing Information and communications technology**

Source: DTI (2004), Fig. 5.2f

Benefits of e-supply chain management

Given, the lack of adoption of e-SCM, particularly in SMEs, which opportunities are being missed that are available to adopters? E-business can be used to improve supply chain management in a number of ways. These are illustrated well by research by IDC (2004) into the challenges facing manufacturers in one sector (electronic component manufacture). This research showed that their main challenges (scored out of 5) were:

- Reduce order-to-delivery time (4.3)
- Reduce costs of manufacturing (4.1)
- Manage inventory more effectively (4.0)
- Improve demand forecasting (3.9)
- Reduce time to introduce new products (3.7)
- Improve aftermarket/post-sales operations (3.2).

We will now consider typical benefits in a little more depth with respect to The B2B Company; they include:

1 *Increased efficiency of individual processes*. Here the cycle time to complete a process and the resources needed to execute it are reduced. If The B2B Company adopts e-procurement this will result in a faster cycle time and lower cost per order as described in *Chapter 7*.
Benefit: reduced cycle time and cost per order as described in *Chapter 7*.
2 *Reduced complexity of the supply chain*. This is the process of disintermediation referred to in *Chapter 2*. Here The B2B Company will offer the facility to sell direct from its e-commerce site rather than through distributors or retailers.
Benefit: reduced cost of channel distribution and sale.
3 *Improved data integration between elements of the supply chain*. The B2B Company can share information with its suppliers on the demand for its products to optimize the supply process in a similar way to that described for Tesco in *Case Study 6.1*.
Benefit: reduced cost of paper processing.
4 *Reduced cost through outsourcing*. The company can outsource or use virtual integration to transfer assets and costs such as inventory holding costs to third-party companies. Technology is also an enabler in forming value networks, and in making it faster to change suppliers on the basis of cost and quality.
Benefits: lower costs through price competition and reduced spend on manufacturing capacity and holding capacity. Better service quality through contractual arrangements?
5 *Innovation*. E-SCM should make it possible to be more flexible in delivering a more diverse range of products and to reduce time to market. For example, The B2B Company may use e-commerce to enable its customers to specify the mixture of chemical compounds and additives used to formulate their plastics and refer to a history of previous formulations.
Benefit: Better customer responsiveness.

Flexibility in adapting to new business requirements is a key capability of e-SCM systems. For example, in 2006, e-business system supplier and integrator SAP (www.sap.com) explained the three key capabilities of its SCM solution as:

- ***Synchronize supply to demand*** *– Balance push and pull network planning processes. Replenish inventory and execute production based on actual demand.*
- ***Sense and respond with an adaptive supply chain network*** *– Drive distribution, transportation, and logistics processes that are integrated with real-time planning processes.*
- ***Provide networkwide visibility****, collaboration, and analytics – Monitor and analyze your extended supply chain.*

Source: www.sap.com/solutions/business-suite/scm.

An alternative perspective on the benefits is to look at the benefits that technology can deliver to customers at the end of the supply chain. For The B2B Company these could include:

- Increased convenience through 24 hours a day, 7 days a week, 365 days a year ordering.
- Increased choice of supplier leading to lower costs.
- Faster lead times and lower costs through reduced inventory holding.
- The facility to tailor products more readily.
- Increased information about products and transactions such as technical data sheets and order histories.

There are two alternative, contradictory implications of supply chains becoming electronically mediated networks. Malone *et al.* (1987) and Steinfield *et al.* (1996) suggest that networks may foster electronic marketplaces that are characterized by more *ephemeral* relationships. In other words, since it is easier to form an electronically mediated relationship, it is also easier for the customer to break it and choose another supplier. Counter to this is the suggestion that electronic networks may *lock in* customers to a particular supplier because of the overhead or risk in changing to another supplier. Here networks are used to strengthen partnerships. An example of this is when the use of an EDI solution is stipulated by a dominant customer.

The popular conception of the introduction of the Internet into a channel is that it will tend to lead to more ephemeral relationships. This may yet prove to be the case as more intermediaries evolve and this becomes an accepted way of buying. However, the review by Steinfield *et al.* (1996) seems to suggest that EDI and the Internet tend to cement existing relationships. Furthermore, research indicates that the use of networks for buying may actually reduce outcomes such as quality, efficiency and satisfaction with suppliers. If the findings of Steinfield *et al.* (1996) are confirmed in practice, then this calls into doubt the future of many B2B marketplaces (*Chapter 7, p. 325*). Personal relationships between the members of the buying unit and the supplier still seem to be important. It will be interesting to see which type of arrangement predominates in the future, or it may well be that there is a role for both according to the nature of the product purchased.

IS-supported upstream supply chain management

The key activities of upstream supply chain management are procurement and upstream logistics. The way in which information systems can be used to support procurement in the e-business is of such importance that a whole chapter is devoted to this (*Chapter 7*). However, in the current chapter we look at some examples of how technologies are used to improve upstream supply chain management.

Many grocery retailers have been at the forefront of using technology to manage their upstream supply chain. The major example we will review here is the system created by Tesco, but other UK retailers have developed such systems as 'Sainsbury Information Direct' and 'Safeway Supplier Information Service'. *Case Study 6.1* illustrates the use of technology to manage the upstream supply chain from the retailer's perspective, but also highlights the benefits for their suppliers. The Tesco Information Exchange (TIE) was developed in conjunction with GE Information Services (GEIS), and is an extranet solution that allows Tesco and its suppliers to collaboratively exchange trading information. *Figure 6.10* shows how TIE is linked to Tesco's key systems to give suppliers access to relevant and up-to-date information such as electronic point of sale (EPOS) data, to track sales and the internal telephone/mail directory, so that suppliers can quickly find the right person to talk to.

RFID (radio-frequency identification microchip)

Radio-frequency identification (RFID)
Microchip-based electronic tags are used for monitoring anything they are attached to, whether inanimate (products) or animate (people).

RFID tags are a relatively recent innovation in e-SCM that are already widely used for logistics purposes. They can be attached to individual product items in a warehouse or in a retail location. With appropriate scanning technology they can then be used to assess stock levels – they can be read at a distance of 1 to 6 metres. However, there are number of issues involved with the implementation of RFID which give a dilemma to managers. These are explored in *Case Study 6.2*.

Case Study 6.2 Tesco develops buy-side e-commerce system for supply chain management

FT

The case summarizes the history of Tesco supermarkets' efforts to encourage electronic trading with their suppliers from EDI to Internet-based purchasing. The benefits and problems of implementing such electronic partnerships are explored.

Retailers have long sought greater collaboration in their supply chains, but few have managed to achieve it. One that has is Tesco, the UK's largest grocery retailer, which has built a reputation as one of Europe's most innovative retailers in its use of information technology.

As with many retailers, Tesco has long used electronic data interchange (EDI) to order goods from suppliers and the network links 1300 of Tesco's 2000 suppliers, representing around 96 per cent by volume of goods sold in Tesco stores.

The EDI system started operating in the 1980s and its use was initially limited to streamlining store replenishment. In 1989, Tesco took its first steps on the road to collaboration and began using its EDI network to help its suppliers better forecast demand.

About 350 suppliers receive EDI messages with details of actual store demand, depot stockholdings and Tesco's weekly sales forecasts.

According to Barry Knichel, Tesco's supply chain director, this forecasting project has been successful as average lead times have fallen from seven to three days. 'Nevertheless, the information flow is strictly one way', he says. 'We still do not know the true value of this sales data because we never get any feedback.'

In 1997, Tesco thus started its Tesco Information Exchange (Tie) project in an attempt to achieve much more sophisticated two-way collaboration in its supply chain.

'This really was a big development for us', he says. 'The guiding principle was to combine our retailing knowledge with the product knowledge of our suppliers.'

A large Tesco store may carry 50,000 products while a supplier will have at most 200. An important aim of the Tie project was thus to shift responsibility for managing products down to the relevant supplier.

'Suppliers clearly have a better understanding of their specific product lines, so if you can engage the supplier to manage the supply chain you are going to get much better product availability and reduce your inventory', says Jorge Castillo, head of retail business for GE Information Services, which developed the extranet technology behind Tie.

Suppliers pay from £100 to £100,000 to join Tie, depending on their size. This then allows them to access the Tie web site and view daily electronic point-of-sale (Pos) data from Tesco stores.

According to Mr Castillo, Tie lets suppliers monitor changes in demand almost in real time and so gives them more time to react. 'Before, Tesco's suppliers would not have seen a problem until Tesco got on the phone to them', he says. 'Now, it is the suppliers who get on the phone to Tesco and they can see much earlier on if a product is not selling well.'

The data can be analysed in a number of ways to allow suppliers to see how sales perform by distribution centre, by individual store or even by TV region – important for promotions.

The management of promotions is a complex process requiring close cooperation between supplier and retailer. However, it has traditionally been difficult to do well because of the lack of shared data to support collaborative decisions.

'Promotions can be a nightmare', says Mr Knichel. Tesco and GEIS added a promotions management module to the service in 1999. It allows retailers and suppliers to collaborate in all stages of the promotion: initial commercial planning, supply chain planning, execution and final evaluation.

According to St Ivel, one of Tesco's bigger food suppliers, Tie has saved 30 per cent of its annual promotional costs.

More than 600 suppliers, representing 70 per cent of Tesco's business, are using Tie today and Tesco aims to have all its suppliers onboard by the end of 2000. Around 40 suppliers are participating in the most recent addition to the Tie system, a collaborative data module.

This aims to allow 'seamless' planning in which the planning data on the screen is jointly filled in by both retailer and supplier. Mr Knichel sees this as radical change for the retail industry as suppliers and retailers have traditionally worked to separate agendas.

He feels Tie has much potential to streamline Tesco's supply chain and to help suppliers improve their service levels and promotions. But retailing is a traditional industry and many suppliers are set in their ways.

'Only two suppliers have fundamentally changed the way they work as a result of Tie. Nevertheless, they can bring products to market much faster than any of their competitors', he says.

Source: Geoffrey Nairn, *Financial Times*, 3 May 2000

Questions

1. What benefits does Tesco's information exchange offer to the retailer and its suppliers?
2. What differences have the use of TIE added over the original EDI system?
3. Discuss reasons why only two of Tesco's suppliers have fundamentally altered the way they work as a result of TIE.

The Tesco case study illustrates the benefits and difficulties of implementing EDI for supply chain optimization from a retailer's perspective. We will now consider it from the perspective of the manufacturer. Fisher (1997) makes the distinction between two strategies that manufacturers can follow according to the type of product and the nature of its demand.

For functional products, particularly those with easily predictable demand, such as consumer goods like toothpaste or shampoo, the product does not need to be modified frequently in response to consumer demand. Here the implication is that the supply chain should be directed at cost reduction and efficiency. For more complex products, including those with less predictable demand, Fisher (1997) gives the example of two contrasting products, skiwear from Sport Obermayer and soup from Campbell. Each year, 95 per cent of Sport Obermayer's products are new designs and demand forecasts may err by over 200 per cent. In contrast, 95 per cent of Campbell's products are similar each year with predictable demand levels. The strategic response for these products is to develop a physically efficient supply chain in the former case and a market-responsive supply chain in the latter case.

Cost cutting within a company such as Campbell may soon give diminishing returns. In these cases the biggest cost savings are possible by reviewing the structure of the supply chain as a whole. In 1991 the company operationalized what it referred to as a 'continuous replenishment programme'. It set up EDI links with major retailers and each morning retailers electronically inform Campbell of their demand for all products. Campbell then uses this information to determine which products require replenishment based on upper and lower limits of inventory agreed with each retailer. Trucks leave Campbell's shipping plants and then arrive at the retailers' distribution centres each day. This approach reduced the inventory of participating retailers from about four weeks to two weeks with the associated cost reductions. This two-week inventory reduction is the equivalent of a 1 per cent increase in sales. This does not sound like a large improvement, but retailers' margins are thin, so this translates to a large increase in profitability on these product lines. This example is instructive since it illustrates not only the savings possible with this approach, but the pitfalls of minimizing inventory through the use of EDI. The problem that Campbell encountered was that when it ran price promotions this could lead to up to five times the demand. This cannot be fulfilled on a short timescale so manufacture and retailer have to cooperate on advanced buying to meet these peaks in demand.

IS-supported downstream supply chain management

The key activities of downstream supply chain management are outbound logistics and fulfilment. It is evident that in a B2B context the benefits for downstream customers are, of course, similar to the benefits that the organization receives through automating its upstream supply chain. These issues are considered from a marketing perspective in *Chapters 8* and *9*, but in this chapter we review the importance of fulfilment in achieving e-commerce success.

We also use the grocery retail market to illustrate the implications of e-commerce for management of the downstream supply chain. In addition to being one of the leaders in using technology to improve upstream supply change management, Tesco is also one of the leaders in using e-commerce for downstream supply chain management. Tesco's downstream supply chain involves selling direct to customers, in other words it is operating a strategy of disintermediation (*Chapter 2, p. 45*) by reducing the role of its branches. Through being an early adopter, Tesco.com has developed as the world's largest online grocery site. By the end of 2000 annualized sales were running at nearly £300 million, with 48,000 orders per week – the most transactions for any online supermarket. In 2005 **Tesco.com** turnover was more than £1 billion.

Outbound logistics management

The importance of outbound logistics relates to the expectations of offering direct sales through a web site. In a nutshell, logistics is crucial to delivering the service promise established on the web site. If a customer is informed on the web site that a book will take two days to arrive, they will not be a repeat customer if the book arrives two weeks later.

A different angle on the importance of logistics and how it relates to the bottom line is illustrated by the fortunes of Amazon, which is infamous for not delivering profitability despite multi-billion-dollar sales. Phillips (2000) reported that the fulfilment mechanism was adding to Amazon's costs because of split shipments, where multiple deliveries of items are necessary from a single order. Evidence suggests that Amazon may require over three shipments to fulfil some orders. This is a particular problem in the USA, which is the source of 86 per cent of Amazon's revenue. Here the distance between population centres requires a network of seven distribution centres for shipments. Phillips (2000) explains that the need to fulfil a single order by shipping items from multiple locations increases costs for postage and the labour to assemble and dispatch goods. The alternative situation of stocking all distribution centres with every product is financially prohibitive. Some analysts suggest that Amazon should change its logistics strategy by separating out its distribution operation as a separate revenue source and outsourcing fulfilment to reduce costs.

A final indication of the importance of logistics is its scale – Phillips (2000) reports that e-fulfilment including warehousing, logistics and dispatch of online orders could be worth £5bn per year in the UK by 2008.

The challenge for distribution companies is to deliver on time and provide services to enable customers to track shipment of products ordered online. While an order-tracking facility has been the reality for international parcel carriers such as Federal Express since the mid-1990s, this is a challenge that needs now to be met by all distribution companies of consumer and business goods. The scale of the challenge can be gauged by looking at van Gend & Loos (vG&L, **www.vgl.nl**), a Dutch distribution company based within the Benelux countries. With over 4,000 employees, a fleet of 1,500 trucks, and annual revenues of approximately $500 million, vG&L wanted to offer its 40,000 customers the ability to track and trace their shipments over the Internet. While some distribution companies offer the facility for the sender to trace a package based on a consignment number, vG&L lets both the sender and the recipient track and trace packages based on date and destination searches. This key feature means that the sending parties can look at their information without the need for a special number, and they can look at all past shipments for the previous two months. At the same time, vG&L customers can also request pick-ups and shipments over the Internet.

IS infrastructure for supply chain management

Supply chain visibility
Access to up-to-date, accurate, relevant information about supply chain processes to different stakeholders.

Information systems need to deliver **supply chain visibility** to different parties who need to access the supply chain information of an organization, whether they be employees within the organization, suppliers, logistics service providers or customers. Information systems have a key role in providing this visibility. Since a huge volume of information defines supply chain processes for each organization, users of this information need to be able to personalize their view of the information according to their needs – customers want to see the status of their order, suppliers want to access the organization's database to know when their customer is next likely to place a major order. Security is also important – if a company has differential pricing, it will not want customers to see price differences.

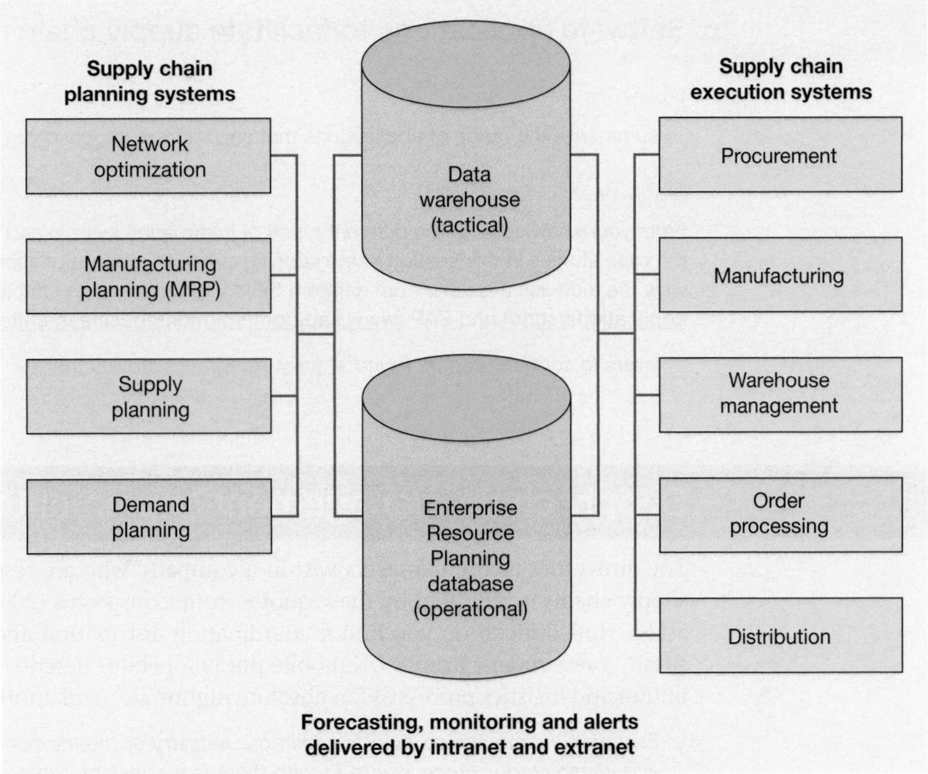

Figure 6.11 **A typical IS infrastructure for supply chain management**

These requirements for delivering supply chain information imply the need for an integrated supply chain database with different personalized views for different parties. A typical integrated information systems infrastructure for delivering supply chain management is illustrated in *Figure 6.11*. It can be seen that applications can be divided into those for planning the supply chain and those to execute the supply chain processes. *Case Studies 6.1* and *6.2* are both good examples of how new technologies are used to collect demand data and transfer data between different databases and applications. A key feature of a modern supply chain infrastructure is the use of a central operational database that enables information to be shared between supply chain processes and applications. This operational database is usually part of an enterprise resource planning system such as SAP, Baan or Prism and is usually purchased with the applications for supply chain planning and execution. Some of the planning applications such as network simulation and optimization are more likely to be supplied by separate software suppliers. The use of Internet technologies to deliver information over a TCP/IP protocol is becoming standard to reduce the costs of proprietary leased line networks (*Chapter 3*). Information needed by managers to intervene in the supply chain process when problems occur is delivered as alerts or through continuous monitoring across secure private intranets of extranets used to link to partners.

To conclude this section on the IS infrastructure to facilitate e-commerce, complete *Activity 6.3* on IS applications for e-commerce.

Activity 6.3 Software applications to facilitate supply chain management

Purpose

To summarize the range of applications that can support supply chain management.

Activity

From your knowledge of the different types of information system and software application, the case studies in this section name specific software applications for SCM. Alternatively, view the modules available from different SCM vendors such as Oracle (www.oracle.com/applications/scm/) and SAP (www.sap.com/solutions/business-suite/scm/).

Answers to activities can be found at www.pearsoned.co.uk/chaffey

Supply chain management implementation

The difficulties facing managers within a company who are responsible for managing supply chains is indicated by these quotes from Conspectus (2000). For example, when asked 'How difficult do you find it coordinating distribution and logistic plans at your sites?', a respondent from a UK mobile phone operator described his company's distribution and logistics process as 'an absolute nightmare', and another commented:

> *Everything is moving so quickly within our industry at the moment that sourcing suppliers and changing our processes to fit with them is a constant battle. We are hoping our SCM software and the roll-out of our extranet will grow end-to-end ROI but it is easy to forget that we must constantly examine the business model to ensure we are doing things right.*

By 2006, the Conspectus report showed that many companies have now invested in e-SCM. A mix of systems is still used, although 92% use the web for some forms of supply chain management, 85% still use fax and 65% traditional EDI. But there are great difficulties in delivering value from these systems. When asked, 'Do you feel you have realized all the benefits that you expected to gain from your supply chain systems?', the responses were:

- No, but may do so in future (56%)
- Yes, have realized some of the benefits (33%)
- Yes, have realized all of the benefits (7%)
- Don't know (4%)
- No, and are unlikely to in future.

If you are unfamiliar with the responsibilities managers tasked with supply chain management face, complete *Activity 6.4*.

Activity 6.4 Who manages the supply chain?

Purpose

To highlight the roles required of staff involved in supply chain management.

Questions

1 Review the job adverts below and for each list the processes that the manager is responsible for and the skills that are required.

2 Discuss the practicality of recruiting a person to this position with the necessary skills and experience.

Advert 1: Supply chain manager – The Healthcare Company

The opportunity

With annual turnover of $27 billion The Healthcare Company is a world leader in healthcare products, servicing over 150 countries in pharmaceutical, consumer diagnostic and professional markets. Manufacturing excellence coupled with exceptional customer service delivery is being met with repeat purchase and new account development. To reinforce business growth and profitability, The Healthcare Company seeks to appoint an experienced supply chain professional to lead a team of supply chain experts.

The challenge

Reporting to the General Manager, UK, you will provide strategic and tactical leadership to the UK operation, reinforcing customer service excellence while simultaneously delivering supply chain profitability. You will be instrumental in developing and implementing supply chain initiatives that impact positively across procurement, product development, manufacturing and distribution supply chains. Your team will be measured against the optimal use of business resources, lead time reductions, access to real-time data, stock turns, working capital costs and on time in full delivery to customers. Through the effective coordination of all business operating departments and the leadership of functional reports, purchasing, master scheduling/manufacturing control and data management, you will be the ambassador of customer service and supply chain excellence.

The solution

An ambitious and commercially mature business professional, your breadth of management exposure will ideally encompass supplier liaison, systems development, implementation and maintenance, material management, sales forecasting and capacity planning. Career progression to date has been enhanced by your ability to lead business professionals in the effective implementation of supply chain systems and their ongoing development (preferably MRPII). Personal qualities should include outstanding communication and influencing skills, combined with excellent analytical skills and a thorough working knowledge of IT business management tools (SAP/Oracle/BPEX) which have allowed your teams to deliver business supply excellence.

£50,000 + bonus + car

Advert 2: Supply chain manager – The Manufacturing Company

The Manufacturing Company is an international manufacturer operating throughout Northern and Continental Europe. The job will involve the management of information channels between customer, company suppliers and partners. The role requires constant monitoring of production against cost to achieve optimum performance levels.

The responsibilities of this role will include:

- The design and implementation of information flows that are consistent and appropriate to achieve minimum cost to the business.
- Manage trade-off between production efficiency, inventory and customer service.
- Analysis of data to ensure that valid business decisions can be made.
- Management of service level agreements to maximize service whilst minimizing inventory.
- Championing the use of IT planning systems.
- The development of team members to ensure standards are set and achieved.

Candidates should have:

- Been educated to a high standard, ideally with a relevant degree.
- Excellent analytical and problem-solving skills, strong systems knowledge (ERP/MRP, finite scheduling) and experience in planning and inventory control preferably in a short-lead-time environment. You should be highly motivated with strong influencing and communication skills.

£40,000 + car allowance

→

Advert 3: Logistics manager – The Engineering Company

A market leader with turnover in excess of £100m and approaching 1,000 employees. The business is engaged in sourcing, manufacturing and direct sales, benefiting from strong brands and a good customer base.

Supply chain and logistics are recognized as critical with 40,000 product lines and 20,000 suppliers. Over 10,000 orders are processed daily with a substantial third-party transport budget.

You will be the logistics champion for the business, coordinating activities between operations and function. Successes will be measured by the achievement of positive change in continuous improvement environment. In addition it will involve direct control of distribution and third parties.

Candidates should be of graduate calibre from a background involving commercial and budget responsibility, customer-focused with character, drive and energy.

To $45,000 plus car

Advert 4: Transport manager – The Food Manufacturer

A long-established, family-owned food manufacturer with an annual turnover of £100m.

Responsible for efficient distribution operation from three sites utilizing a range of owned specialist vehicles supported by approved subcontractors. You will possess extensive transport and management experience, operating a fleet size in excess of 30 vehicles. Analytical and planning skills are essential in order to monitor and optimize fleet efficiency in response to customer requirement.

To £36,000 + benefits

Answers to activities can be found at www.pearsoned.co.uk/chaffey

A new concept is integration managers who enable supply chain partnerships to be redesigned. Approaches include launching 100-day projects to achieve short-term bottom-line results, transfer of best practice between companies and mobilization of joint teams.

The supply chain management strategy process

A strategic approach for supply chain management can also be defined using the SOSTAC™ approach referred to in *Chapters 5* and *8*. *Table 6.2* summarizes a SOSTAC™ approach to supply chain management strategy development based on the guidance of Hughes *et al.* (1998). *Table 6.2* implies a linear approach to strategic thinking, but, as was pointed out in *Chapters 4* and *5*, an iterative approach in which there is a joint development between the organization, the suppliers and other third parties.

Strategies for supply chain improvement have been categorized by Hughes *et al.* (1998) according to the scope of change and the speed of change. These dimensions of change are similar to those that are associated with business process re-engineering and business process improvement (Bocij *et al.*, 2005). *Figure 6.12* illustrates four strategic options for the supply chain. The two strategies that are relatively limited in scope apply to individual processes such as procurement or outbound logistics and can be thought of as delivering improvement at an operational level. These may give

Table 6.2 A SOSTAC™ approach to supply chain management

Strategy element	*SCM approach of Hughes et al. (1998)*
Situation analysis	Gather the data: • Internal assessment of current approaches to the supply chain • External analysis of marketplace trends and customer opportunities
Objective setting	Set the objectives • Definition of required target returns and release of shareholder value
Strategy	Frame the strategies: • Development of supply chain strategies to achieve these goals (actions)
Tactics	Prioritization of operational improvement strategies and quick wins
Actions	Implement the change and challenge the thinking: • Formation of a supply chain strategy forum to assess the needs • Analysis of value-added, cost and cycle time of supply chain activities • Cascade of executive-led project groups to scrutinize key processes • Allocation of business development strategies to sponsor executives
Control	Measure the outcome: • Integration of supply chain measurement in corporation-wide reviews • Baselining to maintain pressure for performance delivery

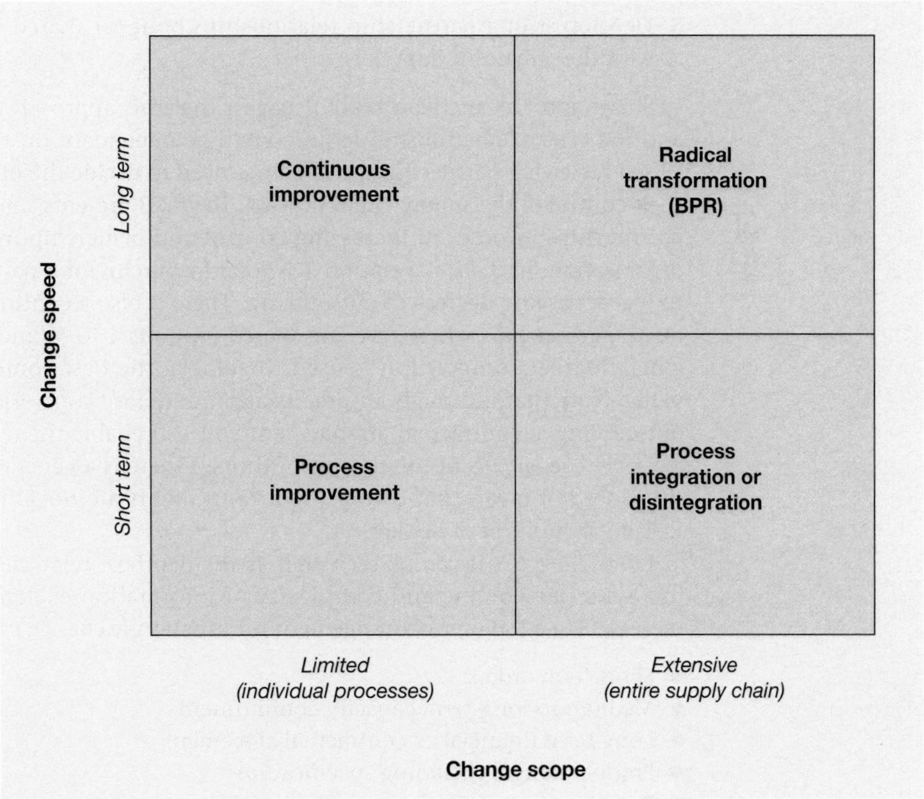

Figure 6.12 Alternative strategies for modification of the e-business supply chain

short-term benefits while minimizing the risk of more radical change. Conversely, where the scope of change is more extensive there is a greater risk, but also greater potential reward. These changes include complete re-engineering of processes or major changes to the supply chain.

Managing partnerships

A key element of restructuring of the supply chain is examining the form of relationships with partners such as suppliers and distributors. This need to review the form of partnership has been accentuated with the globalization enabled by e-commerce. The importance of forming new international partnerships is indicated by the survey of UK manufacturing companies with a turnover greater than £100m reported by Conspectus (2000). This showed that, at the time of the survey, 52 per cent of the sample operated their supply chain at a national level, with 30 per cent at a pan-European level and 18 per cent on a global scale. In this section we consider what forms these partnerships should take and how technology can be used to facilitate them.

Stuart and McCutcheon (2000) state that typically low cost is the main driver for partnership management in supply management (mainly upstream). According to these authors, the modification of supply chain partnerships usually follows what they describe as the 'received wisdom which many practitioners are rigidly following'. This approach requires companies to:

1 Focus on core competencies.
2 Reduce their number of suppliers.
3 Develop strong partnership relationships built on shared information and trust with the remaining suppliers.

Stuart and McCutcheon (2000) suggest that this approach may not suit all needs and the type of relationship required will be dependent on the ultimate objective. When reviewing partnerships, companies need to decide the options for the extent of their control of the supply chain process. *Table 6.3* presents some strategic options for partnerships in order of increasing control and ownership over the process by the organization. In *Table 6.3* option 1 is total insourcing of a particular process while 2 to 9 give varying degrees of outsourcing. There is also a continuum between collaborative partnerships where risks are shared (options 1 to 5) and competitive sourcing where market competition is used to achieve the best combination of price and value. Note that although an organization may lose control of the *process* through outsourcing, a contractual arrangement will still enable them to exert a strong control over the *outputs* of the process. Although there is a general trend to outsourcing, this does not mean that ownership arrangements are not uncommon, such as the Iceland acquisition of Booker.

From *Table 6.3* it can be seen that as the depth of relationship between partners increases, the volume and complexity of information exchange requirements will increase. For a long-term arrangement information exchange can include:

- Short-term orders
- Medium-to-long-term capacity commitments
- Long-term financial or contractual agreement
- Product design, including specifications
- Performance monitoring, standard of product and service quality
- Logistics.

Table 6.3 Strategic options for partnerships

Partnering arrangement	*Technical infrastructure integration*	*Examples*
1 Total ownership (more than 51% equity in company)	Technical issues in merging company systems	Purchase of Booker (distribution company) by Iceland (retailer). Since 1993 Cisco has made over 30 acquisitions (not all SCM-related)
2 Investment stake (less than 49% equity)	Technical issues in merging company systems	Cisco has also made over 40 investments in hardware and software suppliers
3 Strategic alliance	Collaboration tools and groupware for new product development	Cable and Wireless, Compaq and Microsoft new e-business solution called a-Services
4 Profit-sharing partnership	As above	Arrangement sometimes used for IS outsourcing
5 Long-term contract	See above. Tools for managing service level agreements important	ISPs have performance and availability SLAs with penalty clauses
6 Preferred suppliers	Permanent EDI or Internet EDI links set up with preferred partners	Tesco Information Exchange (*Case Study 6.2*)
7 Competitive tendering	Tenders issued at intermediary or buyer's web site	Buyer-arranged auctions, (see *Chapter 2*)
8 Short-term contracts	As above	As above
9 Spot markets and auctions	Auctions at intermediary or buyer's web site	Business-to-business marketplaces, e.g. www.freemarkets.com

For a short-term relationship simple information on transactions only such as the EDI purchase order example in *Chapter 3* are all that are required.

Stuart and McCutcheon (2000) present a more simplified set of partnership choices than those in *Table 6.3*. They suggest that the partnering option chosen should be dependent on the core objective. If this is cost reduction, then a relationship with competitive tension is required (equivalent to options 6 to 9 in *Table 6.3*). Alternatively, if the core objective is value-added benefits such as improved delivery speed, additional design features or the need for customization, then the 'arm's-length' approach of options 6 to 9 may not be appropriate. In this case they suggest a strategic alliance or cooperative partnership is the best option. Stuart and McCutcheon point out that the competitive advantages achieved through cost reduction are likely to be short-lived so companies will increasingly need to turn to value-added benefits. Each supplier has to be considered for whichever type of partnership is most appropriate. For example, ICL, the UK computer supplier, has strategic alliances with only 2 to 3 per cent of suppliers, with the majority in the cost reduction category.

Managing global distribution

Arnold (2000) suggests action that manufacturers should follow as they enter new overseas markets enabled by the Internet. The seven actions are:

1 Select distributors. Do not let them select you.
2 Look for distributors capable of developing markets rather than those with new customer contacts.
3 Treat the local distributors as long-term partners, not temporary market entry vehicles.
4 Support market entry by committing money, managers and proven marketing ideas.
5 From the start, maintain control over marketing strategy.
6 Make sure distributors provide you with detailed market and financial performance data.
7 Build links among national distributors at the earliest opportunity.

Case Study 6.3 RFID: keeping track starts its move to a faster track

FT

Over the years many techniques and technologies have been developed to make supply chains more efficient, but they often fail for the simple reason that it is notoriously difficult to get sufficient accurate information to be useful.

Radio frequency identification (RFID) technology tackles this problem using small radio tags to keep track of goods as they move through the supply chain.

Demand for these tags, which cost around 40 cents each, has soared because of mandates from US and European retailers – Wal-Mart is the best known – and the US Department of Defense which require large suppliers to put tags on pallets and cases as of 2005.

In-Stat, a US research firm, predicts that worldwide revenues from RFID tags will jump from $300m in 2004 to $2.8bn in 2009.

A clear sign that RFID is coming of age is that Nokia recently unveiled a kit to transform one of its phones into a mobile RFID reader. Despite the current hype, RFID is not a new technology. It was first used to identify aircraft in the second world war and has been employed to tag cattle, collect road tolls and open doors for many years.

What is new is the application of RFID to supply chains.

The combination of RFID hardware with a unique number, called the electronic product code (EPC), enables businesses to associate a wealth of information with each tagged object. Not only is the information more detailed than a barcode, it can be read and updated using radio readers.

Early RFID technologies often delivered disappointing performance, but today's tags can be read reliably as packing cases are on a conveyor belt or even if the case is hidden behind others.

'RFID is a barcode on steroids', says Lyle Ginsburg, RFID specialist at Accenture, the management consultancy. 'It promises tremendous productivity gains because you do not have the human intervention and line-of-sight issues that you get with barcodes.'

Many experts believe the combination of RFID and EPC has the potential to transform supply chains: no more inventory counts, no more lost or misdirected shipments, and no more guessing how much is in the supply chain or on the store shelves.

'Just by knowing what is in the store and what is still in the back room, you can get much greater visibility on inventory', says Peter Regen, vice president of global visible commerce at Unisys, the US IT company.

Visibility is sorely lacking from real-world supply chains, which is why companies hold buffer stocks and build warehouses. This lessens the chance of running out, but the annual cost of holding all this inventory – in warehousing, opportunity cost and obsolescence – adds up to $300bn, just in the US.

AMR Research estimates around $3 trillion of inventory is locked in US and European supply chains, which suffer order error rates of 20 per cent. 'There is just too much waste in the supply chain', says Michael Witty, an analyst with Manufacturing Insights, part of the IDC research group.

Even if RFID only manages to reduce inventory levels or error rates by a few percentage points, the benefits to the economy in terms of extra working capital are substantial. In the case of an emerging economy such as China, RFID's potential is even greater.

China's supply chains have not kept pace with the country's rapid rise as a manufacturing nation and bottlenecks now threaten its export-led growth. The Chinese government is keeping a close eye on RFID and officials recently attended a big RFID trade fair in the US.

'In China, there is a lot of interest in RFID, which has really surprised us', says Amar Singh, VP of global RFID initiatives at SAP, the German software giant. In part, this interest is driven by Chinese manufacturers' need to fall in to line with the RFID mandates of western customers, most notably Wal-Mart, which accounts for more than 10 per cent of all US imports from China.

But the Chinese government also sees RFID as a strategic technology that will bring the country's supply chains up to the standards of developed nations. Several projects are underway to test the use of RFID in Chinese port and logistics operations.

In the past three years, ports have become more conscious about security. Shipping companies know they face delays and may be refused entry if they are carrying suspect containers. 'Before 9/11, there was not much concern about what was inside the container', says Scott Brown, general manager for cargo security at GE, the US engineering giant.

GE has developed a 'smart box' that uses RFID to track the movements of maritime containers when they enter ports and sensors to detect if the containers have been opened. The smart box technology has been tested in GE's domestic appliance business, which imports most of its products from China.

'The impetus for doing this was security, but there are also potential supply chain benefits', says Mr Brown. However, he admits that it is difficult to make a case for using RFID on these benefits alone.

This problem affects most RFID initiatives, according to Accenture's Mr Lyle. Unless forced to comply with an RFID mandate, many potential users prefer to wait. Standards are still evolving and the cost of the technology is still too high for many applications. Data security is another big issue.

Burt Kaliski, chief scientist at RSA Laboratories, a US security software firm, fears thieves could quickly discover how to destroy or change the information on RFID tags while hackers could launch 'denial-of-service' attacks with the potential to create chaos in RFID-equipped supply chains.

But the main reason not to jump in yet is that, mandates aside, there are too many hurdles that need to be overcome before RFID can show a clear return on investment.

'The business case for RFID is very challenging', admits Mr Lyle.

Source: Geoffrey Nairn, FT.com site; 20, April 2005, http://search.ft.com/searchArticle?id=050420002433&query=supply+chain+management+rfid&vsc_appId=powerSearch&offset=0&resultsToShow=10&vsc_subjectConcept=&vsc_companyConcept=&state=More&vsc_publicationGroups=FTFT& searchCat=-1

Question

Select a manufacturing sector and then evaluate the benefits and risks of applying RFID in this sector.

Summary

1 Supply chain management involves the coordination of all supply activities of an organization from its suppliers and partners to its customers. Upstream supply chain activities (procurement and inbound logistics) are equivalent to buy-side e-commerce and downstream supply chain activities (sales, outbound logistics and fulfilment) correspond to sell-side e-commerce.

2 There has been a change in supply chain management thinking from a push-oriented supply chain that emphasizes distribution of a product to passive customers to a pull-oriented supply chain that utilizes the supply chain to deliver value to customers who are actively involved in product and service specification.

3 The value chain concept is closely allied to supply chain management. It considers how value can be added both between and within elements of the supply chain and at the interface between them.

4 Electronic communications enable value networks to be created that enable the external value chain to be dynamically updated in response to marketplace variables. →

5 Supply chains and value chains can be revised by disaggregation or re-aggregation. Disaggregation may involve outsourcing core supply chain activities to external parties. As more activities are outsourced a company moves towards becoming a virtual organization.

6 Electronic communications have played a major role in facilitating new models of supply chain management. Technology applications that have facilitated supply chain management are:
- E-mail
- Web-based ordering
- EDI of invoices and payment
- Web-based order tracking.

7 Benefits of deploying these technologies include:
- More efficient, lower-cost execution of processes
- Reduced complexity of the supply chain (disintermediation)
- Improved data integration between elements of the supply chain
- Reduced costs through ease of dynamic outsourcing
- Enabling innovation and customer responsiveness.

8 Intranets connecting internal business applications such as operational enterprise resource planning systems and decision-support-oriented data warehouses enable supply chain management. Such systems increasingly support external links to third parties such as suppliers.

9 Key strategic issues in supply chain management include:
- Redesigning supply chain activities
- Restructuring partnerships which support the supply chain through outsourcing or ownership.

Exercises

Self-assessment questions

1 Define supply chain management; how does it relate to:
- logistics;
- the value chain concept;
- value networks?

2 What is the difference between a push orientation to the value chain and pull orientation?

3 How can information systems support the supply chain?

4 What are the key strategic options in supply chain management?

Essay and discussion questions

1 How does electronic communications enable restructuring of the value chain network?

2 'The concept of a linear value chain is no longer tenable with the advent of electronic commerce.' Discuss.

3 Select an industry of your choice and analyse how business-to-business exchanges will change the supply chain.

4 *'In the end business all comes down to supply chain vs supply chain.'* Discuss.

5 Select a retailer of your choice and analyse their strategy for management of the upstream and downstream supply chain.

Examination questions

1 Explain how the concepts of disintermediation, reintermediation and countermediation apply to the supply chain.

2 You have recently been appointed as supply chain manager for a pharmaceutical company. Summarize the main Internet-based applications you would consider for communicating with your suppliers.

3 How has the increase in electronic communications contributed to the development of value networks?

4 What are the characteristics of a virtual organization? Using examples, explain how e-commerce can support the virtual organization.

5 Explain how information technologies can be employed for different elements of a purchaser–supplier relationship.

6 Using industry examples, summarize three benefits of using e-commerce to streamline the supply chain.

7 How can electronic commerce be used to support restructuring of the supply chain?

8 What are the differences and similarities of using information technology to support:

(a) the upstream supply chain;
(b) the downstream supply chain?

References

Arnold, D. (2000), Seven rules of international distribution. *Harvard Business Review*, November–December, 131–7.

Benjamin, R. and Wigand, R. (1995) Electronic markets and virtual value-chains on the information superhighway. *Sloan Management Review*, Winter, 62–72.

Bocij, P., Chaffey, D., Greasley, A. and Hickie, S. (2005) *Business Information Systems. Technology, Development and Management*, 3rd edn. Financial Times Prentice Hall, Harlow.

Chan, C. and Swatman, P. (2000) From EDI to Internet commerce – the BHP Steel experience. *Internet Research Electronic Networks: Applications and Policy*, 10(1), 77–82.

Conspectus (2000) Supply chain management software issue. Prime Marketing Publications, June. PMP Research www.conspectus.com.

Conspectus (2006) Supply chain management and manufacturing systems. Prime Marketing Publications, June. PMP Research www.conspectus.com.

Davidow, W.H. and Malone, M.S. (1992) *The Virtual Corporation. Structuring and Revitalizing the Corporation for the 21st Century*. HarperCollins, London.

Deise, M., Nowikow, C., King, P. and Wright, A. (2000) *Executive's Guide to E-Business. From Tactics to Strategy*. Wiley, New York.

DTI (2004) Business in the Information Age – International Benchmarking Study 2004. UK Department of Trade and Industry. www.ukonlineforbusiness.gov.uk.

eEurope (2005) Information Society Benchmarking Report. From eEurope (2005) initiative. Published at: http://europa.eu.int/information society/eeurope/i2010/docs/benchmarking/051222%20Final%20Benchmarking%20Report.pdf.

Field, C. (2000). Waterstone's: fully integrated into existing fulfilment systems. *Financial Times*, 3 May.

Fisher, M. (1997) What is the right supply chain for your product? *Harvard Business Review*, March–April, 105–16.

Hagel, J. III and Rayport, J. (1997) The new infomediaries. *McKinsey Quarterly*, no. 4, 54–70.

Hamill, J. and Gregory, K. (1997) Internet marketing in the internationalisation of UK SMEs. *Journal of Marketing Management*, 13, 1–3.

Hayes, R. and Wheelwright, S. (1994) *Restoring our Competitive Edge*. Wiley, New York.

Hughes, J., Ralf, M. and Michels, B. (1998) *Transform Your Supply Chain*. International Thomson Business Press, London.

IDC (2004) Increasing Supply Chain Responsiveness among Configured Electronic Systems Manufacturers, IDC White paper. Author: Meredith Whalen, January.

Kalakota, R. and Robinson, M. (2000) *E-Business. Roadmap for Success*. Addison-Wesley, Reading, MA.

Kraut, R., Chan, A., Butler, B. and Hong, A. (1998) Coordination and virtualisation: the role of electronic networks and personal relationships. *Journal of Computer Mediated Communications*, 3(4).

Magretta, J. (1998) The power of virtual integration. An interview with Michael Dell. *Harvard Business Review*, March–April, 72–84.

Malone, T., Yates, J. and Benjamin, R. (1987) Electronic markets and electronic hierarchies: effects of information technology on market structure and corporate strategies. *Communications of the ACM*, 30(6), 484–97.

Phillips, S. (2000) Retailer's crown jewel is a unique customer database. *Financial Times*, 4 December.

Porter, M. (1980) *Competitive Strategy*. Free Press, New York.

Porter, M. and Millar, V. (1985) How information gives you competitive advantage. *Harvard Business Review*, July–August, 149–60.

Quelch, J. and Klein, L. (1996) The Internet and international marketing. *Sloan Management Review*, Spring, 60–75.

Rayport, J. and Sviokla, J. (1996) Exploiting the virtual value-chain. *McKinsey Quarterly*, no. 1, 20–37.

Steinfield, C., Kraut, R. and Plummer, A. (1996) The impact of interorganizational networks on buyer–seller relationships. *Journal of Computer Mediated Communication*, 1(3).

Stuart, F. and McCutcheon, D. (2000) The manager's guide to supply chain management. *Business Horizons*, March–April, 35–44.

Timmers, P. (1999) *Electronic Commerce Strategies and Models for Business-to-Business Trading*. John Wiley Series in Information Systems. Wiley, Chichester.

Warner, M. (2001) Managing in virtual space. FT Mastering Management. Available online at: www.ftmastering.com/mmo/mmo03_1.htm.

Womack, J. and Jones, D. (1998) *Lean Thinking*. Touchstone, Simon and Schuster, London.

Further reading

Deise, M., Nowikow, C., King, P. and Wright, A. (2000) *Executive's Guide to E-Business. From Tactics to Strategy*. Wiley, New York. See Chapter 5, Industry transformation for description of value networks and partnering arrangements.

Fingar, P., Kumar, H. and Sharma, T. (2000) *Enterprise E-Commerce*. Meghan-Kiffler Press, Tampa, FL. See Chapter 6, Extended supply chain management.

Hughes, J., Ralf, M. and Michels, B. (1998) *Transform Your Supply Chain*. International Thomson Business Press, London An accessible introduction to supply chain management, with many examples. See Chapter 9, The electronic supply chain.

McIvor, R., Humphreys, P. and Huang, G. (2000) Electronic commerce: re-engineering the buyer–supplier interface. *Business Process Management Journal*, 6(2) 122–38. Three case studies showing how SCM has transformed supply chains.

Murillo, L. (2001) Supply chain management and the international dissemination of e-commerce. *Industrial Management and Data Systems*, 101(7), 370–7. An introduction to changes in supply chain management introduced by e-commerce.

Westland, J.C. and Clark, T.H. (2000) *Global Electronic Commerce: Theory and Case Studies*. MIT press, Cambridge, MA. Chapter 4, Supply chain management use – a value chain perspective on the application of e-commerce to SCM.

Web links

CIO Magazine E-commerce resource centre (www.cio.com/forums/ec) One of the best online magazines from a business/technical perspective – see other research centres also, e.g. intranets, knowledge management.

Conspectus (www.conspectus.com) Articles on different e-business applications including supply chain management.

CPFR (Collaborative Planning, Forecasting and Replenishment) www.cpfr.org. CPFR is a concept that allows collaborative processes across the supply chain, using a set of process and technology models. The site includes generic models, white papers and case studies.

Institute of Logistics and Transport (www.iolt.org.uk) Overview of logistics, plus links to related sites.

ITtoolbox (erp.ittoolbox.com) Specialists portal containing news and articles about ERP (enterprise resource planning systems), one application of which is supply chain management.

Oracle SCM introduction (www.oracle.com/applications/scm/) Oracle is one of the biggest providers of SCM applications, here they introduce the benefits of their approach.

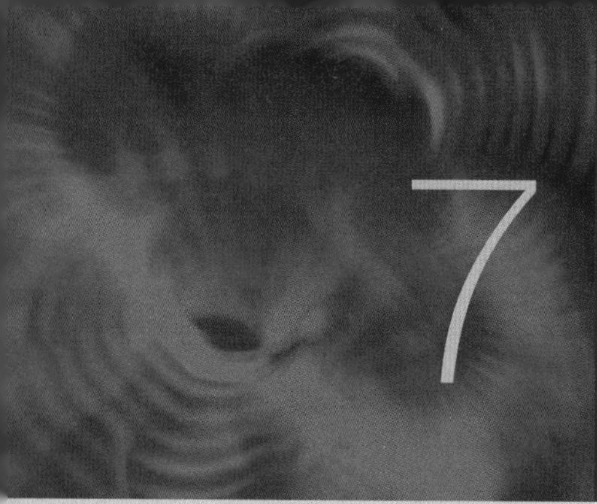

7 E-procurement

Chapter at a glance

Web support

The following additional case studies are available at www.pearsoned.co.uk/chaffey

- Worldwide oil exchange – the Shell perspective
- E-procurement in the aerospace industry

The site also contains a range of study materials designed to help improve your results.

Learning outcomes

After reading this chapter the reader should be able to:

- Identify the benefits and risks of e-procurement
- Analyse procurement methods to evaluate cost savings
- Assess different options for integration of organizations' information systems with e-procurement suppliers.

Management issues

Managers will be concerned with the following e-procurement issues:

- What benefits and risks are associated with e-procurement?
- Which method(s) of e-procurement should we adopt?
- What organizational and technical issues are involved in introducing e-procurement?

Links to other chapters

The main related chapters are:

- *Chapter 2* – introduces business-to-business marketplaces, models of electronic trading and B2B auctions;
- *Chapter 6* – covers the role of purchasing within supply chain management.

Introduction

Procurement has not traditionally been a significant topic for management study in comparison with other areas such as marketing, operations or strategy. The concept of e-business has, however, highlighted its importance as a strategic issue since introducing electronic procurement or e-procurement can achieve significant savings and other benefits which directly impact upon the customer.

The potential importance of online procurement is highlighted by Christa Degnan, a senior analyst at the Aberdeen Group, who explains that purchased goods and services are often the largest expenditure at many companies:

> *We estimate that for every dollar a company earns in revenue, 50 cents to 55 cents is spent on indirect goods and services – things like office supplies and computer equipment. That half dollar represents an opportunity: By driving costs out of the purchasing process, companies can increase profits without having to sell more goods.* (Hildebrand, 2002)

Issues involved with electronic trading between a supplier and its customers are often considered as in *Chapters 8* and *9* from the marketing perspective of the supplier of goods. In this chapter, we consider the same transaction, but from the alternative perspective of the purchaser of goods. It will be seen that there are a wide range of methods of implementing electronic trading with suppliers which will be assessed by purchasing, information systems and marketing managers. Meanwhile, company directors will need to assess the strategic benefits and risks of e-procurement.

In this chapter we consider the benefits and risks of e-procurement together with techniques that can be used to assess these benefits and risks. We also consider the selection of the different types of e-procurement including the hyped business-to-business marketplaces.

What is e-procurement?

Electronic procurement (e-procurement)
The electronic integration and management of all procurement activities including purchase request, authorization, ordering, delivery and payment between a purchaser and a supplier.

Electronic procurement system (EPS)
An electronic system used to automate all or part of the procurement function by enabling the scanning, storage and retrieval of invoices and other documents; management of approvals; routeing of authorization requests; interfaces to other finance systems; and matching of documents to validate transactions.

The terms 'purchasing' and 'procurement' are sometimes used interchangeably, but as Kalakota and Robinson (2000) point out, 'procurement' generally has a broader meaning. 'Procurement' refers to all activities involved with obtaining items from a supplier; this includes purchasing, but also inbound logistics such as transportation, goods-in and warehousing before the item is used. The key procurement activities and associated information flows within an organization are shown in *Figure 7.1*. In this chapter we focus on these activities which include searching and specification of product by the end-user, purchasing by the buyer, payment by an account, and receipt and distribution of goods within a warehouse.

E-procurement should be directed at improving performance for each of the 'five rights of purchasing' (Baily *et al*., 1994), which are sourcing items:

1 at the right price
2 delivered at the right time
3 are of the right quality
4 of the right quantity
5 from the right source.

E-procurement is not new; there have been many attempts to automate the process of procurement for the buyer using electronic procurement systems (EPS), workflow systems and links with suppliers through EDI (*Chapter 3*). These involved online entry, authorization and placing of orders using a combination of data entry

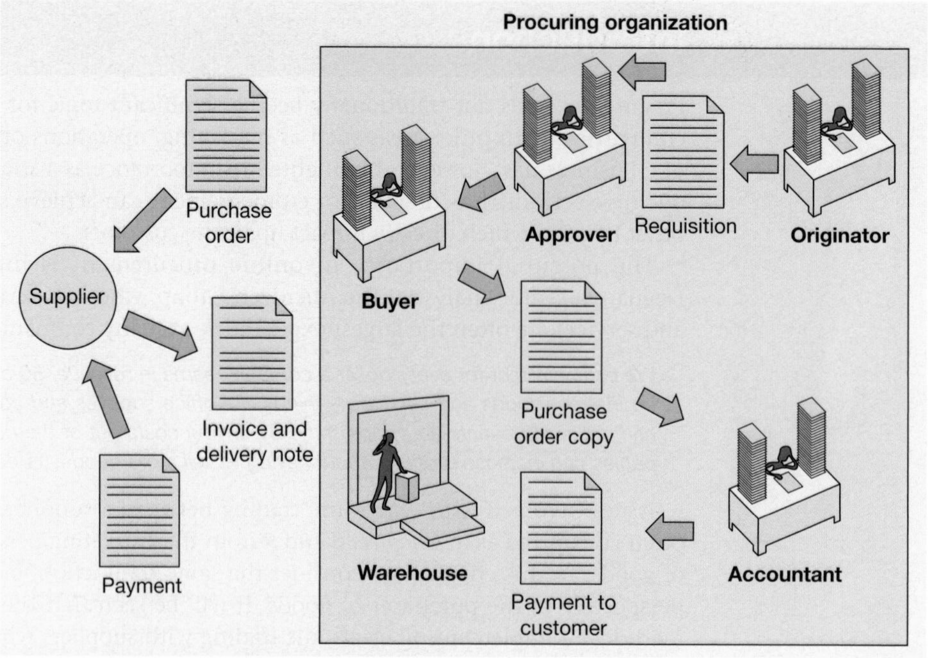

Figure 7.1 **Key procurement activities within an organization**

forms, scanned documents and e-mail-based workflow. It is convenient to refer to these as 'first-generation e-procurement'. *Figure 7.2* is an example of an electronic procurement system that is available through a company intranet.

Read the box *E-procurement at Schlumberger in Paris* to understand how e-procurement occurs within an organization.

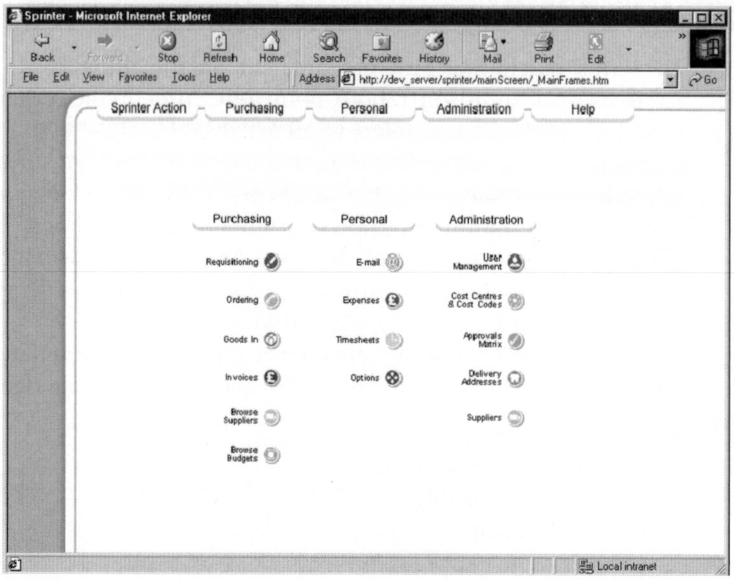

Figure 7.2 **Electronic procurement system**

Source: Tranmit plc

E-procurement at Schlumberger in Paris

Schlumberger is a global company that started its life as a supplier in the oil and gas exploration industry with revenues. In 2000 it had revenues of $8.5 million and 60,000 employees across 100 countries. It now provides a range of information services. This case study describes the installation of an e-procurement system at its largest division, oilfield services. The aim of the new system was to replace existing systems, some paper-based and some computer-based, with a single system that would speed up purchasing. The system has resulted in lower transaction costs for placing orders and also reduced the cost of goods as the price of products has declined through greater competition and negotiation of lower prices for the electronic channel.

With the new system, employees act as purchasing agents, ordering directly via their desktop PCs.

The system runs on the Schlumberger intranet and enables staff to access a simplified catalogue of office supplies and technical equipment. For example, one of the suppliers is OfficeDepot. Although OfficeDepot can post its entire catalogue at an electronic marketplace, employees at Schlumberger only see a subset of relevant products for which special prices have been negotiated. Once the items have been selected, the system automatically produces a requisition that is electronically routed to the person who will approve it, and it is then converted into a purchase order without the intervention of purchasing staff.

The technical solution is based on Commerce One Buysite procurement software for selection and approval and Marketsite from the same supplier for the transaction between Schlumberger and their suppliers. Schlumberger reports that Marketsite tends to give access to a wider range of suppliers than when it used one-to-one EDI transactions with suppliers. The solution was implemented gradually through introducing new items in stages.

Source: Based on a summary of a dialogue between Alain-Michel Diamant-Berger and Andrea Ovans (Ovans, 2000).

Understanding the procurement process

Before the advent of e-procurement, organizational purchasing processes had remained similar for decades. *Table 7.1* highlights the paper-based process. It can be

Table 7.1 **Process flow analysis for traditional procurement (typical cycle time, 5½ days)**

	Task description	*Chart symbols*	*Time*
1	Search for goods	●⇨□D▽	1 hour
2	Fill in paper requisition	●⇨□D▽	10 min
3	Send to buyer	○➡□D▽	1 day
4	In buyer's in-tray	○⇨□◗▽	½ day
5	Buyer enters order number	●⇨□D▽	10 min
6	Buyer authorizes order	●⇨□D▽	10 min
7	Buyer prints order	●⇨□D▽	10 min
8	Order copies to supplier and goods-in	○➡□D▽	1 day
9	Delivery from supplier	○⇨□D▼	1 day
10	Order copy to accounts	○➡□D▽	1 day
11	Three-way invoice match	●⇨□D▽	1 day
12	Cheque payment	●⇨□D▽	10 min

seen that it involves the end-user of the item selecting an item by conducting a search and then filling in a paper requisition form that is sent to a buyer in the purchasing department (often after authorization by a manager, which introduces further delay). The buyer then fills in an order form that is dispatched to the supplier. After the item is delivered, the item and a delivery note are usually reconciled with the order form and an invoice and then payment occurs. Procurement also includes the transport, storage and distribution of goods received within the business – this is referred to as 'inbound logistics'. *Activity 7.1* explains how the procurement process can be simplified through e-procurement.

Activity 7.1 Evaluating the benefits of the e-procurement process for The B2B Company

Purpose

To highlight the tasks involved in organizational purchasing and to indicate the potential time savings from e-procurement.

Introduction

Table 7.1 illustrates a typical traditional procurement process using the flow-process chart symbols that are explained in more detail in *Chapter 11*. It is based on the actual procurement process for Cambridge Consultants described in *Case Study 7.1*. Note that this process is for relatively low-value items that do not need authorization by senior managers. The timings are for a new item rather than a repeat buy for which searching would not be required. *Table 7.2* summarizes the new procurement process.

Table 7.2 **Process flow analysis for new procurement (typical cycle time, 1½ days)**

	Task description	*Chart symbols*	*Time*
1	Search for goods	●⇨□D▽	20 min
2	Order on web	●⇨□D▽	10 min
3	Delivery from supplier	○⇨□D▼	1 day
4	Generate invoice	●⇨□D▽	10 min
5	Cheque payment	●⇨□D▽	10 min

Key to flow process chart symbols

○ Process
⇨ Transport
□ Inspection
D Delay
▽ Inbound goods

Questions

1 Identify inefficiencies in the traditional procurement process (*Table 7.1*).
2 Identify process benefits to *Table 7.1* that would be possible through the automation of a system through an e-mail-based workflow system.
3 Summarize why the e-procurement process in *Table 7.2* is more efficient.

Answers to activities can be found at www.pearsoned.co.uk/chaffey

Types of procurement

To understand the benefits of e-procurement, and also to highlight some of the practical considerations with introducing e-procurement, we need to briefly consider the different types of items that are obtained by procurement (what is bought?) and types of ordering (how is it bought?).

Let us start us by reviewing what is bought by businesses. The B2B Company, for example, will buy everything from steel for manufacturing products, through equipment to help machine products, to paper clips and pens for office use. There are two broad categories of procurement: those that relate to manufacturing of products (*production-related procurement*) and *operating* or *non-production-related procurement* that supports the operations of the whole business and includes office supplies, furniture, information systems, MRO goods and a range of services from catering, buying travel, and professional services such as consulting and training. Raw materials for the production of goods and MRO goods are particularly important since they are critical to the operation of a business. For The B2B Company, they would include manufacturing equipment, network cables and computers to control the process.

MRO
Maintenance, repairs and operations of manufacturing facilities.

Moving to how items are bought, businesses tend to buy by one of two methods:

- *Systematic sourcing* – negotiated contracts with regular suppliers, typically in long-term relationships.
- *Spot sourcing* – fulfilment of an immediate need, typically of a commoditized item for which it is less important to know the credibility of the supplier.

A further characteristic of corporate procurement is that often items such as stationery are purchased repeatedly, either for identical items (straight rebuy) or with some changes (modified rebuy). E-procurement systems can assist in purchase if they make rebuys more straightforward.

Drivers of e-procurement

Case Study 7.1 illustrates many of the reasons why many companies are now introducing e-procurement. The primary driver is cost reduction, in this case from an average of £60 per order to £10 per order. In many cases the cost of ordering exceeds the value of the product purchased. *Internet Business* (1999) indicates that the figures in the case are representative, suggesting that the average cost of ordering is £80. If these types of savings are scaled across the whole of the UK it was estimated that UK businesses could save £100 billion per year and as a result it was estimated that global B2B trading will reach over $1 trillion by 2003 from $60 billion in 1999 (eMarketer, 2000). Savings may also be made through the need for less material in stock because of faster purchase cycle times.

Kluge (1997) and Kalakota and Robinson (2000) consider procurement to be a strategic issue since, as the figures above show, significant savings can be made and these cost reductions should result in greater profitability. Kluge (1997) reports on a survey of electronics companies in which there was a 19 per cent difference in profitability between the most successful and least successful companies. Of this difference, 13 per cent was due to differences in the cost of goods sold of which between 40 and 70 per cent was accounted for by differences in the cost of purchased goods and services.

Direct cost reductions are achieved through efficiencies in the process, as indicated by *Case Study 7.1* and *Tables 7.1* and *7.2*. Process efficiencies result in less staff time spent in searching and ordering products and reconciling deliveries with invoices.

Savings also occur due to automated validation of pre-approved spending budgets for individuals or departments, leading to fewer people processing each order, and in less time. It is also possible to reduce the cost of physical materials such as specially printed order forms and invoices that are important to the process, as is evident from *Figure 7.1*.

There are also indirect benefits from e-procurement; *Tables 7.1* and *7.2* show how the cycle time between order and use of supplies can be reduced. In addition e-procurement may enable greater flexibility in ordering goods from different suppliers according to best value. This is particularly true for *electronic B2B marketplaces (p. 325)*. E-procurement also tends to change the role of buyers in the purchasing department. By removing administrative tasks such as placing orders and reconciling deliveries and invoices with purchase orders, buyers can spend more time on value-adding activities. Such activities may include more time spent with key suppliers to improve product delivery and costs or analysis and control of purchasing behaviour.

Case Study 7.1 Cambridge Consultants reduce costs through e-procurement

Illustrates the potential benefits of e-procurement by reviewing the original and revised process and costs. The e-procurement system in this case is a direct link between the purchaser, Cambridge Consultants, and the web-based catalogue of one its major suppliers, RS Components.

Cambridge Consultants is a manufacturer with 300 employees offering technical product design and development services to commerce and industry. With 120 projects in hand at any one time, Cambridge needs a diverse range of components every day.

Purchasing is centralized across the company and controlled by its Purchasing Manager, Francis Pullen. Because of its varied and often unique requirements, Cambridge has a supplier base of nearly 4000 companies, with 20 new ones added each month. Some of these companies are providing items so specialized that Cambridge purchases from them no more than twice a year. Of the total, only 400 are preferred suppliers. Of those, just 10 per cent – 1 per cent of the overall supplier base – have been graded key supplier by Cambridge. That number includes RS Components. Francis Pullen says, 'We charge our clients by the hour, so if a product is faulty or late we have engineers waiting for new parts to arrive. This doesn't align with our fast time to market business proposition. RS Components' guarantee of service and range of products fits in with our business ethos.'

The existing purchasing process

Pullen has seen many changes and improvements in the company's purchasing process as its suppliers have used new technology to introduce new services. The first was moving to CD-ROM from the paper-based catalogue. Next was an online purchasing card – an account card with detailed line item billing, passwords and controls. Using industry-standard guidelines from the Chartered Institute of Purchasing and Supply (CIPS), Francis Pullen analysed the internal cost of raising an order. This took into account every step, from the engineer raising a paper requisition, through processing by purchasing, the cost of handling the delivery once it arrived, invoice matching and clearance and even the physical cost of a four-part purchase order form. The whole process involved between eight and ten people and cost the company anywhere from £60 to £120, depending on the complexity of the order.

The main cost is in requisitioning, when engineers and consultants spend their revenue-producing time in identifying their needs and raising paperwork. (Centralized purchasing, by contrast, is very efficient, costing around £50 an order.)

Using the RS purchase card removes the need for engineers and consultants to raise a paper requisition. This makes low-value ordering much more cost-efficient. Invoice matching costs are also reduced, since the purchase-card statement lists all purchases made each month.

Although the purchase card is undoubtedly an advance, on its own it does not allow costs to be assigned to jobs in the system each day. The purchase-card statement takes a month to arrive, giving rise to an equivalent lag in showing the real costs on internal project accounts.

The e-procurement process

To enable the company to order online immediately, RS put Cambridge's pre-Internet trading records on the web server. Purchasing agreements and controls were thus automatically set up on the Internet order form, including correct pricing and special payment terms.

The benefit was instantly apparent. The use of the RS purchase card when ordering from the web site meant that the complete order was automatically collated, with all controls in place. Accuracy was assured and the purchase process was speeded up, with the cost per transaction reduced significantly.

Pullen describes the change this has had on Cambridge's purchasing process. 'For the first time in our purchasing history, our financial controllers saw the benefit of distributed purchasing because of the cost savings, reassured by the central purchasing controls as back-up.

'This has benefited us enormously. We have allowed three department heads to have their own purchasing cards, so that they can order independently from the web site.

'We have implemented a very efficient electronic workflow requisition system which is initiated by the purchase card holders and mailed to central purchasing. The orders are held in a mailbox and checked against physical delivery. This has cut out two layers of order activity.

'In purchasing, we no longer spend our time passing on orders that they have raised, and there is no generation of paper during the order process. It doesn't just save time and money – it's also far more environmentally friendly. Passing on low-value orders each day adds very little value, so devolving this function back to our internal customers frees up our time in purchasing to work on higher-value tasks.'

Benefits for staff

Francis Pullen continues: 'Our internal customers are also much happier. We leave at 6 p.m. but the engineers will often work late if they are on a deadline. Because they can order off the web site from their desks (everyone at Cambridge has Internet access), they can add items to the order right up until RS's 8 p.m. deadline without our involvement. We maintain control because of the reporting functions on the site.'

Phase 2 of the rswww.com design has also made it possible for multiple orders to be opened during the day and then put against different cost centres internally.

Results

In the year to June 1999, Cambridge Consultants placed 1200 orders with RS Components, totalling more than £62,000 in value. Of those transactions, 95 per cent went via the Internet. Average order value over the Internet was £34 and accounted for £43,000 of the total business done. The remaining 60 orders were placed though traditional channels but had an average value of £317.

The cost to Cambridge of raising a paper-based order was identified as being £60. Using the combination of the RS purchasing card and rswww.com, this has been reduced to £10 an order. Over a year, this represents a saving of £57,000 to Cambridge. The net effect, therefore, is that its purchases from RS Components now cost it a mere £5,000 a year!

Francis Pullen again: 'RS has demonstrated its commitment to its customers in spending time and investing money in developing a world-class purchasing system that delivers tangible customer cost savings and benefits. We have welcomed their innovative approach to purchasing and believe they are way ahead of their competition in this sector.'

Source: RS Components White Paper (www.rswww.com) © RS Components Ltd 2001

Questions

1. Given the scale of the purchasing operation at Cambridge Consultants, what benefits do you think e-procurement has brought?
2. Why are procurement costs currently as high as £60 to £100 per order?
3. How are procurement costs reduced through e-procurement?
4. What staff benefits accrue to Cambridge Consultants as a result of e-procurement?

Turban *et al.* (2000) summarize the benefits of e-procurement as follows:

- Reduced purchasing cycle time and cost
- Enhanced budgetary control (achieved through rules to limit spending and improved reporting facilities)
- Elimination of administrative errors (correcting errors is traditionally a major part of a buyer's workload)
- Increasing buyers' productivity (enabling them to concentrate on strategic purchasing issues)
- Lowering prices through product standardization and consolidation of buys
- Improving information management (better access to prices from alternative suppliers and summaries of spending)
- Improving the payment process (this does not often occur currently since payment is not always integrated into e-procurement systems).

Focus on estimating e-procurement cost savings

While cost savings are commonly cited as the key benefit of e-procurement, more than half the companies in the Tranmit (1999) survey (54 per cent) did not know the procurement costs of their organization! This suggests that calculating costs is not straightforward, but it is clearly an important part of the cost-justification of introducing an e-procurement system.

The general approach to estimating procurement costs is straightforward. First, we calculate the average procurement cost per item, then we multiply by the average number of requisitions. The Tranmit (1999) report provides some illustrations – typical medium-to-large companies issue between 1,000 and 5,000 requisitions a month and are spending between £600,000 and £3 million annually on the procurement process, based on the £50 median cost per item. In exceptional cases, the number of requisitions was between 30,000 and 40,000 per month. In these cases, the annual cost of procurement could be between £18 million and £43 million!

To calculate cost savings from e-procurement we perform the following calculation:

$$\text{Savings} = \text{No. of requisitions} \times (\text{Original cost} - \text{New cost})$$

For Cambridge Consultants (*Case Study 7.1*) cost savings from orders placed with RS Components alone are as follows:

$$\text{Savings} = 1300 \times (£90 - £10) = £104{,}000$$

These are relative to a typical order value of £70, i.e. savings of £104,000 on purchase item costs of £91,000.

The impact of cost savings on profitability

The study by Kluge (1997) referred to above suggested that cost savings achieved through e-procurement may have a significant effect on profitability. *Activity 7.2* illustrates how the savings will vary between companies according to their buying characteristics. The largest savings and impact on profitability will typically be for manufacturing companies in which procurement is a major cost element and there are many requisitions for relatively low-value items. Service industries have lower potential for savings. The consequence for this is that there will be a wide variation in potential savings according to industry, as illustrated in *Table 7.3*.

Table 7.3 **Procurement as a percentage of costs of goods sold for different industry sectors (estimates from Kluge, 1997)**

Industry	*Procurement costs as a percentage of cost of goods sold*
Consumer electronics	60–70%
Mini and personal computers	50–70%
Consumer goods	50–70%
Automotive	50–60%
Pharmaceuticals	25–50%
Service industry	10–40%

Activity 7.2 Modelling cost savings and profitability arising from e-procurement

Purpose

To explore the different characteristics of purchasing in organizations that will govern the scale of savings made through e-procurement.

Activity

Imagine you are a procurement manager, IS manager or consultant who needs to demonstrate the cost savings of e-procurement to a senior management team in order to obtain approval for investment in an e-procurement system. Develop a spreadsheet model for each of two hypothetical companies to demonstrate the case as follows:

1 *Cost saving calculations*. Using the input parameters for the two companies in *Table 7.4*, develop a spreadsheet model to calculate traditional overall purchasing cost, new overall purchasing cost, percentage change in cost per order and percentage change in overall purchasing cost.
2 *Profitability calculations*. Using input parameters of turnover, traditional purchasing costs, other costs and a 5 per cent reduction in purchasing costs as shown in *Table 7.5* develop a model that calculates the profitability before and after introduction of e-procurement and also shows the change in profitability as an absolute (£) and as a percentage.
3 Analyse the sensitivity of the models to differences in volume of orders and values of purchases (*Table 7.4*) and the balance between traditional purchasing costs and other costs such as salaries and capital by using the parameters (*Table 7.5*). Explain to the managers the typical characteristics of a company that will make significant changes to profitability from introducing e-procurement.

Table 7.4 Input parameters for cost-saving calculations for two companies

Input parameters (Company A)		*Input parameters (Company B)*	
Number of orders	25,000	Number of orders	2,500
Traditional cost per order (average)	£50	Traditional cost per order (average)	£50
New cost per order (average)	£10	New cost per order (average)	£10
Average value of order	£150	Average value of order	£1,500

Table 7.5 Input parameters for profitability calculations for two companies

Parameter	*Company X*	*Company Y*
Turnover	£10,000,000	£10,000,000
Traditional purchasing costs	£5,000,000	£1,000,000
Other costs	£4,000,000	£8,000,000
Reduction in purchasing costs	20%	20%

Answers to activities can be found at www.pearsoned.co.uk/chaffey

Debate 7.1

E-procurement cost-savings

'The cost-saving benefits of e-procurement are theoretical rather than actual since only reduced headcount in procurement can result in savings.'

To conclude this *Focus* on topic, a note of caution should be struck. Many of the models used to calculate savings and return on investment are, of course, only as good as the assumptions they use. Refer to *Activity 7.4, Purchasing ROI myths* to review why savings may be lower than those predicted by models.

Risks and impacts of e-procurement

The Tranmit (1999) report above indicated that in the UK and throughout Europe, adoption of e-procurement is low, with less than a fifth of large companies adopting this technology. It may be possible to explain low adoption through a consideration of the risks and impacts involved with e-procurement. A PricewaterhouseCoopers survey of 400 senior European business leaders indicates that security concerns and lack of faith in trading partners are the most significant factors holding back e-procurement (Potter, 2000). Potter states that authentication of identity is the main issue. He says 'People need to be satisfied about who they are dealing with. They need to know that their messages have not been intercepted or corrupted on the way, and most importantly they are legally non-repudiable – meaning that the other party can't walk away from it in a court of law.' He goes on to say that the security fears are well founded, with nearly two-thirds of companies relying solely on password protection when dealing with suppliers. Trusted third-party certification is required for the level of trust to increase. While the Internet may give the impression of making it readily possible to swap between suppliers and use new suppliers, two-thirds of those interviewed said building a trusted relationship with suppliers is necessary before they would trade using the Internet. The nature and solution of Internet security risks are studied in more detail in *Chapter 11, p. 540.*

Organizational risks

If the cost savings referred to earlier in the chapter are to be achieved it may be necessary to redeploy staff, or in the worst case make them redundant. For a medium-sized company such as Cambridge Consultants the purchasing team of five people was reduced to four. The threat of redundancy or redeployment is likely to lead to resistance to the introduction of the system and this needs to be managed. The purchasing manager will have to carefully explain the reasons for introducing the new system, emphasizing the benefits to the company as a whole and how it should enable more variety to be introduced to the buying role.

Since the cost savings of e-procurement are achieved through empowerment of originators throughout the business to directly purchase their own items rather than through a purchasing department there is a risk that some originators may take advantage of this. This is known as 'maverick or off-contract purchasing', and it has always happened to some extent. Maverick purchasing occurs when items are ordered that are unnecessary or too expensive. Complete *Activity 7.3* to review the mechanisms that can be used to reduce this risk.

Activity 7.3 Avoiding maverick purchasing

Purpose

To identify responses to problems of maverick purchasing.

Activity

To avoid maverick purchasing, businesses introducing e-procurement need to put safeguards into the e-procurement system. Think about the type of rules that could be written into an e-procurement system.

Answers to activities can be found at www.pearsoned.co.uk/chaffey

Failure to achieve real cost reductions

There is a risk that the return on investment (ROI) from introducing e-procurement may be lower than that forecast and the introduction of the e-procurement system may not pay for itself. This may occur if the assumptions used to calculate savings from e-procurement such as those in *Activity 7.2* are too simplistic. Complete *Activity 7.4* to review why savings may be lower than anticipated.

Activity 7.4 Purchasing ROI myths

Purpose

To highlight reasons why not all the benefits of e-procurement may be delivered.

Activity

There are many proponents of the benefits of e-procurement, but a cautionary note is struck by Brian Caffrey of the purchasing web guide on About.com http://purchasing.about.com). Visit this site and review his editorial comments on why caution should be exercised when assessing the financial savings that accrue through e-procurement. The most relevant article is Caffrey (1997). This article also gives a more detailed model from a supplier of how cost savings may be achieved.

Answers to activities can be found at www.pearsoned.co.uk/chaffey

Technology risks

Tranmit (1999) reported the biggest barrier to automation of e-procurement as integration with existing financial systems, according to 60 per cent of respondents.

The section on implementing e-procurement below shows that there is a range of different models for procurement. The models are evolving fast, so it is difficult to know which to select. Likewise there is a range of different marketplaces, many of which have not yet reached critical mass. It will be wasteful to become involved in a marketplace which fails in a year's time. Problems introduced by large-scale ERP systems may also not dispose organizations to e-procurement.

Implementing e-procurement

Hildebrand (2002) illustrates the challenges of implementing e-procurement when he cites a 2002 Forrester Research poll of 50 global 3,500 companies. For these large, international companies, the biggest implementation 'headache' was rated as:

- Training/change management (32%)
- Supplier relationship management (30%)
- Catalogue management (10%)
- Project management (4%).

These problems are also indicated by Carrie Ericson, consultant at e-procurement supplier AT Kearney (www.ebreviate.com) in an interview (logistics.about, 2003). She says that in her experience:

> *Challenges often come down to our classic change management dilemmas: getting folks to change the way they conduct business, disrupting long standing supplier agreements, issues around politics and control.*
>
> *In addition, the up front cost is often a challenge and the ROI* [return on investment] *can be perceived to be risky. I'm sure we've all heard a lot of stories about costly eprocurement implementations. Finally, the buyers are often nervous about perception. Will the new tools reflect that they have been doing a poor job in the past?*

To introduce e-procurement the IS manager and procurement team must work together to find a solution that links together the different people and tasks of procurement shown in *Figure 7.1*. Historically, it has been easier to introduce systems

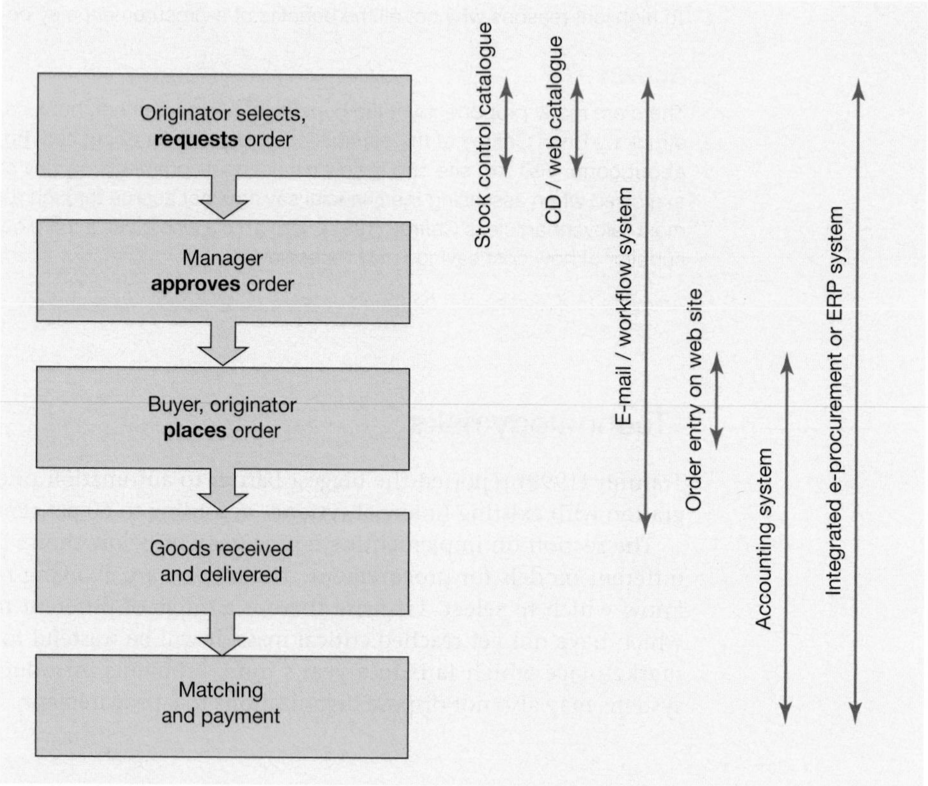

Figure 7.3 **Use of different information systems for different aspects of the fulfilment cycle**

that only cover some parts of the procurement cycle. *Figure 7.3* shows how different types of information system cover different parts of the procurement cycle. The different type of systems are as follows.

- *Stock control system* – this relates mainly to production-related procurement; the system highlights when reordering is required when the number in stock falls below reorder thresholds.
- *CD/web-based catalogue* – paper catalogues have been replaced by electronic forms that make it quicker to find suppliers.
- *E-mail- or database-based workflow systems* integrate the entry of the order by the originator, approval by manager and placement by buyer. The order is routed from one person to the next and will wait in their in box for actioning. Such systems may be extended to accounting systems. *Figure 7.4* shows an e-mail generated by an electronic procurement system as part of a workflow; it shows that a manager has approved the purchase requisition.

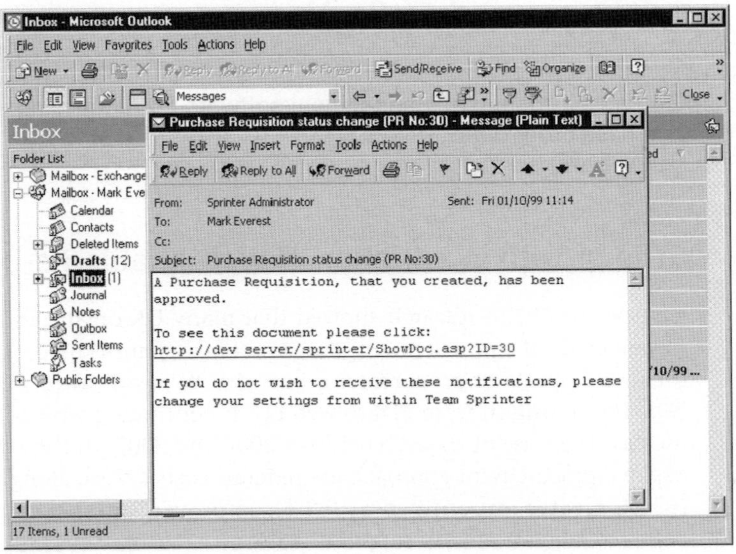

Figure 7.4 E-mail notification of requisition approval

Source: Tranmit plc

- *Order-entry on web site* – the buyer often has the opportunity to order directly on the supplier's web site, but this will involve rekeying and there is no integration with systems for requisitioning or accounting.
- *Accounting systems* – networked accounting systems enable staff in the buying department to enter an order which can then be used by accounting staff to make payment when the invoice arrives.
- *Integrated e-procurement or ERP systems* – these aim to integrate all the facilities above and will also include integration with suppliers' systems. *Figure 7.5* shows document management software as an integrated part of an e-procurement system. Here a paper invoice from a supplier (on the left) has been scanned into the system and is compared to the original electronic order information (on the right).

Companies face a difficult choice in achieving full-cycle e-procurement since they have the option of trying to link different systems or purchasing a single new system that integrates the facilities of the previous systems. Purchasing a new system may be the simplest technical option, but it may be more expensive than trying to integrate existing systems and it also requires retraining in the system.

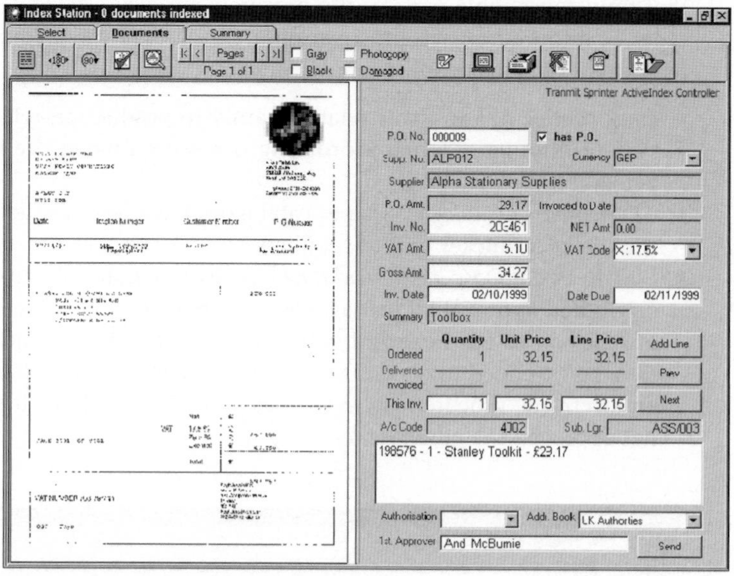

Figure 7.5 **Document management software for reconciling supplier invoice with purchase order data**

Source: Tranmit plc

The growth in adoption of web-enabled e-procurement

Conspectus (2006) research showed that many UK organizations have now invested in web-enabled e-procurement. But, a mix of systems is used, with 92% using the web for some aspects of procurement, but with 85% still using fax and 65% traditional EDI. The transition from EDI to web EDI is continuing with 82% stating they plan to increase their use of the web between 2006 and 2007. In the survey the main benefits of the e-procurement approach are reduced costs (77%), along with improved service (63%), greater responsiveness (63%), improved supplier relationships (63%) and better collaboration with suppliers (55%).

Within SMEs, as would be expected, use of e-procurement is low. FT.com (2006) reported that within SMEs, the use of online procurement is low. A postal survey of 167 SMEs by the Chartered Institute of Purchasing and Supply found that only 37% had used the web to tender for business despite 73% having an Internet connection. The main reason given by those who had not tendered for contracts online was a belief that '*the industry does not use online tendering*' (31%), lack of skills (17%), complexity (14%), lack of opportunity (12%) and mistrust of the process (11%). The benefits cited by SMEs currently selling goods and services online include speed of process (52%), cost savings (26%), reduced paperwork (26%), increased customer satisfaction (18%) and increased productivity (16%).

The results from these surveys suggest that e-procurement is undertaken for some activities, but not all. This is backed up by an earlier survey conducted by AT Kearney, quoted in logistics.about (2003). This showed that although 96% of US companies surveyed were engaged in some form of e-procurement, typically these activities only covered a limited portion, on average 11% of the spend base. While it tends to be higher for indirect materials (up to 15%), it is lower for services (4% on average). However, where e-procurement is used it delivers savings of as much as 40%. These savings come from purchased cost reduction as well as decreased order cycle time and headcount reduction.

Integrating company systems with supplier systems

We saw from the Shell case study in *Chapter 6*, the cost and cycle-time benefits that a company can achieve through linking its systems with those of its suppliers. If integrating systems within a company is difficult, then linking with other companies' systems is more so. This situation arises since suppliers will use different types of systems and different models for integration. As explained in *Chapter 2*, there are three fundamental models for location of B2B e-commerce: sell-side, buy-side and marketplace-based. These alternative options for procurement links with suppliers are summarized in *Figure 7.6* and the advantages and disadvantages of each are summarized in *Table 7.6*.

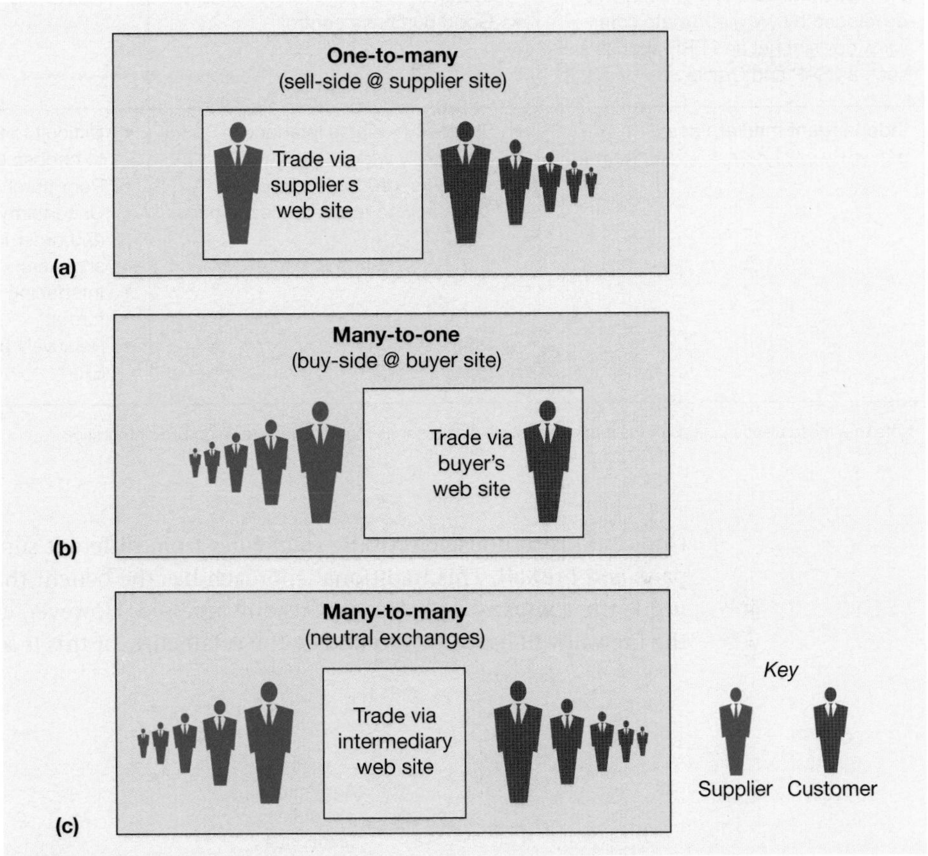

Figure 7.6 **The three main e-procurement model alternatives for buyers**

Chapter 2 explained that companies supplying products and services had to decide which combination of these models would be used to distribute their products. From the buyer's point of view, they will be limited by the selling model their suppliers have adopted.

Figure 7.7 shows options for integration for a buyer who is aiming to integrate an internal system such as an ERP system with external systems. Specialized e-procurement software may be necessary to interface with the ERP system. This could be a special e-procurement application or it could be middleware to interface with an e-procurement component of an ERP system. How does the e-procurement system access price catalogues from suppliers? There are two choices shown on the diagram.

Table 7.6 **Assessment of the procurement model alternatives for buyers**

Procurement model	*Advantages to buyer*	*Disadvantages to buyer*
Sell-side e.g. many catalogue-based B2B suppliers such as www.rswww.com	• Searching • Onus of maintaining data on supplier	• Different interface on each site (catalogue and ordering) • Restricted choice • Poor integration with ERP/procurement systems • Limited purchase control
Buy-side Private exchanges hosted by manufacturers and major suppliers to these manufacturers, e.g. solutions developed by www.ebreviate.com, www.covisint.net and ERP suppliers such as SAP and Oracle	• Simplicity – single interface • Wider choice than sell-side • Integration with ERP/procurement systems • Good purchase control	• Onus of maintaining data is on buyer • Software licence costs • Retraining
Independent marketplace e.g. www.ec21.com, www.eutilia.net	• Simplicity – single interface • Potentially widest choice of suppliers, products and prices • Often unified terms and conditions	• Difficult to know which marketplace to choose (horizontal and vertical) • Poor purchase controls* • Uncertainty on service levels from and order forms unfamiliar suppliers • Interfacing with marketplace data format* • Relatively poor integration with ERP*

* Note that these disadvantages of the marketplace will disappear as marketplaces develop ERP integration.

Choice (a) is to house electronic catalogues from different suppliers inside the company and firewall. This traditional approach has the benefit that the data are housed inside the company and so can be readily accessed. However, electronic links beyond the firewall will be needed to update the catalogues, or this is sometimes achieved via

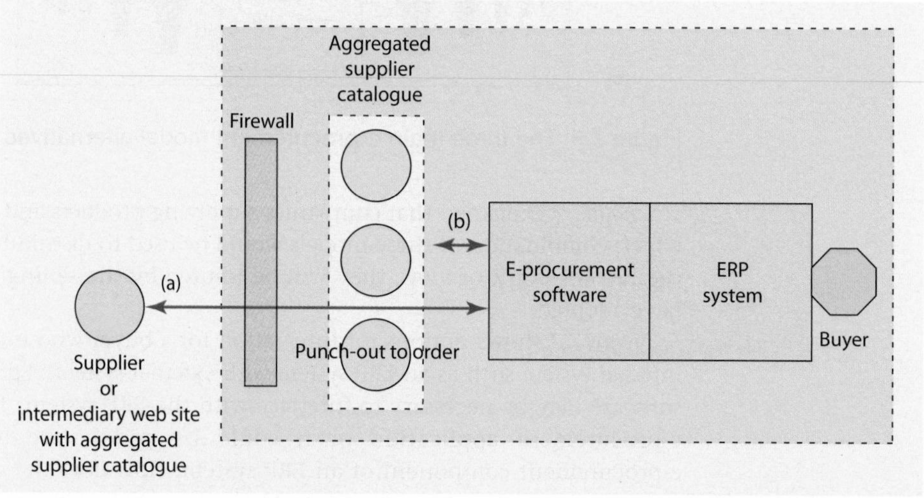

Figure 7.7 **Integration between e-procurement systems and catalogue data**

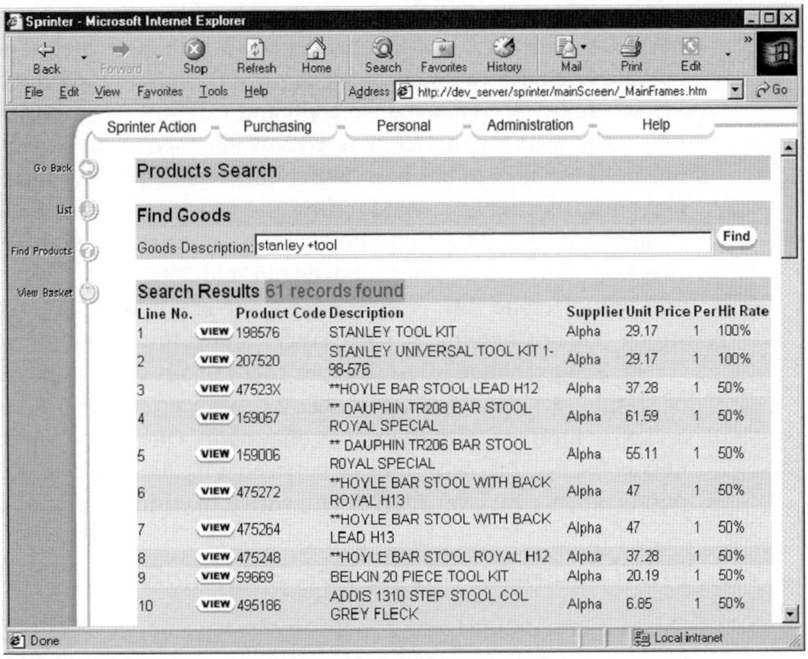

Figure 7.8 An online catalogue of items for purchase

Source: Tranmit plc

delivery of a CD with the updated catalogue. Purchasers will have a single integrated view of products from different suppliers as shown in *Figure 7.8*. Choice (b) is to punch out through the firewall to access catalogues either on a supplier site or at an intermediary site. One of the benefits of linking to an intermediary site such as a B2B exchange is that this has done the work of collecting data from different suppliers and producing it in a consistent format. However, this is also done by suppliers of aggregated data.

Focus on electronic B2B marketplaces

As the new millennium dawned there was a proliferation of B2B marketplaces. A search on 'marketplaces' at the Open Directory (www.dmoz.org) revealed over 100. However, as start-up businesses, many have had difficulty in achieving sustainable business models. This creates a difficult decision for managers exploring the relevance of B2B marketplaces to their organization since they clearly have great potential for achieving greater supplier choice and reduced costs, yet going through the pain of setting up links with B2B marketplaces is only worthwhile if the marketplace is persistent. DTI (2002) showed that in 2002, a significant number of suppliers were now offering their products to customers via marketplaces. For example, Figure 5.5 in this report shows that in the UK, 11% of businesses provide the opportunity for customers to purchase from e-marketplaces, compared with 9% in Sweden and Italy, 8% in Australia and Germany, 7% in France and 6% in Japan.

B2B electronic marketplaces, exchanges and hubs
Virtual locations with facilities to enable trading between buyers and sellers.

Electronic B2B marketplaces are variously known as 'marketplaces, exchanges or hubs'. Typically they are intermediaries that are part of the *reintermediation* (*Chapter 2, p. 46*) phenomenon and are independent of buyers and suppliers.

After a great deal of hype at the turn of the millennium, many B2B marketplaces have closed. Examples of independent B2B exchanges mentioned in the previous edition are Chemdex (www.chemdex.com), Vertical Net (www.vertical.net), CommerceOne Marketsite (www.commerceone.com) and Covisint (www.covisint.net), none of which now exists in its original form. As we saw in *Chapter 5*, in January 2001, Dell shut down one of its business-to-business (B2B) online marketplaces, called Dell Marketplace, only four months after it opened, citing the lack of a mature e-commerce marketplace. *Computer World* (2001a) reported that of an estimated 900 business-to-business web sites that were functioning worldwide in mid-2000, a little more than 400 were left by end-2000. Despite this, enthusiasm for the B2B marketplace concept still seems quite strong. Today, Googling 'B2B Exchanges' shows just a handful are still active.

The B2B exchange intermediaries that remain seem to be mainly for commodities or simple services (for example, EC21 (www.ec21.com), Elance (www.elance.com) and eBay Business (http://business.ebay.com). One of the top categories on eBay business is for tractors, with bids of between $10,000 and $20,000 common; another is photocopiers with over 3,000 listed, with a maximum price of $65,000.

From neutral to private B2B exchanges

So, these new online trading arrangements have not developed as open, neutral marketplaces as predicted by many analysts. This seems to be due to the complexity of business purchase decisions and negotiations and their destabilizing nature on markets. The *Computer World* (2001b) article gives these reasons why what it terms 'private exchanges' are proving successful:

> *First, owners of private exchanges regulate supplier and customer access – and exclude competitors – making the sharing of sensitive information more likely.*
>
> *Second, owners can direct suppliers and customers to use the exchange through price incentives or by mandating changes in the way to conduct business.*
>
> *Third, private exchanges can be secured and tailored to serve specific projects and customers, unlike public exchanges, which must be generic so as to accommodate everyone.*

The article gives the example of IBM which has well-established private marketplaces. IBM has saved about $1.7 billion since 1993 by being able to divulge sensitive price and inventory information over a private exchange built for 25,000 suppliers and customers. As host of the exchange, the company helped defray the cost of connecting suppliers. As a result, on-time delivery of systems to customers increased from around 50% to 90%.

Private B2B exchanges
A manufacturer or major supplier to different manufacturers creates a portal which is used for managing all aspects of procurement.

The approach that has evolved, which few of the analysts seemed to predict in 2001, is that **private B2B exchanges** have developed. These are the buy-side exchanges referred to in *Table 7.1*. These are usually created by an individual manufacturer or supplier and include a 'walled garden of suppliers', i.e. everyone has to be approved as a member, although the forms to register as a supplier to bid in response to a particular Request for Quotation (RFQ) or to participate in a reverse auction are open to all, but with each vetted to avoid competitor involvement.

Case Study 7.2 shows the history of the automotive marketplace Covisint. This pattern of a transition from a marketplace portal to a hosted e-procurement service has been followed by other B2B marketplaces from that time including CommerceOne and Ariba.

Case Study 7.2 Covisint – a typical history of a B2B marketplace?

This case studies a successful marketplace to prompt learning about what makes such a marketplace effective. It also illustrates the importance of online bidding in some industries.

The Covisint marketplace was originally created by Ford, GM and DaimlerChrysler (www.covisint.com). Today, Covisint is not a marketplace, but is described by its owners Compuware as a 'connectivity solution'. Its service is still used by motor manufacturers (www.covisint.com) although they now don't use a single marketplace, rather each manufacturer uses technology to access its suppliers direct.

2002: Covisint used extensively for bidding

Covisint (2002) describes a high-level of activity on the exchange. Taking the example of DaimlerChrysler AG, 512 online bidding events processed through Covisint over a twelve-month period from 2001 to 2002. In total, this amounted to €10 billion. In May 2001, DaimlerChrysler staged the largest online bidding event ever, with an order volume of €3.5 billion in just four days. In total, 43 per cent of the total value of the parts for a future Chrysler model series was negotiated online with over 50 online bidding events in the third quarter of 2001 alone. As well as savings in material purchasing prices, DaimlerChrysler succeeded in reducing throughput times in purchasing by approximately 80 per cent, thus saving on process costs. According to Dr Rüdiger Grube, Deputy Member of the Board of Management responsible for corporate development,

> *the economic effects achieved with e-Procurement in the first year of implementation have already covered the costs of previous investment in e-Business and hold great potential for the future, too. Therefore, we will continue to pursue our e-Business activities to the fullest extent in 2002 as well.*

With the online catalogue system 'eShop' which was part of the Covisint service at that time, DaimlerChrysler would be able to reduce process costs by 50% after the completion of the blanket rollout, which will give approximately 15,000 users the possibility of ordering several millions of articles. By the end of 2002 about 1,500 business partners would be connected to the electronic document exchange system 'eDocs', which would enable them to process approximately 500,000 document transmissions per year. Initital results using the 'FastCar' program for networking change management in automotive development at Chrysler show cuts in communication processes by 60–90%. In 2001, over 600 managers connected to the system developed over 300 product improvement suggestions online with the 'New Product Change Management' used in the development department of Mercedes-Benz.

'e-Business activities are already closely intertwined from development through procurement, logistics, sales and marketing. To a great extent, they are already a part of everyday business', says Olaf Koch, Vice President of Corporate e-Business. Dr Grube: 'We're a good deal closer to our goal of making DaimlerChrysler the first automotive company to be networked throughout the entire value chain.'

2004: Covisint purchased by Compuware

Line56 (2004) summarizes the acquisition of Covisint by B2B software company Compuware. The article quotes Compuware CEO Pete Karmanos as predicting that the messaging and portal part of Covisint will contribute $20 million in 2005, and will eventually become a $100 million-plus business in the automotive industry alone. The primary e-procurement offering of Covisint is as a method of managing purchasing across the many different electronic business document formats including traditional EDI formats like ANSI X12 and EDIFACT along with XML purchasing formats such as OAGIS, STAR, RosettaNet and others. Different suppliers tend to have adopted different exchange formats, so a solution that integrates them is helpful. Covisint continues to offer a portal solution both for manufacturers and their suppliers, who in turn have tier 2 or 3 suppliers. A study for Covisint by AMR Research suggested that the Covisint Communicate service was found to help a company reduce the cost of developing and deploying a portal by up to 80 per cent and reduce the annual cost of maintenance by 50 per cent. You can see the portal solutions at: https://portal.covisint.com/wps/public/tradingPartners/ l/en/, one example is the Ford Supplier portal.

2006: Covisint has 266,000 users in more than 30,000 companies in 96 countries

Today, Covisint describes itself as '*the leading provider of services that enable the integration of vital business information and processes between partners, customers and suppliers*'. The majority of its customers are still in the automotive industry (for example, see *Figure 7.9*), but it also operates within the healthcare industry. For each it has developed specific services particular to data exchange within these industries. Covisint Connect offers EDI and web EDI facilities for e-procurement. Covisint Communicate has over 300 applications available, some typical modules of which are used by DaimlerChrysler AG including:

- **Accounts payable** – enables suppliers to research past and future payment/information, resolve issues prior to payment due dates and download document information to the desktop for further analysis.

→

- **Cooperative raw material acquisition** – provides suppliers with access to a cooperative raw material supply program to leverage customers' purchasing power and maximize operational savings.
- **Product catalogue compilation tool** – collects and distributes information required to produce and update the company's catalogue of products.
- **Request for quote application** – enables customers to issue an online request for quotation process. One example of a customer for the supplier portal is MetalDyne (https://portal.covisint.com/wps/public/metaldyne/ l/en) which is a global producer of automotive components and assemblies. They use this portal to coordinate purchase from their suppliers through issuing RFQs.
- **Supplier profile** – enables customers to maintain an accurate profile consisting of key information about the supplier (e.g. contact information, certifications, key supplier contacts, financial information, minority status).

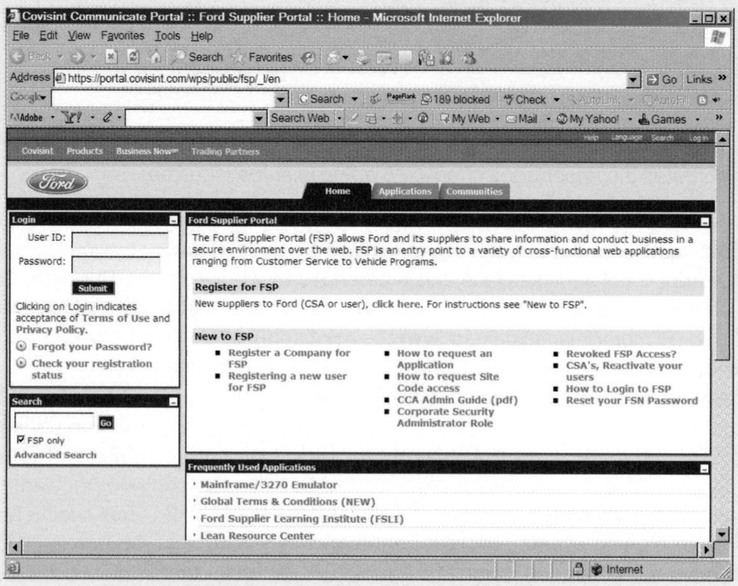

Figure 7.9 Ford supplier portal provided by Covisint
Source: Covisint.com

Sources: Covisint web site (www.covisint.com), Covisint (2002) and Line56 (2004).

Question

By reviewing the case study and examples of the different supplier portals available on Covisint (www.covisint.com) explain why Covisint has prospered as a supplier of e-procurement portals and business document data exchange rather than as a neutral marketplace.

Government marketplace exchanges

In the UK, the government has used reversed auctions on trial, but in 2006 launched two new initiatives which will highlight the value of recruitment. To give more options for small businesses to apply as suppliers to government, the UK government launched the Supplier Route to Government Portal (www.supply2.gov.uk, *Figure 7.10*) as part of its e-government initiative; this is an online marketplace for public-sector procurement valued at less than £100,000. Registered users can receive daily e-mail alerts about contracts appropriate to them, search for contracts online and post details of their offerings. The Office of Government Commerce (OGC) also unveiled an online marketplace for public sector procurement, called Zanzibar Managed Service (www.ogcbuyingsolutions.gov.uk/zanzibar/zanzibar.asp). The Department for Work and Pensions is the first public-sector department to use the system. Zanzibar works in a similar way to other exchanges, with the OGC saying that Zanzibar would only be open to businesses that were either currently allowed to bid for public sector contracts or were invited to do so.

Improved methods for facilitating purchasing using these types of sites will undoubtedly increase the adoption of the Internet for e-commerce since consumers will become aware of the lower prices available by these buying methods. For the business-to-business case this needs to be linked in with methods of making payment easier such as the Open Buying Initiative (www.obi.org).

Debate 7.2

The future for independent B2B marketplaces

'There is no future for independent B2B marketplaces, exchanges or hubs; instead those sponsored by buyers in the industry (for example, Covisint in the car industry) will be dominant.'

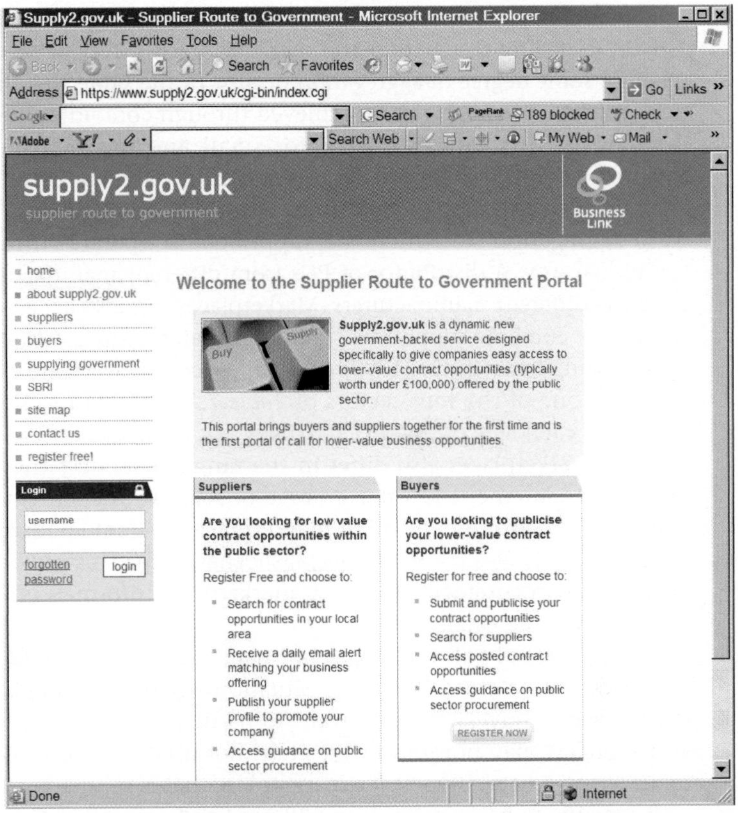

Figure 7.10 **Supplier Route to Government Portal (www.supply2.gov.uk)**

Types of marketplace

Kaplan and Sawhney (2000) have developed a taxonomy of B2B marketplaces by applying existing classifications of corporate purchasing, namely *how* businesses buy (systematic purchasing or spot purchasing) and *what* businesses buy (manufacturing inputs or operating resource inputs). They identify the types of marketplace shown in *Table 7.7*. Note that manufacturing-input marketplaces tend to be vertical market-places set up for a particular industry such as steel, construction or chemicals while operating resources tend to be horizontal marketplaces offering a range of products to differing industries.

Table 7.7 **Types of B2B marketplaces identified by Kaplan and Sawhney (2000) with examples**

How businesses buy	*What businesses buy*	
	Operating resources	*Manufacturing resources*
Systematic sourcing	MRO hubs www.barclaysb2b.com	Catalogue hubs www.sciquest.com
Spot sourcing	Yield managers www.elance.com	Exchanges www.e-steel.com www.plasticsnet.com

Source: Adapted and reprinted by permission of *Harvard Business Review* from table on p. 99 from '*E-hubs: the new B2B marketplaces*,' by Kaplan, S. and Sawhney, M., in *Harvard Business Review*, May–June 2000. Copyright © 2000 by the Harvard Business School Publishing Corporation, all rights reserved.

Kaplan and Sawhney introduce another variation in the way marketplaces differ. This is according to whether the marketplace is direct between buyer and seller or whether some degree of aggregation occurs. In the same way that for consumer products, volume discounts can be achieved through combining the purchasing power of individuals, this can also occur for small and medium businesses. Kaplan and Sawhney refer to this type of aggregation as 'reverse aggregation' since aggregation is back through the supply chain from customers to suppliers. They also identify 'forward aggregation' in which the supply chain operates through distributors in a traditional way. A distributor of PCs from different manufacturers aggregates supply from the different manufacturers. Marketplaces can also act as value chain integrators when they combine supply chain functions referred to in *Chapter 6*.

According to Sawhney (1999) companies looking to create exchanges typically specialize in one of the four sectors of *Table 7.7*, although some B2B marketplaces do offer both catalogue hubs and exchanges.

Some marketplaces also differ in the range of services they offer – some may go beyond procurement to offer a range of services that integrate the supply chain. Sawhney (1999) refers to these marketplaces as **'metamediaries'**. An example of a metamediary is Plastics Net (www.plasticsnet.com). This provides services of supplier evaluation, procurement, tracking, marketplace information, certification monitoring, auctions and catalogues.

Metamediaries
Third parties that provide a single point of contact and deliver a range of services between customers and suppliers.

How successful will exchanges be? Kaplan and Sawhney (2000) note that neutral exchanges face a chicken-and-egg situation when recruiting buyers and suppliers to their service – buyers may not want to participate if there are insufficient suppliers, and suppliers may not join if the site is not used by many purchasers. Procurement managers will naturally select a marketplace that is most active.

It remains to be seen whether B2B marketplaces deliver on their potential. For an update, complete *Activity 7.5*.

Activity 7.5 Reviewing the success of B2B exchanges

A number of B2B exchanges created by buyers were announced or launched in 2000 sponsored by major global companies. Examples include:

- Covisint in the motor industry (Ford, DaimlerChrysler and GM). Here former exchanges created by Ford (AutoXchange) and GM (Tradexchange) have merged. Tait (2000) reports on research that suggests between $1,000 and $3,600 savings on a $26,000 car could be achieved for a car where all purchasing from manufacturer and end-customer is completed electronically. By end-2000 Covisint had already completed $200 million worth of transactions.
- WorldWide Retail Exchange (Kingfisher, Kmart, Marks & Spencer).
- T2 US airline trading exchange.
- GlobalNetExchange (retailers Sears and Carrefour). Note that Transora has been created by fifty of the world's major FMCG suppliers, including Coca-Cola and Kellogg's, in response to retailers.
- PaperX. paper industry exchange designed for one-to-one deals.

Questions

1. Visit the sites of these companies and search news sources (for example, Moreover, www.moreover.com) to summarize the success of these initiatives.
2. Identify other hubs operating in your own country, classify them under the scheme of *Table 7.7*, evaluate their success.

No suggested answer supplied.

The future of e-procurement?

Software (intelligent) agents
Software programs that assist humans by automatically gathering information from the Internet or exchanging data with other agents based on parameters supplied by the user.

In the future, some suggest that the task of searching for suppliers and products may be taken over by software agents which have defined rules or some degree of intelligence that replicates intelligence in humans. An agent is a software program that can perform tasks to assist humans. On the Internet, agents can already be used for marketing research by performing searches using many search engines and in the future they may also be used to search for products or even purchase products. Agents work using predetermined rules or may learn rules using neural network techniques. Such rules will govern whether purchases should be made or not.

Some of the implications of agent technology on marketing are explored by Gatarski and Lundkvist (1998). They suggest that agent technology may create artificial consumers who will undertake supplier search, product evaluation and product selection functions. The authors suggest that such actors in a supplier-to-consumer dialogue will behave in a more rational way than their human equivalents and existing marketing theories may not apply.

Tucker and Jones (2000) also review the use of intelligent agents for sourcing. They foresee agents undertaking evaluation of a wide range of possible alternative suppliers based on predefined quantitative selection criteria including price, availability and delivery. They believe the technology is already available – indeed, similar intelligent software is used for making investments in financial markets. What is not clear is how the software will assess trustworthiness of a supplier or their competence as a business partner or associate.

An example of an exchange using such an agent is TheBuilding-Site.com (www.thebuilding-site.com) which uses Exterprise Activemarket to match online buyers and sellers. The software is intended to look through online alternatives to see which one best meets a business requirement.

As a summary to this chapter, *Activity 7.6* illustrates some of the decisions faced by purchasing managers when deciding how they will link to suppliers through e-procurement.

Activity 7.6 The B2B Company decides how to integrate its procurement with suppliers

Purpose

To highlight issues involved in selecting online suppliers.

Activity

Assume The B2B Company has three favoured suppliers of office items (A, B and C). Supplier A may have set up a web site through which it is possible to place orders, Supplier B may have used a marketplace solution such as Commerce One to sell products and Supplier C may not have developed e-commerce.

Questions

1. Identify the different alternatives for The B2B Company if it wishes to adopt e-procurement.
2. Evaluate the alternatives and recommend your favoured alternative.

Answers to activities can be found at www.pearsoned.co.uk/chaffey

Summary

1 Procurement activities involved with purchasing items from a supplier include purchasing, but also transportation, goods-in and warehousing before the item is used.

2 E-procurement involves the electronic integration of all procurement activities.

3 The numbers of staff and stages involved in procurement are reduced through e-procurement by empowering the originator of orders and changing the role of buying staff.

4 E-procurement is intended to achieve reduced purchasing cycle time and cost savings, principally through reduced staff time spent in procurement and lower inventory.

5 Options for introducing e-procurement include:

- Sell-side e-procurement – purchase direct from a seller's web site that is typically not integrated with the buyer's procurement system.
- Buy-side e-procurement – integration of sellers' catalogues with the buyer's procurement system.
- Marketplace procurement – trading through an intermediary with many suppliers (may or may not be integrated with buyer's procurement system).

6 The main types of electronic marketplace in the terminology of Kaplan and Sawhney (2000) are combinations of:

- Systematic sourcing of operating resources (MRO hubs)
- Systematic sourcing of manufacturing resources (catalogue hubs)
- Spot sourcing of operating resources (yield managers)
- Spot sourcing of manufacturing resources (exchanges).

7 Organizational hurdles involved with the introduction of e-procurement include redeployment or redundancy of staff and overcoming fears of trust in suppliers.

8 The main technical challenges are the integration or replacement of a range of existing purchasing systems with a variety of supplier or marketplace systems.

Exercises

Self-assessment questions

1 Outline the two main methods by which companies purchase supplies and the two broad divisions of supplies needed.

2 Taking your answer from 1, give examples of B2B exchanges that have been created to meet these purchasing needs.

3 Draw a sketch that shows the main stages and people involved in traditional and e-procurement.

4 Outline the main reasons for e-procurement.

5 What is maverick purchasing? What safeguards need to be introduced into e-procurement to avoid this?

6 Explain the differences between the buy-side, sell-side and marketplace options for e-procurement.

7 Outline the benefits and disadvantages of each of the options in 6.

8 What are the organizational implications of introducing e-procurement?

Essay and discussion questions

1 Chris Miller of Shell Chemical (*Case Study 6.1*) has been quoted as saying:

> *'E-procurement is not about screwing suppliers. It's about taking cost out for both suppliers and buyers and reducing institutionalized inefficiencies. Plus it supports smaller buyers and suppliers just as much as larger ones. It's not a big boys' club.'*

Discuss this statement through reviewing the benefits and disadvantages of e-procurement to both buyers and suppliers.

2 For an industry sector of your choice review the current alternative options for, and business adoption of B2B marketplaces available to purchasing and IS professionals and attempt to forecast the situation in five years.

3 Critically assess the claims made for cost savings and increased profitability available from e-procurement.

4 Analyse the procurement process for an organization with which you are familiar. Explain the changes and possible problems involved with introducing e-procurement.

5 'Fully automated end-to-end procurement is not practical.' Discuss.

Examination questions

1 Draw a diagram explaining four types of B2B exchanges that are dependent on the type of purchasing and what is purchased. Give one example of a product that could be purchased at each, and the name of an exchange offering this service.

2 Describe the different elements of an e-procurement system.

3 Draw a diagram that summarizes the main differences in processes within an organization for traditional procurement and e-procurement.

4 Outline the main benefits of e-procurement.

5 Explain the differences between buy-side and sell-side e-procurement. Give an advantage for each type for the purchasing company.

6 Current adoption levels of e-procurement are low. Identify the main reasons for this.

7 Explain how cost savings may arise from e-procurement.

8 Why do some commentators suggest real cost savings from e-procurement may be nearer to 10 per cent than higher figures suggested by e-procurement solutions providers?

References

Baily, P., Farmer, D., Jessop, D. and Jones, D. (1994) *Purchasing Principles and Management*. Pitman, London.

Caffrey, B. (1997) Dispelling e-commerce ROI myths. Published online only at http://purchasing.about.com/industry/purchasing/library/weekly/aa032798.htm, 18 July.

Computer World (2001a) B2B outlook still ominous. By Gary Kadet, 23 April. Available online at www.computerworld.com.

Computer World (2001b) Private exchanges drive B2B success. By Pimm Fox, 7 May. Available online at www.computerworld.com.

Conspectus (2006) Supply chain management and manufacturing systems. Prime Marketing Publications, June. PMP Research www.conspectus.com.

Covisint (2002) Press release, 4 February. Covisint.com.

DTI (2002) *Business in the Information Age – International Benchmarking Study 2002* UK Department of Trade and Industry.

eMarketer (2000) B2B revenues to top US$1 trillion by 2003. Analyst report, 25 July.

FT.com (2006) SMEs miss out on online tendering. Article, published on FT.com site; 3 March.

Gatarski, R. and Lundkvist, A. (1998) Interactive media face artificial customers and marketing theory must rethink. *Journal of Marketing Communications*, 4, 45–59.

Hildebrand, C. (2002) How to: save money with e-procurement, *CIO.com News*. By Carl Hildebrand, 13 August.

Internet Business (1999) A world without e-procurement is costing billions of pounds a year. *Internet Business* magazine, London.

Kalakota, R. and Robinson, M. (2000) *E-Business. Roadmap for Success*. Addison-Wesley, Reading, MA.

Kaplan, S. and Sawhney, M. (2000) E-hubs: the new B2B marketplaces. *Harvard Business Review*, May–June, 97–103.

Kluge, J. (1997) Reducing the cost of goods sold: role of complexity, design relationships. *McKinsey Quarterly*, no. 2, 212–15.

Line56 (2004). Compuware buys last of Covisint. Article by Jim Ericson, *Line56* (www.line56.com), Friday, 6 February.

logistics.about (2003) EProcurement advances chat. Summary by Jeff Ashcroft of interview with Carrie Ericson of AT Kearney (http://logistics.about.com).

Ovans, A. (2000) E-procurement at Schlumberger. *Harvard Business Review*, May–June, 21–3.

Potter, C. (2000) Trust . . . not built at e-speed: trust issues in B2B e-procurement. PricewaterhouseCoopers Report, July, London.

Sawhney, M. (1999) Making new markets. *Business 2.0*, May, 116–21.

Tait, N. (2000) Top dogs push web sales pitch. *Financial Times*, 8 December.

Tranmit plc (1999) *Procurement Management Systems: A Corporate Black Hole. A survey of technology trends and attitudes in British industry*. Tranmit plc, UK. Survey conducted by Byline Research. Report available at www.rswww.com/purchasing.

Tucker, D. and Jones, L. (2000) Leveraging the power of the Internet for optimal supplier sourcing. *International Journal of Physical Distribution and Logistics Management*, 23 May, 30(3/4), 255–67.

Turban, E., Lee, J., King, D. and Chung, H. (2000) *Electronic Commerce: A Managerial Perspective*. Prentice-Hall, Upper Saddle River, NJ.

Further reading

Fingar, P., Kumar, H. and Sharma, T. (2000) *Enterprise E-Commerce*. Meghan-Kiffler Press, Tampa, FL. Chapter 5 covers e-procurement from an applications perspective. E-procurement is described under the heading of 'Vendor management systems'. Chapter 3 describes electronic marketplaces under the heading of 'I-markets'.

Kalakota, R. and Robinson, M. (2000) *E-Business. Roadmap for Success*. Addison-Wesley, Reading, MA. E-procurement is considered in Chapter 9, states procurement to be a senior manager issue and describes implementation of e-procurement from both buy-side and sell-side perspectives.

Turban, E., Lee, J., King, D. and Chung, H. (2000) *Electronic Commerce: A Managerial Perspective*. Prentice-Hall, Upper Saddle River, NJ. Briefly refers to some of the benefits of what they describe as 'procurement re-engineering' in Chapter 6, p. 210.

Web links

Ariba.com (www.ariba.com) Guidelines on B2B e-commerce procurement from this 'spend management provider'.

Buy IT (www.buyitnet.org) UK-based.

The Chartered Institute of Purchasing and Supply (CIPS) (www.cips.org) Industry body in UK. Has research and best-practice advice on e-procurement including a 2006 survey on SME attitudes to e-commerce.

Conspectus (www.conspectus.com) Articles on different aspects of e-business including supply chain management.

Ebreviate (www.ebreviate.com): Articles on e-procurement best practice from solutions provider AT Kearney.

The Logistics web guide on About.com (http://logistics.about.com) Also has collection of links on the benefits and disadvantages of e-procurement.

8 E-marketing

Chapter at a glance

Main topics

Web support

The following additional case studies are available at www.pearsoned.co.uk/chaffey

- ➤ Personalized 'cybercycles' from DBS Oegland, Norway
- ➤ Hamleys e-tail

The site also contains a range of study materials designed to help improve your results.

Learning outcomes

After completing this chapter the reader should be able to:

- **Assess the need for separate e-business and e-marketing strategies**
- **Create an outline e-marketing plan intended to implement the e-marketing strategy**
- **Distinguish between marketing communication characteristics of traditional and new media.**

Management issues

The issues for managers raised in this chapter include:

- **How do we integrate traditional marketing approaches with e-marketing?**
- **How can we use electronic communications to differentiate our products and services?**
- **How do we redefine our marketing and communications mixes to incorporate new media?**

Links to other chapters

The main related chapters are:

- *Chapter 4* – e-environment provides underpinning on the macro-economic factors that support e-marketing planning;
- *Chapter 5* – on e-business strategy acts as an introduction to *Part 2* and the chapters that follow, in particular the section on eight strategic decisions is relevant to this chapter;
- *Chapter 9* – CRM details practical implementation of e-marketing plans through promotional techniques and customer relationship management;
- *Chapter 10* – discusses the change management issues associated with introducing multi-channel marketing within an organization.

Introduction

In *Chapter 5* we explored approaches to developing e-business strategy. In this chapter we examine e-marketing strategy and planning separately since in many organizations a distinct e-marketing plan will often be developed by the marketing or e-commerce team. The e-marketing or Internet marketing plan will help define specific e-marketing objectives and develop strategies to ensure that resources are deployed to take advantage of the marketing opportunities provided by the Internet, and to counter its threats.

Clearly, the e-marketing plan should be informed by the wider business and marketing objectives and e-business strategy to ensure it supports the goals of the organization. *Figure 8.1* shows that typically there is a hierarchy of plans in an organization with the corporate or business plan informing the marketing plan and this then informing specific market plans for different products or geographical markets. There is usually a separate communications plan which details the marketing campaigns that need to be executed to achieve the marketing objectives from the marketing plan.

Chapter structure

This chapter assumes limited previous knowledge of marketing, so we start with an introduction to the marketing concept and explain its relationship to e-business. A structured approach to developing an e-marketing plan is then described which is based on a similar strategy process model to that introduced in *Chapter 5*. The stages reviewed are situation analysis, objective setting, strategy, tactics, action and control. The chapter also reviews how marketing concepts such as target marketing, the marketing mix and branding may require different treatment when we are using digital media such as the Internet, interactive TV and wireless mobile communications.

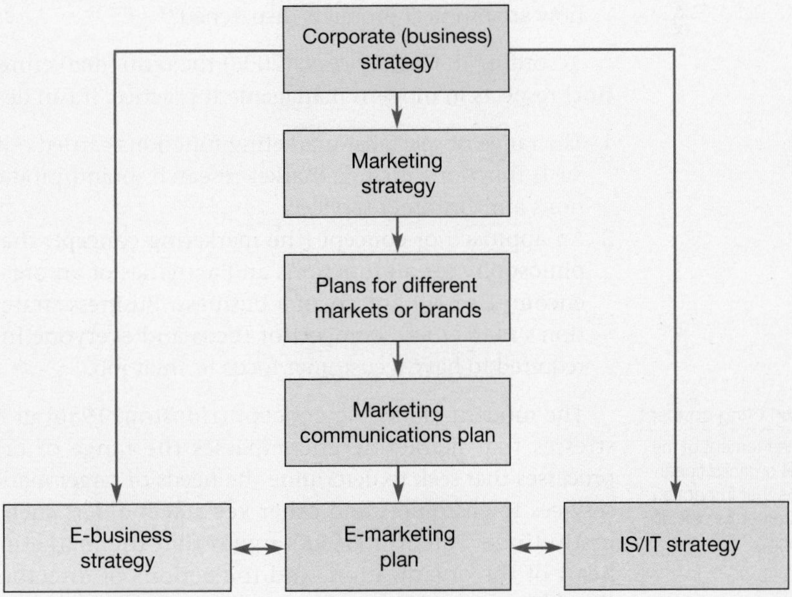

Figure 8.1 **The e-marketing plan in the context of other plans**

What is e-marketing?

Internet marketing has been described simply as *'achieving marketing objectives through applying digital technologies'* (Chaffey *et al.*, 2006). This succinct definition helps remind us that it is the results delivered by technology that should determine investment in Internet marketing, not the adoption of the technology! These digital technologies include Internet media such as web sites and e-mail as well as other digital media such as wireless or mobile and media for delivering digital television such as cable and satellite.

Marketing defined

As with many terms with the 'e' prefix, we need to return to an original definition of the topic to more fully understand what e-marketing involves. The definition of marketing by the UK's Chartered Institute of Marketing is:

> *Marketing is the management process responsible for identifying, anticipating and satisfying customer requirements profitably.*

This definition emphasizes the focus of marketing on the customer, while at the same time implying a need to link to other business operations to achieve this profitability. In this chapter, and in *Chapter 9*, we will focus on how the Internet can be used to achieve the processes implied by this statement:

- *Identifying* – how can the Internet be used for marketing research to find out customers' needs and wants?
- *Anticipating* – we have seen in *Chapter 5* that anticipating the demand for digital services (the online revenue contribution) is key to governing the resource allocation to e-business.
- *Satisfying* – a key issue for e-marketing is how to achieve customer satisfaction through the electronic channel; this raises issues such as: is the site easy to use, does it perform adequately, what is the standard of associated customer service and how are physical products dispatched?

According to Chaffey *et al.* (2006) the term 'marketing' tends to be used in two distinct respects in modern management practice. It can describe:

1. The range of specialist marketing functions carried out within many organizations. Such functions include market research, brand/product management, public relations and customer service.
2. An approach or concept (the marketing concept) that can be used as the guiding philosophy for all functions and activities of an organization. Such a philosophy encompasses all aspects of a business. Business strategy is guided by an organization's market and competitor focus and everyone in the organization should be required to have a customer focus in their job.

The marketing concept
The management of the range of organizational activities that impact on the customer as part of marketing.

The modern **marketing concept** (Houston, 1986) unites these two meanings and stresses that marketing encompasses the range of organizational functions and processes that seek to determine the needs of target markets and deliver products and services to customers and other key stakeholders such as employees and financial institutions. Valentin (1996) argues that the marketing concept should lie at the heart of the organization, and the actions of directors, managers and employees should be guided by its philosophy.

The modern concept of marketing is much broader than the lay person's view of marketing simply as advertising and sales. Modern marketing philosophy also

Marketing orientation
Coordinating all organizational activities that impact on the customer to deliver customer requirements.

requires that organizations be committed to a marketing or customer orientation (Jaworski and Kohli, 1993). This concept involves all parts of the organization coordinating activities to ensure that customer needs are met efficiently, effectively and profitably. The development of e-commerce services in response to changes in market needs is one example of market orientation, as Hughes (2001) has pointed out. In his study of new Internet start-ups and traditional banking operations which use e-commerce, he found that the Internet or e-business start-ups were more involved in conducting research to understand the customer experience and then adapting the service accordingly.

E-marketing defined

E-marketing
Achieving marketing objectives through use of electronic communications technology.

The term 'Internet marketing' tends to refer to an external perspective of how the Internet can be used in conjunction with traditional media to acquire and deliver services to customers. An alternative term is 'e-marketing' (for example, McDonald and Wilson, 1999) which can be considered to have a broader scope since it refers to any use of technology to achieve marketing objectives and has an external and an internal perspective. This is more consistent with the concept of e-business which involves managing both internal and external communications.

Digital marketing is another similar term which is used by online marketing agencies and also the Institute of Direct Marketing (**www.theidm.com**) which offers qualifications in digital marketing.

Chaffey *et al.* (2006) explain the scope and approaches used for digital marketing using this more detailed explanation of digital marketing:

Digital marketing involves:

- *Applying these technologies which form online channels to market:*
  - *Web, e-mail, databases, plus mobile/wireless and digital TV)*
    and these e-communications approaches:
  - *Search engine marketing, affiliate marketing, online advertising, sponsorship and online PR (including blogs, RSS and viral marketing);*
- *To achieve these objectives:*
  - *Support marketing activities aimed at achieving profitable acquisition and retention of customers...within a multi-channel buying process and customer lifecycle*
- *Through using these marketing tactics:*
  - *Recognizing the strategic importance of digital technologies and developing a planned approach to reach and migrate customers to online services through e-communications and traditional communications. Retention is achieved through improving our customer knowledge (of their profiles, behaviour, value and loyalty drivers), then delivering integrated, targeted communications and online services that match their individual needs.*

Customer journey
A description of modern multi-channel buyer behaviour as consumers use different media to select suppliers, make purchases and gain customer support.

Multi-channel marketing strategy
Defines how different marketing channels should integrate and support each other in terms of their proposition development and communications based on their relative merits for the customer and the company.

Customer-centric marketing
An approach to marketing based on detailed knowledge of customer behaviour within the target audience which seeks to fulfil the individual needs and wants of customers.

This extended definition emphasizes that digital media are just part of the customer journey; they are used in conjunction with traditional media when selecting, buying and servicing products, as we saw from the research presented in *Chapter 4*. It follows that an effective approach to using the Internet for marketing is as part of a multi-channel marketing strategy; we also referred to 'right-channelling' in *Chapter 5*. This clarifies how different marketing channels should integrate and support each other in terms of their proposition development and communications based on their relative merits for the customer and the company. The definition also emphasizes the customer-centric approach, by which they mean the capability digital media give marketers to better understand and tailor propositions to individual customers which is one of its greatest appeals as explained in *Chapter 9*.

To help understand the scope of e-marketing, you may also find *Figure 10.1* useful; this summarizes different marketing activities that need to be completed by an online retailer structured according to customer acquisition, conversion and retention activities.

Distinguishing between e-marketing, e-business and e-commerce

Given that the marketing concept implies a broad meaning for marketing, how can we distinguish between e-business and e-marketing? In fact, we can use a similar device to that of *Figure 1.4* to help distinguish between them. The options are:

(a) *Electronic business has some degree of overlap with electronic marketing.* From the discussion of the marketing concept above we can reject this since both e-business and e-marketing are broad topics.

(b) *Electronic business is broadly equivalent to electronic marketing.* This is perhaps more realistic, and indeed some marketers would consider e-business and e-marketing to be synonymous.

(c) *Electronic marketing is a subset of electronic business.* It can be argued that this is most realistic since e-marketing is essentially customer-oriented and it has less emphasis on supply chain and procurement activities in comparison with e-business.

Referring back to *Figure 1.4* once more, you may ask what, if e-commerce is best considered as a subset of e-business and e-marketing is also a subset of e-business, is the relationship between e-commerce and e-marketing? The implication is that they are similar, but e-commerce is perhaps broader than e-marketing since it involves both buy-side and sell-side transactions, whereas e-marketing concentrates on sell-side transactions and communications.

E-marketing planning

E-marketing plan
A plan to achieve the marketing objectives of the e-business strategy.

An **e-marketing plan** is needed in addition to a broader e-business strategy to detail how the sell-side specific objectives of the e-business strategy will be achieved through marketing activities such as marketing research and marketing communications. Since the e-marketing plan is based on the objectives of the e-business or business strategy there is overlap between the elements of each approach, particularly for environment analysis, objective setting and strategic analysis. *Figure 8.1* shows how e-marketing activities will inform the e-business strategy which, in turn, will inform the e-marketing plan.

We will use a similar strategy process model for e-marketing planning to that introduced in *Chapter 5*. In this chapter we use the SOSTAC™ developed by Paul Smith (1999) and this summarizes the different stages that should be involved in a marketing strategy from strategy development to implementation (*Figure 8.2*). The stages involved can be summarized as:

- Situation – where are we now?
- Objectives – where do we want to be?
- Strategy – how do we get there?
- Tactics – how exactly do we get there?
- Action – what is our plan?
- Control – did we get there?

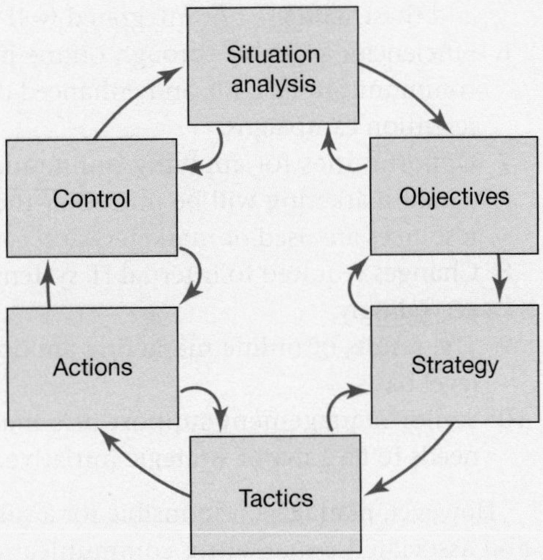

Figure 8.2 **SOSTAC™ – a generic framework for e-marketing planning**

Measurement of the effectiveness of e-marketing is an integral part of the strategy process in order to assess whether objectives have been achieved. The loop is closed by using the analysis of web analytics data (*Chapter 12*) metrics collected as part of the control stage to continuously improve e-marketing through making enhancements to the web site and associated marketing communications.

We will now review the six elements of the SOSTAC™ approach to e-marketing planning. Overlap between this coverage and that in *Chapter 5* is minimized by cross-referencing between these chapters.

Is a separate e-marketing plan required?

If there is a specific resource for e-marketing activities such as an e-marketing or e-commerce manager, then they will be responsible for the e-marketing plan. However, where there is no identified responsibility for e-marketing, which is still the case in many small and medium organizations, there is likely to be no e-marketing plan. This often occurs when marketing managers have limited resources or other priorities and a lack of recognition that a separate e-marketing plan is valuable.

> **Debate 8.1**
>
> **Is a distinct e-marketing plan necessary?**
>
> *'A separate e-marketing plan is not necessary as part of the marketing planning process – e-marketing can and should be integrated into existing marketing plans.'*

These problems are typical and commonplace when there is no clear planning or control for e-marketing:

1. Customer demand for online services will be underestimated if this has not been researched and it is under-resourced and no or unrealistic objectives are set to achieve online marketing share.
2. Existing and start-up competitors will gain market share if insufficient resources are devoted to e-marketing and no clear strategies are defined.
3. Duplication of resources will occur, for example different parts of the marketing organization purchasing different tools or different agencies for performing similar online marketing tasks.
4. Insufficient resource will be devoted to planning and executing e-marketing and there is likely to be a lack of specific specialist e-marketing skills which will make it difficult to respond to competitive threats effectively.

5 Insufficient customer data are collected online as part of relationship building and these data are not integrated well with existing systems.
6 Efficiencies available through online marketing will be missed, for example, lower communications costs and enhanced conversion rates in customer acquisition and retention campaigns.
7 Opportunities for applying online marketing tools such as search marketing or e-mail marketing will be missed or the execution may be inefficient if the wrong resources are used or marketers don't have the right tools.
8 Changes required to internal IT systems by different groups will not be prioritized accordingly.
9 The results of online marketing are not tracked adequately on a detailed or high-level basis.
10 Senior management support of e-marketing is inadequate to drive what often needs to be a major strategic initiative.

However, managers responsible for a substantial investment in an Internet web site and associated e-marketing communications will naturally want to ensure that the correct amount of money is invested and that it is used effectively. For these reasons and to avoid the 10 problems noted above, many leading adopters of e-commerce do have a distinct e-marketing plan, as an E-consultancy survey of UK e-commerce managers shows (*Figure 8.3*).

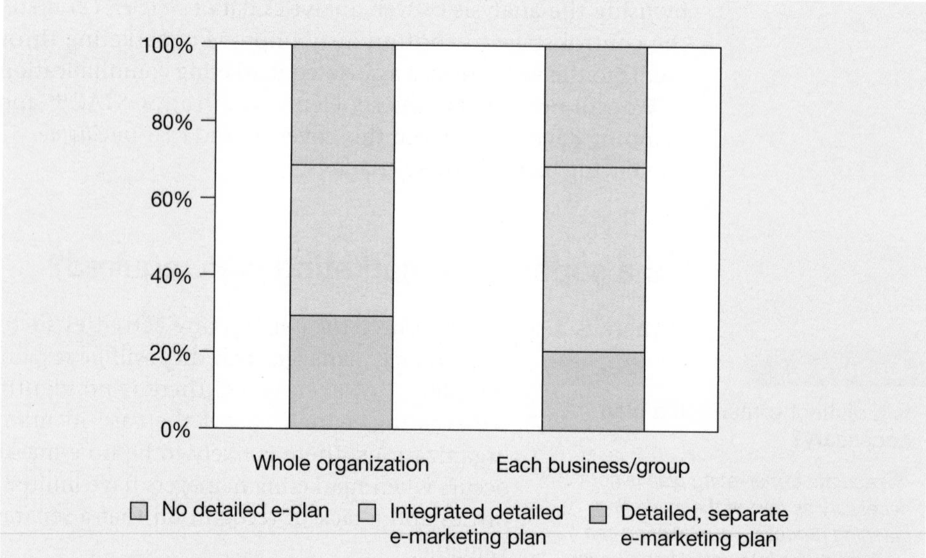

Figure 8.3 Usage of detailed e-marketing plans in UK e-commerce organizations
Source: E-consultancy (2005)

For smaller organizations, the digital plan need not be exhaustive – a two-page summary defining objectives and outlining strategies may be sufficient. The important thing is to set clear objectives and strategies showing how the digital presence should contribute to the sales and marketing process. Specific initiatives that are required such as search marketing, e-mail marketing or features of a web site redesign can be specified.

In the longer term, once an organization has successfully defined its approaches to Internet marketing, it is likely that a separate Internet marketing strategy or e-marketing plan *will not* need to be developed each year since the Internet can be considered as any other communications medium and integrated into existing communications plans as suggested by *Figure 8.3*.

Situation analysis

Situation analysis
Environment analysis and review of internal processes and resources to inform strategy.

The aim of **situation analysis** is to understand the current and future environment in which the company operates in order that the strategic objectives are realistic in light of what is happening in the marketplace. *Figure 8.4* shows the inputs from situation analysis that inform the e-marketing plan. These mainly refer to a company's external environment. The study of an organization's environment was introduced in *Figure 2.1* where it was noted that there was the immediate (micro-)environment of customers, competitors, suppliers and intermediaries and a broader (macro-)environment of social, legal, political, economic and technological characteristics. Situation analysis will involve consideration of all of these factors and will form the basis for defining objectives, strategies and tactics. Consideration of the SLEPT or macro-environment factors is a major topic that is covered in *Chapter 4*. In this chapter we will concentrate on what needs to be analysed about the more immediate market-

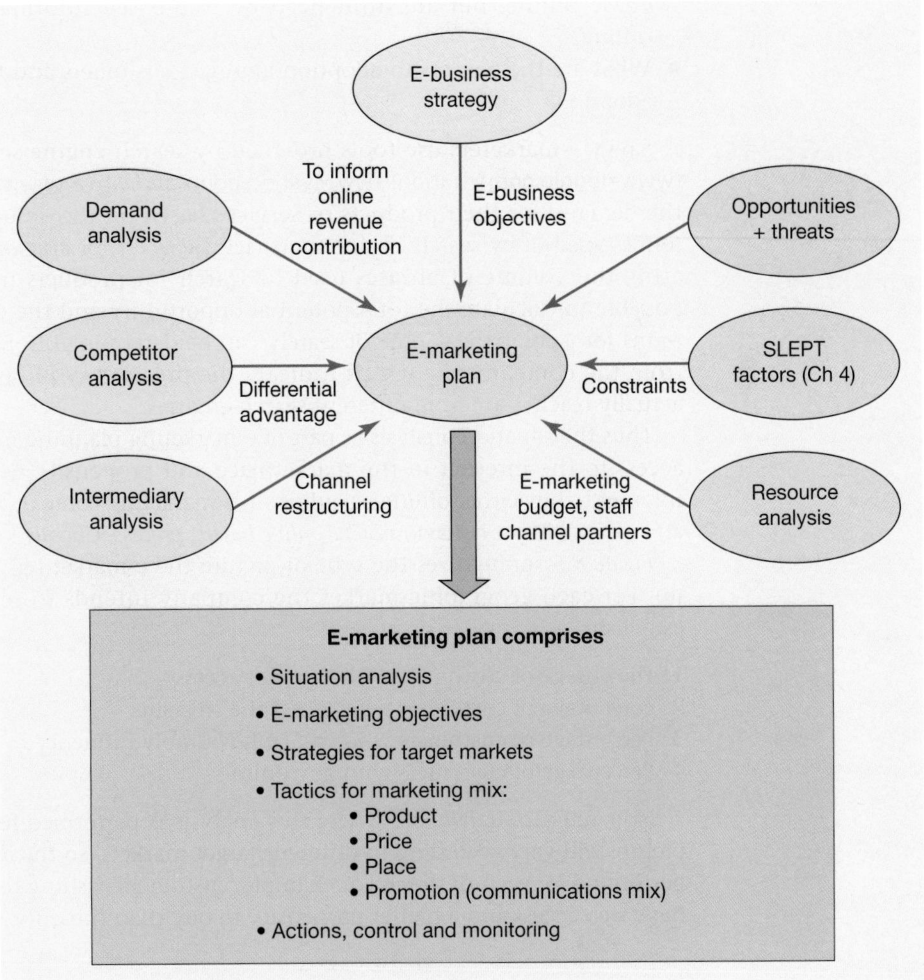

Figure 8.4 **Inputs to the e-marketing plan from situation analysis**

place in terms of customers, competitors, intermediaries and market structure. An internal audit of the capability of the resources of the company such as its people, processes and technology also needs to take place.

Demand analysis

A key factor driving e-marketing and e-business strategy objectives is the current level and future projections of customer demand for e-commerce services in different market segments. (*See Strategic analysis, Chapter 5, p. 212*) This will influence the demand for products online and this, in turn, should govern the resources devoted to different online channels. Demand analysis examines current and projected customer use of each digital channel within different target markets. It can be determined by asking for each market:

Demand analysis for e-business
Assessment of the demand for e-commerce services amongst existing and potential customer segments.

- What percentage of customer businesses have access to the Internet?
- What percentage of members of the buying unit in these businesses have access to the Internet?
- What percentage of customers are prepared to purchase your particular product online?
- What percentage of customers with access to the Internet are not prepared to purchase online, but are influenced by web-based information to buy products offline?
- What are the barriers to adoption amongst customers and how can we encourage adoption?

Savvy e-marketers use tools provided by search engine services such as Google (www.google.com), Yahoo! (www.yahoo.com) and Miva (www.miva.com) to evaluate the demand for their products or services based on the volume of different search terms typed in by search engine users (see *Table 1.1* for an example). Through evaluating the volume of phrases used to search for products in a given market it is possible to calculate the total potential opportunity and the current share of search terms for a company. 'Share of search' can be determined from web analytics reports from the company site which indicate the precise key phrases used by visitors to actually reach a site from different search engines.

Thus the situation analysis as part of e-marketing planning must determine levels of access to the Internet in the marketplace and propensity to be influenced by the Internet to buy either offline or online. In a marketing context, the propensity to buy is an aspect of buyer behaviour (*The online buying process, Chapter 9, p. 400*).

Figure 8.5 summarizes the type of picture the e-marketing planner needs to build up. For each geographic market the company intends to serve research needs to establish:

1. Percentage of customers with Internet access.
2. Percentage of customers who access the web site.
3. Percentage of customers who will be favourably influenced.
4. Percentage of customers who buy online.

Now refer to *Activity 8.1* where this analysis is performed for the car market. This picture will vary according to different target markets, so the analysis will need to be performed for each of these. For example, customers wishing to buy 'luxury cars' may have web access and a higher propensity to buy than those for small cars.

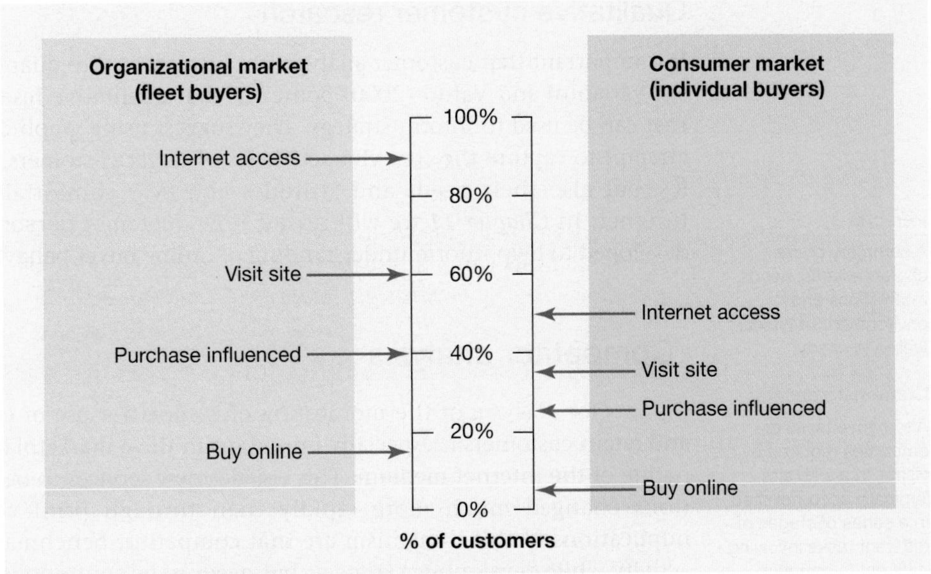

Figure 8.5 **Customer demand analysis for the car market**

Activity 8.1 Customer activity in the car market in your country

Purpose

To illustrate the type of marketing research needed to inform demand analysis for e-marketing planning and approaches to finding this information.

Activity

For your country update *Figure 8.5* to reflect current and future projections:

A. For corporate buyers (known as the 'fleet market') where a specialist manager co-ordinates the purchase and management of company cars for efficiency purposes:

1 Percentage of customers with Internet access.
2 Percentage of customers who access the web site.
3 Percentage of customers who will be favourably influenced (may be difficult to determine).
4 Percentage of customers who buy online.

If possible, try to gauge how these figures vary according to age, sex and social class.

B. For individual buyers (consumers):

1 Percentage of customers with Internet access.
2 Percentage of customers who access the web site.
3 Percentage of customers who will be favourably influenced.
4 Percentage of customers who buy online.

If possible, try to gauge how these figures vary according to companies of different sizes and different members of the buying unit.

Government sources and trade associations for car purchasing can be used to research the data.

No suggested answer supplied.

Qualitative customer research

It is important that customer analysis not be restricted to quantitative demand analysis. Varianini and Vaturi (2000) point out that qualitative research provides insights that can be used to inform strategy. They suggest using graphic profiling, which is an attempt to capture the core characteristics of target customers, not only demographics, but also their needs and attitudes and how comfortable they are with the Internet. In *Chapter 11* we will review how customer personas and scenarios are developed to help inform understanding of online buyer behaviour.

Persona
A summary of the characteristics, needs, motivations and environment of typical web-site users.

Customer scenario
Alternative tasks or outcomes required by a visitor to a web site. Typically accomplished in a series of stages of different tasks involving different information needs or experiences.

Competitor analysis

Competitor analysis for e-business
Review of e-business services offered by existing and new competitors and adoption by their customers.

Competitor analysis or the monitoring of competitor use of e-commerce to acquire and retain customers is especially important in the e-marketplace due to the dynamic nature of the Internet medium. This enables new services to be launched and promotions changed much more rapidly than through print communications. The implications of this dynamism are that competitor benchmarking is not a one-off activity while developing a strategy, but needs to be continuous.

Benchmarking is used to compare e-commerce services within a market. For a retailer, conducting a benchmarking audit of Internet-based competitors may be more difficult than a traditional audit of competitors. Traditionally competitors will be well known. With the Internet and the global marketplace there may be new entrants that have the potential to achieve significant market share. This is particularly the case with retail sales. For example, successful new companies have developed on the Internet that sell books, music, CDs and electronic components. As a consequence, companies need to review the Internet-based performance of both existing and new players. Companies should review:

- well-known local competitors (for example, UK/European competitors for British companies);
- well-known international competitors;
- new Internet companies locally and worldwide (within sector and out of sector).

One form of competitor benchmarking is to use services which compare the number of visitors to a site within a category. Many of these are paid services, but through press releases they also issue sample data for particular sectors. These tools, summarized in *Table 8.1* are a useful tool for student projects as well as e-marketing professionals.

Chase (1998) advocates that, when benchmarking, companies should review competitors' sites, identifying best practices, worst practices and next practices. Next practices are where a company looks beyond their industry sector at what leading Internet companies such as Amazon (www.amazon.com) and Cisco (www.cisco.com) are doing. For instance, a company in the financial services industry could look at what portal sites are providing and see if there are any lessons to be learnt on ways to make information provision easier. When undertaking scanning of competitor sites, the key differences that should be watched out for are:

- new approaches from existing companies;
- new companies starting on the Internet;
- new technologies, design techniques and customer support on the site which may give a competitive advantage.

Deise *et al.* (2000) suggest an 'equation' that can be used in combination to assess competition when benchmarking:

$$\text{Competitive capability} = \frac{\text{Agility} \times \text{Reach}}{\text{Time-to-market}}$$

Table 8.1 Online media consumption benchmarking services

Service	*Description*
1 **Alexa** (www.alexa.com)	Free service owned by Amazon which provides traffic ranking of individual sites relative to all sites. Works best for sites in top 100,000. Sample dependent on users of the Alexa toolbar.
2 **Hitwise** (www.hitwise.com)	Paid service available in some countries to compare audience and search/site usage. Works through monitoring IP traffic to different sites through ISPs.
3 **Netratings** (www.netratings.com)	Panel service based on at-home and at-work users who have agreed to have their web usage tracked by software. Top rankings on site gives examples of most popular sites in several countries.
4 **Comscore** (www.comscore.com)	A similar panel service to Netratings, but focusing on the US and UK.
5 **ABCE Database** (www.abce.org.uk)	The Audit Bureau of Circulation (Electronic) gives free access to its database of portals (not destination sites) who have agreed to have their sites audited to prove traffic volumes to advertisers (Choose ABCE Database).
6 **Key phrase analysis tools** Compilation available from the foot of www.davechaffey.com	These can be used to assess the popularity of brands and their products reflected by the volume of search terms typed into Google and other search engines.

'Agility' refers to the speed at which a company is able to change strategic direction and respond to new customer demands. 'Reach' is the ability to connect to potential and existing customers, or to promote products and generate new business in new markets. 'Time-to-market' is the product lifecycle from concept through to revenue generation.

Deise *et al.* (2000) also suggest a further 'equation' that can be used to appraise competitors from their customers' viewpoint. This is

$$\text{Customer value (brand perception)} = \frac{\text{Product quality} \times \text{Service quality}}{\text{Price} \times \text{Fulfilment time}}$$

Now complete *Activity 8.2* to gain an appreciation of how benchmarking competitor e-business services can be approached.

Activity 8.2 Competitor benchmarking

Purpose

To understand the services of a competitor web site it is useful to benchmark and to assess the value of benchmarking.

Activity

You have been commissioned by a major company to evaluate the *marketing effectiveness* of their online services in comparison with their competitors. You have to present your findings on their services and how they can be improved in a ten-minute PowerPoint presentation.

Choose a B2C industry sector such as airlines, book retailers, book publishers, CDs or clothing or for B2B a sector such as oil companies, chemical companies or construction industry companies.

→

Work individually or in groups to identify the type of information that should be available from the web site (and which parts of the site you will access it from) which will be useful in terms of competitor benchmarking. Once your criteria have been developed, you should then benchmark companies and summarize which you feel is making best use of the Internet medium.

Table 5.8 may also prove useful.

Answers to activities can be found at www.pearsoned.co.uk/chaffey

Intermediary analysis

Chapter 2 highlighted the importance of web-based intermediaries such as portals in driving traffic to an organization's web site. Situation analysis will also involve identifying relevant intermediaries for a particular marketplace. These will be different types of portal such as horizontal and vertical portals which will be assessed for suitability for advertising, PR or partnership. This activity can be used to identify strategic partners or will be performed by a media planner/buyer when executing an online advertising campaign.

For example, a book e-tailer needs to assess which comparison or aggregator services such as Kelkoo (**www.kelkoo.com**) and Shopsmart (**www.shopsmart.com**) it and its competitors are represented on. Questions which are answered by analysis of intermediaries are do competitors have any special sponsorship arrangements and are micro-sites created with intermediaries? The other aspect of situation analysis for intermediaries are to consider the way in which the marketplace is operating. To what extent are competitors using disintermediation or reintermediation? How are existing channel arrangements being changed?

Internal marketing audit

An internal audit will assess the capability of the resources of the company such as its people, processes and technology to deliver e-marketing compared with its competitors. The internal audit will review the way in which a current web site or e-commerce services perform. The audit is likely to review the following elements of an e-commerce site, which are described in more detail in *Focus on measuring and improving performance of e-business systems* in *Chapter 12*:

1 *Business effectiveness*. This will include the contribution of the site to revenue (see Internet contribution section above), profitability and any indications of the corporate mission for the site. The costs of producing and updating the site will also be reviewed, i.e. cost–benefit analysis.
2 *Marketing effectiveness*. These measures may include:
   - leads;
   - sales;
   - retention;
   - market share;
   - brand enhancement and loyalty;
   - customer service.

   These measures will be assessed for each of the different product lines delivered through the web site. The way in which the elements of the marketing mix are utilized will also be reviewed.
3 *Internet effectiveness*. These are specific measures that are used to assess the way in which the web site is used, and the characteristics of the audience. Such measures

include specialist measures such as unique visitors and page impressions that are collected through web analytics, and also traditional research techniques such as focus groups and questionnaires to existing customers. From a marketing point of view, the effectiveness of the value proposition of the site for the customer should also be assessed.

Objective setting

Effective e-marketing plans are based on clearly defined objectives since these will inform the strategies and tactics and help in communicating the strategic aims to the workforce and investors. As with objectives for any business activity, the value of objectives can be tested using the widely used SMART mnemonic, i.e. are they Specific, Measurable, Achievable, Realistic and Time-constrained? Examples of SMART e-marketing objectives are:

- Start-ups – acquiring a specific number of new customers or selling advertising space to generate a specified revenue that will hopefully exceed investment in site creation and promotion!
- Established mobile-phone operator – increase customer retention by reducing churn from 25 per cent to 20 per cent.
- Established media company – increase online revenue, target of 20 per cent online contribution to revenue, by offering new online services and media sales.
- Established business-to-business engineering company – increase overall revenue by 5 per cent, through targeting sales in new international markets.
- Reduce costs of routine customer service by 10 per cent to enable focus on delivery of specialized customer service.

We discussed e-business objectives in *Chapter 5* where we noted the value of using metrics which combined efficiency and effectiveness and could be applied in the context of the balanced scorecard. *Table 8.2* presents detailed e-marketing metrics in this way. The e-marketing plan should define the best framework for reporting on

Table 8.2 **Example Internet marketing objectives within the balanced scorecard framework for a transactional e-commerce site**

Balanced scorecard sector	*Efficiency*	*Effectiveness*
Financial results (business value)	• Channel costs • Channel profitability	• Online contribution (direct) • Online contribution (indirect) • Profit contributed
Customer value	• Online reach (unique visitors as % of potential visitors) • Cost of acquisition or cost per sale (CPA or CPS) • Customer propensity to defect	• Sales and sales per customer • New customers • Online market share • Customer satisfaction ratings • Customer loyalty index
Operational processes	• Conversion rates • Average order value • List size and quality • E-mail-active %	• Fulfilment times • Support response times
Innovation and learning (people and knowledge)	• Novel approaches tested • Internal e-marketing education • Internal satisfaction ratings	• Novel approaches deployed • Performance appraisal review

whether e-marketing goals are being achieved. Another alternative, based on different activities of acquisition, conversion and retention is presented in *Chapter 9*.

The online revenue contribution

It can be suggested that there is a single key objective that should be part of every e-marketing plan. This is the online revenue contribution.

Online revenue contribution
An assessment of the direct contribution of the Internet or other digital media to sales, usually expressed as a percentage of overall sales revenue.

The online revenue contribution is a measure of the extent to which a company's online presence directly impacts on the sales revenue of the organization. Online revenue contribution objectives can be specified for different types of products, customer segments and geographical markets. They can also be set for different digital channels such as web, mobile or interactive digital TV.

Companies that can set a high online revenue contribution objective of, say, 25 per cent for two years' time, will need to provide more resource allocation to the Internet than those companies that anticipate a contribution of 2.5 per cent. Cisco Systems Inc. (**www.cisco.com**), maker of computer networking gear, is now selling over three-quarters of its 20-billion-dollar sales online. This was achieved since senior executives at Cisco identified the significance of the medium, setting aggressive targets for the online revenue contribution and resourcing the e-commerce initiative accordingly. Note that through using the Internet, Cisco has achieved strategic benefits beyond increased revenue. It has also dramatically increased profitability. This has partly been achieved through the web site which is thought to have been responsible for a 20 per cent reduction in overall operating costs.

For some companies such as an FMCG manufacturer like a beverage company, it is unrealistic to expect a high direct online revenue contribution. In this case, an indirect online contribution could be stated. This considers the Internet as part of the promotional mix and its role in influencing a proportion of customers to purchase the product or in building the brand. In this case a company could set an online promotion contribution (reach) of 5 per cent of its target market visiting the web site or seeing banner adverts.

Online promotion contribution (reach)
An assessment of the proportion of customers (new or retained) who use the online information sources and are influenced as a result.

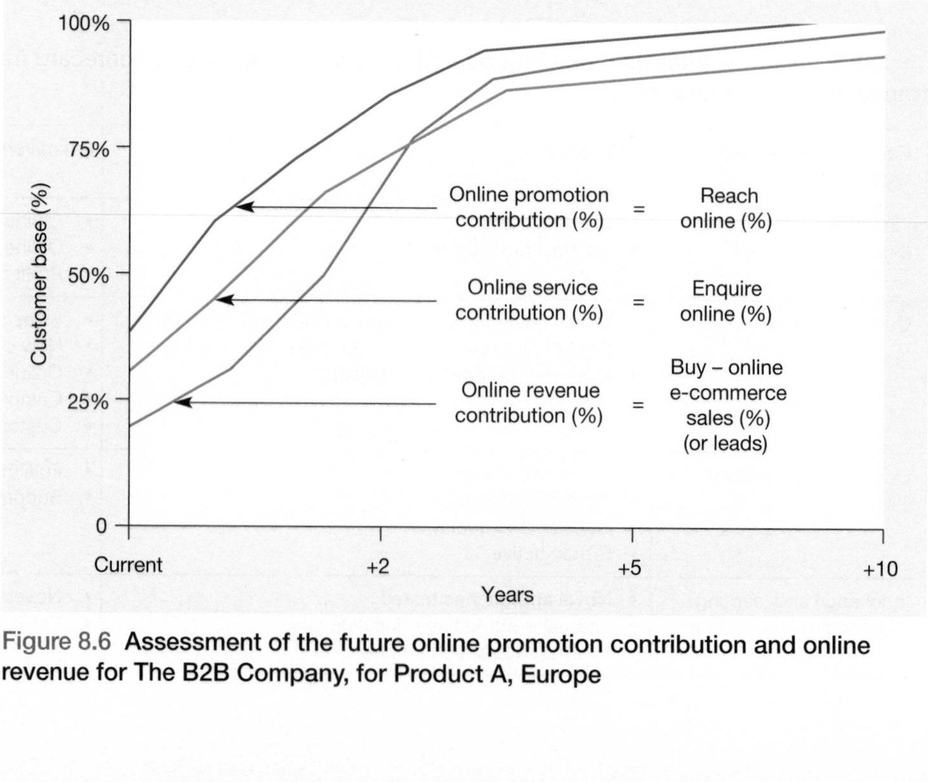

Figure 8.6 Assessment of the future online promotion contribution and online revenue for The B2B Company, for Product A, Europe

Online service contribution
Proportion of customers (new or retained) who use web self-service for different types of service transactions such as invoice checking.

Figure 8.6 combines the online revenue contribution and the online promotion contribution as a forecast based on marketing research of demand analysis and competitor analysis for The B2B Company. It also presents the online service contribution which is important for controlling costs since if a high proportion of customers 'self-serve' this will reduce the costs of replying to phones and e-mail enquiries.

Now complete *Activity 8.3* to look at how the online contribution varies for different types of company.

Activity 8.3 Variations in online revenue contribution

Table 8.3 shows the online revenue contribution for some companies. Note that there is a wide variety in online contribution according to the market sector the company operates in.

Table 8.3 Variations in online revenue contribution

Organization	*Sector*	*Online contribution*	*Overall turnover*
Cisco	Networking hardware	40%	$19bn
EasyJet	Air travel	85%	£264m
Dell	Computers	48%	$25bn
Lands End Clothing	Clothing	11%	$1.3bn
Book Club Associates	Books	10%	£100m
Electrocomponents	Electronics	7%	£761m
Domino's Pizza	Food	3.4%	£76m
Tesco	Grocery	1.4%	£18.4bn
Thomas Cook	Travel	<1%	£1.8bn

Source: Company web sites, end-2000; more recent data not available since most companies are not now separately publishing their Internet-related revenues

Questions

1. Explain the varying percentage contribution to revenue according to the industry sector the companies operate in.
2. Comment on the variation in total Internet-based revenue for the companies shown.
3. What do you think are the strategic implications for other companies operating in a sector if they are not currently leader in Internet contribution?
4. Discuss reasons for the differences between online revenue contribution for the two travel companies.

Answers to activities can be found at www.pearsoned.co.uk/chaffey

Complete *Case Study 8.1* to review how easyJet achieved an online revenue contribution of over 50 per cent.

Case Study 8.1 The e-volution of easyJet's online revenue contribution

This historical case shows how the easyJet web site (Figure 8.7) became the main sales channel for easyJet from its launch in the 1990s. How the Internet was used for service delivery and marketing communications is also described. This case study has been retained since it illustrates the benefits of a planned strategy to the e-channels.

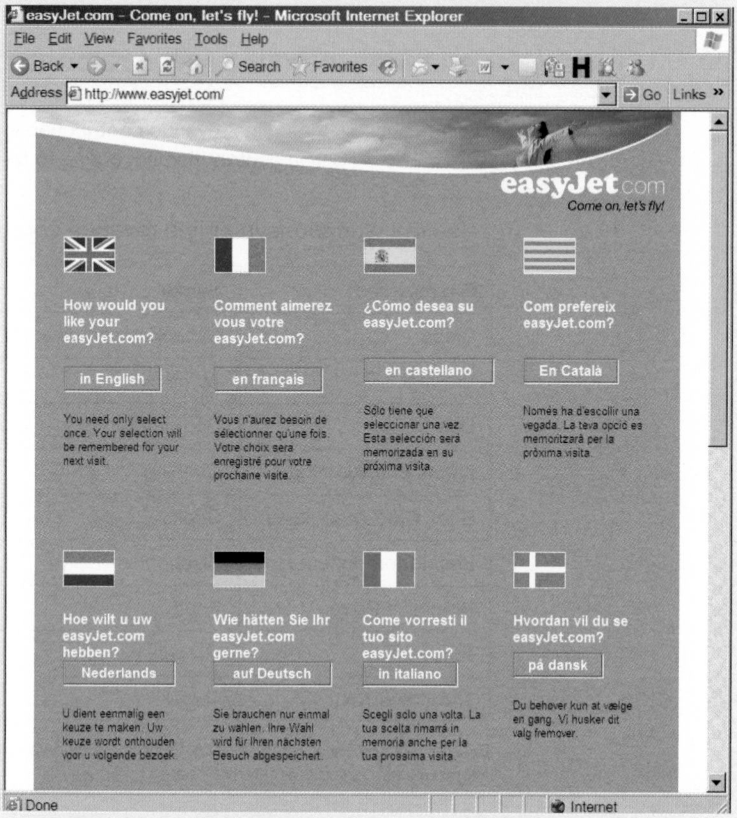

Figure 8.7 **easyJet web site (www.easyjet.com)**

EasyJet was founded by Stelios Haji-Ioannou, the son of a Greek shipping tycoon who reputedly used to 'hate the Internet'. In the mid-1990s Haji-Ioannou reportedly denounced the Internet as something 'for nerds', and swore that it wouldn't do anything for his business. This is no longer the case, since by August 1999 the site accounted for 38 per cent of ticket sales or over 135,000 seats. This was past the company's original Internet contribution target at launch of 30 per cent of sales by 2000. In the period from launch, the site had taken more than 800,000 bookings since it was set up in April 1998 after a shaky start of two sales in the first week and one thousand within the first month. In March 2000 easyJet increased its online discount to £2.50 for a single trip – a higher level of permanent discount than any other airline. By September 2000, Internet sales reached 85% of total sales. Since this time, the growth in proportion of online sales has decreased. By 2003, over 90% of all sales were online.

The articles relate the tale of the owner's office being graced by a photo of the owner with horns on his head and a Mexican moustache on his upper lip. The image was contributed as a complaint by an aggrieved customer. The nature of the entrepreneur was indicated since he sent the customer two free tickets.

The company was originally set up in 1994. As a low-cost airline, looking to undercut traditional carriers such as British Airways, it needed to create a lean operation. To achieve this, Haji-Ioannou decided on a single sales channel in order to survive. He chose the phone. At the time this was groundbreaking, but the owner was encouraged by companies such as Direct Line insurance, and the savings which direct selling would bring.

Although Haji-Ioannou thought at the time that there was no time to worry about the Internet and that one risk was enough, he was adaptable enough to change. When a basic trial site was launched, he kept a close eye on how popular the dedicated information and booking phone line was (having a web-specific phone number advertised on the site can be used to trace the volume of users on the site). A steady rise in the number of calls occurred every week. This early success coincided with the company running out of space at its call centre due to easyJet's growth. Haji-Ioannou related, 'We either had to start selling over the Internet or build a new call centre. So our transactional site became a £10 million decision.'

Although the success of easyJet could be put down solely to the founder's adaptability and vision, the company was helped by the market it operated in and its chosen business model – it was already a 100 per cent direct phone sales operation. This meant it was relatively easy to integrate the web into the central booking system. There were also no potential channel conflicts with intermediaries such as travel agents. The web also fitted in with the low-cost easyJet proposition of no tickets, no travel agents, no network tie-ups and no in-flight meals. Customers are given a PIN number for each order on the web site which they give when they get to the airport.

Sales over the Internet began in April 1998, and although easyJet's new-media operations were then handled by Tableau, a few months ago easyJet took them in-house.

The Internet is important to easyJet since it helps it to reduce running costs, important for a company where each passenger generates a profit of only £1.50. Savings to easyJet made through customers booking online enable it to offer at least £1 off to passengers who book online – this is part of the online proposition. Online buyers also benefit from paying the price of a local call, instead of the standard national rate of easyJet's booking line.

The owner says that 'the savings on the Internet might seem small compared to not serving a meal on a plane, which saves between £5 and £10, but when you think how much it would cost to build a new call centre, pay every easyJet reservation agent 80 pence for each seat sold – not to mention all the middlemen – you're talking much more than the £1 off we give online buyers'.

What about the risks of alienating customers who don't want to book online? This doesn't worry the owner. He says 'I'm sure there are people who live in the middle of nowhere who say they can't use the Internet and will fly Ryanair instead. But I'm more worried about keeping my cost base down, and finding enough people to fill my aeroplanes. I only need six million people a year, not all 56 million.'

Promotion

The Internet marketing gurus say 'put the company URL everywhere'. EasyJet has taken this literally with its web address along the side of its Boeing 737s.

EasyJet frequently varies the mix by running Internet-only promotions in newspapers. EasyJet ran its first Internet-only promotion in a newspaper in *The Times* in February 1999, with impressive results. Some 50,000 seats were offered to readers and 20,000 of them were sold on the first day, rising to 40,000 within three days. And, according to the marketing director, Tony Anderson, most of these were seats that otherwise would have been flying along at 600 mph – empty. The scalability of the Internet helped deal with demand since everyone was directed to the web site rather than the company needing to employ an extra 250 telephone operators. However, risk management did occur with a microsite built for *Times* readers (www.times.easyjet.com) to avoid putting a strain on easyJet's main site.

Anderson says, 'The airline promotions are basically designed to get rid of empty seats.' He adds, 'If we have a flight going to Nice that's leaving in 20 minutes' time, it costs us very little to put some extra people on board, and we can get, say, £15 a head for it.' Flight promotions are intended to avoid attracting people who'd fly with easyJet, so advanced booking schemes are intended to achieve that.

A later five-week promotion within *The Times* and *The Sunday Times* newspapers offered cheap flights to a choice of all easyJet destinations when 18 tokens were collected. In total, 100,000 seats were sold during the promotion, which was worth more than £2m to the airline. Thirty per cent of the seats were sold online, with the rest of the transactions being completed by phone; 13,000 orders were taken over the Internet in the first day alone with over 15,000 people on the site at one point.

The web site also acts as a PR tool. Haji-Ioannou uses its immediacy to keep newspapers informed about new promotions and offers by phoning and e-mailing journalists and referring them to the web site rather than faxing.

The web site is also used as an aggressive tool in what is a very competitive marketplace. Haji-Ioannou says 'Once we had all these people coming to our site, I asked myself: "Why pay a PR company to publicise what we think when we have a captive audience on the site?" For example, easyJet ran a competition in which people had to guess what BA's losses would be on 'Go', its budget rival to easyJet (the figure turned out to be £20m). Within minutes of the BA results being announced on 7 September, the easyJet site had the 50 flight-ticket winners from an incredible 65,000 people who had entered. In a similar vein a section of the site was entitled 'Battle with Swissair', giving easyJet's view that Swissair's head had persuaded the Swiss government to stop easyJet being granted a commercial scheduled licence on the Geneva–Barcelona route. EasyJet also called itself 'The web's favourite airline', in 1999, a direct counterpoint to British Airways' slogan of 'The world's favourite airline' for which it enjoyed a court battle.

EasyEverything

Following the brand extension success of Virgin, easyJet has used the 'easy' prefix to offer additional services as part of the easyGroup:

- easyEverything, a chain of 400-seat-capacity Internet cafés originally offering access at £1 an hour. This is run as an independent company and will charge easyJet for banner ads, but clearly the synergy will help with clickthrough between two and three per cent. The only concession easyEverything makes towards easyJet is that café customers can spend time on the easyJet site for free.
- easyRentacar, a low-cost car rental business offering car rental at £9 a day. These costs are possible through offering a single car type and being an Internet-only business.

Implementation

The articles report that Russell Sheffield, head of new-media agency Tableau, which initially worked with easyJet had an initial problem of colour! 'He says there was a battle to stop him putting his favourite colour all over the site.' The site was intended to be highly functional, simply designed and without any excess baggage. He says 'the home page (orange) only had four options – buy online, news, info, and a topic of the moment such as BA 'go' →

losses – and the site's booking system is simpler to use than some of its competitors'. He adds: 'great effort was put into making the navigation intuitive – for example, users can move directly from the timetables to the booking area, without having to go via the home page'.

The site was designed to be well integrated into easyJet's existing business processes and systems. For example, press releases are fed through an electronic feed into the site, and new destinations appear automatically once they are fed into the company's information system.

Measurement of the effectiveness of the site occurred through the dedicated phone number on the site which showed exactly how many calls the site generated, and the six-month target within six weeks. Web-site log file analysis showed that people were spending an average of eight minutes a time on the site, and better still, almost everyone who called bought a ticket, whereas with the normal phone line, only about one in six callers buys. Instead of having to answer questions, phone operators were doing nothing but sell tickets.

Once the web site generated two-fifths of easyJet business, it was taken in-house and Tableau now acts solely as a strategic adviser.

Source: Based on *Revolution* articles: EasyJet site a success in first month, 1 August 1998; EasyJet promotion sells 30,000 seats, 1 November 1998; Say hello to Mr e-Everything, 13 October 1999. Available in archive at: www.revolution.haynet.com.

Key events in easyJet's history are summarized at: www.easyjet.com/en/ about/infopack history.html

Questions

1 To what extent was the Internet revenue contribution of around 90 per cent achieved 'more by luck than judgement'?

2 Explain the proposition of using the Internet for the customer and define the benefits for the company.

3 Explain how easyJet uses the web site to vary the different elements of the marketing mix and as a marketing communications tool.

4 Use a news source such www.ft.com or review its investors' relations site www.easyjet.com/EN/ about/ investorrelations.html) to find out how easyJet has extended its Internet applications.

Strategy

The strategy element of an e-marketing plan defines how e-marketing objectives will be achieved. Strategy definition has to be tightly integrated into the e-marketing planning process since e-marketing planning is an iterative process from situation analysis to objective setting to strategy definition (*Figure 8.2*). McDonald (1999) points out that models of the stages of strategic marketing planning do not pass sequentially from one stage to the next, rather there is iteration between stages.

Six key decisions in strategy definition for e-business were described in *Chapter 5* (*p. 233*). To avoid significant overlap here, the reader is referred to that section.

The amount invested on the Internet should be based on the anticipated contribution the Internet will make to a business, as explained in the sections on objectives. In *Chapter 5* (*p. 224*) we saw how Kumar (1999) identified four different criteria for deciding whether the Internet would replace or complement other channels to market. In this chapter, we consider an alternative model, the Electronic Shopping Test, for reviewing the likely strategic importance of the Internet to a company as developed by de Kare-Silver (2000).

The Electronic Shopping or ES test

This test was developed by Michael de Kare-Silver to assess the extent to which consumers are likely to purchase a retail product using the Internet. De Kare-Silver suggests factors that should be considered in the ES test:

1 *Product characteristics*. Does the product need to be physically tried or touched before it is bought?

2 *Familiarity and confidence*. Considers the degree the consumer recognizes and trusts the product and brand.
3 *Consumer attributes*. These shape the buyer's behaviour – are they amenable to online purchases in terms of access to the technology skills available and do they no longer wish to shop for a product in a traditional retail environment? For example, a student familiar with technology may buy a CD online because they are comfortable with the technology. An elderly person looking for a classical CD would probably not have access to the technology and might prefer to purchase an item in person.

In his book, de Kare-Silver describes a method for ranking products. Product characteristics, familiarity and confidence are each marked out of 10, and consumer attributes are marked out of 30. Using this method, he scores products as shown in *Table 8.4*.

Table 8.4 **Product scores in de Kare-Silver (2000), electronic shopping potential test**

Product	*1 Product characteristics (10)*	*2 Familiarity and confidence (10)*	*3 Consumer attributes (30)*	**Total**
1 Groceries	4	8	15	27
2 Mortgages	10	1	4	15
3 Travel	10	6	15	31
4 Books	8	7	23	38

De Kare-Silver states that any product scoring over 20 has good potential, since the score for consumer attributes is likely to increase through time. Given this, he suggests companies will regularly need to review the score for their products.

Market and product positioning

The Internet offers new opportunities for selling new products into new markets. These present strategic alternatives that need to be evaluated. These alternatives can be evaluated using the options first stated by Ansoff (1957). The risks involved with the four options of market penetration, market development, product development and both market and product development (diversification) vary, as shown in *Figure 5.22* and explained in the commentary.

There may also be options for new digital products that could include information products that can be delivered over the web. Such products may not be charged for, but will add value to existing products. Ghosh (1998) talks about developing new products or adding 'digital value' to customers. He says companies should ask the following questions:

1 Can I offer additional information or transaction services to my existing customer base?
2 Can I address the needs of new customer segments by repackaging my current information assets or by creating new business propositions using the Internet?
3 Can I use my ability to attract customers to generate new sources of revenue such as advertising or sales of complementary products?
4 Will my current business be significantly harmed by other companies providing some of the value I currently offer?

In addition Ghosh (1998) suggests that companies should provide free digital value to help build an audience. He refers to this process as building a 'customer magnet'; today this would be known as a 'portal' or 'community'. There is good potential for customer magnets in specialized vertical markets served by business-to-business companies.

For example, a customer magnet could be developed for the construction industry, agrochemicals, biotechnology or independent financial advisers.

Target market strategies

We have seen that we need to review the options for using the digital media to reach new markets or develop existing markets. Within both of these markets we need to analyse the target market in more detail to understand their needs and potential and then develop a strategy to satisfy these markets to maximize revenue. This is target marketing strategy and involves the four stages shown in *Figure 8.8*.

Target marketing strategy
Evaluation and selection of appropriate segments and the development of appropriate offers.

Segmentation
Identification of different groups within a target market in order to develop different offerings for the groups.

The first stage in *Figure 8.8* is segmentation. Segmentation involves understanding the groupings of customers in the target market to understand their needs and potential as a revenue source in order to develop a strategy to satisfy these segments while maximizing revenue. Dibb *et al.* (2000) say that:

> *Market segmentation is the key of robust marketing strategy development ... it involves more than simply grouping customers into segments ... identifying segments, targeting, positioning and developing a differential advantage over rivals is the foundation of marketing strategy.*

In an e-marketing planning context market segments will be analysed to assess:

1. Their current market size or value, future projections of size and the organization's current and future market share within the segment.
2. Competitor market shares within the segment.
3. Needs of each segment, in particular unmet needs.
4. Organization and competitor offers and proposition for each segment across all aspects of the buying process.

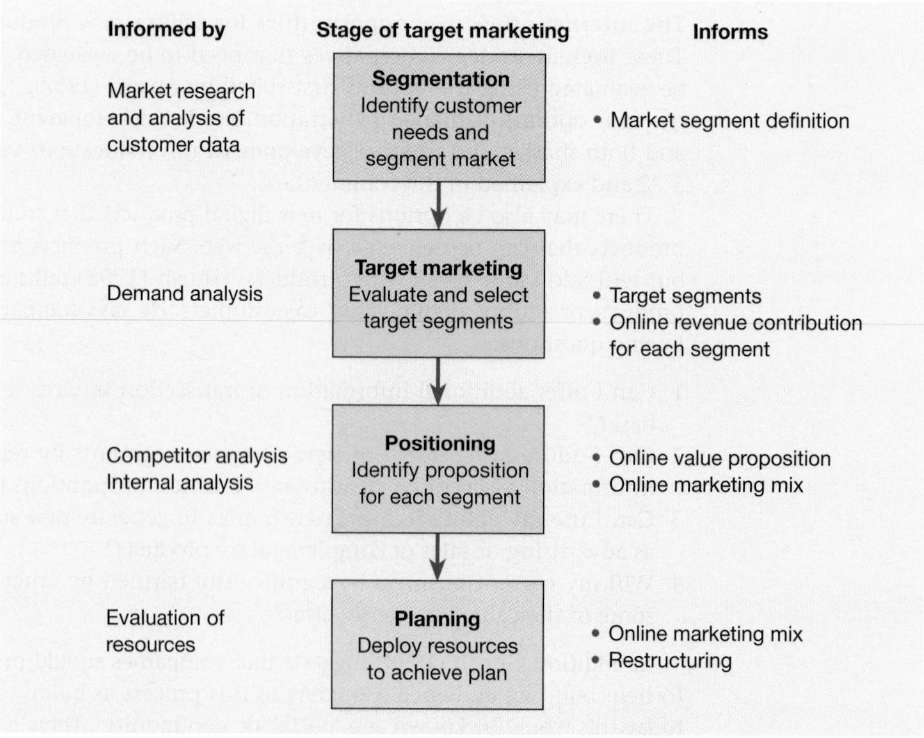

Figure 8.8 **Stages in target marketing strategy development**

Since we do not have time here to detail the process of segmentation, we will spend a little time looking at its significance from an e-marketing planning perspective. Seybold (1999) has identified five questions which she sees as important when developing a customer-centric strategy for e-marketing (in fact, the questions apply equally to marketing). The questions are:

1 Who are our customers?

This involves identifying target segments that share certain characteristics and needs. It was seen in *Chapter 4* that different criteria for identifying segments include demographics and geographical location for the B2C market and organizational characteristics and members of the buying unit for the B2B market.

2 How are their needs changing?

Understanding the needs of different segments when they venture online is important to the next stages of delivering value to the customer. Some segments may have originally been motivated by price, but in the online world, perhaps customer service becomes more important. This is closely related to buyer behaviour (*Chapter 9*).

3 Which do we target?

This is an important strategic decision in e-marketing. Segments for targeting online are selected which are most attractive in terms of growth and profitability. These may be similar to or different from groups targeted offline. Some examples of customer segments that are targeted online include:

- the most profitable customers – using the Internet to provide tailored offers to the top 20 per cent of customers by profit may result in more repeat business and cross-sales;
- larger companies (B2B) – an extranet could be produced to service these customers, and increase their loyalty;
- smaller companies (B2B) – large companies are traditionally serviced through sales representatives and account managers, but smaller companies may not warrant the expense of account managers. However, the Internet can be used to reach smaller companies more cost-effectively. The number of smaller companies that can be reached in this way may be significant, so although the individual revenue of each one is relatively small, the collective revenue achieved through Internet servicing can be large;
- particular members of the buying unit (B2B) – the site should provide detailed information for different interests that support the buying decision, for example technical documentation for users of products, information on savings from e-procurement for IS or purchasing managers and information to establish the credibility of the company for decision makers;
- customers who are difficult to reach using other media – an insurance company looking to target younger drivers could use the web as a vehicle for this;
- customers who are brand-loyal – services to appeal to brand-loyalists can be provided to support them in their role as advocates of a brand;
- customers who are not brand-loyal – conversely, incentives, promotion and a good level of service quality could be provided by the web site to try and retain such customers;
- customers at different stages in their lifecycle – we will see in *Chapter 9* how web and e-mail personalization are used to target customers according to their depth of relationship with a company;
- customers who show intent to purchase – this is the 'sense and respond' approach to targeting detail in *Chapter 9*.

4 How can we add value?

We have seen in *Chapters 5* and *6* that customer value is mainly dependent on the combination of product quality, customer service quality, fulfilment time and price. Companies need to decide for each segment which of these is most important and then seek to adjust these elements accordingly as part of the marketing mix described in the next section.

5 How do we become first choice?

To decide on this it is necessary to know how to position within the marketplace relative to competitor offerings. Positioning is related to how a consumer perceives a product in terms of the elements of value described above. It is stage 3 in *Figure 8.8*. A positioning statement is often developed to encapsulate this. Companies then need to decide how to highlight the benefits as a differential advantage over rivals' products.

Positioning
Influencing the customer's perception of a product within a marketplace.

Differential advantage
A desirable attribute of a product offering that is not currently matched by competitor offerings.

Online value proposition (OVP)
A statement of the benefits of e-commerce services that ideally should not be available in competitor offerings or offline offerings.

In an e-marketing context the differential advantage and positioning can be clarified and communicated by developing an online value proposition (OVP). This is similar to a unique selling proposition, but is developed for e-commerce services. It *builds on the core proposition* for the company's services. In developing a proposition managers should identify:

- A clear differentiation of the proposition from competitors' based on product features or service quality.
- Target market segment(s) that the proposition will appeal to.
- How the proposition will be communicated to site visitors and in all marketing communications. Developing a tag line can help this.
- How the proposition is delivered across different parts of the buying process.
- How the proposition will be delivered and supported by resources – is the proposition genuine? Will resources be internal or external?

Ideally, the e-commerce site should have an additional value proposition to further differentiate the company's products or services. The site design will also need to communicate the core proposition of the brand or products.

Having a clear online value proposition has several benefits:

- it helps distinguish an e-commerce site from its competitors (this should be a website design objective);
- it helps provide a focus to marketing efforts and enables company staff to be clear about the purpose of the site;
- if the proposition is clear it can be used for PR and word-of-mouth recommendations made about the company. For example, the clear proposition of Amazon on its site is that prices are reduced by up to 40 per cent and that a wide range of 3 million titles is available;
- it can be linked to the normal product propositions of a company or its product.

Varianini and Vaturi (2000) have conducted a review of failures in B2C dot-com companies in order to highlight lessons that can be learned. They believe that many of the problems have resulted from a failure to apply established marketing orientation approaches. They summarize their guidelines as follows:

> *First identify customer needs and define a distinctive value proposition that will meet them, at a profit. The value proposition must then be delivered through the right product and service and the right channels and it must be communicated consistently. The ultimate aim is to build a strong, long-lasting brand that delivers value to the company marketing it.*

Conversely, Argrawal *et al.* (2001) suggest that the success of leading e-commerce companies is often due to matching value propositions to segments successfully.

Some of the best taglines have been developed by the start-up companies, for which the OVP is particularly important. For example:

> *'Compare. Buy. Save.' Kelkoo (www.kelkoo.com)*
>
> *'Earth's biggest selection.' Amazon (www.amazon.com)*
>
> *'Search the largest inventory of cars and trucks on the Internet. More than 1.5 million listings, updated daily.' (www.autotrader.com)*

The Citibank site design (www.citibank.com) uses a range of techniques to illustrate its core proposition and OVP. The main messages are:

Welcome to Citibank: The one-stop solution for all your financial needs.

Look for a product or service; Learn about a financial product; Find a location.

Different OVPs can be developed for different products or different segments. For Citibank UK, the OVP for its Internet banking service is:

Bank whenever you want, from wherever you are. Citibank Internet Banking gives you the freedom and flexibility to manage your day-to-day finances. It's secure, convenient and very easy to use.

An OVP can have several elements; easyJet (2003) describes their OVP as follows:

1. *Passengers booking online receive a discount of £2.50 for each leg of a journey. EasyJet pioneered the concept of offering a discount to Internet customers, an initiative that has been widely copied by competitors.*
2. *Any easyJet promotions are exclusive to the Internet, so that customers must get online if they wish to take advantage of discounted fares.*
3. *If customers wish to book seats more than a month in advance of the departure date of their flight, they can only do so by booking online. As fares generally increase as the departure date gets closer, this means that the best fares are available to those who book via the Internet.*

Once e-marketing strategies have been developed as part of the e-marketing plan, tactics need to be implemented to achieve these strategies. These tactics, and in particular the promotion or communications tactics, will be informed by the special marketing characteristics of electronic media. The *Focus on* section below summarizes some of the key differences before we review tactics.

Focus on characteristics of new-media marketing communications

In this section, we explore the main differences between marketing communications in the traditional media such as TV, print and radio and new digital media such as web sites, interactive TV and mobile commerce. This section is based on the summary presented in Chaffey (2000). Recognizing the differences between the Internet and other media is important to achieving success in channel promotion and channel satisfaction, and will lead in turn to positive channel outcomes and profitability.

A useful summary of the differences between the new media and traditional media has been developed by McDonald and Wilson (1999) as the '6 Is' of e-marketing. The '6 Is' are useful since they highlight factors that apply to practical aspects of Internet marketing such as personalization, direct response and marketing research, but also strategic issues of industry restructuring and integrated channel communications. By considering each of these facets of the new media, marketing managers can develop marketing plans that accommodate the characteristics of the new media. This presentation of the '6 Is' is a new interpretation of these factors using new examples and diagrams to illustrate these concepts.

1 Interactivity

Deighton (1996) was one of the first authors to explain that a key characteristic of the Internet was the opportunities that the Internet provided for interactivity. *Figure*

8.9(a) shows how traditional media are predominantly *push media* where the marketing message is broadcast from company *to* customer and other stakeholders. During this process, there is limited interaction with the customer, although interaction is encouraged in some cases such as the direct-response advert or mail-order campaign. On the Internet, it is usually a customer who initiates contact and is *seeking* information on a web site. In other words it is a *'pull'* mechanism unless e-mail is used (this can be considered as a push technique). *Figure 8.9(b)* shows how the Internet should be used to encourage two-way communication; these may be extensions of the direct-response approach. For example, FMCG suppliers such as Nestlé (**www.nescafe.co.uk**) use their web site as a method of generating interaction by providing incentives such as competitions and sales promotions to encourage the customer to respond with their names, addresses and profile information such as age and sex.

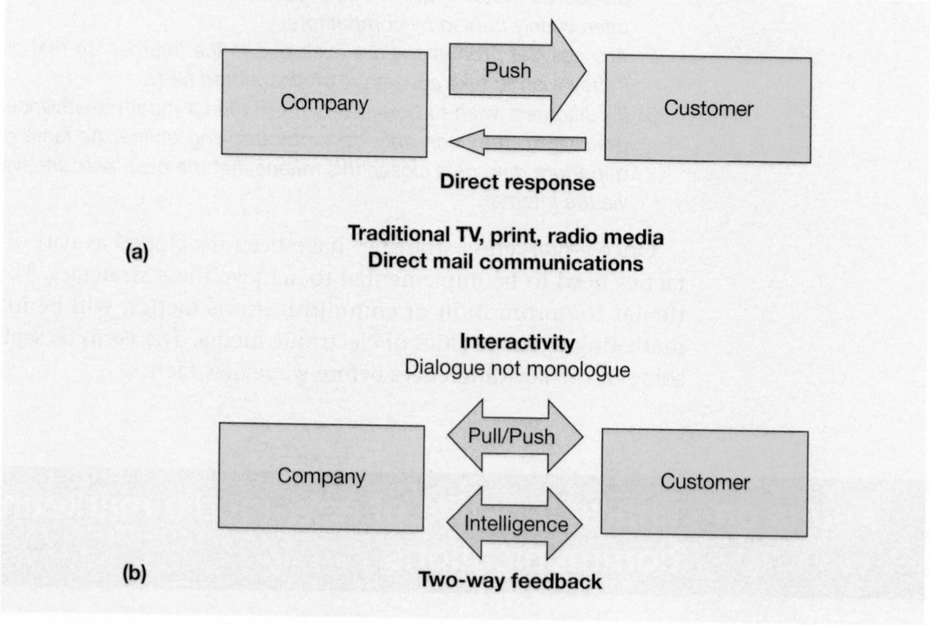

Figure 8.9 Summary of communication models for (a) traditional media, (b) new media

Hoffman and Novak (1997) believe that this change is significant enough to represent a new model for marketing or a new marketing paradigm. They suggest that the facilities of the Internet including the web represent a computer-mediated environment in which the interactions are not between the sender and receiver of information, but with the medium itself. They say:

> *consumers can interact with the medium, firms can provide content to the medium, and in the most radical departure from traditional marketing environments, consumers can provide commercially-oriented content to the media.*

The content customers can provide may be directly commercial such as auctioning of their possessions such as via eBay (**www.ebay.com**) or could include comments on products or suppliers on a neutral site (e.g. **www.bizrate.com**) or a destination site (**www.firebox.com**).

2 Intelligence

The Internet can be used as a relatively low cost method of collecting marketing research, particularly about customer perceptions of products and services. In the competitions referred to above Nestlé is able to profile their customers on the basis of the information received in questionnaires. The Internet can be used to create two-way feedback which does not usually occur in other media. Financial services provider Egg (www.egg.com) collects information about their online service levels through a questionnaire that is continuously available in the customer-service part of their site. What is significant is that the company responds via the web site to the main concerns of the customer; if the length of time it takes to reply to customer-service e-mails is seen as a problem it will explain what the organization is trying to do to resolve this problem.

A wealth of marketing research information is also available from the web site itself, since every time a user clicks on a link this is recorded and can be analysed with the web analytics tools described in *Chapter 12*. Potentially companies can respond in real time to buyer behaviour. For example, banks such as HSBC (www.hsbc.co.uk) and Lloyds TSB (www.lloydstsb.co.uk) use a service from Touch Clarity (www.touchclarity.co.uk) to serve messages according to an evaluation of which offers they are most likely to respond to.

3 Individualization

Another important feature of the interactive marketing communications referred to above is that they can be tailored to the individual (*Figure 8.10 (b)*), unlike traditional media where the same message tends to be broadcast to everyone (*Figure 8.10 (a)*). The process of tailoring is also referred to as *personalization* and is an important aspect of achieving customer relationship management online. Personalization is often achieved through extranets which are set up with key accounts to manage the buying and after-sales processes. Dell (www.dell.com/premier) set up 'Dell Premier' for key accounts such as the Abbey where special offers and bespoke customer support are delivered. Another example of personalization is that achieved by business-to-business e-tailer RS Components (www.rswww.com). Every customer who accesses their system is profiled according to their area of product interest and information describing their role in the buying unit. When they next visit the site information will be displayed relevant to their product interest, for example office products and promotions if this is what was selected. This is an example of what is known as *mass customization* where generic customer information is supplied for particular segments, i.e. the information is not unique to individuals, but to those with a common interest. Amazon (www.amazon.com) is well known for using a *collaborative filtering* approach or Amazon's 'Customers Who bought X ... also bought .... Y'. Amazon also has two other personalization features, 'Customers who shopped for X also SHOPPED for ... ' and 'Customers who searched for X also BOUGHT ...'. You can read about the approach that they use to achieve this in IEE (2003).

4 Integration

The Internet provides further scope for integrated marketing communications. *Figure 8.11* shows how it is just one of many different media channels (these channels are also offered by intermediaries). When assessing the success of a web site, the role of the Internet in communicating with customers and other partners can best be considered from two perspectives. First, organization-to-customer direction: how does the Internet complement other channels in communication of proposition for the

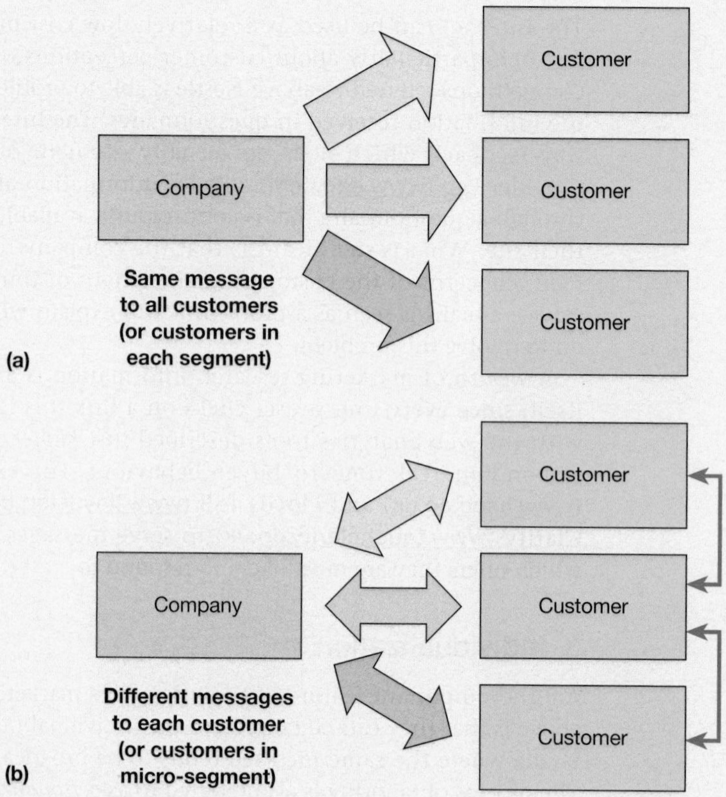

Figure 8.10 **Summary of degree of individualization for (a) traditional media (same message), (b) new media (unique messages and more information exchange between customers)**

company's products and services to new and existing customers with a view to generating new leads and retaining existing customers? Second, customer-to-organization: how can the Internet complement other channels to deliver customer service to these customers? Many companies are now considering how they integrate e-mail response and web-site callback into their existing call-centre or customer-service operation. This may require a substantial investment in training and new software.

Some practical examples of how the Internet can be used as an integrated communications tool are as follows:

- The Internet can be used as a direct-response tool enabling customers to respond to offers and promotions publicized in other media. Dell uses 'E-value codes' which it publishes in magazines and offline material to direct people to specific pages (via a search) when they visit the web site. CapitalOne uses a similar approach. These codes include a media code to assess which offline communications were most effective in driving sales on the web site.
- The web site can have a direct-response or callback facility built into it. The Automobile Association has a feature where a customer service representative will contact a customer by phone when the customer fills in their name, phone number and a suitable time to ring.
- The Internet can be used to support the buying decision even if the purchase does not occur via the web site. For example, Dell has a prominent web-specific phone

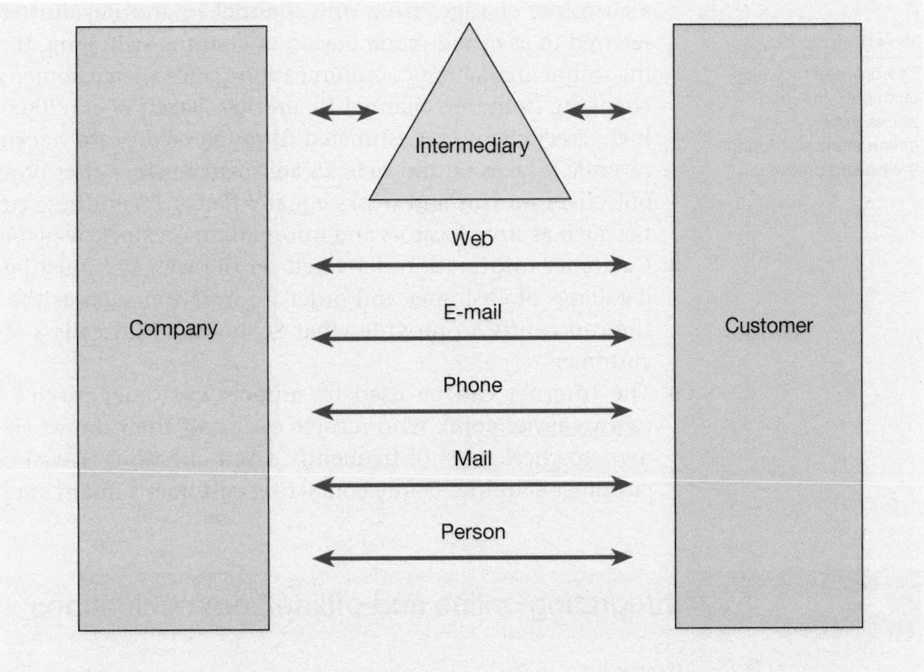

Figure 8.11 **Channels requiring integration as part of integrated e-marketing strategy**

number on their web site that encourages customers to ring a representative in the call centre to place their order. This has the benefits that Dell are less likely to lose the business of customers who are anxious about the security of online ordering and Dell can track sales that result partly from the web site according to the number of callers on this line. This is alternative 3 in *Figure 8.12*. Considering how

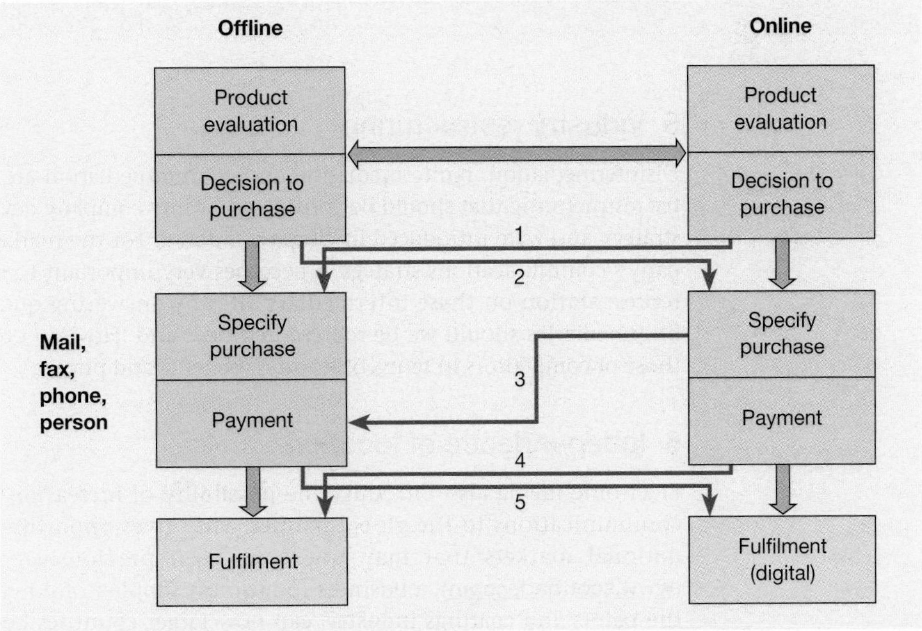

Figure 8.12 **Channel integration required for e-marketing and mixed-mode buying**

a customer changes from one channel to another during the buying process is referred to as mixed-mode buying or channel switching. It is a key aspect of devising online marketing communications since the customer should be supported in changing from one channel to another. Bazett *et al.* (2005) give the example of a high-street chain that estimated (through credit card tracking) that for every £1 of revenue it takes on the web, £3 are spent in-store after browsing online – so it has objectives for this and works equally hard to help these customers through facilities such as store locators and information on stock availability for that store.

Mixed-mode buying
The process by which customer changes between online and offline channels during the buying process.

- Customer information delivered on the web site must be integrated with other databases of customer and order information such as those accessed via staff in the call centre to provide what Seybold (1999) calls a '360 degree view of the customer'.
- The Internet can be used to support customer service. For example, easyJet (www.easyjet.com), who receive over half their orders electronically, encourage users to check a list of frequently asked questions (FAQs) compiled from previous customer enquiries before contacting customer support via phone.

Activity 8.4 Integrating online and offline communications

Purpose

To highlight differences in marketing communications introduced through the use of the Internet as a channel and the need to integrate these communications with existing channels.

Activity

List communications between PC vendor and a home customer over the lifetime of a product such as a PC. Include communications using both the Internet and traditional media. Refer to channel swapping alternatives in the buying decision shown in *Figure 8.11* to develop your answer.

Answers to activities can be found at www.pearsoned.co.uk/chaffey

5 Industry restructuring

Disintermediation, reintermediation and countermediation are key concepts of industry restructuring that should be considered by any company developing an e-marketing strategy and were introduced in *Chapters 2* and *4*. For the marketer defining their company's communications strategy it becomes very important to consider the company's representation on these intermediary sites by answering questions such as 'Which intermediaries should we be represented on?' and 'How do our offerings compare to those of competitors in terms of features, benefits and price?'.

6 Independence of location

Electronic media also introduce the possibility of increasing the reach of company communications to the global market. This gives opportunities to sell into international markets that may not have been previously accessible. Scott Bader (www.scottbader.com), a business-to-business supplier of polymers and chemicals for the paints and coatings industry, can now target countries beyond the forty or so it has traditionally sold to via a network of local agents and franchises. The Internet makes it possible to sell to a country without a local sales or customer service force (although this may still be necessary for some products). In such situations and with the restructuring in conjunction with disintermediation and reintermediation, strategists also need to carefully consider channel conflicts that may arise. If a customer is buying direct from a company in another country rather than via the agent, this will marginalize the business of the local agent who may want some recompense for sales efforts or may look to partner with competitors.

A further appraisal of using the characteristics of new media for effective communications is presented in *Chapter 9*.

Tactics

Marketing tactics to implement strategies and objectives are traditionally based around the elements of the marketing mix. There are other methods for approaching tactics that are detailed in further sections. One approach is to use customer-driven tactics that affect both the design and services provided by an e-commerce site. A further approach to structure e-marketing tactics is that of customer relationship management described in *Chapter 9*.

The marketing mix – the 4 Ps of Product, Price, Place and Promotion originally proposed by Jerome McCarthy (1960) – is used as an essential part of implementing marketing strategy by many practitioners. The 4 Ps have been extended to the 7 Ps by including three further elements that better reflect service delivery: People, Processes and Physical evidence (Booms and Bitner, 1981), although others argue that these are subsumed within the 4 Ps. The marketing mix is applied frequently when developing marketing strategies since it provides a simple framework for varying different elements of the product offering to influence the demand for products within target markets. For example, to increase sales of a product the price can be decreased or the amount or type of promotion changed, or there can be some combination of these elements. E-commerce provides new opportunities for the marketer to vary the marketing mix, so it is worthwhile outlining these. However, it should be noted that many marketers now consider it as only one tool for developing tactics and other approaches such as branding (see *Focus on online branding* below) or a *customer relationship management perspective* (*Chapter 9 p. 424*) can be used to develop tactics, particularly for marketing communications. One difficulty is that the marketing mix is symptomatic of a push approach to marketing and does not recognize the needs of customers. For this reason it is important that mix be backed up by detailed knowledge of buyer behaviour collected through market research. Furthermore, the mix should be adjusted according to different target markets or segments to better meet the needs of customers.

Figure 8.13 summarizes the different sub-elements of the 7 Ps. We will now consider how each element of the marketing mix can be varied or how we 'mix the mix' in more detail. You can also refer to Allen and Fjermestad (2001) for a more detailed assessment.

Before embarking on a review of the role of the Internet on each of the 7 Ps, it is worth briefly restating some of the well known criticisms of applying the marketing mix as a solitary tool for marketing strategy. First, and perhaps most importantly, the marketing mix, because of its origins in the 1960s, is symptomatic of a push approach to marketing and does not explicitly acknowledge the needs of customers. As a consequence, the marketing mix tends to lead to a product rather than a customer orientation – a key concept of market orientation and indeed a key Internet marketing concept. To mitigate this effect, Lautenborn (1990) suggested the 4 Cs framework which considers the 4 Ps from a customer perspective. In an e-commerce context the 4 Cs can be interpreted as follows:

Using the Internet to vary the marketing mix						
Product	**Promotion**	**Price**	**Place**	**People**	**Process**	**Physical evidence**
• Quality • Image • Branding • Features • Variants • Mix • Support • Customer service • Use occasion • Availability • Warranties	• Marketing communications • Personal promotion • Sales promotion • PR • Branding • Direct marketing	• Positioning • List • Discounts • Credit • Payment methods • Free or value-added elements	• Trade channels • Sales support • Channel number • Segmented channels	• Individuals on marketing activities • Individuals on customer contact • Recruitment • Culture/image • Training and skills • Remuneration	• Customer focus • Business-led • IT-supported • Design features • Research and development	• Sales/staff contact experience of brand • Product packaging • Online experience

Figure 8.13 **The elements of the marketing mix**

- Customer needs and wants (from the product) – the web site is a mechanism for explaining how the product proposition meets these needs and wants.
- Cost to the customer (price) – online the customer is likely to be comparing prices to other web sites and traditional purchasing sources.
- Convenience (relative to place) – online this is the quality of customer experience in terms of the ordering process and fulfilment.
- Communication (promotion) – the web site itself coupled with the methods of driving traffic to the site, such as search-engine marketing and e-mail marketing as described in *Chapter 9*.

It follows that the selection of the marketing mix is based on detailed knowledge of buyer behaviour collected through market research. Furthermore, it should be remembered that the mix is often adjusted according to different target markets or segments to better meet the needs of these customer groupings. An increased focus on 'one-to-one marketing' which means tailoring of the offer for specific customers also sits uncomfortably within the 7 Ps framework.

Product variable
The element of the marketing mix that involves researching customers' needs and developing appropriate products.

Product

Core product
The fundamental features of the product that meet the user's needs.

Extended product
Additional features and benefits beyond the core product.

Mass customization
Using economies of scale enabled by technology to offer tailored versions of products to individual customers or groups of customers.

There are many alternatives for varying the Product when a company is developing its online strategy. Internet-related product decisions can be usefully divided into decisions affecting the core product and the extended product. For some companies, there may be options for new digital products which will typically be information products that can be delivered over the web. In some cases, the core product offering has been replaced by information about the product. For example, a company providing oil-drilling equipment focusing instead on analysis and dissemination of information about drilling. In some cases, an online version of the product may be more valuable to customers in that it can be updated more regularly. The advertising directory BRAD (www.brad.co.uk) has been changed from a large paper-based document to an online version with searching facilities that were not available in the paper-based version. The Internet also introduces options for mass customization of products. Levi's provided a truly personal service that dates back to 1994, when Levi Strauss initiated its 'Personal Pair' programme. Women who were prepared to pay up to $15 more than the standard price and wait for delivery could go to Levi's stores and have themselves digitized – that is, have their measurements taken and a pair of custom jeans made and then have their measurements stored on a database for future purchases.

Companies can also consider how the Internet can be used to change the range or combination of products offered. Some companies only offer a subset of products online – for example, WH Smith interactive TV service only offers bestsellers at a discount. Alternatively, a company may have a fuller catalogue available online than is available through offline brochures. Bundling is a further alternative. For example, easyJet has developed a range of complementary travel-related services including flights, packages and car hire.

Bundling
Offering complementary services.

For many companies, using the Internet to vary the extended product is most practical. Smith and Chaffey (2001) suggest these examples of how the Internet can be used to vary the extended product:

- Endorsements
- Awards
- Testimonies
- Customer lists
- Customer comments
- Warranties
- Guarantees
- Money-back offers
- Customer service (see People, Process and Physical evidence)
- Incorporating tools to help users during their use of the product. A good example of this is the Citroën Exceed software which Citroën provides to fleet car managers.

It should also be noted that the Internet can be used to assist in new product development by assessing product needs from web-site logs (*Chapter 12*), testing new concepts, online surveys and focus groups.

Price

Price variable
The element of the marketing mix that involves defining product prices and pricing models.

Pricing models
Describe the form of payment such as outright purchase, auction, rental, volume purchase and credit terms.

The Price element of the marketing mix refers to an organization's pricing policies which are used to define pricing models and, of course, to set prices for products and services. The Internet has dramatic implications for pricing in many sectors and there is a lot of literature in this area. Baker *et al.* (2001) have noted two approaches that have been commonly adopted for pricing on the Internet. Start-up companies have tended to use low prices to gain a customer base, while many existing companies have transferred their existing prices to the web. However, *Case Study 8.1* showed how easyJet discounted online prices in an effort to meet its objectives of online revenue contribution. In this case, price reduction was possible because of the lower overhead of processing a customer transaction online in comparison with on the phone. Similarly, to acquire customers online booksellers may decide to offer a discount of 50 per cent on the top 25 best-selling books in each category, for which no profit is made, but offer a relatively small discount on less popular books to give a profit margin.

The main implications of the Internet for the Price aspect of the mix are as follows.

1 Increased price transparency and its implications on differential pricing

Quelch and Klein (1996) describe two contradictory effects of the Internet on price that are related to price transparency. First, a supplier can use the technology for differential pricing, for example customers in different countries. However, if precautions are not taken about price, the customers may be able to quickly find out about the price discrimination and they will object to it. So, customer knowledge of pricing is enhanced through the Internet. This is particularly the case for standardized goods sold through online retailers. Not only can customers visit sites of rival suppliers, they can visit sites of price-comparison engines provided by intermediaries such as Kelkoo (www.kelkoo.com), or Pricerunner (www.pricerunner.com). These sites will list the best price from suppliers for a particular product ranked from highest to lowest. It is difficult to retain price differentials if all customers are aware of these differences. Currently, this is probably not the case. However, research quoted by Baker *et al.* (2001) suggests that only around 8% of active online consumers are 'aggressive price shoppers'. Furthermore, they note that Internet price brands have remained quite broad. Online booksellers' prices varied by an average of 33% and CD sellers' by 25%.

There appear to be two main reasons for this; first, pricing is only one variable – consumers also decide on suppliers according to other aspects about the brand such as familiarity, trust and perceived service levels. Secondly, consumers often display satisficing behaviour. The term 'satisfice' was coined by Herbert Simon in 1957 when he said that people are only 'rational enough' and that they suspend or relax their rationality if they feel it is no longer required. This is called 'bounded rationality' by cognitive psychologists. In other words, although consumers may seek to minimize some variable (such as price) when making a product or supplier selection, most may not try too hard. Online, this is supported by research by Johnson *et al.* (2004) who showed that by analysing panel data from over 10,000 Internet households and three commodity-like products (books, compact discs (CDs) and air travel services) the amount of online search is actually quite limited. On average, households visit only 1.2 book sites, 1.3 CD sites and 1.8 travel sites during a typical active month in each category. Of course, these averages will reflect a range of behaviour.

Satisficing behaviour
Consumers do not behave entirely rationally in product or supplier selection. They will compare alternatives, but then may make their choice given imperfect information.

A compromise approach used by many companies is to use differential pricing with lower prices or Internet offers for some of their products online. This has been the approach followed by online electrical retailers such as Comet (www.comet.co.uk), travel companies such as Thomson (www.thomson.co.uk) and companies with e-savings products.

2 Downward pressure on price (including commoditization)

For business commodities, auctions on business-to-business exchanges (e.g. Emiliani, 2001) can also have a similar effect of driving down price. Many companies, such as GlaxoSmithKline (pharmaceuticals), Whitbread (entertainment and leisure) and DaimlerChrysler (automotive) have reported that price has been decreased by 10% or more using reverse auctions (see *Case Study 2.1*). Purchase of some products that have not traditionally been thought of as commodities, may become more price-sensitive. This process is known as 'commoditization'. Goods that are becoming commoditized include electrical goods and cars.

Commoditization
The process whereby product selection becomes more dependent on price than on differentiating features, benefits and value-added services.

3 New pricing approaches (including dynamic pricing and auctions)

In addition to the auctions described above, the Internet introduces new opportunities for dynamic pricing, for example new customers could be automatically given discounted purchases for the first three items. Care has to be taken with differential pricing since established customers will be unhappy if significant discounts are given to new customers. Amazon trialled such a discounting scheme in 2000 and it received negative press and had to be withdrawn when people found out that their friends or colleagues had paid less. If the scheme had been a clear introductory promotion this problem may not have arisen.

Dynamic pricing
Prices can be updated in real time according to the type of customer or current market conditions.

A further approach is aggregated buying. This approach was promoted by LetsBuyit.com, but the business model did not prove viable – the cost of creating awareness for the brand and explaining the concept was not offset by the revenue from each transaction.

Aggregated buying
A form of customer union where buyers collectively purchase a number of items at the same price and receive a volume discount.

Finally, it should be remembered that when developing a pricing strategy, the options will be limited by the relative strengths of the seller and buyer (e.g. Pitt *et al.*, 2001). Where the buyer is powerful then reverse auctions are possible. Major car manufacturers fall into this category. Where the seller is more powerful then a negotiation may be more likely where the seller can counter-offer. Nextag.com provides such a service.

4 Alternative pricing structure or policies

Different types of pricing may be possible on the Internet, particularly for digital, downloadable products. Software and music have traditionally been sold for a continuous right to use. The Internet offers new options such as payment per use, rental at a fixed cost per month or a lease arrangement. Bundling options may also be more possible. The use of applications service providers (ASPs) or on-demand services to deliver services such as web-site traffic monitoring also gives new methods of volume pricing. Web analytics companies such as Omniture (www.omniture.com) and Clicktracks (www.clicktracks.com) charge in price bands based on the number of visitors to the purchaser's site.

Further pricing options which could be varied online include:

- Basic price
- Discounts
- Add-ons and extra products and services
- Guarantees and warranties
- Refund policies
- Order cancellation terms.

Place

Allen and Fjermestad (2001) argue that that the Internet has the greatest implications for Place in the marketing mix since the Internet has a global reach. The main implications of the Internet for the Place aspect of the mix, which we will review in this section, are:

Place
The element of the marketing mix that involves distributing products to customers in line with demand and minimizing cost of inventory, transport and storage.

1 Place of purchase

In a B2B context, is e-commerce conducted on the manufacturer's own site, at an intermediary or procured on a customer's site (*Chapter 2, p. 54*).

2 New channel structures

New channel structures such as changes introduced by disintermediation, reintermediation and countermediation referred to in *Chapter 2* (*p. 45*) and *Chapter 5 (p. 240)*

3 Channel conflicts

A significant threat arising from the introduction of an Internet channel is that while disintermediation gives a company the opportunity to sell direct and increase profitability on products, it can also threaten distribution arrangements with existing partners. Such channel conflicts are described by Frazier (1999), and need to be carefully managed. Frazier (1999) identifies some situations when the Internet should only be used as a communications channel. This is particularly the case where manufacturers offer an exclusive, or highly selective, distribution approach. To take an example, a company manufacturing expensive watches costing thousands of pounds will not in the past have sold direct, but will have used a wholesaler to distribute watches via retailers. If this wholesaler is a major player in watch distribution, then it is powerful, and will react against the watch manufacturer selling direct. The wholesaler may even refuse to act as distributor and may threaten to distribute only a competitor's watches, which are not available over the Internet. Furthermore, direct sales may damage the product's brand or change its price positioning.

Further channel conflicts involve other stakeholders including sales representatives and customers. Sales representatives may see the Internet as a direct threat to their livelihood. In some cases such as Avon cosmetics and *Encyclopaedia Britannica* this has proved to be the case with this sales model being partly or completely replaced by the Internet. For many B2B purchases, sales representatives remain an essential method of reaching the customer to support them in the purchase decision. Here, following training of sales staff, the Internet can be used as a sales support and customer education tool. Customers who do not use the online channels may also respond negatively if lower prices are available to their online counterparts. This is less serious than other types of channel conflict.

To assess channel conflicts it is necessary to consider the different forms of channel the Internet can take. These are:

- a communication channel only,
- a distribution channel to intermediaries,
- a direct sales channel to customers,
- any combination of the above.

To avoid channel conflicts, the appropriate combination of channels must be arrived at. For example, Frazier (1999) notes that using the Internet as a direct sales channel may not be wise when a product's price varies considerably across global markets. In the watch manufacturer example, it may be best to use the Internet as a communication channel only.

Internet channel strategy will, of course, depend on the existing arrangements for the market. If a geographical market is new and there are no existing agents or distributors, there is unlikely to be channel conflict, in that there is a choice of distribution through the Internet only or appointments of new agents to support Internet sales, or a combination of the two. Often SMEs will attempt to use the Internet to sell products without appointing agents, but this strategy will only be possible for retail products that need limited pre-sales and after-sales support. For higher-value products such as engineering equipment, which will require skilled sales staff to support the sale and after-sales servicing, agents will have to be appointed.

For existing geographical markets in which a company already has a mechanism for distribution in the form of agents and distributors, the situation is more complex, and there is the threat of channel conflict.

4 Virtual organizations

The concept of virtual organizations was introduced in *Chapter 6*. From an e-marketing perspective, the Internet provides new options for forming partnerships to mutually benefit all parties.

Place tactics will have to review all the types of opportunities and threats described above and decide which are appropriate. In a B2B context they may vary on a case-by-case basis, for example special links may be set up to sell on a large customer's own procurement site. Issues in distribution and fulfilment are described in *Chapter 6*.

Promotion
The element of the marketing mix that involves communication with customers and other stakeholders to inform them about the product and the organization.

Promotion

Specification of the Promotion is usually part of a communications strategy. This will include selection of target markets, positioning and integration of different communications tools. The Internet offers a new, additional marketing communications channel to inform customers of the benefits of a product and assist in the buying decision. One approach for developing promotion tactics is to specify the communications techniques required for different stages of the buying process (see *Online marketing communications, Chapter 9 p. 410*). Another approach is to look at how the Internet can supplement the range of promotional activities such as advertising, sales promotions, PR and direct marketing. How these techniques can be used to drive customer traffic to a web site is described in more detail in *Focus on marketing communications for customer acquisition section* (*Chapter 9*). In *Chapter 9* we also look at how customers can be persuaded to return to a site for future purchases.

The Promotion element of the marketing plan also requires three important decisions about investment for the online promotion or the online communications mix:

1 *Investment in promotion compared to site creation and maintenance.* Since there is often a fixed budget for site creation, maintenance and promotion, the e-marketing plan should specify the budget for each to ensure there is a sensible balance and the promotion of the site is not underfunded.
2 *Investment in online promotion techniques in comparison to offline promotion.* A balance must be struck between these techniques. *Figure 8.14* summarizes the tactical options that companies have. Which do you think would be the best option for an established company as compared to a dot-com company? It seems that in both cases, offline promotion investment often exceeds that for online promotion investment. For existing companies traditional media such as print are used to advertise the sites, while print and TV will also be widely used by dot-com companies to drive traffic to their sites.

   There will naturally be a variation in spend on online marketing tools depending upon on level of adoption of e-commerce by a company and its customers. Research summarised in *Figure 8.15* by E-consultancy (2005) showed there was a wide variation in spend on digital communications, with over 30% of respondents spending less than 5%, but over 30% of respondents spending more than 10%. Factors that will affect the proportion of online media spend in any organization include:

   - Proportion of customers in a segment that can be reached through traditional or digital media.
   - Proportion of customers in target market in researching and purchasing products online.
   - Propensity of customers to purchase products using traditional channels such as phone or in-store.
   - The relative cost effectiveness of different online media such as search engine marketing, affiliate marketing and online advertising (see *Chapter 9* for explanations) in comparison with traditional media such as TV and print.

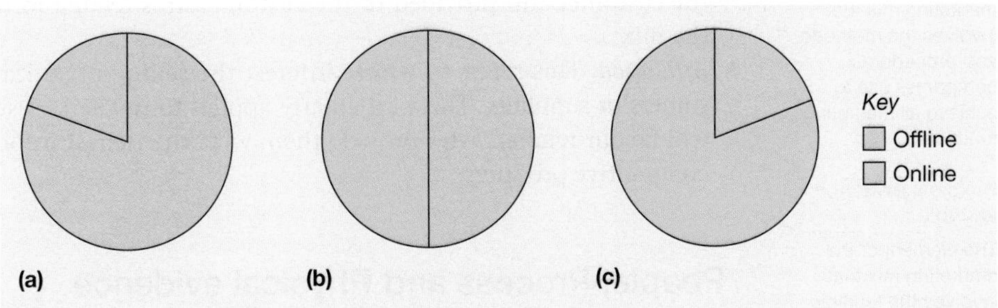

Figure 8.14 **Options for the online vs offline communications mix (a) online > offline, (b) similar online and offline, (c) offline > online**

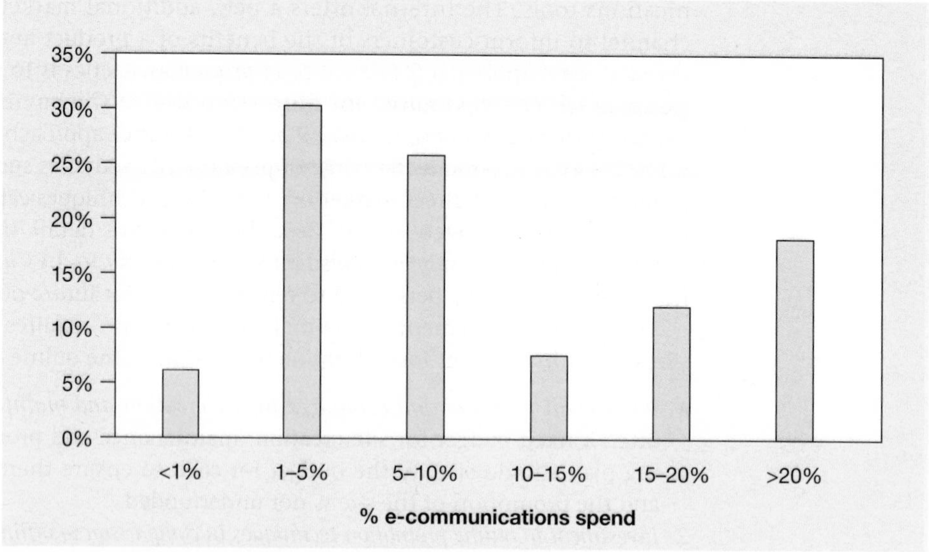

Figure 8.15 **Percent of marketing communications budget spent on e-communications (n = 76)**

Source: E-consultancy (2005)

There is a delicate balance to be struck between driving visitors to a web site where they may be less likely to convert, but the cost of sale will be lower. With any medium there is a point of diminishing returns where more spend on that medium will not result in improved results. It seems that many companies are following a strategy of gradually increasing their digital spend since they want to find this inflection point without overstepping it too far since traditional media buys such as those for TV and print are a known quantity.

3 *Investment in different online promotion techniques*. For example, how much to pay for banner advertising as against online PR about online presence; how much to pay for search engine registration. These and other traffic building techniques are described in *Chapter 9*.

People variable
The element of the marketing mix that involves the delivery of service to customers during interactions with customers.

Process variable
The element of the marketing mix that involves the methods and procedures companies use to achieve all marketing functions.

Physical evidence variable
The element of the marketing mix that involves the tangible expression of a product and how it is purchased and used.

Evans and Wurster (1999) have argued that there are three aspects of online promotion that are key to achieving competitive advantage online. These are:

- *Reach*. This is the potential audience of the e-commerce site. Reach can be increased by moving from a single site to representation with a large number of different intermediaries. Allen and Fjermestad (2001) suggest that niche suppliers can readily reach a much wider market due to search-engine marketing.
- *Richness*. This is the depth or detail of information which is both collected about the customer and provided to the customer. It is related to the Product element of the mix.
- *Affiliation*. This refers to whose interest the selling organization represents – consumers or suppliers. This particularly applies to retailers. It suggests that customers will favour retailers who provide them with the richest information on comparing competitive products.

People, Process and Physical evidence

People, Process and Physical evidence are particularly important for service delivery. Since service delivery is an important aspect of e-commerce sites this is referred to in the *Focus on excelling in e-commerce service quality* in *Chapter 9*; managing organizational change is the focus of *Chapter 10*; and user-centred design is in *Chapter 11*. Enhancing service is also an important element of online branding which is described in the next *Focus on* section. Physical evidence could be applied to site design or the accompanying packaging when products are delivered. Alternatively, these could be interpreted as part of the extended product.

Smith and Chaffey (2001) suggest that online, part of the consideration for the People element of the mix is the consideration of the tactics by which people can be replaced or their work automated. These are some of the options:

- *Autoresponders*. These automatically generate a response when a company e-mails an organization, or submits an online form.
- *E-mail notification*. Automatically generated by a company's systems to update customers on the status of their order, for example, order received, item now in stock, order dispatched.
- *Callback facility*. Customers fill in their phone number on a form and specify a convenient time to be contacted. Dialling from a representative in the call centre occurs automatically at the appointed time and the company pays, which is popular.
- *Frequently asked questions* (FAQs). For these, the art is in compiling and categorizing the questions so customers can easily find (a) the question and (b) a helpful answer.
- *On-site search engines*. These help customers find what they are looking for quickly and are popular when available. Site maps are a related feature.
- *Virtual assistants* come in varying degrees of sophistication and usually help to guide the customer through a maze of choices

Organizations can test actions needed at each stage for different types of scenario, e.g. enquiry from a new or existing customer, enquiry about the web site or e-mails from different stages in the buying process such as pre-sales, sales or post-sales.

Focus on online branding

What comprises a successful online brand? Is it an e-commerce site with high levels of traffic? Is it a brand with good name recognition? Is it a profitable brand? Or is it a site with more modest sales levels, but one that customers perceive as providing good service? Although sites meeting only some of these criteria are often described as successful brands, we will see that a successful brand is dependent on a wide range of factors.

The importance of building an effective online brand is often referred to when start-ups launch e-commerce sites, but what does branding mean in the online context and how important is online branding for existing companies?

Branding
The process of creating and evolving successful brands.

Brand
The sum of the characteristics of a product or service perceived by a user.

Branding seems to be a concept that is difficult to grasp since it is often used in a narrow sense. Many think of branding only in terms of aspects of the brand identity such as the name or logo associated with a company or products, but branding gurus seem agreed that it is much more than that. A brand is described by Leslie de Chernatony and Malcolm McDonald in their classic 1992 book *Creating Powerful Brands* as

> *an identifiable product or service augmented in such a way that the buyer or user perceives relevant unique added values which match their needs most closely. Furthermore, its success results from being able to sustain these added values in the face of competition.*

This definition highlights three essential characteristics of a successful brand:

- brand is dependent on customer perception;
- perception is influenced by the added-value characteristics of the product;
- the added-value characteristics need to be sustainable.

To summarize, a brand is dependent on a customer's psychological affinity for a product, and is much more than the physical name or symbol elements of brand identity.

De Chernatony (2001) has evaluated the relevance of the brand concept on the Internet. He also believes that the main elements of brand values and brand strategy are the same in the Internet environment. However, he suggests that the classical branding model of the Internet where consumers are passive recipients of value is challenged online. Instead, he suggests that consumers on the Internet become active co-producers of value where consumers can contribute feedback through discussion groups to add value to a brand. De Chernatony argues for a looser form of brand control where the company facilitates rather than controls customer discussion.

A further method by which the Internet can change branding that was suggested by Jevons and Gabbott (2000) is that online, '*the first-hand experience of the brand is a more powerful token of trust than the perception of the brand*'. In the online environment, the customer can experience or interact with the brand more frequently and to a greater depth. As Dayal *et al.* (2000) say, '*on the world wide web, the brand is the experience and the experience is the brand*'. They suggest that to build successful online brands, organizations should consider how their proposition can build on these possible brand promises:

Brand experience
The frequency and depth of interactions with a brand can be enhanced through the Internet.

- *the promise of convenience* – making a purchase experience more convenient than the real-world one, or that with rivals;
- *the promise of achievement* – to assist consumers in achieving their goals, for example supporting online investors in their decision or supporting business people in their day-to-day work;
- *the promise of fun and adventure* – this is clearly more relevant for B2C services;
- *the promise of self-expression and recognition* – provided by personalization services such as Yahoo! Geocities where consumers can build their own web site;
- *the promise of belonging* – provided by online communities.

Summarizing the elements of online branding, de Chernatony (2001) suggests successful online branding requires delivering three aspects of a brand: rational values, emotional values and promised experience (based on rational and emotional values).

An alternative perspective on branding is provided by Aaker and Joachimstaler (2000) who refer to 'brand equity' which they define as:

Brand equity
The assets (or liabilities) linked to a brand's name and symbol that add to (or subtract from) a service.

> *a set of brand assets and liabilities linked to a brand, its name and symbol, that add to or subtract from the value provided by a product or service to a firm and/or to that firm's customers.*

So, brand equity indicates the value provided to a company, or its customers through a brand. Assessing brand equity on the web needs to address the unique characteristics of computer-mediated environments, as Christodoulides and de Chernatony (2004) have pointed out. These researchers set out to explore whether additional measures of brand equity were required online. Based on expert interviews they have identified the additional measures of brand equity which are important online, as summarized in *Table 8.5*. As we would expect, this includes attributes of the digital medium such as interactivity and customization which combine to form relevance and a great online brand experience. Content is not stressed separately which is surprising although they do mention its importance under site design and it is also a key aspect of other attributes such as customization, relevance and the overall experience.

Table 8.5 Traditional measures of brand equity and online measures of brand equity

Traditional measures of brand equity (Aaker and Joachimstaler, 2000)	*Online measures of brand equity (from Christodoulides and de Chernatony, 2004)*
Price premium	Online brand experience
Satisfaction/loyalty	Interactivity
Perceived quality	Customization
Leadership popularity	Relevance
Perceived value	Site design
Brand personality	Customer service
Organizational associations	Order fulfilment
Brand awareness	Quality of brand relationships
Market share	Communities
Market price and distribution coverage	Website logs (see *Chapter 9*)

Brand identity

Brand identity
The totality of brand associations including name and symbols that must be communicated.

Aaker and Joachimstaler (2000) also emphasize the importance of developing a plan to communicate the key features of the brand identity and increase brand awareness. Brand identity is again more than the name. These authors refer to it as a set of brand associations that imply a promise to customers from an organisation. See 'Napster.com's brand identity', *Mini Case Study 8.1*, to see the different elements of brand identity which are effectively a checklist of what many e-tailers are looking to achieve.

Mini Case Study 8.1 Napster.com's brand identity

Aaker and Joachimstaler (2000) suggest that the following characteristics of identity need to be defined at the start of a brand-building campaign. Marketing communications can then be developed that create and reinforce this identity. Here, we will apply them to Napster which forms the main case study at the end of this chapter.

- *Brand essence (a summary of what the brand represents)*
  This is not necessarily a tag line, but Napster has been described as an 'All you can eat music service which is fun and affordable'.
- *Core identity (its key features)*
  - choice – millions of tracks
  - value for money – under £10 per month subscription for as many tracks as you can listen to
  - easy-to-use – Napster runs as a separate application built for purpose
  - listen anywhere – on a PC or other computer, MP3 player or mobile phone
  - listen on anything – unlike iPod, Napster is compatible with most MP3 players rather than being tied in to a specific hardware manufacturer.
- *Extended identity*
  - personality – flaunts what is standard for existing music providers thanks to its heritage as a peer-to-peer file-sharing service
  - Personalization – Napster Radio based on particular genres or based on other songs you have downloaded
  - community – facility to share tracks with friends or other Napster members
  - symbols – Napster cat logo.
- *Value proposition*
  - functional benefits – ease of use and personalization

→

- emotional benefits – community, non-conformist
- self-expressive benefit – build your own collection of your tastes.

- *Relationship*
  - customers value and will be loyal to a company that isn't stuffy.

Options for changing brand identity online

A further decision for marketing managers is whether to redefine the name element of brand identity and how to vary associated positioning messages to support the move online. Brands that were newly created for the Internet such as Expedia.com and Zopa.com do not risk damaging existing brands. Existing organizations need to think about how they differentiate their online services and changing the brand identity is part of that. There are four main options for existing organizations migrating their brands online. When a company launches or relaunches an online presence, it has the following choices with regards to brand identity:

1 *Transfer traditional brand online*. This is probably the most common approach. Companies with brands that are well established in the real world can build on the brand by duplicating it online. Sites from companies such as Ford, Argos and Guinness all have consistent brand identities and values that would be expected from experience of their offline brands. The Guinness site has additional brand messages to explain the online value proposition including online merchandise sales. Increasingly, companies will also replicate their offline branding campaigns online. Mobile operator Orange has achieved this since the first edition of this book and others such as Ford have become adept at doing this, but this unified messaging across channels is not achieved by many companies, due to the organizational and technical challenges of integrating messages into the web site. The only risks of migrating existing brands online are that the brand equity may be reduced if the site is of poor quality in terms of performance, structure or information content. There may also be a missed opportunity to use the online channel to add to the experience of the brand as explained below.

2 *Extend traditional brand: variant*. Some companies decide to create a slightly different version of their brand when they create their web site. An early version of the DHL couriers site (www.dhl.co.uk) was based on an online brand 'Red Planet' which was part of a spaceship concept. Through using this approach, the company was able to differentiate itself from similar competing services and this can be used in online and offline promotion to distinguish the site from its rivals. BA used a similar approach with its 2005 'Have You Clicked Yet?' campaign, which sought to showcase arranging a flight and checking in online. The use of an online brand variant helps raise the profile of the web site and helps the customer think of the site in association with the company. Aaker and Joachimstaler (2000) suggest that when a brand variant is created there may still be problems with recognition and also brand trust and quality associations may be damaged.

3 *Partner with existing digital brand*. It may be that a company can best promote its products in association with a strong existing digital or Internet brand such as Yahoo! or MSN. For example, the shopping options for record and book sales on Freeserve are branded as Freeserve although they are actually based on sites from other companies such as record seller Audiostreet.com. Freeserve is given brand prominence since this is to the advantage of both companies.

4 *Create a new digital brand*. It may be necessary to create an entirely new digital brand if the existing offline brand has negative connotations or is too traditional for the

new medium. An example of an entirely new digital brand was the Egg banking service which is part of Prudential, a well established company. Egg can take new approaches without damaging Prudential's brand, and at the same time, not be inhibited by the Prudential brand. Egg is not an entirely online brand since it is primarily accessed by phone. Egg now encourage some of their million-plus customers to perform all their transactions online. Another example of a new digital brand was the Go portal which was created by Disney, who desired to be able to 'own' some of the many online customers who are loyal to one portal. It was felt they could achieve this best through using a completely new brand. The Disney brand might be thought to appeal to a limited younger audience. However, the new brand was not sufficiently powerful to compete with the existing Yahoo! brand and has now failed.

Some of the characteristics of a successful brand name are suggested by de Chernatony and McDonald (1992): ideally it should be simple, distinctive, meaningful and compatible with the product. These principles can be readily applied to web-based brands. Examples of brands that fulfil most of these characteristics are CDNow, CarPoint, BUY.COM and e-STEEL. Others suggest that distinctiveness is most important: Amazon, Yahoo!, Expedia, Quokka.com (extreme sports), E*Trade, and FireandWater (HarperCollins) books.

Ries and Ries (2000) suggest two rules for naming brands. (a) The Law of the Common Name – they say 'The kiss of death for an Internet brand is a common name'. This argues that common names such as Art.com or Advertising.com are poor since they are not sufficiently distinctive. (b) The Law of the Proper Name – they say 'Your name stands alone on the Internet, so you'd better have a good one'. This suggests that proper names are to be preferred to generic names, e.g. Handbag.com against Woman.com or Moreover.com against Business.com. The authors suggest that the best names will follow most of these eight principles: (1) short, (2) simple, (3) suggestive of the category, (4) unique, (5) alliterative, (6) speakable, (7) shocking and (8) personalized. Although these are cast as 'immutable laws' there will of course be exceptions!

The importance of brand online

The Internet presents a 'double-edged sword' to existing brands. We have seen that a consumer who already has knowledge of a brand is more likely to trust it. However, loyalty can be decreased because the Internet encourages consumers to trial other brands. This is suggested by *Figure 8.16*. This trial may well lead to purchase of brands that have not been previously considered.

The BrandNewWorld (2004) survey showed that in some categories, a large proportion of buyers have purchased from different brands to those they initially considered, for example:

- Large home appliances, 47%
- Financial products and services, 39%
- Holidays and travels, 31%
- Mobile phones, 28%
- Cars, 26%.

But, for other types of products, existing brand preferences appear to be more important:

- Clothing/accessories, 22%
- Computer hardware, 21%
- Garden/DIY products, 17%
- Home furnishings, 6%.

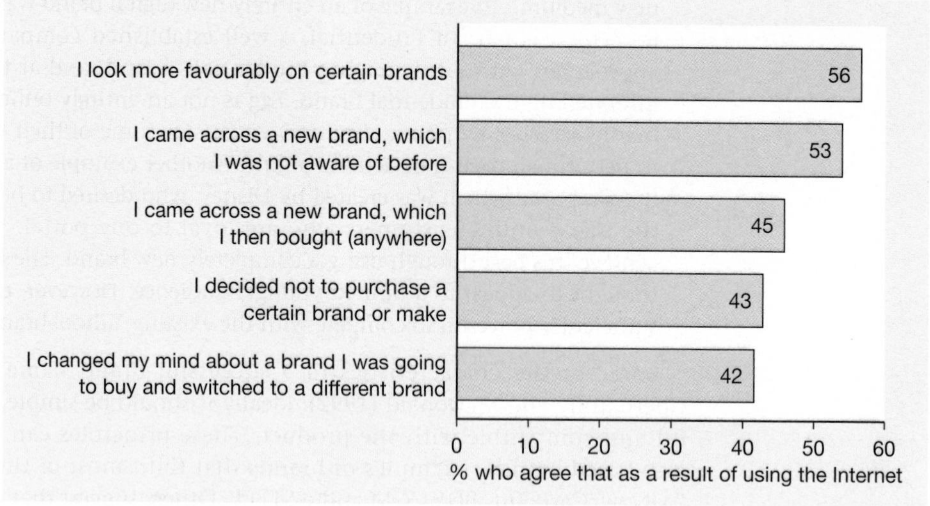

Figure 8.16 Changes to brand perception and behaviour as a result of using the Internet for research

Source: BrandNewWorld: AOL UK/Anne Molen (Cranfield School of Management)/Henley Centre, 2004

The survey also suggested that experienced Internet users were more likely to switch brands (52% agreed they were more likely to switch after researching online) compared to less-experienced users (33%).

Of course, the likelihood of a consumer purchasing from an established brand will depend upon the combination of their knowledge of the retailer brand or product brand. *Figure 8.17* shows that many customers will still buy an unknown manufacturer brand if they are familiar with the retailer brand. This is less true if they don't know the retailer. Significantly, if they don't know the retailer or the brand, it is fairly unlikely they will buy.

When buying online, I will buy a product if...

I am familiar with the retailer	Yes	Yes	No	No
I am familiar with the product brand	Yes	No	Yes	No
	90%	82%	54%	13%

Figure 8.17 The influence of brand knowledge on purchase. Matrix for question 'I will buy a product if ...'

Source: BrandNewWorld: AOL UK/Anne Molen (Cranfield School of Management)/Henley Centre, 2004

Activity 8.5 Applying branding concepts to The B2C Company e-commerce site

Purpose

To illustrate the importance of branding for e-commerce services.

Activity

You are putting together a business plan for a start-up company. Show how each of Aaker's dimensions of brand equity relates to a start-up dot-com. To what extent do these factors also apply to the e-commerce service of an existing company?

Answers to activities can be found at www.pearsoned.co.uk/chaffey

The activity illustrates the importance of building brand awareness for an e-commerce service in a cost-effective manner at the same time as achieving good levels of service quality. This is described further in the *Focus on excelling in e-commerce service* section in *Chapter 9* and summarized in *Table 9.5*. Success factors can be summarized as creating a positive customer experience through:

- Content quality (Can the customer easily find relevant, up-to-date content? Are there errors?)
- Adequate performance of web site infrastructure in terms of availability and download speed
- Ease of contacting a company for support by e-mail or the customer's preferred channel
- Quality of response to e-mail enquiries and fulfilment quality
- Acknowledgement of customer privacy
- Reflecting and supporting the characteristics of the offline brand.

Managing the technology and customer database necessary to deliver service is a key aspect of e-marketing and requires close interaction between marketers and the IS department or external consultants.

Actions

The actions component of e-marketing planning refers to activities conducted by managers to execute the plan. Questions that need to be resolved when specifying actions include:

- What level of investment in the Internet channel is sufficient to deliver these services? What will be the payback?
- What training of staff is required?
- What new responsibilities are required for effective Internet marketing?
- Are changes in organizational structure required to deliver Internet-based services?
- What activities are involved in creating and maintaining the web site?

At this stage an e-marketing plan will be finalized to summarize actions that need to occur. An example of what appears in a typical e-marketing plan is presented in the box *The B2B Company e-marketing plan*. This also acts as a summary for the chapter.

The B2B Company e-marketing plan

1 Situation analysis

Internal audits

- Current Internet marketing audit (business, marketing and Internet marketing effectiveness)
- Audience composition and characteristics
- Reach of web site, contribution to sales and profitability
- Suitability of resources to deliver online services in face of competition.

External audits

- Macro-economic environment (*Chapter 4*)
- Micro-environment – new marketplace structures, predicted customer activity
- Competition – threats from existing rivals, new services, new companies and intermediaries.

Assess opportunities and threats (SWOT analysis)

- Market and product positioning
- Methods of creation of digital value and detailed statement of customer value proposition
- Marketplace positioning (buyer, seller and neutral marketplaces)
- Scope of marketing functions.

2 Objectives statement

- Corporate objectives of online marketing (mission statement)
- Detailed objectives: tangible and intangible benefits, specific critical success factors
- Contribution of online marketing to promotional and sales activities
- Online value proposition.

3 Strategy definition

- Investment and commitment to online channels (mixture of bricks and clicks)
- Market and product positioning – aims for increasing reach, new digital products and new business and revenue models
- Target market strategies – statement of prioritized segments, new segments, online value proposition and differential advantage. Significance of non-customer audiences?
- Change management strategy (Which new processes, structures and responsibilities will be required? *Chapter 10*).

4 Tactics

- *Product*. Creating new core and extended value for customers, options for migrating brand online
- *Promotion*. Specify balance of online and offline promotion methods. Role of CRM (incentivization to acquire new customer registrations and opt-in e-mail to retain customers, *Chapter 9*)
- *Price*. Discounting online sales, options for setting pricing, new pricing options, e.g. auctions
- *Place*. Disintermediation and reintermediation, seller, buyer or neutral sales
- *People, process and physical evidence*. Online service delivery through support and characteristics of web site.

5 Actions

Specify:

- Tasks
- Resources

- Partnering and outsourcing
- Budget including costs for development, promotion and maintenance
- Timescale
- Staff.

Implementation

- Key development tasks (*Chapters 11* and *12*): analysis of business and audience needs, scenario-based design, development of content, integration of databases, migration of data, testing and changeover
- Project and change management (*Chapter 10*)
- Team organization and responsibilities
- Risk assessment (identify risks, measures to counter risks)
- Legal issues
- Development and maintenance process.

6 Control

Identify a measurement process and metrics (*Chapter 12*) covering:

- Business contribution (channel profitability – revenue, costs, return on investment)
- Marketing effectiveness (channel outcomes – leads, sales, conversion rate, channel satisfaction)
- Online marketing effectiveness (channel behaviour – page impressions, visitors, repeat visits, conversion rates).

Control

The control element of the e-marketing plan can be achieved through a combination of traditional techniques such as marketing research to obtain customer views and opinions and novel techniques such as analysis of web-server log files that use technology to monitor whether objectives are achieved. These techniques are reviewed in detail in *Chapter 12* (*p. 605*). Intranets can be used to share information among marketers and consultants within an organization.

Case Study 8.2 The new Napster changes the music marketing mix

This case about the online music subscription service Napster illustrates how different elements of the mix can be varied online. It also highlights success factors for developing an online marketing strategy since Napster's proposition, objectives, competitors and risk factors are all reviewed.

The Napster brand has had a varied history. Its initial incarnation was as the first widely used service for 'free' peer-to-peer (P2P) music sharing. The record companies mounted a legal challenge to Napster due to lost revenues on music sales which eventually forced it to close. But the Napster brand was purchased and its second incarnation (*Figure 8.18*) offers a legal music download service in direct competition with Apple's iTunes. They also offer a music subscription service.

The original Napster

Napster was initially created between 1998 and 1999 by a 19-year-old called Shawn Fanning while he attended Boston's Northeastern University. He wrote the program initially as a way of solving a problem for a friend who wanted to find music downloads more easily online. The name 'Napster' came from Fanning's nickname.

The system was known as 'peer-to-peer' since it enabled music tracks stored on other Internet users' hard disks in MP3 format to be searched and shared with other Internet users. Strictly speaking, the service was not a pure P2P since central services indexed the tracks available and their locations in a similar way to which instant messaging (IM) works.

→

The capability to try a range of tracks proved irresistible and Napster use peaked with 26.4 million users worldwide in February 2001.

It was not long before several major recording companies backed by the RIAA (Recording Industry Association of America) launched a lawsuit. Of course, such an action also gave Napster tremendous PR and more users trialled the service. Some individual bands also responded with lawsuits. Rock band Metallica found that a demo of their song 'I disappear' began circulating on the Napster network and was eventually played on the radio. Other well-known artists who vented their ire on Napster included Madonna and Eminem by posting false 'Cuckoo Egg' files instead of music; Madonna asked the downloader: 'What the fuck do you think you're doing?'! However, not all artists felt the service was negative for them. UK band Radiohead pre-released some tracks of their album *Kid A* on to Napster and subsequently became Number 1 in the US despite failing to achieve this previously.

Eventually, as a result of legal action an injunction was issued on 5 March 2001 ordering Napster to cease trading in copyrighted material. Napster complied with this injunction, but tried to do a deal with the record companies to pay past copyright fees and to turn the service into a legal subscription service.

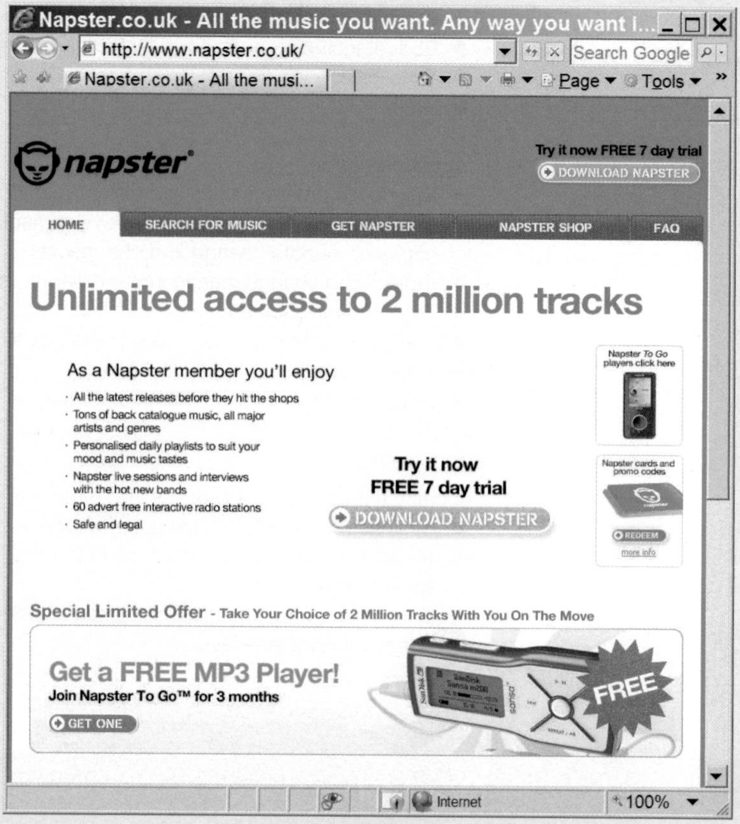

Figure 8.18 Napster (www.napster.co.uk)

In the following year, a deal was agreed with German media company Bertelsmann AG to purchase Napster's assets for $8 million as part of an agreement when Napster filed for Chapter 11 bankruptcy in the United States. This sale was blocked and the web site closed. Eventually, the Napster brand was purchased by Roxio, Inc. which used the brand to rebrand their PressPlay service.

Since this time, other P2P services such as Gnutella, Grokster and Kazaa prospered, which have been more difficult for the copyright owners to pursue in court; however, many individuals have now been sued in the US and Europe and the association of these services with spyware and adware has damaged them, which has reduced the popularity of these services.

New Napster in 2005

Fast-forward to 2005 and Napster now has around 410,000 subscribers in the United States, Canada and the United Kingdom who pay up to £14.95 each month to gain access to about 1.5 million songs. The company is seeking to launch in other countries such as Japan through partnerships.

The online music download environment has also changed with legal music downloading propelled through increasing adoption of broadband, the success of Apple iTunes and its portable music player, the iPod, which by 2005 had achieved around half a billion sales.

Napster gains its main revenues from online subscriptions and permanent music downloads. The Napster service offers subscribers on-demand access to over 2 million tracks that can be streamed or downloaded as well as the ability to purchase individual tracks or albums on an *à la carte* basis. Subscription and permanent download fees are paid by end-user customers in advance via credit card, online payment systems or redemption of pre-paid cards, gift certificates or promotional codes. Napster also periodically licenses merchandising rights and resells hardware that its end-users use to store and replay their music.

BBC (2005) estimated that the global music market is now worth $33 billion (£18.3 billion) a year while the online music market accounted for around 5% of all sales in the first half of 2005. Napster (2005), quoting Forrester Research, estimates that United States purchases of downloadable digital music will exceed $1.9 billion by 2007 and that revenues from online music subscription services such as Napster will exceed $800 million by 2007.

BBC (2005) reports Brad Duea, president of Napster, as saying:

> *The number one brand attribute at the time Napster was shut down was innovation. The second highest characteristic was actually 'free'. The difference now is that the number one attribute is still innovation. Free is now way down on the list. People are able to search for more music than was ever possible at retail, even in the largest megastore.*

The Napster proposition

Napster subscribers can listen to as many tracks as they wish which are contained within the catalogue of over 1 million tracks (the service is sometimes described as 'all you can eat' rather than '*à la carte*'). Napster users can listen to tracks on any compatible device that includes Windows Digital Rights Management software, which includes MP3 players, computers, PDAs and mobile phones.

Duea describes Napster as an 'experience' rather than a retailer. He says this because of features available such as:

- Napster recommendations
- Napster Radio based around songs by particular artists
- Napster Radio playlists based on the songs you have downloaded
- Swapping playlists and recommendations with other users.

iTunes and Napster are probably the two highest-profile services, but they have a quite different model of operating. There are no subscribers to iTunes, where users purchase songs either on a per-track basis or in the form of albums. By mid-2005, over half a billion tracks had been purchased on Napster. Some feel that iTunes locks people into purchasing Apple hardware; as one would expect, Duea of Napster says that Steve Jobs of Apple 'has tricked people into buying a hardware trap'.

But Napster's subscription model has also been criticized since it is a service where subscribers do not 'own' the music unless they purchase it at additional cost, for example to burn it to CD. The music is theirs to play either on a PC or on a portable player, but for only as long as they continue to subscribe to Napster. So it could be argued that Napster achieves lock-in in another form and requires a different approach to music ownership than some of its competitors.

Napster strategy

Napster (2005) describe their strategy as follows. The overall objective is to become the 'leading global provider of consumer digital music services'. They see these strategic initiatives as being important to achieving this:

- *Continue to Build the Napster Consumer Brand* – as well as increasing awareness of the Napster brand identity, this also includes promoting the subscription service which encourages discovery of new music. Napster (2005) say 'We market our Napster service directly to consumers through an integrated offline and online marketing program consistent with the existing strong awareness and perception of the Napster brand. The marketing message is focused on our subscription service, which differentiates our offering from those of many of our competitors. Offline marketing channels include television (including direct-response TV), radio and print advertising. Our online marketing program includes advertising placements on a number of web sites (including affiliate partners) and search engines.'
- *Continue to Innovate by Investing in New Services and Technologies* – this initiative encourages support of a wide range of platforms from portable MP3 players, PCs, cars, mobile phones, etc. The large technical team in Napster shows the importance of this strategy. In the longer term, access to other forms of content such as video may be offered. Napster seems to view their ability to compete as depending substantially upon their intellectual property. They have a number of patents issued, but are also in dispute with other organizations over their patents.
- *Continue to Pursue and Execute Strategic Partnerships* – Napster has already entered strategic partnerships with technology companies (Microsoft and Intel), hardware companies (iRiver, Dell, Creative, Toshiba and IBM), retailers (Best Buy, Blockbuster, Radio Shack, Dixons Group, The Link, PC World, Currys, Target), and others (Molson, Miller, Energizer, Nestlé).
- *Continue to Pursue Strategic Acquisitions and Complementary Technologies* – this is another route to innovation and developing new services.

Customers

Register (2005) reported that in the UK, by mid-2005, Napster UK's 750,000 users had downloaded or streamed 55m tracks since the service launched in May 2004. The company said 80 per cent of its subscribers are over the age of 25, and half of them have kids. Some three-quarters of them are male. Its subscribers buy more music online than folk who buy one-off downloads do and research shows that one in five of them no longer buy CDs, apparently.

Distribution

Napster's online music services are sold directly to end-users through the web site (www.napster.com). Affiliate networks and universities have procured site licences (in the US, a significant proportion of subscribers are university users). Prepaid cards are also available through retail partners such as Dixons in the UK, who also promote the service.

Napster also bundle its service with hardware manufacturers such as iRiver, Dell, Creative Labs, Gateway and Samsung.

→

Competition

Napster see their competitors for online music services in the US as Apple Computer's iTunes, Amazon, RealNetworks, Inc.'s Rhapsody, Yahoo! Unlimited, Sony Connect, AOL Music, MusicNet and MusicNow. In the UK, in 2005, new services with a subscription model were launched by retailers HMV and Virgin. They expect other competitors such MTV Networks to enter the market soon.

Napster (2005) believe that the main competitive factors affecting their market include programming and features, price and performance, quality of customer support, compatibility with popular hardware devices and brand.

Employees

As of 31 March, 2005, Napster had 135 employees, of which 10 directly supported the online music service (maintaining content and providing customer care), 25 were in sales and marketing, 63 were in engineering and product development and 37 were in finance, administration and operations. The costs of managing these staff is evident in *Table 8.6*.

Risk factors

In their annual report submission to the United States Securities and Exchange Commission, Napster is required to give its risk factors, which also give an indication of success factors for the business. Napster (2005) summarizes the main risk factors as follows:

1. The success of our Napster service depends upon our ability to add new subscribers and reduce churn.
2. Our online music distribution business has lower margins than our former consumer software products business. Costs of our online music distribution business as a percentage of the revenue generated by that business are higher than those of our former consumer software products business. The cost of third-party content, in particular, is a substantial portion of revenues we receive from subscribers and end users and is unlikely to decrease significantly over time as a percentage of revenue.
3. We rely on the value of the Napster brand, and our revenues could suffer if we are not able to maintain its high level of recognition in the digital music sector.
4. We face significant competition from traditional retail music distributors, from emerging paid online music services delivered electronically such as ours, and from 'free' peer-to-peer services.
5. Online music distribution services in general are new and rapidly evolving and may not prove to be a profitable or even viable business model.
6. We rely on content provided by third parties, which may not be available to us on commercially reasonable terms or at all.
7. We must provide digital rights management solutions that are acceptable to both content providers and consumers.
8. Our business could be harmed by a lack of availability of popular content.
9. Our success depends on our music service's interoperability with our customer's music playback hardware.
10. We may not successfully develop new products and services.
11. We must maintain and add to our strategic marketing relationships in order to be successful.
12. The growth of our business depends on the increased use of the Internet for communications, electronic commerce and advertising.
13. If broadband technologies do not become widely available or widely adopted, our online music distri-

Table 8.6 Summary of Napster finances from Napster (2005)

	Year ended 31 March	
(in thousands, except per share amounts)	*2005*	*2004*
Net revenues	46,729	11,964
Cost of revenues	37,550	10,530
Gross profit	9,179	1,434
Operating expenses:		
Research and development	12,107	11,940
Sales and marketing	39,215	15,647
General and administrative	23,316	21,217
Restructuring charges	–	1,119
Amortization of intangible assets	1,936	2,172
Stock-based compensation charges(1)	676	904
Total operating expenses	77,250	52,999
Loss from continuing operations	(68,071)	(51,565)
Other income, net	1,091	634
Loss before provision for income taxes	(66,980)	(50,931)
Income tax benefit	15,547	4,515
Loss from continuing operations, after provision for income taxes	(51,433)	(46,416)
Net loss	$ (29,506) $	(44,413)

bution services may not achieve broad market acceptance, and our business may be harmed.

14 Our network is subject to security and stability risks that could harm our business and reputation and expose us to litigation or liability.

15 If we fail to manage expansion effectively, we may not be able to successfully manage our business, which could cause us to fail to meet our customer demand or to attract new customers, which would adversely affect our revenue.

16 We may be subject to intellectual property infringement claims, such as those claimed by SightSound Technologies, which are costly to defend and could limit our ability to use certain technologies in the future.

Finances

Despite growth in subscribers and revenue, Napster has experienced significant net losses since its inception and according to the SEC filing (Napster, 2005), 'we expect to incur net losses for at least the next twelve months and likely continue to experience net losses thereafter'. Since 1 April 2003 Napster has incurred approximately $97.8 million of after-tax losses from continuing operations. A summary of the finances is presented in *Table 8.6*.

Sources: BBC (2005), Napster (2005), Wikipedia (2005), *Register* (2005) and *Wired* (2005). Reprinted by kind permission of Napster, LLC. Napster disclaims any obligation to update or correct any information provided here.

Question

Assess how Napster competes with traditional and online music providers by reviewing the approaches it uses for different elements of the marketing mix.

Summary

1 E-marketing is the application of technology to achieve marketing objectives, defined by the Chartered Institute of Marketing as: '*the management process responsible for identifying, anticipating and satisfying customer requirements profitably*'.

2 E-marketing can be considered a subset of e-business and is equivalent to sell-side e-commerce.

3 An e-marketing plan is often developed separately from an e-business strategy. The SOSTAC™ framework is used to introduce the elements of an e-marketing plan.

4 Situation analysis – involves a consideration of the external environment with the emphasis on levels of customer access to the Internet, benchmarking of competitors and new entrants.

5 Objective setting – a key objective is setting the online revenue contribution or the percentage of sales that will be achieved online. For companies where direct sales are not practical because of the nature of the product companies may set objectives for how the web will affect marketing communications, customer service and cost reductions.

6 Strategies – through evaluating the suitability of product for direct sale a company may define a replacement (product suitable for direct sale, e.g. airline tickets) or complementary strategy (product unsuitable for direct sale, e.g. FMCG or consultancy services). Replacement strategies may involve changing distribution networks. Complementary strategies will involve using the Internet as an additional marketing communications channel.

7 Tactics – e-marketing tactics can be reviewed through varying the elements of the marketing mix: Price, Place, Product, Promotion, People, Processes and Physical evidence.

→

8 Actions – the planning of e-marketing strategy by identifying resources and timescales.

9 Control – control can be achieved through monitoring customer satisfaction and channel performance via the web site and traditional channels.

Exercises

Self-assessment questions

1 Explain the link between e-marketing and e-business and why they may be considered separately.

2 Outline the stages in a strategic e-marketing planning process, for each stage noting two aspects that are of particular importance for e-marketing.

3 What is the Internet contribution and what is its relevance to e-marketing strategy?

4 What factors will govern the Internet contribution that is set for a given organization?

5 Why and how should a company approach benchmarking of online competitors?

6 Describe what is meant by a complementary and replacement Internet channel strategy and give examples of products for which companies follow a particular approach.

7 Summarize new opportunities to vary the marketing mix that arise through deploying the Internet.

8 How can online and offline techniques be used in the control stage of strategy?

Essay and discussion questions

1 Select a particular market sector and assess the past, current and future customer use of the Internet as a medium to select and buy products.

2 Develop an outline strategic e-marketing plan for an organization with which you are familiar.

3 'Traditional strategic planning has no relevance for the start-up company given the dynamism of the marketplace.' Discuss.

4 Assess the value and importance of the Internet contribution in setting e-marketing objectives in relation to other possible objectives.

5 Explain how the e-business can make use of technology to monitor and control its operations.

Examination questions

1 Outline the stages involved in developing a strategic e-marketing plan.

2 Explain what is meant by the Internet contribution and outline how companies will decide on a realistic objective.

3 What opportunities may there be to vary the Price and Place components of the marketing mix when delivering services through the Internet?

4 What is a complementary Internet channel strategy and for which companies will this be most appropriate?

5 What different aspects of e-marketing should be monitored as part of controlling e-marketing? Name three examples of how technology can be used to assist monitoring.

6 Explain the strategic options available for a company currently selling the majority of its products in a single country for product and marketplace positioning.

7 What do the concepts of reintermediation and disintermediation imply for the tactics a company employs for the Promotion and Place elements of the marketing mix?

8 Outline how the electronic medium requires different tactics for effective marketing communications.

References

Aaker, D. and Joachimsthaler, E. (2000) *Brand Leadership*. Free Press, New York.

Agrawal, V., Arjona, V. and Lemmens, R. (2001) E-performance: the path to rational exuberance. *McKinsey Quarterly*, no. 1, 31–43.

Allen, E. and Fjermestad, J. (2001) E-commerce marketing strategies: a framework and case analysis. *Logistics Information Management*, 14 (1/2), 14–23.

Ansoff, H. (1957) Strategies for diversification. *Harvard Business Review*, September–October, 113–24.

Baker, W., Marn, M. and Zawada, C. (2001) Price smarter on the Net. *Harvard Business Review*, February, 2–7.

Bazett, M., Bowden, I., Love, J. Street, R. and Wilson, H. (2005) Measuring multichannel effectiveness using the balanced scorecard. *Interactive Marketing*, 6(3), 224–31.

BBC (2005) Napster boss on life after piracy. By Derren Waters, 22 August. http://news.bbc.co.uk/1/hi/entertainment/music/4165868.stm.

Booms, B. and Bitner, M. (1981) Marketing strategies and organization structure for service firms. In *Marketing of Services*, eds J. Donelly and W. George, American Marketing Association, New York.

BrandNewWorld (2004) AOL Research published at www.brandnewworld.co.uk.

Chaffey, D. (2000) Achieving success in Internet marketing. *Marketing Review*, 1, 1–23.

Chaffey, D., Mayer, R., Johnston, K. and Ellis-Chadwick, F. (2006) *Internet Marketing: Strategy, Implementation and Practice*, 3rd edn. Financial Times Prentice Hall, Harlow.

Chase, L. (1998) *Essential Business Tactics for the Net*. Wiley, New York.

Christodoulides, G. and de Chernatony, L. (2004) Dimensionalising on- and offline brands' composite equity. *Journal of Product and Brand Management*, 13(3), 168–79.

Dayal, S., Landesberg, H. and Zeissberg, M. (2000) Building digital brands. *McKinsey Quarterly*, no. 2.

de Chernatony, L. (2001) Succeeding with brands on the Internet. *Journal of Brand Management*, 8(3), 186–95.

de Chernatony, L. and McDonald, M. (1992) *Creating Powerful Brands*. Butterworth-Heinemann, Oxford.

Deighton, J. (1996) The future of interactive marketing. *Harvard Business Review*, November–December, 151–62.

Deise, M., Nowikow, C., King, P. and Wright, A. (2000) *Executive's Guide to E-Business. From Tactics to Strategy*. Wiley, New York.

de Kare-Silver, M. (2000) *EShock 2000. The Electronic Shopping Revolution: Strategies for Retailers and Manufacturers*. Macmillan, London.

Dibb, S., Simkin, L., Pride, W. and Ferrell, O. (2000) *Marketing. Concepts and Strategies*, 4th edn. Houghton Mifflin, Boston.

easyJet (2003) easyJet Online Infopack. Available at www.easyjet.com/EN/about/infopack_internet.html.

E-consultancy (2005) Managing an E-commerce team. Integrating digital marketing into your organisation. 60-page report. Author: Dave Chaffey. Available from www.e-consultancy.com.

Emiliani, V. (2001) Business-to-business online auctions: key issues for purchasing process improvement. *Supply Chain Management: An International Journal*, 5(4), 176–86.

Evans, P. and Wurster, T. (1999) Getting real about virtual commerce. *Harvard Business Review*, November, 84–94.

Frazier, G. (1999) Organising and managing channels of distribution. *Journal of the Academy of Marketing Science*, 27(2), 222–40.

Ghosh, S. (1998) Making business sense of the Internet. *Harvard Business Review*, March–April, 126–35.

Hoffman, D.L. and Novak, T.P. (1997) A new marketing paradigm for electronic commerce. *The Information Society*, Special issue on electronic commerce, 13 (January–March), 43–54.

Houston, F. (1986) The marketing concept: what it is and what it is not. *Journal of Marketing*, 50 (April), 81–7.

Hughes, S. (2001) Market orientation and the response of UK financial services companies to changes in market conditions as a result of e-commerce. *International Journal of Bank Marketing*, 19(6), 222–31.

IEE (2003) Amazon.com recommendations: item-to-item collaborative filtering. *Internet Computing*, January–February, 76–80. Available online at: http://agents.csie.ntu.edu.tw/~yjhsu/courses/u2010/papers/Amazon%20Recommendations.pdf.

Jaworski, B. and Kohli, A. (1993) Market orientation: antecedents and consequences. *Journal of Marketing*, July, 53–70.

Jevons, C. and Gabbot, M. (2000) Trust, brand equity and brand reality in Internet business relationships: an interdisciplinary approach. *Journal of Marketing Management*, 16, 619–34.

Johnson, E., Moe, W., Fader, P., Bellman, S. and Lohse, G. (2004) On the depth and dynamics of online search behavior. *Management Science*, 50(3), 299–308.

Kumar, N. (1999) Internet distribution strategies: dilemmas for the incumbent. *Financial Times*, Special Issue on Mastering Information Management, no. 7, Electronic Commerce.

Lautenborn, R. (1990) New marketing litany: 4Ps passes, 4Cs takeovers. *Advertising Age*, 1 October, 26.

McCarthy, J. (1960) *Basic Marketing: A Managerial Approach*. Irwin, Homewood, IL.

McDonald, M. (1999) Strategic marketing planning: theory and practice. In *The CIM Marketing Book*, 4th edn, ed. M. Baker. Butterworth-Heinemann, Oxford, 50–77.

McDonald, M. and Wilson, H. (1999) *E-Marketing: Improving Marketing Effectiveness in a Digital World*. Financial Times Prentice Hall, Harlow.

Napster (2005) Annual Report, pubished at Investor relations site (http://investor.napster.com).

Pitt, L., Berthorn, P., Watson, R. and Ewing, M. (2001) Pricing strategy and the Net. *Business Horizons*. March–April, 45–54.

Quelch, J. and Klein, L. (1996) The Internet and international marketing. *Sloan Management Review*, Spring, 60–75.

Register (2005) Napster UK touts subscriber numbers. *The Register*, Tony Smith, 5 September. www.theregister.co.uk/2005/09/05/napster_numbers

Ries, A. and Ries, L. (2000) *The 11 Immutable Laws of Internet Branding*. HarperCollins Business, London.

Seybold, P. (1999) *Customers.com*. Century Business Books, Random House, London.

Simon, Herbert A. (1957) *Models of Man*. Wiley, New York.

Smith, P. (1999) *Marketing Communications: An Integrated Approach*, 2nd edn. Kogan Page, London.

Smith, P. and Chaffey, D. (2001) *EMarketing Excellence – at the Heart of EBusiness*. Butterworth-Heinemann, Oxford.

Valentin, E. (1996) The marketing concept and the conceptualization of marketing strategy. *Journal of Marketing Theory and Practice*, Fall, 16–27.

Varianini, V. and Vaturi, D. (2000) Marketing lessons from e-failures. *McKinsey Quarterly*, no. 4, 86–97.

Wikipedia (2005) Napster. Wikipedia. Wikipedia entry at http://en.wikipedia.org/wiki/Napster.

Wired (2005) The day Napster died. *Wired*. www.wired.com/news/mp3/0,1285, 52540,00.html.

Further reading

Bickerton, P., Bickerton, M. and Pardesi, U. (2000) *CyberMarketing*, 2nd edn. Butterworth-Heinemann, Oxford, Chartered Institute of Marketing series. Considers each element of the marketing mix in a separate chapter.

Chaffey, D., Mayer, R., Johnston, K. and Ellis-Chadwick, F. (2006) *Internet Marketing: Strategy, Implementation and Practice*, 3rd edn. Financial Times Prentice Hall, Harlow. Chapters 2–5 cover e-marketing strategy.

Wilson, H., Hobbs, M., Dolder, C. and McDonald, M. (2004) Optimising multiple channels. *Interactive Marketing*, January–March, 252–68. A review of how companies have to select the best alternative channels.

Web links

Clickz (www.clickz.com/) Has columns on e-mail marketing, e-mail marketing optimization and e-mail marketing case studies.

DaveChaffey.com (www.davechaffey.com/Internet-Marketing) A blog of links and articles about developments in e-marketing and digital communications structured according to the chapter in this book.

E-consultancy (www.e-consultancy.com) Best-practice sections on different e-communications tools and newsletter features interviews with e-commerce practitioners.

Marketing Sherpa (www.marketingsherpa.com) Articles and links on Internet marketing communications including e-mail and online advertising.

What's New in Marketing (www.wnim.com) A monthly newsletter from the Chartered Institute of Marketing including many e-marketing features.

9 Customer relationship management

Chapter at a glance

Main topics

Web support

The following additional case studies are available at www.pearsoned.co.uk/chaffey

- Variations in online buyer behaviour and loyalty
- Worldwide demand for CRM applications
- Digital loyalty networks

The site also contains a range of study material designed to help improve your results.

Learning outcomes

After completing this chapter the reader should be able to:

- **Outline different methods of acquiring customers via electronic media**
- **Evaluate different buyer behaviour amongst online customers**
- **Describe techniques for retaining customers and cross- and up-selling using new media.**

Management issues

Customer relationship management involves these management issues:

- **What is the balance between online and offline investment for customer acquisition?**
- **What technologies can be used to build and maintain the online relationship?**
- **How do we deliver superior service quality to build and maintain relationships?**

Links to other chapters

The main related chapters are:

- *Chapter 4* – CRM techniques are constrained by social, legal and ethical factors;
- *Chapter 5* – CRM supports e-business strategy;
- *Chapter 8* – CRM is one of the tactics aimed at fulfilling the objectives defined in the e-marketing plan.

Introduction

Customer relationship management (CRM)
An approach to building and sustaining long-term business with customers.

The application of technology to achieve customer relationship management (CRM) is a key element of e-business. Building long-term relationships with customers is essential for any sustainable business. Failure to build relationships largely caused the failures of many dot-coms following huge expenditure on customer acquisition as explained in *Chapters 2* and *5*. The importance of customer retention to long-term profitability is well known from modelling of the type referred to in *Chapter 4*. But research summarized by Reicheld and Schefter (2000) shows that acquiring online customers is so expensive (20–30 per cent higher than for traditional businesses) that start-up companies may remain unprofitable for at least two to three years. The research also shows that by retaining just 5 per cent more customers, online companies can boost their profits by 25 per cent to 95 per cent. They say:

> *but if you can keep customers loyal, their profitability accelerates much faster than in traditional businesses. It costs you less and less to service them.*

Note that the relationship between customer loyalty and profitability has been questioned, notably by Reinartz and Kumar (2002), who discovered through analysis of four company databases that:

> *there was little or no evidence to suggest that customers who purchase steadily from a company over time are necessarily cheaper to serve, less price sensitive, or particularly effective at bringing in new business.*

They have suggested that companies that base their marketing focus on the simple assumption that loyal customers are the most profitable will miss opportunities in targeting other potentially profitable customers.

This chapter evaluates different techniques to both initiate and build relationships with customers by using a combination of online and offline techniques. The chapter is structured around the different stages of the classic customer lifecycle of Select, Acquire, Retain, Extend, as is shown in *Figure 9.1*. The figure emphasizes the importance of integrating customer relationship management activities across the appropriate channels.

Customer lifecycle
The stages each customer will pass through in a long-term relationship through acquisition, retention and extension. There are more detailed stages within this.

An alternative view of how CRM can be achieved via a web presence (although e-mail is also important) is the approach Yahoo! has used to build a profitable site. The managers of the site reported at industry conferences that an effective web site should have three characteristics:

- *Magnetic*. Acquisition of visitors by promotion and by making the site attractive.
- *Sticky*. Retention – keeping customers on the site once they arrive and encouraging them to engage in revenue-generating activities.

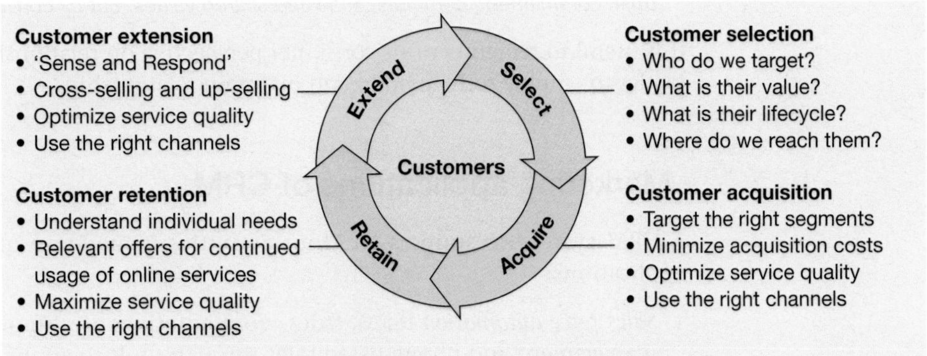

Figure 9.1 **The four classic marketing activities of customer relationship management**

- *Elastic*. Extension – persuading customers to return, particularly for revenue-generating activities.

The four marketing activities that comprise CRM involve the following.

1. **Customer selection** means defining the types of customers that a company will market to. It means identifying different groups of customers for which to develop offerings for and to target during acquisition, retention and extension. Different ways of segmenting customers by value and by their detailed lifecycle with the customer are reviewed. From an e-business perspective, as we see in *Chapter 5*, we may want to selectively target customer types who have adopted e-channels.
2. **Customer acquisition** refers to marketing activities intended to form relationships with new customers while minimizing acquisition costs and targeting high-value customers. Service quality and selecting the right channels for different customers are important at this stage and throughout the lifecycle.
3. **Customer retention** refers to the marketing activities taken by an organization to keep its existing customers. Identifying relevant offerings based on their individual needs and detailed position in the customer lifecycle (e.g. number/value of purchases) is key.
4. **Customer extension** refers to increasing the depth or range of products that a customer purchases from a company. This is often referred to as 'customer development'.

There are a range of customer extension techniques for CRM that are particularly important to online retailers:

(a) **Re-sell**. Selling similar products to existing customers – particularly important in some B2B context as rebuys or modified re-buys.
(b) **Cross-sell**. Sell additional products which may be closely related to the original purchase, but not necessarily so.
(c) **Up-sell**. A sub-set of cross-selling, but in this case, selling more expensive products.
(d) **Reactivation**. Customers who have not purchased for some time, or have lapsed, can be encouraged to purchase again.
(e) **Referrals**. Generating sales from recommendations from existing customers. For example, Member-get-Member deals.

Note that although the concept of CRM is prevalent in current marketing thinking and provides a valuable framework for tactics to increase loyalty and profitability, it should be noted that it may not accurately reflect the way the customer views their dealings with a company. Consumers may simply see their dealings with an organization as an exchange relationship and will not believe that they are tied to any company, i.e they may say 'I don't want a relationship'. O'Malley and Tynan (2001) note that the concept of a long-term relationship or partnership may be more readily applied to B2B marketing than consumer marketing. They say consumers

> *do not consider this false intimacy an interpersonal relationship. It is not driven primarily by trust, commitment, communication and shared values, but by convenience and self-interest.*

It is useful to remember this consumer perspective on relationships when considering tactics to employ to help build and maintain relationships.

Marketing applications of CRM

A CRM system to support the four activities is made up of different marketing applications:

1. *Sales force automation* (SFA). Sales representatives are supported in their account management and phone-based sales through tools to arrange and record customer enquiries and visits.

2 *Customer service management.* Representatives in contact centres respond to customer requests for information by using an intranet to access databases containing information on the customer, products and previous queries.
3 *Managing the sales process.* This can be achieved through e-commerce sites, or in a B2B context by supporting sales representatives by recording the sales process (SFA).
4 *Campaign management.* Managing ad, direct mail, e-mail and other campaigns.
5 *Analysis.* Through technologies such as data warehouses and approaches such as data mining, which are explained later in the chapter, customers' characteristics, their purchase behaviour and campaigns can be analysed in order to optimize the marketing mix.

What is e-CRM?

The interactive nature of the web combined with e-mail communications provides an ideal environment in which to develop customer relationships, and databases provide a foundation for storing information about the relationship and providing information to strengthen it by improved, personalized services. This online approach to CRM is often known as 'e-CRM' or 'electronic customer relationship management', and it is on this we focus in this chapter. Although *Figure 9.1* refers to the whole customer lifecycle, typically it is used to refer to customer retention and extension activities.

Electronic customer relationship management
Using digital communications technologies to maximize sales to existing customers and encourage continued usage of online services.

It is difficult to state where CRM ends and e-CRM starts, since today they both make extensive use of digital technology and media. This is what Smith and Chaffey (2005) say:

> *What is e-CRM? Customer Relations Management with an 'e'? Ultimately, E-CRM cannot be separated from CRM, it needs to be integrated and seamlessly. However, many organisations do have specific E-CRM initiatives or staff responsible for E-CRM. Both CRM and E-CRM are not just about technology and databases, it's not just a process or a way of doing things, it requires, in fact, a complete customer culture.*

More specifically, we can say that important e-CRM challenges and activities which require management are:

- Using the *web site for customer development* from generating leads through to conversion to an online or offline sale using e-mail and web-based information to encourage purchase
- *Managing e-mail list quality* (coverage of e-mail addresses and integration of customer profile information from other databases to enable targeting)
- Applying *e-mail marketing* to support upsell and cross-sell
- *Data mining* to improve targeting
- With a web site with personalization or mass customization facilities to automatically recommend the 'Next-best product'
- Providing *online customer service facilities* (such as Frequently Asked Questions, Call-back and Chat support) that help achieve conversion to sale
- Managing *online service quality* to ensure that first-time buyers have a great customer experience that encourages them to buy again
- Managing the *multi-channel customer experience* as customers use different media as part of the buying process and customer lifecycle.

Personalization
Web-based personalization involves delivering customized content for the individual through web pages, e-mail or push technology.

Mass customization
Mass customization is the creation of tailored marketing messages or products for individual customers or groups of customers typically using technology to retain the economies of scale and the capacity of mass marketing or production.

To help understand the scope of e-marketing, you may also find *Figure 10.2* useful. This summarizes different marketing activities that need to be completed by an online retailer, structured according to customer acquisition, conversion and retention activities.

Customer-centric marketing
The approach to Internet marketing function is based on customer behaviour within the target audience and then seeks to fulfill the needs and wants of each individual customer.

Sense and respond communications
Delivering timely, relevant communications to customers as part of a contact strategy based on assessment of their position in the customer lifecycle and monitoring specific interactions with a company's web site, e-mails and staff.

Sharma and Sheth (2004) have stressed the importance of a trend from mass marketing to what is now widely known as 'one-to-one' or '**customer-centric marketing**' (although many would regard this as a tautology since the modern marketing concept places the customer at the heart of marketing activity). They note that e-channels can have advantages in terms of delivering relevant messages and offers to customers at relatively low cost. It can also be used to support customization of products. These authors give the example of the Dell model where each PC is manufactured and distributed 'on demand' according to the need of a specific customer. This is an example of what they refer to as 'reverse marketing' with the change on marketing execution from product supply to customer need. Another aspect of this transformation is that online, web marketers can track the past and current behaviours of customers in order to customize communications to encourage future purchases. This approach, which is another aspect of reverse marketing and also a key concept with e-CRM, can be characterized as '**sense and respond communications**'. The classic example of this is the personalization facilities provided by Amazon where personal recommendations are provided. Companies can also arrange triggered or follow-up e-mail activity after a customer event such as a quote (as used by insurer More Than, www.morethan.com) or an abandoned shopping basket (as used by Tesco.com) to encourage purchase.

Benefits of e-CRM

Using the Internet for relationship marketing involves integrating the customer database with web sites to make the relationship targeted and personalized. Through doing this marketing can be improved as follows.

- *Targeting more cost-effectively*. Traditional targeting, for direct mail for instance, is often based on mailing lists compiled according to criteria that mean that not everyone contacted is in the target market. For example, a company wishing to acquire new affluent consumers may use postcodes to target areas with appropriate demographics, but within the postal district the population may be heterogeneous. The result of poor targeting will be low response rates, perhaps less than 1 per cent. The Internet has the benefit that the list of contacts is *self-selecting* or pre-qualified. A company will only aim to build relationships with those who have visited a web site and expressed an interest in its products by registering their name and address. The act of visiting the web site and browsing indicates a target customer. Thus the approach to acquiring new customers with whom to build relationships is fundamentally different, as it involves attracting the customers to the web site, where the company provides an offer to make them register.
- *Achieve mass customization of the marketing messages* (and possibly the product). This tailoring process is described in a subsequent section. Technology makes it possible to send tailored e-mails at much lower costs than is possible with direct mail and also to provide tailored web pages to smaller groups of customers (micro-segments).
- *Increase depth, breadth and nature of relationship*. The nature of the Internet medium enables more information to be supplied to customers as required. For example, special pages such as Dell Premier can be set up to provide customers with specific information. The nature of the relationship can be changed in that contact with a customer can be made more frequently. The frequency of contact with the customer can be determined by customers – whenever they have the need to visit their personalized pages – or they can be contacted by e-mail by the company according to their communications preferences.

- *A learning relationship can be achieved using different tools throughout the customer lifecycle.* For example, tools summarize products purchased on site and the searching behaviour that occurred before these products were bought; online feedback forms about the site or products are completed when a customer requests free information; questions asked through forms or e-mails to the online customer service facilities; online questionnaires asking about product category interests and opinions on competitors; new product development evaluation – commenting on prototypes of new products.
- *Lower cost.* Contacting customers by e-mail or through their viewing web pages costs less than using physical mail, but perhaps more importantly, information only needs to be sent to those customers who have expressed a preference for it, resulting in fewer mail-outs. Once personalization technology has been purchased, much of the targeting and communications can be implemented automatically.

Permission marketing

Permission marketing
Customers agree (opt in) to be involved in an organization's marketing activities, usually as a result of an incentive.

Interruption marketing
Marketing communications that disrupt customers' activities.

To understand the thinking and practice behind e-CRM, it is useful to relate it to the concept of permission marketing since this has been a driving force for investment in CRM. 'Permission marketing' is a term coined by Seth Godin. Godin (1999) notes that while research used to show we were bombarded by 500 marketing messages a day, with the advent of the web and digital TV this has now increased to over 3,000 a day! From an organization's viewpoint, this leads to a dilution in the effectiveness of the messages – how can the communications of any one company stand out? From the customer's viewpoint, time is seemingly in ever-shorter supply, customers are losing patience and expect reward for their attention, time and information. Godin refers to the traditional approach as 'interruption marketing'. Permission marketing is about seeking the customer's permission before engaging them in a relationship and providing something in exchange. The classic exchange is based on information or entertainment – a B2B site can offer a free report in exchange for a customer sharing their e-mail address which will be used to maintain a dialogue, while a B2C site can offer a newsletter with valuable content and offers.

Debate 9.1

Is permission marketing the future?

'In the future, all marketing communications, regardless of medium, will be permission-based.'

From an e-commerce perspective, we can think of a customer agreeing to engage in a relationship when they agree by checking a box on a web form to indicate that they agree to receiving further communications from a company. This is referred to as 'opt-in'. This is preferable to opt-out, the situation where a customer has to consciously agree not to receive further information. You may recall from *Chapter 4*, that in many countries data protection laws requiring opt-in before customers receive communications and mandatory inclusion of opt-out have now been introduced in an attempt to stop spamming. Effectively, the law is mandating permission marketing as best practice!

Opt-in
A customer proactively agrees to receive further information.

Opt-out
A customer declines the offer to receive further information.

The importance of incentivization in permission marketing has been emphasized by Seth Godin who likens the process of acquisition and retention to dating someone. Godin (1999) suggests that dating the customer involves:

1 Offering the prospect an *incentive* to volunteer.
2 Using the attention offered by the prospect, offer a curriculum over time, teaching the consumer about your product or service.
3 Reinforce the *incentive* to guarantee that the prospect maintains the permission.
4 Offer additional *incentives* to get even more permission from the consumer.
5 Over time, use the permission to change consumer behaviour towards profits.

Notice the importance of incentives at each stage. The use of incentives at the start of the relationship and throughout it are key to successful relationships. As we shall see in a later section, e-mail is very important in permission marketing to maintain the dialogue between company and customer.

Figure 9.2 summarizes the process of permission marketing in an online context. It shows how different methods are used to drive visitors to a web site (1), incentives are then used to profile the customer (2). Subsequent e-mail communications (3) and direct mail (4) are used to encourage repeat visits to the web site for future purchase or to learn more about the customer and increase the information in the profile (5).

An allied concept to permission marketing is a movement that originated in the USA in 1999, known as the Cluetrain manifesto (www.cluetrain.com). The Cluetrain relates to managers at a large organization who are unable or unprepared to listen or respond to the clues from empowered customers demanding better service and response. Clues might include high churn, rising complaints and the success of more responsive competitors. An idea of the thinking of this movement is that push marketing is inappropriate. The authors, Levine *et al.* (2000), say

> *Conversations among human beings sound human. They are conducted in a human voice. Most corporations, on the other hand, only know how to talk in the soothing, humorless monotone of the mission statement, marketing brochure, and your-call-is-important-to-us busy signal. Same old tone, same old lies. No wonder networked markets have no respect for companies unable or unwilling to speak as they do. Corporate firewalls have kept smart*

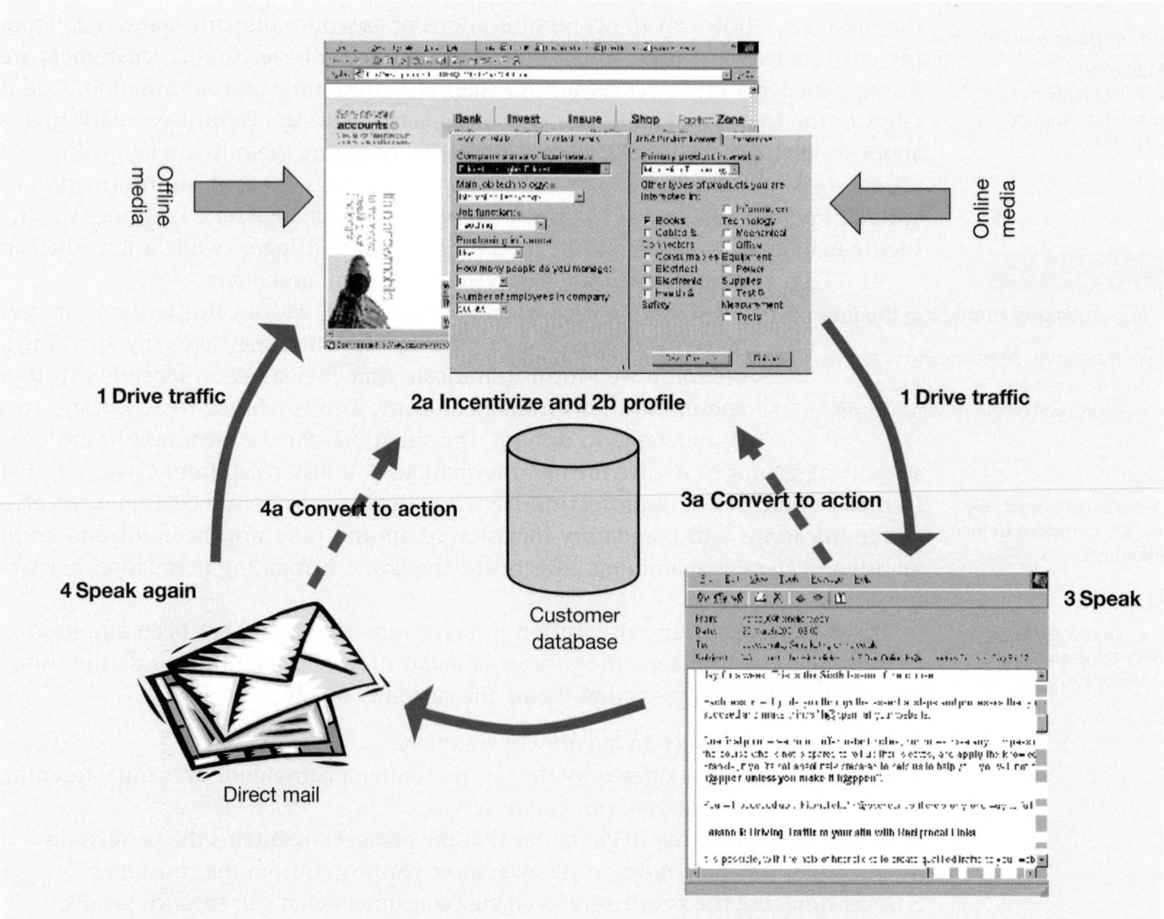

Figure 9.2 A summary of an effective process of online relationship building

employees in and smart markets out. It's going to cause real pain to tear those walls down. But the result will be a new kind of conversation. And it will be the most exciting conversation business has ever engaged in.

It is apparent that the Cluetrain manifesto is encouraging managers to adopt new technology such as Web 2.0 collaborative applications to enable employees of an organization to interact with and listen to their needs in a responsible way. Such techniques include online support forums and online surveys which enable customers to give instant feedback on problems with service quality.

Customer profiling

Qualified lead
Contact information for a customer and an indication of his or her propensity to purchase different products.

Customer profile
Information that can be used to segment a customer.

To engage a customer in an online relationship, the minimum information that needs to be collected in an online form such as in *Figure 9.2* is an e-mail address. This was an initial approach taken by the Peppers and Rogers site (**www.1to1.com**). What we really need, particularly for B2B sites, is a qualified lead that provides us with more information about the customer to help us decide whether that customer is a good prospect who should be targeted with further communications. For B2B this could mean a visit by field sales staff or a follow-up e-mail to arrange this. The Peppers and Rogers site has now been updated to reflect this approach.

To continue the relationship it is essential to build a customer profile that details each customer's product interest, demographics or role in the buying decision. This will affect the type of information and services delivered at the retention stage. For the customer to give this information a company will have to offer an incentive, establish trust and demonstrate credibility. Profiling is also important for selection – to identify potential customers who are likely to be profitable and offer appropriate incentives. Data protection and privacy law sets constraints on what can be collected from the customer, as described in *Chapter 4 (p. 160)*.

Peppers and Rogers (1999) have applied their work on building *one-to-one* relationships with the customer to the web. They suggest the IDIC approach as a framework for using the web effectively to form and build relationships. 'IDIC' represents the following:

1. *Customer identification.* This stresses the need to identify each customer on their first visit and subsequent visits. Common methods for identification are use of cookies or asking the customer to log on to a site.
2. *Customer differentiation.* This refers to building a profile to help segment customers. Characteristics for differentiating customers are described in *Chapter 4 (p. 155)*.
3. *Customer interactions.* These are interactions provided on-site, such as customer service questions or creating a tailored product.
4. *Customization.* This refers to personalization or mass customization of content or e-mails according to the segmentation achieved at the acquisition stage. Approaches for personalization are explained in the section on *customer retention management.*

To consider the practicalities of what is required for customer acquisition in terms of web site design complete *Activity 9.1*. Remember from the section on permission marketing that incentives are key in acquisition and that they should be targeted for selection of the right customers.

Note that although we are suggesting it is vital to capture the registration information, this should not be too 'up-front' since studies reported by Nielsen (2000) show that having to register acts as a barrier to entering sites. So the advice is to delay customer registration as late as possible.

Activity 9.1 **Customer acquisition for the B2B and B2C companies**

Purpose

To identify effective tactics for customer acquisition.

Activity

Visit the site of a B2B company such as RS Components (www.rswww.com) or a B2C company such as (www.virginmega.com) and infer the approach they use to identify customers.

Answers to activities can be found at www.pearsoned.co.uk/chaffey

Conversion marketing

Conversion marketing
Using marketing communications to maximize conversion of potential customers to actual customers and existing customers to repeat customers.

For managers to assess and improve the effectiveness of their customer relationship management implementation, evaluation using the conversion marketing concept is useful. In an online context, this assesses how effective marketing communications are in converting:

- Web browsers or offline audiences to site visitors;
- Site visitors to engaged site visitors who stay on the site and progress beyond the home page;
- Engaged site visitors to prospects (who are profiled for their characteristics and needs);
- Prospects into customers;
- Customers into repeat customers.

A high-level model based on this approach which can be used for planning purposes is presented in *Figure 9.3*. This shows the acquisition part of the process and gives an indication of how the different channels can support each other. At each conversion step, some visitors will switch from one channel to the other, dependent on customers' preferences and marketing messages which encourage customers to switch to other channels for the next conversion step. The dilemma for marketers is that the online channels are cheapest to service, but tend to have a lower conversion rate than traditional channels because of the human element. It follows that it is important to offer phone, live chat or e-mail contact in online channels to help convert customers who need further information or persuading to purchase.

Varianini and Vaturi (2000) suggest that many e-commerce failures have resulted from low conversion as a result of poorly targeted media spending. They suggest the communications mix should be optimized to minimize the cost of acquisition of customers. It can also be suggested that optimization of the conversion to action on-site is important to the success of marketing. Conversion to customer acquisition will be low if the site design, quality of service and marketing communications are not effective in converting visitors to prospects or buyers.

Performance drivers
Critical success factors that govern whether objectives are achieved.

Agrawal *et al.* (2001) have developed a scorecard, assessed using a longitudinal study analysing hundreds of e-commerce sites in the USA and Europe. The scorecard is based on the performance drivers or critical success factors for e-commerce such as the costs for acquisition and retention, conversion rates of visitors to buyers to repeat buyers, together with churn rates. Note that to maximize retention and minimize churn, service-quality-based drivers need to be evaluated.

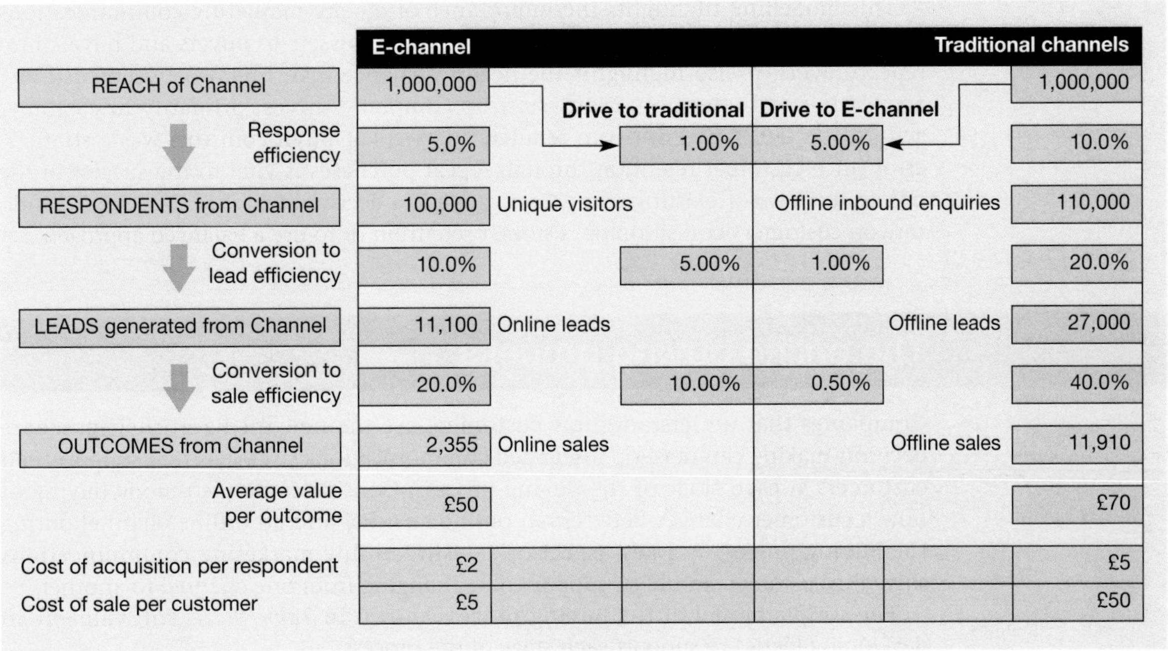

Figure 9.3 **Multi-channel conversion model**

There are three main parts to this scorecard:

1 *Attraction*. Size of visitor's base, visitor acquisition cost and visitor advertising revenue (e.g. media sites).
2 *Conversion*. Customer base, customer acquisition costs, customer conversion rate, number of transactions per customer, revenue per transaction, revenue per customer, customer gross income, customer maintenance cost, customer operating income, customer churn rate, customer operating income before marketing spending.
3 *Retention*. This uses similar measures to those for conversion customers.

The survey performed by Agrawal *et al.* (2001) shows that:

> *companies were successful at luring visitors to their sites, but not at getting these visitors to buy or at turning occasional buyers into frequent ones.*

Agrawal *et al.* (2001) performed a further analysis where they modelled the theoretical change in net present value contributed by an e-commerce site in response to a 10 per cent change in these performance drivers. This shows the relative importance of these drivers, or 'levers' as they refer to them:

Attraction

- Visitor acquisition cost: 0.74% change in Net Present Value (NPV)
- Visitor growth: 3.09% change in NPV.

Conversion

- Customer conversion rate: 0.84% change in NPV
- Revenue per customer: 2.32% change in NPV.

Retention

- Cost of repeat customer: 0.69% change in NPV
- Revenue per repeat customer: 5.78% change in NPV
- Repeat customer churn rate: 6.65% change in NPV
- Repeat customer conversion rate: 9.49% change in NPV.

This modelling highlights the importance of on-site marketing communications and the quality of service delivery in converting browsers to buyers and buyers into repeat buyers. It also highlights the need to balance investment between customer acquisition and retention. Many start-up companies invest primarily in customer acquisition. For failed dot-com retailers such as LetsBuyit.com this was a strategic error since customer retention through repeat purchases is vital to the success of the online service. For existing companies, there is a decision whether to focus expenditure on customer acquisition or customer retention or to use a balanced approach.

The online buying process

Companies that understand how customers use the new media in their purchase decision-making can develop integrated communications strategies that support their customers at each stage of the buying process. Considering mixed-mode buying or how a customer changes between an online channel and an offline channel during the buying process is a key aspect of devising online marketing communications since the customer should be supported in changing from one channel to another.

The simple model of the buying process shown in *Table 9.1* is still valuable in developing tactics to support each stage of the process.

- The relative importance of the Internet in supporting the purchaser through each of the stages of the buying process shown in *Table 9.1* has been illustrated by research by DoubleClick (2003).

Individual preferences for using the web will also differ. Lewis and Lewis (1997) identified five different types of web users who exhibit different searching behaviour according to the purpose of using the web.

- *Directed information-seekers*. Will be looking for product, market or leisure information such as details of their football club's fixtures. This type of user tends to be experienced in using the web and is proficient in using search engines and directories.
- *Undirected information-seekers*. These are the users usually referred to as 'surfers', who like to browse and change sites by following hyperlinks. This group tends to be novice users (but not exclusively so) and they may be more likely to click on banner advertisements. The research in *Figure 9.8* suggests that this behaviour is now less common.
- *Directed buyers*. These buyers are online to purchase specific products. For such users, brokers or cybermediaries who compare product features and prices will be important locations to visit.
- *Bargain hunters*. These users want to use the offers available from sales promotions such as free samples or prizes.
- *Entertainment seekers*. Users looking to interact with the web for enjoyment through entering contests such as quizzes.

These different types of behaviour could be exhibited by the same person in different sessions online, or, less likely, in the same session.

Differences in buyer behaviour in target markets

As explained in *Chapter 4*, in the section *Assessing demand for e-commerce services*, there is great variation in the proportion of user access in different countries. This gives rises to differences in buyer behaviour between different countries or between different segments according to how sophisticated customers are in their use of the Internet.

Table 9.1 Tactics to support customers through different stages of the buying process

Stage	*Tactics*
1 Problem recognition	As the *Focus on marketing communications* section showed, offline advertising and media mentions are important in generating awareness of digital channels as a means by which customers can find, evaluate and purchase products.
2 Information (or supplier) search	We also need to think about different searching behaviours, remembering that surfing, not searching, is more important to groups with a high proportion of non-directed information-seekers such as young adults. By contrast, for the B2B product, directed information-seeking will be the predominant search behaviour. *Figure 9.8* summarizes the relative importance of different techniques for prompting a visit to a web site for research of a purchase.
3 Evaluation	Site content should communicate the features and benefits of the brand in what may be a fleeting visit to the site or an in-depth analysis. We also need to think about how to cater for different customer buying behaviours according to Internet experience.
4 Decision making	To influence decision making other channels can be used to provide mixed-mode messages that reinforce the features and benefits of the product to the customer conveyed on the site. To do this we may need to provide incentives to capture an e-mail or postal address and deliver a more detailed brochure by post, or provide a callback facility so the customer can be contacted to help the decision.
5 Purchase	Once the decision has been made to purchase, we don't want to lose the customer at this stage, so make purchasing straightforward through the user-centred design described in *Chapter 11* and, if the customer has security anxieties, give them the choice of buying through other channels by prompting with a phone number.
6 Post-purchase	Use e-mail and the web site to provide customer service and support. E-mail notifications of an order and its dispatch can help reduce post-purchase dissonance.

Searching behaviours
Approaches to finding information vary from directed to undirected.

Differences between B2C and B2B buyer behaviour

Major differences in buyer behaviour exist between the B2B and B2C markets, and these must be accommodated in e-marketing communications. The main differences are:

1 Market structure
2 Nature of the buying unit
3 Type of purchase
4 Type of buying decision
5 Communication differences.

Market structure

One of the main differences between business-to-business and business-to-consumer, which is important when considering the promotion of a web site is the number of buyers. As Kotler (1997) points out, in B2B there tend to be *far fewer but larger buyers*. What are the implications of this? First, with fewer buyers, the existence of suppliers tends to be well known. This means that efforts to promote the web site using methods such as banner advertising or listing in search engines are less important than for consumer brands. Existing customers can be contacted directly, by post or by e-mail where the e-mail address has been captured or collected, or sales representatives can be used to make customers aware of the web site and how it can help them in their work. Of course, for business-to-business suppliers with many potential customers, then the promotion methods used will correspond more closely to those of the retail market. Second, the existence of larger buyers is likely to mean that each is of great value to the supplier. The supplier therefore needs to understand the buyers' needs from the web site and put effort in to develop the web-based content and services necessary to deliver these services. The type of services to support the customer relationship have been summarized well by Patricia Seybold in her 1999 book *Customers.com* and eight key factors are summarized in *Chapter 11* (*p. 528*) in designing for customer orientation. To implement such principles for a business often implies the development of personalized web content such as Dell Premier which is accessed using an extranet.

To provide potential and existing clients with information each will publish information about new contracts, new products and testimonials from existing customers. This information will also be of great interest to competitors. The web provides a means of finding such information more rapidly and tends to give greater depth of information than other sources. This has led to companies' employing staff specifically to find and summarize information from competitors.

With the need to put information on the web to support customers and encourage loyalty, there is a danger of giving away too much information – 'giving away the crown jewels'. Thus, a careful balance needs to be struck between disclosing too much information and supplying less information than competitors. The use of extranets where businesses have to log-in to find information is one solution to this, but passwords are notoriously insecure. An employee of a customer could be recruited on the basis of their access to a password or knowledge of competitors.

Nature of the buying unit

Business purchases typically involve a more complex decision-making process since more people are involved. Webster and Wind (1972) identified:

- Users
- Influencers
- Buyers
- Deciders
- Gatekeepers.

This complexity is needed for financial control and authorization of what may be expensive products. The implications of this are that the content of the web site should be devised according to the different members of the buying unit who are going to visit the web site. While the site should make the buying process straightforward, the content should be tailored for the users, influencers and deciders. However, for situations where the buyer is the same person as the decider, as may be the case for stationery, it is important to make the whole selection and buying process as easy as possible to encourage repeat purchases. Note that it is not straightforward to tailor content for the different members of the buying unit since it is not practical to label the information under headings such as 'influencer' or 'decider', and their detailed information needs are difficult to identify!

Type of purchase

The type of purchase will vary dramatically according to scale. Companies offering B2B services such as consulting and IT management will have low-volume, high-value orders, while others selling items such as stationery will have high-value, low-volume orders. With the low-volume, high-value purchase the Internet is not likely to be involved in the transaction itself since this will involve a special contract and financing arrangement. The high-value, low-volume orders, however, are suitable for e-commerce transactions and the Internet can offer several benefits over traditional methods of purchase such as mail and fax:

1 Easy for purchaser to assess whether item is in stock.
2 Order can be completed at any time of day or night.
3 Re-buys or repeat orders are easy to specify.
4 Delivery can be tracked online.
5 Purchasing history can be reviewed.

The design of the site should provide facilities such as the modified re-buy or allow the buyer to return to complete a partially complete order. The RS Components web site (www.rswww.com) which focuses on the B2B market highlights these types of facilities.

The buying decision for technical business-to-business products and services will typically be more complicated and lengthy than that for consumer products. There may be a lengthy period of supplier selection and product evaluation. To assist in this, business-to-business exchanges, as described in *Chapter 7* (*p. 325*), have been created.

Customer acquisition management

Customer acquisition
Techniques used to gain new prospects and customers.

In an online context, 'customer acquisition' can have two meanings. First, it may mean the use of the web site to acquire new customers for a company as qualified leads that can hopefully be converted into sales. Second, it may mean encouraging existing customers to *migrate* to using online for purchase or service. Many organizations concentrate on the former, but where acquisition is well managed, campaigns will be used to achieve online conversion. For example, American Express developed a '*Go Paperless*' campaign to persuade customers to receive and review their statements online rather than by post. Phone bank First Direct used call centre representatives to persuade customers of the benefits of bypassing them by reviewing their statements online. They also encourage 'e-advocacy' amongst employees, i.e. encourage them to use the online services so they can better empathize with customer needs.

Before an organization can acquire customers through the content on its site, it must, of course, develop marketing communications strategies to attract visitors to the web site.

Focus on marketing communications for customer acquisition including search engine marketing, online PR, online partnerships, interactive advertising, e-mail marketing and viral marketing

Offline marketing communications
Traditional techniques such as print and TV advertising used to generate web site traffic.

Online marketing communications
Internet-based techniques used to generate web site traffic.

E-commerce managers constantly strive to deliver the most effective mix of communications to drive traffic to their e-commerce sites. The different techniques can be characterized as traditional offline marketing communications or rapidly evolving online communications. From an e-commerce context, the objective of employing these techniques is often to acquire new visitors or 'build traffic' using the techniques summarized in *Figure 9.4*. In *Figure 9.4* the diversity of marketing communications that can be used to encourage site visitors are highlighted. Some additional techniques to promote repeat visits are considered separately in the section on *Customer retention management*.

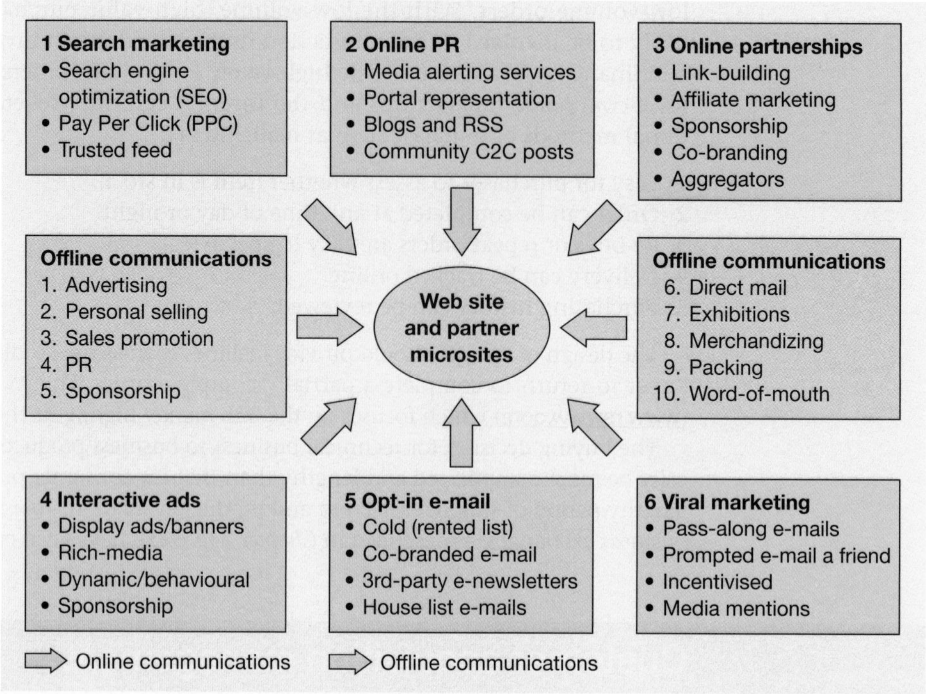

Figure 9.4 **Online and offline communications techniques for e-commerce**

The characteristics of interactive marketing communications

To best exploit the characteristics of digital media, it is important to understand the different communications characteristics of traditional and new media. In this section, we look at eight key differences:

1. From push to pull.
2. From monologue to dialogue.
3. From one-to-many to one-to-some and one-to-one.
4. From one-to-many to many-to-many communications.
5. From 'lean-back' to 'lean-forward'.
6. The medium changes the nature of standard marketing communications tools such as advertising.
7. Increase in communications intermediaries.
8. Integration remains important.

1 From push to pull

Push media
Communications are broadcast from an advertiser to consumers of the message who are passive recipients.

Pull media
The consumer is proactive in selection of the message through actively seeking out a web site.

Traditional media such as print, TV and radio are push media, a one-way street where information is mainly unidirectional, from company to customer unless direct-response elements are built in. In contrast, the web is an example of pull media. This is its biggest strength and its biggest weakness. It is a strength since pull means that prospects and customers only visit a web site when it enters their head to do so – when they have a defined need – they are proactive and self-selecting. But this is a weakness in that online pull means marketers have less control than in traditional communications where the message is pushed out to a defined audience. What are the e-marketing implications of the pull medium? First, we need to provide the physical stimuli to encourage visits to web sites. This may mean traditional ads, direct mail or physical reminders. Second, we need to ensure our site is optimized for search engines – it is registered and is ranked highly on relevant keyword searches. Third, e-mail is important – this is an online push medium, it should be a priority objective of web site design to capture customers' e-mail addresses in order that opt-in e-mail can be used to push relevant and timely messages to customers.

2 From monologue to dialogue

Interactivity
The medium enables a dialogue between company and customer.

Creating a dialogue through **interactivity** is the next important feature of the web and new media. Since the Internet is a digital medium and communications are mediated by software on the web server that hosts the web content, this provides the opportunity for two-way interaction with the customer. This is a distinguishing feature of the medium (Peters, 1998). For example, if a registered customer requests information, or orders a particular product, it will be possible for the supplier to contact them in future using e-mail with details of new offers related to their specific interest. Deighton (1996) proclaimed the interactive benefits of the Internet as a means of developing long-term relationships with customers.

A web site, interactive digital TV and mobile phones all enable marketers to enter dialogue with customers. But digital dialogues have a less obvious benefit also – intelligence. Interactive tools for customer self-help can help collect intelligence – clickstream analysis recorded in web analytics can help us build up valuable pictures of customer preferences and help marketers 'sense and respond'.

3 From one-to-many to one-to-some and one-to-one

Traditional push communications such as TV and print are one-to-many: from one company to many customers, often the same message to different segments and often poorly targeted (although media fragmentation means that reasonably accurate targeting is possible). With new media 'one-to-some' – reaching a niche or micro-segment becomes more practical – e-marketers can afford to tailor and target their message to different segments through providing different site content or e-mail for different audiences through mass customization. We can even move to one-to-one communications where personalized messages can be delivered.

4 From one-to-many to many-to-many communications

New media also enable many-to-many communications. Hoffman and Novak (1996) noted that new media are many-to-many media. Here customers can interact with other customers via your web site or in independent communities. The success of online auctions such as eBay also shows the power of many-to-many communications.

5 From 'lean-back' to 'lean-forward'

New media are also intense media – they are lean-forward media in which the web site usually has the visitor's undivided attention. This intensity means that the customer wants to be in control and wants to experience flow and responsiveness to their needs. First impressions are important.

This contrasts with TV which is more lean-back – the TV may be on, but its audience is not necessarily watching it. An article in the *Financial Times* (2003) entitled 'TV ads "a waste of money"' summarizes new research observing the reaction of consumers to ads. It supports those who argue that many consumers do not watch TV ads. The study found people who watched television with family or friends were far more likely to talk to each other during the commercial breaks than to focus on the ads. Others spent the commercial break doing housework, reading or channel hopping.

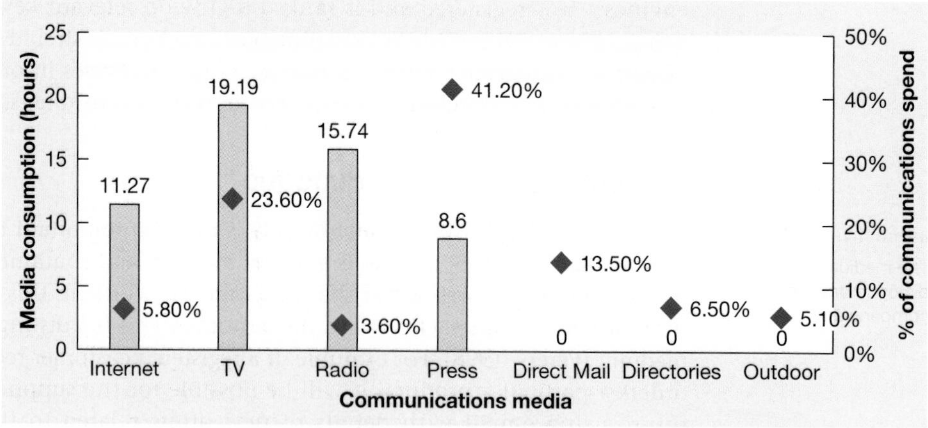

Figure 9.5 **Variation in UK media consumption in hours (bars) compared to percentage media expenditure (squares)**

Source: Compiled from EIAA (2005) and IAB (2005)

Another factor here is the increasing usage of the Internet compared with other media – consider how much time you spend using it each day!

Figure 9.5 shows that in the UK, the Internet is the third most consumed medium after TV (this figure excludes e-mail usage). During the business day, the web is the most frequently consumed medium.

But has this change in media consumption been reflected in changes in advertising expenditure using different media? *Figure 9.5* shows that advertising expenditure for the Internet medium and the radio lags a long way behind expenditure on TV and press advertising (newspapers and magazines) although it has now overtaken radio and outdoor ad spend. This disconnect or mismatch between medium consumption and TV/press advertising expenditure illustrates the core challenge of digital marketing – it is how organizations re-allocate their resources to best maximize their returns from the Internet. However, there is a point at which additional investment in any medium will give diminishing returns.

6 The medium changes the nature of standard marketing communications tools such as advertising

In addition to offering the opportunity for one-to-one marketing, the Internet can be, and still is, widely used for one-to-many advertising. On the Internet the overall message from the advertiser becomes less important, and typically it is detailed information the user is seeking. The web site itself can be considered as similar in function to an advertisement (since it can inform, persuade and remind customers about the offering, although it is not paid for in the same way as a traditional advertisement). Berthon *et al.* (1996) consider a web site as a mix between advertising and direct selling since it can also be used to engage the visitor in a dialogue. Constraints on advertising in traditional mass media such as paying for time or space become less important.

Peters (1998) suggests that communication via the new media is differentiated from communication using traditional media in four different ways. First, *communication style* is changed, with *immediate*, or synchronous transfer of information through online customer service being possible. Asynchronous communication, where there is a time delay between sending and receiving information as through e-mail, also occurs. Second, *social presence* or the feeling that a communications exchange is sociable, warm, personal and active may be lower if a standard web page is delivered, but can be enhanced, perhaps by personalization. Third, the consumer has more *control of contact*, and finally the user has control of *content*, through selection or through personalization facilities.

7 Increase in communications intermediaries

If we consider advertising and PR, with traditional media this occurs through a potentially large number of media owners for TV, radio and print publications. In the Internet era there is a vastly increased range of media owners or publishers through which marketers can promote their services and specifically gain links to their web site. Traditional radio channels, newspapers and print titles have migrated online, but in addition there are a vast number of online-only publishers including horizontal portals (*Chapter 2*) such as search engines and vertical portals such as industry-specific sites. The online marketer needs to select the most appropriate of this plethora of sites which customers visit to drive traffic to their web site.

8 Integration remains important

Although new media have distinct characteristics compared to traditional media, this does not mean we should necessarily concentrate our communications solely on new media. Rather we should combine and integrate new and traditional media according to their strengths. We can then achieve synergy – the sum is greater than its parts. Most of us still spend most of our time in the real world rather than the virtual world, so offline promotion of the proposition of a web site is important. It is also important to support mixed-mode buying. For example, a customer wanting to buy a computer may see a TV ad for a certain brand which raises awareness of the brand and then see a print ad that directs them across to the web site for further information. However, the customer does not want to buy online, preferring the phone, but the site allows for this by prompting with a phone number at the right time. Here all the different communications channels are mutually supporting each other.

Similarly, inbound communications to a company need to be managed. Consider what happens if the customer needs support for an error with their system. They may start by using the onsite diagnostics but these do not solve the problem. They then ring customer support. This process will be much more effective if support staff can access the details of the problem as previously typed in by the customer to the diagnostics package.

Referrer
The source of a web site visit, e.g. paid search, affiliate marketing, online advertising or recorded as 'no referrer', i.e. when a URL is typed in directly.

Cost per acquisition (CPA)
The cost of acquiring a new customer. Typically limited to the communications cost and refers to cost per sale for new customers. May also refer to other outcomes such as cost per quote or enquiry.

Allowable cost per acquisition
A target maximum cost for generating leads or new customers profitably.

Bounce rate
Percentage of visitors entering a site who leave immediately after viewing one page only (known as 'single-page visits')

Assessing marketing communications effectiveness

A campaign will not be successful if it meets its objectives of acquiring site visitors and customers but the cost of achieving this is too high. This constraint is usually imposed simply by having a campaign budget – a necessary component of all campaigns. However, in addition it is also essential to have specific objectives for the cost of getting the visitor to the site using different referrers such as search engine marketing combined with the cost of achieving the outcomes during their visit. This is stated as the cost per acquisition (CPA) (sometimes cost per action). Depending on context and market of a site, CPA may refer to different outcomes. Typical cost targets include:

- cost per acquisition – of a visitor
- cost per acquisition – of a lead
- cost per acquisition – of a sale.

To control costs, it is important for managers to define a target allowable cost per acquisition such as £30 for generating a business lead or £50 for achieving sign-up to a credit card.

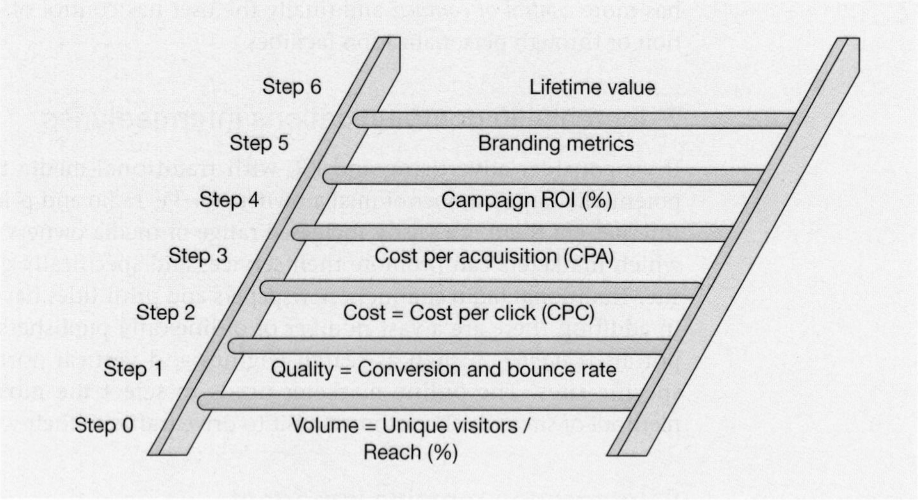

Figure 9.6 **Measures used for setting campaign objectives or assessing campaign success increasing in sophistication from bottom to top**

Figure 9.6 shows the full range of measures used by digital marketers to control communications expenditure from least sophisticated to more sophisticated as follows:

0 *Volume or number of visitors.* This is usually measured as thousands of unique visitors. It is preferable to using page views or hits (see *Chapter 12*) as a measure of effectiveness, since it is opportunities to communicate with individuals. A more sophisticated measure is reach (%) or online audience share. This is only possible using panel data or audience data tools such as www.netratings.com or www.hitwise.com.

Example: An online bank has one million unique visitors per month.

1 *Quality or conversion rates to action.* This shows what proportion of visitors from different sources take specific marketing outcomes on the web such as lead, sale or subscription (see *Figure 9.3*).

Example: Of these visitors 10% convert to an outcome such as logging in to their account or asking for a quote for a product.

2 *Cost (cost per click).* The cost of visitor acquisition is usually measured specific to a particular online marketing tool such as paid search engine marketing since it is difficult to estimate for an entire site with many visitors referred from different sources.

Example: £2 CPC.

3 *Cost (cost per action or acquisition).* When cost of visitor acquisition is combined with conversion to outcomes this is the cost of (customer) acquisition.

Example: £20 CPA (since only one in ten visitors take an action).

4 *Return on investment (ROI).* Return on investment is used to assess the profitability of any marketing activity or indeed any investment. You will also know that there are different forms of ROI, depending on how profitability is calculated. Here we will assume it is just based on sales value or profitability based on the cost per click and conversion rate.

$$\text{ROI} = \frac{\text{Profit generated from referrer}}{\text{Amount spent on advertising with referrer}}$$

A related measure, which does not take profitability into account is return on advertising spend (ROAS) which is calculated as follows:

$$\text{ROAS} = \frac{\text{Total sales revenue generated from referrer}}{\text{Amount spent on advertising with referrer}}$$

5 *Branding metrics*. These tend to be only relevant to interactive advertising or sponsorship. They are the equivalent of offline advertising metrics, i.e. brand awareness (aided and unaided), ad recall, brand favourability and purchase intent. Recorded using tools such as Dynamic Logic (**www.dynamiclogic.com**).

6 *Lifetime-value-based ROI*. Here the value of gaining the customer is not just based on the initial purchase, but the lifetime value (and costs) associated with the customer. This requires more sophisticated models which can be most readily developed for online retailers and online financial services providers.

Example: A bank uses a net present value model for insurance products which looks at the value over 10 years but the main focus is on a 5-year result and takes into account:

- acquisition cost
- retention rates
- claims
- expenses.

This is valuable since it helps give them a realistic 'allowable cost per sale' from different communications tools which is needed to get return over 5 years.

Figure 9.7 shows an example of effectiveness measures for an online ad campaign for an insurance product. Here an opportunity or lead is when a quote is requested. Note that the cost of acquisition is high, but this does not take into account the

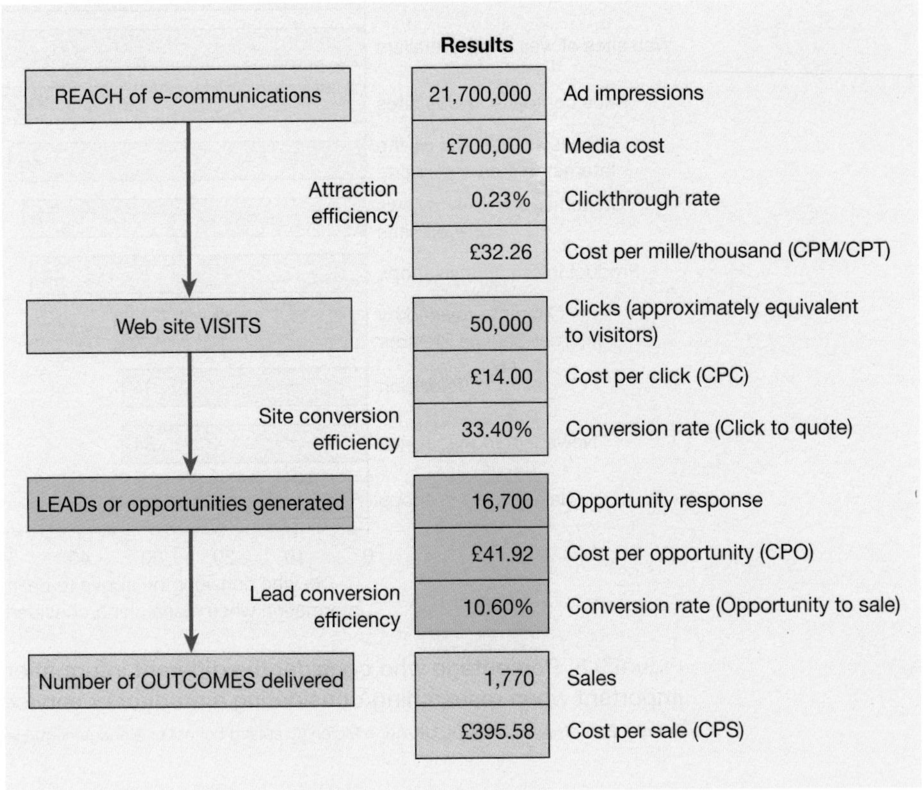

Figure 9.7 **An example of effectiveness measures for an online ad campaign**

synergies of online advertising with offline campaigns, i.e. those who are influenced by the ad, but do not click through immediately.

Online marketing communications

Traffic-building campaign
The use of online and offline promotion techniques such as banner advertising, search engine promotion and reciprocal linking to increase the audience of a site (both new and existing customers).

In this section we will review approaches to online promotion using the different tools of *Figure 9.4* from 1 to 6, including search engine marketing, online advertisements, e-mail and other methods of generating visitors to a web site. These techniques are often combined in what is known as a **'traffic-building campaign'**; this is a method of increasing the audience of a site using different online (and offline) techniques.

A company's investment in the techniques in *Figure 9.4* for customer acquisition should be based on the metrics discussed in the previous section. Most important is minimizing the the cost of acquisition against volume required. As we consider each, think about the strengths and weaknesses of each approach. Another factor is based on assessment of how customers seek product information online. The relative importance of the online promotion techniques we will review in this section are indicated by *Figure 9.8*.

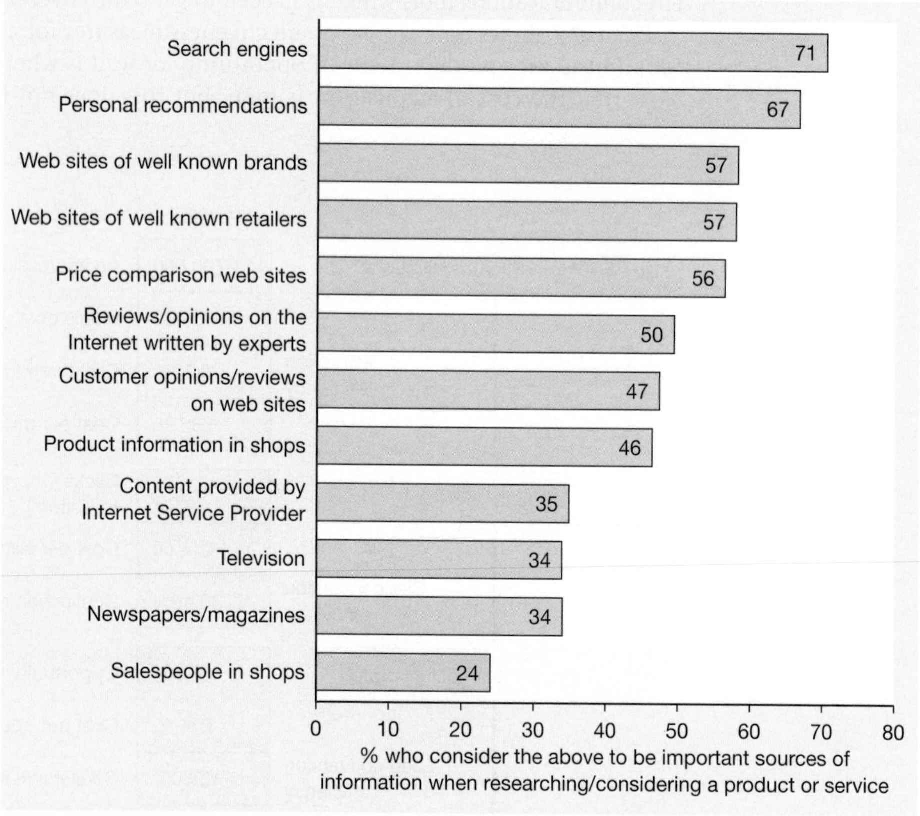

Figure 9.8 **Percentage who consider the different information sources as important when researching/considering a product or service**
Source: BrandNewWorld: AOL UK/Anne Molen (Cranfield School of Management)/Henley Centre, 2004

1 Search-engine marketing (SEM)

Search engines
Provide an index of content on registered sites that can be searched by keyword.

Directories or catalogues
Provide a structured listing of registered web sites and their function in different categories.

As explained in *Chapter 2*, search engines and directories are the primary method of finding information about a company and its products. It follows that if an organization is not prominent in the search engines, then many potential sales could be lost since a company is dependent on the strength of its brand and offline communications to drive visitors to the web site. We will review the first two main types of search engine marketing that are shown in *Figure 9.9*.

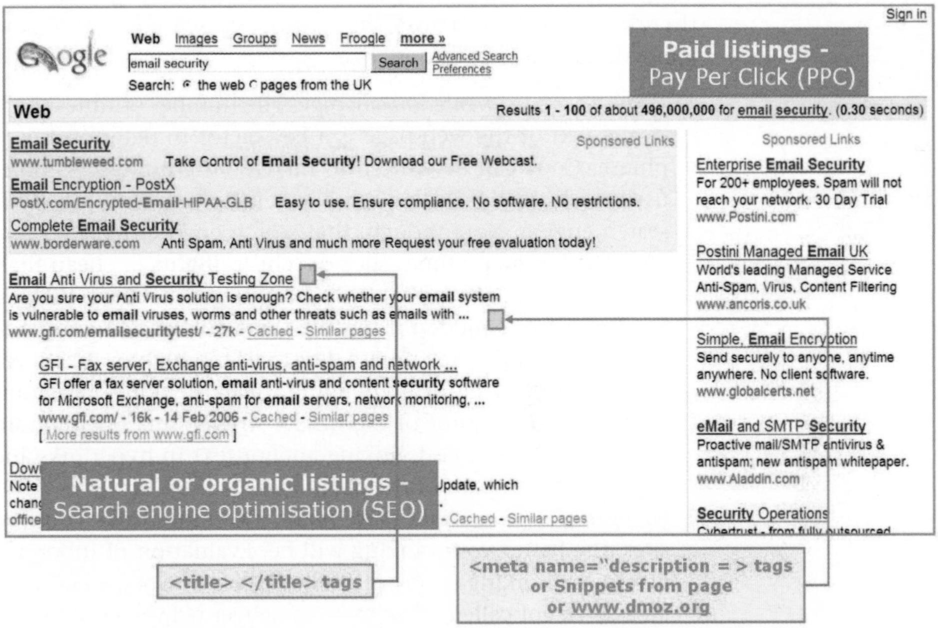

Figure 9.9 **Search engine results page showing the two main methods for achieving visibility**

Source: Screenshot reprinted by permission of Google, Inc

How do we search?

To be successful with SEM requires understanding how consumers use search engines. Search marketing firm iProspect conducted research on how we search; the results are instructive:

- Over half of Internet users search at least once a day.
- 81.7% will start a new search if they cannot find a relevant answer in the first three pages (typically 30 results). So, to some extent, it is a myth that if you are not in the top 10 you will receive no visitors – it depends on the quality and relevance of the listing also. The detailed figures were: 22.6% try another search after first few results; a further 18.6% after reviewing the first page (41.2% cumulative); 25% after checking the first two pages (67% cumulative); and 14.6% the first three pages (81.7% cumulative).
- Users tend to choose the natural search results in preference to the paid search listings. According to a sample; figures for selection of natural search were 60.8% for Yahoo! and 72.3% for Google. These figures increase for experienced users. This suggests that companies that concentrate on paid listings only are limiting their visibility.
- Around half use search toolbars from one of the providers such as Google, Yahoo! or MSN (these are plug-ins for searching which are added to the browser).

Source: iProspect research, Spring 2004 (www.iprospect.com)

Search-engine optimization (SEO)

Search-engine optimization (SEO)
A structured approach used to improve the position of a company or its products in search-engine natural or organic results listings for selected key phrases.

Search-engine optimization (SEO) involves a structured approach used to increase the position of a company or its products in search-engine natural or organic results listings (shown in *Figure 9.9*) for selected key phrases. It also involves controlling index inclusion or ensuring that as many pages of a site as possible are included within the search engine. There may be technical difficulties with this with some content management or e-commerce systems which need to be corrected.

Although each search engine has its own evolving algorithm with hundreds of weighting factors truly only known to the search engineers they employ, fortunately there are common factors that influence search engine rankings. These are, in approximate order of importance:

1 *Frequency of occurrence in body copy*. The number of times the key phrase is repeated in the text of the web page is a key factor in determining the position for a key phrase. Copy can be written to increase the number of times a word or phrase is used (technically, its 'key phrase density') and ultimately boost position in the search engine. Note though, that search engines make checks that a phrase is not repeated too many times such as 'cheap flights ... cheap flights ... cheap flights ... cheap flights ... cheap flights ... cheap flights ... cheap flights ... cheap flights ...' or the key word is hidden using the same colour text and background and will not list the page if this key phrase density is too high or it believes the page creator has tried to mislead the search engine ('search engine spamming'). Relevance is also increased by a gamut of legitimate 'tricks' such as including the key phrase in headings (<H1>, <H2>), linking anchor text in hyperlinks and using a higher density towards the start of the document.

2 *Number of inbound links (page rank)*. The more links you have from good quality sites, the better your ranking will be. Evaluation of inbound links or backlinks to determine ranking is one of the key reasons Google became popular. Google uses an assessment called 'page rank' to deliver relevant results since it counts each link from another site as a vote. However, not all votes are equal – Google gives greater weight to links from pages which themselves have high page rank and which have the same context or topical content as the page they link to. Weighting is also given where hyperlink anchor text or adjacent text contains text relevant to the key phrase, i.e. the linking page must have context.

Page rank
A scale of 0 to 10 used by Google to assess the importance of web sites according to the number of inbound links (link popularity).

Inclusion in directories such as Yahoo! or Business.com (for which a fee is payable) or the Open Directory (**www.dmoz.org**, which is currently free) is important since it can assist in boosting page rank.

3 *Title HTML tag*. The keywords in the title tag of a web page that appears at the top of a browser window are indicated in the HTML code by the <TITLE> keyword. For example, for my site (<title>E-business and Internet marketing articles – DaveChaffey.com</title>). This is significant in search engine listings since if a key phrase appears in a title it is more likely to be listed high than if it is only in the body text of a page. It follows that each page on a site should have a specific title giving the name of a company and the product, service or offer featured on a page. Greater weighting is given to key phrases at the left of the title tag and those with a higher key-phrase density. The Title HTML tag is also vital in search marketing since this is typically the text underlined within the search results page which forms a hyperlink through to your web site. If the Title tag appearing on the search results page is a relevant call-to-action that demonstrates relevance you will receive more clicks, which equals more visits (incidentally, Google will monitor clickthroughs to a site and will determine that your content is relevant too and boost position accordingly).

Meta-tags
Keywords that are part of an HTML page that result in a higher search listing if they match the typed keyword.

4 *Meta-tags*. Meta-tags are part of the HTML source file, typed in by web page creators, which is read by the search engine spider or robot. They are effectively

hidden from users, but are used by some search engines when robots or spiders compile their index. In the past, search engines assigned more relevance to a site containing key phrases in its meta-tags than one that didn't. Search engine spamming of meta-tags resulted in this being an inaccurate method of assessing relevance and Google has reported that it assigns no relevance to meta-tags. However, other search engines such as 'Yahoo! Search' do assign some relevance to meta-tags, so it is best practice to incorporate these and to change them for each page with distinct content. There are two important meta-tags which are specified at the top of an HTML page using the <meta name=""> HTML keyword:

(i) The "keywords" meta-tag highlights the key topics covered on a web page. Example: meta name="keywords" content="E-business, E-commerce, E-marketing">

(ii) The "description" meta-tag denotes the information which will be displayed in the search results page so is very important to describe what the web site offers to encourage searchers to click through to the site.
Example: <meta name="description" content="Your guide to E-business and Internet marketing – DaveChaffey.com">.

5 *Alternative graphic text.* A site that uses a lot of graphical material and/or plug-ins, is less likely to be listed highly. The only text on which the page will be indexed will be the <TITLE> keyword. To improve on this, graphical images can have hidden text associated with them that is not seen by the user (unless graphical images are turned off), but will be seen and indexed by the search engine. For example, text about a company name and products can be assigned to a company logo using the 'ALT' tag as follows:

<IMG NAME= 'Logo' SRC= 'logo.gif' ALT="Internet marketing links and articles – DaveChaffey.com">.

Again, due to search engine spamming this factor is assigned lesser relevance than previously (unless the image is also a link), but it is best practice to use this since it is also required by accessibility law (screen-readers used by the blind and visually impaired read out the text assigned through ALT tags).

Paid search marketing

Paid search marketing or paid listings are similar to conventional advertising; here a relevant text ad with a link to a company page is displayed when the user of a search engine types in a specific phrase. A series of text ads usually labelled as 'sponsored links' are displayed on the right and/or above and below the natural search engine listings. Unlike conventional advertising, the advertiser doesn't pay when the ad is displayed, but only when the ad is clicked on which then leads to a visit to the advertiser's web site – hence this is often known as 'pay-per-click marketing'! Most clicks result in a visit to the site, although there may be a small (usually less than 5–10%) attrition. The relative ranking of these 'paid performance placements' is typically based on the highest bid cost-per-click value for each key phrase. The company which is prepared to pay the most per click gets top spot. Google also takes the relative clickthrough rates of the ads into account when ranking the sponsored links, so ads which do not appear relevant, because fewer people are clicking on them, will drop down or may even disappear off the listing.

Content network
Contextual ads are automatically displayed according to the type of content on partner publisher sites by the search engine. These are typically paid for on a cost-per-click (CPC) basis but ads can also be paid for on a CPM basis.

Cost per thousand (CPM)
Cost per 1,000 ad impressions for a banner advert.

As well as paid search ads within the search engines, text ads are also displayed on third-party sites (for example, the ads on **www.davechaffey.com**) which form a **'content network'** such as Google Adsense (**http://adsense.google.com**) or Content Match on Yahoo! Search where 'contextual ads' are displayed automatically according to the type of content. These are typically paid for on a cost-per-click (CPC) basis but ads can also be paid for on a **CPM** basis. The search networks and publishers share the fees.

Table 9.2 shows how cost-per-click differs between different keywords from generic to specific. It also shows the impact of different conversion rates on the overall CPA. It can be seen that niche terms that better indicate interest in a specific product such as 'women's car insurance' demand a higher fee (this may not be true for less competitive categories where niche terms can be cheaper). The table also shows the cost of PPC search in competitive categories. Advertising just on these four keywords to achieve a high ranking would cost €33,000 in a single day!

The cost per customer acquisition (CPA) can be calculated as follows:

Cost per acquisition = (100 / Conversion rate %) × Cost per click

Table 9.2 **Variation in cost per click for different key phrases in Google UK, 2004**

Keywords	*Clicks / Day*	*Avg. CPC*	*Cost / Day*	*Avg. position*	*CPA @ 25% conversion*	*CPA @ 10% conversion*
Overall	**5,714**	**€5.9**	**€33,317**	**1.3**	**€23.4**	**€58.4**
Insurance	3,800	€5.4	€20,396	1.3	€21.5	€53.7
"Car insurance"	1,700	€6.6	€11,119	1.2	€26.2	€65.5
"Cheap car insurance"	210	€8.4	€1,757	1.1	€33.5	€83.7
"Women's car insurance"	4.1	€10.5	€43	1.0	€42.2	€105.4

Source: Based on Google AdWords™ advertizing program, Traffic Estimator

Given the range in costs, two types of strategy can be pursued in PPC search engine advertising. If budget permits, a premium strategy can be followed to compete with the major competitors who are bidding the highest amounts on popular keywords. Such a strategy is based on being able to achieve an acceptable conversion rate once the customers are driven through to the web site. A lower-cost strategy involves bidding on lower-cost, less-popular phrases, which often show more intent to purchase. These will generate less traffic, so it will be necessary to identify a lot of these phrases to match the traffic from premium keywords.

Beware of the fake clicks!

Whenever the principle of PPC marketing is described to marketers, very soon a light bulb comes on and they ask, 'so we can click on competitors and bankrupt them'? Well, actually no. The PPC ad networks detect multiple clicks from the same computer (IP address) and say they filter them out. However, there are techniques to mimic multiple clicks from different locations such as software tools to fake clicks and even services where you can pay a team of people across the world to click on these links. It is estimated that in competitive markets one in five of the clicks may be fake. While fake clicks can be monitored for and refunds obtained if proved, ultimately this could destroy PPC advertising.

2 Online PR

The UK Institute of PR (IPR) defines PR as:

> *the management of reputation – the planned and sustained effort to establish and maintain goodwill and mutual understanding between an organisation and its publics.*

Online PR
Maximizing favourable mentions of your company, brands, products or web sites on third-party web sites which are likely to be visited by your target audience.

Online PR or e-PR leverages the network effect of the Internet. Remember, Internet is a contraction of 'interconnected networks'! Mentions of a brand or site on other sites are powerful in shaping opinions and driving visitors to your site. The main element of online PR is maximizing favourable mentions of an organization, its brands, products or web sites on third-party web sites which are likely to be visited by its target audience. Furthermore, as we noted in the topic on search engine optimization, the more links there are from other sites to your site, the higher your site will be ranked in the natural or organic listings of the search engines. Minimizing unfavourable mentions through online reputation management is also an aspect of online PR.

Activities which can be considered to be online PR include:

(a) Communicating with media (journalists) online

Communicating with media (journalists) online uses the Internet as a new conduit to disseminate press releases (SEO-optimized) through e-mail and on-site and on third-party sites. Options to consider for a company include: setting up a press-release area on the web site; creating e-mail alerts about news that journalists and other third parties can sign up to; submitting your news stories or releases to online news feeds.

(b) Link building

Link building
A structured activity to include good-quality hyperlinks to your site from relevant sites with a good page rank.

Reciprocal links
Links which are agreed between yours and another's organization.

Link building is a key activity for search engine optimization. It can be considered to be an element of online PR since it is about getting your brand visible on third-party sites. Link building needs to be a structured effort to achieve as many links into a web site as possible from referring web sites (these commonly include reciprocal links). We have also seen that your position in the search engine results pages will be higher if you have quality links into relevant content on your site (not necessarily the home page).

McGaffin (2004) provides a great introduction to implementing a structured link-building programme. The main principle of link-building is as follows. He says: '*Create great content, link to great content and great content will link to you*'. He describes how you should review existing links to your site, links to competitors, set targets and then proactively enquire to suitable site owners for links.

> You can use the syntax 'link:site' in Google to see the number of quality links into a page on your site as judged by Google. e.g. 'link:www.davechaffey.com'.
>
> Note that this also includes internal links. To exclude internal links and include pages with lower page rank or that do not have a true hyperlink, but contain the URL, Google this: 'www.url.com –site:www.url.com'.
>
> For example, 'www.davechaffey.com –site:www.davechaffey.com'

(c) Blogs, podcasting and RSS

Blog
An online diary or news source prepared by an individual or a group of people.

Weblogs or 'blogs' give an easy method of regularly publishing web pages which are best described as online journals, diaries or news or events listings. They may include feedback (traceback) comments from other sites or contributors to the site. Frequency can be hourly, daily, weekly or less frequently, but daily updates are typical.

An example of a useful blog which can keep marketing professionals up-to-date about Internet marketing developments is www.marketingvox.com which is coupled with daily e-mail digests of stories posted. Another example, with news items and articles structured according to the chapters of a book is Davechaffey.com (www.davechaffey.com). Business blogs are created by people within the organization. They can be useful in showing the expertise of those within the organization, but need to be carefully controlled to avoid releasing damaging information. An example of a business blog used to showcase the expertise of its analysts is the Jupiter Research Analyst Weblogs, (http://weblogs.jupiterresearch.com). Technology companies such as Microsoft, Oracle and Sun Microsystems may have several hundreds of bloggers and have a policy to control them to make positive comments.

There are many free services which enable anyone to blog (for example www.blogger.com which was purchased by Google in 2003). Blogs were traditionally accessed through online tools (e.g. www.bloglines.com, www.blogpulse.com – try this to see the popularity trends of discussion about products such as iPods through time) or software readers (www.rssreader.com), but were incorporated into mainstream software in 2006.

Podcasts
Individuals and organizations post online media (audio and video) which can be accessed in the appropriate players including the iPod which first sparked the growth of this technique.

Podcasts are related to blogs since they can potentially be generated by individuals or organizations to voice an opinion either as audio (typically MP3) or less commonly currently as video. They have been successfully used by media organizations such as the BBC which has used them for popular programmes such as film reviews or discussions and for live recording such as the Beethoven symphonies that received over 600,000 downloads in June 2005 alone. Virgin Radio has also used podcasting, but cannot at the time of writing broadcast music due to copyright resrictions, only the presenters! A big challenge for achieving visibility for podcasts is that contents can only currently be recognized by tags and it is difficult to assess quality without listening to the start of a podcast. All the main search engines are working on techniques to make searching of voice and video content practical. In the meantime, some start-ups such as Odeo (www.odeo.com) and Blinkx (www.blinkx.com) are developing solutions.

Online communities and social networks

Companies can also potentially post to forums to promote their services, but it must be done in a sensitive way – it must actually contribute value to the community.

Really Simple Syndication (RSS)

Really Simple Syndication (RSS) (*Chapter 3*) is an extension of blogging where blog, news or any type of content is received by subscribers using the systems mentioned above. It offers a method of receiving news that uses a different broadcast method to e-mail, so is not subject to the same conflicts with spam or spam filters. Many journalists now subscribe to RSS feeds from sources such as the BBC (http://news.bbc.co.uk/2/hi/help/3223484.stm) which publishes RSS feed for different types of content on its site.

(d) Managing how your brand is presented on third-party sites

As part of online PR it is useful to set up monitoring services. It is also necessary to have the resources to deal with negative PR as part of online reputation management. Microsoft's PR agency reputedly has a 'rapid response' unit that can respond to online PR. Examples of alerting service include Googlealert (www.googlealert.com), Google Alerts (www.google.com/alerts) and paid services such as Market Sentinel (www.marketsentinel.com), Mark Monitor (www.markmonitor.com), Reputation Intelligence (www.reputationintelligence.com) and Brand Intelligence (www.brand-intelligence.com).

(e) Creating a buzz – online viral marketing

From a functional point of view, online viral marketing often involves generating word-of-mouth and links through to a web site as outlined in *Chapter 4*, so it can be considered part of online PR.

3 Online partnerships

Partnerships are an important part of today's marketing mix. Smith and Chaffey (2005) say that they are the eighth 'P' (*Chapter 8*). The same is true online. There are three key types of online partnerships which need to be managed: link building (covered in the previous section, this can also be considered to be part of online PR), affiliate marketing and online sponsorship. All should involve a structured approach to managing links through to a site. The important types of partner arrangement are as follows.

(a) Affiliate marketing

Affiliate marketing
A commission-based arrangement where an e-retailer pays sites that link to it for sales, leads (CPA-based) or less commonly visitors (CPC-based).

Affiliate marketing has become very popular with e-retailers since many achieve over 20% of their online sales through affiliates (also known as 'aggregators' since they aggregate offers from different providers). The great thing about affiliate marketing for the e-retailer, is that they, the advertiser, do not pay until the product has been purchased or a lead generated. It is sometimes referred to as 'zero-risk advertising' (*Figure 9.10*).

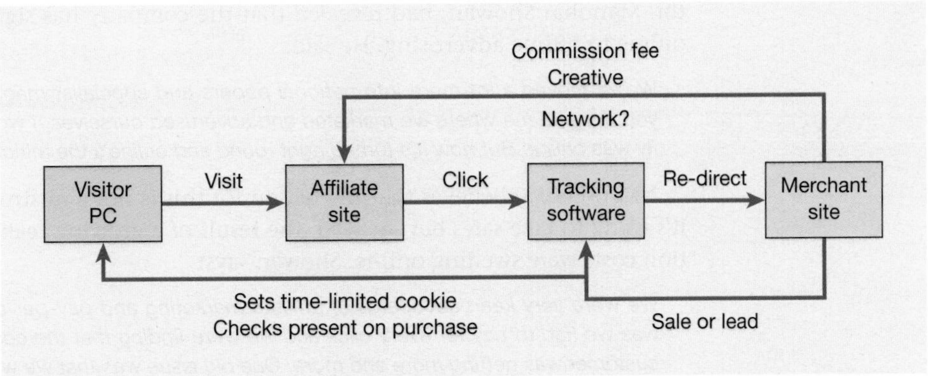

Figure 9.10 **The affiliate marketing model (note that the tracking software and fee payment may be managed through an independent affiliate network manager)**

Amazon was one of the earliest adopters of affiliate marketing and it now has hundreds of thousands of affiliates that drive visitors to Amazon through links in return for commission on products sold. Internet legend records that Jeff Bezos, the creator of Amazon was chatting at a cocktail party to someone who wanted to sell books about divorce via her web site. Subsequently, Amazon.com launched its Associates Program in July 1996 and it is still going strong. To manage the process of finding affiliates, updating product information, tracking clicks and making payments, many companies use an affiliate network or affiliate manager such as Commission Junction (www.cj.com) or Trade Doubler (www.tradedoubler.com).

Some of the issues with balancing spend between affiliate marketing and other online communications techniques and offline communications techniques are illustrated by the mini-case: '*Electronic retailers cut back on their e-communications spend*'.

Mini Case Study 9.1 Electronic retailers cut back on their e-communications spend

Technology e-retailer dabs.com (featured in *Case Study 11.1*) has traditionally used these as their main communications tools:

- Search engine marketing (the main investment)
- Referrals from affiliates (this has been reduced)
- Online display advertising on third-party sites (limited)
- PR.

Jonathan Wall, Dabs marketing director, explains *New Media Age* (2005a) how dabs.com reappraised their use of e-communications tools. He said:

> *We stopped all our affiliate and price-comparison marketing in February because we wanted to see what effect it had on our business and if we were getting value for money. It was proving a very expensive channel for us and we've found [stopping] it has had virtually no effect, because we're seeing that people will still go to Kelkoo to check prices and then come to our site anyway. It's like they're having a look around first and then coming to a brand they know they can trust. We're continuing with paid-for search on Google, but that's all we're doing with online marketing at the moment.*

NMA (2005a) also reported that Empire Direct had adopted a similar approach to its communication mix, reporting that its co-founder and sales and marketing director, Manohar Showan, had revealed that the company has significantly moved from online to offline advertising. He said:

> *We've moved a lot more into national papers and specialist magazines, two years ago, if you'd asked me where we marketed and advertised ourselves, I would have said the majority was online. But now it's turned right round and online's the minority.*

NMA (2005a) believes that the reason for this is not a mistrust of the very medium it's using to take sales but, instead, the result of a growing realization that its acquisition costs were swelling online. Showan says:

> *We were very keen advocates of affiliate marketing and pay-per-click search. The trouble was we had to pay for every click and we were finding that the cost of acquiring each new customer was getting more and more. One big issue was that we were finding people would come to us through affiliates just to check information on a product they'd already bought, so we were basically paying for customers to find out how to hook up their new VCR. We still have affiliates – our main one is Kelkoo – and we still bid for clicks on Google, but not as much as we used to. One of the things we were finding with the search engines is that, with our own search optimisation and because so many people were coming to our site, we were normally very high up the list just through normal searching. In our experience, particularly with Google, if people can see what they want in the main list, they don't look to the right-hand side of the page.*

(b) Online sponsorship

Online sponsorship is not straightforward. It's not just a case of mirroring existing 'real-world' sponsorship arrangements in the 'virtual world' although this is a valid option. There are many additional opportunities for sponsorship online which can be sought out, even if you don't have a big budget at your disposal.

Ryan and Whiteman (2000) define online sponsorship as

> *the linking of a brand with related content or context for the purpose of creating brand awareness and strengthening brand appeal in a form that is clearly distinguishable from a banner, button, or other standardized ad unit.*

For the advertiser, online sponsorship has the benefit that their name is associated with an online brand that the site visitor is already familiar with. So, for users of the ISP Orange with which they are familiar, sponsorship builds on this existing relationship and trust. Closely related is online 'co-branding' where there is an association between two brands.

Paid-for sponsorship of another site, or part of it, especially a portal for an extended period, is another way to develop permanent links. Co-branding is a lower-cost method of sponsorship and can exploit synergies between different companies.

4 Interactive advertising

How positively do you view interactive advertising as a communications tool? Even today, there are relatively few advertisers who have used interactive advertising, partly because of myths promoted about interactive advertising and possibly because of bad experiences. The first 468 by 68 pixels banner ad was placed on Hotwired in 1995 and the call-to-action 'Click here!' generated a clickthough of 25%. Since then, the clickthrough rate (CTR) has fallen dramatically as many consumers like you suffer from 'banner blindness' – they ignore anything on a web site that looks like an ad. The Doubleclick compilation of ad response (www.doubleclick.com) shows that today the average CTR is between 0.2% and 0.3%. This low response rate, combined with relatively high costs of over £20 per thousands of ads served, has seemingly made some marketers prejudiced against interactive advertising. But we will see that there are many innovative approaches to interactive advertising which are proved to increase brand awareness and purchase intent. For example, there are now many other ad formats such as Skyscrapers and MPUs (multi-purpose advertising units) and rich-media ads with animation, audio or video or data capture and interaction. Given these limitations to banner ads, most media owners, digital marketing agencies and industry bodies now refer to 'interactive advertising', which is more suggestive of the range of options for rich-media ads, data-capture ads and large-format ads such as skyscrapers.

Fundamentals of online advertising

Advertising on the web takes place when an advertiser pays to place advertizing content on another web site. The process usually involves ad serving from a different server from that on which the page is hosted (ads can be served on destination sites in a similar way).

Advertising is possible on a range of sites in order to drive traffic to an organization's destination site or alternatively a micro-site or nested ad-content on the media owner's site or on the destination site.

Ad serving
The term for displaying an advertisement on a web site. Often the advertisement will be served from a web server different from the site on which it is placed.

Destination site
The site reached on clickthrough.

Micro-site
A small-scale destination site reached on clickthrough which is part of the media owner's site.

The purpose of interactive advertising

It can be contended that each web site is in itself an advertisement since it can inform, persuade and remind customers about a company or its products and services. However, a company web site is not strictly an advertisement in the conventional sense, since money is not paid for the placement. Although it is often thought that the main aim of interactive advertising is driving traffic to a destination web site, there are other outcomes that a marketing manager may be looking to achieve through an interactive ad campaign. Cartellieri *et al.* (1997) identify the following objectives:

- *Delivering content.* This is the typical case where a clickthrough on a banner advertisement leads through to a destination site giving more detailed information on an offer. This is where a direct response is sought.
- *Enabling transaction.* If a clickthrough leads through to a merchant such as a travel site or an online bookstore this may lead directly to a sale. A direct response is also sought here.
- *Shaping attitudes.* An advertisment that is consistent with a company brand can help build brand awareness.
- *Soliciting response.* An advertisement may be intended to identify new leads or as a start for two-way communication. In these cases an interactive advertisement may encourage a user to type in an e-mail address or other information.
- *Encouraging retention.* The advertisement may be placed as a reminder about the company and its service and may link through to on-site sales promotions such as a prize draw.

Interactive ad targeting options

Online ads can be targeted through placing ads:

1 *On a particular type of site (or part of site)* which has a specific visitor profile or type of content. So a car manufacturer can place ads on the home page of Handbag.com to appeal to a young female audience. A financial services provider can place an ad in the money section of the site to target those interested in these products. To reach large mass-market audiences, place an ad on a large portal home page such as MSN which has millions of visitors each day (sometimes known as a 'road-block' or 'takeover' if they take all ad inventory).
2 *To target a registered user's profile.* A business software provider could advertise on the FT.com to target registrants' profiles such as finance directors or IT managers.
3 At a particular time of day or week.
4 *Online behaviour.* Behavioural ad targeting is all about relevance – dynamically serving relevant content, messaging or ad which matches the interests of a site visitor according to inferences about their characteristics. These inferences are made by anonymously tracking the different types of pages visited by a site user during a single visit to a site or across multiple sessions. Other aspects of the environment used by the visitor can also be determined, such as their location, browser and operating system. For example, FT.com, using software from Revenue Science, can identify users in eight segments: Business Education, Institutional Investor, Information Technology, Luxury and Consumer, Management, Personal Finance, Travel and Private Equity. First, the ad serving system detects whether the visitor is in the target audience (media optimization), then creative optimization occurs to serve the best ad for the viewer type.

Behavioural ad targeting
Enables an advertiser to target ads at a visitor as they move elsewhere on the site or return to the site, thus increasing the frequency or number of impressions served to an individual in the target market.

Interactive ad formats

As well as the classic 468 by 60 rotating GIF banner ad which is decreasing in popularity, media owners now provide a choice of larger, richer formats which web users are more likely to notice. Research has shown that message association and awareness building are much higher for flash-based ads, rich-media ads and larger-format rectangles (multi-purpose units, MPUs) and skyscrapers. View the rich-media ads at www.eyeblaster.com or www.tangozebra.com and you will agree that they definitely can't be ignored.

Other online ad terms you will hear include 'interstitials' (intermediate adverts before another page appears); the more common 'overlays' which appear above content; and of course pop-up windows that are now less widely used because of their intrusion. Online advertisers face a constant battle with users who deploy pop-up blockers or less commonly ad-blocking software, but they will persist in using rich-media formats where they generate the largest response.

Interstitial ads
Ads that appear between one page and the next.

Overlay
Typically an animated ad that moves around the page and is superimposed on the web site content.

Media planning – deciding on the online/offline mix for advertising

This decision is typically taken by the media planner. As we noted in the section on 'Planning integrated marketing communications', the mix between online and offline spend must reflect consumers' media consumption and the cost–response effectiveness of each medium. But, depending on the agency used, they may play it safe by putting the ad spend into what they are familiar with and what may be most rewarding in terms of commission – offline media. Many cross-media optimization studies (XMOS) have shown that the optimal online spend for low-involvement products is surprisingly high at 10–15% of total spend. Although this is not a large amount, it compares to previous spend levels below 1% for many organizations.

Cross-media optimization studies (XMOS)
Studies to determine the optimum spend across different media to produce the best results.

XMOS research is designed to help marketers and their agencies answer the (rather involved) question 'What is the optimal mix of advertising vehicles across different media, in terms of frequency, reach and budget allocation, for a given campaign to achieve its marketing goals?'

The mix between online and offline spend is varied to maximize campaign metrics such as reach, brand awareness and purchase intent. *Table 9.3* summarizes the optimal mix identified for four famous brands. For example, Dove found that increasing the level of interactive advertising to 15% would have resulted in an increase in overall branding metrics of 8%. The proportion of online is small, but remember that many companies are spending less than 1% of their ad budgets online, meaning that offline frequency is too high and they may not be reaching many consumers.

Table 9.3 **Optimum media mix suggested by XMOS® studies**

Brand	*TV*	*Magazine*	*Online*
Colgate	75%	14%	11%
Kleenex	70%	20%	10%
Dove	72%	13%	15%
McDonald's	71%	16% (radio)	13%

Source: Interactive Advertising Bureau (www.iab.net/xmos). XMOS is a registered trademark of the IAB.

The reasons for using and increasing the significance of online in the media mix are similar to those for using any media mix as described by Sissors and Baron (2002):

- Extend reach (adding prospects not exposed by a single medium or other media)
- Flatten frequency distribution (if audience viewing TV ads is exposed too many times, there is a law of diminishing returns and it may be better to reallocate that budget to other media)
- To reach different kinds of audiences
- To provide unique advantages in stressing different benefits based on the different characteristics of each medium
- To allow different creative executions to be implemented
- To add gross impressions if the other media are cost-efficient
- Reinforce message by using different creative stimuli.

All of these factors, and the first three in particular, provide the explanation of why XMOS shows it is worthwhile to put double-digit percentages into online media.

5 E-mail marketing

When devising plans for e-mail marketing communications, marketers need to plan for:

- outbound e-mail marketing, where e-mail campaigns are used as a form of direct marketing to encourage trial and purchases and as part of a CRM dialogue;
- inbound e-mail marketing, where e-mails from customers such as support enquiries are managed.

Outbound e-mail marketing
E-mails are sent to customers and prospects from an organization.

Inbound e-mail marketing
Management of e-mails from customers by an organization.

Despite the increase in spam such that the vast majority of e-mails are spam or viruses (most estimates exceed 80%), e-mail can still drive good response levels, as indicated by *Figure 9.11*. This is particularly the case with in-house lists on which the data in *Figure 9.11* are based, so e-mail communications to customers through e-newsletters or periodic e-mail blasts are today a vital communications technique for companies.

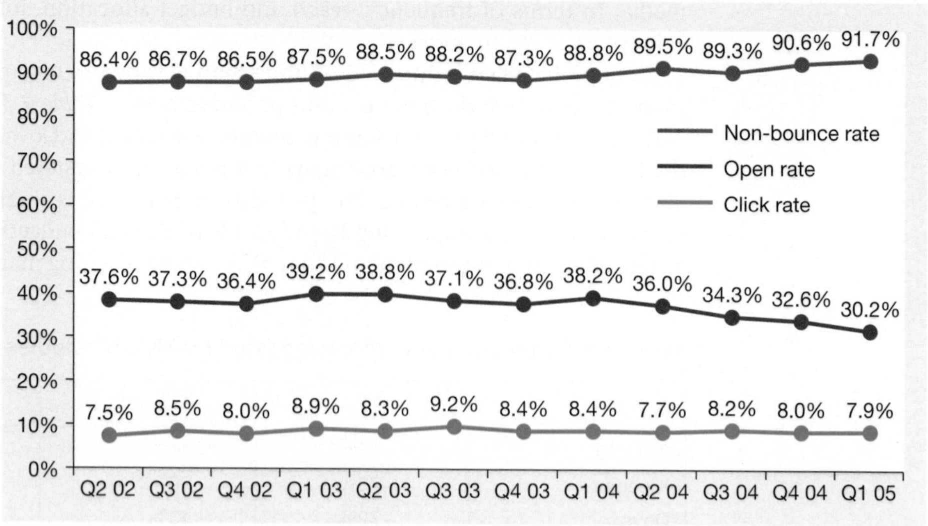

Figure 9.11 E-mail response figures

Source: Epsilon Interactive

Figure 9.11 shows that the key measures for e-mail marketing are:

- *Delivery rate* (here indicated by 'non-bounce rate' – e-mails will bounce if the e-mail address is no longer valid or a spam filter blocks the e-mail. So, online marketers check their 'deliverability' to make sure their messages are not identified as 'false positives' by spam prevention software. Web-based e-mail providers such as Hotmail and Yahoo! Mail have introduced standard authentication techniques known as Sender ID and Domain Keys which make sure the e-mail broadcaster is who they say they are and doesn't spoof their address as many spammers do.
- *Open rate* – this is measured for HTML messages through downloaded images. It is an indication of how many customers open an e-mail, but is not accurate since some users have preview panes in their e-mail readers which load the message even if is deleted without reading and some e-mail readers such as Outlook Express now block images by default (this has resulted in a decline in open rates through time).
- *Clickthrough rate* – this is the number of people who click through on the e-mail of those delivered (strictly unique clicks rather than total clicks). You can see that response rates are quite high at around 10%.

Opt-in e-mail options for customer acquisition

For acquiring new visitors and customers to a site, there are three main options for e-mail marketing. From the point of view of the recipient, these are:

1 *Cold e-mail campaign*. In this case, the recipient receives an opt-in e-mail from an organization that has rented an e-mail list from a consumer e-mail list provider such as Experian (**www.experian.com**), Claritas (**www.claritas.com**) or IPT Limited (**www.myoffers.co.uk**) or a business e-mail list provider such as Mardev (**www.mardev.com**), Corpdata (**www.corpdata.com**) or trade publishers/event providers such as VNU. Although they have agreed to receive offers by e-mail, the e-mail is effectively cold.

2 *Co-branded e-mail*. Here, the recipient receives an e-mail with an offer from a company they have a reasonably strong affinity with. For example, the same credit card company could partner with a mobile service provider such as Vodafone and send out the offer to their customer (who has opted in to receive e-mails from third parties). Although this can be considered a form of cold e-mail, it is warmer since there is a stronger relationship with one of the brands and the subject line and creative will refer to both brands. Co-branded e-mails tend to be more responsive than cold e-mails to rented lists since the relationship exists and fewer offers tend to be given.

3 *Third-party e-newsletter*. In this visitor acquisition option, a company publicizes itself in a third-party e-newsletter. This could be in the form of an ad, sponsorship or PR (editorial) which links through to a destination site. These placements may be set up as part of an interactive advertising ad buy since many e-newsletters also have permanent versions on the web site. Since e-newsletter recipients tend to engage with them by scanning the headlines or reading them if they have time, e-newsletter placements can be relatively cost-effective.

Viral marketing, which is discussed in the next section, also uses e-mail as the mechanism for transferring messages. E-mail is most widely used as a prospect conversion and customer retention tool using an opt-in, or house list of prospects and customers who have given permission to an organization to contact them. For example, Lastminute.com has built a house list of over 10 million prospects and customers across Europe. Successful e-mail marketers adopt a strategic approach to e-mail and develop a contact or touch strategy which plans the frequency and content of e-mail communications as explained in *Chapters 4* and *6*. For customer retention, a house list is built where e-mail is used to communicate to existing customers.

House list
A list of prospect and customer names, e-mail addresses and profile information owned by an organisation.

6 Viral marketing

Viral marketing
E-mail is used to transmit a promotional message to another potential customer.

Viral marketing harnesses the network effect of the Internet and can be effective in reaching a large number of people rapidly in the same way as a natural virus or a computer virus. It is effectively an online form of word-of-mouth communications. Although the best known examples of viral activity are of compromising pictures or jokes being passed around offices worldwide, viral marketing is increasingly being used for commercial purposes. Smith and Chaffey (2005) say ideally viral marketing is a clever idea, a game, a shocking idea, or a highly informative idea which makes compulsive viewing. It can be a video clip, TV ad, cartoon, funny picture, poem, song, political message, or news item. It is so amazing, it makes people want to pass it on. This is a challenge for commercial companies since to be successful, it will need to challenge convention and this may not fit well with the brand.

To make a viral campaign effective, Justin Kirby of viral marketing specialists DMC (www.dmc.co.uk) suggests that three things are needed (Kirby, 2003):

1 *Creative material – the 'viral agent'*. This includes the creative message or offer and how it is spread (text, image, video).
2 *Seeding*. Identifying web sites, blogs or people to send e-mail to start the virus spreading.
3 *Tracking*. To monitor the effect, to assess the return from the cost of developing the viral agent and seeding.

Offline marketing communications

Offline communications will never disappear – they are effective at reaching an audience to encourage them to visit a site, but are also useful as a way of having an impact or explaining a complex proposition as Mini Case Study 9.2 shows.

Mini Case Study 9.2 Offline communications vital for finding the perfect partner at Match.com

UK-based online dating company, Match.com has over 1.5 million members and in 2004 was responsible for 200,000 marriages around the world. Match.com and partner company uDate.com competes against Yahoo! Personals, Dating Direct, traditional players and a host of smaller players. Given the intense competition, Samantha Bedford, UK MD believes it is essential to invest in offline communications for continued growth. In Autumn 2005, Match.com spent over £3 million on a TV advertising campaign since they wanted to generate brand awareness, given that they estimate that by 2008 the value of the online dating market will double. In addition to achieving reach and brand awareness, offline advertising is important because it enables Match.com to communicate a fairly complex message to potential customers. Focus groups showed that many singles felt they didn't need an online dating service and didn't realize how Match.com could help as part of the overall dating experience.

Source: NMA (2005b)

Customer retention management

For an e-commerce site, customer retention has two distinct goals:

1 To retain customers of the organization (repeat customers).
2 To keep customers using the online channel (repeat visits).

These are similar to the two aims of customer acquisition as described in a previous section. Ideally marketing communications should address both aims.

Maintaining online customer relationships is difficult. Laurie Windham (2001) says:

> *That's what's so scary about customer retention in the online space. We've created this empowered, impatient customer who has a short attention span, a lot of choices, and a low barrier to switching.*

To create long-term online customer relationships that build on acquisition, to retain and extend, we need to analyse the drivers of satisfaction amongst these e-customers, since satisfaction drives loyalty and loyalty drives profitability. The relationship is shown in *Figure 9.12*. The objective of marketers is to drive customers up the curve towards the zone of affection. However, it is worth remembering that the majority are not in that zone and to achieve retention marketers must understand why customers defect or are indifferent.

It follows from *Figure 9.12* that we need to understand different factors that affect loyalty. The type of approach that can be taken is highlighted by Reicheld and Schefter (2000). They reported that Dell Computer has created a customer experience council that has researched key loyalty drivers, identified measures to track these and put in place an action plan to improve loyalty (*Table 9.4*).

Since quality of service is so crucial in determining satisfaction and loyalty, see the *Focus on excelling in e-commerce service quality* section later in this chapter.

Now let us consider key e-marketing tools that help retain customers. Repeat visits can be generated by a variety of means and brainstorming sessions can help generate these. Often it may simply be the expedient of regularly updated market and product or technical information that helps customers perform their day-to-day work. Such information can be delivered through extranets such as Dell Premier or through personalization services such as that described for RS Components. Information to help people perform their work is the proposition of the vertical portals such as VerticalNet (**www.vertical.net**) that are essentially online trade papers with industry

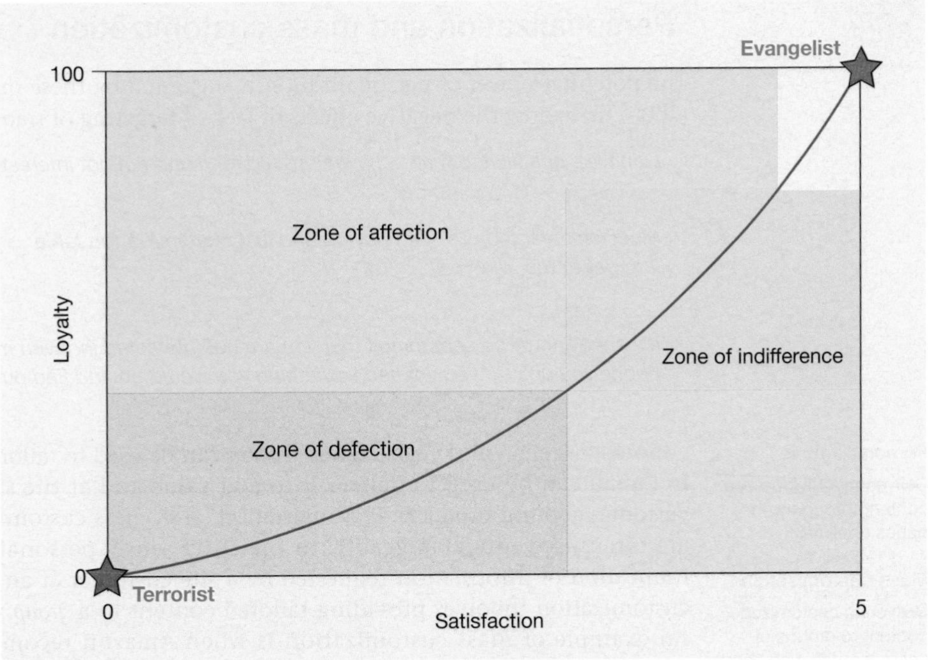

Figure 9.12 Schematic of the relationship between satisfaction and loyalty

Source: Adapted and reprinted by permission of *Harvard Business Review* from graph on p. 167 from 'Putting the service-profit chain to work,' by Heskett, J., Jones, T., Loveman, G., Sasser, W. and Schlesinger, E., in *Harvard Business Review*, March–April 1994. Copyright © 1994 by the Harvard Business School Publishing Corporation, all rights reserved

Table 9.4 Relationship between loyalty drivers and measures to assess their success at Dell Computer

Loyalty drivers	*Summary metric*
1 Order fulfilment	Ship to target. Percentage that ship on time exactly as the customer specified.
2 Product performance	Initial field incident rate – the frequency of problems experienced by customers.
3 Post-sale service and support	On-time, first-time fix – the percentage of problems fixed on the first visit by a service rep who arrives at the time promised.

Source: Reprinted by permission of *Harvard Business Review* from information on pp. 105–13 from 'Your secret weapon on the web', by Reicheld, F. and Schefter, P., in *Harvard Business Review*, July–August 2000. Copyright © 2000 by the Harvard Business School Publishing Corporation, all rights reserved

news and events. However, it adds to this by providing other information such as careers and detailed product information and community. Online communities are popular for both consumer and business markets since users can discuss topical issues or ask for answers to their queries. For example, the UK Net Marketing Group at www.chinwag.com discusses the benefits of new technologies such as mobile commerce and recommends suppliers of Internet services. Many such communities work because they are independent of suppliers, so it may be difficult to introduce these types of facilities on to a corporate site. Finally, traditional sales promotion techniques translate well to the Internet. RS Components use Product of the Week or Month to discount some items and offer competitions and prize draws to encourage repeat visits. These are often publicized in offline mail-outs to encourage repeat visits.

Personalization and mass customization

The potential power of personalization is suggested by these quotes from Evans *et al.* (2000) that show the negative effects of lack of targeting of traditional direct mail:

> *Don't like unsolicited mail ... haven't asked for it and I'm not interested.*
>
> (Female, 25–34)
>
> *Most isn't wanted, it's not relevant and just clutters up the table ... you have to sort through it to get to the 'real mail'.*
>
> (Male, 45–54)
>
> *It's annoying to be sent things that you are not interested in. Even more annoying when they phone you up ... If you wanted something you would go and find out about it.*
>
> (Female, 45–54)

Personalization
Delivering individualized content through web pages or e-mail.

Mass customization
Delivering customized content to groups of users through web pages or e-mail.

Collaborative filtering
Profiling of customer interest coupled with delivery of specific information and offers, often based on the interests of similar customers.

Personalization and **mass customization** can be used to tailor information and opt-in e-mail can be used to deliver it to add value and at the same time remind the customer about a product. 'Personalization' and 'mass customization' are terms that are often used interchangeably. In the strict sense, personalization refers to customization of information requested by a site customer at an *individual* level. Mass customization involves providing tailored content to a *group* with similar interests. An example of mass customization is when Amazon recommends similar books according to what others in a segment have offered, or if it sends a similar e-mail to customers who had an interest in a particular topic such as e-commerce. This approach is sometimes also referred to as '**collaborative filtering**'.

All these personalization techniques take advantage of the dynamic possibilities of web content. Users' preferences are stored in databases and content is taken from a database. Personalization can be achieved through several dynamic variables including:

- the customers' preferences
- the date or time
- particular events
- the location.

Personalization can also be used to offer innovative services. Online bookseller BOL (www.bol.com) allows customers to choose their favourite parts from different types of travel guides, perhaps history from the Rough Guides and maps from the Lonely Planet, but excluding night clubs and restaurants. The personalized book can then be printed on demand on the customer's printer.

A more typical personalization service is that provided by the portals such as Yahoo! and Excite! These enable users to configure their home page so that it delivers the information they are most interested in. Perhaps their regional weather, the results from their soccer team and the prices of shares they have purchased.

Turning to negative aspects of personalization, there are two chief difficulties. First, cost, for the reasons explained in the next section and, second, it may act as a barrier to users. For example, some personalization requires the user to log in. This may be a problem if a customer has mislaid a password. Equally, for a new visitor to the site the need to apply for a password can be offputting and a customer may disappear, never to return. Effective personalization will still enable a new visitor to view a good deal of content even if they do not have a password. Use of *cookies* can avoid the need for the customer to actively log in, with this occurring automatically.

Creating personalization

Personalization of web content is much more expensive than developing static content, since it requires database integration and specialized software tools such as

Broadvision and Bladerunner, which enable users to select the type of content they want, recognize them when they return and then access and display the relevant information from a database.

Extranets

Extranets were introduced in *Chapter 3*. Since they require a user to log in they signify differential services through premium content and services. Many options are possible. A dynamic example of using an extranet is the use of the web to host online events that mirror traditional events such as seminars, trade shows and user group conferences, virtual seminars with a guest speaker by webcast, virtual trade shows where exhibitors, seminar speakers and delegates are linked by the web. Dell Computer has a special brand variant known as Dell Premier that can be used to provide value-added services for key accounts. Other traditional retention methods such as loyalty schemes and sales promotions translate well to the online environment.

The use of extranets presents a barrier to entry, particularly if users lose their passwords. To limit this effect RS Components send out password reminders to help retention. A Dutch insurer combined online and offline techniques to use an extranet to deliver mass customization. Existing customers were divided into six segments and then contacted through a direct mail campaign. Members of each segment were given one of six passwords, so that when they accessed the extranet there were six different versions of content for the web site giving product suggestions and offers consistent with the segment. Extranets provide good traceability of marketing outcomes and tagging of visitors. In this case the effectiveness of the campaign in terms of response rate from the e-mail and conversion to sales could also be monitored for different segments.

Opt-in e-mail

Opt-in e-mail is vital in communicating the retention offers either through regular e-mail communications such as a newsletter or higher-impact irregular e-mail communications such as details of a product launch. Remember that e-mail has the power of traditional push communication. It enables a targeted message to be pushed out to a customer to inform and remind and they are certain to view it within their e-mail inbox; even if it is only deleted, it cannot be ignored. Contrast this with the web – a pull medium where customers will only visit your site if there is a reason or a prompt to do so.

Spam

Unsolicited e-mail (usually bulk-mailed and untargeted).

Despite its potential, use of e-mail for marketing has negative connotations due to spam. Spam is best known as tinned meat, but a modern version of this acronym is 'Sending Persistent Annoying e-Mail'. The negative perception of e-mail derives from the many unsolicited e-mails we have all received from unscrupulous 'get-rich-quick merchants'. The spammers rely on sending out millions of e-mails in the hope that even if there is only a 0.01 per cent response they may make some money, if not get rich.

Many anti-spam activists have formed organizations such as CAUCE (the Coalition Against Unsolicited Commercial Email, **www.cauce.org**). These organizations take a dim view of commercial organizations that send unsolicited mail and prepare a list of all spam perpetrators. They have also been successful in creating legislation to outlaw spam. It is now illegal within Europe, but it is often difficult to trace the originators of spam since they use hijacked e-mail addresses and postal boxes to collect their money.

Spam does not mean that e-mail cannot be used as a marketing tool. As explained in the section on permission marketing, opt-in is the key to successful e-mail marketing. Before starting an e-mail dialogue with customers, according to European law, companies must ask customers to provide their e-mail address and then give them the option of 'opting in' to further communications. Ideally they should proactively opt in by checking a box. E-mail lists can also be purchased where customers have opted in to receive e-mail.

Once an e-mail address has been collected, managers must plan the frequency of e-mail communications. Options include:

- *Regular newsletter type*. For example, once a day, once a week, once a month. It is best if customers are given choice about the frequency.
- *Event-related*. These tend to be less regular and are sent out perhaps every three or six months when there is news of a new product launch or an exceptional offer.
- *E-mail sequence*. Software can be purchased to send out a series of e-mails. For example, after subscription to a trial version of an online magazine, e-mails will be sent out at 3, 10, 25 and 28 days to encourage a subscription before the trial lapses.

To consider the strengths and weaknesses of these techniques in more detail complete *Activity 9.2*.

Activity 9.2 Retention techniques for The B2B Company

Purpose

To develop skills of evaluating technology-led marketing options.

Activity

You have limited resources for investment in the techniques described in the section on customer retention management. Select two techniques from personalization, extranets, opt-in e-mail marketing and online communities, and explain why you have chosen them over the others. Have you chosen technology-led marketing options or marketing-led technology options?

Answers to activities can be found at www.pearsoned.co.uk/chaffey

Online communities

Community
A customer-to-customer interaction delivered via e-mail groups, web-based discussion forums or chat.

Community is a key feature of the new interactive media that distinguishes them from traditional push media. But why is community important? Hagel and Armstrong (1997) say:

> *The rise of virtual communities in online networks has set in motion an unprecedented shift from vendors of goods and services to the customers who buy them. Vendors who understand this transfer of power and choose to capitalize on it by organizing virtual communities will be richly rewarded with both peerless customer loyalty and impressive economic returns.*

What is the reality behind this vision? How can companies deliver the promise of community? The key to successful community is customer-centred communication. It is a customer-to-customer (C2C) interaction. Consumers, not businesses, generate the content of the site, e-mail list or bulletin board. Its success and essential power can be gauged by the millions of customers who used Napster and Gnutella to download MP3 music files using the peer-to-peer (P2P) approach where these companies act as intermediaries to enable users to exchange files – a global swap shop. As well as these high-profile examples of successful C2C community there is also often untapped potential for applying community on any organization's web site. Remember that the C2C approach can be integrated into B2C and B2B sites.

Depending on market sector, an organization has a choice of developing different types of community for B2C, and communities of purpose, position, interest and profession for B2B.

1. *Purpose* – people who are going through the same process or trying to achieve a particular objective. Examples include those researching cars, such as Autotrader (www.autotrader.co.uk), or stocks online, such as the Motley Fool (www.motleyfool.co.uk). Price or product comparison services such as MySimon, Shopsmart and Kelkoo serve this community. At sites such as Bizrate (www.bizrate.com), the Egg Free Zone (www.eggfreezone.com) or Alexa (www.alexa.com), companies can share their comments on companies and their products.
2. *Position*. People who are in a certain circumstance such as having a health disorder or being at a certain stage of life, such as communities set up specifically for young people or old people. Examples are teenage chat site Dobedo (www.dobedo.co.uk), Cennet (www.cennet.co.uk) 'New horizons for the over 50s', www.babycenter.com and www.parentcentre.com for parents and the Pet Channel (www.thepetchannel.com).
3. *Interest*. This community is for people who share an interest or passion such as sport (www.football365.com), music (www.pepsi.com), leisure (www.walkingworld.com) or any other interest (www.deja.com).
4. *Profession*. These are important for companies promoting B2B services. For example, VerticalNet has set up over 50 different communities to appeal to professionals in specific industries such as paints and coatings, the chemical industry or electronics. These B2B vertical portals can be thought of as 'trade papers on steroids'. In fact, in many cases they have been created by publishers of trade papers, for example Emap Business Communications has created Construction Plus for the construction industry. Each has industry and company news and jobs as expected, but also offers online storefronts and auctions for buyers and sellers and community features such as discussion topics. Of course, the trade papers such as Emap's *Construction Weekly* are responding by creating their own portals.

You will notice that most of these examples of community are intermediary sites that are independent of a particular manufacturer or retailer. A key question to ask before embarking on a community-building programme is: '*Can customer interests be best served through a company-independent community?*'.

If the answer to this question is 'yes', then it may be best to form a community that is a brand variant, differentiated from its parent. For example, Boots the chemist has created Handbag.com as a community for its female customers. Another and less costly alternative is to promote your products through sponsorship or co-branding on an independent community site or portal or to get involved in the community discussions.

What tactics can organizations use to foster community? Despite the hype and potential, many communities fail to generate activity, and a silent community is not a community. Parker (2000) suggests eight questions organizations should ask when considering how to create a customer community:

1. What interests, needs or passions do many of your customers have in common?
2. What topics or concerns might your customers like to share with each other?
3. What information is likely to appeal to your customers' friends or colleagues?
4. What other types of business in your area appeal to buyers of your products and services?
5. How can you create packages or offers based on combining offers from two or more affinity partners?
6. What price, delivery, financing or incentives can you afford to offer to friends (or colleagues) which your current customers recommend?
7. What types of incentives or rewards can you afford to provide customers who recommend friends (or colleagues) who make a purchase?
8. How can you best track purchases resulting from word-of-mouth recommendations from friends?

A good approach to avoiding these problems is to think about the problems you may have with your community-building efforts. Typical problems are:

1 *Empty communities*. A community without any people is not a community. The traffic-building techniques mentioned in an earlier section need to be used to communicate the proposition of the community.
2 *Silent communities*. A community may have many registered members, but community is not a community if the conversation flags. This is a tricky problem. You can encourage people to join the community, but how do you get them to participate? Here are some ideas.

- *Seed the community*. Use a moderator to ask questions or have a weekly or monthly question written by the moderator or sourced from customers. Have a resident independent expert to answer questions. Visit the communities on Monster (www.monster.co.uk) to see these approaches in action and think about what distinguishes the quiet communities from the noisy ones.
- *Make it select*. Limit it to key account customers or set it up as an extranet service that is only offered to valued customers as a value-add. Members may be more likely to get involved.

3 *Critical communities*. Many communities on manufacturer or retailer sites can be critical of the brand, see the Egg Free Zone, for example (www.eggfreezone.com). Think about whether this is a bad thing. It could highlight weaknesses in your service offer to customers and competitors, but enlightened companies use community as a means to better understand their customers' needs and failings with their services. Community is a key market research tool. Also, it may be better to control and contain these critical comments on your site rather than their being voiced elsewhere in newsgroups where you may not notice them and can less easily counter them. The computer-oriented newsgroup on Monster shows how the moderator lets criticisms go so far and then counters them or closes them off. Particular criticisms can be removed.

Finally, remember the *lurkers* – those who read the messages but do not actively contribute. There may be ten lurkers for every active participant. The community can also positively influence these people and build brand.

Techniques for managing customer activity and value

Within the online customer base of an organization, there will be customers who have different levels of activity in usage of online services or in sales. A good example is a bank – some customers may use the online account once a week, others much less frequently and some not at all. *Figure 9.13* illustrates the different levels of activity. Another example is a utility (energy) provider of electricity where self-service involves use of e-billing and another is a mobile phone company where customers can check their usage and top up their usage.

To improve the adoption of 'web self-service' which helps reduce costs it is important to define measures which indicate activity levels and then develop tactics to increase activity levels through more frequent use. Objectives and corresponding tactics can be set for:

- Increasing number of *new users* per month and annually (separate objectives will be set for existing bank customers and new bank customers) through promoting online services to drive visitors to the web site.
- Increasing % of *active users* (an appropriate threshold can be used – for some other organizations it could be set at 7, 30 or 90 days). Using direct communications

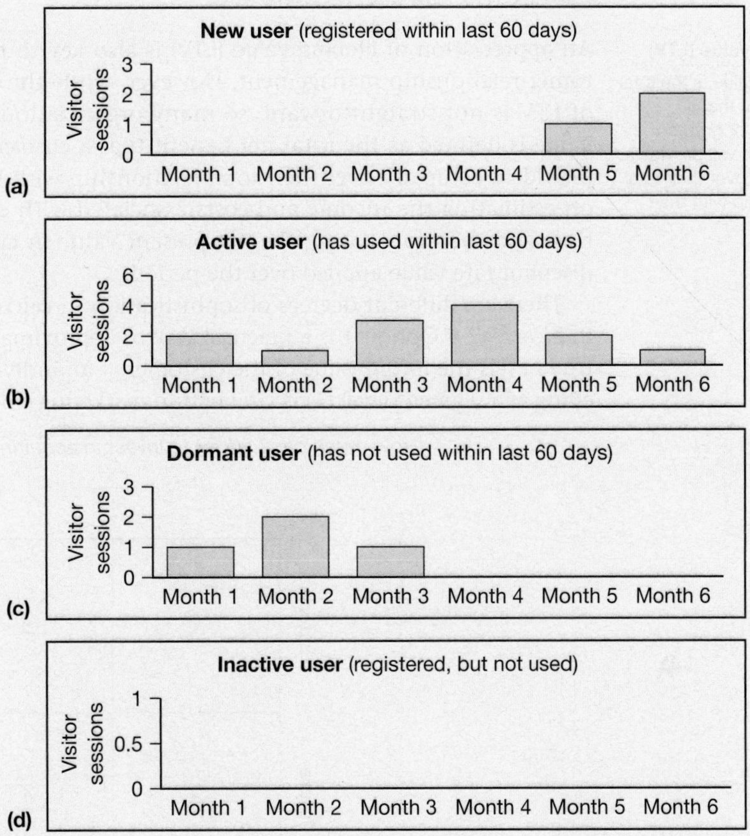

Figure 9.13 **Activity segmentation of a site requiring registration**

such as e-mail, personalized web site messages, direct mail and phone communications to new, dormant and inactive users increases the percentage of active users.

- Decreasing % of *dormant users* (were once new or active, could be sub-categories), but have not used within a time period to be classified as active.
- Decreasing % of *inactive users* (or non-activated) users. These are those who signed up for a service such as online banking and username was issued, but they have not used the service.

You can see that corresponding strategies can be developed for each of these strategies.

Another key metric, in fact the key retention metric for e-commerce sites, refers to repeat business. The importance of retention rate metrics was highlighted by Agrawal *et al.* (2001). The main retention metrics they mention and show the impact on profitability are:

- *Repeat-customer conversion rate* – how many first-time customers purchase a second product.
- *Repeat-customer base* – the proportion of the customer base who have made repeat purchases.
- *Number of transactions per repeat customer* – this indicates the stage of development of the customer in the relationship (another similar measure is number of product categories purchased).
- *Revenue per transaction of repeat customer* – this is a proxy for lifetime value since it gives average order value.

Lifetime value modelling

Lifetime value (LTV)
Lifetime value is the total net benefit that a customer or group of customers will provide a company over their total relationship with the company.

An appreciation of lifetime value (LTV) is also key to the theory and practice of customer relationship management. However, while the term is often used, calculation of LTV is not straightforward, so many organizations do not calculate it. Lifetime value is defined as the total net benefit that a customer or group of customers will provide a company over their total relationship with a company. Modelling is based on estimating the income and costs associated with each customer over a period of time and then calculating the net present value in current monetary terms using a discount rate value applied over the period.

There are different degrees of sophistication in calculating LTV. These are indicated in *Figure 9.14*. Option 1 is a practical way or approximate proxy for future LTV, but the true LTV is the future value of the customer at an individual level. Lifetime value modelling at a segment level (4) is vital within marketing since it answers the question:

How much can I afford to invest in acquiring a new customer?

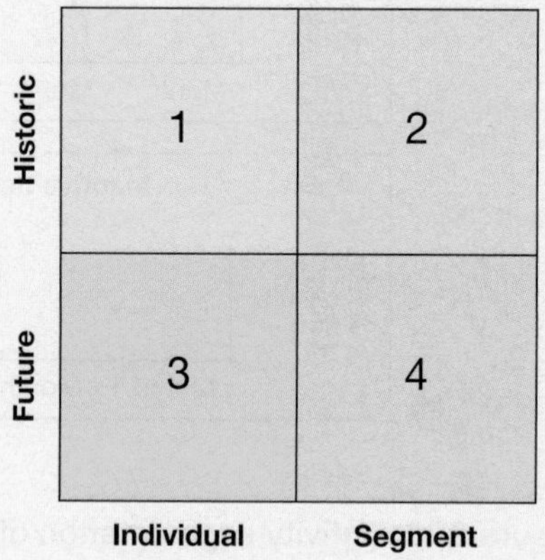

Figure 9.14 **Different representations of lifetime value calculation**

Lifetime value analysis enables marketers to:

- Plan and measure investment in customer acquisition programmes
- Identify and compare critical target segments
- Measure the effectiveness of alternative customer retention strategies
- Establish the true value of a company's customer base
- Make decisions about products and offers
- Make decisions about the value of introducing new e-CRM technologies.

Figure 9.15 gives an example of how LTV can be used to develop a CRM strategy for different customer groups. Four main types of customers are indicated by their current and future value as bronze, silver, gold and platinum. Distinct customer groupings (circles) are identified according to their current value (as indicated by current profitability) and future value as indicated by lifetime value calculations. Each of these groups will have a customer profile signature based on their demographics, so this can be used for customer selection. Different strategies are developed for different customer groups within the four main value groupings. Some bronze customers such as Groups A and B realistically do not have development potential and are typically unprofitable, so the aim is to reduce costs in communications and if they do not remain as customers this is acceptable. Some bronze customers such as Group C

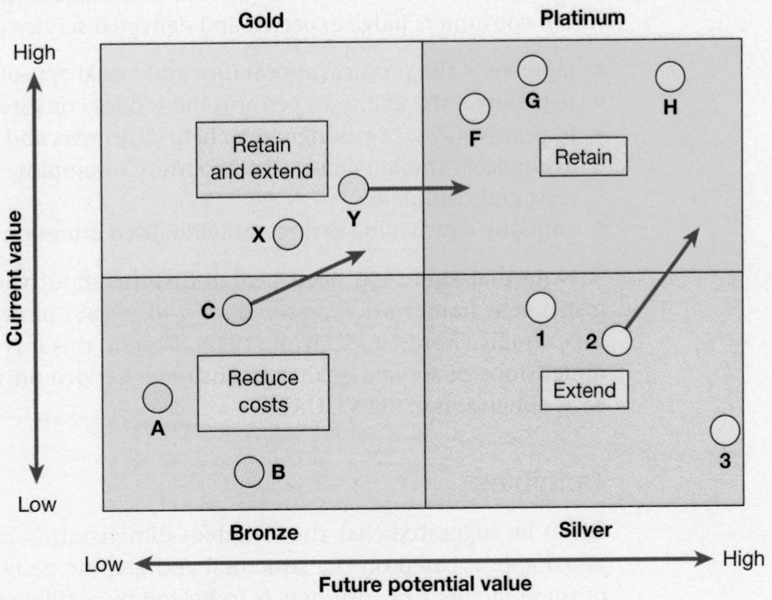

Figure 9.15 **An example of an LTV-based segmentation plan**

may have potential for growth, so for these the strategy is to extend their purchases. Silver customers are targeted with customer extension offers and gold customers are extended where possible although these have relatively little growth potential. Platinum customers are the best customers, so it is important to understand the communication preferences of these customers and not to over-communicate unless there is evidence that they may defect.

Focus on excelling in e-commerce service quality

In the virtual world customer service is a key difference between brands. Jevons and Gabbott (2000) have stressed the importance of service quality in determining brand loyalty with reference to e-commerce. They say: *'the first-hand experience of the brand is a more powerful token of trust than the perception of the brand'*.

Research across industry sectors suggests that the quality of service is a key determinant of loyalty. Feinberg *et al.* (2000) report that if reasons why customers leave a company are considered, over 68 per cent leave because of 'poor service experience', with other factors such as price (10 per cent) and product issues (17 per cent) less significant.

Improving online service quality

Delivering service quality in e-commerce can be assessed through reviewing existing frameworks for determining levels of service quality. Those most frequently used are based on the concept of a 'service-quality gap' that exists between the customers' *expected* level of service (from previous experience and word-of-mouth communication) and their perception of the *actual* level of service delivery.

Parasuraman *et al.* (1985) suggested that these dimensions of service quality on which consumers judge expected and delivered service-quality levels are:

- tangibles – the physical appearance and visual appeal of facilities;
- reliability – the ability to perform the service consistently and accurately;
- responsiveness – a willingness to help customers and provide prompt service;
- assurance – the knowledge and courtesy of employees and their ability to convey trust and confidence;
- empathy – providing caring, individualized attention.

Note that there has been heated dispute about the validity of this SERVQUAL instrument framework (Parasuraman *et al.*, 1985) in determining service quality, see for example Cronin and Taylor (1992). Despite this it is still instructive to apply these dimensions of service quality to customer service on the web. We will now review each dimension of SERVQUAL.

Tangibles

It can be suggested that the tangibles dimension is influenced by ease of use and visual appeal based on the structural and graphic design of the site. The importance of these factors to consumers is indicated by a 1999 study by Forrester Research of 8,600 US consumers that found that the main reason for returning to a site were high-quality content (75 per cent), ease of use (66 per cent), speed to download (58 per cent) and frequency of update (54 per cent); these were the most important aspects of web site quality mentioned.

Reliability

The reliability dimension is dependent on the availability of the web site, or in other words, how easy it is to connect to the web site as a user.

Reliability of e-mail response is also a key issue; Chaffey and Edgar (2000) report on a survey of 361 UK web sites across different sectors. Of those in the sample, 331 (or 92 per cent) were accessible at the time of the survey and, of these, 299 provided an e-mail contact point. E-mail enquiries were sent to all of these 299 web sites; of these, 9 undeliverable mail messages were received. It can be seen that at the time of the survey, service availability is certainly not universal.

Responsiveness

The same survey showed that responsiveness was poor overall: of the 290 successfully delivered e-mails, a 62 per cent response rate occurred within a 28-day period. For over a third of companies there was zero response!

Of the companies that did respond, there was a difference in responsiveness (excluding immediately delivered automated responses) from 8 minutes to over 19 working days! While the mean overall was 2 working days, 5 hours and 11 minutes, the median across all sectors (on the basis of the fastest 50 per cent of responses received) was 1 working day and 34 minutes. The median result suggests that response within one working day represents best practice and could form the basis for consumer expectations.

Responsiveness is also indicated by the performance of the web site – the time it takes for a page request to be delivered to the user's browser as a page impression. Since there is a wide variability in the delivery of information and hence service quality from web servers hosted at ISPs, companies should be careful to monitor this and specify levels of quality with suppliers in service-level agreements (SLAs). Zona

Research (1999) conducted an analysis that suggests that $4.35 billion may be lost in e-commerce revenues due to customer 'bailout' when customers are unwilling to wait for information to download. The report notes that many customers may not be prepared to wait longer than eight seconds!

As explained in *Chapter 7*, effective fulfilment is also an essential part of responsiveness.

Assurance

In an e-mail context, assurance can best be considered as the quality of response. In the survey reported by Chaffey and Edgar (2000), of 180 responses received, 91 per cent delivered a personalized human response with 9 per cent delivering an automated response which did not address the individual enquiry; 40 per cent of responses answered or referred to all three questions with 10 per cent answering two questions, and 22 per cent one. Overall, 38 per cent did not answer any of the specific questions posed!

A further assurance concern of e-commerce web sites is the privacy and security of customer information. A company that adheres to the UK Which? Web Trader (www.which.net/webtrader) or TRUSTe principles (www.truste.org) will provide better assurance than one that does not. The following actions can be suggested to achieve assurance in an e-commerce site:

1. Provide clear and effective privacy statements
2. Follow privacy and consumer protection guidelines in all local markets
3. Make security of customer data a priority
4. Use independent certification bodies
5. Emphasize the excellence of service quality in all communications.

Empathy

Although it might be considered that empathy requires personal human contact, it can still be achieved, to an extent, through e-mail. Chaffey and Edgar (2000) report that of the responses received, 91 per cent delivered a personalized human response, with 29 per cent passing on the enquiry within their organization. Of these 53, 23 further responses were received within the 28-day period and 30 (or 57 per cent) of passed-on queries were not responded to further.

Provision of personalization facilities is also an indication of the empathy provided by the web site, but more research is needed as to customers' perception of the value of web pages that are dynamically created to meet a customer's information needs.

An alternative approach for considering how service quality can be delivered through e-commerce is to consider how the site provides customer service at the different stages of the buying decision shown in *Table 9.1*. Thus quality service is not only dependent on how well the purchase itself is facilitated, but also on how easy it is for customers to select products and on after-sales service, including fulfilment quality. The Epson UK site (www.epson.co.uk) illustrates how the site can be used to help in all stages of the buying process. Interactive tools are available to help users select a particular printer, diagnose and solve faults, and technical brochures can be downloaded. Feedback is solicited on how well these services meet customers' needs.

These SERVQUAL elements have been applied to online banking by Jun and Cai (2001) in a detailed study. This supports the importance of the original SERVQUAL elements in an online setting. For example, it highlights the importance of a timely, accurate response to customer queries. It also uncovers a particular feature of online service – that customers expect to see a continuous improvement to site services, and suggests their satisfaction will be reduced if positive changes are not made.

In summary, it can be suggested that for managers wishing to apply a framework such as SERVQUAL in an e-commerce context there are three stages appropriate to managing the process.

1 *Understanding expectations*. Customer expectations for the e-commerce environment in a particular market sector must be understood. The SERVQUAL framework can be used with market research and benchmarking of other sites, as described in *Chapter 12*, to understand requirements such as responsiveness and empathy. Scenarios can also be used to identify the customer expectations of using services on a site.
2 *Setting and communicating the service promise*. Once expectations are understood, marketing communications can be used to inform the customers of the level of service. This can be achieved through customer service guarantees or promises. It is better to under-promise than over-promise. A book retailer that delivers the book in two days when three days were promised will earn the customer's loyalty better than the retailer that promises one day, but delivers in two! The enlightened company may also explain what it will do if it does not meet its promises – will the customer be recompensed? The service promise must also be communicated internally and combined with training to ensure that the service is delivered.
3 *Delivering the service promise*. Finally, commitments must be delivered through on-site service, support from employees and physical fulfilment. If not, online credibility is destroyed and a customer may never return.

Debate 9.2

Will software replace 'humanware'?

'Some remote customer service contacts will always require personal, human interaction rather than automated electronic responses.'

As a conclusion to this section review *Activity 9.3* to gain an appreciation of solutions that e-commerce sites are using to provide service quality.

Activity 9.3 Delivering customer support on an e-commerce site

Purpose

To review how on-site facilities are used to deliver customer service excellence.

Activity

Visit the web site of an airline and an e-tailer within your country, for example British Airways (www.britishairways.com) and Lands End (www.landsend.com). Review how the site content and in particular the customer support area delivers in the SERVQUAL areas of tangibles, reliability, responsiveness, assurance and empathy. The Landsend live area of the Lands End site provides a good example of state-of-the-art features such as online chat for customer support.

No suggested answer supplied.

Customer extension

Customer extension Deepening the relationship with the customer through increased interaction and product transactions.

Customer extension has the aim of increasing the **lifetime value** of the customer to the company by encouraging cross-sales, for example an Egg credit card customer may be offered the option of a loan or a deposit account. When a customer returns to a web site this is an opportunity for cross-selling and such offers can be communicated. Direct e-mail is also an excellent way for informing a customer about other company products and it is also useful in encouraging repeat visits by publicizing new content or promotions. E-mail is vitally important to achieving online CRM since the web site is a pull medium which the customer will only be exposed to if they decide to visit the web site and they are unlikely to do this unless there is some stimulus. However, e-mail is a push medium where the customer can be reminded about current promotions and offers and why they should visit the web site. This is why it is so important to capture the customer's e-mail address at the acquisition stage. The use of direct e-mail to communicate promotions to customers presents a dilemma to the online marketer since although it is potentially powerful in achieving new orders, as explained in the section on *retention*, if it is used too frequently or e-mail is unsolicited then it may achieve the opposite to the desired effect and the customer will be lost.

Lifetime value (LTV)
The combined revenue attributable to a customer during their relationship with a company.

Many companies are now only proactively marketing to favoured customers. Seth Godin (1999) says '*Focus on share of customer, not market share – fire 70 per cent of your customers and watch your profits go up!*' One UK financial services provider has analysed characteristics of high-churn-rate customers, and when a new prospect fitting this profile contacts the call centre they are actively discouraged. Using these techniques it is possible to increase share of customer.

Share of wallet or share of customer
The proportion of customer expenditure in a particular category that belongs to a single customer.

Advanced online segmentation and targeting techniques

The most sophisticated segmentation and targeting (see *Chapter 8* for an introduction) schemes for extension are often used by e-retailers, who have detailed customer profiling information and purchase history data as they seek to increase customer lifetime value through encouraging increased use of online services over time. However, the general principles of this approach can also be used by other types of companies online. The segmentation and targeting approach used by e-retailers is based on five main elements which in effect are layered on top of each other. The number of options used, and so the sophistication of the approach, will depend on resources available, technology capabilities and opportunities afforded by the list:

1 *Identify customer lifecycle groups. Figure 9.16* illustrates this approach. As visitors use online services they can potentially pass through seven or more stages. Once companies have defined these groups and set up the customer relationship man-

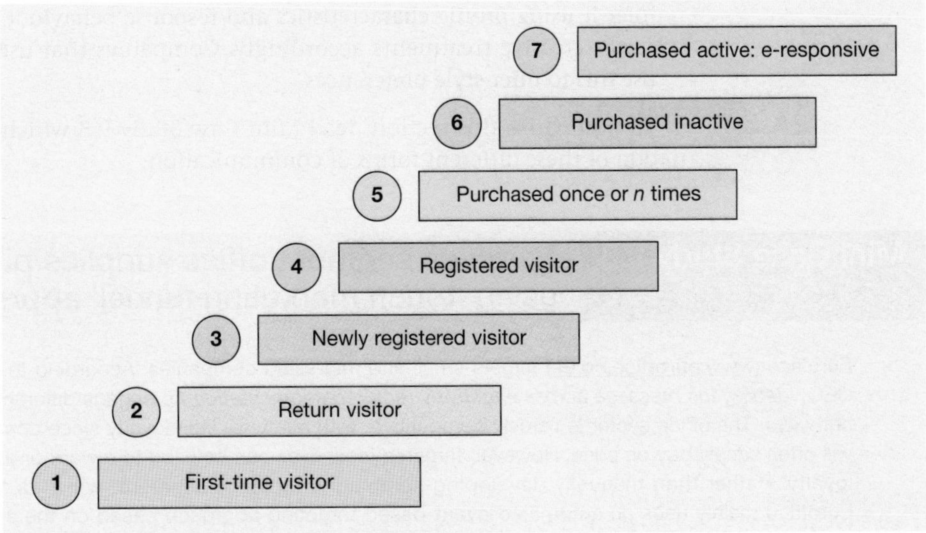

Figure 9.16 **Customer lifecycle segmentation**

agement infrastructure to categorize customers in this way, they can then deliver targeted messages, either by personalized on-site messaging or through e-mails that are triggered automatically due to different rules. First-time visitors can be identified by whether they have a cookie placed on their PC. Once visitors are then registered, they can be tracked through the remaining stages. Two particularly important groups are customers who have purchased one or more times. For many e-retailers, encouraging customers to move from the first purchase to the second purchase and then on to the third purchase is a key challenge. Specific promotions can be used to encourage further purchases. Similarly, once customers become inactive, i.e. they have not purchased for a defined period such as 3 months, they become inactive and further follow-ups are required.

2 *Identify customer profile characteristics*. This is a traditional segmentation based on the type of customer. For B2C e-retailers it will include age, sex and geography. For B2B companies, it will include size of company and the industry sector or application they operate in.
3 *Identify behaviour in response and purchase*. As customers progress through the lifecycle shown in *Figure 9.16*, though analysis of the database, they will be able to build up a detailed response and purchase history which considers the details of recency, frequency, monetary value and category of products purchased. This approach, which is known as 'RFM or FRAC analysis', is reviewed below. See *Case Study 9.1* for how Tesco target their online customers.
4 *Identify multi-channel behaviour* (*channel preference*). Regardless of the enthusiasm of the company for online channels, some customers will prefer using online channels and others will prefer traditional channels. This will, to an extent, be indicated by RFM and response analysis since customers with a preference for online channels will be more responsive and will make more purchases online. Customers that prefer online channels can be targeted mainly by online communications such as e-mail, while customers who prefer traditional channels can be targeted by traditional communications such as direct mail or phone. This is 'right-chanelling', which was introduced in *Chapter 5*.
5 *Tone and style preference*. In a similar manner to channel preference, customers will respond differently to different types of message. Some may like a more rational appeal, in which case a detailed e-mail explaining the benefits of the offer may work best. Others will prefer an emotional appeal based on images and with warmer, less formal copy. Sophisticated companies will test for this in customers or infer it using profile characteristics and response behaviour and then develop different creative treatments accordingly. Companies that use polls can potentially use this to infer style preferences.

To summarize this section, read Mini Case Study 9.3 which illustrates the combination of these different forms of communication.

Mini Case Study 9.3 Euroffice segment office supplies purchasers using 'touch marketing funnel' approach

Euroffice (www.euroffice.co.uk) targets small and mid-sized companies. According to George Karibian, CEO, '*getting the message across effectively required segmentation*' to engage different people in different ways. The office sector is fiercely competitive, with relatively little loyalty since company purchasers will often simply buy on price. However, targeted incentives can be used to reward or encourage buyers' loyalty. Rather than manually developing campaigns for each segment, which is time-consuming, Euroffice mainly uses an automated event-based targeting approach based on the system identifying the stage at which a consumer is in the lifecycle, i.e. how many products they have purchased and the types of product within their purchase history. Karibian calls this a '*touch marketing funnel approach*' approach, i.e. the touch strategy is determined by customer segmentation and response. Three main groups of customers are identified in the lifecycle and these are broken down further according to purchase category. Also layered on this segmentation is breakdown into buyer type – are they a small home-user, an operations manager at a mid-size company or a purchasing manager at a larger company? Each will respond to different promotions.

The first group, at the top of the funnel and the largest are '*Group 1. Trial customers*' who have made one or two purchases. For the first group, Euroffice believes that creating impulse-buying through price promotions is most important. These will be based on categories purchased in the past. The second group, '*Group 2. The nursery*' have made three to eight purchases. A particular issue, as with many e-retailers is encouraging customers from the third to fourth purchase; there is a more significant drop-out at this point which the company uses marketing to control. Karibian says: '*When they get to group two, it's about creating frequency of purchase to ensure they don't forget you*'. Euroffice sends a printed catalogue to Group 2 separately from their merchandise as a reminder about the company. The final group, '*Group 3. Key accounts or "Crown Jewels"*' have made nine or more orders. They also tend to have a higher basket value. 'These people are the Crown Jewels and will spend an average of £135 per order compared to an average of £55 for trial customers'. They have a 90% probability of re-ordering within a six-month period. For this group, tools have been developed on the site to make it easier for them to shop. The intention is that these customers find these tools help them in making their orders and they become reliant on them, so achieving 'soft lock-in'.

Source: Adapted from the company web site press releases and *Revolution* (2005)

Sense, Respond, Adjust – delivering relevant e-communications through monitoring customer behaviour

To be able to identify customers in the categories of value, growth, responsiveness or defection risk we need to characterize them using information about them which indicates their purchase and campaign-response *behaviour*. This is because the past and current actual behaviour is often the best predictor of future behaviour. We can then seek to influence this future behaviour.

Digital marketing enables marketers to create a cycle of:

- Monitoring customer actions or behaviours and then . . .
- Reacting with appropriate messages and offers to encourage desired behaviours
- Monitoring response to these messages and continuing with additional communications and monitoring.

Or, if you prefer, simply:

Sense → Respond → Adjust

The sensing is done through using technology to monitor visits to particular content on a web site or clicking on particular links in an e-mail. Purchase history can also be monitored, but since purchase information is often stored in a legacy sales system it is important to integrate this with systems used for communicating with customers. The response can be done through messages on-site, or in e-mail and then adjustment occurs through further sensing and responding.

This 'Sense and Respond' technique has traditionally been completed by catalogue retailers such as Argos or Littlewoods Index using a technique known as 'RFM analysis'. This technique tends to be little known outside retail circles, but e-CRM gives great potential to applying it in a range of techniques since we can use it not only to analyse purchase history, but also visit or log-in frequency to a site or online service and response rates to e-mail communications.

Recency Frequency Monetary value (RFM) analysis

RFM is sometimes known as 'FRAC', which stands for: **F**requency, **R**ecency, **A**mount, (obviously equivalent to monetary value), **C**ategory (types of product purchased – not included within RFM). We will now give an overview of how RFM approaches can be applied, with special reference to online marketing. We will also look at the related concepts of latency and hurdle rates.

Recency

This is the **R**ecency of customer action, e.g. purchase, site visit, account access, e-mail response, e.g. 3 months ago. Novo (2004) stresses the importance of recency when he says:

> *Recency, or the number of days that have gone by since a customer completed an action (purchase, log-in, download, etc.) is the most powerful predictor of the customer repeating an action ... Recency is why you receive another catalogue from the company shortly after you make your first purchase from them.*

Online applications of analysis of recency include: monitoring through time to identify vulnerable customers and scoring customers to preferentially target more responsive customers for cost savings.

Frequency

Frequency is the number of times an action is completed in the period of a customer action, e.g. purchase, visit, e-mail response, e.g. five purchases per year, five visits per month, five log-ins per week, five e-mail opens per month, five e-mail clicks per year. Online applications of this analysis include combining with Recency for RF targeting.

Monetary value

The **M**onetary value of purchase(s) can be measured in different ways, e.g. average order value of £50, total annual purchase value of £5,000. Generally, customers with higher monetary values tend to have a higher loyalty and potential future value since they have purchased more items historically. One example application would be to exclude these customers from special promotions if their RF scores suggested they were actively purchasing. Frequency is often a proxy for monetary value per year since the more products purchased, the higher the overall monetary value. It is possible then to simplify analysis by just using Recency and Frequency. Monetary value can also skew the analysis for high-value initial purchases.

Latency

Latency is related to Frequency, being the average time between customer events in the customer lifecycle. Examples include the average time between web-site visits, second and third purchase and e-mail clickthroughs. Online applications of latency include putting in place triggers that alert companies to customer behaviour outside the norm, for example increased interest or disinterest, then managing this behaviour using e-communications or traditional communications. For example, a B2B or B2C organization with a long interval between purchases would find that if the average latency increased for a particular customer, then they may be investigating an additional purchase (their recency and frequency would likely increase also). E-mails, phone calls or direct mail could then be used to target this person with relevant offers according to what they were searching for.

Hurdle rate

According to Novo (2004), hurdle rate refers to the percentage of customers in a group (such as in a segment or on a list) who have completed an action. It is a useful concept, although the terminology doesn't really describe its application. Its value is that it can be used to compare the engagement of different groups or to set targets to increase engagement with online channels as the examples below show:

- 20% of customers have visited in the past 6 months
- 5% of customers have made three or more purchases in the year
- 60% of registrants have logged on to the system in the year
- 30% have clicked through on e-mail in the year.

Grouping customers into different RFM categories

In the examples above, each division for Recency, Frequency and Monetary value is placed in an arbitrary position to place a roughly equal number of customers in each group. This approach is also useful since the marketer can set thresholds of value relevant to their understanding of their customers.

RFM analysis involves two techniques for grouping customers:

1 *Statistical RFM analysis*. This involves placing an equal number of customers in each RFM category using quintiles of 20% (10 deciles can also be used for larger databases) as shown in *Figure 9.17*. The figure also shows one application of RFM with a view to using communications channels more effectively. Lower-cost e-communications can be used to communicate with customers who use online services more frequently since they prefer these channels and more expensive communications can be used for customers who seem to prefer traditional channels. This process is sometimes known as 'right-channelling' or 'right-touching'.

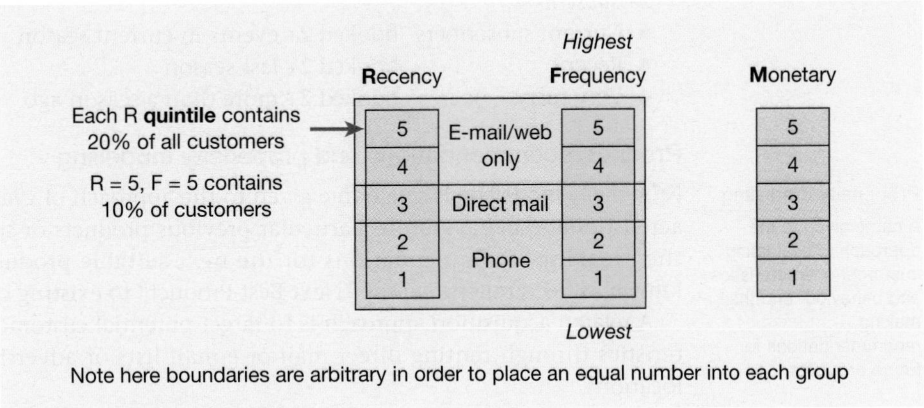

Figure 9.17 **RFM analysis**

2 *Arbitrary divisions of customer database*. This approach is also useful since the marketer can set thresholds of value relevant to their understanding of their customers.

For example, RFM analysis can be applied for targeting using e-mail according to how a customer interacts with an e-commerce site. Values could be assigned to each customer as follows:

Recency:
1 – Over 12 months
2 – Within last 12 months
3 – Within last 6 months
4 – Within last 3 months
5 – Within last 1 month

Frequency:
1 – More than once every 6 months
2 – Every 6 months
3 – Every 3 months
4 – Every 2 months
5 – Monthly

Monetary value:
1 – Less than £10
2 – £10–50
3 – £50–£100
4 – £100–£200
5 – More than £200

Simplified versions of this analysis can be created to make it more manageable, for example a theatre group uses these nine categories for its direct marketing:

Oncers (attended theatre once)
- Recent oncers — attended <12 months
- Rusty oncers — attended >12, <36 months
- Very rusty oncers — attended 36+ months

Twicers:
- Recent twicer — attended < 12 months
- Rusty twicer — attended >12, < 36 months
- Very rusty twicer — attended in 36+ months

2+ subscribers:
- Current subscribers — booked 2+ events in current season
- Recent — booked 2+ last season
- Very rusty — booked 2+ more than a season ago

Product recommendations and propensity modelling

Propensity modelling
A name given to the approach of evaluating customer characteristics and behaviour and then making recommendations for future products.

Propensity modelling is one name given to the approach of evaluating customer characteristics and behaviour, in particular previous products or services purchased, and then making recommendations for the next suitable product. However, it is best known as 'recommending the "Next Best Product" to existing customers'.

A related acquisition approach is to target potential customers with similar characteristics through renting direct mail or e-mail lists or advertising online in similar locations.

The following recommendations are based on those in van Duyne *et al.* (2002).

1 *Create automatic product relationships:* [i.e. Next Best Product] A low-tech approach to this is for each product, to group together products, previously purchased together. Then for each product, rank product by number of times purchased together to find relationships.
2 *Cordon off and minimize the 'real estate' devoted to related products.* An area of screen should be reserved for 'Next-best product prompts' for up-selling and cross-selling.
   However, if these can be made part of the current product they may be more effective.
3 *Use familiar 'trigger words'.* That is, familiar from using other sites such as Amazon. Such phrases include:
   'Related products', 'Your recommendations', 'Similar', 'Customers who bought…', 'Top 3 related products'.
4 *Editorialize about related products* i.e. Within copy about a product.
5 *Allow quick purchase of related products.*

6 *Sell related product during checkout.* And also on post-transaction pages, i.e. after one item has been added to basket or purchased.

Note that techniques do not necessarily require an expensive recommendations engine except for very large sites.

Technology solutions for CRM

Database technology is at the heart of delivering CRM applications. Often the database is accessible through an intranet web site accessed by employees, or an extranet accessed by customers or partners provides an interface with the entire customer relationship management system. Today, on-demand web services such as Siebel CRM On Demand (www.crmondemand.com) and Salesforce.com (www.salesforce.com) are becoming increasingly popular.

E-mail is used to manage many of the inbound, outbound and internal communications managed by the e-CRM system. Using e-mail for communications is a service provided by e-CRM systems such as Epiphany (www.epiphany.com) or Siebel (www.siebel.com), or smaller businesses can use an e-mail marketing ASP service such as EmailReaction (www.emailreaction).

A workflow system is often used for automating CRM processes. For example, a workflow system can remind sales representatives about customer contacts or can be used to manage service delivery such as the many stages of arranging a mortgage. The three main types of customer data held as tables in customer databases for CRM are typically:

1 *Personal and profile data.* These include contact details and characteristics for profiling customers such as age and sex (B2C) and business size, industry sector and individual's role in the buying decision (B2B).
2 *Transaction data.* A record of each purchase transaction including specific product purchased, quantities, category, location, date and time, and channel where purchased.
3 *Communications data.* A record of which customers have been targeted by campaigns, and their response to them (outbound communications). Also includes a record of inbound enquiries and sales representative visits and reports (B2B).

The behavioural data available through 2 and 3 are very important for targeting customers to more closely meet their needs.

Research completed by Stone *et al.* (2001) illustrates how customer data collected through CRM applications can be used for marketing. The types of data that are held, together with the frequency of their usage, are:

Basic customer information	75%
Campaign history	62.5%
Purchase patterns (sales histories)	50%
Market information	42.5%
Competitor information	42.5%
Forecasts	25%

The data within CRM systems that were reported to be used for marketing applications were as follows:

Targeted marketing	80%
Segmentation	65%
Keeping the right customers	47.5%

Trend analysis	45%
Increased loyalty	42.5%
Customized offers	32.5%
Increase share of customer	27.5%

The Hewson Consulting Group (www.hewson.co.uk) identify the following benefits of CRM systems to customers:

- Improved response times to customer requests for information;
- Delivered product meets customer requirements;
- Reduced costs of buying and using a product or service;
- Immediate access to order status and more responsive technical support.

It is apparent that while many of these benefits could be achieved by phoning customer support staff who then access a CRM system, it may increase customer convenience, and reduce costs to the company, if they can access this information through a web interface. This approach is referred to as 'customer self-service'.

Customer self-service
Customers perform information requests and transactions through a web interface rather than contact with customer support staff.

Despite the benefits of CRM described in this chapter, it must be stressed that failure rates are high. Research conducted independently in 2000 by analysts Gartner and the Butler Group suggested that around 60 to 70 per cent of CRM projects fail (Mello, 2001). This is not necessarily indicative of weaknesses in the CRM concept, rather it indicates the difficulty of implementing a complex information system that requires substantial changes to organizations' processes and has major impacts on the staff. Such failure rates occur in many other information systems projects. In addition to the change management issues, discussed in *Chapter 10*, key technical issues for managers selecting e-CRM systems are:

1. Type of applications
2. Integration with back-office systems
3. The choice of single-vendor solutions or a more fragmented choice
4. Data quality.

Types of CRM applications

Figure 9.18 is intended to convey the complexity of providing CRM solutions. The aim of CRM technology is to provide an interface between the customer and the employee that replaces or facilitates direct interaction. From both customer and employee perspectives, the ultimate aim of CRM systems is to enable contact regardless of the communications channel that the customer wants to use, whether this is traditional methods such as phone or fax or newer digital technologies. Thus the ideal CRM system will support multi-channel communication or the customer-preferred channel. Regardless of channel, the customer will have different needs depending on their stage in the buying process (see section on *buyer behaviour*). In the figure, we identify three core needs for the customer – to find out more information about a product, to place an order and to receive post-sales support. Applications must be provided to support each of these needs. Likewise, the employee will have applications requirements to support the customer and the sales and marketing objectives of the organization; in the figure these are sales force automation, to place an order received by phone, by fax or in person and to answer customers' questions via a support system and knowledge base. At the heart of the system is the database storage needed to support these applications. The IT infrastructure described in *Chapter 3* such as servers, middleware and networking is not shown in the figure.

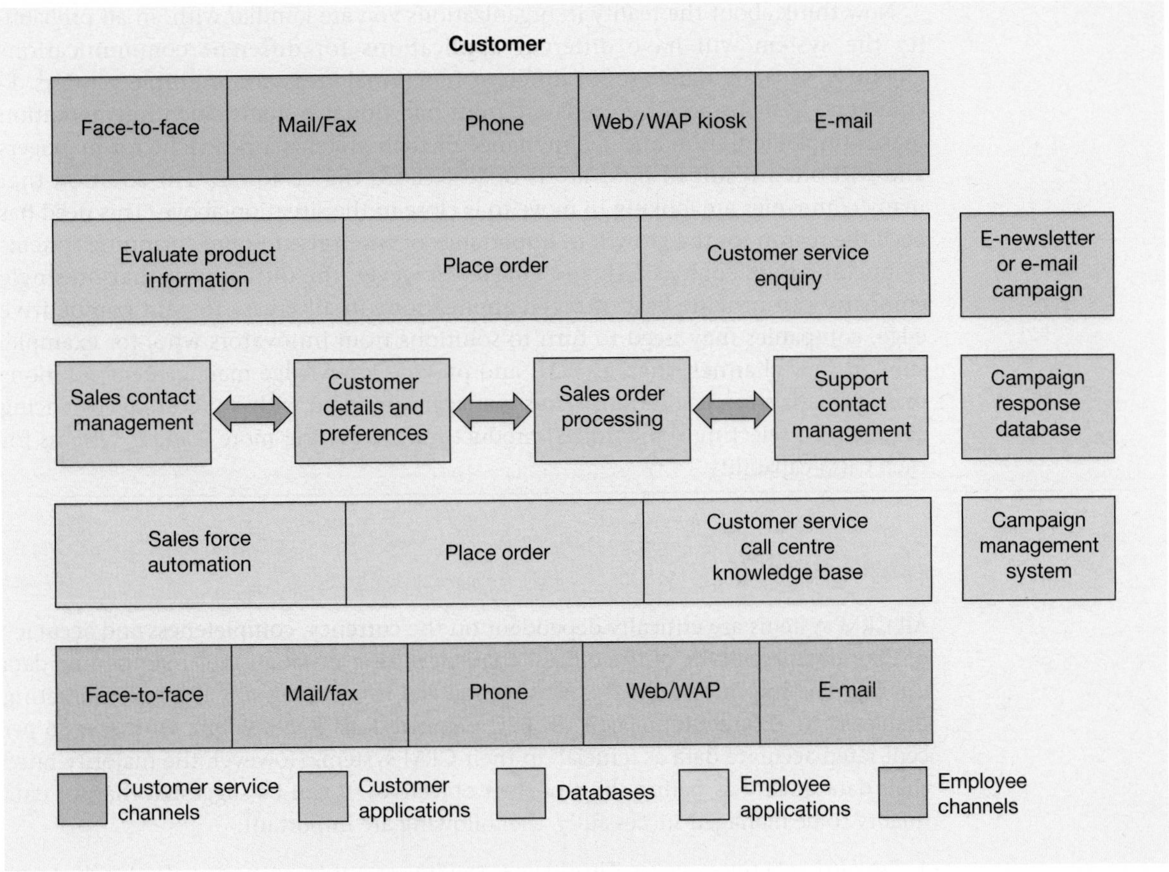

Figure 9.18 An overview of the components of CRM technologies

Integration with back-office systems

When introducing a CRM system to an organization, a company will have previously invested in systems for other key business functions such as sales order processing or customer support. These existing, legacy systems appear at both the applications and database levels in *Figure 9.18*. It will not be financially viable to discard these applications, but integration with them is vital to give visibility of the customer information to everyone in the organization and provide excellent customer support. Thus integration of legacy systems is a vital part of deciding on and implementing CRM systems.

The choice of single-vendor solutions or a more fragmented choice

Figure 9.18 highlights the key issues in deciding on and designing a system to support CRM. Think about the ideal situation; it would be:

- A single customer-facing and employee-facing application that supports all the communications channels;
- A single integrated database such that any employee has total visibility about a customer – they can access all visit, sales and support histories;
- From a single vendor for ease of implementation and support.

Now think about the reality in organizations you are familiar with: in all probability the system will have different applications for different communications channels, separate databases in different functional areas and multiple vendors. E-commerce systems are often separate from traditional systems. Such fragmentation makes implementation and maintenance of such systems a headache for managers and will often result in poor levels of service for the customer. The solution that many companies are looking to move to is close to the situation above. This need has been the reason for the growth in importance of enterprise resource planning systems from companies such as SAP and Oracle. However, the difficulty is that no single company can provide best-of-breed applications in all areas. To gain competitive edge, companies may need to turn to solutions from innovators who, for example, support new channels such as WAP, and provide knowledge management solutions or sales management solutions. Thus managers are faced with a precarious balancing act between selecting standardized products or integrating more leading systems for each CRM capability.

Data quality

All CRM systems are critically dependent on the currency, completeness and accuracy of their databases. One of the biggest challenges after installation is maintaining data quality. The importance of this was recognized in a survey of CRM and marketing managers in 120 medium–large UK B2C organizations (QAS, 2002). Of these, 86 per cent rated accurate data as 'crucial' to their CRM system. However, the majority rated their data quality as falling short of their objectives. It can be suggested that for data quality to be managed successfully, the following are important:

1 *Establish a business owner.* This issue is too important to be managed solely by technologists and it requires management at customer contact points, which are part of the responsibility of marketing. All staff involved with managing customer data should be made clear about their responsibilities.
2 *Optimize quality on capture.* Validation checks can be built in at data entry to check that fields such as postcode are complete and accurate.
3 *Continuously improve quality.* Customer contact details constantly change. Changes of e-mail address are even more difficult to manage than changes of physical address. As a consequence, all contact points, whether with the web site, contact-centre staff, or sales staff should be used to help maintain data quality.
4 *Work towards a single view of customer.* Many errors result because different data are stored in different databases. Unifying the data in a single database is the aim for many organizations, but it is arguably more difficult the older and larger the organization is.
5 *Adopt a data quality policy.* Of the sample in the QAS (2002) survey 40 per cent had no data quality policy, but this is essential to help achieve the four steps above.

As a conclusion to this chapter, read *Case Study 9.1* as an example of how Tesco has used CRM technology to improve their customers' 'share of wallet'. It is estimated that for every £8 spent on groceries £1 is spent at Tesco, which is now seeking its share of all retail category sales.

Case Study 9.1 Tesco.com increases product range and uses triggered communications to support CRM

Context

Tesco, well known as Britain's leading food retail group with a presence in Europe and Asia has also been a pioneer online. By September 2005 online sales in the first half of the year were £401 million, a 31% year-on-year increase, and profit increased by 37% to £21 million. Tesco.com now receives 170,000 orders each week. Soon it should reach an annual turnover of £1 billion online and it is generally recognized as the world's largest online grocer.

Product ranges

The Tesco.com site acts as a portal to most of Tesco's products, including various non-food ranges (for example, books, DVDs and electrical items under the 'Extra' banner), Tesco Personal Finance and the telecoms businesses, as well as services offered in partnership with specialist companies, such as dieting clubs, flights and holidays, music downloads, gas, electricity and DVD rentals. It does not currently sell clothing online but in May 2005 it introduced a clothing web site (www.clothingat-tesco.com), initially to showcase Tesco's clothing brands and link customers to their nearest store with this range.

Competitors

Tesco currently leads the UK's other leading grocery retailers in terms of market share. This pattern is repeated online. The compilation below is from Hitwise (2005) and the figures in brackets show market share for traditional offline retail formats from the Taylor Nelson Softres Super Panel (see http://superpanel.tns-global.com).

1. Tesco Superstore, 27.28% (29% of retail trade)
2. ASDA, 13.36%
3. ASDA @t Home, 10.13% (17.1%)
4. Sainsburys, 8.42%
5. Tesco Wine Warehouse, 8.19%
6. Sainsburys to You, 5.86% (15.9%)
7. Waitrose.com, 3.42% (3.6%)
8. Ocado, 3.32% (owned by Waitrose, 3.6%)
9. Lidl, 2.49% (1.8%)
10. ALDI – UK, 2.10% (2.3%).

Some companies are repeated since their main site and the online shopping site are reported on separately. Asda.com now seems to be performing in a consistent manner online to its offline presence. However, Sainsburys' online performance seems to be significantly lower compared to its offline performance. Some providers such as Ocado which originally just operated within the London area have a strong local performance.

Notably, some of Tesco.com's competitors are absent from the Hitwise listing since their strategy has been to focus on retail formats. These are Morrisons (12.5% retail share), Somerfield (5.5%) and Co-op (5.0%).

Promotion of service

As with other online retailers, Tesco.com relies on in-store advertising and marketing to the supermarket's Clubcard loyalty scheme's customer base to persuade customers to shop online. NMA (2005c) quotes Nigel Dodd, marketing director at Tesco.com, as saying: '*These are invaluable sources as we have such a strong customer base*'. However, for non-food goods the supermarket does advertise online using keyword targeted ads.

For existing customers, e-mail marketing and direct mail marketing to provide special offers and promotions to customers are important.

According to Humby and Hunt (2003), e-retailer Tesco.com uses what he describes as a 'commitment-based segmentation' or 'loyalty ladder' which is based on recency of purchase, frequency of purchase and value which is used to identify six lifecycle categories which are then further divided to target communications:

- 'Logged-on'
- 'Cautionary'
- 'Developing'
- 'Established'
- 'Dedicated'
- 'Logged-off' (the aim here is to win back).

Tesco then uses automated event-triggered messaging to encourage continued purchase. For example, Tesco.com has a touch strategy which includes a sequence of follow-up communications triggered after different events in the customer lifecycle. In the example given below, communications after event 1 are intended to achieve the objective of converting a web-site visitor to action; communications after event 2 are intended to move the customer from a first-time purchaser to a regular purchaser and for event 3 to reactivate lapsed purchasers.

- *Trigger event 1: Customer first registers on site (but does not buy)*
  Auto-response (AR) 1: 2 days after registration e-mail sent offering phone assistance and £5 discount off first purchase to encourage trial.
- *Trigger event 2: Customer first purchases online*
  AR1: Immediate order confirmation.
  AR2: Five days after purchase e-mail sent with link to online customer satisfaction survey asking about quality of service from driver and picker (e.g. item quality and substitutions).
  AR3: Two weeks after first purchase – direct mail offering tips on how to use service and £5 discount on next purchases intended to encourage re-use of online services.

→

AR4: Generic monthly e-newsletter with online exclusive offers encouraging cross-selling.
AR5: Bi-weekly alert with personalised offers for customer.
AR6: After two months – £5 discount for next shop.
AR7: Quarterly mailing of coupons encouraging repeat sales and cross-sales.

- *Trigger event 3: Customer does not purchase for an extended period*
  AR1: Dormancy detected – reactivation e-mail with survey of how the customer is finding the service (to identify any problems) and a £5 incentive.
  AR2: A further discount incentive is used in order to encourage continued usage to shop after the first shop after a break.

Tesco's online product strategy

NMA (2005c) ran a profile of Laura Wade-Gery, CEO of Tesco.com since January 2004, which provides an interesting insight into how the business has run. In her first year, total sales were increased 24% to £719 million. Laura is 40 years old, a keen athlete and has followed a varied career developing through an MA in History at Magdalen College, Oxford, an MBA from Insead; Manager and partner in Kleinwort Benson; Manager and senior consultant, Gemini Consulting; Targeted marketing director (Tesco Clubcard), and Group strategy director, Tesco Stores.

The growth overseen by Wade-Gery has been achieved through a combination of initiatives. Product range development is one key area. In early 2005, Tesco.com fulfilled 150,000 grocery orders a week but now also offers more intangible offerings, such as e-diets and music downloads.

Wade-Gery has also focused on improving the customer experience online – the time it takes for a new customer to complete their first order has been decreased from over an hour to 35 minutes through usability work culminating in a major site revision.

To support the business as it diversifies into new areas, Wade-Gery's strategy was '*to make home delivery part of the DNA of Tesco*' according to NMA (2005c). She continues: '*What we offer is delivery to your home of a Tesco service – it's an obvious extension of the home-delivered groceries concept*'. By May 2005, Tesco.com had 30,000 customers signed up for DVD rental, through partner Video Island (which runs the rival Screenselect service). Over the next year, Wade-Gery's target is to treble this total, while also extending home-delivery services to the likes of bulk wine and white goods.

Wade-Gery looks to achieve synergy between the range of services offered. For example, its partnership with eDiets can be promoted through the Tesco Clubcard loyalty scheme, with mailings to 10m customers a year. In July 2004, Tesco.com Limited paid £2 million for the exclusive licence to eDiets.com in the UK and Ireland under the URLs www.eDietsUK.com and www.eDiets.ie. Through promoting the services through the URLs, Tesco can use the dieting business to grow use of the Tesco.com service and in-store sales.

To help keep focus on home retail delivery, Wade-Gery sold women's portal iVillage (www.ivillage.co.uk) back to its US owners for an undisclosed sum in March 2004. She explained to NMA:

> *It's a very different sort of product to the other services that we're embarking on. In my mind, we stand for providing services and products that you buy, which is slightly different to the world of providing information.*

The implication is that there was insufficient revenue from ad sales on iVillage and insufficient opportunities to promote Tesco.com sales. However, iVillage was a useful learning experience in that there are some parallels with iVillage, such as message boards and community advisers.

Wade-Gery is also director of Tesco Mobile, the joint 'pay-as-you-go' venture with O_2 which is mainly serviced online, although promoted in-store and via direct mail. Tesco also offers broadband and dial-up ISP services, but believe the market for Internet telephony (provided through Skype and Vonage for example) is not sufficiently developed. Tesco.com have concentrated on more traditional services which have the demand, for example Tesco Telecom fixed-line services attracted over a million customers in their first year.

However, this is not to say that Tesco.com will not invest in relatively new services. In November 2004, Tesco introduced a music download service, and just six months later Wade-Gery estimates they have around 10% market share – one of the benefits of launching relatively early. Again, there is synergy, this time with hardware sales. NMA (2005c) reported that as MP3 players were unwrapped, sales went up – even on Christmas Day! She says:

> *The exciting thing about digital is where can you take it in the future. As the technology grows, we'll be able to turn Tesco.com into a digital download store of all sorts, rather than just music. Clearly, film [through video on demand] would be next.*

But it has to be based firmly on analysis of customer demand. Wade-Gery says: '*The number one thing for us is whether the product is something that customers are saying they want, has it reached a point where mass-market customers are interested?*' There also has to be scope for simplification. NMA (2005c) notes that Tesco is built on a core premise of convenience and value and Wade-Gery believes what it's already done with mobile tariffs, broadband packages and music downloads are good examples of the retailer's knack for streamlining propositions. She says: '*We've actually managed to get people joining broadband who have never even had a dial-up service*'.

Sources: Humby and Hunt (2003), NMA (2005c), Hitwise (2005), Wikipedia (2005)

Question

Based on the case study and your own research on competitors, summarize the strategic approaches which have helped Tesco.com achieve success online.

Summary

1 The objective of customer relationship management (CRM) is to increase customer loyalty in order to increase profitability. CRM is aimed at improving all aspects of the level of customer service.

2 CRM tactics can be based around the acquisition–retention–extension model of the ideal relationship between company and customer.

3 In an e-commerce context, acquisition refers to gaining new customers to a company and converting existing customers to online services. To enable an online relationship it is important to profile customers to find out their needs and expectations and obtain an opt-in e-mail agreement to continue the dialogue.

4 Marketing communications techniques to achieve acquisition, retention and extension include traditional online mass-media techniques and specialized online techniques such as search engine registration, link-building, e-mail marketing and banner advertising.

5 Techniques for customer retention include the use of extranets, online communities, online sales promotions and e-mail marketing.

6 Customer extension involves better understanding of the customer through feedback on new product development and encouraging customers to increase the depth of their relationship by offering complementary products for purchase or increasing purchase frequency.

7 Knowledge of online buyer behaviour, and in particular, the differing needs of the customer through the different stages of the buying decision can be used to improve CRM management.

8 Customer service quality is important in achieving loyalty and the SERVQUAL framework can be used to consider how to use the Internet to achieve this.

9 Technology solutions for CRM are aimed at providing interaction between employees and customers across multiple communications channels with all customer information stored in a single database to provide complete visibility of the customer by employees. Managers look to minimize the number of solutions partners they work with to achieve these goals.

10 Specific technology application requirements for CRM are sales-force automation (contact management) and call centre applications which integrate workflow to manage queries and a knowledge base from which queries can be reviewed.

Exercises

Self-assessment questions

1 What are the goals of acquisition and retention in an online context?

2 Outline the differences between permission marketing and interruption marketing including reference to the terms 'opt-in' and 'opt-out'.

→

3 Summarize the main types of online marketing communications for traffic building.

4 Explain why mixed-mode buying needs to be understood by those managing an e-commerce site.

5 Explain a range of techniques for attracting repeat visits to a web site.

6 What is the difference between personalization and mass customization?

7 How can an e-commerce site be used to achieve extension in CRM?

8 What are the management issues in managing data and applications integration in CRM?

Essay and discussion questions

1 On what basis should marketing managers decide on the communications mix for an e-commerce site?

2 Evaluate the current communications mix for an online e-tailer and make recommendations for future communications to achieve customer acquisition and retention.

3 Show how an understanding of the online buying process can be used to revise marketing communications.

4 Explain, using examples, typical differences between a traffic-building campaign for a B2B and a B2C company.

5 Examine the relationship between customer satisfaction, loyalty and sales in relation to a pureplay e-commerce site.

6 Examine the benefits and disadvantages of personalization, community building and direct e-mail. For an organization of your choice recommend a suitable balance between these e-marketing tools.

7 Assess whether a multi-vendor or single (limited number) vendor strategy is best for the implementation of e-CRM systems.

8 Recommend a CRM data and application architecture for The B2C Company that provides integration with related legacy systems.

Examination questions

1 Explain the concept of mixed-mode buying with reference to a pureplay e-commerce bookseller.

2 You are the e-commerce manager for a B2C site. Write an explanation to be included in a report to the managing director of why a permission marketing approach is required.

3 What different types of searching behaviour are exhibited by online users and what are the implications for someone responsible for traffic building on a site?

4 With reference to customer acquisition and retention, explain two goals for each required by an e-commerce site manager.

5 Outline four different methods of building web-site traffic.

6 Explain three factors that will influence the balance of online and offline web-site promotion for an organization.

7 How can an e-commerce site be used to inform new product development?

8 What is a legacy system and what is its relevance to CRM?

References

Agrawal, V., Arjona, V. and Lemmens, R. (2001) E-performance: the path to rational exuberance. *McKinsey Quarterly*, no. 1, 31–43.

Berthon, B., Pitt, L. and Watson, R. (1996) Resurfing W3: research perspectives on marketing communication and buyer behaviour on the World Wide Web. *International Journal of Advertising*, 15, 287–301.

BrandNewWorld (2004) AOL Research published at www.brandnewworld.co.uk.

Cartellieri, C., Parsons, A., Rao, V. and Zeisser, M. (1997) The real impact of Internet advertising. *McKinsey Quarterly*, no. 3, 44–63

Chaffey, D. and Edgar, M. (2000) Measuring online service quality. *Journal of Targeting, Analysis and Measurement for Marketing*, 8(4), 363–78.

Cronin, J. and Taylor, S. (1992) Measuring service quality: a reexamination and extension. *Journal of Marketing*, 56, 55–63.

Deighton, J. (1996) The future of interactive marketing. *Harvard Business Review*, November–December, 151–62.

DoubleClick (2003) Effective marketing sequences in the interactive media age. Summary research paper, 3 March. www.doubleclick.net.

EIAA (2005) European Advertising Association. European media research, October 2004. Research conducted by Millward Brown. Published at www.eiaa.net in 2005.

Evans, M., Patterson, M. and O'Malley, L. (2000) Bridging the direct marketing–direct consumer gap: some solutions from qualitative research. *Proceedings of the Academy of Marketing Annual Conference*, Derby.

Feinberg, R., Trotter, M. and Anton, J. (2000) At any time – from anywhere – in any form. In D. Renner (ed.), *Defying the Limits, Reaching New Heights in Customer Relationship Management*. Report from Montgomery Research Inc, San Francisco, CA. http://feinberg.crmproject.com.

Financial Times (2003) TV ads 'a waste of money', Claire Cozens. Tuesday 4 February.

Forrester Research (1999) Strong content means a loyal audience, Forrester Research report. 27 January.

Godin, S. (1999) *Permission Marketing*. Simon and Schuster, New York.

Hagel, J. and Armstrong, A. (1997) *Net Gain: Expanding Markets through Virtual Communities*. Harvard Business School Press, Cambridge, MA.

Heskett, J., Jones, T., Loveman, G., Sasser, W. and Schlesinger, E. (1994) Putting the service–profit chain to work. *Harvard Business Review*, March–April, 164–74.

Hitwise (2005) Press release: The top UK Grocery and Alcohol websites, week ending 1 October, ranked by market share of web site visits, from Hitwise.co.uk. Press release available at www.hitwise.co.uk.

Hoffman, D.L. and Novak, T.P. (1996) Marketing in Hypermedia computer-mediated environments: conceptual foundations. *Journal of Marketing*, 60 (July) 50–68.

Humby, C. and Hunt, T. (2003) *Scoring Points. How Tesco Is Winning Customer Loyalty*. Kogan Page, London.

IAB (2005) Internet Advertising Bureau. Bi-annual advertising spend study conducted with PricewaterhouseCoopers. Published at www.iabuk.net.

Jevons, C. and Gabbott, M. (2000) Trust, brand equity and brand reality in Internet business relationships: an interdisciplinary approach. *Journal of Marketing Management*, 16(6), 619–34.

Jun, M. and Cai, S. (2001) The key determinants of banking service quality: a content analysis. *International Journal of Bank Marketing*, 19(7), 276–91.

Kirby, J. (2003) Online viral marketing: next big thing or yesterday's fling? *New Media Knowledge*. Published online at www.newmediaknowledge.co.uk.

Kotler, P. (1997) *Marketing Management – Analysis, Planning, Implementation and Control.* Prentice-Hall, Englewood Cliffs, NJ.

Levine, R., Locke, C., Searls, D. and Weinberger, D. (2000) *The Cluetrain Manifesto.* Perseus Books, Cambridge, MA.

Lewis, H. and Lewis, R. (1997) Give your customers what they want. *Selling on the Net. Executive book summaries*, 19(3).

McGraffin, K. (2204) Linking matters: how to create an effective linking strategy to promote your website. Published at www.linkingmatters.com.

Mello, A. (2001) Watch out for CRM's hidden costs. ZdNet online, 15 October. Available online at: http://techupdate.zdnet.com/techupdate/stovies/main/0,14179,2818163,00.html.

NMA (2005a) Product placement. By Sean Hargrave. *New Media Age*, 12 May. www.nma.co.uk.

NMA (2005b) Perfect match. By Greg Brooks, *New Media Age*, 29 September. www.nma.co.uk.

NMA (2005c) Delivering the goods. By Nic Howell, *New Media Age,* 5 May.

Nielsen, J. (2000) Web research: believe the data. *Jakob Nielsen's Alertbox, July 11, 1999*: www.useit.com/alertbox/990711.html.

Novo, J. (2003) *Drilling Down: Turning customer data into profits with a spreadsheet.* Available from www.jimnovo.com.

O'Malley, L. and Tynan, C. (2001) Reframing relationship marketing for consumer markets, *Interactive Marketing*, 2(3), 240–46.

Parasuraman, A., Zeithaml, V. and Berry, L. (1985) A conceptual model of service quality and its implications for future research. *Journal of Marketing*, 49, Fall, 41–50.

Parker, R (2000) *Relationship Marketing on the Web.* Adams Streetwise, Avon, MA.

Peppers, B. and Rogers, P. (1999) *One-to-One Field Book.* Currency/Doubleday, New York.

Peters, L. (1998) The new interactive media: one-to-one but to whom? *Marketing Intelligence and Planning*, 16(1), 22–30.

QAS (2002) Data Quality – the Reality Gap. Executive summary of a report commissioned by QAS. Available online at www.qas.com/uk.

Reicheld, F. and Schefter, P. (2000) E-loyalty, your secret weapon on the web. *Harvard Business Review*, July–August, 105–13.

Reinartz, W. and Kumar. V. (2002) The mismanagement of customer loyalty. *Harvard Business Review*, July, 4–12.

Revolution (2005) E-mail Marketing Report by Justin Pugsley. *Revolution.* September, 2005, 58–60.

Ryan, J. and Whiteman, N. (2000) Online Advertising Glossary: Sponsorships. ClickZ Media Selling Channel, 15 May.

Seybold, P. (1999) *Customers.com.* Century Business Books, Random House, London.

Sharma, A., and Sheth, J. (2004) Web-based marketing: The coming revolution in marketing thought and strategy. *Journal of Business Research*, 57(7) (2004), 696–702.

Sissors, J., and Baron, R. (2002) *Advertising media planning.* McGraw-Hill, Chicago. Sixth edition.

Smith, P.R. and Chaffey, D. (2005) *EMarketing Excellence – at the Heart of EBusiness*, 2nd edn. Butterworth Heinemann, Oxford.

Stone, M., Abbott, J. and Buttle, F. (2001) Integrating customer data into CRM strategy. In B. Foss and M. Stone (eds) *Successful Customer Relationship Marketing.* Wiley, Chichester.

van Duyne, D., Landay, J. and Hong, J. (2002) *The Design of Sites. Patterns, Principles, and Processes for Crafting a Customer-centered Web Experience.* Addison-Wesley, Reading, MA.

Varianini, V. and Vaturi, D. (2000) Marketing lessons from e-failures. *McKinsey Quarterly*, no. 4, 86–97.

Webster, F. and Wind, Y. (1972) *Organizational Buying Behaviour.* Prentice-Hall, Englewood Cliffs, NJ.

Wikipedia (2005) Tesco. *Wikipedia*, the free encyclopedia. http://en.wikipedia.org/wiki/Tesco

Windham, L. (2001) *The Soul of the New Consumer. The Attitudes, Behaviors and Preferences of E-Customers*. Allworth Press, New York.

Zona Research (1999) The economic impacts of unacceptable web-site download speeds. White paper, April (www.zonaresearch.com).

Further reading

Chaffey, D., Mayer, R., Johnston, K. and Ellis-Chadwick, F. (2003) *Internet Marketing: Strategy, Implementation and Practice*, 2nd edn. Financial Times Prentice Hall, Harlow. Chapter 6 covers online relationship building and Chapter 8 interactive communications.

Fill, C. (2002) *Marketing Communications – Contexts, Contents and Strategies*, 3rd edn. Financial Times Prentice Hall, Harlow. Recommended for its integration of theory, concepts and practice of marketing communications.

Møller, K. and Halinen, A. (2000) Relationship marketing theory: its roots and direction. *Journal of Marketing Management*, 16, 29–54.

Sargeant, A. and West, D. (2001) *Direct and Interactive Marketing*. Oxford University Press, Oxford. An excellent coverage of traditional direct marketing, although the specific chapter on e-marketing is brief.

Winer, R. (2001) A framework for Customer Relationship Management. *California Management Review*, 43(4). A good overview of CRM and e-CRM.

Web links

Direct Marketing Association (www.dma.org.uk) Best-practice guidelines and benchmarks of response rates.

DoubleClick (www.doubleclick.net) An e-mail broadcaster and advertising network worldwide, with offices in many countries. Its site provides research of ad and e-mail marketing response rates across its clients.

Internet-advertising-related links

Atlas (www.atlasdmt.com) Ad-serving and tracking provider with research about ad effectiveness.

ClickZ (www.clickz.com/experts/) An excellent collection of articles on online marketing communications. US-focused. Relevant sections for this chapter include: Affiliate marketing, Advertising technology, E-mail marketing, Media buying.

EyeBlaster (www.eyeblaster.com) One of the main providers of rich media ad serving technologies. Its galleries have good examples.

eMarketer (www.emarketer.com) Includes reports on media spend based on compilations of other analysts.

iMediaConnection (www.imediaconnection.com) Media site reporting on best practice in online advertising.

Internet Advertising Bureau (www.iab.net) The widest range of studies about Internet advertising effectiveness. In UK: www.iabuk.net. Internet Advertising Bureau XMOS microsite (www.iab.net/xmos)

Tangozebra (www.tangozebra.co.uk) UK-based provider of ad-serving technology which showcases many of the most recent ad campaigns by industry category.

Search-engine-related links

ClickZ (www.clickz.com/) An excellent collection of articles on online marketing communications. US-focused. Relevant sections for this chapter include: Affiliate marketing, Advertising technology, E-mail marketing, Media buying.

Searchenginewatch (www.searchenginewatch.com) A complete resource on SEO and PPC marketing.

Webmasterworld (www.webmasterworld.com) A forum where search practitioners discuss best practice.

CRM and database marketing

CRM Today (www.crm2day.com) A portal with articles about the practical aspects of deploying CRM Technology.

Database Marketing Institute (www.dbmarketing.com/articles) Good source of articles, some of which refer to e-CRM.

Direct Marketing Association UK (www.dma.org.uk) Source of up-to-date data protection advice and how-to guides about online direct marketing.

Jim Novo (www.jimnovo.com) A site by a US consultant that has a lot of detail on techniques to profile customers online.

Peppers and Rogers One-to-One marketing web site (www.1to1.com) A site containing a lot of information on the techniques and tools of relationship marketing.

Permission marketing (www.permission.com) Site supporting book by Seth Godin of Yahoo! on permission marketing. No content, but four sample chapters.

Part 3

IMPLEMENTATION

Management of e-business implementation is described in Part 3 of the book in which we examine practical management issues involved with creating and maintaining e-business solutions.

10 Change management

Chapter at a glance

Web support

The following additional case studies are available at www.pearsoned.co.uk/chaffey

- ➤ Orange evolves customer services to achieve 12,000 visitors to site each week
- ➤ Staff acquisition and retention at Netdecisions
- ➤ Managing global change at Guinness

The site also contains a range of study material designed to help improve your results.

Learning outcomes

After completing this chapter the reader should be able to:

- **Identify the different types of change that need to be managed for e-commerce**
- **Develop an outline plan for implementing e-commerce change**
- **Describe alternative approaches to organizational structure resulting from organizational change.**

Management issues

The issues for managers raised in this chapter include:

- **What are the success factors in managing change?**
- **Should we change organizational structure in response to e-business? If so, what are the options?**
- **How do we manage the human aspects of the implementation of organizational change?**
- **How do we share knowledge between staff in the light of high staff turnover and rapid changes in market conditions?**

Links to other chapters

The main related chapters to this chapter are:

- Chapters in *Part 2* on strategy development should be read before this chapter since they explain the reasons for change. *Chapter 5* describes structural change for e-business;
- *Chapters 11 and 12* on strategy implementation that follow this chapter describe how the change management approach is implemented through analysis, design and implementation.

Introduction

What we anticipate seldom occurs: what we least expect generally happens.

(Benjamin Disraeli)

Disraeli's quote, referring to changes that need to be responded to in government, could equally be applied to the responses that are necessary from an organization venturing into e-business. Perhaps the greatest challenge faced by both B2B and B2C companies as they adopt e-business practices is how to manage the change that is necessitated by e-business.

However, for managing e-business within a particular organization it is possible to anticipate many of the changes that will be required by learning lessons from the pioneers of e-business. Through applying best practice and adopting risk management, it is possible to be proactive and manage change successfully.

Approaches to managing changes to organizational processes and structures and their impact on organization staff and culture is known as change management. Approaches to managing change associated with e-business is the subject of this chapter.

Change management
Managing process, structural, technical, staff and culture change within an organization.

Business transformation
Significant changes to organizational processes implemented to improve organizational performance.

The introduction of e-business often requires its users to learn how to use new internal information systems, but more significantly it will require new methods of working. The changes experienced by staff tend to be greatest for large-scale projects which are intended to achieve business transformation. For example, the introduction of an e-business system to support online sales or online procurement may introduce major changes for staff working in these areas. Both types of systems represent a potential threat to existing staff. Some staff may have been working face-to-face with customers or suppliers for many years and they are now asked to use technology which decreases the human element of contact. They may consider this reduces the efficiency of the work, they may feel their jobs are less interesting or even that their jobs are under threat.

We start this chapter by reviewing some of the challenges of implementing and managing e-commerce. We then go on to consider different aspects of change management and the chapter is structured around the different aspects of change we need to plan for; these include:

- *Scheduling* – what are the suitable stages for introducing change?
- *Budgeting* – how do we cost e-business?
- *Resources needed* – what type of resources do we need, what are their responsibilities and where do we obtain them?
- *Organizational structures* – do we need to revise organizational structure?
- *Managing the human impact of change* – what is the best way to introduce large-scale e-business change to employees?
- *Technologies to support e-business change* – the roles of knowledge management, groupware and intranets are explored.
- Finally, we summarize different aspects of change management through looking at risk management approaches to e-business-led change.

The challenges of e-business transformation

Figure 10.1 shows key aspects or levers of change that need to be assessed in order to maximize the benefits of e-business. The main change levers required are:

1 Market and business model (described in *Chapter 2*).
2 Business process (described in *Chapter 4*).

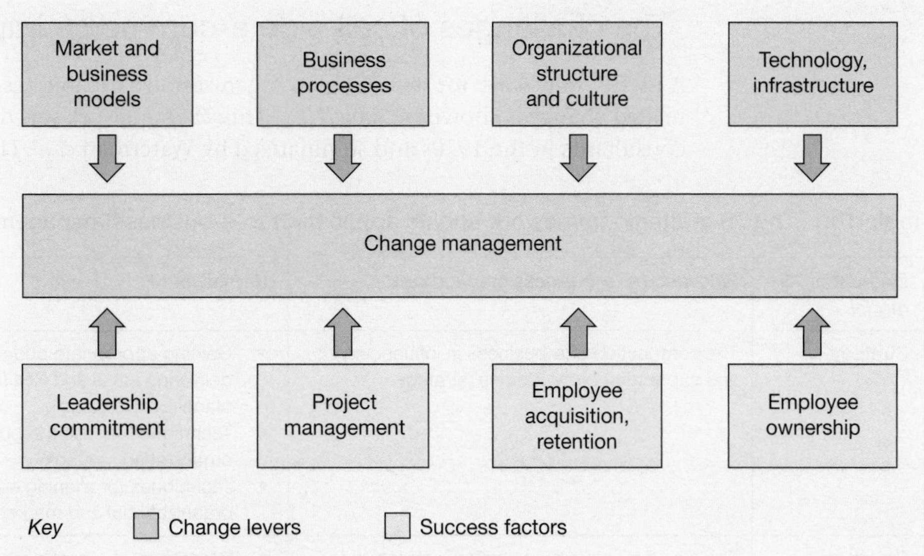

Figure 10.1 **Key factors in achieving change**

3 Organizational structure, culture and staff responsibilities (described in this chapter).
4 Technology infrastructure changes (described in *Chapters 3, 9* and *11*).

These are all major changes that are required in order for an organization to be agile enough to respond to marketplace changes and deliver competitive customer service. To help achieve these different aspects of change, a series of success factors seem to be required. These include:

- management buy-in and ownership;
- effective project management;
- action to attract and keep the right staff to achieve change;
- employee ownership of change.

This chapter focuses on how to best achieve these success factors. *Activity 10.1* introduces some of the changes required by e-business.

Activity 10.1 Managing change at The B2C Company

Purpose

To investigate the impacts of change on employees associated with e-business.

Activity

Speculate how the introduction of changes by a CEO or managing director such as those illustrated by the top four boxes of *Figure 10.1* would affect different employees at The B2C Company. Imagine you are each of the following people. What would your reaction be on a professional and a personal level? What would be your role in affecting change?

- Marketing manager
- Warehouse manager
- HR manager
- IS manager
- Employee in call centre.

Answers to activities can be found at www.pearsoned.co.uk/chaffey

The challenges of sell-side e-commerce implementation

A useful framework for reviewing an organization's capabilities to manage e-business-related change is shown in *Table 10.1*. This 7S framework was developed by McKinsey consultants in the 1970s and summarized by Waterman *et al.* (1980).

Table 10.1 The 7S strategic framework and its application to e-business management

Element of 7S model	*Relevance to e-business management*	*Key issues*
Strategy	The contribution of e-business in influencing and supporting organizations' strategy	• Gaining appropriate budgets and demonstrating/delivering value and ROI from budgets. Annual planning approach • Techniques for using e-business to impact organization strategy • Techniques for aligning e-business strategy with organizational and marketing strategy
Structure	The modification of organizational structure to support e-business	• Integration of e-commerce team with other management, marketing (corporate communications, brand marketing, direct marketing) and IT staff • Use of cross-functional teams and steering groups • Insourcing *vs* outsourcing
Systems	The development of specific processes, procedures or information systems to support Internet marketing	• Campaign planning approach-integration • Managing/sharing customer information • Managing content quality • Unified reporting of digital marketing effectiveness • In-house *vs* external best-of-breed *vs* external integrated technology solutions
Staff	The breakdown of staff in terms of their background, age and sex and characteristics such as IT *vs* Marketing, use of contractors/consultants	• Insourcing *vs* outsourcing • Achieving senior management buy-in/involvement with digital marketing • Staff recruitment and retention. Virtual working • Staff development and training
Style	Includes both the way in which key managers behave in achieving the organization's goals and the cultural style of the organization as a whole	• Relates to role of the e-commerce team in influencing strategy – is it dynamic and influential or conservative and looking for a voice?
Skills	Distinctive capabilities of key staff, but can be interpreted as specific skill-sets of team members	• Staff skills in specific areas: supplier selection, project management, content management, specific e-marketing approaches (search-engine marketing, affiliate marketing, e-mail marketing, online advertising)
Superordinate	The guiding concepts of the e-commerce organization which are also part of shared values and culture. The internal and external perception of these goals may vary	• Improving the perception of the importance and effectiveness of the e-commerce team amongst senior managers and staff it works with (marketing generalists and IT)

Table 10.1 summarizes some of the main issues which need management, but what are the main challenges in implementing strategy? E-consultancy (2005) surveyed UK e-commerce managers to assess their views on the main challenges of managing e-commerce within an organization. In the context of the 7 Ss, we can summarize the main challenges as follows:

- *Strategy* – Limited capabilities to integrate Internet strategy into core marketing and business strategy as discussed in *Chapter 5* is indicated by frustration on gaining appropriate budgets.

- *Structure* – Structural and process issues are indicated by the challenges of gaining resource and buy-in from traditional marketing and IT functions.
- *Skills and staff* –These issues were indicated by difficulties in finding specialist staff or agencies.

E-consultancy research I completed in 2005 highlighted some of the main challenges of implementing e-commerce. My initial sample for interviews were e-commerce managers for transactional sites – for example, mobile phones (Orange, The Carphone Warehouse), travel (Tui and MyTravel), financial services (Lloyds TSB and Bradford and Bingley) and direct marketers such as BCA.

One of the aims of the research was to gain a picture of the organizational processes and activities that need to be managed as part of sell-side e-commerce and the organizational structures that had been created to manage this. *Figure 10.2* gives an indication of the number of operational e-CRM processes that need to be managed across the three core e-CRM areas (acquisition, conversion, retention) which we reviewed in *Chapter 9*. It also shows the management activities needed to support

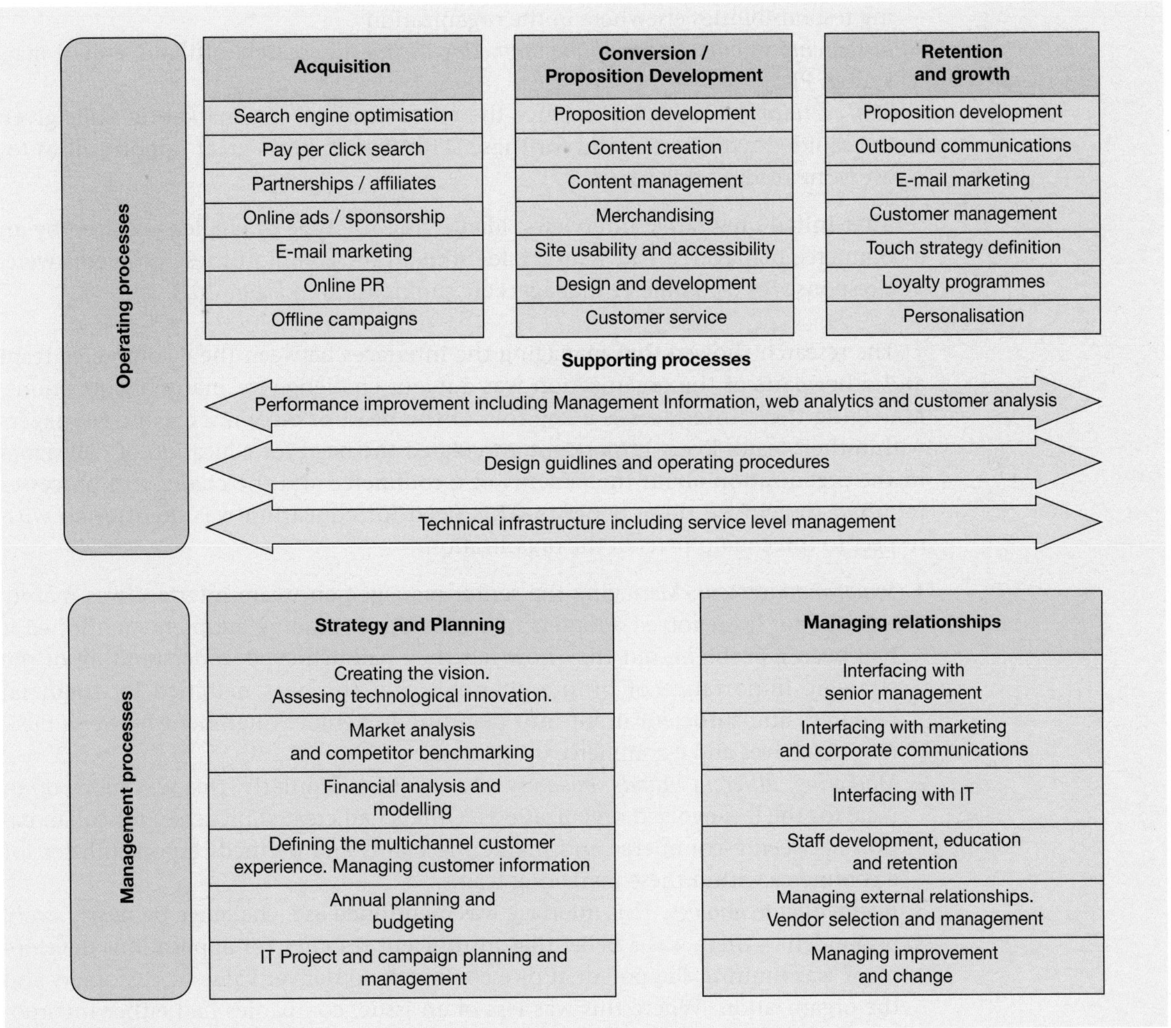

Figure 10.2 **Digital marketing activities that require management as sell-side e-commerce**

Source: E-consultancy (2005)

these. Some large organizations in the study had between 10 and 50 specialist staff managing these activities. For smaller companies, there is also the challenge that only 1 or 2 people are responsible for these activities, so they will need to work smart and outsource many of the activities!

As part of the research, respondents were asked what their main challenges were and these highlighted the issues of gaining sufficient resources for Internet marketing. Their key challenges included:

- *Gaining buy-in and budget* consistent with audience media consumption and value generated
- *Conflicts of ownership and tensions* between a digital marketing team, traditional marketing, IT and finance/senior management
- *Coordination with different channels* in conjunction with teams managing marketing programmes elsewhere in the business
- *Managing and integrating customer information* about characteristics and behaviours collected online
- *Achieving a unified reporting* and performance improvement process throughout the business including reporting, analysis and actioning suggested changes
- *Structuring the specialist digital team* and integrating into the organization by changing responsibilities elsewhere in the organization
- *In-sourcing* vs *outsourcing online marketing tactics,* i.e. search, affiliate, e-mail marketing, PR
- *Staff recruitment and retention* since there is a shortage of e-marketing skills given the rapid growth in demand for these skills, which gives great opportunities for everyone reading this book!

After initial qualitative interviews, identifying the type of challenges faced by an e-commerce manager, a wider survey identified how common these problems were. The responses of e-commerce managers are summarized in *Figure 10.3*.

The research showed that managing the interfaces between the e-commerce team and other parts of the organization was a major challenge for many organizations. Managing these interfaces is a key role of the head of e-commerce and managers within their team. Every respondent articulated the need for education of colleagues in the organization about the benefits of e-commerce and the changes in processes required to achieve these benefits. This need for education was mentioned with respect to three main parts of the organization:

1. *Senior management.* Managing the senior management team interface was mainly an issue for less-evolved adopters of e-commerce. Leading adopters mentioned it had been a problem, but they now felt they had achieved understanding of the strategic importance of online channels and this was matched by financial resources and sufficient input into planning to achieve alignment between business objectives and e-commerce initiatives.
2. *Marketing, different brands, businesses or countries.* Similarly, this was more of an issue for the less-evolved organizations. Others had created processes for collaboration between e-commerce and marketing teams and defined responsibilities for e-commerce within these marketing teams.
3. *Information technology.* This interface was mentioned as a challenge by nearly every respondent – there was a belief that insufficient resource for applications development was limiting the potential of e-commerce to deliver value to customers and the organization. Where this was less of an issue, companies had either incorporated some development function within the e-commerce function, or had outsourced parts of development.

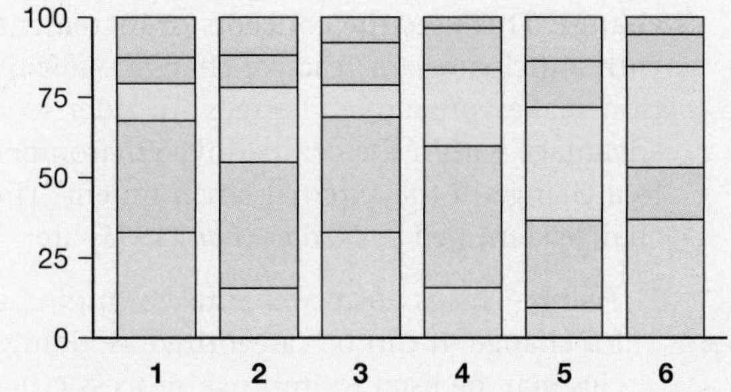

	Strongly agree [1]	Partially agree [2]	Neither agree nor disagree [3]	Partially disagree [4]	Disagree [5]
1 Gaining senior management buy-in/resource	32.14% (27)	35.71% (30)	11.9% (10)	8.33% (7)	11.9% (10)
2 Gaining buy-in/resource from traditional marketing functions/brands	15.48% (13)	39.29% (33)	23.81% (20)	10.71% (9)	10.71% (9)
3 Gaining IT resource/technical support	32.14% (27)	36.9% (31)	10.71% (9)	11.9% (10)	8.33% (7)
4 Finding suitable staff	15.66% (13)	44.58% (37)	22.89% (19)	13.25% (11)	3.61% (3)
5 Finding suitable digital media agencies	9.52% (8)	26.19% (22)	35.71% (30)	15.48% (13)	13.1% (11)
6 Other (please enter challenge)	36.84% (7)	15.79% (3)	31.58% (6)	10.53% (2)	5.26% (1)

Figure 10.3 **The main challenges of managing sell-side e-commerce (n = 84)**

Source: E-consultancy (2005)

Different types of change in business

Incremental change
Relatively small adjustments required by an organization in response to its business environment.

Discontinuous change
Change involving a major transformation in an industry.

Organizational change
Includes both incremental and discontinuous change to organizations.

Viewed at a large-scale across an entire industry, change takes two forms. Incremental change involves relatively small adjustments required by changes in the business environment (*Chapter 4*). Organizations scan their environment and make adjustments according to the introduction of new products from competitors, new laws or long-term changes in customer behaviour such as the increasing spending power of teenagers. Organizations also make changes to improve the efficiency of their processes. More significant discontinuous change or transformational change involves a major change in the business environment which changes the basis for competition. The opportunities and threats presented by widespread availability of low-cost Internet connectivity is a discontinuous change.

Organizational change mirrors that at industry level. It can occur on a continuous or incremental basis or on a discontinuous basis. The introduction of e-business requires organizations to manage both types of change.

Nadler *et al.* (1995) developed a useful way of classifying types of organizational change. This uses the concepts of incremental and discontinuous change together with anticipatory or reactive change. Anticipatory change occurs when an organization makes proactive changes in order to improve its efficiency or to create an advantage within the competitive environment. Reactive change is a direct response to a change in the external environment. The four different forms of organizational change identified by Nadler *et al.* (1995) are:

Anticipatory change
An organization initiates change without an immediate need to respond.

Reactive change
A direct response by an organization to a change in its environment.

1 *Tuning.* This is an incremental form of change when there is no immediate need for change. It can be categorized as 'doing things better'. New procedures or policies may be used to improve process efficiency, e.g. to reduce time to market or reduce costs of doing business. E-business involves 'tuning' as Internet technologies are applied to improve efficiency.
2 *Adaptation.* Also an incremental form of change, but in this case it is in response to an external threat or opportunity. It can also be categorized as 'doing things better'. For example, a competitor may introduce a new product or there may be a merger between two rivals. A response is required, but it does not involve a significant change in the basis for competition. Managing e-business-related change also requires adaptation.
3 *Re-orientation.* A significant change or transformation to the organization is initiated due to discontinuous change. There is not an immediate need for change, but the change is in anticipation of change. When IBM was one of the first organizations to introduce the concept of 'e-business' in the mid-1990s, this was a re-orientation in the way it delivered its service (with an increased focus on consultancy services rather than hardware and software) which helped to spark a wider change in the way businesses worked. Successful adoption of e-business also requires re-orientation for many organizations.
4 *Re-creation.* In re-creation, the senior management team of an organization decides that a fundamental change to the way it operates is required to compete effectively. In the airline industry, established airlines have had to establish change programmes to respond to the low-cost carriers, for example by emphasizing service quality or introducing rival low-cost services. Both re-orientation and re-creation can be categorized as 'doing things differently'. E-business has also caused 're-creation' in the airline industry, with the low-cost airlines now gaining more than 90% of bookings online. However, as we saw in *Chapter 4*, such dramatic change has not been caused in every industry.

Business process management

So, some forms of e-business initiative related to internal processes such as the introduction of a human resources management system are simply about improving efficiency – they involve incremental change. The practice of improving the efficiency of business processes with the assistance of information systems is an important activity in many organizations as is shown by *Case Study 10.1*. It can be seen that the label in vogue at the time of writing is 'business process management' (BPM). This encompasses different scales of improving business process that are introduced above.

Business Process Management (BPM)
An approach supported by software tools intended to increase process efficiency by improving information flows between people as they perform business tasks.

The BPM concept has been defined by Gartner (2003) as follows:

BPM is a methodology, as well a collection of tools that enables enterprises to specify step-by-step business processes. Proper analysis and design of BPM flows require a strong understanding of the atomic business steps that must be performed to complete a business process. As BPM executes a business process, these atomic steps will often correspond to well-known business activities, such as checking credit ratings, updating customer accounts and checking inventory status. In effect, the BPM process flow is often just a sequence of well-known services, executed in a coordinated fashion.

Classic document workflow, which was BPM's predecessor, focused on humans performing the services. Fueled by the power of application integration, BPM focuses on human and automated agents doing the work to deliver the services.

Discontinuous process change

Although BPM often refers to continuous, incremental change, other forms of information-management-related applications such as e-ticketing for an airline will be associated with discontinuous change – with low-cost airlines such as easyJet and Ryanair now selling over 80% of their tickets online this has had a fairly significant impact on the airline industry. The introduction of e-business applications or enterprise resource planning systems described in *Chapter 2* are also often related to transformational change programmes. Three degrees of business-process change are shown in *Table 10.2*.

Business process re-engineering (BPR)

Identifying radical, new ways of carrying out business operations, often enabled by new IT capabilities.

In the early-to-mid-1990s organization-wide transformational change was advocated under the label of 'business process re-engineering' (BPR). It was popularized through the pronouncements of Hammer and Champy (1993) and Davenport (1993). The essence of BPR is the assertion that business processes, organizational structures, team structures and employee responsibilities can be fundamentally altered to improve business performance. Hammer and Champy (1993) defined BPR as:

the fundamental rethinking and radical redesign of business processes to achieve dramatic improvements in critical, contemporary measures of performance, such as cost, quality, service, and speed.

The key terms from this definition that encapsulate the BPR concept are:

- *Fundamental rethinking* – re-engineering usually refers to changing of significant business processes such as customer service, sales order processing or manufacturing.
- *Radical redesign* – re-engineering is not involved with minor, incremental change or automation of existing ways of working. It involves a complete rethinking about the way business processes operate.
- *Dramatic improvements* – the aim of BPR is to achieve improvements measured in tens or hundreds of per cent. With automation of existing processes only single-figure improvements may be possible.
- *Critical contemporary measures of performance* – this point refers to the importance of measuring how well the processes operate in terms of the four important measures of cost, quality, service and speed.

Willcocks and Smith (1995) characterize the typical changes that arise in an organization with process innovation as:

- work units changing from functional departments to process teams;
- jobs changing from simple tasks to multi-dimensional work;
- people's roles changing from controlled to empowered;
- focus of performance changing from activities to results;
- values changing from protective to productive.

In *Re-engineering the Corporation* (1993) Hammer and Champy have a chapter giving examples of how IS can act as a catalyst for change (disruptive technologies). These technologies are familiar from applications of e-business such as those described in *Chapter 2* and include tracking technology, decision support tools, telecommunications networks, teleconferencing and shared databases. Hammer and Champy label these as 'disruptive technologies' which can force companies to reconsider their processes and find new ways of operating. It is arguable though whether technology is commonly disruptive in the sense of achieving major changes such as those in the re-orientation and re-creation categories.

Many re-engineering projects were launched in the 1990s and failed due to their ambitious scale and the problems of managing large information systems projects. Furthermore, BPR was also often linked to downsizing in many organizations, leading to an outflow of staff and knowledge from businesses. As a result BPR as a concept has fallen out of favour and more caution in achieving change is advocated.

Business process improvement (BPI)
Optimizing existing processes, typically coupled with enhancements in information technology.

Less radical approaches to organizational transformation are referred to as '**business process improvement**' **(BPI)** or by Davenport (1993) as 'business process innovation'. Taking the example of a major e-business initiative for supply chain management, an organization would have to decide on the scope of change. For instance, do all supply chain activities need to be revised simultaneously or can certain activities such as procurement or outbound logistics be targeted initially? Modern thinking would suggest that the latter approach is preferable.

Business process automation (BPA)
Automating existing ways of working manually through information technology.

If a less radical approach is adopted, care should be taken not to fall into the trap of simply using technology to automate existing processes which are sub-optimal – in plain words, using information technology 'to do bad things faster'. This approach of using technology to support existing procedures and practices is known as '**business process automation**' **(BPA)**. Although benefits can be achieved through this approach, the improvements may not be sufficient to generate a return on investment.

Table 10.2 Alternative terms for using IS to enhance company performance

Term	*Involves*	*Intention*	*Risk of failure*
Business process re-engineering	Fundamental redesign of all main company processes through organization-wide initiatives	Large gains in performance (>100%?)	Highest
Business process improvement	Targets key processes in sequence for redesign	(<50%)	Medium
Business process automation	Automating existing process. Often uses workflow software (*Chapter 2*)	(<20%)	Lowest

A staged approach to the introduction of BPR has been suggested by Davenport (1993). This can also be applied to e-business change. He suggests the following stages that can be applied to e-business:

- *Identify the process for innovation* – these are the major business processes from the organization's value chain which add most to the value for the customer or achieve the largest efficiency benefits for the company. Examples include customer relationship management, logistics and procurement.
- *Identify the change levers* – these can encourage and help achieve change. The main change levers are innovative technology and, as we have seen, the organization's culture and structure.
- *Develop the process vision* – this involves communication of the reasons for changes and what can be achieved in order to help achieve buy-in throughout the organization.
- *Understand the existing processes* – current business processes are documented. This allows the performance of existing business processes to be benchmarked and so provides a means for measuring the extent to which a re-engineered process has improved business performance.

- *Design and prototype the new process* – the vision is translated into practical new processes which the organization is able to operate. Prototyping the new process operates on two levels. First, simulation and modelling tools can be used to check the logical operation of the process. Second, assuming that the simulation model shows no significant problems, the new process can be given a full operational trial. Needless to say, the implementation must be handled sensitively if it is to be accepted by all parties.

Cope and Waddell (2001) have assessed approaches managers in manufacturing industry in Australia use to introduce e-commerce services. They tested for different stages of transformation from fine-tuning through incremental adjustment, modular transformation and corporate transformation. They found that in this particular industry at the time of the survey, a relatively conservative approach of 'fine tuning' was predominant.

Case Study 10.1 Smoothing the workflow through business process management

FT

This case gives a modern perspective on approaches to improve business processes using information systems. It summarizes the tools, benefits and some of the problems associated with business process management.

With competition becoming seemingly tougher every quarter, companies are starting to experiment with a series of interlinked technologies that allow them to optimise their business processes and to react quickly when market conditions change.

These technologies are collectively known as business process management (BPM). They include tools for business process modelling, workflow management, process monitoring, enterprise application integration and managing organisational change, all of which greatly help information to flow through organisations by co-ordinating and sometimes supplementing companies' key enterprise software packages, such as application suites supplied by SAP, Oracle and Siebel.

A furniture manufacturer, for example, could plan how it wants its customer orders processed, from initial confirmation to cash in the bank, using a process modelling tool that designs each stage in the order's evolution.

This tool then helps the manufacturer to create 'workflow' software that automatically routes the customer order – and all the work associated with it – to the right people and places, in the right order. The workflow application takes decisions on how to advance the order, using pre-defined business rules. It closely monitors the order's progress, and if the order gets held up or seems to encounter problems, it sends an alert in real time to the appropriate manager.

BPM has obvious advantages. Remodelled processes are usually more effective than their predecessors, generating immediate cost savings and competitive advantages. MSB International, an agency supplying workers on temporary contracts to companies, used BPM tools from Metastorm to revamp its contract processing. Previously, each new contract took an hour of a salesperson's time to process after it was agreed. Now the work takes five minutes and is far less prone to error.

Rob Marston, infrastructure manager at MSB, says the business benefit is 'astounding'. The software cost £50,000 and generated a return of £100,000 within a year by making sales people more effective, he says.

Just as importantly, BPM can help businesses change processes more quickly, perhaps with only minor changes to workflow rules, which minimises maintenance costs. 'Hardly a week goes by when we don't change our business processes', says Mr Marston. 'The board recently changed some authorisation procedures, and that took about ten minutes to implement. It sounds small, but in the old days, that would have taken a week.'

BPM can help align IT infrastructures more closely with business needs. 'It helps to break down the traditional barriers between the business way of describing a process and the IT way of implementing a process. That makes it more likely that developers can deliver what the business is asking them to deliver', says Derek Payne, fulfilment technology manager at Leica Microsystems, an optical product manufacturer.

BPM can also help organisations collaborate by aligning their business processes more closely. As web services technologies start to make information flows between organisations easier, supply chains should become shorter and more effective. 'This helps to enhance the ability to work outside your own environment with trading partners', says Mr Payne.

Lastly, by defining processes carefully, BPM clears the way for the radical outsourcing of entire business processes, such as manufacturing or accounting. 'The →

success of BPM will come less from allowing business processes to be redesigned, and more from making it easier to source parts of the business process offshore', predicts Will Cappelli, a research fellow at Forrester Research.

Mr Cappelli sees BPM as a Trojan horse for big IT services companies, enabling them to sell business process outsourcing (BPO) to corporations. BPO is the fastest-growing service in their market, and Mr Cappelli expects IT companies to absorb best-of-breed BPM experts such as Metastorm and Sterling Commerce to support this push.

Nevertheless, BPM is no walkover. As a complex set of technologies that do not always work together easily, it requires great effort and discipline to implement. 'The hardest part is understanding the business processes', warns Mr Marston. 'Initially, we tried to analyse everything about each process, but either the analysis was wrong, or the business had changed by the time it was implemented. So now we evolve our processes continually.'

A big danger is that over-enthusiastic companies may use BPM to create too many new business processes, says David Stephenson, European managing director of supply chain specialist Yantra. 'You can create a proliferation of business processes, and the simplification of your business processes gets lost as a result. You have to keep a tight control over the design process', Mr Stephenson warns.

BPM technologies are also not as sophisticated as some vendors claim. 'Many people are going to be sucked into an idea that sounds very seductive until they get into the detail', warns Rakesh Kumar, a vice president of technology research at analyst Meta Group. 'Integration between technologies is a critical problem. Even if you have the technology problems solved, mapping internal business processes to core IT processes is another problem.'

Gartner, the IT consultancy, said in a research note in December 2002 that corporate satisfaction with BPM is already high and is continuing to rise – making it a rarity in the IT world. Gartner urged clients to adopt BPM, predicting that it would deliver them a 10 to 15 per cent return on their investment over the next two years. BPM 'will hold the key to creating new revenue opportunities and shortening product creation processes', it added.

Nevertheless, BPM is no panacea. Businesses must educate their staff and trading partners carefully about the changes it will bring to the business, or resistance to change – whether conscious or not – will emerge.

Source: Smoothing the workflow. By Douglas Hayward, FT.com site, 15 May, 2003

Questions

1. How does the article suggest that business thinking and practice has evolved since the exhortations for business process re-engineering in the 1990s?
2. Summarize the benefits for BPM discussed in the article.
3. Discuss the need for a concept such as BPM when all new information systems and e-business initiatives are ultimately driven by process improvement.

Planning change

Our starting point for managing change is when the objectives, strategy and tactics for introducing e-business change have already been specified as outlined in *Part 2*. Here, we are concerned with how to implement the strategy to achieve the objectives through the activities performed by the project management team as part of project planning.

The imperative for project governance?

A recent survey of 134 large organizations from the UK, the US and other countries shows both the importance of project management for e-business and IT projects, and its challenges (KPMG, 2002). The research showed that 56 per cent of organizations had experienced failed IT projects in the previous 12 months. The average loss incurred by the businesses surveyed was £8 million per project, with the largest single project failure costing £133 million. Implementation of specific types of information system indicate worse problems. In 2000, it was reported that around 70 per cent of CRM projects failed in terms of delivering a return on investment or completion on time.

It follows that the project governance of e-business projects, like that of other major information systems is essential to success. The COBIT framework provides a good summary of the requirements from a governance approach. COBIT is the widely adopted IT governance model for Control Objectives for Information and related Technology. This definition is also helpful since it highlights some of the success factors in project management which we will cover later in this chapter. Project management is one of the key processes COBIT identifies for the effective governance of IT. It defines its control objective PO10 (COBIT, 2001) as follows – managing projects should:

Satisfy the business requirement:

to set priorities and to deliver on time and within budget

and are enabled by

the organisation identifying and prioritising projects in line with the operational plan and the adoption and application of sound project management techniques for each project undertaken and takes into consideration:

- *business management sponsorship for projects*
- *program management*
- *project management capabilities*
- *user involvement*
- *task breakdown, milestone definition and phase approvals*
- *allocation of responsibilities*
- *rigorous tracking of milestones and deliverables*
- *cost and manpower budgets, balancing internal and external resources*
- *quality assurance plans and methods*
- *program and project risk assessments*
- *transition from development to operations.*

For effective project management the following elements need to be incorporated as part of the project management process as described, for example, by Chaffey and Wood (2005):

- *Estimation* – identifying the activities involved in the project, sometimes referred to as a 'work breakdown structure' (WBS). The sequence of activities for implementation of a typical e-business system are shown in *Figure 10.4*.
- *Resource allocation* – after the initial WBS, appropriate resources can be allocated to the tasks.
- *Schedule/plan* – after resource allocation, the amount of time for each task can be determined according to the availability and skills of the people assigned to the tasks. There are two different concepts. Effort time is the total amount of work that needs to occur to complete a task. Elapsed time indicates how long in time (such as calendar days) the task will take and is dependent on the number of people working on the task, and their skills.
- *Monitoring and control* – monitoring involves ensuring the project is working to plan once it has started. Control is taking corrective action if the project deviates from the plan. In particular the project manager will want to hit milestones – events that need to happen on a particular date are defined for which performance against objectives can be measured (e.g. end of analysis, production of first prototype).

Milestone
Key deadline to be achieved during project, usually with defined deliverable.

The project plan and schedule for an e-business system

The project plan for an e-business system will involve all of the stages shown in *Figure 10.4*. This diagram also shows how the final part of the book is structured.

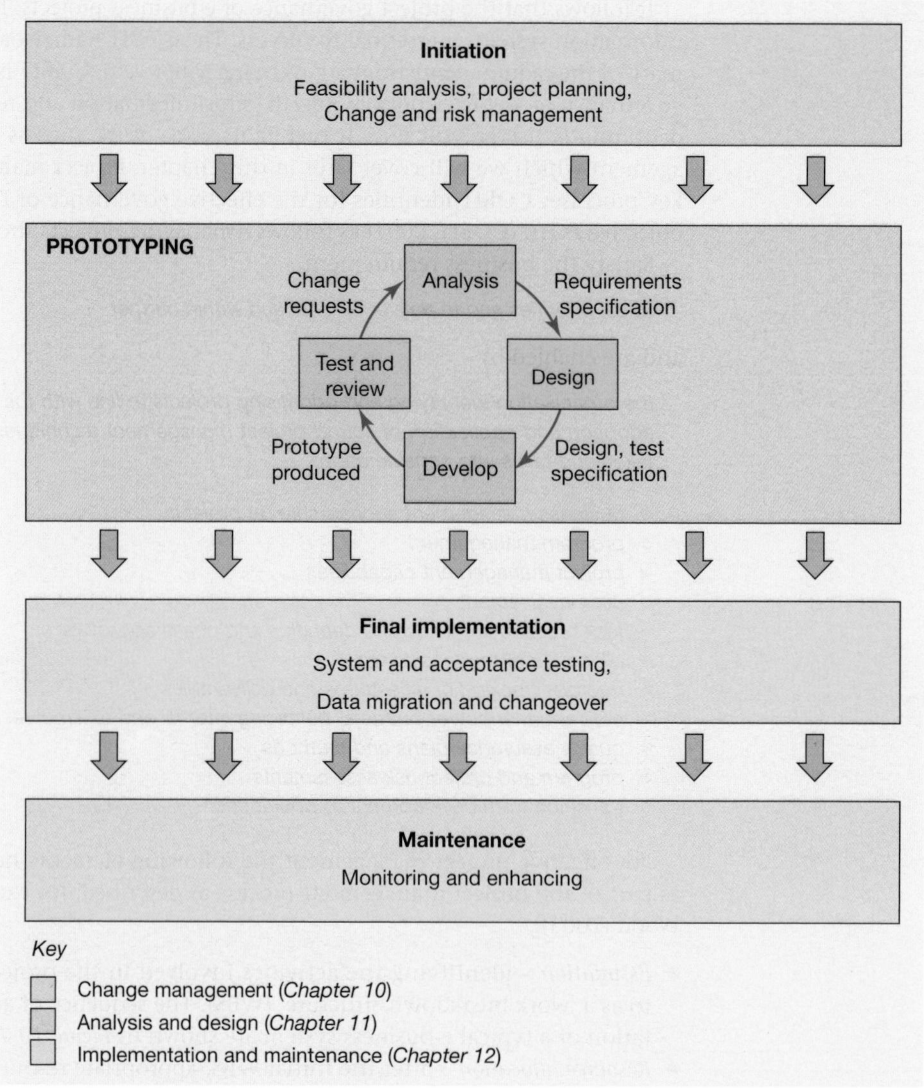

Figure 10.4 **Stages in developing an e-business solution**

Initiation
The start-up phase of the project.

- In *Chapter 10* we review the activities needed during the initiation phase of a project that involves the creation of a change management programme including project planning, managing organizational change and risk management. In this chapter we do not consider feasibility analysis since assessment of the costs and benefits of the e-business system have already been considered as an aspect of strategy as described in *Part 2*.
- In *Chapter 11* the analysis and design phases are described. In these the requirements of the organization and users of the system are defined and translated into a design from which the system can be built. Analysis and design occur in an iterative fashion through prototyping as described in the section that follows.
- In *Chapter 12* the final stages of developing the e-business system are described. These include writing the program code, building the databases, migrating data, testing the system and managing the changeover to the live system. *Chapter 12* also describes the maintenance of the system once it is live. This is monitoring the system and enhancing it as bugs and opportunities arise.

Systems development lifecycle
The sequence in which a system is created from initiation, analysis, design, implementation, build and maintenance.

These stages in developing an e-business system use well established approaches to building IS based on the **systems development lifecycle**. But significant differences project managers need to take into account are:

- The timescales for delivery of the system are compressed compared to traditional applications – the system needs to be developed in 'Internet time'. Prototyping and making activities such as analysis, design and testing which occur in parallel are used to achieve tight deadlines, as is the use of off-the-shelf systems perhaps hosted with an ASP (*Chapter 3*).
- The e-commerce system may be hosted outside of an organization so we need to consider the constraints imposed by hosting the site externally with an ISP and integrating external components of the system with data stored and processes occurring inside the organization.
- The focus of the project is on content and services rather than on application; this means that delivery of information is the key.
- Analysis and design are arguably more closely related in an e-commerce implementation since the usability of the site is critically dependent on the needs of the user and the prototyping approach is used to achieve users' needs.
- Once launched the site is more dynamic than a traditional application: an effective site will be updated continuously in response to customer demands. The solution is never complete.

With the use of tailored off-the-shelf packages such as Siebel's CRM solutions or SAP's supply chain solutions to implement e-business, the analysis, design stages and build tend to be different from bespoke IS implementation. The analysis stage is equally important, but will focus on mapping the facilities of the off-the-shelf software with the existing business practices. A vital decision is the extent to which the company will change or adapt its practices and processes to match the software or the extent it will be possible to tailor the software to match the processes. With a tailored off-the-shelf approach it is inevitable that a move away from the existing business processes and practices will be required.

The design phase will require much less input than for a bespoke system. It will focus on issues of how to tailor the user interface, database structures and security of the off-the-shelf package to the needs of the e-business solution. The build and implementation phases will still be involved and, as for any implementation, the project manager will have to schedule software and database configuration, data migration, testing and training.

An illustration of a typical project schedule for a sell-side e-commerce system is illustrated in the box *A task breakdown and schedule for The B2C Company*. A further example is given in *Figure 12.1*.

A task breakdown and schedule for The B2C Company

This case illustrates the different tasks that need to be performed as part of a sell-side e-commerce implementation for a company that does not have a web-site presence.

The schedule can be structured as followed:

1. *Pre-development tasks.* These include domain name registration and deciding on the company to host the web site. It is important to register the domain name for the site as early as possible – there is then less risk of another company adopting the same name first. It also includes preparing a brief of the aims and objectives of the site, then, if intending to outsource, presenting this to rival companies to bid.
2. *Content planning.* This is the detailed analysis and design of the site, including prototyping.
3. *Content development and testing.* Writing the HTML pages, producing the graphics and testing.
4. *Publishing the site.* This is a relatively short stage.

→

5 Pre-launch promotion. This is the marketing communications techniques described in *Chapter 9*.
6 Ongoing promotion. The schedule should also allow for periodic promotion which might involve discount promotions on the site or competitions. These are often reused each month.

Figure 10.5 gives an indication of the relationship between these tasks, and how long they may take for a typical initial e-commerce site.

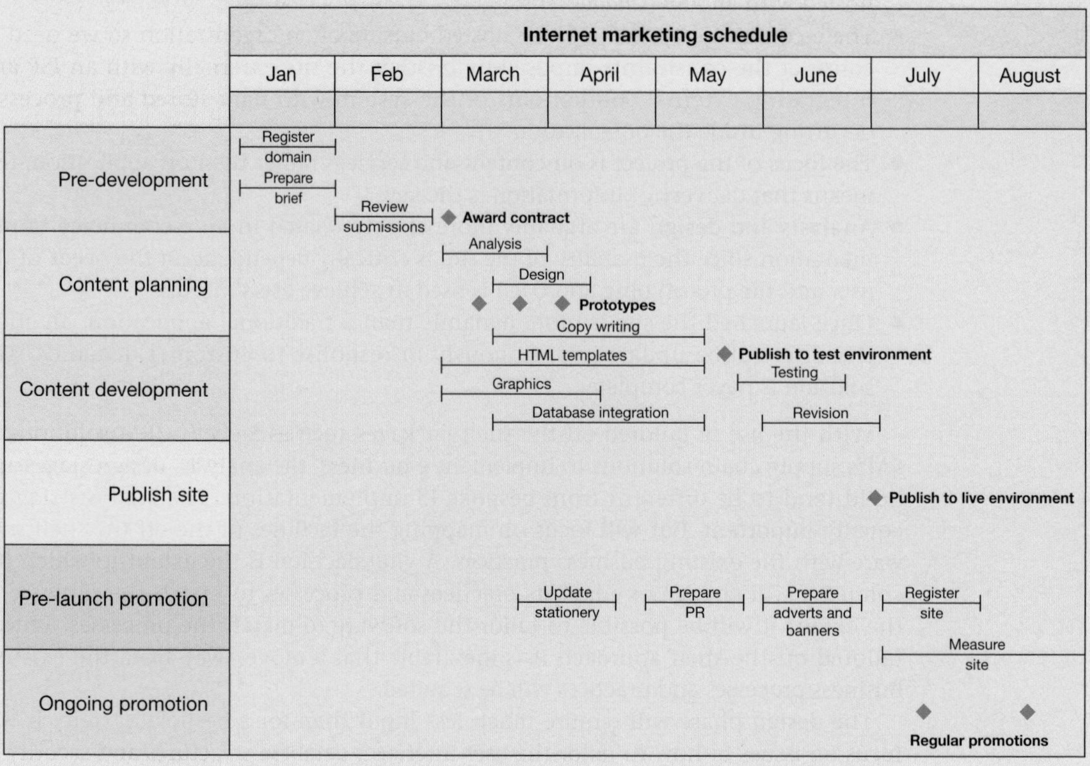

Figure 10.5 An example web site development schedule for The B2C Company

Prototyping

Prototyping
An iterative process in which web site users suggest modifications before further prototypes and the live version of the site are developed.

RAD – Rapid Application Development
An approach to information systems development that includes incremental development using prototypes.

Prototyping is a common approach to the development of e-business systems; its essence is that it is:

- *Rapid* – Prototyping is part of a systems development approach known as **'RAD – Rapid Application Development'** since the time from inception to completion is reduced to months rather than years. More rapid development is achieved through reducing the length of time of the analysis, design and build stages by combining them in conjunction with the use of graphical software tools with which applications can be built quickly from pre-assembled components.
- *Simple* – Skeleton applications are produced as **prototypes** that do not contain all the functions of a system but are a framework which gives a good indication to users of the information available and the look and feel of an application. They can then comment on it and say, for example, 'this information is missing' or 'we like that feature, but it would be nice to do that also' or 'that feature isn't necessary, it's not what we meant'. The prototype may initially be storyboarded as a

Prototype
A preliminary version of part or all of an information system reviewed by its users and business sponsors.

'paper prototype' but is usually produced as a series of screens that can be interacted with, but are not connected to a database.

- *Iterative* – Prototypes are produced often at a frequency of one every few days or weeks so that the comments from the last review can be fed into the evolving system.
- *Incremental* – Each prototype incorporates the feedback from the previous review, so each version of the application has a limited number of new features.
- *User-centred* – Users are involved at all stages of development, in describing the existing system, reviewing the prototypes and testing the system.

The stages involved with prototyping are to first identify the user requirements in outline and then rapidly develop a working prototype which the users operate to check the software proposed is in line with their needs. Once the first prototype has been produced there are several alternatives:

- iterate and produce further refinements, which often occurs throughout the specification stage; when a satisfactory version has been produced other alternatives may follow;
- develop module prototypes – prototype key views of the data from a workflow system or Lotus Notes or important data entry dialogs;
- throw away the prototype and develop a more robust version of the software for the production version. This is often prudent, since in rapid prototyping some corners have to be cut so it may not be optimized for performance or may not have exception handling features.

A frequent general problem with prototyping is to do 'demonstration prototyping' rather than 'hands-on' prototyping. Often prototypes are merely shown by developers to clients for general feedback and not used 'hands-on' until after several iterations of the prototype when many more features are integrated. This causes delays because problems that could have been trapped earlier will only become apparent at a late stage.

The prototyping approach is now ubiquitous since it reduces the risk of major design, functional or informational errors during the construction of the application that may be costly and time-consuming to fix at a later stage in development. Such errors will hopefully be identified early on and then corrected. The iterative approach is intended to be rapid and a site can be produced in a period of months or weeks.

Human resource requirements

E-business implementation requires specialist skills that may not be present within an organization. The range of specialist skill requirements is indicated with *Figure 10.6*. The E-consultancy (2005) research showed that over half of respondents felt it was a challenge, although there were more pressing challenges.

E-business project managers have a choice of building a new skills set within their organization or outsourcing and partnering with other organizations.

Even more problematic than selecting the right type of staff is attracting and retaining e-business staff. If we want effective, experienced staff then these will demand high salaries. We will be competing for these staff with dot-com companies that are trying to recruit and also other established medium-to-large companies that are looking to build an e-business capability. Smaller companies that cannot afford to recruit into each of these areas will have an even trickier problem of needing to find all of these skills rolled into one person!

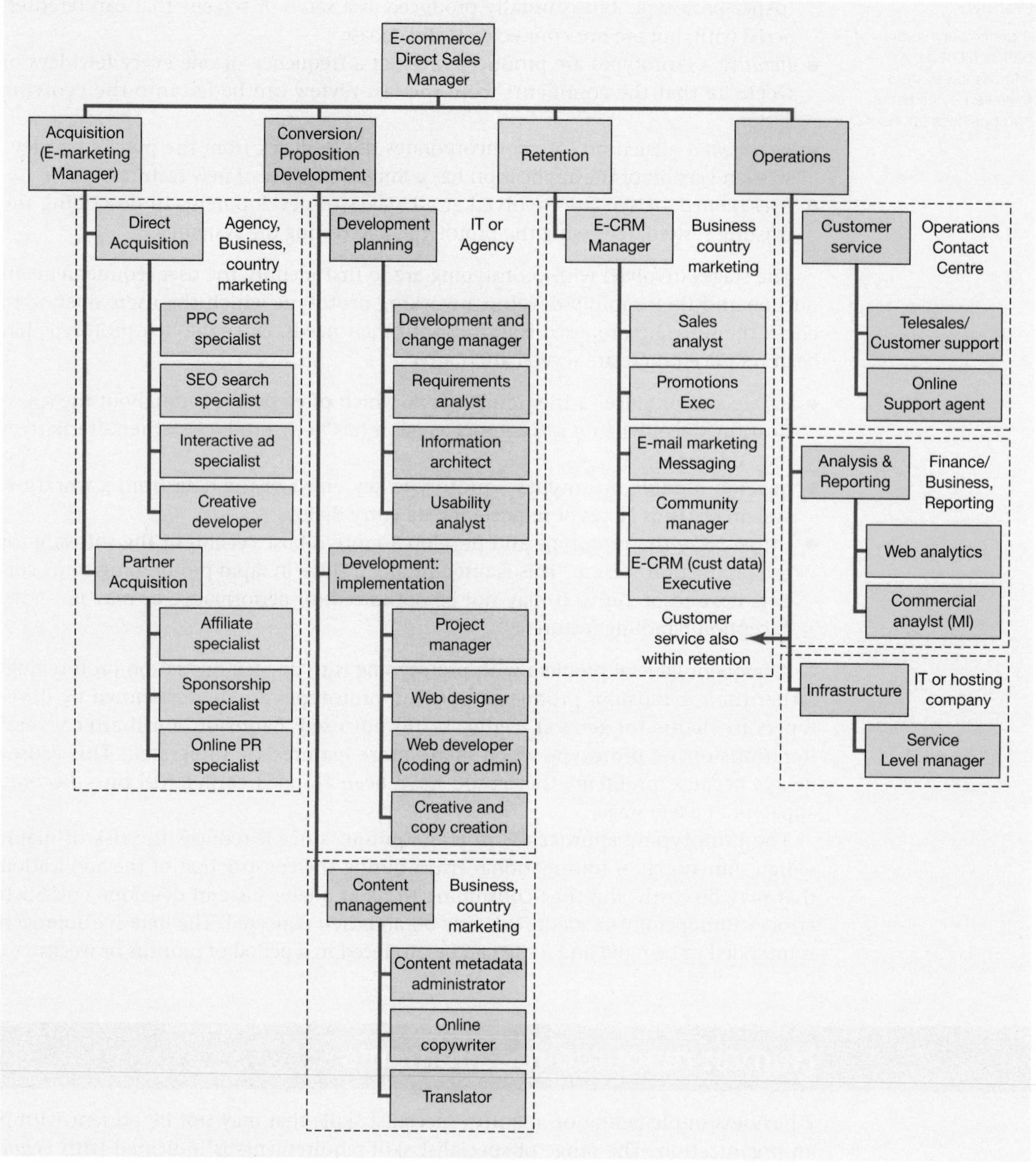

Figure 10.6 Typical structure and responsibilities for a large e-commerce team
Source: E-consultancy (2005)

Staff retention

The difficulties in staff resourcing for e-business do not end with the recruitment of staff. As Crush (2000) says, 'Getting good staff is difficult, keeping them is a nightmare!' Since there is a highly competitive marketplace for e-business staff, many staff will want to move on to further their career. This will often be after the company has spent some time training them. The Job Characteristics model developed by Hackman and Oldham (1980) provides a useful framework for designing jobs that provide a good experience to improve staff motivation and so help retention. The five intrinsic characteristics of a job are:

1 Skill variety.
2 Task identity, how well the work is defined relative to other tasks and whether an employee sees a job through 'from start to finish'.
3 Task significance or the importance of the work.
4 Autonomy or freedom in completing work.
5 Feedback from employer.

To enhance these psychological characteristics Hackman and Oldham (1980) suggest the following approaches can be used:

- *Task combination* – by combining tasks employees see more of the whole task.
- *Natural workgroups* – this also helps in task combination through creating a team to complete task.
- *Establish customer relations* – this helps in task significance.
- *Vertical loading* – employees take responsibility for tasks completed by supervisors.
- *Opening feedback channel* – from internal or external customers, via managers where necessary.

As well as making employees' roles more challenging and enjoyable, another approach is to share the skills between staff, so that if key staff leave, then not all their knowledge will leave with them. Certain types of collaboration referred to in the E-consultancy (2005) report can assist with staff sharing knowledge and experience:

- *Co-locating staff* – including marketing staff in the digital team or e-commerce staff in the marketing team was mentioned.
- *Job-swapping* – a slightly different approach, which also involves co-location, was noted as effective.
- *Interim collaborative teams ('SWAT' teams)* – a temporary multi-disciplinary team (for example, teams from e-commerce, marketing and technology) is formed to drive a particular initiative or performance improvement, e.g. home page improvement, web analytics or supporting customer journeys between channels. This approach is reported to be used by Amazon.
- *Creation of a central 'Centre of Excellence for Digital Marketing'* can provide a clear resource which marketing staff can turn to for advice and best-practice documentation. Members of this team can also be involved in proactively 'spreading the word' through involvement in training or operational campaign planning.
- *Combined planning sessions* – rather than the digital team developing a plan and then discussing with the marketing team who may then incorporate it into their plan, a more collaborative approach is used with both working on creating an integrated plan.

Outsourcing

Given the difficulties of recruiting new business staff referred to above, many companies turn to third parties to assist with their e-business implementation. However, there is a bewildering series of supplier choices. Complete *Activity 10.2* to help understand the choices required.

Activity 10.2 Options for outsourcing different e-business activities

Purpose

To highlight the outsourcing available for e-business implementation and to gain an appreciation of how to choose suppliers.

Activity

The B2C Company is trying to decide which of its sell-side e-business activities it should outsource. Select a single supplier (single tick for each function) that you think can best deliver each of these services indicated in *Table 10.3*. Justify your decision.

Table 10.3 Options for outsourcing different e-business activities

E-marketing function	*Traditional marketing agency*	*New media agency*	*ISP or traditional IT supplier*	*Management consultant*
1. Strategy				
2. Design				
3. Content and service development				
4. Online promotion				
5. Offline promotion				
6. Infrastructure				

Answers to activities can be found at www.pearsoned.co.uk/chaffey

We are seeing a gradual blurring between these types of supplier shown in *Table 10.3* as they recruit expertise so as to deliver a 'one-stop shop' service, though they still tend to be strongest in particular areas. Companies need to decide whether to partner with the best of breed in each, or to compromise and choose the one-stop shop that gives the best balance; this would arguably be the new media agency or perhaps a traditional marketing agency that has an established new media division. Which approach do you think is best?

Observation of the practice of outsourcing suggests that two conflicting patterns are evident:

1 *Outside-in.* The company starts an e-business initiative by outsourcing some activities where there is insufficient in-house expertise. These may be areas such as strategy or online promotion. The company then builds up skills internally to manage these areas as e-business becomes an important contributor to the business. The easyJet case referred to in *Chapter 8* is an example of this approach. The company initially partnered with a digital media agency to offer online services, but once the online contribution to sales exceeded 20 per cent the management of e-commerce was taken inside. The new digital media agency was, however, retained for strategic guidance. An outside-in approach will probably be driven by the need to reduce the costs of outsourcing, poor delivery of services by the supplier or simply a need to concentrate a strategic core resource in-house as is the case with easyJet.

2 *Inside-out*. The company starts to implement e-business using existing resources within the IT department and marketing department in conjunction with recruitment of new media staff. They may then find that there are problems in developing a site that meets customers' needs or in building traffic to the site. At this point they may turn to outsourcing to solve the problems.

These approaches are not mutually exclusive, and an outside-in approach may be used for some e-business functions such as content development, while an inside-out approach is used for other functions such as site promotion. It can also be suggested that these approaches are not planned – they are simply a response to prevailing conditions. However, in order to cost e-business and manage it as a strategic asset it can be argued that the e-business manager should have a long-term picture of which functions to outsource and when to bring them in-house.

The increased use of outsourcing marks a move towards the virtual organization. With the introduction of electronic networks such as the Internet it becomes easier to outsource aspects of the production and distribution of goods to third parties. Employees may work in any time zone and customers are able to purchase tailored products from any location. For example, a digital media agency may use programmers in Asia or Eastern Europe to develop web-based solutions for clients. Alternatively, contact-centre staff responding to voice contacts and e-mails may use overseas staff. Through doing this, they are able to increase the number of hours worked on projects per 24-hour period and also enjoy lower staff costs, even though, for example, Indian employees are well paid in local terms. Hallowell (2001) notes that the degree to which businesses can automate or outsource their human resources is strongly dependent on the type and level of service expected for a particular type of product. This can be significant in governing their **scalability** or capacity for growth without taking on additional staff. He says that customer service in e-commerce are:

Scalability
The ability of an organization or system to adapt to increasing demands being placed on it.

> *described as 'virtual' (either pure information or automated) and 'physical' (requiring some degree of human intervention). ... because the nature and quantity of physical service necessary to deliver value to customers influences the quantity of human intervention required, it also influences a firm's ratio of variable to fixed costs, which alters its 'scalability'. The paradox comes in that while reduced scalability is viewed negatively by many venture capitalists and proponents of ecommerce, the cause of that reduction in scalability, human intervention, may help a firm to differentiate its offering to customers, thus providing a source of competitive advantage.*

He concludes:

> *For firms that are very high on the scalability continuum, the need for physical service does not present a 'scalability' problem. At these firms, information is the core service offering. Physical service is relatively insignificant, both from customers' perspectives (use of physical service is infrequent, if at all) and from the firm's perspective (it represents a very small portion of total costs). Thus, these firms do not rely on physical service (and the employees it requires) to differentiate their offering; their differentiation tends to come from the quality of their content and the ease with which users can access it.*
>
> *In contrast, firms that sell non-information services such as travel, or goods such as books, toys, or antiques require significantly more complex physical service operations. The degree to which they need more physical service is inversely proportional to the degree to which they are 'scalable'.*

Case Study 10.1 explores the extent to which outsourcing of core business processes is possible.

Revising organizational structures

When a company first embarks on e-business, perhaps through creating a new web site to promote its products, it will normally operate within the existing company structure, perhaps using outsourcing to make good a resource deficit. However, as the contribution of the web site to the company increases, the work involved increases and more staff from different parts of the organization are involved in e-business, it may be necessary to adopt new organizational structures and working practices. This issue has been considered by Parsons *et al.* (1996) from a sell-side e-commerce perspective. They recognize four stages in the growth of what they refer to as 'the digital marketing organization':

> **Debate 10.1**
>
> **Organizing for e-business**
>
> *'The introduction of a separate e-business function is necessary in large organizations to effectively implement e-business.'*

1 Ad hoc *activity*. At this stage there is no formal organization related to e-commerce and the skills are dispersed around the organization. At this stage it is likely that there is poor integration between online and offline marketing communications. The web site may not reflect the offline brand, and the web site services may not be featured in the offline marketing communications. A further problem with *ad hoc* activity is that the maintenance of the web site will be informal and errors may occur as information becomes out of date.

2 *Focusing the effort*. At this stage, efforts are made to introduce a controlling mechanism for Internet marketing. Parsons *et al.* (1996) suggest that this is often achieved through a senior executive setting up a steering group which may include interested parties from marketing and IT and legal experts. At this stage the efforts to control the site will be experimental with different approaches being tried to build, promote and manage the site.

3 *Formalization*. At this stage the authors suggest that Internet marketing will have reached a critical mass and there will be a defined group or separate business unit within the company which manages all digital marketing.

4 *Institutionalizing capability*. This stage also involves a formal grouping within the organization, but is distinguished from the previous stage in that there are formal links created between digital marketing and a company's core activities. Baker (1998) argues that a separate e-commerce department may be needed as the company may need to be restructured in order to provide the necessary levels of customer service over the Internet if existing processes and structures do not do this.

Although this is presented as a stage model with evolution implying all companies will move from one stage to the next, many companies will find that true formalization with the creation of a separate e-commerce or e-business department is unnecessary. For small and medium companies with a marketing department numbering a few people and an IT department perhaps consisting of two people, it will not be practical to have a separate group. Even large companies may find it is sufficient to have a single person or small team responsible for e-commerce with their role being to coordinate the different activities within the company using a matrix management approach. That many companies are not ready to move to a separate digital marketing department was indicated by the KPMG report (Baker, 1998). Here it was found that over three-quarters of respondents were against establishing a separate e-commerce department.

Activity 10.3 reviews different types of organizational structures for e-commerce. *Table 10.4* reviews some of the advantages and disadvantages of each.

Table 10.4 **Advantages and disadvantages of the organizational structures shown in *Figure 10.7***

Organizational structure	*Circumstances*	*Advantages*	*Disadvantages*
(a) No formal structure for e-commerce	Initial response to e-commerce or poor leadership with no identification of need for change	Can achieve rapid response to e-commerce service responses (e-mail, phone). Priorities not decided logically. Insufficient resources	Poor-quality site in terms of content quality and customer
(b) A separate committee or department manages and coordinates e-commerce	Identification of problem and response in (a)	Coordination and budgeting and resource allocation possible	May be difficult to get different departments to deliver their input due to other commitments
(c) A separate business unit with independent budgets	Internet contribution (*Chapter 6*) is sizeable (>20%)	As for (b), but can set own targets and not be constrained by resources. Lower-risk option than (d)	Has to respond to corporate strategy. Conflict of interests between department and traditional business
(d) A separate operating company	Major revenue potential or flotation. Need to differentiate from parent	As for (c), but can set strategy independently. Can maximize market potential	High risk if market potential is overestimated due to start-up costs

Activity 10.3 Which is the best organization structure for e-commerce?

Purpose

To review alternative organizational structures for e-commerce.

1 Match the four types of companies and situations to the structures (a) to (d) in *Figure 10.7*.

(a) A separate operating company. *Examples*: Prudential and Egg (www.egg.com).
(b) A separate business unit with independent budgets. *Examples*: RS Components Internet Trading Company (www.rswww.com).
(c) A separate committee or department manages and coordinates e-commerce. *Example*: Derbyshire Building Society (www.derbyshire.co.uk).
(d) No formal structure for e-commerce. *Examples*: many small businesses.

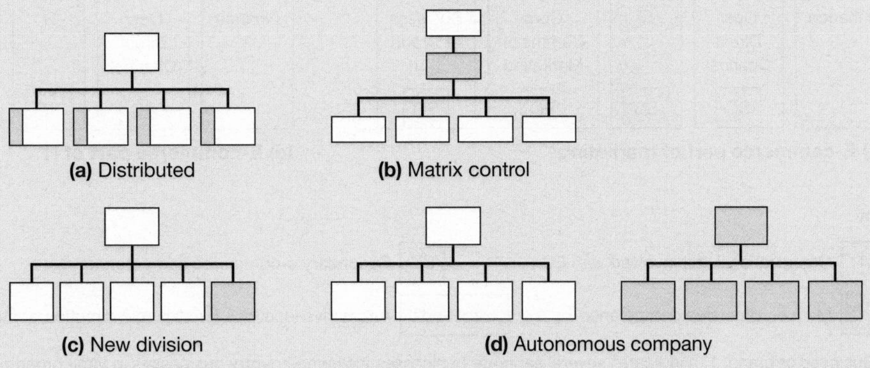

Figure 10.7 **Summary of alternative organizational structures for e-commerce suggested in Parsons *et al.* (1996)**

2 Under which circumstances would each structure be appropriate?
3 Summarize the advantages and disadvantages of each approach.

Answers to activities can be found at www.pearsoned.co.uk/chaffey.

Where the main e-commerce function is internal, the E-consultancy (2005) research suggested that it was typically located in one of four areas (see *Figure 10.8*) in approximate decreasing order of frequency:

(a) Main e-commerce function in separate team.
(b) Main e-commerce function part of operations or direct channel.
(c) Main e-commerce function part of marketing, corporate communications or other central marketing function.
(d) Main e-commerce function part of Information Technology (IT).

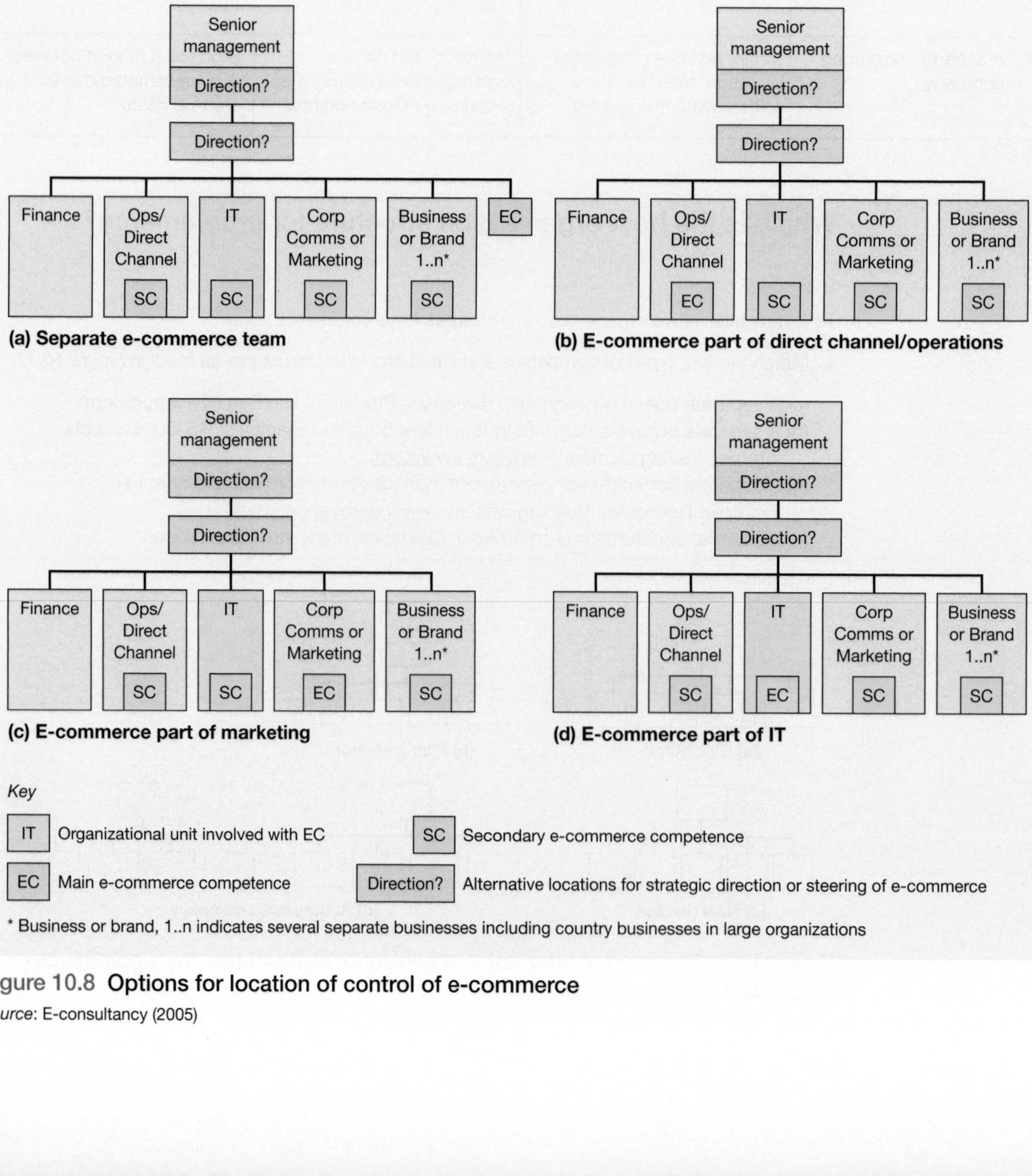

Figure 10.8 Options for location of control of e-commerce
Source: E-consultancy (2005)

There is also often one or several secondary areas of e-commerce competence and resource. For example, IT may have a role in applications development and site build and each business, brand or country may have one or more e-commerce specialists responsible for managing e-commerce in their unit. Consider which of the options would be preferable for organizations you are familiar with, such as your college or university or companies you have worked with. The research suggested that the approach which was appropriate depended strongly on the market(s) the company operated in and their existing channel structures.

Approaches to managing change

Hayes (2002) notes that for external forces of change, it may be difficult for those in an organization to manage and control the impact of change – the deterministic view. However, the voluntarist view is that managers can make an important difference to managing the impact of change. In the case of information systems management, it is clear that much can be done to reduce the impact of change although some negative aspects of change will remain. Change management is conducted by **change agents** who are the managers responsible for controlling change. In the context of e-business, the change agent could be the project manager responsible for implementing a new information system, an e-business manager responsible for increasing adoption of e-business by an organization, or specialist digital marketing or supply chain managers seeking to increase adoption of e-channels.

Change agents
Managers involved in controlling change transitions.

Senior management involvement

Cope and Waddell (2001) have assessed the role of leadership style in e-commerce implementations. They assessed the most common approaches to e-commerce implementation, distinguishing between these approaches:

- *Collaborative* – widespread participation of employees occurs to define the changes required and techniques to achieve them.
- *Consultative* – management takes the final decision, after calling on some employees for input.
- *Directive* – the management team takes the decisions, with the employees generally trusting them to do so and being generally informed.
- *Coercive* – the management team takes the decision with very limited recourse to employees.

Of these approaches, the consultative approach was, as might be expected, most common, but other statements used in the research suggested that there were elements of other approaches.

Models for achieving change

There are many process models for achieving change which can be usefully applied to managing e-business-related change. A classic model for achieving organizational change was suggested by Lewin and Schein. It involves three stages:

1 Unfreeze the present position by creating a climate of change by education, training and motivation of future participants.

2 Quickly move from the present position by developing and implementing the new system.
3 Refreeze by making the system an accepted part of the way the organization works.

Note that Lewin and Schein did not collaborate on developing this model of personal and organizational change. Kurt Lewin developed the model in unpublished work and this was then extended by Edgar Schein (1956) who undertook research into psychology based on Lewin's ideas. More recently, Lewin (1972) has summarized some of his ideas. Later, Schein (1992) concluded that three variables are critical to the success of any organizational change:

1 The degree to which the leaders can break from previous ways of working.
2 The significance and comprehensiveness of the change.
3 The extent to which the head of the organization is actively involved in the change process.

To achieve the unfreeze stages different staff can be identified for different roles by the project manager:

- *System sponsors* are senior managers or board members who have bought into the e-business initiative, are committed to major change and want to achieve success. The sponsors will try to fire up staff with their enthusiasm and stress why introducing the system is important to the business and its workers.
- *System owners* are managers in the organization of key processes such as a procurement manager or marketing manager who will use the e-business system to achieve benefits in their area.
- *System users*. These are staff in the different areas of the business who are actively involved in making the process happen. They could be a buyer in procurement or a brand manager within the marketing department.

Special types of system users can be identified, and it is important for the change manager to try to influence these staff to help achieve commitment among other staff. The three main types of system users that should be influenced are as follows:

- *Stakeholders* should be identified for each of the process areas where change will be introduced. These will be staff who are respected by their co-workers and will again act as a source of enthusiasm for the system. The user representatives used in specification, testing and sign-off are key stakeholders.
- The *legitimizer* protects the norms and values of the system; they are experienced in their job and regarded as the experts by fellow workers; they may initially be resistant to change and therefore need to be involved early.
- *Opinion leaders* are people whom others watch to see whether they accept new ideas and changes. They usually have little formal power, but are regarded as good ideas people who are receptive to change and again need to be involved early in the project.

For e-business implementation these roles will need to be identified for each implementation project as well as the overall change.

A more detailed change model proposed by Jay and Smith (1996) identifies four phases:

1 *Initial orientation*. In the orientation phase, it is necessary that there be a clear understanding of the reasons for bringing about change. This should be identified as part of the e-business, e-marketing or SCM strategies. A change strategy must be developed that includes an indication of how results will be measured, the project milestones, and how objectives would be measured and the change project organized. A skilled change team should be established and committed change sponsors identified.

2 *Preparation*. The preparation phase will involve an analysis of the environment within which the change is to take place. This includes an identification of the critical success factors for change along with a threat analysis. A work-plan for the change process must also be developed that includes detailed tasks and timings. The change direction must be announced to those affected and there should be an emphasis on maximizing communication effectiveness. It is necessary to communicate the future position to a wider audience and the need to make the change and its potential consequences must be clearly specified. The final step in this phase is to provide direction, particularly through strong communication of the goals and how they will be achieved. Hayes (2002) notes the importance of diagnosis at this stage to evaluate the differences, particularly from a staff perspective, between the initial state and the final state. This diagnosis is used to build a case or vision (*Chapter 5*) for change which can be communicated to staff.

   An example of an approach to communicating change to employees is provided by RS Components which, when first introducing an e-commerce site, set aside an area of their staff canteen and put up a stand staffed by members of the electronic commerce team. Other staff were then encouraged to learn about using the Internet and the services that the web site would provide. By doing this all staff understood the purpose of using the Internet and were more supportive of it. Additionally, it helped support the adoption of an in-company intranet. More formal education and training which explains the purpose of the Internet marketing strategy and provides practical training for those involved was also necessary.
3 *Change implementation*. In the third phase, Jay and Smith suggest that the changes are implemented by piloting the change, introducing the new procedures, conducting training and finally rolling out the change. In cases where a new information system is being rolled out to the whole organization at the same time, choosing a pilot department or site may be difficult. However, the organizational aspects as they relate to reporting relationships, job definitions, training schedules, working procedures and reward systems must be still be defined and communicated. Appropriate training should be completed and the implementation must be carried out using a roll-out plan.
4 *A supportive phase*. In the final phase, the change must be stabilized. This means that management must openly commit itself to the change and fine-tune or adjust procedures where necessary. Measuring acceptance and new behaviour and producing a formal report can be used to evaluate the effectiveness of the change. There must be prevention of a relapse, such as an attempt to revert to old systems and practices or even bypassing the new system altogether. Conducting regular review meetings along with continual training and procedure reviews can help this.

   Hayes (2002) has summarized how change managers can facilitate progress through the overall change process and progress through the transitions an individual makes during change. He notes the following general implications of the transition model for change managers:

   - The overall form of the transition curve will take different forms – individual stages may be longer or shorter and the degree of mood change at each stage can vary considerably.
   - There will often be a time lag between the announcement of a change and a reaction to it. It is possible to mistake initial shock and denial for acceptance of the change.
   - Different people and different parts of the organization will pass through the change cycle at different rates and in different ways.
   - Change managers will typically be out of step with other staff since they are involved earlier and deeper.

- The cycle cannot be avoided, but there is much that change managers can do to facilitate people's progress through it.

Hayes (2002) also gives specific advice about how change managers can facilitate change through different change transitions. This advice is summarized in *Table 10.5* together with typical implications for e-business initiatives and applications.

Table 10.5 **Facilitating organizational change through a transition model**

Transition phase	*Typical actions by change managers*	*Implications for e-business implementation*
1 Shock/awareness	Create a climate of receptivity to change. Announcement sufficiently in advance in involving senior managers.	Pre-announcement and involvement are readily practicable for e-business. Announcement and ownership by a senior manager is important.
2 Denial	Diagnosis of the reason for denial is important. Gently support the staff through denial. Repeat message of reason for change and justify. Find ways to get staff involved in change early.	Involvement is typically a requirement of e-business projects, so this is usually practical for some staff; for others communication of the benefits and progress of the project and the implications for them should be considered.
3 Depression	Providing support and listening are required at this stage rather than ignoring complaints.	This stage can be accommodated through prototyping and recording feedback in the live system.
4 Letting go	Continued explanation of the benefits of the new system without denigrating the past approach. Setting targets associated with the new system.	Around this stage prototypes of the new system will be available which will help with the process of letting go since tangible evidence of the new system and, hopefully, its benefits will be available.
5 Testing	Testing is encouraged by encouraging experimentation without blame where problems occur.	Testing corresponds to the testing phase of the system or adoption of the new system dependent on involvement. Positive or negative feedback on the new system should be encouraged, discussed and acted upon where appropriate.
6 Consolidation	This is facilitated by reviewing performance and learning and recognizing, rewarding and communicating benefits.	Improvements achieved through the system should be assessed and communicated.
7 Reflection and learning	This is achieved through structured learning about the change through reviews and encouraging unstructured learning such as feedback about the system.	Post-implementation reviews should occur at this stage, since this acknowledges that no system can be perfect first time and future improvements are planned for. The use of a structured system to log problems with the system or process can also help.

Source: The middle column is based on a summary of the commentary in Hayes (2002)

Organizational culture

Bocij *et al.* (2005) suggest that social relationships in an organization that are part of its culture are important. They say '*the efficiency of any organization is dependent on the complex formal and informal relationships that exist within it*'. Formal relationships include the hierarchical work relationships within and between functional business areas. Informal relationships are created through people working and socializing with

Culture
This concept includes shared values, unwritten rules and assumptions within the organization as well as the practices that all group share. Corporate cultures are created when a group of employees interact over time and are relatively successful in what they undertake.

each other on a regular basis and will cut across functional boundaries. E-business-led change has the capacity to alter both types of relationships as it brings about change within and between functional business areas.

Boddy *et al.* (2001) summarize four different types of cultural orientation that may be identified in different companies. These vary according to the extent to which the company is inward-looking or outward-looking, in other words to what extent it is affected by its environment. They also reflect whether the company is structured and formal or whether it has a more flexible, dynamic, informal character. The four types of cultural orientation are:

1 *Survival (outward-looking, flexible)* – the external environment plays a significant role (an open system) in governing company strategy. The company is likely to be driven by customer demands and will be an innovator. It may have a relatively flat structure.
2 *Productivity (outward-looking, ordered)* – interfaces with the external environment are well structured and the company is typically sales-driven and is likely to have a hierarchical structure.
3 *Human relations (inward-looking, flexible)* – this is the organization as family, with interpersonal relations more important than reporting channels, a flatter structure and staff development, and empowerment is thought of as important by managers.
4 *Stability (inward-looking, ordered)* – the environment is essentially ignored, with managers concentrating on internal efficiency and again management is through a hierarchical stucture.

Now complete *Activity 10.4* to investigate how companies may need to realign their culture to succeed in e-business.

Activity 10.4 Changing the culture for e-business

Purpose

To identify appropriate cultural changes that may be necessary for e-business success.

Activity

Review the four general categories of organizational cultural orientation summarized by Boddy *et al.* (2001) and take each as characterizing four different companies and then suggest which is most appropriate for e-business. State whether you think they are most likely to occur in a small or a larger organization.

Answers to activities can be found at www.pearsoned.co.uk/chaffey

Focus on knowledge management

Knowledge management has an important role within e-business since business success is critically dependent on staff knowledge about all aspects of the micro-environment such as customers, suppliers, intermediaries, competitors and how to shape internal processes to best deliver customer service.

E-business is a significant topic which is only introduced here. A more detailed coverage of how knowledge management can support business processes is available in Chaffey and Wood (2005).

With the move towards globalization and responding more rapidly to changing market conditions knowledge transfer is a key to competitiveness. Knowledge

> **Debate 10.2**
>
> **Knowledge management**
>
> *'Knowledge management is as likely, if not more so, to act as a process of managing people or information than as a practice attuned to facilitating knowledge creation.'*
>
> *(Alvesson and Karreman, 2002)*

management is also a change management response to the problems of staff retention referred to earlier. As Saunders (2000) puts it:

> *Every day, knowledge essential to your business walks out of your door, and much of it never comes back. Employees leave, customers come and go and their knowledge leaves with them. This information drain costs you time, money and customers.*

What is knowledge?

Knowledge
Applying experience to problem solving.

Knowledge management
Techniques and tools disseminating knowledge within an organization.

The concept of knowledge is more difficult to state than that of data or information. However, knowledge can be regarded as the next level of sophistication or business value in the cycle from data through information to knowledge. Knowledge management (KM) seeks to share this experience within a company. Useful summaries have been produced by Mekhilef *et al.* (2004):

> ***Knowledge** is the combination of data and information, to which is added expert opinion, skills and experience, to result in a valuable asset which can be used to aid decision making. Knowledge may be explicit and/or tacit, individual and/or collective.*
>
> ***Knowledge Management** is the management of activities and processes for leveraging knowledge to enhance competitiveness through better use and creation of individual and collective knowledge resources.*

Theorists have identified two different types of knowledge, and different approaches can be used to disseminate each type of knowledge within an organization:

Explicit knowledge
Knowledge that can be readily expressed and recorded within information systems.

Tacit knowledge
Mainly intangible knowledge that is typical intuitive and not recorded since it is part of the human mind.

1 Explicit – details of processes and procedures. Explicit knowledge can be readily detailed in procedural manuals and databases. Examples include records of meetings between sales representatives and key customers, procedures for dealing with customer service queries and management reporting processes.
2 Tacit – less tangible than explicit knowledge, this is experience on how to react to a situation when many different variables are involved. It is more difficult to encapsulate this knowledge, which often resides in the heads of employees. Techniques for sharing this knowledge include learning stories and histories. Examples include knowing how to react when changes occur in the marketplace, such as a competitor launching a new product or a major customer looking to defect. Knowing how to analyse and respond to information in management reports depends on tacit knowledge. To acquire tacit knowledge may rely on sharing knowledge with partners outside the company or others in different sectors. So knowledge management should not be considered solely as confining corporate knowledge within the firewalls.

It follows that one goal of knowledge management is to turn tacit knowledge into explicit knowledge which can then be shared between employees and used to train new employees.

A framework for the different activities that comprise knowledge management is given in *Figure 10.9*. The main activities are:

1 *Identify knowledge.* This is an analysis of the availability of existing knowledge to support the activities forming existing processes and a gap analysis showing what is missing.
2 *Create new knowledge.* This reviews methods to create new knowledge. At the personal and team levels, recommended techniques are through training, process

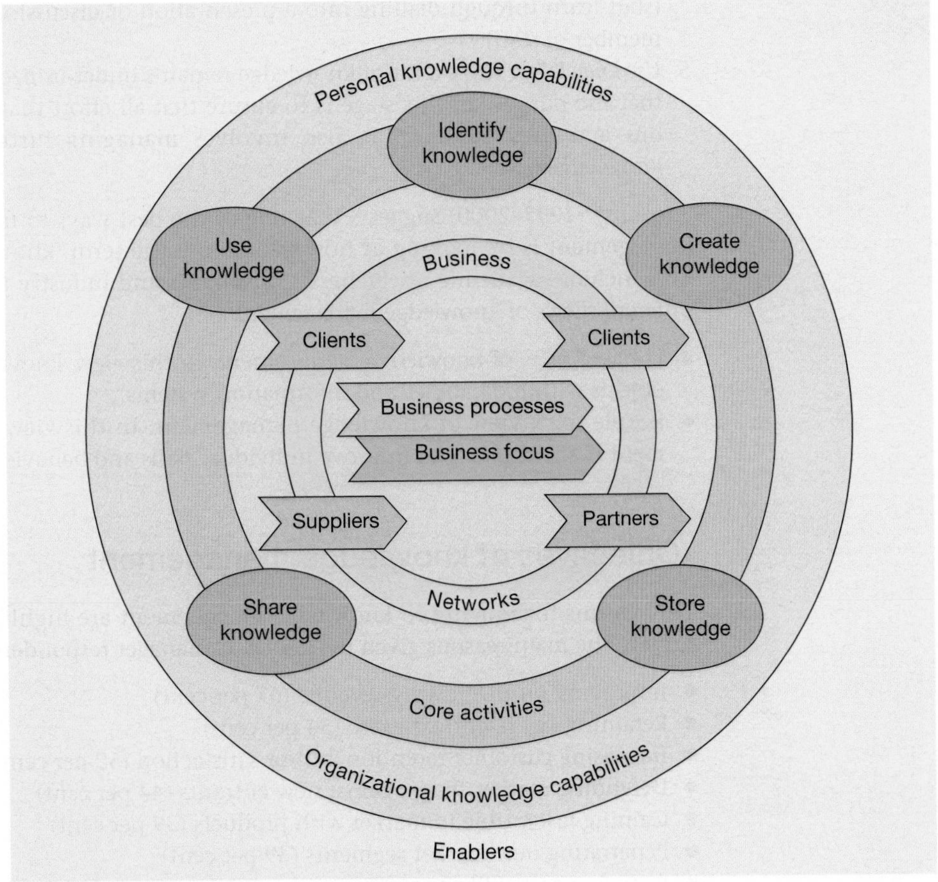

Figure 10.9 Knowledge management framework

problem improvement sessions or brainstorming. At the departmental or organizational levels, knowledge creation can occur through benchmarking against other organizations and through establishing of expert groups known as 'communities of practice' or use of consultants or other companies to acquire new knowledge.

3 *Store knowledge*. Mekhilef *et al.* point out that much knowledge is typically 'stored' in people's brains and so will often remain there as 'tacit knowledge'. Knowledge can also be embedded or become part of the 'organizational memory' through revising processes that form team routines. Storing explicit knowledge requires a structured approach to selecting, updating, organizing or categorizing knowledge within information systems.
4 *Share knowledge*. This increases knowledge availability to ensure it is available in the right context – i.e. for the right person, at the right time to support their current activity. Mekhilef *et al.* (2004) identify the *stock* method of distribution where knowledge is made available through databases and the *flow* method where knowledge is transferred directly from person to person through collaboration, workshops or mentoring.

These authors also say that approaches to support knowledge sharing include: intranets/portals, databases, collaboration, communities of practice, job rotation, coaching, seminars and training. Technology can be used to assist this through making information available through an intranet which enables browsing and searching of document databases or more collaborative approaches such as 'wikis' (a web-based discussion which can be authored by several people) or 'webinars' (staff learn through dialling into a presentation or discussion hosted by an expert member of staff).

5 *Use knowledge*. Since a lot of knowledge remains under-utilized, the authors suggest that the purpose of this stage is to ensure that all effort that is spent in the previous activities pays off! It also involves managing further additions to the knowledge base.

Sveiby (1997–2000) suggests that one of the best ways to understand knowledge management is by looking at how people use the term 'knowledge management'. This includes academic researchers, consultants and industry practitioners. The two different views of knowledge management are:

- IT-based view of knowledge management. In this view, knowledge can be stored as objects within databases and information systems.
- People-track view of knowledge management. In this view, knowledge management is about trying to improve individual skills and behaviour.

Objectives of knowledge management

The reasons for moving to knowledge management are highlighted by a 1999 IDC survey. The main reasons given by 355 US IS manager respondents were:

- Improving profit/growing revenue (67 per cent)
- Retaining key talent/expertise (54 per cent)
- Increasing customer retention and/or satisfaction (52 per cent)
- Defending market share against new entrants (44 per cent)
- Gaining faster time to market with products (39 per cent)
- Penetrating new market segments (39 per cent)
- Reducing costs (38 per cent)
- Developing new products/services (35 per cent).

It is evident that although employee retention is important, knowledge management is also seen as a competitive force for acquiring and retaining customers. Unlike other e-business initiatives cost reduction is relatively unimportant.

Sveiby (1997–2000) identifies an evolution of knowledge management objectives through time starting with a realization around 1992 that many companies were reinventing the wheel by not applying the experience acquired through previous, similar projects. Sharing knowledge was achieved by using best-practice databases using groupware such as Lotus Notes. Later the database was again the focus as companies aimed to learn more about their customers through data warehousing and data mining. The third phase is, he says, associated with sell-side e-commerce and learning more about *interactions* with customers through web-based forms and online purchases.

Implementing knowledge management

The reasons for difficulties in moving to knowledge management (KM) are also highlighted by the 1999 IDC survey. The main problems noted were:

- Lack of understanding of KM and its benefits (55 per cent)
- Lack of employee time for KM (45 per cent)
- Lack of skill in KM techniques (40 per cent)
- Lack of encouragement in the current culture for sharing (35 per cent)
- Lack of incentives/rewards to share (30 per cent)

- Lack of funding for KM initiatives (24 per cent)
- Lack of appropriate technology (18 per cent)
- Lack of commitment from senior management (15 per cent).

Note that lack of the appropriate technology is not a major issue, although selecting the right technology may be important. All the main barriers relate to organizational structure and culture. A key finding seems to be the need to explain the benefits of knowledge management, develop skills and encourage sharing. A quote from Marianne Hedin, Research Manager at IDC Research (IDC, 2000) highlights this. She says:

> *It is impossible to achieve full benefits from knowledge management unless individuals are willing and motivated to share their knowledge or unless organizations lose their structural rigidity to permit information and knowledge flow.*

David Snowden (2002) puts it more simply when he says:

> *Knowledge can only be volunteered – it cannot be conscripted.*

Hansen *et al.* (1999) suggest that incentives are required to encourage staff to share knowledge such as making knowledge sharing a factor in the employees' performance review, assessed by recording of knowledge electronically or transferring it person-to-person. See the box *Implementing knowledge management at Chevron* for a review of how these problems in implementing knowledge management can be overcome.

An example of how staff can be successfully incentivized is provided by ShareNet, a knowledge management system at Siemens where contributors could collect points called ShareNet shares, similar to frequent-flier miles. Users earned shares for entering knowledge objects into the library (20 shares for a success story), answering urgent requests (3 shares), re-using knowledge and rating one another's contributions (single shares). In May 2000, the top 50 point collectors were invited to New York for a conference on ShareNet. Redemption of shares was possible against prizes such as text books, mobile phones, computers, PDAs, business trips. One share was roughly equivalent to one euro at the time. Different countries and business units were then compared on their success in generating shares.

Implementing knowledge management at Chevron

Saunders (2000) suggests that for oil company Chevron, the approach to knowledge management can be summarized as 'connection'. This is the term described by Jeff Stemke, an internal consultant on the knowledge management programme, who refers to himself as 'an evangelist for knowledge management'. The connections Stemke refers to are:

1. Connection to the explicit knowledge via an intranet with a portal with search tools and a directory of information.
2. Connection of people to people with specialized knowledge through an expertise locator – a type of phone directory with people in different expertise categories, again also accessed via search tools.
3. Connection to communities of practice which can help sharing and learning between people.
4. Connection of knowledge and people with processes, products and services.

Further recommendations from Stemke include, again, the need for senior management buy-in; focus on achieving key objectives, in Chevron's case cost-effectiveness; teach and train employees how to share knowledge and put in place a measurement programme. At Chevron, a $2 billion saving in operating costs has occurred. These savings are not all attributable to knowledge management, but development and sharing of best practices has contributed to this. A 50 per cent reduction in incidents and injuries amongst refinery workers has also occurred as a result of the programme.

Technologies for implementing knowledge management

The implementation of e-business applications can support knowledge management through providing different applications which support the five different steps of knowledge management described above. Binney (2001) identifies six different classes of KM applications as follows:

1 *Transactional*. Helpdesk and customer service applications.
2 *Analytical*. Data warehousing and data mining for CRM applications.
3 *Asset management*. Document and content management.
4 *Process support*. Total quality management, benchmarking, BPR, Six Sigma (see www.isixsigma.com for further information).
5 *Developmental*. Enhancing staff skills and competencies – training and e-learning.
6 *Innovation and creation*. Communities, collaboration and virtual teamwork.

Vendors now offer many tools for knowledge management, but it must be recognized that these tools only facilitate knowledge management. Many may simply be re-badged information management tools – do they truly support knowledge management? Major changes to knowledge creation and dissemination processes within the organization are likely to be required to reap the benefits of this technology.

Alternative tools for managing knowledge include:

- Knowledge capture tools such as software for devising knowledge maps and mind maps
- Knowledge sharing techniques such as chat, discussion groups, wikis, webinars and video-conferencing
- Knowledge delivery tools such as intranets and e-mail
- Knowledge storage in document databases or knowledge bases such as Lotus Notes/Domino and content management systems
- Electronic document management systems such as Interleaf publisher
- Expert systems use to capture specific task-based knowledge and deliver a solution.

Chaffey and Wood (2005) point out that intranets have an important role within knowledge management and tend to have three stages of sophistication for knowledge management:

1 *Static*. Basic web pages stored on a web server. Information publishing is centrally controlled. Employees browse and search for information but do not interact. Content is refreshed on an irregular basis. The danger at this stage is that the intranet will become a silo of underused information, employees will not trust the intranet as a tool to assist in knowledge work.
2 *Interaction*. The intranet develops into a dynamic environment developing around the knowledge needs of employees. Publishing becomes a regular process that many employees are involved with. Discussion boards and bulletin boards are introduced. Employees start to develop trust in using the intranet to share and locate knowledge.
3 *Collaborative electronic work space*. The intranet becomes a 'self-service' environment where are all employees are empowered to share knowledge via publishing mechanisms and collaborative tools. It becomes the starting point for discovering explicit knowledge. All core business processes will take place across the intranet platform.

We will now look at some examples of how these different tools have been combined with different strategies for sharing knowledge in organizations. Hansen *et al.* (1999) identify two contrasting approaches for implementing knowledge management which they illustrate through case studies of management consultancies. They refer to these approaches as 'codification' and 'personalization'. They found that companies tend to focus on one approach or the other, although there was some overlap. In the codification approach, used by Andersen Consulting and Ernst & Young, knowledge is codified or translated into a form suitable for searching using a database. Hansen *et al.* (1999) give the example of a partner in the Los Angeles office of Ernst & Young who needed assistance in creating a bid for implementation of an ERP system. Since he did not have this type of implementation he tapped into the knowledge management repository to find similar bids completed by others in the past. The re-use of a previous bid made it possible to complete the bid in half the normal period of four to six weeks, even though the partner was relatively inexperienced in this area. The codification process has been a major initiative at Ernst & Young with over 250 employed at the Center for Business Knowledge to codify information and help others perform searches. In addition, each of Ernst & Young's forty practice areas has a specialist in codifying documents.

The personalization approach has been adopted more by strategy consulting firms such as Bain and McKinsey. Hansen *et al.* (1999) relate the case of a partner in the London office of Bain who had to advise a UK financial institution how to solve a particular strategy dilemma. This assignment required knowledge of different market and geographical sectors and creative input. She used the Bain people-finder system to find those with suitable information, then convened a meeting in Europe that involved video-conferencing with others in Singapore and Sydney. Over the next four months, the partner then consulted regularly through e-mail, video-conferencing and phone. As well as using these technological approaches, McKinsey also fosters knowledge transfer by moving staff between offices, by having directories of experts and by having a culture that encourages prompt return of calls.

Like other strategic initiatives involving significant organizational change and the deployment of new technology, knowledge management has been beset by difficulties of project implementation. Storey and Barnett (2000) review the literature on project failure and report on a detailed case study. They highlight six key learnings:

(1) *Listen very carefully to the expectations, agendas and wants of all parties involved. They may appear to be using the same language and to be supporting the programme but in fact their understandings and plans may be very different.*

(2) *Check continuously that top management support is continuing and is delivered in a practical and public way.*

(3) *Be alert to the potential differences between a paradigm based on knowledge management which is IT-led and infused with priorities relating to knowledge capture, archiving and mining, and one based on the learning organization concept which may be inspired by wider developmental values. If handled with extraordinary skill the two approaches may reinforce each other but this cannot be expected simply to occur by happenchance.*

(4) *It will be found useful to ensure that the purpose and reason for expending effort on knowledge sharing is clarified and understood by everyone involved. It needs to be seen to be useful to those who are, in effect, being asked to behave differently.*

(5) *The interrelationship between knowledge sharing, knowledge creation and organizational change needs to be understood and realized. Reversal to traditional ways of operating based on low trust and direct command are too easily adopted when problems arise as our case demonstrates.*

(6) *If knowledge is to be more widely shared and more readily created and used, there is an implication that innovation in process and probably service or products will also ensue and indeed should be sought. There are different types or levels of organizational KM systems: at the lower level, expert practitioners simply make available their operating routines and information. At the second level, the new knowledge is used as a basis for the shift in the kind of products and services offered to customers.*

Risk management

To conclude this chapter and act as a bridge to the final two chapters we review the problems associated with change when managing an e-business implementation. **Risk management** is intended to identify potential risks in a range of situations and then take actions to minimize the risks. We all unconsciously perform risk management throughout our lives. For example, when crossing a country road we will assess the likely risk of a car approaching, or a silent cyclist approaching around the blind bend, and perhaps increase our pace accordingly. *Activity 10.5* is intended to illustrate these risks. Risk management involves these stages:

Risk management
Evaluating potential risks, developing strategies to reduce risks and learning about future risks.

1 Identify risks, including their probabilities and impacts.
2 Identify possible solutions to these risks.
3 Implement the solutions targeting the highest-impact, most-likely risks.
4 Monitor the risks to learn for future risk assessment.

Activity 10.5 E-business risk management for The B2C Company

Purpose

To highlight risks that are part of an e-business implementation and suggest solutions. This activity acts as a summary of many of the change management concepts reviewed in this chapter.

Activity

Review this chapter with reference to *Chapters 4* and *5* and produce a grid with four columns describing the risk for a company with which you are familiar, or for The B2C Company, assessing its probability on a scale of 0 (no risk) to 10 (very high risk), its impact from a scale of 0 (no impact) to 10 (catastrophic), and possible solutions.

Answers to activities can be found at www.pearsoned.co.uk/chaffey

Table 10.6 Organizational risk exposure factors (from Simon, 1999)

Growth risks	*Culture risks*	*Information management risks*
Pressures for performance (overambitious targets due to external demands)	Rewards for entrepreneurial risk-taking (Nick Leeson syndrome)	Transaction complexity and velocity (a particularly high risk for companies having to purchase or sell raw materials in bulk)
Rate of expansion (expansion difficult to control and recruit new employees)	Executive resistance to bad news (. . . and lack of action)	Gaps in diagnostic performance measures (poor reporting capabilities)
Inexperience of key employees	Levels of internal competition (is the culture cooperative or too competitive?)	Degree of decentralized decision making (lack of central control and management of other risks)

Source: Adapted and reprinted by permission of *Harvard Business Review* from table on p. 87 from 'How risky is your company?', by Simon, R., in *Harvard Business Review*, May–June 1999. Copyright © 1999 by the Harvard Business School Publishing Corporation, all rights reserved

As an alternative view of risks with a wider organization context, Simon (1999) presents a simple risk calculator based on different types of risks faced at a company level (*Table 10.6*). This calculator can be usefully applied to e-business change or a high-growth dot-com company since significant change may accentuate these risks.

Case Study 10.2 Sharing knowledge at the BBC using Internet technologies

FT

A corporate knowledge management system based on the type of technology used in Wikipedia and MySpace might seem a 'Web 2.0' nightmare for the realistic IT manager. But the BBC, one of the UK's biggest organisations, has been doing just this to encourage information sharing between its 28,000 staff – and other big businesses are taking notice.

Euan Semple, head of knowledge management solutions, is the man responsible for this successful and bold experiment which began in 1999 when he was charged with deploying a system. It was the time when large expensive knowledge management platforms were becoming available.

'I think they expected me to go out and buy a big system for hundreds of thousands of pounds, which I studiously avoided doing', he says.

Instead, he bought a cheap piece of bulletin board software for £200. Dubbed talk.gateway, it was set up as an adjunct to the intranet, with two categories: 'Queries and Questions' and 'Discussions'. Any member of staff could register and create new threads.

Today it has 11 topics and includes an interest groups platform, connect.gateway, which all staff can join and set up. It is similar to features in the social networking website MySpace or blog host LiveJournal but, far from being a frivolous distraction, it is an efficient way of sharing information. There are 250 interest groups and as an example, Mr Semple picks the first alphabetical one, which is about Adobe software and has 3,500 members.

'If you wanted to contact all the people who we know use the list, we would have to contact all 3,500 people we know who use it, and risk spamming them', he says.

Wikis were the next step and provided another simple solution – in this case for documents with multiple authors. The BBC again bought a cheap system. The organisation is not allowed to identify products it uses, but there are several dozen types of wiki software available, most of which are open source and include features such as recent changes lists, version control and search.

Blogging is the most recent addition to the BBC's knowledge management suite. So far there are about 200 staff blogs – including one by Richard Sambrook, head of global news. 'It's made him real in a way that most of the other executives aren't', says Mr Semple. The blogs, like the forums and wikis, are kept behind a firewall.

Although the BBC's initiative has attracted interest from several large international companies, Mr Semple accepts that some organisations would not want to adopt such an open approach. The project has encountered opposition from people who question whether the organisation should adopt technologies and processes that are so new and potentially disruptive to the existing structure.

'I tell people that when we hire today's 16-year-olds who have big thumbs and spend all their time texting, they will have to', Mr Semple says.

He believes that if new types of communication technology are not supported within the organisation, they will carry on outside. Staff agree to a fairly standard 'acceptable use' policy to participate in any of the new tools, and are aware that anything they write can be read by management.

Any problematic issues that arise are referred to lawyers, something Mr Semple says happens very occasionally.

He sees the systems he has introduced as much more about organisational culture than technology. 'So much of business has been about treating people like children', he says.

The whole system is still run with very few staff – Mr Semple's colleague John Howard, the technology manager for DigiLab distribution and technology, looks after most of the development, maintenance and support, with some extra development resources for the forums.

The systems they have put in place were chosen to be low-maintenance and, in some ways, self-sustaining. To develop a blogging policy, for example, interested staff were identified via forum topic and used a wiki to develop it. The policy is now up for formal management review.

'I'm solving problems most companies don't even know they have', says Mr Semple.

Source: Encouraging information sharing. By Kate Mackenzie. *Financial Times*, 24 January 2006

Questions

1. Explain how the BBC has been able to exploit low-cost Internet-based tools to support knowledge sharing.
2. Assess the advantages and disadvantages of the tools used in other types of business.

Summary

1 Change as a result of e-business needs to be managed on two levels. First, the change that needs to be managed as part of projects to introduce e-business. Second, organization-wide change is required for e-business. We focus on this change in this chapter.

2 Sound project management is required to achieve change. Traditional project management activities such as estimation, resource allocation, scheduling, planning and monitoring are all important here. A project manager also needs to facilitate change by communicating the need for change.

3 Traditional lifecycle stages – analysis, design and build – can be used to estimate the tasks required for an e-business implementation. Since most e-business solutions will be based on tailoring off-the-shelf packages, there will be a change in balance between the analysis, design, build and implementation phases in comparison with a bespoke solution. Prototyping is essential to achieve the fast timescales required by e-business.

4 Building a team for e-business will require technical, marketing and project management skills. This will be difficult in the face of a competitive marketplace for these scales and high staff turnover. Tactics should be developed to help retain staff in this environment.

5 To implement e-business, a company will need to partner with a variety of companies. The e-business manager will need to decide whether to outsource activities such as strategy, content development and site promotion at the outset of an e-business project and whether it may be necessary to bring these activities back in-house at a later stage.

6 Changes to organizational structures are likely to be required to build the e-business. Coordination of e-business-related activities can be achieved through a working party, e-business manager or separate department. Companies may also spin off sell-side e-commerce to a completely separate business.

7 Managing staff responses to change is an important aspect of change. Managers will need to consider how to achieve commitment and action from senior managers and also how to gain staff acceptance of the new system and new working practices. Techniques that may be used are user education, user involvement and achieving support from respected staff. Companies with an outward-looking cultural orientation will be predisposed to e-business-led change while others that have an inward-facing, inflexible cultural orientation may have to consider changes in culture.

Exercises

Self-assessment questions

1 Summarize the main types of change that need to be managed during introduction of e-business.

2 What approaches must managers take to achieve change management successfully?

3 Outline the main stages of a sell-side e-commerce implementation.

4 Explain the role of prototyping in developing a sell-side e-commerce solutic

5 Describe four different approaches to retaining staff.

6 What alternative approaches are there to structuring e-commerce within an org.

7 Which type of organizational culture is most amenable to e-business-related change?

8 What are some of the risks of e-business change, and how can they be managed?

Essay and discussion questions

1 Write an essay on approaches to managing e-business change.

2 'Total outsourcing of e-business operations is the best method to overcome the skills shortage.' Discuss.

3 Contrast the project management stages involved with sell-side and buy-side e-commerce implementations (referring to *Chapters 11* and *12* will help with this question).

4 'High turnover of technical staff is a fact of life in a buoyant job market and there is little that can be done to reduce turnover.' Discuss.

5 Develop a change management plan for a company you are familiar with.

6 You are the HR manager at a new-media design agency and are evaluating the use of overseas contract workers to help on projects. Write a report summarizing the feasibility of this approach.

7 Write a report on how the knowledge within a company can be better managed. Refer to particular technologies and procedures for managing explicit and tacit knowledge.

8 Assess the merits of virtualization in an organization of your choice.

Examination questions

1 Explain what prototyping is and why it may be used on an e-commerce implementation.

2 Summarize the main human-resource requirements for an e-commerce implementation.

3 A company has implemented a brochureware site without any changes to managerial or organizational structure. They are now seeking to achieve one-third of their revenues via the web site. What changes to managerial and organizational structure would you suggest?

4 Explain how knowledge management differs from information management.

5 Explain the concept of the virtual organization. What are the advantages over a traditional organization?

6 Name four approaches a company can take to increase retention of technical staff.

7 Prioritize, with justification, your recommendations for outsourcing these functions: e-commerce strategy, e-commerce hosting, e-commerce content updating.

8 You are project manager of an e-procurement implementation. How would you maximize acceptance of the new system among staff?

References

Alvesson, M. and Karreman, D. (2002) Odd couple – making sense of the curious concept of knowledge management. *Journal of Management Studies*, 38(7), 995–1018.

Baker, P. (1998) *Electronic Commerce. Research Report 1998*. KPMG Management Consulting.

Binney, D. (2001) The KM spectrum – understanding the KM landscape. *Journal of Knowledge Management*, 5(1) 33–42.

Bocij, P., Chaffey, D., Greasley, A. and Hickie, S. (2005) *Business Information Systems. Technology, Development and Management*, 3rd edn. Financial Times Prentice Hall, Harlow.

Boddy, D., Boonstra, A. and Kennedy, G. (2001) *Managing the Information Revolution*. Financial Times Prentice Hall, Harlow.

Chaffey, D. and Wood, S. (2005) *Business Information Management. Improving Performance Using Information Systems*, Financial Times Prentice Hall, Harlow.

COBIT (2001) Control Objectives. COBIT (3rd edn). Released by the COBIT Steering Committee and the IT Governance Institute. Available online at: www.isacf.org/cobit.

Cope, O. and Waddell, D. (2001) An audit of leadership styles in e-commerce. *Managerial Auditing Journal*, 16(9), 523–9.

Crush, P. (2000) What's my motivation? *Revolution*, 2 August, 34–6.

Davenport, T.H. (1993) *Process Innovation: Re-engineering Work through Information Technology*. Harvard Business School Press, Boston, MA.

E-consultancy (2005) Managing an E-commerce team. Integrating digital marketing into your organisation. 60-page report by Dave Chaffey. Available from www.e-consultancy.com.

Gartner (2003) Gartner Application Integration and Middleware Strategies Research Note T-19-4751, J. Sinur, D. McCoy, J. Thompson, 14 April. The Gartner Group (www.gartner.com).

Hackman, J. and Oldham, G. (1980) *Work Redesign*. Addison-Wesley, Reading, MA.

Hallowell, R. (2001) 'Scalability': the paradox of human resources in e-commerce. *International Journal of Service Industry Management*, 12(1), 34–43.

Hammer, M. and Champy, J. (1993) *Re-engineering the Corporation: A Manifesto for Business Revolution*. HarperCollins, New York.

Hansen, M., Nohria, N. and Tierney, T. (1999) What's your strategy for measuring knowledge? *Harvard Business Review*, May–June, 106–16.

Hayes, J. (2002) *The Theory and Practice of Change Management*. Palgrave, Basingstoke.

IDC (1999) Knowledge Management Survey. IDC Research. (www.idcresearch.com).

IDC (2000) Capitalizing on Knowledge Management. IDC Research Report. (www.idcresearch.com #W18864).

Jay, K.E. and Smith, D.C. (1996) A generic change model for the effective implementation of information systems. *South African Journal of Business Management*, 27(3).

KPMG (2002) KPMG Assurance surveys. Program Management Survey, October. www.kpmg.co.uk/kpmg/uk/services/audit/surveys.cfm.

Lewin, K. (1972) Quasi-stationary social equilibrium and the problems of permanent change. In *Organizational Development: Values, Process, and Technology*, ed. N. Margulies and A. Raia. McGraw-Hill, New York, 65–72.

Mekhilef, M., Kelleher, D. and Oleson, A. (2004) European Guide to Good Practice in Knowledge Management – Chapter 5, Terminology. Published by European Committee for Standardization at www.cenorm.be.

Nadler, D., Shaw, R. and Walton, E. (1995) *Discontinuous Change*. Jossey-Bass, San Francisco.

Parsons, A., Zeisser, M. and Waitman, R. (1996) Organizing for digital marketing. *McKinsey Quarterly*, no. 4, 183–92.

Saunders, R. (2000) Managing knowledge. *Harvard Management Communication Letter*, June, 3–5.

Schein, E. (1956) The Chinese indoctrination program for prisoners of war. *Psychiatry*, 19, 149–72.

Schein, E. (1992) *Organizational Culture and Leadership*. Jossey-Bass, San Francisco.

Simon, R. (1999) How risky is your company? *Harvard Business Review*, May–June, 85–94.

Snowden, D. (2002) Complex acts of knowing – paradox and descriptive self awareness. IBM Global Services, July. www-1.ibm.com/services/files/complex.pdf.

Storey, J. and Barnett, E. (2000) Knowledge management initiatives: learning from failure. *Journal of Knowledge Management*, 4(2), 145–56.

Sveiby, K.E. (1997–2000) *The New Organizational Wealth: Managing and Measuring Knowledge-Based Assets*. Berrett-Koehler, San Francisco. Updated on author's web site (www.sveiby.com.au/KnowledgeManagement.html).

Waterman, R.H., Peters, T.J. and Phillips, J.R. (1980) Structure is not organization. *McKinsey Quarterly*, In-house journal. McKinsey & Co., New York.

Willcocks, L. and Smith, G. (1995) IT enabled business process reengineering: organisational and human resource dimension. *Strategic Information Systems*, 4 (3), 279–301.

Further reading

Boddy, D., Boonstra, A. and Kennedy, G. (2001) *Managing the Information Revolution*. Financial Times Prentice Hall, Harlow. Chapter 5, Information and people, and Chapter 6, Information and structure, are relevant to this chapter and contain good examples.

Chaffey, D. and Wood, S. (2005) *Business Information Management*. Financial Times Prentice Hall, Harlow. Chapter 5 focuses on knowledge management and Chapter 8 on change management.

Rubenstein-Montano, B., Liebowitz, J., Buchwalter, J., McCaw, D., Newman, B. and Rebeck, K. (2001) SMARTVision: a knowledge-management methodology. *Journal of Knowledge Management*, 5(4), 300–10. Reviews different methodologies for implementing knowledge management and suggests a detailed methodology.

Tiwana, A. (2001) *The Essential Guide to Knowledge Management*. Prentice-Hall, Upper Saddle River, NJ. A guide for professionals, applied to e-business and CRM applications.

Web links

BRINT.com (www.brint.com) A Business Researcher's Interests. Extensive portal with articles on e-business, e-commerce, knowledge management, change management and IS strategy.

David Snowdens CYNEFIN Center for Organizational Complexity (www.cynefin.net) Contains a collection of articles by its founder on approaches to knowledge management.

Information Research – an International Journal (http://informationr.net) An online journal focusing on information and knowledge management moderated by staff at the Department of Information Studies, University of Sheffield.

Knowledge Board (www.knowledgeboard.com) Forum focusing on knowledge management with database of articles on the topic.

Knowledge Management Central (www.icasit.org/km/) KM Central provides practical advice and support for business professionals working on knowledge management issues and projects.

Knowledge Management – Ark Group (www.kmmagazine.com) European monthly trade magazine – 'Inside Knowledge'.

Managing Change (www.managingchange.com) Introductory articles.

Office of Government Commerce (www.ogc.gov.uk) Offers good guidelines in the IT Community section on successful IT including project and risk management (www.ogc.gov.uk/index.asp?id=36).

11

Analysis and design

Chapter at a glance

Learning outcomes

After completing this chapter the reader should be able to:

- Summarize approaches for analysing requirements for e-business systems
- Identify key elements of approaches to improve the interface design and security design of e-commerce systems.

Management issues

Analysis and design of e-business systems raises these issues for management:

- What are the critical success factors for analysis and design of e-business systems?
- What is the balance between requirements for usable and secure systems and the costs of designing them in this manner?
- What are the best approaches for incorporating new IS solutions with legacy systems into the architectural design of the e-business?

Links to other chapters

The main related chapters are:

- *Chapter 10* places analysis and design into the context of the change management for e-business as shown in *Figure 10.4*;
- *Chapter 12* – the sections on measurement and marketing research show how the effectiveness of analysis and design are evaluated.

Web support

The following additional case studies are available at www.pearsoned.co.uk/chaffey

- ➤ Legacy data integration
- ➤ User interface enhancements at Waterstones
- ➤ Additional activity – creating a database for The B2C Company

The site also contains a range of study material designed to help improve your results.

Introduction

Analysis and design
Analysis of system requirements and design for creation of a system.

In the context of strategy implementation, analysis and design activities are required to specify the business and user needs for a system and to develop a plan for building it (*Figure 10.4*).

This chapter reviews new approaches to analysis and design required for e-business systems. It does not aim to explain how to follow well established techniques for analysis and design such as data flow diagramming, information flow diagrams and entity relationship diagramming. These have been described many times before, for example in Bocij *et al.* (2005).

The chapter is intended to provide managers with an appreciation of some analysis and design techniques for e-business, to provide familiarity with techniques such as process analysis, data modelling and use-case design. This familiarity should aid collaboration when the managers are involved in discussing the requirements of the system with technical staff.

It is in two main parts. In the first part we review analysis techniques and in particular process analysis for re-engineering which is important in many e-business implementations. We also touch on data modelling, looking at an example from The B2C Company. Data modelling is not described in detail since this is a very well established technique.

The second part looks at the design of e-business systems. The techniques described are aimed at improving the information quality of end-users of e-business systems – ensuring information is timely and secure, has the correct content in terms of accuracy, relevance and completeness, and is in a form that is easy to interpret. The section on architectural design looks at how systems are integrated to improve flow of information and also to achieve timely delivery of information. *Focus on user-centred site design* demonstrates how using use-case analysis and interface design guidelines can be applied to produce usable sell-side or buy-side e-commerce systems with good information quality. *Focus on security design* reviews security requirements for the e-business, reviews generic approaches to security and finally looks at the current usage of e-commerce security techniques.

The importance of analysis and design is such that even if an effective strategy has been developed, its execution can be destroyed by ineffectual analysis and design. Complete *Activity 11.1* to review some of the consequences of poor analysis and design.

Activity 11.1 The consequences of poor analysis and design

Purpose

To highlight the impact of poor analysis and design on customer satisfaction and business performance.

Activity

Form a focus group and discuss your own experiences of online purchasing. What have been your problems and frustrations? Refer to a particular example such as purchasing a book – what are your expectations?

Answers to activities can be found at www.pearsoned.co.uk/chaffey

Analysis for e-business

Analysis for e-business
Using analytical techniques to capture and summarize business and user requirements.

Analysis for e-business is concerned with understanding the business and user requirements for a new system. Typical analysis activity can be broken down into: understanding the current process and then reviewing possible alternatives for implementing the e-business solution. In the following sections we will review different techniques that enable us to summarize the operation of current processes and proposed e-business processes. In this section we focus on using diagrams to demonstrate the business processes. User requirements capture techniques that help determine the function required by a system are described in the *Focus on user-centred site design* section.

Analysts recognize that delivering quality information to employees and partners, or exchanging it between processes, is the key to building information systems that improve efficiency and customer service. Pant and Ravichandran (2001) say:

> *Information is an agent of coordination and control and serves as a glue that holds together organisations, franchises, supply chains and distribution channels. Along with material and other resource flows, information flows must also be handled effectively in any organisation.*

This shows that in the era of e-business analysis should be used as a tool to optimize the flow of information both inside and outside organizations. In this chapter we start by looking at how workflow management is a key to managing time-based information flows. We then review how process modelling is used to analyse information flows to optimize business processes and then look at information storage analysis through a brief review of data modelling.

Workflow management

Workflow management (WFM)
The automation of information flows and provides tools for processing the information according to a set of procedural rules.

Analysing and revising an organization's workflow as part of workflow management (WFM) is a concept that is integral to many e-business applications, so before we look at process analysis techniques, let us look at why workflow is integral to e-business.

WFM is defined by the Workflow Management Coalition (WfMC, 1996) as

> *the automation of a business process, in whole or part during which documents, information or tasks are passed from one participant to another for action, according to a set of procedural rules.*

Workflow systems automate e-business processes by providing a *structured* framework to support a process. Applications of workflow in e-business include actioning queries from external customer queries or internal support queries. These queries may arrive by e-mail, phone or letter. E-mail enquiries can be analysed and routed to the right person depending on their subject. Letters may need to be scanned before being added to the workflow queue.

Workflow helps manage business processes by ensuring that tasks are prioritized to be performed:

→ as soon as possible
→ by the right people
→ in the right order.

The workflow approach gives a consistent, uniform approach for improved efficiency and better customer service. Workflow software provides functions to:

- assign tasks to people
- remind people about their tasks which are part of a workflow queue
- allow collaboration between people sharing tasks

- retrieve information needed to complete the task such as a customer's personal details
- provide an overview for managers of the status of each task and the team's performance.

What type of workflow applications will exist in a company? For The B2B Company, e-business applications of workflow might include:

1 *Administrative workflow*. This concerns internal administrative tasks. Examples include managing purchase orders for procurement and booking holidays and training.
2 *Production workflows*. These are customer-facing or supplier-facing workflows. An intranet- or extranet-based customer support database and stock management system integrated with a supplier's system is an example of production workflow.

Process modelling

Traditional approaches to process analysis use established systems analysis and design methods that are part of methodologies such as Structured Systems Analysis and Design Methodology (SSADM), like the data flow diagram technique outlined in Bocij *et al*. (2005). Such approaches often use a hierarchical method of establishing

- the processes and their constituent sub-processes
- the dependencies between processes
- the inputs (resources) needed by the processes and the outputs.

The processes and sub-processes are essentially the activities or tasks that need to be performed by the business information system, so these are sometime referred to as **'activity-based process definition methods'**. A **process** can be defined at the business level in terms of the main activities of a business. Each process can be broken down further as explained in the section on *Task analysis and task decomposition*. Significant business processes are elements of the value chain; they include inbound logistics (including procurement), manufacture, outbound logistics or distribution, and customer relationship management or sales and marketing activity. Davenport (1993) notes that even for large multinational organizations the number of main processes will rarely exceed ten.

Activity-based process definition methods
Analysis tools used to identify the relationship between tasks within a business process.

Process
Part of a system that has a clearly defined purpose or objective and clearly defined inputs and outputs.

Note that in addition to the approaches shown here, use-case analysis to assist in defining interface requirements is described in the *Focus on user-centred site design* section.

Analysing the efficiency of processes is key to e-business design. Fortunately companies, whether new or start-ups, can tap into existing knowledge about how to improve process efficiency. The Arthur Andersen Global Best Practices knowledge base used standard definitions of processes. There are seven operating processes that can be broken down further:

1 Understand markets and customers.
2 Develop vision and strategy.
3 Design products and services.
4 Market and sell.
5 Produce and deliver services.
6 Produce and deliver services (services organization).
7 Invoice and service customer.

There are also six support and management processes:

1 Develop and manage human resources.
2 Manage information.
3 Manage financial and physical resources.
4 Execute environmental management programme.
5 Manage external relationships.
6 Manage improvement and change.

The performance of all of these processes needs to be analysed for e-business implementation.

Process mapping

Existing business processes often overlap between different functional areas of a business. So, before detailed activities are identified the analyst needs to identify where in the organization processes occur and who is responsible for them. This procedure is often known as 'process mapping'. *Table 11.1* illustrates the activities which occur across functions in a business. Such process mapping is clearly important for identifying potential users of an e-business system. *Table 11.1* shows an outline process map that might be used for The B2B Company to prepare a proposal for a new major account.

Process mapping
Identification of location and responsibilities for processes within an organization.

Task analysis and task decomposition

Before a process such as 'prepare proposal' can be designed and implemented, a more detailed breakdown is required. This is usually referred to as 'task analysis'.

Task analysis
Identification of different tasks, their sequence and how they are broken down.

Table 11.1 Process map for activities with process 'prepare proposal'

Process activity	*Marketing*	*Engineering*	*Finance*	*Senior management*
1 Cost estimation		M		
2 Assess financial risk		m	M	
3 Publicity presentation	M	m		
4 Review	M	M	M	m
5 Authorization			M	M

M = major role in function, m = minor role in function

Noyes and Baber (1999) point out that a difficulty with this type of process or task decomposition is that there are no set rules for what to call the different levels of decomposition or how far to decompose the process. The number of levels and the terminology used for the different levels will vary according to the application you are using and the consultant you may be working with. Georgakoupoulos *et al.* (1995) talk about 'task nesting' of tasks broken down into sub-tasks as part of the activity-based method for describing workflows. They give the example of a workflow process for procurement where the task 'procure materials' is broken down further into the sub-tasks of 'verify status', 'get bids' and 'place order'. Curtis *et al.* (1992) provide a useful framework, referring to *process units* or *elements* at each process level as follows:

Level 1 *business process* are decomposed into:
Level 2 *activities* which are further divided to:
Level 3 *tasks* and finally:
Level 4 *sub-tasks*.

An example of a four-level task decomposition is presented in *Figure 11.1*.

Level 1. Business process:
Obtain listings

Level 2. Activities

1. Register vendor
2. Inspection preparation
3. Inspection appointment
4a. Follow up inspection – IF listing instructions obtained
4b. Follow up inspection – IF listing instructions NOT obtained (exception)
5. Ensure listing obtained

Level 3. Tasks for 'ensure listing obtained'

1. Prepare initial property particulars (48 hours)
2. Remind negotiator to handle sale to contact vendor
3. Send property particulars
4. Instruction to sell with draft PMA (Property Misdescriptions Act 1991) details
5. Contact vendor to obtain PMA on particulars

Level 4. Sub-tasks

1. PMA chase
2. Tenure details
3. Amended details

Key

- Reminder required for negotiator
- Record information (data input)
- Retrieve information (data output)
- IT system used to perform activity
- Letter or form produced (level 4)

Figure 11.1 An example task decomposition for an estate agency
Source: Adapted from Chaffey (1998)

Attempts to standardize the meanings of these terms have been produced by the Workflow Management Coalition, an industry standards body (WfMC, 1996), which describes the different process elements as follows:

1 *Business process*. A set of one or more linked procedures or activities which collectively realize a business objective or policy goal, normally within the context of an organizational structure defining functional roles and relationships.
2 *Activity*. A description of a piece of work that forms one logical step within a process. An activity may be a manual activity, which does not support computer automation, or a workflow (automated) activity. A workflow activity requires human and/or machine resource(s) to support process execution; where human resource is required an activity is allocated to a workflow participant.
3 *Work item*. The representation of the work to be processed (by a workflow participant) in the context of an activity within a process instance. An activity typically generates one or more work items which together constitute the task to be undertaken by the user (a workflow participant) within this activity.

Process dependencies

Process dependencies summarize the order in which activities occur according to the business rules that govern the processes. Normally, activities occur in a sequence and are *serial*; sometimes activities can occur simultaneously, when they are known as *parallel*. Data flow diagrams and flow charts are widely used as diagramming tech-

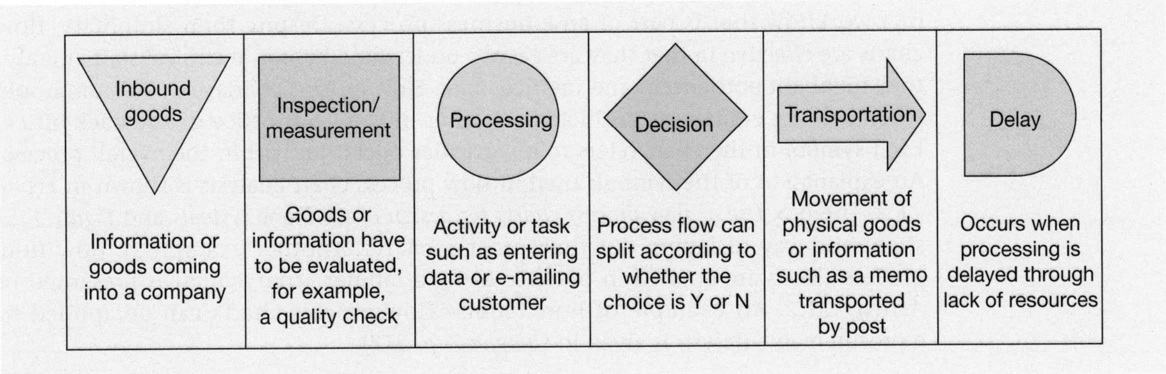

Figure 11.2 **Symbols used for flow process charts**

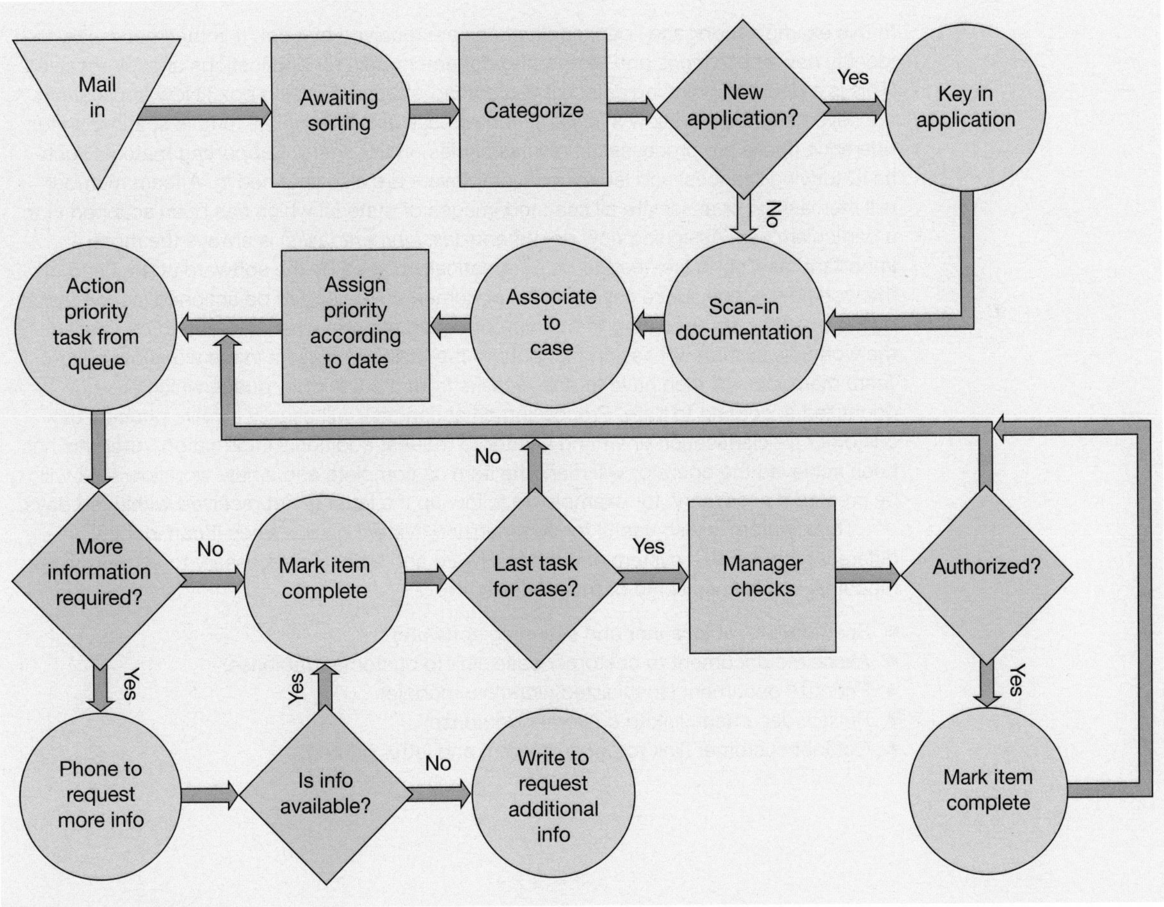

Figure 11.3 **Flow process chart showing the main operations performed by users when working using workflow software**

niques to show process dependencies. In this section we will review three techniques for showing dependencies that are more commonly applied in e-business analysis. These are flow process charts and network diagrams including the EPC (event-driven process chain) standard used by the SAP product.

Flow process charts

A simple flow chart is a good starting point for describing the sequence of activities of a workflow that is part of an e-business process. Despite their simplicity, flow charts are effective in that they are easy to understand by non-technical staff and also they highlight bottlenecks and inefficiencies. Flow process charts are used commonly when solving e-business problems, whether in the front office or the back office. Each symbol in the chart refers to a particular operation within the overall process. An explanation of the symbols used in flow process chart analysis is shown in *Figure 11.2*. The box *Use of flow process charts for design of workflow systems* and *Figure 11.3* show one way of laying out flow process charts. Another example of how flow process charts are applied in practice using a tabular arrangement is presented in *Activity 11.2*. An example of how tabular flow process charts can be applied to e-procurement analysis is given in *Chapter 7 (p. 312)*.

Use of flow process charts for design of workflow systems

In this example mortgage (loan) applications are received by post. It is then necessary to identify *new applications* and supporting documentation for applications already received. (This is a decision point indicated by a diamond-shaped decision box.) New applications are keyed into the workflow system as a new case and the original form is scanned in for reference (these are processes shown as circles on the chart). Supporting material such as ID (driving licences) and letters from employers are also scanned in. A team member will then assign or associate all scanned images of material which has been scanned in to a particular case. Assigning new documents (*assignment tasks*) is always the most important task, so these need to be automatically placed by the software at the head of the workflow queue. Once assigned the documents will need to be actioned (*action tasks*) by the operator, so according to the type of document and when it needs to be chased the workflow system will assign a priority to the task and place it in the workflow queue. Team members will then have to action tasks from the workflow queue which are prioritized according to date. Processing an action task will usually involve phoning the customer for clarification or writing a letter to request additional information. After this has been achieved the operator will mark the item as complete and a new workflow task will be created if necessary: for example, to follow up if a letter is not received within ten days.

This diagram is also useful for summarizing system design since it can identify different modules of a system and the hardware and software necessary to support these modules. In this case some of the modules are:

- Scan document (scanner and scanning software)
- Associate document to customer case (link to customer database)
- Prioritize document (specialized workflow module)
- Review document (link to customer database)
- Contact customer (link to phone system and letter printer).

Activity 11.2 Transforming invoice processing at The B2B Company

Purpose

To illustrate how the flow process chart can be used to simplify a business process.

Background

Table 11.2 has been drawn up following observation of tasks performed during a systems analysis project at The B2B Company. The main problem is the delay currently occurring when the MD has to authorize an invoice of £10,000. The company can obtain a discount of 10 per cent if payment is made in 10 days. This is not achievable currently and the MD wants to use IT to make this possible. As part of this re-engineering, restructuring may be required also – the MD believes that fewer staff are needed for invoice payment.

Table 11.2 Flow process chart for invoice processing – original situation

No.	*Task description*	*Chart symbols*	*Distance (m)*	*Average time (hours)*
1	Receive invoice, stamp date	●⇨□D▼	–	0.1
2	To first payable clerk	○➡□D▽	50	5
3	On first payable clerk's desk	○⇨□◗▽	–	1
4	Write and attach purchase order	●⇨□D▽	–	0.1
5	To cost accountant	○➡□D▽	20	5
6	On cost accountant's desk	○⇨□◗▽	–	5
7	Code to appropriate job number	●⇨□D▽	–	0.1
8	Return to first payable clerk	○➡□D▽	20	5
9	On first payable clerk's desk	○⇨□◗▽	–	1
10	Make copies	●⇨□D▽	–	0.1
11	To Managing Director	○➡□D▽	200	5
12	On Managing Director's desk	○⇨□◗▽	–	48
13	Reviewed and approved by MD	●⇨□D▽	–	0.1
14	To second payable clerk	○➡□D▽	200	5
15	On second payable clerk's desk	○⇨□◗▽	–	1
16	Add vendor number and due date	●⇨□D▽	–	0.1
17	Write to accounts payable ledger in accounting systems	●⇨□D▽	–	0.5
18	Pay invoice – write cheque	●⇨□D▽	–	0.1
19	To file clerk	○➡□D▽	20	5
20	On file clerk's desk	○⇨□◗▽	–	1
21	File invoice	●⇨□D▽	–	0.1

Activity

As a business analyst you have to produce a more efficient way of working. You should restructure the workflow by filling in a blank table. You should also write down assumptions about changed roles and give details of new software needed to support the new workflow. You can assume each member of staff has access to a networked PC and the MD has access to a notebook with fax/modem that they use twice daily.

Table 11.3 Flow process chart for invoice processing – re-engineered process

No.	*Task description*	*Chart symbols*	*Distance (m)*	*Average time (hours)*
1	Receive invoice, stamp and scan	●⇨□D▼	–	0.1
2	E-mail to first payable clerk	○➡□D▽	–	0.1
3	In worklist of first payable clerk	○⇨□◗▽	–	5
4	Fill in purchase order, code job number	●⇨□D▽	–	0.5
5	E-mail to MD	○➡□D▽	–	0.1
6	In MD's worklist	○⇨□◗▽	–	12
7	Review and approval by MD	●⇨□D▽	–	0.1
8	E-mail to second payable clerk	○➡□D▽	–	0.1
9	In worklist of second payable clerk	○⇨□◗▽	–	5
10	Add vendor number and due date	●⇨□D▽	–	0.1
11	Key into accounting system	●⇨□D▽	–	0.1
12	Pay invoice and mark task as complete	●⇨□D▽	–	0.1

Answers to activities can be found at www.pearsoned.co.uk/chaffey

Effort duration analysis

Effort duration analysis is an analytical tool that can be used to calculate the overall efficiency of a process when we have performed a detailed analysis such as that in *Activity 11.2*. To do this, we sum the average time it takes workers to complete every activity making up the overall process, then divide this by the total length of time the whole process takes to occur. The total process time is often much longer since this includes time when the task is not being worked on. Here this is during transport of the forms, and when they are waiting in out-trays and in-trays. The efficiency relationship can be given as:

$$\text{Efficiency} = \frac{\Sigma(\text{T (effort on tasks)})}{\text{T (total process time)}}$$

If we apply effort duration analysis to the first scenario in *Activity 11.2*, with delays and transport not contributing to the overall process, we can see that the efficiency of this extremely inefficient process is barely 2 per cent! This measure can be extended by noting the activities that add value to the customer rather than simply being administrative.

Network diagrams

While data flow diagrams and flow process charts may give a good indication of the sequence in which activities and tasks occur, they often do not give a sufficiently tight, formal definition of the process sequence necessary for input into an e-business, workflow or ERP system. To do this we can use a network diagram known as a GAN (generalized activity network). Here, nodes are added between the boxes representing the tasks, to define precisely the alternatives that exist following completion of a task. The most common situation is that one activity must follow another, for example a check on customer identity must be followed by a credit check. Where alternatives exist, the logic is defined at the node as follows: where a single pathway is taken from two or more alternatives, the node is defined as an OR node, and when several pathways may be followed this is an AND node. Join nodes combine previous activities, and splits determine which activities occur next. Where there are alternatives, business rules are defined as pre-conditions or post-conditions. A summary of the alternative dependencies is given in *Table 11.4*.

Event-driven process chain (EPC) model

One of the most widely used methods for describing business events and processes is the event-driven process chain method (EPC). This has been popularized by its application to re-engineering of enterprises performed using the SAP R/3 ERP product which accounts for worldwide sales of several billion dollars. Over 800 standard business EPCs are defined to support the SAP R/3 system; they are intended to illustrate business rules clearly for interpretation by business users before enactment in the software. The different elements of the EPC model are shown in *Table 11.5*; these include the different types of dependencies previously reviewed in *Table 11.4*. *Figure 11.4* is an EPC meta-model illustrating how the different elements relate to one another. This figure shows how business functions are triggered through transactions on *business objects* which also lead to a *business event*. *Control flows* link the activities, events and logical operators. Entities or information objects are items such as sales orders or invoices.

Table 11.4 Workflow dependencies at a node on a network diagram

Node type	*Description*	*Summary*
AND-SPLIT	Workflow splits into two or more parallel activities which all execute	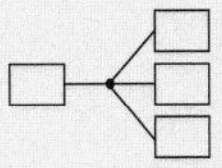
OR-SPLIT	Workflow splits into multiple branches of which only one is followed	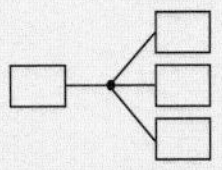
AND-JOIN	Multiple executing activities join into a single thread of control	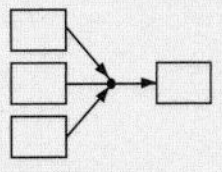
OR-JOIN	An exclusive alternative activity joins into a single thread of execution	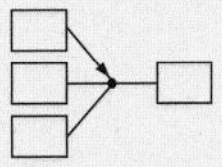
Iteration	Repetition of one or more workflow activities until a condition is met	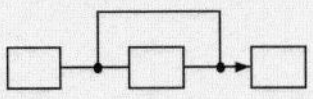
Must follow	No alternative paths exist	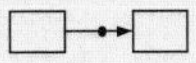

Table 11.5 Elements of the event-driven process chain (EPC) model

EPC symbol	*Description of EPC element*
Business Event	An event occurs when there is a change in the status of a process. It occurs in response to completion of a function
Business Function	A function is an activity or task that is usually completed by a person in the organizational unit responsible for the function. Alternatively it can be completed automatically through the workflow system
xor and or logical operations	Control flow logic between processes is denoted by joins/splits as follows: xor – a single activity follows the completed process(es) and – an and-split gives rises to multiple subsequent functions or – an or-split gives a multiple-choice split
⇨	Control flow forming the process network used to link other elements
Information object	Data needed for completion of a function and acting as input to subsequent functions (workflow relevant data in the WfMC definition). Also known as entity
Organizational unit	The unit responsible for the execution of a function

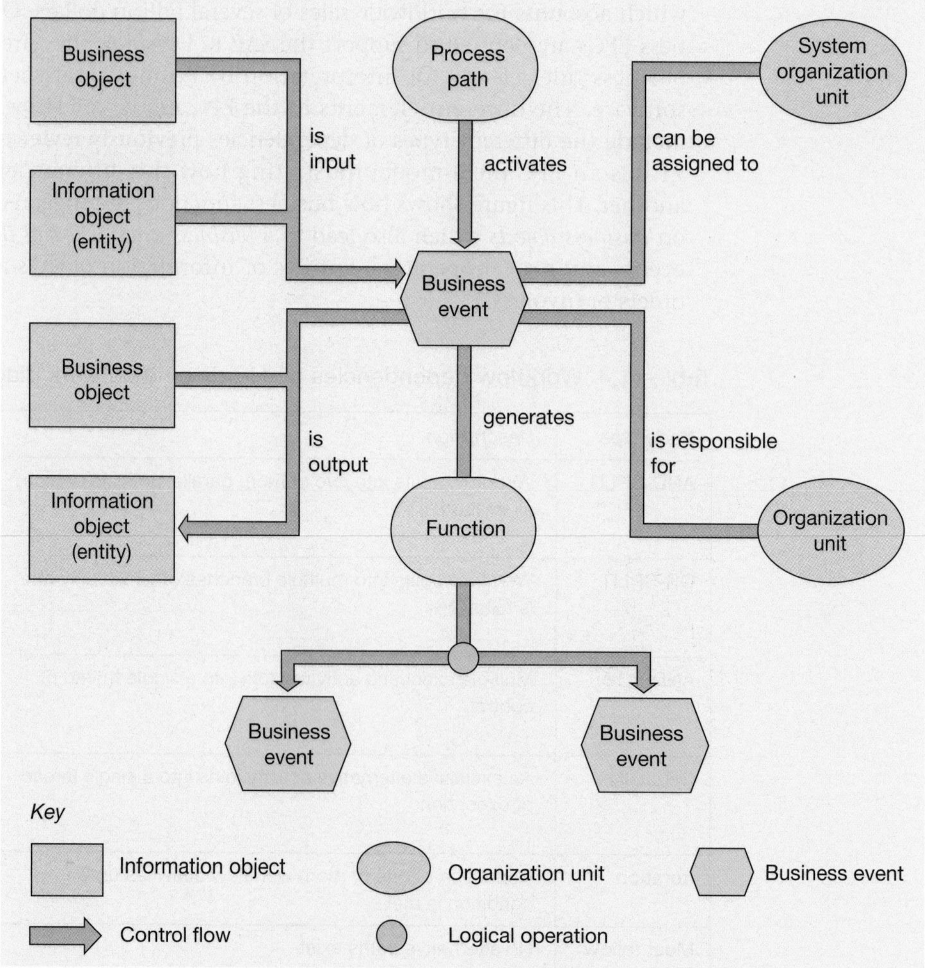

Figure 11.4 General model for the EPC process definition model

Validating a new process model

Whichever method has been used to arrive at the process definition, we need to check that the process definition is realistic. When developing a wish list of process capabilities and corresponding business rules the stages described by David Taylor in his book on concurrent engineering (Taylor, 1995) may be useful. He suggests that once new processes have been established they are sanity checked by performing a 'talk-through, walk-through and run-through'. Here, the design team will describe the proposed business process as a model in which different business objects interact and in the talk-through stage will run through different business scenarios using cards to describe the objects and the services they provide to other business objects. Once the model has been adjusted, the walk-through stage involves more detail in the scenario and the design team will role-play the services the objects provide. The final run-through stage is a quality check in which no on-the-spot debugging occurs – just the interactions between the objects are described. Increasing use is made of simulation software to model alternative scenarios.

Data modelling

Data modelling of e-business and e-commerce systems uses well-established techniques such as normalization that are used for relational database analysis and design. As a consequence, this section is brief in comparison with that on process modelling which introduces some novel techniques. See Bocij *et al.* (2005, Chapter 11) for an introduction to normalization and relational database design. Some basic definitions are given in this section as a reminder of key terms. Before we start it is worth mentioning that the advent of data mining and object-oriented approaches has meant increasing use of non-relational database design. These are outlined further in Chapters 6 and 11 of Bocij *et al.* (2005).

The approach we use to explore data modelling for e-commerce is to use examples that identify typical elements of data modelling for a sell-side e-commerce system (The B2C Company). We will use ER (entity relationship) modelling to review typical structures for these databases. In simple ER modelling there are three main stages.

Entity
A grouping of related data, such as customer entity, implemented as a table.

Database table
Each database comprises several tables.

Attribute
A property or characteristic of an entity, implemented as a field.

Field
Attributes of products, such as date of birth.

Record
A collection of fields for one instance of an entity, such as Customer Smith.

1 Identify entities

Entities define the broad groupings of information such as information about different people, transactions or products. Examples include customer, employee, sales orders, purchase orders. When the design is implemented each design will form a **database table**.

2 Identify attributes for entities

Entities have different properties known as '**attributes**' that describe the characteristics of any single instance of an entity. For example, the customer entity has attributes such as name, phone number and e-mail address. When the design is implemented each attribute will form a **field**, and the collection of fields for one instance of the entity such as a particular customer will form a **record**.

3 Identify relationships between entities

Relationship
Describes how different tables are linked.

Primary key
The field that uniquely identifies each record in a table.

Secondary key
A field that is used to link tables, by linking to a primary key in another table.

The relationships between entities requires identification of which fields are used to link the tables. For example, for each order a customer places we need to know which customer has placed the order and which product they have ordered. As is evident from *Figure 11.5*, the fields customer id and product id are used to relate the order information between the three tables. The fields that are used to relate tables are referred to as 'key fields'. A primary key is used to uniquely identify each instance of an entity and a secondary key is used to link to a primary key in another table. In *Figure 11.5* the primary key of the customer table is customer id, but the field customer id in the order table is here a secondary key that links back to the customer table. This relationship is an example of a one-to-many relationship since each customer may place many orders over the lifetime of the relationship.

Normalization is an additional stage, not covered here, used to optimize the database to minimize redundancy or duplication of information.

If you have previous experience in analysis and design for databases, complete *Activity 11.3* to develop an ER diagram for The B2C Company. If you do not have this experience then refer to the generic answers to gain an appreciation of how databases are structured.

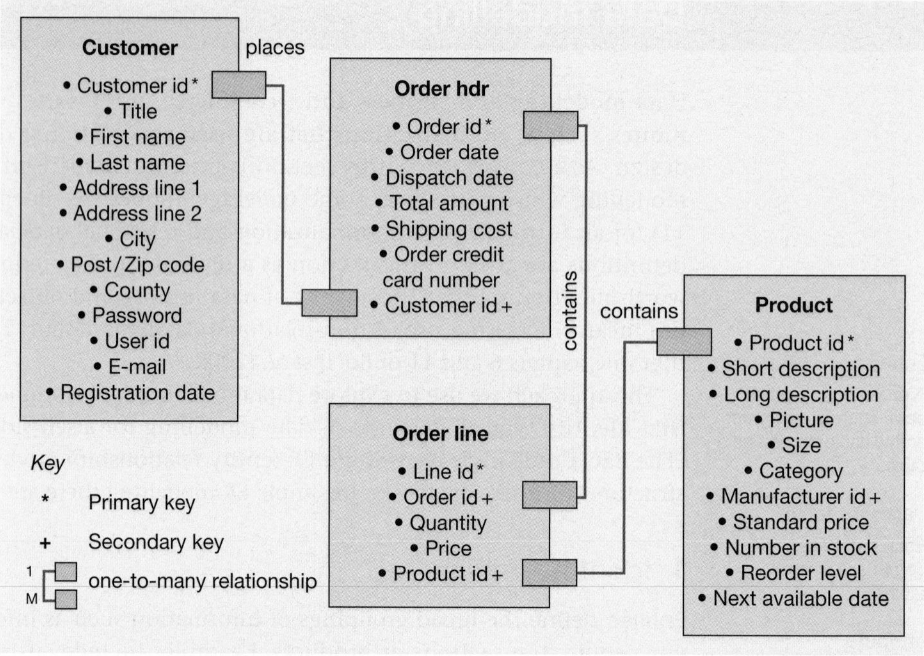

Figure 11.5 Generic B2C ER diagram

Activity 11.3 ER modelling for The B2C Company

Purpose

To gain an understanding of the generic structure for transactional e-commerce databases.

Activity

Create a normalized ER diagram for The B2C Company, or a B2C consumer transactional site.

For answers see Figure 11.5.

Comments

- Customer. May also have a separate delivery address.
- Order. Many items may be required on each order, so each order header can have many line items.
- Product. Includes catalogue information, such as description and a picture.
- Product. Informs the customer the number in stock and when they will be available.
- There will be a separate manufacturer table not shown here.

No suggested answer supplied.

Design for e-business

System design
Defines how an information system will operate.

The **design** element of creating an e-business system involves specifying how the system should be structured.

In the two *Focus on* sections that follow we look at two aspects of design that are of great importance to how e-business systems are perceived by customers – security and interface design. Before that, we consider the overall architectural design of e-business systems.

Architectural design of e-business systems

The starting point for design of e-business systems is to ensure that a common architecture exists across the company in terms of hardware and software technology, applications and business processes. This goal is summarized in *Figure 3.10(b)*.

Client–server model
A system architecture in which end-user machines such as PCs, known as 'clients', run applications while accessing data and possibly programs from a server.

E-business systems follow the same **client–server model** architecture of many business information systems created in the 1990s. For the e-business, the clients are typically employees, suppliers or customers' desktop PCs which give the 'front-end' access point to e-business applications. The clients are connected to a 'back-end' server computer via an intranet, extranet or Internet.

A key design decision in client–server systems is how different tasks involved in delivering a working application to the users are distributed between client and server. The typical situation for these tasks in an e-business system is:

Debate 11.1

E-business *vs* ERP architectures

'Designing an appropriate architecture for e-business is effectively the same as the architecture for enterprise resource planning systems.'

- *Data storage*. Predominantly on server. Client storage is ideally limited to cookies for identification of users and session tracking. Cookie identifiers for each system user are then related to the data for the user which is stored on a database server.
- *Query processing*. Predominantly on the server, although some validation can be performed on the client.
- *Display*. This is largely a client function.
- *Application logic*. Traditionally, in early PC applications this has been a client function, but for e-business systems the design aim is to maximize the application logic processing including the business rules on the server.

Three-tier client–server
The first tier is the client that handles display, second is application logic and business rules, third is database storage.

Thin client
An end-user access device (terminal) where computing requirements such as processing and storage (and so cost) are minimized.

A typical e-business architecture uses a **three-tier client–server** model where the client is mainly used for display with application logic and the business rules partitioned on a server, which is the second tier, and the database server is the third tier. Since most of the processing is executed on the servers rather than the client, this architecture is sometimes referred to as a **'thin client'**, because the size of the executable program is smaller. The application server provider (ASP) described in *Chapter 3* is typically based upon the three-tier model. This is shown in *Figure 11.6*.

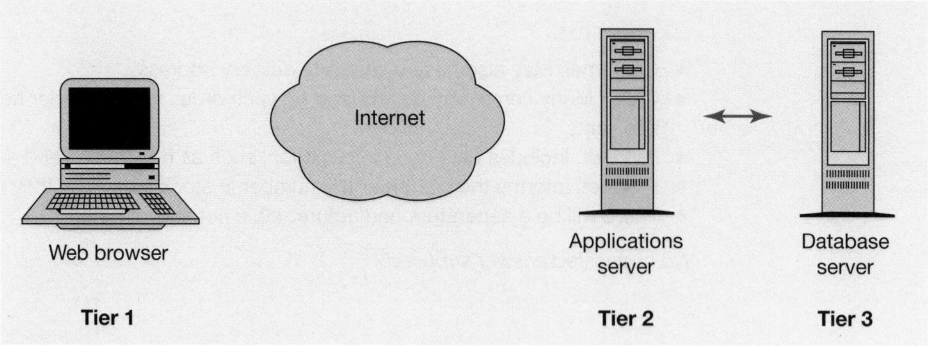

Figure 11.6 Three-tier client server in an e-business environment

Although the three-tier model of an e-business system suggests a relatively simple architectural design, the reality is more complex. Different servers are needed which combine applications logic and database storage for different requirements. These may be physically separate servers or may be combined. *Figure 11.7* shows a typical e-business architecture. The purpose of each of the servers is as follows:

- *Web server.* Manages http requests from client and acts as a passive broker to other servers. Returns or serves web pages.
- *Merchant server.* This is the main location of the application logic and integrates the entire application by making requests to the other server components.
- *Personalization server.* Provides tailored content – may be part of commerce server functionality.
- *Payment commerce server.* Manages payment systems and secure transactions.
- *Catalogue server.* A document management server used to display detailed product information and technical specifications.

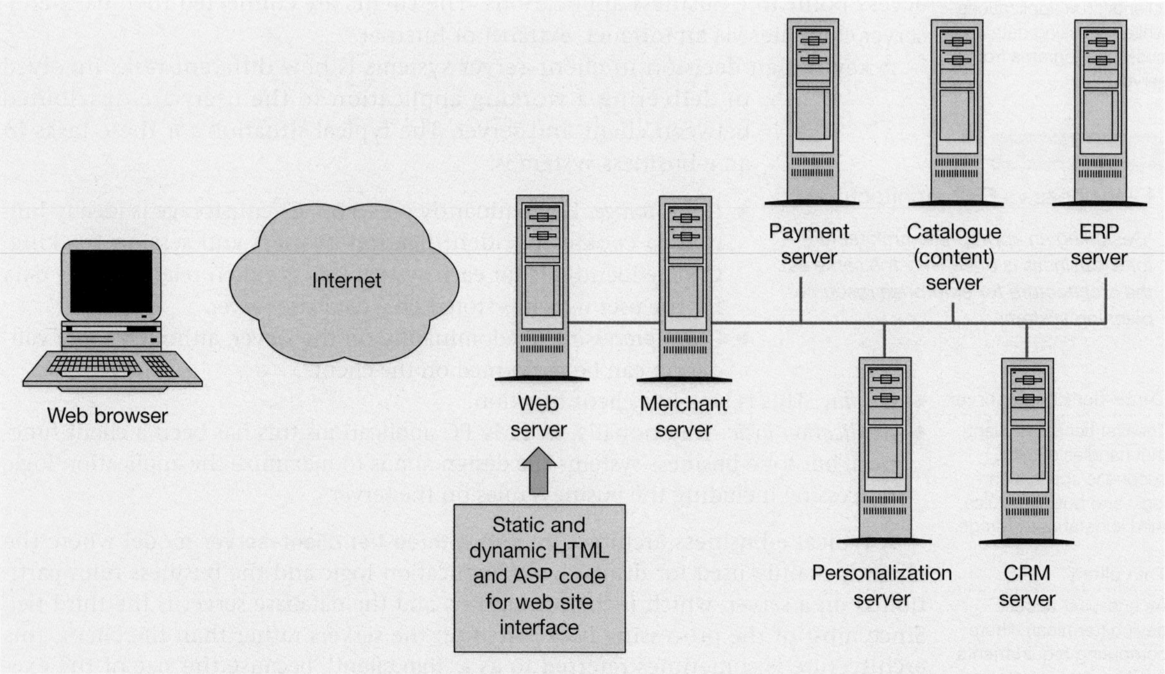

Figure 11.7 E-business architecture for The B2C Company

- *CRM server*. Stores information on all customer contacts.
- *ERP server*. Required for information on stock availability and pricing from the customer. Will also need to be accessed for sales order processing and histories. Logistics for distribution will also be arranged through the ERP server.

It is evident that designing the method of integration between different components is not straightforward – creating a fully integrated e-business is not straightforward! As was discussed in *Chapter 9*, the best approach to simplifying the design is to reduce the number of suppliers of components to improve the ease of data and applications integration.

Focus on user-centred site design

Since e-business systems are often customer- or employee-facing systems, the importance of human–computer interaction is high in the design of web applications. Referring to web-site design, Nigel Bevan says:

> *Unless a web site meets the needs of the intended users it will not meet the needs of the organization providing the web site. Web site development should be user-centred, evaluating the evolving design against user requirements.* (Bevan, 1999a)

Noyes and Baber (1999) explain that user-centred design involves more than user interface design. It can be conceived of as centring on the human, but surrounded concentrically by factors that affect usability such as user interface, computers, workplace and the environment. Here we will be specifically looking at the user interface.

User-centred design
Design based on optimizing the user experience according to all factors, including the user interface, which affect this.

User-centred design starts with understanding the nature and variation within the user groups. According to Bevan (1999a), issues to consider include:

- Who are the important users?
- What is their purpose in accessing the site?
- How frequently will they visit the site?
- What experience and expertise do they have?
- What nationality are they? Can they read English?
- What type of information are they looking for?
- How will they want to use the information: read it on the screen, print it or download it?
- What type of browsers will they use? How fast will their communication links be?
- How large a screen/window will they use, with how many colours?

Usability

Usability
An approach to web-site design intended to enable the completion of user tasks.

Usability is a key concept within user-centred design that is applied to the analysis and design for a range of products which defines how easy they are to use. The British Standard/ISO Standard: Human-centred Design Processes for Interactive Systems (1999) defines usability as the:

> *extent to which a product can be used by specified users to achieve specified goals with effectiveness, efficiency and satisfaction in a specified context of use.*

You can see how the concept can be readily applied to web-site design – web visitors often have defined *goals* such as finding particular information or completing an action such as booking a flight or viewing an account balance.

In Jakob Nielsen's classic book, *Designing Web Usability* (Nielsen, 2000b), he describes usability as follows:

> *An engineering approach to website design to ensure the user interface of the site is learnable, memorable, error free, efficient and gives user satisfaction. It incorporates testing and evaluation to ensure the best use of navigation and links to access information in the shortest possible time. A companion process to information architecture.*

Expert review

An analysis of an existing site or prototype, by an experienced usability expert who will identify deficiencies and improvements to a site based on their knowledge of web design principles and best practice.

Usability/user testing

Representative users are observed performing representative tasks using a system.

In practice, usability involves two key project activities. Expert reviews are often performed at the beginning of a redesign project as a way of identifying problems with a previous design. Usability testing involves:

1 Identifying representative users of the site and identify typical tasks;
2 Asking them to perform specific tasks such as finding a product or completing an order;
3 Observing what they do and how they succeed.

For a site to be successful, the user tasks or actions need to be completed:

- Effectively – web usability specialists measure task completion, for example, only 3 out of 10 visitors to a web site may be able to find a telephone number or other piece of information.
- Efficiently – web usability specialists also measure how long it takes to complete a task on site, or the number of clicks it takes.

Jakob Nielsen explains the imperative for usability best in his 'Usability 101' (www.useit.com/alertbox/20030825.html). He says:

> *On the Web, usability is a necessary condition for survival. If a website is difficult to use, people* ***leave****. If the homepage fails to clearly state what a company offers and what users can do on the site, people* ***leave****. If users get lost on a website, they* ***leave****. If a website's information is hard to read or doesn't answer users' key questions, they* ***leave****. Note a pattern here?*

For these reasons, Nielsen suggests that around 10% of a design project budget should be spent on usability, but often actual spend is significantly less.

Evaluating designs

A test of effective design for usability is, according to Bevan (1999b), dependent on three areas:

1 *Effectiveness* – can users complete their tasks correctly and completely?
2 *Productivity (efficiency)* – are tasks completed in an acceptable length of time?
3 *Satisfaction* – are users satisfied with the interaction?

See *Chapter 12* for further discussion of how the user interface can be created.

Use-case modelling

A user-centred approach to modelling system requirements.

Unified Modelling Language (UML)

A language used to specify, visualize and document the artefacts of an object-oriented system.

Use-case analysis

The use-case method of process analysis and modelling was developed in the early 1990s as part of the development of object-oriented techniques. It is part of a methodology known as 'Unified Modelling Language' (UML) that attempts to unify the approaches that preceded it such as the Booch, OMT and Objectory notations. Jacobsen *et al.* (1994) give an accessible introduction and describe how object modelling can be applied to workflow analysis.

Persona and scenario analysis

Web design personas
A summary of the characteristics, needs, motivations and environment of typical web-site users.

Primary persona
A representation of the typical site user, who is strategically important to the effectiveness of the site, but one which it is challenging to fulfil the needs of.

Customer scenarios (user journeys)
Alternative tasks or outcomes required by a visitor to a web site. Typically accomplished in a series of stages of different tasks involving different information needs or experiences.

Web-site designers and marketers use a similar model to the use-case for web-site design favoured by system analysts and designers, but using different terminology. Marketers create web design personas for typical site visitors; this is a powerful technique for influencing the planning of online campaigns and the usability and customer-centricity of a web site. Forrester (2005) researched the use of personas and found that ethnographic researchers averaged 21 interviews with typical users per project to create with an average of between four and eight personas and this cost between $47,000 and $500,000! Examples included Ford which use three buyer personas at Ford.com. Their 'primary persona' 'Marie' – just beginning car shopping process, hasn't settled on brand, doesn't know about cars and needs help. Staples.com has seven personas for shoppers and Microsoft had seven for Windows XP.

Personas are essentially a 'thumbnail' description of a type of person. They have been used for a long time in research for segmentation and advertising, but in recent years have also proved effective for improving web-site design by companies that have applied this technique.

Customer scenarios are developed for different personas. Patricia Seybold in her book *The Customer Revolution*, (Seybold and Marshak, 2001) explains them as follows:

> *A customer scenario is a set of tasks that a particular customer wants or needs to do in order to accomplish his or her desired outcome.*

You will see that scenarios can be developed for each persona. For an online bank, scenarios might include:

1 New customer – opening an online account
2 Existing customer – transferring an account online
3 Existing customer – finding an additional product.

Each scenario is split up into a series of steps or tasks before the scenario is completed. These steps can be best thought of as a series of questions a visitor asks. By identifying questions web-site designers identify the different information needs of different customer types at different stages in the buying process.

The use of scenarios is a simple, but very powerful web design technique that is still relatively rare in web-site design. They can also be used when benchmarking competitor sites as part of situation analysis.

The customer persona/scenario approach has the benefits of:

- Fostering customer centricity;
- Identifies detailed information needs and steps required by customers;
- Can be used to both test existing web-site designs or prototypes and to devise new designs;
- Can be used to compare and test the strength and clarity of communication of proposition on different web sites.
- Can be linked to specific marketing outcomes required by site owners.

The following are some guidelines and ideas on what can be included when developing a persona. The start or end point is to give each persona a name. The detailed stages are:

1 *Build personal attributes into personas:*
   - Demographic: age, sex, education, occupation and for B2B, company size, position in buying unit
   - Psychographic: goals, tasks, motivation
   - Webographics: web experience (months), usage location (home or work), usage platform (dial-up, broadband), usage frequency, favourite sites.

2 *Remember that personas are only models of characteristics and environment*:
- Design targets
- Stereotypes
- Three or four usually suffice to improve general usability, but more are needed for specific behaviours
- Choose one primary persona which if satisfied, means others are likely to be satisfied.

3 *Different scenarios can be developed for each persona as explained further below.* Write three or four, for example:
- Information-seeking scenario (leads to site registration)
- Purchase scenario – new customer (leads to sale)
- Purchase scenario – existing customer (leads to sale).

Once different personas have been developed that are representative of key site-visitor types or customer types, a primary persona is sometimes identified. Wodtke (2002) says:

> *Your primary persona needs to be a common user type who is both important to the business success of the product and needy from a design point of view – in other words, a beginner user or a technologically challenged one.*

She also says that secondary personas can also be developed such as super-users or complete novices. Complementary personas are those that don't fit into the main categories which display unusual behaviour. Such complementary personas help 'out-of-box thinking' and offer choices or content that may appeal to all users.

Stages in use-case analysis

The following stages are identified by Schneider and Winters (1998) for analysis using the use-case method:

1 Identify actors

Actors
People, software or other devices that interface with a system.

Actors are those objects which are involved in using or interacting with a system. They are not part of the system. The obvious actors are the users of a system. In a customer service application the actors may be a customer and the customer service person at the company. When performing process analysis to define use-cases we ask questions such as 'Who are the actors for this process?', 'What services do these actors provide?', 'What are the actors' tasks?' and 'What changes do they make to the status of the overall process?'. Actors are typically application users such as customers and employers. They may add information to the system or receive it through reporting facilities. Note that an employee who has several roles such as a manager role and an administrator role would be represented by two different actors.

Schneider and Winters (1998) point out that other actors include software and hardware control devices that change the state of the process and external systems that interface with the system under consideration. These are effectively human actors who have been automated through other systems that interface with the current system under consideration. Actors are denoted using the straightforward approach shown in *Figure 11.8*.

2 Identify use-cases

Use-case
The sequence of transactions between an actor and a system that supports the activities of the actor.

Use-cases are the different things users of a system want it to perform. These can be described as activities or tasks that are part of a dialogue between an actor and the system. They summarize the requirements of a system from each actor

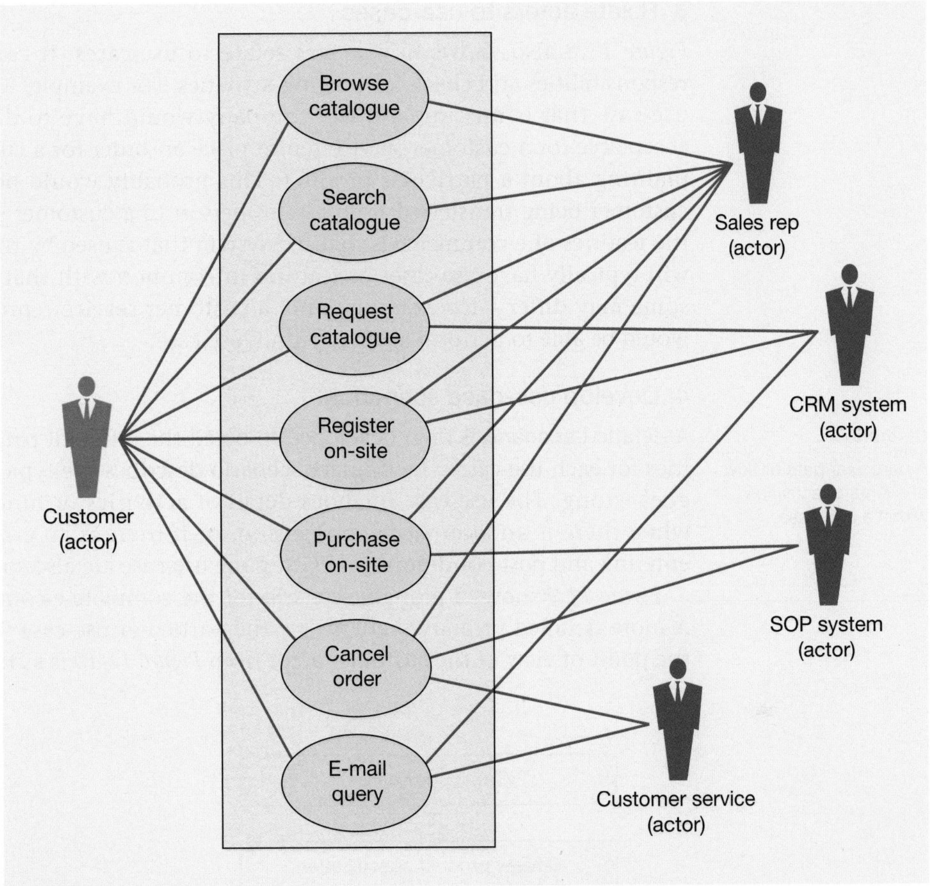

Figure 11.8 Relationship between actors and use-cases for The B2C Company, sell-side e-commerce site

since they describe the functionality that will be provided by the system. Common use-cases are:

- Starting up, shutting down or amending a system.
- Adding or amending information on a system. Examples include placing an e-commerce order or recording a complaint via e-mail.
- Using a system for reporting or decision support.

Some use-cases for The B2C Company are shown in *Figure 11.8*.

Bevan (1999b) also notes the importance of defining key scenarios of use, which is consistent with the use-case approach described above. This stage, often known as 'knowledge elicitation', involves interviewing users and asking them to talk through their current or preferred way of working. Once the scenarios have been established, card sorting techniques, as described by Noyes and Baber (1999), can be used. They describe how after interviewing users, typical tasks or actions were written down on cards. These were then used to identify the sequence of actions users required from a menu system. They explain that the menu system devised was quite different from that envisaged by the software engineers. Card sorting techniques can also be used to check through that no stages have been missed during the **talk-through** – a **walk-through** of the cards is performed. Talk-throughs do not require a physical set-up but walk-throughs do, in the form of a series of cards or use of a prototype of the system.

Talk-through
A user verbally describes their required actions.

Walk-through
A user executes their actions through using a system or mock-up.

3 Relate actors to use-cases

Figure 11.8 also shows how actors relate to use-cases. It can be used to identify responsibilities and check for missing activities. For example, 'Check order status' is a use-case that is missing and the company would have to discuss whether it was acceptable for a customer service rep to place an order for a customer who was complaining about a particular product. This probably would be desirable to avoid a customer being transferred from a sales person to a customer service person. One of the features of e-commerce is that the system that is used by the sales representatives will typically have use-cases or features in common with that for the customer, but some may differ – for example, only a customer service representative or sales rep would be able to perform a 'Give refund' use-case.

4 Develop use-case scenarios

Scenario
A particular path or flow of events or activities within a use-case.

A detailed scenario is then developed to detail the different paths of events and activities for each use-case. The primary scenario describes the typical case where nothing goes wrong. The use-case includes detail of activities or functions, what happens when there is an alternative or decision, or if there is an error. Pre-conditions for entering and post-conditions for exiting the use-case are also specified.

Figure 11.9 shows a primary scenario for the complete e-commerce purchase cycle. A more detailed primary scenario for the particular use-case 'Register' written from the point of view of the customer actor from *Figure 11.10* is as follows:

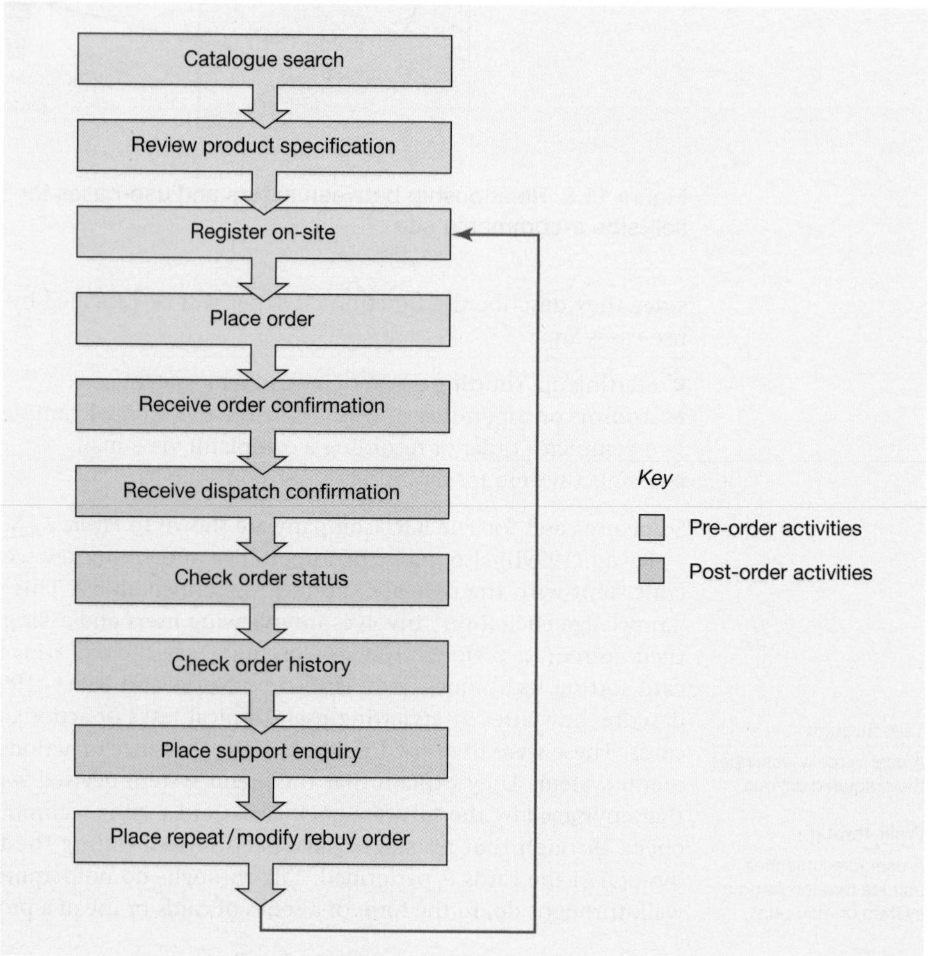

Figure 11.9 Primary use-case scenario for an entire e-commerce purchase cycle

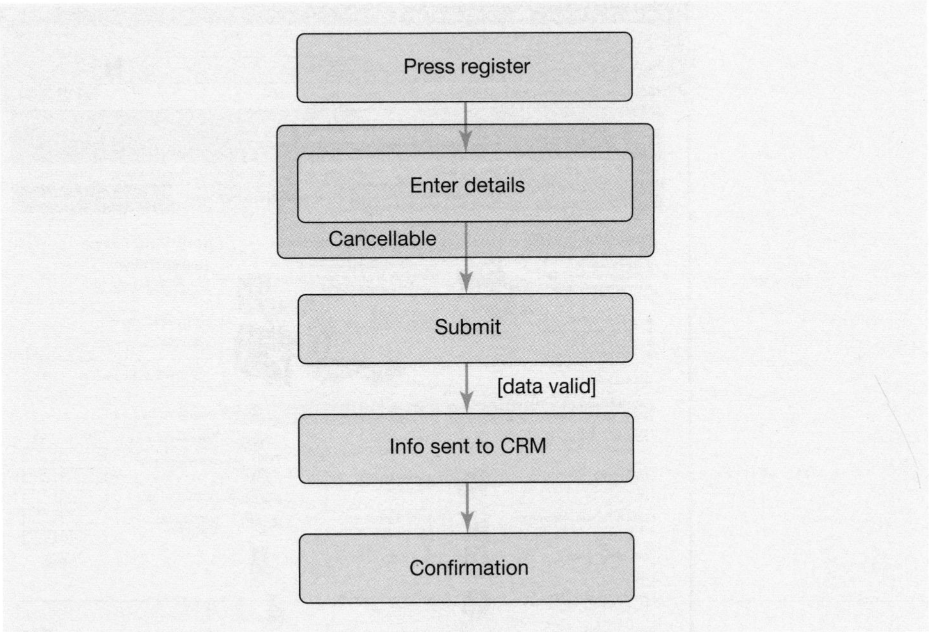

Figure 11.10 Primary scenario for the Register use-cases for The B2C Company

Pre-condition: A user is active on the web site.

Scenario: Register.

Basic path:

1 Use-case starts when customer presses 'register'.
2 Customer enters name, postal address and e-mail.
3 The post/zip code and e-mail address (@ symbol) will be checked for validity after entry and the user prompted if there is an error.
4 The customer will select 'submit'.
5 The system will check all fields are present and the customer information will be passed to the CRM system.
6 A redirect page will be displayed to thank the customer for registering and provide an option to return to the home page, and the use-case ends.

Post-condition: The customer details have been saved.

Alternative paths: The customer can cancel at stages 2 to 4 before pressing 'submit' and the use-case ends.

It can be seen that by stating the use-case in this way different issues can be clarified. For instance, should the validation at stage 3 occur when the entry field loses focus (i.e. tab to next field), or should it wait until stage 4 which is perhaps more conventional? Another issue is whether we should display the customer details at stage 6 with the option to amend them if incorrect. Discussing the options before development saves time when coding prototyping. After the primary scenario is complete, second or alternative scenarios can be developed and added to the primary scenarios as alternatives. For the register scenario, cancel is a secondary scenario; others could include error conditions such as whether the postcode is invalid.

Figure 11.11 illustrates an e-commerce site with clear menu options which is consistent with use-case analysis.

Seybold (2001) also recommends using scenario-based design. She examines the example of how grocery retailer Tesco.com combined both online and offline activity for its online customers. She also give the example of Buzzsaw.com, a B2B service for

Figure 11.11 **Clear user scenario options at the RS Components site (www.rswww.com)**

construction projects where the high-level customer scenario which must be delivered by the web site is:

1 Set project scope, schedule and budget.
2 Gain financial backing.
3 Recruit the team.
4 Develop the design.
5 Produce the plans and specifications.
6 Manage the bidding and negotiations.
7 Manage the construction process.
8 Manage the facility.

In supporting this scenario, the web service also has to support a wide range of participants including the construction manager, architects, engineers and subcontractors.

Designing the information architecture

Information architecture
The combination of organization, labelling and navigation schemes comprising an information system.

Rosenfeld and Morville (2002) emphasize the importance of information architecture to an effective web-site design; they say:

It is important to recognise that every information system, be it a book or an intranet, has an information architecture. 'Well developed' is the key here, as most sites don't have a planned information architecture at all. They are analogous to buildings that weren't architected in advance. Design decisions reflect the personal biases of designers, the space doesn't scale over time, technologies drive the design and not the other way around.

In their book, Rosenfeld and Morville give alternative definitions of an information architecture. They say it is:

1 *The combination of organisation, labelling, and navigation schemes within an information system.*
2 *The structural design of an information space to facilitate task completion and intuitive access to content.*
3 *The art and science of structuring and classifying web sites and intranets to help people find and manage information.*
4 *An emerging discipline and community of practice focused on bringing principles of design and architecture to the digital landscape.*

Essentially, in practice, creation of an information architecture involves creating a plan to group information logically – it involves creating a site structure which is often represented as a site map. Note, though, that whole books have been written on information architecture, so this is necessarily a simplification! A well developed information architecture is very important to usability since it determines navigation options. It is also important to search engine optimization (*Chapter 9*), since it determines how different types of content that users may search for are labelled and grouped.

Site map
A graphical or text depiction of the relationship between different groups of content on a web site.

A planned information architecture is essential to large-scale web sites such as transactional e-commerce sites, media owner sites and relationship-building sites that include a large volume of product or support documentation. Information architectures are less important to small-scale web sites and brand sites, but even here, the principles can be readily applied and can help make the site more visible to search engines and usable.

The benefits of creating an information architecture include:

- A defined structure and categorization of information will support user and organization goals, i.e. it is a vital aspect of usability.
- It helps increase 'flow' on the site – a user's mental model of where to find content should mirror that of the content on the web site.
- Search engine optimization – a higher listing in the search rankings can often be used through structuring and labelling information in a structured way.
- Applicable for integrating offline communications – offline communications such as ads or direct mail can link to a product or campaign landing page to help achieve direct response, sometimes known as 'web response'. A sound URL strategy as explained in *Chapter 8* can help this.
- Related content can be grouped to measure the effectiveness of a web site as part of design for analysis which is also explained below.

Card sorting

Using card sorting is a way users can become actively involved in the development process of information architecture.

Card sorting is a useful approach since web sites are frequently designed from the perspective of the designer rather than the information user, leading to labels, subject grouping and categories that are not intuitive to the user. Card sorting or web classification should categorize web objects (e.g. documents) in order to facilitate information task completion or information goals the user has set.

Card sorting or web classification
The process of arranging a way of organizing objects on the web site in a consistent manner.

Robertson (2003) explains an approach to card sorting which identifies the following questions when using card sorting to aid the process of modelling web classification systems:

- Do the users want to see the information grouped by: subject, task, business or customer groupings, or type of information?
- What are the most important items to put on the main menu?

- How many menu items should there be, and how deep should it go?
- How similar or different are the needs of the users throughout the organization?

Selected groups of users or representatives will be given index cards with the following written on them depending on the aim of the card sorting process:

- Types of documents
- Organizational key words and concepts
- Document titles
- Descriptions of documents
- Navigation labels.

The user groups may then be asked to:

- Group together cards that they feel relate to each other;
- Select cards that accurately reflect a given topic or area;
- Organize cards in terms of hierarchy – high-level terms (broad) to low-level terms.

At the end of session the analyst must take the cards away and map the results into a spreadsheet to find out the most popular terms, descriptions and relationships. If two or more different groups are used the results should be compared and reasons for differences should be analysed.

Blueprints

Blueprints
Show the relationships between pages and other content components, and can be used to portray organization, navigation and labelling systems.

According to Rosenfeld and Morville (2002), **blueprints**:

> *Show the relationships between pages and other content components, and can be used to portray organization, navigation and labelling systems.*

They are often thought of, and referred to, as site maps or site structure diagrams and have much in common with these, except that they are used as a design device clearly showing grouping of information and linkages between pages, rather than a page on the web site to assist navigation.

Refer to *Figure 11.12* for an example of a site structure diagram for a toy manufacturer web site which shows the groupings of content and an indication of the process of task completion also.

Wireframes

Wireframes
Also known as 'schematics', a way of illustrating the layout of an individual web page.

A related technique to blueprints are **wireframes**, which are used by web designers to indicate the eventual layout of a web page. *Figure 11.13* shows that the wireframe is so called because it just consists of an outline of the page with the 'wires' of content separating different areas of content or navigation shown by white space.

Wodtke (2002) describes a wireframe (sometimes known as a 'schematic') as:

> *a basic outline of an individual page, drawn to indicate the elements of a page, their relationships, and their relative importance.*

Tip

Wireframes are useful for agencies and clients to discuss the way a web site will be laid out without getting distracted by colour, style or messaging issues which should be covered separately as a creative planning activity.

A wireframe will be created for all types of similar page groups, identified at the blueprint (site map) stage of creating the information architecture.

Blueprints illustrate how the content of a web site is related and navigated while a wireframe focuses on individual pages, with a wireframe the navigation focus becomes where it will be placed on the page.

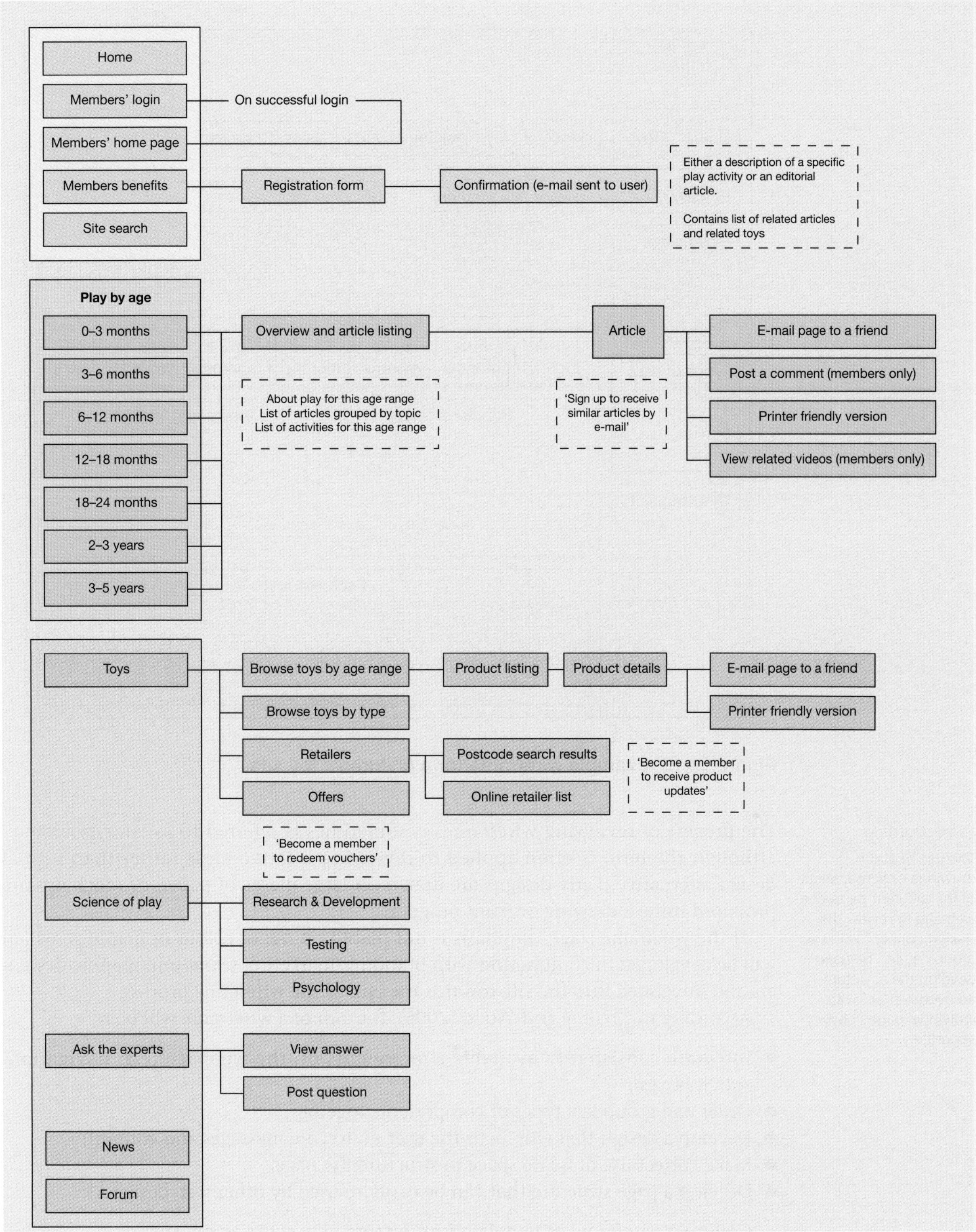

Figure 11.12 Site structure diagram (blueprint) showing layout and relationship between pages

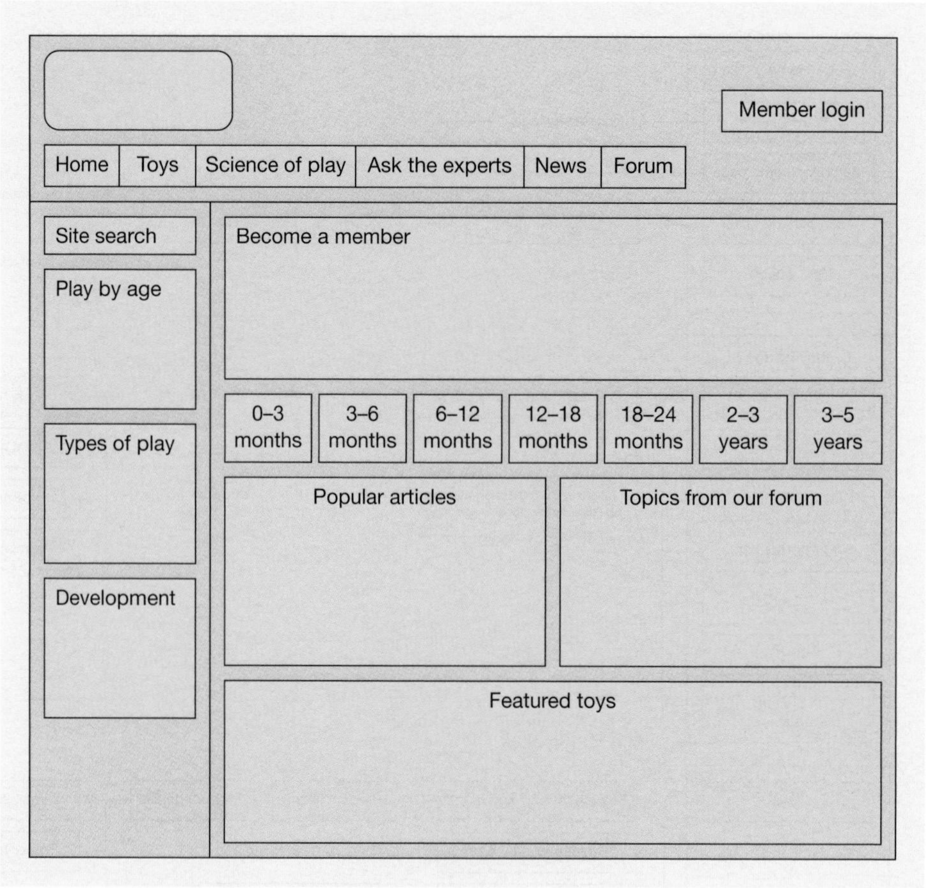

Figure 11.13 Example wireframe for a children's toy site

> **Storyboarding**
> The use of static drawings or screenshots of the different parts of a web site to review the design concept with user groups. It can be used to develop the structure – an overall 'map' with individual pages shown separately.

The process of reviewing wireframes is sometimes is referred to as 'storyboarding', although the term is often applied to reviewing creative ideas rather than formal design alternative. Early designs are drawn on large pieces of paper, or mock-ups are produced using a drawing or paint program.

At the wireframe stage, emphasis is not placed on use of colour or graphics, which will be developed in conjunction with branding/marketing teams and graphic designers and integrated into the site towards the end of the wireframe process.

According to Chaffey and Wood (2005), the aim of a wireframe will be to:

- Integrate consistently available components on the webpage (e.g. navigation, search boxes);
- Order and group key types of components together;
- Develop a design that will focus the user on to core messages and content;
- Make correct use of white space to structure the page;
- Develop a page structure that can be easily re-used by other web designers.

Common wireframe or template features you may come across are:

- Navigation in columns on left or right and at top or bottom.
- Header areas and footer areas.
- 'Slots' or 'portlets' – these are areas of content such as an article or list of articles placed in boxes on the screen. Often slots will be dynamically populated from a content management system.

- Slots on the home page may be used to:
  - Summarize the online value proposition
  - Show promotions
  - Recommend related products
  - Feature news, etc.
  - Contain ads.

Customer orientation

Customer orientation
Developing site content and services to appeal to different customer segments or other members of the audience.

A well designed site will have been developed to achieve **customer orientation** or customer-centricity. This involves the difficult task of trying to provide content and services to appeal to a wide range of audiences. For a B2B company the three main types of audience are customers, other companies and organizations, and staff. The detailed breakdown of these audiences is illustrated in *Figure 11.14*. Visit the Dell web site (www.dell.com) to see how Dell segments its customer base on the home page into:

- Small office and home users
- Small businesses
- Medium businesses
- Large businesses
- Corporates
- Government organizations.

Think about how well this approach works. What would be your reaction to being classified as a mere small-business or home owner? Do you think this is a valid approach? A similar approach, by Microsoft, is to offer specialized content for IS managers to help them in their investment decisions. Is a more straightforward product-centric structure to the web site appropriate?

As well as customer segments, designers also need to take into account variations in the backgrounds of visitors to the site. These can be thought of as four different types of familiarity:

1. *Familiarity with the Internet* – are short cuts provided for those familiar with the Internet? And for novices is there help to lead them through your site? As we saw in *Chapter 4*, users have different levels of familiarity with the web and this should be accommodated within web site designs.
2. *Familiarity with organization* – for customers who do not know the organization, content is needed to explain who the company is and demonstrate credibility through 'About Us' options and customer testimonials.

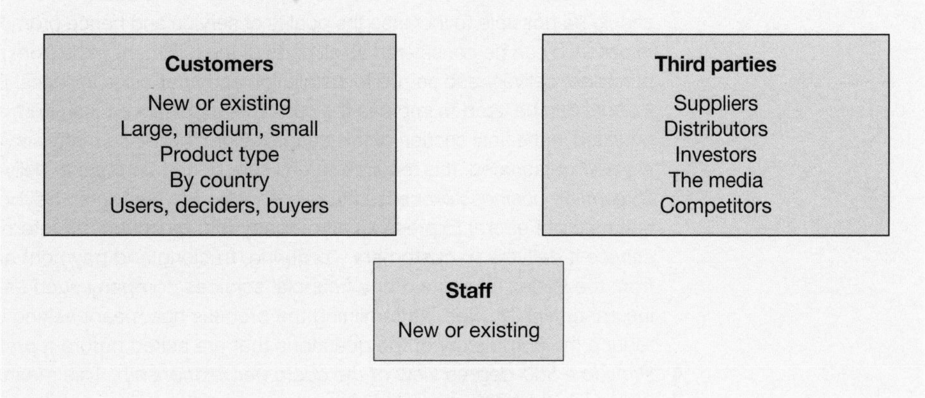

Figure 11.14 Different types of audience for the web site of The B2B Company

3 *Familiarity with organization's products* – even existing customers may not know the full range of your product offering.
4 *Familiarity with your site* – site maps, search and help options are not 'nice to have' options for an e-commerce site, because you may lose potential customers if they cannot be helped when they are lost.

Jakob Nielsen (2000a) says this about novice users:

> *Web users are notoriously fickle: they take one look at a home page and leave after a few seconds if they can't figure it out. The abundance of choice and the ease of going elsewhere puts a huge premium on making it extremely easy to enter a site.*

But he notes that we also need to take account of experts. He says we may eventually move to interfaces where the average site visitor gets a simplified design that is easy to learn and loyal users get an advanced design that is more powerful. But, for now, *'in-depth content and advanced information should be added to sites to provide the depth expected by experts'*.

The principles of customer orientation can be extended from the design of the site to the tactics that are used to deliver services via a web site, as explained through *Activity 11.4*.

Activity 11.4 Applying Patricia Seybold's *Customers.com* approach to customer orientation

Purpose

To highlight how the principles of customer orientation of services offered can be applied to site design.

Activity

Read the extract of the eight success factors outlined by US industry analyst Patricia Seybold in her book, *Customers.com* (Seybold, 1999). Explain how each of these could be applied to customer-oriented site design for The B2B Company.

The eight critical success factors she suggests are:

1 *Target the right customers*. This first and most important principle suggests concentrating on either the most profitable customers, which is one of the tenets of CRM (*Chapter 9*), or those that cannot be reached so well by other media. For example, UK car insurer Swinton wished to target the young-driver market so it trialled a web site with a special 'Streetwise' brand. Alternatively, the right customers in the business-to-business context could be those who make the buying decisions.
2 *Own the customer's total experience*. By managing the customer's entire experience it should be possible to increase the quality of service and hence promote loyalty. The total experience can be considered as all parts of the fulfilment cycle from product selection, purchase, delivery and set-up to installation and after-sales services. Examples of how the Internet can be used to improve the customer experience taken from across this cycle are provided in the final section of this chapter. Note that since many services such as delivery are now outsourced, this requires careful selection of partners to deliver this quality service.
3 *Streamline business processes* that impact on the customer. Seybold (1999) gives the example of Federal Express as a company that has used the Internet to re-engineer the service it delivers to customers – ordering, tracking and payment are now all available from the Fedex web site. For a financial services company such as Eagle Star selling insurance via the web, streamlining the process has meant asking underwriters to reduce the complexity of the questions that are asked before a premium is calculated.
4 *Provide a 360-degree view of the customer relationship*. This means that different parts of the company must have similar information about the customer to provide a

consistent service. It implies integration of the personalization facilities of a web site with other databases holding information about the customer. If these databases are not integrated then customer trust may be lost. If, for example, the web site offers a customer a product they have already purchased offline it will appear that the company does not understand their needs. Integration of call centres with a web site is also an implication of this guideline.

5 *Let customers help themselves*. This has the benefit of reducing costs, while at the same time providing faster, more efficient customer service.
6 *Help customers do their jobs*. This guideline is similar to the previous one, but focuses more on providing them with the information needed to do their jobs. This is again a useful value-added facility of the web site which helps encourage loyalty.
7 *Deliver personalized service*. The importance of delivering personalized service to build a one-to-one relationship with the customer formed the basis for *Chapter 9*.
8 *Foster community*. Business web sites afford good opportunities to create communities of interest since information can be generated which helps customers in their work and again encourages returns to the web site. Independent business community sites are also important places for companies to have representation.

No suggested answers supplied.

Elements of site design

Debate 11.2

Whither web-site design?

'Web-site design is too complex, and too important, to be left to marketers and IT staff untrained in its principles. Specialist usability professionals and psychologists should be present in every large e-commerce team.'

Once the requirements of the user are established we can turn our attention to the design of the human–computer interface. Nielsen (2000b) structures his book on web usability according to three main areas, which can be interpreted as follows:

1 *Site design and structure* – the overall structure of the site.
2 *Page design* – the layout of individual pages.
3 *Content design* – how the text and graphic content on each page is designed.

Site design and structure

The structures created by designers for web sites will vary greatly according to their audience and the site's purpose, but we can make some general observations about design and structure. We will review the factors designers consider in designing the style, organization and navigation schemes for the site.

Site style

An effective web-site design will have a style that is communicated through use of colour, images, typography and layout. This should support the way a product is positioned or its brand.

Site personality

The style elements can be combined to develop a personality for a site. We could describe site personalities in the same way we can describe people, such as 'formal' or 'fun'. This personality has to be consistent with the needs of the target audience. A business audience often requires detailed information and prefers an information-intensive style such as that of the Cisco site (**www.cisco.com**). A consumer site is usually more graphically intensive. Before the designers pass on their creative designs to developers, they also need to consider the constraints on the user experience, such as screen resolution and colour depth, the browser used and download speed. The list of constraints which must be tested is illustrated in *Chapter 12*.

Activity 11.5 Evaluating site organization schemes

Purpose

To assess different forms of information content on e-commerce sites.

Activity

Visit the RS Components web site (www.rswww.com) and the Dell Computer site (www.dell.com) relevant to your country. Which information organization schemes are used?

Answers to activities can be found at www.pearsoned.co.uk/chaffey

Site organization

Information organization schemes
The structure chosen to group and categorize information.

In their book on information architectures for the web, Rosenfeld and Morville (2002) identify several different **information organization schemes**. These can be applied for different aspects of e-commerce sites, from the whole site through to different parts of the site.

Rosenfeld and Morville (2002) identify the following information organization schemes:

1 *Exact.* Here information can be naturally indexed. If we take the example of books, these can alphabetical – by author or title; chronological – by date; or for travel books, for example, geographical – by place. Information on an e-commerce site may be presented alphabetically, but this is not suitable for browsing.

2 *Ambiguous.* Here the information requires classification; again taking the examples of books, the Dewey decimal system is an ambiguous classification scheme since the librarians classify books into arbitrary categories. Such an approach is common on an e-commerce site since products and services can be classified in different ways. Other ambiguous information organization schemes that are commonly used on web sites are where content is broken down by topic, by task or by audience. The use of metaphors is also common; a metaphor is where the web site corresponds to a familiar real-world situation. The Microsoft Windows Explorer, where information is grouped according to Folders, Files and Trash, is an example of a real-world metaphor. The use of the shopping basket metaphor is widespread within e-commerce sites. It should be noted, though, that Nielsen (2000b) believes that metaphors can be confusing if the metaphor is not understood immediately or is misinterpreted.

3 *Hybrid.* Here there will be a mixture of organization schemes, both exact and ambiguous. Rosenfeld and Morville (2002) point out that using different approaches is common on web sites but this can lead to confusion, because the user is not clear what mental model is being followed. We can say that it is probably best to minimize the number of information organization schemes. Now complete *Activity 11.5*.

Site navigation scheme
Tools provided to the user to move between different information on a web site.

Flow
Flow describes how easy it is for users of a site to move between the different pages of content of the site.

Site navigation schemes

Devising a site that is easy to use is critically dependent on the design of the **site navigation scheme**. Hoffman and Novak (1997) stress the importance of the concept of '**flow**' in governing site usability. 'Flow' essentially describes how easy it is for the users to find the information they need as they move from one page of the site to the next, but it also includes other interactions such as filling in on-screen forms. Rettie (2001) summarizes the meaning of flow in an online context and gives guidelines on how this concept can be used to enhance the visitor experience. The concept of flow can be better understood by considering the statements describing flow used originally by Csikszentmihalyi and more recently by Rettie's research to test for a flow experience on a web site:

(1) *My mind isn't wandering. I am not thinking of something else. I am totally involved in what I am doing. My body feels good. I don't seem to hear anything. The world seems to be cut off from me. I am less aware of myself and my problems.*

(2) *My concentration is like breathing. I never think of it. I am really oblivious to my surroundings after I really get going. I think that the phone could ring, and the doorbell could ring, or the house burn down or something like that. When I start, I really do shut out the whole world. Once I stop, I can let it back in again.*

(3) *I am so involved in what I am doing, I don't see myself as separate from what I am doing.*

Rettie (2001) suggests that the following factors limit flow: long download times, delays to download plug-ins, long registration forms, limited stimulation, boring sites, slow responses, sites which are not intuitive, navigation links that fail, challenge greater than skill and irrelevant advertising. Conversely, reversing these factors can improve flow: quick download times, alternative versions (e.g. text and graphics), automatic completion of forms, opportunities for interaction, rapid responses, navigation which creates choices, predictable navigation for control, segmentation by Internet experience.

Most navigation systems are based upon a hierarchical site structure. When creating the structure, designers have to compromise between the two approaches shown in *Figure 11.15*. The narrow and deep approach has the benefit of fewer choices on each page, making it easier for the user to make their selection, but more clicks are

Narrow and deep navigation
Fewer choices, more clicks to reach required content.

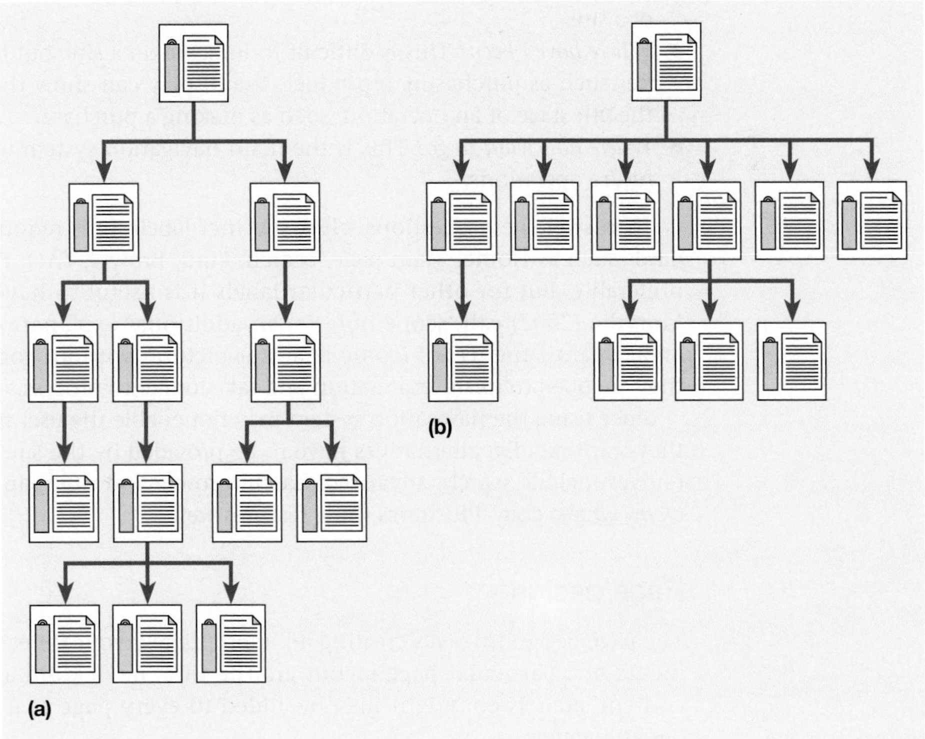

Figure 11.15 (a) Narrow and deep and (b) broad and shallow organization schemes

Broad and shallow navigation
More choices, fewer clicks to reach required content.

required to reach a particular piece of information. The broad and shallow approach requires fewer clicks to reach the same piece of information, but the design of the screen potentially becomes cluttered. *Figure 11.15(a)* depicts the narrow and deep approach and *Figure 11.15(b)* the broad and shallow approach. Note that in these cases the approaches are appropriate for the non-technical and technical audiences respectively. A rule of thumb is that site designers should ensure it only takes three clicks to reach any piece of information on a site. This implies the use of a broad and shallow approach on most large sites. Lynch and Horton (1999) recommend a broad and shallow approach and note that designers should not conceive of a single home page where customers arrive on the site, but of different home pages according to different audience types. Each of the pages in the second row of *Figure 11.15(b)* could be thought of as an example of a home page which the visitors can bookmark if the page appeals to them. Nielsen (2000b) points out that many users will not arrive on the home page, but may be referred from another site or according to a print or TV advert to a particular page such as www.b2b.com/jancomp. He calls this process 'deep linking' and site designers should ensure that navigation and context are appropriate for users arriving on these pages.

Deep linking
Jakob Nielsen's term for a user arriving at a site deep within its structure.

As well as compromises on depth of links within a site it is also necessary to compromise on the amount of space devoted to menus. Nielsen (2000c) points out that some sites devote so much space to navigation bars that the space available for content is limited. Nielsen (2000c) suggests that the designer of navigation systems should consider the following information that a site user wants to know:

- *Where am I?* The user needs to know where they are on the site and this can be indicated by highlighting the current location and clear titling of pages. Chaffey *et al.* (2006) refer to this as *context*. *Consistency* of menu locations on different pages is also required to aid cognition. Users also need to know where they are on the web. This can be indicated by a logo, which by convention is at the top or top left of a site.
- *Where have I been?* This is difficult to indicate on a site, but for task-oriented activities such as purchasing a product, the display can show the user that they are at the *n*th stage of an operation, such as making a purchase.
- *Where do I want to go?* This is the main navigation system which gives options for future operations.

To answer these questions, clear succinct labelling is required. Widely used standards such as Home, Main page, Search, Find, Browse, FAQ, Help and About Us are preferable. But for other particular labels it is useful to have what Rosenfeld and Morville (2002) call 'scope notes' – an additional explanation. These authors also argue against the use of iconic labels or pictures without corresponding text since they are open to misinterpretation and take longer to process.

Since using the navigation system may not enable the user to find the information they want rapidly, alternatives have to be provided by the site designers. These alternatives include search, advanced search, browse and site map facilities. Whatis.com (www.whatis.com) illustrates these features well.

Page design

The page design involves creating an appropriate layout for each page. The main elements of a particular page layout are the title, navigation and content. Standard content such as copyright may be added to every page as a footer. Issues in page design include:

- *Page elements*. The proportion of page devoted to content compared to all other content such as headers, footers and navigation elements. The location of these elements also needs to be considered. It is conventional for the main menu to be at the top or on the left. The use of a menu system at the top of the browser window enables more space for content below.

- *The use of frames*. This is generally discouraged for the reasons given in *Chapter 12*.
- *Resizing*. A good page layout design should allow for the user to change the size of text or work with different monitor resolutions.
- *Consistency*. Page layout should be similar for all areas of the site unless more space is required, for example for a discussion forum or product demonstration. Standards of colour and typography can be enforced through cascading style sheets.
- *Printing*. Layout should allow for printing or provide an alternative printing format.

Content design

Copywriting for the web is an evolving art form, but many of the rules for good copywriting are as for any medium. Common errors we see on web sites are:

- too much knowledge assumed of the visitor about the company, its products and services;
- using internal jargon about products, services or departments – using undecipherable acronyms.

Web copywriters also need to take account of the user reading the content on-screen. Approaches to deal with the limitations imposed by the customer using a monitor include:

- writing more concisely than in brochures;
- chunking or breaking text into units of 5–6 lines at most; this allows users to scan rather than read information on web pages;
- using lists with headline text in larger font;
- never including too much on a single page, except when presenting lengthy information such as a report which may be easier to read on a single page;
- using hyperlinks to decrease page sizes or help achieve flow within copy, either by linking to sections further down a page or linking to another page.

Hofacker (2000) describes five stages of human information processing when a web site is being used. These can be applied to both page design and content design to improve usability and help companies get their message across to consumers. Each of the five stages summarized in *Table 11.6* acts as a hurdle, since if the site design or content is too difficult to process, the customer cannot progress to the next stage. It is useful to consider the stages in order to minimize the difficulties.

The model of Bickerton *et al.* (2000) can still be used to assess the different content and services offered to different audiences of a web site using intranets, extranets and the Internet. The model has three levels:

- *Presentation*. This is the delivery of static information on the web site. It can be thought of as a 'brochureware' site, but may have additional depth of information.
- *Interaction*. This stage involves methods of communicating with the customer such as the use of interactive forms and e-mail or discussion communities.
- *Representation*. Representation occurs where the Internet replaces customer services that are normally delivered by human operators. In the case of a bank this stage would involve a customer performing online money transfers between bank accounts or bill payment. IBM has referred to this concept as 'web self-service'.

Table 11.6 **A summary of information web stages described by Hofacker (2000)**

Stage	*Description*	*Applications*
1 Exposure	Content must be present for long enough to be processed.	Content on banner ads may not be on screen long enough for processing and cognition.
2 Attention	User's eyes will be drawn towards headings and content, not graphics and moving items on a web page (Nielsen, 2000b).	Emphasis and accurate labelling of headings is vital to gain a user's attention. Evidence suggests that users do not notice banner adverts, suffering from 'banner blindness'.
3 Comprehension and perception	The user's interpretation of content.	Designs that use common standards and metaphors and are kept simple will be more readily comprehended.
4 Yielding and acceptance	Is the information (copy) presented accepted by customers?	Copy should reference credible sources and present counter-arguments as necessary.
5 Retention	As for traditional advertising, this describes the extent to which the information is remembered.	An unusual style or high degree of interaction leading to flow and user satisfaction is more likely to be recalled.

Source: Adapted from Hofacker (2001)

Using these layers we can map content across different access levels to produce a site which is integrated across the needs of its audiences (*Table 11.7*). This also relates to the section on security since different access levels may be given for different information.

Now complete *Activity 11.6* so you can apply some of the techniques you have read about in this section.

Table 11.7 **Information and services mapping for The B2B Company**

Stage	*Intranet (employees only)*	*Extranet (favoured partners)*	*Internet (public)*
Presentation	Market research Contacts Sales reports	Technical information sheet Product/pricing information for agents	Company information Product information
Interaction	Access to sales rep reports on company visits Data mining E-mail briefings to staff	Key account user group Order filing	Product availability queries E-mail-based customer service
Representation	Online holiday and claims form submission and processing	Transactional e-commerce on buy-side and sell-side	Transactional e-commerce

Activity 11.6 Use-case analysis for customer service desk at The B2B Company

Purpose

To develop knowledge of the use-case approach by applying it in a particular scenario.

Activity

Develop a primary use-case for the situation when a customer asks a question on the online helpdesk for The B2B Company. State your assumptions about the activities which would be involved. Translate this use-case into an interface design. This activity can be performed in conjunction with *Activity 12.4* which describes the helpdesk requirements in more detail.

Web accessibility

Accessibility
An approach to site design intended to accommodate site usage using different browsers and settings particularly required by the visually impaired.

Web accessibility is another core requirement for web sites. It is about allowing all users of a web site to interact with it regardless of disabilities they may have or the web browser or platform they are using to access the site. The visually impaired are the main audience that designing an accessible web site can help. However, increased usage of mobile or wireless access devices such as Personal Digital Assistants (PDAs) and GPRS or 3G phones also make consideration of accessibility important.

The quote below shows the importance of the accessibility to a visually impaired user of a web site who uses a screen-reader which reads out the navigation options and content on a web site.

> *For me being online is everything. It's my hi-fi, it's my source of income, it's my supermarket, it's my telephone. It's my way in.*
>
> (Lynn Holdsworth, screen-reader user, web developer and programmer, RNIB, www.rnib.org.uk)

Accessibility legislation
Legislation intended to protect users of web sites with disabilities, including those with visual disability.

Remember that many countries now have specific **accessibility legislation** to which web site owners are subject. This is often contained within disability and discrimination acts. In the UK, the relevant act is the Disability and Discrimination Act (DDA) 1995. Recent amendments to the DDA makes it unlawful to discriminate against disabled people in the way in which a company recruits and employs people, provides services or provides education. Providing services is the part of the law that applies to web site design. Providing accessible web sites is a requirement of Part II of the Disability and Discrimination Act published in 1999 and required by law from 2002. In the 2002 code of practice there is a legal requirement for web sites to be accessible. This is most important for sites which provide a service; for example The Code of Practice gives this example:

> *An airline company provides a flight reservation and booking service to the public on its website. This is a provision of a service and is subject to the Act.*

Although there is a moral imperative for accessibility, there is also a business imperative to encourage companies to make their web sites accessibile. The main arguments in favour of accessibility are:

1 *Number of visually impaired people* – in many countries there are millions of visually impaired people varying from 'colour blind' to partially sighted to blind.
2 *Number of users of less popular browsers or variation in screen display resolution.* Microsoft Internet Explorer is now the dominant browser, but there are less well known browsers which have a loyal following amongst the visually impaired (for example screen-readers and Lynx, a text-only browser) and early adopters (for

example Mozilla Firefox, Safari and Opera). If a web site does not display well in these browsers, then you may lose these audiences. Complete *Activity 11.7* to review how much access has varied since this book was published.

3 *More visitors from natural listings of search engines.* Many of the techniques used to make sites more usable also assist in search engine optimisation. For example, clearer navigation, text alternatives for images and site maps can all help improve a site's position in the search engine rankings.

4 *Legal requirements.* In many countries it is a legal requirement to make web sites accessible. For example, the UK has a Disability Discrimination Act that requires this. The requirements of these laws are described in more detail later in this topic.

Activity 11.7 Allowing for the range in access devices

One of the benefits of accessibility requirements is that it helps web site owners and web agencies consider the variation in platforms used to access web sites.

Questions

1 Update the compilation in *Table 11.8* to the latest values using Onestat.com or other data from web analytics providers.

Table 11.8 **Summary of the range in browsers and screen resolutions used at the time of writing**

Web browser popularity		*Screen resolution popularity*	
1 Microsoft IE	86.63 %	1 1024 × 768	57.38%
2 Mozilla Firefox	8.69 %	2 800 × 600	18.23%
3 Apple Safari	1.26 %	3 1280 × 1024	14.18%
4 Netscape	1.08 %	4 1152 × 864	4.95%
5 Opera	1.03 %	5 1600 × 1200	1.67%

Source: Onestat press releases (www.onestat.com)

2 Explain the variations. Which browsers and screen resolutions do you think should be supported?

Guidelines for creating accessible web sites are produced by the governments of different countries and non-government organizations such as charities. Internet standards organizations such as the World Wide Web Consortium have been active in promoting guidelines for web accessibility through its Website Accessibility Initiative (WAI), see **www.w3.org/WAI**. It describes common accessibility problems as:

> *images without alternative text; lack of alternative text for imagemap hot-spots; misleading use of structural elements on pages; uncaptioned audio or undescribed video; lack of alternative information for users who cannot access frames or scripts; tables that are difficult to decipher when linearized; or sites with poor color contrast.*

A fuller checklist for acessibility compliance for web site design and coding using HTML is available from the World Wide Web Consortium (**www.w3.org/TR/WCAG10/full-checklist.html**).

There are three different priority levels which it describes as follows:

- *Priority 1 (Level A)*. A Web content developer must satisfy this checkpoint. Otherwise, one or more groups will find it impossible to access information in the document. Satisfying this checkpoint is a basic requirement for some groups to be able to use Web documents.
- *Priority 2 (Level AA)*. A Web content developer should satisfy this checkpoint. Otherwise, one or more groups will find it difficult to access information in the document. Satisfying this checkpoint will remove significant barriers to accessing Web documents.
- *Priority 3 (Level AAA)*. A Web content developer may address this checkpoint. Otherwise, one or more groups will find it somewhat difficult to access information in the document. Satisfying this checkpoint will improve access to Web documents.

So, for many companies the standard is to meet Priority 1 and Priority 2 or 3 where practical.

Some of the most important Priority 1 elements are indicated by these 'Quick Tips' from the WAI:

Alt tags
Alt tags appear after an image tag and contain a phrase associated with that image. For example: <img src="logo.gif" alt="Company name, company products"/>

- Images and animations: Use **alt tags** to describe the function of each visual.
- Image maps. Use the client-side map and text for hotspots.
- Multimedia. Provide captioning and transcripts of audio, and descriptions of video.

Figure 11.16 HSBC Global home page (www.hsbc.com)

- Hypertext links. Use text that makes sense when read out of context. For example, avoid 'click here'.
- Page organization. Use headings, lists and consistent structure. Use CSS for layout and style where possible.
- Graphs and charts. Summarize or use the longdesc attribute.
- Scripts, applet and plug-ins. Provide alternative content in case active features are inaccessible or unsupported.
- Frames. Use the noframes element and meaningful titles.
- Tables. Make line-by-line reading sensible. Summarize.
- Check your work. Validate. Use the tools, checklist and guidelines at http://www.w3. org/TR/WCAG.

Figure 11.16 is an example of an accessible site which still meets brand and business objectives while supporting accessibility through resizing of screen resolution, text resizing and alternative image text.

Case Study 11.1 dabs.com refines its web store

This case study highlights the importance placed on web-site design as part of the customer experience by dabs.com. It shows the need to upgrade the infrastructure regularly to deliver a satisfactory experience which is competitive with other e-retailers. dabs.com is one of the UK's leading internet retailers of IT and technology products from manufacturers such as Sony, Hewlett-Packard, Toshiba and Microsoft. The case also highlights some of the strategic issues with operating an e-business as it describes the growth of the company.

Company background and history

dabs.com was originally created by entrepreneur David Atherton in partnership with writer Bruce Smith (the name 'Dabs' comes from the combined initials of their two names). Their first venture, Dabs Press was a publisher of technology books. Although David and Bruce remain firm friends, Dabs has been 100% owned by David since 1990.

Dabs Direct was launched in 1990, as a mail order firm which mainly promoted itself through ads in home technology magazines such as *Personal Computer World* and *Computer Shopper*.

dabs.com was launched in 1999 at the height of the dot-com boom, but unlike many dot-com start-up businesses, dabs.com was based on an existing offline business.

In its first year, dabs.com was loss-making with £1.2 million lost in 2000–1, this was partly due to including free delivery as part of the proposition to acquire new customers.

In 2003, the company opened its first 'bricks and mortar' store at Liverpool John Lennon Airport and it has also opened an operation in France (www.dabs.fr). The French site remains, but the retail strategy has now ended since margins were too low, despite a positive effect in building awareness of the brand in retail locations.

Strategy

The importance that dabs.com owners place on customer experience and usability is suggested by their mission statement, which places customer experience at its core together with choice and price. dabs.com's mission is:

> *to provide customers with a quick and easy way of buying the products they want, at the most competitive prices around, delivered directly to their door.*

Growth has been conservatively managed, since as a privately held company dabs.com has to grow profitably rather than take on debts. dabs.com has reviewed the potential of other European countries for distribution and may select a country where broadband access is high such as Sweden or the Netherlands. A country such as Italy where consumers traditionally prefer face-to-face sales, would not be an early candidate to target for an opening.

In terms of products, dabs.com has focused on computers and related products, but is considering expanding into new categories or even ranges. Initially these will be related to what computer users need while they are working.

dabs.com in 2005

In 2005, dabs.com is a £200 million company with 235 staff, holding 15,000 lines for a customer base of almost

1.5 million and processing around 5,000 customer orders every day. dabs.com has 8m visits a month from around 750,000 unique users. Its catalogue contains 20,000 products with laptops, LCD monitors and external hard drives among the main sales lines.

NCC (2005) reports that dabs.com believes that what its customers require is a dynamic site that provides comprehensive information on its product ranges, delivery charges, returns policy, financing services and rewards scheme. It also provides dabs.tv, a video service that allows customers to see more complex products in greater detail.

Jonathan Wall, dabs.com's marketing director, sees security as important as part of the customer experience, and to protect the business, he says:

> *We were one of the first e-businesses to adopt Visa's 'Verified by Visa' 3D secure payment authentication system and we've also implemented MasterCard's SecureCode variant. We've always worked closely with both credit card companies and it's a concern that dates back to our mail order side. The threat of being attacked and defrauded is always in the forefront of our thoughts.*

Delivery

To ensure delivery as promised, Jonathan Wall explains the importance dabs.com attach to IT. 'We invest as much in our highly automated warehouse as we do in our marketing', says Wall. 'Our systems use a sophisticated combination of dynamic bins and unique product numbering. A lot of the management team come from technical backgrounds. Our back office system was written in OpenVMS by our IT director. Our sales processing system was written in-house.'

Staffing

According to NCC (2005), staff skills are viewed as important, from technology staff to product buyers. Wall says:

> *We pay a higher than average salary, and that means we get a higher level of staff. And we really see the effect of that in the way our buyers and merchandisers approach the market.*

dabs.com switched offline sales in September 2001, after online sales reached half of turnover. This enabled it to reduce costs. Although its consumer sales are online, dabs.com does retain a call centre for customer service and account management services for its business clients who spend £15,000 or more per year. Excellence in customer service is also seen as part of the customer experience and helps dabs.com reduce complaints to trading standards officers compared to some of its online rivals such as eBuyer.com.

Europe is the next challenge: the company launched dabs.fr in France in 2004. But all will depend on its ability to adapt quickly to any changes in customer behaviour.

The 2003 site update

In 2003, dabs.com achieved year-on-year profits rise from £2.5m to £5.1m and sales rose from £150m to £200m. It predicted the growth will continue, with sales reaching £350m in 2005. dabs has about one million unique visitors monthly and adds a further 30,000 new users every month. This success has been achieved in just 4 years from the launch of its first transactional site in 1999. The site reassures each visitor, by the scale of its success. On 5 December it read:

- 1,098,412 customers
- 37,093 orders in December
- 21,289 products available for sale.

dabs.com's marketing director, Jonathan Wall, talking to *IT Week* (2003), explained how the initial growth occurred, and how future growth will be sustained: 'We dominate the PC hobbyist/IT professional sector, but our business must evolve. We want to cast our net further so that we are appealing to people who are interested in technology as a whole. New customers need a new approach. We have built a new environment and a new web site for this target audience.'

In mid-2003 dabs.com launched a site to help it achieve sales to the new audience. Research was used to help develop the new site. The usability of the existing web site was tested and the new concept was also shown to a focus group. After analysing the responses dabs.com created a pilot site, which the same focus group then approved. In total, the new site took 10 months to develop and was an investment of £750,000.

The 2005 site update

NCC (2005) says Wall makes the business case for the new site as follows:

> *Our new site will take us right up there to the top of the field, You have to try and stay ahead. We'll have guided navigation, still quite rare on a UK site, which will help customers to find what they're looking for more intuitively. Early e-commerce customers knew that they specifically wanted a Sony Vaio laptop, for example. New customers just know that they want a laptop that's small and fast and costs less than £1,000. Guided navigation means they can search according to a product's attributes rather than specific brands and models.*

Since the average selling price of laptops is going down, slim margins are decreased further. Wall says: 'Selling electronic equipment on the web has traditionally been passive but by redesigning our site we'll be able to show customers what another extra £50 spent on a laptop will buy them.'

Although the previous site was updated only 2 years ago, he describes the need to keep ahead of competitors as 'a cat and mouse thing'.

→

But new site advances must be combined with competitive prices, Wall says: '*Online customers are price-loyal, not retailer-loyal. The customer is only as loyal as the cheapest price they can pay for a product. It means your competitors are only ever one click away. We have to do everything to keep our customers on our site. Getting them to pay that price to you, rather than your competitor, means that you'll need to exploit the constantly-evolving benefits of digital technology to make their buying experience on your site as fluent and satisfactory as possible.*'

On-site search capabilities

Part of the new site is improved on-site search capabilities from Endeca, which powers the search of Wal-mart and Circuit City sites in the US. Search is important to increasing conversion rates, and so increasing sales, since if a user is not presented with a relevant product when they search, they are likely to try another retailer. The search capability should strike a balance between delivering too many results and too few. *Channel Register* (2005) reports that dabs.com hopes to increase conversion rate by up to 50% by updating the site's search and navigation features. Current conversion rate is 3.5% and it is hoped this will be increased to nearer 5%.

Endeca's new search allows users to select products by attributes including price, brand and even size and weight. This method of narrowing down the search should result in the customer being left to choose from a list of 10 or 20 products rather than hundreds.

Another aspect of the business case for the new site is to ensure the customer makes the right decision since product returns are costly for dabs.com and annoying for the customer.

Jonathan Wall explained: 'When we launched the website in 1999 people knew what they wanted. Now we find a large tranche of customers might know the type of product they want to buy but not which model they want. The new site is about guiding them through the process.'

Accessibility

Since dabs.com has tech-savvy customers, it has to support them as they adopt new ways of browsing. Dabs.com found that by 1995 nearly a fifth of its users were using the Mozilla Firefox browser, so a further requirement for the new site was to make it accessible to users browsing with a range of browsers such as Firefox, Opera and Apple's Safari.

Marketing communications

Marketing communications approaches used by dabs.com are summarized in *Chapter 8, p. 417*, in the mini-case 'Electronic retailers cut back on their e-communications spend'. For customer acquisition, the main communications tools that are used are:

- Search engine marketing (the main investment)
- Referrals from affiliates (this has been reduced)
- Online display advertising on third-party sites (limited)
- PR
- Sponsorship (shirt sponsorship for Premiership team Fulham).

Sources: Channel Register (2005), *IT Week* (2003), NCC (2005)

Questions

1. The management of dabs.com have invested in several major upgrades to its online presence in order to improve the online customer experience. Assess the reasons for the need to invest in site upgrades by referring to the dabs.com example. To what extent do you think major, regular site upgrades are inevitable.
2. Compare the quality of the online customer experience of dabs.com by visiting the site and those of its competitors such as www.ebuyer.com and www.euroffice.com. Explain the categories of criteria you have used to make your assessment.

Focus on security design for e-business

Security is a prime concern of e-business managers. The principal concern is the security of information: both about customers and internal company data about finance, logistics, marketing and employees. Indeed we saw in *Chapter 4*, that securing customer information is a legal requirement under data protection laws in many countries. These risks apply to all companies, large and small. Larger companies tend to be more at risk from targeted attacks which are directed at disrupting services.

Information used within e-business systems must be safeguarded from a range of hazards. The range of risks faced by organizations are summarized in *Figure 11.17*. This shows the growing number of security breaches and how they often have the most severe impact on large organizations. You can see that they include both accidental and deliberate modification or deletion of information by people and also natural events which may destroy the media on which it is held.

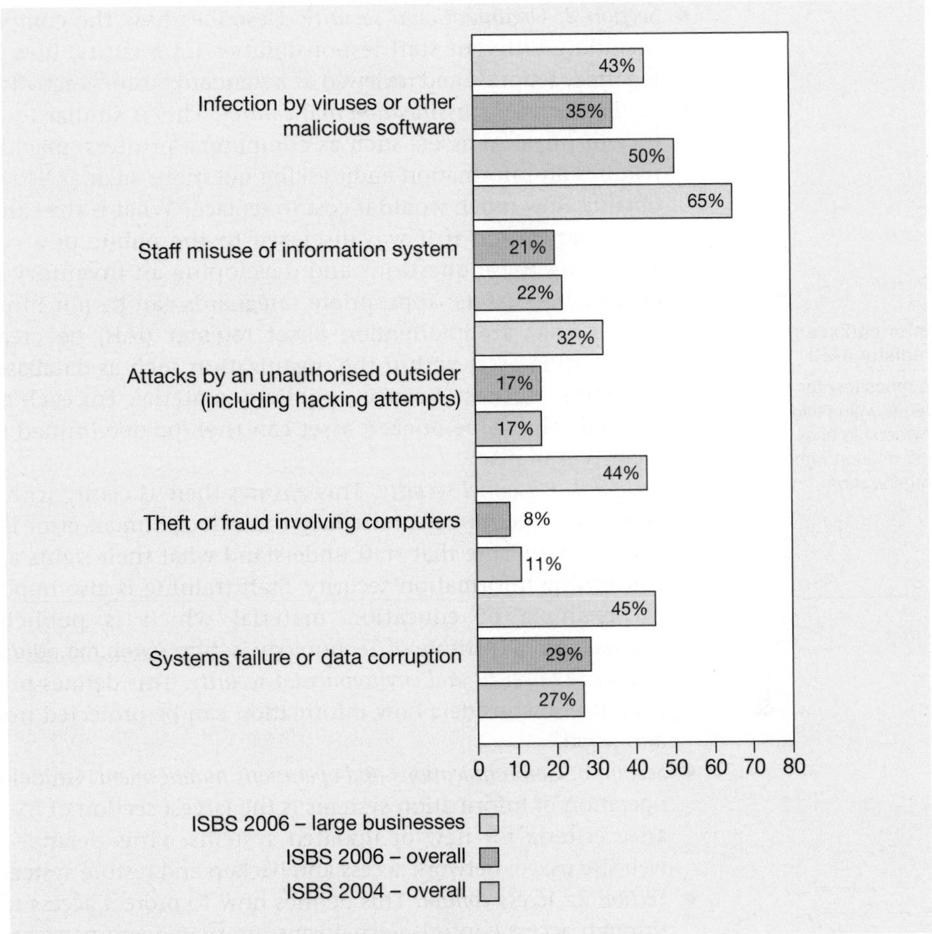

Figure 11.17 UK information security breaches

Source: DTI (2006) Department of Trade and Industry Information Security Breaches Survey. Executive Summary 2006

Information security management system
An organizational process to protect information assets.

Information security policy
A definition of the organizational approaches to information security and the responsibilities of employees in protecting information.

Given the extent of the security risks described in *Figure 11.17 (page 541)*, many organisations now implement a formal information security management system.

The information management strategy will mandate that there is an information security policy. This may be a policy developed in-house, or adoption of a security standard such as British Standard BS7799 which has now been upgraded and ratified as international standard ISO/IEC 17799.

I have based the coverage in this edition of *E-Business and E-Commerce Management* on ISO 17799 since this has comprehensive coverage of different risks and approaches to management of security. It recommends the following processes:

1 *Plan* – perform business risk analysis
2 *Do* – Internal controls to manage the applicable risks
3 *Check* – a management review to verify effectiveness
4 *Act* – action changes required as part of the review as necessary.

ISO 17799/BS 7799 provides an international standard which helps give a framework by which to manage the risks to the information evident from *Figure 11.17*. It requires the following areas of information security management to be defined.

- *Section 1: Security policy*. Describes the organization's requirements and scope of security for different business areas and sites. It also should demonstrate the support of senior management in controlling and owning security.

- *Section 2: Organizational security*. Describes how the company manages security including different staff responsibilities for security, how security incidents are reported, actioned and reviewed as a standard business activity to improve security.
- *Section 3: Asset classification and control*. This is similar to completing an inventory of physical assets such as computers, printers, machinery, vehicles, etc. It requires an information audit asking questions such as 'How much does it cost to obtain? How much would it cost to replace? What is the extent of damage done to the organization if it was disclosed to the public or a competitor?'. Through answering these questions and developing an inventory for different types of information assets, appropriate safeguards can be put in place. BS 7799 recommends that an information asset register (IAR) be created, detailing every information asset within the organization such as databases, personnel records, contracts, software licences, publicity material. For each asset, responsibility is defined. The value of each asset can then be determined to ensure appropriate security is in place.

Information asset register (IAR)
A repository for the types, value and ownership of all information within an organization.

- *Section 4: Personnel security*. This ensures there is clarity within job definitions and employment contracts, to reduce the risk of human error leading to information loss and to ensure that staff understand what their rights and responsibilities are concerning information security. Staff training is also important to achieve this. An example of education material which is publicly available for the Massachusetts Institute of Technology is: http://web.mit.edu/ist/topics/security/.
- *Section 5: Physical and environmental security*. This defines physical access to buildings. It also considers how information can be protected from threats such as fire and flood.
- *Section 6: Communications and operations management*. Guidelines on the day-to-day operation of information systems is the largest section of BS 7799. It covers acceptance criteria for new or updated systems, virus defence software, e-mail and web-site usage, network access and backup and restore systems.
- *Section 7: Access control*. This defines how to protect access to information systems through access control mechanisms (username and password procedures with different security clearance for different applications and types of information).
- *Section 8: System development and maintenance*. This specifies how new systems must be designed and procured with security in mind.
- *Section 9: Business continuity management*. Business continuity management or disaster recovery specifies how the organization will be able to continue to function in the event of a major event such as a fire or flood or other damage to information systems. Use of off-site backups and alternative systems is key to this.

Business continuity management or disaster recovery
Measures taken to ensure that information can be restored and accessed if the original information and access method are destroyed.

- *Section 10: Compliance*. This specifies how an organization will comply with the relevant UK and EU law related to information security management including Health and Safety legislation – The Data Protection Act, The Computer Misuse Act, The Designs, Copyrights and Patents Act, The Human Rights Act. Implementing BS 7799 is is a good way of helping ensure that a business does comply with these requirements. Regular audit and review needs to occur to ensure the organization remains compliant.

We will now cover some of the main threats to security in the e-business which need to be managed.

Managing computer viruses

Computer virus
A program capable of self-replication allowing it to spread from one machine to another. It may be malicious and delete data, or benign.

Computer viruses are a major threat to company and personal information since it is estimated that there are over 60,000 of them.

Types of virus

There are many different mechanisms by which computer viruses spread from one machine to another. All use some technique for the virus to reproduce itself or 'self-replicate' and then pass on to another machine. We will now review the main different types of computer virus which use different techniques to copy or replicate.

Boot-sector virus
Occupies boot record of hard and floppy disks and is activated during computer start-up.

Malicious virus
A virus that causes damage through destruction of data or software.

Worm
A small program that self-replicates and transfers across a network from machine to machine. A form of virus.

1 *Boot-sector virus*. Some of the most successful or most destructive viruses spread when floppy disks were widely used. These boot-sector viruses exist on the first sector on a floppy disk or hard disk known as the Master Boot Record (MBR). If a computer is switched on with an infected floppy disk in the drive this activates the virus which is then transferred to the hard disk and all floppy disks subsequently used in that machine.

   'Brain' was one of the first boot-sector viruses which emerged in 1986. A more recent example from the start of the 1990s is 'Michelangelo' which was one of the most destructive boot-sector viruses. The name was given to it by a researcher who noticed that its trigger date was the same as Michelangelo's birthday, 6 March (1475). This is a malicious virus which overwrites part of the hard disk and floppy disk thus destroying data.
2 *Worms*. A worm is a small computer program that replicates itself and then transfers itself from one machine to the next. One of the first worms was developed in 1988 by Robert Morris and is described in the section on hacking. Since then more malicious worms have been developed which now spread much more widely due to the current scale of the World Wide Web. Since no human interaction is required, worms can spread very rapidly. For example, the 'Code Red' worm replicated itself over 250,000 times in just nine hours on 19 July 2001. In 2003, the 'Slammer' worm exploited a security loophole in the Microsoft SQL server database product and rapidly infected 75,000 machines. Each infected machine sent out so much traffic that many other servers failed also. This was one of the fastest spreading viruses of all time, as *Figure 11.18* shows. In future it seems such worms will bring the Internet to a complete standstill.

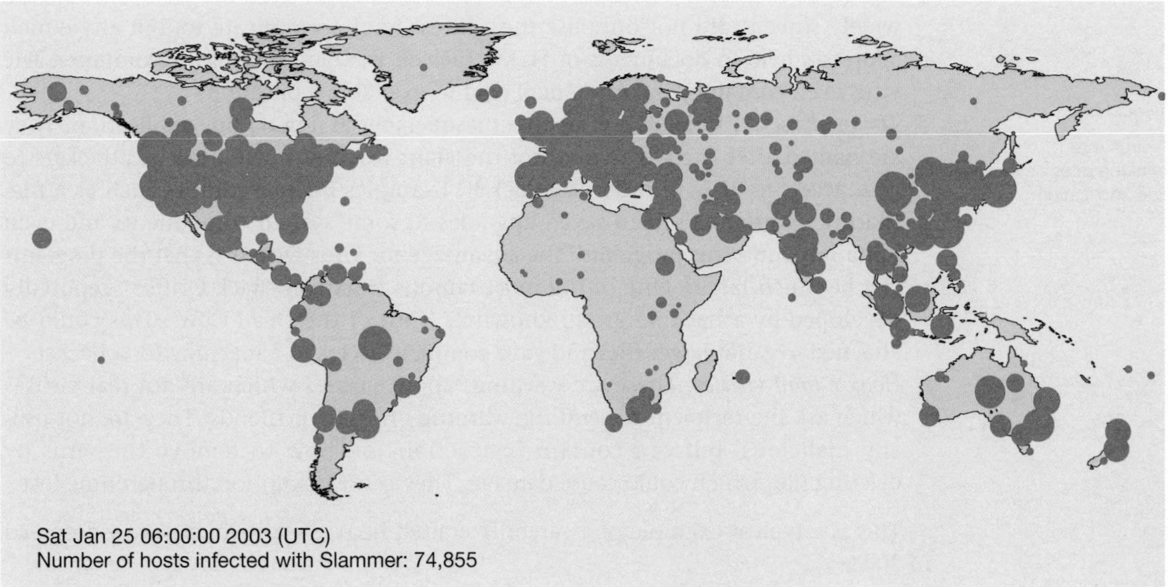

Figure 11.18 The geographic spread of the 'Slammer' worm 30 minutes after release

Source: Code Red (CRv2) Spread Animation. Copyright © 2001 The Regents of the University of California www-cse.ucsd.edu/~savage/papers/IEEESP03.pdf

3 *Macro-viruses*. Macro-viruses are a more recent phenomenon. They piggyback on documents created by office applications such as Microsoft Word and Excel. Office software such as this has a macro-facility to help users record common actions such as formatting or to develop more complex applications in Visual Basic for Applications (VBA). Macro-virus writers develop viruses that spread when a document is opened. Typically it will attach itself to all subsequent documents that are opened. Since documents and spreadsheets are commonly shared in and between offices, these viruses can spread very rapidly.

   One of the first Word macro viruses was the Word 'Concept' virus from 1995. One of the best known macro-viruses is 'Melissa'. This struck in March 1999 and it marked a new trend as it combined a macro virus with one that accessed the address book of Microsoft Outlook to e-mail itself to new victims. This was one of the fastest spreading viruses in history and it is estimated that it affected over a million PCs. In 2002, the author of the 'Melissa' virus, David L. Smith, was sentenced to 20 months in prison in the US.

4 *E-mail attachment viruses*. These viruses are activated when a user of an e-mail program opens an attachment. 'Melissa' is an example of such a virus. They typically replicate by accessing the address book and sending copies of an e-mail with the same attachment to everyone in the address book. Effectively they are then acting as a worm. An even more destructive virus was launched in 2000. The 'Love Bug' virus contains the subject line 'I love you', while the message contains the text 'kindly check the attached LOVELETTER from me' which is an attached file called LOVE-LETTER-FOR-YOU.TXT.VBS. The virus deleted image and audio files and accessed Internet servers to send out different versions of itself. According to Click Z (2003) it was estimated that nearly $9 billion damage was done through this virus. Much of the costs is not the lost of data, but the cost of hiring specialists to rectify the problem or staff time lost.

   More recent e-mail worm viruses have been even more damaging. ClickZ (2003) reports that the e-mail worm viruses such as 'Klez', 'Blaster' and 'So-Big' cause billions of dollars of damage. 'So-Big' alone is estimated to have caused around $30 billion of economic damage. 'So-Big' was activated by an attachment and spread widely since it did not only use the address book to replicate to, but any e-mail addresses held in documents or HTML files on the hard disk of the computer. The virus even contained its own e-mail engine to enable replication.

Trojan
A virus that masquerades as a bona fide application.

5 *Trojan viruses*. A **trojan** is a virus that masquerades as a bona fide application. They are named after the Greek myth of the giant wooden horse used by attackers to gain access to Troy in order to attack it. Examples include utilities such as a file-sharing program, a screen saver, upgrades to some system components and even imitation anti-virus programs. The advantage for virus writers is that the programs can be much larger. One of the most famous trojans is 'Back Orifice', reputedly developed by a hacking group known as 'Cult of the Dead Cow'. This could be attached to other larger files and gave complete access to a machine for a hacker.

6 *Hoax e-mail viruses*. These are warnings about viruses which are not real viruses which ask the recipient to send the warning on to their friends. They are not usually malicious, but can contain instructions on how to remove the virus by deleting files which could cause damage. They cause disruption through time lost.

This is a typical example of a carefully crafted hoax e-mail which was widespread in 2003:

```
To all of my email contacts,

Unfortunately a virus has been passed to me and many other people,
you may already have it from some other source - through an address
book virus which also infected my address book. Since you are in my
address book, you will probably find it in your computer, too. The
virus (called jdbg.exe) is not detected by Norton or McAfee Anti-
virus systems.

The virus sits quietly for 14 days before damaging the system. It
is sent automatically by 'messenger' and by address book, whether
or not you sent e-mail to your contacts. Basically, that means you
will pass it along Unknowingly, as I did. I was sent this email and
am now passing it on to you as to how to check for the virus and
how to get rid of it. Please do this! It's very simple to do and
takes about 3 mins.

1. Go to Start, then click your 'Find' or 'Search' option
2. In the folder option, type the name... jdbgmgr.exe
   <more instructions follow>

If you find the virus, you must contact all the people in your
Address Book so that they may eradicate the virus from their own
address books.

To do this:

1. Open a new e-mail message
2. click the icon Address Book next to 'TO'
3. Highlight every name and add to "BCC"
4. Copy this message and paste to e-mail

This will affect everyone in your address book. So send now!
```

Protecting computer systems against viruses

All organizations require a policy to combat the potential impact of viruses given the frequency with which new, damaging viruses are released. Even individual computer users at home should think through the steps they can take to counter viruses. There are two approaches that can be combined to counter viruses. These are using the right tools and educating staff to change practices.

Anti-virus software
Software to detect and eliminate viruses.

Anti-virus software is well known as a tool to protect systems from viruses. Many businesses and homes now use products such as McAfee Virus Scan and Symantec Norton Anti-Virus to protect themselves against the threat of viruses. Unfortunately, a lot more action is required than initial purchase for the anti-virus software to be effective. We have seen above that new viruses are continually released. It is therefore essential that regular updates be obtained and this often doesn't happen since a process has to be in place to trigger updates such as a monthly update. Typically, updates to the entire software aren't required, but to the signature files which are used to identify viruses. In smaller organizations without a dedicated computer support team it is difficult to maintain up-to-date versions of the signature files. One effective solution is to use tools which provide automatic updates over the Internet as soon as a new release becomes available. This requires continuous access to the Internet to be effective and several new updates may be needed each week.

Companies also need to decide on the frequency of scanning memory and computer files, since a full-scan on start-up can take a long time. Most anti-virus software now seeks to identify viruses when they first arrive (real-time scanning). A further issue is how good the anti-virus tool is at identifying e-mail and macro-viruses, since it is less straightforward for these types of virus to be identified.

Managed e-mail service
Receipt and transmission of e-mails is managed by a third party.

Another approach to countering e-mail viruses is to use an external managed e-mail service which scans e-mails before they arrive in the organization and then scans e-mails for viruses when they are sent. For example, Messagelabs (www.messagelabs.com) scans 30 million e-mails a day for 7,500 companies worldwide. Managed e-mail services are likely to be more effective than using internal anti-virus software since the service providers are experts in this field. They will also be able to identify and respond to e-mail worm attacks more rapidly.

To summarize, organizations need a policy to be developed for use of anti-virus software. This should specify:

1 The preferred anti-virus software to be used on all machines.
2 The frequency and mechanism for updating anti-virus software.
3 The frequency with which the whole end-user PC is system-scanned for viruses.
4 Organizational blocking of attachments with uncommon extensions.
5 Organizational disabling of macros in office applications.
6 Scanning to be performed on mail servers when e-mails are first received and before viruses are sent.
7 Recommendations on use of spam-filtering software.
8 Backup and recovery mechanisms.

Education of staff in identifying and then acting upon the different types of virus can also limit the impact of viruses. Apart from Internet worms which execute automatically, some steps can be taken to reduce the risks from all the types of viruses identified above. Some general instructions can then be developed as part of a policy to reduce the risk of virus infection and transmission. Many of these apply also to home machines; these are:

1 Do not switch off machines when the floppy disk is still in the drive (reduces transmission of boot-sector drives). PCs can also be configured so that they do not boot off the floppy drive.
2 Do not open attachments to e-mails from people you don't know (Reduce transmission of e-mail attachment viruses). Since some viruses will be sent from trusted sources, only open attachments which look legitimate, for example Word documents with relevant names. Some viruses use file extensions that are not common used such as .pif, .scr or .vbs. Viewing documents rather than opening them for editing can also reduce the risk of transmission.
3 Download software only from the official source, and always check for viruses before installing the software (reduces risk of trojan horse viruses).
4 Disable or turn off macros in Word or Excel unless you use them regularly (reduces risk of macro-viruses).
5 Back-up important files daily if this function is not performed by a system administrator.

Controlling information service usage

Issues in controlling information service typically involve one of two problems from the employer's perspective. First, hardware and software resources provided for work purposes are used for personal purposes, thus reducing productivity. Secondly, monitoring the use of information introduces legal issues of surveillance. Monitoring of information service usage includes checking for:

- Use of e-mail for personal purposes.
- Inappropriate use of e-mail, possibly leading to legal action against the company.
- Use of Internet or web sites for personal use.

The problems in e-mail usage are covered in the next section on e-mail management. The extent of these issues, particularly in larger organizations is apparent from *Figure 11.19*.

Monitoring of electronic communications

Employee communications monitoring
Companies monitor staff e-mails and web sites they access.

Employee communications monitoring or surveillance is used by organizations to reduce productivity losses through time wasting. Time can be wasted when a member of staff spends time when they are paid to work checking personal e-mail messages or accessing the Internet for personal interests.

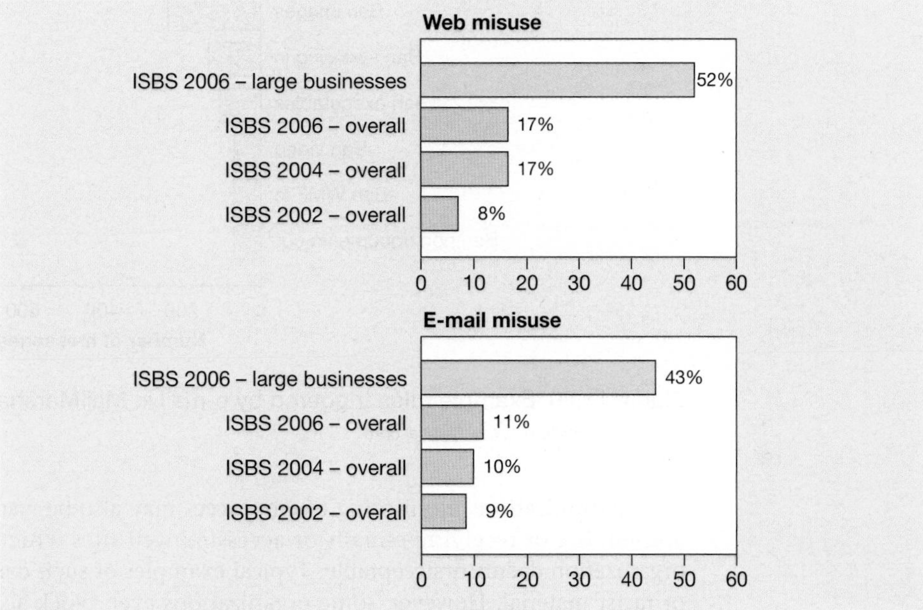

Figure 11.19 Staff misuse of web and e-mail
Source: DTI (2006) *Department of Trade and Industry Information Security Breaches Survey*

Simple calculations highlight the wastage when staff time is spent on non-productive work. If an employee earning £25,000 per year, spends 30 minutes each day of a 5-day week answering personal e-mails or visiting non-work-related web sites, this will cost the company over £1,500 per year. For a company with 100 employees, where the average employee works 46 weeks per year, this amounts to over £150,000 per year or the cost of several new employees! Activities such as using streaming media to view the news or download audio clips can also place strain on the company networks if they are common.

A typical example of alleged time wasting where the company dismissed the employee involved Lois Franxhi, a 28-year-old IT manager who was sacked in July 1998 for making nearly 150 searches over four days in office hours for a holiday. She claimed unfair dismissal – she was pregnant at the time of the dismissal. As with many unfair dismissals, the case was not clear-cut, with Mrs Franxhi claiming the company sacked her because of sex discrimination. The tribunal dismissed these claims, finding that the employee had lied about the use of the Internet, saying she had only used it for one lunchtime when in fact records showed she had used it over four days.

More recently DTI (2006) reported on a member of staff at a small services company who accessed adult web sites at work. He used someone else's computer to conceal his activity. In another case, a lovesick employee at a medium-sized manufacturer spent up to six hours a day on a dating agency web site! The survey reports that

> *What hurts companies is the number of these incidents they suffer, more than one a day on average. While the median was only a few incidents a year, some small companies reported hundreds of e-mail abuses every day.*

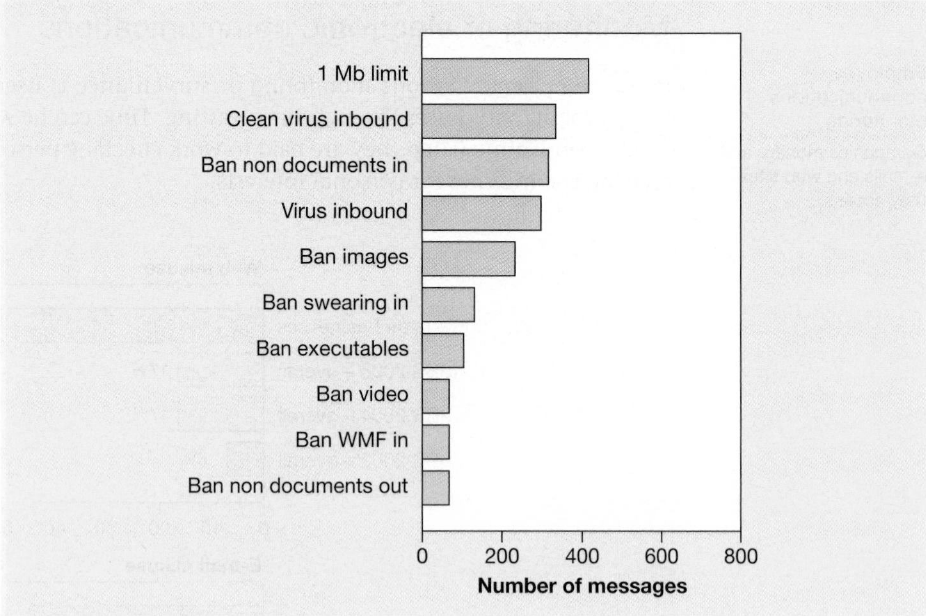

Figure 11.20 **Example rules triggered by e-mail in MailMarshal SMTP from Marshal**
Source: Marshal Ltd. www.marshal.com

Communications monitoring of employees may also be warranted if it is felt they are sending or receiving e-mails or accessing web sites which contain content the organization deems unacceptable. Typical examples of such content are pornography or racist material. However, some organizations even block access to news, sports or web-based e-mail sites because of the amount of time staff spend in accessing them. To define permissible content, many organizations now have acceptable-use policies. For example, many universities, at log-in, or in computer labs and libraries have notices about 'acceptable-use policy'. This will describe the types of material it is not acceptable to access and is also a means of explaining monitoring procedures.

Acceptable-use policy
Statement of employee activities involving use of networked computers that are not considered acceptable by management.

Scanning and filtering are the two most common form of monitoring. Scanning software identifies the content of e-mails sent or received and web pages accessed. Tools such as WebSense or MailMarshal SMTP from Marshal or Web Marshal will look for the occurrence of particular words or images – pornography is indicated by skin colour tones for example. Rules will also be set up, for example to ban e-mail attachments over a particular size or containing swearing as indicated by *Figure 11.20*. Such tools can also give a picture of the most popular types of site or content. This might show, for example, how much time is being wasted accessing news and sports sites.

Scanning software
Identifies e-mail or web-page access that breaches company guidelines or acceptable-use policies.

Such software usually also has blocking or filtering capabilities. Filtering software such as Websense (www.websense.com) can detect and block other activities such as:

Filtering software
Software that blocks specified content or activities.

- Peer-to-peer (P2P) file sharing, for example of MP3 audio files
- Instant messaging using Yahoo! Messenger or Microsoft Instant Messenger
- The use of streaming media (e.g. audio and video) and other high-bandwidth applications
- Accessing specified sites, e.g. some companies block all news sites such as www.bbc.co.uk or www.msn.co.uk since analysis has shown that staff spend so much time using them. Access to personal e-mail programs such as Yahoo! Mail or Hotmail may also be blocked. This would not be popular at universities!
- Spyware which seeks to send out information collected from computers
- Adware programs which place adverts or pop-ups
- Employee hacking.

Websense and similar products can block sites in different categories, for different types of staff, according to the acceptable-use policy of the organization using a database (www.websense.com/products/about/database/categories.cfm) that contains over 1.5 million web sites in many categories of which we list just some to illustrate the degree of control available to the employer. Example of the categories include:

- Abortion or Pro-Choice or Pro-Life
- Adult Material
- Parent category that contains the categories: Adult Content, Lingerie and Swimsuit, Nudity, Sex, Sex Education
- Adult Content
- Advocacy Groups
- Business and Economy
- Financial Data and Services
- Drugs
- Education
- Entertainment
- Gambling
- Games
- Government
- Military – sites sponsored by branches or agencies of the armed services.
- Political Organizations – sites sponsored by or providing information about political parties and interest groups focused on elections or legislation.
- Health
- Information Technology
- Search Engines and Portals – sites that support searching the web, news groups, or indices or
- Web-based E-mail – sites that host web-based e-mail.
- Job Search
- Militancy and Extremist
- News and Media
- Racism and Hate
- Religion
- Shopping
- Professional and Worker Organizations
- Society and Lifestyles
- Hobbies
- Personals and Dating
- Sports
- Travel
- Vehicles
- Violence
- Weapons.

Consider how many of those listed above you may visit when studying, at business or at home. It will be apparent that if an employer wishes, they can block virtually every site. I know of some organizations in the UK that block access to all news sites and have worked in an organization that even blocked access to search engines such as Google and web mail such as Hotmail and Yahoo! Mail. When search engines are blocked, management-grade employees are likely to be restricted in their understanding of the business environment and are restricted from self-development! Employees are likely to view negatively an employer who does not trust them to use their time judiciously.

The extent of monitoring and blocking is indicated by *Figure 11.21*.

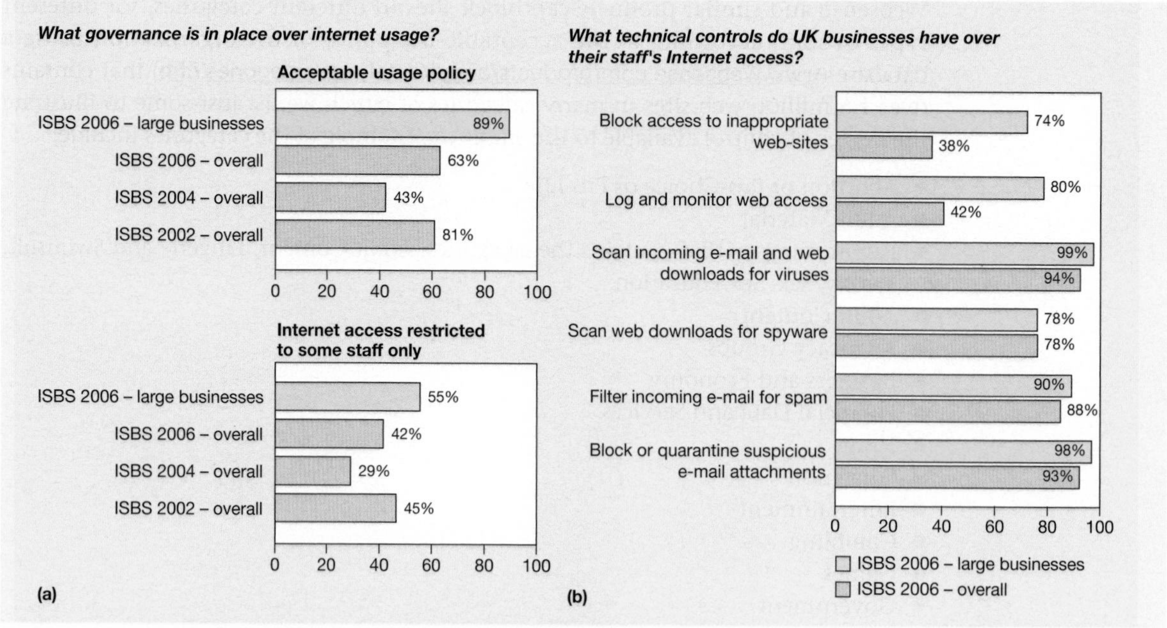

Figure 11.21 Employee controls (a) governance and (b) technical solutions

Source: DTI (2006) *Department of Trade and Industry Information Security Breaches Survey*

Employee monitoring legislation

Although employee monitoring falls within the remit of European data protection law, the Data Protection Act was not originally devised to cover employee monitoring. To help clarify the law on employee monitoring in the UK, in June 2003, the Office of the Information Commissioner published 'Monitoring at Work', the third part of the Employment Practices Data Protection Code. The code provides practical guidance for employers on how they should approach monitoring of employees in the workplace. These guidelines seek to achieve a balance between employees' wishes for privacy and the need for employers to run their businesses efficiently. The code does not prevent monitoring, but is based on the concept of proportionality. Proportionality means that any adverse impacts from monitoring must be justified by the benefits to the employer and others. This addresses an apparent anomaly in that data protection law refers to individual consent for processing of personal data being 'freely given' and it is not normal for employees to give this consent. The code makes it clear that individual consent is not required provided that an organization has undertaken an 'impact assessment' of monitoring activities.

Impact assessment
An assessment of the employee monitoring process in the workplace to identify improvements to minimise infringement of employee privacy.

According to the code, an impact assessment involves:

- *identifying clearly the* ***purpose(s)*** *behind the monitoring arrangement and the benefits it is likely to deliver*
- *identifying any likely* ***adverse impact*** *of the monitoring arrangement*
- *considering* ***alternatives*** *to monitoring or different ways in which it might be carried out*
- *taking into account the* ***obligations*** *that arise from monitoring*
- *judging whether monitoring is* ***justified****.*

The code does not make specific recommendations about monitoring of e-mails or web traffic, but it does refer to them as typical monitoring activities which it suggests may be acceptable if staff are informed of them and an impact assessment has been conducted. The code does ask employers to consider whether alternatives may be better than systematic monitoring. Alternatives may include training or clear communication from managers and analysis of stored e-mails where it is thought an infringement has taken place rather than continuous monitoring. For example, automated monitoring is preferred to IT staff viewing personal e-mails of staff. The code also makes clear that the company should not undertake any covert monitoring; so it should be open about all the types of monitoring that occur. In universities, as mentioned above, at log-in, or in computer labs and libraries there is often a notice about 'acceptable-use policy'. This will describe the types of material it is not acceptable to access and is also a means of explaining monitoring procedures. It does appear, that if an employee was disciplined or dismissed for sending too many personal e-mails for instance, they would have legitimate grounds to appeal if they had not been informed that monitoring was occurring and their managers had not made it clear that this was acceptable practice.

Covert monitoring
Monitoring which the employer undertakes without notification of staff.

Other European countries have different laws on monitoring. Some such as Germany are much more restrictive than the UK in terms of the level of monitoring that organizations are able to perform. Organizations opening offices abroad clearly need to be aware of local variations in legal constraints on employee monitoring and data protection.

E-mail management

E-mail is now an essential business communication tool and is also widely used for personal use. The popularity of e-mail as a communication tool has resulted in billions of messages being sent each day as the box 'E-mail volume' shows. For the individual, managing these communications in their e-mail inbox is rapidly becoming impossible! For the information services manager and indeed any business manager, there are three main controls that need to be considered to reduce the amount of time effectively wasted by staff reading e-mail. Controls can be introduced as part of an e-mail management policy to minimize the volume of:

1. Spam (unsolicited e-mail).
2. Internal business e-mail.
3. External business e-mail.
4. Personal e-mail (friends and family).

Despite the potential time loss through e-mail misuse an AMA (2003) survey suggested that only 34% of employers had a written e-mail retention and deletion policy in place. Furthermore, there are issues of legal liability about what employees say in their e-mail which also need to be considered. We will look at the risk and controls of each e-mail risk in turn.

E-mail volume

Lyman and Varian (2003) compiled research summarizing the volume of e-mail messaging:

- In 2002 it was estimated that there were 31 billion e-mails sent each day or 400,000 terabytes of new information each year worldwide.
- The volume of e-mails amounts to 1,829 terabytes per day or 3.35 terabytes per year.
- By 2006, e-mail volumes were expected to increase to 60 billion per day.
- The number of business e-mails sent each day varies between 10 and 50 per person according to the type of role of the individual. A similar number are received each day for processing.

→

- The volume and proportion of spam has increased dramatically from one in every thousand e-mails in 2001 to one in every three e-mails as is shown in *Figure 11.22*.
- The amount of time spent reading and writing e-mail can amount to over an hour per working day. Incredibly, a 2003 survey by the American Management Association found that the average employee spends 25% of the workday on e-mail, with 8% of workers devoting over four hours a day to e-mail! This highlights the importance of making e-mail use efficient.
- Despite these problems, 86% of respondents still agreed that e-mail has made them more efficient.

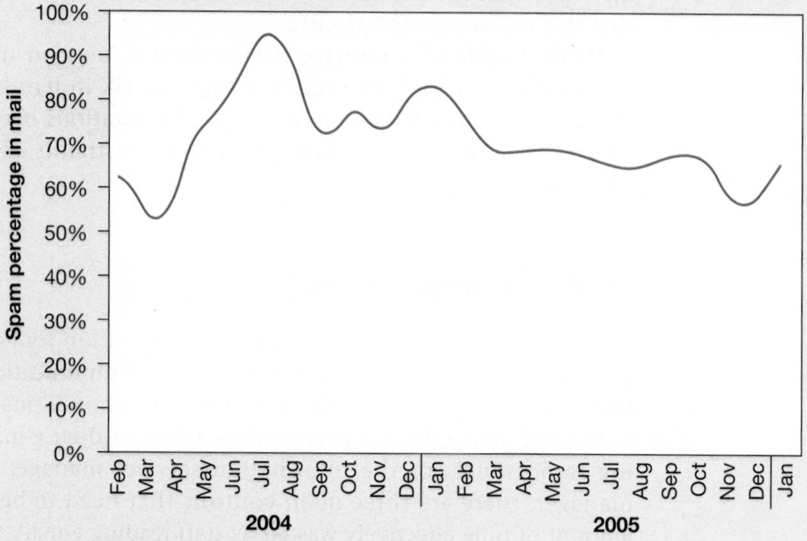

Figure 11.22 Proportion of global e-mail traffic which is spam
Source: MessageLabs (2006)

1 Minimizing spam (unsolicited e-mail)

Spam
Unsolicited e-mail (usually bulk-mailed and untargeted).

Spam is now a potential problem for every company and individual using the Internet as suggested by *Figure 11.22*. At the time of writing over 90% of e-mails were spam or virus-related in some countries and individuals whose inboxes are unprotected can receive hundreds of spam e-mails each day. Originally spam was best known as a tinned meat (a contraction of 'spiced ham'), but a modern acronym that has been devised is 'Sending Persistent Annoying e-Mail'. The negative perception of e-mail derives from the many unsolicited e-mails we all receive from unscrupulous 'get-rich-quick merchants'. The spammers rely on sending out millions of e-mails in the hope that even if there is only a 0.01% response they may make some money, if not necessarily get rich.

Legal measures to combat spam have had limited success. So, many information services managers are now using a range of methods to control spam. *Figure 11.23* summarizes alternative techniques to combat spam. *Figure 11.23(a)* is the original situation where all mail is allowed into an inbox. *Figure 11.23(b)* uses different techniques to reduce the volume of e-mail through identification and blocking of spam. *Figure 11.23(c)* is a closed inbox where only known, trusted e-mails are allowed into an organization.

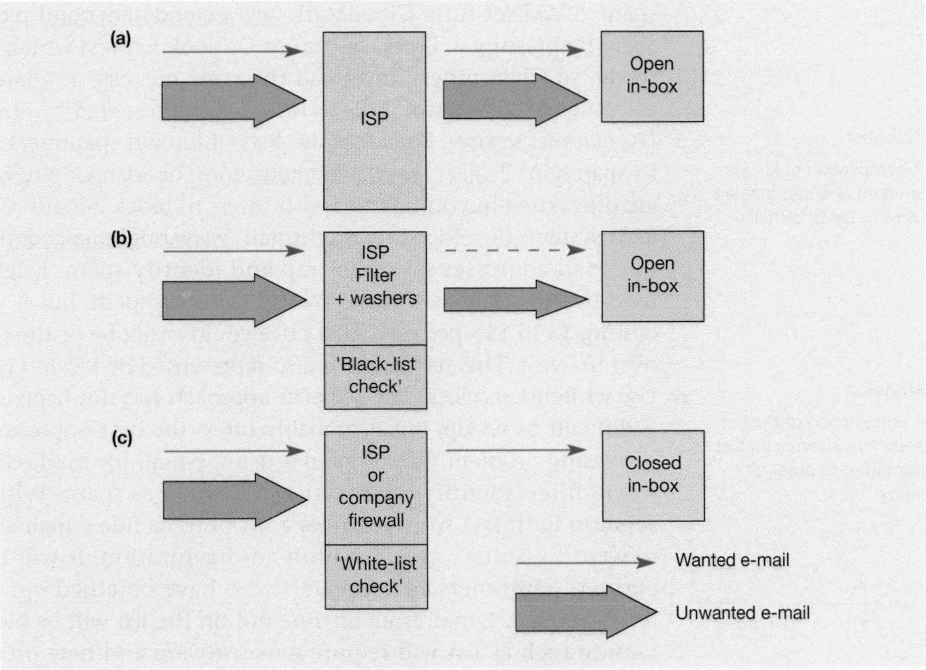

Figure 11.23 Progression of attempts to combat spam

The full range of techniques that can be used in combination to combat spam include:

1 *Avoid harvesting of addresses*. Spammers harvest e-mails from e-mail addresses published on web pages and even the program code used to convert online form content to an e-mail to a company. By reducing the number of e-mail addresses published, or changing their format, the number of e-mail addresses can be reduced.
2 *Educate staff not to reply to spam*. The worst thing an individual can do on receiving spam is to reply to it to complain or to attempt to unsubscribe. This merely confirms to the spammer that the address is valid and they are likely to send more junk e-mail and sell your address on to other spammers. In Microsoft Outlook 2003 images are not enabled since downloading images in an HTML e-mail is a sign to spammers that yours is a valid address.
3 *Use filters*. Filtering software can identify Spam from keywords and phrases such as 'For Free', 'Sex' or 'Viagra' contained in the subject line, from address and body copy of the e-mail. E-mail filters are provided for users of web-based e-mail such as Hotmail and Yahoo! Mail with e-mails placed in a Junk Mail folder. Microsoft Outlook Express has its own filter. Filtering software such as Mailwasher (www.mailwasher.net), Mcaffee Spamkiller (www.mcaffee.com) can also be installed. Unfortunately, many spammers know how to avoid the keywords in the filters. The problem with filters and other services is that there can be 'false positives' or valid e-mails that are classified as junk. Additionally, spammers find ways to work around filters by putting 'gobbeldy gook' in the footer of their messages that is not recognized by the filters or using variants of words such as V1agra, or Via-gra. Review of these may still be necessary. This technique is represented by *Figure 11.23(b)*.
4 *Use 'peer-to-peer' blocking services*. These take advantage of humans being good at identifying spam and then notifying a central server which keeps an index of all

E-mail filter
Software used to identify spam according to its characteristics such as keywords.

spam. SPAMNet from CloudMark (www.cloudmark.com) requires users to identify spam by pressing a 'Block' button in Outlook Express which then updates a central server, so when others download the same message at a later time, it is automatically identified as spam. This technique is represented by *Figure 11.23(b)*.

Blacklist
A compilation of known sources of spam that are used to block e-mail.

5 *Use blacklist services.* **Blacklists** are lists of known spammers such as those reported to Spamhaus Project (www.spamhaus.com) or SpamCop (www.spamcop.net). They are often used in conjunction with filters to block e-mails. One of the most widely used systems developed by Brightmail (www.brightmail.com) uses a global network of e-mail addresses set up to trap and identify spam. Brightmail is increasingly used by ISPs such as BT OpenWorld to block spam, but it is not a cheap service, costing \$5 to \$15 per year. This price could easily be justified by the time staff save over the year. This technique is also represented by *Figure 11.23(b)*.

Whitelist
A compilation of trusted sources of e-mail that is permitted to enter an inbox.

6 Use whitelist services. The **whitelist** approach has not been adopted widely since it is difficult to set up, but it probably offers the best opportunity for the future. An increasing problem for companies using e-mail for marketing is 'false positives' – where filters identify their legitimate e-mail as spam. Whitelist services are one solution to this. A whitelist gives a list of bona fide e-mail addresses that are likely to want to contact people within an organization. It will include all employees, partners, customers and suppliers who have obtained opt-in from employees to receive e-mail. E-mail from anyone not on the list will be blocked. However, maintaining such as list will require new software and new procedures for keeping it up-to-date. One approach that has been developed in the US is the concept of a 'bonded sender' developed by Ironport (www.bondedsender.com). Senders of opt-in e-mail post a financial bond to prove they are a reputable company. Senders of spam would not be able to afford to pay the bond. Recipients who feel they have received an unsolicited e-mail from a bonded sender can complain to their ISP, IT manager or IronPort, and a financial charge is debited from the bond. Another service rapidly gaining acceptance is Habeas (www.habeas.com) where special text (a 'warrant mark') is sent in outbound mail, which allows filtering systems to identify the email as 'not spam'. This technique is represented by *Figure 11.23(c)*.

Providers such as Sendmail (www.sendmail.com), GoodMail (www.goodmail.com) and the Yahoo!-sponsored DomainKeys and Microsoft-sponsored Sender Policy Framework have developed 'sender authentication technology' which allows organizations to verify the source of a message before accepting it by automatically checking if it came from where it claims it did. The raft of measures described in this section should eventually spell the end for spammers, but when is unclear.

Challenge/respond system
An e-mail from an unknown source is challenged by another e-mail which is used to prove the originator is a valid sender.

A further approach is **challenge/respond**. Here, if a message is received from a person who is not on the whitelist, a message is sent to that person requesting that they click on a link to verify that they are a genuine person and not a spammer (spammers would not have time to verify all addresses since it cannot be done automatically). Of course, this presents a problem for legitimate commercial e-mail marketers.

7 *Ensure anti-virus software and blocking is effective.* E-mail viruses are increasingly perpetrated by spammers since they are a method of harvesting e-mail addresses. Virus protection needs to be updated daily with new signatures if addresses are not to be captured through viruses.

2 Minimizing internal business e-mail

The ease and low cost of sending e-mails to a distribution list or copying people in on a message can lead to each person in an organization receiving many messages each day from colleagues within the organization. This problem tends to be worse in large organizations, simply because each individual has a larger address book of colleagues.

A press release from the British Computer Society summarizing research conducted by the Henley Management College released on 20 December 2002 suggested that a lot of time is wasted by managers when processing irrelevant e-mails. It suggested that 'UK management is now suffering acute stress from "Information Overload"' with executives, 'complaining of being deluged by e-mail that demands a daily average of two hours of executive time'; particularly frustrating is that nearly a third of e-mail received is deemed to be irrelevant and much is rated of poor quality. Further findings included:

- Of seven common management tasks, meetings took up 2.8 hours on average, dealing with e-mail came second with an average of 1.7 hours and accessing information from the Internet accounted for a further 0.75 of an hour.
- Respondents reported receiving on average 52 e-mails per day while 7 per cent received 100 e-mails per day or more.
- Managers reported that less than half of e-mails (42 per cent) warranted a response, 35 per cent were read for information only and nearly a quarter were deleted immediately. On average only 30 per cent of e-mails were classified as essential, 37 per cent as important and 33 per cent as irrelevant or unnecessary.
- Despite the reservations about the quality and volume of e-mails received the majority of respondents (81 per cent) regarded e-mail as the communications technology which has had the most positive impact on the way they carried out their job, alongside the Internet and the mobile phone.

To overcome this type of business e-mail overuse, companies are starting to develop e-mail policies which explain best practice. For example, considering the way that the authors of Chaffey and Wood (2005) use their e-mail, we quickly devised these guidelines:

- Only send the e-mail to employees for which it is essential to inform or act upon;
- Banning certain types of e-mails, such as the classic 'e-mail to the person who sits next to you' or individuals in the same office (although there are strong arguments for this since e-mail is an asynchronous medium and colleagues are not always available or don't wish to be disturbed);
- Avoid 'flaming' – these are aggressive e-mails which often put voice to feelings that wouldn't be said face-to-face. If you receive an annoying e-mail it is best to wait 10 minutes to cool down rather than 'flaming' the sender;
- Avoid 'trolls' – these are a species of e-mail closely related to flame-mails. They are postings to a newsgroup deliberately posted to 'wind up' the recipient. They are best ignored;
- Combine items from separate e-mails during the day or week into a single e-mail for the day/week;
- Write clear subject lines;
- Structure e-mails so that they can be scanned quickly using sub-heads and numbered and bulleted lists;
- Make follow-up actions clear;
- When reading e-mail, use folders to categorize e-mails according to content and priority;
- Perform e-mail reading and checking in batches, e.g. once per morning/afternoon rather than being alerted to and opening every e-mail that arrives;
- Delete e-mails which are not required for future reference (large volumes are taken up on servers through staff not deleting e-mails and their attachments);
- etc. – all common-sense guidelines, but often common sense isn't common!

3 Minimizing external business e-mail

As well as spam which is unsolicited and usually untargeted, people within an organization can also receive many e-mails from legitimate suppliers. For example, an IT manager might receive e-mails from hardware and software manufacturers, service providers, event/conference organizers and e-newsletters from magazines. These sources of e-mail are not usually controlled through company e-mail policies; it is usually left to the judgement of the individual employee to select appropriate e-newsletters. The technologies to block e-mails, such as spam filters, will not usually block such messages, but primitive filters may, if they block words such as 'Offer' or 'Free' which also appear in legitimate business e-mails. The challenge/respond system will still enable such e-mails to be received. Additionally, technology described in *Chapter 12* is available to block access to certain web sites such as news or entertainment sites, and this software renders e-newsletters less effective since images are not downloaded from blocked sites. An approach used by many individuals to help control information from these sources is to use a separate e-mail address from the main inbox when opting in. This could be a Hotmail or Yahoo! Mail address and this form of e-newsletter can be read at the office or at home and is also available when the individual changes jobs.

4 Minimizing personal e-mail (friends and family)

Although there are many surveys about the volume of spam and amount of time spent processing e-mail at work, there is relatively little data published on the amount of time spent writing personal e-mails. Most of it is not independent; it is commissioned by vendors of software for monitoring e-mail use. However, using e-mail for personal use is going to occur if there are no measures to stop it.

One example of misuse of e-mails was highlighted in 2003, when UK mobile phone retailer Phones4U became the first UK company to ban the use of internal e-mail across the entire business. This was partly as a result of the use of e-mail for personal purposes and partly due to the management feeling other methods were better for internal communication. *Computer Weekly* (2003) claimed that the move will save each employee three hours a day, adding up to £1m per month. Surprisingly, the article reported that with '13,000 internal e-mails passing through its system every week, individual e-mail accounts were taking up too much of the IT department's time. Communication between Phones4U head office and its stores now occurs by telephone and the company intranet, which is used for ordering equipment and services. This is already showing positive results.'

The move was instigated by John Caudwell, the company's multi-millionaire owner, who believed his 2,500 staff had been spending too much time sending and receiving e-mails and not enough time dealing face-to-face with customers. He was quoted as saying:

> *I saw that email was insidiously invading Phones4U so I banned it immediately, Management and staff at HQ and in the stores were beginning to show signs of being constrained by email proliferation – the ban brought an instant, dramatic and positive effect. Phones4U staff have been told to get off the keyboards, get face-to-face or on the phone to colleagues.*

It doesn't seem as if all companies will follow suit: Charles Dunstone, chief executive of rival Carphone Warehouse, said: 'We trust our people to know how to use email properly'. Similar smaller-scale e-mail bans have come from Nestlé Rowntree and Liverpool City Council.

To minimize this problem and some of the problems of over-using e-mail for business use, the following steps can be taken:

1 Create written guidelines defining the policy on acceptable e-mail use and disciplinary procedures for when guidelines are breached;
2 Use increasing levels of control or sanctions for breaches including performance reviews, verbal warnings, removal of e-mail privileges, termination and legal action.
3 Providing training for staff on acceptable and efficient e-mail use;
4 Monitor e-mails for signatures of personal use and any breaches of the policy, e.g. swearing, and take action accordingly.

Hacking

Hacking

The process of gaining unauthorized access to computer systems, typically across a network.

'Hacking' refers to the process of gaining unauthorized access to computer systems, typically across a network. Hacking can take different forms. Hacking for monetary gain is usually aimed at identity theft where personal details and credit card details are accessed for the purpose of fraud. Hacking could also occur with malicious intent. For example, a former employee might gain access to a network with a view to deleting files or passing information on to a competitor. Some of the notorious hackers who have been prosecuted, but often seem to have ultimately gained from their misdemeanours, are:

- *Robert Morris* – The son of the chief scientist at the US National Computer Security Center, this graduate student created a destructive Internet worm in 1988 which took advantage of a security flaw in the Unix operating system. When unleashed it caused thousands of computers to crash. The disruption was partly accidental and he released instructions to system administrators on how to resolve the problem. He was sentenced to three years of probation, 400 hours of community service and a fine of $10,050. He is now an assistant professor at MIT, where he originally released his worm to disguise its creation at Cornell University.
- *Kevin Poulsen* – In 1990 Poulsen took over all telephone lines into the Los Angeles radio station KIIS-FM, assuring that he would be the 102nd caller. Poulsen won a Porsche 944 S2. This was one of many hacks conducted while he worked for hi-tech company SRI International by day and hacked at night. He was eventually traced and, in June 1994, he pleaded guilty to seven counts of mail, wire and computer fraud, money laundering, and obstruction of justice, and was sentenced to 51 months in prison and ordered to pay $56,000 in restitution. It was the longest sentence ever given for hacking. He is now a computer security journalist.
- *Kevin Mitnick* – The first hacker to be featured on an FBI 'Most wanted' poster, Mitnick was arrested in 1995. He later pleaded guilty to four counts of wire fraud, two counts of computer fraud and one count of illegally intercepting a wire communication. He admitted that he broke into computer systems and stole proprietary software belonging to Motorola, Novell, Fujitsu, Sun Microsystems and other companies. He was sentenced to 46 months. Following his sentence he became a security consultant and is now a leading commentator on security and has made many TV appearances and written books and articles.
- *Vladimir Levin* – A graduate mathematician who was part of a Russian gang that reputedly masterminded a $10 million fraud of Citibank. Arrested by Interpol at Heathrow Airport in 1995.

- *Alexey Ivanov* – A June 2001 indictment against Ivanov alleged that he gained unauthorized access into CTS Network Services, a San Diego-based Internet service provider. Ivanov allegedly used a stolen credit card number to open an account with CTS, and once inside the company's computers hacked the systems to gain control of the computers. He then used CTS computers to launch a series of computer attacks against e-commerce companies, including two credit card processors – Sterling Microsystems of Anaheim and Transmark of Rancho Cucamonga – and NaraBank of Los Angeles. Ivanov allegedly stole customer financial information, such as credit card and bank account numbers, leading to fraud of $25 million. A prison sentence of three years was given.

Hacking may not be directly related to theft or damage, but gaining access to a system may be perceived by the hacker as a technical challenge. The term 'hacking' traditionally refers to the process of creating program code, another form of technical challenge. This can almost be considered as a pastime, albeit an unethical one. While not as popular as watching sports, hacking appears to be more than one or two people in each country. BBC (2003) reports that TruSecure, a US hacking monitoring organization currently tracks more than 11,000 individuals in about 900 different hacking groups and gangs.

Three main forms of gaining unauthorized access to computer systems can be identified. First, the normal entry points to systems through usernames and passwords can be used. For example, many system log-ins have a username of 'administrator' by default. Sometimes the password will be the same. Other common passwords are days of the week or children's names. Tools are available to try different alternative log-ins, although most modern systems will refuse access after several attempts. Hacking can be combined with identity theft to gain an idea of the passwords used.

The second form of hacking exploits known vulnerabilities in systems. Although these vulnerabilities in operating systems such as Windows or Linux or web browsers such as Internet Explorer are publicly known and will be posted on the vendor's web site and specialist security web sites, there will be many system administrators who have not updated their systems with the latest security update or 'patch'. This is partly because there are so many security vulnerabilities, with new ones being announced every week.

Social engineering
Exploiting human behaviour to gain access to computer security information from employees or individuals.

Thirdly, Kevin Mitnick refers to '**social engineering**' which typically involves impersonating employees of an organization to access security details. One example of this, given in Mitnick and Simon (2002), is when the attacker contacts a new employee and advises them of the need to comply with security policies. The attacker then asks the user for their password to check it is in line with the policy of choosing a difficult-to-guess password. Once the user reveals their password, the caller makes recommendations to construct future passwords in such a way that the attacker will be able to guess them.

Protecting computer systems against hackers

Protecting computer systems against hackers involves creating counter-measures to the three main types of hacking outlined above. For gaining access to systems via passwords, policies can be developed to reduce the risk of access. One simple approach is to mandate that new passwords are required every month and that they contain at least one number and a mix of upper and lower case. This prevents users using simple passwords which are easily guessed. Education is required to reduce the risk of passwords falsely obtained through 'social engineering', but this will never completely remove this threat.

Computer systems can also be protected by limiting access at the point the external network enters the company. Firewalls are essential to prevent outside access to confidential company information, particularly where an extranet has been set up. Firewalls are usually created as software mounted on a separate server at the point where the company is connected to the Internet. Firewall software can then be configured to only accept links from trusted domains representing other offices in the company.

Firewall
A specialized software application typically mounted on a server at the point where the company is connected to the Internet. Its purpose is to prevent unauthorized access into the company.

Measures must also be put in place to stop access to systems through published security vulnerabilities. BBC (2003) reported that in 2003 there were 5,500 security vulnerabilities that could be used. A policy on updating operating systems and other software with the latest versions is also required. It is not practical to make all updates, but new vulnerabilities must be monitored and patches applied to the highest-risk categories. This is a specialist task and is often outsourced. TruSecure (www.trusecure.com) is an example of a specialist company that monitors security vulnerabilities and advises organizations on prevention. TruSecure estimates that only 80 or 90 per cent of vulnerabilities are being used regularly, so patches should prioritize on these. TruSecure provides a service for hundreds of organizations to see whether they possess these vulnerabilities. They also employ a team of people who attempt to infiltrate hacker groups to determine the latest techniques. TruSecure gave the FBI over 200 documents about the 'Melissa' virus author. Although they did not know his real name, they knew his three aliases and had built a detailed profile of him.

A further approach organizations use to check their defences against hacking is to employ 'ethical hackers'. These are former hackers who now apply their skills to test the vulnerabilities of existing systems.

Ethical hacker
Hacker employed legitimately to test the quality of system security.

Although all of the examples of hacking above involve computer network, sometimes 'low-tech' techniques can be used to. *Guardian* (2003) reported cases where criminals had impersonated call-centre staff in order to gain access to customer accounts!

'Phishing'

Phishing
Obtaining personal details online through sites and e-mails masquerading as legitimate businesses.

Phishing (fishing) is a specialized form of online identity theft. The most common form of 'phishing' is where a spam e-mail is sent out purporting to be from an organization. Recipients are then invited to visit a web site to update their details after entering their username and password. The web address directs them to a false site appearing to be the same as the organization's site. When the username and password are entered these are then collected and used for removing money from the recipient's real account. Some high-profile companies were subject to this form of attack in 2003, including Barclays Bank and PayPal, the online payment company. Such scams are a modern version of the scam devised by criminals where they install a false ATM in a wall with a card reader to access the person's account details. This form of scam is difficult to counter since the e-mail and web site can be made to appear identical to those of the organization through copying. The main countermeasure is education of users, so banks for instance will tell their customers that they would never send this form of e-mail. However, this will not eradicate the problem since with millions of online customers some will always respond to such scams. A further approach is the use of multiple passwords, such that when an account is first accessed from a new system an additional password is required which can only be obtained through mail or by phone. Of course, this will only work if identity theft hasn't occurred. Earlier this year, the sites barclaysprivate.com and eurocitibank.com – neither of them anything to do with existing banks – were shut down, having been used to garner ID details for fraud.

Denial-of-service attacks

Denial-of-service attacks
Web sites are disabled through bombardment with many requests for information originating from computers around the world that have been hijacked.

Denial-of-service attacks (DOSA) occur where systems are bombarded with many requests for information originating from computers around the world that have been hijacked solely to request information. These distributed DOSA often use thousands of infected home PCs unprotected by firewalls, known as 'zombies'. For example, in 2000 Yahoo! servers suffered a denial-of-service attack where servers were bombarded with a billion hits per minute. This caused direct losses in advertising and online shopping revenue. It is expected that future updates to the law will include new aspects of misuse such as denial-of-service attacks and phishing. Many e-businesses in the gambling market have also been threatened by blackmailers against DOSA, particularly when major sporting events such as the World Cup are taking place when they stand to lose most.

Secure e-commerce transactions

For e-businesses offering online sales there are also additional security risks from the customer or merchant perspective:

(a) Transaction or credit card details stolen in transit.
(b) Customer's credit card details stolen from merchant's server.
(c) Merchant or customer is not who they claim to be.

In this section we assess the measures that can be taken to reduce the risk of these breaches of e-commerce security. We start by reviewing some of the theory of online security and then review the techniques used.

Principles of secure systems

Before we look at the principle of secure systems, it is worth reviewing the standard terminology for the different parties involved in the transaction:

- *Purchasers*. These are the consumers buying the goods.
- *Merchants*. These are the retailers.
- *Certification authority (CA)*. This is a body that issues digital certificates that confirm the identity of purchasers and merchants.
- *Banks*. These are traditional banks.
- *Electronic token issuer*. A virtual bank that issues digital currency.

The basic requirements for security systems from these different parties to the transaction are as follows:

1. *Authentication* – are parties to the transaction who they claim to be (risk (c) above)?
2. *Privacy and confidentiality* – are transaction data protected? The consumer may want to make an anonymous purchase. Are all non-essential traces of a transaction removed from the public network and all intermediary records eliminated (risks (b) and (c) above)?
3. *Integrity* – checks that the message sent is complete, i.e. that it is not corrupted.
4. *Non-repudiability* – ensures sender cannot deny sending message.
5. *Availability* – how can threats to the continuity and performance of the system be eliminated?

Kesh *et al.* (2002) explore the security requirements for e-commerce in more detail.

Approaches to developing secure systems

Digital certificates

Digital certificates (keys)

Consist of keys made up of large numbers that are used to uniquely identify individuals.

There are two main methods of encryption using digital certificates.

1 Secret-key (symmetric) encryption

Symmetric encryption

Both parties to a transaction use the same key to encode and decode messages.

Symmetric encryption involves both parties having an identical (shared) key that is known only to them. Only this key can be used to encrypt and decrypt messages. The secret key has to be passed from one party to the other before use in much the same way as a copy of a secure attaché case key would have to be sent to a receiver of information. This approach has traditionally been used to achieve security between two separate parties, such as major companies conducting EDI. Here the private key is sent out electronically or by courier to ensure it is not copied.

This method is not practical for general e-commerce, as it would not be safe for a purchaser to give a secret key to a merchant since control of it would be lost and it could not then be used for other purposes. A merchant would also have to manage many customer keys.

2 Public-key (asymmetric) encryption

Asymmetric encryption

Both parties use a related but different key to encode and decode messages.

Asymmetric encryption is so called since the keys used by the sender and receiver of information are different. The two keys are related by a numerical code, so only the pair of keys can be used in combination to encrypt and decrypt information. *Figure 11.24* shows how public-key encryption works in an e-commerce context. A customer can place an order with a merchant by automatically looking up the public key of the merchant and then using this key to encrypt the message containing their order. The scrambled message is then sent across the Internet and on receipt by the merchant is read using the merchant's private key. In this way only the merchant who has the only copy of the private key can read the order. In the reverse case the merchant could confirm the customer's identity by reading identity information such as a digital signature encrypted with the private key of the customer using their public key.

Digital signatures

Digital signatures

A method of identifying individuals or companies using public-key encryption.

Digital signatures can be used to create commercial systems by using public key encryption to achieve authentication: the merchant and purchaser can prove they are genuine. The purchaser's digital signature is encrypted before sending a message using their private key and, on receipt, the public key of the purchaser is used to decrypt the digital signature. This proves the customer is genuine. Digital signatures

Figure 11.24 **Public-key or asymmetric encryption**

are not widely used currently due to the difficulty of setting up transactions, but they will become more widespread as the public-key infrastructure (PKI) stabilizes and use of certificate authorities increases.

The public-key infrastructure (PKI) and certificate authorities (CAs)

Certificate and certificate authorities (CAs)

A certificate is a valid copy of a public key of an individual or organization together with identification information. It is issued by a trusted third party (TTP) or certificate authority (CA). CAs make public keys available and also issue private keys.

In order for digital signatures and public-key encryption to be effective it is necessary to be sure that the public key intended for decryption of a document actually belongs to the person you believe is sending you the document. The developing solution to this problem is the issuance by a trusted third party (TTP) of a message containing owner identification information and a copy of the public key of that person. The TTPs are usually referred to as 'certificate authorities' (CAs), and various bodies such as banks and the Post Office are likely to fulfil this role. That message is called a 'certificate'. In reality, as asymmetric encryption is rather slow, it is often only a sample of the message that is encrypted and used as the representative digital signature.

Example certificate information could include:

- user identification data;
- issuing authority identification and digital signature;
- user's public key;
- expiry date of this certificate;
- class of certificate;
- digital identification code of this certificate.

It is proposed that different classes of certificates would exist according to the type of information contained. For example:

1 name, e-mail address
2 driver's licence, national insurance number, date of birth
3 credit check
4 organization-specific security clearance data.

Virtual private networks

Virtual private network

Private network created using the public network infrastructure of the Internet.

A virtual private network (VPN) is a private wide-area network that runs over the public network, rather than a more expensive private network. The technique by which VPN operates is sometimes referred to as 'tunnelling', and involves encrypting both packet headers and content using a secure form of the Internet Protocol known as IPSec. As explained in *Chapter 3*, VPNs enable the global organization to conduct its business securely, but using the public Internet rather than more expensive proprietary systems.

Current approaches to e-commerce security

In this section we review the approaches used by e-commerce sites to achieve security using the techniques described above.

Secure Sockets Layer (SSL)

A commonly used encryption technique for scrambling data as it is passed across the Internet from a customer's web browser to a merchant's web server.

Secure Sockets Layer Protocol (SSL)

SSL is a security protocol, originally developed by Netscape, but now supported by all browsers such as Microsoft Internet Explorer. SSL is used in the majority of B2C e-commerce transactions since it is easy for the customer to use without the need to download additional software or a certificate.

When a customer enters a secure checkout area of an e-commerce site SSL is used and the customer is prompted that 'you are about to view information over a secure connection' and a key symbol is used to denote this security. When encryption is occurring they will see that the web address prefix in the browser changes from 'http://' to 'https://' and a padlock appears at the bottom of the browser window.

How does SSL relate to the different security concepts described above? The main facility it provides is security and confidentiality. SSL enables a private link to be set up between customer and merchant. Encryption is used to scramble the details of an e-commerce transaction as it is passed between sender and receiver and also when the details are held on the computers at each end. It would require a determined attempt to intercept such a message and decrypt it. SSL is more widely used than the rival S-HTTP method.

The detailed stages of SSL are as follows:

1 Client browser sends request for a secure connection.
2 Server responds with a digital certificate which is sent for authentication.
3 Client and server negotiate *session keys*, which are symmetrical keys used only for the duration of the transaction.

Since, with enough computing power, time and motivation, it is possible to decrypt messages encrypted using SSL, much effort is being put into finding more secure methods of encryption such as SET. From a merchant's point of view there is also the problem that authentication of the customer is not possible without resorting to other methods such as credit checks.

Secure Electronic Transaction (SET)
A standard for public-key encryption intended to enable secure e-commerce transactions, lead-development by Mastercard and Visa.

Certificate authorities (CAs)

For secure e-commerce, there is a requirement for the management of the vast number of public keys. This management involves procedures and protocols necessary throughout the lifetime of a key – generation, dissemination, revocation and change – together with the administrative functions of time/date stamping and archiving. The successful establishment of a CA is an immense challenge of trust building and complex management. There are two opposing views on how that challenge should be met.

- *Decentralized*: market-driven, creating brand-name-based 'islands of trust' such as the Consumers Association. There is a practical need for a local physical office to present certificates of attestable value, e.g. passports, drivers' licences. Banks and the Post Office have a huge advantage.
- *Centralized*: in the UK, the Department of Trade and Industry (DTI) has proposed a hierarchical tree leading ultimately to the government.

The best-known commercial CA is Verisign (www.verisign.com) and this is commonly used for merchant verification. For example, the Avon site uses Verisign to prove to its customers that it is the genuine site. Post Offices and telecommunications suppliers are also acting as CAs. Examples in the UK include BT (Trust Wise) and the Post Office (ViaCode).

Pretty Good Privacy (PGP)

PGP is a public-key encryption system used to encrypt e-mail messages.

Reassuring the customer

Once the security measures are in place, content on the merchant's site can be used to reassure the customer, for example Amazon (www.amazon.com) takes customer fears about security seriously, judging by the prominence and amount of content it devotes to this issue. Some of the approaches used indicate good practice in allaying customers' fears. These include:

- use of customer guarantee to safeguard purchase;
- clear explanation of SSL security measures used;
- highlighting the rarity of fraud ('ten million customers have shopped safely without credit card fraud');
- the use of alternative ordering mechanisms such as phone or fax;
- the prominence of information to allay fears – the guarantee is one of the main menu options.

Companies can also use independent third parties that set guidelines for online privacy and security. The best-known international bodies are TRUSTe (www.truste.org) and Verisign for payment authentication (www.verisign.com). Within particular companies there may be other bodies such as, in the UK, Which? Web Trader (www.which.net/webtrader), TrustUK (www.trustuk.org) and ChambersOnline (www.chambersonline.co.uk).

For B2B transactions and B2C transactions, SGS, the Swiss certification agency (www.sgsonline.com), has developed a Gold Seal standard to authenticate e-commerce quality. Founded in 1878 to monitor grain shipments, Société Générale de Surveillance today oversees a vast spectrum of traditional trading activities, ranging from toys to textiles and carbon steel to crude oil.

Case Study 11.2 Building an e-business fortress

FT

In the lead-up to the industrial revolution, many European cities stopped relying on walls that for centuries kept them safe from marauding armies. Cities weighed up the risks and decided trade and collaboration were more important to survival than defence, so expanded beyond the city perimeter.

Businesses today face a similar predicament when it comes to securing computer networks, says Paul Dorey, chief information security officer (CISO) at energy giant BP.

With the growth of outsourcing, managed services, remote working and joint-ventures changing the business landscape, companies can no longer adopt a siege mentality when protecting corporate IT networks, he says.

'Outsourcers, contractors and third parties need to access corporate information. At the same time new technologies, such as wireless and instant messaging, are providing a security headache for those guarding the network perimeter.' Instead of repelling hackers and viruses using firewalls at the network edge, Mr Dorey, and other CISOs from companies including HSBC, ICI, Rolls-Royce and Royal Mail, advocate businesses re-think their security.

They have formed the Jericho Forum, an international pressure group aimed at making vendors listen to user requirements. It plans to lobby for product design changes so companies can trade securely over the internet. By doing so, it hopes businesses will not see electronic assets pillaged or destroyed to the biblical proportions its namesake did.

'The easiest model is something akin to internet banking where you access corporate systems through a highly secure web-portal, using authentication', says Mr Dorey. 'Sensitive data is encrypted and there is a demilitarised zone, so even if one person accessing the system is compromised, the whole system is not', he says.

Pharmaceutical company AstraZeneca is looking at this. In 2004 it spent \$3.8bn (£2.15bn) on drugs research and development through collaboration with research organisations, universities and biotechnology partners. With dozens of organisations and 11,900 employees communicating in the R&D process over multiple networks, protection of intellectual property (IP) was not feasible through a 'walled castle' approach to security. So last year it replaced an in-house collaboration system with electronic vaulting technology from IT security company Cyber-Ark, says Patrick Meehan, lead technical architect at AstraZeneca. The original system had high costs and hindered collaboration, because the virtual private network on which it relied needed software installed on every user's system. By transporting data in an 'electronic safe' AstraZeneca is guarding intellectual property using inbuilt authentication, encryption and firewalls.

Enterprise rights management (ERM) software to restrict who can access, print and e-mail sensitive documents is also used. Paul Stamp, security analyst at Forrester Research believes protecting data assets is an improvement on the 'fortress approach', but current proprietary technologies and differences in global legislation could hamper progress. 'It's not going to happen overnight', he says. 'The Jericho Forum is pushing for open-standards and that's going to be tough for the likes of Microsoft and Cisco to achieve from the very beginning.'

And with countries such as China, Israel, Russia and Saudi Arabia restricting the use of strong data encryption products, ERM is not immediately workable globally, he says.

Steve Wylie, EMEA managing partner at Accenture's security practice, adds that investment in encryption and ERM software could be costly in time spent managing user privileges. 'The negative impact of leaked R&D into drugs will justify the investment, but if employees spend time setting up access rights every time they produce documents like a company newsletter then it could hamper productivity', he says. But while Mr Dorey admits re-defining a company's electronic boundaries has problems, advances in networking and business practices may force the IT industry's hand.

Source: A different approach to protection. By Daniel Thomas. http://news.ft.com/cms/s/43204142-5056-11da-bbd7-0000779e2340,dwp_uuid=b15d54f2-5064-11da-bbd7-0000779e2340,ft_acl=_2_3,s01=1.html Published FT.com: 8 November 2005

Question

Summarize the change in security model needed to protect corporate assets.

Summary

1 Analysis of business and user requirements for e-business systems is important in delivering usable and relevant systems.

2 Process modelling is used to assess existing business processes and suggest revised processes. Techniques such as task analysis and flow process charts from workflow design are useful in understanding tasks that must be supported by the system and weaknesses in the current process.

3 Data modelling for e-business systems mainly involves traditional entity relationship approaches.

4 Architectural designs involve assessing appropriate integration between legacy systems and new e-commerce systems. Such designs are based on the client–server approach.

5 User interface design can be improved through using structured approaches such as use-case and following evolving standards for site structure, page structure and content.

6 Security design is important to maintain trust amongst the customer base. Security solutions target protecting servers from attack and prevent interception of messages when they are in transit.

Exercises

Self-assessment questions

1 What are the risks if analysis and design are not completed adequately?

2 Distinguish between process analysis and data analysis.

3 What are workflow analysis and workflow management systems?

4 What are legacy data and what are the options for their incorporation into an e-commerce system?

5 What are the four requirements of a secure e-commerce site?

6 Explain the concepts of digital keys and digital signatures and how they relate.

7 Explain the notation used for use-case analysis.

8 Summarize the characteristics of a usable web site according to Jakob Nielsen (www.useit.com).

Essay and discussion questions

1 Write a plan for the analysis and design of an e-commerce site, recommending which aspects of process and data analysis should be conducted and explaining how they should be integrated.

2 Write an essay on the significance of workflow systems to e-business, illustrating your answer with examples of organizations of your choice.

3 Write a report summarizing the characteristics of a web site with good usability.

4 How can the concept of customer orientation be translated into e-commerce site design?

5 Assess the success of e-tailers in designing secure e-commerce systems.

Examination questions

1 Summarize the purpose of process analysis.

2 What is meant by 'user-centred design'?

3 Explain the concept of task analysis with reference to a customer placing an order online.

4 Explain the stages involved in use-case analysis with reference to a customer placing an order online.

5 Describe the stages of data modelling with reference to a database for an e-procurement system.

6 Outline the different types of services that need to be provided by different servers on an e-commerce site based on the three-tier client–server system.

7 How do the attributes of a secure e-commerce site differ from customer and company viewpoints?

8 Explain the relationship between analysis, design and implementation for an e-commerce site.

References

AMA (2003) American Managment Association 2003 E-Mail Rules, Policies and Practices Survey. www.amanet.org/research/pdfs/Email_Policies_Practices.pdf.

BBC (2003) Cracking the hacker underground. BBC News Online. http://news.bbc.co.uk/1/hi/technology/3246375.htm.

Bevan, N. (1999a) Usability issues in web site design. *Proceedings of the 6th Interactive Publishing Conference*, November. Available online at www.usability.serco.com.

Bevan, N. (1999b) Common industry format usability tests. *Proceedings of UPA '98*, Usability Professionals Association, Scottsdale, AZ, 29 June–2 July. Available online at www.usability.serco.com.

Bickerton, P., Bickerton, M. and Pardesi, U. (2000) *CyberMarketing*, 2nd edn. Chartered Institute of Marketing series, Butterworth-Heinemann, Oxford.

Bocij, P., Chaffey, D., Greasley, A. and Hickie, S. (2005) *Business Information Systems. Technology, Development and Management*, 3rd edn. Financial Times Prentice Hall, Harlow.

British Standards Institute (1999) BS 13407 Human-centred Design Processes for Interactive Systems.

Chaffey, D. (1998) *Groupware, Workflow and Intranets – Re-engineering the Enterprise with Collaborative Software*. Digital Press, Woburn, MA.

Chaffey, D. and Wood, S. (2005) *Business Information Management. Improving Performance using Information Systems*, Financial Times Prentice Hall, Harlow.

Chaffey, D., Mayer, R., Johnston, K. and Ellis-Chadwick, F. (2006) *Internet Marketing: Strategy, Implementation and Practice*, 3rd edn. Financial Times Prentice Hall, Harlow.

Channel Register (2005) Dabs.com in £500k makeover. By John Leyden. *Channel Register*, 2 September. www.channelregister.co.uk.

ClickZ (2003) Virus damage worst on record for August 2003. By Sharon Gaudin. News alert published online at ClickZ Stats, 2 September. www.clickz.com/stats.

Computer Weekly (2003) Phones4U bans internal e-mail. Daniel Thomas, *Computer Weekly*, 19 September. www.computerweekly.com/articles/article.asp?liArticleID=1250108liArticleTypeID=1&liCategoryID=2&liChannelID-liFlavourID-l&sSearch=&nPage=1.

Curtis, B., Kellner, M. and Over, J. (1992) Process modeling. *Communications of the ACM*, 35(9), 75–90.

Davenport, T.H. (1993) *Process Innovation: Re-engineering Work through Information Technology*. Harvard Business School Press, Boston.

DTI (2006) Identify access and E-mail and Web Usage factsheets. A survey of UK business practice, managed by PricewaterhouseCoopers on behalf of the Department of Trade and Industry (DTI). Published at DTI Information Security Breaches Survey (www.security-survey.gov.uk).

Forrester (2005) Site Design Personas: How Many, How Much. By Harley Manning, 3 June 2005. Forrester Research publication.

Georgakoupoulos, D., Hornick, M. and Sheth, A. (1995) An overview of workflow management: from process modeling to workflow automation infrastructure. *Distributed and Parallel Databases*, 3, 119–53.

Guardian (2003) Hijacked your bank balance, your identity, your life. *The Guardian*, 25 October. www.guardian.co.uk/weekend/story/0,3605,1069646,00.html.

Hofacker, C. (2001) *Internet Marketing*. Wiley, New York.

Hoffman, D.L. and Novak, T.P. (1997) A new marketing paradigm for electronic commerce. *The Information Society*, Special issue on electronic commerce, 13 (Jan.–Mar.), 43–54.

IT Week (2003) E-shop adds to attractions. By David Neal. *IT Week*, 12 September, 24. www.itweek.co.uk.

Jacobsen, I., Ericsson, M. and Jacobsen, A. (1994) *The Object Advantage. Business Process Re-engineering with Object Technology*. Addison-Wesley, Wokingham.

Kesh, S., Ramanujan, S. and Nerur, S. (2002) A framework for analyzing e-commerce security. *Information Management and Computer Security*, 10(4), 149–58.

Lyman, P. and Varian, H. (2003) How Much Information – online research summary. Available online at: www.sims.berkeley.edu/research/projects/how-much-info-2003/.

Lynch, P. and Horton, S. (1999) *Web Style Guide. Basic Design Principles for Creating Web Sites*. Yale University Press, New Haven, CT. Available online at: http://info.med.yale.edu/caim/manual/contents.html.

Messagelabs (2006) Threat Statistics, published monthly at www.messagelabs.com.

Mitnick, K. and Simon, W. (2002) *The Art of Deception: Controlling the Human Element of Security*. Wiley, New York.

NCC (2005) Dabs.com benefits from innovative approach. *Principra*, NCC Members Magazine, no. 37, May/June.

Nielsen, J. (2000a) *Novice vs. Expert Users*. Jakob Nielsen's Alertbox, 6 February. www.useit.com/alertbox/ 20000206.html.

Nielsen, J. (2000b) *Designing Web Usability*. New Riders, San Francisco.

Nielsen, J. (2000c) *Details in Study Methodology Can Give Misleading Results*. Jakob Nielsen's Alertbox, 21 February. www.useit.com/alertbox/990221.html

Noyes, J. and Baber, C. (1999) *User-Centred Design of Systems*. Springer-Verlag, Berlin.

Pant, S. and Ravichandran, T. (2001) A framework for information systems planning for e-business. *Logistics Information Management*, 14(1), 85–98.

Rettie, R. (2001) An exploration of flow during Internet use. *Internet Research: Electronic Networking Applications and Policy*. 11(2), 103–13.

Robertson, J (2003) Information design using card sorting. Step Two. Available online at www.steptwo.com.au/papers/cardsorting/index.html.

Rosenfeld, L. and Morville, P. (2002) *Information Architecture for the World Wide Web*, 2nd edn, O'Reilly, Sebastopol, CA.

Schneider, G. and Winters, J. (1998) *Applying Use Cases. A Practical Guide*. Addison-Wesley, Reading, MA.

Seybold, P. (1999) *Customers.com*. Century Business Books, Random House, London.

Seybold, P. (2001) Get inside the lives of your customers. *Harvard Business Review*, May, 80–9.

Seybold, P. and Marshak, R. (2001) *The Customer Revolution*. Crown Business, London.

Taylor, D. (1995) *Business Engineering with Object Technology*. Wiley, New York.

Wodtke, C. (2002) *Information Architecture: Blueprints for the Web*. New Riders, Indianapolis, IN.

Workflow Management Coalition (WfMC) (1996) Reference model. Version 1. In *The Workflow Management Coalition Specification. Terminology and Glossary*. Workflow Management Coalition, Brussels.

Further reading

Bevan, N. (1999a) Usability issues in web site design. *Proceedings of the 6th Interactive Publishing Conference*, November 1999. Available online at www.usability.serco.com. Accessible, lists of web-design pointers.

Jakob Nielsen's UseIt (www.useit.com). Detailed guidelines (alertboxes) and summaries of research into usability of web media.

Noyes, J. and Baber, C. (1999) *User-Centred Design of Systems*. Springer-Verlag, Berlin. Details the user-centred design approach.

Web links

British web site trade associations BIMA (www.bima.co.uk) and BWDMA (www.bwdma.co.uk) Have good resources for the specialist in this area.

DTI Information Security (www.dti.gov.uk/industries/information_security) Guidelines on information security.

DTI Information Security Breaches Survey (www.security-survey.gov.uk) A survey of security in UK businesses.

Jakob Nielsen's UseIt (www.useit.com) Detailed guidelines (alertboxes) and summaries of research into usability of web media.

Royal National Institute for the Blind (www.rnib.org.uk/accessibility) Web accessibility guidelines.

Usability News (www.usabilitynews.com).

User Interface Engineering (www.uie.com) Articles on usability which often provide a counterpoint to those of Nielsen.

UI Access (www.uiaccess.com/access_links.html) Resources on web site accessibility.

Web Design References (www.d.umn.edu/itss/support/Training/Online/webdesign) A collection from the University of Minnesota Duluth including articles and references on accessibility, information architecture and usability.

Web Style Guide (www.webstyleguide.com) Supporting site for the style guide book of P. Lynch and S. Horton of Yale Medical School. Complete text online.

Worldwide Web consortium web accessibility guidelines (See www.w3.org/ WAI)

12 Implementation and maintenance

Chapter at a glance

Main topics

Focus on ...

Case study

Web support

The following additional case studies are available at www.pearsoned.co.uk/chaffey

➤ Change management at the Woolwich Group

➤ Guide to Smarter Searching

The site also contains a range of study materials designed to help improve your results.

Learning outcomes

After completing this chapter the reader should be able to:

- **Produce a plan to minimize the risks involved with the launch phase of an e-business application**
- **Define a process for the effective maintenance of an e-business system**
- **Produce a simple web page with links to other pages**
- **Create a plan to measure the effectiveness of e-business application using web analytics tools.**

Management issues

Implementation and maintenance of e-business systems raises these issues for management:

- **What actions can we take to minimize the risks of implementation – what are the critical success factors?**
- **How do we achieve transition from previous systems to a new e-business system?**
- **What techniques are available to measure the success of our implementation?**

Links to other chapters

This chapter follows naturally from *Chapters 10* and *11*. The context is given in *Figure 10.4*. The change management plan defined in *Chapter 10* will be enacted in the implementation phase. The coding, testing and changeover aspects of implementation will be based on the analysis and design documentation produced using the techniques described in *Chapter 11*.

Introduction

Implementation
The creation of a system based on analysis and design documentation.

Implementation activities
The creation of the system modules by coding and scripting, module integration and testing and changeover to the live system.

We started *Chapter 11* by considering the typical problems that confront users of e-commerce systems. It was shown that careful analysis and design can help minimize the risks of problems such as difficulties in navigation and slow site response. With good analysis and design, the implementation stage can be relatively straightforward: simply implementing the design. However, even with the best design, it is still necessary to follow implementation activities that test the system thoroughly and manage the transition or changeover from the old system to the new system or the launch of the site. Note that there is also a broader use of the term 'implementation' which is used to describe the implementation of strategy – this includes all aspects of *Part 3*: change management, analysis, design, implementation and maintenance.

Complete *Activity 12.1* to review some of the risks that can occur in the implementation phase.

Activity 12.1 Risks of e-business implementation

Purpose

To highlight the risks of implementation and actions necessary to control them.

Activity

Refer back to *Activity 11.1*. For all the problems of an e-commerce site you identified, which ones may also have occurred because of failings at the implementation phase of the system?

Answers to activities can be found at www.pearsoned.co.uk/chaffey

Maintenance phase
Commences after the system is live.

The dynamic e-business application
The application is continuously updated in response to competitive forces.

Maintenance activities
Involve measurement of an information system's effectiveness and updating to correct errors or introduce new features necessary to improve its value to the organization.

Once an e-business application or e-commerce site is live, the maintenance phase is arguably of more significance than in traditional business application development since a successful application is dynamic. A dynamic e-business application means that content and services will be continuously updated in response to the environmental scanning, as described in *Chapters 4, 5* and *6*. As competitors introduce new services and offers, and as marketing research reveals problems with the site from a customer perspective, or new opportunities, rapid modifications will be required for the e-business to remain competitive.

The relationship between analysis, design, implementation and maintenance was illustrated in *Figure 10.4*. It is evident that implementation activities such as testing and review follow analysis and design during prototyping. These activities also occur before the system becomes live in a final implementation phase. *Figure 12.1* summarizes the sequence of activities in the form of a Gantt chart. It is evident that although analysis and design, implementation and maintenance activities were traditionally conceived of as separate in the systems development lifecycle model, in reality there is a great degree of overlap between these phases and all occur simultaneously as part of the evolutionary prototyping approach (*Chapter 10*). While analysis of requirements is occurring, design and implementation will be occurring simultaneously in order to produce storyboards and prototypes. This prototyping may occur in timeboxes of a certain duration, perhaps 30 days or 60 days, with a prototype produced at the end of each timebox. Web applications such as those produced by Google and Microsoft are continually evolving in what is sometimes called 'perpetual beta' which requires careful testing of different modules before each release is live, or a facility to revert to the previous version if major errors are encountered.

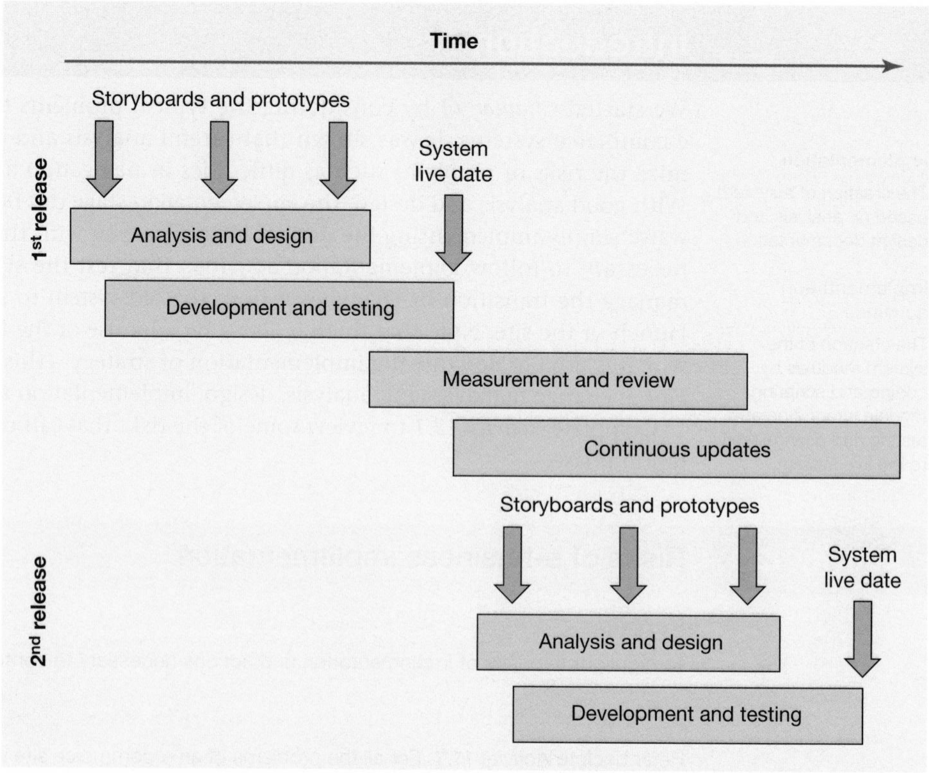

Figure 12.1 Sequencing of implementation and maintenance for the dynamic e-business application

Once the system is live, measurement and review will commence. Measurement of the load and user activity affecting servers can be considered as an extension of pre-launch testing. As soon as the system is live it will be necessary to make minor updates continuously to the content and services. For each update, a small-scale prototyping process involving analysis, design and testing will occur. For more major updates that perhaps may occur every 6, 12 or 18 months another full cycle of analysis and design, development and testing will be required. This is shown at the base of *Figure 12.1* and is completed by the second version of the system going live and the cycle repeating.

Alternatives for acquiring e-business systems

Acquisition method
Defines whether the system is purchased outright or developed from scratch.

Bespoke development
Information system development specifically for purpose.

The basic alternative **acquisition methods** for e-business systems are similar to those for traditional business information systems:

1 *Bespoke development*. With a **bespoke development**, the application is developed from ´scratch' through programming of a solution.
2 *Off-the-shelf*. In a **packaged implementation** a standard existing system is purchased from a solution vendor and installed on servers and clients located within the organization. Alternatively, free or low-cost open-source software may be used. A web design tool such as Dreamweaver is a simple example of an off-the-shelf packaged implementation.
3 *Hosted solution (packaged)*. With a **hosted solution**, a standard system is used, but it is not managed within the company, but using a third-party applications service provider variously known as 'on-demand', 'web services' or a 'managed solution'.

Packaged implementation
Standard software is installed with limited configuration required.

Hosted solution
Standard software which is managed externally on the supplier's server.

Tailored development
The standard solution requires major configuration or integration of different modules.

4 *Tailored development*. In a tailored development, an off-the-shelf system or hosted solution is tailored according to the organization's needs. This form of project is often based on integrating components from one or several vendors.

These acquisition alternatives have been reviewed, for example, in Chaffey and Wood (2005) where it was demonstrated that the prevalent approach is the tailored off-the-shelf or hosted approach, which is often the best compromise between meeting an organization's specific needs and reliability while minimizing cost and development time. Decisions also have to be taken as to whether bespoke development or tailoring occurs in-house or using a consultant who is familiar with the latest e-commerce development tools.

Regardless of the source of the system, the main criteria used to select the solution are common. They are:

1 *Functionality*. The features of the application. Describes how well the e-business application meets the business need.
2 *Ease of use*. Every system takes some time to use, but systems should be intuitive to minimize the time needed to learn how to use them. A well-constructed piece of software will make it fast to conduct common tasks.
3 *Performance*. The speed of the application to perform different functions. This is measured by how long the user has to wait for individual functions to be completed such as data retrieval, calculation and screen display. It will depend on the power of the computer, but can vary significantly between applications.
4 *Scalability*. Scalability is related to performance; it describes how well a system can adapt to higher workloads which arise as a company grows. For example, an ERP system will require more customer details, suppliers and products to be held on it as the company grows. The workload will also be higher as the number of internal and external users of the system increases.
5 *Compatibility or interoperability*. This term refers to how easy it is to integrate the application with other applications. For example, does it have import and export facilities, does it support transfer of data using XML?
6 *Extensibility*. Related to scalability and interoperability, this describes how easy it is to add new functions or features to a package by adding new modules from the original vendor or other vendors.
7 *Stability or reliability*. All applications have errors or bugs and applications vary in the number of times they fail depending on how well they have been tested since they were first introduced.
8 *Security*. Capabilities for restricting access to applications should be assessed. This is particularly important for hosted solutions.
9 *Support*. Levels of support and the cost of support from the software vendor will vary. There is a risk that small companies may cease trading and the product may no longer be supported.

Now complete *Activity 12.2* to consider how these different factors are balanced.

Activity 12.2 Selecting applications software for a small business

Purpose

To aid understanding of the different factors to assess when selecting applications software and the relative importance of them.

→

Activity

A start-up office supplies business which specializes in supply of printers is reviewing its alternatives for different types of e-business system. Form groups with each group selecting one type of e-business service from the list below and then discussing the importance of the nine criteria for selecting software described above. A ranked list of the criteria in order of importance should be produced. These can be put on a whiteboard, with one type of software in each column to assess the commonality in requirements.

E-business service types:

1 Customer relationship management application.
2 Supply chain management application.
3 Employee management system.
4 Web analytics software (see later in chapter).

Development of web-based content and services

The delivery of e-business services via a web interface may initially appear straightforward. Everyone has heard apocryphal tales such as a 12-year-old relation creating a web site to sell used cars. Indeed, the creation of static web content is straightforward as will see. In this example, simple HTML code is used for layout and formatting of information to create a simple catalogue of perhaps ten cars, with a web page for each that is accessed from a home page or simple menu. But imagine the situation for a real car dealership where a customer will want to select from a range of hundreds or thousands of cars with different specifications from different manufacturers. Here, it is impractical for the user to select from a menu of hundreds of cars. At the very least, they will expect the cars to be grouped into categories by manufacturer and perhaps sorted by age. But finding the right car through browsing these categories could take a long time and most users will demand a basic search facility by which they type in, or select, the make of car or an advanced search facility by which they choose the make, plus the specification such as engine size and year of registration. In this case the page delivered to the user will depend on their preferences and will be dynamic web content. Here, it is apparent that more than simple formatting and presentation is required – the site is interactive, that is to say it must accept text input from the user and respond to the request with the appropriate information. The development process will involve coding to accept the user's preferences, passing the request to a database, performing a query, returning the results and formatting them for the user.

Static web content
A web page view that is identical every time it is loaded.

Dynamic web content
A web page view that varies according to user preferences or environment constraints.

In this section we will start by introducing how simple static web pages can be developed using HTML. We will then go on to consider in the section *Focus on HTML* how scripts and databases can be used in conjunction with HTML to produce dynamic content. For each of these we will start by considering the standards used to create the content and then look at tools that facilitate the process.

Creating static web content

HTML (Hypertext Markup Language)
A standard format used to define the text and layout of web pages. HTML files usually have the extension .HTML or .HTM.

HTML or hypertext markup language, which was introduced in *Chapter 3*, is the standard that is most commonly used for producing static web content. HTML files can be written with an ordinary text editor such as the Windows Notepad program or the specialist tools described in a later section.

HTML tags
Markup codes denoted by <start code> and </end code> that instruct the browser to format information or perform a particular operation.

HTML parameters
These occur within the tags to specify particular characteristics of the HTML statement.

The operation of HTML is based on a web browser interpreting **HTML tags** or codes on a web page when it is loaded into the browser. For example, the <TITLE> tag indicates what appears at the top of the web browser window. Each starting tag has a corresponding end tag usually marked by a '/', for example <TITLE>The B2C Company</TITLE>. Tags can be nested or embedded when more than one style of formatting is required. For example, <B><I>highlight</I></B> instructs the browser to display the word 'highlight' as bold and italicized text. The start tags <B> and <I> tell the browser to format all text that appears from that point and the end tags </I></B> instruct the browser to stop using the formatting. Special **HTML parameters** are used to provide more detailed instructions for some HTML tags, for example the 'width' parameter in the code <TABLE width="95%"> instructs the browser that the table should occupy 95 per cent of the screen.

The following *Focus on HTML* section outlines the main features of HTML that are used for constructing web pages.

Focus on HTML

A basic working knowledge of HTML may be useful for managers for two reasons. First, there may be occasions they need to produce a simple page, perhaps to prototype or storyboard a proposal for an enhancement to a web site or perhaps a personal home page for the intranet or at home. Second, it is useful to have an appreciation of the issues involved with creating web pages using HTML in order to be able to plan and manage projects involving creation of web content. Through knowledge of HTML and other development techniques it will be possible to discuss estimates for page development with an internal developer or quotes for page development with an external agency without the 'wool being pulled over your eyes'. For these reasons, and perhaps because it can be fun, a basic introduction to HTML is taught on many college and university courses and for these reasons it is included here.

We will review the elements of HTML by starting with a very simple page and gradually increasing its sophistication by adding different components to the page until a realistic page is produced that could act as the home page for the B2C site. As you review the elements of HTML you can put them into practice by following *Activity 12.3*, creating a web page for The B2C Company.

Activity 12.3 Creating a web page for The B2C Company

Purpose

To learn the basic elements of HTML.

Activity

For each of the examples in the following section create a web page and upload to an ISP so it is published on the web. Use Yahoo Geocities or a similar service to create and host your pages (www.geocities.com).

No suggested answers supplied.

A simple HTML page

<HTML> tag
Denotes an HTML document.

<HEAD> tag
The header part of an HTML document containing titles, meta tags and scripts.

<BODY> tag
The main part of an HTML document containing content.

<TITLE> tag
The text that appears in the browser title bar.

Comment tag <!— —>
Used to document code – text does not appear in browser.

What are the basic elements of an HTML page? First, we need tags to tell the browser this is an HTML page; this is performed by the <HTML> tag. Note that the case used for these tags is not important, but it is now convention for them to be lower-case; however, they are rendered in CAPS in this book to make them clearer. Second, we need tags to show the header and body of the page. This is performed by the <HEAD> and <BODY> tags. Within the <HEAD> part of the HTML document it is possible (but not essential) to add the <TITLE> tag to indicate the text to appear in the title bar of the browser. Within the part of the document tagged by <BODY> </BODY> any text will be displayed as shown below. Comments are denoted by the Comment tag <!— —> . For clarity, the <HTML>, <HEAD> and <BODY> tags will be omitted in the subsequent examples which occur within the <BODY> tags unless otherwise indicated.

HTML code

```
<HTML>
<HEAD>
<TITLE>The B2C
Company</TITLE>
</HEAD>
<BODY> <!—Main content starts
here—>
Welcome to the web site of
The B2C Company
</BODY>
</HTML>
```

Browser display

Welcome to the web site of The B2C Company

Text formatting

<B>, <I> and <U> text formatting
Formats text as bold, italic or underlined.

<P> and <BR> line spacing
Paragraphs are denoted by <B> and line breaks by <BR>.

Text formatting in HTML is straightforward. Bold, italic and underline formatting are applied using the <B>, <I> and <U> text formatting tags. To denote paragraphs use the <P> </P> tags which cause a carriage return (blank line) after each line. To break a line without a space used the break tag
 .

HTML code

```
<P> This text is <B>bold
</B></P>
<P>This text is
<I>italic</I></P><BR>
This text is
<U>underlined</U>
```

Browser display

This text is **bold**

This text is *italic*

This text is underlined

Text justification

<CENTER> tag
Centres enclosed text or other objects.

Text and images are centred by enclosing the text within the <CENTER> alignment tag. For more sophisticated alignment, tables are the best method.

HTML code

```
<CENTER> This text is centred
</CENTER>
```

Browser display

This text is centred

Text size

<H1>, <H2>, <H3>, <H4> heading tags
Produce a heading in bold.

Text size can be crudely controlled by the use of heading tags. The heading style changes the text to bold and increases its size according to the heading number in the range 1 to 4. It also forces a line break following the end tag. These heading styles cannot be readily used to generate a table of contents as in Word, although most HTML editors provide a facility for this.

<FONT> tag
Used to specify font characteristics.

Greater control over text size can be achieved through using the <FONT> tag. Here the style of font such as Arial or Times can be specified together with its colour and relative size. The default font on most browsers is a serifed font such as Times Roman. Serifed fonts are often used for typesetting books such as this one since they make text easier to digest. Sans serif fonts are often used for titles.

HTML code

```
<FONT face="Arial">
<H1> This text is Heading
1</H1>
<H2> This text is Heading
2</H2>
</FONT>
Normal text<BR>
<FONT face ="Verdana, Arial,
Helvetica, sans-serif"
size="-1" color="black">
This is a sans-serif font
</FONT>
<BR><BR>
<CENTER>
Copyright &copy; 2006 The B2C
Company
</CENTER>
```

Browser display

This text is Heading 1

This text is Heading 2

Normal text

This is a sans-serif font

Copyright © 2006 The B2C Company

Lists

Creating lists is straightforward. <LI> is used before each item in a list, and the basic form of the list is determined by the tag at the start and end of the list. The <UL></UL> tag is used to denote the beginning and end of an *unordered (bullet) list* and the <OL></OL>tag is used at the beginning and end of an *ordered (numbered) list.*

HTML code

```
<UL>
  <LI>Item 1
  <LI>Item 2
  <LI>Item 3
</UL>
<OL>
  <LI> Item 1
  <LI> Item 2
  <LI> Item 3
</OL>
```

Browser display

- Item 1
- Item 2
- Item 3

1. Item 1
2. Item 2
3. Item 3

Graphics

<IMG> tag
This is used to insert a graphic into the document by specifying a file name, size and alternative text.

Graphic elements are displayed using the <IMG> tag which refers to a graphic file which is inserted into the displayed page at that point. As explained in *Chapter 3* graphic files are usually .GIF or .JPEG images. The example below shows a .JPG graphic from a graphics subdirectory which is aligned to the right of the page. Note that the specification of width and height is not essential, but it speeds loading. The ALT keyword is important for two reasons. First, if the user has graphics turned off in their browser, or is viewing a page before the graphics are fully loaded, it gives a text indication of what an image shows. Second, it is important for search engines which index the ALT keyword text, but do not know the information contained in the graphic itself. A page made entirely from graphics, but with no ALT text will not be indexed by search engines.

HTML code

```
<IMG
SRC="graphics/car.jpg"WIDTH="
241" HEIGHT="122" ALT="car
picture" ALIGN="RIGHT">
```

Browser display

<Photo appears here on web page>

Links

<A HREF=R""></A> tag
Links to a specified document.

Links, or more strictly hyperlinks, are essential to the function of the web since these enable a user to click on a link text, graphic or button and jump to another part of the same document, a different document on the same site, or a completely different site. The link tag is identified by <A HREF=R""></A> tag and can be thought of as being in two parts as the example below shows. The first part <A HREF="index.htm"> is used to specify the target address or destination page to link to, in this case the home page of the current site. The target destination could also be a graphic, sound or plug-in, although the <EMBED> tag can also be used for this purpose. The second part specifies the form or label used for the hyperlink to link to. This can be a text, graphic or button-based hyperlink. If the hyperlink is text, the text, in this case 'Go to the home page', is specified between the <A HREF=""> tag and the closing </A> tag. If the hyperlink item is a graphic an <IMG> tag is inserted before the </A>. A form-based button (see section on *Forms*) can be used also as the hyperlink as shown below.

HTML code

```
<A HREF="index.htm"> Go to
home page </A><BR>
<A HREF="index.htm"><IMG
SRC="home.gif"></A><BR>
<A HREF="index.htm"><INPUT
TYPE="submit" VALUE="Home
Page"></A>
```

Browser display

Go to home page

Home Page

[Home Page]

Six of the most commonly encountered options for linking to a destination document are shown in *Table 12.1*. All involve the use of the <A HREF=R""></A> tag but specifying different information for the target address.

Tables

<TABLE> table definition tag
Defines table parameters.

<TR> table row tag
Defines a row within a table.

<TD> table data cell definition tag
Defines the characteristics of a cell within a row of a table.

Tables are commonly used in web page implementation, both for formatting data in tables such as a product catalogue on an e-commerce site and also for page layout. Tables are constructed using three tags. To define a table, start with the <TABLE> table definition tag. As the example below shows, parameters of this tag specify the width of the browser window the table will occupy, the style of the border (use 0 for no border) and spacing. Each row in the table is denoted by the <TR> table row tag and the columns are defined by the <TD> table data cell definition tag. In the example below there are three rows, so there are three <TR> table row tags and two columns indicated by six <TD> table cell definition tags. There are six <TD> tags since the columns are defined by individual cells, two cells are nested within each row, making six in total. This approach enables great flexibility in table design, which is especially useful for defining layouts as described in the next section. As in the example below, <TD> table cell definition tags are frequently used when creating tables since the parameters can be used to change the background colour and alignment of the contents of the cells. For example, for the first row the parameter for colour is bgcolor="#c0c0c0" and for alignment is align="center".

Table 12.1 Different forms of the <A HREF> tag to link to other documents

Link to	*Approach used*	*Example*
1 Elsewhere on same page	Define a destination tag using the <A NAME> tag and then link using reference of name preceded by #	<A NAME="Top"></A> <A HREF="#top">Go to top of document</A>
2 Another document on same site, same directory	Use <A HREF> tag with the destination document name specified	<A HREF="destination.htm"> Open page in sub directory </A>
3 Another document on same site, sub-directory document name	Use <A HREF> tag with sub-folder specified followed by / and the document filename	<A HREF="Sub-folder/ destination.htm"> Open page in sub directory</A>
4 Another document sub-folder specified parent directory	Use <A HREF> tag with parent in directory </A> followed by. ./ and the document name	<A HREF="destination.htm"> Open page on same site
5 A home page document on a different web site	Use <A HREF> tag with full site URL of destination site document. No .HTM file to open .htm	<A HREF="http://www.marketing-online.co.uk"> Marketing Online home page</A>
6 A named document on a different site	Use <A HREF> tag with full site URL of destination document including filename	<A HREF="http://www.marketing-online.co.uk/glossind.htm">Marketing Online glossary</A>

HTML code

```
< TABLE width="95% "
border="1"
cellspacing="0"
cellpadding="4">
<TR><!– Row 1 Column 1 –>
  <TD bgcolor="#c0c0c0"
align="center">
       <B>R1C1</B>
  </TD>
  <!– Row 1 Column 2 –>
  <TD bgcolor="#c0c0c0"
align="center">
       <B>R1C2</B>
  </TD>
</TR>
<TR><!– Row 2 Column 1 –>
  <TD align="left">
       R2C1
  </TD>
  <!– Row 2 Column 2 –>
  <TD align="right">
       R2C2
  </TD>
</TR>
<TR>
  <!– Row 3 Column 1 –>
  <TD align="left">
       R3C1
  </TD>
  <!– Row 3 Column 2 –>
  <TD align="right">R3C2</TD>
</TR>
</TABLE>
```

Browser display

R1C1	R1C2
R2C1	R2C2
R3C1	R3C2

Forms

<FORM> tag

Used to accept input from users.

Forms are used to enable interaction. In the example shown in *Figure 12.2*, and the code below, the <Form> tag is used to enable a customer to ask an online customer service question. The question is delivered to the customer service representative as an e-mail.

HTML code

```
<FORM ACTION="/cgi-bin/mailform.cgi" onSubmit="return
validate(this.form)"
METHOD="POST" NAME="enq_form">
<P>
<B>Your name:</B>
<BR><INPUT NAME="user_name" TYPE="text" SIZE="40" VALUE="">
<BR><BR>
```

```
<B>Your e-mail:</B>
<BR><INPUT NAME="e_mail" TYPE="text" size="60"
VALUE="">
<P>
<B>What is the question about?</B>
<BR>
<select name="type">
<option>Product offer</option>
<option>Product return</option>
<option>Other</option>
</select>
<P><B>Your question:</B><BR><TEXTAREA NAME="question"
TYPE="text" rows="6" cols="60" VALUE=""></TEXTAREA>
<P><P>
<INPUT NAME="forwardto" TYPE="hidden" VALUE="dc@marketing-
online.co.uk">
<P>
<INPUT NAME="nextlink" TYPE="hidden" VALUE="http://www.
marketing-online.co.uk/redirect.htm">
<P>
<INPUT TYPE="SUBMIT" Value="Send question">
<INPUT TYPE="RESET">
```

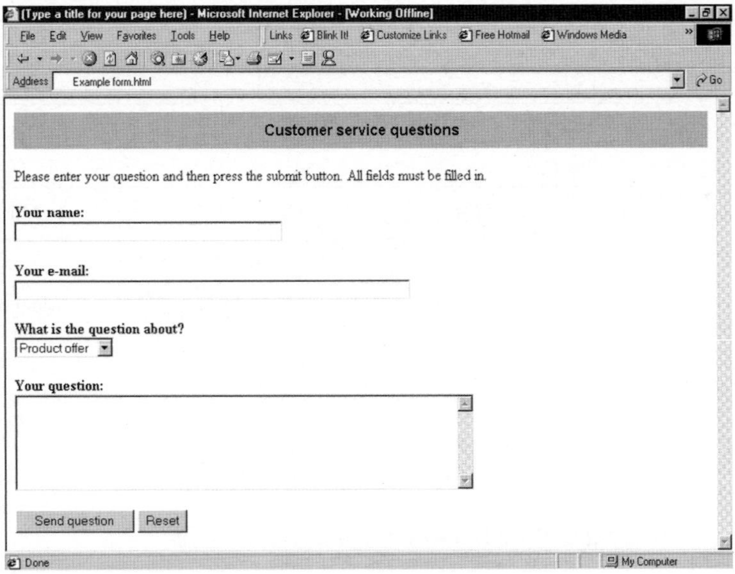

Figure 12.2 **An example online customer service form**

Page layout

The layout for a web page is similar in many ways to the front page of a newspaper. There will be a title area or banner, main content and a footer for each page. In addition, a company logo will usually be displayed together with one or more menus. As was mentioned in *Chapter 11* on *Web interface design*, for ease of use we are usually trying to make the layout consistent between different pages. There are many permutations for laying out a page; some of the more common ones are shown in *Figure 12.3*.

There are two main options for structuring a page such that different content appears in different parts of the page. These are *frames* and *tables*. Frames can be thought of as similar to the choice newspaper editors have for laying out front pages. *Figure 12.3* shows some common frame layouts. A common arrangement is *Figure 12.3(a)*; here one frame on the left has fixed content used for display of company name, logo and menus. When a user selects a menu option this usually causes a new HTML page to be loaded into the main frame window to the right, so this is the only area of screen that is updated. Sometimes as in *(c)* and *(d)* one frame is used for top-level menus that remain fixed and other frames are used to give sub-menu options according to the main menu selection.

<FRAMESET> and <FRAME> tags
Frames are a technical feature of HTML that provide a straightforward means of achieving a standard page layout on screen.

The **<FRAMESET> and <FRAME> tags** are used to produce frames.

HTML code for a two-frame column arrangement such as *Figure 12.3(a)* is shown below. Here, the FRAMESET tag refers to two columns. For horizontal frames the rows parameter can be used. When code such as that below is executed in the browser it will automatically load the content of the frame source indicated by SRC="menu.htm" into the browser. Typically, the user will select a menu option by clicking on a link in the menu and this will update the frame to the right (Main_area) which is known as the 'target frame'.

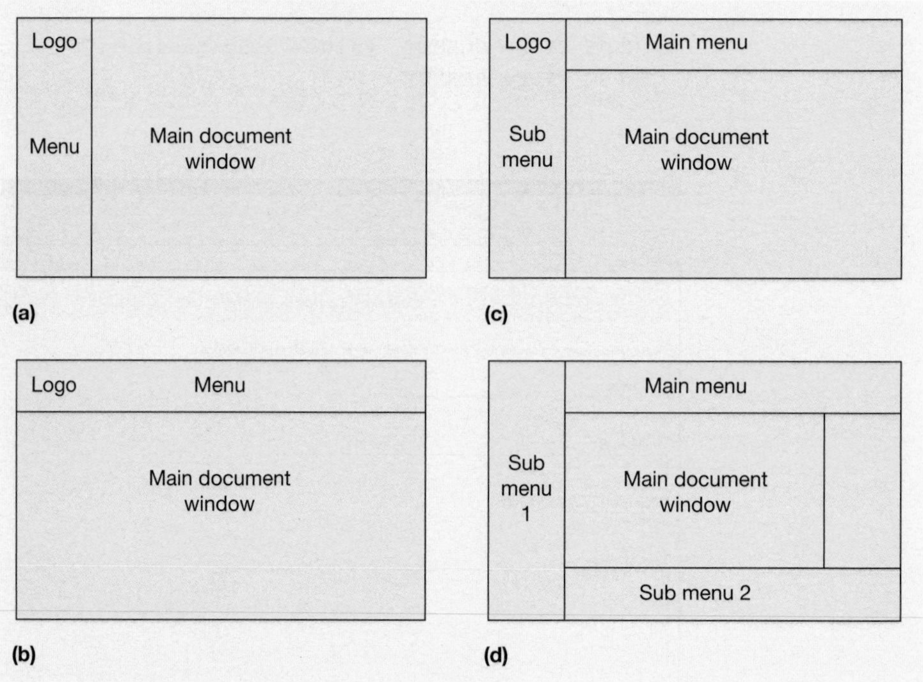

Figure 12.3 **Possible web page layout options**

HTML code

```
<HEAD>
<Frameset cols="30%,*">
<FRAME SRC="menu.htm" scrolling="yes" name="menu_area">
<FRAME SRC="main.htm" scrolling="yes" name="main_area">
</Frameset>
<Noframes>
```

```
This text is displayed if the user doesn't have frames
</Noframes>
</HEAD>
```

Although frames were widely used because they were a convenient technical solution to layout, many companies now use HTML tables to produce a similar effect. Framed sites may not be indexed by search engines and are more difficult for users to bookmark and print. An example of a table-based layout for The B2C Company home page is shown in *Figure 12.4*. The code necessary to achieve this arrangement is shown below.

HTML code

```
<html>
<head>

<table width="100%" border=0 cellspacing=0 cellpadding=0
bgcolor="#99CCFF">
<tr>

<font face="arial" size="12"
color="#000099"><b><center>
 The B2C Company<br> logo area<br></b>
<font face="arial" size="-3">
For your B2C needs</b></center></font>
</td>
<td width=100%>
<font face="arial" size="13"
color="#000099"><b><center>
Banner advert area
<font face="arial" size="-3"
color="#000099"><b></center>
</td>
</tr>
</table>
 <table width="100%" border=0 cellspacing=0 cellpadding=0><tr
valign=top>
 <!– Do not need closing </table> comment here due to nesting –>
 <table width=130 border=0 cellspacing=0 cellpadding=0
bgcolor="#000099">

 <!– Blue menu header on left –>
 <td width=130> <font face="Arial, Helvetica, sans-serif"
size=-1 color="#FFFFFF"><b>Options</b></font><br>
 <img src="images/singpix.gif" width=130
height=1></td></tr>

 </table>
 <!– Blue menu on left –>
 <!– First options –>
 <!– Header 1 –>
 <table width=125 border=0 cellspacing=0 cellpadding=0><tr>
 <td colspan=2>

<form method="get" action="http://search.atomz.com/ search/">
 <input size=15 name="sp-q"><br>
```

→

```
 <input type=submit value="Search">
 <input type=hidden name="sp-a" value="0005390c-sp00000000">
 <font face=Arial size=-1><BR><b>Browse
Products</b></font></td></tr><tr valign=top>

 <!– Suboption –>
 <td>&#149; </td>
 <td width="100%"><font face=Arial size=-1>
 <a href="proda.htm">Spring collection</a>
 </font></td></tr><tr valign=top>

 <!– Suboption –>
 <td>&#149; </td>
 <td width="100%"><font face=Arial size=-1>
 <a href="prodb.htm">Summer collection</a>
 </font></td></tr><tr valign=top>

 <!– Suboption –>
 <td>&#149; </td>
 <td width="100%"><font face=Arial size=-1>
 <a href="prodc.htm">Autumn collection</a>
 </font></td></tr><tr valign=top>

 </table>

 <!– Header 2 –>
 <table width=125 border=0 cellspacing=0 cellpadding=0><tr>
 <td colspan=2><font face=Arial size=-1><b>Customer
 services</b></font></td></tr><tr valign=top>

 <!– Suboption –>
 <td>&#149; </td>
 <td width="100%"><font face=Arial size=-1>
 <a href="faq.htm">Frequently Asked questions</a>
 </font></td></tr><tr valign=top>

 <!– Suboption –>
 <td>&#149; </td>
 <td width="100%"><font face=Arial size=-1>
 <a href="contact.htm">Contact us</a>
 </font></td></tr><tr valign=top>

 <!– Suboption –>
 <td>&#149; </td>
 <td width="100%"><font face=Arial size=-1>
 <a href="about.htm">About Us</a>
 </font></td></tr><tr valign=top>
 </table>
 </td>

 <td width="100%">
 <table border=0 width=100% cellspacing=0 cellpadding=2
bgcolor=#ffffff><tr><td><center></center>
 </td></tr></table>

 <!– Main window –>
 <font face=Arial >
 <table width="100%" border=0 cellspacing=1 cellpadding=0><tr>
 <td height=0 colspan=3>
```

```
<td border=0>

<TITLE>The B2C Company</TITLE>
<table width="100%" border="0" cellpadding="10"
cellspacing="0">
<tr><BR><BR></TR>
<tr>
<td width="100%" ><p align="center"><font size="13"
face="Arial"><b>
Home page and <BR> shopping catalogue area
</b></font></td></p></tr></table>

<!– End main window –>
</td></tr>
<tr><td colspan=3 height=5></td></tr></table>
</table>
<table border=0 width=100% cellspacing=0 cellpadding=2
bgcolor=#ffffff><tr><td><center></center>
</td></tr></table>

<td></td><tr></tr>

 <table width="100%" cellpadding=0 cellspacing=0 border=0><tr>
 <td bgcolor="#003399"><img src="images/singpix.gif" border=0
 width=0 height=2></td></tr></table>
 <table width="100%" cellpadding=5 cellspacing=0 border=0><tr>
 <td align=center><font size=-2 face="arial,helvetica"
 color="#003399">
 <a href="/">&copy; Copyright 2000 The B2C Company – Legal
 notices</a>
 </FONT>
 </td></tr></table>
 </body></html>
```

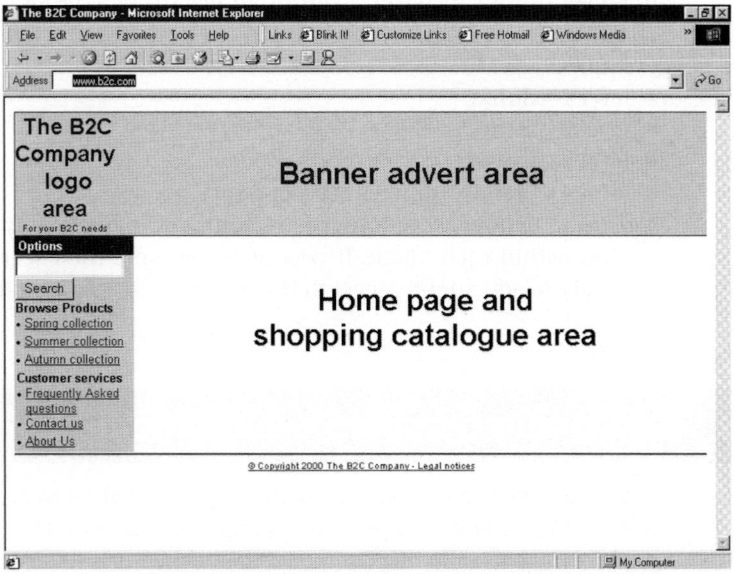

Figure 12.4 Table-based page layout for The B2C Company

Menus

Sites are easier to navigate if there are limited numbers of menu options. It is usually suggested that two or possibly three levels of menus are the most that are desirable. For example, there may be main menu options at the left of the screen that take the user to the different parts of the site and at the bottom of the screen will be specific menu options that refer to that part of the site. (Sub-menus in this form are often referred to as being 'nested'.)

Menu options

Designing and creating the menus to support navigation present several options and these are briefly described. The main options are:

1 *Text menus, buttons or images*. The site user can select menus by clicking on different objects. They can click on a basic text hyperlink, underlined in blue, by default. The use of text menus only may make a site look primitive and reduce its graphic appeal, but some professional sites such as Cisco (www.cisco.com) use this approach. Graphic images or buttons can be used to highlight menu options more distinctly. While these are graphically appealing it may not be obvious that these are menu options until the user positions the mouse over them. A combination of text menu options and either buttons or images is usually the best compromise. This way the user has the visual appeal of buttons or images, but also the faster option of text – they can select these menus if they are waiting for graphical elements to load, or if the images are turned off in the web browser.

2 *Rollovers*. 'Rollover' is the term used to describe where the colour of the menu option changes when the user positions the mouse over the menu option and then changes again when the menu option is selected. Rollovers are useful in that they help achieve the context referred to in the previous section by highlighting the area of the site the user is in.

3 *Positioning*. Menus can be positioned at any of the edges of the screen, with left, bottom or top being conventional for Western cultures. The main design aim is to keep the position consistent between different parts of the site.

4 *Number of levels*. In a hierarchical structure there could be as many as ten different levels, but for simplicity it is normal to try and achieve a site structure with a nesting level of four or fewer. Even in an electronic commerce shopping site with 20,000 products it should be possible to select a product at four menu levels. For example:
   - level 1 – drink
   - level 2 – spirits
   - level 3 – whisky
   - level 4 – brand x (different size options).

5 *Number of options*. Psychologists recommend having only a limited number of choices within each menu. If you are using more than seven, then it is probably necessary to add another level to the hierarchy to accommodate the extra choices.

Focus on developing dynamic web content

Scripting languages
A software standard providing a set of instructions to perform a particular task.

Scripting languages are one of the main tools for creating dynamic web content, a set of instructions intended to perform a particular task. In a web context JavaScript, for example, can be used to display today's date when it is loaded into a browser. Barron (2000) notes that the term probably originated from the use of scripts by actors in

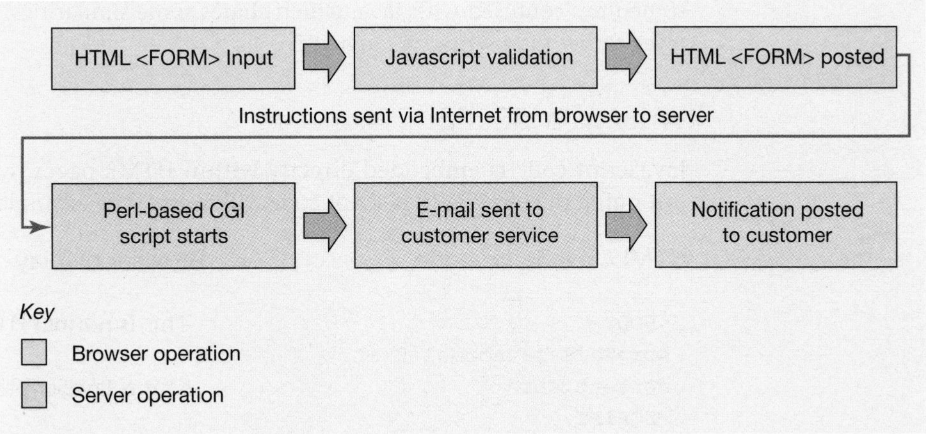

Figure 12.5 Using scripting to produce dynamic web content for form processing

theatre and film. Scripts differ from programs in that they are usually less complex and are executed and run in a single compile-and-run stage. For example, when a web page is loaded, if it contains JavaScript code it is executed or interpreted immediately. This is in contrast to traditional programming languages such as C++ where the program is compiled and checked as part of the development process before executable code is run when the user starts the program.

An early use of web scripting was for processing web forms. HTML contains some tags for accepting data input by a user into a form on the web browser which is then sent to the server for action. For example, a user might type in a question for customer service on the e-commerce site, by typing in their details and the nature of the query. After clicking the submit button, the data is sent to the server where it can be transformed by a CGI script (see later section) into an e-mail to be sent to customer service which is formatted to summarize the nature of the problem and the customer's personal details. The CGI script may then be used to produce a dynamic notification page in the browser that thanks the user for asking a question and says how and when it will be answered. The processing on the server has traditionally been performed by CGI scripts which can be written in a scripting language such as Perl. More recently the JavaScript language has been used to perform some checking or validation of what the user enters within the browser before it is sent to the server. As the example in the section on JavaScript shows, we can use JavaScript in the browser to check whether a valid e-mail address has been entered. The overall process is shown in *Figure 12.5* and explained in more detail in the section on *JavaScript*. This process can be applied to many web interactions from filling in a customer service form to an electronic shopping catalogue.

We will look at one web scripting language, JavaScript, in some detail since this is the most widely used scripting language and illustrates how dynamic web content is developed. When scripting is performed by a script which is executed by the browser, as in the form checking example above, this is referred to as 'client-side scripting', while when the script is run on the server, for example, a CGI script, this is referred to as 'server-side scripting'.

Client-side scripting
Scripts executed on the browser.

Server-side scripting
Scripts executed on the server.

JavaScript

JavaScript
A web-page scripting language that uses an object model.

JavaScript is a scripting language that was originally developed by Netscape, but is now widely used in web development and is supported by all browsers. JavaScript is sometimes confused with Java, which shares some similarities, but Java is a programming rather than scripting language.

Writing JavaScript

JavaScript code is embedded directly within HTML pages, with the <SCRIPT> tag informing the browser that script code will follow. The example below shows this.

HTML/JavaScript code

```
<BODY>
<br>This is normal HTML
content.<br>
<SCRIPT
language="JavaScript">
document.write("This is
JavaScript!")
</SCRIPT>
</BODY>
```

Browser display

This is normal HTML content

This is JavaScript!

From the above example, the reason for using JavaScript may not be clear – we are simply writing a line of text which appears in the browser and we can do this with HTML. The benefits are made clear by the next example where we use JavaScript to display the current date – the page is dynamically updated according to the current date and time.

HTML/JavaScript code

```
<SCRIPT
LANGUAGE="JavaScript"><!– ;
var current_date = new
Date;document.write("The news
at " + current_date.
getHours() + ":"
+ current_date.get Minutes()
1 " on "
+ current_date. getDate() +
"-"
+ current_date. getMonth() +
"-"
+ current_date. getYear()
);
// end hide –></SCRIPT>
```

Browser display

The News at 13:25 on 15-05-2001

Document object model (DOM)

Document object model (DOM)
Enables developers to get and set properties of different document objects such as forms and frames.

JavaScript and other client-side scripting languages enable developers to access different elements of a document to update its properties. The different elements that can be accessed are referred to as the **'document object model' (DOM)**. The Netscape DOM enables the developer to get and change the properties of the current document and specific forms and frames. In the example above a write method is used to update the contents of the document window (document. write();).

JavaScript can also perform simple calculations in response to user entry, thus making the web page interactive. In the following example a user can type in the amount of loan that they require and the script is used to calculate the total repayment. The calculation is defined in a function 'calculation()' in the header section of the HTML page. This function is executed when the user presses the calculate button in the form 'MyForm'. The instruction to perform the calculation is determined by the statement within the input button: OnClick="calculation()". Note that in a mortgage application more complex calculations would probably be performed. The result is displayed for the user as an Alert box using the alert function. Alternatively the result could be written to a new page.

HTML/JavaScript code

```
<HTML><HEAD>
<SCRIPT
LANGUAGE="JavaScript"><!– ;
function calculation() {
var x= 0.05; <!– Interest
rate –>
y =
eval(document.MyForm.loan.val
ue)
var result= y 1 (x * y);
alert('Total repayment: £'
result);
}
// end hide –></SCRIPT>
</HEAD>
<BODY>
<FORM name="MyForm">
Loan amount
<INPUT TYPE="number"
NAME="loan" SIZE="10"
VALUE="500">
<INPUT TYPE="button"
VALUE="Calculate"
OnClick="calculation()">
</FORM>
</BODY></HTML>
```

Browser display

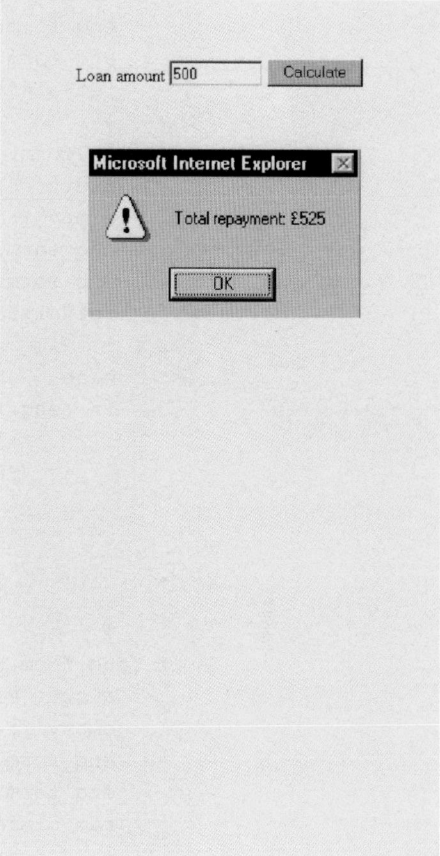

The use of the OnClick statement to execute the calculation in the above example is a common use of JavaScript to increase the interactivity of web pages. OnClick is referred to as an 'event handler'.

Events and event handlers
An event handler monitors and responds to events such as mouse clicks.

Examples of event handlers include the user clicking on a button (OnClick event), the mouse pointer moving across a link (OnMouseOver event), or the mouse pointer moving away from a graphic (OnMouseOut event).

Validation

Form validation
Used to check the validity of form inputs from users.

It is important for any input received from a form on a web site to be checked for validity. JavaScript can also be used for form validation of data entry into a form using the document object model.

In the *Focus on HTML* section we saw how HTML could be used to display an HTML form. In the Form statement the parameter 'onSubmit="return validate(this.form)"' is used to start a function to validate the code. The validation checks that each mandatory field is complete and checks for an e-mail address containing an '@' symbol using the JavaScript code below.

HTML/JavaScript code

```
    <!–
function validate() {
var retVal=true;
if (enq_form.user_name.value == "" ) {
     alert("Please enter your name, this field is empty");
     enq_form.user_name.focus();
     enq_form.user_name.select();
     retVal=false;
     }
if (enq_form.e_mail.value == "" ) {
     alert("Please enter your e-mail address, this field is
     empty");
     enq_form.e_mail.focus();
     enq_form.e_mail.select();
     retVal=false;
     }
     else    {
     if (enq_form.e_mail.value.indexOf('@',0) == -1) {
            alert("You have not entered a valid e-mail address
            (@ missing)");
               enq_form.e_mail.focus();
               enq_form.e_mail.select();
               retVal=false;
                         }
     }
if (enq_form.question.value == "" ) {
     alert("Please enter the nature of your query, this field is
     empty");
     enq_form.question.focus();
     enq_form.question.select();
     retVal=false;
     }
return retVal;
}
//–>
</SCRIPT>
```

VBScript

Like JavaScript, VBScript can be used for client-side scripting. However, it is not as widely used as JavaScript since it is mainly supported by the Microsoft Internet Explorer browser. VBScript's importance is that it is most commonly used for constructing active server pages (ASPs).

Perl

Perl
'Practical Execution and Report Language' is used mainly for server side scripting and producing CGI scripts.

Perl is commonly used as a scripting language on web development projects. Its application is indicated by its full name of 'Practical Execution and Report Language'.

Active server pages (ASPs)

Active server pages (ASPs)
A Microsoft-developed technology that can be used for dynamic web pages, often related to database query and retrieval.

Active server pages are now commonly used to build dynamic content. Although originally developed for Microsoft Internet Information Server, they are increasingly supported by web-server software from other manufacturers. A common application for ASPs is when a user is accessing a shopping trolley on an e-commerce site. ASP is used to manage the user's requests for certain products, information about the products and their availability and adding them to a trolley. ASP can also manage the use of cookies to recognize return visits.

When using a browser you may often see .asp at the end of the browser. When an instruction is sent via http to a web server to load an ASP page the following sequence of operations occurs:

1 The parameters to the ASP statement are interpreted (these are often database query parameters such as the name of an airline, the route to be searched and to show available dates only).
2 The ASP script is executed; this may involve performing a database query, in this example to find available flights. Scripts are typically in VBScript, but other scripting languages can be used.
3 HTML pages are written dynamically to display the flight information returned from the database.

.NET

.NET
Both a business strategy from Microsoft and a supporting collection of programming languages to enable web services to be offered by applications service providers.

.NET, formerly known as 'ASP.net', is not a minor revision to ASP by Microsoft, rather it uses a different programming model to offer improvements in performance, scalability, reliability and security. According to Bill Gates, Microsoft expects that .NET will have as significant an effect on the computing world as the introduction of Windows. This impact is because it is not just a programming language, but a Microsoft business strategy for interoperability or support for web services. Web services are similar in principle to the application service provider applications described in *Chapter 3*. They enable an application to be accessed remotely from the server on which it is running. It is a facility which has encouraged many organizations to plan to use the technology in future. .NET makes it easier to enable different applications within different companies to communicate and transfer data using XML – this will give rise to new supply chain management solutions. The model also supports access using a range of devices and platforms such as PDAs and mobiles. The technology should make it easier for remote workers to access and update company data.

Common Gateway Interface (CGI)

CGI (Common Gateway Interface)
CGI offers a way of providing interactivity through the web.

The CGI (Common Gateway Interface) offers a way of providing interactivity to the web since CGI provides extensions to the web server which allow server-side scripts to be run which process information submitted through web-based forms.

Java
A programming language standard supported by Sun Microsystems which permits complex and graphical customer applications to be written and then accessed from a web browser. An example might be a form for calculating interest on a loan. A competitor to ActiveX.

ActiveX
A programming language standard developed by Microsoft which permits complex and graphical customer applications to be written and then accessed from a web browser. An example might be a form for calculating interest on a loan. A competitor to Java.

Other standards for dynamic content

In addition to the scripting languages described above there are now a range of competing methods which can be used to enable the user to interact with a web site by selecting menu options and entering data. The best known of these standards is the **Java** programming language. Microsoft **ActiveX** is a rival technique. Dynamic content is also increasingly developed using plug-ins from Macromedia such as Flash and Shockwave.

To put into practice some of the techniques for developing static and dynamic content described in the previous section attempt *Activity 12.4*.

Activity 12.4 An intranet for The B2B Company

Purpose

To use HTML to develop a simple site and apply systems analysis and design skills from *Chapter 11*.

Activity

Develop a simple intranet web site for employees of The B2B Company.

1. First outline the requirements based on the extract below. You should include general requirements such as audience, content and services together with a use-case or scenario or storyboard of the structure of the proposed company web site.
2. Implement the web site using HTML and JavaScript. You should write your definition for the company web site based on the description given below plus any other features you feel may be useful.

Outline of requirements

This is a summary of a discussion between the marketing manager for The B2B Company and a junior member of their team who has been asked to develop the specification for the intranet site.

Q. *Who is the intranet intended for?*
A. It will be used by everyone at head office, together with regional offices and overseas distributors and agents. It will not be used directly by customers, but some of the information may be made available through an extranet.

Q. *What is the reason for the business to set up this intranet?*
A. The main aims are:

- Improved information dissemination and feedback within the company and to agents.
- Improve response to queries from customers by employees and agents.
- Improved internal exchange of information for communication and decision making.

Q. *What type of content and services will be on the intranet?*
A. The types of information that The B2B Company wants to provide on the intranet include internal information about product release status, news of past and future events including meetings, trade shows and training seminars, company performance (sales figures) and social information in a monthly newsletter. Some information will be available to all employees and agents, while some such as sales figures will be restricted to certain employees at head office. Details of contact address, position, responsibility and phone numbers for company employees and agents in all countries will also be made available. Similar data will be made available for customers, and these will include their sales history and support questions related to them. Market information such as competitor addresses and market share data will also be provided.

A new database system is required as part of the intranet. Its main purpose is to provide an online question-and-answer forum, or virtual helpdesk. This replaces a manual system where all enquiries were entered in an Excel spreadsheet. It will enable named B2B Company employees and agents to ask a question about a particular product such as product availability, pricing, technical specifications and known problems about products and record where it applies to a particular customer. More general questions can also be asked. This virtual helpdesk will only be available to registered users who have a valid username and password and are on the company-wide address book. They will be able to specify three levels of urgency for the reply. The question will be answered by a named support/helpdesk employee who may include reference in their answer to one or more technical info sheets. The system should record and display the date and time of each question and answer. Support and contact information will also be provided. To enable similar queries to be answered in future, the forum will build up through time to be a knowledge base. So options will be available to search the database by keyword, or a particular employee name, customer name, product name or according to the type of query. To ensure prompt responses to questions all answers will also be e-mailed to employees when answered. It will also be possible for helpdesk staff to sort/order outstanding queries in terms of priority.

No suggested answers supplied.

Tools for web-site development and testing

A variety of software programs are available to help developers of web sites. These can save a lot of time when developing the sites and will also help in site maintenance since they will make it easier for other people not involved in the original development of the web site to be involved in web-site maintenance. Tools are available with different levels of complexity and managers must decide which are most suitable to invest in. The types of tools to choose between are listed below. Although there are many rival tools, the ones here have been used for several years and are widely used, and skills in these tools are often mentioned in adverts for web design staff.

Basic text and graphic editors

Simple text editors can be used to edit HTML tags. Such tools are often low-cost or free, including the Notepad editor included with Windows. They are flexible and all web site developers may need to use them at some stage to develop content since more automated tools may not provide this flexibility and may not support the latest standard commands.

Examples

- Microsoft Windows Notepad (www.microsoft.com)
- Program File Editor (PFE).

Graphics editors are used to create and modify GIF and JPEG pictures.

Examples

- Adobe Photoshop (www.macromedia.com)
- Paintshop Pro (www.jasc.com).

Specialized HTML editors

These tools provide facilities for adding HTML tags automatically. For example, adding the bold text tag <B> </B> to the HTML document will happen when the user clicks the bold tag.

Examples

There are many freeware and shareware editors in this category.

Basic tools

- Arachnoid (www.arachnoid.com) is a good, freely available (careware) tool.
- Microsoft FrontPage (www.microsoft.com).
- Modern versions of word processors such as Microsoft Word now have these facilities through using the Save As Web Page option.

Advanced graphics tools

- Adobe Photoshop (extensively used by graphic designers, www.adobe.com).
- Macromedia Flash and Director-Shockwave (used for graphical animations, www.macromedia.com).

Site management tools

These tools provide the advanced HTML editing facilities of the previous category, but also provide tools to help manage and test the site including graphic layouts of the structure of the site making it easy to find, modify and republish the page by sending the file to the web site using FTP (*Chapter 3*). Scripting with HTML is also possible. Style templates can be applied to produce a consistent look and feel across the site. Tools are also available to create and manage menu options. Many of the tools that started as basic HTML editors have now been developed to incorporate the site management features.

Examples

- ColdFusion (www.allaire.com)
- Dreamweaver (www.macromedia.com)
- Fusion (www.netobjects.com).

Content management systems

Content management system (CMS)
A software tool for creating, editing and updating documents accessed by intranet, extranet, or Internet.

A content management system (CMS) provides a method for non-specialists to update web site pages. Lotus Notes was an early form of enterprise CMS. This is an efficient method of publishing content since the facility can be made available to people throughout the company. Today there are two main forms of CMS, both of which are delivered as web services which can be accessed through a web browser. Enterprise CMS can be used for large, complex sites (and other corporate documents) and as well as the standard page creation and editing facilities, CMS enable version control and review of documents through workflow systems which notify reviewers when new documents are ready for editing.

Content management systems provide these facilities:

- *structure authoring*: the design and maintenance of content structure (sub-components, templates, etc.), web-page structure and web-site structure;
- *link management*: the maintenance of internal and external links through content change and the elimination of dead links;
- *search engine visibility*: the content within the search engine must be stored and linked such that it can be indexed by search engine robots to add it to their index – this was not possible with some first-generation content management systems, but is typical of more recent content management systems;
- *input and syndication*: the loading (spidering) of externally originating content and the aggregation and dissemination of content from a variety of sources;

- *versioning*: the crucial task of controlling which edition of a page, page element or the whole site is published. Typically this will be the most recent, but previous editions should be archived and it should be possible to roll back to a previous version at the page, page element or site level;
- *security and access control*: different permissions can be assigned to different roles of users and some content may only be available through log-in details. In these cases, the CMS maintains a list of users. This facility is useful when a company needs to use the same CMS for an intranet, extranet or public Internet site which may have different levels of permission;
- *publication workflow*: content destined for a web site needs to pass through a publication process to move it from the management environment to the live delivery environment. The process may involve tasks such as format conversion (e.g. to PDF, or to WAP), rendering to HTML, editorial authorization and the construction of composite documents in real time (personalization and selective dissemination);
- *tracking and monitoring*: providing logs and statistical analysis of use to provide performance measures, tune the content according to demand and protect against misuse;
- *navigation and visualization*: providing an intuitive, clear and attractive representation of the nature and location of content using colour, texture, 3D rendering or even virtual reality.

Examples

- Lotus Notes/Domino (www.lotus.com)
- Interwoven (www.interwoven.com)
- RedDot (www.reddot.com)
- Plone (www.plone.org).

Personal CMSs are lower-cost CMSs that can be used by individuals or smaller businesses, often as part of the hosting package. They enable editing and update of content, but do not usually contain version control or workflow facilities. Personal CMSs overlap with blogging services, many of which can be configured for more general site management.

Examples

- Blogger (www.blogger.com)
- Movable Type (www.movabletype.com)
- WordPress (www.wordpress.org)
- Mambo/Jumla (www.mamboserver.com).

Many of these capable CMSs such as Plone, WordPress and Mambo are open source CMSs meaning that the cost of ownership is low.

E-commerce site development tools

These include support for developing catalogue browsing and selection and creation of shopping baskets for transaction e-commerce sites.

Examples

- Actinic (www.actinic.com)
- Intershop (www.intershop.com)
- Imano CommerceNow (www.imano.com).

Testing

Testing
Aims to identify non-conformance in the requirements specification and errors.

Testing has two main objectives: first, to check for non-conformance with the business and user requirements, and, second, to identify bugs or errors. In other words, it checks that the site does what users need and is reliable. Testing is an iterative process that occurs throughout development. As non-conformances are fixed by the development team, there is a risk that the problem may not have been fixed and that new problems have been created. Further testing is required to check that solutions to problems are effective.

The testing process

Test specification
A description of the testing process and tests to be performed.

A structured testing process is necessary in order to identify and solve as many problems as possible before the system is released to users. This testing is conducted in a structured way by using a test specification which is a comprehensive specification of testing in all modules of the system. If the use-case method of analysis described in *Chapter 11* is used then it will specify the different use-cases or scenarios to be tested in detailed test scripts. The comprehensive testing specification will also cover all the different types of test outlined in *Table 12.2*.

Table 12.2 **Types of testing required for an e-commerce site**

Type of testing	*Description*
Developer tests	Code-level tests performed by developers of modules
Feasibility testing	Tests a new approach, often near the start of a project to make sure it is acceptable in terms of user experience
Module (component) tests	Checks individual modules have the correct functionality, i.e. correct outputs are produced for specified inputs (black-box testing)
Integration testing	Checks interactions between groups of modules
System testing	Checks interactions between all modules in the system
Database transaction taken	Can the user connect to the database and are transactions executed correctly?
Performance/capacity testing	Tests the speed of the system under high load
Usability and accessibility testing	Check that the system is easy to use, follows the conventions of user-centred design and meets accessibility requirements described in *Chapter 11*
Acceptance tests	Checks the system is acceptable for the party that commissioned it
Content or copy testing	Tests the acceptability of copy from a marketing view

Testing in the web environment requires new constraints. Unfortunately the list of constraints is long and sometimes neglected to disastrous effect. Retailer Boo.com used a complex graphic to display clothes that was too time-consuming to use for visitors to the site. If there are a thousand potential users of an e-commerce site, all of the following constraints on design may exclude a proportion:

- *Speed of access* – everyone has used sites with huge graphics that take minutes to download. Good designers will optimize graphics for speed and then test using a slow modem across phone lines. Yahoo! downloads in just one second, so this is the performance that users expect from other sites.
- *Screen resolutions* – designing for different screen resolutions is necessary since some users with laptops may be operating at low resolution such as 640 by 480 pixels, the majority at 800 by 600 pixels, a few at higher resolutions of 1064 by 768 pixels or greater. If the designers have designed the site using PCs with high resolutions, they may be difficult to read for the majority.
- *Number of colours* – some users may have monitors capable of displaying 16 million colours giving photo-realism while others may only have the PC set up to display 256 colours.
- *Changing font size* – choosing large fonts on some sites causes unsightly overlap between the different design elements – depends on the type of web browser used.
- *Different browsers* such as Microsoft Internet Explorer and Netscape Navigator and different versions of browsers such as version 4.0 or 5.0 may display graphics or text slightly differently or process JavaScript differently, so it is essential to test on a range of browser platforms.
- *Plug-ins such as Macromedia Flash and Shockwave* – if a site requires plug-ins that the user doesn't have, then a business will be cutting down its audience by the number of people who are unable or unprepared to download these plug-ins.

Testing environments

Development environment
Software and hardware used to create a system.

Test environment
Separate software and hardware used to test a system.

Production or live environment
Software and hardware used to host operational system.

Testing occurs in different environments during the project. Prototypes are tested in a development environment which involves programmers' testing data across a network on a shared server. In the implementation phase a special test environment may be set up which simulates the final operating environment for the system. This test environment will be used for early user training and testing and for system testing. Finally, the production or live environment is that in which the system will be used operationally. This will be used for user acceptance testing and when the system becomes live.

Changeover

Changeover
The term used to describe moving from the old to the new information system.

Soft launch
A preliminary site launch with limited promotion to provide initial feedback and testing of an e-commerce site.

Migration or changeover from a previous information system to a new system is particularly important for mission-critical e-business systems where errors in management of changeover will result in a negative customer experience or disruption to the supply chain.

In this section we look at significant issues involved in managing this transition from previous systems to e-business systems and the transition from one version of an e-business system to the next. When introducing a new sell-side e-commerce system there are two basic choices. First, the company can fully test the system in a controlled environment before it goes live and thus minimize the risk of adverse publicity due to problems with the site. Second, the company can perform what is known as a 'soft launch'. Here, after initial testing, the site will be tested in a live environment where customers can use it.

The alternatives for migrating from different versions of a system are reviewed in Bocij *et al.* (2005) and summarized in *Table 12.3*. Complete *Activity 12.5* to review the relative merits of these approaches.

Table 12.3 **Advantages and disadvantages of the different methods of implementation**

Method	*Main advantages*	*Main disadvantages*
1 **Immediate cutover.** Straight from old system to new system on a single date	Rapid, lowest cost	High risk. Major disruption if serious errors with system
2 **Parallel running.** Old system and new system run side-by-side for a period	Lower risk than immediate cutover	Slower and higher cost than immediate cutover
3 **Phased implementation.** Different modules of the system are introduced sequentially	Good compromise between methods 1 and 2	Difficult to achieve technically due to interdependencies between modules
4 **Pilot system.** Trial implementation occurs before widespread deployment	Essential for multinational or national rollouts	Has to be used in combination with the other methods
5 **'Perpetual beta'**	Used by on-demand service providers such as the search engines to introduce new functionality in modules	Errors not identified in testing may impact large numbers of users, but can be updated to users rapidly

Activity 12.5 Understanding e-commerce and e-business

Purpose

Highlight the most suitable techniques for changeover.

Activity

1. Identify the variables which will determine the choice of changeover method.
2. What alternative would you recommend for The B2B Company as it introduces the new intranet-based virtual helpdesk described in *Activity 12.4*?
3. Justify your answer by analysing in a table the degree of risk, from high to low for each factor across each approach.

Answers to activities can be found at www.pearsoned.co.uk/chaffey

Database creation and data migration

Data migration
Transfer of data from old systems to new systems.

A final aspect of changeover that should be mentioned, and is often underestimated, is data migration. For an e-commerce system for a bank, for example, this would involve transferring or exporting data on existing customers and importing them to the new system. This is sometimes also referred to as 'populating the database'. Alternatively, a middleware layer may be set up such that the new system accesses customers from the original legacy database. Before migration occurs it is also necessary for a member of the development team known as 'the database administrator' to create the e-commerce databases. This can be time-consuming since it involves:

- Creating the different tables by entering the field definitions arising from the data modelling described in *Chapter 11*.
- Creating the different roles of users such as their security rights or access privileges. These need to be created for internal and external users.

Deployment plan
A schedule which defines all the tasks that need to occur in order for changeover to occur successfully. This includes putting in place all the infrastructure such as cabling and hardware.

Systems integrator
A company that organizes the procurement and installation of hardware and software needed for implementation.

- Creating stored procedures and triggers, which is effectively server-side coding to implement business rules.
- Optimizing the database for performance.

Deployment planning

A **deployment plan** is needed to put in place the hardware and software infrastructure in time for user acceptance testing. This is not a trivial task since often a range of equipment will be required from a variety of manufacturers. Although the project manager is ultimately responsible for deployment planning, many companies employ **systems integrators** to coordinate these activities, particularly where there is a national rollout.

Content management and maintenance

Sell-side e-commerce sites are continuously under development, even when they become live. The sites need to be dynamic to deal with errors reported by customers and in response to innovations by competitors. Additionally the content, such as information about different events or new product launches and price promotions, will need to be updated if the site is to generate repeat visits from customers.

Buy-side e-commerce sites are less dynamic and are more akin to traditional business information systems, so in this section we will focus on maintenance of e-commerce sites, although this description will also apply to e-business implementations of intranets and extranets.

What are the management issues involved with maintenance? We will review the following:

- Deciding on the frequency and scope of content updating
- Processes for managing maintenance of the site and responsibilities for updating
- Selection of content management system
- Testing and communicating changes made
- Integration with monitoring and measurement systems
- Managing content in the global organization.

Frequency and scope of content updating

The moment an e-commerce system is live it will require updates to the content and services. Different types of content updating can be identified, and a different approach will be required for each. We can apply the fault taxonomy of Jorgenson (1995) to an e-commerce site to decide on the timing of the action required according to the type of problem. We can see that the approach is quite different from that for a traditional information system or packaged software that is distributed to thousands of customers. For example, with a mild problem such as a spelling mistake within software, it would be too costly to update and redistribute the software. With the e-commerce site, a spelling mistake, although trivial, can be updated immediately by correcting it on the web page or in the database/content management system where it is stored. Indeed, minor problems need to be corrected because they reduce the credibility of the site.

For more major errors, it is essential to fix the problems as soon as possible since revenue will be lost, both from customers who are unable to complete their current purchases, and from users who will be unprepared to use the site in future because of their bad experience. Data from transactional e-commerce sites show that very few have continuous availability. Problems can occur from bugs in the e-commerce software or problems with the web-server hardware and software. Some are as bad as 90 per cent. If the site revenue for a 24-hours, 7-days-a-week site is £10 million per week then if availability falls to 95 per cent this is the equivalent of losing £500,000 before

Table 12.4 Fault taxonomy described in Jorgensen (1995) applied to an e-commerce site

Category	*Example*	*Action – traditional BIS or packaged software*	*Action – e-commerce site*
1 Mild	Misspelled word	Ignore or fix when next major release occurs	Fix immediately
2 Moderate	Misleading or redundant information. Problem with font readability	Ignore or defer to next major release	Fix immediately
3 Annoying	Truncated text, failed JavaScript, but site still usable	Defer to next major release	Fix immediately
4 Disturbing	Some transactions not processed correctly, intermittent crashes in one module	Defer to next maintenance release	Urgent patch required for module
5 Serious	Lost transactions	Defer to next maintenance release. May need immediate fix and release	Urgent patch required for module
6 Very serious	Crash occurs regularly in one module	Immediate solution needed	Urgent patch required for module, revert to previous version
7 Extreme	Frequent very serious errors	Immediate solution needed	Urgent patch required for module, revert to previous version
8 Intolerable	Database corruption	Immediate solution needed	Urgent patch required for module, revert to previous version
9 Catastrophic	System crashes, cannot be restarted – system unusable	Immediate solution needed	Urgent patch required for module, revert to previous version
10 Infectious	Catastrophic problem also causes failure of other systems	Immediate solution needed	Revert to previous version

Source: Copyright © 1995 from *Software Testing: A Craftsman's Approach* by Paul C. Jorgensen. Reproduced by permission of Routledge/Taylor & Francis Group, LLC the loss of future revenues from disgruntled customers is taken into account. A modular or component-based approach to e-commerce systems should enable the location of the problem module or cartridge to be identified rapidly and the problem in the module to be fixed, or possibly to revert to the previous version.

As well as fixing the problems shown in *Table 12.4* companies will also wish to update the functionality of the e-commerce system in response to customer demands, sales promotions or competitor innovations. Again a component-based approach can enable self-contained, discrete, new modules or cartridges to be plugged into the system which are designed to provide new functionality with only minimal changes to existing modules. For each such update, a small-scale prototyping process involving analysis, design and testing will need to occur.

Maintenance process and responsibilities

Debate 12.1

Control of web content

'Web site content organization and standards for page design and copy must be centrally controlled to achieve consistency across any organization, regardless of size.'

For efficient updating of an e-commerce system, it is vital to have a clearly defined process for content and service changes. Different processes will apply depending on the scope of the change, as described in the previous section. We can identify two different types of changes – routine content changes such as updates to documents on the site or new documents and major changes where we make changes to the structure, navigation or services on the site.

Process for routine content changes

The process for routine content changes should be communicated to all staff providing content to the site, with responsibilities clearly identified in their job descriptions. The main stages involved in producing an updated web page are to design it, write it, test it and publish it. A more detailed process is indicated here which distinguishes between review of the content and technical testing of the completed web page. A simple model of the work involved in maintenance is shown in *Figure 12.6*. It is assumed that the needs of the users and design features of the site had already been defined when the site was originally created as described in *Chapter 8*. The model only applies to minor updates to copy, or perhaps updating product or company information.

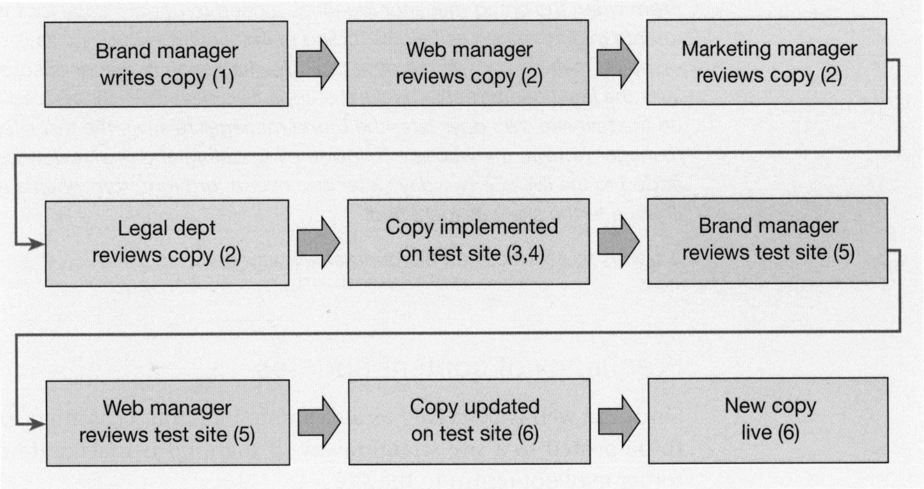

Figure 12.6 **A content update review process**

According to Chaffey *et al.* (2006), the different tasks involved in the maintenance process for new copy are as follows:

1 *Write*. This stage involves writing copy and, if necessary, designing the layout of copy and associated images.
2 *Review*. An independent review of the copy is necessary to check for errors before a document is published. Depending on the size of organization, review may be necessary by one person or several people covering different aspects of site quality such as corporate image, marketing copy, branding and legality.
3 *Correct*. This stage is straightforward and involves updates necessary as a result of stage 2.
4 *Publish (to test environment)*. The publication stage involves putting the corrected copy on a web page which can be checked further. This will be in a test environment that can only be viewed from inside the company.
5 *Test*. Before the completed web page is made available over the World Wide Web a final test will be required for technical issues such as whether the page loads successfully on different browsers.
6 *Publish (to live environment)*. Once the material has been reviewed and tested and is signed off as satisfactory it will be published to the main web site and will be accessible by customers.

The difficulty is that all these stages are required for quality control, but if different people are involved then rapid, responsive publication is not possible. *Activity 12.6* illustrates a typical problem of content maintenance, involving the six stages described above and assesses changes that could be made to improve the situation.

Activity 12.6 Optimizing the content review process at The B2C Company

Purpose

Assess how quality control and efficiency can be balanced for revisions to web content.

Activity

The extract below and *Figure 12.7* illustrate a problem of updating encountered by The B2C Company. How can they solve this problem?

Problem description

From when the brand manager identifies a need to update copy for their product, the update might happen as follows: brand manager writes copy (½ day), one day later the web manager reviews copy, three days later the marketing manager checks the copy, seven days later the legal department checks the copy, two days later the revised copy is implemented on the test site, two days later the brand manager reviews the test site, the next day the web manager reviews the web site followed by updating and final review before the copy is added to the live site two days later and over a fortnight from when a relatively minor change to the site was identified!

Answers to activities can be found at www.pearsoned.co.uk/chaffey

Frequency of content updates

Since the web is perceived as a dynamic medium, customers expect new information to be posted to a site straightaway. If material is inaccurate or 'stale' then the customer may not return to the site.

As information on a web page becomes outdated and will need to be updated, it is important to have a mechanism defining what triggers this update process. Trigger

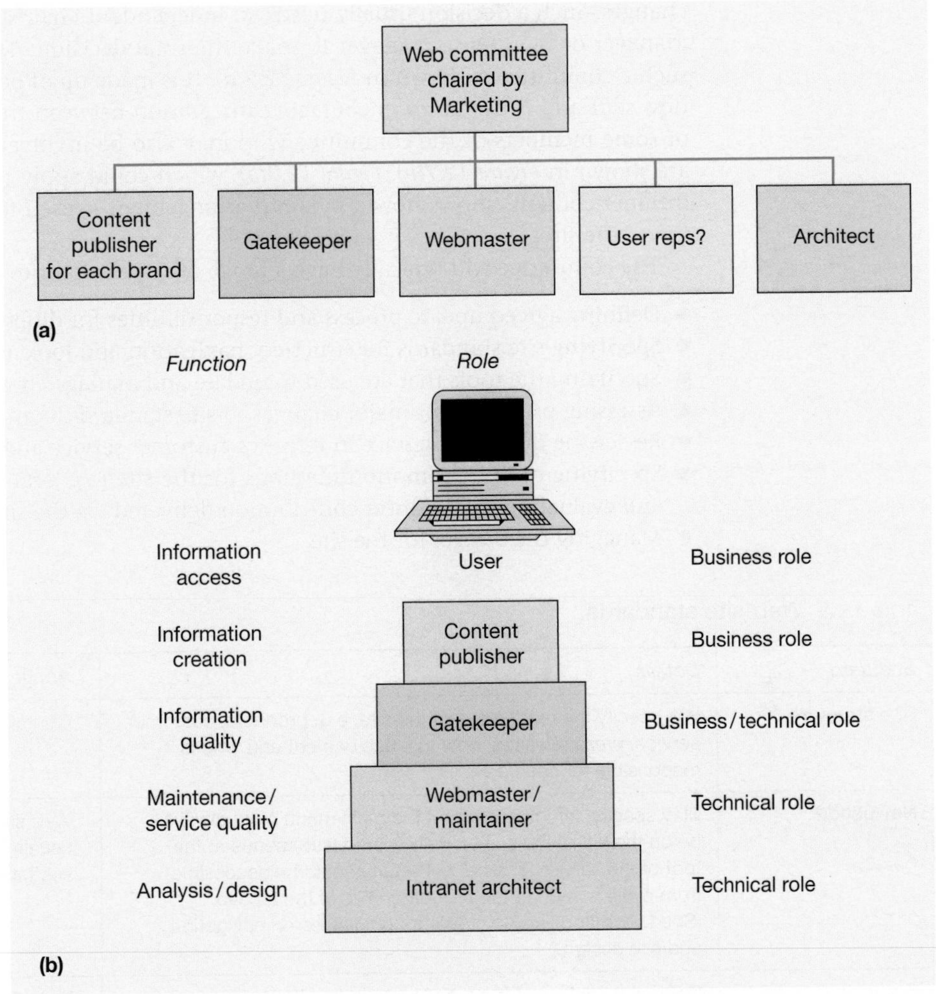

Figure 12.7 **Typical structures of an e-commerce site steering group**

procedures should be developed such that when price changes, PR release or product specifications are updated in promotional leaflets or catalogues, these changes are also reflected on the web site. Without procedures of this type, it is easy for there to be mismatches between online and offline content.

As part of defining a web-site update process and standards, a company may want to issue guidelines which suggest how often content is updated. This may specify that content is updated as follows:

- within two days of a factual error being identified;
- a new 'news' item is added at least once a month;
- when product information has been static for two months.

Process for major changes

For major changes to a web site, such as changing the menu structure, adding a new section of content or changing the services for users, a different process is required. Such changes will involve a larger investment and there will be limited funds for investment, so priorities for these major changes must be agreed. To achieve this the approach that is usually used is to set up a steering committee to ratify proposed changes. Such a decision usually needs an independent chair such as the e-commerce manager or marketing manager to make the final decision. The typical structure of such a committee is shown in *Figure 12.7(a)*. It is made up of both technical and business staff and is useful for encouraging integration between these roles. Typical roles of some members of the committee who may also be involved in update of the site are shown in *Figure 12.7(b)*. *Figure 12.7(a)*, which could apply to Internet, extranet or intranet content, shows how a pyramid arrangement is used to ensure content quality on the site.

The committee will typically have a range of responsibilities such as:

- Defining agreed update process and responsibilities for different types of changes
- Specifying site standards for structure, navigation and look and feel (*Table 12.5*)
- Specifying the tools that are used to update and manage content
- Assessing proposals for major changes to site standards, content and services
- Reviewing quality of service in terms of customer service and security
- Specifying online promotion methods for the site (e.g. search engine registration) and evaluating the business contribution delivered via the site
- Managing the budget for the site.

Table 12.5 **Web-site standards**

Standard	*Details*	*Applies to*
Site structure	Will specify the main areas of the site, e.g. products, customer service, press releases, how to place content and who is responsible for each area.	Content developers
Navigation	May specify, for instance, that the main menu must always be on the left of the screen with nested (sub)menus at the foot of the screen. The home button should be accessible from every screen at the top-left corner of the screen. (See Lynch and Horton (1999) for guidelines on navigation and site design.)	Web site designer/webmaster usually achieves these through site templates
Copy style	General guidelines, for example, reminding those writing copy that copy for the web needs to be briefer than its paper equivalent. Where detail is required, perhaps with product specifications, it should be broken up into chunks that are digestible on screen.	Individual content developers
Testing standards	Check site functions for: • different browser types and versions • plug-ins and invalid links • speed of download of graphics • spellchecking each page.	Web site designer/webmaster
Corporate branding and graphic design	Specifies the appearance of company logos and the colours and typefaces used to convey the brand message.	Web site designer/webmaster
Process	The sequence of events for publishing a new web page or updating an existing page. Who is responsible for reviewing and updating?	All
Performance	Availability and download speed figures.	Webmaster and designers

Initiatives to keep content fresh

It is often said that up-to-date content is crucial to site 'stickiness', but fresh content will not happen by accident, so companies have to consider approaches that can be used to control the quality of documents and in particular to keep them up-to-date and relevant. Generic approaches that I have seen which can work well are:

- Assign responsibility for particular content types or site sections to individuals.
- Make the quality of web content produced part of employee's performance appraisal.
- Produce a target schedule for publication of content.
- Identify events which trigger the publication of new content, e.g. a new product launch, price change or a press release.
- Identify stages and responsibilities in updating – who specifies, who creates, who reviews, who checks, who publishes.
- Measure the usage of content through web analytics or get feedback from site users.
- Publish a league table of content to highlight when content is out-of-date.
- Audit and publish content to show which is up-to-date.

Managing content for a global site

The issues in developing content management policies that are described above are complicated for a large organization with many lines of business and particularly for a multinational company. Centralization can give economies of scale and can achieve consistency in the way brand values are communicated nationally and internationally. However, content will need to be developed locally for regional audiences and this may require variations from central guidelines. Some regional autonomy needs to be allowed to enable buy-in from the different regions. It can be suggested that the following are required at an international level:

1 *Technology platform*. A common software system (CMS) will reduce costs of purchase, update and training. Integration with common software for customer relationship management (*Chapter 9*) and evaluation and measurement systems (see later in this chapter) will also be most efficient.
2 *System architecture*. A consistent architecture will avoid 'reinventing the wheel' in each country and will enable staff, partners and customers who need to access the CMS in different countries to be immediately familiar with it. Standards include:
   - Common page layout and navigation through templates
   - Common directory structures and consistent URL structure
   - Programming standard and languages and version control systems.
3 *Process/standards*. Update procedures for review of content for marketing, data protection and legal reasons as described in previous sections. Backup and archiving policies will also be required.

Focus on measuring and improving performance of e-business systems

We review measuring the effectiveness of e-commerce system in detail since it is a key part of managing an e-commerce initiative. Often a large investment will have been made in the site and senior managers will want to ensure that the investment is delivering its objectives. They will also want to find and rectify problems with the site or exploit approaches that are working well. We focus on measurement of sell-side e-commerce, since the approach is most advanced for this sector, but the principles and practice can be readily applied to other types of e-business system such as intranets and extranets.

Companies that have a successful approach to e-commerce often seem to share a common characteristic. They attach great importance and devote resources to monitoring the success of their online marketing and putting in place the processes to continuously improve the performance of their digital channels. This culture of measurement is visible in the UK bank, Alliance and Leicester, which in 2004 reported that they spent over 20% of their £80 million marketing communications budget on online marketing. Stephen Leonard, head of e-commerce, described their process as 'Test, Learn, Refine' (*Revolution*, 2004). Graeme Findlay, senior manager, customer acquisition of e-commerce at A&L, explains further: '*Our online approach is integrated with our offline brand and creative strategy, with a focus on direct, straightforward presentation of strong, value-led messages. Everything we do online, including creative, is driven by an extensive and dynamic testing process.*' Seth Romanow, Director of Customer Knowledge at Hewlett-Packard, speaking at the 2004 E-metrics summit, described their process as 'Measure, Report, Analyse, Optimize'. Amazon refers to their approach as 'The Culture of Metrics' (see *Case Study 12.1*). Jim Sterne, who convenes an annual event devoted to improving online performance (**www.emetrics.org**) has summarized his view on the required approach in his book *Web Metrics* (Sterne, 2002) as 'TIMITI' which stands for 'Try It! Measure It! Tweak It!', i.e. online content should be reviewed and improved continuously rather than as a periodic or ad-hoc process. The importance of defining an appropriate approach to measurement and improvement is such that the term 'web analytics' has developed to describe this key Internet marketing activity. A web analytics association (**www.waa.org**) has been developed by vendors, consultants and researchers in this area. Eric Petersen, an analyst specializing in web analytics, defines it as follows:

Web analytics
Techniques used to assess and improve the contribution of e-marketing to a business including reviewing traffic volume, referrals, clickstreams, online reach data, customer satisfaction surveys, leads and sales.

> *Web analytics is the assessment of a variety of data, including web traffic, web-based transactions, web server performance, usability studies, user submitted information [i.e. surveys], and related sources to help create a generalised understanding of the visitor experience online.* (Petersen, 2004)

You can see that in addition to what are commonly referred to as 'site statistics' about web traffic, sales transactions, usability and researching customers' views through surveys are also included. We believe, though, that the definition can be improved further – it suggests analysis for the sake of it – whereas the business purpose of analytics should be emphasized. The definition could also refer to comparison of site visitor volumes and demographics relative to competitors using panels and ISP collected data. Our definition is:

> *Web analytics is the customer-centred evaluation of the effectiveness of Internet-based marketing in order to improve the business contribution of online channels to an organisation.*

A more recent definition from the Web Analytics Association (WAA, **www.webanalyticsassociation.org**) in 2005 is:

> *Web Analytics is the objective tracking, collection, measurement, reporting and analysis of quantitative Internet data to optimize websites and web marketing initiatives.*

Principles of performance management and improvement

To improve results for any aspect of any business, performance management is vital. As Bob Napier, Chief Information Officer, Hewlett-Packard, was reported to have said back in the 1960s,

> *You can't manage what you can't measure.*

The processes and systems intended to monitor and improve the performance of an organization and specific management activities such as Internet marketing are widely known as 'performance management systems' and are based on the study of performance measurement systems.

Performance measurement system
The process by which metrics are defined, collected, disseminated and actioned.

Performance management system
A process used to evaluate and improve the efficiency and effectiveness of an organisation and its processes.

Design for analysis (DFA)
The required measures from a site are considered during design to better understand the audience of a site and their decision points.

Although we have stated that measurement is an important part of maintaining a web site, it is worth noting that the reality is that measurement is often neglected when a web site is first created. Measurement is often highlighted as an issue once early versions of a site have been 'up and running' for a few months or even years, and employees start to ask questions such as *'How many customers are visiting our site, how many sales are we achieving as a result of our site and how can we improve the site to achieve a return on investment?'* The consequence of this is that performance measurement is something that is often built into an online presence retrospectively. Of course it is preferable if measurement is built into site management from the start since then a more accurate approach can be developed and it is more readily possible to apply a technique known as 'design for analysis' (DFA). Here, the site is designed so companies can better understand the types of audience and their decision points. For example, for Dell (www.dell.com), the primary navigation on the home page is by business type. This is a simple example of DFA since it enables Dell to estimate the proportion of different audiences to their site and at the same time connect them with relevant content. Other examples of DFA include:

- Breaking up a long page or form into different parts, so you can see which parts people are interested in.
- A URL policy used to recommend entry pages for printed material.
- Group content by audience type or buying decision and setting up content groups of related content within web analytics systems.
- Measure attrition at different points in a customer journey, e.g. exit points on a five-page buying cycle.

Internet marketing metrics
Measures that indicate the effectiveness of Internet marketing activities in meeting customer, business and marketing objectives.

In this section, we will review approaches to performance management by examining three key elements of an e-commerce performance improvement system. These are, first, the *process* for improvement, secondly, the measurement framework which specifies groups of relevant Internet marketing metrics and, finally, an assessment of the suitability of tools and techniques for collecting, analysing, disseminating and actioning results. We will review three stages of creating and implementing a performance management system.

Stage 1: Creating a performance management system

The essence of performance *management* is suggested by the definition for performance *measurement* used by Andy Neely of Cranfield School of Management's Centre for Business Performance. He defines performance measurement as

> *the process of quantifying the efficiency and effectiveness of past actions through acquisition, collation, sorting, analysis, interpretation and dissemination of appropriate data.* (Neely *et al*., 2002)

Effectiveness
Meeting process objectives, delivering the required outputs and outcomes. 'Doing the right thing.'

Efficiency
Minimising resources or time needed to complete a process. 'Doing the thing right.'

Performance management extends this definition to the process of analysis and actioning change in order to drive business performance and returns. Online marketers can apply many of the approaches of business performance management to Internet marketing. As you can see from the definition, performance is measured primarily through information on process effectiveness and efficiency as introduced in *Chapter 5* in the section on objective setting where we noted that it is important to include both effectiveness and efficiency measures.

The need for a structured performance management process is clear if we examine the repercussions if an organization does not have one. These include: poor linkage of measures with strategic objectives or even absence of objectives; key data not collected; data inaccuracies; data not disseminated or analysed; or no corrective action. Many of the barriers to improvement of measurement systems reported by respondents in Adams *et al.* (2000) also indicate the lack of an effective process. The barriers can be grouped as follows:

- *senior management myopia* – performance measurement not seen as a priority, not understood or targeted at the wrong targets – reducing costs rather than improving performance;
- *unclear responsibilities for delivering and improving the measurement system;*
- *resourcing issues* – lack of time (perhaps suggesting lack of staff motivation), the necessary technology and integrated systems;
- *data problems* – data overload or of poor quality, limited data for benchmarking.

To avoid these pitfalls, a coordinated, structured measurement process such as that shown in *Figure 12.8* is required. *Figure 12.8* indicates four key stages in a measurement process. These were defined as key aspects of annual plan control by Kotler (1997). Stage 1 is a goal-setting stage where the aims of the measurement system are defined – this will usually take the strategic Internet marketing objectives as an input to the measurement system. The aim of the measurement system will be to assess whether these goals are achieved and specify corrective marketing actions to reduce variance between target and actual key performance indicators. Stage 2, performance measurement, involves collecting data to determine the different metrics that are part of a measurement framework as discussed in the next section. Stage 3, performance diagnosis, is the analysis of results to understand the reasons for variance from objectives (the 'performance gap' of Friedman and Furey, 1999) and selection of marketing solutions to reduce variance. The purpose of Stage 4, corrective action, according to Wisner and Fawcett (1991), is

> *to identify competitive position, locate problem areas, assist the firm in updating strategic objectives and making tactical decisions to achieve these objectives and supply feedback after the decisions are implemented.*

In an Internet marketing context, corrective action is the implementation of these solutions as updates to web-site content, design and associated marketing communications. At this stage the continuous cycle repeats, possibly with modified goals. Bourne *et al.* (2000) and Plant (2000) suggest that in addition to reviewing objectives, the suitability of the metrics should also be reviewed and revised.

Measurement is not something that can occur on an ad hoc basis because if it is left to the individual they may forget to collect the data needed. A 'measurement culture' is one in which each employee is aware of the need to collect data on how well the company is performing and on how well it is meeting its customers' needs.

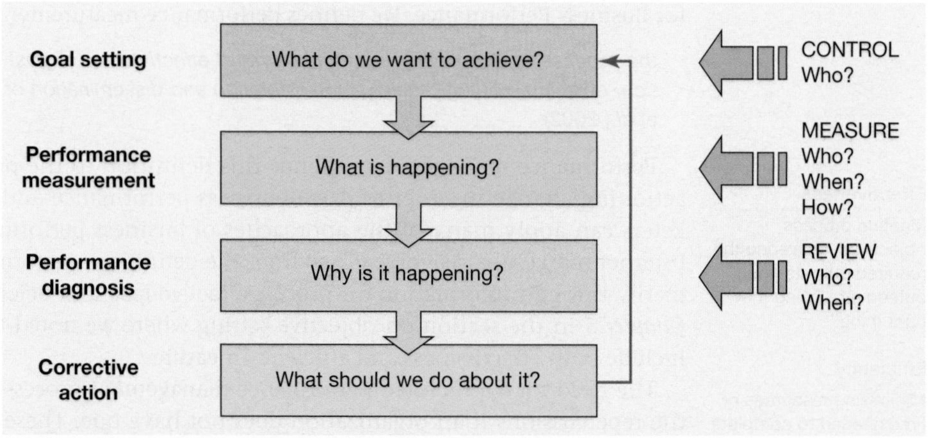

Figure 12.8 **A summary of the performance measurement process**

Stage 2: Defining the performance metrics framework

Measurement for assessing the effectiveness of Internet marketing can be thought of as answering these questions:

1 Are corporate objectives identified in the Internet marketing strategy being met?
2 Are marketing objectives defined in the Internet marketing strategy and plan achieved?
3 Are marketing communications objectives identified in the Internet marketing plan achieved? How efficient are the different promotional techniques used to attract visitors to a site?

These measures can also be related to the different levels of marketing control specified by Kotler (1997). These include strategic control (question 1), profitability control (question 1), annual-plan control (question 2) and efficiency control (question 3).

Efficiency measures are more concerned with minimizing the costs of online marketing while maximizing the returns for different areas of focus such as acquiring visitors to a web site, converting visitors to outcome or achieving repeat business.

Chaffey (2000) suggests that organizations define a measurement framework which defines groupings of specific metrics used to assess Internet marketing performance. He suggests that suitable measurement frameworks will fulfil these criteria:

A. Include both macro-level effectiveness metrics which assess whether strategic goals are achieved and indicate to what extent e-marketing contributes to the business (revenue contribution and return on investment). This criterion covers the different levels of marketing control specified by Kotler (1997) including strategic control, profitability control and annual-plan control.

B. Include micro-level metrics which assess the efficiency of e-marketing tactics and implementation. Wisner and Fawcett (1991) note that typically organizations use a hierarchy of measures and they should check that the lower-level measures support the macro-level strategic objectives. Such measures are often referred to as *performance drivers*, since achieving targets for these measures will assist in achieving strategic objectives. E-marketing performance drivers help optimize e-marketing by attracting more site visitors and increasing conversion to desired marketing outcomes. These achieve the marketing efficiency control specified by Kotler (1997). The research by Agrawal *et al.* (2001), who assessed companies on metrics defined in three categories of attraction, conversion and retention as part of an e-performance scorecard, uses a combination of macro- and micro-level metrics.

C. Assess the impact of the e-marketing on the satisfaction, loyalty and contribution of key stakeholders (customers, investors, employees and partners) as suggested by Adams *et al.* (2000).

D. The framework must be flexible enough to be applied to different forms of online presence whether business-to-consumer, business-to-business, not-for-profit or transactional e-tail, CRM-oriented or brand-building. Much discussion of e-marketing measurement is limited to a transactional e-tail presence. Adams *et al.* (2000) note that a 'one-size-fits-all' framework is not desirable.

E. Enable comparison of performance of different e-channels with other channels as suggested by Friedman and Furey (1999).

F. The framework can be used to assess e-marketing performance against competitors' or out-of-sector best practice.

When identifying metrics it is common practice to apply the widely used SMART mnemonic and it is also useful to consider three levels – business measures, marketing measures and specific Internet marketing measures (see objective setting section in *Chapter 4*).

Chaffey (2000) presents a framework of measures, shown in *Figure 12.9* which can be applied to a range of different companies. Metrics for the categories are generated as objectives from Internet marketing planning which then need to be monitored to assess the success of strategy and its implementation. Objectives can be devised in a top-down fashion, starting with strategic objectives for business contribution and marketing outcomes leading to tactical objectives for customer satisfaction, behaviour and site promotion. An alternative perspective is bottom-up – success in achieving objectives for site promotion, on-site customer behaviour and customer satisfaction lead sequentially to achieving objectives for marketing outcomes and business contribution.

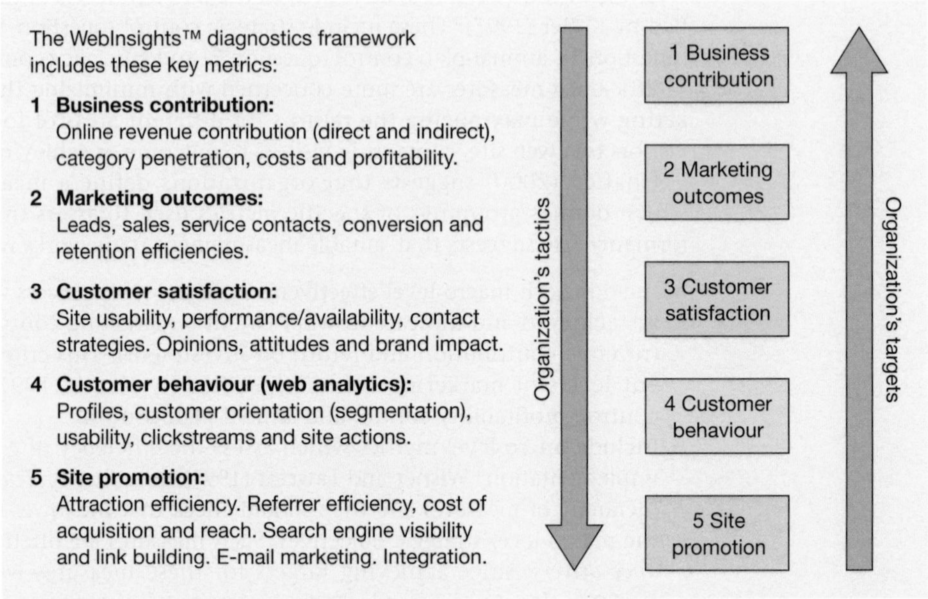

Figure 12.9 **The five diagnostic categories for e-marketing measurement from the framework presented by Chaffey (2000)**

1 Channel promotion

Channel promotion
Measures that assess why customers visit a site – which adverts they have seen, which sites they have been referred from.

Referrer
The site that a visitor previously visited before following a link.

Channel-promotion measures consider where the web site users originate – online or offline, and what are the sites or offline media that have prompted their visit. Log file analysis can be used to assess which intermediary sites customers are referred from and even which keywords they typed into search engines when trying to locate product information. Promotion is successful if traffic is generated that meets objectives of volume and quality. Quality will be determined by whether visitors are in the target market and have a propensity for the service offered (conversion rates for different referrers). Overall hits or page views are not enough – inspection of log files for companies shows that a high proportion of visitors get no further than the home page! Differences in costs of acquiring customers via different channels also need to be assessed.

Key measure: Referral mix. For each referral source such as offline or banner ads online it should be possible to calculate:

- % of all referrals (or visitors);
- cost of acquisition;
- contribution to sales or other outcomes.

2 Channel buyer behaviour

Channel buyer behaviour
Describes which content is visited, time and duration.

Once customers have been attracted to the site we can monitor content accessed, when they visit and how long they stay, and whether this interaction with content leads to satisfactory marketing outcomes such as new leads or sales. If visitors are incentivized to register on-site it is possible to build up profiles of behaviour for different segments. It is also important to recognize return visitors for whom cookies or log-in are used.

Key measures are:

Bounce rates for different pages, i.e. proportion of single page visits

	Home page views/All page views e.g.	20%	= (2,358/11,612)
Stickiness	Page views/visitor sessions e.g.	6	= 11,612/2,048
Repeats	Visitor sessions/visitors e.g.	2	= 2,048/970

Stickiness
An indication of how long a visitor stays on-site.

3 Channel satisfaction

Channel satisfaction
Evaluation of the customer's opinion of the service quality on the site and supporting services such as e-mail.

Customer satisfaction with the online experience is vital in achieving the desired channel outcomes, although it is difficult to set specific objectives. Online methods such as online questionnaires, focus groups and interviews can be used to assess customers' opinions of the web site content and customer service and how it has affected overall perception of brand.

Key measure: Customer satisfaction indices. These are discussed in *Chapter 7* and include ease of use, site availability and performance, and e-mail response. To compare customer satisfaction with other sites, benchmarking services can be used.

4 Channel outcomes

Channel outcomes
Record customer actions taken as a consequence of a site visit.

Conversion rate
Percentage of site visitors who perform a particular action such as making a purchase.

Traditional marketing objectives such as number of sales, number of leads, conversion rates and targets for customer acquisition and retention should be set and then compared to other channels. Dell Computer (www.dell.com) records on-site sales and also orders generated as a result of site visits, but placed by phone. This is achieved by monitoring calls to a specific phone number unique to the site.

Key measure: Channel contribution (direct and indirect).

A widely used method of assessing channel outcomes is to review the conversion rate, which gives an indication of the percentage of site visitors who take a particular outcome. For example:

Conversion rate, visitors to purchase = 2% (10,000 visitors, of which 200 make purchases).

Conversion rate, visitors to registration = 5% (10,000 visitors, of which 500 register).

Attrition rate
Percentage of site visitors who are lost at each stage in making a purchase.

A related concept is the attrition rate which describes how many visitors are lost at each stage of visiting a site. *Figure 12.10* shows that for a set time period, only a proportion of site visitors will make their way to product information, a small proportion will add an item to a basket and a smaller proportion still will actually make the purchase. A key feature of e-commerce sites is that there is a high attrition rate between a customer's adding an item to a basket and subsequently making a purchase. Online marketers work to decrease this 'shopping basket abandonment rate' through improving usability and modifying messaging to persuade visitors to continue the 'user journey'.

Channel profitability
The profitability of the web site, taking into account revenue and cost and discounted cash flow.

5 Channel profitability

A contribution to business profitability is always the ultimate aim of e-commerce. To assess this, leading companies set an Internet contribution target of achieving a

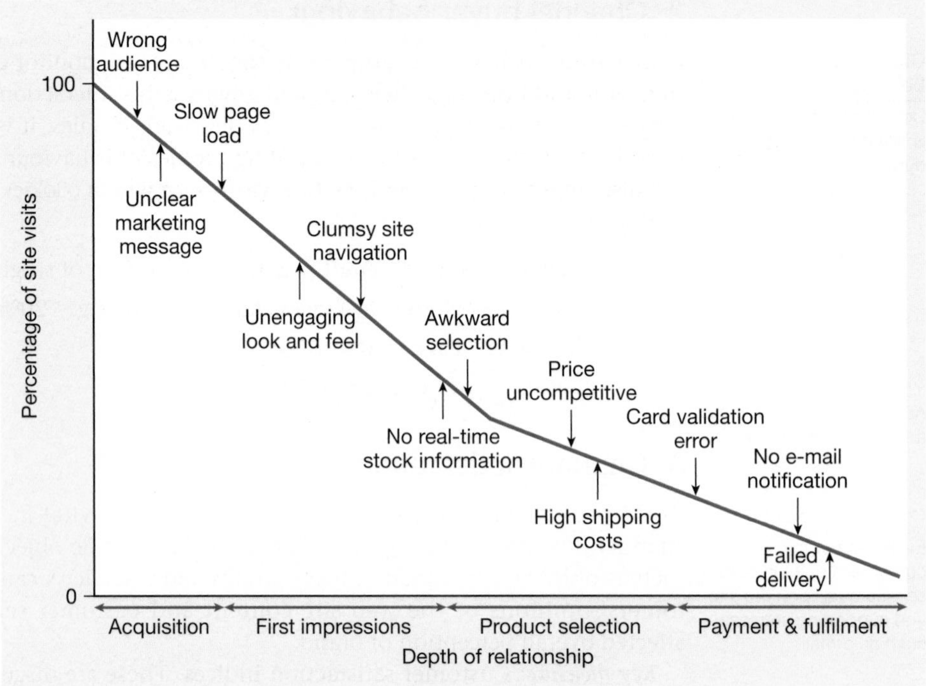

Figure 12.10 **Attrition through e-commerce site activities**

certain proportion of sales via the channel. When easyJet (www.easyjet.com) launched its e-commerce facility in 1998, it set an Internet contribution target of 30% by 2000. They put the resources and communications plan in place to achieve this and their target was reached in 1999. Assessing contribution is more difficult for a company that cannot sell products online, but the role of the Internet in influencing purchase should be assessed. Discounted cash flow techniques are used to assess the rate of return over time. Service contribution from e-channels should also be assessed.

Stage 3: Tools and techniques for collecting metrics and summarizing results

Techniques to collect metrics include the collection of site-visitor activity data such as that collected from site log-files, the collection of metrics about outcomes such as online sales or e-mail enquiries and traditional marketing research techniques such as questionnaires and focus groups which collect information on the customer's experience on the web site. We start by describing methods for collecting site visitor activity and then review more traditional techniques of market research which assess the customer experience.

Collecting site-visitor activity data

Site-visitor activity data
Information on content and services accessed by e-commerce site visitors.

Site-visitor activity data captured in web analytics systems records the number of visitors on the site and the paths or clickstreams they take through the site as they visit different content. There are a wide variety of technical terms to describe these activity data which Internet marketers need to be conversant with.

Hit
Recorded for each graphic or text file requested from a web server. It is not a reliable measure for the number of people viewing a page.

Log file analyser
A separate program such as WebTrends that is used to summarize the information on customer activity in a log file.

Page impression
A more reliable measure than a hit, denoting one person viewing one page.

Unique visitors
Individual visitors to a site measured through cookies or IP addresses on an individual computer.

Traditionally this information has been collected using a log file analysis web analytics tool. The server-based log file is added to every time a user downloads a piece of information (a **hit**) and is analysed using a **log file analyser** as illustrated by *Figure 3.7*. Examples of transactions within a log file are:

www.davechaffey.com – [05/Oct/2006:00:00:49 -000] "GET /index.html HTTP/1.0" 200 33362

www.davechaffey.com – [05/Oct/2006:00:00:49 -000] "GET /logo.gif HTTP/1.0" 200 54342

Despite their wide use in the media, hits are not a useful measure of web site effectiveness since if a page consists of 10 graphics, plus text, this is recorded as 11 hits. **Page impressions** or **page views** and **unique visitors** are better measures of site activity. Auditing companies such as ABC electronic (**www.abce.org.uk**) that audit sites for the purpose of proving the number of visitors to a site to advertisers use unique visitors and page impression as the main measures.

An example of visitor volume to a web site using different measures based on real, representative data for one month is presented in *Figure 12.11* You can see how hits are much higher than page views and unique visitors and are quite misleading in terms of the 'opportunities to see' a message. We can also learn from the ratio between some of these measures – the figure indicates:

- *Pages per visit (PPV)* – the average number of pages viewed per visitor to a site (this is indicative of engagement with a site since the longer a visitor stays on a 'sticky site', the higher this value will be). PPV is a more accurate indication of stickiness than duration on a site in minutes since this figure is skewed upwards by visitors who arrive on a site and are inactive before their session times out at 30 minutes.
- *Visits per (unique) visitor (VPV)* – this suggests the frequency of site visits. Readers will realize that this value is dependent on the period that data are collected over. These data are reported for a month, during which time one would not expect many returning visitors. So it is often more relevant to present these data across a quarter or a year.

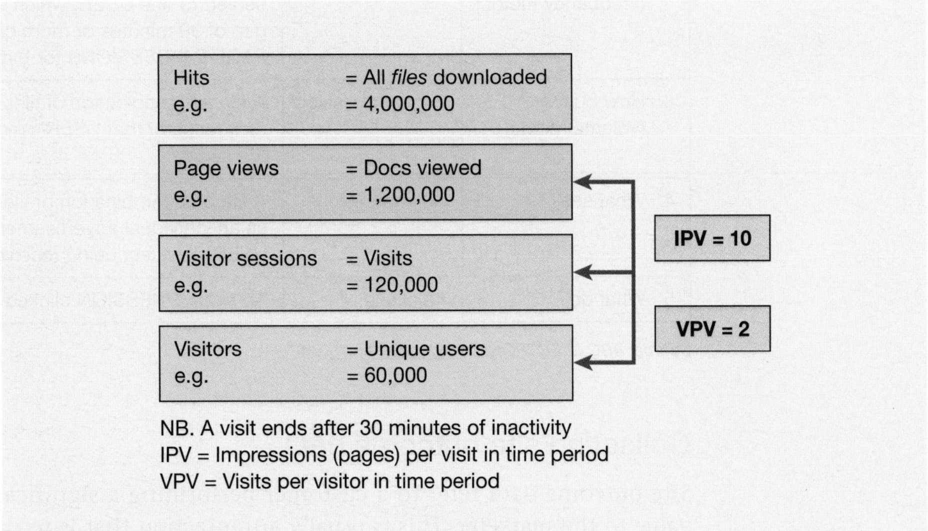

Figure 12.11 Examples of different measures of visitor volume to a web site

Other information giving detailed knowledge of customer behaviour that can be reported by any web analytics package include:

- Top pages;
- Entry and exit pages;
- Path or clickstream analysis showing the sequence of pages viewed;
- country of visitor's origin (actually dependent on the location of their ISP);
- browser and operating system used;
- referring URL and domain (where the visitor came from).

Comparing apples to oranges?

With hundreds of different web analytics tools being used on different sites, it is important that there be standards for measuring visitor volumes. In particular, there are different techniques for measuring unique visitors which can be measured through IP addresses, but this is more accurate if it is combined with cookies and browser types. International standards bodies such as the IFABC (www.ifabc.org) and Web Analytics Association (www.webanalyticsassociation.org) and UK organizations such as ABC ELECTRONIC (www.abce.org.uk) and JICWEBS (www.jicwebs.org) have worked to standardize the meaning and data collection methods for different measures. See *Table 12.6* or visit these sites for the latest precise definition of the terms in this section. Media buyers are particularly interested in accurate audited figures of media sites and organizations such as ABC electronic are important for this.

Table 12.6 **Terminology for key web-site volume measures**

Measure	*Measure*	*Definition*
1 How many? (Audience reach)	Unique users	A unique and valid identifier [for a site visitor]. Sites may use (i) IP + user-agent, (ii) cookie and/or (iii) registration ID
2 How often? (Frequency metric)	Visit	A series of one or more PAGE IMPRESSIONS, served to one USER, which ends when there is a gap of 30 minutes or more between successive PAGE IMPRESSIONS for that USER
3 How busy? (Volume metric)	Page impression	A file, or combination of files, sent to a valid USER as a result of that USER's request being received by the server
4 What see?	Ad impressions	A file or a combination of files sent to a valid USER as an individual advertisement as a result of that USER's request being received by the server
5 What do?	Ad clicks	An AD IMPRESSION clicked on by a valid USER

Source: *ABC ELECTRONIC* (www.abce.org.uk)

Collecting site outcome data

Site outcome data refer to a customer performing a significant action which is of value to the marketer. This is usually a transaction that is recorded. It involves more than downloading of a web page, and is proactive. Key marketing outcomes include:

- registration to site or subscriptions to an e-mail newsletter;
- requests for further information such as a brochure or a request for a callback from a customer service representative;

- responding to a promotion such as an online competition;
- a sale influenced by a visit to the site;
- a sale on-site.

When reviewing the efficiency of different e-communications tools referred to in *Chapter 9*, such as search engine marketing, online advertising and affiliate marketing it is important to assess the outcomes generated. Measuring quantity of clickthroughs to a site is simplistic, it is conversion to these outcomes which should be used to assess the quality of traffic. To achieve this 'end-to-end' tracking, two main tools are used: first, using cookies to identify the visitor across different sessions and, secondly, using tracking IDs within URLs to identify a user session.

An important aspect of measures collected offline is that the marketing outcomes may be recorded in different media according to how the customer has performed mixed-mode buying. For example, a new customer enquiry could arrive by e-mail, fax or phone. Similarly, an order could be placed online using a credit card, or by phone, fax or post. For both these cases what we are really interested in is whether the web site influenced the enquiry or sale. This is a difficult question to answer unless steps are put in place to answer it. For all contact points with customers staff need to be instructed to ask how they found out about the company, or made their decision to buy. Although this is valuable information it is often intrusive, and a customer placing an order may be annoyed to be asked such a question. To avoid alienating the customer, these questions about the role of the web site can be asked later, perhaps when the customer is filling in a registration or warranty card. Another device that can be used to identify use of the web site is to use a specific phone number on the web site, so when a customer rings to place an order, it is known that the number was obtained from the web site. This approach is used by Dell on its site.

It will be apparent that to collect some of these measures we may need to integrate different information systems. Where customers provide details such as an e-mail address and name in response to an offer, these are known as 'leads' and they may need to be passed on to a direct-sales team or recorded in a customer relationship management system. For full visibility of customer behaviour, the outcomes from these systems need to be integrated with the site-visitor activity data.

Selecting a web analytics tool

There are a bewildering range of hundreds of web analytics tools varying from shareware packages with often primitive reporting through to complex systems which may cost hundreds of thousands of dollars a year for a popular site. Given this, it is difficult for the Internet marketer to select the best tool or tools to meet their needs. One of the first issues to consider is the different types of measures that need to integrated within the performance management system. *Figure 12.12* gives an indication of the types of data that need to be integrated which include:

1. *Operational data.* Data would be ideally collected and reported within a single tool at this level, but unfortunately to obtain the best reporting it is often necessary to resort to four different types of tools or data source:

   - Referrer data from acquisition campaigns such as search marketing or online advertising. Separate tools are often also required for retention e-mail marketing.
   - Site-centric data about visitor volume and clickstream behaviour on the web site.
   - Customer response and profile data.
   - Transactional data about leads and sales which is often obtained from separate legacy systems.

2 *Tactical data*. These data are typically models of required response such as:
- Reach models with online audience share data for different demographic groupings from sources such as Hitwise and Netratings.
- Lifetime value models which are created to assess profitability of visitors to the site from different sources and so need to integrate with operational data.

3 *Strategic data*. Performance management systems for senior managers will give the big picture presented as scorecards or dashboards showing the contribution of digital channels to the organization in terms of sales, revenue and profitability for different products. These data indicate trends and relative performance within the company and to competitors such that the Internet marketing strategy can be reviewed for effectiveness. The efficiency of the processes may be indicated, through, for example, the cost of acquisition of customers in different markets and their conversion and retention rates.

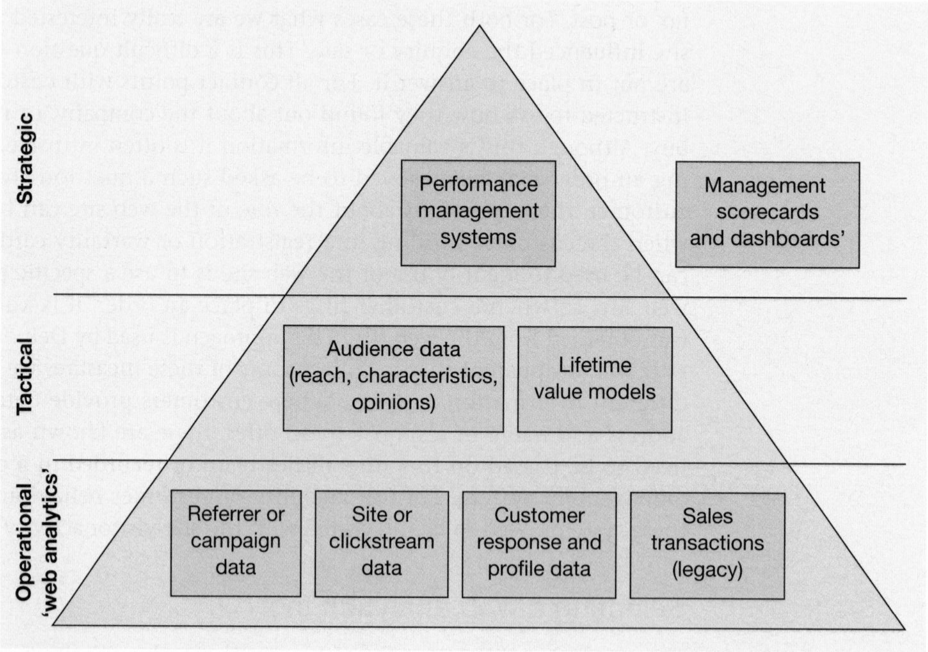

Figure 12.12 **Different types of data within a performance management system for Internet marketing**

So an important requirement of a web analytics tool is that it should seek to integrate all these different data sources. The other main requirements of a web analytics tool to consider include:

- Reporting of marketing performance (many are technical tools which do not clearly report on results from a marketing perspective)
- Accuracy of technique
- Analysis tools
- Integration with other marketing information systems (export)
- Ease of use and configuration
- Cost which often varies according to site visitor volumes and number of system users
- Suitability for reporting on e-marketing campaigns.

Many online tracking tools were originally developed to report on the performance of the site and the pages accessed rather than specifically to report on e-marketing campaigns. It is therefore important that companies have an excellent campaign reporting capability. When online marketers are reviewing the capability of tools, they should be able to answer these questions:

1 *Can the tool track through to point entry on site through to outcome such as site registration or sale?* For example, to outcomes such as registration, lead or sale? Integration with data to reflect actual leads or sales in a legacy system should also be reported.
2 *Can the tool track and compare a range of online media types?* These were explained in *Chapter 8*, for example, interactive (banner) ads, affiliates, e-mail marketing natural and paid search.
3 *Can return-on-investment models can be constructed?* For example, by entering costs and profitability for each product?
4 *Can reports be produced at both a detailed level and a summary level?* This enables comparison of performance for different campaigns and different parts of the business.
5 *Capability to track clickthroughs at an individual respondent level for e-mail campaigns.* This is important for follow-up marketing activities such as a phone call, direct mail or e-mail after an e-mail list member has expressed interest in a product through clicking on a promotion link.
6 *Are post-view responses tracked for ads?* Cookies can be used to assess visitors who arrive on the site at a later point in time, rather than immediately.
7 *Are post-click responses tracked for affiliates?* Similarly, visitors from affiliates may buy the product not on their first visit, but on a later visit.
8 *Do e-mail campaign summaries give unique clicks as well as total clicks?* If an e-mail communication such as a newsletter contains multiple links, then total clicks will be higher.
9 *Is real-time reporting available?* Is immediate access to campaign performance data available (this is usually possible with browser or tag-based campaign tracking solutions)?
10 *Is cross-campaign and cross-product or content reporting available?* Is it readily possible to compare campaigns and sales levels across different products or different parts of the site rather than an aggregate?

Table 12.7 Inaccuracies caused by server-based log-file analysis

Sources of undercounting	*Sources of overcounting*
Caching in user's web browsers (when a user accesses a previously accessed file, it is loaded from the user's on a server-based cache on their PC) Caching on proxy servers (proxy servers are used within organizations or ISPs to reduce Internet traffic by storing copies of frequently used pages) Firewalls (these do not usually exclude page impressions, but they usually assign a single IP address for the user of the page, rather than referring to an individual's PC) Dynamically generated pages, generated 'on-the-fly', are difficult to assess with server-based log files	Frames (a user viewing a framed page with three frames will be recorded as three page impressions system) Spiders and robots (traversing of a site by spiders from different search engines is recorded as page impressions. These spiders can be excluded, but this is time-consuming) Executable files (these can also be recorded as hits or page impressions unless excluded)

Accuracy is another an important aspect of web analytics tool and managers need to be aware of some of the weaknesses of web analytics tools based on log file analysis. Perhaps the worst problems are the problems of undercounting or overcounting. These are reviewed in *Table 12.7*.

A relatively new approach to the problems of undercounting and overcounting of server-based log file analysis described in *Table 12.7* is to use the alternative *browser-based* or *tag-based* measurement system that records access to web pages every time a page is loaded into a user's web browser through running a short script, program or tag inserted into the web page. The key benefit of the browser-based approach is that potentially it is more accurate than server-based approaches for the reasons explained in *Table 12.7*. This approach usually runs as a hosted solution with the metrics recorded on a remote server. An example of the output reporting from a web analytics service is shown in Figure *12.13*.

Internet-based market research

The use of online questionnaires and focus groups to assess customer perceptions of a web site or broader marketing issues.

In addition to the quantitative web analytics measurement approaches discussed, traditional marketing research can be used to help determine the influence of the web-site and related communications on customer perception of the company and its products and services. The options for conducting survey research include interviews, questionnaires, focus groups and mystery shoppers. Each of these techniques can be conducted offline or online. The advantages and disadvantages of the different approaches are shown in *Table 12.8*.

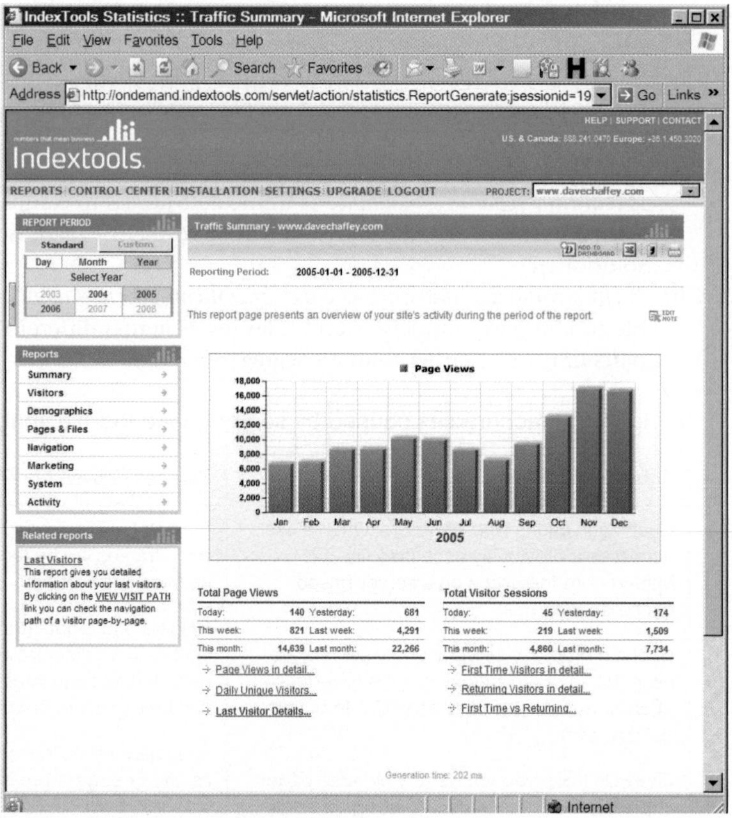

Figure 12.13 **Web analytics tool IndexTools used to assess page popularity in Dave Chaffey's site (www.davechaffey.com)**

Table 12.8 A comparison of different online metrics collection methods

Technique	*Strengths*	*Weaknesses*
1 **Server-based log-file analysis of site activity**	Directly records customer behaviour on site plus where they were referred from Low cost	Not based around marketing outcomes such as leads, sales Size, even summaries may be over 50 pages long Doesn't directly record channel satisfaction Undercounting and overcounting Misleading unless interpreted carefully
2 **Browser-based site activity data**	Greater accuracy than server-based analysis Count all users, cf. panel approach	Relatively expensive method Similar weaknesses to server-based technique apart from accuracy Limited demographic information
3 **Panel activity and demographic data**	Provide competitor comparisons Give demographic profiling Avoid undercounting and overcounting	Depend on extrapolation from limited sample that may not be representative
4 **Outcome data**, e.g. enquiries, customer service e-mails	Record marketing outcomes	Difficulty of integrating data with other methods of data collection when collected manually or in other information systems
5 **Online questionnaires.** Customers are prompted randomly – every *n*th customer or after customer activity or by e-mail	Can record customer satisfaction and profiles Relatively cheap to create and analyse	Difficulty of recruiting respondents who complete accurately Sample bias – tend to be advocates or disgruntled customers who complete
6 **Online focus groups.** Synchronous recording	Relatively cheap to create	Difficult to moderate and coordinate No visual cues, as from offline focus groups
7 **Mystery shoppers.** Customers are recruited to evaluate the site, e.g. www.emysteryshopper.com	Structured tests give detailed feedback Also tests integration with other channels such as e-mail and phone	Relatively expensive Sample must be representative

Budgeting

To estimate profitability and return on investment of e-channels as part of budgeting, companies need to consider both tangible and intangible costs and benefits. A suggested checklist of these is shown in the box *Suggested worksheet for calculating return on investment for an e-commerce site.*

Suggested worksheet for calculating return on investment for an e-commerce site

Tangible business benefits

1 *Reduced costs*
 (a) Promotional materials, including catalogues – creative, printing, paper, distribution
 (b) Product support materials – creation, printing, paper, distribution
 (c) Lower infrastructure or communication costs – fewer outbound calls required
 (d) Support staff savings
 (e) Sales staff savings
 (f) Order inaccuracies
 (g) Lower cost of supporting channel

→

2 *Increased revenue*
- (a) New sales to new geo-demographic segments
- (b) Penetration/retention/repeat orders
- (c) Cross-sales to existing purchasers
- (d) Penetration/cross-sales to new purchasers in an organization

Intangible business benefits

3 *Faster time to market*
Reduce product introduction by *n* weeks

4 *Improved customer satisfaction/brand equity*
Also an intangible factor, how does this affect retention?

Tangible costs

1 *Physical costs*
- (a) Hardware, software
- (b) Network costs

2 *Planning costs*

3 *Implementation costs*
- (a) Project management
- (b) Software development, testing
- (c) Data migration
- (d) Training
- (e) Promotion (online and offline)

4 *Operational costs*
- (a) Hardware and software maintenance
- (b) Network maintenance
- (c) Technical staff costs
- (d) Content maintenance staff costs
- (e) Support staff costs
- (f) Management staff costs
- (g) Ongoing promotional costs (online and offline)

This worksheet was originally based on White Paper 'A Return on Investment Guide for Business-to-Business Internet Commerce' provided by E-commerce solution provider Openmarket (www.openmarket.com)

A similar approach can be used to calculating the ROI of enhancements to an e-commerce site. Hanson (2000) suggests an approach to this which requires identification of revenue from the site, costs from site and costs from supporting it via a call centre. These are related to profit as follows:

Operating profit = Net income from sales – E-commerce site costs – Call centre costs

Net income from sales = (Product price – Unit cost) × Sales – Fixed product costs

E-commerce site costs = Site fixed costs + ((% site support contacts) × Cost site support contact × Sales)

Call centre (CC) costs = CC fixed costs + ((% CC support contacts) × Cost CC support contact × Sales)

Different approaches for estimating costs are recommended by Bayne (1997):

- *Last year's Internet marketing budget*. This is assuming the site has been up and running for some time.
- *Percentage of company sales*. It is again difficult to establish this for the first iteration of a site.

- *Percentage of total marketing budget*. This is a common approach. Typically the percentage will start small (less than 5 per cent, or even 1 per cent), but will rise as the impact of the Internet increases.
- *Reallocation of marketing dollars*. The money for e-marketing will often be taken by cutting back other marketing activities.
- *What other companies in your industry are spending*. This is definitely necessary in order to assess and meet competitive threats, but it may be possible that competitors are over-investing.
- *Creating an effective online presence*. In this model of 'paying whatever it takes', a company spends sufficient money to create a web site which is intended to achieve their objectives. This may be a costly option, but for industries in which the Internet is having a significant impact, it may be the wise option. A larger than normal marketing budget will be necessary to achieve this.
- *A graduated plan tied into measurable results*. This implies an ongoing programme in which investment each year is tied into achieving the results established in a measurement programme.
- *A combination of approaches*. Since the first budget will be based on many intangibles it is best to use several methods and present high, medium and low expenditure options for executives with expected results related to costs.

As a summary to this section, complete *Activity 12.7*.

Activity 12.7 Creating a measurement plan for The B2C Company

Purpose

To develop skills in selecting appropriate techniques for measuring e-business effectiveness.

Activity

This activity acts as a summary to this section on e-business measurement. Review *Table 12.9* and assess the frequency with which metrics in each of the following categories should be reported for a sell-side e-commerce site and acted upon. For each column, place an R in the column for the frequency with which you think the data should be recorded.

Table 12.9 Alternative timescales for reporting e-commerce site performance

	Promotion	*Behaviour*	*Satisfaction*	*Outcomes*	*Profitability*
Hour					
Day					
Week					
Month					
Quarter					
Relaunch					

Answers to activities can be found at www.pearsoned.co.uk/chaffey

In *Chapter 1*, we started this book with a case study of the world's largest e-business retailer. We conclude with a case of the world's second largest e-retailer, showing how the culture of test, learn, refine is key to their success.

Case Study 12.1 Learning from Amazon's culture of metrics

Context

Why a case study on Amazon? Surely everyone knows about who Amazon are and what they do? Yes, well, that's maybe true, but this case goes beyond the surface to review some of the 'insider secrets' of Amazon's success.

Like eBay, Amazon.com was born in 1995. The name reflected the vision of Jeff Bezos to produce a large-scale phenomenon like the Amazon river. This ambition has proved justified since, just 8 years later, Amazon passed the $5 billion sales mark – it took Wal-Mart 20 years to achieve this.

By 2005 Amazon was a global brand with over 41 million active customers accounts and order fulfilment to more than 200 countries. Despite this volume of sales, at 31 December 2004 Amazon employed approximately 9,000 full-time and part-time employees.

Vision and strategy

In their 2005 SEC filing, Amazon describes the vision of their business as to:

> *Relentlessly focus on customer experience by offering our customers low prices, convenience, and a wide selection of merchandise.*

The vision is to offer Earth's biggest selection and to be Earth's most customer-centric company. Consider how these core marketing messages summarizing the Amazon online value proposition are communicated both on-site and through offline communications.

Of course, achieving customer loyalty and repeat purchases has been key to Amazon's success. Many dot-coms failed because they succeeded in achieving awareness, but not loyalty. Amazon achieved both. In their SEC filing they stress how they seek to achieve this. They say:

> *We work to earn repeat purchases by providing easy-to-use functionality, fast and reliable fulfillment, timely customer service, feature rich content, and a trusted transaction environment. Key features of our websites include editorial and customer reviews; manufacturer product information; Web pages tailored to individual preferences, such as recommendations and notifications; 1-Click® technology; secure payment systems; image uploads; searching on our websites as well as the Internet; browsing; and the ability to view selected interior pages and citations, and search the entire contents of many of the books we offer with our "Look Inside the Book" and "Search Inside the Book" features. Our community of online customers also creates feature-rich content, including product reviews, online recommendation lists, wish lists, buying guides, and wedding and baby registries.*

In practice, as is the practice for many online retailers, the lowest prices are for the most popular products, with less popular products commanding higher prices and a greater margin for Amazon. Free shipping offers are used to encourage increase in basket size since customers have to spend over a certain amount to receive free shipping. The level at which free shipping is set is critical to profitability and Amazon has changed it as competition has changed and for promotional reasons.

Amazon communicates the fulfilment promise in several ways including presentation of latest inventory availability information, delivery date estimates, and options for expedited delivery, as well as delivery shipment notifications and update facilities.

This focus on the customer has translated to excellence in service with the 2004 American Customer Satisfaction Index giving Amazon.com a score of 88, which was at the time the highest customer satisfaction score ever recorded in any service industry, online or offline.

Round (2004) notes that Amazon focuses on customer satisfaction metrics. Each site is closely monitored with standard service availability monitoring (for example, using Keynote or Mercury Interactive) site availability and download speed. Interestingly, it also monitors per-minute site revenue upper/lower bounds – Round describes an alarm system rather like a power plant where if revenue on a site falls below $10,000 per minute, alarms go off! There are also internal performance service-level agreements for web services where *T*% of the time, different pages must return in *X* seconds.

Competition

In its SEC (2005) filing Amazon describes the environment for its products and services as 'intensely competitive'. It views its main current and potential competitors as: (1) physical-world retailers, catalogue retailers, publishers, vendors, distributors and manufacturers of products, many of which possess significant brand awareness, sales volume and customer bases, and some of which currently sell, or may sell, products or services through the Internet, mail order or direct marketing; (2) other online e-commerce sites; (3) a number of indirect competitors, including media companies, web portals, comparison shopping web sites, and web search engines, either directly or in collaboration with other retailers; and (4) companies that provide e-commerce services, including web site development; third-party fulfilment and customer service.

It believes the main competitive factors in its market segments include 'selection, price, availability, convenience, information, discovery, brand recognition, personalized services, accessibility, customer service, reliability, speed of fulfillment, ease of use, and ability to adapt to changing conditions, as well as our customers' overall experience and trust in transactions with us and facilitated by us on behalf of third-party sellers'.

For services offered to business and individual sellers, additional competitive factors include the quality of their services and tools, their ability to generate sales for third parties they serve, and the speed of performance for their services.

From auctions to marketplaces

Amazon auctions (known as zShops) were launched in March 1999, in large part as a response to the success of eBay. They were promoted heavily from the home page, category pages and individual product pages. Despite this, a year after launch they had only achieved a 3.2% share of the online auction compared to 58% for eBay and it only declined from this point.

Today, competitive prices of products are available through third-party sellers in the 'Amazon Marketplace' which are integrated within the standard product listings. The strategy to offer such an auction facility was initially driven by the need to compete with eBay, but now the strategy has been adjusted such that Amazon describes it as part of the approach of low pricing.

Although it might be thought that Amazon would lose out on enabling its merchants to sell products at lower prices, in fact Amazon makes greater margin on these sales since merchants are charged a commission on each sale and it is the merchant who bears the cost of storing inventory and fulfilling the product to customers. As with eBay, Amazon is just facilitating the exchange of bits and bytes between buyers and sellers without the need to distribute physical products.

How 'the culture of metrics' started

A common theme in Amazon's development is the drive to use a measured approach to all aspects of the business, beyond the finance. Marcus (2004) describes an occasion at a corporate 'boot-camp' in January 1997 when Amazon CEO Jeff Bezos 'saw the light'. '*At Amazon, we will have a Culture of Metrics*', he said while addressing his senior staff. He went on to explain how web-based business gave Amazon an '*amazing window into human behavior*'. Marcus says: '*Gone were the fuzzy approximations of focus groups, the anecdotal fudging and smoke blowing from the marketing department. A company like Amazon could (and did) record every move a visitor made, every last click and twitch of the mouse. As the data piled up into virtual heaps, hummocks and mountain ranges, you could draw all sorts of conclusions about their chimerical nature, the consumer. In this sense, Amazon was not merely a store, but an immense repository of facts. All we needed were the right equations to plug into them.*'

James Marcus then goes on to give a fascinating insight into a breakout group discussion of how Amazon could better use measures to improve its performance. Marcus was in the Bezos group, brainstorming customer-centric metrics. Marcus (2004) summarizes the dialogue, led by Bezos:

> *'First, we figure out which things we'd like to measure on the site', he said. 'For example, let's say we want a metric for customer enjoyment. How could we calculate that?*
>
> *There was silence. Then somebody ventured: 'How much time each customer spends on the site?'*
> *'Not specific enough', Jeff said.*
>
> *'How about the average number of minutes each customer spends on the site per session', someone else suggested. 'If that goes up, they're having a blast.'*
>
> *'But how do we factor in purchase?', I [Marcus] said feeling proud of myself. 'Is that a measure of enjoyment'?*
>
> *'I think we need to consider frequency of visits, too', said a dark-haired woman I didn't recognize. 'Lot of folks are still accessing the web with those creepy-crawly modems. Four short visits from them might be just as good as one visit from a guy with a T-1. Maybe better.'*
>
> *'Good point', Jeff said. 'And anyway, enjoyment is just the start. In the end, we should be measuring customer ecstasy.'*

It is interesting that Amazon was having this debate about the elements of RFM analysis (described in Chaffey *et al.*, 2006 Chapter 6) in 1997, after already having achieved $16 million of revenue in the previous year. Of course, this is a miniscule amount compared with today's billions of dollar turnover. The important point was that this was the start of a focus on metrics which can be seen through the description of Matt Round's work later in this case study.

From human to software-based recommendations

Amazon has developed internal tools to support this 'culture of metrics'. Marcus (2004) describes how the 'Creator Metrics' tool shows content creators how well their product listings and product copy are working. For each content editor such as Marcus, it retrieves all recently posted documents including articles, interviews, booklists and features. For each one it then gives a conversion rate to sale plus the number of page views, adds (added to basket) and repels (content requested, but the back button then used). In time, the work of editorial reviewers such as Marcus was marginalized since Amazon found that the majority of visitors used the search tools rather than read editorials and they responded to the personalized recommendations as the matching technology improved (Marcus likens early recommendations techniques to 'going shopping with the village idiot').

Experimentation and testing at Amazon

The 'culture of metrics' also led to a test-driven approach to improving results at Amazon. Matt Round, speaking at E-metrics 2004 when he was director of personalization at →

Amazon, describes the philosophy as *'data trumps intuitions'*. He explained how Amazon used to have a lot of arguments about which content and promotion should go on the all-important home page or category pages. He described how every category VP wanted top-centre and how the Friday meetings about placements for next week were getting 'too long, too loud, and lacked performance data'.

But today 'automation replaces intuitions' and real-time experimentation tests are always run to answer these questions since actual consumer behaviour is the best way to decide upon tactics.

Marcus (2004) also notes that Amazon has a culture of *experiments,* of which A/B tests are key components. Examples where A/B tests are used include new home page design, moving features around the page, different algorithms for recommendations, changing search relevance rankings. These involve testing a new treatment against a previous control for a limited time of a few days or a week. The system will randomly show one or more treatments to visitors and measure a range of parameters such as units sold and revenue by category (and total), session time, session length, etc. The new features will usually be launched if the desired metrics are statistically significantly better. Statistical tests are a challenge though, as distributions are not normal (they have a large mass at zero for example, of no purchase). There are other challenges since multiple A/B tests are running every day and A/B tests may overlap and so conflict. There are also longer-term effects where some features are 'cool' for the first two weeks and the opposite effect where changing navigation may degrade performance temporarily. Amazon also finds that as its users evolve in their online experience the way they act online has changed. This means that Amazon has to constantly test and evolve its features.

Technology

It follows that the Amazon technology infrastructure must readily support this culture of experimentation and this can be difficult to achieve with standardized content management. Amazon has achieved its competitive advantage through developing its technology internally and with a significant investment in this which may not be available to other organizations without the right focus on the online channels. As Amazon explains in SEC (2005),

> *using primarily our own proprietary technologies, as well as technology licensed from third parties, we have implemented numerous features and functionality that simplify and improve the customer shopping experience, enable third parties to sell on our platform, and facilitate our fulfillment and customer service operations. Our current strategy is to focus our development efforts on continuous innovation by creating and enhancing the specialized, proprietary software that is unique to our business, and to license or acquire commercially-developed technology for other applications where available and appropriate. We continually invest in several areas of technology, including our seller platform; A9.com, our wholly-owned subsidiary focused on search technology on www.A9.com and other Amazon sites; web services; and digital initiatives.*

Round (2004) describes the technology approach as 'distributed development and deployment'. Pages such as the home page have a number of content 'pods' or 'slots' which call web services for features. This makes it relatively easy to change the content in these pods and even change the location of the pods on-screen. Amazon uses a flowable or fluid page design unlike many sites, which enables it to make the most of real estate on-screen.

Technology also supports more standard e-retail facilities. SEC (2005) states:

> *We use a set of applications for accepting and validating customer orders, placing and tracking orders with suppliers, managing and assigning inventory to customer orders, and ensuring proper shipment of products to customers. Our transaction-processing systems handle millions of items, a number of different status inquiries, multiple shipping addresses, gift-wrapping requests, and multiple shipment methods. These systems allow the customer to choose whether to receive single or several shipments based on availability and to track the progress of each order. These applications also manage the process of accepting, authorizing, and charging customer credit cards.*

Data-driven automation

Round (2004) said that 'data is king at Amazon'. He gave many examples of data-driven automation including customer channel preferences, managing the way content is displayed to different user types such as new releases and top-sellers, merchandizing and recommendation (showing related products and promotions) and also advertising through paid search (automatic ad generation and bidding).

The automated search advertising and bidding system for paid search has had a big impact at Amazon. Sponsored links were initially done by humans, but this was unsustainable due to the range of products at Amazon. The automated programme generates keywords, writes ad creative, determines best landing page, manages bids, and measures conversion rates, profit per converted visitor and updates bids. Again the problem of volume is there, Matt Round described how the book *How to Make Love like a Porn Star* by Jenna Jameson received tens of thousands of clicks from pornography-related searches, but few actually purchased the book. So the update cycle must be quick to avoid large losses.

There is also an automated e-mail measurement and optimization system. The campaign calendar used to be manually managed with relatively weak measurement and it was costly to schedule and use. A new system:

- Automatically optimizes content to improve customer experience
- Avoids sending an e-mail campaign that has low click-through or high unsubscribe rate
- Includes inbox management (avoid sending multiple e-mails/per week)
- Has a growing library of automated e-mail programmes covering new releases and recommendations
- But there are challenges if promotions are too successful if inventory isn't available.

Your recommendations

'Customers Who Bought X ..., also bought Y' is Amazon's signature feature. Round (2004) describes how Amazon relies on acquiring and then crunching a massive amount of data. Every purchase, every page viewed and every search is recorded. So there are now two new versions, 'Customers who shopped for X also shopped for Y and 'Customers who searched for X also bought Y'. They also have a system codenamed 'Goldbox' which is a cross-sell and awareness-raising tool. Items are discounted to encourage purchases in new categories!

He also describes the challenge of techniques for sifting patterns from noise (sensitivity filtering) and clothing and toy catalogues change frequently so recommendations become out of date. The main challenges though are the massive data size arising from millions of customers, millions of items and recommendations made in real time.

Partnership strategy

As Amazon grew, its share price growth enabled partnership or acquisition with a range of companies in different sectors. Marcus (2004) describes how Amazon partnered with Drugstore.com (pharmacy), Living.com (furniture), Pets.com (pet supplies), Wineshopper.com (wines), HomeGrocer.com (groceries), Sothebys.com (auctions) and Kozmo.com (urban home delivery). In most cases, Amazon purchased an equity stake in these partners, so that it would share in their prosperity. It also charged them fees for placements on the Amazon site to promote and drive traffic to their sites. Similarly, Amazon charged publishers for prime-position to promote books on its site which caused an initial hue-and-cry, but this abated when it was realized that paying for prominent placements was widespread in traditional booksellers and supermarkets. Many of these new online companies failed in 1999 and 2000, but Amazon had covered the potential for growth and was not pulled down by these partners, even though for some such as Pets.com it had an investment of 50%.

Analysts sometimes refer to 'Amazoning a sector', meaning that one company becomes dominant in an online sector such as book retail such that it becomes very difficult for others to achieve market share. In addition to developing, communicating and delivering a very strong proposition, Amazon has been able to consolidate its strength in different sectors through its partnership arrangements and through using technology to facilitate product promotion and distribution via these partnerships. The Amazon retail platform enables other retailers to sell products online using the Amazon user interface and infrastructure through their 'Syndicated Stores' programme. For example, in the UK, Waterstones (www.waterstones.co.uk) is one of the largest traditional bookstores. It found competition with online so expensive and challenging that eventually it entered a partnership arrangement where Amazon markets and distributes its books online in return for a commission. Similarly, in the US, Borders, a large book retailer, uses the Amazon merchant platform for distributing its products. Toy retailer Toys 'R Us has a similar arrangement. Such partnerships help Amazon extends its reach into the customer base of other suppliers, and of course, customers who buy in one category such as books can be encouraged to purchase from other areas such as clothing or electronics.

Another form of partnership referred to above is the Amazon Marketplace which enables Amazon customers and other retailers to sell their new and used books and other goods alongside the regular retail listings. A similar partnership approach is the Amazon 'Merchants@' programme which enables third-party merchants (typically larger than those who sell via the Amazon Marketplace) to sell their products via Amazon. Amazon earns fees either as fixed fees or as sales commissions per unit. This arrangement can help customers who get a wider choice of products from a range of suppliers with the convenience of purchasing them through a single checkout process.

Finally, Amazon has also facilitated formation of partnerships with smaller companies through its affiliates programme. Internet legend records that Jeff Bezos, the creator of Amazon, was chatting at a cocktail party to someone who wanted to sell books about divorce via her web site. Subsequently, Amazon.com launched its Associates Program in July 1996 and it is still going strong. Googling www.google.com/search?q=www.amazon.com+-site%3Awww.amazon.com for sites that link to the US site shows over 4 million pages, many of which will be affiliates. Amazon does not use an affiliate network which would take commissions from sale, but thanks to the strength of its brand has developed its own affiliate programme. Amazon has created tiered performance-based incentives to encourage affiliates to sell more Amazon products.

Marketing communications

In their SEC filings Amazon state that the aims of their communications strategy are (unsurprisingly) to:

1. Increase customer traffic to their web sites
2. Create awareness of their products and services
3. Promote repeat purchases
4. Develop incremental product and service revenue opportunities
5. Strengthen and broaden the Amazon.com brand name. →

Amazon also believes that their most effective marketing communications are a consequence of their focus on continuously improving the customer experience. This then creates word-of-mouth promotion which is effective in acquiring new customers and may also encourage repeat customer visits.

As well as this, Marcus (2004) describes how Amazon used the personalization enabled through technology to reach out to a difficult-to-reach market which Bezos originally called 'the hard middle'. Bezos's view was that it was easy to reach 10 people (you called them on the phone) or the ten million people who bought the most popular products (you placed a superbowl ad), but more difficult to reach those in between. The search facilities in the search engine and on the Amazon site, together with its product recommendation features meant that Amazon could connect its products with the interests of these people.

Online advertising techniques include paid search marketing, interactive ads on portals, e-mail campaigns and search engine optimization. These are automated as far as possible as described earlier in the case study. As previously mentioned, the affiliate programme is also important in driving visitors to Amazon and Amazon offers a wide range of methods of linking to its site to help improve conversion. For example, affiliates can use straight text links leading direct to a product page and they also offer a range of dynamic banners which feature different content such as books about Internet marketing or a search box.

Amazon also uses cooperative advertising arrangements, better known as 'contra-deals' with some vendors and other third parties. For example, a print advertisement in 2005 for a particular product such as a wireless router with a free wireless laptop card promotion was to feature a specific Amazon URL in the ad. In product fulfilment packs, Amazon may include a leaflet for a non-competing online company such as Figleaves.com (lingerie) or Expedia (travel). In return, Amazon leaflets may be included in customer communications from the partner brands.

Amazon's associates programme directs customers to its web sites by enabling independent web sites to make millions of products available to its audiences with

	Year ended 31 December				
	2004	2003	2002	2001	2000
	(in thousands, except per share data)				
Net sales	$ 6,921,124	$ 5,263,699	$ 3,932,936	$ 3,122,433	$ 2,761,983
Income (loss) before change in accounting principle	588,451	35,282	(149,933)	(556,754)	(1,411,273)
Cumulative effect of change in accounting principle	—	—	801	(10,523)	
Net income (loss)	588,451	35,282	(149,132)	(567,277)	(1,411,273)
Basic earnings per share (1):					
Prior to cumulative effect of change in accounting principal	$ 1.45	$ 0.09	$ (0.40)	$ (1.53)	$ (4.02)
Cumulative effect of change in accounting principal	—	—	0.01	(0.03)	—
Basic earnings per share (1)	$ 1.45	$ 0.09	$ (0.39)	$ (1.56)	$ (4.02)
Diluted earnings per share (1):					
Prior to cumulative effect of change in accounting principal	$ 1.39	$ 0.08	$ (0.40)	$ (1.53)	$ (4.02)
Cumulative effect of change in accounting principal	—	—	0.01	(0.03)	—
Diluted earnings per share (1)	$ 1.39	$ 0.08	$ (0.39)	$ (1.56)	$ (4.02)
Shares used in computation of earnings (loss) per share:					
Basic	405,926	395,479	378,363	364,211	350,873
Diluted	424,757	419,352	378,363	364,211	350,873
Balance Sheet and Other Data:					
Total assets	$ 3,248,508	$ 2,162,033	$ 1,990,449	$ 1,637,547	$ 2,135,169
Long-term debt and other	1,855,319	1,945,439	2,277,305	2,156,133	2,127,464

fulfilment performed by Amazon or third parties. It pays commissions to hundreds of thousands of participants in its associates programme when its customer referrals result in product sales.

In addition, it offers everyday free shipping options worldwide and recently announced Amazon.com Prime in the US, its first membership programme in which members receive free two-day shipping and discounted overnight shipping. Although marketing expenses do not include the costs of free shipping or promotional offers, it views such offers as effective marketing tools.

Sources: *Internet Retailer* (2004), Marcus (2004), Round (2004), SEC (2005)

Questions

1 By referring to the case study, Amazon's web site for your country and your experience of Amazon offline communications evaluate how well Amazon communicates its core proposition and promotional offers.

2 Using the case study, characterize Amazon's approach to marketing communications.

3 Explain what distinguishes Amazon in its uses of technology for competitive advantage.

4 How does the Amazon 'culture of metrics' differ from that in other organizations from your experience.

Summary

1 Implementation is an iterative process of managing changes involving analysis, design, testing and review as part of an evolutionary prototyping process.

2 Maintenance is a continuous process of monitoring, assessing required changes and then implanting them using evolutionary prototyping.

3 Simple web pages are developed in static HTML. Most e-business systems require dynamic pages that are implemented using client- and server-side scripting, of which the most popular are JavaScript and ASP.

4 Testing has two main objectives: first, to check for non-conformance with the business and user requirements, and second, to identify bugs or errors. There are many specialized techniques to test either part of the system (component testing) or all of the system (system testing).

5 Changeover has to be managed to include elements of piloting, phased implementation, immediate cutover and parallel running.

6 Content management requires a clearly defined update process and responsibilities according to different types of changes required.

7 Measurement also requires process and responsibilities and also a measurement framework. A suggested framework for sell-side e-commerce assesses channel promotion, channel behaviour, channel satisfaction, channel outcomes and channel profitability. Selection of appropriate web analytics tools is important to assess the effectiveness of e-commerce.

Exercises

Self-assessment questions

1 Summarize how the activities involved with implementation and maintenance relate to analysis and design activities in previous chapters.

2 What are the risks of launching a new e-commerce site if implementation is not conducted effectively?

3 Distinguish between static and dynamic content and methods of achieving them.

4 What are the objectives of testing? How do these relate to an e-commerce site?

5 Summarize the advantages and disadvantages of the different changeover methods.

6 What are the issues for managers of content management?

7 What are the main elements of an e-commerce site measurement plan?

8 What are the elements of a budget for an e-commerce site enhancement?

Essay and discussion questions

1 Write a report to a manager recommending particular techniques that should/should not be implemented on an e-commerce site. Examples may include frames, Flash or Shockwave plug-ins, JavaScript, Java and active server pages.

2 Develop a plan for measuring the marketing effectiveness of an e-commerce site.

3 Discuss the balance of using a web site and traditional methods for marketing research.

4 Choose an example of a simple brochureware web site. Develop an implementation plan for this site, recommending development techniques that will be used to enhance the site.

Examination questions

1 You are developing a testing plan for an e-commerce site. Outline five key aspects of the site you would test.

2 Data migration is often overlooked in implementation planning. Explain what data migration is and explain when it may need to occur for creation of an e-commerce site for an existing business.

3 Analyse the advantages and disadvantages of a soft versus hard web site launch.

4 Explain the following terms and suggest which is the most useful in measuring the effectiveness of a web site.

(a) hit
(b) page impression
(c) site visit.

5 Why are conversion and attrition rates important in evaluating the performance of an e-commerce site?

6 Suggest three key measures that indicate the contribution of an e-commerce site to overall business performance for a company with online and offline presence.

References

Adams, C., Kapashi, N., Neely, A. and Marr, B. (2000) Managing with measures. Measuring ebusiness performance. *Accenture white paper*. Survey conducted in conjunction with Cranfield School of Management.

Agrawal, V., Arjana, V. and Lemmens, R. (2001) E-performance: the path to rational exuberance. *McKinsey Quarterly*, no. 1, 31–43.

Barron, D. (2000) *The World of Scripting Languages*. Wiley, Chichester.

Bayne, K. (1997) *The Internet Marketing Plan*. Wiley, New York.

Bocij, P., Chaffey, D., Greasley, A. and Hickie, S. (2005) *Business Information Systems. Technology, Development and Management*, 3rd edn. Financial Times Prentice Hall, Harlow.

Bourne, M., Mills, J., Willcox, M., Neely, A and Platts, K. (2000) Designing, implementing and updating performance measurement systems. *International Journal of Operations and Production Management*, 20(7), 754–71.

Chaffey, D. (2000) Achieving Internet marketing success. *Marketing Review*, 1(1), 35–60.

Chaffey, D. and Wood, S. (2005) *Business Information Management. Improving Performance Using Information Systems*, Financial Times Prentice Hall, Harlow.

Chaffey, D., Mayer, R., Johnston, K. and Ellis-Chadwick, F. (2006) *Internet Marketing: Strategy, Implementation and Practice*, 3rd edn. Financial Times Prentice Hall, Harlow.

Friedman, L. and Furey, T. (1999) *The Channel Advantage*. Butterworth Heinemenn, Oxford.

Hanson, W. (2000) *Principles of Internet Marketing*. South Western College Publishing, Cincinnati, OH.

Internet Retailer (2004) The New Wal-Mart? By Paul Demery. *Internet Retailer,* 1 May. www.internetretailer.com.

Jorgenson, P. (1995) *Software Testing: A Craftsman's Approach*. CRC Press, Boca Raton, FL.

Kotler, P. (1997) *Marketing Management – Analysis, Planning, Implementation and Control*. Prentice-Hall, Englewood Cliffs, NJ.

Lynch, P. and Horton, S. (1999) *Web Style Guide. Basic Design Principles for Creating Web Sites*. Yale University Press, New Haven, CT.

Marcus, J. (2004) *Amazonia. Five Years at the Epicentre of the Dot-com Juggernaut*. The New Press, New York.

Neely, A., Adams, C. and Kennerley, M. (2002) *The Performance Prism. The Scorecard for Measuring and Managing Business Success*. Financial Times. Prentice Hall. Harlow.

Petersen, E. (2004) *Web Analytics Demystified*. Self-published. Available from www.webanalyticsdemystified.com.

Plant, R. (2000) *ECommerce: Formulation of Strategy*, Prentice-Hall, Upper Saddle River, NJ.

Revolution (2004) Alliance and Leicester Banks on E-commerce. *Revolution*. Article by Philip Buxton. www.revolutionmagazine.com, 28 July.

Round, M. (2004) Presentation to E-metrics, London, May. www.emetrics.org.

SEC (2005) United States Securities And Exchange Commission submission Form 10-K from Amazon. For the fiscal year ended 31 December 2004.

Sterne, J. *Web Metrics: Proven Methods for Measuring Web Site Success*. Wiley, New York.

Wisner, J. and Fawcett, S. (1991) Link firm strategy to operating decisions through performance measurement. *Production and Inventory Management Journal*, Third Quarter, 5–11.

Further reading

Barron, D. (2000) *The World of Scripting Languages*. Wiley, Chichester. An accessible introduction to scripting languages such as Perl and JavaScript.

Deitel, H., Deitel, P. and Nieto, T. (2001) *E-Business and E-Commerce. How to Program*. Prentice-Hall, Upper Saddle River, NJ. An excellent guide to creating static and dynamic pages and many other issues of e-business technology.

Friedlein, A. (2002) *Maintaining and Evolving Successful Commercial Web Sites*. Morgan Kaufmann, San Francisco. An excellent book for professionals covering managing change, content, customer relationships and site measurement.

Inan, H. (2002) *Measuring the Success of Your Website: A Customer-centric Approach to Website Management*. Pearson Education/Prentice Hall, Frenchs Forest, NSW. A detailed guide to online measurement options.

Sterne, J. (2002) *Web Metrics: Proven Methods for Measuring Web Site Success*. Wiley, New York. A guide to measurement online, with many case studies and examples of tools.

Web links

ABC ELECTRONIC (www.abce.org.uk) Audited Bureau of Circulation is standard for magazines in the UK. This is the electronic auditing part. Useful for definitions and examples of traffic for UK organizations.

E-consultancy (www.e-consultancy.com) Has a section on web analytics including buyers' guides to the tools available.

E-metrics (www.emetrics.org) Jim Sternes's site has many resources for online marketing metrics.

Gerry McGovern content management New Thinking (www.gerrymcgovern.com/new thinking.htm) Newsletter focusing on user-centric content management.

Web Analytics Association (WAA, www.webanalyticsassociation.org) The site of the trade association for web analytics has useful definitions, articles and forums on this topic.

Web Analytics Demystified (www.webanalyticsdemystified.com) A site to support Eric Petersen's books with a range of content.

Web Design/HTML About.com (http://webdesign.about.com) Portal of HTML resources.

Web Reference.com (www.webreference.com) Mainly developer news but some good guidelines on e-commerce.

Glossary

.NET
.NET is both a business strategy from Microsoft and a supporting collection of programming languages to enable **web services** to be offered by **applications service providers**.

3G
Third generation of mobile phone technology based on UMTS standard with high-speed data transfer enabling video calling and download.

4G
Fourth-generation wireless, expected to deliver wireless broadband at 20–40 Mbps (about 10–20 times the current rate of ADSL broadband services).

Acceptable-use policy
Statement of employee activities involving use of networked computers that are not considered acceptable by management.

Accessibility
An approach to site design intended to accommodate site usage using different browsers and settings particularly required by the visually impaired.

Accessibility legislation
Legislation intended to protect users of web sites with disabilities, including those with visual disability.

Acquisition method
Defines whether the system is purchased outright or developed from scratch.

Active Server Pages (ASPs)
A Microsoft-developed technology that can be used for dynamic web pages, often related to database query and retrieval.

ActiveX
A programming language standard developed by Microsoft which permits complex and graphical customer applications to be written and then accessed from a web browser. An example might be a form for calculating interest on a loan. A competitor to **Java**.

Activity-based process definition methods
Analysis tools used to identify the relationship between tasks within a business process.

Actors
People, software or other devices that interface with a system. See **use-case**.

Ad serving
The term for displaying an advertisement on a web site. Often the advertisement will be served from a web server different from the site on which it is placed.

Affiliate marketing
A commission-based arrangement where an e-retailer pays sites that link to it for sales, leads (CPA-based) or less commonly visitors (CPC-based).

Affiliate networks
An e-tailer pays commission on sales referred from other sites.

Agents
Software programs that assist humans by automatically gathering information from the Internet or exchanging data with other agents based on parameters supplied by the user.

Aggregated buying
A form of customer union where buyers collectively purchase a number of items at the same price and receive a volume discount.

Allowable cost per acquisition
A target maximum cost for generating leads or new customers profitably.

Alt tags
Alt tags appear after an image tag and contain a phrase associated with that image. For example: <img src="logo.gif" alt="Company name, company products"/>

Analysis and design
Analysis of system requirements and design for creation of a system.

Analysis for e-business
Using analytical techniques to capture and summarize business and user requirements.

Anticipatory change
An organization initiates change without an immediate need to respond.

Anti-virus software
Software to detect and eliminate viruses.

Application server
An application server provides a business application on a server remote from the user.

Application service provider (ASP)
A provider of business applications such as e-mail, workflow or groupware or any business application on a server remote from the user. A service often offered by ISPs.

Archie
A tool important before the advent of the web for storing and searching documents on the Internet. Has largely been superseded by the web which provides better searching and more sophisticated document publishing.

Asymmetric encryption
Both parties use a related but different key to encode and decode messages.

Attribute
A property or characteristic of an entity, implemented as a field; see **database**.

Attrition rate
Percentage of site visitors that are lost at each stage in making a purchase.

Auction
A buying model where traders make **offers** and **bids** to sell or buy under certain conditions.

B2B electronic marketplace
Virtual locations with facilities to enable trading between buyers and sellers.

Backbones
High-speed communications links used to enable Internet communications across a country and internationally.

Back-office systems
Processes or systems adopted within a company which were traditionally conducted separately from 'front-office' systems used to link to external partners.

Balanced scorecard
A framework for setting and monitoring business performance. Metrics are structured according to customer issues, internal efficiency measures, financial measures and innovation.

Bandwidth
Indicates the speed at which data are transferred using a particular network media. It is measured in bits per second (bps).

Behavioural ad targeting
Enables an advertiser to target ads at a visitor as they move elsewhere on the site or return to the site, thus increasing the frequency or number of impressions served to an individual in the target market.

Bespoke development
Information system development specifically for a purpose.

Bid
A commitment by a trader to *purchase* under certain conditions. See **auction**.

BitTorrent
A peer-to-peer file-sharing technology used to enable sharing of large audio and video files.

Blacklist
A compilation of known sources of **spam** that is used to block e-mail.

Blog
An online diary or news source prepared by an individual or a group of people.

Blueprints
Show the relationships between pages and other content components, and can be used to portray organization, labelling and navigation systems.

Bluetooth
A wireless standard for transmission of data between devices over short ranges (less than 100 m).

Boot-sector virus
Occupies boot record of hard and floppy disks and is activated during computer start-up.

Bounce rate
Percentage of visitors entering a site who leave immediately after viewing one page only (known as 'single-page visits').

Brand
The sum of the characteristics of a product or service perceived by a user.

Brand equity
A brand's assets (or liabilities) linked to the brand's name and symbol that add to (or subtract from) a service.

Brand experience
The frequency and depth of interactions with a brand can be enhanced through the Internet.

Brand identity
The totality of brand associations including name and symbols that must be communicated.

Branding
The process of creating and developing successful brands.

Bricks and mortar
A traditional organization with limited online presence.

Broad and shallow navigation
More choices, fewer clicks to reach required content.

Broadband connection
Access to the Internet via phone lines using a digital data transfer mechanism.

Brochureware
Brochureware describes a web site in which a company has migrated its existing paper-based promotional literature on to the Internet without recognizing the differences required by this medium.

Browser See **Web browsers**

Bundling
Offering complementary services.

Burn rate
The speed at which dot-coms spend investors' money.

Business alignment IS strategy
The IS strategy is generated from the business strategy through techniques such as CSF analysis.

Business continuity management
Measures taken to ensure that information can be restored and accessed if the original information and access method are destroyed.

Business-impacting IS strategy
IS strategy analyses opportunities for new technologies and processes to favourably impact the business strategy.

Business information systems
Information systems used to support the functional areas of business. For example, an organization might use specialized information systems to support sales, marketing and human resource management activities.

Business model
A summary of how a company will generate revenue identifying its product offering, value-added services, revenue sources and target customers.

Business process automation (BPA)
Automating existing ways of working manually through information technology.

Business process improvement (BPI)
Optimizing existing processes typically coupled with enhancements in information technology.

Business process management (BPM)
An approach supported by software tools intended to increase process efficiency by improving information flows between people as they perform business tasks.

Business process re-engineering (BPR)
Identifying radical, new ways of carrying out business operations, often enabled by new IT capabilities.

Business rule
A rule defines the actions that need to occur in a business when a particular situation arises. For example, a business rule may state that if a customer requests credit and they have a history of defaulting on payments, then credit will not be issued. A business rule is broken down into an event which triggers the rule with test conditions which result in defined actions.

Business-to-business (B2B)
Commercial transactions between an organization and other organizations.

Business-to-consumer (B2C)
Commercial transactions between an organization and consumers.

Business transformation
Significant changes to organizational processes implemented to improve organizational performance.

Buy-side e-commerce
E-commerce transactions between a purchasing organization, its suppliers and partners.

Card sorting
The process of arranging a way of organizing objects on a web site in a consistent manner.

Catalogues
Structured listing of registered sites in different categories.

ccTLD
There are some 250 country-code top-level **domains** (ccTLD).

Certificate and certificate authorities (CAs)
A certificate is a valid copy of a public key of an individual or organization together with identification information. It is issued by a trusted third party (TTP) or certificate authority (CA). CAs make public keys available and also issue private keys.

CGI (Common Gateway Interface)
CGI offers a way of providing interactivity through the web.

Challenge/respond system
An e-mail from an unknown source is challenged by another e-mail which is used to prove the originator is a valid sender.

Change agents
Managers involved in controlling change transitions.

Change management
Managing process, structural, technical, staff and culture change within an organization.

Changeover
The term used to describe moving from the old information system to the new information system.

Churn rate
The proportion of customers (typically subscribers) that no longer purchase a company's products in a time period.

'Clicks and mortar'
A business combining an online and offline presence.

Clicks-only or Internet pureplay
An organization with principally an online presence.

Client–server
The client–server architecture consists of **client** computers such as PCs sharing resources such as a database stored on more powerful **server** computers.

Client–server model
A system architecture in which end-user machines such as PCs known as clients run applications while accessing data and possibly programs from a server.

Client-side scripting
Scripts executed on the browser.

Cold list
Data about individuals that are rented or sold by a third party.

Collaborative filtering
Profiling of customer interest coupled with delivery of specific information and offers, often based on the interests of similar customers.

Commoditization
The process whereby product selection becomes more dependent on price than on differentiating features, benefits and value-added services.

Community
A customer-to-customer interaction delivered via e-mail groups, web-based discussion forums or chat.

Competitive intelligence (CI)
A process that transforms disaggregated information into relevant, accurate and usable strategic knowledge about competitors, position, performance, capabilities and intentions.

Competitor analysis for e-business
Review of e-business services offered by existing and new competitors and adoption by their customers.

Computer virus
A program capable of self-replication allowing it to spread from one machine to another. It may be malicious and delete data, or benign.

Consumer-to-business (C2B)
Customer is proactive in making an offer to a business, e.g. the price they are prepared to pay for an airline ticket.

Consumer-to-consumer (C2C)
Interactions between customers on a web site, e.g. posting and reading of topics on an electronic bulletin board.

Content
Content is the design, text and graphical information which forms a web page. Good content is the key to attracting customers to a web site and retaining their interest or achieving repeat visits.

Content management system (CMS)
Software used to manage creation, editing and review of web-based content.

Content network
Contextual ads are automatically displayed according to the type of content on partner publisher sites by the search engine. These are typically paid for on a cost-per-click (CPC) basis but ads can also be paid for on a CPM basis.

Convergence
A trend in which different hardware devices such as TVs, computers and phones merge and have similar functions.

Conversion marketing
Using marketing communications to maximize conversion of potential customers to actual customers and existing customers to repeat customers.

Conversion rate
Percentage of site visitors that perform a particular action such as making a purchase.

Cookies
Cookies are small text files stored on an end-user's computer to enable web sites to identity them.

Core competencies
Resources, including skills or technologies that provide a particular benefit to customers.

Core product
The fundamental features of the product that meet the user's needs.

Cost per acquisition (CPA)
The cost of acquiring a new customer. Typically limited to the communications cost and refers to cost per sale for new customers. May also refer to other outcomes such as cost per quote or enquiry.

CPC (cost per click)
The cost to the advertiser (or the revenue received by the publisher) of each click of a link to a thrd-party site.

Cost per thousand (CPM)
Cost per 1000 ad impressions for a banner advert.

Countermediation
Creation of a new intermediary by an established company.

Covert monitoring
Monitoring which the employer undertakes without notification of staff.

Cross-media optimization studies (XMOS)
Studies to determine the optimum spend across different media to produce the best results.

Culture
This concept includes shared values,.e cultures are created when a group of employees interact over time and are relatively successful in what they undertake.

Customer acquisition
Techniques used to gain new prospects and customers.

Customer-centric marketing
An approach to marketing based on detailed knowledge of customer behaviour within the target audience which seeks to fulfil the individual needs and wants of customers.

Customer extension
Techniques to encourage customers to increase their involvement with an organization.

Customer journey
A description of modern multi-channel behaviour as consumers use different media to select suppliers, make purchases and gain customer support.

Customer lifecycle
The stages each customer will pass through in a long-term relationship through acquisition, retention and extension. There are more detailed stages within this.

Customer orientation
Developing site content and services to appeal to different customer segments or other members of the audience.

Customer profile
Information that can be used to segment a customer.

Customer relationship management (CRM)
An approach to building and sustaining long-term business with customers.

Customer retention
Techniques to maintain relationships with existing customers.

Customer scenario
Alternative tasks or outcomes required by a visitor to a web site. Typically accomplished in a series of stages of different tasks involving different information needs or experiences.

Customer selection
Picking the ideal customers for acquisition, retention and extension.

Customer self-service
Customers perform information requests and transactions through a web interface rather than contact with customer support staff.

Customer value
Dependent on product quality, service quality, price and fulfilment time.

Data controller
Each company must have a defined person responsible for data protection.

Data migration
Transfer of data from old to new systems.

Data mining
This involves searching organizational databases in order to uncover hidden patterns or relationships in groups of data. Data mining software attempts to represent information in new ways so that previously unseen patterns or trends can be identified.

Data modelling
Data modelling involves considering how to represent data objects within a system, both logically and physically. The entity relationship diagram is used to model the data.

Data protection legislation
Law intended to protect the privacy of consumers' data through defining how organizations can gather, store, process and disclose personal information.

Data subject
The individual whose privacy is protected through data protection legislation.

Data warehouses
Data warehouses are large database systems (often measured in gigabytes or terabytes) containing detailed company data on sales transactions which are analysed to assist in improving the marketing and financial performance of companies.

Database
A database can be defined as a collection of related information. The information held in the database is stored in an organized way so that specific items can be selected and retrieved quickly. See **Database management system**.

Database management system (DBMS)
The information held in an electronic database is accessed via a database management system. A DBMS can be defined as one or more computer programs that allow users to enter, store, organize, manipulate and retrieve data from a database. For many users, the terms *database* and *database management system* are interchangeable. A *relational database management system (RDBMS)* is an extension of a DBMS and allows data to be combined from a variety of sources.

Database table
Each database comprises several tables.

Decision support system
Decision support systems provide managers with information needed to support semi-structured or unstructured decisions.

Dedicated server
Server only contains content and applications for a single company.

Deep linking
Jakob Nielsen's term for a user arriving at a site deep within its structure.

Demand analysis
Assessment of the demand for e-commerce services amongst existing and potential customer segments.

Demographic characteristics
Variations in attributes of the populations such as age, sex and social class.

Denial-of-service attacks
Web sites are disabled through bombardment with many requests for information originating from computers around the world that have been hijacked.

Deployment plan
A deployment plan is a schedule which defines all the tasks that need to occur in order for changeover to occur successfully. This includes putting in place all the infrastructure such as cabling and hardware.

Design for analysis (DFA)
The required measures from a site are considered during design to better understand the audience of a site and their decision points.

Destination site
Typically a retailer or manufacturer site with sales and service information. Intermediaries such as media sites may be destination sites for some.

Development environment
Software and hardware used to create a system.

Dial-up connection
Access to the Internet via phone lines using analogue modems.

Differential advantage
A desirable attribute of a product offering that is not currently matched by competitor offerings.

Digital certificates (keys)
Consist of keys made up of large numbers that are used to uniquely identify individuals.

Digital rights management (DRM)
The use of different technologies to protect the distribution of digital services or content such as software, music, movies or other digital data.

Digital signatures
A method of identifying individuals or companies using public-key encryption.

Directories or catalogues
Structured listings of registered sites in different categories such as Yahoo! categories.

Disaster recovery
See **Business continuity management**

Discontinuous change
Change involving a major transformation in an industry.

Disintermediation
The removal of intermediaries such as distributors or brokers that formerly linked a company to its customers.

Disruptive Internet technologies
New Internet-based communications approaches which change the way in which information about products is exchanged, which impact the basis for competition in a marketplace.

Document object model (DOM)
Enables developers to get and set properties of different document (web page) objects such as forms and frames.

Domain name
The domain name refers to the name of the web server and it is usually selected to be the same as the name of the company, e.g. www.<company-name>.com, and the extension will indicate its type.

Dot-coms
Businesses whose main trading presence is on the Internet.

Downstream supply chain
Transactions between an organization and its customers and intermediaries, equivalent to sell-side e-commerce.

Dynamic pricing
Prices can be updated in real time according to the type of customer or current market conditions.

The dynamic e-business application
The application is continuously updated in response to competitive forces.

Dynamic web content
A page that is created in real time, often with reference to a database query, in response to a user request.

Early adopter
Company or department that invests in new technologies and techniques.

Early (first) mover
An early entrant into the marketplace.

EDGE Evolved Data for GSM Evolution
Intermediate mobile standard between **GSM** and **UMTS**.

Effectiveness
Meeting process objectives, delivering the required outputs and outcomes: 'doing the right thing'.

Efficiency
Minimizing resources or time needed to complete a process: 'doing the thing right'.

Efficient consumer response (ECR)
A model for retail logistics to achieve rapid restocking in line with customer needs.

Electronic business (e-business)
All electronically mediated information exchanges, both within an organization and with external stakeholders supporting the range of business processes.

E-business applications infrastructure
Applications that provide access to services and information inside and beyond an organization.

Electronic business (e-business) infrastructure
The architecture of hardware, software, content and data used to deliver e-business services to employees, customers and partners.

Electronic business (e-business) strategy
Definition of the approach by which applications of internal and external electronic communications can support and influence corporate strategy.

E-channel service contribution
The proportion of service-type processes that are completed using electronic channels.

Electronic channel (e-channel) strategies
Define how a company should set specific objectives and develop specific differential strategies for communicating with its customers and partners through electronic media such as the Internet, e-mails and wireless media.

Electronic commerce (e-commerce)
All electronically mediated information exchanges between an organization and its external stakeholders. See **Sell-side** and **Buy-side e-commerce**.

Electronic customer relationship management (e-CRM)
Using digital communications technologies to maximize sales to existing customers and encourage continued usage of online services.

Electronic data interchange (EDI)
The exchange, using digital media, of structured business information, particularly for sales transactions, such as purchase orders and invoices between buyers and sellers.

Electronic economy (e-economy)
The dynamic system of interactions between a nation's citizens, businesses and government that capitalize upon online technology to achieve a social or economic good.

Electronic funds transfer (EFT)
Automated digital transmissions of money between organizations and banks.

Electronic government (e-government)
The use of Internet technologies to provide government services to citizens.

Electronic mail (e-mail)
Sending messages or documents, such as news about a new product or sales promotion between individuals. A primitive form of 'push' channel. See **Inbound**, **Outbound e-mail**.

Electronic mail (e-mail) filter
Software used to identify **spam** according to its characteristics such as keywords.

Electronic marketing (e-marketing)
Achieving marketing objectives through use of electronic communications technology.

Electronic marketing (e-marketing) plan
A plan to achieve the marketing objectives of the e-business strategy.

Electronic marketplace
A virtual marketplace such as the Internet in which no direct contact occurs between buyers and sellers.

Electronic procurement (e-procurement)
The electronic integration and management of all procurement activities including purchase request, authorization, ordering, delivery and payment between a purchaser and a supplier.

Electronic procurement systems (EPSs)
An electronic system used to automate all or part of the procurement function by enabling the scanning, storage and retrieval of invoices and other documents; management of approvals; routing of authorization requests; interfaces to other finance systems; and matching of documents to validate transactions.

Electronic tokens
Units of digital currency that are in a standard electronic format.

Emergent strategy
Strategic analysis, strategic development and strategy implementation are interrelated and are developed together.

Employee communications monitoring
Companies monitor staff e-mails and web sites they access.

Encryption
See **Asymmetric encryption** and **Symmetric encryption**

Enterprise application integration (EAI)
Software used to facilitate communications between business applications including data transfer and control.

Enterprise resource planning (ERP) applications
Enterprise applications used to manage information about organizational resources such as raw materials, products, staff and customers as part of delivery of a product or service.

Entity
A grouping of related data, such as a customer entity. Implemented as a table.

Environmental scanning and analysis
The process of continuously monitoring the environment and events and responding accordingly.

Ethical hacker
Hacker employed legitimately to test the quality of system security.

Ethical standards
Practice or behaviour which is morally acceptable to society.

Events and event handlers
An event handler monitors and responds to events such as a mouse click.

Exchange
See **B2B electronic marketplace**

Expert review
An analysis of an existing site or prototype by an experienced usability expert who will identify deficiencies and improvements to a site based on their knowledge of web design principles and best practice.

Explicit knowledge
Knowledge that can be readily expressed and recorded within information systems.

Extended product
Additional features and benefits beyond the core product.

Extranet
Formed by extending an intranet beyond a company to customers, suppliers and collaborators.

Field
Attributes of products, such as date of birth. See **Database**.

Filtering software
Software that blocks specified content or activities.

Financial EDI
Aspect of electronic payment mechanism involving transfer of funds from the bank of a buyer to a seller. See **Electronic data exchange**.

Firewall
A specialized software application mounted on a server at the point where the company is connected to the Internet. Its purpose is to prevent unauthorized access into the company from outsiders.

First-party cookies
Served by the site you are currently using – typical for e-commerce sites.

Flow
Flow describes how easy it is for users of a site to move between the different pages of content of the site.

Form validation
Used to check the validity of online form inputs from users.

FTP (File Transfer Protocol)
The File Transfer Protocol is used as a standard for moving files across the Internet. FTP is available as a feature of web browsers that is used for marketing applications such as downloading files such as product price lists or specifications. Also used to update HTML files on web pages.

Gbps
One gigabit per second or 1,000,000,000 bps; fibre-optic or satellite links operate at Gbps.

GIF (Graphics Interchange Format)
A graphics format and compression algorithm best used for simple graphics.

Globalization
The increase of international trading and shared social and cultural values.

Global System for Mobile (GSM) communications
The most widely used digital mobile phone system in Europe before the emergence of 3G.

Gophers
A tool important before the advent of the web for storing and searching documents on the Internet. Has largely been superseded by the web which provides better searching and more sophisticated document publishing.

Governance
Control of the operation and use of the Internet.

gTLD (generic Top-Level Domain)
gTLDs are part of a **domain name**:

- **.com** represents an international or American company such as www.travelagency.com
- **.co.uk** represents a company based in the UK, such as www.thomascook.co.uk
- **.ac.uk** is a UK university (e.g. www.derby. ac.uk)
- **.org.uk** and **.org** are not-for-profit organizations (e.g. www.greenpeace.org)
- **.net** is a network provider such as www.virgin.net

Hacking
The process of gaining unauthorized access to computer systems, typically across a network.

Hardware
Describes the physical components of a computer system. The hardware of a computer system can be said to consist of: input devices, memory, central processing unit, output devices and storage devices.

Hit
Recorded for each graphic or text file requested from a web server. It is not a reliable measure for the number of people viewing a page.

Hosted solution
Standard software which is managed externally on the supplier's server.

House list
Data about existing customers used to market products to encourage future purchase.

HTML (Hypertext Markup Language)
HTML is a standard format used to define the text and layout of web pages. HTML files usually have the extension .HTML or .HTM.

HTML tags
Markup codes denoted by <start code> and </end code> that instruct the browser to format information or perform a particular operation.

HTML parameters
These occur within the tags to specify particular characteristics of the HTML statement.

HTTP (Hypertext Transfer Protocol)
HTTP or Hypertext Transfer Protocol is a standard which defines the way information is transmitted across the Internet between web browsers and web servers.

Hub See **B2B electronic marketplace**

Hype cycle
A graphic representation of the maturity, adoption and business application of specific technologies.

Hyperlink
A method of moving between one web site page and another, indicated to the user by an image or text highlighted by underlining and/or a different colour.

Identity theft
The misappropriation of the identity of another person, without their knowledge or consent.

i-Mode
A mobile access platform that enables display of colour graphics and content subscription services.

Impact assessment
An assessment of the **employee monitoring** process in the workplace to identify improvements to minimize infringement of employee privacy.

Implementation
The creation of a system based on analysis and design documentation.

Implementation activities
The creation of the system modules by coding and scripting, module integration and testing and changeover to the live system.

Inbound e-mail
E-mail received from outside the organization such as customer and supplier enquiries.

Inbound e-mail marketing
Management of e-mails from customers by an organization.

Inbound logistics
The management of material resources entering an organization from its suppliers and other partners.

Incremental change
Relatively small adjustments required by an organization in response to its business environment.

Infomediary
A business whose main source of revenue derives from capturing consumer information and developing detailed profiles of individual customers for use by third parties.

Information
Data that have been processed so that they are meaningful.

Information and communication technology (ICT or IT)
The software applications, computer hardware and networks used to create e-business systems.

Information architecture
The combination of organization, labelling and navigation schemes comprising an information system.

Information asset register
A repository for the types, value and ownership of all information within an organization.

Information organization schemes
The structure chosen to group and categorize information.

Information security management system
An organizational process to protect information assets.

Information security policy
A definition of the organizational approaches to information security and the responsibilities of employees in protecting information.

Information society
A society with widespread access and transfer of digital information within business and the community.

Information system
A system designed to produce information that can be used to support the activities of managers and other workers.

Initiation
The start-up phase of the project.

Instant Messaging (IM)
Immediate text-based communication via computer or mobile phone.

Intellectual property rights (IPR)
Protect the intangible property created by corporations or individuals that is protected under copyright, trade secret and patent laws.

Intelligent agents
Software programs that assist humans by automatically gathering information from the Internet or exchanging data with other agents based on parameters supplied by the user.

Interactive digital TV (iDTV)
TV that enables interaction with viewers through handset or keyboard.

Interactivity
The medium enables a dialogue between company and customer.

Intermediary
An organization or e-commerce site that typically brings buyers and sellers together.

Internet
The Internet refers to the physical network that links computers across the globe. It consists of the infrastructure of network servers and communication links between them that are used to hold and transport information between the client PCs and web servers.

Internet-based market research
The use of online questionnaires and focus groups to assess customer perceptions of a web site or broader marketing issues.

Internet EDI
Use of **EDI** data standards delivered across non-proprietary IP networks.

Internet governance
Control of the operation and use of the Internet.

Internet marketing metrics
Measures that indicate the effectiveness of Internet marketing activities in meeting customer, business and marketing objectives.

Internet pureplay
An organization with principally an online presence.

Internet Relay Chat (IRC)
This is a synchronous communications tool which allows a text-based 'chat' between different users who are logged on at the same time. Of limited use for marketing purposes.

Internet service provider (ISP)
A provider enabling home or business users a connection to access the Internet. They can also host web-based applications.

Interruption marketing
Marketing communications that disrupt customers' activities.

Interstitial ads
Ads that appear between one page and the next.

Intranet
A private network within a single company using Internet standards to enable employees to share information using e-mail and web publishing.

IP address
The unique numerical address of a computer.

IP/TV
Digital TV channels are made available via broadband Internet either as streamed live broadcasts or as archived broadcasts of TV programmes.

Java
A programming language standard supported by Sun Microsystems which permits complex and graphical customer applications to be written and then accessed from a web browser. An example might be a form for calculating interest on a loan. A competitor to **ActiveX**.

JavaScript
A web-page scripting language that uses an object model.

JPEG (Joint Photographics Experts Group)
A graphics format and compression algorithm best used for photographs.

kbps
One kilobit per second or 1,000 bps (a modem operates at up to 56.6 kbps).

Key See **Primary key** and **Secondary key** or **Digital certificates, Encryption**

Knowledge
Applying experience to problem solving.

Knowledge management
Techniques and tools for disseminating knowledge within an organization.

Landing page
Part of a web site used for direct responses from an e-mail campaign.

Lead See **Qualified lead**

Lifetime value (LTV)
Lifetime value is the total net benefit that a customer or group of customers will provide a company over their total relationship with the company.

Link building
A structured activity to include good-quality hyperlinks to your site from relevant sites with a good **page rank**.

Localization
Tailoring of web-site information for individual countries or regions.

Log file See **Transaction log files**
A web server file that records all page requests.

Log file analyser
A log file analyser is a separate program such as Webtrends that is used to summarize the information on customer activity contained in a log file.

Logistics
See **Inbound logistics** and **Outbound logistics**

Maintenance activities
Involve measurement of an information system's effectiveness and updating to correct errors or introduce new features necessary to improve its value to the organization.

Maintenance phase
Commences after the system is live.

Malicious virus
A virus that causes damage through destruction of data or software.

Managed e-mail service
Receipt and transmission of e-mails is managed by a third party.

Marketing concept
The management of the range of organizational activities that impact on the customer as part of marketing.

Marketing orientation
Meeting customer requirements through the coordination of all organizational activities that impact the customer.

Marketplace
See **B2B electronic marketplace**

Mass customization
Delivering customized content to groups of users through web pages or e-mail.

Mbps
One megabit per second or 1,000,000 bps (company networks operate at 10 or more Mbps).

Meta-data
A definition of the structure and content of a collection of data or documents. 'Data about data'.

Metamediaries
Third parties that provide a single point of contact and deliver a range of services between customers and suppliers.

Meta-tags
Keywords that are part of an HTML page that result in a higher search listing if they match the typed keyword.

Micropayments
Small-denomination payments.

Middleware
Software used to facilitate communication between business applications including data transfer control.

Milestone
Key deadline to be achieved during project, usually with defined deliverable criteria.

Micro-site
A small-scale destination site reached on clickthrough which is part of the media owner's site.

Mixed-mode buying
The process by which a customer changes between online and offline channels during the buying process.

Mobile commerce (m-commerce)
Electronic transactions and communications conducted using mobile devices such as laptops, PDAs and mobile phones, and typically with a wireless connection.

MRO
Maintenance, repairs and operations of manufacturing facilities.

Multi-channel e-business strategy
Defines how different marketing and supply chain channels should integrate and support each other to drive business efficiency and effectiveness.

Multi-channel marketing strategy
Defines how different marketing channels should integrate and support each other in terms of their proposition development and communications based on their relative merits for the customer and the company.

Narrow and deep navigation
Fewer choices, more clicks to reach required content.

Navigation scheme
Tools provided to the user to move between different information on a web site.

Newsgroup
See **Usenet newsgroup**

Notification
The process whereby companies register with the data protection registrar to inform about their data holdings.

Offer
A commitment by a trader to sell under certain conditions. See **Auction**.

Offline marketing communications
Traditional techniques such as print and TV advertising used to generate web-site traffic.

On-demand computing
This term was coined by IBM to describe managed services.

Online buyer behaviour
An assessment of how consumers and business people use the Internet in combination with other communications channels when selecting and buying products and services.

Online intermediaries
Web sites which help connect web users with content they are seeking on **destination sites**. Include new online intermediaries such as search engines and shopping comparison sites and traditional brokers, directories and newspaper and magazine publishers that now have an online presence.

Online marketing communications
Internet-based techniques used to generate web-site traffic.

Online PR
Maximizing favourable mentions of your company, brands, products or web sites on third-party web sites which are likely to be visited by your target audience.

Online promotion contribution
An assessment of the proportion of customers (new or retained) who use the online information sources and are influenced as a result.

Online revenue contribution (ORC)
An assessment of the direct contribution of the Internet or other digital media to sales, usually expressed as a percentage of overall sales revenue.

Online service contribution
Proportion of customers (new or retained) who use web self-service for different types of service transactions such as invoice checking.

Online value proposition (OVP)
A statement of the benefits of e-commerce services that ideally should not be available in competitor offerings or offline offerings.

Open-source software
Software that is developed collaboratively, independent of a vendor, by a community of software developers and users.

Opt-in
A customer proactively agrees to receive further information.

Opt-out
A customer declines the offer to receive further information.

Organizational change
Includes both **incremental** and **discontinuous change** to an organization.

Outbound e-mail
E-mail sent from the company to other organizations.

Outbound e-mail marketing
E-mails are sent to customers and prospects from an organization.

Outbound logistics
The management of resources supplied from an organization to its customers and intermediaries such as retailers and distributors.

Outsourcing
Contracting of functional tasks to a third party.

Overlay
Typically an animated ad that moves around the page and is superimposed on the web site content.

Packaged implementation
Standard software is installed with limited configuration required.

Packet
Each Internet message such as an e-mail or http request is broken down into smaller parts for ease of transmission.

Page impression (view)
A more reliable measure than a hit denoting one person viewing one page.

Page rank
A scale of 0 to 10 used by Google to assess the importance of web sites according to the number of inbound links (link popularity).

Payment systems
Methods of transferring funds from a customer to a merchant.

Pay-per-click (PPC) search marketing
A company pays for text adverts to be displayed on the search engine results pages when a specific key phrase is entered by the search users. It is so called since the marketer pays for each time the hypertext link in the ad is clicked on.

People variable
The element of the marketing mix that involves the delivery of service to customers during interactions with customers.

Performance drivers
Critical success factors that govern whether objectives are achieved.

Performance management system
A process used to evaluate and improve the **efficiency** and **effectiveness** of an organization and its processes.

Performance management system
A process used to evaluate and improve the efficiency and effectiveness of an organisation and its processes.

Perl
Practical Execution and Report Language used mainly for server-side scripting and producing CGI scripts.

Permission marketing
Customers agree (opt in) to be involved in an organization's marketing activities, usually as a result of an incentive.

Persistent cookies
Cookies that remain on the computer after a visitor session has ended. Used to recognize returning visitors.

Persona
A summary of the characteristics, needs, motivations and environment of typical web-site users.

Personal data
Any information about an individual stored by companies concerning their customers or employees.

Personalization
Delivering individualized content through web pages or e-mail.

Phishing
Obtaining personal details online through sites and e-mails masquerading as legitimate businesses.

Physical evidence variable
The element of the marketing mix that involves the tangible expression of a product and how it is purchased and used.

Place variable
The element of the marketing mix that involves distributing products to customers in line with demand and minimizing cost of inventory, transport and storage.

Plug-in
An add-on program to a web browser providing extra functionality such as animation.

Podcasts
Individuals and organizations post online media (audio and video) which can be accessed in the appropriate players including the iPod which first sparked the growth of this technique.

Portal
An **intermediary site** focused on providing a gateway to other information on other sites, but often also providing its own content and services. Examples include search engines, ISPs and online newspapers and magazines.

Positioning
Influencing the customer's perception of a product within a marketplace.

Prescriptive strategy
The three core areas of strategic analysis, strategic development and strategy implementation are linked together sequentially.

Price variable
The element of the marketing mix that involves defining product prices and pricing models.

Pricing models
Describe the form of payment such as outright purchase, auction, rental, volume purchase and credit terms.

Primary key
The field that uniquely identifies each record in a table. See **Database**.

Primary persona
A representation of the typical web site user, who is strategically important to the effectiveness of the site, but one which it is challenging to fulfil the needs of.

Privacy
The right of an individual to control the information held about them by third parties.

Privacy and Electronic Communications Regulations (PECR) Act
A law intended to control the distribution of e-mail and other online communications including **cookies**.

Privacy statement
A web page explaining how personal data will be collected, stored, disseminated and updated.

Private B2B exchanges
A manufacturer or major supplier to different manufacturers creates a **portal** which is used for managing all aspects of procurement.

Private key See **Encryption**

Process
Part of a system that has a clearly defined purpose or objective and clearly defined inputs and outputs.

Process mapping
Identification of location and responsibilities for processes within an organization.

Process variable
The element of the marketing mix that involves the methods and procedures companies use to achieve all marketing functions.

Product variable
The element of the marketing mix that involves researching customers' needs and developing appropriate products.

Production or live environment
Software and hardware used to host an operational system.

Productivity paradox
Research results indicating a poor correlation between organizational investment in information systems and organizational performance measured by return on equity.

Promotion variable
The element of the marketing mix that involves communication with customers and other stakeholders to inform them about the product and the organization.

Propensity modelling
A name given to the approach of evaluating customer characteristics and behaviour and then making recommendations for future products.

Prototype
A preliminary version of part or all of an information system reviewed by its users and business sponsors.

Prototyping
Prototyping is an iterative process whereby web-site users suggest modifications before further prototypes and the live version of the site are developed.

Psychographic segmentation
A breakdown of customers according to different characteristics.

Public key See **Encryption**

Pull media
The consumer is proactive in selection of the message through actively seeking out a web site.

Pull supply chain
An emphasis on using the supply chain to deliver value to customers who are actively involved in product and service specification.

Push channel
Information is broadcast over the Internet or an intranet and received using a web browser or special program for which a subscription to this channel has been set up. This technique is still used for automated software distribution, but has not proved popular as a method for accessing web content by users.

Push media
Communications are broadcast from an advertiser to consumers of the message who are passive recipients.

Push supply chain
A supply chain that emphasizes distribution of a product to passive customers.

Qualified lead
Contact information for a customer and an indication of their propensity to purchase different products.

RAD – Rapid Application Development
An approach to information systems development that includes incremental development using **prototypes**.

Radio-frequency identification (RFID)
Microchip-based electronic tags are used for monitoring anything they are attached to, whether inanimate (products) or animate (people).

Reactive change
A direct response by an organization to a change in its environment.

Reciprocal links
An exchange of links between two site owners.

Record
A collection of fields for one instance of an entity, such as Customer Smith. See **Database**.

Referrer
The source of a web site visit, e.g. paid search, affiliate marketing, online advertising or recorded as 'no referrer', i.e. when a URL is typed in directly.

Reintermediation
The creation of new intermediaries between customers and suppliers providing services such as supplier search and product evaluation.

Relationship
Describes how different tables are linked. See **Database**.

Repurposing
Developing content for a new access platform which was previously used for a different platform such as the web.

Resource analysis
Review of the technological, financial and human resources of an organization and how they are utilized in business processes.

Return path
An interaction where the customer sends information to the provider using a phone line or cable.

Revenue models
Describe methods of generating income for an organization.

Right-channelling
This is selective adoption of e-channels by business for some products or markets in order to best generate value for the organization according to stakeholder preferences.

Risk management
Evaluating potential risks, developing strategies to reduce risks and learning about future risks.

Robots
Automated tools known as 'spiders' or 'robots' index registered sites. Users search by typing keywords into a search engine and are presented with a list of pages.

Satisficing behaviour
Consumers do not behave entirely rationally in product or supplier selection. They will compare alternatives, but then may make their choice given imperfect information.

Scalability
The ability of an organization or system to adapt to increasing demands being placed on it.

Scanning software
Identifies e-mail or web-site access that breaches company guidelines or **acceptable-use policies**.

Scenario
A particular path or flow of events or activities within a use-case.

Scenario-based analysis
Models of the future environment are developed from different starting points.

Schematics
See **Wireframes**

Scripting languages
A software standard providing a set of instructions to perform a particular task.

Search engines
Automated tools known as 'spiders' or 'robots' index registered sites. Users use search engines by typing keywords and are presented with a list of ranked pages from the index.

Search-engine optimization (SEO)
A structured approach used to increase the position of a company or its products in search-engine results according to selected keywords.

Searching behaviours
Approaches to finding information vary from directed to undirected.

Secondary key
A field that is used to link tables, by linking to a primary key in another table. See **Database**.

Secure Electronic Transaction (SET)
A standard for public-key encryption intended to enable secure e-commerce transactions, lead-developed by Mastercard and Visa.

Secure Sockets Layer (SSL)
A commonly used encryption technique for scrambling data as they are passed across the Internet from a customer's web browser to a merchant's web server.

Segmentation
Identification of different groups within a target market in order to develop different offerings for the groups.

Sell-side e-commerce
E-commerce transactions between a supplier organization and its customers.

Semantic web
Interrelated content including data with defined meaning, enabling better exchange of information between computers and between people and computers.

Sense and respond communications
Delivering timely, relevant communications to customers as part of a contact strategy based on assessment of their position in the customer lifecycle and monitoring specific interactions with a company's web site, e-mails and staff.

Servers See **Web servers**

Server-side scripting
Scripts executed on a server.

Service-level agreement
A contractual specification of service standards a contractor must meet.

Service-oriented architecture (SOA)
A service-oriented architecture is a collection of services that communicate with each other as part of a distributed systems architecture comprising different services.

Session cookies
Cookies used to manage a single visitor session.

Share of wallet or share of customer
The proportion of customer expenditure in a particular category that belongs to a single customer.

Site map
A graphical or text depiction of the relationship between different groups of content on a web site.

Site navigation scheme
Tools provided to the user to move between different information on a web site.

Site-visitor activity data
Information on content and services accessed by e-commerce site visitors.

Situation analysis
Environment analysis and review of internal processes and resources to inform strategy.

SMS (Short Message Services)
The formal name for text messaging.

Social engineering
Exploiting human behaviour to gain access to computer security information from employees or individuals.

Social network
A site-facilitating exchange of text, audio or video content.

Soft launch
A preliminary site launch with limited promotion to provide initial feedback and testing of an e-commerce site.

Soft lock-in
Customers or suppliers continue to use online services because of the switching costs.

Software
A series of detailed instructions that control the operation of a computer system. Software exists as programs which are developed by computer programmers.

Software (intelligent) agents
Software programs that assist humans by automatically gathering information from the Internet or exchanging data with other agents based on parameters supplied by the user.

Spam
Unsolicited e-mail (usually bulk mailed and untargeted).

Spamming
Bulk e-mailing of unsolicited mail.

Spiders
Automated tools known as 'spiders' or 'robots' index registered sites. Users search by typing keywords and are presented with a list of pages.

Static web content
A page on the web server that is invariant.

Stickiness
An indication of how long a visitor stays on a site.

Storyboarding
The use of static drawings or screenshots of the different parts of a web site to review the design concept with user groups. It can be used to develop the structure – an overall 'map' with individual pages shown separately.

Strategic analysis
Collection and review of information about an organization's internal processes and resources and external marketplace factors in order to inform strategy definition.

Strategic objectives
Statement and communication of an organization's mission, vision and objectives.

Strategy
Definition of the future direction and actions of a company defined as approaches to achieve specific objectives. See **Prescriptive** and **Emergent strategy**.

Strategy definition
Formulation, review and selection of strategies to achieve strategic objectives.

Strategy implementation
Planning, actions and controls needed to achieve strategic goals.

Strategy process model
A framework for approaching strategy development.

Streaming media
Sound and video that can be experienced within a web browser before the whole clip is downloaded.

Subject access request
A request by a **data subject** to view **personal data** from an organization.

Supply chain management (SCM)
The coordination of all supply activities of an organization from its suppliers and partners to its customers. See **Upstream** and **Downstream supply chain**.

Supply chain network
The links between an organization and all partners involved with multiple supply chains.

Supply chain visibility
Access to up-to-date, accurate, relevant information about supply chains process to different stakeholders.

SWOT analysis
Strengths, weaknesses, opportunities and threats.

Symmetric encryption
Both parties to a transaction use the same key to encode and decode messages.

System
A system can be defined as a collection of interrelated components that work together towards a collective goal.

System design
Defines how an information system will operate.

Systems development lifecycle
The sequence in which a system is created through initiation, analysis, design, implementation, build and maintenance.

Systems integrator
A company that organizes the procurement and installation of hardware and software needed for implementation.

Systems software
This form of software manages and controls the operation of the computer system as it performs tasks on behalf of the user.

Table
Each database comprises several tables. See **Database**.

Tacit knowledge
Mainly intangible knowledge that is typical intuitive and not recorded since it is part of the human mind.

Tagging
Tracking of origin of site visitors and their spending patterns.

Tailored development
The standard solution requires major configuration or integration of different modules.

Talk-through
A user verbally describes his or her required actions.

Target marketing strategy
Evaluation and selection of appropriate segments and the development of appropriate offers.

Task analysis
Identification of different tasks, their sequence and how they are broken down.

TCP/IP
The Transmission Control Protocol is a transport-layer protocol that moves data between applications. The Internet Protocol is a network-layer protocol that moves data (**packets**) across networks.

Technology convergence
A trend in which different hardware devices such as TVs, computers and phones merge and have similar functions.

TELNET
This allows remote access to computer systems. For example, a retailer could check to see whether an item was in stock in a warehouse using a TELNET application.

Test environment
Separate software and hardware used to test a system.

Test specification
A description of the testing process and tests to be performed.

Testing
Aims to identify non-conformance in the requirements specification and errors.

Thin client
An end-user device (terminal) where computing requirements such as processing and storage (and so cost) are minimized.

Third-party cookies
Served by another site to the one you are visiting – typical for **portals** where an ad network will track remotely or where the web analytics software places a **cookie**.

Three-tier client–server
The first tier is the client that handles display, second is application logic and business rules, third is database storage.

Total cost of ownership (TCO)
The sum of all cost elements of managing information systems for end-users including purchase, support *and* maintenance.

Trademark
A trademark is a unique word or phrase that distinguishes your company. The mark can be registered as plain or designed text, artwork or a combination. In theory, colours, smells and sounds can also be trademarks.

Trading hub See **B2B electronic marketplace**

Traffic-building campaign
The use of online and offline promotion techniques such as banner advertising, search engine promotion and reciprocal linking to increase the audience of a site (both new and existing customers).

Transaction log files
A web server file that records all page requests.

Transaction processing systems (TPS)
Transaction processing systems (TPS) manage the frequent external and internal transactions such as orders for goods and services which serve the operational level of the organization.

Trojan
A virus that masquerades as a bona fide application.

UMTS (Universal Mobile Telecommunications System)
The standard for **3G** mobile access.

Unified Modelling Language (UML)
A language used to specify, visualize and document the artefacts of an object-oriented system.

Uniform (universal) resource locators (URL)
A web address used to locate a web page on a web server.

Unique visitors
Individual visitors to a site measured through cookies or IP addresses on an individual computer.

Upstream supply chain
Transactions between an organization and its suppliers and intermediaries, equivalent to buy-side e-commerce.

URL (uniform or universal resource locator)
A web address used to locate a web page on a web server.

Usability
An approach to web site design intended to enable the completion of user tasks.

Usability/user testing
Representative users are observed performing representative tasks using a system.

Use-case
The sequence of transactions between an actor and a system that supports the activities of the actor.

Use-case modelling
A user-centred approach to modelling system requirements.

Usenet newsgroups
A widely used electronic bulletin board used to discuss a particular topic such as a sport, hobby or business area. Traditionally accessed by special newsreader software, can now be accessed via a web browser from www.deja.com.

User-centred design
Design based on optimizing the user experience according to all factors, including the user interface, which affect this.

Utility computing
IT resources and in particular software and hardware are utilized on a pay-per-use basis and are managed externally as 'managed services'.

Validation
This is a test of the design where we check that the design fulfils the requirements of the business users which are defined in the requirements specification.

Value-added network (VAN)
A secure wide-area network that uses proprietary rather than Internet technology.

Value chain
A model for analysis of how supply chain activities can add value to products and services delivered to the customer.

Value network
The links between an organization and its strategic and non-strategic partners that form its external value chain.

Value stream
The combination of actions required to deliver value to the customer as products and services.

Vertical integration
The extent to which supply chain activities are undertaken and controlled within the organization.

Viral marketing
In an online context, 'Forward to a Friend' e-mail is used to transmit a promotional message from one person to another. 'Online word of mouth'.

Virtual integration
The majority of supply chain activities are undertaken and controlled outside the organization by third parties.

Virtual organization
An organization which uses information and communications technology to allow it to operate without clearly defined physical boundaries between different functions. It provides customized services by outsourcing production and other functions to third parties.

Virtual private network (VPN)
A secure, encrypted (tunnelled) connection between two points using the Internet, typically created by ISPs for organizations wanting to conduct secure Internet trading.

Virtualization
The process of a company developing more of the characteristics of the virtual organization.

Voice over IP (VOIP)
Voice data is transferred across the Internet – it enables phone calls to be made over the Internet.

WAIS
A tool important before the advent of the web for storing and searching documents on the Internet. Has largely been superseded by the web which provides better searching and more sophisticated document publishing.

Walk-through
A user executes their actions through using a system or mock-up.

Web 2.0 concept
Web 2.0 refers to a collection of web services which facilitate certain behaviours online such as community participation and user-generated content, rating and tagging.

Web address See **URL**

Web analytics
Techniques used to assess and improve the contribution of e-marketing to a business including reviewing traffic volume, referrals, clickstreams, online reach data, customer satisfaction surveys, leads and sales.

Web browsers
Browsers such as Microsoft Internet Explorer provide an easy method of accessing and viewing information stored as web documents on different servers.

Web classification
See **Card sorting**

Web design personas
A summary of the characteristics, needs, motivations and environment of typical web-site users.

Web logs
Web logs or blogs are a method of publishing web pages, particularly those with news listings.

Web page See **Static web page**, **Dynamic web page** and **Web servers**

Web servers
Store and present the web pages accessed by web browsers.

Web services
Business applications and software services are provided through Internet and web protocols with the application managed on a separate server to where it is accessed.

Web-site persona
A summary of the characteristics, needs, motivations and environment of typical web site users.

Whitelist
A compilation of trusted sources of e-mail that is permitted to enter an inbox.

Wi-Fi ('wireless-fidelity')
A high-speed wireless local-area network enabling wireless access to the Internet for mobile, office and home users.

Wireframes
Also known as 'schematics' – a way of illustrating the layout of an individual web page.

Wireless Application Protocol (WAP)
WAP is a technical standard for transferring information to wireless devices, such as mobile phones.

Wireless communications
Electronic transactions and communications conducted using mobile devices such as laptops, personal digital assistants (PDAs) and mobile phones (and fixed access platforms) with different forms of wireless connection.

Wireless Markup Language (WML)
Standard for displaying mobile pages such as transferred by WAP.

Workflow management
Workflow management (WFM) is the automation of information flows and provides tools for processing the information according to a set of procedural rules.

World Wide Web (WWW)
The most common technique for publishing information on the Internet. It is accessed through web browsers which display web pages of embedded graphics and HTML/XML encoded text.

Worm
A small program that self-replicates and transfers across a network from machine to machine. A form of virus.

XML or eXtensible Markup Language
A standard for transferring structured data, unlike HTML which is purely presentational.

Index